PEARSON

ALWAYS LEARNING

Hugh D. Young • Roger A. Freedman •
Contributions by A. Lewis Ford

Sears and Zemansky's University Physics

with Modern Physics

Technology Update
Volume B

Fourth Custom Edition for the University of British Columbia

Taken from:
*Sears and Zemansky's University Physics with Modern Physics:
Technology Update*, Thirteenth Edition
by Hugh D. Young and Roger A. Freedman
with Contributions by A. Lewis Ford

Cover Art: "Commercial Alternator" courtesy of Corbis; "Lightning" courtesy of Ralph Wetmore/Getty Images.

Taken from:

Sears and Zemansky's University Physics with Modern Physics: Technology Update, Thirteenth Edition
by Hugh D. Young and Roger A. Freedman
with Contributions by A. Lewis Ford
Copyright © 2014, 2012, 2008 by Pearson Education, Inc.
San Francisco, California 94111

This special edition published in cooperation with Pearson Learning Solutions.

All trademarks, service marks, registered trademarks, and registered service marks are the property of their respective owners and are used herein for identification purposes only.

Pearson Learning Solutions, 501 Boylston Street, Suite 900, Boston, MA 02116
A Pearson Education Company
www.pearsoned.com

Printed in Canada

1 2 3 4 5 6 7 8 9 10 XXXX 17 16 15 14 13

000200010271796028

BK/MB

ISBN 10: 1-269-42331-2
ISBN 13: 978-1-269-42331-1

DETAILED CONTENTS

ELECTRIC CHARGE AND ELECTRIC FIELD

? Water makes life possible: The cells of your body could not function without water in which to dissolve essential biological molecules. What electrical properties of water make it such a good solvent?

LEARNING GOALS

By studying this chapter, you will learn:

- The nature of electric charge, and how we know that electric charge is conserved.

- How objects become electrically charged.

- How to use Coulomb's law to calculate the electric force between charges.

- The distinction between electric force and electric field.

- How to calculate the electric field due to a collection of charges.

- How to use the idea of electric field lines to visualize and interpret electric fields.

- How to calculate the properties of electric dipoles.

In Chapter 5 we mentioned the four kinds of fundamental forces. To this point the only one of these forces that we have examined in any detail is gravity. Now we are ready to examine the force of *electromagnetism,* which encompasses both electricity and magnetism. Electromagnetic phenomena will occupy our attention for most of the remainder of this book.

Electromagnetic interactions involve particles that have a property called *electric charge,* an attribute that is as fundamental as mass. Just as objects with mass are accelerated by gravitational forces, so electrically charged objects are accelerated by electric forces. The shock you feel when you scuff your shoes across a carpet and then reach for a metal doorknob is due to charged particles leaping between your finger and the doorknob. Electric currents are simply streams of charged particles flowing within wires in response to electric forces. Even the forces that hold atoms together to form solid matter, and that keep the atoms of solid objects from passing through each other, are fundamentally due to electric interactions between the charged particles within atoms.

We begin our study of electromagnetism in this chapter by examining the nature of electric charge. We'll find that charge is quantized and obeys a conservation principle. When charges are at rest in our frame of reference, they exert *electrostatic* forces on each other. These forces are of tremendous importance in chemistry and biology and have many technological applications. Electrostatic forces are governed by a simple relationship known as *Coulomb's law* and are most conveniently described by using the concept of *electric field.* In later chapters we'll expand our discussion to include electric charges in motion. This will lead us to an understanding of magnetism and, remarkably, of the nature of light.

While the key ideas of electromagnetism are conceptually simple, applying them to practical problems will make use of many of your mathematical skills, especially your knowledge of geometry and integral calculus. For this reason you may find this chapter and those that follow to be more mathematically demanding than earlier chapters. The reward for your extra effort will be a deeper understanding of principles that are at the heart of modern physics and technology.

21.1 Electric Charge

The ancient Greeks discovered as early as 600 B.C. that after they rubbed amber with wool, the amber could attract other objects. Today we say that the amber has acquired a net **electric charge,** or has become *charged.* The word "electric" is derived from the Greek word *elektron,* meaning amber. When you scuff your shoes across a nylon carpet, you become electrically charged, and you can charge a comb by passing it through dry hair.

Plastic rods and fur (real or fake) are particularly good for demonstrating **electrostatics,** the interactions between electric charges that are at rest (or nearly so). After we charge both plastic rods in Fig. 21.1a by rubbing them with the piece of fur, we find that the rods repel each other.

When we rub glass rods with silk, the glass rods also become charged and repel each other (Fig. 21.1b). But a charged plastic rod *attracts* a charged glass rod; furthermore, the plastic rod and the fur attract each other, and the glass rod and the silk attract each other (Fig. 21.1c).

These experiments and many others like them have shown that there are exactly two kinds of electric charge: the kind on the plastic rod rubbed with fur and the kind on the glass rod rubbed with silk. Benjamin Franklin (1706–1790) suggested calling these two kinds of charge *negative* and *positive,* respectively, and these names are still used. The plastic rod and the silk have negative charge; the glass rod and the fur have positive charge.

> **Two positive charges or two negative charges repel each other. A positive charge and a negative charge attract each other.**

CAUTION **Electric attraction and repulsion** The attraction and repulsion of two charged objects are sometimes summarized as "Like charges repel, and opposite charges attract." But keep in mind that the phrase "like charges" does *not* mean that the two charges are exactly identical, only that both charges have the same algebraic *sign* (both positive or both negative). "Opposite charges" means that both objects have an electric charge, and those charges have different signs (one positive and the other negative).

21.1 Experiments in electrostatics. (a) Negatively charged objects repel each other. (b) Positively charged objects repel each other. (c) Positvely charged objects and negatively charged objects attract each other.

(a) Interaction between plastic rods rubbed on fur

Plain plastic rods neither attract nor repel each other ...

Fur   Plastic

... but after being rubbed with fur, the rods repel each other.

(b) Interaction between glass rods rubbed on silk

Plain glass rods neither attract nor repel each other ...

Silk   Glass

... but after being rubbed with silk, the rods repel each other.

(c) Interaction between objects with opposite charges

The fur-rubbed plastic rod and the silk-rubbed glass rod attract each other ...

... and the fur and silk each attracts the rod it rubbed.

21.2 Schematic diagram of the operation of a laser printer.

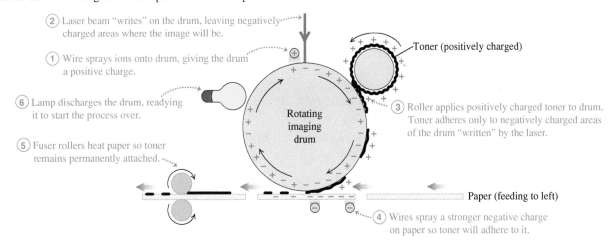

(2) Laser beam "writes" on the drum, leaving negatively charged areas where the image will be.

(1) Wire sprays ions onto drum, giving the drum a positive charge.

(6) Lamp discharges the drum, readying it to start the process over.

(5) Fuser rollers heat paper so toner remains permanently attached.

Rotating imaging drum

Toner (positively charged)

(3) Roller applies positively charged toner to drum. Toner adheres only to negatively charged areas of the drum "written" by the laser.

Paper (feeding to left)

(4) Wires spray a stronger negative charge on paper so toner will adhere to it.

One application of forces between charged bodies is in a laser printer (Fig. 21.2). The printer's light-sensitive imaging drum is given a positive charge. As the drum rotates, a laser beam shines on selected areas of the drum, leaving those areas with a *negative* charge. Positively charged particles of toner adhere only to the areas of the drum "written" by the laser. When a piece of paper is placed in contact with the drum, the toner particles stick to the paper and form an image.

Electric Charge and the Structure of Matter

When you charge a rod by rubbing it with fur or silk as in Fig. 21.1, there is no visible change in the appearance of the rod. What, then, actually happens to the rod when you charge it? To answer this question, we must look more closely at the structure of atoms, the building blocks of ordinary matter.

The structure of atoms can be described in terms of three particles: the negatively charged **electron**, the positively charged **proton**, and the uncharged **neutron** (Fig. 21.3). The proton and neutron are combinations of other entities called *quarks*, which have charges of $\pm\frac{1}{3}$ and $\pm\frac{2}{3}$ times the electron charge. Isolated quarks have not been observed, and there are theoretical reasons to believe that it is impossible in principle to observe a quark in isolation.

The protons and neutrons in an atom make up a small, very dense core called the **nucleus,** with dimensions of the order of 10^{-15} m. Surrounding the nucleus are the electrons, extending out to distances of the order of 10^{-10} m from the nucleus. If an atom were a few kilometers across, its nucleus would be the size of a tennis ball. The negatively charged electrons are held within the atom by the attractive electric forces exerted on them by the positively charged nucleus. (The protons and neutrons are held within stable atomic nuclei by an attractive interaction, called the *strong nuclear force,* that overcomes the electric repulsion of the protons. The strong nuclear force has a short range, and its effects do not extend far beyond the nucleus.)

The masses of the individual particles, to the precision that they are presently known, are

$$\text{Mass of electron} = m_{e} = 9.10938215(45) \times 10^{-31} \text{ kg}$$

$$\text{Mass of proton} = m_{p} = 1.672621637(83) \times 10^{-27} \text{ kg}$$

$$\text{Mass of neutron} = m_{n} = 1.674927211(84) \times 10^{-27} \text{ kg}$$

The numbers in parentheses are the uncertainties in the last two digits. Note that the masses of the proton and neutron are nearly equal and are roughly 2000 times

21.3 The structure of an atom. The particular atom depicted here is lithium (see Fig. 21.4a).

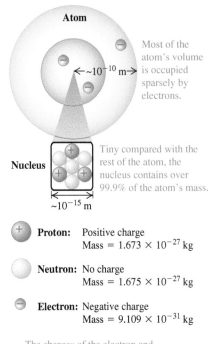

Atom

Most of the atom's volume is occupied sparsely by electrons.

$\leftarrow\sim10^{-10}$ m $\rightarrow$

Nucleus

Tiny compared with the rest of the atom, the nucleus contains over 99.9% of the atom's mass.

$\sim10^{-15}$ m

⊕ **Proton:** Positive charge
Mass $= 1.673 \times 10^{-27}$ kg

◯ **Neutron:** No charge
Mass $= 1.675 \times 10^{-27}$ kg

⊖ **Electron:** Negative charge
Mass $= 9.109 \times 10^{-31}$ kg

The charges of the electron and proton are equal in magnitude.

21.4 (a) A neutral atom has as many electrons as it does protons. (b) A positive ion has a deficit of electrons. (c) A negative ion has an excess of electrons. (The electron "shells" are a schematic representation of the actual electron distribution, a diffuse cloud many times larger than the nucleus.)

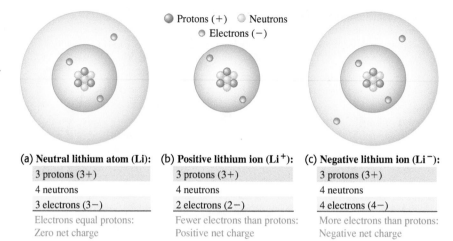

Protons (+) Neutrons
Electrons (−)

(a) Neutral lithium atom (Li):
3 protons (3+)
4 neutrons
3 electrons (3−)
Electrons equal protons:
Zero net charge

(b) Positive lithium ion (Li⁺):
3 protons (3+)
4 neutrons
2 electrons (2−)
Fewer electrons than protons:
Positive net charge

(c) Negative lithium ion (Li⁻):
3 protons (3+)
4 neutrons
4 electrons (4−)
More electrons than protons:
Negative net charge

the mass of the electron. Over 99.9% of the mass of any atom is concentrated in its nucleus.

The negative charge of the electron has (within experimental error) *exactly* the same magnitude as the positive charge of the proton. In a neutral atom the number of electrons equals the number of protons in the nucleus, and the net electric charge (the algebraic sum of all the charges) is exactly zero (Fig. 21.4a). The number of protons or electrons in a neutral atom of an element is called the **atomic number** of the element. If one or more electrons are removed from an atom, what remains is called a **positive ion** (Fig. 21.4b). A **negative ion** is an atom that has *gained* one or more electrons (Fig. 21.4c). This gain or loss of electrons is called **ionization.**

When the total number of protons in a macroscopic body equals the total number of electrons, the total charge is zero and the body as a whole is electrically neutral. To give a body an excess negative charge, we may either *add negative* charges to a neutral body or *remove positive* charges from that body. Similarly, we can create an excess positive charge by either *adding positive* charge or *removing negative* charge. In most cases, negatively charged (and highly mobile) electrons are added or removed, and a "positively charged body" is one that has lost some of its normal complement of electrons. When we speak of the charge of a body, we always mean its *net* charge. The net charge is always a very small fraction (typically no more than 10^{-12}) of the total positive charge or negative charge in the body.

Electric Charge Is Conserved

Implicit in the foregoing discussion are two very important principles. First is the **principle of conservation of charge:**

The algebraic sum of all the electric charges in any closed system is constant.

If we rub together a plastic rod and a piece of fur, both initially uncharged, the rod acquires a negative charge (since it takes electrons from the fur) and the fur acquires a positive charge of the *same* magnitude (since it has lost as many electrons as the rod has gained). Hence the total electric charge on the two bodies together does not change. In any charging process, charge is not created or destroyed; it is merely *transferred* from one body to another.

Conservation of charge is thought to be a *universal* conservation law. No experimental evidence for any violation of this principle has ever been observed. Even in high-energy interactions in which particles are created and destroyed, such as the creation of electron–positron pairs, the total charge of any closed system is exactly constant.

The second important principle is:

The magnitude of charge of the electron or proton is a natural unit of charge.

Every observable amount of electric charge is always an integer multiple of this basic unit. We say that charge is *quantized*. A familiar example of quantization is money. When you pay cash for an item in a store, you have to do it in one-cent increments. Cash can't be divided into amounts smaller than one cent, and electric charge can't be divided into amounts smaller than the charge of one electron or proton. (The quark charges, $\pm\frac{1}{3}$ and $\pm\frac{2}{3}$ of the electron charge, are probably not observable as isolated charges.) Thus the charge on any macroscopic body is always either zero or an integer multiple (negative or positive) of the electron charge.

Understanding the electric nature of matter gives us insight into many aspects of the physical world (Fig. 21.5). The chemical bonds that hold atoms together to form molecules are due to electric interactions between the atoms. They include the strong ionic bonds that hold sodium and chlorine atoms together to make table salt and the relatively weak bonds between the strands of DNA that record your body's genetic code. The normal force exerted on you by the chair in which you're sitting arises from electric forces between charged particles in the atoms of your seat and in the atoms of your chair. The tension force in a stretched string and the adhesive force of glue are likewise due to the electric interactions of atoms.

Test Your Understanding of Section 21.1 (a) Strictly speaking, does the plastic rod in Fig. 21.1 weigh more, less, or the same after rubbing it with fur? (b) What about the glass rod after rubbing it with silk? What about (c) the fur and (d) the silk? ❙

21.2 Conductors, Insulators, and Induced Charges

Some materials permit electric charge to move easily from one region of the material to another, while others do not. For example, Fig. 21.6a shows a copper wire supported by a nylon thread. Suppose you touch one end of the wire to a charged plastic rod and attach the other end to a metal ball that is initially uncharged; you then remove the charged rod and the wire. When you bring another charged body up close to the ball (Figs. 21.6b and 21.6c), the ball is attracted or repelled, showing that the ball has become electrically charged. Electric charge has been transferred through the copper wire between the ball and the surface of the plastic rod.

The copper wire is called a **conductor** of electricity. If you repeat the experiment using a rubber band or nylon thread in place of the wire, you find that *no* charge is transferred to the ball. These materials are called **insulators.** Conductors permit the easy movement of charge through them, while insulators do not. (The supporting nylon threads shown in Fig. 21.6 are insulators, which prevents charge from leaving the metal ball and copper wire.)

As an example, carpet fibers on a dry day are good insulators. As you walk across a carpet, the rubbing of your shoes against the fibers causes charge to build up on you, and this charge remains on you because it can't flow through the insulating fibers. If you then touch a conducting object such as a doorknob, a rapid charge transfer takes place between your finger and the doorknob, and you feel a shock. One way to prevent this is to wind some of the carpet fibers around conducting cores so that any charge that builds up on you can be transferred harmlessly to the carpet. Another solution is to coat the carpet fibers with an anti-static layer that does not easily transfer electrons to or from your shoes; this prevents any charge from building up on you in the first place.

21.5 Most of the forces on this water skier are electric. Electric interactions between adjacent molecules give rise to the force of the water on the ski, the tension in the tow rope, and the resistance of the air on the skier's body. Electric interactions also hold the atoms of the skier's body together. Only one wholly nonelectric force acts on the skier: the force of gravity.

PhET: Balloons and Static Electricity
PhET: John Travoltage

21.6 Copper is a good conductor of electricity; nylon is a good insulator. **(a)** The copper wire conducts charge between the metal ball and the charged plastic rod to charge the ball negatively. Afterward, the metal ball is **(b)** repelled by a negatively charged plastic rod and **(c)** attracted to a positively charged glass rod.

(a)

Insulating nylon threads

Charged plastic rod

Metal ball

Copper wire

The wire conducts charge from the negatively charged plastic rod to the metal ball.

(b)

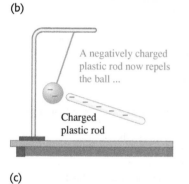

A negatively charged plastic rod now repels the ball ...

Charged plastic rod

(c)

... and a positively charged glass rod attracts the ball.

Charged glass rod

Most metals are good conductors, while most nonmetals are insulators. Within a solid metal such as copper, one or more outer electrons in each atom become detached and can move freely throughout the material, just as the molecules of a gas can move through the spaces between the grains in a bucket of sand. The other electrons remain bound to the positively charged nuclei, which themselves are bound in nearly fixed positions within the material. In an insulator there are no, or very few, free electrons, and electric charge cannot move freely through the material. Some materials called *semiconductors* are intermediate in their properties between good conductors and good insulators.

Charging by Induction

We can charge a metal ball using a copper wire and an electrically charged plastic rod, as in Fig. 21.6a. In this process, some of the excess electrons on the rod are transferred from it to the ball, leaving the rod with a smaller negative charge. But there is a different technique in which the plastic rod can give another body a charge of *opposite* sign without losing any of its own charge. This process is called charging by **induction.**

Figure 21.7 shows an example of charging by induction. An uncharged metal ball is supported on an insulating stand (Fig. 21.7a). When you bring a negatively charged rod near it, without actually touching it (Fig. 21.7b), the free electrons in the metal ball are repelled by the excess electrons on the rod, and they shift toward the right, away from the rod. They cannot escape from the ball because the supporting stand and the surrounding air are insulators. So we get excess negative charge at the right surface of the ball and a deficiency of negative charge (that is, a net positive charge) at the left surface. These excess charges are called **induced charges.**

Not all of the free electrons move to the right surface of the ball. As soon as any induced charge develops, it exerts forces toward the *left* on the other free electrons. These electrons are repelled by the negative induced charge on the right and attracted toward the positive induced charge on the left. The system reaches an equilibrium state in which the force toward the right on an electron, due to the charged rod, is just balanced by the force toward the left due to the induced charge. If we remove the charged rod, the free electrons shift back to the left, and the original neutral condition is restored.

What happens if, while the plastic rod is nearby, you touch one end of a conducting wire to the right surface of the ball and the other end to the earth (Fig. 21.7c)? The earth is a conductor, and it is so large that it can act as a practically infinite source of extra electrons or sink of unwanted electrons. Some of the negative charge flows through the wire to the earth. Now suppose you disconnect the wire (Fig. 21.7d) and then remove the rod (Fig. 21.7e); a net positive charge is left on the ball. The charge on the negatively charged rod has not changed during this process. The earth acquires a negative charge that is equal in magnitude to the induced positive charge remaining on the ball.

21.7 Charging a metal ball by induction.

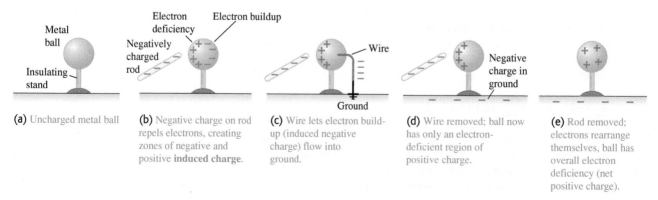

(a) Uncharged metal ball

(b) Negative charge on rod repels electrons, creating zones of negative and positive **induced charge.**

(c) Wire lets electron build-up (induced negative charge) flow into ground.

(d) Wire removed; ball now has only an electron-deficient region of positive charge.

(e) Rod removed; electrons rearrange themselves, ball has overall electron deficiency (net positive charge).

21.8 The charges within the molecules of an insulating material can shift slightly. As a result, a comb with either sign of charge attracts a neutral insulator. By Newton's third law the neutral insulator exerts an equal-magnitude attractive force on the comb.

(a) A charged comb picking up uncharged pieces of plastic

(b) How a negatively charged comb attracts an insulator

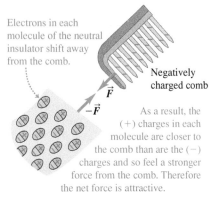

Electrons in each molecule of the neutral insulator shift away from the comb.

Negatively charged comb

$\vec{F}$

$-\vec{F}$

As a result, the (+) charges in each molecule are closer to the comb than are the (−) charges and so feel a stronger force from the comb. Therefore the net force is attractive.

(c) How a positively charged comb attracts an insulator

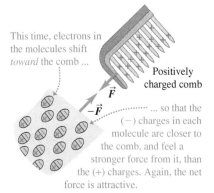

This time, electrons in the molecules shift *toward* the comb ...

Positively charged comb

$\vec{F}$

$-\vec{F}$

... so that the (−) charges in each molecule are closer to the comb, and feel a stronger force from it, than the (+) charges. Again, the net force is attractive.

Electric Forces on Uncharged Objects

Finally, we note that a charged body can exert forces even on objects that are *not* charged themselves. If you rub a balloon on the rug and then hold the balloon against the ceiling, it sticks, even though the ceiling has no net electric charge. After you electrify a comb by running it through your hair, you can pick up uncharged bits of paper or plastic with the comb (Fig. 21.8a). How is this possible?

This interaction is an induced-charge effect. Even in an insulator, electric charges can shift back and forth a little when there is charge nearby. This is shown in Fig. 21.8b; the negatively charged plastic comb causes a slight shifting of charge within the molecules of the neutral insulator, an effect called *polarization*. The positive and negative charges in the material are present in equal amounts, but the positive charges are closer to the plastic comb and so feel an attraction that is stronger than the repulsion felt by the negative charges, giving a net attractive force. (In Section 21.3 we will study how electric forces depend on distance.) Note that a neutral insulator is also attracted to a *positively* charged comb (Fig. 21.8c). Now the charges in the insulator shift in the opposite direction; the negative charges in the insulator are closer to the comb and feel an attractive force that is stronger than the repulsion felt by the positive charges in the insulator. Hence a charged object of *either* sign exerts an attractive force on an uncharged insulator. Figure 21.9 shows an industrial application of this effect.

Test Your Understanding of Section 21.2   You have two lightweight metal spheres, each hanging from an insulating nylon thread. One of the spheres has a net negative charge, while the other sphere has no net charge. (a) If the spheres are close together but do not touch, will they (i) attract each other, (ii) repel each other, or (iii) exert no force on each other? (b) You now allow the two spheres to touch. Once they have touched, will the two spheres (i) attract each other, (ii) repel each other, or (iii) exert no force on each other?

Video Tutor Demo

21.9 The electrostatic painting process (compare Figs. 21.7b and 21.7c). A metal object to be painted is connected to the earth ("ground"), and the paint droplets are given an electric charge as they exit the sprayer nozzle. Induced charges of the opposite sign appear in the object as the droplets approach, just as in Fig. 21.7b, and they attract the droplets to the surface. This process minimizes overspray from clouds of stray paint particles and gives a particularly smooth finish.

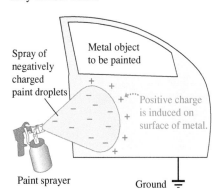

Spray of negatively charged paint droplets

Metal object to be painted

Positive charge is induced on surface of metal.

Paint sprayer

Ground

21.3 Coulomb's Law

Charles Augustin de Coulomb (1736–1806) studied the interaction forces of charged particles in detail in 1784. He used a torsion balance (Fig. 21.10a) similar to the one used 13 years later by Cavendish to study the much weaker gravitational interaction, as we discussed in Section 13.1. For **point charges,** charged

ActivPhysics 11.1: Electric Force: Coulomb's Law
ActivPhysics 11.2: Electric Force: Superposition Principle
ActivPhysics 11.3: Electric Force: Superposition (Quantitative)

Application Electric Forces, Sweat, and Cystic Fibrosis

One way to test for the genetic disease cystic fibrosis (CF) is by measuring the salt content of a person's sweat. Sweat is a mixture of water and ions, including the sodium (Na^+) and chloride (Cl^-) ions that make up ordinary salt ($NaCl$). When sweat is secreted by epithelial cells, some of the Cl^- ions flow from the sweat back into these cells (a process called reabsorption). The electric attraction between negative and positive charges pulls Na^+ ions along with the Cl^-. Water molecules cannot flow back into the epithelial cells, so sweat on the skin has a low salt content. However, in persons with CF the reabsorption of Cl^- ions is blocked. Hence the sweat of persons with CF is unusually salty, with up to four times the normal concentration of Cl^- and Na^+.

bodies that are very small in comparison with the distance r between them, Coulomb found that the electric force is proportional to $1/r^2$. That is, when the distance r doubles, the force decreases to one-quarter of its initial value; when the distance is halved, the force increases to four times its initial value.

The electric force between two point charges also depends on the quantity of charge on each body, which we will denote by q or Q. To explore this dependence, Coulomb divided a charge into two equal parts by placing a small charged spherical conductor into contact with an identical but uncharged sphere; by symmetry, the charge is shared equally between the two spheres. (Note the essential role of the principle of conservation of charge in this procedure.) Thus he could obtain one-half, one-quarter, and so on, of any initial charge. He found that the forces that two point charges q_1 and q_2 exert on each other are proportional to each charge and therefore are proportional to the *product* $q_1 q_2$ of the two charges.

Thus Coulomb established what we now call **Coulomb's law:**

> **The magnitude of the electric force between two point charges is directly proportional to the product of the charges and inversely proportional to the square of the distance between them.**

In mathematical terms, the magnitude F of the force that each of two point charges q_1 and q_2 a distance r apart exerts on the other can be expressed as

$$F = k \frac{|q_1 q_2|}{r^2} \qquad (21.1)$$

where k is a proportionality constant whose numerical value depends on the system of units used. The absolute value bars are used in Eq. (21.1) because the charges q_1 and q_2 can be either positive or negative, while the force magnitude F is always positive.

The directions of the forces the two charges exert on each other are always along the line joining them. When the charges q_1 and q_2 have the same sign, either both positive or both negative, the forces are repulsive; when the charges have opposite signs, the forces are attractive (Fig. 21.10b). The two forces obey Newton's third law; they are always equal in magnitude and opposite in direction, even when the charges are not equal in magnitude.

21.10 (a) Measuring the electric force between point charges. (b) The electric forces between point charges obey Newton's third law: $\vec{F}_{1 \text{ on } 2} = -\vec{F}_{2 \text{ on } 1}$.

(a) A torsion balance of the type used by Coulomb to measure the electric force

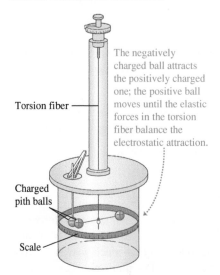

Torsion fiber

The negatively charged ball attracts the positively charged one; the positive ball moves until the elastic forces in the torsion fiber balance the electrostatic attraction.

Charged pith balls

Scale

(b) Interactions between point charges

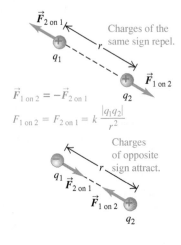

$\vec{F}_{2 \text{ on } 1}$

Charges of the same sign repel.

q_1 r

$\vec{F}_{1 \text{ on } 2}$ q_2

$\vec{F}_{1 \text{ on } 2} = -\vec{F}_{2 \text{ on } 1}$

$F_{1 \text{ on } 2} = F_{2 \text{ on } 1} = k \dfrac{|q_1 q_2|}{r^2}$

Charges of opposite sign attract.

q_1 r

$\vec{F}_{2 \text{ on } 1}$

$\vec{F}_{1 \text{ on } 2}$ q_2

The proportionality of the electric force to $1/r^2$ has been verified with great precision. There is no reason to suspect that the exponent is different from precisely 2. Thus the form of Eq. (21.1) is the same as that of the law of gravitation. But electric and gravitational interactions are two distinct classes of phenomena. Electric interactions depend on electric charges and can be either attractive or repulsive, while gravitational interactions depend on mass and are always attractive (because there is no such thing as negative mass).

Fundamental Electric Constants

The value of the proportionality constant k in Coulomb's law depends on the system of units used. In our study of electricity and magnetism we will use SI units exclusively. The SI electric units include most of the familiar units such as the volt, the ampere, the ohm, and the watt. (There is *no* British system of electric units.) The SI unit of electric charge is called one **coulomb** (1 C). In SI units the constant k in Eq. (21.1) is

$$k = 8.987551787 \times 10^9 \, \text{N} \cdot \text{m}^2/\text{C}^2 \cong 8.988 \times 10^9 \, \text{N} \cdot \text{m}^2/\text{C}^2$$

The value of k is known to such a large number of significant figures because this value is closely related to the speed of light in vacuum. (We will show this in Chapter 32 when we study electromagnetic radiation.) As we discussed in Section 1.3, this speed is *defined* to be exactly $c = 2.99792458 \times 10^8 \, \text{m/s}$. The numerical value of k is defined in terms of c to be precisely

$$k = (10^{-7} \, \text{N} \cdot \text{s}^2/\text{C}^2)c^2$$

You should check this expression to confirm that k has the right units.

In principle we can measure the electric force F between two equal charges q at a measured distance r and use Coulomb's law to determine the charge. Thus we could regard the value of k as an operational definition of the coulomb. For reasons of experimental precision it is better to define the coulomb instead in terms of a unit of electric *current* (charge per unit time), the *ampere,* equal to 1 coulomb per second. We will return to this definition in Chapter 28.

In SI units we usually write the constant k in Eq. (21.1) as $1/4\pi\epsilon_0$, where ϵ_0 ("epsilon-nought" or "epsilon-zero") is another constant. This appears to complicate matters, but it actually simplifies many formulas that we will encounter in later chapters. From now on, we will usually write Coulomb's law as

$$F = \frac{1}{4\pi\epsilon_0} \frac{|q_1 q_2|}{r^2} \qquad \text{(Coulomb's law: force between two point charges)} \qquad \text{(21.2)}$$

The constants in Eq. (21.2) are approximately

$$\epsilon_0 = 8.854 \times 10^{-12} \, \text{C}^2/\text{N} \cdot \text{m}^2 \quad \text{and} \quad \frac{1}{4\pi\epsilon_0} = k = 8.988 \times 10^9 \, \text{N} \cdot \text{m}^2/\text{C}^2$$

In examples and problems we will often use the approximate value

$$\frac{1}{4\pi\epsilon_0} = 9.0 \times 10^9 \, \text{N} \cdot \text{m}^2/\text{C}^2$$

which is within about 0.1% of the correct value.

As we mentioned in Section 21.1, the most fundamental unit of charge is the magnitude of the charge of an electron or a proton, which is denoted by e. The most precise value available as of the writing of this book is

$$e = 1.602176487(40) \times 10^{-19} \, \text{C}$$

One coulomb represents the negative of the total charge of about 6×10^{18} electrons. For comparison, a copper cube 1 cm on a side contains about 2.4×10^{24}

electrons. About 10^{19} electrons pass through the glowing filament of a flashlight bulb every second.

In electrostatics problems (that is, problems that involve charges at rest), it's very unusual to encounter charges as large as 1 coulomb. Two 1-C charges separated by 1 m would exert forces on each other of magnitude 9×10^9 N (about 1 million tons)! The total charge of all the electrons in a copper one-cent coin is even greater, about 1.4×10^5 C, which shows that we can't disturb electric neutrality very much without using enormous forces. More typical values of charge range from about 10^{-9} to about 10^{-6} C. The microcoulomb $(1 \text{ mC} = 10^{-6} \text{ C})$ and the nanocoulomb $(1 \text{ nC} = 10^{-9} \text{ C})$ are often used as practical units of charge.

Example 21.1 Electric force versus gravitational force

An α particle (the nucleus of a helium atom) has mass $m = 6.64 \times 10^{-27}$ kg and charge $q = +2e = 3.2 \times 10^{-19}$ C. Compare the magnitude of the electric repulsion between two α ("alpha") particles with that of the gravitational attraction between them.

SOLUTION

IDENTIFY and SET UP: This problem involves Newton's law for the gravitational force F_g between particles (see Section 13.1) and Coulomb's law for the electric force F_e between point charges. To compare these forces, we make our target variable the ratio F_e/F_g. We use Eq. (21.2) for F_e and Eq. (13.1) for F_g.

21.11 Our sketch for this problem.

$q = 3.2 \times 10^{-19}$ C
$m = 6.64 \times 10^{-27}$ kg

EXECUTE: Figure 21.11 shows our sketch. From Eqs. (21.2) and (13.1),

$$ F_e = \frac{1}{4\pi\epsilon_0} \frac{q^2}{r^2} \qquad F_g = G\frac{m^2}{r^2} $$

These are both inverse-square forces, so the r^2 factors cancel when we take the ratio:

$$ \frac{F_e}{F_g} = \frac{1}{4\pi\epsilon_0 G} \frac{q^2}{m^2} $$

$$ = \frac{9.0 \times 10^9 \text{ N} \cdot \text{m}^2/\text{C}^2}{6.67 \times 10^{-11} \text{ N} \cdot \text{m}^2/\text{kg}^2} \frac{(3.2 \times 10^{-19} \text{ C})^2}{(6.64 \times 10^{-27} \text{ kg})^2} $$

$$ = 3.1 \times 10^{35} $$

EVALUATE: This astonishingly large number shows that the gravitational force in this situation is completely negligible in comparison to the electric force. This is always true for interactions of atomic and subnuclear particles. But within objects the size of a person or a planet, the positive and negative charges are nearly equal in magnitude, and the net electric force is usually much *smaller* than the gravitational force.

Superposition of Forces

Coulomb's law as we have stated it describes only the interaction of two *point* charges. Experiments show that when two charges exert forces simultaneously on a third charge, the total force acting on that charge is the *vector sum* of the forces that the two charges would exert individually. This important property, called the **principle of superposition of forces,** holds for any number of charges. By using this principle, we can apply Coulomb's law to *any* collection of charges. Two of the examples at the end of this section use the superposition principle.

Strictly speaking, Coulomb's law as we have stated it should be used only for point charges *in a vacuum.* If matter is present in the space between the charges, the net force acting on each charge is altered because charges are induced in the molecules of the intervening material. We will describe this effect later. As a practical matter, though, we can use Coulomb's law unaltered for point charges in air. At normal atmospheric pressure, the presence of air changes the electric force from its vacuum value by only about one part in 2000.

Problem-Solving Strategy 21.1   Coulomb's Law

IDENTIFY *the relevant concepts:* Coulomb's law describes the electric force between charged particles.

SET UP *the problem* using the following steps:
1. Sketch the locations of the charged particles and label each particle with its charge.
2. If the charges do not all lie on a single line, set up an *xy*-coordinate system.
3. The problem will ask you to find the electric force on one or more particles. Identify which these are.

EXECUTE *the solution* as follows:
1. For each particle that exerts an electric force on a given particle of interest, use Eq. (21.2) to calculate the magnitude of that force.
2. Using those magnitudes, sketch a free-body diagram showing the electric force vectors acting on each particle of interest. The force exerted by particle 1 on particle 2 points from particle 2 toward particle 1 if the charges have opposite signs, but points from particle 2 directly away from particle 1 if the charges have the same sign.
3. Use the principle of superposition to calculate the total electric force—a *vector* sum—on each particle of interest. (Review the vector algebra in Sections 1.7 through 1.9. The method of components is often helpful.)
4. Use consistent units; SI units are completely consistent. With $1/4\pi\epsilon_0 = 9.0 \times 10^9 \ \text{N}\cdot\text{m}^2/\text{C}^2$, distances must be in meters, charges in coulombs, and forces in newtons.
5. Some examples and problems in this and later chapters involve *continuous* distributions of charge along a line, over a surface, or throughout a volume. In these cases the vector sum in step 3 becomes a vector *integral*. We divide the charge distribution into infinitesimal pieces, use Coulomb's law for each piece, and integrate to find the vector sum. Sometimes this can be done without actual integration.
6. Exploit any symmetries in the charge distribution to simplify your problem solving. For example, two identical charges q exert zero net electric force on a charge Q midway between them, because the forces on Q have equal magnitude and opposite direction.

EVALUATE *your answer:* Check whether your numerical results are reasonable. Confirm that the direction of the net electric force agrees with the principle that charges of the same sign repel and charges of opposite sign attract.

Example 21.2   Force between two point charges

Two point charges, $q_1 = +25$ nC and $q_2 = -75$ nC, are separated by a distance $r = 3.0$ cm (Fig. 21.12a). Find the magnitude and direction of the electric force (a) that q_1 exerts on q_2 and (b) that q_2 exerts on q_1.

SOLUTION

IDENTIFY and SET UP: This problem asks for the electric forces that two charges exert on each other. We use Coulomb's law, Eq. (21.2), to calculate the magnitudes of the forces. The signs of the charges will determine the directions of the forces.

EXECUTE: (a) After converting the units of r to meters and the units of q_1 and q_2 to coulombs, Eq. (21.2) gives us

$$F_{1 \text{ on } 2} = \frac{1}{4\pi\epsilon_0}\frac{|q_1 q_2|}{r^2}$$

$$= (9.0 \times 10^9 \ \text{N}\cdot\text{m}^2/\text{C}^2)\frac{|(+25 \times 10^{-9} \ \text{C})(-75 \times 10^{-9} \ \text{C})|}{(0.030 \ \text{m})^2}$$

$$= 0.019 \ \text{N}$$

The charges have opposite signs, so the force is attractive (to the left in Fig. 21.12b); that is, the force that acts on q_2 is directed toward q_1 along the line joining the two charges.

21.12 What force does q_1 exert on q_2, and what force does q_2 exert on q_1? Gravitational forces are negligible.

(a) The two charges   (b) Free-body diagram for charge q_2 (c) Free-body diagram for charge q_1

(b) Proceeding as in part (a), we have

$$F_{1 \text{ on } 2} = \frac{1}{4\pi\epsilon_0}\frac{|q_2 q_1|}{r^2} = F_{2 \text{ on } 1} = 0.019 \ \text{N}$$

The attractive force that acts on q_1 is to the right, toward q_2 (Fig. 21.12c).

EVALUATE: Newton's third law applies to the electric force. Even though the charges have different magnitudes, the magnitude of the force that q_2 exerts on q_1 is the same as the magnitude of the force that q_1 exerts on q_2, and these two forces are in opposite directions.

Example 21.3   Vector addition of electric forces on a line

Two point charges are located on the *x*-axis of a coordinate system: $q_1 = 1.0$ nC is at $x = +2.0$ cm, and $q_2 = -3.0$ nC is at $x = +4.0$ cm. What is the total electric force exerted by q_1 and q_2 on a charge $q_3 = 5.0$ nC at $x = 0$?

SOLUTION

IDENTIFY and SET UP: Figure 21.13a shows the situation. To find the total force on q_3, our target variable, we find the vector sum of the two electric forces on it.

Continued

EXECUTE: Figure 21.13b is a free-body diagram for q_3, which is repelled by q_1 (which has the same sign) and attracted to q_2 (which has the opposite sign): $\vec{F}_{1\text{ on }3}$ is in the $-x$-direction and $\vec{F}_{2\text{ on }3}$ is in the $+x$-direction. After unit conversions, we have from Eq. (21.2)

$$F_{1\text{ on }3} = \frac{1}{4\pi\epsilon_0}\frac{|q_1 q_3|}{r_{13}^2}$$

$$= (9.0 \times 10^9 \text{ N}\cdot\text{m}^2/\text{C}^2)\frac{(1.0 \times 10^{-9}\text{ C})(5.0 \times 10^{-9}\text{C})}{(0.020\text{ m})^2}$$

$$= 1.12 \times 10^{-4}\text{ N} = 112\ \mu\text{N}$$

In the same way you can show that $F_{2\text{ on }3} = 84\ \mu\text{N}$. We thus have $\vec{F}_{1\text{ on }3} = (-112\ \mu\text{N})\hat{\imath}$ and $\vec{F}_{2\text{ on }3} = (84\ \mu\text{N})\hat{\imath}$. The net force on q_3 is

$$\vec{F}_3 = \vec{F}_{1\text{ on }3} + \vec{F}_{2\text{ on }3} = (-112\ \mu\text{N})\hat{\imath} + (84\ \mu\text{N})\hat{\imath} = (-28\ \mu\text{N})\hat{\imath}$$

21.13 Our sketches for this problem.

(a) Our diagram of the situation   **(b)** Free-body diagram for q_3

EVALUATE: As a check, note that the magnitude of q_2 is three times that of q_1, but q_2 is twice as far from q_3 as q_1. Equation (21.2) then says that $F_{2\text{ on }3}$ must be $3/2^2 = 3/4 = 0.75$ as large as $F_{1\text{ on }3}$. This agrees with our calculated values: $F_{2\text{ on }3}/F_{1\text{ on }3} = (84\ \mu\text{N})/(112\ \mu\text{N}) = 0.75$. Because $F_{2\text{ on }3}$ is the weaker force, the direction of the net force is that of $\vec{F}_{1\text{ on }3}$—that is, in the negative x-direction.

Example 21.4 **Vector addition of electric forces in a plane**

Two equal positive charges $q_1 = q_2 = 2.0\ \mu\text{C}$ are located at $x = 0$, $y = 0.30$ m and $x = 0$, $y = -0.30$ m, respectively. What are the magnitude and direction of the total electric force that q_1 and q_2 exert on a third charge $Q = 4.0\ \mu\text{C}$ at $x = 0.40$ m, $y = 0$?

SOLUTION

IDENTIFY and SET UP: As in Example 21.3, we must compute the force that each charge exerts on Q and then find the vector sum of those forces. Figure 21.14 shows the situation. Since the three charges do not all lie on a line, the best way to calculate the forces is to use components.

21.14 Our sketch for this problem.

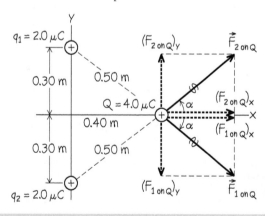

EXECUTE: Figure 21.14 shows the forces $\vec{F}_{1\text{ on }Q}$ and $\vec{F}_{2\text{ on }Q}$ due to the identical charges q_1 and q_2, which are at equal distances from Q. From Coulomb's law, *both* forces have magnitude

$$F_{1\text{ or }2\text{ on }Q} = (9.0 \times 10^9 \text{ N}\cdot\text{m}^2/\text{C}^2)$$

$$\times \frac{(4.0 \times 10^{-6}\text{ C})(2.0 \times 10^{-6}\text{ C})}{(0.50\text{ m})^2} = 0.29\text{ N}$$

The x-components of the two forces are equal:

$$(F_{1\text{ or }2\text{ on }Q})_x = (F_{1\text{ or }2\text{ on }Q})\cos\alpha = (0.29\text{ N})\frac{0.40\text{ m}}{0.50\text{ m}} = 0.23\text{ N}$$

From symmetry we see that the y-components of the two forces are equal and opposite. Hence their sum is zero and the total force $\vec{F}$ on Q has only an x-component $F_x = 0.23$ N $+ 0.23$ N $= 0.46$ N. The total force on Q is in the $+x$-direction, with magnitude 0.46 N.

EVALUATE: The total force on Q points neither directly away from q_1 nor directly away from q_2. Rather, this direction is a compromise that points away from the *system* of charges q_1 and q_2. Can you see that the total force would *not* be in the $+x$-direction if q_1 and q_2 were not equal or if the geometrical arrangement of the changes were not so symmetric?

Test Your Understanding of Section 21.3 Suppose that charge q_2 in Example 21.4 were $-2.0\ \mu\text{C}$. In this case, the total electric force on Q would be (i) in the positive x-direction; (ii) in the negative x-direction; (iii) in the positive y-direction; (iv) in the negative y-direction; (v) zero; (vi) none of these.

21.4 Electric Field and Electric Forces

When two electrically charged particles in empty space interact, how does each one know the other is there? We can begin to answer this question, and at the same time reformulate Coulomb's law in a very useful way, by using the concept of *electric field*.

Electric Field

To introduce this concept, let's look at the mutual repulsion of two positively charged bodies A and B (Fig. 21.15a). Suppose B has charge q_0, and let $\vec{F}_0$ be the electric force of A on B. One way to think about this force is as an "action-at-a-distance" force—that is, as a force that acts across empty space without needing any matter (such as a push rod or a rope) to transmit it through the intervening space. (Gravity can also be thought of as an "action-at-a-distance" force.) But a more fruitful way to visualize the repulsion between A and B is as a two-stage process. We first envision that body A, as a result of the charge that it carries, somehow *modifies the properties of the space around it.* Then body B, as a result of the charge that *it* carries, senses how space has been modified at its position. The response of body B is to experience the force $\vec{F}_0$.

To elaborate how this two-stage process occurs, we first consider body A by itself: We remove body B and label its former position as point P (Fig. 21.15b). We say that the charged body A produces or causes an **electric field** at point P (and at all other points in the neighborhood). This electric field is present at P even if there is no charge at P; it is a consequence of the charge on body A only. If a point charge q_0 is then placed at point P, it experiences the force $\vec{F}_0$. We take the point of view that this force is exerted on q_0 *by the field* at P (Fig. 21.15c). Thus the electric field is the intermediary through which A communicates its presence to q_0. Because the point charge q_0 would experience a force at *any* point in the neighborhood of A, the electric field that A produces exists at all points in the region around A.

We can likewise say that the point charge q_0 produces an electric field in the space around it and that this electric field exerts the force $-\vec{F}_0$ on body A. For each force (the force of A on q_0 and the force of q_0 on A), one charge sets up an electric field that exerts a force on the second charge. We emphasize that this is an *interaction* between *two* charged bodies. A single charge produces an electric field in the surrounding space, but this electric field cannot exert a net force on the charge that created it; as we discussed in Section 4.3, a body cannot exert a net force on itself. (If this wasn't true, you would be able to lift yourself to the ceiling by pulling up on your belt!)

> **The electric force on a charged body is exerted by the electric field created by *other* charged bodies.**

To find out experimentally whether there is an electric field at a particular point, we place a small charged body, which we call a **test charge,** at the point (Fig. 21.15c). If the test charge experiences an electric force, then there is an electric field at that point. This field is produced by charges other than q_0.

Force is a vector quantity, so electric field is also a vector quantity. (Note the use of vector signs as well as boldface letters and plus, minus, and equals signs in the following discussion.) We define the *electric field* $\vec{E}$ at a point as the electric force $\vec{F}_0$ experienced by a test charge q_0 at the point, divided by the charge q_0. That is, the electric field at a certain point is equal to the *electric force per unit charge* experienced by a charge at that point:

$$\vec{E} = \frac{\vec{F}_0}{q_0} \quad \text{(definition of electric field as electric force per unit charge)} \quad (21.3)$$

In SI units, in which the unit of force is 1 N and the unit of charge is 1 C, the unit of electric field magnitude is 1 newton per coulomb ($1\ \text{N/C}$).

If the field $\vec{E}$ at a certain point is known, rearranging Eq. (21.3) gives the force $\vec{F}_0$ experienced by a point charge q_0 placed at that point. This force is just equal to the electric field $\vec{E}$ produced at that point by charges other than q_0, multiplied by the charge q_0:

$$\vec{F}_0 = q_0 \vec{E} \quad \text{(force exerted on a point charge } q_0 \text{ by an electric field } \vec{E}) \quad (21.4)$$

21.15 A charged body creates an electric field in the space around it.

(a) A and B exert electric forces on each other.

(b) Remove body B ...

... and label its former position as P.

(c) Body A sets up an electric field $\vec{E}$ at point P.

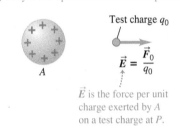

$\vec{E}$ is the force per unit charge exerted by A on a test charge at P.

Application Sharks and the "Sixth Sense"
Sharks have the ability to locate prey (such as flounder and other bottom-dwelling fish) that are completely hidden beneath the sand at the bottom of the ocean. They do this by sensing the weak electric fields produced by muscle contractions in their prey. Sharks derive their sensitivity to electric fields (a "sixth sense") from jelly-filled canals in their bodies. These canals end in pores on the shark's skin (shown in this photograph). An electric field as weak as 5×10^{-7} N/C causes charge flow within the canals and triggers a signal in the shark's nervous system. Because the shark has canals with different orientations, it can measure different components of the electric-field vector and hence determine the direction of the field.

21.16 The force $\vec{F}_0 = q_0 \vec{E}$ exerted on a point charge q_0 placed in an electric field $\vec{E}$.

The force on a positive test charge q_0 points in the direction of the electric field.

The force on a negative test charge q_0 points opposite to the electric field.

ActivPhysics 11.4: Electric Field: Point Charge
ActivPhysics 11.9: Motion of a Charge in an Electric Field: Introduction
ActivPhysics 11.10: Motion in an Electric Field: Problems

The charge q_0 can be either positive or negative. If q_0 is *positive,* the force $\vec{F}_0$ experienced by the charge is the same direction as $\vec{E}$; if q_0 is *negative,* $\vec{F}_0$ and $\vec{E}$ are in opposite directions (Fig. 21.16).

While the electric field concept may be new to you, the basic idea—that one body sets up a field in the space around it and a second body responds to that field—is one that you've actually used before. Compare Eq. (21.4) to the familiar expression for the gravitational force $\vec{F}_g$ that the earth exerts on a mass m_0:

$$\vec{F}_g = m_0\vec{g} \qquad (21.5)$$

In this expression, $\vec{g}$ is the acceleration due to gravity. If we divide both sides of Eq. (21.5) by the mass m_0, we obtain

$$\vec{g} = \frac{\vec{F}_g}{m_0}$$

Thus $\vec{g}$ can be regarded as the gravitational force per unit mass. By analogy to Eq. (21.3), we can interpret $\vec{g}$ as the *gravitational field.* Thus we treat the gravitational interaction between the earth and the mass m_0 as a two-stage process: The earth sets up a gravitational field $\vec{g}$ in the space around it, and this gravitational field exerts a force given by Eq. (21.5) on the mass m_0 (which we can regard as a *test mass*). The gravitational field $\vec{g}$, or gravitational force per unit mass, is a useful concept because it does not depend on the mass of the body on which the gravitational force is exerted; likewise, the electric field $\vec{E}$, or electric force per unit charge, is useful because it does not depend on the charge of the body on which the electric force is exerted.

CAUTION $\vec{F}_0 = q_0 \vec{E}_0$ **is for *point* test charges only** The electric force experienced by a test charge q_0 can vary from point to point, so the electric field can also be different at different points. For this reason, Eq. (21.4) can be used only to find the electric force on a *point* charge. If a charged body is large enough in size, the electric field $\vec{E}$ may be noticeably different in magnitude and direction at different points on the body, and calculating the net electric force on the body can become rather complicated.

Electric Field of a Point Charge

If the source distribution is a point charge q, it is easy to find the electric field that it produces. We call the location of the charge the **source point,** and we call the point P where we are determining the field the **field point.** It is also useful to introduce a *unit vector* $\hat{r}$ that points along the line from source point to field point (Fig. 21.17a). This unit vector is equal to the displacement vector $\vec{r}$ from the source point to the field point, divided by the distance $r = |\vec{r}|$ between these two points; that is, $\hat{r} = \vec{r}/r$. If we place a small test charge q_0 at the field point P, at a

21.17 The electric field $\vec{E}$ produced at point P by an isolated point charge q at S. Note that in both (b) and (c), $\vec{E}$ is *produced* by q [see Eq. (21.7)] but *acts* on the charge q_0 at point P [see Eq. (21.4)].

(a)

Unit vector $\hat{r}$ points from source point S to field point P.

(b)

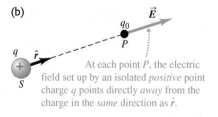

At each point P, the electric field set up by an isolated *positive* point charge q points directly *away* from the charge in the *same* direction as $\hat{r}$.

(c)

At each point P, the electric field set up by an isolated *negative* point charge q points directly *toward* the charge in the *opposite* direction from $\hat{r}$.

distance r from the source point, the magnitude F_0 of the force is given by Coulomb's law, Eq. (21.2):

$$F_0 = \frac{1}{4\pi\epsilon_0} \frac{|qq_0|}{r^2}$$

From Eq. (21.3) the magnitude E of the electric field at P is

$$E = \frac{1}{4\pi\epsilon_0} \frac{|q|}{r^2} \quad \text{(magnitude of electric field of a point charge)} \quad (21.6)$$

Using the unit vector $\hat{r}$, we can write a *vector* equation that gives both the magnitude and direction of the electric field $\vec{E}$:

$$\vec{E} = \frac{1}{4\pi\epsilon_0} \frac{q}{r^2} \hat{r} \quad \text{(electric field of a point charge)} \quad (21.7)$$

By definition, the electric field of a point charge always points *away from* a positive charge (that is, in the same direction as $\hat{r}$; see Fig. 21.17b) but *toward* a negative charge (that is, in the direction opposite $\hat{r}$; see Fig. 21.17c).

We have emphasized calculating the electric field $\vec{E}$ at a certain point. But since $\vec{E}$ can vary from point to point, it is not a single vector quantity but rather an *infinite* set of vector quantities, one associated with each point in space. This is an example of a **vector field.** Figure 21.18 shows a number of the field vectors produced by a positive or negative point charge. If we use a rectangular (x, y, z) coordinate system, each component of $\vec{E}$ at any point is in general a function of the coordinates (x, y, z) of the point. We can represent the functions as $E_x(x, y, z)$, $E_y(x, y, z)$, and $E_z(x, y, z)$. Vector fields are an important part of the language of physics, not just in electricity and magnetism. One everyday example of a vector field is the velocity $\vec{v}$ of wind currents; the magnitude and direction of $\vec{v}$, and hence its vector components, vary from point to point in the atmosphere.

In some situations the magnitude and direction of the field (and hence its vector components) have the same values everywhere throughout a certain region; we then say that the field is *uniform* in this region. An important example of this is the electric field inside a *conductor*. If there is an electric field within a conductor, the field exerts a force on every charge in the conductor, giving the free charges a net motion. By definition an electrostatic situation is one in which the charges have *no* net motion. We conclude that *in electrostatics the electric field at every point within the material of a conductor must be zero.* (Note that we are not saying that the field is necessarily zero in a *hole* inside a conductor.)

In summary, our description of electric interactions has two parts. First, a given charge distribution acts as a source of electric field. Second, the electric field exerts a force on any charge that is present in the field. Our analysis often has two corresponding steps: first, calculating the field caused by a source charge distribution; second, looking at the effect of the field in terms of force and motion. The second step often involves Newton's laws as well as the principles of electric interactions. In the next section we show how to calculate fields caused by various source distributions, but first here are three examples of calculating the field due to a point charge and of finding the force on a charge due to a given field $\vec{E}$.

21.18 A point charge q produces an electric field $\vec{E}$ at *all* points in space. The field strength decreases with increasing distance.

(a) The field produced by a positive point charge points *away from* the charge.

(b) The field produced by a negative point charge points *toward* the charge.

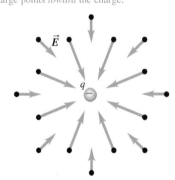

Example 21.5   **Electric-field magnitude for a point charge**

What is the magnitude of the electric field $\vec{E}$ at a field point 2.0 m from a point charge $q = 4.0$ nC?

SOLUTION

IDENTIFY and SET UP: This problem concerns the electric field due to a point charge. We are given the magnitude of the charge

Continued

and the distance from the charge to the field point, so we use Eq. (21.6) to calculate the field magnitude E.

EXECUTE: From Eq. (21.6),

$$E = \frac{1}{4\pi\epsilon_0}\frac{|q|}{r^2} = (9.0 \times 10^9 \text{ N} \cdot \text{m}^2/\text{C}^2)\frac{4.0 \times 10^{-9} \text{ C}}{(2.0 \text{ m})^2}$$

$$= 9.0 \text{ N/C}$$

EVALUATE: Our result $E = 9.0$ N/C means that if we placed a 1.0-C charge at a point 2.0 m from q, it would experience a 9.0-N force. The force on a 2.0-C charge at that point would be $(2.0 \text{ C})(9.0 \text{ N/C}) = 18$ N, and so on.

Example 21.6 Electric-field vector for a point charge

A point charge $q = -8.0$ nC is located at the origin. Find the electric-field vector at the field point $x = 1.2$ m, $y = -1.6$ m.

SOLUTION

IDENTIFY and SET UP: We must find the electric-field *vector* $\vec{E}$ due to a point charge. Figure 21.19 shows the situation. We use Eq. (21.7); to do this, we must find the distance r from the source point S (the position of the charge q, which in this example is at the origin O) to the field point P, and we must obtain an expression for the unit vector $\hat{r} = \vec{r}/r$ that points from S to P.

EXECUTE: The distance from S to P is

$$r = \sqrt{x^2 + y^2} = \sqrt{(1.2 \text{ m})^2 + (-1.6 \text{ m})^2} = 2.0 \text{ m}$$

The unit vector $\hat{r}$ is then

$$\hat{r} = \frac{\vec{r}}{r} = \frac{x\hat{i} + y\hat{j}}{r}$$

$$= \frac{(1.2 \text{ m})\hat{i} + (-1.6 \text{ m})\hat{j}}{2.0 \text{ m}} = 0.60\hat{i} - 0.80\hat{j}$$

Then, from Eq. (21.7),

$$\vec{E} = \frac{1}{4\pi\epsilon_0}\frac{q}{r^2}\hat{r}$$

$$= (9.0 \times 10^9 \text{ N} \cdot \text{m}^2/\text{C}^2)\frac{(-8.0 \times 10^{-9} \text{ C})}{(2.0 \text{ m})^2}(0.60\hat{i} - 0.80\hat{j})$$

$$= (-11 \text{ N/C})\hat{i} + (14 \text{ N/C})\hat{j}$$

EVALUATE: Since q is negative, $\vec{E}$ points from the field point to the charge (the source point), in the direction opposite to $\hat{r}$ (compare Fig. 21.17c). We leave the calculation of the magnitude and direction of $\vec{E}$ to you (see Exercise 21.36).

21.19 Our sketch for this problem.

Example 21.7 Electron in a uniform field

When the terminals of a battery are connected to two parallel conducting plates with a small gap between them, the resulting charges on the plates produce a nearly uniform electric field $\vec{E}$ between the plates. (In the next section we'll see why this is.) If the plates are 1.0 cm apart and are connected to a 100-volt battery as shown in Fig. 21.20, the field is vertically upward and has magnitude $E = 1.00 \times 10^4$ N/C. (a) If an electron (charge $-e = -1.60 \times 10^{-9}$ C, mass $m = 9.11 \times 10^{-31}$ kg) is released from rest at the upper plate, what is its acceleration? (b) What speed and kinetic energy does it acquire while traveling 1.0 cm to the lower plate? (c) How long does it take to travel this distance?

SOLUTION

IDENTIFY and SET UP: This example involves the relationship between electric field and electric force. It also involves the relationship between force and acceleration, the definition of kinetic energy, and the kinematic relationships among acceleration, distance, velocity, and time. Figure 21.20 shows our coordinate system. We are given the electric field, so we use Eq. (21.4) to find the force on the electron and Newton's second law to find its acceleration. Because the field is uniform, the force is constant and we can use the constant-acceleration formulas from Chapter 2 to find the electron's velocity and travel time. We find the kinetic energy using $K = \frac{1}{2}mv^2$.

21.20 A uniform electric field between two parallel conducting plates connected to a 100-volt battery. (The separation of the plates is exaggerated in this figure relative to the dimensions of the plates.)

The thin arrows represent the uniform electric field.

EXECUTE: (a) Although $\vec{E}$ is upward (in the $+y$-direction), $\vec{F}$ is downward (because the electron's charge is negative) and so F_y is negative. Because F_y is constant, the electron's acceleration is constant:

$$a_y = \frac{F_y}{m} = \frac{-eE}{m} = \frac{(-1.60 \times 10^{-19} \text{ C})(1.00 \times 10^4 \text{ N/C})}{9.11 \times 10^{-31} \text{ kg}}$$

$$= -1.76 \times 10^{15} \text{ m/s}^2$$

(b) The electron starts from rest, so its motion is in the y-direction only (the direction of the acceleration). We can find the electron's speed at any position y using the constant-acceleration Eq. (2.13), $v_y^2 = v_{0y}^2 + 2a_y(y - y_0)$. We have $v_{0y} = 0$ and $y_0 = 0$, so at $y = -1.0 \text{ cm} = -1.0 \times 10^{-2} \text{ m}$ we have

$$|v_y| = \sqrt{2a_y y} = \sqrt{2(-1.76 \times 10^{15} \text{ m/s}^2)(-1.0 \times 10^{-2} \text{ m})}$$

$$= 5.9 \times 10^6 \text{ m/s}$$

The velocity is downward, so $v_y = -5.9 \times 10^6$ m/s. The electron's kinetic energy is

$$K = \tfrac{1}{2}mv^2 = \tfrac{1}{2}(9.11 \times 10^{-31} \text{ kg})(5.9 \times 10^6 \text{ m/s})^2$$

$$= 1.6 \times 10^{-17} \text{ J}$$

(c) From Eq. (2.8) for constant acceleration, $v_y = v_{0y} + a_y t$,

$$t = \frac{v_y - v_{0y}}{a_y} = \frac{(-5.9 \times 10^6 \text{ m/s}) - (0 \text{ m/s})}{-1.76 \times 10^{15} \text{ m/s}^2}$$

$$= 3.4 \times 10^{-9} \text{ s}$$

EVALUATE: Our results show that in problems concerning subatomic particles such as electrons, many quantities—including acceleration, speed, kinetic energy, and time—will have *very* different values from those typical of everyday objects such as baseballs and automobiles.

Test Your Understanding of Section 21.4 (a) A negative point charge moves along a straight-line path directly toward a stationary positive point charge. Which aspect(s) of the electric force on the negative point charge will remain constant as it moves? (i) magnitude; (ii) direction; (iii) both magnitude and direction; (iv) neither magnitude nor direction. (b) A negative point charge moves along a circular orbit around a positive point charge. Which aspect(s) of the electric force on the negative point charge will remain constant as it moves? (i) magnitude; (ii) direction; (iii) both magnitude and direction; (iv) neither magnitude nor direction. ❙

21.5 Electric-Field Calculations

Equation (21.7) gives the electric field caused by a single point charge. But in most realistic situations that involve electric fields and forces, we encounter charge that is *distributed* over space. The charged plastic and glass rods in Fig. 21.1 have electric charge distributed over their surfaces, as does the imaging drum of a laser printer (Fig. 21.2). In this section we'll learn to calculate electric fields caused by various distributions of electric charge. Calculations of this kind are of tremendous importance for technological applications of electric forces. To determine the trajectories of atomic nuclei in an accelerator for cancer radiotherapy or of charged particles in a semiconductor electronic device, you have to know the detailed nature of the electric field acting on the charges.

ActivPhysics 11.5: Electric Field Due to a Dipole
ActivPhysics 11.6: Electric Field: Problems

The Superposition of Electric Fields

To find the field caused by a charge distribution, we imagine the distribution to be made up of many point charges $q_1, q_2, q_3, \ldots$. (This is actually quite a realistic description, since we have seen that charge is carried by electrons and protons that are so small as to be almost pointlike.) At any given point P, each point charge produces its own electric field $\vec{E}_1, \vec{E}_2, \vec{E}_3, \ldots$, so a test charge q_0 placed at P experiences a force $\vec{F}_1 = q_0\vec{E}_1$ from charge q_1, a force $\vec{F}_2 = q_0\vec{E}_2$ from charge q_2, and so on. From the principle of superposition of forces discussed in Section 21.3, the *total* force $\vec{F}_0$ that the charge distribution exerts on q_0 is the vector sum of these individual forces:

$$\vec{F}_0 = \vec{F}_1 + \vec{F}_2 + \vec{F}_3 + \cdots = q_0\vec{E}_1 + q_0\vec{E}_2 + q_0\vec{E}_3 + \cdots$$

The combined effect of all the charges in the distribution is described by the *total* electric field $\vec{E}$ at point P. From the definition of electric field, Eq. (21.3), this is

$$\vec{E} = \frac{\vec{F}_0}{q_0} = \vec{E}_1 + \vec{E}_2 + \vec{E}_3 + \cdots$$

21.21 Illustrating the principle of superposition of electric fields.

The total electric field $\vec{E}$ at point P is the vector sum of $\vec{E}_1$ and $\vec{E}_2$.

The total electric field at P is the vector sum of the fields at P due to each point charge in the charge distribution (Fig. 21.21). This is the **principle of superposition of electric fields.**

When charge is distributed along a line, over a surface, or through a volume, a few additional terms are useful. For a line charge distribution (such as a long, thin, charged plastic rod), we use λ (the Greek letter lambda) to represent the **linear charge density** (charge per unit length, measured in C/m). When charge is distributed over a surface (such as the surface of the imaging drum of a laser printer), we use σ (sigma) to represent the **surface charge density** (charge per unit area, measured in C/m^2). And when charge is distributed through a volume, we use ρ (rho) to represent the **volume charge density** (charge per unit volume, C/m^3).

Some of the calculations in the following examples may look fairly intricate. After you've worked through the examples one step at a time, the process will seem less formidable. We will use many of the calculational techniques in these examples in Chapter 28 to calculate the *magnetic* fields caused by charges in motion.

Problem-Solving Strategy 21.2 | **Electric-Field Calculations**

IDENTIFY *the relevant concepts:* Use the principle of superposition to calculate the electric field due to a discrete or continuous charge distribution.

SET UP *the problem* using the following steps:
1. Make a drawing showing the locations of the charges and your choice of coordinate axes.
2. On your drawing, indicate the position of the *field point P* (the point at which you want to calculate the electric field $\vec{E}$).

EXECUTE *the solution* as follows:
1. Use consistent units. Distances must be in meters and charge must be in coulombs. If you are given centimeters or nanocoulombs, don't forget to convert.
2. Distinguish between the source point S and the field point P. The field produced by a point charge always points from S to P if the charge is positive, and from P to S if the charge is negative.
3. Use *vector* addition when applying the principle of superposition; review the treatment of vector addition in Chapter 1 if necessary.

4. Simplify your calculations by exploiting any symmetries in the charge distribution.
5. If the charge distribution is continuous, define a small element of charge that can be considered as a point, find its electric field at P, and find a way to add the fields of all the charge elements by doing an integral. Usually it is easiest to do this for each component of $\vec{E}$ separately, so you may need to evaluate more than one integral. Ensure that the limits on your integrals are correct; especially when the situation has symmetry, don't count a charge twice.

EVALUATE *your answer:* Check that the direction of $\vec{E}$ is reasonable. If your result for the electric-field magnitude E is a function of position (say, the coordinate x), check your result in any limits for which you know what the magnitude should be. When possible, check your answer by calculating it in a different way.

Example 21.8 | **Field of an electric dipole**

Point charges $q_1 = +12$ nC and $q_2 = -12$ nC are 0.100 m apart (Fig. 21.22). (Such pairs of point charges with equal magnitude and opposite sign are called *electric dipoles*.) Compute the electric field caused by q_1, the field caused by q_2, and the total field (a) at point a; (b) at point b; and (c) at point c.

SOLUTION

IDENTIFY and SET UP: We must find the total electric field at various points due to two point charges. We use the principle of superposition: $\vec{E} = \vec{E}_1 + \vec{E}_2$. Figure 21.22 shows the coordinate system and the locations of the field points a, b, and c.

EXECUTE: At each field point, $\vec{E}$ depends on $\vec{E}_1$ and $\vec{E}_2$ there; we first calculate the magnitudes E_1 and E_2 at each field point. At a the magnitude of the field $\vec{E}_{1a}$ caused by q_1 is

$$E_{1a} = \frac{1}{4\pi\epsilon_0}\frac{|q_1|}{r^2} = (9.0 \times 10^9 \text{ N}\cdot\text{m}^2/\text{C}^2)\frac{12 \times 10^{-9} \text{ C}}{(0.060 \text{ m})^2}$$

$$= 3.0 \times 10^4 \text{ N/C}$$

We calculate the other field magnitudes in a similar way. The results are

$$E_{1a} = 3.0 \times 10^4 \text{ N/C} \qquad E_{1b} = 6.8 \times 10^4 \text{ N/C}$$
$$E_{1c} = 6.39 \times 10^3 \text{ N/C}$$

$$E_{2a} = 6.8 \times 10^4 \text{ N/C} \qquad E_{2b} = 0.55 \times 10^4 \text{ N/C}$$
$$E_{2c} = E_{1c} = 6.39 \times 10^3 \text{ N/C}$$

The *directions* of the corresponding fields are in all cases *away* from the positive charge q_1 and *toward* the negative charge q_2.

21.22 Electric field at three points, a, b, and c, set up by charges q_1 and q_2, which form an electric dipole.

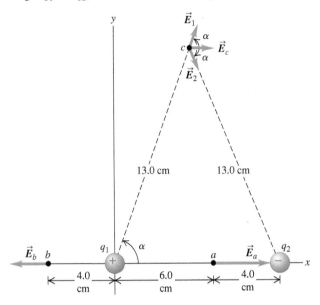

(a) At a, $\vec{E}_{1a}$ and $\vec{E}_{2a}$ are both directed to the right, so

$$\vec{E}_a = E_{1a}\hat{\imath} + E_{2a}\hat{\imath} = (9.8 \times 10^4 \text{ N/C})\hat{\imath}$$

(b) At b, $\vec{E}_{1b}$ is directed to the left and $\vec{E}_{2b}$ is directed to the right, so

$$\vec{E}_b = -E_{1b}\hat{\imath} + E_{2b}\hat{\imath} = (-6.2 \times 10^4 \text{ N/C})\hat{\imath}$$

(c) Figure 21.22 shows the directions of $\vec{E}_1$ and $\vec{E}_2$ at c. Both vectors have the same x-component:

$$E_{1cx} = E_{2cx} = E_{1c}\cos\alpha = (6.39 \times 10^3 \text{ N/C})\left(\tfrac{5}{13}\right)$$

$$= 2.46 \times 10^3 \text{ N/C}$$

From symmetry, E_{1y} and E_{2y} are equal and opposite, so their sum is zero. Hence

$$\vec{E}_c = 2(2.46 \times 10^3 \text{ N/C})\hat{\imath} = (4.9 \times 10^3 \text{ N/C})\hat{\imath}$$

EVALUATE: We can also find $\vec{E}_c$ using Eq. (21.7) for the field of a point charge. The displacement vector $\vec{r}_1$ from q_1 to point c is $\vec{r}_1 = r\cos\alpha\hat{\imath} + r\sin\alpha\hat{\jmath}$. Hence the unit vector that points from q_1 to point c is $\hat{r}_1 = \vec{r}_1/r = \cos\alpha\hat{\imath} + \sin\alpha\hat{\jmath}$. By symmetry, the unit vector that points from q_2 to point c has the opposite x-component but the same y-component: $\hat{r}_2 = -\cos\alpha\hat{\imath} + \sin\alpha\hat{\jmath}$. We can now use Eq. (21.7) to write the fields $\vec{E}_{1c}$ and $\vec{E}_{2c}$ at c in vector form, then find their sum. Since $q_2 = -q_1$ and the distance r to c is the same for both charges,

$$\vec{E}_c = \vec{E}_{1c} + \vec{E}_{2c} = \frac{1}{4\pi\epsilon_0}\frac{q_1}{r^2}\hat{r}_1 + \frac{1}{4\pi\epsilon_0}\frac{q_2}{r^2}\hat{r}_2$$

$$= \frac{1}{4\pi\epsilon_0 r^2}(q_1\hat{r}_1 + q_2\hat{r}_2) = \frac{q_1}{4\pi\epsilon_0 r^2}(\hat{r}_1 - \hat{r}_2)$$

$$= \frac{1}{4\pi\epsilon_0}\frac{q_1}{r^2}(2\cos\alpha\hat{\imath})$$

$$= 2(9.0 \times 10^9 \text{ N}\cdot\text{m}^2/\text{C}^2)\frac{12 \times 10^{-9} \text{ C}}{(0.13 \text{ m})^2}\left(\tfrac{5}{13}\right)\hat{\imath}$$

$$= (4.9 \times 10^3 \text{ N/C})\hat{\imath}$$

This is the same as we calculated in part (c).

Example 21.9   Field of a ring of charge

Charge Q is uniformly distributed around a conducting ring of radius a (Fig. 21.23). Find the electric field at a point P on the ring axis at a distance x from its center.

SOLUTION

IDENTIFY and SET UP: This is a problem in the superposition of electric fields. Each bit of charge around the ring produces an electric field at an arbitrary point on the x-axis; our target variable is the total field at this point due to all such bits of charge.

21.23 Calculating the electric field on the axis of a ring of charge. In this figure, the charge is assumed to be positive.

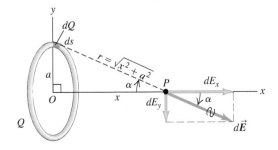

EXECUTE: We divide the ring into infinitesimal segments ds as shown in Fig. 21.23. In terms of the linear charge density $\lambda = Q/2\pi a$, the charge in a segment of length ds is $dQ = \lambda\, ds$. Consider two identical segments, one as shown in the figure at $y = a$ and another halfway around the ring at $y = -a$. From Example 21.4, we see that the net force $d\vec{F}$ they exert on a point test charge at P, and thus their net field $d\vec{E}$, are directed along the x-axis. The same is true for any such pair of segments around the ring, so the *net* field at P is along the x-axis: $\vec{E} = E_x\hat{\imath}$.

To calculate E_x, note that the square of the distance r from a single ring segment to the point P is $r^2 = x^2 + a^2$. Hence the magnitude of this segment's contribution $d\vec{E}$ to the electric field at P is

$$dE = \frac{1}{4\pi\epsilon_0}\frac{dQ}{x^2 + a^2}$$

The x-component of this field is $dE_x = dE\cos\alpha$. We know $dQ = \lambda\, ds$ and Fig. 21.23 shows that $\cos\alpha = x/r = x/(x^2 + a^2)^{1/2}$, so

$$dE_x = dE\cos\alpha = \frac{1}{4\pi\epsilon_0}\frac{dQ}{x^2 + a^2}\frac{x}{\sqrt{x^2 + a^2}}$$

$$= \frac{1}{4\pi\epsilon_0}\frac{\lambda x}{(x^2 + a^2)^{3/2}}ds$$

Continued

To find E_x we integrate this expression over the entire ring—that is, for s from 0 to $2\pi a$ (the circumference of the ring). The integrand has the same value for all points on the ring, so it can be taken outside the integral. Hence we get

$$E_x = \int dE_x = \frac{1}{4\pi\epsilon_0}\frac{\lambda x}{(x^2 + a^2)^{3/2}}\int_0^{2\pi a} ds$$

$$= \frac{1}{4\pi\epsilon_0}\frac{\lambda x}{(x^2 + a^2)^{3/2}}(2\pi a)$$

$$\vec{E} = E_x\hat{i} = \frac{1}{4\pi\epsilon_0}\frac{Qx}{(x^2 + a^2)^{3/2}}\hat{i} \qquad (21.8)$$

EVALUATE: Equation (21.8) shows that $\vec{E} = 0$ at the center of the ring ($x = 0$). This makes sense; charges on opposite sides of the ring push in opposite directions on a test charge at the center, and the vector sum of each such pair of forces is zero. When the field point P is much farther from the ring than the ring's radius, we have $x \gg a$ and the denominator in Eq. (21.8) becomes approximately equal to x^3. In this limit the electric field at P is

$$\vec{E} = \frac{1}{4\pi\epsilon_0}\frac{Q}{x^2}\hat{i}$$

That is, when the ring is so far away that its radius is negligible in comparison to the distance x, its field is the same as that of a point charge.

Example 21.10 Field of a charged line segment

Positive charge Q is distributed uniformly along the y-axis between $y = -a$ and $y = +a$. Find the electric field at point P on the x-axis at a distance x from the origin.

SOLUTION

IDENTIFY and SET UP: Figure 21.24 shows the situation. As in Example 21.9, we must find the electric field due to a continuous distribution of charge. Our target variable is an expression for the electric field at P as a function of x. The x-axis is a perpendicular bisector of the segment, so we can use a symmetry argument.

EXECUTE: We divide the line charge of length $2a$ into infinitesimal segments of length dy. The linear charge density is $\lambda = Q/2a$, and the charge in a segment is $dQ = \lambda\, dy = (Q/2a)dy$. The distance r from a segment at height y to the field point P is $r = (x^2 + y^2)^{1/2}$, so the magnitude of the field at P due to the segment at height y is

$$dE = \frac{1}{4\pi\epsilon_0}\frac{dQ}{r^2} = \frac{1}{4\pi\epsilon_0}\frac{Q}{2a}\frac{dy}{(x^2 + y^2)}$$

Figure 21.24 shows that the x- and y-components of this field are $dE_x = dE\cos\alpha$ and $dE_y = -dE\sin\alpha$, where $\cos\alpha = x/r$ and $\sin\alpha = y/r$. Hence

$$dE_x = \frac{1}{4\pi\epsilon_0}\frac{Q}{2a}\frac{x\,dy}{(x^2 + y^2)^{3/2}}$$

$$dE_y = \frac{1}{4\pi\epsilon_0}\frac{Q}{2a}\frac{y\,dy}{(x^2 + y^2)^{3/2}}$$

To find the total field at P, we must sum the fields from all segments along the line—that is, we must integrate from $y = -a$ to $y = +a$. You should work out the details of the integration (a table of integrals will help). The results are

$$E_x = \frac{1}{4\pi\epsilon_0}\frac{Q}{2a}\int_{-a}^{+a}\frac{x\,dy}{(x^2 + y^2)^{3/2}} = \frac{Q}{4\pi\epsilon_0}\frac{1}{x\sqrt{x^2 + a^2}}$$

$$E_y = \frac{1}{4\pi\epsilon_0}\frac{Q}{2a}\int_{-a}^{+a}\frac{y\,dy}{(x^2 + y^2)^{3/2}} = 0$$

or, in vector form,

$$\vec{E} = \frac{1}{4\pi\epsilon_0}\frac{Q}{x\sqrt{x^2 + a^2}}\hat{i} \qquad (21.9)$$

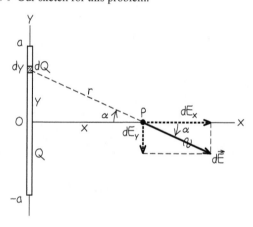

21.24 Our sketch for this problem.

$\vec{E}$ points away from the line of charge if λ is positive and toward the line of charge if λ is negative.

EVALUATE: Using a symmetry argument as in Example 21.9, we could have guessed that E_y would be zero; if we place a positive test charge at P, the upper half of the line of charge pushes downward on it, and the lower half pushes up with equal magnitude. Symmetry also tells us that the upper and lower halves of the segment contribute equally to the total field at P.

If the segment is very *short* (or the field point is very far from the segment) so that $x \gg a$, we can neglect a in the denominator of Eq. (21.9). Then the field becomes that of a point charge, just as in Example 21.9:

$$\vec{E} = \frac{1}{4\pi\epsilon_0}\frac{Q}{x^2}\hat{i}$$

To see what happens if the segment is very *long* (or the field point is very close to it) so that $a \gg x$, we first rewrite Eq. (21.9) slightly:

$$\vec{E} = \frac{1}{2\pi\epsilon_0}\frac{\lambda}{x\sqrt{(x^2/a^2) + 1}}\hat{i} \qquad (21.10)$$

In the limit $a \gg x$ we can neglect x^2/a^2 in the denominator of Eq. (21.10), so

$$\vec{E} = \frac{\lambda}{2\pi\epsilon_0 x}\hat{i}$$

This is the field of an *infinitely long* line of charge. At any point P at a perpendicular distance r from the line in *any* direction, $\vec{E}$ has magnitude

$$E = \frac{\lambda}{2\pi\epsilon_0 r} \qquad \text{(infinite line of charge)}$$

Note that this field is proportional to $1/r$ rather than to $1/r^2$ as for a point charge.

There's really no such thing in nature as an infinite line of charge. But when the field point is close enough to the line, there's very little difference between the result for an infinite line and the real-life finite case. For example, if the distance r of the field point from the center of the line is 1% of the length of the line, the value of E differs from the infinite-length value by less than 0.02%.

Example 21.11 Field of a uniformly charged disk

A nonconducting disk of radius R has a uniform positive surface charge density σ. Find the electric field at a point along the axis of the disk a distance x from its center. Assume that x is positive.

SOLUTION

IDENTIFY and SET UP: Figure 21.25 shows the situation. We represent the charge distribution as a collection of concentric rings of charge dQ. In Example 21.9 we obtained Eq. (21.8) for the field on the axis of a single uniformly charged ring, so all we need do here is integrate the contributions of our rings.

EXECUTE: A typical ring has charge dQ, inner radius r, and outer radius $r + dr$. Its area is approximately equal to its width dr times its circumference $2\pi r$, or $dA = 2\pi r\, dr$. The charge per unit area is $\sigma = dQ/dA$, so the charge of the ring is $dQ = \sigma\, dA = 2\pi\sigma r\, dr$. We use dQ in place of Q in Eq. (21.8), the expression for the field due to a ring that we found in Example 21.9, and replace the ring radius a with r. Then the field component dE_x at point P due to this ring is

$$dE_x = \frac{1}{4\pi\epsilon_0} \frac{2\pi\sigma rx\, dr}{(x^2 + r^2)^{3/2}}$$

21.25 Our sketch for this problem.

To find the total field due to all the rings, we integrate dE_x over r from $r = 0$ to $r = R$ (*not* from $-R$ to R):

$$E_x = \int_0^R \frac{1}{4\pi\epsilon_0} \frac{(2\pi\sigma r\, dr)x}{(x^2 + r^2)^{3/2}} = \frac{\sigma x}{4\epsilon_0} \int_0^R \frac{2r\, dr}{(x^2 + r^2)^{3/2}}$$

You can evaluate this integral by making the substitution $t = x^2 + r^2$ (which yields $dt = 2r\, dr$); you can work out the details. The result is

$$E_x = \frac{\sigma x}{2\epsilon_0}\left[-\frac{1}{\sqrt{x^2 + R^2}} + \frac{1}{x} \right]$$

$$= \frac{\sigma}{2\epsilon_0}\left[1 - \frac{1}{\sqrt{(R^2/x^2) + 1}} \right] \qquad (21.11)$$

EVALUATE: If the disk is very large (or if we are very close to it), so that $R \gg x$, the term $1/\sqrt{(R^2/x^2) + 1}$ in Eq. (21.11) is very much less than 1. Then Eq. (21.11) becomes

$$E = \frac{\sigma}{2\epsilon_0} \qquad (21.12)$$

Our final result does not contain the distance x from the plane. Hence the electric field produced by an *infinite* plane sheet of charge is *independent of the distance from the sheet*. The field direction is everywhere perpendicular to the sheet, away from it. There is no such thing as an infinite sheet of charge, but if the dimensions of the sheet are much larger than the distance x of the field point P from the sheet, the field is very nearly given by Eq. (21.12).

If P is to the *left* of the plane ($x < 0$), the result is the same except that the direction of $\vec{E}$ is to the left instead of the right. If the surface charge density is negative, the directions of the fields on both sides of the plane are toward it rather than away from it.

Example 21.12 Field of two oppositely charged infinite sheets

Two infinite plane sheets with uniform surface charge densities $+\sigma$ and $-\sigma$ are placed parallel to each other with separation d (Fig. 21.26). Find the electric field between the sheets, above the upper sheet, and below the lower sheet.

SOLUTION

IDENTIFY and SET UP: Equation (21.12) gives the electric field due to a single infinite plane sheet of charge. To find the field due to *two* such sheets, we combine the fields using the principle of superposition (Fig. 21.26).

21.26 Finding the electric field due to two oppositely charged infinite sheets. The sheets are seen edge-on; only a portion of the infinite sheets can be shown!

Continued

EXECUTE: From Eq. (21.12), both $\vec{E}_1$ and $\vec{E}_2$ have the same magnitude at all points, independent of distance from either sheet:

$$E_1 = E_2 = \frac{\sigma}{2\epsilon_0}$$

From Example 21.11, $\vec{E}_1$ is everywhere directed away from sheet 1, and $\vec{E}_2$ is everywhere directed toward sheet 2.

Between the sheets, $\vec{E}_1$ and $\vec{E}_2$ reinforce each other; above the upper sheet and below the lower sheet, they cancel each other. Thus the total field is

$$\vec{E} = \vec{E}_1 + \vec{E}_2 = \begin{cases} \mathbf{0} & \text{above the upper sheet} \\ \dfrac{\sigma}{\epsilon_0}\hat{\boldsymbol{j}} & \text{between the sheets} \\ \mathbf{0} & \text{below the lower sheet} \end{cases}$$

EVALUATE: Because we considered the sheets to be infinite, our result does not depend on the separation d. Our result shows that the field between oppositely charged plates is essentially uniform if the plate separation is much smaller than the dimensions of the plates. We actually used this result in Example 21.7 (Section 21.4).

CAUTION **Electric fields are not "flows"** You may have thought that the field $\vec{E}_1$ of sheet 1 would be unable to "penetrate" sheet 2, and that field $\vec{E}_2$ caused by sheet 2 would be unable to "penetrate" sheet 1. You might conclude this if you think of the electric field as some kind of physical substance that "flows" into or out of charges. But in fact there is no such substance, and the electric fields $\vec{E}_1$ and $\vec{E}_2$ depend only on the individual charge distributions that create them. The *total* field at every point is just the vector sum of $\vec{E}_1$ and $\vec{E}_2$. ▮

Test Your Understanding of Section 21.5 Suppose that the line of charge in Fig. 21.25 (Example 21.11) had charge $+Q$ distributed uniformly between $y = 0$ and $y = +a$ and had charge $-Q$ distributed uniformly between $y = 0$ and $y = -a$. In this situation, the electric field at P would be (i) in the positive x-direction; (ii) in the negative x-direction; (iii) in the positive y-direction; (iv) in the negative y-direction; (v) zero; (vi) none of these. ▮

21.6 Electric Field Lines

21.27 The direction of the electric field at any point is tangent to the field line through that point.

PhET: Charges and Fields
PhET: Electric Field of Dreams
PhET: Electric Field Hockey

The concept of an electric field can be a little elusive because you can't see an electric field directly. Electric field *lines* can be a big help for visualizing electric fields and making them seem more real. An **electric field line** is an imaginary line or curve drawn through a region of space so that its tangent at any point is in the direction of the electric-field vector at that point. Figure 21.27 shows the basic idea. (We used a similar concept in our discussion of fluid flow in Section 12.5. A *streamline* is a line or curve whose tangent at any point is in the direction of the velocity of the fluid at that point. However, the similarity between electric field lines and fluid streamlines is a mathematical one only; there is nothing "flowing" in an electric field.) The English scientist Michael Faraday (1791–1867) first introduced the concept of field lines. He called them "lines of force," but the term "field lines" is preferable.

Electric field lines show the direction of $\vec{E}$ at each point, and their spacing gives a general idea of the *magnitude* of $\vec{E}$ at each point. Where $\vec{E}$ is strong, we draw lines bunched closely together; where $\vec{E}$ is weaker, they are farther apart. At any particular point, the electric field has a unique direction, so only one field line can pass through each point of the field. In other words, *field lines never intersect*.

Figure 21.28 shows some of the electric field lines in a plane containing (a) a single positive charge; (b) two equal-magnitude charges, one positive and one negative (a dipole); and (c) two equal positive charges. Diagrams such as these are sometimes called *field maps;* they are cross sections of the actual three-dimensional patterns. The direction of the total electric field at every point in each diagram is along the tangent to the electric field line passing through the point. Arrowheads indicate the direction of the $\vec{E}$-field vector along each field line. The actual field vectors have been drawn at several points in each pattern. Notice that in general, the magnitude of the electric field is different at different points on a given field line; a field line is *not* a curve of constant electric-field magnitude!

Figure 21.28 shows that field lines are directed *away* from positive charges (since close to a positive point charge, $\vec{E}$ points away from the charge) and

21.28 Electric field lines for three different charge distributions. In general, the magnitude of $\vec{E}$ is different at different points along a given field line.

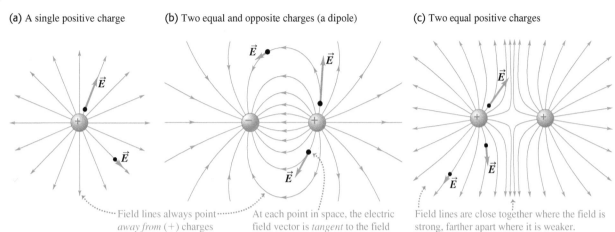

(a) A single positive charge

(b) Two equal and opposite charges (a dipole)

(c) Two equal positive charges

············ Field lines always point ············
away from (+) charges
and *toward* (−) charges.

At each point in space, the electric field vector is *tangent* to the field line passing through that point.

Field lines are close together where the field is strong, farther apart where it is weaker.

toward negative charges (since close to a negative point charge, $\vec{E}$ points toward the charge). In regions where the field magnitude is large, such as between the positive and negative charges in Fig. 21.28b, the field lines are drawn close together. In regions where the field magnitude is small, such as between the two positive charges in Fig. 21.28c, the lines are widely separated. In a *uniform* field, the field lines are straight, parallel, and uniformly spaced, as in Fig. 21.20.

Figure 21.29 is a view from above of a demonstration setup for visualizing electric field lines. In the arrangement shown here, the tips of two positively charged wires are inserted in a container of insulating liquid, and some grass seeds are floated on the liquid. The grass seeds are electrically neutral insulators, but the electric field of the two charged wires causes *polarization* of the grass seeds; there is a slight shifting of the positive and negative charges within the molecules of each seed, like that shown in Fig. 21.8. The positively charged end of each grass seed is pulled in the direction of $\vec{E}$ and the negatively charged end is pulled opposite $\vec{E}$. Hence the long axis of each grass seed tends to orient parallel to the electric field, in the direction of the field line that passes through the position of the seed (Fig. 21.29b).

> **CAUTION** **Electric field lines are not the same as trajectories** It's a common misconception that if a charged particle of charge q is in motion where there is an electric field, the particle must move along an electric field line. Because $\vec{E}$ at any point is tangent to the field line that passes through that point, it is indeed true that the *force* $\vec{F} = q\vec{E}$ on the particle, and hence the particle's acceleration, are tangent to the field line. But we learned in Chapter 3 that when a particle moves on a curved path, its acceleration *cannot* be tangent to the path. So in general, the trajectory of a charged particle is *not* the same as a field line. ▮

Test Your Understanding of Section 21.6 Suppose the electric field lines in a region of space are straight lines. If a charged particle is released from rest in that region, will the trajectory of the particle be along a field line? ▮

21.7 Electric Dipoles

An **electric dipole** is a pair of point charges with equal magnitude and opposite sign (a positive charge q and a negative charge $-q$) separated by a distance d. We introduced electric dipoles in Example 21.8 (Section 21.5); the concept is worth exploring further because many physical systems, from molecules to TV antennas, can be described as electric dipoles. We will also use this concept extensively in our discussion of dielectrics in Chapter 24.

21.29 (a) Electric field lines produced by two equal point charges. The pattern is formed by grass seeds floating on a liquid above two charged wires. Compare this pattern with Fig. 21.28c. (b) The electric field causes polarization of the grass seeds, which in turn causes the seeds to align with the field.

(a)

(b)

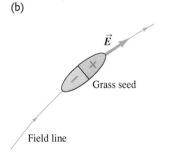

21.30 (a) A water molecule is an example of an electric dipole. (b) Each test tube contains a solution of a different substance in water. The large electric dipole moment of water makes it an excellent solvent.

(a) A water molecule, showing positive charge as red and negative charge as blue

The electric dipole moment $\vec{p}$ is directed from the negative end to the positive end of the molecule.

(b) Various substances dissolved in water

21.31 The net force on this electric dipole is zero, but there is a torque directed into the page that tends to rotate the dipole clockwise.

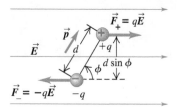

Figure 21.30 a shows a molecule of water (H_2O), which in many ways behaves like an electric dipole. The water molecule as a whole is electrically neutral, but the chemical bonds within the molecule cause a displacement of charge; the result is a net negative charge on the oxygen end of the molecule and a net positive charge on the hydrogen end, forming an electric dipole. The effect is equivalent to shifting one electron only about 4×10^{-11} m (about the radius of a hydrogen atom), but the consequences of this shift are profound. Water is an excellent solvent for ionic substances such as table salt (sodium chloride, NaCl) precisely because the water molecule is an electric dipole (Fig. 21.30b). When dissolved in water, salt dissociates into a positive sodium ion (Na^+) and a negative chlorine ion (Cl^-), which tend to be attracted to the negative and positive ends, respectively, of water molecules; this holds the ions in solution. If water molecules were not electric dipoles, water would be a poor solvent, and almost all of the chemistry that occurs in aqueous solutions would be impossible. This includes all of the biochemical reactions that occur in all of the life on earth. In a very real sense, your existence as a living being depends on electric dipoles!

We examine two questions about electric dipoles. First, what forces and torques does an electric dipole experience when placed in an external electric field (that is, a field set up by charges outside the dipole)? Second, what electric field does an electric dipole itself produce?

Force and Torque on an Electric Dipole

To start with the first question, let's place an electric dipole in a *uniform* external electric field $\vec{E}$, as shown in Fig. 21.31. The forces $\vec{F}_+$ and $\vec{F}_-$ on the two charges both have magnitude qE, but their directions are opposite, and they add to zero. *The net force on an electric dipole in a uniform external electric field is zero.*

However, the two forces don't act along the same line, so their *torques* don't add to zero. We calculate torques with respect to the center of the dipole. Let the angle between the electric field $\vec{E}$ and the dipole axis be ϕ; then the lever arm for both $\vec{F}_+$ and $\vec{F}_-$ is $(d/2) \sin \phi$. The torque of $\vec{F}_+$ and the torque of $\vec{F}_-$ both have the same magnitude of $(qE)(d/2) \sin \phi$, and both torques tend to rotate the dipole clockwise (that is, $\vec{\tau}$ is directed into the page in Fig. 21.31). Hence the magnitude of the net torque is twice the magnitude of either individual torque:

$$\tau = (qE)(d \sin \phi) \qquad [21.13]$$

where $d \sin \phi$ is the perpendicular distance between the lines of action of the two forces.

The product of the charge q and the separation d is the magnitude of a quantity called the **electric dipole moment**, denoted by p:

$$p = qd \qquad \text{(magnitude of electric dipole moment)} \qquad [21.14]$$

The units of p are charge times distance (C·m). For example, the magnitude of the electric dipole moment of a water molecule is $p = 6.13 \times 10^{-30}$ C·m.

CAUTION **The symbol p has multiple meanings** Be careful not to confuse dipole moment with momentum or pressure. There aren't as many letters in the alphabet as there are physical quantities, so some letters are used several times. The context usually makes it clear what we mean, but be careful.

We further define the electric dipole moment to be a *vector* quantity $\vec{p}$. The magnitude of $\vec{p}$ is given by Eq. (21.14), and its direction is along the dipole axis from the negative charge to the positive charge as shown in Fig. 21.31.

In terms of p, Eq. (21.13) for the magnitude τ of the torque exerted by the field becomes

$$\tau = pE \sin\phi \quad \text{(magnitude of the torque on an electric dipole)} \quad (21.15)$$

Since the angle ϕ in Fig. 21.31 is the angle between the directions of the vectors $\vec{p}$ and $\vec{E}$, this is reminiscent of the expression for the magnitude of the *vector product* discussed in Section 1.10. (You may want to review that discussion.) Hence we can write the torque on the dipole in vector form as

$$\vec{\tau} = \vec{p} \times \vec{E} \quad \text{(torque on an electric dipole, in vector form)} \quad (21.16)$$

You can use the right-hand rule for the vector product to verify that in the situation shown in Fig. 21.31, $\vec{\tau}$ is directed into the page. The torque is greatest when $\vec{p}$ and $\vec{E}$ are perpendicular and is zero when they are parallel or antiparallel. The torque always tends to turn $\vec{p}$ to line it up with $\vec{E}$. The position $\phi = 0$, with $\vec{p}$ parallel to $\vec{E}$, is a position of stable equilibrium, and the position $\phi = \pi$, with $\vec{p}$ and $\vec{E}$ antiparallel, is a position of unstable equilibrium. The polarization of a grass seed in the apparatus of Fig. 21.29b gives it an electric dipole moment; the torque exerted by $\vec{E}$ then causes the seed to align with $\vec{E}$ and hence with the field lines.

Potential Energy of an Electric Dipole

When a dipole changes direction in an electric field, the electric-field torque does *work* on it, with a corresponding change in potential energy. The work dW done by a torque τ during an infinitesimal displacement $d\phi$ is given by Eq. (10.19): $dW = \tau \, d\phi$. Because the torque is in the direction of decreasing ϕ, we must write the torque as $\tau = -pE \sin\phi$, and

$$dW = \tau \, d\phi = -pE \sin\phi \, d\phi$$

In a finite displacement from ϕ_1 to ϕ_2 the total work done on the dipole is

$$W = \int_{\phi_1}^{\phi_2} (-pE \sin\phi) \, d\phi$$
$$= pE \cos\phi_2 - pE \cos\phi_1$$

The work is the negative of the change of potential energy, just as in Chapter 7: $W = U_1 - U_2$. So a suitable definition of potential energy U for this system is

$$U(\phi) = -pE \cos\phi \quad (21.17)$$

In this expression we recognize the *scalar product* $\vec{p} \cdot \vec{E} = pE \cos\phi$, so we can also write

$$U = -\vec{p} \cdot \vec{E} \quad \text{(potential energy for a dipole in an electric field)} \quad (21.18)$$

The potential energy has its minimum (most negative) value $U = -pE$ at the stable equilibrium position, where $\phi = 0$ and $\vec{p}$ is parallel to $\vec{E}$. The potential energy is maximum when $\phi = \pi$ and $\vec{p}$ is antiparallel to $\vec{E}$; then $U = +pE$. At $\phi = \pi/2$, where $\vec{p}$ is perpendicular to $\vec{E}$, U is zero. We could define U differently so that it is zero at some other orientation of $\vec{p}$, but our definition is simplest.

Equation (21.18) gives us another way to look at the effect shown in Fig. 21.29. The electric field $\vec{E}$ gives each grass seed an electric dipole moment, and the grass seed then aligns itself with $\vec{E}$ to minimize the potential energy.

PhET: Microwaves

Example 21.13 Force and torque on an electric dipole

Figure 21.32a shows an electric dipole in a uniform electric field of magnitude 5.0×10^5 N/C that is directed parallel to the plane of the figure. The charges are $\pm 1.6 \times 10^{-19}$ C; both lie in the plane and are separated by 0.125 nm $= 0.125 \times 10^{-9}$ m. Find (a) the net force exerted by the field on the dipole; (b) the magnitude and

Continued

21.32 (a) An electric dipole. (b) Directions of the electric dipole moment, electric field, and torque ($\vec{\tau}$ points out of the page).

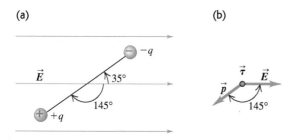

(a)   (b)

direction of the electric dipole moment; (c) the magnitude and direction of the torque; (d) the potential energy of the system in the position shown.

SOLUTION

IDENTIFY and SET UP: This problem uses the ideas of this section about an electric dipole placed in an electric field. We use the relationship $\vec{F} = q\vec{E}$ for each point charge to find the force on the dipole as a whole. Equation (21.14) gives the dipole moment, Eq. (21.16) gives the torque on the dipole, and Eq. (21.18) gives the potential energy of the system.

EXECUTE: (a) The field is uniform, so the forces on the two charges are equal and opposite. Hence the total force on the dipole is zero.

(b) The magnitude p of the electric dipole moment $\vec{p}$ is

$$p = qd = (1.6 \times 10^{-19} \text{ C})(0.125 \times 10^{-9} \text{ m})$$
$$= 2.0 \times 10^{-29} \text{ C} \cdot \text{m}$$

The direction of $\vec{p}$ is from the negative to the positive charge, 145° clockwise from the electric-field direction (Fig. 21.32b).

(c) The magnitude of the torque is

$$\tau = pE \sin\phi = (2.0 \times 10^{-29} \text{ C})(5.0 \times 10^5 \text{ N/C})(\sin 145°)$$
$$= 5.7 \times 10^{-24} \text{ N} \cdot \text{m}$$

From the right-hand rule for vector products (see Section 1.10), the direction of the torque $\vec{\tau} = \vec{p} \times \vec{E}$ is out of the page. This corresponds to a counterclockwise torque that tends to align $\vec{p}$ with $\vec{E}$.

(d) The potential energy

$$U = -pE \cos\phi$$
$$= -(2.0 \times 10^{-29} \text{ C} \cdot \text{m})(5.0 \times 10^5 \text{ N/C})(\cos 145°)$$
$$= 8.2 \times 10^{-24} \text{ J}$$

EVALUATE: The charge magnitude, the distance between the charges, the dipole moment, and the potential energy are all very small, but are all typical of molecules.

In this discussion we have assumed that $\vec{E}$ is uniform, so there is no net force on the dipole. If $\vec{E}$ is not uniform, the forces at the ends may not cancel completely, and the net force may not be zero. Thus a body with zero net charge but an electric dipole moment can experience a net force in a nonuniform electric field. As we mentioned in Section 21.1, an uncharged body can be polarized by an electric field, giving rise to a separation of charge and an electric dipole moment. This is how uncharged bodies can experience electrostatic forces (see Fig. 21.8).

Field of an Electric Dipole

Now let's think of an electric dipole as a *source* of electric field. What does the field look like? The general shape of things is shown by the field map of Fig. 21.28b. At each point in the pattern the total $\vec{E}$ field is the vector sum of the fields from the two individual charges, as in Example 21.8 (Section 21.5). Try drawing diagrams showing this vector sum for several points.

To get quantitative information about the field of an electric dipole, we have to do some calculating, as illustrated in the next example. Notice the use of the principle of superposition of electric fields to add up the contributions to the field of the individual charges. Also notice that we need to use approximation techniques even for the relatively simple case of a field due to two charges. Field calculations often become very complicated, and computer analysis is typically used to determine the field due to an arbitrary charge distribution.

Example 21.14   **Field of an electric dipole, revisited**

An electric dipole is centered at the origin, with $\vec{p}$ in the direction of the $+y$-axis (Fig. 21.33). Derive an approximate expression for the electric field at a point P on the y-axis for which y is much larger than d. To do this, use the binomial expansion $(1 + x)^n \cong 1 + nx + n(n - 1)x^2/2 + \cdots$ (valid for the case $|x| < 1$).

SOLUTION

IDENTIFY and SET UP: We use the principle of superposition: The total electric field is the vector sum of the field produced by the positive charge and the field produced by the negative charge. At the field point P shown in Fig. 21.33, the field $\vec{E}_+$ of the positive charge has a positive (upward) y-component and the field $\vec{E}_-$ of

21.33 Finding the electric field of an electric dipole at a point on its axis.

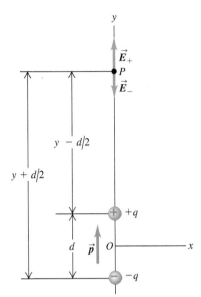

the negative charge has a negative (downward) y-component. We add these components to find the total field and then apply the approximation that y is much greater than d.

EXECUTE: The total y-component E_y of electric field from the two charges is

$$E_y = \frac{q}{4\pi\epsilon_0}\left[\frac{1}{(y-d/2)^2} - \frac{1}{(y+d/2)^2}\right]$$

$$= \frac{q}{4\pi\epsilon_0 y^2}\left[\left(1-\frac{d}{2y}\right)^{-2} - \left(1+\frac{d}{2y}\right)^{-2}\right]$$

We used this same approach in Example 21.8 (Section 21.5). Now the approximation: When we are far from the dipole compared to its size, so $y \gg d$, we have $d/2y \ll 1$. With $n = -2$ and with $d/2y$ replacing x in the binomial expansion, we keep only the first two terms (the terms we discard are much smaller). We then have

$$\left(1-\frac{d}{2y}\right)^{-2} \cong 1 + \frac{d}{y} \quad \text{and} \quad \left(1+\frac{d}{2y}\right)^{-2} \cong 1 - \frac{d}{y}$$

Hence E_y is given approximately by

$$E_y \cong \frac{q}{4\pi\epsilon_0 y^2}\left[1 + \frac{d}{y} - \left(1 - \frac{d}{y}\right)\right] = \frac{qd}{2\pi\epsilon_0 y^3} = \frac{p}{2\pi\epsilon_0 y^3}$$

EVALUATE: An alternative route to this result is to put the fractions in the first expression for E_y over a common denominator, add, and then approximate the denominator $(y - d/2)^2(y + d/2)^2$ as y^4. We leave the details to you (see Exercise 21.60).

For points P off the coordinate axes, the expressions are more complicated, but at *all* points far away from the dipole (in any direction) the field drops off as $1/r^3$. We can compare this with the $1/r^2$ behavior of a point charge, the $1/r$ behavior of a long line charge, and the independence of r for a large sheet of charge. There are charge distributions for which the field drops off even more quickly. At large distances, the field of an *electric quadrupole*, which consists of two equal dipoles with opposite orientation, separated by a small distance, drops off as $1/r^4$.

Test Your Understanding of Section 21.7 An electric dipole is placed in a region of uniform electric field $\vec{E}$, with the electric dipole moment $\vec{p}$, pointing in the direction opposite to $\vec{E}$. Is the dipole (i) in stable equilibrium, (ii) in unstable equilibrium, or (iii) neither? (*Hint:* You many want to review Section 7.5.)

Electric charge, conductors, and insulators: The fundamental quantity in electrostatics is electric charge. There are two kinds of charge, positive and negative. Charges of the same sign repel each other; charges of opposite sign attract. Charge is conserved; the total charge in an isolated system is constant.

All ordinary matter is made of protons, neutrons, and electrons. The positive protons and electrically neutral neutrons in the nucleus of an atom are bound together by the nuclear force; the negative electrons surround the nucleus at distances much greater than the nuclear size. Electric interactions are chiefly responsible for the structure of atoms, molecules, and solids.

Conductors are materials in which charge moves easily; in insulators, charge does not move easily. Most metals are good conductors; most nonmetals are insulators.

Coulomb's law: For charges q_1 and q_2 separated by a distance r, the magnitude of the electric force on either charge is proportional to the product $q_1 q_2$ and inversely proportional to r^2. The force on each charge is along the line joining the two charges—repulsive if q_1 and q_2 have the same sign, attractive if they have opposite signs. In SI units the unit of electric charge is the coulomb, abbreviated C. (See Examples 21.1 and 21.2.)

When two or more charges each exert a force on a charge, the total force on that charge is the vector sum of the forces exerted by the individual charges. (See Examples 21.3 and 21.4.)

$$F = \frac{1}{4\pi\epsilon_0} \frac{|q_1 q_2|}{r^2} \quad (21.2)$$

$$\frac{1}{4\pi\epsilon_0} = 8.988 \times 10^9 \ \text{N} \cdot \text{m}^2/\text{C}^2$$

Electric field: Electric field $\vec{E}$, a vector quantity, is the force per unit charge exerted on a test charge at any point. The electric field produced by a point charge is directed radially away from or toward the charge. (See Examples 21.5–21.7.)

$$\vec{E} = \frac{\vec{F}_0}{q_0} \quad (21.3)$$

$$\vec{E} = \frac{1}{4\pi\epsilon_0} \frac{q}{r^2} \hat{r} \quad (21.7)$$

Superposition of electric fields: The electric field $\vec{E}$ of any combination of charges is the vector sum of the fields caused by the individual charges. To calculate the electric field caused by a continuous distribution of charge, divide the distribution into small elements, calculate the field caused by each element, and then carry out the vector sum, usually by integrating. Charge distributions are described by linear charge density λ, surface charge density σ, and volume charge density ρ. (See Examples 21.8–21.12.)

Electric field lines: Field lines provide a graphical representation of electric fields. At any point on a field line, the tangent to the line is in the direction of $\vec{E}$ at that point. The number of lines per unit area (perpendicular to their direction) is proportional to the magnitude of $\vec{E}$ at the point.

Electric dipoles: An electric dipole is a pair of electric charges of equal magnitude q but opposite sign, separated by a distance d. The electric dipole moment $\vec{p}$ has magnitude $p = qd$. The direction of $\vec{p}$ is from negative toward positive charge. An electric dipole in an electric field $\vec{E}$ experiences a torque $\vec{\tau}$ equal to the vector product of $\vec{p}$ and $\vec{E}$. The magnitude of the torque depends on the angle ϕ between $\vec{p}$ and $\vec{E}$. The potential energy U for an electric dipole in an electric field also depends on the relative orientation of $\vec{p}$ and $\vec{E}$. (See Examples 21.13 and 21.14.)

$$\tau = pE \sin\phi \quad (21.15)$$

$$\vec{\tau} = \vec{p} \times \vec{E} \quad (21.16)$$

$$U = -\vec{p} \cdot \vec{E} \quad (21.18)$$

Calculating Electric Field: Half a Ring of Charge

Positive charge Q is uniformly distributed around a semicircle of radius a as shown in Fig. 21.34. Find the magnitude and direction of the resulting electric field at point P, the center of curvature of the semicircle.

SOLUTION GUIDE

See MasteringPhysics® study area for a Video Tutor solution.

IDENTIFY and SET UP

1. The target variables are the components of the electric field at P.
2. Divide the semicircle into infinitesimal segments, each of which is a short circular arc of radius a and angle $d\theta$. What is the length of such a segment? How much charge is on a segment?

21.34

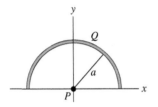

3. Consider an infinitesimal segment located at an angular position θ on the semicircle, measured from the lower right corner of the semicircle at $x = a$, $y = 0$. (Thus $\theta = \pi/2$ at $x = 0$, $y = a$ and $\theta = \pi$ at $x = -a$, $y = 0$.) What are the x- and y-components of the electric field at P (dE_x and dE_y) produced by just this segment?

EXECUTE

4. Integrate your expressions for dE_x and dE_y from $\theta = 0$ to $\theta = \pi$. The results will be the x-component and y-component of the electric field at P.
5. Use your results from step 4 to find the magnitude and direction of the field at P.

EVALUATE

6. Does your result for the electric-field magnitude have the correct units?
7. Explain how you could have found the x-component of the electric field using a symmetry argument.
8. What would be the electric field at P if the semicircle were extended to a full circle centered at P?

Problems

For instructor-assigned homework, go to MasteringPhysics®.

•, ••, •••: Problems of increasing difficulty. **CP**: Cumulative problems incorporating material from earlier chapters. **CALC**: Problems requiring calculus. **BIO**: Biosciences problems.

DISCUSSION QUESTIONS

Q21.1 If you peel two strips of transparent tape off the same roll and immediately let them hang near each other, they will repel each other. If you then stick the sticky side of one to the shiny side of the other and rip them apart, they will attract each other. Give a plausible explanation, involving transfer of electrons between the strips of tape, for this sequence of events.

Q21.2 Two metal spheres are hanging from nylon threads. When you bring the spheres close to each other, they tend to attract. Based on this information alone, discuss all the possible ways that the spheres could be charged. Is it possible that after the spheres touch, they will cling together? Explain.

Q21.3 The electric force between two charged particles becomes weaker with increasing distance. Suppose instead that the electric force were *independent* of distance. In this case, would a charged comb still cause a neutral insulator to become polarized as in Fig. 21.8? Why or why not? Would the neutral insulator still be attracted to the comb? Again, why or why not?

Q21.4 Your clothing tends to cling together after going through the dryer. Why? Would you expect more or less clinging if all your clothing were made of the same material (say, cotton) than if you dried different kinds of clothing together? Again, why? (You may want to experiment with your next load of laundry.)

Q21.5 An uncharged metal sphere hangs from a nylon thread. When a positively charged glass rod is brought close to the metal sphere, the sphere is drawn toward the rod. But if the sphere touches the rod, it suddenly flies away from the rod. Explain why the sphere is first attracted and then repelled.

Q21.6 The free electrons in a metal are gravitationally attracted toward the earth. Why, then, don't they all settle to the bottom of the conductor, like sediment settling to the bottom of a river?

Q21.7 • Figure Q21.7 shows some of the electric field lines due to three point charges arranged along the vertical axis. All three charges have the same magnitude. (a) What are the signs of the three charges? Explain your reasoning. (b) At what point(s) is the magnitude of the electric field the smallest? Explain your reasoning. Explain how the fields produced by each individual point charge combine to give a small net field at this point or points.

Figure **Q21.7**

Q21.8 Good electrical conductors, such as metals, are typically good conductors of heat; electrical insulators, such as wood, are typically poor conductors of heat. Explain why there should be a relationship between electrical conduction and heat conduction in these materials.

Q21.9 • Suppose the charge shown in Fig. 21.28a is fixed in position. A small, positively charged particle is then placed at some point in the figure and released. Will the trajectory of the particle follow an electric field line? Why or why not? Suppose instead that the particle is placed at some point in Fig. 21.28b and released (the positive and negative charges shown in the figure are fixed in position). Will its trajectory follow an electric field line? Again, why or why not? Explain any differences between your answers for the two different situations.

Q21.10 Two identical metal objects are mounted on insulating stands. Describe how you could place charges of opposite sign but exactly equal magnitude on the two objects.

Q21.11 You can use plastic food wrap to cover a container by stretching the material across the top and pressing the overhanging material against the sides. What makes it stick? (*Hint:* The answer involves the electric force.) Does the food wrap stick to itself with equal tenacity? Why or why not? Does it work with metallic containers? Again, why or why not?

Q21.12 If you walk across a nylon rug and then touch a large metal object such as a doorknob, you may get a spark and a shock. Why does this tend to happen more on dry days than on humid days? (*Hint:* See Fig. 21.30.) Why are you less likely to get a shock if you touch a *small* metal object, such as a paper clip?

Q21.13 You have a negatively charged object. How can you use it to place a net negative charge on an insulated metal sphere? To place a net positive charge on the sphere?

Q21.14 When two point charges of equal mass and charge are released on a frictionless table, each has an initial acceleration a_0. If instead you keep one fixed and release the other one, what will be its initial acceleration: a_0, $2a_0$, or $a_0/2$? Explain.

Q21.15 A point charge of mass m and charge Q and another point charge of mass m but charge $2Q$ are released on a frictionless table. If the charge Q has an initial acceleration a_0, what will be the acceleration of $2Q$: a_0, $2a_0$, $4a_0$, $a_0/2$, or $a_0/4$? Explain.

Q21.16 A proton is placed in a uniform electric field and then released. Then an electron is placed at this same point and released. Do these two particles experience the same force? The same acceleration? Do they move in the same direction when released?

Q21.17 In Example 21.1 (Section 21.3) we saw that the electric force between two α particles is of the order of 10^{35} times as strong as the gravitational force. So why do we readily feel the gravity of the earth but no electrical force from it?

Q21.18 What similarities do electrical forces have with gravitational forces? What are the most significant differences?

Q21.19 Two irregular objects A and B carry charges of opposite sign. Figure Q21.19 shows the electric field lines near each of these objects. (a) Which object is positive, A or B? How do you know? (b) Where is the electric field stronger, close to A or close to B? How do you know?

Figure **Q21.19**

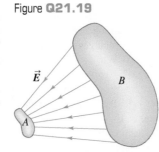

Q21.20 Atomic nuclei are made of protons and neutrons. This shows that there must be another kind of interaction in addition to gravitational and electric forces. Explain.

Q21.21 Sufficiently strong electric fields can cause atoms to become positively ionized—that is, to lose one or more electrons. Explain how this can happen. What determines how strong the field must be to make this happen?

Q21.22 The electric fields at point P due to the positive charges q_1 and q_2 are shown in Fig. Q21.22. Does the fact that they cross each other violate the statement in Section 21.6 that electric field lines never cross? Explain.

Figure **Q21.22**

Q21.23 The air temperature and the velocity of the air have different values at different places in the earth's atmosphere. Is the air velocity a vector field? Why or why not? Is the air temperature a vector field? Again, why or why not?

EXERCISES

Section 21.3 Coulomb's Law

21.1 •• Excess electrons are placed on a small lead sphere with mass 8.00 g so that its net charge is -3.20×10^{-9} C. (a) Find the number of excess electrons on the sphere. (b) How many excess electrons are there per lead atom? The atomic number of lead is 82, and its atomic mass is 207 g/mol.

21.2 • Lightning occurs when there is a flow of electric charge (principally electrons) between the ground and a thundercloud. The maximum rate of charge flow in a lightning bolt is about 20,000 C/s; this lasts for 100 μs or less. How much charge flows between the ground and the cloud in this time? How many electrons flow during this time?

21.3 •• **BIO** Estimate how many electrons there are in your body. Make any assumptions you feel are necessary, but clearly state what they are. (*Hint:* Most of the atoms in your body have equal numbers of electrons, protons, and neutrons.) What is the combined charge of all these electrons?

21.4 • **Particles in a Gold Ring.** You have a pure (24-karat) gold ring with mass 17.7 g. Gold has an atomic mass of 197 g/mol and an atomic number of 79. (a) How many protons are in the ring, and what is their total positive charge? (b) If the ring carries no net charge, how many electrons are in it?

21.5 • **BIO Signal Propagation in Neurons.** *Neurons* are components of the nervous system of the body that transmit signals as electrical impulses travel along their length. These impulses propagate when charge suddenly rushes into and then out of a part of the neuron called an *axon*. Measurements have shown that, during the inflow part of this cycle, approximately 5.6×10^{11} Na^+ (sodium ions) per meter, each with charge $+e$, enter the axon. How many coulombs of charge enter a 1.5-cm length of the axon during this process?

21.6 • Two small spheres spaced 20.0 cm apart have equal charge. How many excess electrons must be present on each sphere if the magnitude of the force of repulsion between them is 4.57×10^{-21} N?

21.7 •• An average human weighs about 650 N. If two such generic humans each carried 1.0 coulomb of excess charge, one positive and one negative, how far apart would they have to be for the electric attraction between them to equal their 650-N weight?

21.8 •• Two small aluminum spheres, each having mass 0.0250 kg, are separated by 80.0 cm. (a) How many electrons does each sphere contain? (The atomic mass of aluminum is 26.982 g/mol, and its atomic number is 13.) (b) How many electrons would have to be removed from one sphere and added to the other to cause an attractive force between the spheres of magnitude 1.00×10^4 N (roughly 1 ton)? Assume that the spheres may be treated as point charges. (c) What fraction of all the electrons in each sphere does this represent?

21.9 •• Two small plastic spheres are given positive electrical charges. When they are 15.0 cm apart, the repulsive force between them has magnitude 0.220 N. What is the charge on each sphere (a) if the two charges are equal and (b) if one sphere has four times the charge of the other?

21.10 •• **What If We Were Not Neutral?** A 75-kg person holds out his arms so that his hands are 1.7 m apart. Typically, a person's hand makes up about 1.0% of his or her body weight. For round numbers, we shall assume that all the weight of each hand is due to the calcium in the bones, and we shall treat the hands as point charges. One mole of Ca contains 40.18 g, and each atom has 20 protons and 20 electrons. Suppose that only 1.0% of the positive charges in each hand were unbalanced by negative charge. (a) How many Ca atoms does each hand contain? (b) How many coulombs of unbalanced charge does each hand contain? (c) What force would the person's arms have to exert on his hands to prevent them from flying off? Does it seem likely that his arms are capable of exerting such a force?

21.11 •• Two very small 8.55-g spheres, 15.0 cm apart from center to center, are charged by adding equal numbers of electrons to each of them. Disregarding all other forces, how many electrons would you have to add to each sphere so that the two spheres will accelerate at $25.0g$ when released? Which way will they accelerate?

21.12 •• **Just How Strong Is the Electric Force?** Suppose you had two small boxes, each containing 1.0 g of protons. (a) If one were placed on the moon by an astronaut and the other were left on the earth, and if they were connected by a very light (and very long!) string, what would be the tension in the string? Express your answer in newtons and in pounds. Do you need to take into account the gravitational forces of the earth and moon on the protons? Why? (b) What gravitational force would each box of protons exert on the other box?

21.13 • In an experiment in space, one proton is held fixed and another proton is released from rest a distance of 2.50 mm away. (a) What is the initial acceleration of the proton after it is released? (b) Sketch qualitative (no numbers!) acceleration–time and velocity–time graphs of the released proton's motion.

21.14 • A negative charge of $-0.550\ \mu$C exerts an upward 0.200-N force on an unknown charge 0.300 m directly below it. (a) What is the unknown charge (magnitude and sign)? (b) What are the magnitude and direction of the force that the unknown charge exerts on the -0.550-μC charge?

21.15 •• Three point charges are arranged on a line. Charge $q_3 = +5.00$ nC and is at the origin. Charge $q_2 = -3.00$ nC and is at $x = +4.00$ cm. Charge q_1 is at $x = +2.00$ cm. What is q_1 (magnitude and sign) if the net force on q_3 is zero?

21.16 •• In Example 21.4, suppose the point charge on the y-axis at $y = -0.30$ m has negative charge $-2.0\ \mu$C, and the other charges remain the same. Find the magnitude and direction of the net force on Q. How does your answer differ from that in Example 21.4? Explain the differences.

21.17 •• In Example 21.3, calculate the net force on charge q_1.

21.18 •• In Example 21.4, what is the net force (magnitude and direction) on charge q_1 exerted by the other two charges?

21.19 •• Three point charges are arranged along the x-axis. Charge $q_1 = +3.00\ \mu$C is at the origin, and charge $q_2 = -5.00\ \mu$C is at $x = 0.200$ m. Charge $q_3 = -8.00\ \mu$C. Where is q_3 located if the net force on q_1 is 7.00 N in the $-x$-direction?

21.20 •• Repeat Exercise 21.19 for $q_3 = +8.00\ \mu$C.

21.21 •• Two point charges are located on the y-axis as follows: charge $q_1 = -1.50$ nC at $y = -0.600$ m, and charge $q_2 = +3.20$ nC at the origin ($y = 0$). What is the total force (magnitude and direction) exerted by these two charges on a third charge $q_3 = +5.00$ nC located at $y = -0.400$ m?

21.22 •• Two point charges are placed on the x-axis as follows: Charge $q_1 = +4.00$ nC is located at $x = 0.200$ m, and charge $q_2 = +5.00$ nC is at $x = -0.300$ m. What are the magnitude and direction of the total force exerted by these two charges on a negative point charge $q_3 = -6.00$ nC that is placed at the origin?

21.23 •• **BIO Base Pairing in DNA, I.** The two sides of the DNA double helix are connected by pairs of bases (adenine, thymine, cytosine, and guanine). Because of the geometric shape of these molecules, adenine bonds with thymine and cytosine bonds with guanine. Figure E21.23 shows the thymine–adenine bond. Each charge shown is $\pm e$, and the H—N distance is 0.110 nm. (a) Calculate the *net* force that thymine exerts on adenine. Is it attractive or repulsive? To keep the calculations fairly simple, yet reasonable, consider only the forces due to the O—H—N and the N—H—N combinations, assuming that these two combinations are parallel to each other. Remember, however, that in the O—H—N set, the O$^-$ exerts a force on both the H$^+$ and the N$^-$, and likewise along the N—H—N set. (b) Calculate the force on the electron in the hydrogen atom, which is 0.0529 nm from the proton. Then compare the strength of the bonding force of the electron in hydrogen with the bonding force of the adenine–thymine molecules.

Figure **E21.23**

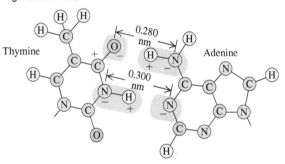

21.24 •• **BIO Base Pairing in DNA, II.** Refer to Exercise 21.23. Figure E21.24 shows the bonding of the cytosine and guanine molecules. The O—H and H—N distances are each 0.110 nm. In this case, assume that the bonding is due only to the forces along the O—H—O, N—H—N, and O—H—N combinations, and assume also that these three combinations are parallel to each other. Calculate the *net* force that cytosine exerts on guanine due to the preceding three combinations. Is this force attractive or repulsive?

Figure **E21.24**

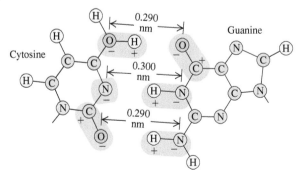

Section 21.4 Electric Field and Electric Forces

21.25 • **CP** A proton is placed in a uniform electric field of 2.75×10^3 N/C. Calculate: (a) the magnitude of the electric force felt by the proton; (b) the proton's acceleration; (c) the proton's speed after 1.00 μs in the field, assuming it starts from rest.

21.26 • A particle has charge -3.00 nC. (a) Find the magnitude and direction of the electric field due to this particle at a point 0.250 m directly above it. (b) At what distance from this particle does its electric field have a magnitude of 12.0 N/C?

21.27 • **CP** A proton is traveling horizontally to the right at 4.50×10^6 m/s. (a) Find the magnitude and direction of the weakest electric field that can bring the proton uniformly to rest over a distance of 3.20 cm. (b) How much time does it take the proton to stop after entering the field? (c) What minimum field (magnitude and direction) would be needed to stop an electron under the conditions of part (a)?

21.28 • **CP** An electron is released from rest in a uniform electric field. The electron accelerates vertically upward, traveling 4.50 m in the first 3.00 μs after it is released. (a) What are the magnitude and direction of the electric field? (b) Are we justified in ignoring the effects of gravity? Justify your answer quantitatively.

21.29 •• (a) What must the charge (sign and magnitude) of a 1.45-g particle be for it to remain stationary when placed in a downward-directed electric field of magnitude 650 N/C? (b) What is the magnitude of an electric field in which the electric force on a proton is equal in magnitude to its weight?

21.30 •• A point charge is placed at each corner of a square with side length a. The charges all have the same magnitude q. Two of the charges are positive and two are negative, as shown in Fig. E21.30. What is the direction of the net electric field at the center of the square due to the four charges, and what is its magnitude in terms of q and a?

Figure **E21.30**

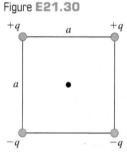

21.31 • Two point charges are separated by 25.0 cm (Fig. E21.31). Find the net electric field these charges produce at (a) point A and (b) point B. (c) What would be the magnitude and direction of the electric force this combination of charges would produce on a proton at A?

Figure **E21.31**

21.32 •• **Electric Field of the Earth.** The earth has a net electric charge that causes a field at points near its surface equal to 150 N/C and directed in toward the center of the earth. (a) What magnitude and sign of charge would a 60-kg human have to acquire to overcome his or her weight by the force exerted by the earth's electric field? (b) What would be the force of repulsion between two people each with the charge calculated in part (a) and separated by a distance of 100 m? Is use of the earth's electric field a feasible means of flight? Why or why not?

21.33 •• **CP** An electron is projected with an initial speed $v_0 = 1.60 \times 10^6$ m/s into the uniform field between the parallel plates in Fig. E21.33. Assume that the field between the plates is uniform and directed vertically downward, and that the field outside the plates is zero. The electron enters the field at a point

Figure **E21.33**

midway between the plates. (a) If the electron just misses the upper plate as it emerges from the field, find the magnitude of the electric field. (b) Suppose that in Fig. E21.33 the electron is replaced by a proton with the same initial speed v_0. Would the proton hit one of the plates? If the proton would not hit one of the plates, what would be the magnitude and direction of its vertical displacement as it exits the region between the plates? (c) Compare the paths traveled by the electron and the proton and explain the differences. (d) Discuss whether it is reasonable to ignore the effects of gravity for each particle.

21.34 •• Point charge $q_1 = -5.00$ nC is at the origin and point charge $q_2 = +3.00$ nC is on the x-axis at $x = 3.00$ cm. Point P is on the y-axis at $y = 4.00$ cm. (a) Calculate the electric fields $\vec{E}_1$ and $\vec{E}_2$ at point P due to the charges q_1 and q_2. Express your results in terms of unit vectors (see Example 21.6). (b) Use the results of part (a) to obtain the resultant field at P, expressed in unit vector form.

21.35 •• **CP** In Exercise 21.33, what is the speed of the electron as it emerges from the field?

21.36 • (a) Calculate the magnitude and direction (relative to the $+x$-axis) of the electric field in Example 21.6. (b) A -2.5-nC point charge is placed at point P in Fig. 21.19. Find the magnitude and direction of (i) the force that the -8.0-nC charge at the origin exerts on this charge and (ii) the force that this charge exerts on the -8.0-nC charge at the origin.

21.37 •• If two electrons are each 1.50×10^{-10} m from a proton, as shown in Fig. E21.37, find the magnitude and direction of the net electric force they will exert on the proton.

Figure **E21.37**

21.38 •• **CP** A uniform electric field exists in the region between two oppositely charged plane parallel plates. A proton is released from rest at the surface of the positively charged plate and strikes the surface of the opposite plate, 1.60 cm distant from the first, in a time interval of 1.50×10^{-6} s. (a) Find the magnitude of the electric field. (b) Find the speed of the proton when it strikes the negatively charged plate.

21.39 • A point charge is at the origin. With this point charge as the source point, what is the unit vector $\hat{r}$ in the direction of (a) the field point at $x = 0$, $y = -1.35$ m; (b) the field point at $x = 12.0$ cm, $y = 12.0$ cm; (c) the field point at $x = -1.10$ m, $y = 2.60$ m? Express your results in terms of the unit vectors $\hat{i}$ and $\hat{j}$.

21.40 •• A $+8.75$-μC point charge is glued down on a horizontal frictionless table. It is tied to a -6.50-μC point charge by a light, nonconducting 2.50-cm wire. A uniform electric field of magnitude 1.85×10^8 N/C is directed parallel to the wire, as shown in Fig. E21.40. (a) Find the tension in the wire. (b) What would the tension be if both charges were negative?

Figure **E21.40**

21.41 •• (a) An electron is moving east in a uniform electric field of 1.50 N/C directed to the west. At point A, the velocity of the electron is 4.50×10^5 m/s toward the east. What is the speed of the electron when it reaches point B, 0.375 m east of point A? (b) A proton is moving in the uniform electric field of part (a). At point A, the velocity of the proton is 1.90×10^4 m/s, east. What is the speed of the proton at point B?

Section 21.5 Electric-Field Calculations

21.42 • Two point charges Q and $+q$ (where q is positive) produce the net electric field shown at point P in Fig. E21.42. The field points parallel to the line connecting the two charges. (a) What can you conclude about the sign and magnitude of Q? Explain your reasoning. (b) If the lower charge were negative instead, would it be possible for the field to have the direction shown in the figure? Explain your reasoning.

Figure **E21.42**

21.43 •• Two positive point charges q are placed on the x-axis, one at $x = a$ and one at $x = -a$. (a) Find the magnitude and direction of the electric field at $x = 0$. (b) Derive an expression for the electric field at points on the x-axis. Use your result to graph the x-component of the electric field as a function of x, for values of x between $-4a$ and $+4a$.

21.44 • The two charges q_1 and q_2 shown in Fig. E21.44 have equal magnitudes. What is the direction of the net electric field due to these two charges at points A (midway between the charges), B, and C if (a) both charges are negative, (b) both charges are positive, (c) q_1 is positive and q_2 is negative.

Figure **E21.44**

21.45 • A $+2.00$-nC point charge is at the origin, and a second -5.00-nC point charge is on the x-axis at $x = 0.800$ m. (a) Find the electric field (magnitude and direction) at each of the following points on the x-axis: (i) $x = 0.200$ m; (ii) $x = 1.20$ m; (iii) $x = -0.200$ m. (b) Find the net electric force that the two charges would exert on an electron placed at each point in part (a).

21.46 •• Repeat Exercise 21.44, but now let $q_1 = -4.00$ nC.

21.47 • Three negative point charges lie along a line as shown in Fig. E21.47. Find the magnitude and direction of the electric field this combination of charges produces at point P, which lies 6.00 cm from the -2.00-μC charge measured perpendicular to the line connecting the three charges.

Figure **E21.47**

21.48 •• **BIO** **Electric Field of Axons.** A nerve signal is transmitted through a neuron when an excess of Na^+ ions suddenly enters the axon, a long cylindrical part of the neuron. Axons are approximately 10.0 μm in diameter, and measurements show that about 5.6×10^{11} Na^+ ions per meter (each of charge $+e$) enter during this process. Although the axon is a long cylinder, the charge does not all enter everywhere at the same time. A plausible model would be a series of point charges moving along the axon. Let us look at a 0.10-mm length of the axon and model it as a point charge. (a) If the charge that enters each meter of the axon gets distributed uniformly along it, how many coulombs of charge enter a 0.10-mm length of the axon? (b) What electric field (magnitude and direction) does the sudden influx of charge produce at the surface of the body if the axon is 5.00 cm below the skin? (c) Certain sharks can respond to electric fields as weak as 1.0 μN/C.

How far from this segment of axon could a shark be and still detect its electric field?

21.49 • In a rectangular coordinate system a positive point charge $q = 6.00 \times 10^{-9}$ C is placed at the point $x = +0.150$ m, $y = 0$, and an identical point charge is placed at $x = -0.150$ m, $y = 0$. Find the x- and y-components, the magnitude, and the direction of the electric field at the following points: (a) the origin; (b) $x = 0.300$ m, $y = 0$; (c) $x = 0.150$ m, $y = -0.400$ m; (d) $x = 0$, $y = 0.200$ m.

21.50 •• A point charge $q_1 = -4.00$ nC is at the point $x = 0.600$ m, $y = 0.800$ m, and a second point charge $q_2 = +6.00$ nC is at the point $x = 0.600$ m, $y = 0$. Calculate the magnitude and direction of the net electric field at the origin due to these two point charges.

21.51 •• Repeat Exercise 21.49 for the case where the point charge at $x = +0.150$ m, $y = 0$ is positive and the other is negative, each with magnitude 6.00×10^{-9} C.

21.52 •• A very long, straight wire has charge per unit length 1.50×10^{-10} C/m. At what distance from the wire is the electric-field magnitude equal to 2.50 N/C?

21.53 • A ring-shaped conductor with radius $a = 2.50$ cm has a total positive charge $Q = +0.125$ nC uniformly distributed around it, as shown in Fig. 21.23. The center of the ring is at the origin of coordinates O. (a) What is the electric field (magnitude and direction) at point P, which is on the x-axis at $x = 40.0$ cm? (b) A point charge $q = -2.50$ μC is placed at the point P described in part (a). What are the magnitude and direction of the force exerted *by* the charge q *on* the ring?

21.54 •• A straight, nonconducting plastic wire 8.50 cm long carries a charge density of $+175$ nC/m distributed uniformly along its length. It is lying on a horizontal tabletop. (a) Find the magnitude and direction of the electric field this wire produces at a point 6.00 cm directly above its midpoint. (b) If the wire is now bent into a circle lying flat on the table, find the magnitude and direction of the electric field it produces at a point 6.00 cm directly above its center.

21.55 •• A charge of -6.50 nC is spread uniformly over the surface of one face of a nonconducting disk of radius 1.25 cm. (a) Find the magnitude and direction of the electric field this disk produces at a point P on the axis of the disk a distance of 2.00 cm from its center. (b) Suppose that the charge were all pushed away from the center and distributed uniformly on the outer rim of the disk. Find the magnitude and direction of the electric field at point P. (c) If the charge is all brought to the center of the disk, find the magnitude and direction of the electric field at point P. (d) Why is the field in part (a) stronger than the field in part (b)? Why is the field in part (c) the strongest of the three fields?

Section 21.7 Electric Dipoles

21.56 • The ammonia molecule (NH_3) has a dipole moment of 5.0×10^{-30} C·m. Ammonia molecules in the gas phase are placed in a uniform electric field $\vec{E}$ with magnitude 1.6×10^6 N/C. (a) What is the change in electric potential energy when the dipole moment of a molecule changes its orientation with respect to $\vec{E}$ from parallel to perpendicular? (b) At what absolute temperature T is the average translational kinetic energy $\frac{3}{2}kT$ of a molecule equal to the change in potential energy calculated in part (a)? (*Note:* Above this temperature, thermal agitation prevents the dipoles from aligning with the electric field.)

21.57 • Point charges $q_1 = -4.5$ nC and $q_2 = +4.5$ nC are separated by 3.1 mm, forming an electric dipole. (a) Find the electric dipole moment (magnitude and direction). (b) The charges are in a uniform electric field whose direction makes an angle of 36.9° with the line connecting the charges. What is the magnitude of this field if the torque exerted on the dipole has magnitude 7.2×10^{-9} N·m?

21.58 • The dipole moment of the water molecule (H_2O) is 6.17×10^{-30} C·m. Consider a water molecule located at the origin whose dipole moment $\vec{p}$ points in the $+x$-direction. A chlorine ion (Cl^-), of charge -1.60×10^{-19} C, is located at $x = 3.00 \times 10^{-9}$ m. Find the magnitude and direction of the electric force that the water molecule exerts on the chlorine ion. Is this force attractive or repulsive? Assume that x is much larger than the separation d between the charges in the dipole, so that the approximate expression for the electric field along the dipole axis derived in Example 21.14 can be used.

21.59 • **Torque on a Dipole.** An electric dipole with dipole moment $\vec{p}$ is in a uniform electric field $\vec{E}$. (a) Find the orientations of the dipole for which the torque on the dipole is zero. (b) Which of the orientations in part (a) is stable, and which is unstable? (*Hint:* Consider a small displacement away from the equilibrium position and see what happens.) (c) Show that for the stable orientation in part (b), the dipole's own electric field tends to oppose the external field.

21.60 •• Consider the electric dipole of Example 21.14. (a) Derive an expression for the magnitude of the electric field produced by the dipole at a point on the x-axis in Fig. 21.33. What is the direction of this electric field? (b) How does the electric field at points on the x-axis depend on x when x is very large?

21.61 • Three charges are at the corners of an isosceles triangle as shown in Fig. E21.61. The ± 5.00-μC charges form a dipole. (a) Find the force (magnitude and direction) the -10.00-μC charge exerts on the dipole. (b) For an axis perpendicular to the line connecting the ± 5.00-μC charges at the midpoint of this line, find the torque (magnitude and direction) exerted on the dipole by the -10.00-μC charge.

Figure **E21.61**

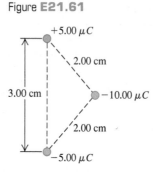

21.62 • A dipole consisting of charges $\pm e$, 220 nm apart, is placed between two very large (essentially infinite) sheets carrying equal but opposite charge densities of 125 μC/m². (a) What is the maximum potential energy this dipole can have due to the sheets, and how should it be oriented relative to the sheets to attain this value? (b) What is the maximum torque the sheets can exert on the dipole, and how should it be oriented relative to the sheets to attain this value? (c) What net force do the two sheets exert on the dipole?

PROBLEMS

21.63 ••• Four identical charges Q are placed at the corners of a square of side L. (a) In a free-body diagram, show all of the forces that act on one of the charges. (b) Find the magnitude and direction of the total force exerted on one charge by the other three charges.

21.64 ••• Two charges, one of 2.50 μC and the other of -3.50 μC, are placed on the x-axis, one at the origin and the other at $x = 0.600$ m, as shown in Fig. P21.64. Find the position on the x-axis where the net force on a small charge $+q$ would be zero.

Figure **P21.64**

21.65 •• Three point charges are arranged along the x-axis. Charge $q_1 = -4.50$ nC is located at $x = 0.200$ m, and charge $q_2 = +2.50$ nC is at $x = -0.300$ m. A positive point charge q_3 is located at the origin. (a) What must the value of q_3 be for the net force on this point charge to have magnitude 4.00 μN? (b) What is the direction of the net force on q_3? (c) Where along the x-axis can q_3 be placed and the net force on it be zero, other than the trivial answers of $x = +\infty$ and $x = -\infty$?

21.66 •• A charge $q_1 = +5.00$ nC is placed at the origin of an xy-coordinate system, and a charge $q_2 = -2.00$ nC is placed on the positive x-axis at $x = 4.00$ cm. (a) If a third charge $q_3 = +6.00$ nC is now placed at the point $x = 4.00$ cm, $y = 3.00$ cm, find the x- and y-components of the total force exerted on this charge by the other two. (b) Find the magnitude and direction of this force.

21.67 •• CP Two positive point charges Q are held fixed on the x-axis at $x = a$ and $x = -a$. A third positive point charge q, with mass m, is placed on the x-axis away from the origin at a coordinate x such that $|x| \ll a$. The charge q, which is free to move along the x-axis, is then released. (a) Find the frequency of oscillation of the charge q. (*Hint:* Review the definition of simple harmonic motion in Section 14.2. Use the binomial expansion $(1 + z)^n = 1 + nz + n(n-1)z^2/2 + \cdots$, valid for the case $|z| < 1$.) (b) Suppose instead that the charge q were placed on the y-axis at a coordinate y such that $|y| \ll a$, and then released. If this charge is free to move anywhere in the xy-plane, what will happen to it? Explain your answer.

21.68 •• CP Two identical spheres with mass m are hung from silk threads of length L, as shown in Fig. P21.68. Each sphere has the same charge, so $q_1 = q_2 = q$. The radius of each sphere is very small compared to the distance between the spheres, so they may be treated as point charges. Show that if the angle θ is small, the equilibrium separation d between the spheres is $d = (q^2 L/2\pi\epsilon_0 mg)^{1/3}$. (*Hint:* If θ is small, then $\tan \theta \cong \sin \theta$.)

Figure **P21.68**

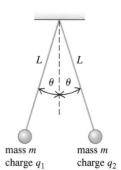

mass m charge q_1 mass m charge q_2

21.69 ••• CP Two small spheres with mass $m = 15.0$ g are hung by silk threads of length $L = 1.20$ m from a common point (Fig. P21.68). When the spheres are given equal quantities of negative charge, so that $q_1 = q_2 = q$, each thread hangs at $\theta = 25.0°$ from the vertical. (a) Draw a diagram showing the forces on each sphere. Treat the spheres as point charges. (b) Find the magnitude of q. (c) Both threads are now shortened to length $L = 0.600$ m, while the charges q_1 and q_2 remain unchanged. What new angle will each thread make with the vertical? (*Hint:* This part of the problem can be solved numerically by using trial values for θ and adjusting the values of θ until a self-consistent answer is obtained.)

21.70 •• **CP** Two identical spheres are each attached to silk threads of length $L = 0.500$ m and hung from a common point (Fig. P21.68). Each sphere has mass $m = 8.00$ g. The radius of each sphere is very small compared to the distance between the spheres, so they may be treated as point charges. One sphere is given positive charge q_1, and the other a different positive charge q_2; this causes the spheres to separate so that when the spheres are in equilibrium, each thread makes an angle $\theta = 20.0°$ with the vertical. (a) Draw a free-body diagram for each sphere when in equilibrium, and label all the forces that act on each sphere. (b) Determine the magnitude of the electrostatic force that acts on each sphere, and determine the tension in each thread. (c) Based on the information you have been given, what can you say about the magnitudes of q_1 and q_2? Explain your answers. (d) A small wire is now connected between the spheres, allowing charge to be transferred from one sphere to the other until the two spheres have equal charges; the wire is then removed. Each thread now makes an angle of $30.0°$ with the vertical. Determine the original charges. (*Hint:* The total charge on the pair of spheres is conserved.)

21.71 •• Sodium chloride (NaCl, ordinary table salt) is made up of positive sodium ions (Na^+) and negative chloride ions (Cl^-). (a) If a point charge with the same charge and mass as all the Na^+ ions in 0.100 mol of NaCl is 2.00 cm from a point charge with the same charge and mass as all the Cl^- ions, what is the magnitude of the attractive force between these two point charges? (b) If the positive point charge in part (a) is held in place and the negative point charge is released from rest, what is its initial acceleration? (See Appendix D for atomic masses.) (c) Does it seem reasonable that the ions in NaCl could be separated in this way? Why or why not? (In fact, when sodium chloride dissolves in water, it breaks up into Na^+ and Cl^- ions. However, in this situation there are additional electric forces exerted by the water molecules on the ions.)

21.72 •• A -5.00-nC point charge is on the x-axis at $x = 1.20$ m. A second point charge Q is on the x-axis at -0.600 m. What must be the sign and magnitude of Q for the resultant electric field at the origin to be (a) 45.0 N/C in the $+x$-direction, (b) 45.0 N/C in the $-x$-direction?

21.73 •• **CP** A small 12.3-g plastic ball is tied to a very light 28.6-cm string that is attached to the vertical wall of a room (Fig. P21.73). A uniform horizontal electric field exists in this room. When the ball has been given an excess charge of -1.11 μC, you observe that it remains suspended, with the string making an angle of $17.4°$ with the wall. Find the magnitude and direction of the electric field in the room.

Figure **P21.73**

17.4°

21.74 •• **CP** At $t = 0$ a very small object with mass 0.400 mg and charge $+9.00$ μC is traveling at 125 m/s in the $-x$-direction. The charge is moving in a uniform electric field that is in the $+y$-direction and that has magnitude $E = 895$ N/C. The gravitational force on the particle can be neglected. How far is the particle from the origin at $t = 7.00$ ms?

21.75 •• Two particles having charges $q_1 = 0.500$ nC and $q_2 = 8.00$ nC are separated by a distance of 1.20 m. At what point along the line connecting the two charges is the total electric field due to the two charges equal to zero?

21.76 ••• Two point charges q_1 and q_2 are held in place 4.50 cm apart. Another point charge $Q = -1.75$ μC of mass 5.00 g is initially located 3.00 cm from each of these charges (Fig. P21.76) and released from rest. You observe that the initial acceleration of Q is 324 m/s^2 upward, parallel to the line connecting the two point charges. Find q_1 and q_2.

Figure **P21.76**

21.77 • Three identical point charges q are placed at each of three corners of a square of side L. Find the magnitude and direction of the net force on a point charge $-3q$ placed (a) at the center of the square and (b) at the vacant corner of the square. In each case, draw a free-body diagram showing the forces exerted on the $-3q$ charge by each of the other three charges.

21.78 ••• Three point charges are placed on the y-axis: a charge q at $y = a$, a charge $-2q$ at the origin, and a charge q at $y = -a$. Such an arrangement is called an electric quadrupole. (a) Find the magnitude and direction of the electric field at points on the positive x-axis. (b) Use the binomial expansion to find an approximate expression for the electric field valid for $x \gg a$. Contrast this behavior to that of the electric field of a point charge and that of the electric field of a dipole.

21.79 •• **CP Strength of the Electric Force.** Imagine two 1.0-g bags of protons, one at the earth's north pole and the other at the south pole. (a) How many protons are in each bag? (b) Calculate the gravitational attraction and the electrical repulsion that each bag exerts on the other. (c) Are the forces in part (b) large enough for you to feel if you were holding one of the bags?

21.80 • **Electric Force Within the Nucleus.** Typical dimensions of atomic nuclei are of the order of 10^{-15} m (1 fm). (a) If two protons in a nucleus are 2.0 fm apart, find the magnitude of the electric force each one exerts on the other. Express the answer in newtons and in pounds. Would this force be large enough for a person to feel? (b) Since the protons repel each other so strongly, why don't they shoot out of the nucleus?

21.81 •• **If Atoms Were Not Neutral . . .** Because the charges on the electron and proton have the same absolute value, atoms are electrically neutral. Suppose this were not precisely true, and the absolute value of the charge of the electron were less than the charge of the proton by 0.00100%. (a) Estimate what the net charge of this textbook would be under these circumstances. Make any assumptions you feel are justified, but state clearly what they are. (*Hint:* Most of the atoms in this textbook have equal numbers of electrons, protons, and neutrons.) (b) What would be the magnitude of the electric force between two textbooks placed 5.0 m apart? Would this force be attractive or repulsive? Estimate what the acceleration of each book would be if the books were 5.0 m apart and there were no non-electric forces on them. (c) Discuss how the fact that ordinary matter is stable shows that the absolute values of the charges on the electron and proton must be identical to a *very* high level of accuracy.

21.82 ••• **CP** Two tiny spheres of mass 6.80 mg carry charges of equal magnitude,

Figure **P21.82**

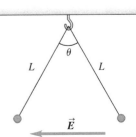

72.0 nC, but opposite sign. They are tied to the same ceiling hook by light strings of length 0.530 m. When a horizontal uniform electric field E that is directed to the left is turned on, the spheres hang at rest with the angle θ between the strings equal to $50.0°$ (Fig. P21.82). (a) Which ball (the one on the right or the one on the left) has positive charge? (b) What is the magnitude E of the field?

21.83 •• **CP** Consider a model of a hydrogen atom in which an electron is in a circular orbit of radius $r = 5.29 \times 10^{-11}$ m around a stationary proton. What is the speed of the electron in its orbit?

21.84 •• **CP** A small sphere with mass $9.00\ \mu g$ and charge $-4.30\ \mu C$ is moving in a circular orbit around a stationary sphere that has charge $+7.50\ \mu C$. If the speed of the small sphere is 5.90×10^3 m/s, what is the radius of its orbit? Treat the spheres as point charges and ignore gravity.

21.85 •• Two small copper spheres each have radius 1.00 mm. (a) How many atoms does each sphere contain? (b) Assume that each copper atom contains 29 protons and 29 electrons. We know that electrons and protons have charges of exactly the same magnitude, but let's explore the effect of small differences (see also Problem 21.81). If the charge of a proton is $+e$ and the magnitude of the charge of an electron is 0.100% smaller, what is the net charge of each sphere and what force would one sphere exert on the other if they were separated by 1.00 m?

21.86 ••• **CP** **Operation of an Inkjet Printer.** In an inkjet printer, letters are built up by squirting drops of ink at the paper from a rapidly moving nozzle. The ink drops, which have a mass of 1.4×10^{-8} g each, leave the nozzle and travel toward the paper at 20 m/s, passing through a charging unit that gives each drop a positive charge q by removing some electrons from it. The drops then pass between parallel deflecting plates 2.0 cm long where there is a uniform vertical electric field with magnitude 8.0×10^4 N/C. If a drop is to be deflected 0.30 mm by the time it reaches the end of the deflection plates, what magnitude of charge must be given to the drop?

21.87 •• **CP** A proton is projected into a uniform electric field that points vertically upward and has magnitude E. The initial velocity of the proton has a magnitude v_0 and is directed at an angle α below the horizontal. (a) Find the maximum distance h_{max} that the proton descends vertically below its initial elevation. You can ignore gravitational forces. (b) After what horizontal distance d does the proton return to its original elevation? (c) Sketch the trajectory of the proton. (d) Find the numerical values of h_{max} and d if $E = 500$ N/C, $v_0 = 4.00 \times 10^5$ m/s, and $\alpha = 30.0°$.

21.88 • A negative point charge $q_1 = -4.00$ nC is on the x-axis at $x = 0.60$ m. A second point charge q_2 is on the x-axis at $x = -1.20$ m. What must the sign and magnitude of q_2 be for the net electric field at the origin to be (a) 50.0 N/C in the $+x$-direction and (b) 50.0 N/C in the $-x$-direction?

21.89 •• **CALC** Positive charge Q is distributed uniformly along the x-axis from $x = 0$ to $x = a$. A positive point charge q is located on the positive x-axis at $x = a + r$, a distance r to the right of the end of Q (Fig. P21.89). (a) Calculate the x- and y-components of the electric field produced by the charge distribution Q at points on the positive x-axis where $x > a$. (b) Calculate the force (magnitude and direction) that the charge distribution Q exerts on q. (c) Show that if $r \gg a$, the magnitude of the force in part (b) is approximately $Qq/4\pi\epsilon_0 r^2$. Explain why this result is obtained.

Figure **P21.89**

21.90 •• **CALC** Positive charge Q is distributed uniformly along the positive y-axis between $y = 0$ and $y = a$. A negative point charge $-q$ lies on the positive x-axis, a distance x from the origin (Fig. P21.90). (a) Calculate the x- and y-components of the electric field produced by the charge distribution Q at points on the positive x-axis. (b) Calculate the x- and y-components of the force that the charge distribution Q exerts on q. (c) Show that if $x \gg a$, $F_x \cong -Qq/4\pi\epsilon_0 x^2$ and $F_y \cong +Qqa/8\pi\epsilon_0 x^3$. Explain why this result is obtained.

Figure **P21.90**

21.91 •• A charged line like that shown in Fig. 21.24 extends from $y = 2.50$ cm to $y = -2.50$ cm. The total charge distributed uniformly along the line is -7.00 nC. (a) Find the electric field (magnitude and direction) on the x-axis at $x = 10.0$ cm. (b) Is the magnitude of the electric field you calculated in part (a) larger or smaller than the electric field 10.0 cm from a point charge that has the same total charge as this finite line of charge? In terms of the approximation used to derive $E = Q/4\pi\epsilon_0 x^2$ for a point charge from Eq. (21.9), explain why this is so. (c) At what distance x does the result for the finite line of charge differ by 1.0% from that for the point charge?

21.92 • **CP** **A Parallel Universe.** Imagine a parallel universe in which the electric force has the same properties as in our universe but there is no gravity. In this parallel universe, the sun carries charge Q, the earth carries charge $-Q$, and the electric attraction between them keeps the earth in orbit. The earth in the parallel universe has the same mass, the same orbital radius, and the same orbital period as in our universe. Calculate the value of Q. (Consult Appendix F as needed.)

21.93 ••• A uniformly charged disk like the disk in Fig. 21.25 has radius 2.50 cm and carries a total charge of 7.0×10^{-12} C. (a) Find the electric field (magnitude and direction) on the x-axis at $x = 20.0$ cm. (b) Show that for $x \gg R$, Eq. (21.11) becomes $E = Q/4\pi\epsilon_0 x^2$, where Q is the total charge on the disk. (c) Is the magnitude of the electric field you calculated in part (a) larger or smaller than the electric field 20.0 cm from a point charge that has the same total charge as this disk? In terms of the approximation used in part (b) to derive $E = Q/4\pi\epsilon_0 x^2$ for a point charge from Eq. (21.11), explain why this is so. (d) What is the percent difference between the electric fields produced by the finite disk and by a point charge with the same charge at $x = 20.0$ cm and at $x = 10.0$ cm?

21.94 •• **BIO** **Electrophoresis.** Electrophoresis is a process used by biologists to separate different biological molecules (such as proteins) from each other according to their ratio of charge to size. The materials to be separated are in a viscous solution that produces a drag force F_D proportional to the size and speed of the molecule. We can express this relationship as $F_D = KRv$, where R is the radius of the molecule (modeled as being spherical), v is its speed, and K is a constant that depends on the viscosity of the

Figure **P21.94**

solution. The solution is placed in an external electric field E so that the electric force on a particle of charge q is $F = qE$. (a) Show that when the electric field is adjusted so that the two forces (electric and viscous drag) just balance, the ratio of q to R is Kv/E. (b) Show that if we leave the electric field on for a time T, the distance x that the molecule moves during that time is $x = (ET/k)(q/R)$. (c) Suppose you have a sample containing three different biological molecules for which the molecular ratio q/R for material 2 is twice that of material 1 and the ratio for material 3 is three times that of material 1. Show that the distances migrated by these molecules after the same amount of time are $x_2 = 2x_1$ and $x_3 = 3x_1$. In other words, material 2 travels twice as far as material 1, and material 3 travels three times as far as material 1. Therefore, we have separated these molecules according to their ratio of charge to size. In practice, this process can be carried out in a special gel or paper, along which the biological molecules migrate. (Fig. P21.94). The process can be rather slow, requiring several hours for separations of just a centimeter or so.

21.95 • **CALC** Positive charge $+Q$ is distributed uniformly along the $+x$-axis from $x = 0$ to $x = a$. Negative charge $-Q$ is distributed uniformly along the $-x$-axis from $x = 0$ to $x = -a$. (a) A positive point charge q lies on the positive y-axis, a distance y from the origin. Find the force (magnitude and direction) that the positive and negative charge distributions together exert on q. Show that this force is proportional to y^{-3} for $y \gg a$. (b) Suppose instead that the positive point charge q lies on the positive x-axis, a distance $x > a$ from the origin. Find the force (magnitude and direction) that the charge distribution exerts on q. Show that this force is proportional to x^{-3} for $x \gg a$.

21.96 •• **CP** A small sphere with mass m carries a positive charge q and is attached to one end of a silk fiber of length L. The other end of the fiber is attached to a large vertical insulating sheet that has a positive surface charge density σ. Show that when the sphere is in equilibrium, the fiber makes an angle equal to arctan $(q\sigma/2mg\epsilon_0)$ with the vertical sheet.

21.97 •• **CALC** Negative charge $-Q$ is distributed uniformly around a quarter-circle of radius a that lies in the first quadrant, with the center of curvature at the origin. Find the x- and y-components of the net electric field at the origin.

21.98 •• **CALC** A semicircle of radius a is in the first and second quadrants, with the center of curvature at the origin. Positive charge $+Q$ is distributed uniformly around the left half of the semicircle, and negative charge $-Q$ is distributed uniformly around the right half of the semicircle (Fig. P21.98). What are the magnitude and direction of the net electric field at the origin produced by this distribution of charge?

Figure **P21.98**

21.99 •• Two 1.20-m nonconducting wires meet at a right angle. One segment carries $+2.50~\mu C$ of charge distributed uniformly along its length, and the other carries $-2.50~\mu C$ distributed uniformly along it, as shown in Fig. P21.99.

Figure **P21.99**

(a) Find the magnitude and direction of the electric field these wires produce at point P, which is 60.0 cm from each wire. (b) If an electron is released at P, what are the magnitude and direction of the net force that these wires exert on it?

21.100 • Two very large parallel sheets are 5.00 cm apart. Sheet A carries a uniform surface charge density of $-9.50\mu C/m^2$, and sheet B, which is to the right of A, carries a uniform charge density of $-11.6~\mu C/m^2$. Assume the sheets are large enough to be treated as infinite. Find the magnitude and direction of the net electric field these sheets produce at a point (a) 4.00 cm to the right of sheet A; (b) 4.00 cm to the left of sheet A; (c) 4.00 cm to the right of sheet B.

21.101 • Repeat Problem 21.100 for the case where sheet B is positive.

21.102 • Two very large horizontal sheets are 4.25 cm apart and carry equal but opposite uniform surface charge densities of magnitude σ. You want to use these sheets to hold stationary in the region between them an oil droplet of mass 324 μg that carries an excess of five electrons. Assuming that the drop is in vacuum, (a) which way should the electric field between the plates point, and (b) what should σ be?

21.103 •• An infinite sheet with positive charge per unit area σ lies in the xy-plane. A second infinite sheet with negative charge per unit area $-\sigma$ lies in the yz-plane. Find the net electric field at all points that do not lie in either of these planes. Express your answer in terms of the unit vectors $\hat{i}$, $\hat{j}$, and $\hat{k}$.

21.104 •• **CP** A thin disk with a circular hole at its center, called an *annulus*, has inner radius R_1 and outer radius R_2 (Fig. P21.104). The disk has a uniform positive surface charge density σ on its surface. (a) Determine the total electric charge on the annulus. (b) The annulus lies in the yz-plane, with its center at the origin. For an arbitrary point on the x-axis (the axis of the annulus), find the magnitude and direction of the electric field $\vec{E}$. Consider points both above and below the annulus in Fig. P21.104. (c) Show that at points on the x-axis that are sufficiently close to the origin, the magnitude of the electric field is approximately proportional to the distance between the center of the annulus and the point. How close is "sufficiently close"? (d) A point particle with mass m and negative charge $-q$ is free to move along the x-axis (but cannot move off the axis). The particle is originally placed at rest at $x = 0.01R_1$ and released. Find the frequency of oscillation of the particle. (*Hint:* Review Section 14.2. The annulus is held stationary.)

Figure **P21.104**

CHALLENGE PROBLEMS

21.105 ••• Three charges are placed as shown in Fig. P21.105. The magnitude of q_1 is 2.00 μC, but its sign and the value of the charge q_2 are not known. Charge q_3 is $+4.00~\mu C$, and the net force $\vec{F}$ on q_3 is entirely in the negative x-direction. (a) Considering the different possible signs of q_1, there are four possible force diagrams representing the forces $\vec{F}_1$ and $\vec{F}_2$ that q_1 and q_2 exert on q_3. Sketch these four possible force configurations.

Figure **P21.105**

(b) Using the sketches from part (a) and the direction of $\vec{F}$, deduce the signs of the charges q_1 and q_2. (c) Calculate the magnitude of q_2. (d) Determine F, the magnitude of the net force on q_3.

21.106 ••• Two charges are placed as shown in Fig. P21.106. The magnitude of q_1 is 3.00 μC, but its sign and the value of the charge q_2 are not known. The direction of the net electric field $\vec{E}$ at point P is entirely in the negative y-direction. (a) Considering the different possible signs of q_1 and q_2, there are four possible diagrams that could represent the electric fields $\vec{E}_1$ and $\vec{E}_2$ produced by q_1 and q_2. Sketch the four possible electric-field configurations. (b) Using the sketches from part (a) and the direction of $\vec{E}$, deduce the signs of q_1 and q_2. (c) Determine the magnitude of $\vec{E}$.

Figure **P21.106**

21.107 ••• **CALC** Two thin rods of length L lie along the x-axis, one between $x = a/2$ and $x = a/2 + L$ and the other between $x = -a/2$ and $x = -a/2 - L$. Each rod has positive charge Q distributed uniformly along its length. (a) Calculate the electric field produced by the second rod at points along the positive x-axis. (b) Show that the magnitude of the force that one rod exerts on the other is

$$F = \frac{Q^2}{4\pi\epsilon_0 L^2}\ln\left[\frac{(a+L)^2}{a(a+2L)}\right]$$

(c) Show that if $a \gg L$, the magnitude of this force reduces to $F = Q^2/4\pi\epsilon_0 a^2$. (*Hint:* Use the expansion $\ln(1 + z) = z - z^2/2 + z^3/3 - \cdots$, valid for $|z| \ll 1$. Carry *all* expansions to at least order L^2/a^2.) Interpret this result.

Answers

Chapter Opening Question ?

Water molecules have a permanent electric dipole moment: One end of the molecule has a positive charge and the other end has a negative charge. These ends attract negative and positive ions, respectively, holding the ions apart in solution. Water is less effective as a solvent for materials whose molecules do not ionize (called *nonionic* substances), such as oils.

Test Your Understanding Questions

21.1 Answers: (a) the plastic rod weighs more, (b) the glass rod weighs less, (c) the fur weighs less, (d) the silk weighs more The plastic rod gets a negative charge by taking electrons from the fur, so the rod weighs a little more and the fur weighs a little less after the rubbing. By contrast, the glass rod gets a positive charge by giving electrons to the silk. Hence, after they are rubbed together, the glass rod weighs a little less and the silk weighs a little more. The weight change is *very* small: The number of electrons transferred is a small fraction of a mole, and a mole of electrons has a mass of only $(6.02 \times 10^{23}$ electrons$)(9.11 \times 10^{-31}$ kg/electron$) = 5.48 \times 10^{-7}$ kg $= 0.548$ milligram!

21.2 Answers: (a) (i), (b) (ii) Before the two spheres touch, the negatively charged sphere exerts a repulsive force on the electrons in the other sphere, causing zones of positive and negative induced charge (see Fig. 21.7b). The positive zone is closer to the negatively charged sphere than the negative zone, so there is a net force of attraction that pulls the spheres together, like the comb and insulator in Fig. 21.8b. Once the two metal spheres touch, some of the excess electrons on the negatively charged sphere will flow onto the other sphere (because metals are conductors). Then both spheres will have a net negative charge and will repel each other.

21.3 Answer: (iv) The force exerted by q_1 on Q is still as in Example 21.4. The magnitude of the force exerted by q_2 on Q is still equal to $F_{1 \text{ on } Q}$, but the direction of the force is now *toward* q_2 at an angle α below the x-axis. Hence the x-components of the two forces cancel while the (negative) y-components add together, and the total electric force is in the negative y-direction.

21.4 Answers: (a) (ii), (b) (i) The electric field $\vec{E}$ produced by a positive point charge points directly away from the charge (see Fig. 21.18a) and has a magnitude that depends on the distance r from the charge to the field point. Hence a second, negative point charge $q < 0$ will feel a force $\vec{F} = q\vec{E}$ that points directly toward the positive charge and has a magnitude that depends on the distance r between the two charges. If the negative charge moves directly toward the positive charge, the direction of the force remains the same but the force magnitude increases as the distance r decreases. If the negative charge moves in a circle around the positive charge, the force magnitude stays the same (because the distance r is constant) but the force direction changes.

21.5 Answer: (iv) Think of a pair of segments of length dy, one at coordinate $y > 0$ and the other at coordinate $-y < 0$. The upper segment has a positive charge and produces an electric field $d\vec{E}$ at P that points away from the segment, so this $d\vec{E}$ has a positive x-component and a negative y-component, like the vector $d\vec{E}$ in Fig. 21.24. The lower segment has the same amount of negative charge. It produces a $d\vec{E}$ that has the same magnitude but points *toward* the lower segment, so it has a negative x-component and a negative y-component. By symmetry, the two x-components are equal but opposite, so they cancel. Thus the total electric field has only a negative y-component.

21.6 Answer: yes If the field lines are straight, $\vec{E}$ must point in the same direction throughout the region. Hence the force $\vec{F} = q\vec{E}$ on a particle of charge q is always in the same direction. A particle released from rest accelerates in a straight line in the direction of $\vec{F}$, and so its trajectory is a straight line along a field line.

21.7 Answer: (ii) Equations (21.17) and (21.18) tell us that the potential energy for a dipole in an electric field is $U = -\vec{p} \cdot \vec{E} = -pE\cos\phi$, where ϕ is the angle between the directions of $\vec{p}$ and $\vec{E}$. If $\vec{p}$ and $\vec{E}$ point in opposite directions, so that $\phi = 180°$, we have $\cos\phi = -1$ and $U = +pE$. This is the maximum value that U can have. From our discussion of energy diagrams in Section 7.5, it follows that this is a situation of unstable equilibrium.

Bridging Problem

Answer: $E = 2kQ/\pi a^2$ in the $-y$-direction

GAUSS'S LAW

? This child acquires an electric charge by touching the charged metal sphere. The charged hairs on the child's head repel and stand out. If the child stands *inside* a large, charged metal sphere, will her hair stand on end?

LEARNING GOALS

By studying this chapter, you will learn:

- How you can determine the amount of charge within a closed surface by examining the electric field on the surface.

- What is meant by electric flux, and how to calculate it.

- How Gauss's law relates the electric flux through a closed surface to the charge enclosed by the surface.

- How to use Gauss's law to calculate the electric field due to a symmetric charge distribution.

- Where the charge is located on a charged conductor.

Often, there are both an easy way and a hard way to do a job; the easy way may involve nothing more than using the right tools. In physics, an important tool for simplifying problems is the *symmetry properties* of systems. Many physical systems have symmetry; for example, a cylindrical body doesn't look any different after you've rotated it around its axis, and a charged metal sphere looks just the same after you've turned it about any axis through its center.

Gauss's law is part of the key to using symmetry considerations to simplify electric-field calculations. For example, the field of a straight-line or plane-sheet charge distribution, which we derived in Section 21.5 using some fairly strenuous integrations, can be obtained in a few lines with the help of Gauss's law. But Gauss's law is more than just a way to make certain calculations easier. Indeed, it is a fundamental statement about the relationship between electric charges and electric fields. Among other things, Gauss's law can help us understand how electric charge distributes itself over conducting bodies.

Here's what Gauss's law is all about. Given any general distribution of charge, we surround it with an imaginary surface that encloses the charge. Then we look at the electric field at various points on this imaginary surface. Gauss's law is a relationship between the field at *all* the points on the surface and the total charge enclosed within the surface. This may sound like a rather indirect way of expressing things, but it turns out to be a tremendously useful relationship. Above and beyond its use as a calculational tool, Gauss's law can help us gain deeper insights into electric fields. We will make use of these insights repeatedly in the next several chapters as we pursue our study of electromagnetism.

22.1 Charge and Electric Flux

In Chapter 21 we asked the question, "Given a charge distribution, what is the electric field produced by that distribution at a point *P*?" We saw that the answer could be found by representing the distribution as an assembly of point charges,

The discussion of Gauss's law in this section is based on and inspired by the innovative ideas of Ruth W. Chabay and Bruce A. Sherwood in *Electric and Magnetic Interactions* (John Wiley & Sons, 1994).

22.1 How can you measure the charge inside a box without opening it?

(a) A box containing an unknown amount of charge

(b) Using a test charge outside the box to probe the amount of charge inside the box

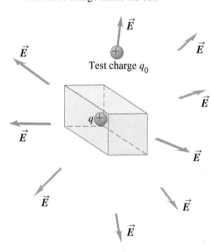

each of which produces an electric field $\vec{E}$ given by Eq. (21.7). The total field at P is then the vector sum of the fields due to all the point charges.

But there is an alternative relationship between charge distributions and electric fields. To discover this relationship, let's stand the question of Chapter 21 on its head and ask, "If the electric field pattern is known in a given region, what can we determine about the charge distribution in that region?"

Here's an example. Consider the box shown in Fig. 22.1a, which may or may not contain electric charge. We'll imagine that the box is made of a material that has no effect on any electric fields; it's of the same breed as the massless rope and the frictionless incline. Better still, let the box represent an *imaginary* surface that may or may not enclose some charge. We'll refer to the box as a **closed surface** because it completely encloses a volume. How can you determine how much (if any) electric charge lies within the box?

Knowing that a charge distribution produces an electric field and that an electric field exerts a force on a test charge, you move a test charge q_0 around the vicinity of the box. By measuring the force $\vec{F}$ experienced by the test charge at different positions, you make a three-dimensional map of the electric field $\vec{E} = \vec{F}/q_0$ outside the box. In the case shown in Fig. 22.1b, the map turns out to be the same as that of the electric field produced by a positive point charge (Fig. 21.28a). From the details of the map, you can find the exact value of the point charge inside the box.

To determine the contents of the box, we actually need to measure $\vec{E}$ only on the *surface* of the box. In Fig. 22.2a there is a single *positive* point charge inside the box, and in Fig. 22.2b there are two such charges. The field patterns on the surfaces of the boxes are different in detail, but in each case the electric field points *out* of the box. Figures 22.2c and 22.2d show cases with one and two *negative* point charges, respectively, inside the box. Again, the details of $\vec{E}$ are different for the two cases, but the electric field points *into* each box.

Electric Flux and Enclosed Charge

In Section 21.4 we mentioned the analogy between electric-field vectors and the velocity vectors of a fluid in motion. This analogy can be helpful, even though an electric field does not actually "flow." Using this analogy, in Figs. 22.2a and 22.2b, in which the electric field vectors point out of the surface, we say that there is an *outward* **electric flux.** (The word "flux" comes from a Latin word meaning "flow.") In Figs. 22.2c and 22.2d the $\vec{E}$ vectors point into the surface, and the electric flux is *inward.*

Figure 22.2 suggests a simple relationship: Positive charge inside the box goes with an outward electric flux through the box's surface, and negative charge inside goes with an inward electric flux. What happens if there is *zero* charge

22.2 The electric field on the surface of boxes containing (a) a single positive point charge, (b) two positive point charges, (c) a single negative point charge, or (d) two negative point charges.

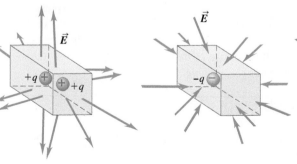

(a) Positive charge inside box, outward flux

(b) Positive charges inside box, outward flux

(c) Negative charge inside box, inward flux

(d) Negative charges inside box, inward flux

inside the box? In Fig. 22.3a the box is empty and $\vec{E} = 0$ everywhere, so there is no electric flux into or out of the box. In Fig. 22.3b, one positive and one negative point charge of equal magnitude are enclosed within the box, so the *net* charge inside the box is zero. There is an electric field, but it "flows into" the box on half of its surface and "flows out of" the box on the other half. Hence there is no *net* electric flux into or out of the box.

The box is again empty in Fig. 22.3c. However, there is charge present *outside* the box; the box has been placed with one end parallel to a uniformly charged infinite sheet, which produces a uniform electric field perpendicular to the sheet (as we learned in Example 21.11 of Section 21.5). On one end of the box, $\vec{E}$ points into the box; on the opposite end, $\vec{E}$ points out of the box; and on the sides, $\vec{E}$ is parallel to the surface and so points neither into nor out of the box. As in Fig. 22.3b, the inward electric flux on one part of the box exactly compensates for the outward electric flux on the other part. So in all of the cases shown in Fig. 22.3, there is no *net* electric flux through the surface of the box, and no *net* charge is enclosed in the box.

Figures 22.2 and 22.3 demonstrate a connection between the *sign* (positive, negative, or zero) of the *net* charge enclosed by a closed surface and the sense (outward, inward, or none) of the net electric flux through the surface. There is also a connection between the *magnitude* of the net charge inside the closed surface and the *strength* of the net "flow" of $\vec{E}$ over the surface. In both Figs. 22.4a and 22.4b there is a single point charge inside the box, but in Fig. 22.4b the magnitude of the charge is twice as great, and so $\vec{E}$ is everywhere twice as great in magnitude as in Fig. 22.4a. If we keep in mind the fluid-flow analogy, this means that the net outward electric flux is also twice as great in Fig. 22.4b as in Fig. 22.4a. This suggests that the net electric flux through the surface of the box is *directly proportional* to the magnitude of the net charge enclosed by the box.

This conclusion is independent of the size of the box. In Fig. 22.4c the point charge $+q$ is enclosed by a box with twice the linear dimensions of the box in Fig. 22.4a. The magnitude of the electric field of a point charge decreases with distance according to $1/r^2$, so the average magnitude of $\vec{E}$ on each face of the large box in Fig. 22.4c is just $\frac{1}{4}$ of the average magnitude on the corresponding face in Fig. 22.4a. But each face of the large box has exactly four times the area of the corresponding face of the small box. Hence the outward electric flux is the *same* for the two boxes if we *define* electric flux as follows: For each face of the box, take the product of the average perpendicular component of $\vec{E}$ and the area of that face; then add up the results from all faces of the box. With this definition the net electric flux due to a single point charge inside the box is independent of the size of the box and depends only on the net charge inside the box.

22.3 Three cases in which there is zero *net* charge inside a box and no net electric flux through the surface of the box. (a) An empty box with $\vec{E} = 0$. (b) A box containing one positive and one equal-magnitude negative point charge. (c) An empty box immersed in a uniform electric field.

(a) No charge inside box, zero flux

(b) Zero *net* charge inside box, inward flux cancels outward flux.

(c) No charge inside box, inward flux cancels outward flux.

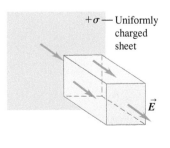

22.4 (a) A box enclosing a positive point charge $+q$. (b) Doubling the charge causes the magnitude of $\vec{E}$ to double, and it doubles the electric flux through the surface. (c) If the charge stays the same but the dimensions of the box are doubled, the flux stays the same. The magnitude of $\vec{E}$ on the surface decreases by a factor of $\frac{1}{4}$, but the area through which $\vec{E}$ "flows" increases by a factor of 4.

(a) A box containing a charge

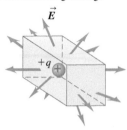

(b) Doubling the enclosed charge doubles the flux.

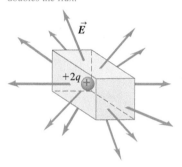

(c) Doubling the box dimensions *does not change* the flux.

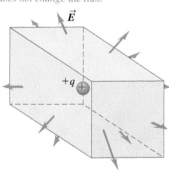

To summarize, for the special cases of a closed surface in the shape of a rectangular box and charge distributions made up of point charges or infinite charged sheets, we have found:

1. Whether there is a net outward or inward electric flux through a closed surface depends on the sign of the enclosed charge.
2. Charges *outside* the surface do not give a net electric flux through the surface.
3. The net electric flux is directly proportional to the net amount of charge enclosed within the surface but is otherwise independent of the size of the closed surface.

These observations are a qualitative statement of *Gauss's law*.

Do these observations hold true for other kinds of charge distributions and for closed surfaces of arbitrary shape? The answer to these questions will prove to be yes. But to explain why this is so, we need a precise mathematical statement of what we mean by electric flux. We develop this in the next section.

Test Your Understanding of Section 22.1 If all of the dimensions of the box in Fig. 22.2a are increased by a factor of 3, what effect will this change have on the electric flux through the box? (i) The flux will be $3^2 = 9$ times greater; (ii) the flux will be 3 times greater; (iii) the flux will be unchanged; (iv) the flux will be $\frac{1}{3}$ as great; (v) the flux will be $\left(\frac{1}{3}\right)^2 = \frac{1}{9}$ as great; (vi) not enough information is given to decide.

22.2 Calculating Electric Flux

In the preceding section we introduced the concept of *electric flux*. We used this to give a rough qualitative statement of Gauss's law: The net electric flux through a closed surface is directly proportional to the net charge inside that surface. To be able to make full use of this law, we need to know how to *calculate* electric flux. To do this, let's again make use of the analogy between an electric field $\vec{E}$ and the field of velocity vectors $\vec{v}$ in a flowing fluid. (Again, keep in mind that this is only an analogy; an electric field is *not* a flow.)

Flux: Fluid-Flow Analogy

Figure 22.5 shows a fluid flowing steadily from left to right. Let's examine the volume flow rate dV/dt (in, say, cubic meters per second) through the wire rectangle with area A. When the area is perpendicular to the flow velocity $\vec{v}$ (Fig. 22.5a) and the flow velocity is the same at all points in the fluid, the volume flow rate dV/dt is the area A multiplied by the flow speed v:

$$\frac{dV}{dt} = vA$$

When the rectangle is tilted at an angle ϕ (Fig. 22.5b) so that its face is not perpendicular to $\vec{v}$, the area that counts is the silhouette area that we see when we look in the direction of $\vec{v}$. This area, which is outlined in red and labeled $A_\perp$ in Fig. 22.5b, is the *projection* of the area A onto a surface perpendicular to $\vec{v}$. Two sides of the projected rectangle have the same length as the original one, but the other two are foreshortened by a factor of $\cos\phi$, so the projected area $A_\perp$ is equal to $A\cos\phi$. Then the volume flow rate through A is

$$\frac{dV}{dt} = vA\cos\phi$$

If $\phi = 90°$, $dV/dt = 0$; the wire rectangle is edge-on to the flow, and no fluid passes through the rectangle.

Also, $v \cos \phi$ is the component of the vector $\vec{v}$ perpendicular to the plane of the area A. Calling this component $v_\perp$, we can rewrite the volume flow rate as

$$\frac{dV}{dt} = v_\perp A$$

We can express the volume flow rate more compactly by using the concept of *vector area $\vec{A}$*, a vector quantity with magnitude A and a direction perpendicular to the plane of the area we are describing. The vector area $\vec{A}$ describes both the size of an area and its orientation in space. In terms of $\vec{A}$, we can write the volume flow rate of fluid through the rectangle in Fig. 22.5b as a scalar (dot) product:

$$\frac{dV}{dt} = \vec{v} \cdot \vec{A}$$

Flux of a Uniform Electric Field

Using the analogy between electric field and fluid flow, we now define electric flux in the same way as we have just defined the volume flow rate of a fluid; we simply replace the fluid velocity $\vec{v}$ by the electric field $\vec{E}$. The symbol that we use for electric flux is Φ_E (the capital Greek letter phi; the subscript E is a reminder that this is *electric* flux). Consider first a flat area A perpendicular to a uniform electric field $\vec{E}$ (Fig. 22.6a). We define the electric flux through this area to be the product of the field magnitude E and the area A:

$$\Phi_E = EA$$

Roughly speaking, we can picture Φ_E in terms of the field lines passing through A. Increasing the area means that more lines of $\vec{E}$ pass through the area, increasing the flux; a stronger field means more closely spaced lines of $\vec{E}$ and therefore more lines per unit area, so again the flux increases.

If the area A is flat but not perpendicular to the field $\vec{E}$, then fewer field lines pass through it. In this case the area that counts is the silhouette area that we see when looking in the direction of $\vec{E}$. This is the area $A_\perp$ in Fig. 22.6b and is equal to $A \cos \phi$ (compare to Fig. 22.5b). We generalize our definition of electric flux for a uniform electric field to

$$\Phi_E = EA \cos \phi \qquad \text{(electric flux for uniform } \vec{E}\text{, flat surface)} \qquad (22.1)$$

Since $E \cos \phi$ is the component of $\vec{E}$ perpendicular to the area, we can rewrite Eq. (22.1) as

$$\Phi_E = E_\perp A \qquad \text{(electric flux for uniform } \vec{E}\text{, flat surface)} \qquad (22.2)$$

In terms of the vector area $\vec{A}$ perpendicular to the area, we can write the electric flux as the scalar product of $\vec{E}$ and $\vec{A}$:

$$\Phi_E = \vec{E} \cdot \vec{A} \qquad \text{(electric flux for uniform } \vec{E}\text{, flat surface)} \qquad (22.3)$$

Equations (22.1), (22.2), and (22.3) express the electric flux for a *flat* surface and a *uniform* electric field in different but equivalent ways. The SI unit for electric flux is $1 \ \text{N} \cdot \text{m}^2/\text{C}$. Note that if the area is edge-on to the field, $\vec{E}$ and $\vec{A}$ are perpendicular and the flux is zero (Fig. 22.6c).

We can represent the direction of a vector area $\vec{A}$ by using a *unit vector $\hat{n}$* perpendicular to the area; $\hat{n}$ stands for "normal." Then

$$\vec{A} = A\hat{n} \qquad (22.4)$$

A surface has two sides, so there are two possible directions for $\hat{n}$ and $\vec{A}$. We must always specify which direction we choose. In Section 22.1 we related the charge inside a *closed* surface to the electric flux through the surface. With a closed surface we will always choose the direction of $\hat{n}$ to be *outward*, and we

22.5 The volume flow rate of fluid through the wire rectangle (a) is vA when the area of the rectangle is perpendicular to $\vec{v}$ and (b) is $vA \cos \phi$ when the rectangle is tilted at an angle ϕ.

(a) A wire rectangle in a fluid

(b) The wire rectangle tilted by an angle ϕ

Application Flux Through a Basking Shark's Mouth

Unlike aggressive carnivorous sharks such as great whites, a basking shark feeds passively on plankton in the water that passes through the shark's gills as it swims. To survive on these tiny organisms requires a huge flux of water through a basking shark's immense mouth, which can be up to a meter across. The water flux—the product of the shark's speed through the water and the area of its mouth—can be up to $0.5 \ \text{m}^3/\text{s}$ (500 liters per second, or almost 5×10^5 gallons per hour). In a similar way, the flux of electric field through a surface depends on the magnitude of the field and the area of the surface (as well as the relative orientation of the field and surface).

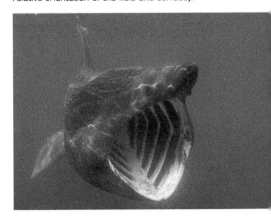

22.6 A flat surface in a uniform electric field. The electric flux Φ_E through the surface equals the scalar product of the electric field $\vec{E}$ and the area vector $\vec{A}$.

(a) Surface is face-on to electric field:
• $\vec{E}$ and $\vec{A}$ are parallel (the angle between $\vec{E}$ and $\vec{A}$ is $\phi = 0$).
• The flux $\Phi_E = \vec{E} \cdot \vec{A} = EA$.

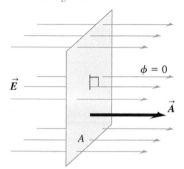

(b) Surface is tilted from a face-on orientation by an angle ϕ:
• The angle between $\vec{E}$ and $\vec{A}$ is ϕ.
• The flux $\Phi_E = \vec{E} \cdot \vec{A} = EA \cos \phi$.

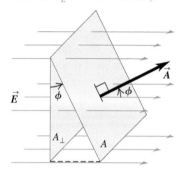

(c) Surface is edge-on to electric field:
• $\vec{E}$ and $\vec{A}$ are perpendicular (the angle between $\vec{E}$ and $\vec{A}$ is $\phi = 90°$).
• The flux $\Phi_E = \vec{E} \cdot \vec{A} = EA \cos 90° = 0$.

will speak of the flux *out of* a closed surface. Thus what we called "outward electric flux" in Section 22.1 corresponds to a *positive* value of Φ_E, and what we called "inward electric flux" corresponds to a *negative* value of Φ_E.

Flux of a Nonuniform Electric Field

What happens if the electric field $\vec{E}$ isn't uniform but varies from point to point over the area A? Or what if A is part of a curved surface? Then we divide A into many small elements dA, each of which has a unit vector $\hat{n}$ perpendicular to it and a vector area $d\vec{A} = \hat{n}\, dA$. We calculate the electric flux through each element and integrate the results to obtain the total flux:

$$\Phi_E = \int E \cos \phi \, dA = \int E_\perp \, dA = \int \vec{E} \cdot d\vec{A} \quad \begin{array}{l}\text{(general definition} \\ \text{of electric flux)}\end{array} \quad (22.5)$$

We call this integral the **surface integral** of the component $E_\perp$ over the area, or the surface integral of $\vec{E} \cdot d\vec{A}$. In specific problems, one form of the integral is sometimes more convenient than another. Example 22.3 at the end of this section illustrates the use of Eq. (22.5).

In Eq. (22.5) the electric flux $\int E_\perp \, dA$ is equal to the *average* value of the perpendicular component of the electric field, multiplied by the area of the surface. This is the same definition of electric flux that we were led to in Section 22.1, now expressed more mathematically. In the next section we will see the connection between the total electric flux through *any* closed surface, no matter what its shape, and the amount of charge enclosed within that surface.

Example 22.1 **Electric flux through a disk**

A disk of radius 0.10 m is oriented with its normal unit vector $\hat{n}$ at 30° to a uniform electric field $\vec{E}$ of magnitude 2.0×10^3 N/C (Fig. 22.7). (Since this isn't a closed surface, it has no "inside" or "outside." That's why we have to specify the direction of $\hat{n}$ in the figure.) (a) What is the electric flux through the disk? (b) What is the flux through the disk if it is turned so that $\hat{n}$ is perpendicular to $\vec{E}$? (c) What is the flux through the disk if $\hat{n}$ is parallel to $\vec{E}$?

22.7 The electric flux Φ_E through a disk depends on the angle between its normal $\hat{n}$ and the electric field $\vec{E}$.

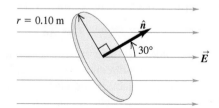

IDENTIFY and SET UP: This problem is about a flat surface in a uniform electric field, so we can apply the ideas of this section. We calculate the electric flux using Eq. (22.1).

EXECUTE: (a) The area is $A = \pi(0.10 \text{ m})^2 = 0.0314 \text{ m}^2$ and the angle between $\vec{E}$ and $\vec{A} = A\hat{n}$ is $\phi = 30°$, so from Eq. (22.1),

$$\Phi_E = EA\cos\phi = (2.0 \times 10^3 \text{ N/C})(0.0314 \text{ m}^2)(\cos 30°)$$
$$= 54 \text{ N} \cdot \text{m}^2/\text{C}$$

(b) The normal to the disk is now perpendicular to $\vec{E}$, so $\phi = 90°$, $\cos\phi = 0$, and $\Phi_E = 0$.

(c) The normal to the disk is parallel to $\vec{E}$, so $\phi = 0$ and $\cos\phi = 1$:

$$\Phi_E = EA\cos\phi = (2.0 \times 10^3 \text{ N/C})(0.0314 \text{ m}^2)(1)$$
$$= 63 \text{ N} \cdot \text{m}^2/\text{C}$$

EVALUATE: As a check on our results, note that our answer to part (b) is smaller than that to part (a), which is in turn smaller than that to part (c). Is all this as it should be?

Electric flux through a cube

An imaginary cubical surface of side L is in a region of uniform electric field $\vec{E}$. Find the electric flux through each face of the cube and the total flux through the cube when (a) it is oriented with two of its faces perpendicular to $\vec{E}$ (Fig. 22.8a) and (b) the cube is turned by an angle θ about a vertical axis (Fig. 22.8b).

IDENTIFY and SET UP: Since $\vec{E}$ is uniform and each of the six faces of the cube is flat, we find the flux Φ_{Ei} through each face using Eqs. (22.3) and (22.4). The total flux through the cube is the sum of the six individual fluxes.

EXECUTE: (a) Figure 22.8a shows the unit vectors $\hat{n}_1$ through $\hat{n}_6$ for each face; each unit vector points *outward* from the cube's closed surface. The angle between $\vec{E}$ and $\hat{n}_1$ is 180°, the angle between $\vec{E}$

22.8 Electric flux of a uniform field $\vec{E}$ through a cubical box of side L in two orientations.

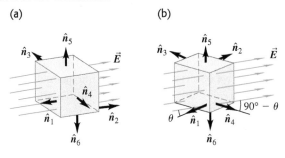

and $\hat{n}_2$ is 0°, and the angle between $\vec{E}$ and each of the other four unit vectors is 90°. Each face of the cube has area L^2, so the fluxes through the faces are

$$\Phi_{E1} = \vec{E} \cdot \hat{n}_1 A = EL^2\cos 180° = -EL^2$$
$$\Phi_{E2} = \vec{E} \cdot \hat{n}_2 A = EL^2\cos 0° = +EL^2$$
$$\Phi_{E3} = \Phi_{E4} = \Phi_{E5} = \Phi_{E6} = EL^2\cos 90° = 0$$

The flux is negative on face 1, where $\vec{E}$ is directed into the cube, and positive on face 2, where $\vec{E}$ is directed out of the cube. The total flux through the cube is

$$\Phi_E = \Phi_{E1} + \Phi_{E2} + \Phi_{E3} + \Phi_{E4} + \Phi_{E5} + \Phi_{E6}$$
$$= -EL^2 + EL^2 + 0 + 0 + 0 + 0 = 0$$

(b) The field $\vec{E}$ is directed into faces 1 and 3, so the fluxes through them are negative; $\vec{E}$ is directed out of faces 2 and 4, so the fluxes through them are positive. We find

$$\Phi_{E1} = \vec{E} \cdot \hat{n}_1 A = EL^2\cos(180° - \theta) = -EL^2\cos\theta$$
$$\Phi_{E2} = \vec{E} \cdot \hat{n}_2 A = +EL^2\cos\theta$$
$$\Phi_{E3} = \vec{E} \cdot \hat{n}_3 A = EL^2\cos(90° + \theta) = -EL^2\sin\theta$$
$$\Phi_{E4} = \vec{E} \cdot \hat{n}_4 A = EL^2\cos(90° - \theta) = +EL^2\sin\theta$$
$$\Phi_{E5} = \Phi_{E6} = EL^2\cos 90° = 0$$

The total flux $\Phi_E = \Phi_{E1} + \Phi_{E2} + \Phi_{E3} + \Phi_{E4} + \Phi_{E5} + \Phi_{E6}$ through the surface of the cube is again zero.

EVALUATE: We came to the same conclusion in our discussion of Fig. 22.3c: There is zero net flux of a uniform electric field through a closed surface that contains no electric charge.

Electric flux through a sphere

A point charge $q = +3.0 \ \mu\text{C}$ is surrounded by an imaginary sphere of radius $r = 0.20$ m centered on the charge (Fig. 22.9). Find the resulting electric flux through the sphere.

IDENTIFY and SET UP: The surface is not flat and the electric field is not uniform, so to calculate the electric flux (our target variable)

we must use the general definition, Eq. (22.5). We use Eq. (22.5) to calculate the electric flux (our target variable). Because the sphere is centered on the point charge, at any point on the spherical surface, $\vec{E}$ is directed out of the sphere perpendicular to the surface. The positive direction for both $\hat{n}$ and $E_\perp$ is outward, so $E_\perp = E$ and the flux through a surface element dA is $\vec{E} \cdot d\vec{A} = E\,dA$. This greatly simplifies the integral in Eq. (22.5).

Continued

22.9 Electric flux through a sphere centered on a point charge.

EXECUTE: We must evaluate the integral of Eq. (22.5), $\Phi_E = \int E\, dA$. At any point on the sphere of radius r the electric field has the same magnitude $E = q/4\pi\epsilon_0 r^2$. Hence E can be taken outside the integral, which becomes $\Phi_E = E\int dA = EA$, where A is the

area of the spherical surface: $A = 4\pi r^2$. Hence the total flux through the sphere is

$$\Phi_E = EA = \frac{q}{4\pi\epsilon_0 r^2}4\pi r^2 = \frac{q}{\epsilon_0}$$

$$= \frac{3.0 \times 10^{-6}\text{ C}}{8.85 \times 10^{-12}\text{ C}^2/\text{N}\cdot\text{m}^2} = 3.4 \times 10^5\text{ N}\cdot\text{m}^2/\text{C}$$

EVALUATE: The radius r of the sphere cancels out of the result for Φ_E. We would have obtained the same flux with a sphere of radius 2.0 m or 200 m. We came to essentially the same conclusion in our discussion of Fig. 22.4 in Section 22.1, where we considered rectangular closed surfaces of two different sizes enclosing a point charge. There we found that the flux of $\vec{E}$ was independent of the size of the surface; the same result holds true for a spherical surface. Indeed, the flux through *any* surface enclosing a single point charge is independent of the shape or size of the surface, as we'll soon see.

Test Your Understanding of Section 22.2 Rank the following surfaces in order from most positive to most negative electric flux. (i) a flat rectangular surface with vector area $\vec{A} = (6.0\text{ m}^2)\hat{\imath}$ in a uniform electric field $\vec{E} = (4.0\text{ N/C})\hat{\jmath}$; (ii) a flat circular surface with vector area $\vec{A} = (3.0\text{ m}^2)\hat{\jmath}$ in a uniform electric field $\vec{E} = (4.0\text{ N/C})\hat{\imath} + (2.0\text{ N/C})\hat{\jmath}$; (iii) a flat square surface with vector area $\vec{A} = (3.0\text{ m}^2)\hat{\imath} + (7.0\text{ m}^2)\hat{\jmath}$ in a uniform electric field $\vec{E} = (4.0\text{ N/C})\hat{\imath} - (2.0\text{ N/C})\hat{\jmath}$; (iv) a flat oval surface with vector area $\vec{A} = (3.0\text{ m}^2)\hat{\imath} - (7.0\text{ m}^2)\hat{\jmath}$ in a uniform electric field $\vec{E} = (4.0\text{ N/C})\hat{\imath} - (2.0\text{ N/C})\hat{\jmath}$.

22.3 Gauss's Law

22.10 Carl Friedrich Gauss helped develop several branches of mathematics, including differential geometry, real analysis, and number theory. The "bell curve" of statistics is one of his inventions. Gauss also made state-of-the-art investigations of the earth's magnetism and calculated the orbit of the first asteroid to be discovered.

Gauss's law is an alternative to Coulomb's law. While completely equivalent to Coulomb's law, Gauss's law provides a different way to express the relationship between electric charge and electric field. It was formulated by Carl Friedrich Gauss (1777–1855), one of the greatest mathematicians of all time (Fig. 22.10).

Point Charge Inside a Spherical Surface

Gauss's law states that the total electric flux through any closed surface (a surface enclosing a definite volume) is proportional to the total (net) electric charge inside the surface. In Section 22.1 we observed this relationship qualitatively for certain special cases; now we'll develop it more rigorously. We'll start with the field of a single positive point charge q. The field lines radiate out equally in all directions. We place this charge at the center of an imaginary spherical surface with radius R. The magnitude E of the electric field at every point on the surface is given by

$$E = \frac{1}{4\pi\epsilon_0}\frac{q}{R^2}$$

At each point on the surface, $\vec{E}$ is perpendicular to the surface, and its magnitude is the same at every point, just as in Example 22.3 (Section 22.2). The total electric flux is the product of the field magnitude E and the total area $A = 4\pi R^2$ of the sphere:

$$\Phi_E = EA = \frac{1}{4\pi\epsilon_0}\frac{q}{R^2}(4\pi R^2) = \frac{q}{\epsilon_0} \qquad (22.6)$$

The flux is independent of the radius R of the sphere. It depends only on the charge q enclosed by the sphere.

We can also interpret this result in terms of field lines. Figure 22.11 shows two spheres with radii R and $2R$ centered on the point charge q. Every field line that passes through the smaller sphere also passes through the larger sphere, so the total flux through each sphere is the same.

What is true of the entire sphere is also true of any portion of its surface. In Fig. 22.11 an area dA is outlined on the sphere of radius R and then projected onto the sphere of radius $2R$ by drawing lines from the center through points on the boundary of dA. The area projected on the larger sphere is clearly $4\,dA$. But since the electric field due to a point charge is inversely proportional to r^2, the field magnitude is $\frac{1}{4}$ as great on the sphere of radius $2R$ as on the sphere of radius R. Hence the electric flux is the same for both areas and is independent of the radius of the sphere.

Point Charge Inside a Nonspherical Surface

This projection technique shows us how to extend this discussion to nonspherical surfaces. Instead of a second sphere, let us surround the sphere of radius R by a surface of irregular shape, as in Fig. 22.12a. Consider a small element of area dA on the irregular surface; we note that this area is *larger* than the corresponding element on a spherical surface at the same distance from q. If a normal to dA makes an angle ϕ with a radial line from q, two sides of the area projected onto the spherical surface are foreshortened by a factor $\cos\phi$ (Fig. 22.12b). The other two sides are unchanged. Thus the electric flux through the spherical surface element is equal to the flux $E\,dA\cos\phi$ through the corresponding irregular surface element.

We can divide the entire irregular surface into elements dA, compute the electric flux $E\,dA\cos\phi$ for each, and sum the results by integrating, as in Eq. (22.5). Each of the area elements projects onto a corresponding spherical surface element. Thus the *total* electric flux through the irregular surface, given by any of the forms of Eq. (22.5), must be the same as the total flux through a sphere, which Eq. (22.6) shows is equal to q/ϵ_0. Thus, for the irregular surface,

$$\Phi_E = \oint \vec{E} \cdot d\vec{A} = \frac{q}{\epsilon_0} \qquad (22.7)$$

Equation (22.7) holds for a surface of *any* shape or size, provided only that it is a *closed* surface enclosing the charge q. The circle on the integral sign reminds us that the integral is always taken over a *closed* surface.

The area elements $d\vec{A}$ and the corresponding unit vectors $\hat{n}$ always point *out of* the volume enclosed by the surface. The electric flux is then positive in areas

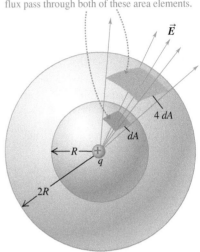

22.11 Projection of an element of area dA of a sphere of radius R onto a concentric sphere of radius $2R$. The projection multiplies each linear dimension by 2, so the area element on the larger sphere is $4\,dA$.

The same number of field lines and the same flux pass through both of these area elements.

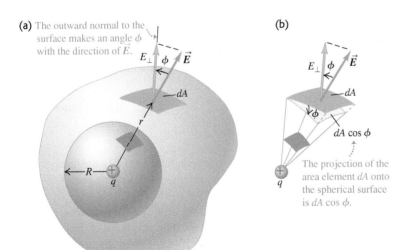

(a) The outward normal to the surface makes an angle ϕ with the direction of $\vec{E}$.

(b)

The projection of the area element dA onto the spherical surface is $dA\cos\phi$.

22.12 Calculating the electric flux through a nonspherical surface.

where the electric field points out of the surface and negative where it points inward. Also, $E_\perp$ is positive at points where $\vec{E}$ points out of the surface and negative at points where $\vec{E}$ points into the surface.

If the point charge in Fig. 22.12 is negative, the $\vec{E}$ field is directed radially *inward;* the angle ϕ is then greater than 90°, its cosine is negative, and the integral in Eq. (22.7) is negative. But since q is also negative, Eq. (22.7) still holds.

For a closed surface enclosing *no* charge,

$$\Phi_E = \oint \vec{E} \cdot d\vec{A} = 0$$

This is the mathematical statement that when a region contains no charge, any field lines caused by charges *outside* the region that enter on one side must leave again on the other side. (In Section 22.1 we came to the same conclusion by considering the special case of a rectangular box in a uniform field.) Figure 22.13 illustrates this point. *Electric field lines can begin or end inside a region of space only when there is charge in that region.*

General Form of Gauss's Law

Now comes the final step in obtaining the general form of Gauss's law. Suppose the surface encloses not just one point charge q but several charges q_1, q_2, q_3, ... The total (resultant) electric field $\vec{E}$ at any point is the vector sum of the $\vec{E}$ fields of the individual charges. Let Q_{encl} be the *total* charge enclosed by the surface: $Q_{encl} = q_1 + q_2 + q_3 + \cdots$. Also let $\vec{E}$ be the *total* field at the position of the surface area element $d\vec{A}$, and let $E_\perp$ be its component perpendicular to the plane of that element (that is, parallel to $d\vec{A}$). Then we can write an equation like Eq. (22.7) for each charge and its corresponding field and add the results. When we do, we obtain the general statement of Gauss's law:

$$\Phi_E = \oint \vec{E} \cdot d\vec{A} = \frac{Q_{encl}}{\epsilon_0} \qquad \text{(Gauss's law)} \qquad (22.8)$$

The total electric flux through a closed surface is equal to the total (net) electric charge inside the surface, divided by ϵ_0.

CAUTION **Gaussian surfaces are imaginary** Remember that the closed surface in Gauss's law is *imaginary;* there need not be any material object at the position of the surface. We often refer to a closed surface used in Gauss's law as a **Gaussian surface.**

Using the definition of Q_{encl} and the various ways to express electric flux given in Eq. (22.5), we can express Gauss's law in the following equivalent forms:

$$\Phi_E = \oint E\cos\phi \, dA = \oint E_\perp \, dA = \oint \vec{E} \cdot d\vec{A} = \frac{Q_{encl}}{\epsilon_0} \quad \begin{array}{l}\text{(various forms}\\ \text{of Gauss's law)}\end{array} \quad (22.9)$$

As in Eq. (22.5), the various forms of the integral all express the same thing, the total electric flux through the Gaussian surface, in different terms. One form is sometimes more convenient than another.

As an example, Fig. 22.14a shows a spherical Gaussian surface of radius r around a positive point charge $+q$. The electric field points out of the Gaussian surface, so at every point on the surface $\vec{E}$ is in the same direction as $d\vec{A}$, $\phi = 0$, and $E_\perp$ is equal to the field magnitude $E = q/4\pi\epsilon_0 r^2$. Since E is the same at all points

22.13 A point charge *outside* a closed surface that encloses no charge. If an electric field line from the external charge enters the surface at one point, it must leave at another.

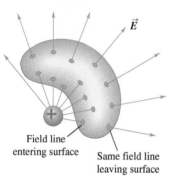

Field line entering surface

Same field line leaving surface

$\vec{E}$

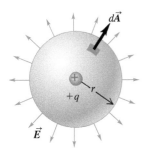

(a) Gaussian surface around positive charge: positive (outward) flux

(b) Gaussian surface around negative charge: negative (inward) flux

22.14 Spherical Gaussian surfaces around **(a)** a positive point charge and **(b)** a negative point charge.

on the surface, we can take it outside the integral in Eq. (22.9). Then the remaining integral is $\int dA = A = 4\pi r^2$, the area of the sphere. Hence Eq. (22.9) becomes

$$\Phi_E = \oint E_\perp \, dA = \oint \left(\frac{q}{4\pi\epsilon_0 r^2}\right) dA = \frac{q}{4\pi\epsilon_0 r^2} \oint dA = \frac{q}{4\pi\epsilon_0 r^2} 4\pi r^2 = \frac{q}{\epsilon_0}$$

The enclosed charge Q_{encl} is just the charge $+q$, so this agrees with Gauss's law. If the Gaussian surface encloses a *negative* point charge as in Fig. 22.14b, then $\vec{E}$ points *into* the surface at each point in the direction opposite $d\vec{A}$. Then $\phi = 180°$ and $E_\perp$ is equal to the negative of the field magnitude: $E_\perp = -E = -|-q|/4\pi\epsilon_0 r^2 = -q/4\pi\epsilon_0 r^2$. Equation (22.9) then becomes

$$\Phi_E = \oint E_\perp \, dA = \oint \left(\frac{-q}{4\pi\epsilon_0 r^2}\right) dA = \frac{-q}{4\pi\epsilon_0 r^2} \oint dA = \frac{-q}{4\pi\epsilon_0 r^2} 4\pi r^2 = \frac{-q}{\epsilon_0}$$

This again agrees with Gauss's law because the enclosed charge in Fig. 22.14b is $Q_{\text{encl}} = -q$.

In Eqs. (22.8) and (22.9), Q_{encl} is always the algebraic sum of all the positive and negative charges enclosed by the Gaussian surface, and $\vec{E}$ is the *total* field at each point on the surface. Also note that in general, this field is caused partly by charges inside the surface and partly by charges outside. But as Fig. 22.13 shows, the outside charges do *not* contribute to the total (net) flux through the surface. So Eqs. (22.8) and (22.9) are correct even when there are charges outside the surface that contribute to the electric field at the surface. When $Q_{\text{encl}} = 0$, the total flux through the Gaussian surface must be zero, even though some areas may have positive flux and others may have negative flux (see Fig. 22.3b).

Gauss's law is the definitive answer to the question we posed at the beginning of Section 22.1: "If the electric field pattern is known in a given region, what can we determine about the charge distribution in that region?" It provides a relationship between the electric field on a closed surface and the charge distribution within that surface. But in some cases we can use Gauss's law to answer the reverse question: "If the charge distribution is known, what can we determine about the electric field that the charge distribution produces?" Gauss's law may seem like an unappealing way to address this question, since it may look as though evaluating the integral in Eq. (22.8) is a hopeless task. Sometimes it is, but other times it is surprisingly easy. Here's an example in which *no* integration is involved at all; we'll work out several more examples in the next section.

Conceptual Example 22.4 **Electric flux and enclosed charge**

Figure 22.15 shows the field produced by two point charges $+q$ and $-q$ (an electric dipole). Find the electric flux through each of the closed surfaces A, B, C, and D.

SOLUTION

Gauss's law, Eq. (22.8), says that the total electric flux through a closed surface is equal to the total enclosed charge divided by ϵ_0. In

Continued

Fig. 22.15, surface A (shown in red) encloses the positive charge, so $Q_{encl} = +q$; surface B (in blue) encloses the negative charge, so $Q_{encl} = -q$; surface C (in purple) encloses *both* charges, so $Q_{encl} = +q + (-q) = 0$; and surface D (in yellow) encloses no charges, so $Q_{encl} = 0$. Hence, without having to do any integration, we have $\Phi_{EA} = +q/\epsilon_0$, $\Phi_{EB} = -q/\epsilon_0$, and $\Phi_{EC} = \Phi_{ED} = 0$. These results depend only on the charges enclosed within each Gaussian surface, not on the precise shapes of the surfaces.

We can draw similar conclusions by examining the electric field lines. All the field lines that cross surface A are directed out of the surface, so the flux through A must be positive. Similarly, the flux through B must be negative since all of the field lines that cross that surface point inward. For both surface C and surface D, there are as many field lines pointing into the surface as there are field lines pointing outward, so the flux through each of these surfaces is zero.

22.15 The net number of field lines leaving a closed surface is proportional to the total charge enclosed by that surface.

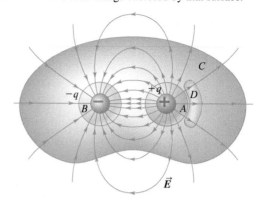

22.16 Five Gaussian surfaces and six point charges.

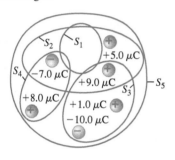

Test Your Understanding of Section 22.3 Figure 22.16 shows six point charges that all lie in the same plane. Five Gaussian surfaces—S_1, S_2, S_3, S_4, and S_5—each enclose part of this plane, and Fig. 22.16 shows the intersection of each surface with the plane. Rank these five surfaces in order of the electric flux through them, from most positive to most negative.

22.4 Applications of Gauss's Law

Gauss's law is valid for *any* distribution of charges and for *any* closed surface. Gauss's law can be used in two ways. If we know the charge distribution, and if it has enough symmetry to let us evaluate the integral in Gauss's law, we can find the field. Or if we know the field, we can use Gauss's law to find the charge distribution, such as charges on conducting surfaces.

In this section we present examples of both kinds of applications. As you study them, watch for the role played by the symmetry properties of each system. We will use Gauss's law to calculate the electric fields caused by several simple charge distributions; the results are collected in a table in the chapter summary.

In practical problems we often encounter situations in which we want to know the electric field caused by a charge distribution on a conductor. These calculations are aided by the following remarkable fact: *When excess charge is placed on a solid conductor and is at rest, it resides entirely on the surface, not in the interior of the material.* (By *excess* we mean charges other than the ions and free electrons that make up the neutral conductor.) Here's the proof. We know from Section 21.4 that in an electrostatic situation (with all charges at rest) the electric field $\vec{E}$ at every point in the interior of a conducting material is zero. If $\vec{E}$ were *not* zero, the excess charges would move. Suppose we construct a Gaussian surface inside the conductor, such as surface A in Fig. 22.17. Because $\vec{E} = \mathbf{0}$ everywhere on this surface, Gauss's law requires that the net charge inside the surface is zero. Now imagine shrinking the surface like a collapsing balloon until it encloses a region so small that we may consider it as a point P; then the charge at that point must be zero. We can do this anywhere inside the conductor, so *there can be no excess charge at any point within a solid conductor; any excess charge must reside on the conductor's surface.* (This result is for a *solid* conductor. In the next section we'll discuss what can happen if the conductor has cavities in its interior.) We will make use of this fact frequently in the examples that follow.

22.17 Under electrostatic conditions (charges not in motion), any excess charge on a solid conductor resides entirely on the conductor's surface.

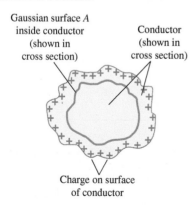

Gaussian surface A inside conductor (shown in cross section)

Conductor (shown in cross section)

Charge on surface of conductor

Problem-Solving Strategy 22.1   Gauss's Law

IDENTIFY *the relevant concepts:* Gauss's law is most useful when the charge distribution has spherical, cylindrical, or planar symmetry. In these cases the symmetry determines the direction of $\vec{E}$. Then Gauss's law yields the magnitude of $\vec{E}$ if we are given the charge distribution, and vice versa. In either case, begin the analysis by asking the question: What is the symmetry?

SET UP *the problem* using the following steps:
1. List the known and unknown quantities and identify the target variable.
2. Select the appropriate closed, imaginary Gaussian surface. For spherical symmetry, use a concentric spherical surface. For cylindrical symmetry, use a coaxial cylindrical surface with flat ends perpendicular to the axis of symmetry (like a soup can). For planar symmetry, use a cylindrical surface (like a tuna can) with its flat ends parallel to the plane.

EXECUTE *the solution* as follows:
1. Determine the appropriate size and placement of your Gaussian surface. To evaluate the field magnitude at a particular point, the surface must include that point. It may help to place one end of a can-shaped surface within a conductor, where $\vec{E}$ and therefore Φ are zero, or to place its ends equidistant from a charged plane.
2. Evaluate the integral $\oint E_\perp\, dA$ in Eq. (22.9). In this equation $E_\perp$ is the perpendicular component of the *total* electric field at each point on the Gaussian surface. A well-chosen Gaussian surface should make integration trivial or unnecessary. If the surface comprises several separate surfaces, such as the sides and ends

of a cylinder, the integral $\oint E_\perp\, dA$ over the entire closed surface is the sum of the integrals $\int E_\perp\, dA$ over the separate surfaces. Consider points 3–6 as you work.

3. If $\vec{E}$ is *perpendicular* (normal) at every point to a surface with area A, if it points *outward* from the interior of the surface, and if it has the same *magnitude* at every point on the surface, then $E_\perp = E = $ constant, and $\int E_\perp\, dA$ over that surface is equal to EA. (If $\vec{E}$ is inward, then $E_\perp = -E$ and $\int E_\perp\, dA = -EA$.) This should be the case for part or all of your Gaussian surface. If $\vec{E}$ is tangent to a surface at every point, then $E_\perp = 0$ and the integral over that surface is zero. This may be the case for parts of a cylindrical Gaussian surface. If $\vec{E} = 0$ at every point on a surface, the integral is zero.
4. Even when there is *no* charge within a Gaussian surface, the field at any given point on the surface is not necessarily zero. In that case, however, the total electric flux through the surface is always zero.
5. The flux integral $\oint E_\perp\, dA$ can be approximated as the difference between the numbers of electric lines of force leaving and entering the Gaussian surface. In this sense the flux gives the sign of the enclosed charge, but is only proportional to it; zero flux corresponds to zero enclosed charge.
6. Once you have evaluated $\oint E_\perp\, dA$, use Eq. (22.9) to solve for your target variable.

EVALUATE *your answer:* If your result is a *function* that describes how the magnitude of the electric field varies with position, ensure that it makes sense.

Example 22.5   Field of a charged conducting sphere

We place a total positive charge q on a solid conducting sphere with radius R (Fig. 22.18). Find $\vec{E}$ at any point inside or outside the sphere.

22.18 Calculating the electric field of a conducting sphere with positive charge q. Outside the sphere, the field is the same as if all of the charge were concentrated at the center of the sphere.

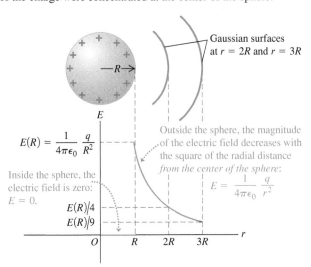

$$E(R) = \frac{1}{4\pi\epsilon_0}\frac{q}{R^2}$$

Inside the sphere, the electric field is zero: $E = 0$.

Outside the sphere, the magnitude of the electric field decreases with the square of the radial distance *from the center of the sphere*: $E = \frac{1}{4\pi\epsilon_0}\frac{q}{r^2}$

SOLUTION

IDENTIFY and SET UP: As we discussed earlier in this section, all of the charge must be on the surface of the sphere. The charge is free to move on the conductor, and there is no preferred position on the surface; the charge is therefore distributed *uniformly* over the surface, and the system is spherically symmetric. To exploit this symmetry, we take as our Gaussian surface a sphere of radius r centered on the conductor. We can calculate the field inside or outside the conductor by taking $r < R$ or $r > R$, respectively. In either case, the point at which we want to calculate $\vec{E}$ lies on the Gaussian surface.

EXECUTE: The spherical symmetry means that the direction of the electric field must be radial; that's because there is no preferred direction parallel to the surface, so $\vec{E}$ can have no component parallel to the surface. There is also no preferred orientation of the sphere, so the field magnitude E can depend only on the distance r from the center and must have the same value at all points on the Gaussian surface.

For $r > R$ the entire conductor is within the Gaussian surface, so the enclosed charge is q. The area of the Gaussian surface is $4\pi r^2$, and $\vec{E}$ is uniform over the surface and perpendicular to it at each point. The flux integral $\oint E_\perp\, dA$ is then just $E(4\pi r^2)$, and Eq. (22.8) gives

Continued

$$E(4\pi r^2) = \frac{q}{\epsilon_0} \quad \text{and}$$

$$E = \frac{1}{4\pi\epsilon_0} \frac{q}{r^2} \quad \text{(outside a charged conducting sphere)}$$

This expression is the same as that for a point charge; outside the charged sphere, its field is the same as though the entire charge were concentrated at its center. Just outside the surface of the sphere, where $r = R$,

$$E = \frac{1}{4\pi\epsilon_0} \frac{q}{R^2} \quad \text{(at the surface of a charged conducting sphere)}$$

CAUTION **Flux can be positive or negative** Remember that we have chosen the charge q to be *positive*. If the charge is negative, the electric field is radially *inward* instead of radially outward, and the electric flux through the Gaussian surface is negative. The electric-field magnitudes outside and at the surface of the sphere are given by the same expressions as above, except that q denotes the *magnitude* (absolute value) of the charge. |

For $r < R$ we again have $E(4\pi r^2) = Q_{encl}/\epsilon_0$. But now our Gaussian surface (which lies entirely within the conductor)

encloses *no* charge, so $Q_{encl} = 0$. The electric field inside the conductor is therefore zero.

EVALUATE: We already knew that $\vec{E} = 0$ inside a solid conductor (whether spherical or not) when the charges are at rest. Figure 22.18 shows E as a function of the distance r from the center of the sphere. Note that in the limit as $R \rightarrow 0$, the sphere becomes a point charge; there is then only an "outside," and the field is everywhere given by $E = q/4\pi\epsilon_0 r^2$. Thus we have deduced Coulomb's law from Gauss's law. (In Section 22.3 we deduced Gauss's law from Coulomb's law; the two laws are equivalent.)

We can also use this method for a conducting spherical *shell* (a spherical conductor with a concentric spherical hole inside) if there is no charge inside the hole. We use a spherical Gaussian surface with radius r less than the radius of the hole. If there *were* a field inside the hole, it would have to be radial and spherically symmetric as before, so $E = Q_{encl}/4\pi\epsilon_0 r^2$. But now there is no enclosed charge, so $Q_{encl} = 0$ and $E = 0$ inside the hole.

Can you use this same technique to find the electric field in the region between a charged sphere and a concentric hollow conducting sphere that surrounds it?

Example 22.6 **Field of a uniform line charge**

Electric charge is distributed uniformly along an infinitely long, thin wire. The charge per unit length is λ (assumed positive). Find the electric field using Gauss's law.

SOLUTION

IDENTIFY and SET UP: We found in Example 21.10 (Section 21.5) that the field $\vec{E}$ of a uniformly charged, infinite wire is radially outward if λ is positive and radially inward if λ is negative, and that the field magnitude E depends only on the radial distance from the wire. This suggests that we use a *cylindrical* Gaussian surface, of radius r and arbitrary length l, coaxial with the wire and with its ends perpendicular to the wire (Fig. 22.19).

EXECUTE: The flux through the flat ends of our Gaussian surface is zero because the radial electric field is parallel to these ends, and so $\vec{E} \cdot \hat{n} = 0$. On the cylindrical part of our surface we have $\vec{E} \cdot \hat{n} = E_\perp = E$ everywhere. (If λ were negative, we would have

22.19 A coaxial cylindrical Gaussian surface is used to find the electric field outside an infinitely long, charged wire.

$\vec{E} \cdot \hat{n} = E_\perp = -E$ everywhere.) The area of the cylindrical surface is $2\pi rl$, so the flux through it—and hence the total flux Φ_E through the Gaussian surface—is $EA = 2\pi rlE$. The total enclosed charge is $Q_{encl} = \lambda l$, and so from Gauss's law, Eq. (22.8),

$$\Phi_E = 2\pi rlE = \frac{\lambda l}{\epsilon_0} \quad \text{and}$$

$$E = \frac{1}{2\pi\epsilon_0} \frac{\lambda}{r} \quad \text{(field of an infinite line of charge)}$$

We found this same result in Example 21.10 with *much* more effort.

If λ is *negative*, $\vec{E}$ is directed radially inward, and in the above expression for E we must interpret λ as the absolute value of the charge per unit length.

EVALUATE: We saw in Example 21.10 that the *entire* charge on the wire contributes to the field at any point, and yet we consider only that part of the charge $Q_{encl} = \lambda l$ within the Gaussian surface when we apply Gauss's law. There's nothing inconsistent here; it takes the entire charge to give the field the properties that allow us to calculate Φ_E so easily, and Gauss's law always applies to the enclosed charge only. If the wire is short, the symmetry of the infinite wire is lost, and E is not uniform over a coaxial, cylindrical Gaussian surface. Gauss's law then *cannot* be used to find Φ_E; we must solve the problem the hard way, as in Example 21.10.

We can use the Gaussian surface in Fig. 22.19 to show that the field outside a long, uniformly charged cylinder is the same as though all the charge were concentrated on a line along its axis (see Problem 22.42). We can also calculate the electric field in the space between a charged cylinder and a coaxial hollow conducting cylinder surrounding it (see Problem 22.39).

Example 22.7 Field of an infinite plane sheet of charge

Use Gauss's law to find the electric field caused by a thin, flat, infinite sheet with a uniform positive surface charge density σ.

SOLUTION

IDENTIFY and SET UP: In Example 21.11 (Section 21.5) we found that the field $\vec{E}$ of a uniformly charged infinite sheet is normal to the sheet, and that its magnitude is independent of the distance from the sheet. To take advantage of these symmetry properties, we use a cylindrical Gaussian surface with ends of area A and with its axis perpendicular to the sheet of charge (Fig. 22.20).

22.20 A cylindrical Gaussian surface is used to find the field of an infinite plane sheet of charge.

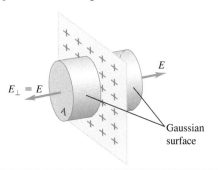

EXECUTE: The flux through the cylindrical part of our Gaussian surface is zero because $\vec{E} \cdot \hat{\boldsymbol{n}} = 0$ everywhere. The flux through each flat end of the surface is $+EA$ because $\vec{E} \cdot \hat{\boldsymbol{n}} = E_\perp = E$ everywhere, so the total flux through both ends—and hence the total flux Φ_E through the Gaussian surface—is $+2EA$. The total enclosed charge is $Q_{\text{encl}} = \sigma A$, and so from Gauss's law,

$$2EA = \frac{\sigma A}{\epsilon_0} \quad \text{and}$$

$$E = \frac{\sigma}{2\epsilon_0} \quad \text{(field of an infinite sheet of charge)}$$

In Example 21.11 we found this same result using a much more complex calculation.

If σ is negative, $\vec{E}$ is directed *toward* the sheet, the flux through the Gaussian surface in Fig. 22.20 is negative, and σ in the expression $E = \sigma/2\epsilon_0$ denotes the magnitude (absolute value) of the charge density.

EVALUATE: Again we see that, given favorable symmetry, we can deduce electric fields using Gauss's law much more easily than using Coulomb's law.

Example 22.8 Field between oppositely charged parallel conducting plates

Two large plane parallel conducting plates are given charges of equal magnitude and opposite sign; the surface charge densities are $+\sigma$ and $-\sigma$. Find the electric field in the region between the plates.

SOLUTION

IDENTIFY and SET UP: Figure 22.21a shows the field. Because opposite charges attract, most of the charge accumulates at the opposing faces of the plates. A small amount of charge resides on the *outer* surfaces of the plates, and there is some spreading or "fringing" of

the field at the edges. But if the plates are very large in comparison to the distance between them, the amount of charge on the outer surfaces is negligibly small, and the fringing can be neglected except near the edges. In this case we can assume that the field is uniform in the interior region between the plates, as in Fig. 22.21b, and that the charges are distributed uniformly over the opposing surfaces. To exploit this symmetry, we can use the shaded Gaussian surfaces S_1, S_2, S_3, and S_4. These surfaces are cylinders with flat ends of area A; one end of each surface lies *within* a plate.

22.21 Electric field between oppositely charged parallel plates.

(a) Realistic drawing

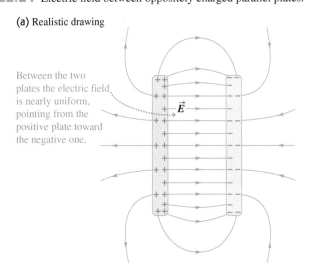

Between the two plates the electric field is nearly uniform, pointing from the positive plate toward the negative one.

(b) Idealized model

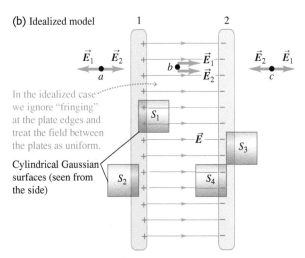

In the idealized case we ignore "fringing" at the plate edges and treat the field between the plates as uniform.

Cylindrical Gaussian surfaces (seen from the side)

Continued

EXECUTE: The left-hand end of surface S_1 is within the positive plate 1. Since the field is zero within the volume of any solid conductor under electrostatic conditions, there is no electric flux through this end. The electric field between the plates is perpendicular to the right-hand end, so on that end, $E_\perp$ is equal to E and the flux is EA; this is positive, since $\vec{E}$ is directed out of the Gaussian surface. There is no flux through the side walls of the cylinder, since these walls are parallel to $\vec{E}$. So the total flux integral in Gauss's law is EA. The net charge enclosed by the cylinder is σA, so Eq. (22.8) yields $EA = \sigma A/\epsilon_0$; we then have

$$E = \frac{\sigma}{\epsilon_0} \text{ (field between oppositely charged conducting plates)}$$

Example 22.9 Field of a uniformly charged sphere

Positive electric charge Q is distributed uniformly *throughout the volume* of an *insulating* sphere with radius R. Find the magnitude of the electric field at a point P a distance r from the center of the sphere.

SOLUTION

IDENTIFY and SET UP: As in Example 22.5, the system is spherically symmetric. Hence we can use the conclusions of that example about the direction and magnitude of $\vec{E}$. To make use of the spherical symmetry, we choose as our Gaussian surface a sphere with radius r, concentric with the charge distribution.

EXECUTE: From symmetry, the direction of $\vec{E}$ is radial at every point on the Gaussian surface, so $E_\perp = E$ and the field magnitude E is the same at every point on the surface. Hence the total electric flux through the Gaussian surface is the product of E and the total area of the surface $A = 4\pi r^2$—that is, $\Phi_E = 4\pi r^2 E$.

The amount of charge enclosed within the Gaussian surface depends on r. To find E *inside* the sphere, we choose $r < R$. The volume charge density ρ is the charge Q divided by the volume of the entire charged sphere of radius R:

$$\rho = \frac{Q}{4\pi R^3/3}$$

The volume V_{encl} enclosed by the Gaussian surface is $\frac{4}{3}\pi r^3$, so the total charge Q_{encl} enclosed by that surface is

$$Q_{encl} = \rho V_{encl} = \left(\frac{Q}{4\pi R^3/3}\right)\left(\tfrac{4}{3}\pi r^3\right) = Q\frac{r^3}{R^3}$$

Then Gauss's law, Eq. (22.8), becomes

$$4\pi r^2 E = \frac{Q}{\epsilon_0}\frac{r^3}{R^3} \text{ or}$$

$$E = \frac{1}{4\pi\epsilon_0}\frac{Qr}{R^3} \quad \text{(field inside a uniformly charged sphere)}$$

The field magnitude is proportional to the distance r of the field point from the center of the sphere (see the graph of E versus r in Fig. 22.22).

To find E *outside* the sphere, we take $r > R$. This surface encloses the entire charged sphere, so $Q_{encl} = Q$, and Gauss's law gives

$$4\pi r^2 E = \frac{Q}{\epsilon_0} \text{ or}$$

$$E = \frac{1}{4\pi\epsilon_0}\frac{Q}{r^2} \quad \text{(field outside a uniformly charged sphere)}$$

The field is uniform and perpendicular to the plates, and its magnitude is independent of the distance from either plate. The Gaussian surface S_4 yields the same result. Surfaces S_2 and S_3 yield $E = 0$ to the left of plate 1 and to the right of plate 2, respectively. We leave these calculations to you (see Exercise 22.29).

EVALUATE: We obtained the same results in Example 21.11 by using the principle of superposition of electric fields. The fields due to the two sheets of charge (one on each plate) are $\vec{E}_1$ and $\vec{E}_2$; from Example 22.7, both of these have magnitude $\sigma/2\epsilon_0$. The total electric field at any point is the vector sum $\vec{E} = \vec{E}_1 + \vec{E}_2$. At points a and c in Fig. 22.21b, $\vec{E}_1$ and $\vec{E}_2$ point in opposite directions, and their sum is zero. At point b, $\vec{E}_1$ and $\vec{E}_2$ are in the same direction; their sum has magnitude $E = \sigma/\epsilon_0$, just as we found above using Gauss's law.

22.22 The magnitude of the electric field of a uniformly charged insulating sphere. Compare this with the field for a conducting sphere (see Fig. 22.18).

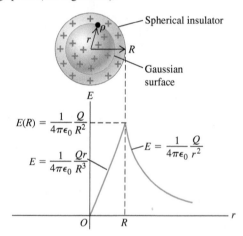

The field outside *any* spherically symmetric charged body varies as $1/r^2$, as though the entire charge were concentrated at the center. This is graphed in Fig. 22.22.

If the charge is *negative*, $\vec{E}$ is radially *inward* and in the expressions for E we interpret Q as the absolute value of the charge.

EVALUATE: Notice that if we set $r = R$ in either expression for E, we get the same result $E = Q/4\pi\epsilon_0 R^2$ for the magnitude of the field at the surface of the sphere. This is because the magnitude E is a *continuous* function of r. By contrast, for the charged conducting sphere of Example 22.5 the electric-field magnitude is *discontinuous* at $r = R$ (it jumps from $E = 0$ just inside the sphere to $E = Q/4\pi\epsilon_0 R^2$ just outside the sphere). In general, the electric field $\vec{E}$ is discontinuous in magnitude, direction, or both wherever there is a *sheet* of charge, such as at the surface of a charged conducting sphere (Example 22.5), at the surface of an infinite charged sheet (Example 22.7), or at the surface of a charged conducting plate (Example 22.8).

The approach used here can be applied to *any* spherically symmetric distribution of charge, even if it is not radially uniform, as it was here. Such charge distributions occur within many atoms and atomic nuclei, so Gauss's law is useful in atomic and nuclear physics.

Example 22.10 **Charge on a hollow sphere**

A thin-walled, hollow sphere of radius 0.250 m has an unknown charge distributed uniformly over its surface. At a distance of 0.300 m from the center of the sphere, the electric field points radially inward and has magnitude 1.80×10^2 N/C. How much charge is on the sphere?

SOLUTION

IDENTIFY and SET UP: The charge distribution is spherically symmetric. As in Examples 22.5 and 22.9, it follows that the electric field is radial everywhere and its magnitude is a function only of the radial distance r from the center of the sphere. We use a spherical Gaussian surface that is concentric with the charge distribution and has radius $r = 0.300$ m. Our target variable is $Q_{encl} = q$.

EXECUTE: The charge distribution is the same as if the charge were on the surface of a 0.250-m-radius conducting sphere. Hence we can borrow the results of Example 22.5. We note that the electric

field here is directed toward the sphere, so that q must be *negative*. Furthermore, the electric field is directed into the Gaussian surface, so that $E_\perp = -E$ and $\Phi_E = \oint E_\perp \, dA = -E(4\pi r^2)$.

By Gauss's law, the flux is equal to the charge q on the sphere (all of which is enclosed by the Gaussian surface) divided by ϵ_0. Solving for q, we find

$$q = -E(4\pi\epsilon_0 r^2) = -(1.80 \times 10^2 \text{ N/C})(4\pi)$$
$$\times (8.854 \times 10^{-12} \text{ C}^2/\text{N} \cdot \text{m}^2)(0.300 \text{ m})^2$$
$$= -1.80 \times 10^{-9} \text{ C} = -1.80 \text{ nC}$$

EVALUATE: To determine the charge, we had to know the electric field at *all* points on the Gaussian surface so that we could calculate the flux integral. This was possible here because the charge distribution is highly symmetric. If the charge distribution is irregular or lacks symmetry, Gauss's law is not very useful for calculating the charge distribution from the field, or vice versa.

Test Your Understanding of Section 22.4 You place a known amount of charge Q on the irregularly shaped conductor shown in Fig. 22.17. If you know the size and shape of the conductor, can you use Gauss's law to calculate the electric field at an arbitrary position outside the conductor?

22.5 **Charges on Conductors**

We have learned that in an electrostatic situation (in which there is no net motion of charge) the electric field at every point within a conductor is zero and that any excess charge on a solid conductor is located entirely on its surface (Fig. 22.23a). But what if there is a *cavity* inside the conductor (Fig. 22.23b)? If there is no charge within the cavity, we can use a Gaussian surface such as A (which lies completely within the material of the conductor) to show that the *net* charge on the *surface of the cavity* must be zero, because $\vec{E} = 0$ everywhere on the Gaussian surface. In fact, we can prove in this situation that there can't be any charge *anywhere* on the cavity surface. We will postpone detailed proof of this statement until Chapter 23.

Suppose we place a small body with a charge q inside a cavity within a conductor (Fig. 22.23c). The conductor is uncharged and is insulated from the charge q. Again $\vec{E} = 0$ everywhere on surface A, so according to Gauss's law the *total* charge inside this surface must be zero. Therefore there must be a charge $-q$ distributed on the surface of the cavity, drawn there by the charge q inside the cavity. The *total* charge on the conductor must remain zero, so a charge $+q$ must appear

Application Charge Distribution Inside a Nerve Cell

The interior of a human nerve cell contains both positive potassium ions (K^+) and negatively charged protein molecules (Pr^-). Potassium ions can flow out of the cell through the cell membrane, but the much larger protein molecules cannot. The result is that the interior of the cell has a net negative charge. (The fluid outside the cell has a positive charge that balances this.) The fluid within the cell is a good conductor, so the Pr^- molecules distribute themselves on the outer surface of the fluid—that is, on the inner surface of the cell membrane, which is an insulator. This is true no matter what the shape of the cell.

22.23 Finding the electric field within a charged conductor.

(a) Solid conductor with charge q_C

The charge q_C resides entirely on the surface of the conductor. The situation is electrostatic, so $\vec{E} = 0$ within the conductor.

(b) The same conductor with an internal cavity

Because $\vec{E} = 0$ at all points within the conductor, the electric field at all points on the Gaussian surface must be zero.

(c) An isolated charge q placed in the cavity

For $\vec{E}$ to be zero at all points on the Gaussian surface, the surface of the cavity must have a total charge $-q$.

either on its outer surface or inside the material. But we showed that in an electrostatic situation there can't be any excess charge within the material of a conductor. So we conclude that the charge $+q$ must appear on the outer surface. By the same reasoning, if the conductor originally had a charge q_C, then the total charge on the outer surface must be $q_C + q$ after the charge q is inserted into the cavity.

Conceptual Example 22.11   A conductor with a cavity

A solid conductor with a cavity carries a total charge of $+7$ nC. Within the cavity, insulated from the conductor, is a point charge of -5 nC. How much charge is on each surface (inner and outer) of the conductor?

SOLUTION

Figure 22.24 shows the situation. If the charge in the cavity is $q = -5$ nC, the charge on the inner cavity surface must be $-q = -(-5$ nC$) = +5$ nC. The conductor carries a *total* charge of $+7$ nC, none of which is in the interior of the material. If $+5$ nC is on the inner surface of the cavity, then there must be $(+7$ nC$) - (+5$ nC$) = +2$ nC on the outer surface of the conductor.

22.24 Our sketch for this problem. There is zero electric field inside the bulk conductor and hence zero flux through the Gaussian surface shown, so the charge on the cavity wall must be the opposite of the point charge.

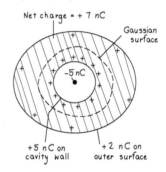

Testing Gauss's Law Experimentally

We can now consider a historic experiment, shown in Fig. 22.25. We mount a conducting container on an insulating stand. The container is initially uncharged. Then we hang a charged metal ball from an insulating thread (Fig. 22.25a), lower it into the container, and put the lid on (Fig. 22.25b). Charges are induced on the walls of the container, as shown. But now we let the ball *touch* the inner wall (Fig. 22.25c). The surface of the ball becomes part of the cavity surface. The situation is now the same as Fig. 22.23b; if Gauss's law is correct, the net charge on the cavity surface must be zero. Thus the ball must lose all its charge. Finally, we pull the ball out; we find that it has indeed lost all its charge.

This experiment was performed in the 19th century by the English scientist Michael Faraday, using a metal icepail with a lid, and it is called **Faraday's icepail experiment.** The result confirms the validity of Gauss's law and therefore of

22.25 (a) A charged conducting ball suspended by an insulating thread outside a conducting container on an insulating stand. (b) The ball is lowered into the container, and the lid is put on. (c) The ball is touched to the inner surface of the container.

Charged ball induces charges on the interior and exterior of the container.

Once the ball touches the container, it is part of the interior surface; all the charge moves to the container's exterior.

22.26 Cutaway view of the essential parts of a Van de Graaff electrostatic generator. The electron sink at the bottom draws electrons from the belt, giving it a positive charge; at the top the belt attracts electrons away from the conducting shell, giving the shell a positive charge.

Coulomb's law. Faraday's result was significant because Coulomb's experimental method, using a torsion balance and dividing of charges, was not very precise; it is very difficult to confirm the $1/r^2$ dependence of the electrostatic force by direct force measurements. By contrast, experiments like Faraday's test the validity of Gauss's law, and therefore of Coulomb's law, with much greater precision. Modern versions of this experiment have shown that the exponent 2 in the $1/r^2$ of Coulomb's law does not differ from precisely 2 by more than 10^{-16}. So there is no reason to believe it is anything other than exactly 2.

The same principle behind Faraday's icepail experiment is used in a *Van de Graaff electrostatic generator* (Fig. 22.26). A charged belt continuously carries charge to the inside of a conducting shell. By Gauss's law, there can never be any charge on the inner surface of this shell, so the charge is immediately carried away to the outside surface of the shell. As a result, the charge on the shell and the electric field around it can become very large very rapidly. The Van de Graaff generator is used as an accelerator of charged particles and for physics demonstrations.

This principle also forms the basis for *electrostatic shielding*. Suppose we have a very sensitive electronic instrument that we want to protect from stray electric fields that might cause erroneous measurements. We surround the instrument with a conducting box, or we line the walls, floor, and ceiling of the room with a conducting material such as sheet copper. The external electric field redistributes the free electrons in the conductor, leaving a net positive charge on the outer surface in some regions and a net negative charge in others (Fig. 22.27). This charge distribution causes an additional electric field such that the *total* field at every point inside the box is zero, as Gauss's law says it must be. The charge distribution on the box also alters the shapes of the field lines near the box, as the figure shows. Such a setup is often called a *Faraday cage*. The same physics tells

22.27 (a) A conducting box (a Faraday cage) immersed in a uniform electric field. The field of the induced charges on the box combines with the uniform field to give zero total field inside the box. (b) This person is inside a Faraday cage, and so is protected from the powerful electric discharge.

(a)

Field pushes electrons toward left side.   Net positive charge remains on right side.

$\vec{E}$ $\vec{E} = 0$ $\vec{E}$

Field perpendicular to conductor surface

(b)

you that one of the safest places to be in a lightning storm is inside an automobile; if the car is struck by lightning, the charge tends to remain on the metal skin of the vehicle, and little or no electric field is produced inside the passenger compartment.

Field at the Surface of a Conductor

Finally, we note that there is a direct relationship between the $\vec{E}$ field at a point just outside any conductor and the surface charge density σ at that point. In general, σ varies from point to point on the surface. We will show in Chapter 23 that at any such point, the direction of $\vec{E}$ is always *perpendicular* to the surface. (You can see this effect in Fig. 22.27a.)

To find a relationship between σ at any point on the surface and the perpendicular component of the electric field at that point, we construct a Gaussian surface in the form of a small cylinder (Fig. 22.28). One end face, with area A, lies within the conductor and the other lies just outside. The electric field is zero at all points within the conductor. Outside the conductor the component of $\vec{E}$ perpendicular to the side walls of the cylinder is zero, and over the end face the perpendicular component is equal to $E_\perp$. (If σ is positive, the electric field points out of the conductor and $E_\perp$ is positive; if σ is negative, the field points inward and $E_\perp$ is negative.) Hence the total flux through the surface is $E_\perp A$. The charge enclosed within the Gaussian surface is σA, so from Gauss's law,

22.28 The field just outside a charged conductor is perpendicular to the surface, and its perpendicular component $E_\perp$ is equal to σ/ϵ_0.

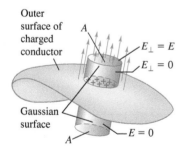

Outer surface of charged conductor

A

$E_\perp = E$

$E_\perp = 0$

Gaussian surface

A $E = 0$

$$E_\perp A = \frac{\sigma A}{\epsilon_0} \quad \text{and} \quad E_\perp = \frac{\sigma}{\epsilon_0} \quad \begin{array}{l}\text{(field at the surface} \\ \text{of a conductor)}\end{array} \quad (22.10)$$

We can check this with the results we have obtained for spherical, cylindrical, and plane surfaces.

We showed in Example 22.8 that the field magnitude between two infinite flat oppositely charged conducting plates also equals σ/ϵ_0. In this case the field magnitude E is the same at *all* distances from the plates, but in all other cases E decreases with increasing distance from the surface.

Conceptual Example 22.12 Field at the surface of a conducting sphere

Verify Eq. (22.10) for a conducting sphere with radius R and total charge q.

SOLUTION

In Example 22.5 (Section 22.4) we showed that the electric field just outside the surface is

$$E = \frac{1}{4\pi\epsilon_0} \frac{q}{R^2}$$

The surface charge density is uniform and equal to q divided by the surface area of the sphere:

$$\sigma = \frac{q}{4\pi R^2}$$

Comparing these two expressions, we see that $E = \sigma/\epsilon_0$, which verifies Eq. (22.10).

Example 22.13 Electric field of the earth

The earth (a conductor) has a net electric charge. The resulting electric field near the surface has an average value of about 150 N/C, directed toward the center of the earth. (a) What is the corresponding surface charge density? (b) What is the *total* surface charge of the earth?

SOLUTION

IDENTIFY and SET UP: We are given the electric-field magnitude at the surface of the conducting earth. We can calculate the surface charge density σ using Eq. (22.10). The total charge Q on the earth's surface is then the product of σ and the earth's surface area.

EXECUTE: (a) The direction of the field means that σ is negative (corresponding to $\vec{E}$ being directed *into* the surface, so $E_\perp$ is negative). From Eq. (22.10),

$$\sigma = \epsilon_0 E_\perp = (8.85 \times 10^{-12} \text{ C}^2/\text{N} \cdot \text{m}^2)(-150 \text{ N/C})$$
$$= -1.33 \times 10^{-9} \text{ C/m}^2 = -1.33 \text{ nC/m}^2$$

(b) The earth's surface area is $4\pi R_E^2$, where $R_E = 6.38 \times 10^6$ m is the radius of the earth (see Appendix F). The total charge Q is the product $4\pi R_E^2 \sigma$, or

$$Q = 4\pi(6.38 \times 10^6 \text{ m})^2(-1.33 \times 10^{-9} \text{ C/m}^2)$$
$$= -6.8 \times 10^5 \text{ C} = -680 \text{ kC}$$

EVALUATE: You can check our result in part (b) using the result of Example 22.5. Solving for Q, we find

$$Q = 4\pi\epsilon_0 R^2 E_\perp$$
$$= \frac{1}{9.0 \times 10^9 \text{ N} \cdot \text{m}^2/\text{C}^2}(6.38 \times 10^6 \text{ m})^2 (-150 \text{ N/C})$$
$$= -6.8 \times 10^5 \text{ C}$$

One electron has a charge of -1.60×10^{-19} C. Hence this much excess negative electric charge corresponds to there being $(-6.8 \times 10^5 \text{ C})/(-1.60 \times 10^{-19} \text{ C}) = 4.2 \times 10^{24}$ excess electrons on the earth, or about 7 moles of excess electrons. This is compensated by an equal *deficiency* of electrons in the earth's upper atmosphere, so the combination of the earth and its atmosphere is electrically neutral.

Test Your Understanding of Section 22.5 A hollow conducting sphere has no net charge. There is a positive point charge q at the center of the spherical cavity within the sphere. You connect a conducting wire from the outside of the sphere to ground. Will you measure an electric field outside the sphere?

Electric flux: Electric flux is a measure of the "flow" of electric field through a surface. It is equal to the product of an area element and the perpendicular component of $\vec{E}$, integrated over a surface. (See Examples 22.1–22.3.)

$$\Phi_E = \int E \cos\phi \, dA$$

$$= \int E_\perp \, dA = \int \vec{E} \cdot d\vec{A} \quad (22.5)$$

Gauss's law: Gauss's law states that the total electric flux through a closed surface, which can be written as the surface integral of the component of $\vec{E}$ normal to the surface, equals a constant times the total charge Q_{encl} enclosed by the surface. Gauss's law is logically equivalent to Coulomb's law, but its use greatly simplifies problems with a high degree of symmetry. (See Examples 22.4–22.10.)

When excess charge is placed on a conductor and is at rest, it resides entirely on the surface, and $\vec{E} = 0$ everywhere in the material of the conductor. (See Examples 22.11–22.13.)

$$\Phi_E = \oint E \cos\phi \, dA$$

$$= \oint E_\perp \, dA = \oint \vec{E} \cdot d\vec{A}$$

$$= \frac{Q_{encl}}{\epsilon_0} \quad (22.8), (22.9)$$

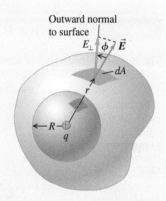

Electric field of various symmetric charge distributions: The following table lists electric fields caused by several symmetric charge distributions. In the table, q, Q, λ, and σ refer to the *magnitudes* of the quantities.

Charge Distribution	Point in Electric Field	Electric Field Magnitude
Single point charge q	Distance r from q	$E = \dfrac{1}{4\pi\epsilon_0}\dfrac{q}{r^2}$
Charge q on surface of conducting sphere with radius R	Outside sphere, $r > R$	$E = \dfrac{1}{4\pi\epsilon_0}\dfrac{q}{r^2}$
	Inside sphere, $r < R$	$E = 0$
Infinite wire, charge per unit length λ	Distance r from wire	$E = \dfrac{1}{2\pi\epsilon_0}\dfrac{\lambda}{r}$
Infinite conducting cylinder with radius R, charge per unit length λ	Outside cylinder, $r > R$	$E = \dfrac{1}{2\pi\epsilon_0}\dfrac{\lambda}{r}$
	Inside cylinder, $r < R$	$E = 0$
Solid insulating sphere with radius R, charge Q distributed uniformly throughout volume	Outside sphere, $r > R$	$E = \dfrac{1}{4\pi\epsilon_0}\dfrac{Q}{r^2}$
	Inside sphere, $r < R$	$E = \dfrac{1}{4\pi\epsilon_0}\dfrac{Qr}{R^3}$
Infinite sheet of charge with uniform charge per unit area σ	Any point	$E = \dfrac{\sigma}{2\epsilon_0}$
Two oppositely charged conducting plates with surface charge densities $+\sigma$ and $-\sigma$	Any point between plates	$E = \dfrac{\sigma}{\epsilon_0}$
Charged conductor	Just outside the conductor	$E = \dfrac{\sigma}{\epsilon_0}$

BRIDGING PROBLEM **Electric Field Inside a Hydrogen Atom**

A hydrogen atom is made up of a proton of charge $+Q = 1.60 \times 10^{-19}$ C and an electron of charge $-Q = -1.60 \times 10^{-19}$ C. The proton may be regarded as a point charge at $r = 0$, the center of the atom. The motion of the electron causes its charge to be "smeared out" into a spherical distribution around the proton, so that the electron is equivalent to a charge per unit volume of $\rho(r) = -(Q/\pi a_0^3)e^{-2r/a_0}$, where $a_0 = 5.29 \times 10^{-11}$ m is called the *Bohr radius*. (a) Find the total amount of the hydrogen atom's charge that is enclosed within a sphere with radius r centered on the proton. (b) Find the electric field (magnitude and direction) caused by the charge of the hydrogen atom as a function of r. (c) Make a graph as a function of r of the ratio of the electric-field magnitude E to the magnitude of the field due to the proton alone.

SOLUTION GUIDE

See MasteringPhysics® study area for a Video Tutor solution.

IDENTIFY and SET UP

1. The charge distribution in this problem is spherically symmetric, just as in Example 22.9, so you can solve it using Gauss's law.
2. The charge within a sphere of radius r includes the proton charge $+Q$ plus the portion of the electron charge distribution that lies within the sphere. The difference from Example 22.9 is that the electron charge distribution is *not* uniform, so the charge enclosed within a sphere of radius r is *not* simply the charge density multiplied by the volume $4\pi r^3/3$ of the sphere. Instead, you'll have to do an integral.

3. Consider a thin spherical shell centered on the proton, with radius r' and infinitesimal thickness dr'. Since the shell is so thin, every point within the shell is at essentially the same radius from the proton. Hence the amount of electron charge within this shell *is* equal to the electron charge density $\rho(r')$ at this radius multiplied by the volume dV of the shell. What is dV in terms of r'?
4. The total electron charge within a radius r equals the integral of $\rho(r')dV$ from $r' = 0$ to $r' = r$. Set up this integral (but don't solve it yet), and use it to write an expression for the total charge (including the proton) within a sphere of radius r.

EXECUTE

5. Integrate your expression from step 4 to find the charge within radius r. *Hint:* Integrate by substitution: Change the integration variable from r' to $x = 2r'/a_0$. You can calculate the integral $\int x^2 e^{-x}\,dx$ using integration by parts, or you can look it up in a table of integrals or on the World Wide Web.
6. Use Gauss's law and your results from step 5 to find the electric field at a distance r from the proton.
7. Find the ratio referred to in part (c) and graph it versus r. (You'll actually find it simplest to graph this function versus the quantity r/a_0.)

EVALUATE

8. How do your results for the enclosed charge and the electric-field magnitude behave in the limit $r \to 0$? In the limit $r \to \infty$? Explain your results.

Problems For instructor-assigned homework, go to MasteringPhysics®.

•, ••, •••: Problems of increasing difficulty. **CP**: Cumulative problems incorporating material from earlier chapters. **CALC**: Problems requiring calculus. **BIO**: Biosciences problems.

DISCUSSION QUESTIONS

Q22.1 A rubber balloon has a single point charge in its interior. Does the electric flux through the balloon depend on whether or not it is fully inflated? Explain your reasoning.

Q22.2 Suppose that in Fig. 22.15 both charges were positive. What would be the fluxes through each of the four surfaces in the example?

Q22.3 In Fig. 22.15, suppose a third point charge were placed outside the purple Gaussian surface C. Would this affect the electric flux through any of the surfaces A, B, C, or D in the figure? Why or why not?

Q22.4 A certain region of space bounded by an imaginary closed surface contains no charge. Is the electric field always zero everywhere on the surface? If not, under what circumstances is it zero on the surface?

Q22.5 A spherical Gaussian surface encloses a point charge q. If the point charge is moved from the center of the sphere to a point away from the center, does the electric field at a point on the surface change? Does the total flux through the Gaussian surface change? Explain.

Q22.6 You find a sealed box on your doorstep. You suspect that the box contains several charged metal spheres packed in insulating material. How can you determine the total net charge inside the box without opening the box? Or isn't this possible?

Q22.7 A solid copper sphere has a net positive charge. The charge is distributed uniformly over the surface of the sphere, and the electric field inside the sphere is zero. Then a negative point charge outside the sphere is brought close to the surface of the sphere. Is all the net charge on the sphere still on its surface? If so, is this charge still distributed uniformly over the surface? If it is not uniform, how is it distributed? Is the electric field inside the sphere still zero? In each case justify your answers.

Q22.8 If the electric field of a point charge were proportional to $1/r^3$ instead of $1/r^2$, would Gauss's law still be valid? Explain your reasoning. (*Hint:* Consider a spherical Gaussian surface centered on a single point charge.)

Q22.9 In a conductor, one or more electrons from each atom are free to roam throughout the volume of the conductor. Does this contradict the statement that any excess charge on a solid conductor must reside on its surface? Why or why not?

Q22.10 You charge up the van de Graaff generator shown in Fig. 22.26, and then bring an identical but uncharged hollow conducting sphere near it, without letting the two spheres touch. Sketch the distribution of charges on the second sphere. What is the net flux through the second sphere? What is the electric field inside the second sphere?

Q22.11 A lightning rod is a rounded copper rod mounted on top of a building and welded to a heavy copper cable running down into the ground. Lightning rods are used to protect houses and barns from lightning; the lightning current runs through the copper rather than through the building. Why? Why should the end of the rod be rounded?

Q22.12 A solid conductor has a cavity in its interior. Would the presence of a point charge inside the cavity affect the electric field outside the conductor? Why or why not? Would the presence of a point charge outside the conductor affect the electric field inside the cavity? Again, why or why not?

Q22.13 Explain this statement: "In a static situation, the electric field at the surface of a conductor can have no component parallel to the surface because this would violate the condition that the charges on the surface are at rest." Would this same statement be valid for the electric field at the surface of an *insulator*? Explain your answer and the reason for any differences between the cases of a conductor and an insulator.

Q22.14 In a certain region of space, the electric field $\vec{E}$ is uniform. (a) Use Gauss's law to prove that this region of space must be electrically neutral; that is, the volume charge density ρ must be zero. (b) Is the converse true? That is, in a region of space where there is no charge, must $\vec{E}$ be uniform? Explain.

Q22.15 (a) In a certain region of space, the volume charge density ρ has a uniform positive value. Can $\vec{E}$ be uniform in this region? Explain. (b) Suppose that in this region of uniform positive ρ there is a "bubble" within which $\rho = 0$. Can $\vec{E}$ be uniform within this bubble? Explain.

EXERCISES

Section 22.2 Calculating Electric Flux

22.1 • A flat sheet of paper of area 0.250 m² is oriented so that the normal to the sheet is at an angle of 60° to a uniform electric field of magnitude 14 N/C. (a) Find the magnitude of the electric flux through the sheet. (b) Does the answer to part (a) depend on the shape of the sheet? Why or why not? (c) For what angle ϕ between the normal to the sheet and the electric field is the magnitude of the flux through the sheet (i) largest and (ii) smallest? Explain your answers.

22.2 •• A flat sheet is in the shape of a rectangle with sides of lengths 0.400 m and 0.600 m. The sheet is immersed in a uniform electric field of magnitude 75.0 N/C that is directed at 20° from the plane of the sheet (Fig. E22.2). Find the magnitude of the electric flux through the sheet.

Figure **E22.2**

22.3 • You measure an electric field of 1.25×10^6 N/C at a distance of 0.150 m from a point charge. There is no other source of electric field in the region other than this point charge. (a) What is the electric flux through the surface of a sphere that has this charge

at its center and that has radius 0.150 m? (b) What is the magnitude of this charge?

22.4 • It was shown in Example 21.11 (Section 21.5) that the electric field due to an infinite line of charge is perpendicular to the line and has magnitude $E = \lambda/2\pi\epsilon_0 r$. Consider an imaginary cylinder with radius $r = 0.250$ m and length $l = 0.400$ m that has an infinite line of positive charge running along its axis. The charge per unit length on the line is $\lambda = 3.00 \, \mu\text{C/m}$. (a) What is the electric flux through the cylinder due to this infinite line of charge? (b) What is the flux through the cylinder if its radius is increased to $r = 0.500$ m? (c) What is the flux through the cylinder if its length is increased to $l = 0.800$ m?

22.5 •• A hemispherical surface with radius r in a region of uniform electric field $\vec{E}$ has its axis aligned parallel to the direction of the field. Calculate the flux through the surface.

22.6 • The cube in Fig. E22.6 has sides of length $L =10.0$ cm. The electric field is uniform, has magnitude $E = 4.00 \times 10^3$ N/C, and is parallel to the xy-plane at an angle of 53.1° measured from the $+x$-axis toward the $+y$-axis. (a) What is the electric flux through each of the six cube faces S_1, S_2, S_3, S_4, S_5, and S_6? (b) What is the total electric flux through all faces of the cube?

Figure **E22.6**

Section 22.3 Gauss's Law

22.7 • **BIO** As discussed in Section 22.5, human nerve cells have a net negative charge and the material in the interior of the cell is a good conductor. If a cell has a net charge of -8.65 pC, what are the magnitude and direction (inward or outward) of the net flux through the cell boundary?

22.8 • The three small spheres shown in Fig. E22.8 carry charges $q_1 = 4.00$ nC, $q_2 = -7.80$ nC, and $q_3 = 2.40$ nC. Find the net electric flux through each of the following closed surfaces shown in cross section in the figure: (a) S_1; (b) S_2; (c) S_3; (d) S_4; (e) S_5. (f) Do your answers to parts (a)–(e) depend on how the charge is distributed over each small sphere? Why or why not?

Figure **E22.8**

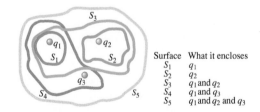

Surface	What it encloses
S_1	q_1
S_2	q_2
S_3	q_1 and q_2
S_4	q_1 and q_3
S_5	q_1 and q_2 and q_3

22.9 •• A charged paint is spread in a very thin uniform layer over the surface of a plastic sphere of diameter 12.0 cm, giving it a charge of $-35.0 \, \mu\text{C}$. Find the electric field (a) just inside the paint layer; (b) just outside the paint layer; (c) 5.00 cm outside the surface of the paint layer.

22.10 • A point charge $q_1 = 4.00$ nC is located on the x-axis at $x = 2.00$ m, and a second point charge $q_2 = -6.00$ nC is on the y-axis at $y = 1.00$ m. What is the total electric flux due to these two point charges through a spherical surface centered at the origin and with radius (a) 0.500 m, (b) 1.50 m, (c) 2.50 m?

22.11 • A 6.20-μC point charge is at the center of a cube with sides of length 0.500 m. (a) What is the electric flux through one of the six faces of the cube? (b) How would your answer to part (a) change if the sides were 0.250 m long? Explain.

22.12 • **Electric Fields in an Atom.** The nuclei of large atoms, such as uranium, with 92 protons, can be modeled as spherically symmetric spheres of charge. The radius of the uranium nucleus is approximately 7.4×10^{-15} m. (a) What is the electric field this nucleus produces just outside its surface? (b) What magnitude of electric field does it produce at the distance of the electrons, which is about 1.0×10^{-10} m? (c) The electrons can be modeled as forming a uniform shell of negative charge. What net electric field do they produce at the location of the nucleus?

22.13 • A point charge of +5.00 μC is located on the x-axis at $x = 4.00$ m, next to a spherical surface of radius 3.00 m centered at the origin. (a) Calculate the magnitude of the electric field at $x = 3.00$ m. (b) Calculate the magnitude of the electric field at $x = -3.00$ m. (c) According to Gauss's law, the net flux through the sphere is zero because it contains no charge. Yet the field due to the external charge is much stronger on the near side of the sphere (i.e., at $x = 3.00$ m) than on the far side (at $x = -3.00$ m). How, then, can the flux into the sphere (on the near side) equal the flux out of it (on the far side)? Explain. A sketch will help.

Section 22.4 Applications of Gauss's Law and Section 22.5 Charges on Conductors

22.14 •• A solid metal sphere with radius 0.450 m carries a net charge of 0.250 nC. Find the magnitude of the electric field (a) at a point 0.100 m outside the surface of the sphere and (b) at a point inside the sphere, 0.100 m below the surface.

22.15 •• Two very long uniform lines of charge are parallel and are separated by 0.300 m. Each line of charge has charge per unit length +5.20 μC/m. What magnitude of force does one line of charge exert on a 0.0500-m section of the other line of charge?

22.16 • Some planetary scientists have suggested that the planet Mars has an electric field somewhat similar to that of the earth, producing a net electric flux of 3.63×10^{16} N·m²/C at the planet's surface, directed toward the center of the planet. Calculate: (a) the total electric charge on the planet; (b) the electric field at the planet's surface (refer to the astronomical data inside the back cover); (c) the charge density on Mars, assuming all the charge is uniformly distributed over the planet's surface.

22.17 •• How many excess electrons must be added to an isolated spherical conductor 32.0 cm in diameter to produce an electric field of 1150 N/C just outside the surface?

22.18 •• The electric field 0.400 m from a very long uniform line of charge is 840 N/C. How much charge is contained in a 2.00-cm section of the line?

22.19 •• A very long uniform line of charge has charge per unit length 4.80 μC/m and lies along the x-axis. A second long uniform line of charge has charge per unit length −2.40 μC/m and is parallel to the x-axis at $y = 0.400$ m. What is the net electric field (magnitude and direction) at the following points on the y-axis: (a) $y = 0.200$ m and (b) $y = 0.600$ m?

22.20 • (a) At a distance of 0.200 cm from the center of a charged conducting sphere with radius 0.100 cm, the electric field is 480 N/C. What is the electric field 0.600 cm from the center of the sphere? (b) At a distance of 0.200 cm from the axis of a very long charged conducting cylinder with radius 0.100 cm, the electric field is 480 N/C. What is the electric field 0.600 cm from the axis of the cylinder? (c) At a distance of 0.200 cm from a large uniform sheet of charge, the electric field is 480 N/C. What is the electric field 1.20 cm from the sheet?

22.21 •• A hollow, conducting sphere with an outer radius of 0.250 m and an inner radius of 0.200 m has a uniform surface charge density of $+6.37 \times 10^{-6}$ C/m². A charge of −0.500 μC is now introduced into the cavity inside the sphere. (a) What is the new charge density on the outside of the sphere? (b) Calculate the strength of the electric field just outside the sphere. (c) What is the electric flux through a spherical surface just inside the inner surface of the sphere?

22.22 •• A point charge of −2.00 μC is located in the center of a spherical cavity of radius 6.50 cm inside an insulating charged solid. The charge density in the solid is $\rho = 7.35 \times 10^{-4}$ C/m³. Calculate the electric field inside the solid at a distance of 9.50 cm from the center of the cavity.

22.23 •• The electric field at a distance of 0.145 m from the surface of a solid insulating sphere with radius 0.355 m is 1750 N/C. (a) Assuming the sphere's charge is uniformly distributed, what is the charge density inside it? (b) Calculate the electric field inside the sphere at a distance of 0.200 m from the center.

22.24 •• CP A very small object with mass 8.20×10^{-9} kg and positive charge 6.50×10^{-9} C is projected directly toward a very large insulating sheet of positive charge that has uniform surface charge density 5.90×10^{-8} C/m². The object is initially 0.400 m from the sheet. What initial speed must the object have in order for its closest distance of approach to the sheet to be 0.100 m?

22.25 •• CP At time $t = 0$ a proton is a distance of 0.360 m from a very large insulating sheet of charge and is moving parallel to the sheet with speed 9.70×10^2 m/s. The sheet has uniform surface charge density 2.34×10^{-9} C/m². What is the speed of the proton at $t = 5.00 \times 10^{-8}$ s?

22.26 •• CP An electron is released from rest at a distance of 0.300 m from a large insulating sheet of charge that has uniform surface charge density $+2.90 \times 10^{-12}$ C/m². (a) How much work is done on the electron by the electric field of the sheet as the electron moves from its initial position to a point 0.050 m from the sheet? (b) What is the speed of the electron when it is 0.050 m from the sheet?

22.27 ••• CP CALC An insulating sphere of radius $R = 0.160$ m has uniform charge density $\rho = +7.20 \times 10^{-9}$ C/m³. A small object that can be treated as a point charge is released from rest just outside the surface of the sphere. The small object has positive charge $q = 3.40 \times 10^{-6}$ C. How much work does the electric field of the sphere do on the object as the object moves to a point very far from the sphere?

22.28 • A conductor with an inner cavity, like that shown in Fig. 22.23c, carries a total charge of +5.00 nC. The charge within the cavity, insulated from the conductor, is −6.00 nC. How much charge is on (a) the inner surface of the conductor and (b) the outer surface of the conductor?

22.29 • Apply Gauss's law to the Gaussian surfaces S_2, S_3, and S_4 in Fig. 22.21b to calculate the electric field between and outside the plates.

22.30 • A square insulating sheet 80.0 cm on a side is held horizontally. The sheet has 7.50 nC of charge spread uniformly over its area. (a) Calculate the electric field at a point 0.100 mm above the center of the sheet. (b) Estimate the electric field at a point 100 m above the center of the sheet. (c) Would the answers to parts (a) and (b) be different if the sheet were made of a conducting material? Why or why not?

22.31 • An infinitely long cylindrical conductor has radius R and uniform surface charge density σ. (a) In terms of σ and R, what is the charge per unit length λ for the cylinder? (b) In terms of σ, what is the magnitude of the electric field produced by the charged cylinder at a distance $r > R$ from its axis? (c) Express the result of part (b) in terms of λ and show that the electric field outside the cylinder is the same as if all the charge were on the axis. Compare your result to the result for a line of charge in Example 22.6 (Section 22.4).

22.32 • Two very large, nonconducting plastic sheets, each 10.0 cm thick, carry uniform charge densities σ_1, σ_2, σ_3, and σ_4 on their surfaces, as shown in Fig. E22.32. These surface charge densities have the values $\sigma_1 = -6.00\ \mu\text{C/m}^2$, $\sigma_2 = +5.00\ \mu\text{C/m}^2$, $\sigma_3 = +2.00\ \mu\text{C/m}^2$, and $\sigma_4 = +4.00\ \mu\text{C/m}^2$. Use Gauss's law to find the magnitude and direction of the electric field at the following points, far from

Figure **E22.32**

the edges of these sheets: (a) point A, 5.00 cm from the left face of the left-hand sheet; (b) point B, 1.25 cm from the inner surface of the right-hand sheet; (c) point C, in the middle of the right-hand sheet.

22.33 • A negative charge $-Q$ is placed inside the cavity of a hollow metal solid. The outside of the solid is grounded by connecting a conducting wire between it and the earth. (a) Is there any excess charge induced on the inner surface of the piece of metal? If so, find its sign and magnitude. (b) Is there any excess charge on the outside of the piece of metal? Why or why not? (c) Is there an electric field in the cavity? Explain. (d) Is there an electric field within the metal? Why or why not? Is there an electric field outside the piece of metal? Explain why or why not. (e) Would someone outside the solid measure an electric field due to the charge $-Q$? Is it reasonable to say that the grounded conductor has *shielded* the region from the effects of the charge $-Q$? In principle, could the same thing be done for gravity? Why or why not?

PROBLEMS

22.34 •• A cube has sides of length $L = 0.300$ m. It is placed with one corner at the origin as shown in Fig. E22.6. The electric field is not uniform but is given by $\vec{E} = (-5.00\ \text{N/C}\cdot\text{m})x\hat{\imath} + (3.00\ \text{N/C}\cdot\text{m})z\hat{k}$. (a) Find the electric flux through each of the six cube faces S_1, S_2, S_3, S_4, S_5, and S_6. (b) Find the total electric charge inside the cube.

22.35 • The electric field $\vec{E}$ in Fig. P22.35 is everywhere parallel to the x-axis, so the components E_y and E_z are zero. The x-component of the field E_x depends on x but not on y and z. At points in the yz-plane (where $x = 0$), $E_x = 125$ N/C. (a) What is the electric flux through surface I in Fig. P22.35? (b) What is the electric flux through surface II? (c) The volume shown in the figure is a small section of a

Figure **P22.35**

very large insulating slab 1.0 m thick. If there is a total charge of -24.0 nC within the volume shown, what are the magnitude and direction of $\vec{E}$ at the face opposite surface I? (d) Is the electric field produced only by charges within the slab, or is the field also due to charges outside the slab? How can you tell?

22.36 •• **CALC** In a region of space there is an electric field $\vec{E}$ that is in the z-direction and that has magnitude $E = (964\ \text{N}/(\text{C}\cdot\text{m}))x$. Find the flux for this field through a square in the xy-plane at $z = 0$ and with side length 0.350 m. One side of the square is along the $+x$-axis and another side is along the $+y$-axis.

22.37 •• The electric field $\vec{E}_1$ at one face of a parallelepiped is uniform over the entire face and is directed out of the face. At the opposite face, the electric field $\vec{E}_2$ is also uniform over the entire face and is directed into that face (Fig. P22.37). The two faces in question are inclined at 30.0° from the horizontal, while $\vec{E}_1$ and $\vec{E}_2$ are both horizontal; $\vec{E}_1$ has a magnitude of 2.50×10^4 N/C, and $\vec{E}_2$ has a magnitude of 7.00×10^4 N/C. (a) Assuming that no other electric field lines cross the surfaces of the parallelepiped, determine the net charge contained within. (b) Is the electric field produced only by the charges within the parallelepiped, or is the field also due to charges outside the parallelepiped? How can you tell?

Figure **P22.37**

22.38 • A long line carrying a uniform linear charge density $+50.0\ \mu\text{C/m}$ runs parallel to and 10.0 cm from the surface of a large, flat plastic sheet that has a uniform surface charge density of $-100\ \mu\text{C/m}^2$ on one side. Find the location of all points where an α particle would feel no force due to this arrangement of charged objects.

22.39 • **The Coaxial Cable.** A long coaxial cable consists of an inner cylindrical conductor with radius a and an outer coaxial cylinder with inner radius b and outer radius c. The outer cylinder is mounted on insulating supports and has no net charge. The inner cylinder has a uniform positive charge per unit length λ. Calculate the electric field (a) at any point between the cylinders a distance r from the axis and (b) at any point outside the outer cylinder. (c) Graph the magnitude of the electric field as a function of the distance r from the axis of the cable, from $r = 0$ to $r = 2c$. (d) Find the charge per unit length on the inner surface and on the outer surface of the outer cylinder.

22.40 • A very long conducting tube (hollow cylinder) has inner radius a and outer radius b. It carries charge per unit length $+\alpha$, where α is a positive constant with units of C/m. A line of charge lies along the axis of the tube. The line of charge has charge per unit length $+\alpha$. (a) Calculate the electric field in terms of α and the distance r from the axis of the tube for (i) $r < a$; (ii) $a < r < b$; (iii) $r > b$. Show your results in a graph of E as a function of r. (b) What is the charge per unit length on (i) the inner surface of the tube and (ii) the outer surface of the tube?

22.41 • Repeat Problem 22.40, but now let the conducting tube have charge per unit length $-\alpha$. As in Problem 22.40, the line of charge has charge per unit length $+\alpha$.

22.42 • A very long, solid cylinder with radius R has positive charge uniformly distributed throughout it, with charge per unit volume ρ. (a) Derive the expression for the electric field inside the volume at a distance r from the axis of the cylinder in terms of the charge density ρ. (b) What is the electric field at a point outside the volume in terms of the charge per unit length λ in the cylinder? (c) Compare the answers to parts (a) and (b) for $r = R$. (d) Graph the electric-field magnitude as a function of r from $r = 0$ to $r = 3R$.

22.43 •• **CP** A small sphere with a mass of 4.00×10^{-6} kg and carrying a charge of 5.00×10^{-8} C hangs from a thread near a very large, charged insulating

Figure **P22.43**

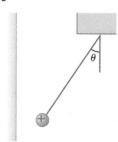

sheet, as shown in Fig. P22.43. The charge density on the surface of the sheet is uniform and equal to $2.50 \times 10^{-9} \, \text{C/m}^2$. Find the angle of the thread.

22.44 • **A Sphere in a Sphere.** A solid conducting sphere carrying charge q has radius a. It is inside a concentric hollow conducting sphere with inner radius b and outer radius c. The hollow sphere has no net charge. (a) Derive expressions for the electric-field magnitude in terms of the distance r from the center for the regions $r < a$, $a < r < b$, $b < r < c$, and $r > c$. (b) Graph the magnitude of the electric field as a function of r from $r = 0$ to $r = 2c$. (c) What is the charge on the inner surface of the hollow sphere? (d) On the outer surface? (e) Represent the charge of the small sphere by four plus signs. Sketch the field lines of the system within a spherical volume of radius $2c$.

22.45 • A solid conducting sphere with radius R that carries positive charge Q is concentric with a very thin insulating shell of radius $2R$ that also carries charge Q. The charge Q is distributed uniformly over the insulating shell. (a) Find the electric field (magnitude and direction) in each of the regions $0 < r < R$, $R < r < 2R$, and $r > 2R$. (b) Graph the electric-field magnitude as a function of r.

22.46 • A conducting spherical shell with inner radius a and outer radius b has a positive point charge Q located at its center. The total charge on the shell is $-3Q$, and it is insulated from its surroundings (Fig. P22.46). (a) Derive expressions for the electric-field magnitude in terms of the distance r from the center for the regions $r < a$, $a < r < b$, and $r > b$. (b) What is the surface charge density on the inner surface of the conducting shell? (c) What is the surface charge density on the outer surface of the conducting shell? (d) Sketch the electric field lines and the location of all charges. (e) Graph the electric-field magnitude as a function of r.

Figure **P22.46**

22.47 • **Concentric Spherical Shells.** A small conducting spherical shell with inner radius a and outer radius b is concentric with a larger conducting spherical shell with inner radius c and outer radius d (Fig. P22.47). The inner shell has total charge $+2q$, and the outer shell has charge $+4q$. (a) Calculate the electric field (magnitude and direction) in terms of q and the distance r from the common center of the two shells for (i) $r < a$; (ii) $a < r < b$; (iii) $b < r < c$; (iv) $c < r < d$; (v) $r > d$. Show your results in a graph of the radial component of $\vec{E}$ as a function of r. (b) What is the total charge on the (i) inner surface of the small shell; (ii) outer surface of the small shell; (iii) inner surface of the large shell; (iv) outer surface of the large shell?

Figure **P22.47**

22.48 • Repeat Problem 22.47, but now let the outer shell have charge $-2q$. As in Problem 22.47, the inner shell has charge $+2q$.

22.49 • Repeat Problem 22.47, but now let the outer shell have charge $-4q$. As in Problem 22.47, the inner shell has charge $+2q$.

22.50 • A solid conducting sphere with radius R carries a positive total charge Q. The sphere is surrounded by an insulating shell with inner radius R and outer radius $2R$. The insulating shell has a uniform charge density ρ. (a) Find the value of ρ so that the net charge of the entire system is zero. (b) If ρ has the value found in part (a), find the electric field (magnitude and direction) in each of the regions $0 < r < R$, $R < r < 2R$, and $r > 2R$. Show your results in a graph of the radial component of $\vec{E}$ as a function of r. (c) As a general rule, the electric field is discontinuous only at locations where there is a thin sheet of charge. Explain how your results in part (b) agree with this rule.

22.51 • Negative charge $-Q$ is distributed uniformly over the surface of a thin spherical insulating shell with radius R. Calculate the force (magnitude and direction) that the shell exerts on a positive point charge q located (a) a distance $r > R$ from the center of the shell (outside the shell) and (b) a distance $r < R$ from the center of the shell (inside the shell).

22.52 •• (a) How many excess electrons must be distributed uniformly within the volume of an isolated plastic sphere 30.0 cm in diameter to produce an electric field of 1390 N/C just outside the surface of the sphere? (b) What is the electric field at a point 10.0 cm outside the surface of the sphere?

22.53 ••• **CALC** An insulating hollow sphere has inner radius a and outer radius b. Within the insulating material the volume charge density is given by $\rho(r) = \frac{\alpha}{r}$, where α is a positive constant. (a) In terms of α and a, what is the magnitude of the electric field at a distance r from the center of the shell, where $a < r < b$? (b) A point charge q is placed at the center of the hollow space, at $r = 0$. In terms of α and a, what value must q have (sign and magnitude) in order for the electric field to be constant in the region $a < r < b$, and what then is the value of the constant field in this region?

22.54 •• **CP Thomson's Model of the Atom.** In the early years of the 20th century, a leading model of the structure of the atom was that of the English physicist J. J. Thomson (the discoverer of the electron). In Thomson's model, an atom consisted of a sphere of positively charged material in which were embedded negatively charged electrons, like chocolate chips in a ball of cookie dough. Consider such an atom consisting of one electron with mass m and charge $-e$, which may be regarded as a point charge, and a uniformly charged sphere of charge $+e$ and radius R. (a) Explain why the equilibrium position of the electron is at the center of the nucleus. (b) In Thomson's model, it was assumed that the positive material provided little or no resistance to the motion of the electron. If the electron is displaced from equilibrium by a distance less than R, show that the resulting motion of the electron will be simple harmonic, and calculate the frequency of oscillation. (*Hint:* Review the definition of simple harmonic motion in Section 14.2. If it can be shown that the net force on the electron is of this form, then it follows that the motion is simple harmonic. Conversely, if the net force on the electron does not follow this form, the motion is not simple harmonic.) (c) By Thomson's time, it was known that excited atoms emit light waves of only certain frequencies. In his model, the frequency of emitted light is the same as the oscillation frequency of the electron or electrons in the atom. What would the radius of a Thomson-model atom have to be for it to produce red light of frequency 4.57×10^{14} Hz? Compare your answer to the radii of real atoms, which are of the order of 10^{-10} m (see Appendix F for data about the electron). (d) If the electron were displaced from equilibrium by a distance greater than R, would the electron oscillate? Would its motion be simple harmonic? Explain your reasoning. (*Historical note:* In 1910, the atomic nucleus was discovered, proving the Thomson model to be incorrect. An atom's positive charge is not spread over its volume as Thomson supposed, but is concentrated in the tiny nucleus of radius 10^{-14} to 10^{-15} m.)

22.55 • **Thomson's Model of the Atom, Continued.** Using Thomson's (outdated) model of the atom described in Problem 22.54, consider an atom consisting of two electrons, each of charge $-e$, embedded in a sphere of charge $+2e$ and radius R. In

Figure **P22.55**

equilibrium, each electron is a distance d from the center of the atom (Fig. P22.55). Find the distance d in terms of the other properties of the atom.

22.56 • **A Uniformly Charged Slab.** A slab of insulating material has thickness $2d$ and is oriented so that its faces are parallel to the yz-plane and given by the planes $x = d$ and $x = -d$. The y- and z-dimensions of the slab are very large compared to d and may be treated as essentially infinite. The slab has a uniform positive charge density ρ. (a) Explain why the electric field due to the slab is zero at the center of the slab ($x = 0$). (b) Using Gauss's law, find the electric field due to the slab (magnitude and direction) at all points in space.

22.57 • **CALC** **A Nonuniformly Charged Slab.** Repeat Problem 22.56, but now let the charge density of the slab be given by $\rho(x) = \rho_0 (x/d)^2$, where ρ_0 is a positive constant.

22.58 • **CALC** A nonuniform, but spherically symmetric, distribution of charge has a charge density $\rho(r)$ given as follows:

$$\rho(r) = \rho_0(1 - 4r/3R) \qquad \text{for } r \leq R$$
$$\rho(r) = 0 \qquad \text{for } r \geq R$$

where ρ_0 is a positive constant. (a) Find the total charge contained in the charge distribution. (b) Obtain an expression for the electric field in the region $r \geq R$. (c) Obtain an expression for the electric field in the region $r \leq R$. (d) Graph the electric-field magnitude E as a function of r. (e) Find the value of r at which the electric field is maximum, and find the value of that maximum field.

22.59 • **CP CALC** **Gauss's Law for Gravitation.** The gravitational force between two point masses separated by a distance r is proportional to $1/r^2$, just like the electric force between two point charges. Because of this similarity between gravitational and electric interactions, there is also a Gauss's law for gravitation. (a) Let $\vec{g}$ be the acceleration due to gravity caused by a point mass m at the origin, so that $\vec{g} = -(Gm/r^2)\hat{r}$. Consider a spherical Gaussian surface with radius r centered on this point mass, and show that the flux of $\vec{g}$ through this surface is given by

$$\oint \vec{g} \cdot d\vec{A} = -4\pi Gm$$

(b) By following the same logical steps used in Section 22.3 to obtain Gauss's law for the electric field, show that the flux of $\vec{g}$ through *any* closed surface is given by

$$\oint \vec{g} \cdot d\vec{A} = -4\pi GM_{\text{encl}}$$

where M_{encl} is the total mass enclosed within the closed surface.

22.60 • **CP** **Applying Gauss's Law for Gravitation.** Using Gauss's law for gravitation (derived in part (b) of Problem 22.59), show that the following statements are true: (a) For any spherically symmetric mass distribution with total mass M, the acceleration due to gravity outside the distribution is the same as though all the mass were concentrated at the center. (*Hint:* See Example 22.5 in Section 22.4.) (b) At any point inside a spherically symmetric shell of mass, the acceleration due to gravity is zero. (*Hint:* See Example 22.5.) (c) If we could drill a hole through a spherically symmetric planet to its center, and if the density were uniform, we would find that the magnitude of $\vec{g}$ is directly proportional to the distance r from the center. (*Hint:* See Example 22.9 in Section 22.4.) We proved these results in Section 13.6 using some fairly strenuous analysis; the proofs using Gauss's law for gravitation are *much* easier.

22.61 • (a) An insulating sphere with radius a has a uniform charge density ρ. The sphere is not centered at the origin but at $\vec{r} = \vec{b}$. Show that the electric field inside the sphere is given by

$\vec{E} = \rho(\vec{r} - \vec{b})/3\epsilon_0$. (b) An insulating sphere of radius R has a spherical hole of radius a located within its volume and centered a distance b from the center of the sphere, where $a < b < R$ (a cross section of the sphere is shown in Fig. P22.61). The solid part of the sphere has a uniform volume charge density ρ. Find the magnitude and direction of the electric field $\vec{E}$ inside the hole, and show that $\vec{E}$ is uniform over the entire hole. [*Hint:* Use the principle of superposition and the result of part (a).]

Figure **P22.61**

Charge density ρ

22.62 • A very long, solid insulating cylinder with radius R has a cylindrical hole with radius a bored along its entire length. The axis of the hole is a distance b from the axis of the cylinder, where $a < b < R$ (Fig. P22.62). The solid material of the cylinder has a uniform volume charge density ρ. Find the magnitude and direction of the electric field $\vec{E}$ inside the hole, and show that $\vec{E}$ is uniform over the entire hole. (*Hint:* See Problem 22.61.)

Figure **P22.62**

Charge density ρ

22.63 • Positive charge Q is distributed uniformly over each of two spherical volumes with radius R. One sphere of charge is centered at the origin and the other at $x = 2R$ (Fig. P22.63). Find the magnitude and direction of the net electric field due to these two distributions of charge at the following points on the x-axis: (a) $x = 0$; (b) $x = R/2$; (c) $x = R$; (d) $x = 3R$.

Figure **P22.63**

22.64 • Repeat Problem 22.63, but now let the left-hand sphere have positive charge Q and let the right-hand sphere have negative charge $-Q$.

22.65 •• **CALC** A nonuniform, but spherically symmetric, distribution of charge has a charge density $\rho(r)$ given as follows:

$$\rho(r) = \rho_0(1 - r/R) \qquad \text{for } r \leq R$$
$$\rho(r) = 0 \qquad \text{for } r \geq R$$

where $\rho_0 = 3Q/\pi R^3$ is a positive constant. (a) Show that the total charge contained in the charge distribution is Q. (b) Show that the electric field in the region $r \geq R$ is identical to that produced by a point charge Q at $r = 0$. (c) Obtain an expression for the electric field in the region $r \leq R$. (d) Graph the electric-field magnitude E as a function of r. (e) Find the value of r at which the electric field is maximum, and find the value of that maximum field.

CHALLENGE PROBLEMS

22.66 ••• **CP CALC** A region in space contains a total positive charge Q that is distributed spherically such that the volume charge density $\rho(r)$ is given by

$$\rho(r) = \alpha \qquad \text{for } r \leq R/2$$
$$\rho(r) = 2\alpha(1 - r/R) \qquad \text{for } R/2 \leq r \leq R$$
$$\rho(r) = 0 \qquad \text{for } r \geq R$$

Here α is a positive constant having units of C/m^3. (a) Determine α in terms of Q and R. (b) Using Gauss's law, derive an expression for the magnitude of $\vec{E}$ as a function of r. Do this separately for all three regions. Express your answers in terms of the total charge Q. Be sure to check that your results agree on the boundaries of the regions. (c) What fraction of the total charge is contained within the region $r \leq R/2$? (d) If an electron with charge $q' = -e$ is oscillating back and forth about $r = 0$ (the center of the distribution) with an amplitude less than $R/2$, show that the motion is simple harmonic. (*Hint:* Review the discussion of simple harmonic motion in Section 14.2. If, and only if, the net force on the electron is proportional to its displacement from equilibrium, then the motion is simple harmonic.) (e) What is the period of the motion in part (d)? (f) If the amplitude of the motion described in part (e) is greater than $R/2$, is the motion still simple harmonic? Why or why not?

22.67 ••• CP CALC A region in space contains a total positive charge Q that is distributed spherically such that the volume charge density $\rho(r)$ is given by

$$\rho(r) = 3\alpha r/(2R) \qquad \text{for } r \leq R/2$$
$$\rho(r) = \alpha[1 - (r/R)^2] \qquad \text{for } R/2 \leq r \leq R$$
$$\rho(r) = 0 \qquad \text{for } r \geq R$$

Here α is a positive constant having units of C/m^3. (a) Determine α in terms of Q and R. (b) Using Gauss's law, derive an expression for the magnitude of the electric field as a function of r. Do this separately for all three regions. Express your answers in terms of the total charge Q. (c) What fraction of the total charge is contained within the region $R/2 \leq r \leq R$? (d) What is the magnitude of $\vec{E}$ at $r = R/2$? (e) If an electron with charge $q' = -e$ is released from rest at any point in any of the three regions, the resulting motion will be oscillatory but not simple harmonic. Why? (See Challenge Problem 22.66.)

Answers

Chapter Opening Question ?

No. The electric field inside a cavity within a conductor is zero, so there is no electric effect on the child. (See Section 22.5.)

Test Your Understanding Questions

22.1 Answer: (iii) Each part of the surface of the box will be three times farther from the charge $+q$, so the electric field will be $(\frac{1}{3})^2 = \frac{1}{9}$ as strong. But the area of the box will increase by a factor of $3^2 = 9$. Hence the electric flux will be multiplied by a factor of $(\frac{1}{9})(9) = 1$. In other words, the flux will be unchanged.

22.2 Answer: (iv), (ii), (i), (iii) In each case the electric field is uniform, so the flux is $\Phi_E = \vec{E} \cdot \vec{A}$. We use the relationships for the scalar products of unit vectors: $\hat{\imath} \cdot \hat{\imath} = \hat{\jmath} \cdot \hat{\jmath} = 1$, $\hat{\imath} \cdot \hat{\jmath} = 0$. In case (i) we have $\Phi_E = (4.0 \text{ N/C})(6.0 \text{ m}^2)\hat{\imath} \cdot \hat{\jmath} = 0$ (the electric field and vector area are perpendicular, so there is zero flux). In case (ii) we have $\Phi_E [(4.0 \text{ N/C})\hat{\imath} + (2.0 \text{ N/C})\hat{\jmath}] \cdot (3.0 \text{ m}^2)\hat{\jmath} = (2.0 \text{ N/C}) \cdot (3.0 \text{ m}^2) = 6.0 \text{ N} \cdot \text{m}^2/\text{C}$. Similarly, in case (iii) we have $\Phi_E = [(4.0 \text{ N/C})\hat{\imath} - (2.0 \text{ N/C})\hat{\jmath}] \cdot [(3.0 \text{ m}^2)\hat{\imath} + (7.0 \text{ m}^2)\hat{\jmath}] = (4.0 \text{ N/C})(3.0 \text{ m}^2) - (2.0 \text{ N/C})(7.0 \text{ m}^2) = -2 \text{ N} \cdot \text{m}^2/\text{C}$, and in case (iv) we have $\Phi_E = [(4.0 \text{ N/C})\hat{\imath} - (2.0 \text{ N/C})\hat{\jmath}] \cdot [(3.0 \text{ m}^2)\hat{\imath} - (7.0 \text{ m}^2)\hat{\jmath}] = (4.0 \text{ N/C})(3.0 \text{ m}^2) + (2.0 \text{ N/C}) \cdot (7.0 \text{ m}^2) = 26 \text{ N} \cdot \text{m}^2/\text{C}$.

22.3 Answer: S_2, S_5, S_4, S_1 **and** S_3 **(tie)** Gauss's law tells us that the flux through a closed surface is proportional to the amount of charge enclosed within that surface. So an ordering of these surfaces by their fluxes is the same as an ordering by the amount of enclosed charge. Surface S_1 encloses no charge, surface S_2 encloses $9.0 \mu\text{C} + 5.0 \mu\text{C} + (-7.0 \mu\text{C}) = 7.0 \mu\text{C}$, surface S_3 encloses $9.0 \mu\text{C} + 1.0 \mu\text{C} + (-10.0 \mu\text{C}) = 0$, surface S_4 encloses $8.0 \mu\text{C} + (-7.0 \mu\text{C}) = 1.0 \mu\text{C}$, and surface S_5 encloses $8.0 \mu\text{C} + (-7.0 \mu\text{C}) + (-10.0 \mu\text{C}) + (1.0 \mu\text{C}) + (9.0 \mu\text{C}) + (5.0 \mu\text{C}) = 6.0 \mu\text{C}$.

22.4 Answer: no You might be tempted to draw a Gaussian surface that is an enlarged version of the conductor, with the same shape and placed so that it completely encloses the conductor.

While you know the flux through this Gaussian surface (by Gauss's law, it's $\Phi_E = Q/\epsilon_0$), the direction of the electric field need not be perpendicular to the surface and the magnitude of the field need not be the same at all points on the surface. It's not possible to do the flux integral $\oint E_\perp \, dA$, and we can't calculate the electric field. Gauss's law is useful for calculating the electric field only when the charge distribution is *highly* symmetric.

22.5 Answer: no Before you connect the wire to the sphere, the presence of the point charge will induce a charge $-q$ on the inner surface of the hollow sphere and a charge q on the outer surface (the net charge on the sphere is zero). There will be an electric field outside the sphere due to the charge on the outer surface. Once you touch the conducting wire to the sphere, however, electrons will flow from ground to the outer surface of the sphere to neutralize the charge there (see Fig. 21.7c). As a result the sphere will have no charge on its outer surface and no electric field outside.

Bridging Problem

Answers: (a) $Q(r) = Qe^{-2r/a_0}[2(r/a_0)^2 + 2(r/a_0) + 1]$

(b) $E = \dfrac{kQe^{-2r/a_0}}{r^2}[2(r/a_0)^2 + 2(r/a_0) + 1]$

(c)

23 ELECTRIC POTENTIAL

LEARNING GOALS

By studying this chapter, you will learn:

- How to calculate the electric potential energy of a collection of charges.

- The meaning and significance of electric potential.

- How to calculate the electric potential that a collection of charges produces at a point in space.

- How to use equipotential surfaces to visualize how the electric potential varies in space.

- How to use electric potential to calculate the electric field.

? In one type of welding, electric charge flows between the welding tool and the metal pieces that are to be joined together. This produces a glowing arc whose high temperature fuses the pieces together. Why must the tool be held close to the pieces being welded?

This chapter is about energy associated with electrical interactions. Every time you turn on a light, listen to an MP3 player, or talk on a mobile phone, you are using electrical energy, an indispensable ingredient of our technological society. In Chapters 6 and 7 we introduced the concepts of *work* and *energy* in the context of mechanics; now we'll combine these concepts with what we've learned about electric charge, electric forces, and electric fields. Just as we found for many problems in mechanics, using energy ideas makes it easier to solve a variety of problems in electricity.

When a charged particle moves in an electric field, the field exerts a force that can do *work* on the particle. This work can always be expressed in terms of electric potential energy. Just as gravitational potential energy depends on the height of a mass above the earth's surface, electric potential energy depends on the position of the charged particle in the electric field. We'll describe electric potential energy using a new concept called *electric potential,* or simply *potential.* In circuits, a difference in potential from one point to another is often called *voltage.* The concepts of potential and voltage are crucial to understanding how electric circuits work and have equally important applications to electron beams used in cancer radiotherapy, high-energy particle accelerators, and many other devices.

23.1 Electric Potential Energy

The concepts of work, potential energy, and conservation of energy proved to be extremely useful in our study of mechanics. In this section we'll show that these concepts are just as useful for understanding and analyzing electrical interactions.

Let's begin by reviewing three essential points from Chapters 6 and 7. First, when a force $\vec{F}$ acts on a particle that moves from point a to point b, the work $W_{a \to b}$ done by the force is given by a *line integral:*

$$W_{a \to b} = \int_a^b \vec{F} \cdot d\vec{l} = \int_a^b F \cos \phi \, dl \quad \text{(work done by a force)} \tag{23.1}$$

where $d\vec{l}$ is an infinitesimal displacement along the particle's path and ϕ is the angle between $\vec{F}$ and $d\vec{l}$ at each point along the path.

Second, if the force $\vec{F}$ is *conservative,* as we defined the term in Section 7.3, the work done by $\vec{F}$ can always be expressed in terms of a **potential energy** U. When the particle moves from a point where the potential energy is U_a to a point where it is U_b, the change in potential energy is $\Delta U = U_b - U_a$ and the work $W_{a \to b}$ done by the force is

$$W_{a \to b} = U_a - U_b = -(U_b - U_a) = -\Delta U \quad \begin{array}{l}\text{(work done by a} \\ \text{conservative force)}\end{array} \tag{23.2}$$

When $W_{a \to b}$ is positive, U_a is greater than U_b, ΔU is negative, and the potential energy *decreases.* That's what happens when a baseball falls from a high point (a) to a lower point (b) under the influence of the earth's gravity; the force of gravity does positive work, and the gravitational potential energy decreases (Fig. 23.1). When a tossed ball is moving upward, the gravitational force does negative work during the ascent, and the potential energy increases.

Third, the work–energy theorem says that the change in kinetic energy $\Delta K = K_b - K_a$ during a displacement equals the *total* work done on the particle. If only conservative forces do work, then Eq. (23.2) gives the total work, and $K_b - K_a = -(U_b - U_a)$. We usually write this as

$$K_a + U_a = K_b + U_b \tag{23.3}$$

That is, the total mechanical energy (kinetic plus potential) is *conserved* under these circumstances.

23.1 The work done on a baseball moving in a uniform gravitational field.

Object moving in a uniform gravitational field

$\vec{w} = m\vec{g}$

The work done by the gravitational force is the same for any path from a to b:
$W_{a \to b} = -\Delta U = mgh$

Electric Potential Energy in a Uniform Field

Let's look at an electrical example of these basic concepts. In Fig. 23.2 a pair of charged parallel metal plates sets up a uniform, downward electric field with magnitude E. The field exerts a downward force with magnitude $F = q_0 E$ on a positive test charge q_0. As the charge moves downward a distance d from point a to point b, the force on the test charge is constant and independent of its location. So the work done by the electric field is the product of the force magnitude and the component of displacement in the (downward) direction of the force:

$$W_{a \to b} = Fd = q_0 Ed \tag{23.4}$$

This work is positive, since the force is in the same direction as the net displacement of the test charge.

The y-component of the electric force, $F_y = -q_0 E$, is constant, and there is no x- or z-component. This is exactly analogous to the gravitational force on a mass m near the earth's surface; for this force, there is a constant y-component $F_y = -mg$ and the x- and z-components are zero. Because of this analogy, we can conclude that the force exerted on q_0 by the uniform electric field in Fig. 23.2 is *conservative,* just as is the gravitational force. This means that the work $W_{a \to b}$ done by the field is independent of the path the particle takes from a to b. We can represent this work with a *potential-energy* function U, just as we did for gravitational potential energy

23.2 The work done on a point charge moving in a uniform electric field. Compare with Fig. 23.1.

Point charge moving in a uniform electric field

$\vec{E}$

q_0

$\vec{F} = q_0\vec{E}$

The work done by the electric force is the same for any path from a to b:
$W_{a \to b} = -\Delta U = q_0 Ed$

23.3 A positive charge moving **(a)** in the direction of the electric field $\vec{E}$ and **(b)** in the direction opposite $\vec{E}$.

(a) Positive charge moves in the direction of $\vec{E}$:
• Field does *positive* work on charge.
• *U decreases.*

(b) Positive charge moves opposite $\vec{E}$:
• Field does *negative* work on charge.
• *U increases.*

in Section 7.1. The potential energy for the gravitational force $F_y = -mg$ was $U = mgy$; hence the potential energy for the electric force $F_y = -q_0E$ is

$$U = q_0Ey \tag{23.5}$$

When the test charge moves from height y_a to height y_b, the work done on the charge by the field is given by

$$W_{a \to b} = -\Delta U = -(U_b - U_a) = -(q_0Ey_b - q_0Ey_a) = q_0E(y_a - y_b) \tag{23.6}$$

When y_a is greater than y_b (Fig. 23.3a), the positive test charge q_0 moves downward, in the same direction as $\vec{E}$; the displacement is in the same direction as the force $\vec{F} = q_0\vec{E}$, so the field does positive work and U decreases. [In particular, if $y_a - y_b = d$ as in Fig. 23.2, Eq. (23.6) gives $W_{a \to b} = q_0Ed$, in agreement with Eq. (23.4).] When y_a is less than y_b (Fig. 23.3b), the positive test charge q_0 moves upward, in the opposite direction to $\vec{E}$; the displacement is opposite the force, the field does negative work, and U increases.

If the test charge q_0 is *negative*, the potential energy increases when it moves with the field and decreases when it moves against the field (Fig. 23.4).

Whether the test charge is positive or negative, the following general rules apply: *U increases* if the test charge q_0 moves in the direction *opposite* the electric force $\vec{F} = q_0\vec{E}$ (Figs. 23.3b and 23.4a); *U decreases* if q_0 moves in the *same*

23.4 A negative charge moving **(a)** in the direction of the electric field $\vec{E}$ and **(b)** in the direction opposite $\vec{E}$. Compare with Fig. 23.3.

(a) Negative charge moves in the direction of $\vec{E}$:
• Field does *negative* work on charge.
• *U increases.*

(b) Negative charge moves opposite $\vec{E}$:
• Field does *positive* work on charge.
• *U decreases.*

direction as $\vec{F} = q_0\vec{E}$ (Figs. 23.3a and 23.4b). This is the same behavior as for gravitational potential energy, which increases if a mass m moves upward (opposite the direction of the gravitational force) and decreases if m moves downward (in the same direction as the gravitational force).

CAUTION **Electric potential energy** The relationship between electric potential energy change and motion in an electric field is an important one that we'll use often, but that takes some effort to truly understand. Take the time to carefully study the preceding paragraph as well as Figs. 23.3 and 23.4. Doing so now will help you tremendously later!

Electric Potential Energy of Two Point Charges

The idea of electric potential energy isn't restricted to the special case of a uniform electric field. Indeed, we can apply this concept to a point charge in *any* electric field caused by a static charge distribution. Recall from Chapter 21 that we can represent any charge distribution as a collection of point charges. Therefore it's useful to calculate the work done on a test charge q_0 moving in the electric field caused by a single, stationary point charge q.

We'll consider first a displacement along the *radial* line in Fig. 23.5. The force on q_0 is given by Coulomb's law, and its radial component is

23.5 Test charge q_0 moves along a straight line extending radially from charge q. As it moves from a to b, the distance varies from r_a to r_b.

$$F_r = \frac{1}{4\pi\epsilon_0}\frac{qq_0}{r^2} \quad (23.7)$$

If q and q_0 have the same sign ($+$ or $-$) the force is repulsive and F_r is positive; if the two charges have opposite signs, the force is attractive and F_r is negative. The force is *not* constant during the displacement, and we have to integrate to calculate the work $W_{a\rightarrow b}$ done on q_0 by this force as q_0 moves from a to b:

$$W_{a\rightarrow b} = \int_{r_a}^{r_b} F_r\, dr = \int_{r_a}^{r_b} \frac{1}{4\pi\epsilon_0}\frac{qq_0}{r^2}\, dr = \frac{qq_0}{4\pi\epsilon_0}\left(\frac{1}{r_a} - \frac{1}{r_b}\right) \quad (23.8)$$

The work done by the electric force for this particular path depends only on the endpoints.

Now let's consider a more general displacement (Fig. 23.6) in which a and b do *not* lie on the same radial line. From Eq. (23.1) the work done on q_0 during this displacement is given by

$$W_{a\rightarrow b} = \int_{r_a}^{r_b} F\cos\phi\, dl = \int_{r_a}^{r_b} \frac{1}{4\pi\epsilon_0}\frac{qq_0}{r^2}\cos\phi\, dl$$

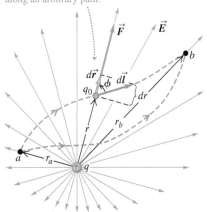

23.6 The work done on charge q_0 by the electric field of charge q does not depend on the path taken, but only on the distances r_a and r_b.

Test charge q_0 moves from a to b along an arbitrary path.

But Fig. 23.6 shows that $\cos\phi\, dl = dr$. That is, the work done during a small displacement $d\vec{l}$ depends only on the change dr in the distance r between the charges, which is the *radial component* of the displacement. Thus Eq. (23.8) is valid even for this more general displacement; the work done on q_0 by the electric field $\vec{E}$ produced by q depends only on r_a and r_b, not on the details of the path. Also, if q_0 returns to its starting point a by a different path, the total work done in the round-trip displacement is zero (the integral in Eq. (23.8) is from r_a back to r_a). These are the needed characteristics for a conservative force, as we defined it in Section 7.3. Thus the force on q_0 is a *conservative* force.

We see that Eqs. (23.2) and (23.8) are consistent if we define the potential energy to be $U_a = qq_0/4\pi\epsilon_0 r_a$ when q_0 is a distance r_a from q, and to be $U_b = qq_0/4\pi\epsilon_0 r_b$ when q_0 is a distance r_b from q. Thus the potential energy U when the test charge q_0 is at *any* distance r from charge q is

$$U = \frac{1}{4\pi\epsilon_0}\frac{qq_0}{r} \qquad \text{(electric potential energy of two point charges } q \text{ and } q_0) \quad (23.9)$$

23.7 Graphs of the potential energy U of two point charges q and q_0 versus their separation r.

(a) q and q_0 have the same sign.

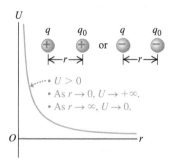

- $U > 0$
- As $r \to 0$, $U \to +\infty$.
- As $r \to \infty$, $U \to 0$.

(b) q and q_0 have opposite signs.

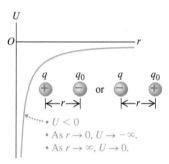

- $U < 0$
- As $r \to 0$, $U \to -\infty$.
- As $r \to \infty$, $U \to 0$.

Equation (23.9) is valid no matter what the signs of the charges q and q_0. The potential energy is positive if the charges q and q_0 have the same sign (Fig. 23.7a) and negative if they have opposite signs (Fig. 23.7b).

CAUTION **Electric potential energy vs. electric force** Don't confuse Eq. (23.9) for the potential energy of two point charges with the similar expression in Eq. (23.7) for the radial component of the electric force that one charge exerts on the other. Potential energy U is proportional to $1/r$, while the force component F_r is proportional to $1/r^2$.

Potential energy is always defined relative to some reference point where $U = 0$. In Eq. (23.9), U is zero when q and q_0 are infinitely far apart and $r = \infty$. Therefore U represents the work that would be done on the test charge q_0 by the field of q if q_0 moved from an initial distance r to infinity. If q and q_0 have the same sign, the interaction is repulsive, this work is positive, and U is positive at any finite separation (Fig. 23.7a). If the charges have opposite signs, the interaction is attractive, the work done is negative, and U is negative (Fig. 23.7b).

We emphasize that the potential energy U given by Eq. (23.9) is a *shared* property of the two charges. If the distance between q and q_0 is changed from r_a to r_b, the change in potential energy is the same whether q is held fixed and q_0 is moved or q_0 is held fixed and q is moved. For this reason, we never use the phrase "the electric potential energy *of* a point charge." (Likewise, if a mass m is at a height h above the earth's surface, the gravitational potential energy is a shared property of the mass m and the earth. We emphasized this in Sections 7.1 and 13.3.)

Equation (23.9) also holds if the charge q_0 is outside a spherically symmetric charge *distribution* with total charge q; the distance r is from q_0 to the center of the distribution. That's because Gauss's law tells us that the electric field outside such a distribution is the same as if all of its charge q were concentrated at its center (see Example 22.9 in Section 22.4).

Example 23.1 **Conservation of energy with electric forces**

A positron (the electron's antiparticle) has mass 9.11×10^{-31} kg and charge $q_0 = +e = +1.60 \times 10^{-19}$ C. Suppose a positron moves in the vicinity of an α (alpha) particle, which has charge $q = +2e = 3.20 \times 10^{-19}$ C and mass 6.64×10^{-27} kg. The α particle's mass is more than 7000 times that of the positron, so we assume that the α particle remains at rest. When the positron is 1.00×10^{-10} m from the α particle, it is moving directly away from the α particle at 3.00×10^6 m/s. (a) What is the positron's speed when the particles are 2.00×10^{-10} m apart? (b) What is the positron's speed when it is very far from the α particle? (c) Suppose the initial conditions are the same but the moving particle is an electron (with the same mass as the positron but charge $q_0 = -e$). Describe the subsequent motion.

SOLUTION

IDENTIFY and SET UP: The electric force between a positron (or an electron) and an α particle is conservative, so mechanical energy (kinetic plus potential) is conserved. Equation (23.9) gives the potential energy U at any separation r: The potential-energy function for parts (a) and (b) looks like that of Fig. 23.7a, and the function for part (c) looks like that of Fig. 23.7b. We are given the positron speed $v_a = 3.00 \times 10^6$ m/s when the separation between the particles is $r_a = 1.00 \times 10^{-10}$ m. In parts (a) and (b) we use Eqs. (23.3) and (23.9) to find the speed for $r = r_b = 2.00 \times 10^{-10}$ m and $r = r_c \to \infty$, respectively. In part (c) we replace the positron with an electron and reconsider the problem.

EXECUTE: (a) Both particles have positive charge, so the positron speeds up as it moves away from the α particle. From the energy-conservation equation, Eq. (23.3), the final kinetic energy is

$$K_b = \tfrac{1}{2}mv_b^2 = K_a + U_a - U_b$$

In this expression,

$$K_a = \tfrac{1}{2}mv_a^2 = \tfrac{1}{2}(9.11 \times 10^{-31}\text{ kg})(3.00 \times 10^6\text{ m/s})^2$$

$$= 4.10 \times 10^{-18}\text{ J}$$

$$U_a = \frac{1}{4\pi\epsilon_0}\frac{qq_0}{r_a} = (9.0 \times 10^9\text{ N}\cdot\text{m}^2/\text{C}^2)$$

$$\times \frac{(3.20 \times 10^{-19}\text{ C})(1.60 \times 10^{-19}\text{ C})}{1.00 \times 10^{-10}\text{ m}}$$

$$= 4.61 \times 10^{-18}\text{ J}$$

$$U_b = \frac{1}{4\pi\epsilon_0}\frac{qq_0}{r_b} = 2.30 \times 10^{-18}\text{ J}$$

Hence the positron kinetic energy and speed at $r = r_b = 2.00 \times 10^{-10}$ m are

$$K_b = \tfrac{1}{2}mv_b^2 = 4.10 \times 10^{-18}\text{ J} + 4.61 \times 10^{-18}\text{ J} - 2.30 \times 10^{-18}\text{ J}$$

$$= 6.41 \times 10^{-18}\text{ J}$$

$$v_b = \sqrt{\frac{2K_b}{m}} = \sqrt{\frac{2(6.41 \times 10^{-18}\text{ J})}{9.11 \times 10^{-31}\text{ kg}}} = 3.8 \times 10^6\text{ m/s}$$

(b) When the positron and α particle are very far apart so that $r = r_c \to \infty$, the final potential energy U_c approaches zero. Again from energy conservation, the final kinetic energy and speed of the positron in this case are

$$K_c = K_a + U_a - U_c = 4.10 \times 10^{-18}\,\text{J} + 4.61 \times 10^{-18}\,\text{J} - 0$$
$$= 8.71 \times 10^{-18}\,\text{J}$$
$$v_c = \sqrt{\frac{2K_c}{m}} = \sqrt{\frac{2(8.71 \times 10^{-18}\,\text{J})}{9.11 \times 10^{-31}\,\text{kg}}} = 4.4 \times 10^6\,\text{m/s}$$

(c) The electron and α particle have opposite charges, so the force is attractive and the electron slows down as it moves away. Changing the moving particle's sign from $+e$ to $-e$ means that the initial potential energy is now $U_a = -4.61 \times 10^{-18}$ J, which makes the total mechanical energy *negative*:

$$K_a + U_a = (4.10 \times 10^{-18}\,\text{J}) - (4.61 \times 10^{-18}\,\text{J})$$
$$= -0.51 \times 10^{-18}\,\text{J}$$

The total mechanical energy would have to be positive for the electron to move infinitely far away from the α particle. Like a rock thrown upward at low speed from the earth's surface, it will reach a maximum separation $r = r_d$ from the α particle before reversing direction. At this point its speed and its kinetic energy K_d are zero, so at separation r_d we have

$$U_d = K_a + U_a - K_d = (-0.51 \times 10^{-18}\,\text{J}) - 0$$
$$U_d = \frac{1}{4\pi\epsilon_0}\frac{qq_0}{r_d} = -0.51 \times 10^{-18}\,\text{J}$$
$$r_d = \frac{1}{U_d}\frac{qq_0}{4\pi\epsilon_0}$$
$$= \frac{(9.0 \times 10^9\,\text{N}\cdot\text{m}^2/\text{C}^2)}{-0.51 \times 10^{-18}\,\text{J}}(3.20 \times 10^{-19}\,\text{C})(-1.60 \times 10^{-19}\text{C})$$
$$= 9.0 \times 10^{-10}\,\text{m}$$

For $r_b = 2.00 \times 10^{-10}$ m we have $U_b = -2.30 \times 10^{-18}$ J, so the electron kinetic energy and speed at this point are

$$K_b = \tfrac{1}{2}mv_b^2 = 4.10 \times 10^{-18}\,\text{J} + (-4.61 \times 10^{-18}\,\text{J})$$
$$- (-2.30 \times 10^{-18}\,\text{J}) = 1.79 \times 10^{-18}\,\text{J}$$
$$v_b = \sqrt{\frac{2K_b}{m}} = \sqrt{\frac{2(1.79 \times 10^{-18}\,\text{J})}{9.11 \times 10^{-31}\,\text{kg}}} = 2.0 \times 10^6\,\text{m/s}$$

EVALUATE: Both particles behave as expected as they move away from the α particle: The positron speeds up, and the electron slows down and eventually turns around. How fast would an electron have to be moving at $r_a = 1.00 \times 10^{-10}$ m to travel infinitely far from the α particle? (*Hint:* See Example 13.4 in Section 13.3.)

Electric Potential Energy with Several Point Charges

Suppose the electric field $\vec{E}$ in which charge q_0 moves is caused by *several* point charges $q_1, q_2, q_3, \ldots$ at distances $r_1, r_2, r_3, \ldots$ from q_0, as in Fig. 23.8. For example, q_0 could be a positive ion moving in the presence of other ions (Fig. 23.9). The total electric field at each point is the *vector sum* of the fields due to the individual charges, and the total work done on q_0 during any displacement is the sum of the contributions from the individual charges. From Eq. (23.9) we conclude that the potential energy associated with the test charge q_0 at point a in Fig. 23.8 is the *algebraic* sum (*not* a vector sum):

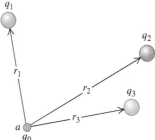

23.8 The potential energy associated with a charge q_0 at point a depends on the other charges q_1, q_2, and q_3 and on their distances r_1, r_2, and r_3 from point a.

$$U = \frac{q_0}{4\pi\epsilon_0}\left(\frac{q_1}{r_1} + \frac{q_2}{r_2} + \frac{q_3}{r_3} + \cdots\right) = \frac{q_0}{4\pi\epsilon_0}\sum_i \frac{q_i}{r_i} \quad \begin{array}{l}\text{(point charge } q_0 \\ \text{and collection} \quad \text{(23.10)} \\ \text{of charges } q_i)\end{array}$$

When q_0 is at a different point b, the potential energy is given by the same expression, but $r_1, r_2, \ldots$ are the distances from $q_1, q_2, \ldots$ to point b. The work done on charge q_0 when it moves from a to b along any path is equal to the difference $U_a - U_b$ between the potential energies when q_0 is at a and at b.

We can represent *any* charge distribution as a collection of point charges, so Eq. (23.10) shows that we can always find a potential-energy function for *any* static electric field. It follows that **for every electric field due to a static charge distribution, the force exerted by that field is conservative.**

Equations (23.9) and (23.10) define U to be zero when all the distances $r_1, r_2, \ldots$ are infinite—that is, when the test charge q_0 is very far away from all the charges that produce the field. As with any potential-energy function, the point where $U = 0$ is arbitrary; we can always add a constant to make U equal zero at any point we choose. In electrostatics problems it's usually simplest to choose this point to be at infinity. When we analyze electric circuits in Chapters 25 and 26, other choices will be more convenient.

23.9 This ion engine for spacecraft uses electric forces to eject a stream of positive xenon ions (Xe^+) at speeds in excess of 30 km/s. The thrust produced is very low (about 0.09 newton) but can be maintained continuously for days, in contrast to chemical rockets, which produce a large thrust for a short time (see Fig. 8.33). Such ion engines have been used for maneuvering interplanetary spacecraft.

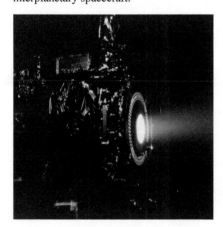

Equation (23.10) gives the potential energy associated with the presence of the test charge q_0 in the $\vec{E}$ field produced by $q_1, q_2, q_3, \ldots$. But there is also potential energy involved in assembling these charges. If we start with charges $q_1, q_2, q_3, \ldots$ all separated from each other by infinite distances and then bring them together so that the distance between q_i and q_j is r_{ij}, the *total* potential energy U is the sum of the potential energies of interaction for each pair of charges. We can write this as

$$U = \frac{1}{4\pi\epsilon_0} \sum_{i<j} \frac{q_i q_j}{r_{ij}} \tag{23.11}$$

This sum extends over all *pairs* of charges; we don't let $i = j$ (because that would be an interaction of a charge with itself), and we include only terms with $i < j$ to make sure that we count each pair only once. Thus, to account for the interaction between q_3 and q_4, we include a term with $i = 3$ and $j = 4$ but not a term with $i = 4$ and $j = 3$.

Interpreting Electric Potential Energy

As a final comment, here are two viewpoints on electric potential energy. We have defined it in terms of the work done *by the electric field* on a charged particle moving in the field, just as in Chapter 7 we defined potential energy in terms of the work done by gravity or by a spring. When a particle moves from point a to point b, the work done on it by the electric field is $W_{a \to b} = U_a - U_b$. Thus the potential-energy difference $U_a - U_b$ equals *the work that is done by the electric force when the particle moves from a to b*. When U_a is greater than U_b, the field does positive work on the particle as it "falls" from a point of higher potential energy (a) to a point of lower potential energy (b).

An alternative but equivalent viewpoint is to consider how much work we would have to do to "raise" a particle from a point b where the potential energy is U_b to a point a where it has a greater value U_a (pushing two positive charges closer together, for example). To move the particle slowly (so as not to give it any kinetic energy), we need to exert an additional external force $\vec{F}_{ext}$ that is equal and opposite to the electric-field force and does positive work. The potential-energy difference $U_a - U_b$ is then defined as *the work that must be done by an external force to move the particle slowly from b to a against the electric force*. Because $\vec{F}_{ext}$ is the negative of the electric-field force and the displacement is in the opposite direction, this definition of the potential difference $U_a - U_b$ is equivalent to that given above. This alternative viewpoint also works if U_a is less than U_b, corresponding to "lowering" the particle; an example is moving two positive charges away from each other. In this case, $U_a - U_b$ is again equal to the work done by the external force, but now this work is negative.

We will use both of these viewpoints in the next section to interpret what is meant by electric *potential*, or potential energy per unit charge.

Example 23.2	**A system of point charges**

Two point charges are located on the x-axis, $q_1 = -e$ at $x = 0$ and $q_2 = +e$ at $x = a$. (a) Find the work that must be done by an external force to bring a third point charge $q_3 = +e$ from infinity to $x = 2a$. (b) Find the total potential energy of the system of three charges.

infinity to $x = 2a$. We do this by using Eq. (23.10) to find the potential energy associated with q_3 in the presence of q_1 and q_2. In part (b) we use Eq. (23.11), the expression for the potential energy of a collection of point charges, to find the total potential energy of the system.

SOLUTION

IDENTIFY and SET UP: Figure 23.10 shows the final arrangement of the three charges. In part (a) we need to find the work W that must be done on q_3 by an external force $\vec{F}_{ext}$ to bring q_3 in from

23.10 Our sketch of the situation after the third charge has been brought in from infinity.

$$q_1 = -e \qquad q_2 = +e \qquad q_3 = +e$$
$$\xrightarrow{\ominus \qquad\qquad \oplus \qquad\qquad \oplus\ } x$$
$$x = 0 \qquad\quad x = a \qquad\quad x = 2a$$

EXECUTE: (a) The work W equals the difference between (i) the potential energy U associated with q_3 when it is at $x = 2a$ and (ii) the potential energy when it is infinitely far away. The second of these is zero, so the work required is equal to U. The distances between the charges are $r_{13} = 2a$ and $r_{23} = a$, so from Eq. (23.10),

$$W = U = \frac{q_3}{4\pi\epsilon_0}\left(\frac{q_1}{r_{13}} + \frac{q_2}{r_{23}}\right) = \frac{+e}{4\pi\epsilon_0}\left(\frac{-e}{2a} + \frac{+e}{a}\right) = \frac{+e^2}{8\pi\epsilon_0 a}$$

This is positive, just as we should expect. If we bring q_3 in from infinity along the $+x$-axis, it is attracted by q_1 but is repelled more strongly by q_2. Hence we must do positive work to push q_3 to the position at $x = 2a$.

(b) From Eq. (23.11), the total potential energy of the three-charge system is

$$U = \frac{1}{4\pi\epsilon_0}\sum_{i<j}\frac{q_i q_j}{r_{ij}} = \frac{1}{4\pi\epsilon_0}\left(\frac{q_1 q_2}{r_{12}} + \frac{q_1 q_3}{r_{13}} + \frac{q_2 q_3}{r_{23}}\right)$$

$$= \frac{1}{4\pi\epsilon_0}\left[\frac{(-e)(e)}{a} + \frac{(-e)(e)}{2a} + \frac{(e)(e)}{a}\right] = \frac{-e^2}{8\pi\epsilon_0 a}$$

EVALUATE: Our negative result in part (b) means that the system has lower potential energy than it would if the three charges were infinitely far apart. An external force would have to do *negative* work to bring the three charges from infinity to assemble this entire arrangement and would have to do *positive* work to move the three charges back to infinity.

Test Your Understanding of Section 23.1   Consider the system of three point charges in Example 21.4 (Section 21.3) and shown in Fig. 21.14. (a) What is the sign of the total potential energy of this system? (i) positive; (ii) negative; (iii) zero. (b) What is the sign of the total amount of work you would have to do to move these charges infinitely far from each other? (i) positive; (ii) negative; (iii) zero.   ▮

23.2 Electric Potential

In Section 23.1 we looked at the potential energy U associated with a test charge q_0 in an electric field. Now we want to describe this potential energy on a "per unit charge" basis, just as electric field describes the force per unit charge on a charged particle in the field. This leads us to the concept of *electric potential,* often called simply *potential.* This concept is very useful in calculations involving energies of charged particles. It also facilitates many electric-field calculations because electric potential is closely related to the electric field $\vec{E}$. When we need to determine an electric field, it is often easier to determine the potential first and then find the field from it.

Potential is *potential energy per unit charge.* We define the potential V at any point in an electric field as the potential energy U *per unit charge* associated with a test charge q_0 at that point:

$$V = \frac{U}{q_0} \quad \text{or} \quad U = q_0 V \tag{23.12}$$

Potential energy and charge are both scalars, so potential is a scalar. From Eq. (23.12) its units are the units of energy divided by those of charge. The SI unit of potential, called one **volt** (1 V) in honor of the Italian electrical experimenter Alessandro Volta (1745–1827), equals 1 joule per coulomb:

$$1\text{ V} = 1\text{ volt} = 1\text{ J/C} = 1\text{ joule/coulomb}$$

Let's put Eq. (23.2), which equates the work done by the electric force during a displacement from a to b to the quantity $-\Delta U = -(U_b - U_a)$, on a "work per unit charge" basis. We divide this equation by q_0, obtaining

$$\frac{W_{a\to b}}{q_0} = -\frac{\Delta U}{q_0} = -\left(\frac{U_b}{q_0} - \frac{U_a}{q_0}\right) = -(V_b - V_a) = V_a - V_b \tag{23.13}$$

where $V_a = U_a/q_0$ is the potential energy per unit charge at point a and similarly for V_b. We call V_a and V_b the *potential at point a* and *potential at point b*, respectively. Thus the work done per unit charge by the electric force when a charged body moves from a to b is equal to the potential at a minus the potential at b.

PhET: Charges and Fields
ActivPhysics 11.13: Electrical Potential Energy and Potential

23.11 The voltage of this battery equals the difference in potential $V_{ab} = V_a - V_b$ between its positive terminal (point a) and its negative terminal (point b).

Point a (positive terminal)

$V_{ab} = 1.5$ volts

Point b (negative terminal)

The difference $V_a - V_b$ is called the *potential of a with respect to b*; we sometimes abbreviate this difference as $V_{ab} = V_a - V_b$ (note the order of the subscripts). This is often called the potential difference between a and b, but that's ambiguous unless we specify which is the reference point. In electric circuits, which we will analyze in later chapters, the potential difference between two points is often called **voltage** (Fig. 23.11). Equation (23.13) then states: V_{ab}, **the potential of a with respect to b, equals the work done by the electric force when a UNIT charge moves from a to b.**

Another way to interpret the potential difference V_{ab} in Eq. (23.13) is to use the alternative viewpoint mentioned at the end of Section 23.1. In that viewpoint, $U_a - U_b$ is the amount of work that must be done by an *external* force to move a particle of charge q_0 slowly from b to a against the electric force. The work that must be done *per unit charge* by the external force is then $(U_a - U_b)/q_0 = V_a - V_b = V_{ab}$. In other words: V_{ab}, **the potential of a with respect to b, equals the work that must be done to move a UNIT charge slowly from b to a against the electric force.**

An instrument that measures the difference of potential between two points is called a *voltmeter.* (In Chapter 26 we'll discuss how these devices work.) Voltmeters that can measure a potential difference of 1 μV are common, and sensitivities down to 10^{-12} V can be attained.

Calculating Electric Potential

To find the potential V due to a single point charge q, we divide Eq. (23.9) by q_0:

$$V = \frac{U}{q_0} = \frac{1}{4\pi\epsilon_0}\frac{q}{r} \quad \text{(potential due to a point charge)} \quad (23.14)$$

where r is the distance from the point charge q to the point at which the potential is evaluated. If q is positive, the potential that it produces is positive at all points; if q is negative, it produces a potential that is negative everywhere. In either case, V is equal to zero at $r = \infty$, an infinite distance from the point charge. Note that potential, like electric field, is independent of the test charge q_0 that we use to define it.

Similarly, we divide Eq. (23.10) by q_0 to find the potential due to a collection of point charges:

$$V = \frac{U}{q_0} = \frac{1}{4\pi\epsilon_0}\sum_i \frac{q_i}{r_i} \quad \begin{array}{l}\text{(potential due to a collection}\\\text{of point charge)}\end{array} \quad (23.15)$$

In this expression, r_i is the distance from the ith charge, q_i, to the point at which V is evaluated. Just as the electric field due to a collection of point charges is the *vector* sum of the fields produced by each charge, the electric potential due to a collection of point charges is the *scalar* sum of the potentials due to each charge. When we have a continuous distribution of charge along a line, over a surface, or through a volume, we divide the charge into elements dq, and the sum in Eq. (23.15) becomes an integral:

Application Electrocardiography
The electrodes used in an electrocardiogram—EKG or ECG for short—measure the potential differences (typically no greater than 1 mV = 10^{-3} V) between different parts of the patient's skin. These are indicative of the potential differences between regions of the heart, and so provide a sensitive way to detect any abnormalities in the electrical activity that drives cardiac function.

$$V = \frac{1}{4\pi\epsilon_0}\int \frac{dq}{r} \quad \begin{array}{l}\text{(potential due to a continuous}\\\text{distribution of charge)}\end{array} \quad (23.16)$$

where r is the distance from the charge element dq to the field point where we are finding V. We'll work out several examples of such cases. The potential defined by Eqs. (23.15) and (23.16) is zero at points that are infinitely far away from *all* the charges. Later we'll encounter cases in which the charge distribution itself extends to infinity. We'll find that in such cases we cannot set $V = 0$ at infinity, and we'll need to exercise care in using and interpreting Eqs. (23.15) and (23.16).

CAUTION **What is electric potential?** Before getting too involved in the details of how to calculate electric potential, you should stop and remind yourself what potential is. The electric *potential* at a certain point is the potential energy that would be associated with a *unit* charge placed at that point. That's why potential is measured in joules per coulomb, or volts. Keep in mind, too, that there doesn't have to be a charge at a given point for a potential V to exist at that point. (In the same way, an electric field can exist at a given point even if there's no charge there to respond to it.)

Finding Electric Potential from Electric Field

When we are given a collection of point charges, Eq. (23.15) is usually the easiest way to calculate the potential V. But in some problems in which the electric field is known or can be found easily, it is easier to determine V from $\vec{E}$. The force $\vec{F}$ on a test charge q_0 can be written as $\vec{F} = q_0\vec{E}$, so from Eq. (23.1) the work done by the electric force as the test charge moves from a to b is given by

$$W_{a\to b} = \int_a^b \vec{F} \cdot d\vec{l} = \int_a^b q_0\vec{E} \cdot d\vec{l}$$

If we divide this by q_0 and compare the result with Eq. (23.13), we find

$$V_a - V_b = \int_a^b \vec{E} \cdot d\vec{l} = \int_a^b E\cos\phi\, dl \qquad \begin{array}{l}\text{(potential difference}\\ \text{as an integral of } \vec{E})\end{array} \quad \text{(23.17)}$$

The value of $V_a - V_b$ is independent of the path taken from a to b, just as the value of $W_{a\to b}$ is independent of the path. To interpret Eq. (23.17), remember that $\vec{E}$ is the electric force per unit charge on a test charge. If the line integral $\int_a^b \vec{E} \cdot d\vec{l}$ is positive, the electric field does positive work on a positive test charge as it moves from a to b. In this case the electric potential energy decreases as the test charge moves, so the potential energy per unit charge decreases as well; hence V_b is less than V_a and $V_a - V_b$ is positive.

As an illustration, consider a positive point charge (Fig. 23.12a). The electric field is directed away from the charge, and $V = q/4\pi\epsilon_0 r$ is positive at any finite distance from the charge. If you move away from the charge, in the direction of $\vec{E}$, you move toward lower values of V; if you move toward the charge, in the direction opposite $\vec{E}$, you move toward greater values of V. For the negative point charge in Fig. 23.12b, $\vec{E}$ is directed toward the charge and $V = q/4\pi\epsilon_0 r$ is negative at any finite distance from the charge. In this case, if you move toward the charge, you are moving in the direction of $\vec{E}$ and in the direction of decreasing (more negative) V. Moving away from the charge, in the direction opposite $\vec{E}$, moves you toward increasing (less negative) values of V. The general rule, valid for *any* electric field, is: Moving *with* the direction of $\vec{E}$ means moving in the direction of *decreasing V*, and moving *against* the direction of $\vec{E}$ means moving in the direction of *increasing V*.

Also, a positive test charge q_0 experiences an electric force in the direction of $\vec{E}$, toward lower values of V; a negative test charge experiences a force opposite $\vec{E}$, toward higher values of V. Thus a positive charge tends to "fall" from a high-potential region to a lower-potential region. The opposite is true for a negative charge.

Notice that Eq. (23.17) can be rewritten as

$$V_a - V_b = -\int_b^a \vec{E} \cdot d\vec{l} \qquad \text{(23.18)}$$

This has a negative sign compared to the integral in Eq. (23.17), and the limits are reversed; hence Eqs. (23.17) and (23.18) are equivalent. But Eq. (23.18) has a slightly different interpretation. To move a unit charge slowly against the electric

23.12 If you move in the direction of $\vec{E}$, electric potential V decreases; if you move in the direction opposite $\vec{E}$, V increases.

(a) A positive point charge

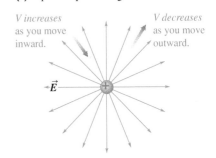

V increases as you move inward.

V decreases as you move outward.

(b) A negative point charge

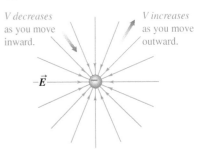

V decreases as you move inward.

V increases as you move outward.

force, we must apply an *external* force per unit charge equal to $-\vec{E}$, equal and opposite to the electric force per unit charge $\vec{E}$. Equation (23.18) says that $V_a - V_b = V_{ab}$, the potential of a with respect to b, equals the work done per unit charge by this external force to move a unit charge from b to a. This is the same alternative interpretation we discussed under Eq. (23.13).

Equations (23.17) and (23.18) show that the unit of potential difference (1 V) is equal to the unit of electric field (1 N/C) multiplied by the unit of distance (1 m). Hence the unit of electric field can be expressed as 1 *volt per meter* (1 V/m), as well as 1 N/C:

$$1 \text{ V/m} = 1 \text{ volt/meter} = 1 \text{ N/C} = 1 \text{ newton/coulomb}$$

In practice, the volt per meter is the usual unit of electric-field magnitude.

Electron Volts

The magnitude e of the electron charge can be used to define a unit of energy that is useful in many calculations with atomic and nuclear systems. When a particle with charge q moves from a point where the potential is V_b to a point where it is V_a, the change in the potential energy U is

$$U_a - U_b = q(V_a - V_b) = qV_{ab}$$

If the charge q equals the magnitude e of the electron charge, 1.602×10^{-19} C, and the potential difference is $V_{ab} = 1$ V, the change in energy is

$$U_a - U_b = (1.602 \times 10^{-19} \text{ C})(1 \text{ V}) = 1.602 \times 10^{-19} \text{ J}$$

This quantity of energy is defined to be 1 **electron volt** (1 eV):

$$1 \text{ eV} = 1.602 \times 10^{-19} \text{ J}$$

The multiples meV, keV, MeV, GeV, and TeV are often used.

CAUTION **Electron volts vs. volts** Remember that the electron volt is a unit of energy, *not* a unit of potential or potential difference!

When a particle with charge e moves through a potential difference of 1 volt, the change in potential *energy* is 1 eV. If the charge is some multiple of e—say Ne—the change in potential energy in electron volts is N times the potential difference in volts. For example, when an alpha particle, which has charge $2e$, moves between two points with a potential difference of 1000 V, the change in potential energy is $2(1000 \text{ eV}) = 2000$ eV. To confirm this, we write

$$U_a - U_b = qV_{ab} = (2e)(1000 \text{ V}) = (2)(1.602 \times 10^{-19} \text{ C})(1000 \text{ V})$$

$$= 3.204 \times 10^{-16} \text{ J} = 2000 \text{ eV}$$

Although we have defined the electron volt in terms of *potential* energy, we can use it for *any* form of energy, such as the kinetic energy of a moving particle. When we speak of a "one-million-electron-volt proton," we mean a proton with a kinetic energy of one million electron volts (1 MeV), equal to $(10^6)(1.602 \times 10^{-19} \text{ J}) = 1.602 \times 10^{-13}$ J. The Large Hadron Collider near Geneva, Switzerland, is designed to accelerate protons to a kinetic energy of 7 TeV (7×10^{12} eV).

Example 23.3 **Electric force and electric potential**

A proton (charge $+e = 1.602 \times 10^{-19}$ C) moves a distance $d = 0.50$ m in a straight line between points a and b in a linear accelerator. The electric field is uniform along this line, with mag- nitude $E = 1.5 \times 10^7$ V/m $= 1.5 \times 10^7$ N/C in the direction from a to b. Determine (a) the force on the proton; (b) the work done on it by the field; (c) the potential difference $V_a - V_b$.

SOLUTION

IDENTIFY and SET UP: This problem uses the relationship between electric field and electric force. It also uses the relationship among force, work, and potential-energy difference. We are given the electric field, so it is straightforward to find the electric force on the proton. Calculating the work is also straightforward because $\vec{E}$ is uniform, so the force on the proton is constant. Once the work is known, we find $V_a - V_b$ using Eq. (23.13).

EXECUTE: (a) The force on the proton is in the same direction as the electric field, and its magnitude is

$$F = qE = (1.602 \times 10^{-19}\,\text{C})(1.5 \times 10^7\,\text{N/C})$$
$$= 2.4 \times 10^{-12}\,\text{N}$$

(b) The force is constant and in the same direction as the displacement, so the work done on the proton is

$$W_{a \to b} = Fd = (2.4 \times 10^{-12}\,\text{N})(0.50\,\text{m}) = 1.2 \times 10^{-12}\,\text{J}$$

$$= (1.2 \times 10^{-12}\,\text{J})\frac{1\,\text{eV}}{1.602 \times 10^{-19}\,\text{J}}$$

$$= 7.5 \times 10^6\,\text{eV} = 7.5\,\text{MeV}$$

(c) From Eq. (23.13) the potential difference is the work per unit charge, which is

$$V_a - V_b = \frac{W_{a \to b}}{q} = \frac{1.2 \times 10^{-12}\,\text{J}}{1.602 \times 10^{-19}\,\text{C}}$$

$$= 7.5 \times 10^6\,\text{J/C} = 7.5 \times 10^6\,\text{V}$$

$$= 7.5\,\text{MV}$$

We can get this same result even more easily by remembering that 1 electron volt equals 1 volt multiplied by the charge e. The work done is 7.5×10^6 eV and the charge is e, so the potential difference is $(7.5 \times 10^6\,\text{eV})/e = 7.5 \times 10^6$ V.

EVALUATE: We can check our result in part (c) by using Eq. (23.17) or Eq. (23.18). The angle ϕ between the constant field $\vec{E}$ and the displacement is zero, so Eq. (23.17) becomes

$$V_a - V_b = \int_a^b E \cos \phi \, dl = \int_a^b E \, dl = E \int_a^b dl$$

The integral of dl from a to b is just the distance d, so we again find

$$V_a - V_b = Ed = (1.5 \times 10^7\,\text{V/m})(0.50\,\text{m}) = 7.5 \times 10^6\,\text{V}$$

Example 23.4   **Potential due to two point charges**

An electric dipole consists of point charges $q_1 = +12$ nC and $q_2 = -12$ nC placed 10.0 cm apart (Fig. 23.13). Compute the electric potentials at points a, b, and c.

SOLUTION

IDENTIFY and SET UP: This is the same arrangement as in Example 21.8, in which we calculated the electric *field* at each point by doing a *vector* sum. Here our target variable is the electric *potential* V at three points, which we find by doing the *algebraic* sum in Eq. (23.15).

EXECUTE: At point a we have $r_1 = 0.060$ m and $r_2 = 0.040$ m, so Eq. (23.15) becomes

$$V_a = \frac{1}{4\pi\epsilon_0}\sum_i \frac{q_i}{r_i} = \frac{1}{4\pi\epsilon_0}\frac{q_1}{r_1} + \frac{1}{4\pi\epsilon_0}\frac{q_2}{r_2}$$

$$= (9.0 \times 10^9\,\text{N}\cdot\text{m}^2/\text{C}^2)\frac{12 \times 10^{-9}\,\text{C}}{0.060\,\text{m}}$$

$$+ (9.0 \times 10^9\,\text{N}\cdot\text{m}^2/\text{C}^2)\frac{(-12 \times 10^{-9}\,\text{C})}{0.040\,\text{m}}$$

$$= 1800\,\text{N}\cdot\text{m/C} + (-2700\,\text{N}\cdot\text{m/C})$$

$$= 1800\,\text{V} + (-2700\,\text{V}) = -900\,\text{V}$$

In a similar way you can show that the potential at point b (where $r_1 = 0.040$ m and $r_2 = 0.140$ m) is $V_b = 1930$ V and that the potential at point c (where $r_1 = r_2 = 0.130$ m) is $V_c = 0$.

EVALUATE: Let's confirm that these results make sense. Point a is closer to the -12-nC charge than to the $+12$-nC charge, so the potential at a is negative. The potential is positive at point b, which

23.13 What are the potentials at points a, b, and c due to this electric dipole?

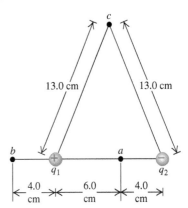

is closer to the $+12$-nC charge than the -12-nC charge. Finally, point c is equidistant from the $+12$-nC charge and the -12-nC charge, so the potential there is zero. (The potential is also equal to zero at a point infinitely far from both charges.)

Comparing this example with Example 21.8 shows that it's much easier to calculate electric potential (a scalar) than electric field (a vector). We'll take advantage of this simplification whenever possible.

Example 23.5 Potential and potential energy

Compute the potential energy associated with a +4.0-nC point charge if it is placed at points *a*, *b*, and *c* in Fig. 23.13.

SOLUTION

IDENTIFY and SET UP: The potential energy U associated with a point charge q at a location where the electric potential is V is $U = qV$. We use the values of V from Example 23.4.

EXECUTE: At the three points we find

$$U_a = qV_a = (4.0 \times 10^{-9}\,\text{C})(-900\,\text{J/C}) = -3.6 \times 10^{-6}\,\text{J}$$
$$U_b = qV_b = (4.0 \times 10^{-9}\,\text{C})(1930\,\text{J/C}) = 7.7 \times 10^{-6}\,\text{J}$$
$$U_c = qV_c = 0$$

All of these values correspond to U and V being zero at infinity.

EVALUATE: Note that *zero* net work is done on the 4.0-nC charge if it moves from point *c* to infinity *by any path*. In particular, let the path be along the perpendicular bisector of the line joining the other two charges q_1 and q_2 in Fig. 23.13. As shown in Example 21.8 (Section 21.5), at points on the bisector, the direction of $\vec{E}$ is perpendicular to the bisector. Hence the force on the 4.0-nC charge is perpendicular to the path, and no work is done in any displacement along it.

Example 23.6 Finding potential by integration

By integrating the electric field as in Eq. (23.17), find the potential at a distance *r* from a point charge *q*.

SOLUTION

IDENTIFY and SET UP: We let point *a* in Eq. (23.17) be at distance *r* and let point *b* be at infinity (Fig. 23.14). As usual, we choose the potential to be zero at an infinite distance from the charge *q*.

EXECUTE: To carry out the integral, we can choose any path we like between points *a* and *b*. The most convenient path is a radial line as shown in Fig. 23.14, so that $d\vec{l}$ is in the radial direction and has magnitude dr. Writing $d\vec{l} = \hat{r}dr$, we have from Eq. (23.17)

$$V - 0 = V = \int_r^\infty \vec{E} \cdot d\vec{l}$$
$$= \int_r^\infty \frac{1}{4\pi\epsilon_0}\frac{q}{r^2}\hat{r} \cdot \hat{r}dr = \int_r^\infty \frac{q}{4\pi\epsilon_0 r^2}dr$$
$$= -\frac{q}{4\pi\epsilon_0 r}\Big|_r^\infty = 0 - \left(-\frac{q}{4\pi\epsilon_0 r}\right)$$
$$V = \frac{q}{4\pi\epsilon_0 r}$$

23.14 Calculating the potential by integrating $\vec{E}$ for a single point charge.

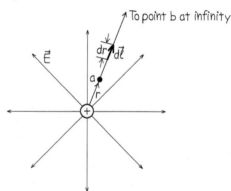

EVALUATE: Our result agrees with Eq. (23.14) and is correct for positive or negative *q*.

Example 23.7 Moving through a potential difference

In Fig. 23.15 a dust particle with mass $m = 5.0 \times 10^{-9}$ kg $= 5.0\,\mu$g and charge $q_0 = 2.0$ nC starts from rest and moves in a straight line from point *a* to point *b*. What is its speed v at point *b*?

SOLUTION

IDENTIFY and SET UP: Only the conservative electric force acts on the particle, so mechanical energy is conserved: $K_a + U_a = K_b + U_b$. We get the potential energies U from the

23.15 The particle moves from point *a* to point *b*; its acceleration is not constant.

corresponding potentials V using Eq. (23.12): $U_a = q_0V_a$ and $U_b = q_0V_b$.

EXECUTE: We have $K_a = 0$ and $K_b = \frac{1}{2}mv^2$. We substitute these and our expressions for U_a and U_b into the energy-conservation equation, then solve for v. We find

$$0 + q_0 V_a = \tfrac{1}{2}mv^2 + q_0 V_b$$

$$v = \sqrt{\frac{2q_0(V_a - V_b)}{m}}$$

We calculate the potentials using Eq. (23.15), $V = q/4\pi\epsilon_0 r$:

$$V_a = (9.0 \times 10^9 \text{ N} \cdot \text{m}^2/\text{C}^2)\left(\frac{3.0 \times 10^{-9}\text{ C}}{0.010 \text{ m}} \right.$$

$$\left. + \frac{(-3.0 \times 10^{-9}\text{ C})}{0.020 \text{ m}} \right)$$

$$= 1350 \text{ V}$$

$$V_b = (9.0 \times 10^9 \text{ N} \cdot \text{m}^2/\text{C}^2)\left(\frac{3.0 \times 10^{-9}\text{ C}}{0.020 \text{ m}} \right.$$

$$\left. + \frac{(-3.0 \times 10^{-9}\text{ C})}{0.010 \text{ m}} \right)$$

$$= -1350 \text{ V}$$

$$V_a - V_b = (1350 \text{ V}) - (-1350 \text{ V}) = 2700 \text{ V}$$

Finally,

$$v = \sqrt{\frac{2(2.0 \times 10^{-9}\text{ C})(2700 \text{ V})}{5.0 \times 10^{-9}\text{ kg}}} = 46 \text{ m/s}$$

EVALUATE: Our result makes sense: The positive test charge speeds up as it moves away from the positive charge and toward the negative charge. To check unit consistency in the final line of the calculation, note that $1 \text{ V} = 1 \text{ J/C}$, so the numerator under the radical has units of J or kg $\cdot$ m^2/s^2.

Test Your Understanding of Section 23.2 If the electric *potential* at a certain point is zero, does the electric *field* at that point have to be zero? (*Hint:* Consider point c in Example 23.4 and Example 21.8.)

23.3 Calculating Electric Potential

When calculating the potential due to a charge distribution, we usually follow one of two routes. If we know the charge distribution, we can use Eq. (23.15) or (23.16). Or if we know how the electric field depends on position, we can use Eq. (23.17), defining the potential to be zero at some convenient place. Some problems require a combination of these approaches.

As you read through these examples, compare them with the related examples of calculating electric *field* in Section 21.5. You'll see how much easier it is to calculate scalar electric potentials than vector electric fields. The moral is clear: Whenever possible, solve problems using an energy approach (using electric potential and electric potential energy) rather than a dynamics approach (using electric fields and electric forces).

Problem-Solving Strategy 23.1 **Calculating Electric Potential**

IDENTIFY *the relevant concepts:* Remember that electric potential is *potential energy per unit charge.*

SET UP *the problem* using the following steps:
1. Make a drawing showing the locations and values of the charges (which may be point charges or a continuous distribution of charge) and your choice of coordinate axes.
2. Indicate on your drawing the position of the point at which you want to calculate the electric potential V. Sometimes this position will be an arbitrary one (say, a point a distance r from the center of a charged sphere).

EXECUTE *the solution* as follows:
1. To find the potential due to a collection of point charges, use Eq. (23.15). If you are given a continuous charge distribution, devise a way to divide it into infinitesimal elements and use Eq. (23.16). Carry out the integration, using appropriate limits to include the entire charge distribution.
2. If you are given the electric field, or if you can find it using any of the methods presented in Chapter 21 or 22, it may be

easier to find the potential difference between points a and b using Eq. (23.17) or (23.18). When appropriate, make use of your freedom to define V to be zero at some convenient place, and choose this place to be point b. (For point charges, this will usually be at infinity. For other distributions of charge—especially those that themselves extend to infinity—it may be necessary to define V_b to be zero at some finite distance from the charge distribution.) Then the potential at any other point, say a, can by found from Eq. (23.17) or (23.18) with $V_b = 0$.
3. Although potential V is a *scalar* quantity, you may have to use components of the vectors $\vec{E}$ and $d\vec{l}$ when you use Eq. (23.17) or (23.18) to calculate V.

EVALUATE *your answer:* Check whether your answer agrees with your intuition. If your result gives V as a function of position, graph the function to see whether it makes sense. If you know the electric field, you can make a rough check of your result for V by verifying that V decreases if you move in the direction of $\vec{E}$.

Example 23.8 | **A charged conducting sphere**

A solid conducting sphere of radius R has a total charge q. Find the electric potential everywhere, both outside and inside the sphere.

SOLUTION

IDENTIFY and SET UP: In Example 22.5 (Section 22.4) we used Gauss's law to find the electric *field* at all points for this charge distribution. We can use that result to determine the corresponding potential.

EXECUTE: From Example 22.5, the field *outside* the sphere is the same as if the sphere were removed and replaced by a point charge q. We take $V = 0$ at infinity, as we did for a point charge. Then the potential at a point outside the sphere at a distance r from its center is the same as that due to a point charge q at the center:

$$V = \frac{1}{4\pi\epsilon_0}\frac{q}{r}$$

The potential at the surface of the sphere is $V_{surface} = q/4\pi\epsilon_0 R$.

Inside the sphere, $\vec{E}$ is zero everywhere. Hence no work is done on a test charge that moves from any point to any other point inside the sphere. This means that the potential is the same at every point inside the sphere and is equal to its value $q/4\pi\epsilon_0 R$ at the surface.

EVALUATE: Figure 23.16 shows the field and potential for a positive charge q. In this case the electric field points radially away from the sphere. As you move away from the sphere, in the direction of $\vec{E}$, V decreases (as it should).

23.16 Electric-field magnitude E and potential V at points inside and outside a positively charged spherical conductor.

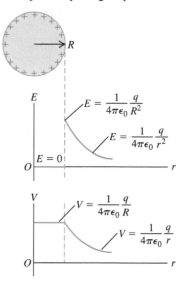

Ionization and Corona Discharge

The results of Example 23.8 have numerous practical consequences. One consequence relates to the maximum potential to which a conductor in air can be raised. This potential is limited because air molecules become *ionized,* and air becomes a conductor, at an electric-field magnitude of about 3×10^6 V/m. Assume for the moment that q is positive. When we compare the expressions in Example 23.8 for the potential $V_{surface}$ and field magnitude $E_{surface}$ at the surface of a charged conducting sphere, we note that $V_{surface} = E_{surface}R$. Thus, if E_m represents the electric-field magnitude at which air becomes conductive (known as the *dielectric strength* of air), then the maximum potential V_m to which a spherical conductor can be raised is

$$V_m = RE_m$$

For a conducting sphere 1 cm in radius in air, $V_m = (10^{-2}\,\text{m})(3 \times 10^6\,\text{V/m}) = 30{,}000$ V. No amount of "charging" could raise the potential of a conducting sphere of this size in air higher than about 30,000 V; attempting to raise the potential further by adding extra charge would cause the surrounding air to become ionized and conductive, and the extra added charge would leak into the air.

To attain even higher potentials, high-voltage machines such as Van de Graaff generators use spherical terminals with very large radii (see Fig. 22.26 and the photograph that opens Chapter 22). For example, a terminal of radius $R = 2$ m has a maximum potential $V_m = (2\,\text{m})(3 \times 10^6\,\text{V/m}) = 6 \times 10^6\,\text{V} = 6\,\text{MV}$.

Our result in Example 23.8 also explains what happens with a charged conductor with a very *small* radius of curvature, such as a sharp point or thin wire. Because the maximum potential is proportional to the radius, even relatively small potentials applied to sharp points in air produce sufficiently high fields just outside the point to ionize the surrounding air, making it become a conductor. The resulting current and its associated glow (visible in a dark room) are called *corona*. Laser printers and photocopying machines use corona from fine wires to spray charge on the imaging drum (see Fig. 21.2).

A large-radius conductor is used in situations where it's important to *prevent* corona. An example is the metal ball at the end of a car radio antenna, which prevents the static that would be caused by corona. Another example is the blunt end of a metal lightning rod (Fig. 23.17). If there is an excess charge in the atmosphere, as happens during thunderstorms, a substantial charge of the opposite sign can build up on this blunt end. As a result, when the atmospheric charge is discharged through a lightning bolt, it tends to be attracted to the charged lightning rod rather than to other nearby structures that could be damaged. (A conducting wire connecting the lightning rod to the ground then allows the acquired charge to dissipate harmlessly.) A lightning rod with a sharp end would allow less charge buildup and hence would be less effective.

23.17 The metal mast at the top of the Empire State Building acts as a lightning rod. It is struck by lightning as many as 500 times each year.

Example 23.9   Oppositely charged parallel plates

Find the potential at any height y between the two oppositely charged parallel plates discussed in Section 23.1 (Fig. 23.18).

SOLUTION

IDENTIFY and SET UP: We discussed this situation in Section 23.1. From Eq. (23.5), we know the electric *potential energy* U for a test charge q_0 is $U = q_0 E y$. (We set $y = 0$ and $U = 0$ at the bottom plate.) We use Eq. (23.12), $U = q_0 V$, to find the electric *potential* V as a function of y.

EXECUTE: The potential $V(y)$ at coordinate y is the potential energy per unit charge:

$$V(y) = \frac{U(y)}{q_0} = \frac{q_0 E y}{q_0} = E y$$

The potential decreases as we move in the direction of $\vec{E}$ from the upper to the lower plate. At point a, where $y = d$ and $V(y) = V_a$,

$$V_a - V_b = Ed \quad \text{and} \quad E = \frac{V_a - V_b}{d} = \frac{V_{ab}}{d}$$

where V_{ab} is the potential of the positive plate with respect to the negative plate. That is, the electric field equals the potential difference between the plates divided by the distance between them. For a given potential difference V_{ab}, the smaller the distance d between the two plates, the greater the magnitude E of the electric field. (This relationship between E and V_{ab} holds *only* for the planar geometry

23.18 The charged parallel plates from Fig. 23.2.

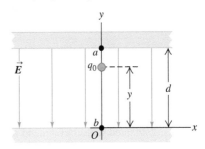

we have described. It does *not* work for situations such as concentric cylinders or spheres in which the electric field is not uniform.)

EVALUATE: Our result shows that $V = 0$ at the bottom plate (at $y = 0$). This is consistent with our choice that $U = q_0 V = 0$ for a test charge placed at the bottom plate.

CAUTION **"Zero potential" is arbitrary** You might think that if a conducting body has zero potential, it must necessarily also have zero net charge. But that just isn't so! As an example, the plate at $y = 0$ in Fig. 23.18 has zero potential ($V = 0$) but has a nonzero charge per unit area $-\sigma$. There's nothing particularly special about the place where potential is zero; we can *define* this place to be wherever we want it to be.

Example 23.10   An infinite line charge or charged conducting cylinder

Find the potential at a distance r from a very long line of charge with linear charge density (charge per unit length) λ.

SOLUTION

IDENTIFY and SET UP: In both Example 21.10 (Section 21.5) and Example 22.6 (Section 22.4) we found that the electric field at a

radial distance r from a long straight-line charge (Fig. 23.19a) has only a radial component given by $E_r = \lambda/2\pi\epsilon_0 r$. We use this expression to find the potential by integrating $\vec{E}$ as in Eq. (23.17).

EXECUTE: Since the field has only a radial component, we have $\vec{E} \cdot d\vec{l} = E_r \, dr$. Hence from Eq. (23.17) the potential of any point a

Continued

with respect to any other point b, at radial distances r_a and r_b from the line of charge, is

$$V_a - V_b = \int_a^b \vec{E} \cdot d\vec{l} = \int_a^b E_r \, dr = \frac{\lambda}{2\pi\epsilon_0} \int_{r_a}^{r_b} \frac{dr}{r} = \frac{\lambda}{2\pi\epsilon_0} \ln\frac{r_b}{r_a}$$

If we take point b at infinity and set $V_b = 0$, we find that V_a is *infinite* for any finite distance r_a from the line charge: $V_a = (\lambda/2\pi\epsilon_0)\ln(\infty/r_a) = \infty$. This is *not* a useful way to define V for this problem! The difficulty is that the charge distribution itself extends to infinity.

Instead, as recommended in Problem-Solving Strategy 23.1, we set $V_b = 0$ at point b at an arbitrary but *finite* radial distance r_0. Then the potential $V = V_a$ at point a at a radial distance r is given by $V - 0 = (\lambda/2\pi\epsilon_0)\ln(r_0/r)$, or

$$V = \frac{\lambda}{2\pi\epsilon_0}\ln\frac{r_0}{r}$$

EVALUATE: According to our result, if λ is positive, then V decreases as r increases. This is as it should be: V decreases as we move in the direction of $\vec{E}$.

From Example 22.6, the expression for E_r with which we started also applies outside a long, charged conducting cylinder with charge per unit length λ (Fig. 23.19b). Hence our result also gives the potential for such a cylinder, but only for values

23.19 Electric field outside **(a)** a long, positively charged wire and **(b)** a long, positively charged cylinder.

of r (the distance from the cylinder axis) equal to or greater than the radius R of the cylinder. If we choose r_0 to be the cylinder radius R, so that $V = 0$ when $r = R$, then at any point for which $r > R$,

$$V = \frac{\lambda}{2\pi\epsilon_0}\ln\frac{R}{r}$$

Inside the cylinder, $\vec{E} = 0$, and V has the same value (zero) as on the cylinder's surface.

Example 23.11   **A ring of charge**

Electric charge Q is distributed uniformly around a thin ring of radius a (Fig. 23.20). Find the potential at a point P on the ring axis at a distance x from the center of the ring.

SOLUTION

IDENTIFY and SET UP: We divide the ring into infinitesimal segments and use Eq. (23.16) to find V. All parts of the ring (and therefore all elements of the charge distribution) are at the same distance from P.

EXECUTE: Figure 23.20 shows that the distance from each charge element dq to P is $r = \sqrt{x^2 + a^2}$. Hence we can take the factor $1/r$ outside the integral in Eq. (23.16), and

$$V = \frac{1}{4\pi\epsilon_0}\int\frac{dq}{r} = \frac{1}{4\pi\epsilon_0}\frac{1}{\sqrt{x^2 + a^2}}\int dq = \frac{1}{4\pi\epsilon_0}\frac{Q}{\sqrt{x^2 + a^2}}$$

EVALUATE: When x is much larger than a, our expression for V becomes approximately $V = Q/4\pi\epsilon_0 x$, which is the potential at a distance x from a point charge Q. Very far away from a charged

23.20 All the charge in a ring of charge Q is the same distance r from a point P on the ring axis.

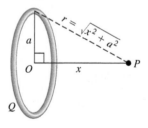

ring, its electric potential looks like that of a point charge. We drew a similar conclusion about the electric *field* of a ring in Example 21.9 (Section 21.5).

We know the electric field at all points along the x-axis from Example 21.9 (Section 21.5), so we can also find V along this axis by integrating $\vec{E} \cdot d\vec{l}$ as in Eq. (23.17).

Example 23.12   **Potential of a line of charge**

Positive electric charge Q is distributed uniformly along a line of length $2a$ lying along the y-axis between $y = -a$ and $y = +a$ (Fig. 23.21). Find the electric potential at a point P on the x-axis at a distance x from the origin.

SOLUTION

IDENTIFY and SET UP: This is the same situation as in Example 21.10 (Section 21.5), where we found an expression for the electric field $\vec{E}$ at an arbitrary point on the x-axis. We can find V at point P by integrating over the charge distribution using Eq. (23.16). Unlike the situation in Example 23.11, each charge element dQ is a *different* distance from point P, so the integration will take a little more effort.

EXECUTE: As in Example 21.10, the element of charge dQ corresponding to an element of length dy on the rod is $dQ = (Q/2a)dy$. The distance from dQ to P is $\sqrt{x^2 + y^2}$, so the contribution dV that the charge element makes to the potential at P is

$$dV = \frac{1}{4\pi\epsilon_0}\frac{Q}{2a}\frac{dy}{\sqrt{x^2 + y^2}}$$

To find the potential at P due to the entire rod, we integrate dV over the length of the rod from $y = -a$ to $y = a$:

$$V = \frac{1}{4\pi\epsilon_0}\frac{Q}{2a}\int_{-a}^{a}\frac{dy}{\sqrt{x^2 + y^2}}$$

You can look up the integral in a table. The final result is

$$V = \frac{1}{4\pi\epsilon_0}\frac{Q}{2a}\ln\left(\frac{\sqrt{a^2 + x^2} + a}{\sqrt{a^2 + x^2} - a}\right)$$

23.21 Our sketch for this problem.

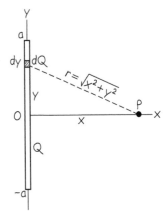

EVALUATE: We can check our result by letting x approach infinity. In this limit the point P is infinitely far from all of the charge, so we expect V to approach zero; you can verify that it does.

We know the electric field at all points along the x-axis from Example 21.10. We invite you to use this information to find V along this axis by integrating $\vec{E}$ as in Eq. (23.17).

Test Your Understanding of Section 23.3 If the electric *field* at a certain point is zero, does the electric *potential* at that point have to be zero? (*Hint:* Consider the center of the ring in Example 23.11 and Example 21.9.)

23.4 Equipotential Surfaces

Field lines (see Section 21.6) help us visualize electric fields. In a similar way, the potential at various points in an electric field can be represented graphically by *equipotential surfaces*. These use the same fundamental idea as topographic maps like those used by hikers and mountain climbers (Fig. 23.22). On a topographic map, contour lines are drawn through points that are all at the same elevation. Any number of these could be drawn, but typically only a few contour lines are shown at equal spacings of elevation. If a mass m is moved over the terrain along such a contour line, the gravitational potential energy mgy does not change because the elevation y is constant. Thus contour lines on a topographic map are really curves of constant gravitational potential energy. Contour lines are close together where the terrain is steep and there are large changes in elevation over a small horizontal distance; the contour lines are farther apart where the terrain is gently sloping. A ball allowed to roll downhill will experience the greatest downhill gravitational force where contour lines are closest together.

By analogy to contour lines on a topographic map, an **equipotential surface** is a three-dimensional surface on which the *electric potential V* is the same at every point. If a test charge q_0 is moved from point to point on such a surface, the *electric potential energy* q_0V remains constant. In a region where an electric field is present, we can construct an equipotential surface through any point. In diagrams we usually show only a few representative equipotentials, often with equal potential differences between adjacent surfaces. No point can be at two different potentials, so equipotential surfaces for different potentials can never touch or intersect.

23.22 Contour lines on a topographic map are curves of constant elevation and hence of constant gravitational potential energy.

Equipotential Surfaces and Field Lines

Because potential energy does not change as a test charge moves over an equipotential surface, the electric field can do no work on such a charge. It follows that $\vec{E}$ must be perpendicular to the surface at every point so that the electric force $q_0\vec{E}$ is always perpendicular to the displacement of a charge moving on the surface.

23.23 Cross sections of equipotential surfaces (blue lines) and electric field lines (red lines) for assemblies of point charges. There are equal potential differences between adjacent surfaces. Compare these diagrams to those in Fig. 21.28, which showed only the electric field lines.

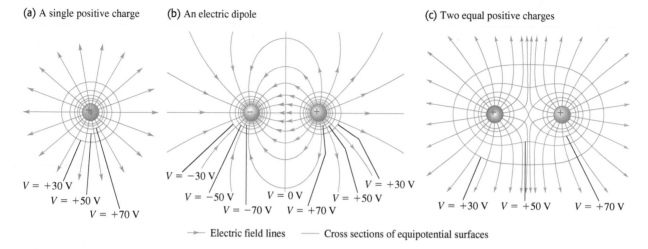

(a) A single positive charge

$V = +30$ V
$V = +50$ V
$V = +70$ V

(b) An electric dipole

$V = -30$ V
$V = -50$ V
$V = 0$ V
$V = -70$ V
$V = +30$ V
$V = +50$ V
$V = +70$ V

(c) Two equal positive charges

$V = +30$ V $V = +50$ V $V = +70$ V

→ Electric field lines   —— Cross sections of equipotential surfaces

Field lines and equipotential surfaces are always mutually perpendicular. In general, field lines are curves, and equipotentials are curved surfaces. For the special case of a *uniform* field, in which the field lines are straight, parallel, and equally spaced, the equipotentials are parallel *planes* perpendicular to the field lines.

Figure 23.23 shows three arrangements of charges. The field lines in the plane of the charges are represented by red lines, and the intersections of the equipotential surfaces with this plane (that is, cross sections of these surfaces) are shown as blue lines. The actual equipotential surfaces are three-dimensional. At each crossing of an equipotential and a field line, the two are perpendicular.

In Fig. 23.23 we have drawn equipotentials so that there are equal potential differences between adjacent surfaces. In regions where the magnitude of $\vec{E}$ is large, the equipotential surfaces are close together because the field does a relatively large amount of work on a test charge in a relatively small displacement. This is the case near the point charge in Fig. 23.23a or between the two point charges in Fig. 23.23b; note that in these regions the field lines are also closer together. This is directly analogous to the downhill force of gravity being greatest in regions on a topographic map where contour lines are close together. Conversely, in regions where the field is weaker, the equipotential surfaces are farther apart; this happens at larger radii in Fig. 23.23a, to the left of the negative charge or the right of the positive charge in Fig. 23.23b, and at greater distances from both charges in Fig. 23.23c. (It may appear that two equipotential surfaces intersect at the center of Fig. 23.23c, in violation of the rule that this can never happen. In fact this is a single figure-8–shaped equipotential surface.)

CAUTION   *E need not be constant over an equipotential surface* On a given equipotential surface, the potential V has the same value at every point. In general, however, the electric-field magnitude E is *not* the same at all points on an equipotential surface. For instance, on the equipotential surface labeled "$V = -30$ V" in Fig. 23.23b, the magnitude E is less to the left of the negative charge than it is between the two charges. On the figure-8–shaped equipotential surface in Fig. 23.23c, $E = 0$ at the middle point halfway between the two charges; at any other point on this surface, E is nonzero. ▮

**Video Tutor
Demo**

Equipotentials and Conductors

Here's an important statement about equipotential surfaces: **When all charges are at rest, the surface of a conductor is always an equipotential surface.**

Since the electric field $\vec{E}$ is always perpendicular to an equipotential surface, we can prove this statement by proving that **when all charges are at rest, the electric field just outside a conductor must be perpendicular to the surface at every point** (Fig. 23.24). We know that $\vec{E} = 0$ everywhere inside the conductor; otherwise, charges would move. In particular, at any point just inside the surface the component of $\vec{E}$ tangent to the surface is zero. It follows that the tangential component of $\vec{E}$ is also zero just *outside* the surface. If it were not, a charge could move around a rectangular path partly inside and partly outside (Fig. 23.25) and return to its starting point with a net amount of work having been done on it. This would violate the conservative nature of electrostatic fields, so the tangential component of $\vec{E}$ just outside the surface must be zero at every point on the surface. Thus $\vec{E}$ is perpendicular to the surface at each point, proving our statement.

It also follows that **when all charges are at rest, the entire solid volume of a conductor is at the same potential.** Equation (23.17) states that the potential difference between two points a and b within the conductor's solid volume, $V_a - V_b$, is equal to the line integral $\int_a^b \vec{E} \cdot d\vec{l}$ of the electric field from a to b. Since $\vec{E} = 0$ everywhere inside the conductor, the integral is guaranteed to be zero for any two such points a and b. Hence the potential is the same for any two points within the solid volume of the conductor. We describe this by saying that the solid volume of the conductor is an *equipotential volume.*

Finally, we can now prove a theorem that we quoted without proof in Section 22.5. The theorem is as follows: In an electrostatic situation, if a conductor contains a cavity and if no charge is present inside the cavity, then there can be no net charge *anywhere* on the surface of the cavity. This means that if you're inside a charged conducting box, you can safely touch any point on the inside walls of the box without being shocked. To prove this theorem, we first prove that *every point in the cavity is at the same potential.* In Fig. 23.26 the conducting surface A of the cavity is an equipotential surface, as we have just proved. Suppose point P in the cavity is at a different potential; then we can construct a different equipotential surface B including point P.

Now consider a Gaussian surface, shown in Fig. 23.26, between the two equipotential surfaces. Because of the relationship between $\vec{E}$ and the equipotentials, we know that the field at every point between the equipotentials is from A toward B, or else at every point it is from B toward A, depending on which equipotential surface is at higher potential. In either case the flux through this Gaussian surface is certainly not zero. But then Gauss's law says that the charge enclosed by the Gaussian surface cannot be zero. This contradicts our initial assumption that there is *no* charge in the cavity. So the potential at P cannot be different from that at the cavity wall.

The entire region of the cavity must therefore be at the same potential. But for this to be true, *the electric field inside the cavity must be zero everywhere.* Finally, Gauss's law shows that the electric field at any point on the surface of a conductor is proportional to the surface charge density σ at that point. We conclude that *the surface charge density on the wall of the cavity is zero at every point.* This chain of reasoning may seem tortuous, but it is worth careful study.

CAUTION **Equipotential surfaces vs. Gaussian surfaces** Don't confuse equipotential surfaces with the Gaussian surfaces we encountered in Chapter 22. Gaussian surfaces have relevance only when we are using Gauss's law, and we can choose *any* Gaussian surface that's convenient. We are *not* free to choose the shape of equipotential surfaces; the shape is determined by the charge distribution.

Test Your Understanding of Section 23.4 Would the shapes of the equipotential surfaces in Fig. 23.23 change if the sign of each charge were reversed?

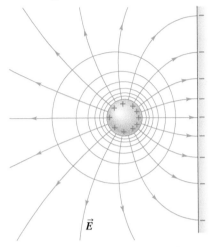

23.24 When charges are at rest, a conducting surface is always an equipotential surface. Field lines are perpendicular to a conducting surface.

$\vec{E}$

—— Cross sections of equipotential surfaces

→ Electric field lines

23.25 At all points on the surface of a conductor, the electric field must be perpendicular to the surface. If $\vec{E}$ had a tangential component, a net amount of work would be done on a test charge by moving it around a loop as shown here—which is impossible because the electric force is conservative.

An impossible electric field
If the electric field just outside a conductor had a tangential component $E_\parallel$, a charge could move in a loop with net work done.

$\vec{E}$

$E_\perp$ $E_\parallel$

Vacuum

$\vec{E} = 0$ Conductor

23.26 A cavity in a conductor. If the cavity contains no charge, every point in the cavity is at the same potential, the electric field is zero everywhere in the cavity, and there is no charge anywhere on the surface of the cavity.

Cross section of equipotential surface through P

Gaussian surface (in cross section)

B

P

Surface of cavity

A

Conductor

Application Potential Gradient Across a Cell Membrane
The interior of a human cell is at a lower electric potential V than the exterior. (The potential difference when the cell is inactive is about −70 mV in neurons and about −95 mV in skeletal muscle cells.) Hence there is a potential gradient $\vec{\nabla}V$ that points from the *interior* to the *exterior* of the cell membrane, and an electric field $\vec{E} = -\vec{\nabla}V$ that points from the *exterior* to the *interior*. This field affects how ions flow into or out of the cell through special channels in the membrane.

Calcium (Ca)

Potassium (K)

Sodium (Na)

23.5 Potential Gradient

Electric field and potential are closely related. Equation (23.17), restated here, expresses one aspect of that relationship:

$$V_a - V_b = \int_a^b \vec{E} \cdot d\vec{l}$$

If we know $\vec{E}$ at various points, we can use this equation to calculate potential differences. In this section we show how to turn this around; if we know the potential V at various points, we can use it to determine $\vec{E}$. Regarding V as a function of the coordinates (x, y, z) of a point in space, we will show that the components of $\vec{E}$ are related to the *partial derivatives* of V with respect to x, y, and z.

In Eq. (23.17), $V_a - V_b$ is the potential of a with respect to b—that is, the change of potential encountered on a trip from b to a. We can write this as

$$V_a - V_b = \int_b^a dV = -\int_a^b dV$$

where dV is the infinitesimal change of potential accompanying an infinitesimal element $d\vec{l}$ of the path from b to a. Comparing to Eq. (23.17), we have

$$-\int_a^b dV = \int_a^b \vec{E} \cdot d\vec{l}$$

These two integrals must be equal for *any* pair of limits a and b, and for this to be true the *integrands* must be equal. Thus, for *any* infinitesimal displacement $d\vec{l}$,

$$-dV = \vec{E} \cdot d\vec{l}$$

To interpret this expression, we write $\vec{E}$ and $d\vec{l}$ in terms of their components: $\vec{E} = \hat{\imath}\,E_x + \hat{\jmath}\,E_y + \hat{k}\,E_z$ and $d\vec{l} = \hat{\imath}\,dx + \hat{\jmath}\,dy + \hat{k}\,dz$. Then we have

$$-dV = E_x\,dx + E_y\,dy + E_z\,dz$$

Suppose the displacement is parallel to the x-axis, so $dy = dz = 0$. Then $-dV = E_x\,dx$ or $E_x = -(dV/dx)_{y,\,z \text{ constant}}$, where the subscript reminds us that only x varies in the derivative; recall that V is in general a function of x, y, and z. But this is just what is meant by the partial derivative $\partial V/\partial x$. The y- and z-components of $\vec{E}$ are related to the corresponding derivatives of V in the same way, so we have

$$E_x = -\frac{\partial V}{\partial x} \qquad E_y = -\frac{\partial V}{\partial y} \qquad E_z = -\frac{\partial V}{\partial z} \qquad \begin{array}{l}\text{(components of } \vec{E} \\ \text{in terms of } V)\end{array} \qquad (23.19)$$

This is consistent with the units of electric field being V/m. In terms of unit vectors we can write $\vec{E}$ as

$$\vec{E} = -\left(\hat{\imath}\frac{\partial V}{\partial x} + \hat{\jmath}\frac{\partial V}{\partial y} + \hat{k}\frac{\partial V}{\partial z}\right) \qquad (\vec{E} \text{ in terms of } V) \qquad (23.20)$$

In vector notation the following operation is called the **gradient** of the function f:

$$\vec{\nabla}f = \left(\hat{\imath}\frac{\partial}{\partial x} + \hat{\jmath}\frac{\partial}{\partial y} + \hat{k}\frac{\partial}{\partial z}\right)f \qquad (23.21)$$

The operator denoted by the symbol $\vec{\nabla}$ is called "grad" or "del." Thus in vector notation,

$$\vec{E} = -\vec{\nabla}V \qquad (23.22)$$

This is read "$\vec{E}$ is the negative of the gradient of V" or "$\vec{E}$ equals negative grad V." The quantity $\vec{\nabla}V$ is called the *potential gradient*.

At each point, the potential gradient points in the direction in which V *increases* most rapidly with a change in position. Hence at each point the direction of $\vec{E}$ is the direction in which V *decreases* most rapidly and is always perpendicular to the equipotential surface through the point. This agrees with our observation in Section 23.2 that moving in the direction of the electric field means moving in the direction of decreasing potential.

Equation (23.22) doesn't depend on the particular choice of the zero point for V. If we were to change the zero point, the effect would be to change V at every point by the same amount; the derivatives of V would be the same.

If $\vec{E}$ is radial with respect to a point or an axis and r is the distance from the point or the axis, the relationship corresponding to Eqs. (23.19) is

$$E_r = -\frac{\partial V}{\partial r} \quad \text{(radial electric field)} \qquad (23.23)$$

Often we can compute the electric field caused by a charge distribution in either of two ways: directly, by adding the $\vec{E}$ fields of point charges, or by first calculating the potential and then taking its gradient to find the field. The second method is often easier because potential is a *scalar* quantity, requiring at worst the integration of a scalar function. Electric field is a *vector* quantity, requiring computation of components for each element of charge and a separate integration for each component. Thus, quite apart from its fundamental significance, potential offers a very useful computational technique in field calculations. Below, we present two examples in which a knowledge of V is used to find the electric field.

We stress once more that if we know $\vec{E}$ as a function of position, we can calculate V using Eq. (23.17) or (23.18), and if we know V as a function of position, we can calculate $\vec{E}$ using Eq. (23.19), (23.20), or (23.23). Deriving V from $\vec{E}$ requires integration, and deriving $\vec{E}$ from V requires differentiation.

Example 23.13   Potential and field of a point charge

From Eq. (23.14) the potential at a radial distance r from a point charge q is $V = q/4\pi\epsilon_0 r$. Find the vector electric field from this expression for V.

SOLUTION

IDENTIFY and SET UP: This problem uses the general relationship between the electric potential as a function of position and the electric-field vector. By symmetry, the electric field here has only a radial component E_r. We use Eq. (23.23) to find this component.

EXECUTE: From Eq. (23.23),

$$E_r = -\frac{\partial V}{\partial r} = -\frac{\partial}{\partial r}\left(\frac{1}{4\pi\epsilon_0}\frac{q}{r}\right) = \frac{1}{4\pi\epsilon_0}\frac{q}{r^2}$$

so the vector electric field is

$$\vec{E} = \hat{r}E_r = \frac{1}{4\pi\epsilon_0}\frac{q}{r^2}\hat{r}$$

EVALUATE: Our result agrees with Eq. (21.7), as it must.

An alternative approach is to ignore the radial symmetry, write the radial distance as $r = \sqrt{x^2 + y^2 + z^2}$, and take the derivatives of V with respect to x, y, and z as in Eq. (23.20). We find

$$\frac{\partial V}{\partial x} = \frac{\partial}{\partial x}\left(\frac{1}{4\pi\epsilon_0}\frac{q}{\sqrt{x^2 + y^2 + z^2}}\right) = -\frac{1}{4\pi\epsilon_0}\frac{qx}{(x^2 + y^2 + z^2)^{3/2}}$$

$$= -\frac{qx}{4\pi\epsilon_0 r^3}$$

and similarly

$$\frac{\partial V}{\partial y} = -\frac{qy}{4\pi\epsilon_0 r^3} \qquad \frac{\partial V}{\partial z} = -\frac{qz}{4\pi\epsilon_0 r^3}$$

Then from Eq. (23.20),

$$\vec{E} = -\left[\hat{i}\left(-\frac{qx}{4\pi\epsilon_0 r^3}\right) + \hat{j}\left(-\frac{qy}{4\pi\epsilon_0 r^3}\right) + \hat{k}\left(-\frac{qz}{4\pi\epsilon_0 r^3}\right)\right]$$

$$= \frac{1}{4\pi\epsilon_0}\frac{q}{r^2}\left(\frac{x\hat{i} + y\hat{j} + z\hat{k}}{r}\right) = \frac{1}{4\pi\epsilon_0}\frac{q}{r^2}\hat{r}$$

This approach gives us the same answer, but with more effort. Clearly it's best to exploit the symmetry of the charge distribution whenever possible.

Example 23.14 **Potential and field of a ring of charge**

In Example 23.11 (Section 23.3) we found that for a ring of charge with radius a and total charge Q, the potential at a point P on the ring's symmetry axis a distance x from the center is

$$V = \frac{1}{4\pi\epsilon_0} \frac{Q}{\sqrt{x^2 + a^2}}$$

Find the electric field at P.

SOLUTION

IDENTIFY and SET UP: Figure 23.20 shows the situation. We are given V as a function of x along the x-axis, and we wish to find the electric field at a point on this axis. From the symmetry of the charge distribution, the electric field along the symmetry (x-) axis of the ring can have only an x-component. We find it using the first of Eqs. (23.19).

EXECUTE: The x-component of the electric field is

$$E_x = -\frac{\partial V}{\partial x} = \frac{1}{4\pi\epsilon_0} \frac{Qx}{(x^2 + a^2)^{3/2}}$$

EVALUATE: This agrees with our result in Example 21.9.

CAUTION **Don't use expressions where they don't apply** In this example, V is not a function of y or z on the ring axis, so that $\partial V/\partial y = \partial V/\partial z = 0$ and $E_y = E_z = 0$. But that does not mean that it's true *everywhere*; our expressions for V and E_x are valid *only on the ring axis*. If we had an expression for V valid at *all* points in space, we could use it to find the components of $\vec{E}$ at any point using Eqs. (23.19).

Test Your Understanding of Section 23.5 In a certain region of space the potential is given by $V = A + Bx + Cy^3 + Dxy$, where A, B, C, and D are positive constants. Which of these statements about the electric field $\vec{E}$ in this region of space is correct? (There may be more than one correct answer.) (i) Increasing the value of A will increase the value of $\vec{E}$ at all points; (ii) increasing the value of A will decrease the value of $\vec{E}$ at all points; (iii) $\vec{E}$ has no z-component; (iv) the electric field is zero at the origin ($x = 0, y = 0, z = 0$).

Electric potential energy: The electric force caused by any collection of charges at rest is a conservative force. The work W done by the electric force on a charged particle moving in an electric field can be represented by the change in a potential-energy function U.

The electric potential energy for two point charges q and q_0 depends on their separation r. The electric potential energy for a charge q_0 in the presence of a collection of charges q_1, q_2, q_3 depends on the distance from q_0 to each of these other charges. (See Examples 23.1 and 23.2.)

$$W_{a \to b} = U_a - U_b \quad (23.2)$$

$$U = \frac{1}{4\pi\epsilon_0}\frac{qq_0}{r} \quad (23.9)$$
(two point charges)

$$U = \frac{q_0}{4\pi\epsilon_0}\left(\frac{q_1}{r_1} + \frac{q_2}{r_2} + \frac{q_3}{r_3} + \cdots\right)$$
$$= \frac{q_0}{4\pi\epsilon_0}\sum_i \frac{q_i}{r_i} \quad (23.10)$$
(q_0 in presence of other point charges)

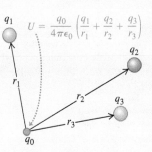

Electric potential: Potential, denoted by V, is potential energy per unit charge. The potential difference between two points equals the amount of work that would be required to move a unit positive test charge between those points. The potential V due to a quantity of charge can be calculated by summing (if the charge is a collection of point charges) or by integrating (if the charge is a distribution). (See Examples 23.3, 23.4, 23.5, 23.7, 23.11, and 23.12.)

The potential difference between two points a and b, also called the potential of a with respect to b, is given by the line integral of $\vec{E}$. The potential at a given point can be found by first finding $\vec{E}$ and then carrying out this integral. (See Examples 23.6, 23.8, 23.9, and 23.10.)

$$V = \frac{U}{q_0} = \frac{1}{4\pi\epsilon_0}\frac{q}{r} \quad (23.14)$$
(due to a point charge)

$$V = \frac{U}{q_0} = \frac{1}{4\pi\epsilon_0}\sum_i \frac{q_i}{r_i} \quad (23.15)$$
(due to a collection of point charges)

$$V = \frac{1}{4\pi\epsilon_0}\int \frac{dq}{r} \quad (23.16)$$
(due to a charge distribution)

$$V_a - V_b = \int_a^b \vec{E} \cdot d\vec{l} = \int_a^b E\cos\phi\, dl \quad (23.17)$$

Equipotential surfaces: An equipotential surface is a surface on which the potential has the same value at every point. At a point where a field line crosses an equipotential surface, the two are perpendicular. When all charges are at rest, the surface of a conductor is always an equipotential surface and all points in the interior of a conductor are at the same potential. When a cavity within a conductor contains no charge, the entire cavity is an equipotential region and there is no surface charge anywhere on the surface of the cavity.

Finding electric field from electric potential: If the potential V is known as a function of the coordinates x, y, and z, the components of electric field $\vec{E}$ at any point are given by partial derivatives of V. (See Examples 23.13 and 23.14.)

$$E_x = -\frac{\partial V}{\partial x} \quad E_y = -\frac{\partial V}{\partial y} \quad E_z = -\frac{\partial V}{\partial z} \quad (23.19)$$

$$\vec{E} = -\left(\hat{i}\frac{\partial V}{\partial x} + \hat{j}\frac{\partial V}{\partial y} + \hat{k}\frac{\partial V}{\partial z}\right) \quad (23.20)$$
(vector form)

BRIDGING PROBLEM **A Point Charge and a Line of Charge**

Positive electric charge Q is distributed uniformly along a thin rod of length $2a$. The rod lies along the x-axis between $x = -a$ and $x = +a$. Calculate how much work you must do to bring a positive point charge q from infinity to the point $x = +L$ on the x-axis, where $L > a$.

SOLUTION GUIDE

See MasteringPhysics® study area for a Video Tutor solution.

IDENTIFY and SET UP

1. In this problem you must first calculate the potential V at $x = +L$ due to the charged rod. You can then find the change in potential energy involved in bringing the point charge q from infinity (where $V = 0$) to $x = +L$.

2. To find V, divide the rod into infinitesimal segments of length dx'. How much charge is on such a segment? Consider one such segment located at $x = x'$, where $-a \le x' \le a$. What is the potential dV at $x = +L$ due to this segment?

3. The total potential at $x = +L$ is the integral of dV, including contributions from all of the segments for x' from $-a$ to $+a$. Set up this integral.

EXECUTE

4. Integrate your expression from step 3 to find the potential V at $x = +L$. A simple, standard substitution will do the trick; use a table of integrals only as a last resort.

5. Use your result from step 4 to find the potential energy for a point charge q placed at $x = +L$.

6. Use your result from step 5 to find the work you must do to bring the point charge from infinity to $x = +L$.

EVALUATE

7. What does your result from step 5 become in the limit $a \to 0$? Does this make sense?

8. Suppose the point charge q were negative rather than positive. How would this affect your result in step 4? In step 5?

Problems

For instructor-assigned homework, go to MasteringPhysics®.

•, ••, •••: Problems of increasing difficulty. **CP**: Cumulative problems incorporating material from earlier chapters. **CALC**: Problems requiring calculus. **BIO**: Biosciences problems.

DISCUSSION QUESTIONS

Q23.1 A student asked, "Since electrical potential is always proportional to potential energy, why bother with the concept of potential at all?" How would you respond?

Q23.2 The potential (relative to a point at infinity) midway between two charges of equal magnitude and opposite sign is zero. Is it possible to bring a test charge from infinity to this midpoint in such a way that no work is done in any part of the displacement? If so, describe how it can be done. If it is not possible, explain why.

Q23.3 Is it possible to have an arrangement of two point charges separated by a finite distance such that the electric potential energy of the arrangement is the same as if the two charges were infinitely far apart? Why or why not? What if there are three charges? Explain your reasoning.

Q23.4 Since potential can have any value you want depending on the choice of the reference level of zero potential, how does a voltmeter know what to read when you connect it between two points?

Q23.5 If $\vec{E}$ is zero everywhere along a certain path that leads from point A to point B, what is the potential difference between those two points? Does this mean that $\vec{E}$ is zero everywhere along *any* path from A to B? Explain.

Q23.6 If $\vec{E}$ is zero throughout a certain region of space, is the potential necessarily also zero in this region? Why or why not? If not, what *can* be said about the potential?

Q23.7 If you carry out the integral of the electric field $\int \vec{E} \cdot d\vec{l}$ for a *closed* path like that shown in Fig. Q23.7, the integral will *always* be equal to zero, independent of the shape of the

Figure **Q23.7**

path and independent of where charges may be located relative to the path. Explain why.

Q23.8 The potential difference between the two terminals of an AA battery (used in flashlights and portable stereos) is 1.5 V. If two AA batteries are placed end to end with the positive terminal of one battery touching the negative terminal of the other, what is the potential difference between the terminals at the exposed ends of the combination? What if the two positive terminals are touching each other? Explain your reasoning.

Q23.9 It is easy to produce a potential difference of several thousand volts between your body and the floor by scuffing your shoes across a nylon carpet. When you touch a metal doorknob, you get a mild shock. Yet contact with a power line of comparable voltage would probably be fatal. Why is there a difference?

Q23.10 If the electric potential at a single point is known, can $\vec{E}$ at that point be determined? If so, how? If not, why not?

Q23.11 Because electric field lines and equipotential surfaces are always perpendicular, two equipotential surfaces can never cross; if they did, the direction of $\vec{E}$ would be ambiguous at the crossing points. Yet two equipotential surfaces appear to cross at the center of Fig. 23.23c. Explain why there is no ambiguity about the direction of $\vec{E}$ in this particular case.

Q23.12 A uniform electric field is directed due east. Point B is 2.00 m west of point A, point C is 2.00 m east of point A, and point D is 2.00 m south of A. For each point, B, C, and D, is the potential at that point larger, smaller, or the same as at point A? Give the reasoning behind your answers.

Q23.13 We often say that if point A is at a higher potential than point B, A is at positive potential and B is at negative potential. Does it necessarily follow that a point at positive potential is positively charged, or that a point at negative potential is negatively charged? Illustrate your answers with clear, simple examples.

Q23.14 A conducting sphere is to be charged by bringing in positive charge a little at a time until the total charge is Q. The total work required for this process is alleged to be proportional to Q^2. Is this correct? Why or why not?

Q23.15 Three pairs of parallel metal plates (A, B, and C) are connected as shown in Fig. Q23.15, and a battery maintains a potential of 1.5 V across ab. What can you say about the potential difference across each pair of plates? Why?

Figure **Q23.15**

Q23.16 A conducting sphere is placed between two charged parallel plates such as those shown in Fig. 23.2. Does the electric field inside the sphere depend on precisely where between the plates the sphere is placed? What about the electric potential inside the sphere? Do the answers to these questions depend on whether or not there is a net charge on the sphere? Explain your reasoning.

Q23.17 A conductor that carries a net charge Q has a hollow, empty cavity in its interior. Does the potential vary from point to point within the material of the conductor? What about within the cavity? How does the potential inside the cavity compare to the potential within the material of the conductor?

Q23.18 A high-voltage dc power line falls on a car, so the entire metal body of the car is at a potential of 10,000 V with respect to the ground. What happens to the occupants (a) when they are sitting in the car and (b) when they step out of the car? Explain your reasoning.

Q23.19 When a thunderstorm is approaching, sailors at sea sometimes observe a phenomenon called "St. Elmo's fire," a bluish flickering light at the tips of masts. What causes this? Why does it occur at the tips of masts? Why is the effect most pronounced when the masts are wet? (*Hint:* Seawater is a good conductor of electricity.)

Q23.20 A positive point charge is placed near a very large conducting plane. A professor of physics asserted that the field caused by this configuration is the same as would be obtained by removing the plane and placing a negative point charge of equal magnitude in the mirror-image position behind the initial position of the plane. Is this correct? Why or why not? (*Hint:* Inspect Fig. 23.23b.)

Q23.21 In electronics it is customary to define the potential of ground (thinking of the earth as a large conductor) as zero. Is this consistent with the fact that the earth has a net electric charge that is not zero? (Refer to Exercise 21.32.)

EXERCISES

Section 23.1 Electric Potential Energy

23.1 •• A point charge $q_1 = +2.40\ \mu$C is held stationary at the origin. A second point charge $q_2 = -4.30\ \mu$C moves from the point $x = 0.150$ m, $y = 0$ to the point $x = 0.250$ m, $y = 0.250$ m. How much work is done by the electric force on q_2?

23.2 • A point charge q_1 is held stationary at the origin. A second charge q_2 is placed at point a, and the electric potential energy of the pair of charges is $+5.4 \times 10^{-8}$ J. When the second charge is moved to point b, the electric force on the charge does -1.9×10^{-8} J of work. What is the electric potential energy of the pair of charges when the second charge is at point b?

23.3 •• **Energy of the Nucleus.** How much work is needed to assemble an atomic nucleus containing three protons (such as Be) if we model it as an equilateral triangle of side 2.00×10^{-15} m

with a proton at each vertex? Assume the protons started from very far away.

23.4 •• (a) How much work would it take to push two protons very slowly from a separation of 2.00×10^{-10} m (a typical atomic distance) to 3.00×10^{-15} m (a typical nuclear distance)? (b) If the protons are both released from rest at the closer distance in part (a), how fast are they moving when they reach their original separation?

23.5 •• A small metal sphere, carrying a net charge of $q_1 = -2.80\ \mu$C, is held in a stationary position by insulating supports. A second small metal sphere, with a net charge of $q_2 = -7.80\ \mu$C and mass 1.50 g, is projected toward q_1. When the two spheres are 0.800 m apart, q_2 is moving toward q_1 with speed 22.0 m/s (Fig. E23.5). Assume that the two spheres can be treated as point charges. You can ignore the force of gravity. (a) What is the speed of q_2 when the spheres are 0.400 m apart? (b) How close does q_2 get to q_1?

Figure **E23.5**

23.6 •• **BIO Energy of DNA Base Pairing, I.** (See Exercise 21.23.) (a) Calculate the electric potential energy of the adenine–thymine bond, using the same combinations of molecules (O − H − N and N − H − N) as in Exercise 21.23. (b) Compare this energy with the potential energy of the proton–electron pair in the hydrogen atom.

23.7 •• **BIO Energy of DNA Base Pairing, II.** (See Exercise 21.24.) Calculate the electric potential energy of the guanine–cytosine bond, using the same combinations of molecules (O − H − O, N − H − N, and O − H − N) as in Exercise 21.24.

23.8 •• Three equal 1.20-μC point charges are placed at the corners of an equilateral triangle whose sides are 0.500 m long. What is the potential energy of the system? (Take as zero the potential energy of the three charges when they are infinitely far apart.)

23.9 •• Two protons are released from rest when they are 0.750 nm apart. (a) What is the maximum speed they will reach? When does this speed occur? (b) What is the maximum acceleration they will achieve? When does this acceleration occur?

23.10 •• Four electrons are located at the corners of a square 10.0 nm on a side, with an alpha particle at its midpoint. How much work is needed to move the alpha particle to the midpoint of one of the sides of the square?

23.11 •• Three point charges, which initially are infinitely far apart, are placed at the corners of an equilateral triangle with sides d. Two of the point charges are identical and have charge q. If zero net work is required to place the three charges at the corners of the triangle, what must the value of the third charge be?

23.12 •• Starting from a separation of several meters, two protons are aimed directly toward each other by a cyclotron accelerator with speeds of 1000 km/s, measured relative to the earth. Find the maximum electrical force that these protons will exert on each other.

Section 23.2 Electric Potential

23.13 • A small particle has charge $-5.00\ \mu$C and mass 2.00×10^{-4} kg. It moves from point A, where the electric potential is $V_A = +200$ V, to point B, where the electric potential is $V_B = +800$ V. The electric force is the only force acting on the particle. The particle has speed 5.00 m/s at point A. What is its speed at point B? Is it moving faster or slower at B than at A? Explain.

23.14 • A particle with a charge of +4.20 nC is in a uniform electric field $\vec{E}$ directed to the left. It is released from rest and moves to the left; after it has moved 6.00 cm, its kinetic energy is found to be $+1.50 \times 10^{-6}$ J. (a) What work was done by the electric force? (b) What is the potential of the starting point with respect to the end point? (c) What is the magnitude of $\vec{E}$?

23.15 • A charge of 28.0 nC is placed in a uniform electric field that is directed vertically upward and has a magnitude of 4.00×10^4 V/m. What work is done by the electric force when the charge moves (a) 0.450 m to the right; (b) 0.670 m upward; (c) 2.60 m at an angle of 45.0° downward from the horizontal?

23.16 • Two stationary point charges +3.00 nC and +2.00 nC are separated by a distance of 50.0 cm. An electron is released from rest at a point midway between the two charges and moves along the line connecting the two charges. What is the speed of the electron when it is 10.0 cm from the +3.00-nC charge?

23.17 •• Point charges $q_1 = +2.00 \ \mu$C and $q_2 = -2.00 \ \mu$C are placed at adjacent corners of a square for which the length of each side is 3.00 cm. Point a is at the center of the square, and point b is at the empty corner closest to q_2. Take the electric potential to be zero at a distance far from both charges. (a) What is the electric potential at point a due to q_1 and q_2? (b) What is the electric potential at point b? (c) A point charge $q_3 = -5.00 \ \mu$C moves from point a to point b. How much work is done on q_3 by the electric forces exerted by q_1 and q_2? Is this work positive or negative?

23.18 • Two charges of equal magnitude Q are held a distance d apart. Consider only points on the line passing through both charges. (a) If the two charges have the same sign, find the location of all points (if there are any) at which (i) the potential (relative to infinity) is zero (is the electric field zero at these points?), and (ii) the electric field is zero (is the potential zero at these points?). (b) Repeat part (a) for two charges having opposite signs.

23.19 • Two point charges $q_1 = +2.40$ nC and $q_2 = -6.50$ nC are 0.100 m apart. Point A is midway between them; point B is 0.080 m from q_1 and 0.060 m from q_2 (Fig. E23.19). Take the electric potential to be zero at infinity. Find (a) the potential at point A; (b) the potential at point B; (c) the work done by the electric field on a charge of 2.50 nC that travels from point B to point A.

Figure **E23.19**

23.20 • A positive charge $+q$ is located at the point $x = 0$, $y = -a$, and a negative charge $-q$ is located at the point $x = 0$, $y = +a$. (a) Derive an expression for the potential V at points on the y-axis as a function of the coordinate y. Take V to be zero at an infinite distance from the charges. (b) Graph V at points on the y-axis as a function of y over the range from $y = -4a$ to $y = +4a$. (c) Show that for $y > a$, the potential at a point on the positive y-axis is given by $V = -(1/4\pi\epsilon_0)2qa/y^2$. (d) What are the answers to parts (a) and (c) if the two charges are interchanged so that $+q$ is at $y = +a$ and $-q$ is at $y = -a$?

23.21 •• A positive charge q is fixed at the point $x = 0$, $y = 0$, and a negative charge $-2q$ is fixed at the point $x = a$, $y = 0$. (a) Show the positions of the charges in a diagram. (b) Derive an expression for the potential V at points on the x-axis as a function of the coordinate x. Take V to be zero at an infinite distance from the charges. (c) At which positions on the x-axis is $V = 0$? (d) Graph V at points on the x-axis as a function of x in the range from $x = -2a$ to $x = +2a$. (e) What does the answer to part (b) become when $x \gg a$? Explain why this result is obtained.

23.22 •• Consider the arrangement of point charges described in Exercise 23.21. (a) Derive an expression for the potential V at points on the y-axis as a function of the coordinate y. Take V to be zero at an infinite distance from the charges. (b) At which positions on the y-axis is $V = 0$? (c) Graph V at points on the y-axis as a function of y in the range from $y = -2a$ to $y = +2a$. (d) What does the answer to part (a) become when $y > a$? Explain why this result is obtained.

23.23 •• (a) An electron is to be accelerated from 3.00×10^6 m/s to 8.00×10^6 m/s. Through what potential difference must the electron pass to accomplish this? (b) Through what potential difference must the electron pass if it is to be slowed from 8.00×10^6 m/s to a halt?

23.24 • At a certain distance from a point charge, the potential and electric-field magnitude due to that charge are 4.98 V and 12.0 V/m, respectively. (Take the potential to be zero at infinity.) (a) What is the distance to the point charge? (b) What is the magnitude of the charge? (c) Is the electric field directed toward or away from the point charge?

23.25 • A uniform electric field has magnitude E and is directed in the negative x-direction. The potential difference between point a (at $x = 0.60$ m) and point b (at $x = 0.90$ m) is 240 V. (a) Which point, a or b, is at the higher potential? (b) Calculate the value of E. (c) A negative point charge $q = -0.200 \ \mu$C is moved from b to a. Calculate the work done on the point charge by the electric field.

23.26 • For each of the following arrangements of two point charges, find all the points along the line passing through both charges for which the electric potential V is zero (take $V = 0$ infinitely far from the charges) and for which the electric field E is zero: (a) charges $+Q$ and $+2Q$ separated by a distance d, and (b) charges $-Q$ and $+2Q$ separated by a distance d. (c) Are both V and E zero at the same places? Explain.

Section 23.3 Calculating Electric Potential

23.27 •• A thin spherical shell with radius $R_1 = 3.00$ cm is concentric with a larger thin spherical shell with radius $R_2 = 5.00$ cm. Both shells are made of insulating material. The smaller shell has charge $q_1 = +6.00$ nC distributed uniformly over its surface, and the larger shell has charge $q_2 = -9.00$ nC distributed uniformly over its surface. Take the electric potential to be zero at an infinite distance from both shells. (a) What is the electric potential due to the two shells at the following distance from their common center: (i) $r = 0$; (ii) $r = 4.00$ cm; (iii) $r = 6.00$ cm? (b) What is the magnitude of the potential difference between the surfaces of the two shells? Which shell is at higher potential: the inner shell or the outer shell?

23.28 • A total electric charge of 3.50 nC is distributed uniformly over the surface of a metal sphere with a radius of 24.0 cm. If the potential is zero at a point at infinity, find the value of the potential at the following distances from the center of the sphere: (a) 48.0 cm; (b) 24.0 cm; (c) 12.0 cm.

23.29 •• A uniformly charged, thin ring has radius 15.0 cm and total charge +24.0 nC. An electron is placed on the ring's axis a distance 30.0 cm from the center of the ring and is constrained to stay on the axis of the ring. The electron is then released from rest. (a) Describe the subsequent motion of the electron. (b) Find the speed of the electron when it reaches the center of the ring.

23.30 •• An infinitely long line of charge has linear charge density 5.00×10^{-12} C/m. A proton (mass 1.67×10^{-27} kg, charge $+1.60 \times 10^{-19}$ C) is 18.0 cm from the line and moving directly toward the line at 1.50×10^3 m/s. (a) Calculate the proton's initial kinetic energy. (b) How close does the proton get to the line of charge?

23.31 • A very long wire carries a uniform linear charge density λ. Using a voltmeter to measure potential difference, you find that when one probe of the meter is placed 2.50 cm from the wire and the other probe is 1.00 cm farther from the wire, the meter reads 575 V. (a) What is λ? (b) If you now place one probe at 3.50 cm from the wire and the other probe 1.00 cm farther away, will the voltmeter read 575 V? If not, will it read more or less than 575 V? Why? (c) If you place both probes 3.50 cm from the wire but 17.0 cm from each other, what will the voltmeter read?

23.32 •• A very long insulating cylinder of charge of radius 2.50 cm carries a uniform linear density of 15.0 nC/m. If you put one probe of a voltmeter at the surface, how far from the surface must the other probe be placed so that the voltmeter reads 175 V?

23.33 •• A very long insulating cylindrical shell of radius 6.00 cm carries charge of linear density 8.50 μC/m spread uniformly over its outer surface. What would a voltmeter read if it were connected between (a) the surface of the cylinder and a point 4.00 cm above the surface, and (b) the surface and a point 1.00 cm from the central axis of the cylinder?

23.34 • A ring of diameter 8.00 cm is fixed in place and carries a charge of +5.00 μC uniformly spread over its circumference. (a) How much work does it take to move a tiny +3.00-μC charged ball of mass 1.50 g from very far away to the center of the ring? (b) Is it necessary to take a path along the axis of the ring? Why? (c) If the ball is slightly displaced from the center of the ring, what will it do and what is the maximum speed it will reach?

23.35 •• A very small sphere with positive charge $q = +8.00 \mu$C is released from rest at a point 1.50 cm from a very long line of uniform linear charge density $\lambda = +3.00 \mu$C/m. What is the kinetic energy of the sphere when it is 4.50 cm from the line of charge if the only force on it is the force exerted by the line of charge?

23.36 • Charge $Q = 5.00 \mu$C is distributed uniformly over the volume of an insulating sphere that has radius $R = 12.0$ cm. A small sphere with charge $q = +3.00 \mu$C and mass 6.00×10^{-5} kg is projected toward the center of the large sphere from an initial large distance. The large sphere is held at a fixed position and the small sphere can be treated as a point charge. What minimum speed must the small sphere have in order to come within 8.00 cm of the surface of the large sphere?

23.37 • BIO **Axons.** Neurons are the basic units of the nervous system. They contain long tubular structures called *axons* that propagate electrical signals away from the ends of the neurons. The axon contains a solution of potassium (K^+) ions and large negative organic ions. The axon membrane prevents the large ions from leaking out, but the smaller K^+ ions are able to penetrate the membrane to some degree (Fig. E23.37). This leaves an excess negative charge on the inner surface of the axon membrane and an excess positive charge on the outer surface, resulting in a potential difference across the membrane that prevents further K^+ ions from leaking out. Measurements show that this potential difference is typically about 70 mV. The thickness of the axon membrane itself varies from about 5 to 10 nm, so we'll use an average of 7.5 nm. We can model the membrane as a large sheet having equal and opposite charge densities on its faces. (a) Find the electric field inside the axon membrane, assuming (not too realistically) that it is filled with air. Which way does it point: into or out of the axon?

Figure **E23.37**

(b) Which is at a higher potential: the inside surface or the outside surface of the axon membrane?

23.38 • CP Two large, parallel conducting plates carrying opposite charges of equal magnitude are separated by 2.20 cm. (a) If the surface charge density for each plate has magnitude 47.0 nC/m², what is the magnitude of $\vec{E}$ in the region between the plates? (b) What is the potential difference between the two plates? (c) If the separation between the plates is doubled while the surface charge density is kept constant at the value in part (a), what happens to the magnitude of the electric field and to the potential difference?

23.39 • Two large, parallel, metal plates carry opposite charges of equal magnitude. They are separated by 45.0 mm, and the potential difference between them is 360 V. (a) What is the magnitude of the electric field (assumed to be uniform) in the region between the plates? (b) What is the magnitude of the force this field exerts on a particle with charge +2.40 nC? (c) Use the results of part (b) to compute the work done by the field on the particle as it moves from the higher-potential plate to the lower. (d) Compare the result of part (c) to the change of potential energy of the same charge, computed from the electric potential.

23.40 • BIO **Electrical Sensitivity of Sharks.** Certain sharks can detect an electric field as weak as 1.0 μV/m. To grasp how weak this field is, if you wanted to produce it between two parallel metal plates by connecting an ordinary 1.5-V AA battery across these plates, how far apart would the plates have to be?

23.41 •• (a) Show that V for a spherical shell of radius R, that has charge q distributed uniformly over its surface, is the same as V for a solid conductor with radius R and charge q. (b) You rub an inflated balloon on the carpet and it acquires a potential that is 1560 V lower than its potential before it became charged. If the charge is uniformly distributed over the surface of the balloon and if the radius of the balloon is 15 cm, what is the net charge on the balloon? (c) In light of its 1200-V potential difference relative to you, do you think this balloon is dangerous? Explain.

23.42 •• (a) How much excess charge must be placed on a copper sphere 25.0 cm in diameter so that the potential of its center, relative to infinity, is 1.50 kV? (b) What is the potential of the sphere's surface relative to infinity?

23.43 • The electric field at the surface of a charged, solid, copper sphere with radius 0.200 m is 3800 N/C, directed toward the center of the sphere. What is the potential at the center of the sphere, if we take the potential to be zero infinitely far from the sphere?

Section 23.4 Equipotential Surfaces and Section 23.5 Potential Gradient

23.44 • A very large plastic sheet carries a uniform charge density of -6.00 nC/m² on one face. (a) As you move away from the sheet along a line perpendicular to it, does the potential increase or decrease? How do you know, without doing any calculations? Does your answer depend on where you choose the reference point for potential? (b) Find the spacing between equipotential surfaces that differ from each other by 1.00 V. What type of surfaces are these?

23.45 • CALC In a certain region of space, the electric potential is $V(x, y, z) = Axy - Bx^2 + Cy$, where A, B, and C are positive constants. (a) Calculate the x-, y-, and z-components of the electric field. (b) At which points is the electric field equal to zero?

23.46 • CALC In a certain region of space the electric potential is given by $V = +Ax^2y - Bxy^2$, where $A = 5.00$ V/m³ and $B = 8.00$ V/m³. Calculate the magnitude and direction of the electric field at the point in the region that has coordinates $x = 2.00$ m, $y = 0.400$ m, and $z = 0$.

23.47 •• CALC A metal sphere with radius r_a is supported on an insulating stand at the center of a hollow, metal, spherical shell with radius r_b. There is charge $+q$ on the inner sphere and charge $-q$ on the outer spherical shell. (a) Calculate the potential $V(r)$ for (i) $r < r_a$; (ii) $r_a < r < r_b$; (iii) $r > r_b$. (*Hint:* The net potential is the sum of the potentials due to the individual spheres.) Take V to be zero when r is infinite. (b) Show that the potential of the inner sphere with respect to the outer is

$$V_{ab} = \frac{q}{4\pi\epsilon_0}\left(\frac{1}{r_a} - \frac{1}{r_b}\right)$$

(c) Use Eq. (23.23) and the result from part (a) to show that the electric field at any point between the spheres has magnitude

$$E(r) = \frac{V_{ab}}{(1/r_a - 1/r_b)}\frac{1}{r^2}$$

(d) Use Eq. (23.23) and the result from part (a) to find the electric field at a point outside the larger sphere at a distance r from the center, where $r > r_b$. (e) Suppose the charge on the outer sphere is not $-q$ but a negative charge of different magnitude, say $-Q$. Show that the answers for parts (b) and (c) are the same as before but the answer for part (d) is different.

23.48 • A metal sphere with radius $r_a = 1.20$ cm is supported on an insulating stand at the center of a hollow, metal, spherical shell with radius $r_b = 9.60$ cm. Charge $+q$ is put on the inner sphere and charge $-q$ on the outer spherical shell. The magnitude of q is chosen to make the potential difference between the spheres 500 V, with the inner sphere at higher potential. (a) Use the result of Exercise 23.47(b) to calculate q. (b) With the help of the result of Exercise 23.47(a), sketch the equipotential surfaces that correspond to 500, 400, 300, 200, 100, and 0 V. (c) In your sketch, show the electric field lines. Are the electric field lines and equipotential surfaces mutually perpendicular? Are the equipotential surfaces closer together when the magnitude of $\vec{E}$ is largest?

23.49 • A very long cylinder of radius 2.00 cm carries a uniform charge density of 1.50 nC/m. (a) Describe the shape of the equipotential surfaces for this cylinder. (b) Taking the reference level for the zero of potential to be the surface of the cylinder, find the radius of equipotential surfaces having potentials of 10.0 V, 20.0 V, and 30.0 V. (c) Are the equipotential surfaces equally spaced? If not, do they get closer together or farther apart as r increases?

PROBLEMS

23.50 • CP A point charge $q_1 = +5.00\ \mu C$ is held fixed in space. From a horizontal distance of 6.00 cm, a small sphere with mass 4.00×10^{-3} kg and charge $q_2 = +2.00\ \mu C$ is fired toward the fixed charge with an initial speed of 40.0 m/s. Gravity can be neglected. What is the acceleration of the sphere at the instant when its speed is 25.0 m/s?

23.51 ••• A point charge $q_1 = 4.00$ nC is placed at the origin, and a second point charge $q_2 = -3.00$ nC is placed on the x-axis at $x = +20.0$ cm. A third point charge $q_3 = 2.00$ nC is to be placed on the x-axis between q_1 and q_2. (Take as zero the potential energy of the three charges when they are infinitely far apart.) (a) What is the potential energy of the system of the three charges if q_3 is placed at $x = +10.0$ cm? (b) Where should q_3 be placed to make the potential energy of the system equal to zero?

23.52 ••• A small sphere with mass 5.00×10^{-7} kg and charge $+3.00\ \mu C$ is released from rest a distance of 0.400 m above a large horizontal insulating sheet of charge that has uniform surface charge density $\sigma = +8.00$ pC/m^2. Using energy methods, calculate the speed of the sphere when it is 0.100 m above the sheet of charge?

23.53 •• **Determining the Size of the Nucleus.** When radium-226 decays radioactively, it emits an alpha particle (the nucleus of helium), and the end product is radon-222. We can model this decay by thinking of the radium-226 as consisting of an alpha particle emitted from the surface of the spherically symmetric radon-222 nucleus, and we can treat the alpha particle as a point charge. The energy of the alpha particle has been measured in the laboratory and has been found to be 4.79 MeV when the alpha particle is essentially infinitely far from the nucleus. Since radon is much heavier than the alpha particle, we can assume that there is no appreciable recoil of the radon after the decay. The radon nucleus contains 86 protons, while the alpha particle has 2 protons and the radium nucleus has 88 protons. (a) What was the electric potential energy of the alpha–radon combination just before the decay, in MeV and in joules? (b) Use your result from part (a) to calculate the radius of the radon nucleus.

23.54 •• CP A proton and an alpha particle are released from rest when they are 0.225 nm apart. The alpha particle (a helium nucleus) has essentially four times the mass and two times the charge of a proton. Find the maximum *speed* and maximum *acceleration* of each of these particles. When do these maxima occur: just following the release of the particles or after a very long time?

23.55 • A particle with charge $+7.60$ nC is in a uniform electric field directed to the left. Another force, in addition to the electric force, acts on the particle so that when it is released from rest, it moves to the right. After it has moved 8.00 cm, the additional force has done 6.50×10^{-5} J of work and the particle has 4.35×10^{-5} J of kinetic energy. (a) What work was done by the electric force? (b) What is the potential of the starting point with respect to the end point? (c) What is the magnitude of the electric field?

23.56 • CP In the *Bohr model* of the hydrogen atom, a single electron revolves around a single proton in a circle of radius r. Assume that the proton remains at rest. (a) By equating the electric force to the electron mass times its acceleration, derive an expression for the electron's speed. (b) Obtain an expression for the electron's kinetic energy, and show that its magnitude is just half that of the electric potential energy. (c) Obtain an expression for the total energy, and evaluate it using $r = 5.29 \times 10^{-11}$ m. Give your numerical result in joules and in electron volts.

23.57 •• CALC A vacuum tube diode consists of concentric cylindrical electrodes, the negative cathode and the positive anode. Because of the accumulation of charge near the cathode, the electric potential between the electrodes is not a linear function of the position, even with planar geometry, but is given by

$$V(x) = Cx^{4/3}$$

where x is the distance from the cathode and C is a constant, characteristic of a particular diode and operating conditions. Assume that the distance between the cathode and anode is 13.0 mm and the potential difference between electrodes is 240 V. (a) Determine the value of C. (b) Obtain a formula for the electric field between the electrodes as a function of x. (c) Determine the force on an electron when the electron is halfway between the electrodes.

23.58 •• Two oppositely charged, identical insulating spheres, each 50.0 cm in diameter and carrying a uniform charge of magnitude 250 μC, are placed 1.00 m apart center to center (Fig. P23.58). (a) If a voltmeter is connected between the nearest points (a and b) on their surfaces, what will it read? (b) Which point, a or b, is at the higher potential? How can you know this without any calculations?

Figure **P23.58**

23.59 •• **An Ionic Crystal.** Figure P23.59 shows eight point charges arranged at the corners of a cube with sides of length d. The values of the charges are $+q$ and $-q$, as shown. This is a model of one cell of a cubic ionic crystal. In sodium chloride (NaCl), for instance, the positive ions are Na$^+$ and the negative ions are Cl$^-$. (a) Calculate the potential energy U of this arrangement. (Take as zero the potential energy of the eight charges when they are infinitely far apart.) (b) In part (a), you should have found that $U < 0$. Explain the relationship between this result and the observation that such ionic crystals exist in nature.

Figure **P23.59**

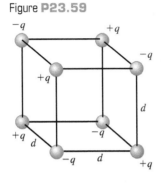

23.60 • (a) Calculate the potential energy of a system of two small spheres, one carrying a charge of 2.00 μC and the other a charge of -3.50 μC, with their centers separated by a distance of 0.250 m. Assume zero potential energy when the charges are infinitely separated. (b) Suppose that one of the spheres is held in place and the other sphere, which has a mass of 1.50 g, is shot away from it. What minimum initial speed would the moving sphere need in order to escape completely from the attraction of the fixed sphere? (To escape, the moving sphere would have to reach a velocity of zero when it was infinitely distant from the fixed sphere.)

23.61 •• **The H$_2^+$ Ion.** The H$_2^+$ ion is composed of two protons, each of charge $+e = 1.60 \times 10^{-19}$ C, and an electron of charge $-e$ and mass 9.11×10^{-31} kg. The separation between the protons is 1.07×10^{-10} m. The protons and the electron may be treated as point charges. (a) Suppose the electron is located at the point midway between the two protons. What is the potential energy of the interaction between the electron and the two protons? (Do not include the potential energy due to the interaction between the two protons.) (b) Suppose the electron in part (a) has a velocity of magnitude 1.50×10^6 m/s in a direction along the perpendicular bisector of the line connecting the two protons. How far from the point midway between the two protons can the electron move? Because the masses of the protons are much greater than the electron mass, the motions of the protons are very slow and can be ignored. (*Note:* A realistic description of the electron motion requires the use of quantum mechanics, not Newtonian mechanics.)

23.62 •• **CP** A small sphere with mass 1.50 g hangs by a thread between two parallel vertical plates 5.00 cm apart (Fig. P23.62). The plates are insulating and have uniform

Figure **P23.62**

surface charge densities $+\sigma$ and $-\sigma$. The charge on the sphere is $q = 8.90 \times 10^{-6}$ C. What potential difference between the plates will cause the thread to assume an angle of 30.0° with the vertical?

23.63 • **CALC Coaxial Cylinders.** A long metal cylinder with radius a is supported on an insulating stand on the axis of a long, hollow, metal tube with radius b. The positive charge per unit length on the inner cylinder is λ, and there is an equal negative charge per unit length on the outer cylinder. (a) Calculate the potential $V(r)$ for (i) $r < a$; (ii) $a < r < b$; (iii) $r > b$. (*Hint:* The net potential is the sum of the potentials due to the individual conductors.) Take $V = 0$ at $r = b$. (b) Show that the potential of the inner cylinder with respect to the outer is

$$V_{ab} = \frac{\lambda}{2\pi\epsilon_0} \ln\frac{b}{a}$$

(c) Use Eq. (23.23) and the result from part (a) to show that the electric field at any point between the cylinders has magnitude

$$E(r) = \frac{V_{ab}}{\ln(b/a)} \frac{1}{r}$$

(d) What is the potential difference between the two cylinders if the outer cylinder has no net charge?

23.64 •• A *Geiger counter* detects radiation such as alpha particles by using the fact that the radiation ionizes the air along its path. A thin wire lies on the axis of a hollow metal cylinder and is insulated from it (Fig. P23.64). A large potential difference is established between the wire and the outer cylinder, with the wire at higher potential; this sets up a strong electric field directed radially outward. When ionizing radiation enters the device, it ionizes a few air molecules. The free electrons produced are accelerated by the electric field toward the wire and, on the way there, ionize many more air molecules. Thus a current pulse is produced that can be detected by appropriate electronic circuitry and converted to an audible "click." Suppose the radius of the central wire is 145 μm and the radius of the hollow cylinder is 1.80 cm. What potential difference between the wire and the cylinder produces an electric field of 2.00×10^4 V/m at a distance of 1.20 cm from the axis of the wire? (The wire and cylinder are both very long in comparison to their radii, so the results of Problem 23.63 apply.)

Figure **P23.64**

23.65 • **CP Deflection in a CRT.** Cathode-ray tubes (CRTs) are often found in oscilloscopes and computer monitors. In Fig. P23.65 an electron with an initial speed of 6.50×10^6 m/s is projected along the axis midway between the deflection plates of a cathode-ray tube. The potential difference between the two plates is 22.0 V and the lower plate is the one at higher potential. (a) What is the force (magnitude and direction) on the electron when it is between the plates? (b) What is the acceleration of the electron (magnitude and direction) when acted on by the force in part (a)? (c) How far below the axis has the electron moved when it reaches the end of the plates? (d) At what angle with the axis is it moving as it leaves the plates? (e) How far below the axis will it strike the fluorescent screen S?

Figure **P23.65**

23.66 •• **CP** **Deflecting Plates of an Oscilloscope.** The vertical deflecting plates of a typical classroom oscilloscope are a pair of parallel square metal plates carrying equal but opposite charges. Typical dimensions are about 3.0 cm on a side, with a separation of about 5.0 mm. The potential difference between the plates is 25.0 V. The plates are close enough that we can ignore fringing at the ends. Under these conditions: (a) how much charge is on each plate, and (b) how strong is the electric field between the plates? (c) If an electron is ejected at rest from the negative plate, how fast is it moving when it reaches the positive plate?

23.67 •• *Electrostatic precipitators* use electric forces to remove pollutant particles from smoke, in particular in the smokestacks of coal-burning power plants. One form of precipitator consists of a vertical, hollow, metal cylinder with a thin wire, insulated from the cylinder, running along its axis (Fig. P23.67). A large potential difference is established between the wire and the outer cylinder, with the wire at lower potential. This sets up a strong radial electric field directed inward. The field produces a region of ionized air near the wire. Smoke enters the precipitator at the bottom, ash and dust in it pick up electrons, and the charged pollutants are accelerated toward the outer cylinder wall by the electric field. Suppose the radius of the central wire is 90.0 μm, the radius of the cylinder is 14.0 cm, and a potential difference of 50.0 kV is established between the wire and the cylinder. Also assume that the wire and cylinder are both very long in comparison to the cylinder radius, so the results of Problem 23.63 apply. (a) What is the magnitude of the electric field midway between the wire and the cylinder wall? (b) What magnitude of charge must a 30.0-μg ash particle have if the electric field computed in part (a) is to exert a force ten times the weight of the particle?

Figure **P23.67**

23.68 •• **CALC** A disk with radius R has uniform surface charge density σ. (a) By regarding the disk as a series of thin concentric rings, calculate the electric potential V at a point on the disk's axis a distance x from the center of the disk. Assume that the potential is zero at infinity. (*Hint:* Use the result of Example 23.11 in Section 23.3.) (b) Calculate $-\partial V / \partial x$. Show that the result agrees with the expression for E_x calculated in Example 21.11 (Section 21.5).

23.69 •• **CALC** (a) From the expression for E obtained in Problem 22.42, find the expressions for the electric potential V as a function of r, both inside and outside the cylinder. Let $V = 0$ at the surface of the cylinder. In each case, express your result in terms of the charge per unit length λ of the charge distribution. (b) Graph V and E as functions of r from $r = 0$ to $r = 3R$.

23.70 • **CALC** A thin insulating rod is bent into a semicircular arc of radius a, and a total electric charge Q is distributed uniformly along the rod. Calculate the potential at the center of curvature of the arc if the potential is assumed to be zero at infinity.

23.71 ••• **CALC** **Self-Energy of a Sphere of Charge.** A solid sphere of radius R contains a total charge Q distributed uniformly throughout its volume. Find the energy needed to assemble this charge by bringing infinitesimal charges from far away. This energy is called the "self-energy" of the charge distribution. (*Hint:* After you have assembled a charge q in a sphere of radius r, how much energy would it take to add a spherical shell of thickness dr having charge dq? Then integrate to get the total energy.)

23.72 •• **CALC** (a) From the expression for E obtained in Example 22.9 (Section 22.4), find the expression for the electric potential V as a function of r both inside and outside the uniformly charged sphere. Assume that $V = 0$ at infinity. (b) Graph V and E as functions of r from $r = 0$ to $r = 3R$.

23.73 •• Charge $Q = +4.00\ \mu$C is distributed uniformly over the volume of an insulating sphere that has radius $R = 5.00$ cm. What is the potential difference between the center of the sphere and the surface of the sphere?

23.74 • An insulating spherical shell with inner radius 25.0 cm and outer radius 60.0 cm carries a charge of $+150.0\ \mu$C uniformly distributed over its outer surface (see Exercise 23.41). Point a is at the center of the shell, point b is on the inner surface, and point c is on the outer surface. (a) What will a voltmeter read if it is connected between the following points: (i) a and b; (ii) b and c; (iii) c and infinity; (iv) a and c? (b) Which is at higher potential: (i) a or b; (ii) b or c; (iii) a or c? (c) Which, if any, of the answers would change sign if the charge were $-150\ \mu$C?

23.75 •• Exercise 23.41 shows that, outside a spherical shell with uniform surface charge, the potential is the same as if all the charge were concentrated into a point charge at the center of the sphere. (a) Use this result to show that for two uniformly charged insulating shells, the force they exert on each other and their mutual electrical energy are the same as if all the charge were concentrated at their centers. (*Hint:* See Section 13.6.) (b) Does this same result hold for solid insulating spheres, with charge distributed uniformly throughout their volume? (c) Does this same result hold for the force between two charged conducting shells? Between two charged solid conductors? Explain.

23.76 •• **CP** Two plastic spheres, each carrying charge uniformly distributed throughout its interior, are initially placed in contact and then released. One sphere is 60.0 cm in diameter, has mass 50.0 g, and contains $-10.0\ \mu$C of charge. The other sphere is 40.0 cm in diameter, has mass 150.0 g, and contains $-30.0\ \mu$C of charge. Find the maximum acceleration and the maximum speed achieved by each sphere (relative to the fixed point of their initial location in space), assuming that no other forces are acting on them. (*Hint:* The uniformly distributed charges behave as though they were concentrated at the centers of the two spheres.)

23.77 • **CALC** Use the electric field calculated in Problem 22.45 to calculate the potential difference between the solid conducting sphere and the thin insulating shell.

23.78 • **CALC** Consider a solid conducting sphere inside a hollow conducting sphere, with radii and charges specified in Problem 22.44. Take $V = 0$ as $r \to \infty$. Use the electric field calculated in Problem 22.44 to calculate the potential V at the following values of r: (a) $r = c$ (at the outer surface of the hollow sphere); (b) $r = b$ (at the inner surface of the hollow sphere); (c) $r = a$ (at the surface of the solid sphere); (d) $r = 0$ (at the center of the solid sphere).

23.79 • **CALC** Electric charge is distributed uniformly along a thin rod of length a, with total charge Q. Take the potential to be zero at infinity. Find the potential at the following points (Fig. P23.79): (a) point P, a distance x to the right of the rod, and (b) point R, a distance y above the right-hand end of the rod. (c) In parts (a) and (b), what does your result reduce to as x or y becomes much larger than a?

Figure **P23.79**

23.80 • (a) If a spherical raindrop of radius 0.650 mm carries a charge of -3.60 pC uniformly distributed over its volume, what is the potential at its surface? (Take the potential to be zero at an infinite distance from the raindrop.) (b) Two identical raindrops, each with radius and charge specified in part (a), collide and merge into one larger raindrop. What is the radius of this larger drop, and what is the potential at its surface, if its charge is uniformly distributed over its volume?

23.81 •• Two metal spheres of different sizes are charged such that the electric potential is the same at the surface of each. Sphere A has a radius three times that of sphere B. Let Q_A and Q_B be the charges on the two spheres, and let E_A and E_B be the electric-field magnitudes at the surfaces of the two spheres. What are (a) the ratio Q_B/Q_A and (b) the ratio E_B/E_A?

23.82 • An alpha particle with kinetic energy 11.0 MeV makes a head-on collision with a lead nucleus at rest. What is the distance of closest approach of the two particles? (Assume that the lead nucleus remains stationary and that it may be treated as a point charge. The atomic number of lead is 82. The alpha particle is a helium nucleus, with atomic number 2.)

23.83 • A metal sphere with radius R_1 has a charge Q_1. Take the electric potential to be zero at an infinite distance from the sphere. (a) What are the electric field and electric potential at the surface of the sphere? This sphere is now connected by a long, thin conducting wire to another sphere of radius R_2 that is several meters from the first sphere. Before the connection is made, this second sphere is uncharged. After electrostatic equilibrium has been reached, what are (b) the total charge on each sphere; (c) the electric potential at the surface of each sphere; (d) the electric field at the surface of each sphere? Assume that the amount of charge on the wire is much less than the charge on each sphere.

23.84 ••• CALC Use the charge distribution and electric field calculated in Problem 22.65. (a) Show that for $r \geq R$ the potential is identical to that produced by a point charge Q. (Take the potential to be zero at infinity.) (b) Obtain an expression for the electric potential valid in the region $r \leq R$.

23.85 •• CP **Nuclear Fusion in the Sun.** The source of the sun's energy is a sequence of nuclear reactions that occur in its core. The first of these reactions involves the collision of two protons, which fuse together to form a heavier nucleus and release energy. For this process, called *nuclear fusion,* to occur, the two protons must first approach until their surfaces are essentially in contact. (a) Assume both protons are moving with the same speed and they collide head-on. If the radius of the proton is 1.2×10^{-15} m, what is the minimum speed that will allow fusion to occur? The charge distribution within a proton is spherically symmetric, so the electric field and potential outside a proton are the same as if it were a point charge. The mass of the proton is 1.67×10^{-27} kg. (b) Another nuclear fusion reaction that occurs in the sun's core involves a collision between two helium nuclei, each of which has 2.99 times the mass of the proton, charge $+2e$, and radius 1.7×10^{-15} m. Assuming the same collision geometry as in part (a), what minimum speed is required for this fusion reaction to take place if the nuclei must approach a center-to-center

distance of about 3.5×10^{-15} m? As for the proton, the charge of the helium nucleus is uniformly distributed throughout its volume. (c) In Section 18.3 it was shown that the average translational kinetic energy of a particle with mass m in a gas at absolute temperature T is $\frac{3}{2}kT$, where k is the Boltzmann constant (given in Appendix F). For two protons with kinetic energy equal to this average value to be able to undergo the process described in part (a), what absolute temperature is required? What absolute temperature is required for two average helium nuclei to be able to undergo the process described in part (b)? (At these temperatures, atoms are completely ionized, so nuclei and electrons move separately.) (d) The temperature in the sun's core is about 1.5×10^7 K. How does this compare to the temperatures calculated in part (c)? How can the reactions described in parts (a) and (b) occur at all in the interior of the sun? (*Hint:* See the discussion of the distribution of molecular speeds in Section 18.5.)

23.86 • CALC The electric potential V in a region of space is given by

$$V(x, y, z) = A(x^2 - 3y^2 + z^2)$$

where A is a constant. (a) Derive an expression for the electric field $\vec{E}$ at any point in this region. (b) The work done by the field when a 1.50-μC test charge moves from the point $(x, y, z) = (0, 0, 0.250$ m$)$ to the origin is measured to be 6.00×10^{-5} J. Determine A. (c) Determine the electric field at the point $(0, 0, 0.250$ m$)$. (d) Show that in every plane parallel to the xz-plane the equipotential contours are circles. (e) What is the radius of the equipotential contour corresponding to $V = 1280$ V and $y = 2.00$ m?

23.87 •• **Nuclear Fission.** The unstable nucleus of uranium-236 can be regarded as a uniformly charged sphere of charge $Q = +92e$ and radius $R = 7.4 \times 10^{-15}$ m. In nuclear fission, this can divide into two smaller nuclei, each with half the charge and half the volume of the original uranium-236 nucleus. This is one of the reactions that occurred in the nuclear weapon that exploded over Hiroshima, Japan, in August 1945. (a) Find the radii of the two "daughter" nuclei of charge $+46e$. (b) In a simple model for the fission process, immediately after the uranium-236 nucleus has undergone fission, the "daughter" nuclei are at rest and just touching, as shown in Fig. P23.87. Calculate the kinetic energy that each of the "daughter" nuclei will have when they are very far apart. (c) In this model the sum of the kinetic energies of the two "daughter" nuclei, calculated in part (b), is the energy released by the fission of one uranium-236 nucleus. Calculate the energy released by the fission of 10.0 kg of uranium-236. The atomic mass of uranium-236 is 236 u, where 1 u = 1 atomic mass unit = 1.66×10^{-24} kg. Express your answer both in joules and in kilotons of TNT (1 kiloton of TNT releases 4.18×10^{12} J when it explodes). (d) In terms of this model, discuss why an atomic bomb could just as well be called an "electric bomb."

Figure **P23.87**

$Q = +92e$

BEFORE

$Q = +46e$ $Q = +46e$

AFTER

CHALLENGE PROBLEMS

23.88 ••• CP CALC In a certain region, a charge distribution exists that is spherically symmetric but nonuniform. That is, the volume charge density $\rho(r)$ depends on the distance r from the center of the distribution but not on the spherical polar angles θ and ϕ. The electric potential $V(r)$ due to this charge distribution is

$$V(r) = \begin{cases} \dfrac{\rho_0 a^2}{18\epsilon_0}\left[1 - 3\left(\dfrac{r}{a}\right)^2 + 2\left(\dfrac{r}{a}\right)^3\right] & \text{for } r \le a \\ 0 & \text{for } r \ge a \end{cases}$$

where ρ_0 is a constant having units of C/m^3 and a is a constant having units of meters. (a) Derive expressions for $\vec{E}$ for the regions $r \le a$ and $r \ge a$. [*Hint:* Use Eq. (23.23).] Explain why $\vec{E}$ has only a radial component. (b) Derive an expression for $\rho(r)$ in each of the two regions $r \le a$ and $r \ge a$. [*Hint:* Use Gauss's law for two spherical shells, one of radius r and the other of radius $r + dr$. The charge contained in the infinitesimal spherical shell of radius dr is $dq = 4\pi r^2 \rho(r)\, dr$.] (c) Show that the net charge contained in the volume of a sphere of radius greater than or equal to a is zero. [*Hint:* Integrate the expressions derived in part (b) for $\rho(r)$ over a spherical volume of radius greater than or equal to a.] Is this result consistent with the electric field for $r > a$ that you calculated in part (a)?

23.89 ••• CP In experiments in which atomic nuclei collide, head-on collisions like that described in Problem 23.82 do happen, but "near misses" are more common. Suppose the alpha particle in Problem 23.82 was not "aimed" at the center of the lead nucleus, but had an initial nonzero angular momentum (with respect to the stationary lead nucleus) of magnitude $L = p_0 b$, where p_0 is the magnitude of the initial momentum of the alpha particle and $b = 1.00 \times 10^{-12}$ m. What is the distance of closest approach? Repeat for $b = 1.00 \times 10^{-13}$ m and $b = 1.00 \times 10^{-14}$ m.

23.90 ••• CALC A hollow, thin-walled insulating cylinder of radius R and length L (like the cardboard tube in a roll of toilet paper) has charge Q uniformly distributed over its surface. (a) Calculate the electric potential at all points along the axis of the tube. Take the origin to be at the center of the tube, and take the potential to be zero at infinity. (b) Show that if $L \ll R$, the result of part (a) reduces to the potential on the axis of a ring of charge of radius R. (See Example 23.11 in Section 23.3.) (c) Use the result of part (a) to find the electric field at all points along the axis of the tube.

23.91 ••• **The Millikan Oil-Drop Experiment.** The charge of an electron was first measured by the American physicist Robert Millikan during 1909–1913. In his experiment, oil is sprayed in very fine drops (around 10^{-4} mm in diameter) into the space between two parallel horizontal plates separated by a distance d. A potential difference V_{AB} is maintained between the parallel plates, causing a downward electric field between them. Some of the oil drops acquire a negative charge because of frictional effects or because of ionization of the surrounding air by x rays or radioactivity. The drops are observed through a microscope. (a) Show that an oil drop of radius r at rest between the plates will remain at rest if the magnitude of its charge is

$$q = \frac{4\pi}{3}\frac{\rho r^3 g d}{V_{AB}}$$

where ρ is the density of the oil. (Ignore the buoyant force of the air.) By adjusting V_{AB} to keep a given drop at rest, the charge on that drop can be determined, provided its radius is known. (b) Millikan's oil drops were much too small to measure their radii directly. Instead, Millikan determined r by cutting off the electric field and measuring the *terminal speed* v_t of the drop as it fell. (We discussed the concept of terminal speed in Section 5.3.) The viscous force F on a sphere of radius r moving with speed v through a fluid with viscosity η is given by Stokes's law: $F = 6\pi\eta rv$. When the drop is falling at v_t, the viscous force just balances the weight $w = mg$ of the drop. Show that the magnitude of the charge on the drop is

$$q = 18\pi\frac{d}{V_{AB}}\sqrt{\frac{\eta^3 v_t^3}{2\rho g}}$$

Within the limits of their experimental error, every one of the thousands of drops that Millikan and his coworkers measured had a charge equal to some small integer multiple of a basic charge e. That is, they found drops with charges of $\pm 2e$, $\pm 5e$, and so on, but none with values such as $0.76e$ or $2.49e$. A drop with charge $-e$ has acquired one extra electron; if its charge is $-2e$, it has acquired two extra electrons, and so on. (c) A charged oil drop in a Millikan oil-drop apparatus is observed to fall 1.00 mm at constant speed in 39.3 s if $V_{AB} = 0$. The same drop can be held at rest between two plates separated by 1.00 mm if $V_{AB} = 9.16$ V. How many excess electrons has the drop acquired, and what is the radius of the drop? The viscosity of air is 1.81×10^{-5} N·s/m², and the density of the oil is 824 kg/m³.

23.92 •• CP Two point charges are moving to the right along the x-axis. Point charge 1 has charge $q_1 = 2.00\ \mu\text{C}$, mass $m_1 = 6.00 \times 10^{-5}$ kg, and speed v_1. Point charge 2 is to the right of q_1 and has charge $q_2 = -5.00\ \mu\text{C}$, mass $m_2 = 3.00 \times 10^{-5}$ kg, and speed v_2. At a particular instant, the charges are separated by a distance of 9.00 mm and have speeds $v_1 = 400$ m/s and $v_2 = 1300$ m/s. The only forces on the particles are the forces they exert on each other. (a) Determine the speed v_{cm} of the center of mass of the system. (b) The *relative energy* E_{rel} of the system is defined as the total energy minus the kinetic energy contributed by the motion of the center of mass:

$$E_{\text{rel}} = E - \tfrac{1}{2}(m_1 + m_2)v_{\text{cm}}^2$$

where $E = \tfrac{1}{2}m_1 v_1^2 + \tfrac{1}{2}m_2 v_2^2 + q_1 q_2/4\pi\epsilon_0 r$ is the total energy of the system and r is the distance between the charges. Show that $E_{\text{rel}} = \tfrac{1}{2}\mu v^2 + q_1 q_2/4\pi\epsilon_0 r$, where $\mu = m_1 m_2/(m_1 + m_2)$ is called the *reduced mass* of the system and $v = v_2 - v_1$ is the relative speed of the moving particles. (c) For the numerical values given above, calculate the numerical value of E_{rel}. (d) Based on the result of part (c), for the conditions given above, will the particles escape from one another? Explain. (e) If the particles do escape, what will be their final relative speed when $r \to \infty$? If the particles do not escape, what will be their distance of maximum separation? That is, what will be the value of r when $v = 0$? (f) Repeat parts (c)–(e) for $v_1 = 400$ m/s and $v_2 = 1800$ m/s when the separation is 9.00 mm.

Answers

Chapter Opening Question ?

A large, constant potential difference V_{ab} is maintained between the welding tool (a) and the metal pieces to be welded (b). From Example 23.9 (Section 23.3) the electric field between two conductors separated by a distance d has magnitude $E = V_{ab}/d$. Hence d must be small in order for the field magnitude E to be large enough to ionize the gas between the conductors a and b (see Section 23.3) and produce an arc through this gas.

Test Your Understanding Questions

23.1 Answers: (a) (i), (b) (ii) The three charges q_1, q_2, and q_3 are all positive, so all three of the terms in the sum in Eq. (23.11)—q_1q_2/r_{12}, q_1q_3/r_{13}, and q_2q_3/r_{23}—are positive. Hence the total electric potential energy U is positive. This means that it would take positive work to bring the three charges from infinity to the positions shown in Fig. 21.14, and hence *negative* work to move the three charges from these positions back to infinity.

23.2 Answer: no If $V = 0$ at a certain point, $\vec{E}$ does *not* have to be zero at that point. An example is point c in Figs. 21.23 and 23.13, for which there is an electric field in the $+x$-direction (see Example 21.9 in Section 21.5) even though $V = 0$ (see Example 23.4). This isn't a surprising result because V and $\vec{E}$ are quite different quantities: V is the net amount of work required to bring a unit charge from infinity to the point in question, whereas $\vec{E}$ is the electric force that acts on a unit charge when it arrives at that point.

23.3 Answer: no If $\vec{E} = 0$ at a certain point, V does *not* have to be zero at that point. An example is point O at the center of the charged ring in Figs. 21.23 and 23.21. From Example 21.9 (Section 21.5), the electric field is zero at O because the electric-field contributions from different parts of the ring completely cancel. From Example 23.11, however, the potential at O is *not* zero: This point corresponds to $x = 0$, so $V = (1/4\pi\epsilon_0)(Q/a)$. This value of V corresponds to the work that would have to be done to move a unit positive test charge along a path from infinity to point O; it is nonzero because the charged ring repels the test charge, so positive work must be done to move the test charge toward the ring.

23.4 Answer: no If the positive charges in Fig. 23.23 were replaced by negative charges, and vice versa, the equipotential surfaces would be the same but the sign of the potential would be reversed. For example, the surfaces in Fig. 23.23b with potential $V = +30$ V and $V = -50$ V would have potential $V = -30$ V and $V = +50$ V, respectively.

23.5 Answer: (iii) From Eqs. (23.19), the components of the electric field are $E_x = -\partial V/\partial x = B + Dy$, $E_y = -\partial V/\partial y = 3Cy^2 + Dx$, and $E_z = -\partial V/\partial z = 0$. The value of A has no effect, which means that we can add a constant to the electric potential at all points without changing $\vec{E}$ or the potential difference between two points. The potential does not depend on z, so the z-component of $\vec{E}$ is zero. Note that at the origin the electric field is not zero because it has a nonzero x-component: $E_x = B$, $E_y = 0$, $E_z = 0$.

Bridging Problem

Answer: $\dfrac{qQ}{8\pi\epsilon_0 a} \ln\left(\dfrac{L + a}{L - a}\right)$

24 CAPACITANCE AND DIELECTRICS

LEARNING GOALS

By studying this chapter, you will learn:

- The nature of capacitors, and how to calculate a quantity that measures their ability to store charge.

- How to analyze capacitors connected in a network.

- How to calculate the amount of energy stored in a capacitor.

- What dielectrics are, and how they make capacitors more effective.

? The energy used in a camera's flash unit is stored in a capacitor, which consists of two closely spaced conductors that carry opposite charges. If the amount of charge on the conductors is doubled, by what factor does the stored energy increase?

When you set an old-fashioned spring mousetrap or pull back the string of an archer's bow, you are storing mechanical energy as elastic potential energy. A capacitor is a device that stores *electric* potential energy and electric charge. To make a capacitor, just insulate two conductors from each other. To store energy in this device, transfer charge from one conductor to the other so that one has a negative charge and the other has an equal amount of positive charge. Work must be done to move the charges through the resulting potential difference between the conductors, and the work done is stored as electric potential energy.

Capacitors have a tremendous number of practical applications in devices such as electronic flash units for photography, pulsed lasers, air bag sensors for cars, and radio and television receivers. We'll encounter many of these applications in later chapters (particularly Chapter 31, in which we'll see the crucial role played by capacitors in the alternating-current circuits that pervade our technological society). In this chapter, however, our emphasis is on the fundamental properties of capacitors. For a particular capacitor, the ratio of the charge on each conductor to the potential difference between the conductors is a constant, called the *capacitance*. The capacitance depends on the sizes and shapes of the conductors and on the insulating material (if any) between them. Compared to the case in which there is only vacuum between the conductors, the capacitance increases when an insulating material (a *dielectric*) is present. This happens because a redistribution of charge, called *polarization*, takes place within the insulating material. Studying polarization will give us added insight into the electrical properties of matter.

Capacitors also give us a new way to think about electric potential energy. The energy stored in a charged capacitor is related to the electric field in the space between the conductors. We will see that electric potential energy can be regarded as being stored *in the field itself*. The idea that the electric field is itself a storehouse of energy is at the heart of the theory of electromagnetic waves and our modern understanding of the nature of light, to be discussed in Chapter 32.

24.1 Capacitors and Capacitance

Any two conductors separated by an insulator (or a vacuum) form a **capacitor** (Fig. 24.1). In most practical applications, each conductor initially has zero net charge and electrons are transferred from one conductor to the other; this is called *charging* the capacitor. Then the two conductors have charges with equal magnitude and opposite sign, and the *net* charge on the capacitor as a whole remains zero. We will assume throughout this chapter that this is the case. When we say that a capacitor has charge Q, or that a charge Q is *stored* on the capacitor, we mean that the conductor at higher potential has charge $+Q$ and the conductor at lower potential has charge $-Q$ (assuming that Q is positive). Keep this in mind in the following discussion and examples.

In circuit diagrams a capacitor is represented by either of these symbols:

In either symbol the vertical lines (straight or curved) represent the conductors and the horizontal lines represent wires connected to either conductor. One common way to charge a capacitor is to connect these two wires to opposite terminals of a battery. Once the charges Q and $-Q$ are established on the conductors, the battery is disconnected. This gives a fixed *potential difference* V_{ab} between the conductors (that is, the potential of the positively charged conductor a with respect to the negatively charged conductor b) that is just equal to the voltage of the battery.

The electric field at any point in the region between the conductors is proportional to the magnitude Q of charge on each conductor. It follows that the potential difference V_{ab} between the conductors is also proportional to Q. If we double the magnitude of charge on each conductor, the charge density at each point doubles, the electric field at each point doubles, and the potential difference between conductors doubles; however, the *ratio* of charge to potential difference does not change. This ratio is called the **capacitance** C of the capacitor:

$$C = \frac{Q}{V_{ab}} \quad \text{(definition of capacitance)} \quad (24.1)$$

The SI unit of capacitance is called one **farad** (1 F), in honor of the 19th-century English physicist Michael Faraday. From Eq. (24.1), one farad is equal to one *coulomb per volt* (1 C/V):

$$1\ \text{F} = 1\ \text{farad} = 1\ \text{C/V} = 1\ \text{coulomb/volt}$$

CAUTION **Capacitance vs. coulombs** Don't confuse the symbol C for capacitance (which is always in italics) with the abbreviation C for coulombs (which is never italicized).

The greater the capacitance C of a capacitor, the greater the magnitude Q of charge on either conductor for a given potential difference V_{ab} and hence the greater the amount of stored energy. (Remember that potential is potential energy per unit charge.) Thus *capacitance is a measure of the ability of a capacitor to store energy.* We will see that the value of the capacitance depends only on the shapes and sizes of the conductors and on the nature of the insulating material between them. (The above remarks about capacitance being independent of Q and V_{ab} do not apply to certain special types of insulating materials. We won't discuss these materials in this book, however.)

Calculating Capacitance: Capacitors in Vacuum

We can calculate the capacitance C of a given capacitor by finding the potential difference V_{ab} between the conductors for a given magnitude of charge Q and

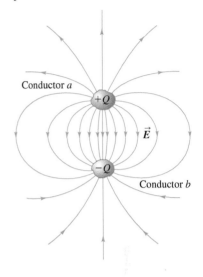

24.1 Any two conductors a and b insulated from each other form a capacitor.

(MP)

ActivPhysics 11.11.6: Electric Potential: Qualitative Introduction
ActivPhysics 11.12.1 and 11.12.3: Electric Potential, Field, and Force

24.2 A charged parallel-plate capacitor.

(a) Arrangement of the capacitor plates

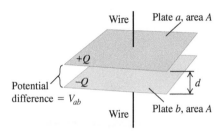

(b) Side view of the electric field $\vec{E}$

When the separation of the plates is small compared to their size, the fringing of the field is slight.

24.3 Inside a condenser microphone is a capacitor with one rigid plate and one flexible plate. The two plates are kept at a constant potential difference V_{ab}. Sound waves cause the flexible plate to move back and forth, varying the capacitance C and causing charge to flow to and from the capacitor in accordance with the relationship $C = Q/V_{ab}$. Thus a sound wave is converted to a charge flow that can be amplified and recorded digitally.

then using Eq. (24.1). For now we'll consider only *capacitors in vacuum;* that is, we'll assume that the conductors that make up the capacitor are separated by empty space.

The simplest form of capacitor consists of two parallel conducting plates, each with area A, separated by a distance d that is small in comparison with their dimensions (Fig. 24.2a). When the plates are charged, the electric field is almost completely localized in the region between the plates (Fig. 24.2b). As we discussed in Example 22.8 (Section 22.4), the field between such plates is essentially *uniform,* and the charges on the plates are uniformly distributed over their opposing surfaces. We call this arrangement a **parallel-plate capacitor.**

We worked out the electric-field magnitude E for this arrangement in Example 21.12 (Section 21.5) using the principle of superposition of electric fields and again in Example 22.8 (Section 22.4) using Gauss's law. It would be a good idea to review those examples. We found that $E = \sigma/\epsilon_0$, where σ is the magnitude (absolute value) of the surface charge density on each plate. This is equal to the magnitude of the total charge Q on each plate divided by the area A of the plate, or $\sigma = Q/A$, so the field magnitude E can be expressed as

$$E = \frac{\sigma}{\epsilon_0} = \frac{Q}{\epsilon_0 A}$$

The field is uniform and the distance between the plates is d, so the potential difference (voltage) between the two plates is

$$V_{ab} = Ed = \frac{1}{\epsilon_0}\frac{Qd}{A}$$

From this we see that the capacitance C of a parallel-plate capacitor in vacuum is

$$C = \frac{Q}{V_{ab}} = \epsilon_0 \frac{A}{d} \quad \begin{matrix}\text{(capacitance of a parallel-plate} \\ \text{capacitor in vacuum)}\end{matrix} \quad \text{(24.2)}$$

The capacitance depends only on the geometry of the capacitor; it is directly proportional to the area A of each plate and inversely proportional to their separation d. The quantities A and d are constants for a given capacitor, and ϵ_0 is a universal constant. Thus in vacuum the capacitance C is a constant independent of the charge on the capacitor or the potential difference between the plates. If one of the capacitor plates is flexible, the capacitance C changes as the plate separation d changes. This is the operating principle of a condenser microphone (Fig. 24.3).

When matter is present between the plates, its properties affect the capacitance. We will return to this topic in Section 24.4. Meanwhile, we remark that if the space contains air at atmospheric pressure instead of vacuum, the capacitance differs from the prediction of Eq. (24.2) by less than 0.06%.

In Eq. (24.2), if A is in square meters and d in meters, C is in farads. The units of ϵ_0 are $C^2/N \cdot m^2$, so we see that

$$1\ F = 1\ C^2/N \cdot m = 1\ C^2/J$$

Because $1\ V = 1\ J/C$ (energy per unit charge), this is consistent with our definition $1\ F = 1\ C/V$. Finally, the units of ϵ_0 can be expressed as $1\ C^2/N \cdot m^2 = 1\ F/m$, so

$$\epsilon_0 = 8.85 \times 10^{-12}\ F/m$$

This relationship is useful in capacitance calculations, and it also helps us to verify that Eq. (24.2) is dimensionally consistent.

One farad is a very large capacitance, as the following example shows. In many applications the most convenient units of capacitance are the *microfarad*

($1 \mu F = 10^{-6}$ F) and the *picofarad* (1 pF $= 10^{-12}$ F). For example, the flash unit in a point-and-shoot camera uses a capacitor of a few hundred microfarads (Fig. 24.4), while capacitances in a radio tuning circuit are typically from 10 to 100 picofarads.

For *any* capacitor in vacuum, the capacitance C depends only on the shapes, dimensions, and separation of the conductors that make up the capacitor. If the conductor shapes are more complex than those of the parallel-plate capacitor, the expression for capacitance is more complicated than in Eq. (24.2). In the following examples we show how to calculate C for two other conductor geometries.

24.4 A commercial capacitor is labeled with the value of its capacitance. For these capacitors, $C = 2200 \mu F$, $1000 \mu F$, and $470 \mu F$.

Example 24.1 Size of a 1-F capacitor

The parallel plates of a 1.0-F capacitor are 1.0 mm apart. What is their area?

SOLUTION

IDENTIFY and SET UP: This problem uses the relationship among the capacitance C, plate separation d, and plate area A (our target variable) for a parallel-plate capacitor. We solve Eq. (24.2) for A.

EXECUTE: From Eq. (24.2),

$$A = \frac{Cd}{\epsilon_0} = \frac{(1.0 \text{ F})(1.0 \times 10^{-3} \text{ m})}{8.85 \times 10^{-12} \text{ F/m}} = 1.1 \times 10^8 \text{ m}^2$$

EVALUATE: This corresponds to a square about 10 km (about 6 miles) on a side! The volume of such a capacitor would be at least $Ad = 1.1 \times 10^5$ m^3, equivalent to that of a cube about 50 m on a side. In fact, it's possible to make 1-F capacitors a few *centimeters* on a side. The trick is to have an appropriate substance between the plates rather than a vacuum, so that (among other things) the plate separation d can greatly reduced. We'll explore this further in Section 24.4.

Example 24.2 Properties of a parallel-plate capacitor

The plates of a parallel-plate capacitor in vacuum are 5.00 mm apart and 2.00 m^2 in area. A 10.0-kV potential difference is applied across the capacitor. Compute (a) the capacitance; (b) the charge on each plate; and (c) the magnitude of the electric field between the plates.

SOLUTION

IDENTIFY and SET UP: We are given the plate area A, the plate spacing d, and the potential difference $V_{ab} = 1.00 \times 10^4$ V for this parallel-plate capacitor. Our target variables are the capacitance C, the charge Q on each plate, and the electric-field magnitude E. We use Eq. (24.2) to calculate C and then use Eq. (24.1) and V_{ab} to find Q. We use $E = Q/\epsilon_0 A$ to find E.

EXECUTE: (a) From Eq. (24.2),

$$C = \epsilon_0 \frac{A}{d} = (8.85 \times 10^{-12} \text{ F/m}) \frac{(2.00 \text{ m}^2)}{5.00 \times 10^{-3} \text{ m}}$$

$$= 3.54 \times 10^{-9} \text{ F} = 0.00354 \mu F$$

(b) The charge on the capacitor is

$$Q = CV_{ab} = (3.54 \times 10^{-9} \text{ C/V})(1.00 \times 10^4 \text{ V})$$

$$= 3.54 \times 10^{-5} \text{ C} = 35.4 \mu C$$

The plate at higher potential has charge $+35.4 \mu C$, and the other plate has charge $-35.4 \mu C$.

(c) The electric-field magnitude is

$$E = \frac{\sigma}{\epsilon_0} = \frac{Q}{\epsilon_0 A} = \frac{3.54 \times 10^{-5} \text{ C}}{(8.85 \times 10^{-12} \text{ C}^2/\text{N} \cdot \text{m}^2)(2.00 \text{ m}^2)}$$

$$= 2.00 \times 10^6 \text{ N/C}$$

EVALUATE: We can also find E by recalling that the electric field is equal in magnitude to the potential gradient [Eq. (23.22)]. The field between the plates is uniform, so

$$E = \frac{V_{ab}}{d} = \frac{1.00 \times 10^4 \text{ V}}{5.00 \times 10^{-3} \text{ m}} = 2.00 \times 10^6 \text{ V/m}$$

(Remember that 1 N/C = 1 V/m.)

Example 24.3 **A spherical capacitor**

Two concentric spherical conducting shells are separated by vacuum (Fig. 24.5). The inner shell has total charge $+Q$ and outer radius r_a, and the outer shell has charge $-Q$ and inner radius r_b. Find the capacitance of this spherical capacitor.

SOLUTION

IDENTIFY and SET UP: By definition, the capacitance C is the magnitude Q of the charge on either sphere divided by the potential difference V_{ab} between the spheres. We first find V_{ab}, and then use Eq. (24.1) to find the capacitance $C = Q/V_{ab}$.

EXECUTE: Using a Gaussian surface such as that shown in Fig. 24.5, we found in Example 22.5 (Section 22.4) that the charge on a conducting sphere produces zero field *inside* the sphere, so the outer sphere makes no contribution to the field between the spheres. Therefore the electric field *and* the electric potential

24.5 A spherical capacitor.

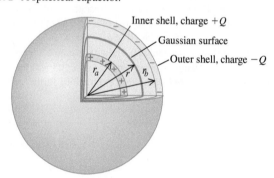

Inner shell, charge $+Q$

Gaussian surface

Outer shell, charge $-Q$

between the shells are the same as those outside a charged conducting sphere with charge $+Q$. We considered that problem in Example 23.8 (Section 23.3), so the same result applies here: The potential at any point between the spheres is $V = Q/4\pi\epsilon_0 r$. Hence the potential of the inner (positive) conductor at $r = r_a$ with respect to that of the outer (negative) conductor at $r = r_b$ is

$$V_{ab} = V_a - V_b = \frac{Q}{4\pi\epsilon_0 r_a} - \frac{Q}{4\pi\epsilon_0 r_b}$$

$$= \frac{Q}{4\pi\epsilon_0}\left(\frac{1}{r_a} - \frac{1}{r_b}\right) = \frac{Q}{4\pi\epsilon_0}\frac{r_b - r_a}{r_a r_b}$$

The capacitance is then

$$C = \frac{Q}{V_{ab}} = 4\pi\epsilon_0 \frac{r_a r_b}{r_b - r_a}$$

As an example, if $r_a = 9.5$ cm and $r_b = 10.5$ cm,

$$C = 4\pi(8.85 \times 10^{-12} \text{ F/m})\frac{(0.095 \text{ m})(0.105 \text{ m})}{0.010 \text{ m}}$$

$$= 1.1 \times 10^{-10} \text{ F} = 110 \text{ pF}$$

EVALUATE: We can relate our expression for C to that for a parallel-plate capacitor. The quantity $4\pi r_a r_b$ is intermediate between the areas $4\pi r_a^2$ and $4\pi r_b^2$ of the two spheres; in fact, it's the *geometric mean* of these two areas, which we can denote by A_{gm}. The distance between spheres is $d = r_b - r_a$, so we can write $C = 4\pi\epsilon_0 r_a r_b/(r_b - r_a) = \epsilon_0 A_{\text{gm}}/d$. This has the same form as for parallel plates: $C = \epsilon_0 A/d$. If the distance between spheres is very small in comparison to their radii, their capacitance is the same as that of parallel plates with the same area and spacing.

Example 24.4 **A cylindrical capacitor**

Two long, coaxial cylindrical conductors are separated by vacuum (Fig. 24.6). The inner cylinder has radius r_a and linear charge density $+\lambda$. The outer cylinder has inner radius r_b and linear charge density $-\lambda$. Find the capacitance per unit length for this capacitor.

SOLUTION

IDENTIFY and SET UP: As in Example 24.3, we use the definition of capacitance, $C = Q/V_{ab}$. We use the result of Example 23.10

24.6 A long cylindrical capacitor. The linear charge density λ is assumed to be positive in this figure. The magnitude of charge in a length L of either cylinder is λL.

$-\lambda$

$+\lambda$

r_a

r_b

L

(Section 23.3) to find the potential difference V_{ab} between the cylinders, and find the charge Q on a length L of the cylinders from the linear charge density. We then find the corresponding capacitance C using Eq. (24.1). Our target variable is this capacitance divided by L.

EXECUTE: As in Example 24.3, the potential V between the cylinders is not affected by the presence of the charged outer cylinder. Hence our result in Example 23.10 for the potential outside a charged conducting cylinder also holds in this example for potential in the space between the cylinders:

$$V = \frac{\lambda}{2\pi\epsilon_0}\ln\frac{r_0}{r}$$

Here r_0 is the arbitrary, *finite* radius at which $V = 0$. We take $r_0 = r_b$, the radius of the inner surface of the outer cylinder. Then the potential at the outer surface of the inner cylinder (at which $r = r_a$) is just the potential V_{ab} of the inner (positive) cylinder a with respect to the outer (negative) cylinder b:

$$V_{ab} = \frac{\lambda}{2\pi\epsilon_0}\ln\frac{r_b}{r_a}$$

If λ is positive as in Fig. 24.6, then V_{ab} is positive as well: The inner cylinder is at higher potential than the outer.

The total charge Q in a length L is $Q = \lambda L$, so from Eq. (24.1) the capacitance C of a length L is

$$C = \frac{Q}{V_{ab}} = \frac{\lambda L}{\dfrac{\lambda}{2\pi\epsilon_0}\ln\dfrac{r_b}{r_a}} = \frac{2\pi\epsilon_0 L}{\ln(r_b/r_a)}$$

The capacitance per unit length is

$$\frac{C}{L} = \frac{2\pi\epsilon_0}{\ln(r_b/r_a)}$$

Substituting $\epsilon_0 = 8.85 \times 10^{-12}$ F/m $= 8.85$ pF/m, we get

$$\frac{C}{L} = \frac{55.6 \text{ pF/m}}{\ln(r_b/r_a)}$$

EVALUATE: The capacitance of coaxial cylinders is determined entirely by their dimensions, just as for parallel-plate and spherical capacitors. Ordinary coaxial cables are made like this but with an insulating material instead of vacuum between the conductors. A typical cable used for connecting a television to a cable TV feed has a capacitance per unit length of 69 pF/m.

Test Your Understanding of Section 24.1   A capacitor has vacuum in the space between the conductors. If you double the amount of charge on each conductor, what happens to the capacitance? (i) It increases; (ii) it decreases; (iii) it remains the same; (iv) the answer depends on the size or shape of the conductors.

24.2 Capacitors in Series and Parallel

Capacitors are manufactured with certain standard capacitances and working voltages (Fig. 24.7). However, these standard values may not be the ones you actually need in a particular application. You can obtain the values you need by combining capacitors; many combinations are possible, but the simplest combinations are a series connection and a parallel connection.

Capacitors in Series

Figure 24.8a is a schematic diagram of a **series connection.** Two capacitors are connected in series (one after the other) by conducting wires between points a and b. Both capacitors are initially uncharged. When a constant positive potential difference V_{ab} is applied between points a and b, the capacitors become charged; the figure shows that the charge on *all* conducting plates has the same magnitude. To see why, note first that the top plate of C_1 acquires a positive charge Q. The electric field of this positive charge pulls negative charge up to the bottom plate of C_1 until all of the field lines that begin on the top plate end on the bottom plate. This requires that the bottom plate have charge $-Q$. These negative charges had to come from the top plate of C_2, which becomes positively charged with charge $+Q$. This positive charge then pulls negative charge $-Q$ from the connection at point b onto the bottom plate of C_2. The total charge on the lower plate of C_1 and the upper plate of C_2 together must always be zero because these plates aren't connected to anything except each other. Thus *in a series connection the magnitude of charge on all plates is the same.*

Referring to Fig. 24.8a, we can write the potential differences between points a and c, c and b, and a and b as

$$V_{ac} = V_1 = \frac{Q}{C_1} \qquad V_{cb} = V_2 = \frac{Q}{C_2}$$

$$V_{ab} = V = V_1 + V_2 = Q\left(\frac{1}{C_1} + \frac{1}{C_2}\right)$$

and so

$$\frac{V}{Q} = \frac{1}{C_1} + \frac{1}{C_2} \tag{24.3}$$

Following a common convention, we use the symbols V_1, V_2, and V to denote the potential *differences* V_{ac} (across the first capacitor), V_{cb} (across the second capacitor), and V_{ab} (across the entire combination of capacitors), respectively.

24.7 An assortment of commercially available capacitors.

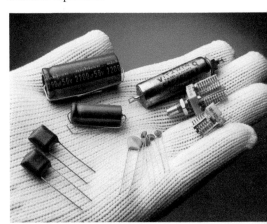

24.8 A series connection of two capacitors.

(a) Two capacitors in series

(b) The equivalent single capacitor

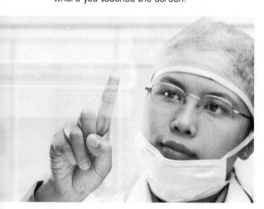

The **equivalent capacitance** C_{eq} of the series combination is defined as the capacitance of a *single* capacitor for which the charge Q is the same as for the combination, when the potential difference V is the same. In other words, the combination can be replaced by an *equivalent capacitor* of capacitance C_{eq}. For such a capacitor, shown in Fig. 24.8b,

$$C_{eq} = \frac{Q}{V} \quad \text{or} \quad \frac{1}{C_{eq}} = \frac{V}{Q} \tag{24.4}$$

Combining Eqs. (24.3) and (24.4), we find

$$\frac{1}{C_{eq}} = \frac{1}{C_1} + \frac{1}{C_2}$$

We can extend this analysis to any number of capacitors in series. We find the following result for the *reciprocal* of the equivalent capacitance:

$$\frac{1}{C_{eq}} = \frac{1}{C_1} + \frac{1}{C_2} + \frac{1}{C_3} + \cdots \quad \text{(capacitors in series)} \tag{24.5}$$

The reciprocal of the equivalent capacitance of a series combination equals the sum of the reciprocals of the individual capacitances. In a series connection the equivalent capacitance is always *less than* any individual capacitance.

CAUTION **Capacitors in series** The magnitude of charge is the same on all plates of all the capacitors in a series combination; however, the potential differences of the individual capacitors are *not* the same unless their individual capacitances are the same. The potential differences of the individual capacitors add to give the total potential difference across the series combination: $V_{total} = V_1 + V_2 + V_3 + \cdots$. ▮

Capacitors in Parallel

24.9 A parallel connection of two capacitors.

(a) Two capacitors in parallel

Capacitors in parallel:
• The capacitors have the same potential V.
• The charge on each capacitor depends on its capacitance: $Q_1 = C_1V$, $Q_2 = C_2V$.

(b) The equivalent single capacitor

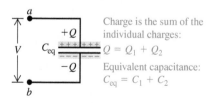

Charge is the sum of the individual charges:
$Q = Q_1 + Q_2$

Equivalent capacitance:
$C_{eq} = C_1 + C_2$

The arrangement shown in Fig. 24.9a is called a **parallel connection.** Two capacitors are connected in parallel between points a and b. In this case the upper plates of the two capacitors are connected by conducting wires to form an equipotential surface, and the lower plates form another. Hence *in a parallel connection the potential difference for all individual capacitors is the same* and is equal to $V_{ab} = V$. The charges Q_1 and Q_2 are not necessarily equal, however, since charges can reach each capacitor independently from the source (such as a battery) of the voltage V_{ab}. The charges are

$$Q_1 = C_1V \quad \text{and} \quad Q_2 = C_2V$$

The *total* charge Q of the combination, and thus the total charge on the equivalent capacitor, is

$$Q = Q_1 + Q_2 = (C_1 + C_2)V$$

so

$$\frac{Q}{V} = C_1 + C_2 \tag{24.6}$$

The parallel combination is equivalent to a single capacitor with the same total charge $Q = Q_1 + Q_2$ and potential difference V as the combination (Fig. 24.9b). The equivalent capacitance of the combination, C_{eq}, is the same as the capacitance Q/V of this single equivalent capacitor. So from Eq. (24.6),

$$C_{eq} = C_1 + C_2$$

In the same way we can show that for any number of capacitors in parallel,

$$C_{eq} = C_1 + C_2 + C_3 + \cdots \qquad \text{(capacitors in parallel)} \qquad (24.7)$$

The equivalent capacitance of a parallel combination equals the *sum* of the individual capacitances. In a parallel connection the equivalent capacitance is always *greater than* any individual capacitance.

CAUTION **Capacitors in parallel** The potential differences are the same for all the capacitors in a parallel combination; however, the charges on individual capacitors are *not* the same unless their individual capacitances are the same. The charges on the individual capacitors add to give the total charge on the parallel combination: $Q_{total} = Q_1 + Q_2 + Q_3 + \cdots$. [Compare these statements to those in the "Caution" paragraph following Eq. (24.5).]

Video Tutor
Demo

Problem-Solving Strategy 24.1 **Equivalent Capacitance**

(MP)

IDENTIFY *the relevant concepts:* The concept of equivalent capacitance is useful whenever two or more capacitors are connected.

SET UP *the problem* using the following steps:
1. Make a drawing of the capacitor arrangement.
2. Identify all groups of capacitors that are connected in series or in parallel.
3. Keep in mind that when we say a capacitor "has charge Q," we mean that the plate at higher potential has charge $+Q$ and the other plate has charge $-Q$.

EXECUTE *the solution* as follows:
1. Use Eq. (24.5) to find the equivalent capacitance of capacitors connected in series, as in Fig. 24.8. Such capacitors each have the *same charge* if they were uncharged before they were connected; that charge is the same as that on the equivalent capacitor. The potential difference across the combination is the sum of the potential differences across the individual capacitors.

2. Use Eq. (24.7) to find the equivalent capacitance of capacitors connected in parallel, as in Fig. 24.9. Such capacitors all have the *same potential difference* across them; that potential difference is the same as that across the equivalent capacitor. The total charge on the combination is the sum of the charges on the individual capacitors.
3. After replacing all the series or parallel groups you initially identified, you may find that more such groups reveal themselves. Replace those groups using the same procedure as above until no more replacements are possible. If you then need to find the charge or potential difference for an individual original capacitor, you may have to retrace your steps.

EVALUATE *your answer:* Check whether your result makes sense. If the capacitors are connected in series, the equivalent capacitance C_{eq} must be *smaller* than any of the individual capacitances. If the capacitors are connected in parallel, C_{eq} must be *greater* than any of the individual capacitances.

Example 24.5 **Capacitors in series and in parallel**

In Figs. 24.8 and 24.9, let $C_1 = 6.0 \ \mu\text{F}$, $C_2 = 3.0 \ \mu\text{F}$, and $V_{ab} = 18 \ \text{V}$. Find the equivalent capacitance and the charge and potential difference for each capacitor when the capacitors are connected (a) in series (see Fig. 24.8) and (b) in parallel (see Fig. 24.9).

SOLUTION

IDENTIFY and SET UP: In both parts of this example a target variable is the equivalent capacitance C_{eq}, which is given by Eq. (24.5) for the series combination in part (a) and by Eq. (24.7) for the parallel combination in part (b). In each part we find the charge and potential difference using the definition of capacitance, Eq. (24.1), and the rules outlined in Problem-Solving Strategy 24.1.

EXECUTE: (a) From Eq. (24.5) for a series combination,

$$\frac{1}{C_{eq}} = \frac{1}{C_1} + \frac{1}{C_2} = \frac{1}{6.0 \ \mu\text{F}} + \frac{1}{3.0 \ \mu\text{F}} \qquad C_{eq} = 2.0 \ \mu\text{F}$$

The charge Q on each capacitor in series is the same as that on the equivalent capacitor:

$$Q = C_{eq}V = (2.0 \ \mu\text{F})(18 \ \text{V}) = 36 \ \mu\text{C}$$

The potential difference across each capacitor is inversely proportional to its capacitance:

$$V_{ac} = V_1 = \frac{Q}{C_1} = \frac{36 \ \mu\text{C}}{6.0 \ \mu\text{F}} = 6.0 \ \text{V}$$

$$V_{cb} = V_2 = \frac{Q}{C_2} = \frac{36 \ \mu\text{C}}{3.0 \ \mu\text{F}} = 12.0 \ \text{V}$$

(b) From Eq. (24.7) for a parallel combination,
$$C_{eq} = C_1 + C_2 = 6.0 \ \mu\text{F} + 3.0 \ \mu\text{F} = 9.0 \ \mu\text{F}$$

The potential difference across each of the capacitors is the same as that across the equivalent capacitor, 18 V. The charge on each capacitor is directly proportional to its capacitance:

$$Q_1 = C_1V = (6.0 \ \mu\text{F})(18 \ \text{V}) = 108 \ \mu\text{C}$$
$$Q_2 = C_2V = (3.0 \ \mu\text{F})(18 \ \text{V}) = 54 \ \mu\text{C}$$

EVALUATE: As expected, the equivalent capacitance C_{eq} for the series combination in part (a) is less than either C_1 or C_2, while

Continued

that for the parallel combination in part (b) is greater than either C_1 or C_2. For two capacitors in series, as in part (a), the charge is the same on either capacitor and the *larger* potential difference appears across the capacitor with the *smaller* capacitance. Furthermore, the sum of the potential differences across the individual capacitors in series equals the potential difference across the

equivalent capacitor: $V_{ac} + V_{cb} = V_{ab} = 18$ V. By contrast, for two capacitors in parallel, as in part (b), each capacitor has the same potential difference and the *larger* charge appears on the capacitor with the *larger* capacitance. Can you show that the total charge $Q_1 + Q_2$ on the parallel combination is equal to the charge $Q = C_{eq}V$ on the equivalent capacitor?

Example 24.6   **A capacitor network**

Find the equivalent capacitance of the five-capacitor network shown in Fig. 24.10a.

SOLUTION

IDENTIFY and SET UP: These capacitors are neither all in series nor all in parallel. We can, however, identify portions of the arrangement that *are* either in series or parallel. We combine these as described in Problem-Solving Strategy 24.1 to find the net equivalent capacitance, using Eq. (24.5) for series connections and Eq. (24.7) for parallel connections.

EXECUTE: The caption of Fig. 24.10 outlines our procedure. We first use Eq. (24.5) to replace the 12-μF and 6-μF series combination by its equivalent capacitance C':

$$\frac{1}{C'} = \frac{1}{12\ \mu\text{F}} + \frac{1}{6\ \mu\text{F}} \qquad C' = 4\ \mu\text{F}$$

This gives us the equivalent combination of Fig. 24.10b. Now we see three capacitors in parallel, and we use Eq. (24.7) to replace them with their equivalent capacitance C'':

$$C'' = 3\ \mu\text{F} + 11\ \mu\text{F} + 4\ \mu\text{F} = 18\ \mu\text{F}$$

This gives us the equivalent combination of Fig. 24.10c, which has two capacitors in series. We use Eq. (24.5) to replace them with their equivalent capacitance C_{eq}, which is our target variable (Fig. 24.10d):

$$\frac{1}{C_{eq}} = \frac{1}{18\ \mu\text{F}} + \frac{1}{9\ \mu\text{F}} \qquad C_{eq} = 6\ \mu\text{F}$$

EVALUATE: If the potential difference across the entire network in Fig. 24.10a is $V_{ab} = 9.0$ V, the net charge on the network is $Q = C_{eq}V_{ab} = (6\ \mu\text{F})(9.0\ \text{V}) = 54\ \mu\text{C}$. Can you find the charge on, and the voltage across, each of the five individual capacitors?

24.10 (a) A capacitor network between points a and b. (b) The 12-μF and 6-μF capacitors in series in (a) are replaced by an equivalent 4-μF capacitor. (c) The 3-μF, 11-μF, and 4-μF capacitors in parallel in (b) are replaced by an equivalent 18-μF capacitor. (d) Finally, the 18-μF and 9-μF capacitors in series in (c) are replaced by an equivalent 6-μF capacitor.

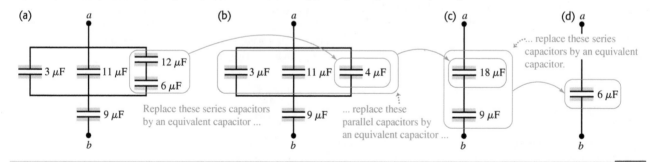

Test Your Understanding of Section 24.2 You want to connect a 4-μF capacitor and an 8-μF capacitor. (a) With which type of connection will the 4-μF capacitor have a greater potential difference across it than the 8-μF capacitor? (i) series; (ii) parallel; (iii) either series or parallel; (iv) neither series nor parallel. (b) With which type of connection will the 4-μF capacitor have a greater charge than the 8-μF capacitor? (i) series; (ii) parallel; (iii) either series or parallel; (iv) neither series nor parallel.

24.3 Energy Storage in Capacitors and Electric-Field Energy

Many of the most important applications of capacitors depend on their ability to store energy. The electric potential energy stored in a charged capacitor is just equal to the amount of work required to charge it—that is, to separate opposite charges and place them on different conductors. When the capacitor is discharged, this stored energy is recovered as work done by electrical forces.

We can calculate the potential energy U of a charged capacitor by calculating the work W required to charge it. Suppose that when we are done charging the capacitor, the final charge is Q and the final potential difference is V. From Eq. (24.1) these quantities are related by

$$V = \frac{Q}{C}$$

Let q and v be the charge and potential difference, respectively, at an intermediate stage during the charging process; then $v = q/C$. At this stage the work dW required to transfer an additional element of charge dq is

$$dW = v\, dq = \frac{q\, dq}{C}$$

The total work W needed to increase the capacitor charge q from zero to a final value Q is

$$W = \int_0^W dW = \frac{1}{C} \int_0^Q q\, dq = \frac{Q^2}{2C} \quad \text{(work to charge a capacitor)} \quad \text{(24.8)}$$

This is also equal to the total work done by the electric field on the charge when the capacitor discharges. Then q *decreases* from an initial value Q to zero as the elements of charge dq "fall" through potential differences v that vary from V down to zero.

If we define the potential energy of an *uncharged* capacitor to be zero, then W in Eq. (24.8) is equal to the potential energy U of the charged capacitor. The final stored charge is $Q = CV$, so we can express U (which is equal to W) as

$$U = \frac{Q^2}{2C} = \tfrac{1}{2}CV^2 = \tfrac{1}{2}QV \quad \begin{array}{l}\text{(potential energy stored} \\ \text{in a capacitor)}\end{array} \quad \text{(24.9)}$$

When Q is in coulombs, C in farads (coulombs per volt), and V in volts (joules per coulomb), U is in joules.

The last form of Eq. (24.9), $U = \tfrac{1}{2}QV$, shows that the total work W required to charge the capacitor is equal to the total charge Q multiplied by the *average* potential difference $\tfrac{1}{2}V$ during the charging process.

The expression $U = \tfrac{1}{2}(Q^2/C)$ in Eq. (24.9) shows that a charged capacitor is the electrical analog of a stretched spring with elastic potential energy $U = \tfrac{1}{2}kx^2$. The charge Q is analogous to the elongation x, and the *reciprocal* of the capacitance, $1/C$, is analogous to the force constant k. The energy supplied to a capacitor in the charging process is analogous to the work we do on a spring when we stretch it.

Equations (24.8) and (24.9) tell us that capacitance measures the ability of a capacitor to store both energy and charge. If a capacitor is charged by connecting it to a battery or other source that provides a fixed potential difference V, then increasing the value of C gives a greater charge $Q = CV$ and a greater amount of stored energy $U = \tfrac{1}{2}CV^2$. If instead the goal is to transfer a given quantity of charge Q from one conductor to another, Eq. (24.8) shows that the work W required is inversely proportional to C; the greater the capacitance, the easier it is to give a capacitor a fixed amount of charge.

Applications of Capacitors: Energy Storage

Most practical applications of capacitors take advantage of their ability to store and release energy. In electronic flash units used by photographers, the energy stored in a capacitor (see Fig. 24.4) is released by depressing the camera's shutter button. This provides a conducting path from one capacitor plate to the other through the flash tube. Once this path is established, the stored energy is rapidly converted into a brief but intense flash of light. An extreme example of the same principle is the Z machine at Sandia National Laboratories in New Mexico,

24.11 The Z machine uses a large number of capacitors in parallel to give a tremendous equivalent capacitance C (see Section 24.2). Hence a large amount of energy $U = \frac{1}{2}CV^2$ can be stored with even a modest potential difference V. The arcs shown here are produced when the capacitors discharge their energy into a target, which is no larger than a spool of thread. This heats the target to a temperature higher than 2×10^9 K.

which is used in experiments in controlled nuclear fusion (Fig. 24.11). A bank of charged capacitors releases more than a million joules of energy in just a few billionths of a second. For that brief space of time, the power output of the Z machine is 2.9×10^{14} W, or about 80 times the power output of all the electric power plants on earth combined!

In other applications, the energy is released more slowly. Springs in the suspension of an automobile help smooth out the ride by absorbing the energy from sudden jolts and releasing that energy gradually; in an analogous way, a capacitor in an electronic circuit can smooth out unwanted variations in voltage due to power surges. We'll discuss these circuits in detail in Chapter 26.

Electric-Field Energy

We can charge a capacitor by moving electrons directly from one plate to another. This requires doing work against the electric field between the plates. Thus we can think of the energy as being stored *in the field* in the region between the plates. To develop this relationship, let's find the energy *per unit volume* in the space between the plates of a parallel-plate capacitor with plate area A and separation d. We call this the **energy density,** denoted by u. From Eq. (24.9) the total stored potential energy is $\frac{1}{2}CV^2$ and the volume between the plates is just Ad; hence the energy density is

$$u = \text{Energy density} = \frac{\frac{1}{2}CV^2}{Ad} \qquad (24.10)$$

From Eq. (24.2) the capacitance C is given by $C = \epsilon_0 A/d$. The potential difference V is related to the electric-field magnitude E by $V = Ed$. If we use these expressions in Eq. (24.10), the geometric factors A and d cancel, and we find

$$u = \tfrac{1}{2}\epsilon_0 E^2 \qquad \text{(electric energy density in a vacuum)} \qquad (24.11)$$

Although we have derived this relationship only for a parallel-plate capacitor, it turns out to be valid for any capacitor in vacuum and indeed *for any electric field configuration in vacuum.* This result has an interesting implication. We think of vacuum as space with no matter in it, but vacuum can nevertheless have electric fields and therefore energy. Thus "empty" space need not be truly empty after all. We will use this idea and Eq. (24.11) in Chapter 32 in connection with the energy transported by electromagnetic waves.

CAUTION **Electric-field energy is electric potential energy** It's a common misconception that electric-field energy is a new kind of energy, different from the electric potential energy described before. This is *not* the case; it is simply a different way of interpreting electric potential energy. We can regard the energy of a given system of charges as being a shared property of all the charges, or we can think of the energy as being a property of the electric field that the charges create. Either interpretation leads to the same value of the potential energy.

Example 24.7 **Transferring charge and energy between capacitors**

We connect a capacitor $C_1 = 8.0\ \mu\text{F}$ to a power supply, charge it to a potential difference $V_0 = 120$ V, and disconnect the power supply (Fig. 24.12). Switch S is open. (a) What is the charge Q_0 on C_1? (b) What is the energy stored in C_1? (c) Capacitor $C_2 = 4.0\ \mu\text{F}$ is initially uncharged. We close switch S. After charge no longer flows, what is the potential difference across each capacitor, and what is the charge on each capacitor? (d) What is the final energy of the system?

24.12 When the switch S is closed, the charged capacitor C_1 is connected to an uncharged capacitor C_2. The center part of the switch is an insulating handle; charge can flow only between the two upper terminals and between the two lower terminals.

SOLUTION

IDENTIFY and SET UP: In parts (a) and (b) we find the charge Q_0 and stored energy $U_{initial}$ for the single charged capacitor C_1 using Eqs. (24.1) and (24.9), respectively. After we close switch S, one wire connects the upper plates of the two capacitors and another wire connects the lower plates; the capacitors are now connected in parallel. In part (c) we use the character of the parallel connection to determine how Q_0 is shared between the two capacitors. In part (d) we again use Eq. (24.9) to find the energy stored in capacitors C_1 and C_2; the energy of the system is the sum of these values.

EXECUTE: (a) The initial charge Q_0 on C_1 is

$$Q_0 = C_1V_0 = (8.0\ \mu\text{F})(120\ \text{V}) = 960\ \mu\text{C}$$

(b) The energy initially stored in C_1 is

$$U_{initial} = \tfrac{1}{2}Q_0V_0 = \tfrac{1}{2}(960 \times 10^{-6}\ \text{C})(120\ \text{V}) = 0.058\ \text{J}$$

(c) When we close the switch, the positive charge Q_0 is distributed over the upper plates of both capacitors and the negative charge $-Q_0$ is distributed over the lower plates. Let Q_1 and Q_2 be the magnitudes of the final charges on the capacitors. Conservation

of charge requires that $Q_1 + Q_2 = Q_0$. The potential difference V between the plates is the same for both capacitors because they are connected in parallel, so the charges are $Q_1 = C_1V$ and $Q_2 = C_2V$. We now have three independent equations relating the three unknowns Q_1, Q_2, and V. Solving these, we find

$$V = \frac{Q_0}{C_1 + C_2} = \frac{960\ \mu\text{C}}{8.0\ \mu\text{F} + 4.0\ \mu\text{F}} = 80\ \text{V}$$

$$Q_1 = 640\ \mu\text{C} \qquad Q_2 = 320\ \mu\text{C}$$

(d) The final energy of the system is

$$U_{final} = \tfrac{1}{2}Q_1V + \tfrac{1}{2}Q_2V = \tfrac{1}{2}Q_0V$$

$$= \tfrac{1}{2}(960 \times 10^{-6}\ \text{C})(80\ \text{V}) = 0.038\ \text{J}$$

EVALUATE: The final energy is less than the initial energy; the difference was converted to energy of some other form. The conductors become a little warmer because of their resistance, and some energy is radiated as electromagnetic waves. We'll study the behavior of capacitors in more detail in Chapters 26 and 31.

Example 24.8 Electric-field energy

(a) What is the magnitude of the electric field required to store 1.00 J of electric potential energy in a volume of 1.00 m³ in vacuum? (b) If the field magnitude is 10 times larger than that, how much energy is stored per cubic meter?

SOLUTION

IDENTIFY and SET UP: We use the relationship between the electric-field magnitude E and the energy density u. In part (a) we use the given information to find u; then we use Eq. (24.11) to find the corresponding value of E. In part (b), Eq. (24.11) tells us how u varies with E.

EXECUTE: (a) The desired energy density is $u = 1.00\ \text{J/m}^3$. Then from Eq. (24.11),

$$E = \sqrt{\frac{2u}{\epsilon_0}} = \sqrt{\frac{2(1.00\ \text{J/m}^3)}{8.85 \times 10^{-12}\ \text{C}^2/\text{N} \cdot \text{m}^2}}$$

$$= 4.75 \times 10^5\ \text{N/C} = 4.75 \times 10^5\ \text{V/m}$$

(b) Equation (24.11) shows that u is proportional to E^2. If E increases by a factor of 10, u increases by a factor of $10^2 = 100$, so the energy density becomes $u = 100\ \text{J/m}^3$.

EVALUATE: Dry air can sustain an electric field of about $3 \times 10^6\ \text{V/m}$ without experiencing *dielectric breakdown*, which we will discuss in Section 24.4. There we will see that field magnitudes in practical insulators can be as great as this or even larger.

Example 24.9 Two ways to calculate energy stored in a capacitor

The spherical capacitor described in Example 24.3 (Section 24.1) has charges $+Q$ and $-Q$ on its inner and outer conductors. Find the electric potential energy stored in the capacitor (a) by using the capacitance C found in Example 24.3 and (b) by integrating the electric-field energy density u.

SOLUTION

IDENTIFY and SET UP: We can determine the energy U stored in a capacitor in two ways: in terms of the work done to put the charges on the two conductors, and in terms of the energy in the electric field between the conductors. The descriptions are equivalent, so they must give us the same result. In Example 24.3 we found the capacitance C and the field magnitude E in the space between the conductors. (The electric field is zero inside the inner sphere and is also zero outside the inner surface of the outer sphere, because a Gaussian surface with radius $r < r_a$ or $r > r_b$ encloses zero net

charge. Hence the energy density is nonzero only in the space between the spheres, $r_a < r < r_b$.) In part (a) we use Eq. (24.9) to find U. In part (b) we use Eq. (24.11) to find u, which we integrate over the volume between the spheres to find U.

EXECUTE: (a) From Example 24.3, the spherical capacitor has capacitance

$$C = 4\pi\epsilon_0 \frac{r_a r_b}{r_b - r_a}$$

where r_a and r_b are the radii of the inner and outer conducting spheres, respectively. From Eq. (24.9) the energy stored in this capacitor is

$$U = \frac{Q^2}{2C} = \frac{Q^2}{8\pi\epsilon_0} \frac{r_b - r_a}{r_a r_b}$$

Continued

(b) The electric field in the region $r_a < r < r_b$ between the two conducting spheres has magnitude $E = Q/4\pi\epsilon_0 r^2$. The energy density in this region is

$$u = \tfrac{1}{2}\epsilon_0 E^2 = \tfrac{1}{2}\epsilon_0\left(\frac{Q}{4\pi\epsilon_0 r^2}\right)^2 = \frac{Q^2}{32\pi^2\epsilon_0 r^4}$$

The energy density is *not* uniform; it decreases rapidly with increasing distance from the center of the capacitor. To find the total electric-field energy, we integrate u (the energy per unit volume) over the region $r_a < r < r_b$. We divide this region into spherical shells of radius r, surface area $4\pi r^2$, thickness dr, and volume $dV = 4\pi r^2\,dr$. Then

$$U = \int u\,dV = \int_{r_a}^{r_b}\left(\frac{Q^2}{32\pi^2\epsilon_0 r^4}\right)4\pi r^2\,dr$$

$$= \frac{Q^2}{8\pi\epsilon_0}\int_{r_a}^{r_b}\frac{dr}{r^2} = \frac{Q^2}{8\pi\epsilon_0}\left(-\frac{1}{r_b} + \frac{1}{r_a}\right)$$

$$= \frac{Q^2}{8\pi\epsilon_0}\frac{r_b - r_a}{r_a r_b}$$

EVALUATE: Electric potential energy can be regarded as being associated with either the *charges,* as in part (a), or the *field,* as in part (b); the calculated amount of stored energy is the same in either case.

Test Your Understanding of Section 24.3   You want to connect a 4-μF capacitor and an 8-μF capacitor. With which type of connection will the 4-μF capacitor have a greater amount of *stored energy* than the 8-μF capacitor? (i) series; (ii) parallel; (iii) either series or parallel; (iv) neither series nor parallel.

24.4 Dielectrics

24.13 A common type of capacitor uses dielectric sheets to separate the conductors.

Conductor
(metal foil)

Conductor
(metal foil)

Dielectric
(plastic sheets)

Most capacitors have a nonconducting material, or **dielectric,** between their conducting plates. A common type of capacitor uses long strips of metal foil for the plates, separated by strips of plastic sheet such as Mylar. A sandwich of these materials is rolled up, forming a unit that can provide a capacitance of several microfarads in a compact package (Fig. 24.13).

Placing a solid dielectric between the plates of a capacitor serves three functions. First, it solves the mechanical problem of maintaining two large metal sheets at a very small separation without actual contact.

Second, using a dielectric increases the maximum possible potential difference between the capacitor plates. As we described in Section 23.3, any insulating material, when subjected to a sufficiently large electric field, experiences a partial ionization that permits conduction through it. This is called **dielectric breakdown.** Many dielectric materials can tolerate stronger electric fields without breakdown than can air. Thus using a dielectric allows a capacitor to sustain a higher potential difference V and so store greater amounts of charge and energy.

Third, the capacitance of a capacitor of given dimensions is *greater* when there is a dielectric material between the plates than when there is vacuum. We can demonstrate this effect with the aid of a sensitive *electrometer,* a device that measures the potential difference between two conductors without letting any appreciable charge flow from one to the other. Figure 24.14a shows an electrometer connected across a charged capacitor, with magnitude of charge Q on each plate and potential difference V_0. When we insert an uncharged sheet of dielectric, such as glass, paraffin, or polystyrene, between the plates, experiment shows that the potential difference *decreases* to a smaller value V (Fig. 24.14b). When we remove the dielectric, the potential difference returns to its original value V_0, showing that the original charges on the plates have not changed.

The original capacitance C_0 is given by $C_0 = Q/V_0$, and the capacitance C with the dielectric present is $C = Q/V$. The charge Q is the same in both cases, and V is less than V_0, so we conclude that the capacitance C with the dielectric present is *greater* than C_0. When the space between plates is completely filled by the dielectric, the ratio of C to C_0 (equal to the ratio of V_0 to V) is called the **dielectric constant** of the material, K:

$$K = \frac{C}{C_0} \qquad \text{(definition of dielectric constant)} \qquad (24.12)$$

When the charge is constant, $Q = C_0V_0 = CV$ and $C/C_0 = V_0/V$. In this case, Eq. (24.12) can be rewritten as

$$V = \frac{V_0}{K} \quad \text{(when } Q \text{ is constant)} \tag{24.13}$$

With the dielectric present, the potential difference for a given charge Q is *reduced* by a factor K.

The dielectric constant K is a pure number. Because C is always greater than C_0, K is always greater than unity. Some representative values of K are given in Table 24.1. For vacuum, $K = 1$ by definition. For air at ordinary temperatures and pressures, K is about 1.0006; this is so nearly equal to 1 that for most purposes an air capacitor is equivalent to one in vacuum. Note that while water has a very large value of K, it is usually not a very practical dielectric for use in capacitors. The reason is that while pure water is a very poor conductor, it is also an excellent ionic solvent. Any ions that are dissolved in the water will cause charge to flow between the capacitor plates, so the capacitor discharges.

Table 24.1 Values of Dielectric Constant K at 20°C

Material	K	Material	K
Vacuum	1	Polyvinyl chloride	3.18
Air (1 atm)	1.00059	Plexiglas®	3.40
Air (100 atm)	1.0548	Glass	5–10
Teflon	2.1	Neoprene	6.70
Polyethylene	2.25	Germanium	16
Benzene	2.28	Glycerin	42.5
Mica	3–6	Water	80.4
Mylar	3.1	Strontium titanate	310

No real dielectric is a perfect insulator. Hence there is always some *leakage current* between the charged plates of a capacitor with a dielectric. We tacitly ignored this effect in Section 24.2 when we derived expressions for the equivalent capacitances of capacitors in series, Eq. (24.5), and in parallel, Eq. (24.7). But if a leakage current flows for a long enough time to substantially change the charges from the values we used to derive Eqs. (24.5) and (24.7), those equations may no longer be accurate.

Induced Charge and Polarization

When a dielectric material is inserted between the plates while the charge is kept constant, the potential difference between the plates decreases by a factor K. Therefore the electric field between the plates must decrease by the same factor. If E_0 is the vacuum value and E is the value with the dielectric, then

$$E = \frac{E_0}{K} \quad \text{(when } Q \text{ is constant)} \tag{24.14}$$

Since the electric-field magnitude is smaller when the dielectric is present, the surface charge density (which causes the field) must be smaller as well. The surface charge on the conducting plates does not change, but an *induced* charge of the opposite sign appears on each surface of the dielectric (Fig. 24.15). The dielectric was originally electrically neutral and is still neutral; the induced surface charges arise as a result of *redistribution* of positive and negative charge within the dielectric material, a phenomenon called **polarization.** We first encountered polarization in Section 21.2, and we suggest that you reread the discussion of Fig. 21.8. We will assume that the induced surface charge is *directly proportional* to the electric-field magnitude E in the material; this is indeed the case for many common dielectrics. (This direct proportionality is analogous to

24.14 Effect of a dielectric between the plates of a parallel-plate capacitor. (a) With a given charge, the potential difference is V_0. (b) With the same charge but with a dielectric between the plates, the potential difference V is smaller than V_0.

(a)

(b)

··· Adding the dielectric *reduces* the potential difference across the capacitor.

24.15 Electric field lines with (a) vacuum between the plates and (b) dielectric between the plates.

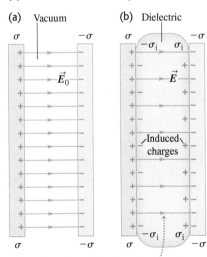

For a given charge density σ, the induced charges on the dielectric's surfaces reduce the electric field between the plates.

Hooke's law for a spring.) In that case, K is a constant for any particular material. When the electric field is very strong or if the dielectric is made of certain crystalline materials, the relationship between induced charge and the electric field can be more complex; we won't consider such cases here.

We can derive a relationship between this induced surface charge and the charge on the plates. Let's denote the magnitude of the charge per unit area induced on the surfaces of the dielectric (the induced surface charge density) by σ_i. The magnitude of the surface charge density on the capacitor plates is σ, as usual. Then the *net* surface charge on each side of the capacitor has magnitude $(\sigma - \sigma_i)$, as shown in Fig. 24.15b. As we found in Example 21.12 (Section 21.5) and in Example 22.8 (Section 22.4), the field between the plates is related to the net surface charge density by $E = \sigma_{net}/\epsilon_0$. Without and with the dielectric, respectively, we have

$$E_0 = \frac{\sigma}{\epsilon_0} \qquad E = \frac{\sigma - \sigma_i}{\epsilon_0} \qquad (24.15)$$

Using these expressions in Eq. (24.14) and rearranging the result, we find

$$\sigma_i = \sigma\left(1 - \frac{1}{K}\right) \qquad \text{(induced surface charge density)} \qquad (24.16)$$

This equation shows that when K is very large, σ_i is nearly as large as σ. In this case, σ_i nearly cancels σ, and the field and potential difference are much smaller than their values in vacuum.

The product $K\epsilon_0$ is called the **permittivity** of the dielectric, denoted by ϵ:

$$\epsilon = K\epsilon_0 \qquad \text{(definition of permittivity)} \qquad (24.17)$$

In terms of ϵ we can express the electric field within the dielectric as

$$E = \frac{\sigma}{\epsilon} \qquad (24.18)$$

The capacitance when the dielectric is present is given by

$$C = KC_0 = K\epsilon_0\frac{A}{d} = \epsilon\frac{A}{d} \qquad \begin{array}{l}\text{(parallel-plate capacitor,}\\\text{dielectric between plates)}\end{array} \qquad (24.19)$$

We can repeat the derivation of Eq. (24.11) for the energy density u in an electric field for the case in which a dielectric is present. The result is

$$u = \tfrac{1}{2}K\epsilon_0E^2 = \tfrac{1}{2}\epsilon E^2 \qquad \text{(electric energy density in a dielectric)} \qquad (24.20)$$

In empty space, where $K = 1$, $\epsilon = \epsilon_0$ and Eqs. (24.19) and (24.20) reduce to Eqs. (24.2) and (24.11), respectively, for a parallel-plate capacitor in vacuum. For this reason, ϵ_0 is sometimes called the "permittivity of free space" or the "permittivity of vacuum." Because K is a pure number, ϵ and ϵ_0 have the same units, $C^2/N \cdot m^2$ or F/m.

Equation (24.19) shows that extremely high capacitances can be obtained with plates that have a large surface area A and are separated by a small distance d by a dielectric with a large value of K. In an *electrolytic double-layer capacitor*, tiny carbon granules adhere to each plate: The value of A is the combined surface area of the granules, which can be tremendous. The plates with granules attached are separated by a very thin dielectric sheet. A capacitor of this kind can have a capacitance of 5000 farads yet fit in the palm of your hand (compare Example 24.1 in Section 24.1).

Several practical devices make use of the way in which a capacitor responds to a change in dielectric constant. One example is an electric stud finder, used by home repair workers to locate metal studs hidden behind a wall's surface. It consists of a metal plate with associated circuitry. The plate acts as one half of a capacitor, with the wall acting as the other half. If the stud finder moves over a metal stud, the effective dielectric constant for the capacitor changes, changing the capacitance and triggering a signal.

Problem-Solving Strategy 24.2 Dielectrics

IDENTIFY *the relevant concepts:* The relationships in this section are useful whenever there is an electric field in a dielectric, such as a dielectric between charged capacitor plates. Typically you must relate the potential difference V_{ab} between the plates, the electric field magnitude E in the capacitor, the charge density σ on the capacitor plates, and the induced charge density σ_i on the surfaces of the capacitor.

SET UP *the problem* using the following steps:
1. Make a drawing of the situation.
2. Identify the target variables, and choose which equations from this section will help you solve for those variables.

EXECUTE *the solution* as follows:
1. In problems such as the next example, it is easy to get lost in a blizzard of formulas. Ask yourself at each step what kind of

quantity each symbol represents. For example, distinguish clearly between charges and charge densities, and between electric fields and electric potential differences.
2. Check for consistency of units. Distances must be in meters. A microfarad is 10^{-6} farad, and so on. Don't confuse the numerical value of ϵ_0 with the value of $1/4\pi\epsilon_0$. Electric-field magnitude can be expressed in both N/C and V/m. The units of ϵ_0 are $C^2/N \cdot m^2$ or F/m.

EVALUATE *your answer:* With a dielectric present, (a) the capacitance is greater than without a dielectric; (b) for a given charge on the capacitor, the electric field and potential difference are less than without a dielectric; and (c) the magnitude of the induced surface charge density σ_i on the dielectric is less than that of the charge density σ on the capacitor plates.

Example 24.10 A capacitor with and without a dielectric

Suppose the parallel plates in Fig. 24.15 each have an area of 2000 cm² (2.00×10^{-1} m²) and are 1.00 cm (1.00×10^{-2} m) apart. We connect the capacitor to a power supply, charge it to a potential difference $V_0 = 3.00$ kV, and disconnect the power supply. We then insert a sheet of insulating plastic material between the plates, completely filling the space between them. We find that the potential difference decreases to 1.00 kV while the charge on each capacitor plate remains constant. Find (a) the original capacitance C_0; (b) the magnitude of charge Q on each plate; (c) the capacitance C after the dielectric is inserted; (d) the dielectric constant K of the dielectric; (e) the permittivity ϵ of the dielectric; (f) the magnitude of the induced charge Q_i on each face of the dielectric; (g) the original electric field E_0 between the plates; and (h) the electric field E after the dielectric is inserted.

SOLUTION

IDENTIFY and SET UP: This problem uses most of the relationships we have discussed for capacitors and dielectrics. (Energy relationships are treated in Example 24.11.) Most of the target variables can be obtained in several ways. The methods used below are a sample; we encourage you to think of others and compare your results.

EXECUTE: (a) With vacuum between the plates, we use Eq. (24.19) with $K = 1$:

$$C_0 = \epsilon_0 \frac{A}{d} = (8.85 \times 10^{-12} \text{ F/m}) \frac{2.00 \times 10^{-1} \text{ m}^2}{1.00 \times 10^{-2} \text{ m}}$$

$$= 1.77 \times 10^{-10} \text{ F} = 177 \text{ pF}$$

(b) From the definition of capacitance, Eq. (24.1),

$$Q = C_0 V_0 = (1.77 \times 10^{-10} \text{ F})(3.00 \times 10^3 \text{ V})$$
$$= 5.31 \times 10^{-7} \text{ C} = 0.531 \ \mu\text{C}$$

(c) When the dielectric is inserted, Q is unchanged but the potential difference decreases to $V = 1.00$ kV. Hence from Eq. (24.1), the new capacitance is

$$C = \frac{Q}{V} = \frac{5.31 \times 10^{-7} \text{ C}}{1.00 \times 10^3 \text{ V}} = 5.31 \times 10^{-10} \text{ F} = 531 \text{ pF}$$

(d) From Eq. (24.12), the dielectric constant is

$$K = \frac{C}{C_0} = \frac{5.31 \times 10^{-10} \text{ F}}{1.77 \times 10^{-10} \text{ F}} = \frac{531 \text{ pF}}{177 \text{ pF}} = 3.00$$

Alternatively, from Eq. (24.13),

$$K = \frac{V_0}{V} = \frac{3000 \text{ V}}{1000 \text{ V}} = 3.00$$

(e) Using K from part (d) in Eq. (24.17), the permittivity is

$$\epsilon = K\epsilon_0 = (3.00)(8.85 \times 10^{-12} \text{ C}^2/\text{N} \cdot \text{m}^2)$$
$$= 2.66 \times 10^{-11} \text{ C}^2/\text{N} \cdot \text{m}^2$$

(f) Multiplying both sides of Eq. (24.16) by the plate area A gives the induced charge $Q_i = \sigma_i A$ in terms of the charge $Q = \sigma A$ on each plate:

$$Q_i = Q\left(1 - \frac{1}{K}\right) = (5.31 \times 10^{-7} \text{ C})\left(1 - \frac{1}{3.00}\right)$$
$$= 3.54 \times 10^{-7} \text{ C}$$

Continued

(g) Since the electric field between the plates is uniform, its magnitude is the potential difference divided by the plate separation:

$$E_0 = \frac{V_0}{d} = \frac{3000 \text{ V}}{1.00 \times 10^{-2} \text{ m}} = 3.00 \times 10^5 \text{ V/m}$$

(h) After the dielectric is inserted,

$$E = \frac{V}{d} = \frac{1000 \text{ V}}{1.00 \times 10^{-2} \text{ m}} = 1.00 \times 10^5 \text{ V/m}$$

or, from Eq. (24.18),

$$E = \frac{\sigma}{\epsilon} = \frac{Q}{\epsilon A} = \frac{5.31 \times 10^{-7} \text{ C}}{(2.66 \times 10^{-11} \text{ C}^2/\text{N} \cdot \text{m}^2)(2.00 \times 10^{-1} \text{ m}^2)}$$

$$= 1.00 \times 10^5 \text{ V/m}$$

or, from Eq. (24.15),

$$E = \frac{\sigma - \sigma_i}{\epsilon_0} = \frac{Q - Q_i}{\epsilon_0 A}$$

$$= \frac{(5.31 - 3.54) \times 10^{-7} \text{ C}}{(8.85 \times 10^{-12} \text{ C}^2/\text{N} \cdot \text{m}^2)(2.00 \times 10^{-1} \text{ m}^2)}$$

$$= 1.00 \times 10^5 \text{ V/m}$$

or, from Eq. (24.14),

$$E = \frac{E_0}{K} = \frac{3.00 \times 10^5 \text{ V/m}}{3.00} = 1.00 \times 10^5 \text{ V/m}$$

EVALUATE: Inserting the dielectric increased the capacitance by a factor of $K = 3.00$ and reduced the electric field between the plates by a factor of $1/K = 1/3.00$. It did so by developing induced charges on the faces of the dielectric of magnitude $Q(1 - 1/K) = Q(1 - 1/3.00) = 0.667Q$.

Example 24.11 **Energy storage with and without a dielectric**

Find the energy stored in the electric field of the capacitor in Example 24.10 and the energy density, both before and after the dielectric sheet is inserted.

SOLUTION

IDENTIFY and SET UP: We now consider the ideas of energy stored in a capacitor and of electric-field energy density. We use Eq. (24.9) to find the stored energy and Eq. (24.20) to find the energy density.

EXECUTE: From Eq. (24.9), the stored energies U_0 and U without and with the dielectric in place are

$$U_0 = \tfrac{1}{2}C_0 V_0^2 = \tfrac{1}{2}(1.77 \times 10^{-10} \text{ F})(3000 \text{ V})^2 = 7.97 \times 10^{-4} \text{ J}$$

$$U = \tfrac{1}{2}C V^2 = \tfrac{1}{2}(5.31 \times 10^{-10} \text{ F})(1000 \text{ V})^2 = 2.66 \times 10^{-4} \text{ J}$$

The final energy is one-third of the original energy.

Equation (24.20) gives the energy densities without and with the dielectric:

$$u_0 = \tfrac{1}{2}\epsilon_0 E_0^2 = \tfrac{1}{2}(8.85 \times 10^{-12} \text{ C}^2/\text{N} \cdot \text{m}^2)(3.00 \times 10^5 \text{ N/C})^2$$

$$= 0.398 \text{ J/m}^3$$

$$u = \tfrac{1}{2}\epsilon E^2 = \tfrac{1}{2}(2.66 \times 10^{-11} \text{ C}^2/\text{N} \cdot \text{m}^2)(1.00 \times 10^5 \text{ N/C})^2$$

$$= 0.133 \text{ J/m}^3$$

The energy density with the dielectric is one-third of the original energy density.

EVALUATE: We can check our answer for u_0 by noting that the volume between the plates is $V = (0.200 \text{ m}^2)(0.0100 \text{ m}) =$

0.00200 m³. Since the electric field between the plates is uniform, u_0 is uniform as well and the energy density is just the stored energy divided by the volume:

$$u_0 = \frac{U_0}{V} = \frac{7.97 \times 10^{-4} \text{ J}}{0.00200 \text{ m}^3} = 0.398 \text{ J/m}^3$$

This agrees with our earlier answer. You can use the same approach to check our result for u.

In general, when a dielectric is inserted into a capacitor while the charge on each plate remains the same, the permittivity ϵ increases by a factor of K (the dielectric constant), and the electric field E and the energy density $u = \tfrac{1}{2}\epsilon E^2$ decrease by a factor of $1/K$. Where does the energy go? The answer lies in the fringing field at the edges of a real parallel-plate capacitor. As Fig. 24.16 shows, that field tends to pull the dielectric into the space between the plates, doing work on it as it does so. We could attach a spring to the left end of the dielectric in Fig. 24.16 and use this force to stretch the spring. Because work is done by the field, the field energy density decreases.

24.16 The fringing field at the edges of the capacitor exerts forces $\vec{F}_{-i}$ and $\vec{F}_{+i}$ on the negative and positive induced surface charges of a dielectric, pulling the dielectric into the capacitor.

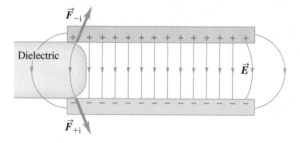

Dielectric Breakdown

We mentioned earlier that when a dielectric is subjected to a sufficiently strong electric field, *dielectric breakdown* takes place and the dielectric becomes a conductor. This occurs when the electric field is so strong that electrons are ripped loose from their molecules and crash into other molecules, liberating even more electrons. This avalanche of moving charge forms a spark or arc discharge. Lightning is a dramatic example of dielectric breakdown in air.

Because of dielectric breakdown, capacitors always have maximum voltage ratings. When a capacitor is subjected to excessive voltage, an arc may form through a layer of dielectric, burning or melting a hole in it. This arc creates a conducting path (a short circuit) between the conductors. If a conducting path remains after the arc is extinguished, the device is rendered permanently useless as a capacitor.

The maximum electric-field magnitude that a material can withstand without the occurrence of breakdown is called its **dielectric strength.** This quantity is affected significantly by temperature, trace impurities, small irregularities in the metal electrodes, and other factors that are difficult to control. For this reason we can give only approximate figures for dielectric strengths. The dielectric strength of dry air is about 3×10^6 V/m. Table 24.2 lists the dielectric strengths of a few common insulating materials. Note that the values are all substantially greater than the value for air. For example, a layer of polycarbonate 0.01 mm thick (about the smallest practical thickness) has 10 times the dielectric strength of air and can withstand a maximum voltage of about $(3 \times 10^7 \text{ V/m})(1 \times 10^{-5} \text{ m}) = 300$ V.

Table 24.2 Dielectric Constant and Dielectric Strength of Some Insulating Materials

Material	Dielectric Constant, K	Dielectric Strength, E_m (V/m)
Polycarbonate	2.8	3×10^7
Polyester	3.3	6×10^7
Polypropylene	2.2	7×10^7
Polystyrene	2.6	2×10^7
Pyrex glass	4.7	1×10^7

Test Your Understanding of Section 24.4 The space between the plates of an isolated parallel-plate capacitor is filled by a slab of dielectric with dielectric constant K. The two plates of the capacitor have charges Q and $-Q$. You pull out the dielectric slab. If the charges do not change, how does the energy in the capacitor change when you remove the slab? (i) It increases; (ii) it decreases; (iii) it remains the same.

24.5 Molecular Model of Induced Charge

In Section 24.4 we discussed induced surface charges on a dielectric in an electric field. Now let's look at how these surface charges can arise. If the material were a *conductor*, the answer would be simple. Conductors contain charge that is free to move, and when an electric field is present, some of the charge redistributes itself on the surface so that there is no electric field inside the conductor. But an ideal dielectric has *no* charges that are free to move, so how can a surface charge occur?

To understand this, we have to look again at rearrangement of charge at the *molecular* level. Some molecules, such as H_2O and N_2O, have equal amounts of positive and negative charges but a lopsided distribution, with excess positive charge concentrated on one side of the molecule and negative charge on the other. As we described in Section 21.7, such an arrangement is called an *electric dipole*, and the molecule is called a *polar molecule*. When no electric field is present in a gas or liquid with polar molecules, the molecules are oriented randomly (Fig. 24.17a). When they are placed in an electric field, however, they tend to orient themselves as in Fig. 24.17b, as a result of the electric-field torques described in Section 21.7. Because of thermal agitation, the alignment of the molecules with $\vec{E}$ is not perfect.

Application Dielectric Cell Membrane
The membrane of a living cell behaves like a dielectric between the plates of a capacitor. The membrane is made of two sheets of lipid molecules, with their water-insoluble ends in the middle and their water-soluble ends (shown in red) on the surfaces of the membrane. The conductive fluids on either side of the membrane (water with negative ions inside the cell, water with positive ions outside) act as charged capacitor plates, and the nonconducting membrane acts as a dielectric with K of about 10. The potential difference V across the membrane is about 0.07 V and the membrane thickness d is about 7×10^{-9} m, so the electric field $E = V/d$ in the membrane is about 10^7 V/m—close to the dielectric strength of the membrane. If the membrane were made of air, V and E would be larger by a factor of $K \approx 10$ and dielectric breakdown would occur.

24.17 Polar molecules (a) without and (b) with an applied electric field $\vec{E}$.

(a)

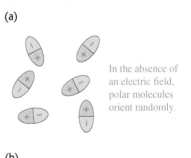

In the absence of an electric field, polar molecules orient randomly.

(b)

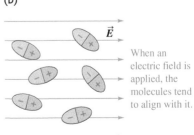

When an electric field is applied, the molecules tend to align with it.

24.18 Nonpolar molecules (a) without and (b) with an applied electric field $\vec{E}$.

(a)

In the absence of an electric field, nonpolar molecules are not electric dipoles.

(b)

An electric field causes the molecules' positive and negative charges to separate slightly, making the molecule effectively polar.

Even a molecule that is *not* ordinarily polar *becomes* a dipole when it is placed in an electric field because the field pushes the positive charges in the molecules in the direction of the field and pushes the negative charges in the opposite direction. This causes a redistribution of charge within the molecule (Fig. 24.18). Such dipoles are called *induced* dipoles.

With either polar or nonpolar molecules, the redistribution of charge caused by the field leads to the formation of a layer of charge on each surface of the dielectric material (Fig. 24.19). These layers are the surface charges described in Section 24.4; their surface charge density is denoted by σ_i. The charges are *not* free to move indefinitely, as they would be in a conductor, because each charge is bound to a molecule. They are in fact called **bound charges** to distinguish them from the **free charges** that are added to and removed from the conducting capacitor plates. In the interior of the material the net charge per unit volume remains zero. As we have seen, this redistribution of charge is called *polarization*, and we say that the material is *polarized*.

The four parts of Fig. 24.20 show the behavior of a slab of dielectric when it is inserted in the field between a pair of oppositely charged capacitor plates. Figure 24.20a shows the original field. Figure 24.20b is the situation after the dielectric has been inserted but before any rearrangement of charges has occurred. Figure 24.20c shows by thinner arrows the additional field set up in the dielectric by its induced surface charges. This field is *opposite* to the original field, but it is not great enough to cancel the original field completely because the charges in the dielectric are not free to move indefinitely. The resultant field

24.19 Polarization of a dielectric in an electric field $\vec{E}$ gives rise to thin layers of bound charges on the surfaces, creating surface charge densities σ_i and $-\sigma_i$. The sizes of the molecules are greatly exaggerated for clarity.

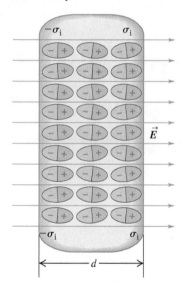

24.20 (a) Electric field of magnitude E_0 between two charged plates. (b) Introduction of a dielectric of dielectric constant K. (c) The induced surface charges and their field. (d) Resultant field of magnitude E_0/K.

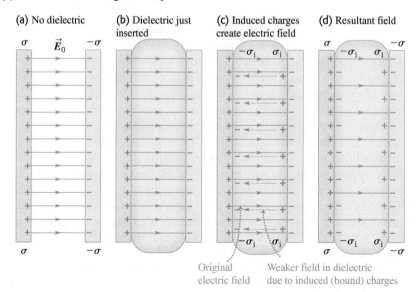

(a) No dielectric

(b) Dielectric just inserted

(c) Induced charges create electric field

(d) Resultant field

Original electric field

Weaker field in dielectric due to induced (bound) charges

in the dielectric, shown in Fig. 24.20d, is therefore decreased in magnitude. In the field-line representation, some of the field lines leaving the positive plate go through the dielectric, while others terminate on the induced charges on the faces of the dielectric.

As we discussed in Section 21.2, polarization is also the reason a charged body, such as an electrified plastic rod, can exert a force on an *uncharged* body such as a bit of paper or a pith ball. Figure 24.21 shows an uncharged dielectric sphere B in the radial field of a positively charged body A. The induced positive charges on B experience a force toward the right, while the force on the induced negative charges is toward the left. The negative charges are closer to A, and thus are in a stronger field, than are the positive charges. The force toward the left is stronger than that toward the right, and B is attracted toward A, even though its net charge is zero. The attraction occurs whether the sign of A's charge is positive or negative (see Fig. 21.8). Furthermore, the effect is not limited to dielectrics; an uncharged conducting body would be attracted in the same way.

Test Your Understanding of Section 24.5   A parallel-plate capacitor has charges Q and $-Q$ on its two plates. A dielectric slab with $K = 3$ is then inserted into the space between the plates as shown in Fig. 24.20. Rank the following electric-field magnitudes in order from largest to smallest. (i) the field before the slab is inserted; (ii) the resultant field after the slab is inserted; (iii) the field due to the bound charges. ❙

24.6 Gauss's Law in Dielectrics

We can extend the analysis of Section 24.4 to reformulate Gauss's law in a form that is particularly useful for dielectrics. Figure 24.22 is a close-up view of the left capacitor plate and left surface of the dielectric in Fig. 24.15b. Let's apply Gauss's law to the rectangular box shown in cross section by the purple line; the surface area of the left and right sides is A. The left side is embedded in the conductor that forms the left capacitor plate, and so the electric field everywhere on that surface is zero. The right side is embedded in the dielectric, where the electric field has magnitude E, and $E_\perp = 0$ everywhere on the other four sides. The total charge enclosed, including both the charge on the capacitor plate and the induced charge on the dielectric surface, is $Q_{encl} = (\sigma - \sigma_i)A$, so Gauss's law gives

$$EA = \frac{(\sigma - \sigma_i)A}{\epsilon_0} \qquad (24.21)$$

This equation is not very illuminating as it stands because it relates two unknown quantities: E inside the dielectric and the induced surface charge density σ_i. But now we can use Eq. (24.16), developed for this same situation, to simplify this equation by eliminating σ_i. Equation (24.16) is

$$\sigma_i = \sigma\left(1 - \frac{1}{K}\right) \quad \text{or} \quad \sigma - \sigma_i = \frac{\sigma}{K}$$

Combining this with Eq. (24.21), we get

$$EA = \frac{\sigma A}{K\epsilon_0} \quad \text{or} \quad KEA = \frac{\sigma A}{\epsilon_0} \qquad (24.22)$$

Equation (24.22) says that the flux of $K\vec{E}$, not $\vec{E}$, through the Gaussian surface in Fig. 24.22 is equal to the enclosed *free* charge σA divided by ϵ_0. It turns out that for *any* Gaussian surface, whenever the induced charge is proportional to the electric field in the material, we can rewrite Gauss's law as

$$\oint K\vec{E} \cdot d\vec{A} = \frac{Q_{encl\text{-}free}}{\epsilon_0} \qquad \text{(Gauss's law in a dielectric)} \qquad (24.23)$$

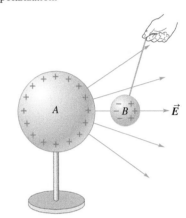

24.21 A neutral sphere B in the radial electric field of a positively charged sphere A is attracted to the charge because of polarization.

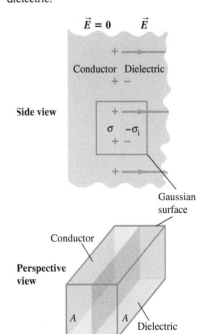

24.22 Gauss's law with a dielectric. This figure shows a close-up of the left-hand capacitor plate in Fig. 24.15b. The Gaussian surface is a rectangular box that lies half in the conductor and half in the dielectric.

where $Q_{\text{encl-free}}$ is the total *free* charge (not bound charge) enclosed by the Gaussian surface. The significance of these results is that the right sides contain only the *free* charge on the conductor, not the bound (induced) charge. In fact, although we have not proved it, Eq. (24.23) remains valid even when different parts of the Gaussian surface are embedded in dielectrics having different values of K, provided that the value of K in each dielectric is independent of the electric field (usually the case for electric fields that are not too strong) and that we use the appropriate value of K for each point on the Gaussian surface.

Example 24.12 **A spherical capacitor with dielectric**

Use Gauss's law to find the capacitance of the spherical capacitor of Example 24.3 (Section 24.1) if the volume between the shells is filled with an insulating oil with dielectric constant K.

SOLUTION

IDENTIFY and SET UP: The spherical symmetry of the problem is not changed by the presence of the dielectric, so as in Example 24.3, we use a concentric spherical Gaussian surface of radius r between the shells. Since a dielectric is present, we use Gauss's law in the form of Eq. (24.23).

EXECUTE: From Eq. (24.23),

$$\oint K\vec{E} \cdot d\vec{A} = \oint KE\, dA = KE \oint dA = (KE)(4\pi r^2) = \frac{Q}{\epsilon_0}$$

$$E = \frac{Q}{4\pi K\epsilon_0 r^2} = \frac{Q}{4\pi\epsilon r^2}$$

where $\epsilon = K\epsilon_0$. Compared to the case in which there is vacuum between the shells, the electric field is reduced by a factor of $1/K$. The potential difference V_{ab} between the shells is reduced by the same factor, and so the capacitance $C = Q/V_{ab}$ is *increased* by a factor of K, just as for a parallel-plate capacitor when a dielectric is inserted. Using the result of Example 24.3, we find that the capacitance with the dielectric is

$$C = \frac{4\pi K\epsilon_0 r_a r_b}{r_b - r_a} = \frac{4\pi\epsilon r_a r_b}{r_b - r_a}$$

EVALUATE: If the dielectric fills the volume between the two conductors, the capacitance is just K times the value with no dielectric. The result is more complicated if the dielectric only partially fills this volume (see Challenge Problem 24.78).

Test Your Understanding of Section 24.6 A single point charge q is imbedded in a dielectric of dielectric constant K. At a point inside the dielectric a distance r from the point charge, what is the magnitude of the electric field? (i) $q/4\pi\epsilon_0 r^2$; (ii) $Kq/4\pi\epsilon_0 r^2$; (iii) $q/4\pi K\epsilon_0 r^2$; (iv) none of these.

Capacitors and capacitance: A capacitor is any pair of conductors separated by an insulating material. When the capacitor is charged, there are charges of equal magnitude Q and opposite sign on the two conductors, and the potential V_{ab} of the positively charged conductor with respect to the negatively charged conductor is proportional to Q. The capacitance C is defined as the ratio of Q to V_{ab}. The SI unit of capacitance is the farad (F): $1\ \text{F} = 1\ \text{C/V}$.

A parallel-plate capacitor consists of two parallel conducting plates, each with area A, separated by a distance d. If they are separated by vacuum, the capacitance depends only on A and d. For other geometries, the capacitance can be found by using the definition $C = Q/V_{ab}$. (See Examples 24.1–24.4.)

$$C = \frac{Q}{V_{ab}} \quad (24.1)$$

$$C = \frac{Q}{V_{ab}} = \epsilon_0 \frac{A}{d} \quad (24.2)$$

Capacitors in series and parallel: When capacitors with capacitances $C_1, C_2, C_3, \ldots$ are connected in series, the reciprocal of the equivalent capacitance C_{eq} equals the sum of the reciprocals of the individual capacitances. When capacitors are connected in parallel, the equivalent capacitance C_{eq} equals the sum of the individual capacitances. (See Examples 24.5 and 24.6.)

$$\frac{1}{C_{eq}} = \frac{1}{C_1} + \frac{1}{C_2} + \frac{1}{C_3} + \cdots \quad (24.5)$$
(capacitors in series)

$$C_{eq} = C_1 + C_2 + C_3 + \cdots \quad (24.7)$$
(capacitors in parallel)

Energy in a capacitor: The energy U required to charge a capacitor C to a potential difference V and a charge Q is equal to the energy stored in the capacitor. This energy can be thought of as residing in the electric field between the conductors; the energy density u (energy per unit volume) is proportional to the square of the electric-field magnitude. (See Examples 24.7–24.9.)

$$U = \frac{Q^2}{2C} = \tfrac{1}{2}CV^2 = \tfrac{1}{2}QV \quad (24.9)$$

$$u = \tfrac{1}{2}\epsilon_0 E^2 \quad (24.11)$$

Dielectrics: When the space between the conductors is filled with a dielectric material, the capacitance increases by a factor K, called the dielectric constant of the material. The quantity $\epsilon = K\epsilon_0$ is called the permittivity of the dielectric. For a fixed amount of charge on the capacitor plates, induced charges on the surface of the dielectric decrease the electric field and potential difference between the plates by the same factor K. The surface charge results from polarization, a microscopic rearrangement of charge in the dielectric. (See Example 24.10.)

Under sufficiently strong fields, dielectrics become conductors, a situation called dielectric breakdown. The maximum field that a material can withstand without breakdown is called its dielectric strength.

In a dielectric, the expression for the energy density is the same as in vacuum but with ϵ_0 replaced by $\epsilon = K\epsilon$. (See Example 24.11.)

Gauss's law in a dielectric has almost the same form as in vacuum, with two key differences: $\vec{E}$ is replaced by $K\vec{E}$ and Q_{encl} is replaced by $Q_{encl\text{-}free}$, which includes only the free charge (not bound charge) enclosed by the Gaussian surface. (See Example 24.12.)

$$C = KC_0 = K\epsilon_0 \frac{A}{d} = \epsilon \frac{A}{d}$$
(parallel-plate capacitor filled with dielectric)
$$\quad (24.19)$$

$$u = \tfrac{1}{2}K\epsilon_0 E^2 = \tfrac{1}{2}\epsilon E^2 \quad (24.20)$$

$$\oint K\vec{E} \cdot d\vec{A} = \frac{Q_{encl\text{-}free}}{\epsilon_0} \quad (24.23)$$

Dielectric between plates

BRIDGING PROBLEM | **Electric-Field Energy and Capacitance of a Conducting Sphere**

A solid conducting sphere of radius R carries a charge Q. Calculate the electric-field energy density at a point a distance r from the center of the sphere for (a) $r < R$ and (b) $r > R$. (c) Calculate the total electric-field energy associated with the charged sphere. (d) How much work is required to assemble the charge Q on the sphere? (e) Use the result of part (c) to find the capacitance of the sphere. (You can think of the second conductor as a hollow conducting shell of infinite radius.)

SOLUTION GUIDE

See MasteringPhysics® study area for a Video Tutor solution

IDENTIFY and SET UP

1. You know the electric field for this situation at all values of r from Example 22.5 (Section 22.4). You'll use this to find the electric-field energy density u and the *total* electric-field energy U. You can then find the capacitance from the relationship $U = Q^2/2C$.
2. To find U, consider a spherical shell of radius r and thickness dr that has volume $dV = 4\pi r^2 dr$. The energy stored in this volume

is $u\,dV$, and the total energy is the integral of $u\,dV$ from $r = 0$ to $r \to \infty$. Set up this integral.

EXECUTE

3. Find u for $r < R$ and for $r > R$.
4. Substitute your results from step 3 into the expression from step 2. Then calculate the integral to find the total electric-field energy U.
5. Use your understanding of the energy stored in a charge distribution to find the work required to assemble the charge Q.
6. Find the capacitance of the sphere.

EVALUATE

7. Where is the electric-field energy density greatest? Where is it least?
8. How would the results be affected if the solid sphere were replaced by a hollow conducting sphere of the same radius R?
9. You can find the potential difference between the sphere and infinity from $C = Q/V$. Does this agree with the result of Example 23.8 (Section 23.3)?

Problems

For instructor-assigned homework, go to MasteringPhysics®.

•, ••, •••: Problems of increasing difficulty. **CP**: Cumulative problems incorporating material from earlier chapters. **CALC**: Problems requiring calculus. **BIO**: Biosciences problems.

DISCUSSION QUESTIONS

Q24.1 Equation (24.2) shows that the capacitance of a parallel-plate capacitor becomes larger as the plate separation d decreases. However, there is a practical limit to how small d can be made, which places limits on how large C can be. Explain what sets the limit on d. (*Hint:* What happens to the magnitude of the electric field as $d \to 0$?)

Q24.2 Suppose several different parallel-plate capacitors are charged up by a constant-voltage source. Thinking of the actual movement and position of the charges on an atomic level, why does it make sense that the capacitances are proportional to the surface areas of the plates? Why does it make sense that the capacitances are *inversely* proportional to the distance between the plates?

Q24.3 Suppose the two plates of a capacitor have different areas. When the capacitor is charged by connecting it to a battery, do the charges on the two plates have equal magnitude, or may they be different? Explain your reasoning.

Q24.4 At the Fermi National Accelerator Laboratory (Fermilab) in Illinois, protons are accelerated around a ring 2 km in radius to speeds that approach that of light. The energy for this is stored in capacitors the size of a house. When these capacitors are being charged, they make a very loud creaking sound. What is the origin of this sound?

Q24.5 In the parallel-plate capacitor of Fig. 24.2, suppose the plates are pulled apart so that the separation d is much larger than the size of the plates. (a) Is it still accurate to say that the electric field between the plates is uniform? Why or why not? (b) In the sit-

uation shown in Fig. 24.2, the potential difference between the plates is $V_{ab} = Qd/\epsilon_0 A$. If the plates are pulled apart as described above, is V_{ab} more or less than this formula would indicate? Explain your reasoning. (c) With the plates pulled apart as described above, is the capacitance more than, less than, or the same as that given by Eq. (24.2)? Explain your reasoning.

Q24.6 A parallel-plate capacitor is charged by being connected to a battery and is kept connected to the battery. The separation between the plates is then doubled. How does the electric field change? The charge on the plates? The total energy? Explain your reasoning.

Q24.7 A parallel-plate capacitor is charged by being connected to a battery and is then disconnected from the battery. The separation between the plates is then doubled. How does the electric field change? The potential difference? The total energy? Explain your reasoning.

Q24.8 Two parallel-plate capacitors, identical except that one has twice the plate separation of the other, are charged by the same voltage source. Which capacitor has a stronger electric field between the plates? Which capacitor has a greater charge? Which has greater energy density? Explain your reasoning.

Q24.9 The charged plates of a capacitor attract each other, so to pull the plates farther apart requires work by some external force. What becomes of the energy added by this work? Explain your reasoning.

Q24.10 The two plates of a capacitor are given charges $\pm Q$. The capacitor is then disconnected from the charging device so that the charges on the plates can't change, and the capacitor is immersed in a tank of oil. Does the electric field between the plates increase, decrease, or stay the same? Explain your reasoning. How can this field be measured?

Q24.11 As shown in Table 24.1, water has a very large dielectric constant $K = 80.4$. Why do you think water is not commonly used as a dielectric in capacitors?

Q24.12 Is dielectric strength the same thing as dielectric constant? Explain any differences between the two quantities. Is there a simple relationship between dielectric strength and dielectric constant (see Table 24.2)?

Q24.13 A capacitor made of aluminum foil strips separated by Mylar film was subjected to excessive voltage, and the resulting dielectric breakdown melted holes in the Mylar. After this, the capacitance was found to be about the same as before, but the breakdown voltage was much less. Why?

Q24.14 Suppose you bring a slab of dielectric close to the gap between the plates of a charged capacitor, preparing to slide it between the plates. What force will you feel? What does this force tell you about the energy stored between the plates once the dielectric is in place, compared to before the dielectric is in place?

Q24.15 The freshness of fish can be measured by placing a fish between the plates of a capacitor and measuring the capacitance. How does this work? (*Hint:* As time passes, the fish dries out. See Table 24.1.)

Q24.16 *Electrolytic* capacitors use as their dielectric an extremely thin layer of nonconducting oxide between a metal plate and a conducting solution. Discuss the advantage of such a capacitor over one constructed using a solid dielectric between the metal plates.

Q24.17 In terms of the dielectric constant K, what happens to the electric flux through the Gaussian surface shown in Fig. 24.22 when the dielectric is inserted into the previously empty space between the plates? Explain.

Q24.18 A parallel-plate capacitor is connected to a power supply that maintains a fixed potential difference between the plates. (a) If a sheet of dielectric is then slid between the plates, what happens to (i) the electric field between the plates, (ii) the magnitude of charge on each plate, and (iii) the energy stored in the capacitor? (b) Now suppose that before the dielectric is inserted, the charged capacitor is disconnected from the power supply. In this case, what happens to (i) the electric field between the plates, (ii) the magnitude of charge on each plate, and (iii) the energy stored in the capacitor? Explain any differences between the two situations.

Q24.19 Liquid dielectrics that have polar molecules (such as water) always have dielectric constants that decrease with increasing temperature. Why?

Q24.20 A conductor is an extreme case of a dielectric, since if an electric field is applied to a conductor, charges are free to move within the conductor to set up "induced charges." What is the dielectric constant of a perfect conductor? Is it $K = 0$, $K \rightarrow \infty$, or something in between? Explain your reasoning.

EXERCISES

Section 24.1 Capacitors and Capacitance

24.1 • The plates of a parallel-plate capacitor are 2.50 mm apart, and each carries a charge of magnitude 80.0 nC. The plates are in vacuum. The electric field between the plates has a magnitude of 4.00×10^6 V/m. (a) What is the potential difference between the plates? (b) What is the area of each plate? (c) What is the capacitance?

24.2 • The plates of a parallel-plate capacitor are 3.28 mm apart, and each has an area of 12.2 cm^2. Each plate carries a charge of magnitude 4.35×10^{-8} C. The plates are in vacuum. (a) What is the capacitance? (b) What is the potential difference between the plates? (c) What is the magnitude of the electric field between the plates?

24.3 • A parallel-plate air capacitor of capacitance 245 pF has a charge of magnitude 0.148 μC on each plate. The plates are 0.328 mm apart. (a) What is the potential difference between the plates? (b) What is the area of each plate? (c) What is the electric-field magnitude between the plates? (d) What is the surface charge density on each plate?

24.4 •• **Capacitance of an Oscilloscope.** Oscilloscopes have parallel metal plates inside them to deflect the electron beam. These plates are called the *deflecting plates*. Typically, they are squares 3.0 cm on a side and separated by 5.0 mm, with vacuum in between. What is the capacitance of these deflecting plates and hence of the oscilloscope? (*Note:* This capacitance can sometimes have an effect on the circuit you are trying to study and must be taken into consideration in your calculations.)

24.5 • A 10.0-μF parallel-plate capacitor with circular plates is connected to a 12.0-V battery. (a) What is the charge on each plate? (b) How much charge would be on the plates if their separation were doubled while the capacitor remained connected to the battery? (c) How much charge would be on the plates if the capacitor were connected to the 12.0-V battery after the radius of each plate was doubled without changing their separation?

24.6 • A 10.0-μF parallel-plate capacitor is connected to a 12.0-V battery. After the capacitor is fully charged, the battery is disconnected without loss of any of the charge on the plates. (a) A voltmeter is connected across the two plates without discharging them. What does it read? (b) What would the voltmeter read if (i) the plate separation were doubled; (ii) the radius of each plate were doubled but their separation was unchanged?

24.7 •• How far apart would parallel pennies have to be to make a 1.00-pF capacitor? Does your answer suggest that you are justified in treating these pennies as infinite sheets? Explain.

24.8 • A 5.00-pF, parallel-plate, air-filled capacitor with circular plates is to be used in a circuit in which it will be subjected to potentials of up to 1.00×10^2 V. The electric field between the plates is to be no greater than 1.00×10^4 N/C. As a budding electrical engineer for Live-Wire Electronics, your tasks are to (a) design the capacitor by finding what its physical dimensions and separation must be; (b) find the maximum charge these plates can hold.

24.9 • A parallel-plate air capacitor is to store charge of magnitude 240.0 pC on each plate when the potential difference between the plates is 42.0 V. (a) If the area of each plate is 6.80 cm^2, what is the separation between the plates? (b) If the separation between the two plates is double the value calculated in part (a), what potential difference is required for the capacitor to store charge of magnitude 240.0 pC on each plate?

24.10 • A cylindrical capacitor consists of a solid inner conducting core with radius 0.250 cm, surrounded by an outer hollow conducting tube. The two conductors are separated by air, and the length of the cylinder is 12.0 cm. The capacitance is 36.7 pF. (a) Calculate the inner radius of the hollow tube. (b) When the capacitor is charged to 125 V, what is the charge per unit length λ on the capacitor?

24.11 • A capacitor is made from two hollow, coaxial, iron cylinders, one inside the other. The inner cylinder is negatively charged and the outer is positively charged; the magnitude of the charge on each is 10.0 pC. The inner cylinder has radius 0.50 mm, the outer one has radius 5.00 mm, and the length of each cylinder is 18.0 cm. (a) What is the capacitance? (b) What applied potential difference is necessary to produce these charges on the cylinders?

24.12 •• A cylindrical capacitor has an inner conductor of radius 1.5 mm and an outer conductor of radius 3.5 mm. The two conductors are separated by vacuum, and the entire capacitor is 2.8 m long. (a) What is the capacitance per unit length? (b) The potential of the inner conductor is 350 mV higher than that of the outer conductor. Find the charge (magnitude and sign) on both conductors.

24.13 •• A spherical capacitor contains a charge of 3.30 nC when connected to a potential difference of 220 V. If its plates are separated by vacuum and the inner radius of the outer shell is 4.00 cm, calculate: (a) the capacitance; (b) the radius of the inner sphere; (c) the electric field just outside the surface of the inner sphere.

24.14 • A spherical capacitor is formed from two concentric, spherical, conducting shells separated by vacuum. The inner sphere has radius 15.0 cm and the capacitance is 116 pF. (a) What is the radius of the outer sphere? (b) If the potential difference between the two spheres is 220 V, what is the magnitude of charge on each sphere?

Section 24.2 Capacitors in Series and Parallel

24.15 • BIO **Electric Eels.** Electric eels and electric fish generate large potential differences that are used to stun enemies and prey. These potentials are produced by cells that each can generate 0.10 V. We can plausibly model such cells as charged capacitors. (a) How should these cells be connected (in series or in parallel) to produce a total potential of more than 0.10 V? (b) Using the connection in part (a), how many cells must be connected together to produce the 500-V surge of the electric eel?

24.16 • For the system of capacitors shown in Fig. E24.16, find the equivalent capacitance (a) between b and c, and (b) between a and c.

24.17 • In Fig. E24.17, each capacitor has $C = 4.00 \ \mu F$ and $V_{ab} = +28.0$ V. Calculate (a) the charge on each capacitor; (b) the potential difference across each capacitor; (c) the potential difference between points a and d.

24.18 • In Fig. 24.8a, let $C_1 = 3.00 \ \mu F$, $C_2 = 5.00 \ \mu F$, and $V_{ab} = +52.0$ V. Calculate (a) the charge on each capacitor and (b) the potential difference across each capacitor.

24.19 • In Fig. 24.9a, let $C_1 = 3.00 \ \mu F$, $C_2 = 5.00 \ \mu F$, and $V_{ab} = +52.0$ V. Calculate (a) the charge on each capacitor and (b) the potential difference across each capacitor.

24.20 • In Fig. E24.20, $C_1 = 6.00 \ \mu F$, $C_2 = 3.00 \ \mu F$, and $C_3 = 5.00 \ \mu F$. The capacitor network is connected to an applied potential V_{ab}. After the charges on the capacitors have reached their final values, the charge on C_2 is 40.0 μC. (a) What are the charges on capacitors C_1 and C_3? (b) What is the applied voltage V_{ab}?

24.21 •• For the system of capacitors shown in Fig. E24.21, a potential difference of 25 V is maintained across ab. (a) What is the equivalent capacitance of this system between a and b? (b) How much charge is stored by this system? (c) How much charge does the 6.5-nF capacitor store? (d) What is the potential difference across the 7.5-nF capacitor?

24.22 • Figure E24.22 shows a system of four capacitors, where the potential difference across ab is 50.0 V. (a) Find the equivalent capacitance of this system between a and b. (b) How much charge is stored by this combination of capacitors? (c) How much charge is stored in each of the 10.0-μF and the 9.0-μF capacitors?

24.23 •• Suppose the 3-μF capacitor in Fig. 24.10a were removed and replaced by a different one, and that this changed the equivalent capacitance between points a and b to 8 μF. What would be the capacitance of the replacement capacitor?

Section 24.3 Energy Storage in Capacitors and Electric-Field Energy

24.24 • A parallel-plate air capacitor has a capacitance of 920 pF. The charge on each plate is 2.55 μC. (a) What is the potential difference between the plates? (b) If the charge is kept constant, what will be the potential difference between the plates if the separation is doubled? (c) How much work is required to double the separation?

24.25 • A 5.80-μF, parallel-plate, air capacitor has a plate separation of 5.00 mm and is charged to a potential difference of 400 V. Calculate the energy density in the region between the plates, in units of J/m³.

24.26 • An air capacitor is made from two flat parallel plates 1.50 mm apart. The magnitude of charge on each plate is 0.0180 μC when the potential difference is 200 V. (a) What is the capacitance? (b) What is the area of each plate? (c) What maximum voltage can be applied without dielectric breakdown? (Dielectric breakdown for air occurs at an electric-field strength of 3.0×10^6 V/m.) (d) When the charge is 0.0180 μC, what total energy is stored?

24.27 • A parallel-plate vacuum capacitor with plate area A and separation x has charges $+Q$ and $-Q$ on its plates. The capacitor is disconnected from the source of charge, so the charge on each plate remains fixed. (a) What is the total energy stored in the capacitor? (b) The plates are pulled apart an additional distance dx. What is the change in the stored energy? (c) If F is the force with

Figure **E24.16**

Figure **E24.17**

Figure **E24.20**

Figure **E24.21**

Figure **E24.22**

which the plates attract each other, then the change in the stored energy must equal the work $dW = F\,dx$ done in pulling the plates apart. Find an expression for F. (d) Explain why F is *not* equal to QE, where E is the electric field between the plates.

24.28 •• A parallel-plate vacuum capacitor has 8.38 J of energy stored in it. The separation between the plates is 2.30 mm. If the separation is decreased to 1.15 mm, what is the energy stored (a) if the capacitor is disconnected from the potential source so the charge on the plates remains constant, and (b) if the capacitor remains connected to the potential source so the potential difference between the plates remains constant?

24.29 • You have two identical capacitors and an external potential source. (a) Compare the total energy stored in the capacitors when they are connected to the applied potential in series and in parallel. (b) Compare the maximum amount of charge stored in each case. (c) Energy storage in a capacitor can be limited by the maximum electric field between the plates. What is the ratio of the electric field for the series and parallel combinations?

24.30 • For the capacitor network shown in Fig. E24.30, the potential difference across ab is 36 V. Find (a) the total charge stored in this network; (b) the charge on each capacitor; (c) the total energy stored in the network; (d) the energy stored in each capacitor; (e) the potential differences across each capacitor.

Figure **E24.30**

24.31 • For the capacitor network shown in Fig. E24.31, the potential difference across ab is 220 V. Find (a) the total charge stored in this network; (b) the charge on each capacitor; (c) the total energy stored in the network; (d) the energy stored in each capacitor; (e) the potential difference across each capacitor.

Figure **E24.31**

24.32 • A 0.350-m-long cylindrical capacitor consists of a solid conducting core with a radius of 1.20 mm and an outer hollow conducting tube with an inner radius of 2.00 mm. The two conductors are separated by air and charged to a potential difference of 6.00 V. Calculate (a) the charge per length for the capacitor; (b) the total charge on the capacitor; (c) the capacitance; (d) the energy stored in the capacitor when fully charged.

24.33 • A cylindrical air capacitor of length 15.0 m stores 3.20×10^{-9} J of energy when the potential difference between the two conductors is 4.00 V. (a) Calculate the magnitude of the charge on each conductor. (b) Calculate the ratio of the radii of the inner and outer conductors.

24.34 •• A capacitor is formed from two concentric spherical conducting shells separated by vacuum. The inner sphere has radius 12.5 cm, and the outer sphere has radius 14.8 cm. A potential difference of 120 V is applied to the capacitor. (a) What is the energy density at $r = 12.6$ cm, just outside the inner sphere? (b) What is the energy density at $r = 14.7$ cm, just inside the outer sphere? (c) For a parallel-plate capacitor the energy density is uniform in the region between the plates, except near the edges of the plates. Is this also true for a spherical capacitor?

Section 24.4 Dielectrics

24.35 • A 12.5-μF capacitor is connected to a power supply that keeps a constant potential difference of 24.0 V across the plates. A piece of material having a dielectric constant of 3.75 is placed between the plates, completely filling the space between them. (a) How much energy is stored in the capacitor before and after the dielectric is inserted? (b) By how much did the energy change during the insertion? Did it increase or decrease?

24.36 • A parallel-plate capacitor has capacitance $C_0 = 5.00$ pF when there is air between the plates. The separation between the plates is 1.50 mm. (a) What is the maximum magnitude of charge Q that can be placed on each plate if the electric field in the region between the plates is not to exceed 3.00×10^4 V/m? (b) A dielectric with $K = 2.70$ is inserted between the plates of the capacitor, completely filling the volume between the plates. Now what is the maximum magnitude of charge on each plate if the electric field between the plates is not to exceed 3.00×10^4 V/m?

24.37 • Two parallel plates have equal and opposite charges. When the space between the plates is evacuated, the electric field is $E = 3.20 \times 10^5$ V/m. When the space is filled with dielectric, the electric field is $E = 2.50 \times 10^5$ V/m. (a) What is the charge density on each surface of the dielectric? (b) What is the dielectric constant?

24.38 • A budding electronics hobbyist wants to make a simple 1.0-nF capacitor for tuning her crystal radio, using two sheets of aluminum foil as plates, with a few sheets of paper between them as a dielectric. The paper has a dielectric constant of 3.0, and the thickness of one sheet of it is 0.20 mm. (a) If the sheets of paper measure 22×28 cm and she cuts the aluminum foil to the same dimensions, how many sheets of paper should she use between her plates to get the proper capacitance? (b) Suppose for convenience she wants to use a single sheet of posterboard, with the same dielectric constant but a thickness of 12.0 mm, instead of the paper. What area of aluminum foil will she need for her plates to get her 1.0 nF of capacitance? (c) Suppose she goes high-tech and finds a sheet of Teflon of the same thickness as the posterboard to use as a dielectric. Will she need a larger or smaller area of Teflon than of posterboard? Explain.

24.39 • The dielectric to be used in a parallel-plate capacitor has a dielectric constant of 3.60 and a dielectric strength of 1.60×10^7 V/m. The capacitor is to have a capacitance of 1.25×10^{-9} F and must be able to withstand a maximum potential difference of 5500 V. What is the minimum area the plates of the capacitor may have?

24.40 •• **BIO** **Potential in Human Cells.** Some cell walls in the human body have a layer of negative charge on the inside surface and a layer of positive charge of equal magnitude on the outside surface. Suppose that the charge density on either surface is $\pm 0.50 \times 10^{-3}$ C/m^2, the cell wall is 5.0 nm thick, and the cell-wall material is air. (a) Find the magnitude of $\vec{E}$ in the wall between the two layers of charge. (b) Find the potential difference between the inside and the outside of the cell. Which is at the higher potential? (c) A typical cell in the human body has a volume of 10^{-16} m^3. Estimate the total electric-field energy stored in the wall of a cell of this size. (*Hint:* Assume that the cell is spherical, and calculate the volume of the cell wall.) (d) In reality, the cell wall is made up, not of air, but of tissue with a dielectric constant of 5.4. Repeat parts (a) and (b) in this case.

24.41 • A capacitor has parallel plates of area 12 cm^2 separated by 2.0 mm. The space between the plates is filled with polystyrene (see Table 24.2). (a) Find the permittivity of polystyrene. (b) Find the maximum permissible voltage across the capacitor to avoid dielectric breakdown. (c) When the voltage equals the value found in part (b), find the surface charge density on each plate and the induced surface charge density on the surface of the dielectric.

24.42 • A constant potential difference of 12 V is maintained between the terminals of a 0.25-μF, parallel-plate, air capacitor. (a) A sheet of Mylar is inserted between the plates of the capacitor, completely filling the space between the plates. When this is done, how much additional charge flows onto the positive plate of the capacitor (see Table 24.1)? (b) What is the total induced charge on either face of the Mylar sheet? (c) What effect does the Mylar sheet have on the electric field between the plates? Explain how you can reconcile this with the increase in charge on the plates, which acts to *increase* the electric field.

24.43 • When a 360-nF air capacitor $(1 \text{ nF} = 10^{-9}$ F$)$ is connected to a power supply, the energy stored in the capacitor is 1.85×10^{-5} J. While the capacitor is kept connected to the power supply, a slab of dielectric is inserted that completely fills the space between the plates. This increases the stored energy by 2.32×10^{-5} J. (a) What is the potential difference between the capacitor plates? (b) What is the dielectric constant of the slab?

24.44 • A parallel-plate capacitor has capacitance $C = 12.5$ pF when the volume between the plates is filled with air. The plates are circular, with radius 3.00 cm. The capacitor is connected to a battery, and a charge of magnitude 25.0 pC goes onto each plate. With the capacitor still connected to the battery, a slab of dielectric is inserted between the plates, completely filling the space between the plates. After the dielectric has been inserted, the charge on each plate has magnitude 45.0 pC. (a) What is the dielectric constant K of the dielectric? (b) What is the potential difference between the plates before and after the dielectric has been inserted? (c) What is the electric field at a point midway between the plates before and after the dielectric has been inserted?

Section 24.6 Gauss's Law in Dielectrics

24.45 • A parallel-plate capacitor has the volume between its plates filled with plastic with dielectric constant K. The magnitude of the charge on each plate is Q. Each plate has area A, and the distance between the plates is d. (a) Use Gauss's law as stated in Eq. (24.23) to calculate the magnitude of the electric field in the dielectric. (b) Use the electric field determined in part (a) to calculate the potential difference between the two plates. (c) Use the result of part (b) to determine the capacitance of the capacitor. Compare your result to Eq. (24.12).

24.46 • A parallel-plate capacitor has plates with area 0.0225 m^2 separated by 1.00 mm of Teflon. (a) Calculate the charge on the plates when they are charged to a potential difference of 12.0 V. (b) Use Gauss's law (Eq. 24.23) to calculate the electric field inside the Teflon. (c) Use Gauss's law to calculate the electric field if the voltage source is disconnected and the Teflon is removed.

PROBLEMS

24.47 • Electronic flash units for cameras contain a capacitor for storing the energy used to produce the flash. In one such unit, the flash lasts for $\frac{1}{675}$ s with an average light power output of 2.70×10^5 W. (a) If the conversion of electrical energy to light is 95% efficient (the rest of the energy goes to thermal energy), how much energy must be stored in the capacitor for one flash? (b) The capacitor has a potential difference between its plates of 125 V when the stored energy equals the value calculated in part (a). What is the capacitance?

24.48 • A parallel-plate air capacitor is made by using two plates 16 cm square, spaced 3.7 mm apart. It is connected to a 12-V battery. (a) What is the capacitance? (b) What is the charge on each plate? (c) What is the electric field between the plates? (d) What is the energy stored in the capacitor? (e) If the battery is disconnected and then the plates are pulled apart to a separation of 7.4 mm, what are the answers to parts (a)–(d)?

24.49 •• Suppose the battery in Problem 24.48 remains connected while the plates are pulled apart. What are the answers then to parts (a)–(d) after the plates have been pulled apart?

24.50 ••• **BIO Cell Membranes.** Cell membranes (the walled enclosure around a cell) are typically about 7.5 nm thick. They are partially permeable to allow charged material to pass in and out, as needed. Equal but opposite charge densities build up on the inside and outside faces of such a membrane, and these charges prevent additional charges from passing through the cell wall. We can model a cell membrane as a parallel-plate capacitor, with the membrane itself containing proteins embedded in an organic material to give the membrane a dielectric constant of about 10. (See Fig. P24.50.) (a) What is the capacitance per square centimeter of such a cell wall? (b) In its normal resting state, a cell has a potential difference of 85 mV across its membrane. What is the electric field inside this membrane?

Figure **P24.50**

24.51 • A capacitor is made from two hollow, coaxial copper cylinders, one inside the other. There is air in the space between the cylinders. The inner cylinder has net positive charge and the outer cylinder has net negative charge. The inner cylinder has radius 2.50 mm, the outer cylinder has radius 3.10 mm, and the length of each cylinder is 36.0 cm. If the potential difference between the surfaces of the two cylinders is 80.0 V, what is the magnitude of the electric field at a point between the two cylinders that is a distance of 2.80 mm from their common axis and midway between the ends of the cylinders?

24.52 ••• In one type of computer keyboard, each key holds a small metal plate that serves as one plate of a parallel-plate, air-filled capacitor. When the key is depressed, the plate separation decreases and the capacitance increases. Electronic circuitry detects the change in capacitance and thus detects that the key has been pressed. In one particular keyboard, the area of each metal plate is 42.0 mm^2, and the separation between the plates is 0.700 mm before the key is depressed. (a) Calculate the capacitance before the key is depressed. (b) If the circuitry can detect a change in capacitance of 0.250 pF, how far must the key be depressed before the circuitry detects its depression?

24.53 •• A 20.0-μF capacitor is charged to a potential difference of 800 V. The terminals of the charged capacitor are then connected to those of an uncharged 10.0-μF capacitor. Compute (a) the original charge of the system, (b) the final potential difference across each capacitor, (c) the final energy of the system, and (d) the decrease in energy when the capacitors are connected.

24.54 •• In Fig. 24.9a, let $C_1 = 9.0 \ \mu$F, $C_2 = 4.0 \ \mu$F, and $V_{ab} = 36$ V. Suppose the charged capacitors are disconnected from the source and from each other, and then reconnected to each other with plates of *opposite* sign together. By how much does the energy of the system decrease?

24.55 • For the capacitor network shown in Fig. P24.55, the potential difference across ab is 12.0 V. Find (a) the total energy stored in this network and (b) the energy stored in the 4.80-μF capacitor.

Figure **P24.55**

24.56 ·· Several 0.25-μF capacitors are available. The voltage across each is not to exceed 600 V. You need to make a capacitor with capacitance 0.25 μF to be connected across a potential difference of 960 V. (a) Show in a diagram how an equivalent capacitor with the desired properties can be obtained. (b) No dielectric is a perfect insulator that would not permit the flow of any charge through its volume. Suppose that the dielectric in one of the capacitors in your diagram is a moderately good conductor. What will happen in this case when your combination of capacitors is connected across the 960-V potential difference?

24.57 · In Fig. P24.57, $C_1 = C_5 = 8.4$ μF and $C_2 = C_3 = C_4 = 4.2$ μF. The applied potential is $V_{ab} = 220$ V. (a) What is the equivalent capacitance of the network between points a and b? (b) Calculate the charge on each capacitor and the potential difference across each capacitor.

Figure **P24.57**

24.58 ·· You are working on an electronics project requiring a variety of capacitors, but you have only a large supply of 100-nF capacitors available. Show how you can connect these capacitors to produce each of the following equivalent capacitances: (a) 50 nF; (b) 450 nF; (c) 25 nF; (d) 75 nF.

24.59 ·· In Fig. E24.20, $C_1 = 3.00$ μF and $V_{ab} = 150$ V. The charge on capacitor C_1 is 150 μC and the charge on C_3 is 450 μC. What are the values of the capacitances of C_2 and C_3?

24.60 · The capacitors in Fig. P24.60 are initially uncharged and are connected, as in the diagram, with switch S open. The applied potential difference is $V_{ab} = +210$ V. (a) What is the potential difference V_{cd}? (b) What is the potential difference across each capacitor after switch S is closed? (c) How much charge flowed through the switch when it was closed?

Figure **P24.60**

24.61 ·· Three capacitors having capacitances of 8.4, 8.4, and 4.2 μF are connected in series across a 36-V potential difference. (a) What is the charge on the 4.2-μF capacitor? (b) What is the total energy stored in all three capacitors? (c) The capacitors are disconnected from the potential difference without allowing them to discharge. They are then reconnected in parallel with each other, with the positively charged plates connected together. What is the voltage across each capacitor in the parallel combination? (d) What is the total energy now stored in the capacitors?

24.62 · **Capacitance of a Thundercloud.** The charge center of a thundercloud, drifting 3.0 km above the earth's surface, contains 20 C of negative charge. Assuming the charge center has a radius of 1.0 km, and modeling the charge center and the earth's surface as parallel plates, calculate: (a) the capacitance of the system; (b)

the potential difference between charge center and ground; (c) the average strength of the electric field between cloud and ground; (d) the electrical energy stored in the system.

24.63 ·· In Fig. P24.63, each capacitance C_1 is 6.9 μF, and each capacitance C_2 is 4.6 μF. (a) Compute the equivalent capacitance of the network between points a and b. (b) Compute the charge on each of the three capacitors nearest a and b when $V_{ab} = 420$ V. (c) With 420 V across a and b, compute V_{cd}.

Figure **P24.63**

24.64 · Each combination of capacitors between points a and b in Fig. P24.64 is first connected across a 120-V battery, charging the combination to 120 V. These combinations are then connected to make the circuits shown. When the switch S is thrown, a surge of charge for the discharging capacitors flows to trigger the signal device. How much charge flows through the signal device in each case?

Figure **P24.64**

(a)

(b)

24.65 · A parallel-plate capacitor with only air between the plates is charged by connecting it to a battery. The capacitor is then disconnected from the battery, without any of the charge leaving the plates. (a) A voltmeter reads 45.0 V when placed across the capacitor. When a dielectric is inserted between the plates, completely filling the space, the voltmeter reads 11.5 V. What is the dielectric constant of this material? (b) What will the voltmeter read if the dielectric is now pulled partway out so it fills only one-third of the space between the plates?

24.66 ·· An air capacitor is made by using two flat plates, each with area A, separated by a distance d. Then a metal slab having thickness a (less than d) and the same shape and size as the plates is inserted between them, parallel to the plates and not touching either plate (Fig. P24.66). (a) What is the capacitance of this arrangement? (b) Express the capacitance as a multiple of the capacitance C_0 when the metal slab is not present. (c) Discuss what happens to the capacitance in the limits $a \to 0$ and $a \to d$.

Figure **P24.66**

24.67 ·· **Capacitance of the Earth.** Consider a spherical capacitor with one conductor being a solid conducting sphere of radius R and the other conductor being at infinity. (a) Use Eq. (24.1) and what you know about the potential at the surface of a conducting sphere with charge Q to derive an expression for the capacitance of the charged sphere. (b) Use your result in part (a) to calculate the capacitance of the earth. The earth is a good conductor and has a radius of 6380 km. Compare your results to the capacitance of typical capacitors used in electronic circuits, which ranges from 10 pF to 100 pF.

24.68 ·· A potential difference $V_{ab} = 48.0$ V is applied across the capacitor network of Fig. E24.17. If $C_1 = C_2 = 4.00$ μF and

$C_4 = 8.00 \ \mu F$, what must the capacitance C_3 be if the network is to store 2.90×10^{-3} J of electrical energy?

24.69 • **Earth-Ionosphere Capacitance.** The earth can be considered as a single-conductor capacitor (see Problem 24.67). It can also be considered in combination with a charged layer of the atmosphere, the ionosphere, as a spherical capacitor with two plates, the surface of the earth being the negative plate. The ionosphere is at a level of about 70 km, and the potential difference between earth and ionosphere is about 350,000 V. Calculate: (a) the capacitance of this system; (b) the total charge on the capacitor; (c) the energy stored in the system.

24.70 • **CALC** The inner cylinder of a long, cylindrical capacitor has radius r_a and linear charge density $+\lambda$. It is surrounded by a coaxial cylindrical conducting shell with inner radius r_b and linear charge density $-\lambda$ (see Fig. 24.6). (a) What is the energy density in the region between the conductors at a distance r from the axis? (b) Integrate the energy density calculated in part (a) over the volume between the conductors in a length L of the capacitor to obtain the total electric-field energy per unit length. (c) Use Eq. (24.9) and the capacitance per unit length calculated in Example 24.4 (Section 24.1) to calculate U/L. Does your result agree with that obtained in part (b)?

24.71 •• **CP** A capacitor has a potential difference of 2.25×10^3 V between its plates. A short aluminum wire with initial temperature $23.0°C$ is connected between the plates of the capacitor and all the energy stored in the capacitor goes into heating the wire. The wire has mass 12.0 g. If no heat is lost to the surroundings and the final temperature of the wire is $34.2°C$, what is the capacitance of the capacitor?

24.72 •• A parallel-plate capacitor is made from two plates 12.0 cm on each side and 4.50 mm apart. Half of the space between these plates contains only air, but the other half is filled with Plexiglas® of dielectric constant 3.40 (Fig. P24.72). An 18.0-V battery is connected across the plates. (a) What is the capacitance of this combination? (*Hint:* Can you think of this capacitor as equivalent to two capacitors in parallel?) (b) How much energy is stored in the capacitor? (c) If we remove the Plexiglas® but change nothing else, how much energy will be stored in the capacitor?

Figure **P24.72**

24.73 •• A parallel-plate capacitor has square plates that are 8.00 cm on each side and 3.80 mm apart. The space between the plates is completely filled with two square slabs of dielectric, each 8.00 cm on a side and 1.90 mm thick. One slab is pyrex glass and the other is polystyrene. If the potential difference between the plates is 86.0 V, how much electrical energy is stored in the capacitor?

24.74 •• A fuel gauge uses a capacitor to determine the height of the fuel in a tank. The effective dielectric constant K_{eff} changes from a value of 1 when the tank is empty to a value of K, the dielectric constant of the fuel, when the tank is full. The appropriate electronic circuitry can determine the effective dielectric constant of the combined air and fuel between the capacitor plates. Each of the two rectangular plates has a width

Figure **P24.74**

w and a length L (Fig. P24.74). The height of the fuel between the plates is h. You can ignore any fringing effects. (a) Derive an expression for K_{eff} as a function of h. (b) What is the effective dielectric constant for a tank $\frac{1}{4}$ full, $\frac{1}{2}$ full, and $\frac{3}{4}$ full if the fuel is gasoline $(K = 1.95)$? (c) Repeat part (b) for methanol $(K = 33.0)$? (d) For which fuel is this fuel gauge more practical?

24.75 •• Three square metal plates A, B, and C, each 12.0 cm on a side and 1.50 mm thick, are arranged as in Fig. P24.75. The plates are separated by sheets of paper 0.45 mm thick and with dielectric constant 4.2. The outer plates are connected together and connected to point b. The inner plate is connected to point a. (a) Copy the diagram and show by plus and minus signs the charge distribution on the plates when point a is maintained at a positive potential relative to point b. (b) What is the capacitance between points a and b?

Figure **P24.75**

CHALLENGE PROBLEMS

24.76 ••• **CP** The parallel-plate air capacitor in Fig. P24.76 consists of two horizontal conducting plates of equal area A. The bottom plate rests on a fixed support, and the top plate is suspended by four springs with spring constant k, positioned at each of the four corners of the top plate as shown in the figure. When uncharged, the plates are separated by a distance z_0. A battery is connected to the plates and produces a potential difference V between them. This causes the plate separation to decrease to z. Neglect any fringing effects. (a) Show that the electrostatic force between the charged plates has a magnitude $\epsilon_0 AV^2/2z^2$. (*Hint:* See Exercise 24.27.) (b) Obtain an expression that relates the plate separation z to the potential difference V. The resulting equation will be cubic in z. (c) Given the values $A = 0.300 \ m^2$, $z_0 = 1.20$ mm, $k = 25.0$ N/m, and $V = 120$ V, find the two values of z for which the top plate will be in equilibrium. (*Hint:* You can solve the cubic equation by plugging a trial value of z into the equation and then adjusting your guess until the equation is satisfied to three significant figures. Locating the roots of the cubic equation graphically can help you pick starting values of z for this trial-and-error procedure. One root of the cubic equation has a nonphysical negative value.) (d) For each of the two values of z found in part (c), is the equilibrium stable or unstable? For stable equilibrium a small displacement of the object will give rise to a net force tending to return the object to the equilibrium position. For unstable equilibrium a small displacement gives rise to a net force that takes the object farther away from equilibrium.

Figure **P24.76**

24.77 ••• Two square conducting plates with sides of length L are separated by a distance D. A dielectric slab with constant K with dimensions $L \times L \times D$ is inserted a distance x into the space between the plates, as shown in Fig. P24.77. (a) Find the capacitance

C of this system. (b) Suppose that the capacitor is connected to a battery that maintains a constant potential difference V between the plates. If the dielectric slab is inserted an additional distance dx into the space between the plates, show that the change in stored energy is

$$dU = +\frac{(K-1)\epsilon_0 V^2 L}{2D}dx$$

Figure **P24.77**

Dielectric slab, constant K

(c) Suppose that before the slab is moved by dx, the plates are disconnected from the battery, so that the charges on the plates remain constant. Determine the magnitude of the charge on each plate, and then show that when the slab is moved dx farther into the space between the plates, the stored energy changes by an amount that is the *negative* of the expression for dU given in part (b). (d) If F is the force exerted on the slab by the charges on the plates, then dU should equal the work done *against* this force to move the slab a distance dx. Thus $dU = -F\,dx$. Show that applying this expression to the result of part (b) suggests that the electric force on the slab pushes it *out* of the capacitor, while the result of part (c) suggests that the force

pulls the slab *into* the capacitor. (e) Figure 24.16 shows that the force in fact pulls the slab into the capacitor. Explain why the result of part (b) gives an incorrect answer for the direction of this force, and calculate the magnitude of the force. (This method does not require knowledge of the nature of the fringing field.)

24.78 ••• An isolated spherical capacitor has charge $+Q$ on its inner conductor (radius r_a) and charge $-Q$ on its outer conductor (radius r_b). Half of the volume between the two conductors is then filled with a liquid dielectric of constant K, as shown in cross section in Fig. P24.78. (a) Find the capacitance of the half-filled capacitor. (b) Find the magnitude of $\vec{E}$ in the volume between the two conductors as a function of the distance r from the center of the capacitor. Give answers for both the upper and lower halves of this volume. (c) Find the surface density of free charge on the upper and lower halves of the inner and outer conductors. (d) Find the surface density of bound charge on the inner ($r = r_a$) and outer ($r = r_b$) surfaces of the dielectric. (e) What is the surface density of bound charge on the flat surface of the dielectric? Explain.

Figure **P24.78**

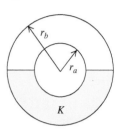

Answers

Chapter Opening Question ?

Equation (24.9) shows that the energy stored in a capacitor with capacitance C and charge Q is $U = Q^2/2C$. If the charge Q is doubled, the stored energy increases by a factor of $2^2 = 4$. Note that if the value of Q is too great, the electric-field magnitude inside the capacitor will exceed the dielectric strength of the material between the plates and dielectric breakdown will occur (see Section 24.4). This puts a practical limit on the amount of energy that can be stored.

Test Your Understanding Questions

24.1 Answer: (iii) The capacitance does not depend on the value of the charge Q. Doubling the value of Q causes the potential difference V_{ab} to double, so the capacitance $C = Q/V_{ab}$ remains the same. These statements are true no matter what the geometry of the capacitor.

24.2 Answers: (a) (i), (b) (iv) In a series connection the two capacitors carry the same charge Q but have different potential differences $V_{ab} = Q/C$; the capacitor with the smaller capacitance C has the greater potential difference. In a parallel connection the two capacitors have the same potential difference V_{ab} but carry different charges $Q = CV_{ab}$; the capacitor with the larger capacitance C has the greater charge. Hence a 4-μF capacitor will have a greater potential difference than an 8-μF capacitor if the two are connected in series. The 4-μF capacitor cannot carry more charge than the 8-μF capacitor no matter how they are connected: In a series connection they will carry the same charge, and in a parallel connection the 8-μF capacitor will carry more charge.

24.3 Answer: (i) Capacitors connected in series carry the same charge Q. To compare the amount of energy stored, we use the expression $U = Q^2/2C$ from Eq. (24.9); it shows that the capacitor with the *smaller* capacitance ($C = 4\,\mu$F) has more stored

energy in a series combination. By contrast, capacitors in parallel have the same potential difference V, so to compare them we use $U = \frac{1}{2}CV^2$ from Eq. (24.9). It shows that in a parallel combination, the capacitor with the *larger* capacitance ($C = 8\,\mu$F) has more stored energy. (If we had instead used $U = \frac{1}{2}CV^2$ to analyze the series combination, we would have to account for the different potential differences across the two capacitors. Likewise, using $U = Q^2/2C$ to study the parallel combination would require us to account for the different charges on the capacitors.)

24.4 Answer: (i) Here Q remains the same, so we use $U = Q^2/2C$ from Eq. (24.9) for the stored energy. Removing the dielectric lowers the capacitance by a factor of $1/K$; since U is inversely proportional to C, the stored energy *increases* by a factor of K. It takes work to pull the dielectric slab out of the capacitor because the fringing field tries to pull the slab back in (Fig. 24.16). The work that you do goes into the energy stored in the capacitor.

24.5 Answer: (i), (iii), (ii) Equation (24.14) says that if E_0 is the initial electric-field magnitude (before the dielectric slab is inserted), then the resultant field magnitude after the slab is inserted is $E_0/K = E_0/3$. The magnitude of the resultant field equals the difference between the initial field magnitude and the magnitude E_i of the field due to the bound charges (see Fig. 24.20). Hence $E_0 - E_i = E_0/3$ and $E_i = 2E_0/3$.

24.6 Answer: (iii) Equation (24.23) shows that this situation is the same as an isolated point charge in vacuum but with $\vec{E}$ replaced by $K\vec{E}$. Hence KE at the point of interest is equal to $q/4\pi\epsilon_0 r^2$, and so $E = q/4\pi K\epsilon_0 r^2$. As in Example 24.12, filling the space with a dielectric reduces the electric field by a factor of $1/K$.

Bridging Problem

Answers: (a) 0   **(b)** $Q^2/32\pi^2\epsilon_0 r^4$ **(c)** $Q^2/8\pi\epsilon_0 R$
       (d) $Q^2/8\pi\epsilon_0 R$ **(e)** $C = 4\pi\epsilon_0 R$

CURRENT, RESISTANCE, AND ELECTROMOTIVE FORCE

LEARNING GOALS

By studying this chapter, you will learn:

- The meaning of electric current, and how charges move in a conductor.

- What is meant by the resistivity and conductivity of a substance.

- How to calculate the resistance of a conductor from its dimensions and its resistivity.

- How an electromotive force (emf) makes it possible for current to flow in a circuit.

- How to do calculations involving energy and power in circuits.

? In a flashlight, is the amount of current that flows out of the bulb less than, greater than, or equal to the amount of current that flows into the bulb?

I n the past four chapters we studied the interactions of electric charges *at rest;* now we're ready to study charges *in motion.* An *electric current* consists of charges in motion from one region to another. If the charges follow a conducting path that forms a closed loop, the path is called an *electric circuit.*

Fundamentally, electric circuits are a means for conveying *energy* from one place to another. As charged particles move within a circuit, electric potential energy is transferred from a source (such as a battery or generator) to a device in which that energy is either stored or converted to another form: into sound in a stereo system or into heat and light in a toaster or light bulb. Electric circuits are useful because they allow energy to be transported without any moving parts (other than the moving charged particles themselves). They are at the heart of flashlights, computers, radio and television transmitters and receivers, and household and industrial power distribution systems. Your nervous system is a specialized electric circuit that carries vital signals from one part of your body to another.

In Chapter 26 we will see how to analyze electric circuits and will examine some practical applications of circuits. Before we can do so, however, you must understand the basic properties of electric currents. These properties are the subject of this chapter. We'll begin by describing the nature of electric conductors and considering how they are affected by temperature. We'll learn why a short, fat, cold copper wire is a better conductor than a long, skinny, hot steel wire. We'll study the properties of batteries and see how they cause current and energy transfer in a circuit. In this analysis we will use the concepts of current, potential difference (or voltage), resistance, and electromotive force. Finally, we'll look at electric current in a material from a microscopic viewpoint.

25.1 Current

A **current** is any motion of charge from one region to another. In this section we'll discuss currents in conducting materials. The vast majority of technological applications of charges in motion involve currents of this kind.

In electrostatic situations (discussed in Chapters 21 through 24) the electric field is zero everywhere within the conductor, and there is *no* current. However, this does not mean that all charges within the conductor are at rest. In an ordinary metal such as copper or alumium, some of the electrons are free to move within the conducting material. These free electrons move randomly in all directions, somewhat like the molecules of a gas but with much greater speeds, of the order of 10^6 m/s. The electrons nonetheless do not escape from the conducting material, because they are attracted to the positive ions of the material. The motion of the electrons is random, so there is no *net* flow of charge in any direction and hence no current.

Now consider what happens if a constant, steady electric field $\vec{E}$ is established inside a conductor. (We'll see later how this can be done.) A charged particle (such as a free electron) inside the conducting material is then subjected to a steady force $\vec{F} = q\vec{E}$. If the charged particle were moving in *vacuum*, this steady force would cause a steady acceleration in the direction of $\vec{F}$, and after a time the charged particle would be moving in that direction at high speed. But a charged particle moving in a *conductor* undergoes frequent collisions with the massive, nearly stationary ions of the material. In each such collision the particle's direction of motion undergoes a random change. The net effect of the electric field $\vec{E}$ is that in addition to the random motion of the charged particles within the conductor, there is also a very slow net motion or *drift* of the moving charged particles as a group in the direction of the electric force $\vec{F} = q\vec{E}$ (Fig. 25.1). This motion is described in terms of the **drift velocity** $\vec{v}_d$ of the particles. As a result, there is a net current in the conductor.

While the random motion of the electrons has a very fast average speed of about 10^6 m/s, the drift speed is very slow, often on the order of 10^{-4} m/s. Given that the electrons move so slowly, you may wonder why the light comes on immediately when you turn on the switch of a flashlight. The reason is that the electric field is set up in the wire with a speed approaching the speed of light, and electrons start to move all along the wire at very nearly the same time. The time that it takes any individual electron to get from the switch to the light bulb isn't really relevant. A good analogy is a group of soldiers standing at attention when the sergeant orders them to start marching; the order reaches the soldiers' ears at the speed of sound, which is much faster than their marching speed, so all the soldiers start to march essentially in unison.

The Direction of Current Flow

The drift of moving charges through a conductor can be interpreted in terms of work and energy. The electric field $\vec{E}$ does work on the moving charges. The resulting kinetic energy is transferred to the material of the conductor by means of collisions with the ions, which vibrate about their equilibrium positions in the crystalline structure of the conductor. This energy transfer increases the average vibrational energy of the ions and therefore the temperature of the material. Thus much of the work done by the electric field goes into heating the conductor, *not* into making the moving charges move ever faster and faster. This heating is sometimes useful, as in an electric toaster, but in many situations is simply an unavoidable by-product of current flow.

In different current-carrying materials, the charges of the moving particles may be positive or negative. In metals the moving charges are always (negative) electrons, while in an ionized gas (plasma) or an ionic solution the moving charges may include both electrons and positively charged ions. In a semiconductor

25.1 If there is no electric field inside a conductor, an electron moves randomly from point P_1 to point P_2 in a time Δt. If an electric field $\vec{E}$ is present, the electric force $\vec{F} = q\vec{E}$ imposes a small drift (greatly exaggerated here) that takes the electron to point P_2', a distance $v_d\Delta t$ from P_2 in the direction of the force.

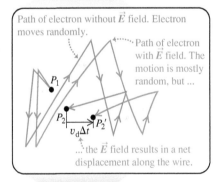

Conductor without internal $\vec{E}$ field

Path of electron without $\vec{E}$ field. Electron moves randomly.

Path of electron with $\vec{E}$ field. The motion is mostly random, but ...

P_1

P_2

P_2'

$v_d\Delta t$

...the $\vec{E}$ field results in a net displacement along the wire.

Conductor with internal $\vec{E}$ field

$\vec{E}$ $\vec{F} = q\vec{E}$ $\vec{E}$

An electron has a negative charge q, so the force on it due to the $\vec{E}$ field is in the direction opposite to $\vec{E}$.

25.2 The same current can be produced by (a) positive charges moving in the direction of the electric field $\vec{E}$ or (b) the same number of negative charges moving at the same speed in the direction opposite to $\vec{E}$.

(a)

A **conventional current** is treated as a flow of positive charges, regardless of whether the free charges in the conductor are positive, negative, or both.

(b)

In a metallic conductor, the moving charges are electrons — but the *current* still points in the direction positive charges would flow.

25.3 The current I is the time rate of charge transfer through the cross-sectional area A. The random component of each moving charged particle's motion averages to zero, and the current is in the same direction as $\vec{E}$ whether the moving charges are positive (as shown here) or negative (see Fig. 25.2b).

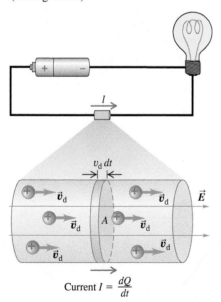

Current $I = \dfrac{dQ}{dt}$

material such as germanium or silicon, conduction is partly by electrons and partly by motion of *vacancies,* also known as *holes;* these are sites of missing electrons and act like positive charges.

Figure 25.2 shows segments of two different current-carrying materials. In Fig. 25.2a the moving charges are positive, the electric force is in the same direction as $\vec{E}$, and the drift velocity $\vec{v}_d$ is from left to right. In Fig. 25.2b the charges are negative, the electric force is opposite to $\vec{E}$, and the drift velocity $\vec{v}_d$ is from right to left. In both cases there is a net flow of positive charge from left to right, and positive charges end up to the right of negative ones. We *define* the current, denoted by I, to be in the direction in which there is a flow of *positive* charge. Thus we describe currents as though they consisted entirely of positive charge flow, even in cases in which we know that the actual current is due to electrons. Hence the current is to the right in both Figs. 25.2a and 25.2b. This choice or convention for the direction of current flow is called **conventional current.** While the direction of the conventional current is *not* necessarily the same as the direction in which charged particles are actually moving, we'll find that the sign of the moving charges is of little importance in analyzing electric circuits.

Figure 25.3 shows a segment of a conductor in which a current is flowing. We consider the moving charges to be *positive,* so they are moving in the same direction as the current. We define the current through the cross-sectional area A to be *the net charge flowing through the area per unit time.* Thus, if a net charge dQ flows through an area in a time dt, the current I through the area is

$$I = \frac{dQ}{dt} \qquad \text{(definition of current)} \qquad (25.1)$$

CAUTION **Current is not a vector** Although we refer to the *direction* of a current, current as defined by Eq. (25.1) is *not* a vector quantity. In a current-carrying wire, the current is always along the length of the wire, regardless of whether the wire is straight or curved. No single vector could describe motion along a curved path, which is why current is not a vector. We'll usually describe the direction of current either in words (as in "the current flows clockwise around the circuit") or by choosing a current to be positive if it flows in one direction along a conductor and negative if it flows in the other direction.

The SI unit of current is the **ampere;** one ampere is defined to be *one coulomb per second* (1 A = 1 C/s). This unit is named in honor of the French scientist André Marie Ampère (1775–1836). When an ordinary flashlight (D-cell size) is turned on, the current in the flashlight is about 0.5 to 1 A; the current in the wires of a car engine's starter motor is around 200 A. Currents in radio and television circuits are usually expressed in *milliamperes* ($1 \text{ mA} = 10^{-3}$ A) or *microamperes* ($1\ \mu\text{A} = 10^{-6}$ A), and currents in computer circuits are expressed in *nanoamperes* ($1 \text{ nA} = 10^{-9}$ A) or *picoamperes* ($1 \text{ pA} = 10^{-12}$ A).

Current, Drift Velocity, and Current Density

We can express current in terms of the drift velocity of the moving charges. Let's consider again the situation of Fig. 25.3 of a conductor with cross-sectional area A and an electric field $\vec{E}$ directed from left to right. To begin with, we'll assume that the free charges in the conductor are positive; then the drift velocity is in the same direction as the field.

Suppose there are n moving charged particles per unit volume. We call n the **concentration** of particles; its SI unit is m^{-3}. Assume that all the particles move with the same drift velocity with magnitude v_d. In a time interval dt, each particle moves a distance $v_d\,dt$. The particles that flow out of the right end of the shaded cylinder with length $v_d\,dt$ during dt are the particles that were within this cylinder at the beginning of the interval dt. The volume of the cylinder is $Av_d\,dt$, and the number of particles within it is $nAv_d\,dt$. If each particle has a charge q, the charge dQ that flows out of the end of the cylinder during time dt is

$$dQ = q(nAv_d \, dt) = nqv_d A \, dt$$

and the current is

$$I = \frac{dQ}{dt} = nqv_d A$$

The current *per unit cross-sectional area* is called the **current density** J:

$$J = \frac{I}{A} = nqv_d$$

The units of current density are amperes per square meter (A/m^2).

If the moving charges are negative rather than positive, as in Fig. 25.2b, the drift velocity is opposite to $\vec{E}$. But the *current* is still in the same direction as $\vec{E}$ at each point in the conductor. Hence the current I and current density J don't depend on the sign of the charge, and so in the above expressions for I and J we replace the charge q by its absolute value $|q|$:

$$I = \frac{dQ}{dt} = n|q|v_d A \qquad \text{(general expression for current)} \qquad (25.2)$$

$$J = \frac{I}{A} = n|q|v_d \qquad \text{(general expression for current density)} \qquad (25.3)$$

The current in a conductor is the product of the concentration of moving charged particles, the magnitude of charge of each such particle, the magnitude of the drift velocity, and the cross-sectional area of the conductor.

We can also define a *vector* current density $\vec{J}$ that includes the direction of the drift velocity:

$$\vec{J} = nq\vec{v}_d \qquad \text{(vector current density)} \qquad (25.4)$$

There are *no* absolute value signs in Eq. (25.4). If q is positive, $\vec{v}_d$ is in the same direction as $\vec{E}$; if q is negative, $\vec{v}_d$ is opposite to $\vec{E}$. In either case, $\vec{J}$ is in the same direction as $\vec{E}$. Equation (25.3) gives the *magnitude J* of the vector current density $\vec{J}$.

CAUTION **Current density vs. current** Note that current density $\vec{J}$ is a vector, but current I is not. The difference is that the current density $\vec{J}$ describes how charges flow at a certain point, and the vector's direction tells you about the direction of the flow at that point. By contrast, the current I describes how charges flow through an extended object such as a wire. For example, I has the same value at all points in the circuit of Fig. 25.3, but $\vec{J}$ does not: The current density is directed downward in the left-hand side of the loop and upward in the right-hand side. The magnitude of $\vec{J}$ can also vary around a circuit. In Fig. 25.3 the current density magnitude $J = I/A$ is less in the battery (which has a large cross-sectional area A) than in the wires (which have a small cross-sectional area).

25.4 Part of the electric circuit that includes this light bulb passes through a beaker with a solution of sodium chloride. The current in the solution is carried by both positive charges (Na^+ ions) and negative charges (Cl^- ions).

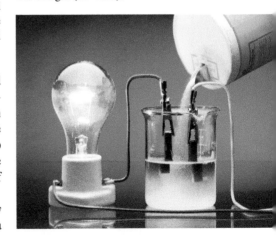

In general, a conductor may contain several different kinds of moving charged particles having charges $q_1, q_2, \ldots$, concentrations $n_1, n_2, \ldots$, and drift velocities with magnitudes $v_{d1}, v_{d2}, \ldots$. An example is current flow in an ionic solution (Fig. 25.4). In a sodium chloride solution, current can be carried by both positive sodium ions and negative chlorine ions; the total current I is found by adding up the currents due to each kind of charged particle, using Eq. (25.2). Likewise, the total vector current density $\vec{J}$ is found by using Eq. (25.4) for each kind of charged particle and adding the results.

We will see in Section 25.4 that it is possible to have a current that is *steady* (that is, one that is constant in time) only if the conducting material forms a closed loop, called a *complete circuit.* In such a steady situation, the total charge in every segment of the conductor is constant. Hence the rate of flow of charge *out* at one end of a segment at any instant equals the rate of flow of charge *in* at the other end of the segment, and *the current is the same at all cross sections of the circuit.* We'll make use of this observation when we analyze electric circuits later in this chapter.

In many simple circuits, such as flashlights or cordless electric drills, the direction of the current is always the same; this is called *direct current.* But home appliances such as toasters, refrigerators, and televisions use *alternating current,* in which the current continuously changes direction. In this chapter we'll consider direct current only. Alternating current has many special features worthy of detailed study, which we'll examine in Chapter 31.

Example 25.1 Current density and drift velocity in a wire

An 18-gauge copper wire (the size usually used for lamp cords), with a diameter of 1.02 mm, carries a constant current of 1.67 A to a 200-W lamp. The free-electron density in the wire is 8.5×10^{28} per cubic meter. Find (a) the current density and (b) the drift speed.

SOLUTION

IDENTIFY and SET UP: This problem uses the relationships among current I, current density J, and drift speed v_d. We are given I and the wire diameter d, so we use Eq. (25.3) to find J. We use Eq. (25.3) again to find v_d from J and the known electron density n.

EXECUTE: (a) The cross-sectional area is

$$A = \frac{\pi d^2}{4} = \frac{\pi (1.02 \times 10^{-3} \text{ m})^2}{4} = 8.17 \times 10^{-7} \text{ m}^2$$

The magnitude of the current density is then

$$J = \frac{I}{A} = \frac{1.67 \text{ A}}{8.17 \times 10^{-7} \text{ m}^2} = 2.04 \times 10^6 \text{ A/m}^2$$

(b) From Eq. (25.3) for the drift velocity magnitude v_d, we find

$$v_d = \frac{J}{n|q|} = \frac{2.04 \times 10^6 \text{ A/m}^2}{(8.5 \times 10^{28} \text{ m}^{-3})|-1.60 \times 10^{-19} \text{ C}|}$$
$$= 1.5 \times 10^{-4} \text{ m/s} = 0.15 \text{ mm/s}$$

EVALUATE: At this speed an electron would require 6700 s (almost 2 h) to travel 1 m along this wire. The speeds of random motion of the electrons are roughly 10^6 m/s, around 10^{10} times the drift speed. Picture the electrons as bouncing around frantically, with a very slow drift!

Test Your Understanding of Section 25.1 Suppose we replaced the wire in Example 25.1 with 12-gauge copper wire, which has twice the diameter of 18-gauge wire. If the current remains the same, what effect would this have on the magnitude of the drift velocity v_d? (i) none—v_d would be unchanged; (ii) v_d would be twice as great; (iii) v_d would be four times greater; (iv) v_d would be half as great; (v) v_d would be one-fourth as great.

25.2 Resistivity

The current density $\vec{J}$ in a conductor depends on the electric field $\vec{E}$ and on the properties of the material. In general, this dependence can be quite complex. But for some materials, especially metals, at a given temperature, $\vec{J}$ is nearly *directly proportional* to $\vec{E}$, and the ratio of the magnitudes of E and J is constant. This relationship, called Ohm's law, was discovered in 1826 by the German physicist Georg Simon Ohm (1787–1854). The word "law" should actually be in quotation marks, since **Ohm's law,** like the ideal-gas equation and Hooke's law, is an *idealized model* that describes the behavior of some materials quite well but is not a general description of *all* matter. In the following discussion we'll assume that Ohm's law is valid, even though there are many situations in which it is not. The situation is comparable to our representation of the behavior of the static and kinetic friction forces; we treated these friction forces as being directly proportional to the normal force, even though we knew that this was at best an approximate description.

Table 25.1 Resistivities at Room Temperature (20°C)

	Substance	ρ ($\Omega \cdot$ m)	Substance	ρ ($\Omega \cdot$ m)
Conductors			**Semiconductors**	
Metals	Silver	1.47×10^{-8}	Pure carbon (graphite)	3.5×10^{-5}
	Copper	1.72×10^{-8}	Pure germanium	0.60
	Gold	2.44×10^{-8}	Pure silicon	2300
	Aluminum	2.75×10^{-8}	**Insulators**	
	Tungsten	5.25×10^{-8}	Amber	5×10^{14}
	Steel	20×10^{-8}	Glass	10^{10}–10^{14}
	Lead	22×10^{-8}	Lucite	$>10^{13}$
	Mercury	95×10^{-8}	Mica	10^{11}–10^{15}
Alloys	Manganin (Cu 84%, Mn 12%, Ni 4%)	44×10^{-8}	Quartz (fused)	75×10^{16}
	Constantan (Cu 60%, Ni 40%)	49×10^{-8}	Sulfur	10^{15}
	Nichrome	100×10^{-8}	Teflon	$>10^{13}$
			Wood	10^{8}–10^{11}

We define the **resistivity** ρ of a material as the ratio of the magnitudes of electric field and current density:

$$\rho = \frac{E}{J} \quad \text{(definition of resistivity)} \quad (25.5)$$

The greater the resistivity, the greater the field needed to cause a given current density, or the smaller the current density caused by a given field. From Eq. (25.5) the units of ρ are $(\text{V/m})/(\text{A/m}^2) = \text{V} \cdot \text{m/A}$. As we will discuss in the next section, 1 V/A is called one *ohm* (1 Ω; we use the Greek letter Ω, or omega, which is alliterative with "ohm"). So the SI units for ρ are $\Omega \cdot$ m (ohm-meters). Table 25.1 lists some representative values of resistivity. A perfect conductor would have zero resistivity, and a perfect insulator would have an infinite resistivity. Metals and alloys have the smallest resistivities and are the best conductors. The resistivities of insulators are greater than those of the metals by an enormous factor, on the order of 10^{22}.

The reciprocal of resistivity is **conductivity.** Its units are $(\Omega \cdot \text{m})^{-1}$. Good conductors of electricity have larger conductivity than insulators. Conductivity is the direct electrical analog of thermal conductivity. Comparing Table 25.1 with Table 17.5 (Thermal Conductivities), we note that good electrical conductors, such as metals, are usually also good conductors of heat. Poor electrical conductors, such as ceramic and plastic materials, are also poor thermal conductors. In a metal the free electrons that carry charge in electrical conduction also provide the principal mechanism for heat conduction, so we should expect a correlation between electrical and thermal conductivity. Because of the enormous difference in conductivity between electrical conductors and insulators, it is easy to confine electric currents to well-defined paths or circuits (Fig. 25.5). The variation in *thermal* conductivity is much less, only a factor of 10^3 or so, and it is usually impossible to confine heat currents to that extent.

Semiconductors have resistivities intermediate between those of metals and those of insulators. These materials are important because of the way their resistivities are affected by temperature and by small amounts of impurities.

A material that obeys Ohm's law reasonably well is called an *ohmic* conductor or a *linear* conductor. For such materials, at a given temperature, ρ is a *constant* that does not depend on the value of E. Many materials show substantial departures from Ohm's-law behavior; they are *nonohmic*, or *nonlinear*. In these materials, J depends on E in a more complicated manner.

Analogies with fluid flow can be a big help in developing intuition about electric current and circuits. For example, in the making of wine or maple syrup, the product is sometimes filtered to remove sediments. A pump forces the fluid through the filter under pressure; if the flow rate (analogous to J) is proportional to the pressure difference between the upstream and downstream sides (analogous to E), the behavior is analogous to Ohm's law.

25.5 The copper "wires," or traces, on this circuit board are printed directly onto the surface of the dark-colored insulating board. Even though the traces are very close to each other (only about a millimeter apart), the board has such a high resistivity (and low conductivity) that no current can flow between the traces.

Conducting paths (traces)

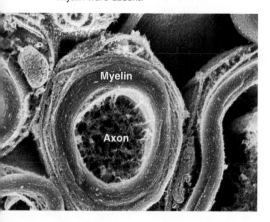

Resistivity and Temperature

The resistivity of a *metallic* conductor nearly always increases with increasing temperature, as shown in Fig. 25.6a. As temperature increases, the ions of the conductor vibrate with greater amplitude, making it more likely that a moving electron will collide with an ion as in Fig. 25.1; this impedes the drift of electrons through the conductor and hence reduces the current. Over a small temperature range (up to 100 C° or so), the resistivity of a metal can be represented approximately by the equation

$$\rho(T) = \rho_0[1 + \alpha(T - T_0)] \qquad \text{(temperature dependence of resistivity)} \qquad (25.6)$$

where ρ_0 is the resistivity at a reference temperature T_0 (often taken as 0°C or 20°C) and $\rho(T)$ is the resistivity at temperature T, which may be higher or lower than T_0. The factor α is called the **temperature coefficient of resistivity.** Some representative values are given in Table 25.2. The resistivity of the alloy manganin is practically independent of temperature.

Table 25.2 Temperature Coefficients of Resistivity (Approximate Values Near Room Temperature)

Material	$\alpha\,[(°C)^{-1}]$	Material	$\alpha\,[(°C)^{-1}]$
Aluminum	0.0039	Lead	0.0043
Brass	0.0020	Manganin	0.00000
Carbon (graphite)	−0.0005	Mercury	0.00088
Constantan	0.00001	Nichrome	0.0004
Copper	0.00393	Silver	0.0038
Iron	0.0050	Tungsten	0.0045

The resistivity of graphite (a nonmetal) *decreases* with increasing temperature, since at higher temperatures, more electrons are "shaken loose" from the atoms and become mobile; hence the temperature coefficient of resistivity of graphite is negative. This same behavior occurs for semiconductors (Fig. 25.6b). Measuring the resistivity of a small semiconductor crystal is therefore a sensitive measure of temperature; this is the principle of a type of thermometer called a *thermistor.*

Some materials, including several metallic alloys and oxides, show a phenomenon called *superconductivity.* As the temperature decreases, the resistivity at first decreases smoothly, like that of any metal. But then at a certain critical temperature T_c a phase transition occurs and the resistivity suddenly drops to zero, as shown in Fig. 25.6c. Once a current has been established in a superconducting ring, it continues indefinitely without the presence of any driving field.

Superconductivity was discovered in 1911 by the Dutch physicist Heike Kamerlingh Onnes (1853–1926). He discovered that at very low temperatures, below 4.2 K, the resistivity of mercury suddenly dropped to zero. For the next 75 years, the highest T_c attained was about 20 K. This meant that superconductivity occurred only when the material was cooled using expensive liquid helium, with a boiling-point temperature of 4.2 K, or explosive liquid hydrogen, with a boiling point of 20.3 K. But in 1986 Karl Müller and Johannes Bednorz discovered an oxide of barium, lanthanum, and copper with a T_c of nearly 40 K, and the race was on to develop "high-temperature" superconducting materials.

By 1987 a complex oxide of yttrium, copper, and barium had been found that has a value of T_c well above the 77 K boiling temperature of liquid nitrogen, a refrigerant that is both inexpensive and safe. The current (2010) record for T_c at atmospheric pressure is 138 K, and materials that are superconductors at room temperature may become a reality. The implications of these discoveries for power-distribution systems, computer design, and transportation are enormous. Meanwhile, superconducting electromagnets cooled by liquid helium are used in particle accelerators and some experimental magnetic-levitation railroads.

25.6 Variation of resistivity ρ with absolute temperature T for **(a)** a normal metal, **(b)** a semiconductor, and **(c)** a superconductor. In **(a)** the linear approximation to ρ as a function of T is shown as a green line; the approximation agrees exactly at $T = T_0$, where $\rho = \rho_0$.

(a)

Metal: Resistivity increases with increasing temperature.

Slope = $\rho_0\alpha$

(b)

Semiconductor: Resistivity decreases with increasing temperature.

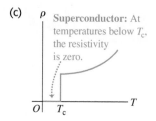

(c)

Superconductor: At temperatures below T_c, the resistivity is zero.

Superconductors have other exotic properties that require an understanding of magnetism to explore; we will discuss these further in Chapter 29.

Test Your Understanding of Section 25.2   You maintain a constant electric field inside a piece of semiconductor while lowering the semiconductor's temperature. What happens to the current density in the semiconductor? (i) It increases; (ii) it decreases; (iii) it remains the same.

25.3 Resistance

PhET: Resistance in a Wire

For a conductor with resistivity ρ, the current density $\vec{J}$ at a point where the electric field is $\vec{E}$ is given by Eq. (25.5), which we can write as

$$\vec{E} = \rho \vec{J} \qquad (25.7)$$

When Ohm's law is obeyed, ρ is constant and independent of the magnitude of the electric field, so $\vec{E}$ is directly proportional to $\vec{J}$. Often, however, we are more interested in the total current in a conductor than in $\vec{J}$ and more interested in the potential difference between the ends of the conductor than in $\vec{E}$. This is so largely because current and potential difference are much easier to measure than are $\vec{J}$ and $\vec{E}$.

Suppose our conductor is a wire with uniform cross-sectional area A and length L, as shown in Fig. 25.7. Let V be the potential difference between the higher-potential and lower-potential ends of the conductor, so that V is positive. The *direction* of the current is always from the higher-potential end to the lower-potential end. That's because current in a conductor flows in the direction of $\vec{E}$, no matter what the sign of the moving charges (Fig. 25.2), and because $\vec{E}$ points in the direction of *decreasing* electric potential (see Section 23.2). As the current flows through the potential difference, electric potential energy is lost; this energy is transferred to the ions of the conducting material during collisions.

We can also relate the *value* of the current I to the potential difference between the ends of the conductor. If the magnitudes of the current density $\vec{J}$ and the electric field $\vec{E}$ are uniform throughout the conductor, the total current I is given by $I = JA$, and the potential difference V between the ends is $V = EL$. When we solve these equations for J and E, respectively, and substitute the results in Eq. (25.7), we obtain

$$\frac{V}{L} = \frac{\rho I}{A} \quad \text{or} \quad V = \frac{\rho L}{A} I \qquad (25.8)$$

This shows that when ρ is constant, the total current I is proportional to the potential difference V.

The ratio of V to I for a particular conductor is called its **resistance** R:

$$R = \frac{V}{I} \qquad (25.9)$$

Comparing this definition of R to Eq. (25.8), we see that the resistance R of a particular conductor is related to the resistivity ρ of its material by

$$R = \frac{\rho L}{A} \qquad \begin{array}{l}\text{(relationship between}\\\text{resistance and resistivity)}\end{array} \qquad (25.10)$$

If ρ is constant, as is the case for ohmic materials, then so is R.

The equation

$$V = IR \qquad \begin{array}{l}\text{(relationship among voltage,}\\\text{current, and resistance)}\end{array} \qquad (25.11)$$

is often called Ohm's law, but it is important to understand that the real content of Ohm's law is the direct proportionality (for some materials) of V to I or of J to E.

25.7 A conductor with uniform cross section. The current density is uniform over any cross section, and the electric field is constant along the length.

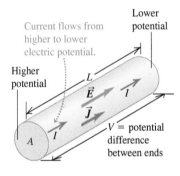

Current flows from higher to lower electric potential.

Higher potential

Lower potential

L

$\vec{E}$

$\vec{J}$

I

A

V = potential difference between ends

25.8 A long fire hose offers substantial resistance to water flow. To make water pass through the hose rapidly, the upstream end of the hose must be at much higher pressure than the end where the water emerges. In an analogous way, there must be a large potential difference between the ends of a long wire in order to cause a substantial electric current through the wire.

25.9 This resistor has a resistance of 5.7 kΩ with a precision (tolerance) of ±10%.

Second digit   Multiplier

First digit   Tolerance

Table 25.3 Color Codes for Resistors

Color	Value as Digit	Value as Multiplier
Black	0	1
Brown	1	10
Red	2	10^2
Orange	3	10^3
Yellow	4	10^4
Green	5	10^5
Blue	6	10^6
Violet	7	10^7
Gray	8	10^8
White	9	10^9

Equation (25.9) or (25.11) *defines* resistance R for *any* conductor, whether or not it obeys Ohm's law, but only when R is constant can we correctly call this relationship Ohm's law.

Interpreting Resistance

Equation (25.10) shows that the resistance of a wire or other conductor of uniform cross section is directly proportional to its length and inversely proportional to its cross-sectional area. It is also proportional to the resistivity of the material of which the conductor is made.

The flowing-fluid analogy is again useful. In analogy to Eq. (25.10), a narrow water hose offers more resistance to flow than a fat one, and a long hose has more resistance than a short one (Fig. 25.8). We can increase the resistance to flow by stuffing the hose with cotton or sand; this corresponds to increasing the resistivity. The flow rate is approximately proportional to the pressure difference between the ends. Flow rate is analogous to current, and pressure difference is analogous to potential difference ("voltage"). Let's not stretch this analogy too far, though; the water flow rate in a pipe is usually *not* proportional to its cross-sectional area (see Section 14.6).

The SI unit of resistance is the **ohm,** equal to one volt per ampere (1 Ω = 1 V/A). The *kilohm* (1 kΩ = 10^3 Ω) and the *megohm* (1 MΩ = 10^6 Ω) are also in common use. A 100-m length of 12-gauge copper wire, the size usually used in household wiring, has a resistance at room temperature of about 0.5 Ω. A 100-W, 120-V light bulb has a resistance (at operating temperature) of 140 Ω. If the same current I flows in both the copper wire and the light bulb, the potential difference $V = IR$ is much greater across the light bulb, and much more potential energy is lost per charge in the light bulb. This lost energy is converted by the light bulb filament into light and heat. You don't want your household wiring to glow white-hot, so its resistance is kept low by using wire of low resistivity and large cross-sectional area.

Because the resistivity of a material varies with temperature, the resistance of a specific conductor also varies with temperature. For temperature ranges that are not too great, this variation is approximately a linear relationship, analogous to Eq. (25.6):

$$R(T) = R_0[1 + \alpha(T - T_0)] \qquad (25.12)$$

In this equation, $R(T)$ is the resistance at temperature T and R_0 is the resistance at temperature T_0, often taken to be 0°C or 20°C. The *temperature coefficient of resistance* α is the same constant that appears in Eq. (25.6) if the dimensions L and A in Eq. (25.10) do not change appreciably with temperature; this is indeed the case for most conducting materials (see Problem 25.67). Within the limits of validity of Eq. (25.12), the *change* in resistance resulting from a temperature change $T - T_0$ is given by $R_0\alpha(T - T_0)$.

A circuit device made to have a specific value of resistance between its ends is called a **resistor.** Resistors in the range 0.01 to 10^7 Ω can be bought off the shelf. Individual resistors used in electronic circuitry are often cylindrical, a few millimeters in diameter and length, with wires coming out of the ends. The resistance may be marked with a standard code using three or four color bands near one end (Fig. 25.9), according to the scheme shown in Table 25.3. The first two bands (starting with the band nearest an end) are digits, and the third is a power-of-10 multiplier, as shown in Fig. 25.9. For example, green–violet–red means 57×10^2 Ω, or 5.7 kΩ. The fourth band, if present, indicates the precision (tolerance) of the value; no band means ±20%, a silver band ±10%, and a gold band ±5%. Another important characteristic of a resistor is the maximum *power* it can dissipate without damage. We'll return to this point in Section 25.5.

25.10 Current–voltage relationships for two devices. Only for a resistor that obeys Ohm's law as in (a) is current I proportional to voltage V.

(a)

Ohmic resistor (e.g., typical metal wire): At a given temperature, current is proportional to voltage.

(b)

Semiconductor diode: a nonohmic resistor

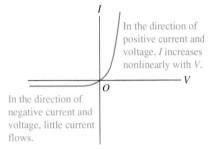

For a resistor that obeys Ohm's law, a graph of current as a function of potential difference (voltage) is a straight line (Fig. 25.10a). The slope of the line is $1/R$. If the sign of the potential difference changes, so does the sign of the current produced; in Fig. 25.7 this corresponds to interchanging the higher- and lower-potential ends of the conductor, so the electric field, current density, and current all reverse direction. In devices that do not obey Ohm's law, the relationship of voltage to current may not be a direct proportion, and it may be different for the two directions of current. Figure 25.10b shows the behavior of a semiconductor *diode*, a device used to convert alternating current to direct current and to perform a wide variety of logic functions in computer circuitry. For positive potentials V of the anode (one of two terminals of the diode) with respect to the cathode (the other terminal), I increases exponentially with increasing V; for negative potentials the current is extremely small. Thus a positive V causes a current to flow in the positive direction, but a potential difference of the other sign causes little or no current. Hence a diode acts like a one-way valve in a circuit.

Example 25.2   **Electric field, potential difference, and resistance in a wire**

The 18-gauge copper wire of Example 25.1 has a cross-sectional area of $8.20 \times 10^{-7} \, \mathrm{m^2}$. It carries a current of 1.67 A. Find (a) the electric-field magnitude in the wire; (b) the potential difference between two points in the wire 50.0 m apart; (c) the resistance of a 50.0-m length of this wire.

SOLUTION

IDENTIFY and SET UP: We are given the cross-sectional area A and current I. Our target variables are the electric-field magnitude E, potential difference V, and resistance R. The current density is $J = I/A$. We find E from Eq. (25.5), $E = \rho J$ (Table 25.1 gives the resistivity ρ for copper). The potential difference is then the product of E and the length of the wire. We can use either Eq. (25.10) or Eq. (25.11) to find R.

EXECUTE: (a) From Table 25.1, $\rho = 1.72 \times 10^{-8} \, \Omega \cdot \mathrm{m}$. Hence, using Eq. (25.5),

$$E = \rho J = \frac{\rho I}{A} = \frac{(1.72 \times 10^{-8} \, \Omega \cdot \mathrm{m})(1.67 \, \mathrm{A})}{8.20 \times 10^{-7} \, \mathrm{m^2}}$$

$$= 0.0350 \, \mathrm{V/m}$$

(b) The potential difference is

$$V = EL = (0.0350 \, \mathrm{V/m})(50.0 \, \mathrm{m}) = 1.75 \, \mathrm{V}$$

(c) From Eq. (25.10) the resistance of 50.0 m of this wire is

$$R = \frac{\rho L}{A} = \frac{(1.72 \times 10^{-8} \, \Omega \cdot \mathrm{m})(50.0 \, \mathrm{m})}{8.20 \times 10^{-7} \, \mathrm{m^2}} = 1.05 \, \Omega$$

Alternatively, we can find R using Eq. (25.11):

$$R = \frac{V}{I} = \frac{1.75 \, \mathrm{V}}{1.67 \, \mathrm{A}} = 1.05 \, \Omega$$

EVALUATE: We emphasize that the resistance of the wire is *defined* to be the ratio of voltage to current. If the wire is made of nonohmic material, then R is different for different values of V but is always given by $R = V/I$. Resistance is also always given by $R = \rho L/A$; if the material is nonohmic, ρ is not constant but depends on E (or, equivalently, on $V = EL$).

828

| Example 25.3 | **Temperature dependence of resistance** |

Suppose the resistance of a copper wire is 1.05 Ω at 20°C. Find the resistance at 0°C and 100°C.

SOLUTION

IDENTIFY and SET UP: We are given the resistance $R_0 = 1.05$ Ω at a reference temperature $T_0 = 20$°C. We use Eq. (25.12) to find the resistances at $T = 0$°C and $T = 100$°C (our target variables), taking the temperature coefficient of resistivity from Table 25.2.

EXECUTE: From Table 25.2, $\alpha = 0.00393$ (C°)$^{-1}$ for copper. Then from Eq. (25.12),

$$R = R_0[1 + \alpha(T - T_0)]$$
$$= (1.05 \text{ Ω})\{1 + [0.00393 \text{ (C°)}^{-1}][0°\text{C} - 20°\text{C}]\}$$
$$= 0.97 \text{ Ω at } T = 0°\text{C}$$

$$R = (1.05 \text{ Ω})\{1 + [0.00393 \text{ (C°)}^{-1}][100°\text{C} - 20°\text{C}]\}$$
$$= 1.38 \text{ Ω at } T = 100°\text{C}$$

EVALUATE: The resistance at 100°C is greater than that at 0°C by a factor of (1.38 Ω)/(0.97 Ω) = 1.42: Raising the temperature of copper wire from 0°C to 100°C increases its resistance by 42%. From Eq. (25.11), $V = IR$, this means that 42% more voltage is required to produce the same current at 100°C than at 0°C. Designers of electric circuits that must operate over a wide temperature range must take this substantial effect into account.

Test Your Understanding of Section 25.3 Suppose you increase the voltage across the copper wire in Examples 25.2 and 25.3. The increased voltage causes more current to flow, which makes the temperature of the wire increase. (The same thing happens to the coils of an electric oven or a toaster when a voltage is applied to them. We'll explore this issue in more depth in Section 25.5.) If you double the voltage across the wire, the current in the wire increases. By what factor does it increase? (i) 2; (ii) greater than 2; (iii) less than 2.

25.4 Electromotive Force and Circuits

25.11 If an electric field is produced inside a conductor that is *not* part of a complete circuit, current flows for only a very short time.

(a) An electric field $\vec{E}_1$ produced inside an isolated conductor causes a current.

(b) The current causes charge to build up at the ends.

The charge buildup produces an opposing field $\vec{E}_2$, thus reducing the current.

(c) After a very short time $\vec{E}_2$ has the same magnitude as $\vec{E}_1$; then the total field is $\vec{E}_{\text{total}} = 0$ and the current stops completely.

For a conductor to have a steady current, it must be part of a path that forms a closed loop or **complete circuit.** Here's why. If you establish an electric field $\vec{E}_1$ inside an isolated conductor with resistivity ρ that is *not* part of a complete circuit, a current begins to flow with current density $\vec{J} = \vec{E}_1/\rho$ (Fig. 25.11a). As a result a net positive charge quickly accumulates at one end of the conductor and a net negative charge accumulates at the other end (Fig. 25.11b). These charges themselves produce an electric field $\vec{E}_2$ in the direction opposite to $\vec{E}_1$, causing the total electric field and hence the current to decrease. Within a very small fraction of a second, enough charge builds up on the conductor ends that the total electric field $\vec{E} = \vec{E}_1 + \vec{E}_2 = 0$ inside the conductor. Then $\vec{J} = 0$ as well, and the current stops altogether (Fig. 25.11c). So there can be no steady motion of charge in such an *incomplete* circuit.

To see how to maintain a steady current in a *complete* circuit, we recall a basic fact about electric potential energy: If a charge q goes around a complete circuit and returns to its starting point, the potential energy must be the same at the end of the round trip as at the beginning. As described in Section 25.3, there is always a *decrease* in potential energy when charges move through an ordinary conducting material with resistance. So there must be some part of the circuit in which the potential energy *increases*.

The problem is analogous to an ornamental water fountain that recycles its water. The water pours out of openings at the top, cascades down over the terraces and spouts (moving in the direction of decreasing gravitational potential energy), and collects in a basin in the bottom. A pump then lifts it back to the top (increasing the potential energy) for another trip. Without the pump, the water would just fall to the bottom and stay there.

Electromotive Force

In an electric circuit there must be a device somewhere in the loop that acts like the water pump in a water fountain (Fig. 25.12). In this device a charge travels "uphill," from lower to higher potential energy, even though the electrostatic force is trying to push it from higher to lower potential energy. The direction of current in such a device is from lower to higher potential, just the opposite of what happens in an ordinary conductor. The influence that makes current flow from lower to higher potential is called **electromotive force** (abbreviated **emf** and pronounced "ee-em-eff"). This is a poor term because emf is *not* a force but an energy-per-unit-charge quantity, like potential. The SI unit of emf is the same as that for potential, the volt $(1\ \text{V} = 1\ \text{J/C})$. A typical flashlight battery has an emf of 1.5 V; this means that the battery does 1.5 J of work on every coulomb of charge that passes through it. We'll use the symbol $\mathcal{E}$ (a script capital E) for emf.

Every complete circuit with a steady current must include some device that provides emf. Such a device is called a **source of emf.** Batteries, electric generators, solar cells, thermocouples, and fuel cells are all examples of sources of emf. All such devices convert energy of some form (mechanical, chemical, thermal, and so on) into electric potential energy and transfer it into the circuit to which the device is connected. An *ideal* source of emf maintains a constant potential difference between its terminals, independent of the current through it. We define electromotive force quantitatively as the magnitude of this potential difference. As we will see, such an ideal source is a mythical beast, like the frictionless plane and the massless rope. We will discuss later how real-life sources of emf differ in their behavior from this idealized model.

Figure 25.13 is a schematic diagram of an ideal source of emf that maintains a potential difference between conductors a and b, called the *terminals* of the device. Terminal a, marked +, is maintained at *higher* potential than terminal b, marked −. Associated with this potential difference is an electric field $\vec{E}$ in the region around the terminals, both inside and outside the source. The electric field inside the device is directed from a to b, as shown. A charge q within the source experiences an electric force $\vec{F}_e = q\vec{E}$. But the source also provides an additional influence, which we represent as a nonelectrostatic force $\vec{F}_n$. This force, operating inside the device, pushes charge from b to a in an "uphill" direction against the electric force $\vec{F}_e$. Thus $\vec{F}_n$ maintains the potential difference between the terminals. If $\vec{F}_n$ were not present, charge would flow between the terminals until the potential difference was zero. The origin of the additional influence $\vec{F}_n$ depends on the kind of source. In a generator it results from magnetic-field forces on moving charges. In a battery or fuel cell it is associated with diffusion processes and varying electrolyte concentrations resulting from chemical reactions. In an electrostatic machine such as a Van de Graaff generator (see Fig. 22.26), an actual mechanical force is applied by a moving belt or wheel.

If a positive charge q is moved from b to a inside the source, the nonelectrostatic force $\vec{F}_n$ does a positive amount of work $W_n = q\mathcal{E}$ on the charge. This displacement is *opposite* to the electrostatic force $\vec{F}_e$, so the potential energy associated with the charge *increases* by an amount equal to qV_{ab}, where $V_{ab} = V_a - V_b$ is the (positive) potential of point a with respect to point b. For the ideal source of emf that we've described, $\vec{F}_e$ and $\vec{F}_n$ are equal in magnitude but opposite in direction, so the total work done on the charge q is zero; there is an increase in potential energy but *no* change in the kinetic energy of the charge. It's like lifting a book from the floor to a high shelf at constant speed. The increase in potential energy is just equal to the nonelectrostatic work W_n, so $q\mathcal{E} = qV_{ab}$, or

$$V_{ab} = \mathcal{E} \qquad \text{(ideal source of emf)} \qquad (25.13)$$

Now let's make a complete circuit by connecting a wire with resistance R to the terminals of a source (Fig. 25.14). The potential difference between terminals a and b sets up an electric field within the wire; this causes current to flow around the loop from a toward b, from higher to lower potential. Where the wire bends, equal amounts of positive and negative charge persist on the "inside" and "outside"

25.12 Just as a water fountain requires a pump, an electric circuit requires a source of electromotive force to sustain a steady current.

25.13 Schematic diagram of a source of emf in an "open-circuit" situation. The electric-field force $\vec{F}_e = q\vec{E}$ and the nonelectrostatic force $\vec{F}_n$ are shown for a positive charge q.

When the emf source is not part of a closed circuit, $F_n = F_e$ and there is no net motion of charge between the terminals.

PhET: Battery Voltage
PhET: Signal Circuit
ActivPhysics 12.1: DC Series Circuits (Qualitative)

25.14 Schematic diagram of an ideal source of emf in a complete circuit. The electric-field force $\vec{F}_e = q\vec{E}$ and the non-electrostatic force $\vec{F}_n$ are shown for a positive charge q. The current is in the direction from a to b in the external circuit and from b to a within the source.

Potential across terminals creates electric field in circuit, causing charges to move.

Ideal emf source

V_a

$V_{ab} = \mathcal{E}$

V_b

When a real (as opposed to ideal) emf source is connected to a circuit, V_{ab} and thus F_e fall, so that $F_n > F_e$ and $\vec{F}_n$ does work on the charges.

Application **Danger: Electric Ray!**
Electric rays deliver electric shocks to stun their prey and to discourage predators. (In ancient Rome, physicians practiced a primitive form of electroconvulsive therapy by placing electric rays on their patients to cure headaches and gout.) The shocks are produced by specialized flattened cells called electroplaques. Such a cell moves ions across membranes to produce an emf of about 0.05 V. Thousands of electroplaques are stacked on top of each other, so their emfs add to a total of as much as 200 V. These stacks make up more than half of an electric ray's body mass. A ray can use these to deliver an impressive current of up to 30 A for a few milliseconds.

of the bend. These charges exert the forces that cause the current to follow the bends in the wire.

From Eq. (25.11) the potential difference between the ends of the wire in Fig. 25.14 is given by $V_{ab} = IR$. Combining with Eq. (25.13), we have

$$\mathcal{E} = V_{ab} = IR \qquad \text{(ideal source of emf)} \qquad (25.14)$$

That is, when a positive charge q flows around the circuit, the potential *rise* $\mathcal{E}$ as it passes through the ideal source is numerically equal to the potential *drop* $V_{ab} = IR$ as it passes through the remainder of the circuit. Once $\mathcal{E}$ and R are known, this relationship determines the current in the circuit.

CAUTION **Current is not "used up" in a circuit** It's a common misconception that in a closed circuit, current is something that squirts out of the positive terminal of a battery and is consumed or "used up" by the time it reaches the negative terminal. In fact the current is the *same* at every point in a simple loop circuit like that in Fig. 25.14, even if the thickness of the wires is different at different points in the circuit. This happens because charge is conserved (that is, it can be neither created nor destroyed) and because charge cannot accumulate in the circuit devices we have described. If charge did accumulate, the potential differences would change with time. It's like the flow of water in an ornamental fountain; water flows out of the top of the fountain at the same rate at which it reaches the bottom, no matter what the dimensions of the fountain. None of the water is "used up" along the way!

Internal Resistance

Real sources of emf in a circuit don't behave in exactly the way we have described; the potential difference across a real source in a circuit is *not* equal to the emf as in Eq. (25.14). The reason is that charge moving through the material of any real source encounters *resistance*. We call this the **internal resistance** of the source, denoted by r. If this resistance behaves according to Ohm's law, r is constant and independent of the current I. As the current moves through r, it experiences an associated drop in potential equal to Ir. Thus, when a current is flowing through a source from the negative terminal b to the positive terminal a, the potential difference V_{ab} between the terminals is

$$V_{ab} = \mathcal{E} - Ir \qquad \begin{array}{l}\text{(terminal voltage, source}\\ \text{with internal resistance)}\end{array} \qquad (25.15)$$

The potential V_{ab}, called the **terminal voltage,** is less than the emf $\mathcal{E}$ because of the term Ir representing the potential drop across the internal resistance r. Expressed another way, the increase in potential energy qV_{ab} as a charge q moves from b to a within the source is now less than the work $q\mathcal{E}$ done by the nonelectrostatic force $\vec{F}_n$, since some potential energy is lost in traversing the internal resistance.

A 1.5-V battery has an emf of 1.5 V, but the terminal voltage V_{ab} of the battery is equal to 1.5 V only if no current is flowing through it so that $I = 0$ in Eq. (25.15). If the battery is part of a complete circuit through which current is flowing, the terminal voltage will be less than 1.5 V. *For a real source of emf, the terminal voltage equals the emf only if no current is flowing through the source* (Fig. 25.15). Thus we can describe the behavior of a source in terms of two properties: an emf $\mathcal{E}$, which supplies a constant potential difference independent of current, in series with an internal resistance r.

The current in the external circuit connected to the source terminals a and b is still determined by $V_{ab} = IR$. Combining this with Eq. (25.15), we find

$$\mathcal{E} - Ir = IR \quad \text{or} \quad I = \frac{\mathcal{E}}{R + r} \qquad \begin{array}{l}\text{(current, source with}\\ \text{internal resistance)}\end{array} \qquad (25.16)$$

That is, the current equals the source emf divided by the *total* circuit resistance $(R + r)$.

CAUTION   **A battery is not a "current source"**   You might have thought that a battery or other source of emf always produces the same current, no matter what circuit it's used in. Equation (25.16) shows that this isn't so! The greater the resistance R of the external circuit, the less current the source will produce. It's analogous to pushing an object through a thick, viscous liquid such as oil or molasses; if you exert a certain steady push (emf), you can move a small object at high speed (small R, large I) or a large object at low speed (large R, small I).

Symbols for Circuit Diagrams

An important part of analyzing any electric circuit is drawing a schematic *circuit diagram.* Table 25.4 shows the usual symbols used in circuit diagrams. We will use these symbols extensively in this chapter and the next. We usually assume that the wires that connect the various elements of the circuit have negligible resistance; from Eq. (25.11), $V = IR$, the potential difference between the ends of such a wire is zero.

Table 25.4 includes two *meters* that are used to measure the properties of circuits. Idealized meters do not disturb the circuit in which they are connected. A **voltmeter,** introduced in Section 23.2, measures the potential difference between its terminals; an idealized voltmeter has infinitely large resistance and measures potential difference without having any current diverted through it. An ammeter measures the current passing through it; an idealized **ammeter** has zero resistance and has no potential difference between its terminals. Because meters act as part of the circuit in which they are connected, these properties are important to remember.

25.15 The emf of this battery—that is, the terminal voltage when it's not connected to anything—is 12 V. But because the battery has internal resistance, the terminal voltage of the battery is less than 12 V when it is supplying current to a light bulb.

Table 25.4 **Symbols for Circuit Diagrams**

	Conductor with negligible resistance
R	Resistor
$+\ \ \mathcal{E}$	Source of emf (longer vertical line always represents the positive terminal, usually the terminal with higher potential)
$\mathcal{E}\ +$ or $+\ \mathcal{E}$	Source of emf with internal resistance r (r can be placed on either side)
V	Voltmeter (measures potential difference between its terminals)
A	Ammeter (measures current through it)

Conceptual Example 25.4   **A source in an open circuit**

Figure 25.16 shows a source (a battery) with emf $\mathcal{E} = 12$ V and internal resistance $r = 2\ \Omega$. (For comparison, the internal resistance of a commercial 12-V lead storage battery is only a few thousandths of an ohm.) The wires to the left of a and to the right of the ammeter A are not connected to anything. Determine the respective readings V_{ab} and I of the idealized voltmeter V and the idealized ammeter A.

25.16 A source of emf in an open circuit.

V_{ab}

a b

$r = 2\ \Omega,\ \mathcal{E} = 12$ V

Continued

SOLUTION

There is *zero* current because there is no complete circuit. (Our idealized voltmeter has an infinitely large resistance, so no current flows through it.) Hence the ammeter reads $I = 0$. Because there is no current through the battery, there is no potential difference across

its internal resistance. From Eq. (25.15) with $I = 0$, the potential difference V_{ab} across the battery terminals is equal to the emf. So the voltmeter reads $V_{ab} = \mathcal{E} = 12$ V. The terminal voltage of a real, nonideal source equals the emf *only* if there is no current flowing through the source, as in this example.

Example 25.5   **A source in a complete circuit**

We add a 4-Ω resistor to the battery in Conceptual Example 25.4, forming a complete circuit (Fig. 25.17). What are the voltmeter and ammeter readings V_{ab} and I now?

SOLUTION

IDENTIFY and SET UP: Our target variables are the current I through the circuit $aa'b'b$ and the potential difference V_{ab}. We first find I using Eq. (25.16). To find V_{ab}, we can use either Eq. (25.11) or Eq. (25.15).

25.17 A source of emf in a complete circuit.

EXECUTE: The ideal ammeter has zero resistance, so the total resistance external to the source is $R = 4\ \Omega$. From Eq. (25.16), the current through the circuit $aa'b'b$ is then

$$I = \frac{\mathcal{E}}{R + r} = \frac{12\ \text{V}}{4\ \Omega + 2\ \Omega} = 2\ \text{A}$$

Our idealized conducting wires and the idealized ammeter have zero resistance, so there is no potential difference between points a and a' or between points b and b'; that is, $V_{ab} = V_{a'b'}$. We find V_{ab} by considering a and b as the terminals of the resistor: From Ohm's law, Eq. (25.11), we then have

$$V_{a'b'} = IR = (2\ \text{A})(4\ \Omega) = 8\ \text{V}$$

Alternatively, we can consider a and b as the terminals of the source. Then, from Eq. (25.15),

$$V_{ab} = \mathcal{E} - Ir = 12\ \text{V} - (2\ \text{A})(2\ \Omega) = 8\ \text{V}$$

Either way, we see that the voltmeter reading is 8 V.

EVALUATE: With current flowing through the source, the terminal voltage V_{ab} is less than the emf $\mathcal{E}$. The smaller the internal resistance r, the less the difference between V_{ab} and $\mathcal{E}$.

Conceptual Example 25.6   **Using voltmeters and ammeters**

We move the voltmeter and ammeter in Example 25.5 to different positions in the circuit. What are the readings of the ideal voltmeter and ammeter in the situations shown in (a) Fig. 25.18a and (b) Fig. 25.18b?

SOLUTION

(a) The voltmeter now measures the potential difference between points a' and b'. As in Example 25.5, $V_{ab} = V_{a'b'}$, so the voltmeter reads the same as in Example 25.5: $V_{a'b'} = 8$ V.

25.18 Different placements of a voltmeter and an ammeter in a complete circuit.

(a)   (b)

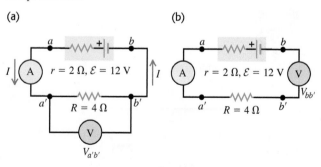

CAUTION   Current in a simple loop As charges move through a resistor, there is a decrease in electric potential energy, but there is *no* change in the current. *The current in a simple loop is the same at every point;* it is not "used up" as it moves through a resistor. Hence the ammeter in Fig. 25.17 ("downstream" of the 4-Ω resistor) and the ammeter in Fig. 25.18b ("upstream" of the resistor) both read $I = 2$ A.

(b) There is no current through the ideal voltmeter because it has infinitely large resistance. Since the voltmeter is now part of the circuit, there is no current at all in the circuit, and the ammeter reads $I = 0$.

The voltmeter measures the potential difference $V_{bb'}$ between points b and b'. Since $I = 0$, the potential difference across the resistor is $V_{a'b'} = IR = 0$, and the potential difference between the ends a and a' of the idealized ammeter is also zero. So $V_{bb'}$ is equal to V_{ab}, the terminal voltage of the source. As in Conceptual Example 25.4, there is no current, so the terminal voltage equals the emf, and the voltmeter reading is $V_{ab} = \mathcal{E} = 12$ V.

This example shows that ammeters and voltmeters are circuit elements, too. Moving the voltmeter from the position in Fig. 25.18a to that in Fig. 25.18b makes large changes in the current and potential differences in the circuit. If you want to measure the potential difference between two points in a circuit without disturbing the circuit, use a voltmeter as in Fig. 25.17 or 25.18a, *not* as in Fig. 25.18b.

Example 25.7 A source with a short circuit

In the circuit of Example 25.5 we replace the 4-Ω resistor with a zero-resistance conductor. What are the meter readings now?

SOLUTION

IDENTIFY and SET UP: Figure 25.19 shows the new circuit. Our target variables are again I and V_{ab}. There is now a zero-resistance path between points a and b, through the lower loop, so the potential difference between these points must be zero.

25.19 Our sketch for this problem.

EXECUTE: We must have $V_{ab} = IR = I(0) = 0$, no matter what the current. We can therefore find the current I from Eq. (25.15):

$$V_{ab} = \mathcal{E} - Ir = 0$$

$$I = \frac{\mathcal{E}}{r} = \frac{12 \text{ V}}{2 \text{ }\Omega} = 6 \text{ A}$$

EVALUATE: The current has a different value than in Example 25.5, even though the same battery is used; the current depends on both the internal resistance r and the resistance of the external circuit.

The situation here is called a *short circuit*. The external-circuit resistance is zero, because terminals of the battery are connected directly to each other. The short-circuit current is equal to the emf $\mathcal{E}$ divided by the internal resistance r. *Warning:* Short circuits can be dangerous! An automobile battery or a household power line has very small internal resistance (much less than in these examples), and the short-circuit current can be great enough to melt a small wire or cause a storage battery to explode.

Potential Changes Around a Circuit

The net change in potential energy for a charge q making a round trip around a complete circuit must be zero. Hence the net change in *potential* around the circuit must also be zero; in other words, the algebraic sum of the potential differences and emfs around the loop is zero. We can see this by rewriting Eq. (25.16) in the form

$$\mathcal{E} - Ir - IR = 0$$

A potential gain of $\mathcal{E}$ is associated with the emf, and potential drops of Ir and IR are associated with the internal resistance of the source and the external circuit, respectively. Figure 25.20 is a graph showing how the potential varies as we go around the complete circuit of Fig. 25.17. The horizontal axis doesn't necessarily represent actual distances, but rather various points in the loop. If we take the potential to be zero at the negative terminal of the battery, then we have a rise $\mathcal{E}$ and a drop Ir in the battery and an additional drop IR in the external resistor, and as we finish our trip around the loop, the potential is back where it started.

In this section we have considered only situations in which the resistances are ohmic. If the circuit includes a nonlinear device such as a diode (see Fig. 25.10b), Eq. (25.16) is still valid but cannot be solved algebraically because R is not a constant. In such a situation, the current I can be found by using numerical techniques.

Finally, we remark that Eq. (25.15) is not always an adequate representation of the behavior of a source. The emf may not be constant, and what we have described as an internal resistance may actually be a more complex voltage–current relationship that doesn't obey Ohm's law. Nevertheless, the concept of internal resistance frequently provides an adequate description of batteries, generators, and other energy converters. The principal difference between a fresh flashlight battery and an old one is not in the emf, which decreases only slightly with use, but in the internal resistance, which may increase from less than an ohm when the battery is fresh to as much as 1000 Ω or more after long use. Similarly, a car battery can deliver less current to the starter motor on a cold morning than when the battery is warm, not because the emf is appreciably less but because the internal resistance increases with decreasing temperature.

25.20 Potential rises and drops in a circuit.

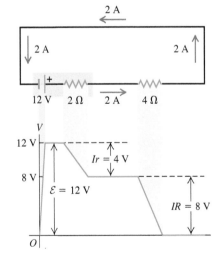

Rank the following circuits in order from highest to lowest current. (i) a 1.4-Ω resistor connected to a 1.5-V battery that has an internal resistance of 0.10 Ω; (ii) a 1.8-Ω resistor connected to a 4.0-V battery that has a terminal voltage of 3.6 V but an unknown internal resistance; (iii) an unknown resistor connected to a 12.0-V battery that has an internal resistance of 0.20 Ω and a terminal voltage of 11.0 V.

25.5 Energy and Power in Electric Circuits

25.21 The power input to the circuit element between a and b is $P = (V_a - V_b)I = V_{ab}I$.

PhET: Battery-Resistor Circuit
PhET: Circuit Construction Kit (AC+DC)
PhET: Circuit Construction Kit (DC Only)
PhET: Ohm's Law

Let's now look at some energy and power relationships in electric circuits. The box in Fig. 25.21 represents a circuit element with potential difference $V_a - V_b = V_{ab}$ between its terminals and current I passing through it in the direction from a toward b. This element might be a resistor, a battery, or something else; the details don't matter. As charge passes through the circuit element, the electric field does work on the charge. In a source of emf, additional work is done by the force $\vec{F}_n$ that we mentioned in Section 25.4.

As an amount of charge q passes through the circuit element, there is a change in potential energy equal to qV_{ab}. For example, if $q > 0$ and $V_{ab} = V_a - V_b$ is positive, potential energy decreases as the charge "falls" from potential V_a to lower potential V_b. The moving charges don't gain *kinetic* energy, because the current (the rate of charge flow) out of the circuit element must be the same as the current into the element. Instead, the quantity qV_{ab} represents energy transferred into the circuit element. This situation occurs in the coils of a toaster or electric oven, in which electrical energy is converted to thermal energy.

If the potential at a is lower than at b, then V_{ab} is negative and there is a net transfer of energy *out* of the circuit element. The element then acts as a source, delivering electrical energy into the circuit to which it is attached. This is the usual situation for a battery, which converts chemical energy into electrical energy and delivers it to the external circuit. Thus qV_{ab} can denote either a quantity of energy delivered to a circuit element or a quantity of energy extracted from that element.

In electric circuits we are most often interested in the *rate* at which energy is either delivered to or extracted from a circuit element. If the current through the element is I, then in a time interval dt an amount of charge $dQ = I\,dt$ passes through the element. The potential energy change for this amount of charge is $V_{ab}\,dQ = V_{ab}I\,dt$. Dividing this expression by dt, we obtain the *rate* at which energy is transferred either into or out of the circuit element. The time rate of energy transfer is *power*, denoted by P, so we write

$$P = V_{ab}I \qquad \text{(rate at which energy is delivered to or extracted from a circuit element)} \qquad (25.17)$$

The unit of V_{ab} is one volt, or one joule per coulomb, and the unit of I is one ampere, or one coulomb per second. Hence the unit of $P = V_{ab}I$ is one watt, as it should be:

$$(1\ \text{J/C})(1\ \text{C/s}) = 1\ \text{J/s} = 1\ \text{W}$$

Let's consider a few special cases.

Power Input to a Pure Resistance

If the circuit element in Fig. 25.21 is a resistor, the potential difference is $V_{ab} = IR$. From Eq. (25.17) the electrical power delivered to the resistor by the circuit is

Video Tutor Demo

$$P = V_{ab}I = I^2R = \frac{V_{ab}^2}{R} \qquad \text{(power delivered to a resistor)} \qquad (25.18)$$

In this case the potential at a (where the current enters the resistor) is always higher than that at b (where the current exits). Current enters the higher-potential terminal of the device, and Eq. (25.18) represents the rate of transfer of electric potential energy *into* the circuit element.

What becomes of this energy? The moving charges collide with atoms in the resistor and transfer some of their energy to these atoms, increasing the internal energy of the material. Either the temperature of the resistor increases or there is a flow of heat out of it, or both. In any of these cases we say that energy is *dissipated* in the resistor at a rate I^2R. Every resistor has a *power rating,* the maximum power the device can dissipate without becoming overheated and damaged. Some devices, such as electric heaters, are designed to get hot and transfer heat to their surroundings. But if the power rating is exceeded, even such a device may melt or even explode.

Power Output of a Source

The upper rectangle in Fig. 25.22a represents a source with emf $\mathcal{E}$ and internal resistance r, connected by ideal (resistanceless) conductors to an external circuit represented by the lower box. This could describe a car battery connected to one of the car's headlights (Fig. 25.22b). Point a is at higher potential than point b, so $V_a > V_b$ and V_{ab} is positive. Note that the current I is *leaving* the source at the higher-potential terminal (rather than entering there). Energy is being delivered to the external circuit, at a rate given by Eq. (25.17):

$$P = V_{ab}I$$

For a source that can be described by an emf $\mathcal{E}$ and an internal resistance r, we may use Eq. (25.15):

$$V_{ab} = \mathcal{E} - Ir$$

Multiplying this equation by I, we find

$$P = V_{ab}I = \mathcal{E}I - I^2r \qquad (25.19)$$

What do the terms $\mathcal{E}I$ and I^2r mean? In Section 25.4 we defined the emf $\mathcal{E}$ as the work per unit charge performed on the charges by the nonelectrostatic force as the charges are pushed "uphill" from b to a in the source. In a time dt, a charge $dQ = I\,dt$ flows through the source; the work done on it by this nonelectrostatic force is $\mathcal{E}\,dQ = \mathcal{E}I\,dt$. Thus $\mathcal{E}I$ is the *rate* at which work is done on the circulating charges by whatever agency causes the nonelectrostatic force in the source. This term represents the rate of conversion of nonelectrical energy to electrical energy within the source. The term I^2r is the rate at which electrical energy is *dissipated* in the internal resistance of the source. The difference $\mathcal{E}I - I^2r$ is the *net* electrical power output of the source—that is, the rate at which the source delivers electrical energy to the remainder of the circuit.

Power Input to a Source

Suppose that the lower rectangle in Fig. 25.22a is itself a source, with an emf *larger* than that of the upper source and with its emf opposite to that of the upper source. Figure 25.23 shows a practical example, an automobile battery (the upper circuit element) being charged by the car's alternator (the lower element). The current I in the circuit is then *opposite* to that shown in Fig. 25.22; the lower source is pushing current backward through the upper source. Because of this reversal of current, instead of Eq. (25.15) we have for the upper source

$$V_{ab} = \mathcal{E} + Ir$$

and instead of Eq. (25.19), we have

$$P = V_{ab}I = \mathcal{E}I + I^2r \qquad (25.20)$$

25.22 Energy conversion in a simple circuit.

(a) Diagrammatic circuit

- The emf source converts nonelectrical to electrical energy at a rate $\mathcal{E}I$.
- Its internal resistance *dissipates* energy at a rate I^2r.
- The difference $\mathcal{E}I - I^2r$ is its power output.

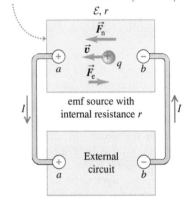

(b) A real circuit of the type shown in (a)

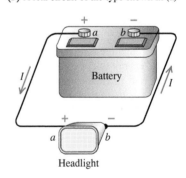

Headlight

25.23 When two sources are connected in a simple loop circuit, the source with the larger emf delivers energy to the other source.

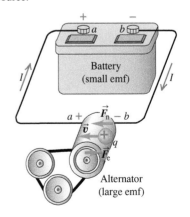

Battery (small emf)

Alternator (large emf)

Work is being done *on,* rather than *by,* the agent that causes the nonelectrostatic force in the upper source. There is a conversion of electrical energy into nonelectrical energy in the upper source at a rate $\mathcal{E}I$. The term I^2r in Eq. (25.20) is again the rate of dissipation of energy in the internal resistance of the upper source, and the sum $\mathcal{E}I + I^2r$ is the total electrical power *input* to the upper source. This is what happens when a rechargeable battery (a storage battery) is connected to a charger. The charger supplies electrical energy to the battery; part of it is converted to chemical energy, to be reconverted later, and the remainder is dissipated (wasted) in the battery's internal resistance, warming the battery and causing a heat flow out of it. If you have a power tool or laptop computer with a rechargeable battery, you may have noticed that it gets warm while it is charging.

Problem-Solving Strategy 25.1 | **Power and Energy in Circuits**

IDENTIFY *the relevant concepts:* The ideas of electric power input and output can be applied to any electric circuit. Many problems will ask you to explicitly consider power or energy.

SET UP *the problem* using the following steps:
1. Make a drawing of the circuit.
2. Identify the circuit elements, including sources of emf and resistors. We will introduce other circuit elements later, including capacitors (Chapter 26) and inductors (Chapter 30).
3. Identify the target variables. Typically they will be the power input or output for each circuit element, or the total amount of energy put into or taken out of a circuit element in a given time.

EXECUTE *the solution* as follows:
1. A source of emf $\mathcal{E}$ delivers power $\mathcal{E}I$ into a circuit when current I flows through the source in the direction from $-$ to $+$. (For example, energy is converted from chemical energy in a battery, or from mechanical energy in a generator.) In this case there is a *positive* power output to the circuit or, equivalently, a *negative* power input to the source.
2. A source of emf takes power $\mathcal{E}I$ from a circuit when current passes through the source from $+$ to $-$. (This occurs in charging a storage battery, when electrical energy is converted to chemical energy.) In this case there is a *negative* power output

to the circuit or, equivalently, a *positive* power input to the source.
3. There is always a *positive* power input to a resistor through which current flows, irrespective of the direction of current flow. This process removes energy from the circuit, converting it to heat at the rate $VI = I^2R = V^2/R$, where V is the potential difference across the resistor.
4. Just as in item 3, there always is a positive power input to the internal resistance r of a source through which current flows, irrespective of the direction of current flow. This process likewise removes energy from the circuit, converting it into heat at the rate I^2r.
5. If the power into or out of a circuit element is constant, the energy delivered to or extracted from that element is the product of power and elapsed time. (In Chapter 26 we will encounter situations in which the power is not constant. In such cases, calculating the total energy requires an integral over the relevant time interval.)

EVALUATE *your answer:* Check your results; in particular, check that energy is conserved. This conservation can be expressed in either of two forms: "net power input = net power output" or "the algebraic sum of the power inputs to the circuit elements is zero."

Example 25.8 | **Power input and output in a complete circuit**

For the circuit that we analyzed in Example 25.5, find the rates of energy conversion (chemical to electrical) and energy dissipation in the battery, the rate of energy dissipation in the 4-Ω resistor, and the battery's net power output.

SOLUTION

IDENTIFY and SET UP: Figure 25.24 shows the circuit, gives values of quantities known from Example 25.5, and indicates how we find the target variables. We use Eq. (25.19) to find the battery's net power output, the rate of chemical-to-electrical energy conversion, and the rate of energy dissipation in the battery's internal resistance. We use Eq. (25.18) to find the power delivered to (and dissipated in) the 4-Ω resistor.

EXECUTE: From the first term in Eq. (25.19), the rate of energy conversion in the battery is

$$\mathcal{E}I = (12 \text{ V})(2 \text{ A}) = 24 \text{ W}$$

25.24 Our sketch for this problem.

From the second term in Eq. (25.19), the rate of dissipation of energy in the battery is

$$I^2r = (2 \text{ A})^2(2 \text{ }\Omega) = 8 \text{ W}$$

The *net* electrical power output of the battery is the difference between these: $\mathcal{E}I - I^2r = 16$ W. From Eq. (25.18), the electrical power input to, and the equal rate of dissipation of electrical energy in, the 4-Ω resistor are

$$V_{a'b'}I = (8 \text{ V})(2 \text{ A}) = 16 \text{ W} \quad \text{and}$$
$$I^2R = (2 \text{ A})^2(4 \text{ }\Omega) = 16 \text{ W}$$

EVALUATE: The rate $V_{a'b'}I$ at which energy is supplied to the 4-Ω resistor equals the rate I^2R at which energy is dissipated there. This is also equal to the battery's net power output: $P = V_{ab}I = (8 \text{ V})(2 \text{ A}) = 16$ W. In summary, the rate at which the source of emf supplies energy is $\mathcal{E}I = 24$ W, of which $I^2r = 8$ W is dissipated in the battery's internal resistor and $I^2R = 16$ W is dissipated in the external resistor.

Example 25.9   **Increasing the resistance**

Suppose we replace the external 4-Ω resistor in Fig. 25.24 with an 8-Ω resistor. Hiow does this affect the electrical power dissipated in this resistor?

SOLUTION

IDENTIFY and SET UP: Our target variable is the power dissipated in the resistor to which the battery is connected. The situation is the same as in Example 25.8, but with a higher external resistance R.

EXECUTE: According to Eq. (25.18), the power dissipated in the resistor is $P = I^2R$. You might conclude that making the resistance R twice as great as in Example 25.8 should also make the power twice as great, or $2(16 \text{ W}) = 32$ W. If instead you used the formula $P = V_{ab}^2/R$, you might conclude that the power should be one-half as great as in the preceding example, or $(16 \text{ W})/2 = 8$ W. Which answer is correct?

In fact, *both* of these answers are *incorrect*. The first is wrong because changing the resistance R also changes the current in the circuit (remember, a source of emf does *not* generate the same current in all situations). The second answer is wrong because the potential difference V_{ab} across the resistor changes when the current changes. To get the correct answer, we first find the current just as we did in Example 25.5:

$$I = \frac{\mathcal{E}}{R + r} = \frac{12 \text{ V}}{8 \text{ }\Omega + 2 \text{ }\Omega} = 1.2 \text{ A}$$

The greater resistance causes the current to decrease. The potential difference across the resistor is

$$V_{ab} = IR = (1.2 \text{ A})(8 \text{ }\Omega) = 9.6 \text{ V}$$

which is greater than that with the 4-Ω resistor. We can then find the power dissipated in the resistor in either of two ways:

$$P = I^2R = (1.2 \text{ A})^2(8 \text{ }\Omega) = 12 \text{ W} \quad \text{or}$$
$$P = \frac{V_{ab}^2}{R} = \frac{(9.6 \text{ V})^2}{8 \text{ }\Omega} = 12 \text{ W}$$

EVALUATE: Increasing the resistance R causes a *reduction* in the power input to the resistor. In the expression $P = I^2R$ the decrease in current is more important than the increase in resistance; in the expression $P = V_{ab}^2/R$ the increase in resistance is more important than the increase in V_{ab}. This same principle applies to ordinary light bulbs; a 50-W light bulb has a greater resistance than does a 100-W light bulb.

Can you show that replacing the 4-Ω resistor with an 8-Ω resistor decreases both the rate of energy conversion (chemical to electrical) in the battery and the rate of energy dissipation in the battery?

Example 25.10   **Power in a short circuit**

For the short-circuit situation of Example 25.7, find the rates of energy conversion and energy dissipation in the battery and the net power output of the battery.

SOLUTION

IDENTIFY and SET UP: Our target variables are again the power inputs and outputs associated with the battery. Figure 25.25 shows

25.25 Our sketch for this problem.

the circuit. This is the same situation as in Example 25.8, but now the external resistance R is zero.

EXECUTE: We found in Example 25.7 that the current in this situation is $I = 6$ A. From Eq. (25.19), the rate of energy conversion (chemical to electrical) in the battery is then

$$\mathcal{E}I = (12 \text{ V})(6 \text{ A}) = 72 \text{ W}$$

and the rate of dissipation of energy in the battery is

$$I^2r = (6 \text{ A})^2(2 \text{ }\Omega) = 72 \text{ W}$$

The net power output of the source is $\mathcal{E}I - I^2r = 0$. We get this same result from the expression $P = V_{ab}I$, because the terminal voltage V_{ab} of the source is zero.

EVALUATE: With ideal wires and an ideal ammeter, so that $R = 0$, *all* of the converted energy from the source is dissipated within the source. This is why a short-circuited battery is quickly ruined and may explode.

25.6 Theory of Metallic Conduction

25.26 Random motions of an electron in a metallic crystal (a) with zero electric field and (b) with an electric field that causes drift. The curvatures of the paths are greatly exaggerated.

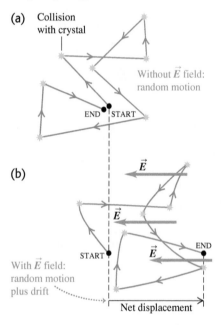

(a) Collision with crystal

Without $\vec{E}$ field: random motion

END   START

(b)

$\vec{E}$

$\vec{E}$

START $\vec{E}$ END

With $\vec{E}$ field: random motion plus drift

Net displacement

PhET: Conductivity

25.27 The motion of a ball rolling down an inclined plane and bouncing off pegs in its path is analogous to the motion of an electron in a metallic conductor with an electric field present.

We can gain additional insight into electrical conduction by looking at the microscopic origin of conductivity. We'll consider a very simple model that treats the electrons as classical particles and ignores their quantum-mechanical behavior in solids. Using this model, we'll derive an expression for the resistivity of a metal. Even though this model is not entirely correct, it will still help you to develop an intuitive idea of the microscopic basis of conduction.

In the simplest microscopic model of conduction in a metal, each atom in the metallic crystal gives up one or more of its outer electrons. These electrons are then free to move through the crystal, colliding at intervals with the stationary positive ions. The motion of the electrons is analogous to the motion of molecules of a gas moving through a porous bed of sand.

If there is no electric field, the electrons move in straight lines between collisions, the directions of their velocities are random, and on average they never get anywhere (Fig. 25.26a). But if an electric field is present, the paths curve slightly because of the acceleration caused by electric-field forces. Figure 25.26b shows a few paths of an electron in an electric field directed from right to left. As we mentioned in Section 25.1, the average speed of random motion is of the order of 10^6 m/s, while the average drift speed is *much* slower, of the order of 10^{-4} m/s. The average time between collisions is called the **mean free time,** denoted by τ. Figure 25.27 shows a mechanical analog of this electron motion.

We would like to derive from this model an expression for the resistivity ρ of a material, defined by Eq. (25.5):

$$\rho = \frac{E}{J} \qquad (25.21)$$

where E and J are the magnitudes of electric field and current density, respectively. The current density $\vec{J}$ is in turn given by Eq. (25.4):

$$\vec{J} = nq\vec{v}_{\mathrm{d}} \qquad (25.22)$$

where n is the number of free electrons per unit volume, $q = -e$ is the charge of each, and $\vec{v}_{\mathrm{d}}$ is their average drift velocity.

We need to relate the drift velocity $\vec{v}_{\mathrm{d}}$ to the electric field $\vec{E}$. The value of $\vec{v}_{\mathrm{d}}$ is determined by a steady-state condition in which, on average, the velocity *gains* of the charges due to the force of the $\vec{E}$ field are just balanced by the velocity *losses* due to collisions. To clarify this process, let's imagine turning on the two effects one at a time. Suppose that before time $t = 0$ there is no field. The electron motion is then completely random. A typical electron has velocity $\vec{v}_0$ at time $t = 0$, and the value of $\vec{v}_0$ averaged over many electrons (that is, the initial velocity of an average electron) is zero: $(\vec{v}_0)_{\mathrm{av}} = \mathbf{0}$. Then at time $t = 0$ we turn on a constant electric field $\vec{E}$. The field exerts a force $\vec{F} = q\vec{E}$ on each charge, and this causes an acceleration $\vec{a}$ in the direction of the force, given by

$$\vec{a} = \frac{\vec{F}}{m} = \frac{q\vec{E}}{m}$$

where m is the electron mass. *Every* electron has this acceleration.

We wait for a time τ, the average time between collisions, and then "turn on" the collisions. An electron that has velocity $\vec{v}_0$ at time $t = 0$ has a velocity at time $t = \tau$ equal to

$$\vec{v} = \vec{v}_0 + \vec{a}\tau$$

The velocity $\vec{v}_{av}$ of an *average* electron at this time is the sum of the averages of the two terms on the right. As we have pointed out, the initial velocity $\vec{v}_0$ is zero for an average electron, so

$$\vec{v}_{av} = \vec{a}\tau = \frac{q\tau}{m}\vec{E} \qquad (25.23)$$

After time $t = \tau$, the tendency of the collisions to decrease the velocity of an average electron (by means of randomizing collisions) just balances the tendency of the $\vec{E}$ field to increase this velocity. Thus the velocity of an average electron, given by Eq. (25.23), is maintained over time and is equal to the drift velocity $\vec{v}_d$:

$$\vec{v}_d = \frac{q\tau}{m}\vec{E}$$

Now we substitute this equation for the drift velocity $\vec{v}_d$ into Eq. (25.22):

$$\vec{J} = nq\vec{v}_d = \frac{nq^2\tau}{m}\vec{E}$$

Comparing this with Eq. (25.21), which we can rewrite as $\vec{J} = \vec{E}/\rho$, and substituting $q = -e$ for an electron, we see that the resistivity ρ is given by

$$\rho = \frac{m}{ne^2\tau} \qquad (25.24)$$

If n and τ are independent of $\vec{E}$, then the resistivity is independent of $\vec{E}$ and the conducting material obeys Ohm's law.

Turning the interactions on one at a time may seem artificial. But the derivation would come out the same if each electron had its own clock and the $t = 0$ times were different for different electrons. If τ is the average time between collisions, then $\vec{v}_d$ is still the average electron drift velocity, even though the motions of the various electrons aren't actually correlated in the way we postulated.

What about the temperature dependence of resistivity? In a perfect crystal with no atoms out of place, a correct quantum-mechanical analysis would let the free electrons move through the crystal with no collisions at all. But the atoms vibrate about their equilibrium positions. As the temperature increases, the amplitudes of these vibrations increase, collisions become more frequent, and the mean free time τ decreases. So this theory predicts that the resistivity of a metal increases with temperature. In a superconductor, roughly speaking, there are no inelastic collisions, τ is infinite, and the resistivity ρ is zero.

In a pure semiconductor such as silicon or germanium, the number of charge carriers per unit volume, n, is not constant but increases very rapidly with increasing temperature. This increase in n far outweighs the decrease in the mean free time, and in a semiconductor the resistivity always decreases rapidly with increasing temperature. At low temperatures, n is very small, and the resistivity becomes so large that the material can be considered an insulator.

Electrons gain energy between collisions through the work done on them by the electric field. During collisions they transfer some of this energy to the atoms of the material of the conductor. This leads to an increase in the material's internal energy and temperature; that's why wires carrying current get warm. If the electric field in the material is large enough, an electron can gain enough energy between collisions to knock off electrons that are normally bound to atoms in the material. These can then knock off more electrons, and so on, leading to an avalanche of current. This is the basis of dielectric breakdown in insulators (see Section 24.4).

Example 25.11 **Mean free time in copper**

Calculate the mean free time between collisions in copper at room temperature.

SOLUTION

IDENTIFY and SET UP: We can obtain an expression for mean free time τ in terms of n, ρ, e, and m by rearranging Eq. (25.24). From Example 25.1 and Table 25.1, for copper $n = 8.5 \times 10^{28}$ m^{-3} and $\rho = 1.72 \times 10^{-8}$ $\Omega \cdot$m. In addition, $e = 1.60 \times 10^{-19}$ C and $m = 9.11 \times 10^{-31}$ kg for electrons.

EXECUTE: From Eq. (25.24), we get

$$\tau = \frac{m}{ne^2\rho}$$

$$= \frac{9.11 \times 10^{-31} \text{ kg}}{(8.5 \times 10^{28} \text{ m}^{-3})(1.60 \times 10^{-19} \text{ C})^2(1.72 \times 10^{-8} \ \Omega \cdot \text{m})}$$

$$= 2.4 \times 10^{-14} \text{ s}$$

EVALUATE: The mean free time is the average time between collisions for a given electron. Taking the reciprocal of this time, we find that each electron averages $1/\tau = 4.2 \times 10^{13}$ collisions per second!

Test Your Understanding of Section 25.6 Which of the following factors will, if increased, make it more difficult to produce a certain amount of current in a conductor? (There may be more than one correct answer.) (i) the mass of the moving charged particles in the conductor; (ii) the number of moving charged particles per cubic meter; (iii) the amount of charge on each moving particle; (iv) the average time between collisions for a typical moving charged particle.

Current and current density: Current is the amount of charge flowing through a specified area, per unit time. The SI unit of current is the ampere (1 A = 1 C/s). The current I through an area A depends on the concentration n and charge q of the charge carriers, as well as on the magnitude of their drift velocity $\vec{v}_d$. The current density is current per unit cross-sectional area. Current is usually described in terms of a flow of positive charge, even when the charges are actually negative or of both signs. (See Example 25.1.)

$$I = \frac{dQ}{dt} = n|q|v_d A \qquad (25.2)$$

$$\vec{J} = nq\vec{v}_d \qquad (25.4)$$

Resistivity: The resistivity ρ of a material is the ratio of the magnitudes of electric field and current density. Good conductors have small resistivity; good insulators have large resistivity. Ohm's law, obeyed approximately by many materials, states that ρ is a constant independent of the value of E. Resistivity usually increases with temperature; for small temperature changes this variation is represented approximately by Eq. (25.6), where α is the temperature coefficient of resistivity.

$$\rho = \frac{E}{J} \qquad (25.5)$$

$$\rho(T) = \rho_0[1 + \alpha(T - T_0)] \qquad (25.6)$$

Metal: ρ increases with increasing T.

Resistors: The potential difference V across a sample of material that obeys Ohm's law is proportional to the current I through the sample. The ratio $V/I = R$ is the resistance of the sample. The SI unit of resistance is the ohm (1 Ω = 1 V/A). The resistance of a cylindrical conductor is related to its resistivity ρ, length L, and cross-sectional area A. (See Examples 25.2 and 25.3.)

$$V = IR \qquad (25.11)$$

$$R = \frac{\rho L}{A} \qquad (25.10)$$

Circuits and emf: A complete circuit has a continuous current-carrying path. A complete circuit carrying a steady current must contain a source of electromotive force (emf) $\mathcal{E}$. The SI unit of electromotive force is the volt (1 V). Every real source of emf has some internal resistance r, so its terminal potential difference V_{ab} depends on current. (See Examples 25.4–25.7.)

$$V_{ab} = \mathcal{E} - Ir \qquad (25.15)$$
(source with internal resistance)

Energy and power in circuits: A circuit element with a potential difference $V_a - V_b = V_{ab}$ and a current I puts energy into a circuit if the current direction is from lower to higher potential in the device, and it takes energy out of the circuit if the current is opposite. The power P equals the product of the potential difference and the current. A resistor always takes electrical energy out of a circuit. (See Examples 25.8–25.10.)

$$P = V_{ab}I \qquad (25.17)$$
(general circuit element)

$$P = V_{ab}I = I^2R = \frac{V_{ab}^2}{R} \qquad (25.18)$$
(power into a resistor)

Conduction in metals: The microscopic basis of conduction in metals is the motion of electrons that move freely through the metallic crystal, bumping into ion cores in the crystal. In a crude classical model of this motion, the resistivity of the material can be related to the electron mass, charge, speed of random motion, density, and mean free time between collisions. (See Example 25.11.)

BRIDGING PROBLEM | **Resistivity, Temperature, and Power**

A toaster using a Nichrome heating element operates on 120 V. When it is switched on at 20°C, the heating element carries an initial current of 1.35 A. A few seconds later the current reaches the steady value of 1.23 A. (a) What is the final temperature of the element? The average value of the temperature coefficient of resistivity for Nichrome over the relevant temperature range is 4.5×10^{-4} (C°)$^{-1}$. (b) What is the power dissipated in the heating element initially and when the current reaches 1.23 A?

SOLUTION GUIDE

See MasteringPhysics® study area for a Video Tutor solution.

IDENTIFY and SET UP

1. A heating element acts as a resistor that converts electrical energy into thermal energy. The resistivity ρ of Nichrome depends on temperature, and hence so does the resistance $R = \rho L/A$ of the heating element and the current $I = V/R$ that it carries.

2. We are given $V = 120$ V and the initial and final values of I. Select an equation that will allow you to find the initial and

final values of resistance, and an equation that relates resistance to temperature [the target variable in part (a)].

3. The power P dissipated in the heating element depends on I and V. Select an equation that will allow you to calculate the initial and final values of P.

EXECUTE

4. Combine your equations from step 2 to give a relationship between the initial and final values of I and the initial and final temperatures (20°C and T_{final}).

5. Solve your expression from step 4 for T_{final}.

6. Use your equation from step 3 to find the initial and final powers.

EVALUATE

7. Is the final temperature greater than or less than 20°C? Does this make sense?

8. Is the final resistance greater than or less than the initial resistance? Again, does this make sense?

9. Is the final power greater than or less than the initial power? Does this agree with your observations in step 8?

Problems

For instructor-assigned homework, go to MasteringPhysics®.

•, ••, •••: Problems of increasing difficulty. **CP**: Cumulative problems incorporating material from earlier chapters. **CALC**: Problems requiring calculus. **BIO**: Biosciences problems.

DISCUSSION QUESTIONS

Q25.1 The definition of resistivity ($\rho = E/J$) implies that an electric field exists inside a conductor. Yet we saw in Chapter 21 that there can be no electric field inside a conductor. Is there a contradiction here? Explain.

Q25.2 A cylindrical rod has resistance R. If we triple its length and diameter, what is its resistance, in terms of R?

Q25.3 A cylindrical rod has resistivity ρ. If we triple its length and diameter, what is its resistivity, in terms of ρ?

Q25.4 Two copper wires with different diameters are joined end to end. If a current flows in the wire combination, what happens to electrons when they move from the larger-diameter wire into the smaller-diameter wire? Does their drift speed increase, decrease, or stay the same? If the drift speed changes, what is the force that causes the change? Explain your reasoning.

Q25.5 When is a 1.5-V AAA battery *not* actually a 1.5-V battery? That is, when do its terminals provide a potential difference of less than 1.5 V?

Q25.6 Can the potential difference between the terminals of a battery ever be opposite in direction to the emf? If it can, give an example. If it cannot, explain why not.

Q25.7 A rule of thumb used to determine the internal resistance of a source is that it is the open-circuit voltage divided by the short-circuit current. Is this correct? Why or why not?

Q25.8 Batteries are always labeled with their emf; for instance, an AA flashlight battery is labeled "1.5 volts." Would it also be appropriate to put a label on batteries stating how much current they provide? Why or why not?

Q25.9 We have seen that a coulomb is an enormous amount of charge; it is virtually impossible to place a charge of 1 C on an object. Yet, a current of 10 A, 10 C/s, is quite reasonable. Explain this apparent discrepancy.

Q25.10 Electrons in an electric circuit pass through a resistor. The wire on either side of the resistor has the same diameter. (a) How does the drift speed of the electrons before entering the resistor compare to the speed after leaving the resistor? Explain your reasoning. (b) How does the potential energy for an electron before entering the resistor compare to the potential energy after leaving the resistor? Explain your reasoning.

Q25.11 Current causes the temperature of a real resistor to increase. Why? What effect does this heating have on the resistance? Explain.

Q25.12 Which of the graphs in Fig. Q25.12 best illustrates the current I in a real resistor as a function of the potential difference V across it? Explain. (*Hint:* See Discussion Question Q25.11.)

Figure **Q25.12**

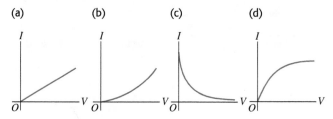

Q25.13 Why does an electric light bulb nearly always burn out just as you turn on the light, almost never while the light is shining?

Q25.14 A light bulb glows because it has resistance. The brightness of a light bulb increases with the electrical power dissipated in the bulb. (a) In the circuit shown in Fig. Q25.14a, the two bulbs *A* and *B* are identical. Compared to bulb *A*, does bulb *B* glow more brightly, just as brightly, or less brightly? Explain your reasoning. (b) Bulb *B* is removed from the circuit and the circuit is completed as shown in Fig. Q25.14b. Compared to the brightness of bulb *A* in Fig. Q25.14a, does bulb *A* now glow more brightly, just as brightly, or less brightly? Explain your reasoning.

Figure **Q25.14**

Q25.15 (See Discussion Question Q25.14.) An ideal ammeter A is placed in a circuit with a battery and a light bulb as shown in Fig. Q25.15a, and the ammeter reading is noted. The circuit is then reconnected as in Fig. Q25.15b, so that the positions of the ammeter and light bulb are reversed. (a) How does the ammeter reading in the situation shown in Fig. Q25.15a compare to the reading in the situation shown in Fig. Q25.15b? Explain your reasoning. (b) In which situation does the light bulb glow more brightly? Explain your reasoning.

Figure **Q25.15**

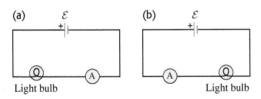

Q25.16 (See Discussion Question Q25.14.) Will a light bulb glow more brightly when it is connected to a battery as shown in Fig. Q25.16a, in which an ideal ammeter A is placed in the circuit, or when it is connected as shown in Fig. 25.16b, in which an ideal voltmeter *V* is placed in the circuit? Explain your reasoning.

Figure **Q25.16**

Q25.17 The energy that can be extracted from a storage battery is always less than the energy that goes into it while it is being charged. Why?

Q25.18 Eight flashlight batteries in series have an emf of about 12 V, similar to that of a car battery. Could they be used to start a car with a dead battery? Why or why not?

Q25.19 Small aircraft often have 24-V electrical systems rather than the 12-V systems in automobiles, even though the electrical power requirements are roughly the same in both applications. The explanation given by aircraft designers is that a 24-V system weighs less than a 12-V system because thinner wires can be used. Explain why this is so.

Q25.20 Long-distance, electric-power, transmission lines always operate at very high voltage, sometimes as much as 750 kV. What are the advantages of such high voltages? What are the disadvantages?

Q25.21 Ordinary household electric lines in North America usually operate at 120 V. Why is this a desirable voltage, rather than a value considerably larger or smaller? On the other hand, automobiles usually have 12-V electrical systems. Why is this a desirable voltage?

Q25.22 A fuse is a device designed to break a circuit, usually by melting when the current exceeds a certain value. What characteristics should the material of the fuse have?

Q25.23 High-voltage power supplies are sometimes designed intentionally to have rather large internal resistance as a safety precaution. Why is such a power supply with a large internal resistance safer than a supply with the same voltage but lower internal resistance?

Q25.24 The text states that good thermal conductors are also good electrical conductors. If so, why don't the cords used to connect toasters, irons, and similar heat-producing appliances get hot by conduction of heat from the heating element?

EXERCISES

Section 25.1 Current

25.1 • **Lightning Strikes.** During lightning strikes from a cloud to the ground, currents as high as 25,000 A can occur and last for about 40 μs. How much charge is transferred from the cloud to the earth during such a strike?

25.2 • A silver wire 2.6 mm in diameter transfers a charge of 420 C in 80 min. Silver contains 5.8×10^{28} free electrons per cubic meter. (a) What is the current in the wire? (b) What is the magnitude of the drift velocity of the electrons in the wire?

25.3 • A 5.00-A current runs through a 12-gauge copper wire (diameter 2.05 mm) and through a light bulb. Copper has 8.5×10^{28} free electrons per cubic meter. (a) How many electrons pass through the light bulb each second? (b) What is the current density in the wire? (c) At what speed does a typical electron pass by any given point in the wire? (d) If you were to use wire of twice the diameter, which of the above answers would change? Would they increase or decrease?

25.4 • An 18-gauge copper wire (diameter 1.02 mm) carries a current with a current density of 1.50×10^6 A/m^2. The density of free electrons for copper is 8.5×10^{28} electrons per cubic meter. Calculate (a) the current in the wire and (b) the drift velocity of electrons in the wire.

25.5 •• Copper has 8.5×10^{28} free electrons per cubic meter. A 71.0-cm length of 12-gauge copper wire that is 2.05 mm in diameter carries 4.85 A of current. (a) How much time does it take for an electron to travel the length of the wire? (b) Repeat part (a) for 6-gauge copper wire (diameter 4.12 mm) of the same length that carries the same current. (c) Generally speaking, how does changing the diameter of a wire that carries a given amount of current affect the drift velocity of the electrons in the wire?

25.6 • Consider the 18-gauge wire in Example 25.1. How many atoms are in 1.00 m^3 of copper? With the density of free electrons given in the example, how many free electrons are there per copper atom?

25.7 • **CALC** The current in a wire varies with time according to the relationship $I = 55$ A $- (0.65$ A/s$^2)t^2$. (a) How many coulombs of charge pass a cross section of the wire in the time interval between $t = 0$ and $t = 8.0$ s? (b) What constant current would transport the same charge in the same time interval?

25.8 • Current passes through a solution of sodium chloride. In 1.00 s, 2.68×10^{16} Na$^+$ ions arrive at the negative electrode and 3.92×10^{16} Cl$^-$ ions arrive at the positive electrode. (a) What is the current passing between the electrodes? (b) What is the direction of the current?

25.9 • **BIO** **Transmission of Nerve Impulses.** Nerve cells transmit electric signals through their long tubular axons. These signals propagate due to a sudden rush of Na$^+$ ions, each with charge $+e$, into the axon. Measurements have revealed that typically about 5.6×10^{11} Na$^+$ ions enter each meter of the axon during a time of 10 ms. What is the current during this inflow of charge in a meter of axon?

Section 25.2 Resistivity and Section 25.3 Resistance

25.10 • (a) At room temperature what is the strength of the electric field in a 12-gauge copper wire (diameter 2.05 mm) that is needed to cause a 2.75-A current to flow? (b) What field would be needed if the wire were made of silver instead?

25.11 •• A 1.50-m cylindrical rod of diameter 0.500 cm is connected to a power supply that maintains a constant potential difference of 15.0 V across its ends, while an ammeter measures the current through it. You observe that at room temperature (20.0°C) the ammeter reads 18.5 A, while at 92.0°C it reads 17.2 A. You can ignore any thermal expansion of the rod. Find (a) the resistivity at 20.0°C and (b) the temperature coefficient of resistivity at 20°C for the material of the rod.

25.12 • A copper wire has a square cross section 2.3 mm on a side. The wire is 4.0 m long and carries a current of 3.6 A. The density of free electrons is $8.5 \times 10^{28}/$m^3. Find the magnitudes of (a) the current density in the wire and (b) the electric field in the wire. (c) How much time is required for an electron to travel the length of the wire?

25.13 • A 14-gauge copper wire of diameter 1.628 mm carries a current of 12.5 mA. (a) What is the potential difference across a 2.00-m length of the wire? (b) What would the potential difference in part (a) be if the wire were silver instead of copper, but all else were the same?

25.14 •• A wire 6.50 m long with diameter of 2.05 mm has a resistance of 0.0290 Ω. What material is the wire most likely made of?

25.15 •• A cylindrical tungsten filament 15.0 cm long with a diameter of 1.00 mm is to be used in a machine for which the temperature will range from room temperature (20°C) up to 120°C. It will carry a current of 12.5 A at all temperatures (consult Tables 25.1 and 25.2). (a) What will be the maximum electric field in this filament, and (b) what will be its resistance with that field? (c) What will be the maximum potential drop over the full length of the filament?

25.16 •• A ductile metal wire has resistance R. What will be the resistance of this wire in terms of R if it is stretched to three times its original length, assuming that the density and resistivity of the material do not change when the wire is stretched? (*Hint:* The amount of metal does not change, so stretching out the wire will affect its cross-sectional area.)

25.17 • In household wiring, copper wire 2.05 mm in diameter is often used. Find the resistance of a 24.0-m length of this wire.

25.18 •• What diameter must a copper wire have if its resistance is to be the same as that of an equal length of aluminum wire with diameter 3.26 mm?

25.19 • You need to produce a set of cylindrical copper wires 3.50 m long that will have a resistance of 0.125 Ω each. What will be the mass of each of these wires?

25.20 • A tightly coiled spring having 75 coils, each 3.50 cm in diameter, is made of insulated metal wire 3.25 mm in diameter. An ohmmeter connected across its opposite ends reads 1.74 Ω. What is the resistivity of the metal?

25.21 • An aluminum cube has sides of length 1.80 m. What is the resistance between two opposite faces of the cube?

25.22 • You apply a potential difference of 4.50 V between the ends of a wire that is 2.50 m in length and 0.654 mm in radius. The resulting current through the wire is 17.6 A. What is the resistivity of the wire?

25.23 • A current-carrying gold wire has diameter 0.84 mm. The electric field in the wire is 0.49 V/m. What are (a) the current carried by the wire; (b) the potential difference between two points in the wire 6.4 m apart; (c) the resistance of a 6.4-m length of this wire?

25.24 • A hollow aluminum cylinder is 2.50 m long and has an inner radius of 3.20 cm and an outer radius of 4.60 cm. Treat each surface (inner, outer, and the two end faces) as an equipotential surface. At room temperature, what will an ohmmeter read if it is connected between (a) the opposite faces and (b) the inner and outer surfaces?

25.25 • (a) What is the resistance of a Nichrome wire at 0.0°C if its resistance is 100.00 Ω at 11.5°C? (b) What is the resistance of a carbon rod at 25.8°C if its resistance is 0.0160 Ω at 0.0°C?

25.26 • A carbon resistor is to be used as a thermometer. On a winter day when the temperature is 4.0°C, the resistance of the carbon resistor is 217.3 Ω. What is the temperature on a spring day when the resistance is 215.8 Ω? (Take the reference temperature T_0 to be 4.0°C.)

25.27 • A strand of wire has resistance 5.60 $\mu\Omega$. Find the net resistance of 120 such strands if they are (a) placed side by side to form a cable of the same length as a single strand, and (b) connected end to end to form a wire 120 times as long as a single strand.

Section 25.4 Electromotive Force and Circuits

25.28 • Consider the circuit shown in Fig. E25.28. The terminal voltage of the 24.0-V battery is 21.2 V. What are (a) the internal resistance r of the battery and (b) the resistance R of the circuit resistor?

Figure **E25.28**

25.29 • A copper transmission cable 100 km long and 10.0 cm in diameter carries a current of 125 A. (a) What is the potential drop across the cable? (b) How much electrical energy is dissipated as thermal energy every hour?

25.30 • An idealized ammeter is connected to a battery as shown in Fig. E25.30. Find (a) the reading of the ammeter, (b) the current through the 4.00-Ω resistor, (c) the terminal voltage of the battery.

Figure **E25.30**

25.31 • An ideal voltmeter V is connected to a 2.0-Ω resistor and a battery with emf 5.0 V and internal resistance 0.5 Ω as shown in Fig. E25.31. (a) What is the current in the 2.0-Ω resistor? (b) What is the terminal voltage of the battery? (c) What is the reading on the voltmeter? Explain your answers.

Figure **E25.31**

0.5 Ω 5.0 V
2.0 Ω

25.32 • The circuit shown in Fig. E25.32 contains two batteries, each with an emf and an internal resistance, and two resistors. Find (a) the current in the circuit (magnitude *and* direction); (b) the terminal voltage V_{ab} of the 16.0-V battery; (c) the potential difference V_{ac} of point a with respect to point c. (d) Using Fig. 25.20 as a model, graph the potential rises and drops in this circuit.

Figure **E25.32**

1.6 Ω 16.0 V
a b
5.0 Ω 9.0 Ω
1.4 Ω 8.0 V
c

25.33 • When switch S in Fig. E25.33 is open, the voltmeter V of the battery reads 3.08 V. When the switch is closed, the voltmeter reading drops to 2.97 V, and the ammeter A reads 1.65 A. Find the emf, the internal resistance of the battery, and the circuit resistance R. Assume that the two meters are ideal, so they don't affect the circuit.

Figure **E25.33**

r $\mathcal{E}$
R
S

25.34 • In the circuit of Fig. E25.32, the 5.0-Ω resistor is removed and replaced by a resistor of unknown resistance R. When this is done, an ideal voltmeter connected across the points b and c reads 1.9 V. Find (a) the current in the circuit and (b) the resistance R. (c) Graph the potential rises and drops in this circuit (see Fig. 25.20).

25.35 • In the circuit shown in Fig. E25.32, the 16.0-V battery is removed and reinserted with the opposite polarity, so that its negative terminal is now next to point a. Find (a) the current in the circuit (magnitude *and* direction); (b) the terminal voltage V_{ba} of the 16.0-V battery; (c) the potential difference V_{ac} of point a with respect to point c. (d) Graph the potential rises and drops in this circuit (see Fig. 25.20).

25.36 • The following measurements were made on a Thyrite resistor:

I (A)	0.50	1.00	2.00	4.00
V_{ab} (V)	2.55	3.11	3.77	4.58

(a) Graph V_{ab} as a function of I. (b) Does Thyrite obey Ohm's law? How can you tell? (c) Graph the resistance $R = V_{ab}/I$ as a function of I.

25.37 • The following measurements of current and potential difference were made on a resistor constructed of Nichrome wire:

I (A)	0.50	1.00	2.00	4.00
V_{ab} (V)	1.94	3.88	7.76	15.52

(a) Graph V_{ab} as a function of I. (b) Does Nichrome obey Ohm's law? How can you tell? (c) What is the resistance of the resistor in ohms?

25.38 •• The circuit shown in Fig. E25.38 contains two batteries, each with an emf and an internal resistance, and two resistors. Find

(a) the current in the circuit (magnitude and direction) and (b) the terminal voltage V_{ab} of the 16.0-V battery.

Figure **E25.38**

1.6 Ω 16.0 V
a b
5.0 Ω 9.0 Ω
1.4 Ω 8.0 V

Section 25.5 Energy and Power in Electric Circuits

25.39 • **Light Bulbs.** The power rating of a light bulb (such as a 100-W bulb) is the power it dissipates when connected across a 120-V potential difference. What is the resistance of (a) a 100-W bulb and (b) a 60-W bulb? (c) How much current does each bulb draw in normal use?

25.40 • If a "75-W" bulb (see Problem 25.39) is connected across a 220-V potential difference (as is used in Europe), how much power does it dissipate?

25.41 • **European Light Bulb.** In Europe the standard voltage in homes is 220 V instead of the 120 V used in the United States. Therefore a "100-W" European bulb would be intended for use with a 220-V potential difference (see Problem 25.40). (a) If you bring a "100-W" European bulb home to the United States, what should be its U.S. power rating? (b) How much current will the 100-W European bulb draw in normal use in the United States?

25.42 • A battery-powered global positioning system (GPS) receiver operating on 9.0 V draws a current of 0.13 A. How much electrical energy does it consume during 1.5 h?

25.43 • Consider a resistor with length L, uniform cross-sectional area A, and uniform resistivity ρ that is carrying a current with uniform current density J. Use Eq. (25.18) to find the electrical power dissipated per unit volume, p. Express your result in terms of (a) E and J; (b) J and ρ; (c) E and ρ.

25.44 • BIO **Electric Eels.** Electric eels generate electric pulses along their skin that can be used to stun an enemy when they come into contact with it. Tests have shown that these pulses can be up to 500 V and produce currents of 80 mA (or even larger). A typical pulse lasts for 10 ms. What power and how much energy are delivered to the unfortunate enemy with a single pulse, assuming a steady current?

25.45 • BIO **Treatment of Heart Failure.** A heart defibrillator is used to enable the heart to start beating if it has stopped. This is done by passing a large current of 12 A through the body at 25 V for a very short time, usually about 3.0 ms. (a) What power does the defibrillator deliver to the body, and (b) how much energy is transferred?

25.46 • Consider the circuit of Fig. E25.32. (a) What is the total rate at which electrical energy is dissipated in the 5.0-Ω and 9.0-Ω resistors? (b) What is the power output of the 16.0-V battery? (c) At what rate is electrical energy being converted to other forms in the 8.0-V battery? (d) Show that the power output of the 16.0-V battery equals the overall rate of dissipation of electrical energy in the rest of the circuit.

25.47 •• The capacity of a storage battery, such as those used in automobile electrical systems, is rated in ampere-hours (A·h). A 50-A·h battery can supply a current of 50 A for 1.0 h, or 25 A for 2.0 h, and so on. (a) What total energy can be supplied by a 12-V, 60-A·h battery if its internal resistance is negligible? (b) What volume (in liters) of gasoline has a total heat of combustion equal to the energy obtained in part (a)? (See Section 17.6; the density of gasoline is 900 kg/m³.) (c) If a generator with an average electrical power output of 0.45 kW is connected to the battery, how much time will be required for it to charge the battery fully?

25.48 • In the circuit analyzed in Example 25.8 the 4.0-Ω resistor is replaced by a 8.0-Ω resistor, as in Example 25.9. (a) Calculate the rate of conversion of chemical energy to electrical energy in the battery. How does your answer compare to the result calculated in Example 25.8? (b) Calculate the rate of electrical energy dissipation in the internal resistance of the battery. How does your answer compare to the result calculated in Example 25.8? (c) Use the results of parts (a) and (b) to calculate the net power output of the battery. How does your result compare to the electrical power dissipated in the 8.0-Ω resistor as calculated for this circuit in Example 25.9?

25.49 •• A 25.0-Ω bulb is connected across the terminals of a 12.0-V battery having 3.50 Ω of internal resistance. What percentage of the power of the battery is dissipated across the internal resistance and hence is not available to the bulb?

25.50 • An idealized voltmeter is connected across the terminals of a 15.0-V battery, and a 75.0-Ω appliance is also connected across its terminals. If the voltmeter reads 11.3 V: (a) how much power is being dissipated by the appliance, and (b) what is the internal resistance of the battery?

25.51 • In the circuit in Fig. E25.51, find (a) the rate of conversion of internal (chemical) energy to electrical energy within the battery; (b) the rate of dissipation of electrical energy in the battery; (c) the rate of dissipation of electrical energy in the external resistor.

Figure **E25.51**

25.52 •• A typical small flashlight contains two batteries, each having an emf of 1.5 V, connected in series with a bulb having resistance 17 Ω. (a) If the internal resistance of the batteries is negligible, what power is delivered to the bulb? (b) If the batteries last for 5.0 h, what is the total energy delivered to the bulb? (c) The resistance of real batteries increases as they run down. If the initial internal resistance is negligible, what is the combined internal resistance of both batteries when the power to the bulb has decreased to half its initial value? (Assume that the resistance of the bulb is constant. Actually, it will change somewhat when the current through the filament changes, because this changes the temperature of the filament and hence the resistivity of the filament wire.)

25.53 • A "540-W" electric heater is designed to operate from 120-V lines. (a) What is its resistance? (b) What current does it draw? (c) If the line voltage drops to 110 V, what power does the heater take? (Assume that the resistance is constant. Actually, it will change because of the change in temperature.) (d) The heater coils are metallic, so that the resistance of the heater decreases with decreasing temperature. If the change of resistance with temperature is taken into account, will the electrical power consumed by the heater be larger or smaller than what you calculated in part (c)? Explain.

Section 25.6 Theory of Metallic Conduction

25.54 •• Pure silicon contains approximately 1.0×10^{16} free electrons per cubic meter. (a) Referring to Table 25.1, calculate the mean free time τ for silicon at room temperature. (b) Your answer in part (a) is much greater than the mean free time for copper given in Example 25.11. Why, then, does pure silicon have such a high resistivity compared to copper?

PROBLEMS

25.55 • An electrical conductor designed to carry large currents has a circular cross section 2.50 mm in diameter and is 14.0 m long. The resistance between its ends is 0.104 Ω. (a) What is the resistivity of the material? (b) If the electric-field magnitude in the conductor is 1.28 V/m, what is the total current? (c) If the material has 8.5×10^{28} free electrons per cubic meter, find the average drift speed under the conditions of part (b).

25.56 •• A plastic tube 25.0 m long and 3.00 cm in diameter is dipped into a silver solution, depositing a layer of silver 0.100 mm thick uniformly over the outer surface of the tube. If this coated tube is then connected across a 12.0-V battery, what will be the current?

25.57 •• On your first day at work as an electrical technician, you are asked to determine the resistance per meter of a long piece of wire. The company you work for is poorly equipped. You find a battery, a voltmeter, and an ammeter, but no meter for directly measuring resistance (an ohmmeter). You put the leads from the voltmeter across the terminals of the battery, and the meter reads 12.6 V. You cut off a 20.0-m length of wire and connect it to the battery, with an ammeter in series with it to measure the current in the wire. The ammeter reads 7.00 A. You then cut off a 40.0-m length of wire and connect it to the battery, again with the ammeter in series to measure the current. The ammeter reads 4.20 A. Even though the equipment you have available to you is limited, your boss assures you of its high quality: The ammeter has very small resistance, and the voltmeter has very large resistance. What is the resistance of 1 meter of wire?

25.58 • A 2.0-mm length of wire is made by welding the end of a 120-cm-long silver wire to the end of an 80-cm-long copper wire. Each piece of wire is 0.60 mm in diameter. The wire is at room temperature, so the resistivities are as given in Table 25.1. A potential difference of 5.0 V is maintained between the ends of the 2.0-m composite wire. (a) What is the current in the copper section? (b) What is the current in the silver section? (c) What is the magnitude of $\vec{E}$ in the copper? (d) What is the magnitude of $\vec{E}$ in the silver? (e) What is the potential difference between the ends of the silver section of wire?

25.59 • A 3.00-m length of copper wire at 20°C has a 1.20-m-long section with diameter 1.60 mm and a 1.80-m-long section with diameter 0.80 mm. There is a current of 2.5 mA in the 1.60-mm-diameter section. (a) What is the current in the 0.80-mm-diameter section? (b) What is the magnitude of $\vec{E}$ in the 1.60-mm-diameter section? (c) What is the magnitude of $\vec{E}$ in the 0.80-mm-diameter section? (d) What is the potential difference between the ends of the 3.00-m length of wire?

25.60 • **Critical Current Density in Superconductors.** One problem with some of the newer high-temperature superconductors is getting a large enough current density for practical use without causing the resistance to reappear. The maximum current density for which the material will remain a superconductor is called the critical current density of the material. In 1987, IBM research labs had produced thin films with critical current densities of 1.0×10^5 A/cm². (a) How much current could an 18-gauge wire (see Example 25.1 in Section 25.1) of this material carry and still remain superconducting? (b) Researchers are trying to develop superconductors with critical current densities of 1.0×10^6 A/cm². What diameter cylindrical wire of such a material would be needed to carry 1000 A without losing its superconductivity?

25.61 •• **CP** A Nichrome heating element that has resistance 28.0 Ω is connected to a battery that has emf 96.0 V and internal resistance 1.2 Ω. An aluminum cup with mass 0.130 kg contains 0.200 kg of water. The heating element is placed in the water and the electrical energy dissipated in the resistance of the heating element all goes into the cup and water. The element itself has very small mass. How much time does it take for the temperature of the cup and water to rise from 21.2°C to 34.5°C? (The change of the resistance of the Nichrome due to its temperature change can be neglected.)

25.62 •• A resistor with resistance R is connected to a battery that has emf 12.0 V and internal resistance $r = 0.40$ Ω. For what two values of R will the power dissipated in the resistor be 80.0 W?

25.63 •• **CP BIO Struck by Lightning.** Lightning strikes can involve currents as high as 25,000 A that last for about 40 μs. If a person is struck by a bolt of lightning with these properties, the current will pass through his body. We shall assume that his mass is 75 kg, that he is wet (after all, he is in a rainstorm) and therefore has a resistance of 1.0 kΩ, and that his body is all water (which is reasonable for a rough, but plausible, approximation). (a) By how many degrees Celsius would this lightning bolt increase the temperature of 75 kg of water? (b) Given that the internal body temperature is about 37°C, would the person's temperature actually increase that much? Why not? What would happen first?

25.64 •• In the Bohr model of the hydrogen atom, the electron makes 6.0×10^{15} rev/s around the nucleus. What is the average current at a point on the orbit of the electron?

25.65 • **CALC** A material of resistivity ρ is formed into a solid, truncated cone of height h and radii r_1 and r_2 at either end (Fig. P25.65). (a) Calculate the resistance of the cone between the two flat end faces. (*Hint:* Imagine slicing the cone into very many thin disks, and calculate the resistance of one such disk.) (b) Show that your result agrees with Eq. (25.10) when $r_1 = r_2$.

Figure **P25.65**

25.66 • **CALC** The region between two concentric conducting spheres with radii a and b is filled with a conducting material with resistivity ρ. (a) Show that the resistance between the spheres is given by

$$R = \frac{\rho}{4\pi}\left(\frac{1}{a} - \frac{1}{b}\right)$$

(b) Derive an expression for the current density as a function of radius, in terms of the potential difference V_{ab} between the spheres. (c) Show that the result in part (a) reduces to Eq. (25.10) when the separation $L = b - a$ between the spheres is small.

25.67 ••• The temperature coefficient of resistance α in Eq. (25.12) equals the temperature coefficient of resistivity α in Eq. (25.6) only if the coefficient of thermal expansion is small. A cylindrical column of mercury is in a vertical glass tube. At 20°C, the length of the mercury column is 12.0 cm. The diameter of the mercury column is 1.6 mm and doesn't change with temperature because glass has a small coefficient of thermal expansion. The coefficient of volume expansion of the mercury is given in Table 17.2, its resistivity at 20°C is given in Table 25.1, and its temperature coefficient of resistivity is given in Table 25.2. (a) At 20°C, what is the resistance between the ends of the mercury column? (b) The mercury column is heated to 60°C. What is the change in its resistivity? (c) What is the change in its length? Explain why the coefficient of volume expansion, rather than the coefficient of linear expansion, determines the change in length. (d) What is the change in its resistance? (*Hint:* Since the percentage changes in ρ and L are small, you may find it helpful to derive from Eq. (25.10) an

equation for ΔR in terms of $\Delta\rho$ and ΔL.) (e) What is the temperature coefficient of resistance α for the mercury column, as defined in Eq. (25.12)? How does this value compare with the temperature coefficient of resistivity? Is the effect of the change in length important?

25.68 • (a) What is the potential difference V_{ad} in the circuit of Fig. P25.68? (b) What is the terminal voltage of the 4.00-V battery? (c) A battery with emf 10.30 V and internal resistance 0.50 Ω is inserted in the circuit at d, with its negative terminal connected to the negative terminal of the 8.00-V battery. What is the difference of potential V_{bc} between the terminals of the 4.00-V battery now?

Figure **P25.68**

25.69 • The potential difference across the terminals of a battery is 8.40 V when there is a current of 1.50 A in the battery from the negative to the positive terminal. When the current is 3.50 A in the reverse direction, the potential difference becomes 10.20 V. (a) What is the internal resistance of the battery? (b) What is the emf of the battery?

25.70 •• **BIO** A person with body resistance between his hands of 10 kΩ accidentally grasps the terminals of a 14-kV power supply. (a) If the internal resistance of the power supply is 2000 Ω, what is the current through the person's body? (b) What is the power dissipated in his body? (c) If the power supply is to be made safe by increasing its internal resistance, what should the internal resistance be for the maximum current in the above situation to be 1.00 mA or less?

25.71 • **BIO** The average bulk resistivity of the human body (apart from surface resistance of the skin) is about 5.0 Ω·m. The conducting path between the hands can be represented approximately as a cylinder 1.6 m long and 0.10 m in diameter. The skin resistance can be made negligible by soaking the hands in salt water. (a) What is the resistance between the hands if the skin resistance is negligible? (b) What potential difference between the hands is needed for a lethal shock current of 100 mA? (Note that your result shows that small potential differences produce dangerous currents when the skin is damp.) (c) With the current in part (b), what power is dissipated in the body?

25.72 • A typical cost for electric power is $0.120 per kilowatt-hour. (a) Some people leave their porch light on all the time. What is the yearly cost to keep a 75-W bulb burning day and night? (b) Suppose your refrigerator uses 400 W of power when it's running, and it runs 8 hours a day. What is the yearly cost of operating your refrigerator?

25.73 •• A 12.6-V car battery with negligible internal resistance is connected to a series combination of a 3.2-Ω resistor that obeys Ohm's law and a thermistor that does not obey Ohm's law but instead has a current–voltage relationship $V = \alpha I + \beta I^2$, with $\alpha = 3.8$ Ω and $\beta = 1.3$ Ω/A. What is the current through the 3.2-Ω resistor?

25.74 •• A cylindrical copper cable 1.50 km long is connected across a 220.0-V potential difference. (a) What should be its diameter so that it produces heat at a rate of 75.0 W? (b) What is the electric field inside the cable under these conditions?

25.75 •• **A Nonideal Ammeter.** Unlike the idealized ammeter described in Section 25.4, any real ammeter has a nonzero resistance. (a) An ammeter with resistance R_A is connected in series with a resistor R and a battery of emf $\mathcal{E}$ and internal resistance r. The current measured by the ammeter is I_A. Find the current through the circuit if the ammeter is removed so that the battery and the resistor form a complete circuit. Express your answer in terms of I_A, r, R_A, and R. The more "ideal" the ammeter, the smaller the difference between this current and the current I_A. (b) If $R = 3.80$ Ω, $\mathcal{E} = 7.50$ V, and $r = 0.45$ Ω, find the maximum value of the ammeter resistance R_A so that I_A is within 1.0% of the current in the circuit when the ammeter is absent. (c) Explain why your answer in part (b) represents a *maximum* value.

25.76 • **CALC** A 1.50-m cylinder of radius 1.10 cm is made of a complicated mixture of materials. Its resistivity depends on the distance x from the left end and obeys the formula $\rho(x) = a + bx^2$, where a and b are constants. At the left end, the resistivity is 2.25×10^{-8} $\Omega \cdot$m, while at the right end it is 8.50×10^{-8} $\Omega \cdot$m. (a) What is the resistance of this rod? (b) What is the electric field at its midpoint if it carries a 1.75-A current? (c) If we cut the rod into two 75.0-cm halves, what is the resistance of each half?

25.77 •• According to the U.S. National Electrical Code, copper wire used for interior wiring of houses, hotels, office buildings, and industrial plants is permitted to carry no more than a specified maximum amount of current. The table below shows the maximum current I_{max} for several common sizes of wire with varnished cambric insulation. The "wire gauge" is a standard used to describe the diameter of wires. Note that the larger the diameter of the wire, the *smaller* the wire gauge.

Wire gauge	Diameter (cm)	I_{max} (A)
14	0.163	18
12	0.205	25
10	0.259	30
8	0.326	40
6	0.412	60
5	0.462	65
4	0.519	85

(a) What considerations determine the maximum current-carrying capacity of household wiring? (b) A total of 4200 W of power is to be supplied through the wires of a house to the household electrical appliances. If the potential difference across the group of appliances is 120 V, determine the gauge of the thinnest permissible wire that can be used. (c) Suppose the wire used in this house is of the gauge found in part (b) and has total length 42.0 m. At what rate is energy dissipated in the wires? (d) The house is built in a community where the consumer cost of electric energy is $0.11 per kilowatt-hour. If the house were built with wire of the next larger diameter than that found in part (b), what would be the savings in electricity costs in one year? Assume that the appliances are kept on for an average of 12 hours a day.

25.78 •• **Compact Fluorescent Bulbs.** Compact fluorescent bulbs are much more efficient at producing light than are ordinary incandescent bulbs. They initially cost much more, but they last far longer and use much less electricity. According to one study of these bulbs, a compact bulb that produces as much light as a 100-W incandescent bulb uses only 23 W of power. The compact bulb lasts 10,000 hours, on the average, and costs $11.00, whereas the incandescent bulb costs only $0.75, but lasts just 750 hours. The study assumed that electricity costs $0.080 per kilowatt-hour and that the bulbs are on for 4.0 h per day. (a) What is the total cost (including the price of the bulbs) to run each bulb for 3.0 years? (b) How much do you save over 3.0 years if you use a compact fluorescent bulb instead of an incandescent bulb? (c) What is the resistance of a "100-W" fluorescent bulb? (Remember, it actually uses only 23 W of power and operates across 120 V.)

25.79 • In the circuit of Fig. P25.79, find (a) the current through the 8.0-Ω resistor and (b) the total rate of dissipation of electrical energy in the 8.0-Ω resistor and in the internal resistance of the batteries. (c) In one of the batteries, chemical energy is being converted into electrical energy. In which one is this happening, and at what rate? (d) In one of the batteries, electrical energy is being converted into chemical energy. In which one is this happening, and at what rate? (e) Show that the overall rate of production of electrical energy equals the overall rate of consumption of electrical energy in the circuit.

Figure **P25.79**

$\mathcal{E}_1 = 12.0$ V $\quad r_1 = 1.0$ Ω

$R = 8.0$ Ω

$\mathcal{E}_2 = 8.0$ V $\quad r_2 = 1.0$ Ω

25.80 • A lightning bolt strikes one end of a steel lightning rod, producing a 15,000-A current burst that lasts for 65 μs. The rod is 2.0 m long and 1.8 cm in diameter, and its other end is connected to the ground by 35 m of 8.0-mm-diameter copper wire. (a) Find the potential difference between the top of the steel rod and the lower end of the copper wire during the current burst. (b) Find the total energy deposited in the rod and wire by the current burst.

25.81 • A 12.0-V battery has an internal resistance of 0.24 Ω and a capacity of 50.0 A $\cdot$ h (see Exercise 25.47). The battery is charged by passing a 10-A current through it for 5.0 h. (a) What is the terminal voltage during charging? (b) What total electrical energy is supplied to the battery during charging? (c) What electrical energy is dissipated in the internal resistance during charging? (d) The battery is now completely discharged through a resistor, again with a constant current of 10 A. What is the external circuit resistance? (e) What total electrical energy is supplied to the external resistor? (f) What total electrical energy is dissipated in the internal resistance? (g) Why are the answers to parts (b) and (e) not the same?

25.82 • Repeat Problem 25.81 with charge and discharge currents of 30 A. The charging and discharging times will now be 1.7 h rather than 5.0 h. What differences in performance do you see?

25.83 •• **CP** Consider the circuit shown in Fig. P25.83. The emf source has negligible internal resistance. The resistors have resistances $R_1 = 6.00$ Ω and $R_2 = 4.00$ Ω. The capacitor has capacitance $C = 9.00$ μF. When the capacitor is fully charged, the magnitude of the charge on its plates is $Q = 36.0$ μC. Calculate the emf $\mathcal{E}$.

Figure **P25.83**

R_2

$\mathcal{E}$ $\quad R_1$ $\quad C$

25.84 •• **CP** Consider the circuit shown in Fig. P25.84. The battery has emf 60.0 V and negligible internal resistance. $R_2 = 2.00$ Ω, $C_1 = 3.00$ μF, and $C_2 = 6.00$ μF. After the capacitors have attained their final charges, the charge on C_1 is $Q_1 = 18.0$ μC . (a) What is the final charge on C_2? (b) What is the resistance R_1?

Figure **P25.84**

R_1

$\mathcal{E}$ $\quad R_2$ $\quad C_1$ $\quad C_2$

CHALLENGE PROBLEMS

25.85 ••• The *Tolman-Stewart ex-periment* in 1916 demonstrated that the free charges in a metal have negative charge and pro-vided a quantitative measurement of their charge-to-mass ratio, $|q|/m$. The experiment consisted of abruptly stopping a rapidly rotating spool of wire and measuring the potential difference that this produced between the ends of the wire. In a simplified model of this experiment, consider a metal rod of length L that is given a uniform acceleration $\vec{a}$ to the right. Initially the free charges in the metal lag behind the rod's motion, thus setting up an electric field $\vec{E}$ in the rod. In the steady state this field exerts a force on the free charges that makes them accelerate along with the rod. (a) Apply $\sum \vec{F} = m\vec{a}$ to the free charges to obtain an expression for $|q|/m$ in terms of the magnitudes of the induced electric field $\vec{E}$ and the acceleration $\vec{a}$. (b) If all the free charges in the metal rod have the same acceleration, the electric field $\vec{E}$ is the same at all points in the rod. Use this fact to rewrite the expression for $|q|/m$ in terms of the potential V_{bc} between the ends of the rod (Fig. P25.85). (c) If the free charges have negative charge, which end of the rod, b or c, is at higher potential? (d) If the rod is 0.50 m long and the free

Figure **P25.85**

charges are electrons (charge $q = -1.60 \times 10^{-19}$ C, mass 9.11×10^{-31} kg), what magnitude of acceleration is required to produce a potential difference of 1.0 mV between the ends of the rod? (e) Discuss why the actual experiment used a rotating spool of thin wire rather than a moving bar as in our simplified analysis.

25.86 ••• CALC A source with emf $\mathcal{E}$ and internal resistance r is connected to an external circuit. (a) Show that the power output of the source is maximum when the current in the circuit is one-half the short-circuit current of the source. (b) If the external circuit consists of a resistance R, show that the power output is maximum when $R = r$ and that the maximum power is $\mathcal{E}^2/4r$.

25.87 ••• CALC The resistivity of a semiconductor can be modi-fied by adding different amounts of impurities. A rod of semicon-ducting material of length L and cross-sectional area A lies along the x-axis between $x = 0$ and $x = L$. The material obeys Ohm's law, and its resistivity varies along the rod according to $\rho(x) = \rho_0 \exp(-x/L)$. The end of the rod at $x = 0$ is at a potential V_0 greater than the end at $x = L$. (a) Find the total resistance of the rod and the current in the rod. (b) Find the electric-field magnitude $E(x)$ in the rod as a function of x. (c) Find the electric potential $V(x)$ in the rod as a function of x. (d) Graph the functions $\rho(x)$, $E(x)$, and $V(x)$ for values of x between $x = 0$ and $x = L$.

Answers

Chapter Opening Question ?

The current out equals the current in. In other words, charge must enter the bulb at the same rate as it exits the bulb. It is not "used up" or consumed as it flows through the bulb.

Test Your Understanding Questions

25.1 Answer: (v) Doubling the diameter increases the cross-sectional area A by a factor of 4. Hence the current-density magni-tude $J = I/A$ is reduced to $\frac{1}{4}$ of the value in Example 25.1, and the magnitude of the drift velocity $v_d = J/n|q|$ is reduced by the same factor. The new magnitude is $v_d = (0.15 \text{ mm/s})/4 = 0.038 \text{ mm/s}$. This behavior is the same as that of an incompressible fluid, which slows down when it moves from a narrow pipe to a broader one (see Section 14.4).

25.2 Answer: (ii) Figure 25.6b shows that the resistivity ρ of a semiconductor increases as the temperature decreases. From Eq. (25.5), the magnitude of the current density is $J = E/\rho$, so the cur-rent density decreases as the temperature drops and the resistivity increases.

25.3 Answer: (iii) Solving Eq. (25.11) for the current shows that $I = V/R$. If the resistance R of the wire remained the same, dou-bling the voltage V would make the current I double as well. How-ever, we saw in Example 25.3 that the resistance is *not* constant: As the current increases and the temperature increases, R increases as well. Thus doubling the voltage produces a current that is *less* than double the original current. An ohmic conductor is one for which $R = V/I$ has the same value no matter what the voltage, so the wire is *nonohmic*. (In many practical problems the temperature

change of the wire is so small that it can be ignored, so we can safely regard the wire as being ohmic. We do so in almost all examples in this book.)

25.4 Answer: (iii), (ii), (i) For circuit (i), we find the current from Eq. (25.16): $I = \mathcal{E}/(R + r) = (1.5 \text{ V})/(1.4\ \Omega + 0.10\ \Omega) = 1.0 \text{ A}$. For circuit (ii), we note that the terminal voltage $v_{ab} = 3.6 \text{ V}$ equals the voltage IR across the 1.8-Ω resistor: $V_{ab} = IR$, so $I = V_{ab}/R = (3.6 \text{ V})/(1.8\ \Omega) = 2.0 \text{ A}$. For circuit (iii), we use Eq. (25.15) for the terminal voltage: $V_{ab} = \mathcal{E} - Ir$, so $I = (\mathcal{E} - V_{ab})/r = (12.0 \text{ V} - 11.0 \text{ V})/(0.20\ \Omega) = 5.0 \text{ A}$.

25.5 Answer: (iii), (ii), (i) These are the same circuits that we ana-lyzed in Test Your Understanding of Section 25.4. In each case the net power output of the battery is $P = V_{ab}I$, where V_{ab} is the bat-tery terminal voltage. For circuit (i), we found that $I = 1.0 \text{ A}$, so $V_{ab} = \mathcal{E} - Ir = 1.5 \text{ V} - (1.0 \text{ A})(0.10\ \Omega) = 1.4 \text{ V}$, so $P = (1.4 \text{ V})(1.0 \text{ A}) = 1.4 \text{ W}$. For circuit (ii), we have $V_{ab} = 3.6 \text{ V}$ and found that $I = 2.0 \text{ A}$, so $P = (3.6 \text{ V})(2.0 \text{ A}) = 7.2 \text{ W}$. For circuit (iii), we have $V_{ab} = 11.0 \text{ V}$ and found that $I = 5.0 \text{ A}$, so $P = (11.0 \text{ V})(5.0 \text{ A}) = 55 \text{ A}$.

25.6 Answer: (i) The difficulty of producing a certain amount of current increases as the resistivity ρ increases. From Eq. (25.24), $\rho = m/ne^2\tau$, so increasing the mass m will increase the resistivity. That's because a more massive charged particle will respond more sluggishly to an applied electric field and hence drift more slowly. To produce the same current, a greater electric field would be needed. (Increasing n, e, or τ would decrease the resistivity and make it easier to produce a given current.)

Bridging Problem

Answers: **(a)** 237°C   **(b)** 162 W initially, 148 W at 1.23 A

DIRECT-CURRENT CIRCUITS

By studying this chapter, you will learn:

• How to analyze circuits with multiple resistors in series or parallel.

• Rules that you can apply to any circuit with more than one loop.

• How to use an ammeter, voltmeter, ohmmeter, or potentiometer in a circuit.

• How to analyze circuits that include both a resistor and a capacitor.

• How electric power is distributed in the home.

? In a complex circuit like the one on this circuit board, is it possible to connect several resistors with different resistances so that they all have the same potential difference? If so, will the current be the same through all of the resistors?

If you look inside your TV, your computer, or under the hood of a car, you will find circuits of much greater complexity than the simple circuits we studied in Chapter 25. Whether connected by wires or integrated in a semiconductor chip, these circuits often include several sources, resistors, and other circuit elements interconnected in a *network*.

In this chapter we study general methods for analyzing such networks, including how to find voltages and currents of circuit elements. We'll learn how to determine the equivalent resistance for several resistors connected in series or in parallel. For more general networks we need two rules called *Kirchhoff's rules*. One is based on the principle of conservation of charge applied to a junction; the other is derived from energy conservation for a charge moving around a closed loop. We'll discuss instruments for measuring various electrical quantities. We'll also look at a circuit containing resistance and capacitance, in which the current varies with time.

Our principal concern in this chapter is with **direct-current** (dc) circuits, in which the direction of the current does not change with time. Flashlights and automobile wiring systems are examples of direct-current circuits. Household electrical power is supplied in the form of **alternating current** (ac), in which the current oscillates back and forth. The same principles for analyzing networks apply to both kinds of circuits, and we conclude this chapter with a look at household wiring systems. We'll discuss alternating-current circuits in detail in Chapter 31.

ActivPhysics 12.1: DC Series Circuits (Qualitative)

26.1 Resistors in Series and Parallel

Resistors turn up in all kinds of circuits, ranging from hair dryers and space heaters to circuits that limit or divide current or reduce or divide a voltage. Such circuits often contain several resistors, so it's appropriate to consider *combinations* of resistors. A simple example is a string of light bulbs used for holiday decorations;

each bulb acts as a resistor, and from a circuit-analysis perspective the string of bulbs is simply a combination of resistors.

Suppose we have three resistors with resistances R_1, R_2, and R_3. Figure 26.1 shows four different ways in which they might be connected between points a and b. When several circuit elements such as resistors, batteries, and motors are connected in sequence as in Fig. 26.1a, with only a single current path between the points, we say that they are connected in **series.** We studied *capacitors* in series in Section 24.2; we found that, because of conservation of charge, capacitors in series all have the same charge if they are initially uncharged. In circuits we're often more interested in the *current,* which is charge flow per unit time.

The resistors in Fig. 26.1b are said to be connected in **parallel** between points a and b. Each resistor provides an alternative path between the points. For circuit elements that are connected in parallel, the *potential difference* is the same across each element. We studied capacitors in parallel in Section 24.2.

In Fig. 26.1c, resistors R_2 and R_3 are in parallel, and this combination is in series with R_1. In Fig. 26.1d, R_2 and R_3 are in series, and this combination is in parallel with R_1.

For any combination of resistors we can always find a *single* resistor that could replace the combination and result in the same total current and potential difference. For example, a string of holiday light bulbs could be replaced by a single, appropriately chosen light bulb that would draw the same current and have the same potential difference between its terminals as the original string of bulbs. The resistance of this single resistor is called the **equivalent resistance** of the combination. If any one of the networks in Fig. 26.1 were replaced by its equivalent resistance R_{eq}, we could write

$$V_{ab} = IR_{eq} \quad \text{or} \quad R_{eq} = \frac{V_{ab}}{I}$$

where V_{ab} is the potential difference between terminals a and b of the network and I is the current at point a or b. To compute an equivalent resistance, we assume a potential difference V_{ab} across the actual network, compute the corresponding current I, and take the ratio V_{ab}/I.

Resistors in Series

We can derive general equations for the equivalent resistance of a series or parallel combination of resistors. If the resistors are in *series,* as in Fig. 26.1a, the current I must be the same in all of them. (As we discussed in Section 25.4, current is *not* "used up" as it passes through a circuit.) Applying $V = IR$ to each resistor, we have

$$V_{ax} = IR_1 \qquad V_{xy} = IR_2 \qquad V_{yb} = IR_3$$

The potential differences across each resistor need not be the same (except for the special case in which all three resistances are equal). The potential difference V_{ab} across the entire combination is the sum of these individual potential differences:

$$V_{ab} = V_{ax} + V_{xy} + V_{yb} = I(R_1 + R_2 + R_3)$$

and so

$$\frac{V_{ab}}{I} = R_1 + R_2 + R_3$$

The ratio V_{ab}/I is, by definition, the equivalent resistance R_{eq}. Therefore

$$R_{eq} = R_1 + R_2 + R_3$$

It is easy to generalize this to any number of resistors:

$$R_{eq} = R_1 + R_2 + R_3 + \cdots \qquad \text{(resistors in series)} \qquad \text{(26.1)}$$

26.1 Four different ways of connecting three resistors.

(a) R_1, R_2, and R_3 in series

(b) R_1, R_2, and R_3 in parallel

(c) R_1 in series with parallel combination of R_2 and R_3

(d) R_1 in parallel with series combination of R_2 and R_3

The equivalent resistance of *any number* of resistors in series equals the sum of their individual resistances.

The equivalent resistance is *greater than* any individual resistance.

Let's compare this result with Eq. (24.5) for *capacitors* in series. Resistors in series add directly because the voltage across each is directly proportional to its resistance and to the common current. Capacitors in series add reciprocally because the voltage across each is directly proportional to the common charge but *inversely* proportional to the individual capacitance.

Resistors in Parallel

If the resistors are in *parallel*, as in Fig. 26.1b, the current through each resistor need not be the same. But the potential difference between the terminals of each resistor must be the same and equal to V_{ab} (Fig. 26.2). (Remember that the potential difference between any two points does not depend on the path taken between the points.) Let's call the currents in the three resistors I_1, I_2, and I_3. Then from $I = V/R$,

$$I_1 = \frac{V_{ab}}{R_1} \qquad I_2 = \frac{V_{ab}}{R_2} \qquad I_3 = \frac{V_{ab}}{R_3}$$

In general, the current is different through each resistor. Because charge is not accumulating or draining out of point a, the total current I must equal the sum of the three currents in the resistors:

$$I = I_1 + I_2 + I_3 = V_{ab}\left(\frac{1}{R_1} + \frac{1}{R_2} + \frac{1}{R_3}\right) \quad \text{or}$$

$$\frac{I}{V_{ab}} = \frac{1}{R_1} + \frac{1}{R_2} + \frac{1}{R_3}$$

But by the definition of the equivalent resistance R_{eq}, $I/V_{ab} = 1/R_{eq}$, so

$$\frac{1}{R_{eq}} = \frac{1}{R_1} + \frac{1}{R_2} + \frac{1}{R_3}$$

Again it is easy to generalize to *any number* of resistors in parallel:

$$\frac{1}{R_{eq}} = \frac{1}{R_1} + \frac{1}{R_2} + \frac{1}{R_3} + \cdots \qquad \text{(resistors in parallel)} \qquad (26.2)$$

For *any number* of resistors in parallel, the *reciprocal* of the equivalent resistance equals the *sum of the reciprocals* of their individual resistances.

The equivalent resistance is always *less than* any individual resistance.

Compare this with Eq. (24.7) for *capacitors* in parallel. Resistors in parallel add reciprocally because the current in each is proportional to the common voltage across them and *inversely* proportional to the resistance of each. Capacitors in parallel add directly because the charge on each is proportional to the common voltage across them and *directly* proportional to the capacitance of each.

For the special case of *two* resistors in parallel,

$$\frac{1}{R_{eq}} = \frac{1}{R_1} + \frac{1}{R_2} = \frac{R_1 + R_2}{R_1 R_2} \quad \text{and}$$

$$R_{eq} = \frac{R_1 R_2}{R_1 + R_2} \qquad \text{(two resistors in parallel)} \qquad (26.3)$$

26.2 A car's headlights and taillights are connected in parallel. Hence each light is exposed to the full potential difference supplied by the car's electrical system, giving maximum brightness. Another advantage is that if one headlight or taillight burns out, the other one keeps shining (see Example 26.2).

ActivPhysics 12.2: DC Parallel Circuits

Video Tutor Demo

Because $V_{ab} = I_1 R_1 = I_2 R_2$, it follows that

$$\frac{I_1}{I_2} = \frac{R_2}{R_1} \quad \text{(two resistors in parallel)} \qquad (26.4)$$

This shows that the currents carried by two resistors in parallel are *inversely proportional* to their resistances. More current goes through the path of least resistance.

Problem-Solving Strategy 26.1 **Resistors in Series and Parallel**

IDENTIFY *the relevant concepts:* As in Fig. 26.1, many resistor networks are made up of resistors in series, in parallel, or a combination thereof. Such networks can be replaced by a single equivalent resistor. The logic is similar to that of Problem-Solving Strategy 24.1 for networks of capacitors.

SET UP *the problem* using the following steps:
1. Make a drawing of the resistor network.
2. Identify groups of resistors connected in series or parallel.
3. Identify the target variables. They could include the equivalent resistance of the network, the potential difference across each resistor, or the current through each resistor.

EXECUTE *the solution* as follows:
1. Use Eq. (26.1) or (26.2), respectively, to find the equivalent resistance for series or parallel combinations.
2. If the network is more complex, try reducing it to series and parallel combinations. For example, in Fig. 26.1c we first replace the parallel combination of R_2 and R_3 with its equivalent resistance;

this then forms a series combination with R_1. In Fig. 26.1d, the combination of R_2 and R_3 in series forms a parallel combination with R_1.
3. Keep in mind that the total potential difference across resistors connected in series is the sum of the individual potential differences. The potential difference across resistors connected in parallel is the same for every resistor and equals the potential difference across the combination.
4. The current through resistors connected in series is the same through every resistor and equals the current through the combination. The total current through resistors connected in parallel is the sum of the currents through the individual resistors.

EVALUATE *your answer:* Check whether your results are consistent. The equivalent resistance of resistors connected in series should be greater than that of any individual resistor; that of resistors in parallel should be less than that of any individual resistor.

Example 26.1 **Equivalent resistance**

Find the equivalent resistance of the network in Fig. 26.3a and the current in each resistor. The source of emf has negligible internal resistance.

SOLUTION

IDENTIFY and SET UP: This network of three resistors is a *combination* of series and parallel resistances, as in Fig. 26.1c. We determine

26.3 Steps in reducing a combination of resistors to a single equivalent resistor and finding the current in each resistor.

Continued

the equivalent resistance of the parallel 6-Ω and 3-Ω resistors, and then that of their series combination with the 4-Ω resistor: This is the equivalent resistance R_{eq} of the network as a whole. We then find the current in the emf, which is the same as that in the 4-Ω resistor. The potential difference is the same across each of the parallel 6-Ω and 3-Ω resistors; we use this to determine how the current is divided between these.

EXECUTE: Figures 26.3b and 26.3c show successive steps in reducing the network to a single equivalent resistance R_{eq}. From Eq. (26.2), the 6-Ω and 3-Ω resistors in parallel in Fig. 26.3a are equivalent to the single 2-Ω resistor in Fig. 26.3b:

$$\frac{1}{R_{6\,\Omega+3\,\Omega}} = \frac{1}{6\,\Omega} + \frac{1}{3\,\Omega} = \frac{1}{2\,\Omega}$$

[Equation (26.3) gives the same result.] From Eq. (26.1) the series combination of this 2-Ω resistor with the 4-Ω resistor is equivalent to the single 6-Ω resistor in Fig. 26.3c.

We reverse these steps to find the current in each resistor of the original network. In the circuit shown in Fig. 26.3d (identical to Fig. 26.3c), the current is $I = V_{ab}/R = (18\text{ V})/(6\,\Omega) = 3$ A. So the current in the 4-Ω and 2-Ω resistors in Fig. 26.3e (identical to Fig. 26.3b) is also 3 A. The potential difference V_{cb} across the 2-Ω resistor is therefore $V_{cb} = IR = (3\text{ A})(2\,\Omega) = 6$ V. This potential difference must also be 6 V in Fig. 26.3f (identical to Fig. 26.3a). From $I = V_{cb}/R$, the currents in the 6-Ω and 3-Ω resistors in Fig. 26.3f are respectively $(6\text{ V})/(6\,\Omega) = 1$ A and $(6\text{ V})/(3\,\Omega) = 2$ A.

EVALUATE: Note that for the two resistors in parallel between points c and b in Fig. 26.3f, there is twice as much current through the 3-Ω resistor as through the 6-Ω resistor; more current goes through the path of least resistance, in accordance with Eq. (26.4). Note also that the total current through these two resistors is 3 A, the same as it is through the 4-Ω resistor between points a and c.

Example 26.2 Series versus parallel combinations

Two identical light bulbs, each with resistance $R = 2\,\Omega$, are connected to a source with $\mathcal{E} = 8$ V and negligible internal resistance. Find the current through each bulb, the potential difference across each bulb, and the power delivered to each bulb and to the entire network if the bulbs are connected (a) in series and (b) in parallel. (c) Suppose one of the bulbs burns out; that is, its filament breaks and current can no longer flow through it. What happens to the other bulb in the series case? In the parallel case?

SOLUTION

IDENTIFY and SET UP: The light bulbs are just resistors in simple series and parallel connections (Figs. 26.4a and 26.4b). Once we find the current I through each bulb, we can find the power delivered to each bulb using Eq. (25.18), $P = I^2R = V^2/R$.

EXECUTE: (a) From Eq. (26.1) the equivalent resistance of the two bulbs between points a and c in Fig. 26.4a is $R_{eq} = 2R = 2(2\,\Omega) = 4\,\Omega$. In series, the current is the same through each bulb:

$$I = \frac{V_{ac}}{R_{eq}} = \frac{8\text{ V}}{4\,\Omega} = 2\text{ A}$$

Since the bulbs have the same resistance, the potential difference is the same across each bulb:

$$V_{ab} = V_{bc} = IR = (2\text{ A})(2\,\Omega) = 4\text{ V}$$

From Eq. (25.18), the power delivered to each bulb is

$$P = I^2R = (2\text{ A})^2(2\,\Omega) = 8\text{ W} \qquad \text{or}$$

$$P = \frac{V_{ab}^2}{R} = \frac{V_{bc}^2}{R} = \frac{(4\text{ V})^2}{2\,\Omega} = 8\text{ W}$$

The total power delivered to both bulbs is $P_{tot} = 2P = 16$ W.

(b) If the bulbs are in parallel, as in Fig. 26.4b, the potential difference V_{de} across each bulb is the same and equal to 8 V, the terminal voltage of the source. Hence the current through each light bulb is

$$I = \frac{V_{de}}{R} = \frac{8\text{ V}}{2\,\Omega} = 4\text{ A}$$

and the power delivered to each bulb is

$$P = I^2R = (4\text{ A})^2(2\,\Omega) = 32\text{ W} \qquad \text{or}$$

$$P = \frac{V_{de}^2}{R} = \frac{(8\text{ V})^2}{2\,\Omega} = 32\text{ W}$$

Both the potential difference across each bulb and the current through each bulb are twice as great as in the series case. Hence the power delivered to each bulb is *four* times greater, and each bulb is brighter.

The total power delivered to the parallel network is $P_{total} = 2P = 64$ W, four times greater than in the series case. The

26.4 Our sketches for this problem.

(a) Light bulbs in series

(b) Light bulbs in parallel

26.5 When connected to the same source, two light bulbs in series (shown at top) draw less power and glow less brightly than when they are in parallel (shown at bottom).

increased power compared to the series case isn't obtained "for free"; energy is extracted from the source four times more rapidly in the parallel case than in the series case. If the source is a battery, it will be used up four times as fast.

(c) In the series case the same current flows through both bulbs. If one bulb burns out, there will be no current in the circuit, and neither bulb will glow.

In the parallel case the potential difference across either bulb is unchanged if a bulb burns out. The current through the functional bulb and the power delivered to it are unchanged.

EVALUATE: Our calculation isn't completely accurate, because the resistance $R = V/I$ of real light bulbs depends on the potential difference V across the bulb. That's because the filament resistance increases with increasing operating temperature and therefore with increasing V. But bulbs connected in series across a source do in fact glow less brightly than when connected in parallel across the same source (Fig. 26.5).

Test Your Understanding of Section 26.1 Suppose all three of the resistors shown in Fig. 26.1 have the same resistance, so $R_1 = R_2 = R_3 = R$. Rank the four arrangements shown in parts (a)–(d) of Fig. 26.1 in order of their equivalent resistance, from highest to lowest.

26.2 Kirchhoff's Rules

Many practical resistor networks cannot be reduced to simple series-parallel combinations. Figure 26.6a shows a dc power supply with emf $\mathcal{E}_1$ charging a battery with a smaller emf $\mathcal{E}_2$ and feeding current to a light bulb with resistance R. Figure 26.6b is a "bridge" circuit, used in many different types of measurement and control systems. (Problem 26.81 describes one important application of a "bridge" circuit.) To compute the currents in these networks, we'll use the techniques developed by the German physicist Gustav Robert Kirchhoff (1824–1887).

First, here are two terms that we will use often. A **junction** in a circuit is a point where three or more conductors meet. A **loop** is any closed conducting path. In Fig. 26.6a points a and b are junctions, but points c and d are not; in Fig. 26.6b the points a, b, c, and d are junctions, but points e and f are not. The blue lines in Figs. 26.6a and 26.6b show some possible loops in these circuits.

Kirchhoff's rules are the following two statements:

Kirchhoff's junction rule: *The algebraic sum of the currents into any junction is zero.* That is,

$$\sum I = 0 \quad \text{(junction rule, valid at any junction)} \quad (26.5)$$

Kirchhoff's loop rule: *The algebraic sum of the potential differences in any loop,* including those associated with emfs and those of resistive elements, *must equal zero.* That is,

$$\sum V = 0 \quad \text{(loop rule, valid for any closed loop)} \quad (26.6)$$

26.6 Two networks that cannot be reduced to simple series-parallel combinations of resistors.

(a)

(b)
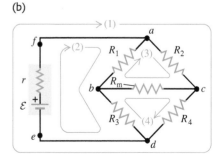

26.7 Kirchhoff's junction rule states that as much current flows into a junction as flows out of it.

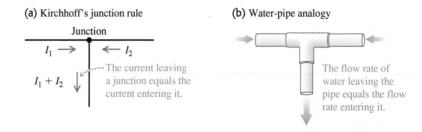

(a) Kirchhoff's junction rule

Junction

$I_1 \rightarrow$ $\leftarrow I_2$

$I_1 + I_2 \downarrow$ The current leaving a junction equals the current entering it.

(b) Water-pipe analogy

The flow rate of water leaving the pipe equals the flow rate entering it.

The junction rule is based on *conservation of electric charge.* No charge can accumulate at a junction, so the total charge entering the junction per unit time must equal the total charge leaving per unit time (Fig. 26.7a). Charge per unit time is current, so if we consider the currents entering a junction to be positive and those leaving to be negative, the algebraic sum of currents into a junction must be zero. It's like a T branch in a water pipe (Fig. 26.7b); if you have a total of 1 liter per minute coming in the two pipes, you can't have 3 liters per minute going out the third pipe. We may as well confess that we used the junction rule (without saying so) in Section 26.1 in the derivation of Eq. (26.2) for resistors in parallel.

The loop rule is a statement that the electrostatic force is *conservative.* Suppose we go around a loop, measuring potential differences across successive circuit elements as we go. When we return to the starting point, we must find that the *algebraic sum* of these differences is zero; otherwise, we could not say that the potential at this point has a definite value.

Sign Conventions for the Loop Rule

In applying the loop rule, we need some sign conventions. Problem-Solving Strategy 26.2 describes in detail how to use these, but here's a quick overview. We first assume a direction for the current in each branch of the circuit and mark it on a diagram of the circuit. Then, starting at any point in the circuit, we imagine traveling around a loop, adding emfs and *IR* terms as we come to them. When we travel through a source in the direction from $-$ to $+$, the emf is considered to be *positive;* when we travel from $+$ to $-$, the emf is considered to be *negative* (Fig. 26.8a). When we travel through a resistor in the *same* direction as the assumed current, the *IR* term is *negative* because the current goes in the direction of decreasing potential. When we travel through a resistor in the direction *opposite* to the assumed current, the *IR* term is *positive* because this represents a rise of potential (Fig. 26.8b).

Kirchhoff's two rules are all we need to solve a wide variety of network problems. Usually, some of the emfs, currents, and resistances are known, and others are unknown. We must always obtain from Kirchhoff's rules a number of independent equations equal to the number of unknowns so that we can solve the equations simultaneously. Often the hardest part of the solution is not understanding the basic principles but keeping track of algebraic signs!

26.8 Use these sign conventions when you apply Kirchhoff's loop rule. In each part of the figure "Travel" is the direction that we imagine going around the loop, which is not necessarily the direction of the current.

(a) Sign conventions for emfs

$+\mathcal{E}$: Travel direction from $-$ to $+$:

— Travel →

$\mathcal{E}$

$-\mathcal{E}$: Travel direction from $+$ to $-$:

← Travel —

$\mathcal{E}$

(b) Sign conventions for resistors

$+IR$: Travel *opposite to* current direction:

— Travel →

R

$-IR$: Travel *in* current direction:

← Travel —

R

Problem-Solving Strategy 26.2 Kirchhoff's Rules

IDENTIFY *the relevant concepts:* Kirchhoff's rules are useful for analyzing any electric circuit.

SET UP *the problem* using the following steps:
1. Draw a circuit diagram, leaving room to label all quantities, known and unknown. Indicate an assumed direction for each unknown current and emf. (Kirchhoff's rules will yield the magnitudes *and directions* of unknown currents and emfs. If the actual direction of a quantity is opposite to your assumption, the resulting quantity will have a negative sign.)
2. As you label currents, it helpful to use Kirchhoff's junction rule, as in Fig. 26.9, so as to express the currents in terms of as few quantities as possible.
3. Identify the target variables.

EXECUTE *the solution* as follows:
1. Choose any loop in the network and choose a direction (clockwise or counterclockwise) to travel around the loop as you apply Kirchhoff's loop rule. The direction need not be the same as any assumed current direction.

2. Travel around the loop in the chosen direction, adding potential differences algebraically as you cross them. Use the sign conventions of Fig. 26.8.
3. Equate the sum obtained in step 2 to zero in accordance with the loop rule.
4. If you need more independent equations, choose another loop and repeat steps 1–3; continue until you have as many independent equations as unknowns or until every circuit element has been included in at least one loop.
5. Solve the equations simultaneously to determine the unknowns.
6. You can use the loop-rule bookkeeping system to find the potential V_{ab} of any point *a* with respect to any other point *b*. Start at *b* and add the potential changes you encounter in going from *b* to *a*, using the same sign rules as in step 2. The algebraic sum of these changes is $V_{ab} = V_a - V_b$.

EVALUATE *your answer:* Check all the steps in your algebra. Apply steps 1 and 2 to a loop you have not yet considered; if the sum of potential drops isn't zero, you've made an error somewhere.

26.9 Applying the junction rule to point *a* reduces the number of unknown currents from three to two.

(a) Three unknown currents: I_1, I_2, I_3

(b) Applying the junction rule to point *a* eliminates I_3.

Example 26.3 A single-loop circuit

The circuit shown in Fig. 26.10a contains two batteries, each with an emf and an internal resistance, and two resistors. Find (a) the current in the circuit, (b) the potential difference V_{ab}, and (c) the power output of the emf of each battery.

SOLUTION

IDENTIFY and SET UP: There are no junctions in this single-loop circuit, so we don't need Kirchhoff's junction rule. To apply Kirchhoff's loop rule, we first assume a direction for the current; let's assume a counterclockwise direction as shown in Fig. 26.10a.

EXECUTE: (a) Starting at *a* and traveling counterclockwise with the current, we add potential increases and decreases and equate the sum to zero as in Eq. (26.6):

$$-I(4\ \Omega) - 4\ \text{V} - I(7\ \Omega) + 12\ \text{V} - I(2\ \Omega) - I(3\ \Omega) = 0$$

Collecting like terms and solving for *I*, we find

$$8\ \text{V} = I(16\ \Omega) \quad \text{and} \quad I = 0.5\ \text{A}$$

The positive result for *I* shows that our assumed current direction is correct.

(b) To find V_{ab}, the potential at *a* with respect to *b*, we start at *b* and add potential changes as we go toward *a*. There are two paths from *b* to *a*; taking the lower one, we find

$$V_{ab} = (0.5\ \text{A})(7\ \Omega) + 4\ \text{V} + (0.5\ \text{A})(4\ \Omega)$$
$$= 9.5\ \text{V}$$

Point *a* is at 9.5 V higher potential than *b*. All the terms in this sum, including the *IR* terms, are positive because each represents an *increase* in potential as we go from *b* to *a*. Taking the upper path, we find

$$V_{ab} = 12\ \text{V} - (0.5\ \text{A})(2\ \Omega) - (0.5\ \text{A})(3\ \Omega)$$
$$= 9.5\ \text{V}$$

Here the *IR* terms are negative because our path goes in the direction of the current, with potential decreases through the resistors. The results for V_{ab} are the same for both paths, as they must be in order for the total potential change around the loop to be zero.

Continued

(c) The power outputs of the emf of the 12-V and 4-V batteries are

$$P_{12V} = \mathcal{E}I = (12 \text{ V})(0.5 \text{ A}) = 6 \text{ W}$$

$$P_{4V} = \mathcal{E}I = (-4 \text{ V})(0.5 \text{ A}) = -2 \text{ W}$$

The negative sign in $\mathcal{E}$ for the 4-V battery appears because the current actually runs from the higher-potential side of the battery to the lower-potential side. The negative value of P means that we are *storing* energy in that battery; the 12-V battery is *recharging* it (if it is in fact rechargeable; otherwise, we're destroying it).

EVALUATE: By applying the expression $P = I^2R$ to each of the four resistors in Fig. 26.10a, you can show that the total power

dissipated in all four resistors is 4 W. Of the 6 W provided by the emf of the 12-V battery, 2 W goes into storing energy in the 4-V battery and 4 W is dissipated in the resistances.

The circuit shown in Fig. 26.10a is much like that used when a fully charged 12-V storage battery (in a car with its engine running) is used to "jump-start" a car with a run-down battery (Fig. 26.10b). The run-down battery is slightly recharged in the process. The 3-Ω and 7-Ω resistors in Fig. 26.10a represent the resistances of the jumper cables and of the conducting path through the automobile with the run-down battery. (The values of the resistances in actual automobiles and jumper cables are considerably lower.)

26.10 (a) In this example we travel around the loop in the same direction as the assumed current, so all the *IR* terms are negative. The potential decreases as we travel from + to − through the bottom emf but increases as we travel from − to + through the top emf. (b) A real-life example of a circuit of this kind.

Example 26.4 | **Charging a battery**

In the circuit shown in Fig. 26.11, a 12-V power supply with unknown internal resistance r is connected to a run-down rechargeable battery with unknown emf $\mathcal{E}$ and internal resistance 1 Ω and to an indicator light bulb of resistance 3 Ω carrying a current of 2 A. The current through the run-down battery is 1 A in the direction shown. Find r, $\mathcal{E}$, and the current I through the power supply.

SOLUTION

IDENTIFY and SET UP: This circuit has more than one loop, so we must apply both the junction and loop rules. We assume the direction of the current through the 12-V power supply, and the polarity of the run-down battery, to be as shown in Fig. 26.11. There are three target variables, so we need three equations.

26.11 In this circuit a power supply charges a run-down battery and lights a bulb. An assumption has been made about the polarity of the emf $\mathcal{E}$ of the run-down battery. Is this assumption correct?

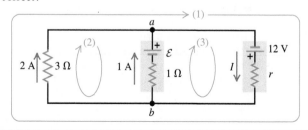

EXECUTE: We apply the junction rule, Eq. (26.5), to point a:

$$-I + 1 \text{ A} + 2 \text{ A} = 0 \quad \text{so} \quad I = 3 \text{ A}$$

To determine r, we apply the loop rule, Eq. (26.6), to the large, outer loop (1):

$$12 \text{ V} - (3 \text{ A})r - (2 \text{ A})(3 \text{ }\Omega) = 0 \quad \text{so} \quad r = 2 \text{ }\Omega$$

To determine $\mathcal{E}$, we apply the loop rule to the left-hand loop (2):

$$-\mathcal{E} + (1 \text{ A})(1 \text{ }\Omega) - (2 \text{ A})(3 \text{ }\Omega) = 0 \quad \text{so} \quad \mathcal{E} = -5 \text{ V}$$

The negative value for $\mathcal{E}$ shows that the actual polarity of this emf is opposite to that shown in Fig. 26.11. As in Example 26.3, the battery is being recharged.

EVALUATE: Try applying the junction rule at point b instead of point a, and try applying the loop rule by traveling counterclockwise rather than clockwise around loop (1). You'll get the same results for I and r. We can check our result for $\mathcal{E}$ by using the right-hand loop (3):

$$12 \text{ V} - (3 \text{ A})(2 \text{ }\Omega) - (1 \text{ A})(1 \text{ }\Omega) + \mathcal{E} = 0$$

which again gives us $\mathcal{E} = -5$ V.

As an additional check, we note that $V_{ba} = V_b - V_a$ equals the voltage across the 3-Ω resistance, which is $(2 \text{ A})(3 \text{ }\Omega) = 6$ V. Going from a to b by the top branch, we encounter potential differences $+12 \text{ V} - (3 \text{ A})(2 \text{ }\Omega) = +6$ V, and going by the middle branch, we find $-(-5 \text{ V}) + (1 \text{ A})(1 \text{ }\Omega) = +6$ V. The three ways of getting V_{ba} give the same results.

Example 26.5 Power in a battery-charging circuit

In the circuit of Example 26.4 (shown in Fig. 26.11), find the power delivered by the 12-V power supply and by the battery being recharged, and find the power dissipated in each resistor.

SOLUTION

IDENTIFY and SET UP: We use the results of Section 25.5, in which we found that the power delivered *from* an emf to a circuit is $\mathcal{E}I$ and the power delivered *to* a resistor from a circuit is $V_{ab}I = I^2R$. We know the values of all relevant quantities from Example 26.4.

EXECUTE: The power output P_s from the emf of the power supply is

$$P_{supply} = \mathcal{E}_{supply}I_{supply} = (12\text{ V})(3\text{ A}) = 36\text{ W}$$

The power dissipated in the power supply's internal resistance r is

$$P_{r-supply} = I_{supply}^2 r_{supply} = (3\text{ A})^2(2\text{ }\Omega) = 18\text{ W}$$

so the power supply's *net* power output is $P_{net} = 36\text{ W} - 18\text{ W} = 18\text{ W}$. Alternatively, from Example 26.4 the terminal voltage of the battery is $V_{ba} = 6$ V, so the net power output is

$$P_{net} = V_{ba}I_{supply} = (6\text{ V})(3\text{ A}) = 18\text{ W}$$

The power output of the emf $\mathcal{E}$ of the battery being charged is

$$P_{emf} = \mathcal{E}I_{battery} = (-5\text{ V})(1\text{ A}) = -5\text{ W}$$

This is negative because the 1-A current runs through the battery from the higher-potential side to the lower-potential side. (As we mentioned in Example 26.4, the polarity assumed for this battery in Fig. 26.11 was wrong.) We are storing energy in the battery as we charge it. Additional power is dissipated in the battery's internal resistance; this power is

$$P_{r-battery} = I_{battery}^2 r_{battery} = (1\text{ A})^2(1\text{ }\Omega) = 1\text{ W}$$

The total power input to the battery is thus $1\text{ W} + |-5\text{ W}| = 6\text{ W}$. Of this, 5 W represents useful energy stored in the battery; the remainder is wasted in its internal resistance.

The power dissipated in the light bulb is

$$P_{bulb} = I_{bulb}^2 R_{bulb} = (2\text{ A})^2(3\text{ }\Omega) = 12\text{ W}$$

EVALUATE: As a check, note that all of the power from the supply is accounted for. Of the 18 W of net power from the power supply, 5 W goes to recharge the battery, 1 W is dissipated in the battery's internal resistance, and 12 W is dissipated in the light bulb.

Example 26.6 A complex network

Figure 26.12 shows a "bridge" circuit of the type described at the beginning of this section (see Fig. 26.6b). Find the current in each resistor and the equivalent resistance of the network of five resistors.

SOLUTION

IDENTIFY and SET UP: This network is neither a series combination nor a parallel combination. Hence we must use Kirchhoff's rules to find the values of the target variables. There are five unknown currents, but by applying the junction rule to junctions a and b, we can represent them in terms of three unknown currents I_1, I_2, and I_3, as shown in Fig. 26.12.

26.12 A network circuit with several resistors.

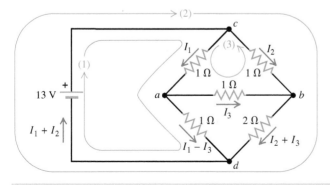

EXECUTE: We apply the loop rule to the three loops shown:

$$13\text{ V} - I_1(1\text{ }\Omega) - (I_1 - I_3)(1\text{ }\Omega) = 0 \quad (1)$$
$$-I_2(1\text{ }\Omega) - (I_2 + I_3)(2\text{ }\Omega) + 13\text{ V} = 0 \quad (2)$$
$$-I_1(1\text{ }\Omega) - I_3(1\text{ }\Omega) + I_2(1\text{ }\Omega) = 0 \quad (3)$$

One way to solve these simultaneous equations is to solve Eq. (3) for I_2, obtaining $I_2 = I_1 + I_3$, and then substitute this expression into Eq. (2) to eliminate I_2. We then have

$$13\text{ V} = I_1(2\text{ }\Omega) - I_3(1\text{ }\Omega) \quad (1')$$
$$13\text{ V} = I_1(3\text{ }\Omega) + I_3(5\text{ }\Omega) \quad (2')$$

Now we can eliminate I_3 by multiplying Eq. (1') by 5 and adding the two equations. We obtain

$$78\text{ V} = I_1(13\text{ }\Omega) \qquad I_1 = 6\text{ A}$$

We substitute this result into Eq. (1') to obtain $I_3 = -1$ A, and from Eq. (3) we find $I_2 = 5$ A. The negative value of I_3 tells us that its direction is opposite to the direction we assumed.

The total current through the network is $I_1 + I_2 = 11$ A, and the potential drop across it is equal to the battery emf, 13 V. The equivalent resistance of the network is therefore

$$R_{eq} = \frac{13\text{ V}}{11\text{ A}} = 1.2\text{ }\Omega$$

EVALUATE: You can check our results for I_1, I_2, and I_3 by substituting them back into Eqs. (1)–(3). What do you find?

Example 26.7 **A potential difference in a complex network**

In the circuit of Example 26.6 (Fig. 26.12), find the potential difference V_{ab}.

SOLUTION

IDENTIFY and SET UP: Our target variable $V_{ab} = V_a - V_b$ is the potential at point a with respect to point b. To find it, we start at point b and follow a path to point a, adding potential rises and drops as we go. We can follow any of several paths from b to a; the result must be the same for all such paths, which gives us a way to check our result.

EXECUTE: The simplest path is through the center 1-Ω resistor. In Example 26.6 we found $I_3 = -1$ A, showing that the actual current direction through this resistor is from right to left. Thus, as we go from b to a, there is a *drop* of potential with magnitude $|I_3|R = (1 \text{ A})(1 \text{ }\Omega) = 1$ V. Hence $V_{ab} = -1$ V, and the potential at a is 1 V less than at point b.

EVALUATE: To check our result, let's try a path from b to a that goes through the lower two resistors. The currents through these are

$$I_2 + I_3 = 5 \text{ A} + (-1 \text{ A}) = 4 \text{ A} \quad \text{and}$$
$$I_1 - I_3 = 6 \text{ A} - (-1 \text{ A}) = 7 \text{ A}$$

and so

$$V_{ab} = -(4 \text{ A})(2 \text{ }\Omega) + (7 \text{ A})(1 \text{ }\Omega) = -1 \text{ V}$$

You can confirm this result using some other paths from b to a.

26.13 This ammeter (top) and voltmeter (bottom) are both d'Arsonval galvanometers. The difference has to do with their internal connections (see Fig. 26.15).

Test Your Understanding of Section 26.2 Subtract Eq. (1) from Eq. (2) in Example 26.6. To which loop in Fig. 26.12 does this equation correspond? Would this equation have simplified the solution of Example 26.6? ∎

26.3 Electrical Measuring Instruments

We've been talking about potential difference, current, and resistance for two chapters, so it's about time we said something about how to *measure* these quantities. Many common devices, including car instrument panels, battery chargers, and inexpensive electrical instruments, measure potential difference (voltage), current, or resistance using a **d'Arsonval galvanometer** (Fig. 26.13). In the following discussion we'll often call it just a *meter*. A pivoted coil of fine wire is placed in the magnetic field of a permanent magnet (Fig. 26.14). Attached to the coil is a spring, similar to the hairspring on the balance wheel of a watch. In the equilibrium position, with no current in the coil, the pointer is at zero. When there is a current in the coil, the magnetic field exerts a torque on the coil that is proportional to the current. (We'll discuss this magnetic interaction in detail in Chapter 27.) As the coil turns, the spring exerts a restoring torque that is proportional to the angular displacement.

Thus the angular deflection of the coil and pointer is directly proportional to the coil current, and the device can be calibrated to measure current. The maximum deflection, typically 90° or so, is called *full-scale deflection*. The essential electrical characteristics of the meter are the current I_{fs} required for full-scale deflection (typically on the order of 10 μA to 10 mA) and the resistance R_c of the coil (typically on the order of 10 to 1000 Ω).

The meter deflection is proportional to the *current* in the coil. If the coil obeys Ohm's law, the current is proportional to the *potential difference* between the terminals of the coil, and the deflection is also proportional to this potential difference. For example, consider a meter whose coil has a resistance $R_c = 20.0 \text{ }\Omega$ and that deflects full scale when the current in its coil is $I_{fs} = 1.00$ mA. The corresponding potential difference for full-scale deflection is

$$V = I_{fs}R_c = (1.00 \times 10^{-3} \text{ A})(20.0 \text{ }\Omega) = 0.0200 \text{ V}$$

26.14 A d'Arsonval galvanometer, showing a pivoted coil with attached pointer, a permanent magnet supplying a magnetic field that is uniform in magnitude, and a spring to provide restoring torque, which opposes magnetic-field torque.

Magnetic-field torque tends to push pointer away from zero.

Spring torque tends to push pointer toward zero.

Spring

Magnetic field

Permanent magnet   Soft-iron core   Pivoted coil

Ammeters

A current-measuring instrument is usually called an **ammeter** (or milliammeter, microammeter, and so forth, depending on the range). *An ammeter always measures the current passing through it.* An *ideal* ammeter, discussed in Section 25.4, would have *zero* resistance, so including it in a branch of a circuit would not affect the current in that branch. Real ammeters always have some finite resistance, but it is always desirable for an ammeter to have as little resistance as possible.

We can adapt any meter to measure currents that are larger than its full-scale reading by connecting a resistor in parallel with it (Fig. 26.15a) so that some of the current bypasses the meter coil. The parallel resistor is called a **shunt resistor** or simply a *shunt,* denoted as R_{sh}.

Suppose we want to make a meter with full-scale current I_{fs} and coil resistance R_c into an ammeter with full-scale reading I_a. To determine the shunt resistance R_{sh} needed, note that at full-scale deflection the total current through the parallel combination is I_a, the current through the coil of the meter is I_{fs}, and the current through the shunt is the difference $I_a - I_{fs}$. The potential difference V_{ab} is the same for both paths, so

$$I_{fs}R_c = (I_a - I_{fs})R_{sh} \quad \text{(for an ammeter)} \quad (26.7)$$

26.15 Using the same meter to measure (a) current and (b) voltage.

(a) Moving-coil ammeter

(b) Moving-coil voltmeter

Example 26.8 **Designing an ammeter**

What shunt resistance is required to make the 1.00-mA, 20.0-Ω meter described above into an ammeter with a range of 0 to 50.0 mA?

SOLUTION

IDENTIFY and SET UP: Since the meter is being used as an ammeter, its internal connections are as shown in Fig. 26.15a. Our target variable is the shunt resistance R_{sh}, which we will find using Eq. (26.7). The ammeter must handle a maximum current $I_a = 50.0 \times 10^{-3}$ A. The coil resistance is $R_c = 20.0$ Ω, and the meter shows full-scale deflection when the current through the coil is $I_{fs} = 1.00 \times 10^{-3}$ A.

EXECUTE: Solving Eq. (26.7) for R_{sh}, we find

$$R_{sh} = \frac{I_{fs}R_c}{I_a - I_{fs}} = \frac{(1.00 \times 10^{-3}\,\text{A})(20.0\,\Omega)}{50.0 \times 10^{-3}\,\text{A} - 1.00 \times 10^{-3}\,\text{A}}$$
$$= 0.408\ \Omega$$

EVALUATE: It's useful to consider the equivalent resistance R_{eq} of the ammeter as a whole. From Eq. (26.2),

$$R_{eq} = \left(\frac{1}{R_c} + \frac{1}{R_{sh}}\right)^{-1} = \left(\frac{1}{20.0\,\Omega} + \frac{1}{0.408\,\Omega}\right)^{-1}$$
$$= 0.400\ \Omega$$

The shunt resistance is so small in comparison to the coil resistance that the equivalent resistance is very nearly equal to the shunt resistance. The result is an ammeter with a low equivalent resistance and the desired 0–50.0-mA range. At full-scale deflection, $I = I_a = 50.0$ mA, the current through the galvanometer is 1.00 mA, the current through the shunt resistor is 49.0 mA, and $V_{ab} = 0.0200$ V. If the current I is *less* than 50.0 mA, the coil current and the deflection are proportionally less.

Voltmeters

This same basic meter may also be used to measure potential difference or *voltage.* A voltage-measuring device is called a **voltmeter.** A voltmeter always measures the potential difference between two points, and its terminals must be connected to these points. (Example 25.6 in Section 25.4 described what can happen if a voltmeter is connected incorrectly.) As we discussed in Section 25.4, an ideal voltmeter would have *infinite* resistance, so connecting it between two points in a circuit would not alter any of the currents. Real voltmeters always have finite resistance, but a voltmeter should have large enough resistance that connecting it in a circuit does not change the other currents appreciably.

For the meter described in Example 26.8 the voltage across the meter coil at full-scale deflection is only $I_{fs}R_c = (1.00 \times 10^{-3}\,\text{A})(20.0\,\Omega) = 0.0200$ V. We can extend this range by connecting a resistor R_s in *series* with the coil (Fig. 26.15b). Then only a fraction of the total potential difference appears across the coil itself, and the remainder appears across R_s. For a voltmeter with full-scale reading V_V, we need a series resistor R_s in Fig. 26.15b such that

$$V_V = I_{fs}(R_c + R_s) \quad \text{(for a voltmeter)} \quad (26.8)$$

Application Electromyography

A fine needle containing two electrodes is being inserted into a muscle in this patient's hand. By using a sensitive voltmeter to measure the potential difference between these electrodes, a physician can probe the muscle's electrical activity. This is an important technique for diagnosing neurological and neuromuscular diseases.

Example 26.9 Designing a voltmeter

What series resistance is required to make the 1.00-mA, 20.0-Ω meter described above into a voltmeter with a range of 0 to 10.0 V?

SOLUTION

IDENTIFY and SET UP: Since this meter is being used as a voltmeter, its internal connections are as shown in Fig. 26.15b. Our target variable is the series resistance R_s. The maximum allowable voltage across the voltmeter is $V_V = 10.0$ V. We want this to occur when the current through the coil is $I_{fs} = 1.00 \times 10^{-3}$ A. Our target variable is the series resistance R_s, which we find using Eq. (26.8).

EXECUTE: From Eq. (26.8),

$$R_s = \frac{V_V}{I_{fs}} - R_c = \frac{10.0 \text{ V}}{0.00100 \text{ A}} - 20.0 \ \Omega = 9980 \ \Omega$$

EVALUATE: At full-scale deflection, $V_{ab} = 10.0$ V, the voltage across the meter is 0.0200 V, the voltage across R_s is 9.98 V, and the current through the voltmeter is 0.00100 A. Most of the voltage appears across the series resistor. The meter's equivalent resistance is a desirably high $R_{eq} = 20.0 \ \Omega + 9980 \ \Omega = 10,000 \ \Omega$. Such a meter is called a "1000 ohms-per-volt" meter, referring to the ratio of resistance to full-scale deflection. In normal operation the current through the circuit element being measured (I in Fig. 26.15b) is much greater than 0.00100 A, and the resistance between points a and b in the circuit is much less than 10,000 Ω. The voltmeter draws off only a small fraction of the current and thus disturbs the circuit being measured only slightly.

ActivPhysics 12.4: Using Ammeters and Voltmeters

Ammeters and Voltmeters in Combination

A voltmeter and an ammeter can be used together to measure *resistance* and *power.* The resistance R of a resistor equals the potential difference V_{ab} between its terminals divided by the current I; that is, $R = V_{ab}/I$. The power input P to any circuit element is the product of the potential difference across it and the current through it: $P = V_{ab}I$. In principle, the most straightforward way to measure R or P is to measure V_{ab} and I simultaneously.

With practical ammeters and voltmeters this isn't quite as simple as it seems. In Fig. 26.16a, ammeter A reads the current I in the resistor R. Voltmeter V, however, reads the *sum* of the potential difference V_{ab} across the resistor and the potential difference V_{bc} across the ammeter. If we transfer the voltmeter terminal from c to b, as in Fig. 26.16b, then the voltmeter reads the potential difference V_{ab} correctly, but the ammeter now reads the *sum* of the current I in the resistor and the current I_V in the voltmeter. Either way, we have to correct the reading of one instrument or the other unless the corrections are small enough to be negligible.

26.16 Ammeter–voltmeter method for measuring resistance.

Example 26.10 Measuring resistance I

The voltmeter in the circuit of Fig. 26.16a reads 12.0 V and the ammeter reads 0.100 A. The meter resistances are $R_V = 10,000 \ \Omega$ (for the voltmeter) and $R_A = 2.00 \ \Omega$ (for the ammeter). What are the resistance R and the power dissipated in the resistor?

SOLUTION

IDENTIFY and SET UP: The ammeter reads the current $I = 0.100$ A through the resistor, and the voltmeter reads the potential difference between a and c. If the ammeter were *ideal* (that is, if $R_A = 0$), there would be zero potential difference between b and c, the voltmeter reading $V = 12.0$ V would be equal to the potential difference V_{ab} across the resistor, and the resistance would simply be equal to $R = V/I = (12.0 \text{ V})/(0.100 \text{ A}) = 120 \ \Omega$. The ammeter is *not* ideal, however (its resistance is $R_A = 2.00 \ \Omega$), so the voltmeter reading V is actually the sum of the potential differences V_{bc} (across the ammeter) and V_{ab} (across the resistor). We use Ohm's law to find the voltage V_{bc} from the known current and ammeter resistance. Then we solve for V_{ab} and the resistance R. Given these, we are able to calculate the power P into the resistor.

EXECUTE: From Ohm's law, $V_{bc} = IR_A = (0.100 \text{ A})(2.00 \text{ }\Omega) = 0.200$ V and $V_{ab} = IR$. The sum of these is $V = 12.0$ V, so the potential difference across the resistor is $V_{ab} = V - V_{bc} = (12.0 \text{ V}) - (0.200 \text{ V}) = 11.8$ V. Hence the resistance is

$$R = \frac{V_{ab}}{I} = \frac{11.8 \text{ V}}{0.100 \text{ A}} = 118 \text{ }\Omega$$

The power dissipated in this resistor is

$$P = V_{ab}I = (11.8 \text{ V})(0.100 \text{ A}) = 1.18 \text{ W}$$

EVALUATE: You can confirm this result for the power by using the alternative formula $P = I^2R$. Do you get the same answer?

Example 26.11   **Measuring resistance II**

Suppose the meters of Example 26.10 are connected to a different resistor as shown in Fig. 26.16b, and the readings obtained on the meters are the same as in Example 26.10. What is the value of this new resistance R, and what is the power dissipated in the resistor?

SOLUTION

IDENTIFY and SET UP: In Example 26.10 the ammeter read the actual current through the resistor, but the voltmeter reading was not the same as the potential difference across the resistor. Now the situation is reversed: The voltmeter reading $V = 12.0$ V shows the actual potential difference V_{ab} across the resistor, but the ammeter reading $I_A = 0.100$ A is *not* equal to the current I through the resistor. Applying the junction rule at b in Fig. 26.16b shows that $I_A = I + I_V$, where I_V is the current through the voltmeter. We find I_V from the given values of V and the voltmeter resistance R_V, and we use this value to find the resistor current I. We then determine the resistance R from I and the voltmeter reading, and calculate the power as in Example 26.10.

EXECUTE: We have $I_V = V/R_V = (12.0 \text{ V})/(10,000 \text{ }\Omega) = 1.20$ mA. The actual current I in the resistor is $I = I_A - I_V = 0.100 \text{ A} - 0.0012 \text{ A} = 0.0988$ A, and the resistance is

$$R = \frac{V_{ab}}{I} = \frac{12.0 \text{ V}}{0.0988 \text{ A}} = 121 \text{ }\Omega$$

The power dissipated in the resistor is

$$P = V_{ab}I = (12.0 \text{ V})(0.0988 \text{ A}) = 1.19 \text{ W}$$

EVALUATE: Had the meters been ideal, our results would have been $R = 12.0 \text{ V}/0.100 \text{ A} = 120 \text{ }\Omega$ and $P = VI = (12.0 \text{ V}) \times (0.100 \text{ A}) = 1.2$ W both here and in Example 26.10. The actual (correct) results are not too different in either case. That's because the ammeter and voltmeter are nearly ideal: Compared with the resistance R under test, the ammeter resistance R_A is very small and the voltmeter resistance R_V is very large. Under these conditions, treating the meters as ideal yields pretty good results; accurate work requires calculations as in these two examples.

Ohmmeters

An alternative method for measuring resistance is to use a d'Arsonval meter in an arrangement called an **ohmmeter.** It consists of a meter, a resistor, and a source (often a flashlight battery) connected in series (Fig. 26.17). The resistance R to be measured is connected between terminals x and y.

The series resistance R_s is variable; it is adjusted so that when terminals x and y are short-circuited (that is, when $R = 0$), the meter deflects full scale. When nothing is connected to terminals x and y, so that the circuit between x and y is *open* (that is, when $R \rightarrow \infty$), there is no current and hence no deflection. For any intermediate value of R the meter deflection depends on the value of R, and the meter scale can be calibrated to read the resistance R directly. Larger currents correspond to smaller resistances, so this scale reads backward compared to the scale showing the current.

In situations in which high precision is required, instruments containing d'Arsonval meters have been supplanted by electronic instruments with direct digital readouts. Digital voltmeters can be made with extremely high internal resistance, of the order of 100 MΩ. Figure 26.18 shows a digital *multimeter,* an instrument that can measure voltage, current, or resistance over a wide range.

The Potentiometer

The *potentiometer* is an instrument that can be used to measure the emf of a source without drawing any current from the source; it also has a number of other useful applications. Essentially, it balances an unknown potential difference against an adjustable, measurable potential difference.

26.17 Ohmmeter circuit. The resistor R_s has a variable resistance, as is indicated by the arrow through the resistor symbol. To use the ohmmeter, first connect x directly to y and adjust R_s until the meter reads zero. Then connect x and y across the resistor R and read the scale.

26.18 This digital multimeter can be used as a voltmeter (red arc), ammeter (yellow arc), or ohmmeter (green arc).

26.19 A potentiometer.

(a) Potentiometer circuit

(b) Circuit symbol for potentiometer (variable resistor)

The principle of the potentiometer is shown schematically in Fig. 26.19a. A resistance wire *ab* of total resistance R_{ab} is permanently connected to the terminals of a source of known emf $\mathcal{E}_1$. A sliding contact *c* is connected through the galvanometer G to a second source whose emf $\mathcal{E}_2$ is to be measured. As contact *c* is moved along the resistance wire, the resistance R_{cb} between points *c* and *b* varies; if the resistance wire is uniform, R_{cb} is proportional to the length of wire between *c* and *b*. To determine the value of $\mathcal{E}_2$, contact *c* is moved until a position is found at which the galvanometer shows no deflection; this corresponds to zero current passing through $\mathcal{E}_2$. With $I_2 = 0$, Kirchhoff's loop rule gives

$$\mathcal{E}_2 = IR_{cb}$$

With $I_2 = 0$, the current I produced by the emf $\mathcal{E}_1$ has the same value no matter what the value of the emf $\mathcal{E}_2$. We calibrate the device by replacing $\mathcal{E}_2$ by a source of known emf; then any unknown emf $\mathcal{E}_2$ can be found by measuring the length of wire *cb* for which $I_2 = 0$. Note that for this to work, V_{ab} must be greater than $\mathcal{E}_2$.

The term *potentiometer* is also used for any variable resistor, usually having a circular resistance element and a sliding contact controlled by a rotating shaft and knob. The circuit symbol for a potentiometer is shown in Fig. 26.19b.

Test Your Understanding of Section 26.3   You want to measure the current through and the potential difference across the 2-Ω resistor shown in Fig. 26.12 (Example 26.6 in Section 26.2). (a) How should you connect an ammeter and a voltmeter to do this? (i) ammeter and voltmeter both in series with the 2-Ω resistor; (ii) ammeter in series with the 2-Ω resistor and voltmeter connected between points *b* and *d*; (iii) ammeter connected between points *b* and *d* and voltmeter in series with the 2-Ω resistor; (iv) ammeter and voltmeter both connected between points *b* and *d*. (b) What resistances should these meters have? (i) Ammeter and voltmeter resistances should both be much greater than 2 Ω; (ii) ammeter resistance should be much greater than 2 Ω and voltmeter resistance should be much less than 2 Ω; (iii) ammeter resistance should be much less than 2 Ω and voltmeter resistance should be much greater than 2 Ω; (iv) ammeter and voltmeter resistances should both be much less than 2 Ω.

26.4 *R-C* Circuits

In the circuits we have analyzed up to this point, we have assumed that all the emfs and resistances are *constant* (time independent) so that all the potentials, currents, and powers are also independent of time. But in the simple act of charging or discharging a capacitor we find a situation in which the currents, voltages, and powers *do* change with time.

Many devices incorporate circuits in which a capacitor is alternately charged and discharged. These include flashing traffic lights, automobile turn signals, and electronic flash units. Understanding what happens in such circuits is thus of great practical importance.

Charging a Capacitor

Figure 26.20 shows a simple circuit for charging a capacitor. A circuit such as this that has a resistor and a capacitor in series is called an ***R-C* circuit.** We idealize the battery (or power supply) to have a constant emf $\mathcal{E}$ and zero internal resistance $(r = 0)$, and we neglect the resistance of all the connecting conductors.

We begin with the capacitor initially uncharged (Fig. 26.20a); then at some initial time $t = 0$ we close the switch, completing the circuit and permitting current around the loop to begin charging the capacitor (Fig. 26.20b). For all practical purposes, the current begins at the same instant in every conducting part of the circuit, and at each instant the current is the same in every part.

CAUTION **Lowercase means time-varying** Up to this point we have been working with constant potential differences (voltages), currents, and charges, and we have used *capital* letters *V*, *I*, and *Q*, respectively, to denote these quantities. To distinguish between quantities that vary with time and those that are constant, we will use *lowercase* letters *v*, *i*, and *q* for time-varying voltages, currents, and charges, respectively. We suggest that you follow this same convention in your own work. ▌

Because the capacitor in Fig. 26.20 is initially uncharged, the potential difference v_{bc} across it is zero at $t = 0$. At this time, from Kirchhoff's loop law, the voltage v_{ab} across the resistor R is equal to the battery emf $\mathcal{E}$. The initial ($t = 0$) current through the resistor, which we will call I_0, is given by Ohm's law: $I_0 = v_{ab}/R = \mathcal{E}/R$.

As the capacitor charges, its voltage v_{bc} increases and the potential difference v_{ab} across the resistor decreases, corresponding to a decrease in current. The sum of these two voltages is constant and equal to $\mathcal{E}$. After a long time the capacitor becomes fully charged, the current decreases to zero, and the potential difference v_{ab} across the resistor becomes zero. Then the entire battery emf $\mathcal{E}$ appears across the capacitor and $v_{bc} = \mathcal{E}$.

Let q represent the charge on the capacitor and i the current in the circuit at some time t after the switch has been closed. We choose the positive direction for the current to correspond to positive charge flowing onto the left-hand capacitor plate, as in Fig. 26.20b. The instantaneous potential differences v_{ab} and v_{bc} are

$$v_{ab} = iR \qquad v_{bc} = \frac{q}{C}$$

Using these in Kirchhoff's loop rule, we find

$$\mathcal{E} - iR - \frac{q}{C} = 0 \qquad (26.9)$$

The potential drops by an amount iR as we travel from a to b and by q/C as we travel from b to c. Solving Eq. (26.9) for i, we find

$$i = \frac{\mathcal{E}}{R} - \frac{q}{RC} \qquad (26.10)$$

At time $t = 0$, when the switch is first closed, the capacitor is uncharged, and so $q = 0$. Substituting $q = 0$ into Eq. (26.10), we find that the *initial* current I_0 is given by $I_0 = \mathcal{E}/R$, as we have already noted. If the capacitor were not in the circuit, the last term in Eq. (26.10) would not be present; then the current would be *constant* and equal to $\mathcal{E}/R$.

As the charge q increases, the term q/RC becomes larger and the capacitor charge approaches its final value, which we will call Q_f. The current decreases and eventually becomes zero. When $i = 0$, Eq. (26.10) gives

$$\frac{\mathcal{E}}{R} = \frac{Q_f}{RC} \qquad Q_f = C\mathcal{E} \qquad (26.11)$$

Note that the final charge Q_f does not depend on R.

Figure 26.21 shows the current and capacitor charge as functions of time. At the instant the switch is closed ($t = 0$), the current jumps from zero to its initial value $I_0 = \mathcal{E}/R$; after that, it gradually approaches zero. The capacitor charge starts at zero and gradually approaches the final value given by Eq. (26.11), $Q_f = C\mathcal{E}$.

We can derive general expressions for the charge q and current i as functions of time. With our choice of the positive direction for current (Fig. 26.20b), i equals the rate at which positive charge arrives at the left-hand (positive)

26.20 Charging a capacitor. (a) Just before the switch is closed, the charge q is zero. (b) When the switch closes (at $t = 0$), the current jumps from zero to $\mathcal{E}/R$. As time passes, q approaches Q_f and the current i approaches zero.

(a) Capacitor initially uncharged

(b) Charging the capacitor

When the switch is closed, the charge on the capacitor increases over time while the current decreases.

26.21 Current i and capacitor charge q as functions of time for the circuit of Fig. 26.20. The initial current is I_0 and the initial capacitor charge is zero. The current asymptotically approaches zero, and the capacitor charge asymptotically approaches a final value of Q_f.

(a) Graph of current versus time for a charging capacitor

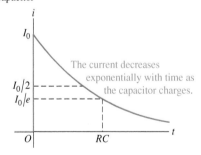

The current decreases exponentially with time as the capacitor charges.

(b) Graph of capacitor charge versus time for a charging capacitor

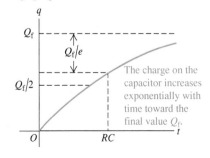

The charge on the capacitor increases exponentially with time toward the final value Q_f.

plate of the capacitor, so $i = dq/dt$. Making this substitution in Eq. (26.10), we have

$$\frac{dq}{dt} = \frac{\mathcal{E}}{R} - \frac{q}{RC} = -\frac{1}{RC}(q - C\mathcal{E})$$

We can rearrange this to

$$\frac{dq}{q - C\mathcal{E}} = -\frac{dt}{RC}$$

and then integrate both sides. We change the integration variables to q' and t' so that we can use q and t for the upper limits. The lower limits are $q' = 0$ and $t' = 0$:

$$\int_0^q \frac{dq'}{q' - C\mathcal{E}} = -\int_0^t \frac{dt'}{RC}$$

When we carry out the integration, we get

$$\ln\left(\frac{q - C\mathcal{E}}{-C\mathcal{E}}\right) = -\frac{t}{RC}$$

Exponentiating both sides (that is, taking the inverse logarithm) and solving for q, we find

$$\frac{q - C\mathcal{E}}{-C\mathcal{E}} = e^{-t/RC}$$

PhET: Circuit Construction Kit (AC+DC)
PhET: Circuit Construction Kit (DC Only)
ActivPhysics 12.6: Capacitance
ActivPhysics 12.7: Series and Parallel Capacitors
ActivPhysics 12.8: Circuit Time Constants

$$q = C\mathcal{E}(1 - e^{-t/RC}) = Q_f(1 - e^{-t/RC}) \qquad \begin{array}{l}\text{(R-C circuit, charging} \\ \text{capacitor)}\end{array} \qquad (26.12)$$

The instantaneous current i is just the time derivative of Eq. (26.12):

$$i = \frac{dq}{dt} = \frac{\mathcal{E}}{R}e^{-t/RC} = I_0 e^{-t/RC} \qquad \begin{array}{l}\text{(R-C circuit, charging} \\ \text{capacitor)}\end{array} \qquad (26.13)$$

The charge and current are both *exponential* functions of time. Figure 26.21a is a graph of Eq. (26.13) and Fig. 26.21b is a graph of Eq. (26.12).

Time Constant

After a time equal to RC, the current in the R-C circuit has decreased to $1/e$ (about 0.368) of its initial value. At this time, the capacitor charge has reached $(1 - 1/e) = 0.632$ of its final value $Q_f = C\mathcal{E}$. The product RC is therefore a measure of how quickly the capacitor charges. We call RC the **time constant,** or the **relaxation time,** of the circuit, denoted by τ:

$$\tau = RC \qquad \text{(time constant for R-C circuit)} \qquad (26.14)$$

When τ is small, the capacitor charges quickly; when it is larger, the charging takes more time. If the resistance is small, it's easier for current to flow, and the capacitor charges more quickly. If R is in ohms and C in farads, τ is in seconds.

In Fig. 26.21a the horizontal axis is an *asymptote* for the curve. Strictly speaking, i never becomes exactly zero. But the longer we wait, the closer it gets. After a time equal to $10RC$, the current has decreased to 0.000045 of its initial value. Similarly, the curve in Fig. 26.21b approaches the horizontal dashed line labeled Q_f as an asymptote. The charge q never attains exactly this value, but after a time equal to $10RC$, the difference between q and Q_f is only 0.000045 of Q_f. We invite you to verify that the product RC has units of time.

Application Pacemakers and Capacitors

This x-ray image shows a pacemaker implanted in a patient with a malfunctioning sinoatrial node, the part of the heart that generates the electrical signal to trigger heartbeats. The pacemaker circuit contains a battery, a capacitor, and a computer-controlled switch. To maintain regular beating, once per second the switch discharges the capacitor and sends an electrical pulse along the lead to the heart. The switch then flips to allow the capacitor to recharge for the next pulse.

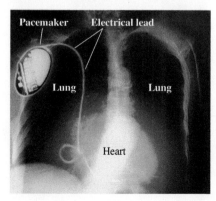

Discharging a Capacitor

Now suppose that after the capacitor in Fig. 26.21b has acquired a charge Q_0, we remove the battery from our *R-C* circuit and connect points a and c to an open switch (Fig. 26.22a). We then close the switch and at the same instant reset our stopwatch to $t = 0$; at that time, $q = Q_0$. The capacitor then *discharges* through the resistor, and its charge eventually decreases to zero.

Again let i and q represent the time-varying current and charge at some instant after the connection is made. In Fig. 26.22b we make the same choice of the positive direction for current as in Fig. 26.20b. Then Kirchhoff's loop rule gives Eq. (26.10) but with $\mathcal{E} = 0$; that is,

$$i = \frac{dq}{dt} = -\frac{q}{RC} \qquad (26.15)$$

The current i is now negative; this is because positive charge q is leaving the left-hand capacitor plate in Fig. 26.22b, so the current is in the direction opposite to that shown in the figure. At time $t = 0$, when $q = Q_0$, the initial current is $I_0 = -Q_0/RC$.

To find q as a function of time, we rearrange Eq. (26.15), again change the names of the variables to q' and t', and integrate. This time the limits for q' are Q_0 to q. We get

$$\int_{Q_0}^{q} \frac{dq'}{q'} = -\frac{1}{RC} \int_0^t dt'$$

$$\ln \frac{q}{Q_0} = -\frac{t}{RC}$$

$$q = Q_0 e^{-t/RC} \qquad (\textit{R-C circuit, discharging capacitor}) \qquad (26.16)$$

The instantaneous current i is the derivative of this with respect to time:

$$i = \frac{dq}{dt} = -\frac{Q_0}{RC} e^{-t/RC} = I_0 e^{-t/RC} \qquad \begin{array}{l}(\textit{R-C circuit,} \\ \textit{discharging capacitor})\end{array} \qquad (26.17)$$

We graph the current and the charge in Fig. 26.23; both quantities approach zero exponentially with time. Comparing these results with Eqs. (26.12) and (26.13), we note that the expressions for the current are identical, apart from the sign of I_0. The capacitor charge approaches zero asymptotically in Eq. (26.16), while the *difference* between q and Q approaches zero asymptotically in Eq. (26.12).

Energy considerations give us additional insight into the behavior of an *R-C* circuit. While the capacitor is charging, the instantaneous rate at which the battery delivers energy to the circuit is $P = \mathcal{E}i$. The instantaneous rate at which electrical energy is dissipated in the resistor is i^2R, and the rate at which energy is stored in the capacitor is $iv_{bc} = iq/C$. Multiplying Eq. (26.9) by i, we find

$$\mathcal{E}i = i^2R + \frac{iq}{C} \qquad (26.18)$$

This means that of the power $\mathcal{E}i$ supplied by the battery, part (i^2R) is dissipated in the resistor and part (iq/C) is stored in the capacitor.

The *total* energy supplied by the battery during charging of the capacitor equals the battery emf $\mathcal{E}$ multiplied by the total charge Q_f, or $\mathcal{E}Q_f$. The total energy stored in the capacitor, from Eq. (24.9), is $Q_f\mathcal{E}/2$. Thus, of the energy supplied by the battery, *exactly half* is stored in the capacitor, and the other half is dissipated in the resistor. This half-and-half division of energy doesn't depend on C, R, or $\mathcal{E}$. You can verify this result by taking the integral over time of each of the power quantities in Eq. (26.18) (see Problem 26.88).

26.22 Discharging a capacitor. **(a)** Before the switch is closed at time $t = 0$, the capacitor charge is Q_0 and the current is zero. **(b)** At time t after the switch is closed, the capacitor charge is q and the current is i. The actual current direction is opposite to the direction shown; i is negative. After a long time, q and i both approach zero.

(a) Capacitor initially charged

(b) Discharging the capacitor

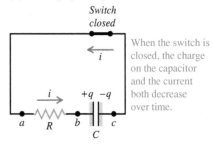

When the switch is closed, the charge on the capacitor and the current both decrease over time.

26.23 Current i and capacitor charge q as functions of time for the circuit of Fig. 26.22. The initial current is I_0 and the initial capacitor charge is Q_0. Both i and q asymptotically approach zero.

(a) Graph of current versus time for a discharging capacitor

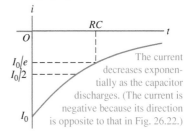

The current decreases exponentially as the capacitor discharges. (The current is negative because its direction is opposite to that in Fig. 26.22.)

(b) Graph of capacitor charge versus time for a discharging capacitor

The charge on the capacitor decreases exponentially as the capacitor discharges.

Example 26.12 Charging a capacitor

A 10-MΩ resistor is connected in series with a 1.0-μF capacitor and a battery with emf 12.0 V. Before the switch is closed at time $t = 0$, the capacitor is uncharged. (a) What is the time constant? (b) What fraction of the final charge Q_f is on the capacitor at $t = 46$ s? (c) What fraction of the initial current I_0 is still flowing at $t = 46$ s?

SOLUTION

IDENTIFY and SET UP: This is the same situation as shown in Fig. 26.20, with $R = 10$ MΩ, $C = 1.0$ μF, and $\mathcal{E} = 12.0$ V. The charge q and current i vary with time as shown in Fig. 26.21. Our target variables are (a) the time constant τ, (b) the ratio q/Q_f at $t = 46$ s, and (c) the ratio i/I_0 at $t = 46$ s. Equation (26.14) gives τ. For a capacitor being charged, Eq. (26.12) gives q and Eq. (26.13) gives i.

EXECUTE: (a) From Eq. (26.14),

$$\tau = RC = (10 \times 10^6 \ \Omega)(1.0 \times 10^{-6} \ \text{F}) = 10 \ \text{s}$$

(b) From Eq. (26.12),

$$\frac{q}{Q_f} = 1 - e^{-t/RC} = 1 - e^{-(46 \ \text{s})/(10 \ \text{s})} = 0.99$$

(c) From Eq. (26.13),

$$\frac{i}{I_0} = e^{-t/RC} = e^{-(46 \ \text{s})/(10 \ \text{s})} = 0.010$$

EVALUATE: After 4.6 time constants the capacitor is 99% charged and the charging current has decreased to 1.0% of its initial value. The circuit would charge more rapidly if we reduced the time constant by using a smaller resistance.

Example 26.13 Discharging a capacitor

The resistor and capacitor of Example 26.12 are reconnected as shown in Fig. 26.22. The capacitor has an initial charge of 5.0 μC and is discharged by closing the switch at $t = 0$. (a) At what time will the charge be equal to 0.50 μC? (b) What is the current at this time?

SOLUTION

IDENTIFY and SET UP: Now the capacitor is being discharged, so q and i vary with time as in Fig. 26.23, with $Q_0 = 5.0 \times 10^{-6}$ C. Again we have $RC = \tau = 10$ s. Our target variables are (a) the value of t at which $q = 0.50$ μC and (b) the value of i at this time. We first solve Eq. (26.16) for t, and then solve Eq. (26.17) for i.

EXECUTE: (a) Solving Eq. (26.16) for the time t gives

$$t = -RC \ \ln\frac{q}{Q_0} = -(10 \ \text{s}) \ln\frac{0.50 \ \mu\text{C}}{5.0 \ \mu\text{C}} = 23 \ \text{s} = 2.3\tau$$

(b) From Eq. (26.17), with $Q_0 = 5.0$ μC $= 5.0 \times 10^{-6}$ C,

$$i = -\frac{Q_0}{RC}e^{-t/RC} = -\frac{5.0 \times 10^{-6} \ \text{C}}{10 \ \text{s}}e^{-2.3} = -5.0 \times 10^{-8} \ \text{A}$$

EVALUATE: The current in part (b) is negative because i has the opposite sign when the capacitor is discharging than when it is charging. Note that we could have avoided evaluating $e^{-t/RC}$ by noticing that at the time in question, $q = 0.10Q_0$; from Eq. (26.16) this means that $e^{-t/RC} = 0.10$.

Test Your Understanding of Section 26.4 The energy stored in a capacitor is equal to $q^2/2C$. When a capacitor is discharged, what fraction of the initial energy remains after an elapsed time of one time constant? (i) $1/e$; (ii) $1/e^2$; (iii) $1 - 1/e$; (iv) $(1 - 1/e)^2$; (v) answer depends on how much energy was stored initially.

26.5 Power Distribution Systems

We conclude this chapter with a brief discussion of practical household and automotive electric-power distribution systems. Automobiles use direct-current (dc) systems, while nearly all household, commercial, and industrial systems use alternating current (ac) because of the ease of stepping voltage up and down with transformers. Most of the same basic wiring concepts apply to both. We'll talk about alternating-current circuits in greater detail in Chapter 31.

The various lamps, motors, and other appliances to be operated are always connected in *parallel* to the power source (the wires from the power company for houses, or from the battery and alternator for a car). If appliances were connected in series, shutting one appliance off would shut them all off (see Example 26.2 in Section 26.1). Figure 26.24 shows the basic idea of house wiring. One side of the "line," as the pair of conductors is called, is called the *neutral* side; it is always connected to

26.24 Schematic diagram of part of a house wiring system. Only two branch circuits are shown; an actual system might have four to thirty branch circuits. Lamps and appliances may be plugged into the outlets. The grounding wires, which normally carry no current, are not shown.

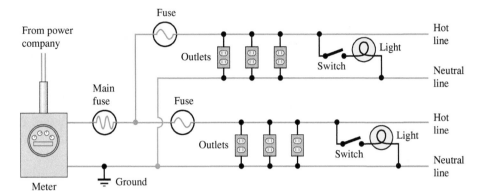

"ground" at the entrance panel. For houses, *ground* is an actual electrode driven into the earth (which is usually a good conductor) or sometimes connected to the household water pipes. Electricians speak of the "hot" side and the "neutral" side of the line. Most modern house wiring systems have *two* hot lines with opposite polarity with respect to the neutral. We'll return to this detail later.

Household voltage is nominally 120 V in the United States and Canada, and often 240 V in Europe. (For alternating current, which varies sinusoidally with time, these numbers represent the *root-mean-square* voltage, which is $1/\sqrt{2}$ times the peak voltage. We'll discuss this further in Section 31.1.) The amount of current I drawn by a given device is determined by its power input P, given by Eq. (25.17): $P = VI$. Hence $I = P/V$. For example, the current in a 100-W light bulb is

$$I = \frac{P}{V} = \frac{100 \text{ W}}{120 \text{ V}} = 0.83 \text{ A}$$

The power input to this bulb is actually determined by its resistance R. Using Eq. (25.18), which states that $P = VI = I^2R = V^2/R$ for a resistor, the resistance of this bulb at operating temperature is

$$R = \frac{V}{I} = \frac{120 \text{ V}}{0.83 \text{ A}} = 144 \text{ }\Omega \qquad \text{or} \qquad R = \frac{V^2}{P} = \frac{(120 \text{ V})^2}{100 \text{ W}} = 144 \text{ }\Omega$$

Similarly, a 1500-W waffle iron draws a current of $(1500 \text{ W})/(120 \text{ V}) = 12.5$ A and has a resistance, at operating temperature, of 9.6 Ω. Because of the temperature dependence of resistivity, the resistances of these devices are considerably less when they are cold. If you measure the resistance of a 100-W light bulb with an ohmmeter (whose small current causes very little temperature rise), you will probably get a value of about 10 Ω. When a light bulb is turned on, this low resistance causes an initial surge of current until the filament heats up. That's why a light bulb that's ready to burn out nearly always does so just when you turn it on.

Circuit Overloads and Short Circuits

The maximum current available from an individual circuit is limited by the resistance of the wires. As we discussed in Section 25.5, the I^2R power loss in the wires causes them to become hot, and in extreme cases this can cause a fire or melt the wires. Ordinary lighting and outlet wiring in houses usually uses 12-gauge wire. This has a diameter of 2.05 mm and can carry a maximum current of 20 A safely (without overheating). Larger-diameter wires of the same length have lower resistance [see Eq. (25.10)]. Hence 8-gauge (3.26 mm) or 6-gauge (4.11 mm) are used for high-current appliances such as clothes dryers, and 2-gauge (6.54 mm) or larger is used for the main power lines entering a house.

26.25 (a) Excess current will melt the thin wire of lead–tin alloy that runs along the length of a fuse, inside the transparent housing. (b) The switch on this circuit breaker will flip if the maximum allowable current is exceeded.

(a)

(b)

Protection against overloading and overheating of circuits is provided by fuses or circuit breakers. A *fuse* contains a link of lead–tin alloy with a very low melting temperature; the link melts and breaks the circuit when its rated current is exceeded (Fig. 26.25a). A *circuit breaker* is an electromechanical device that performs the same function, using an electromagnet or a bimetallic strip to "trip" the breaker and interrupt the circuit when the current exceeds a specified value (Fig. 26.25b). Circuit breakers have the advantage that they can be reset after they are tripped, while a blown fuse must be replaced.

If your system has fuses and you plug too many high-current appliances into the same outlet, the fuse blows. *Do not* replace the fuse with one of larger rating; if you do, you risk overheating the wires and starting a fire. The only safe solution is to distribute the appliances among several circuits. Modern kitchens often have three or four separate 20-A circuits.

Contact between the hot and neutral sides of the line causes a *short circuit*. Such a situation, which can be caused by faulty insulation or by any of a variety of mechanical malfunctions, provides a very low-resistance current path, permitting a very large current that would quickly melt the wires and ignite their insulation if the current were not interrupted by a fuse or circuit breaker (see Example 25.10 in Section 25.5). An equally dangerous situation is a broken wire that interrupts the current path, creating an *open circuit*. This is hazardous because of the sparking that can occur at the point of intermittent contact.

In approved wiring practice, a fuse or breaker is placed *only* in the hot side of the line, never in the neutral side. Otherwise, if a short circuit should develop because of faulty insulation or other malfunction, the ground-side fuse could blow. The hot side would still be live and would pose a shock hazard if you touched the live conductor and a grounded object such as a water pipe. For similar reasons the wall switch for a light fixture is always in the hot side of the line, never the neutral side.

Further protection against shock hazard is provided by a third conductor called the *grounding wire,* included in all present-day wiring. This conductor corresponds to the long round or U-shaped prong of the three-prong connector plug on an appliance or power tool. It is connected to the neutral side of the line at the entrance panel. The grounding wire normally carries no current, but it connects the metal case or frame of the device to ground. If a conductor on the hot side of the line accidentally contacts the frame or case, the grounding conductor provides a current path, and the fuse blows. Without the ground wire, the frame could become "live"—that is, at a potential 120 V above ground. Then if you touched it and a water pipe (or even a damp basement floor) at the same time, you could get a dangerous shock (Fig. 26.26). In some situations, especially outlets located outdoors or near a sink or other water pipes, a special kind of circuit breaker called a *ground-fault interrupter* (GFI or GFCI) is used. This device senses the difference in current between the hot and neutral conductors (which is normally zero) and trips when this difference exceeds some very small value, typically 5 mA.

Household and Automotive Wiring

Most modern household wiring systems actually use a slight elaboration of the system described above. The power company provides *three* conductors. One is neutral; the other two are both at 120 V with respect to the neutral but with opposite polarity, giving a voltage between them of 240 V. The power company calls this a *three-wire line,* in contrast to the 120-V two-wire (plus ground wire) line described above. With a three-wire line, 120-V lamps and appliances can be connected between neutral and either hot conductor, and high-power devices requiring 240 V, such as electric ranges and clothes dryers, are connected between the two hot lines.

All of the above discussion can be applied directly to automobile wiring. The voltage is about 13 V (direct current); the power is supplied by the battery and by

(a) Two-prong plug   (b) Three-prong plug

26.26 (a) If a malfunctioning electric drill is connected to a wall socket via a two-prong plug, a person may receive a shock. (b) When the drill malfunctions when connected via a three-prong plug, a person touching it receives no shock, because electric charge flows through the ground wire (shown in green) to the third prong and into the ground rather than into the person's body. If the ground current is appreciable, the fuse blows.

the alternator, which charges the battery when the engine is running. The neutral side of each circuit is connected to the body and frame of the vehicle. For this low voltage a separate grounding conductor is not required for safety. The fuse or circuit breaker arrangement is the same in principle as in household wiring. Because of the lower voltage (less energy per charge), more current (a greater number of charges per second) is required for the same power; a 100-W headlight bulb requires a current of about $(100 \text{ W})/(13 \text{ V}) = 8$ A.

Although we spoke of *power* in the above discussion, what we buy from the power company is *energy*. Power is energy transferred per unit time, so energy is average power multiplied by time. The usual unit of energy sold by the power company is the kilowatt-hour $(1 \text{ kW} \cdot \text{h})$:

$$1 \text{ kW} \cdot \text{h} = (10^3 \text{ W})(3600 \text{ s}) = 3.6 \times 10^6 \text{ W} \cdot \text{s} = 3.6 \times 10^6 \text{ J}$$

In the United States, one kilowatt-hour typically costs 8 to 27 cents, depending on the location and quantity of energy purchased. To operate a 1500-W (1.5-kW) waffle iron continuously for 1 hour requires $1.5 \text{ kW} \cdot \text{h}$ of energy; at 10 cents per kilowatt-hour, the energy cost is 15 cents. The cost of operating any lamp or appliance for a specified time can be calculated in the same way if the power rating is known. However, many electric cooking utensils (including waffle irons) cycle on and off to maintain a constant temperature, so the average power may be less than the power rating marked on the device.

Example 26.14   A kitchen circuit

An 1800-W toaster, a 1.3-kW electric frying pan, and a 100-W lamp are plugged into the same 20-A, 120-V circuit. (a) What current is drawn by each device, and what is the resistance of each device? (b) Will this combination trip the circuit breaker?

SOLUTION

IDENTIFY and SET UP: When plugged into the same circuit, the three devices are connected in parallel, so the voltage across each appliance is $V = 120$ V. We find the current I drawn by each device using the relationship $P = VI$, where P is the power input of the device. To find the resistance R of each device we use the relationship $P = V^2/R$.

EXECUTE: (a) To simplify the calculation of current and resistance, we note that $I = P/V$ and $R = V^2/P$. Hence

$$I_{\text{toaster}} = \frac{1800 \text{ W}}{120 \text{ V}} = 15 \text{ A} \qquad R_{\text{toaster}} = \frac{(120 \text{ V})^2}{1800 \text{ W}} = 8 \text{ }\Omega$$

$$I_{\text{frying pan}} = \frac{1300 \text{ W}}{120 \text{ V}} = 11 \text{ A} \qquad R_{\text{frying pan}} = \frac{(120 \text{ V})^2}{1300 \text{ W}} = 11 \text{ }\Omega$$

$$I_{\text{lamp}} = \frac{100 \text{ W}}{120 \text{ V}} = 0.83 \text{ A} \qquad R_{\text{lamp}} = \frac{(120 \text{ V})^2}{100 \text{ W}} = 144 \text{ }\Omega$$

For constant voltage the device with the *least* resistance (in this case the toaster) draws the most current and receives the most power.

Continued

(b) The total current through the line is the sum of the currents drawn by the three devices:

$$I = I_{\text{toaster}} + I_{\text{frying pan}} + I_{\text{lamp}}$$
$$= 15 \text{ A} + 11 \text{ A} + 0.83 \text{ A} = 27 \text{ A}$$

This exceeds the 20-A rating of the line, and the circuit breaker will indeed trip.

EVALUATE: We could also find the total current by using $I = P/V$ and dividing the total power P delivered to all three devices by the voltage:

$$I = \frac{P_{\text{toaster}} + P_{\text{frying pan}} + P_{\text{lamp}}}{V}$$
$$= \frac{1800 \text{ W} + 1300 \text{ W} + 100 \text{ W}}{120 \text{ V}} = 27 \text{ A}$$

A third way to determine I is to use $I = V/R_{\text{eq}}$, where R_{eq} is the equivalent resistance of the three devices in parallel:

$$I = \frac{V}{R_{\text{eq}}} = (120 \text{ V})\left(\frac{1}{8 \ \Omega} + \frac{1}{11 \ \Omega} + \frac{1}{144 \ \Omega}\right) = 27 \text{ A}$$

Appliances with such current demands are common, so modern kitchens have more than one 20-A circuit. To keep currents safely below 20 A, the toaster and frying pan should be plugged into different circuits.

Test Your Understanding of Section 26.5 To prevent the circuit breaker in Example 26.14 from blowing, a home electrician replaces the circuit breaker with one rated at 40 A. Is this a reasonable thing to do? ❙

Resistors in series and parallel: When several resistors $R_1, R_2, R_3, \ldots$ are connected in series, the equivalent resistance R_{eq} is the sum of the individual resistances. The same *current* flows through all the resistors in a series connection. When several resistors are connected in parallel, the reciprocal of the equivalent resistance R_{eq} is the sum of the reciprocals of the individual resistances. All resistors in a parallel connection have the same *potential difference* between their terminals. (See Examples 26.1 and 26.2.)

$$R_{eq} = R_1 + R_2 + R_3 + \cdots \quad (26.1)$$
(resistors in series)

$$\frac{1}{R_{eq}} = \frac{1}{R_1} + \frac{1}{R_2} + \frac{1}{R_3} + \cdots \quad (26.2)$$
(resistors in parallel)

Kirchhoff's rules: Kirchhoff's junction rule is based on conservation of charge. It states that the algebraic sum of the currents into any junction must be zero. Kirchhoff's loop rule is based on conservation of energy and the conservative nature of electrostatic fields. It states that the algebraic sum of potential differences around any loop must be zero. Careful use of consistent sign rules is essential in applying Kirchhoff's rules. (See Examples 26.3–26.7.)

$$\sum I = 0 \quad \text{(junction rule)} \quad (26.5)$$
$$\sum V = 0 \quad \text{(loop rule)} \quad (26.6)$$

Electrical measuring instruments: In a d'Arsonval galvanometer, the deflection is proportional to the current in the coil. For a larger current range, a shunt resistor is added, so some of the current bypasses the meter coil. Such an instrument is called an ammeter. If the coil and any additional series resistance included obey Ohm's law, the meter can also be calibrated to read potential difference or voltage. The instrument is then called a voltmeter. A good ammeter has very low resistance; a good voltmeter has very high resistance. (See Examples 26.8–26.11.)

R-C circuits: When a capacitor is charged by a battery in series with a resistor, the current and capacitor charge are not constant. The charge approaches its final value asymptotically and the current approaches zero asymptotically. The charge and current in the circuit are given by Eqs. (26.12) and (26.13). After a time $\tau = RC$, the charge has approached within $1/e$ of its final value. This time is called the time constant or relaxation time of the circuit. When the capacitor discharges, the charge and current are given as functions of time by Eqs. (26.16) and (26.17). The time constant is the same for charging and discharging. (See Examples 26.12 and 26.13.)

Capacitor charging:
$$q = C\mathcal{E}\left(1 - e^{-t/RC}\right)$$
$$= Q_f\left(1 - e^{-t/RC}\right) \quad (26.12)$$
$$i = \frac{dq}{dt} = \frac{\mathcal{E}}{R}e^{-t/RC}$$
$$= I_0 e^{-t/RC} \quad (26.13)$$

Capacitor discharging:
$$q = Q_0 e^{-t/RC} \quad (26.16)$$
$$i = \frac{dq}{dt} = -\frac{Q_0}{RC}e^{-t/RC}$$
$$= I_0 e^{-t/RC} \quad (26.17)$$

Household wiring: In household wiring systems, the various electrical devices are connected in parallel across the power line, which consists of a pair of conductors, one "hot" and the other "neutral." An additional "ground" wire is included for safety. The maximum permissible current in a circuit is determined by the size of the wires and the maximum temperature they can tolerate. Protection against excessive current and the resulting fire hazard is provided by fuses or circuit breakers. (See Example 26.14.)

BRIDGING PROBLEM **Two Capacitors and Two Resistors**

A 2.40-μF capacitor and a 3.60-μF capacitor are connected in series. (a) A charge of 5.20 mC is placed on each capacitor. What is the energy stored in the capacitors? (b) A 655-Ω resistor is connected to the terminals of the capacitor combination, and a voltmeter with resistance 4.58×10^4 Ω is connected across the resistor. What is the rate of change of the energy stored in the capacitors just after the connection is made? (c) How long after the connection is made has the energy stored in the capacitors decreased to $1/e$ of its initial value? (d) At the instant calculated in part (c), what is the rate of change of the energy stored in the capacitors?

SOLUTION GUIDE

See MasteringPhysics® study area for a Video Tutor solution.

IDENTIFY and SET UP

1. The two capacitors act as a single equivalent capacitor (see Section 24.2), and the resistor and voltmeter act as a single equivalent resistor. Select equations that will allow you to calculate the values of these equivalent circuit elements.

2. Equation (24.9) gives the energy stored in a capacitor. Equations (26.16) and (26.17) give the capacitor charge and current as functions of time. Use these to set up the solutions to the various parts of this problem. (*Hint:* The rate at which energy is lost by the capacitors equals the rate at which energy is dissipated in the resistances.)

EXECUTE

3. Find the stored energy at $t = 0$.
4. Find the rate of change of the stored energy at $t = 0$.
5. Find the value of t at which the stored energy has $1/e$ of the value you found in step 3.
6. Find the rate of change of the stored energy at the time you found in step 5.

EVALUATE

7. Check your results from steps 4 and 6 by calculating the rate of change in a different way. (*Hint:* The rate of change of the stored energy U is dU/dt.)

Problems   For instructor-assigned homework, go to MasteringPhysics®.

•, ••, •••: Problems of increasing difficulty. **CP:** Cumulative problems incorporating material from earlier chapters. **CALC:** Problems requiring calculus. **BIO:** Biosciences problems.

DISCUSSION QUESTIONS

Q26.1 In which 120-V light bulb does the filament have greater resistance: a 60-W bulb or a 120-W bulb? If the two bulbs are connected to a 120-V line in series, through which bulb will there be the greater voltage drop? What if they are connected in parallel? Explain your reasoning.

Q26.2 Two 120-V light bulbs, one 25-W and one 200-W, were connected in series across a 240-V line. It seemed like a good idea at the time, but one bulb burned out almost immediately. Which one burned out, and why?

Q26.3 You connect a number of identical light bulbs to a flashlight battery. (a) What happens to the brightness of each bulb as more and more bulbs are added to the circuit if you connect them (i) in series and (ii) in parallel? (b) Will the battery last longer if the bulbs are in series or in parallel? Explain your reasoning.

Q26.4 In the circuit shown in Fig. Q26.4, three identical light bulbs are connected to a flashlight battery. How do the brightnesses of the bulbs compare? Which light bulb has the greatest current passing through it? Which light bulb has the greatest potential difference between its terminals? What happens if bulb A is unscrewed? Bulb B? Bulb C? Explain your reasoning.

Figure **Q26.4**

Q26.5 If two resistors R_1 and R_2 ($R_2 > R_1$) are connected in series as shown in Fig. Q26.5, which of the following must be true? In each case justify your answer. (a) $I_1 = I_2 = I_3$. (b) The current is greater in R_1 than in R_2. (c) The electrical power consumption is the same for both resistors. (d) The electrical power consumption is greater in R_2 than in R_1.

Figure **Q26.5**

(e) The potential drop is the same across both resistors. (f) The potential at point a is the same as at point c. (g) The potential at point b is lower than at point c. (h) The potential at point c is lower than at point b.

Q26.6 If two resistors R_1 and R_2 ($R_2 > R_1$) are connected in parallel as shown in Fig. Q26.6, which of the following must be true? In each case justify your answer. (a) $I_1 = I_2$. (b) $I_3 = I_4$. (c) The current is greater in R_1 than in R_2. (d) The rate of electrical energy consumption is the same for both resistors. (e) The rate of electrical energy consumption is greater in R_2 than in R_1. (f) $V_{cd} = V_{ef} = V_{ab}$. (g) Point c is at higher potential than point d. (h) Point f is at higher potential than point e. (i) Point c is at higher potential than point e.

Figure **Q26.6**

Q26.7 Why do the lights on a car become dimmer when the starter is operated?

Q26.8 A resistor consists of three identical metal strips connected as shown in Fig. Q26.8. If one of the strips is cut out, does the ammeter reading increase, decrease, or stay the same? Why?

Figure **Q26.8**

Q26.9 A light bulb is connected in the circuit shown in Fig. Q26.9. If we close the switch S, does the bulb's brightness increase, decrease, or remain the same? Explain why.

Figure **Q26.9**

Q26.10 A real battery, having nonnegligible internal resistance, is connected across a light bulb as shown in Fig. Q26.10. When the switch S is closed, what happens to the brightness of the bulb? Why?

Figure **Q26.10**

Q26.11 If the battery in Discussion Question Q26.10 is ideal with no internal resistance, what will happen to the brightness of the bulb when S is closed? Why?

Q26.12 For the circuit shown in Fig. Q26.12 what happens to the brightness of the bulbs when the switch S is closed if the battery (a) has no internal resistance and (b) has nonnegligible internal resistance? Explain why.

Figure **Q26.12**

Q26.13 Is it possible to connect resistors together in a way that cannot be reduced to some combination of series and parallel combinations? If so, give examples. If not, state why not.

Q26.14 The direction of current in a battery can be reversed by connecting it to a second battery of greater emf with the positive terminals of the two batteries together. When the direction of current is reversed in a battery, does its emf also reverse? Why or why not?

Q26.15 In a two-cell flashlight, the batteries are usually connected in series. Why not connect them in parallel? What possible advantage could there be in connecting several identical batteries in parallel?

Q26.16 The greater the diameter of the wire used in household wiring, the greater the maximum current that can safely be carried by the wire. Why is this? Does the maximum permissible current depend on the length of the wire? Does it depend on what the wire is made of? Explain your reasoning.

Q26.17 The emf of a flashlight battery is roughly constant with time, but its internal resistance increases with age and use. What sort of meter should be used to test the freshness of a battery?

Q26.18 Is it possible to have a circuit in which the potential difference across the terminals of a battery in the circuit is zero? If so, give an example. If not, explain why not.

Q26.19 Verify that the time constant RC has units of time.

Q26.20 For very large resistances it is easy to construct R-C circuits that have time constants of several seconds or minutes. How might this fact be used to measure very large resistances, those that are too large to measure by more conventional means?

Q26.21 Whan a capacitor, battery, and resistor are connected in series, does the resistor affect the maximum charge stored on the capacitor? Why or why not? What purpose does the resistor serve?

EXERCISES

Section 26.1 Resistors in Series and Parallel

26.1 •• A uniform wire of resistance R is cut into three equal lengths. One of these is formed into a circle and connected between the other two (Fig. E26.1). What is the resistance between the opposite ends a and b?

Figure **E26.1**

26.2 •• A machine part has a resistor X protruding from an opening in the side. This resistor is connected to three other resistors, as shown in Fig. E26.2. An ohmmeter connected across a and b reads 2.00 Ω. What is the resistance of X?

Figure **E26.2**

26.3 • A resistor with $R_1 = 25.0\ \Omega$ is connected to a battery that has negligible internal resistance and electrical energy is dissipated by R_1 at a rate of 36.0 W. If a second resistor with $R_2 = 15.0\ \Omega$ is connected in series with R_1, what is the total rate at which electrical energy is dissipated by the two resistors?

26.4 • A 32-Ω resistor and a 20-Ω resistor are connected in parallel, and the combination is connected across a 240-V dc line. (a) What is the resistance of the parallel combination? (b) What is the total current through the parallel combination? (c) What is the current through each resistor?

26.5 • A triangular array of resistors is shown in Fig. E26.5. What current will this array draw from a 35.0-V battery having negligible internal resistance if we connect it across (a) ab; (b) bc; (c) ac? (d) If the battery has an internal resistance of 3.00 Ω, what current will the array draw if the battery is connected across bc?

Figure **E26.5**

26.6 •• For the circuit shown in Fig. E26.6 both meters are idealized, the battery has no appreciable internal resistance, and the ammeter reads 1.25 A. (a) What does the voltmeter read? (b) What is the emf $\mathcal{E}$ of the battery?

Figure **E26.6**

26.7 •• For the circuit shown in Fig. E26.7 find the reading of the idealized ammeter if the battery has an internal resistance of 3.26 Ω.

Figure **E26.7**

26.8 • Three resistors having resistances of 1.60 Ω, 2.40 Ω, and 4.80 Ω are connected in parallel to a 28.0-V battery that has negligible internal resistance. Find (a) the equivalent resistance of the combination; (b) the current in each resistor; (c) the total current through the battery; (d) the voltage across each resistor; (e) the power dissipated in each resistor. (f) Which resistor dissipates the most power: the one with the greatest resistance or the least resistance? Explain why this should be.

26.9 • Now the three resistors of Exercise 26.8 are connected in series to the same battery. Answer the same questions for this situation.

26.10 •• **Power Rating of a Resistor.** The *power rating* of a resistor is the maximum power the resistor can safely dissipate without too great a rise in temperature and hence damage to the resistor. (a) If the power rating of a 15-kΩ resistor is 5.0 W, what is the maximum allowable potential difference across the terminals of the resistor? (b) A 9.0-kΩ resistor is to be connected across a 120-V potential difference. What power rating is required? (c) A 100.0-Ω and a 150.0-Ω resistor, both rated at 2.00 W, are connected in series across a variable potential difference. What is the greatest this potential difference can be without overheating either resistor, and what is the rate of heat generated in each resistor under these conditions?

26.11 • In Fig. E26.11, $R_1 = 3.00\ \Omega$, $R_2 = 6.00\ \Omega$, and $R_3 = 5.00\ \Omega$. The battery has negligible internal resistance. The current I_2 through R_2 is 4.00 A. (a) What are the currents I_1 and I_3? (b) What is the emf of the battery?

Figure **E26.11**

26.12 •• In Fig. E26.11 the battery has emf 25.0 V and negligible internal resistance. R_1 = 5.00 Ω. The current through R_1 is 1.50 A and the current through R_3 = 4.50 A. What are the resistances R_2 and R_3?

26.13 • Compute the equivalent resistance of the network in Fig. E26.13, and find the current in each resistor. The battery has negligible internal resistance.

Figure **E26.13**

$\mathcal{E}$ = 60.0 V, r = 0

3.00 Ω   12.0 Ω

6.00 Ω   4.00 Ω

26.14 • Compute the equivalent resistance of the network in Fig. E26.14, and find the current in each resistor. The battery has negligible internal resistance.

Figure **E26.14**

$\mathcal{E}$ = 48.0 V, r = 0

1.00 Ω   3.00 Ω

7.00 Ω   5.00 Ω

26.15 • In the circuit of Fig. E26.15, each resistor represents a light bulb. Let $R_1 = R_2 = R_3 = R_4 = 4.50$ Ω and $\mathcal{E}$ = 9.00 V. (a) Find the current in each bulb. (b) Find the power dissipated in each bulb. Which bulb or bulbs glow the brightest? (c) Bulb R_4 is now removed from the circuit, leaving a break in the wire at its position. Now what is the current in each of the remaining bulbs R_1, R_2, and R_3? (d) With bulb R_4 removed, what is the power dissipated in each of the remaining bulbs? (e) Which light bulb(s) glow brighter as a result of removing R_4? Which bulb(s) glow less brightly? Discuss why there are different effects on different bulbs.

Figure **E26.15**

R_1

$\mathcal{E}$ R_2 R_3 R_4

26.16 • Consider the circuit shown in Fig. E26.16. The current through the 6.00-Ω resistor is 4.00 A, in the direction shown. What are the currents through the 25.0-Ω and 20.0-Ω resistors?

Figure **E26.16**

4.00 A   6.00 Ω

25.0 Ω

8.00 Ω

20.0 Ω

$\mathcal{E}$

26.17 • In the circuit shown in Fig. E26.17, the voltage across the 2.00-Ω resistor is 12.0 V. What are the emf of the battery and the current through the 6.00-Ω resistor?

Figure **E26.17**

$\mathcal{E}$

1.00 Ω   2.00 Ω

6.00 Ω

26.18 • **A Three-Way Light Bulb.** A three-way light bulb has three brightness settings (low, medium, and high) but only two filaments. (a) A particular three-way light bulb connected across a 120-V line can dissipate 60 W, 120 W, or 180 W. Describe how the two filaments are arranged in the bulb, and calculate the resistance of each filament. (b) Suppose the filament with the higher resistance burns out. How much power will the bulb dissipate on each of the three brightness settings? What will be the brightness (low, medium, or high) on each setting? (c) Repeat part (b) for the situation in which the filament with the lower resistance burns out.

26.19 •• **Working Late!** You are working late in your electronics shop and find that you need various resistors for a project. But alas, all you have is a big box of 10.0-Ω resistors. Show how you can make each of the following equivalent resistances by a combination of your 10.0-Ω resistors: (a) 35 Ω, (b) 1.0 Ω, (c) 3.33 Ω, (d) 7.5 Ω.

26.20 • In the circuit shown in Fig. E26.20, the rate at which R_1 is dissipating electrical energy is 20.0 W. (a) Find R_1 and R_2. (b) What is the emf of the battery? (c) Find the current through both R_2 and the 10.0-Ω resistor. (d) Calculate the total electrical power consumption in all the resistors and the electrical power delivered

Figure **E26.20**

3.50 A

$\mathcal{E}$ 10.0 Ω R_2 R_1

2.00 A

by the battery. Show that your results are consistent with conservation of energy.

26.21 • **Light Bulbs in Series and in Parallel.** Two light bulbs have resistances of 400 Ω and 800 Ω. If the two light bulbs are connected in series across a 120-V line, find (a) the current through each bulb; (b) the power dissipated in each bulb; (c) the total power dissipated in both bulbs. The two light bulbs are now connected in parallel across the 120-V line. Find (d) the current through each bulb; (e) the power dissipated in each bulb; (f) the total power dissipated in both bulbs. (g) In each situation, which of the two bulbs glows the brightest? (h) In which situation is there a greater total light output from both bulbs combined?

26.22 • **Light Bulbs in Series.** A 60-W, 120-V light bulb and a 200-W, 120-V light bulb are connected in series across a 240-V line. Assume that the resistance of each bulb does not vary with current. (*Note:* This description of a light bulb gives the power it dissipates when connected to the stated potential difference; that is, a 25-W, 120-V light bulb dissipates 25 W when connected to a 120-V line.) (a) Find the current through the bulbs. (b) Find the power dissipated in each bulb. (c) One bulb burns out very quickly. Which one? Why?

26.23 •• **CP** In the circuit in Fig. E26.23, a 20.0-Ω resistor is inside 100 g of pure water that is surrounded by insulating styrofoam. If the water is initially at 10.0°C, how long will it take for its temperature to rise to 58.0°C?

Figure **E26.23**

10.0 Ω   10.0 Ω
20.0 Ω   10.0 Ω 10.0 Ω
Water   5.0 Ω 5.0 Ω
30.0 V   5.0 Ω

Section 26.2 Kirchhoff's Rules

26.24 •• The batteries shown in the circuit in Fig. E26.24 have negligibly small internal resistances. Find the current through (a) the 30.0-Ω resistor; (b) the 20.0-Ω resistor; (c) the 10.0-V battery.

Figure **E26.24**

10.0 V   30.0 Ω   20.0 Ω   5.00 V

26.25 • In the circuit shown in Fig. E26.25 find (a) the current in resistor R; (b) the resistance R; (c) the unknown emf $\mathcal{E}$. (d) If the circuit is broken at point x, what is the current in resistor R?

Figure **E26.25**

28.0 V R
$\mathcal{E}$ 4.00 A
x 6.00 Ω
6.00 A
3.00 Ω

26.26 • Find the emfs $\mathcal{E}_1$ and $\mathcal{E}_2$ in the circuit of Fig. E26.26, and find the potential difference of point b relative to point a.

Figure **E26.26**

1.00 Ω   20.0 V   6.00 Ω
1.00 A
4.00 Ω   1.00 Ω $\mathcal{E}_1$
a b
2.00 A   1.00 Ω $\mathcal{E}_2$
2.00 Ω

26.27 • In the circuit shown in Fig. E26.27, find (a) the current in the 3.00-Ω resistor; (b) the unknown emfs $\mathcal{E}_1$ and $\mathcal{E}_2$; (c) the resistance R. Note that three currents are given.

Figure **E26.27**

Figure **E26.28**

26.28 •• In the circuit shown in Fig. E26.28, find (a) the current in each branch and (b) the potential difference V_{ab} of point a relative to point b.

26.29 • The 10.00-V battery in Fig. E26.28 is removed from the circuit and reinserted with the opposite polarity, so that its positive terminal is now next to point a. The rest of the circuit is as shown in the figure. Find (a) the current in each branch and (b) the potential difference V_{ab} of point a relative to point b.

26.30 • The 5.00-V battery in Fig. E26.28 is removed from the circuit and replaced by a 20.00-V battery, with its negative terminal next to point b. The rest of the circuit is as shown in the figure. Find (a) the current in each branch and (b) the potential difference V_{ab} of point a relative to point b.

26.31 •• In the circuit shown in Fig. E26.31 the batteries have negligible internal resistance and the meters are both idealized. With the switch S open, the voltmeter reads 15.0 V. (a) Find the emf $\mathcal{E}$ of the battery. (b) What will the ammeter read when the switch is closed?

Figure **E26.31**

26.32 •• In the circuit shown in Fig. E26.32 both batteries have insignificant internal resistance and the idealized ammeter reads 1.50 A in the direction shown. Find the emf $\mathcal{E}$ of the battery. Is the polarity shown correct?

Figure **E26.32**

26.33 • In the circuit shown in Fig. E26.33 all meters are idealized and the batteries have no appreciable internal resistance. (a) Find the reading of the voltmeter with the switch S open. Which point is at a higher potential: a or b?

Figure **E26.33**

(b) With the switch closed, find the reading of the voltmeter and the ammeter. Which way (up or down) does the current flow through the switch?

26.34 •• In the circuit shown in Fig. E26.34, the 6.0-Ω resistor is consuming energy at a rate of 24 J/s when the current through it flows as shown. (a) Find the current through the ammeter A. (b) What are the polarity and emf $\mathcal{E}$ of the battery, assuming it has negligible internal resistance?

Figure **E26.34**

Section 26.3 Electrical Measuring Instruments

26.35 • The resistance of a galvanometer coil is 25.0 Ω, and the current required for full-scale deflection is 500 μA. (a) Show in a diagram how to convert the galvanometer to an ammeter reading 20.0 mA full scale, and compute the shunt resistance. (b) Show how to convert the galvanometer to a voltmeter reading 500 mV full scale, and compute the series resistance.

26.36 • The resistance of the coil of a pivoted-coil galvanometer is 9.36 Ω, and a current of 0.0224 A causes it to deflect full scale. We want to convert this galvanometer to an ammeter reading 20.0 A full scale. The only shunt available has a resistance of 0.0250 Ω. What resistance R must be connected in series with the coil (Fig. E26.36)?

Figure **E26.36**

26.37 • A circuit consists of a series combination of 6.00-kΩ and 5.00-kΩ resistors connected across a 50.0-V battery having negligible internal resistance. You want to measure the true potential difference (that is, the potential difference without the meter present) across the 5.00-kΩ resistor using a voltmeter having an internal resistance of 10.0 kΩ. (a) What potential difference does the voltmeter measure across the 5.00-kΩ resistor? (b) What is the *true* potential difference across this resistor when the meter is not present? (c) By what percentage is the voltmeter reading in error from the true potential difference?

26.38 • A galvanometer having a resistance of 25.0 Ω has a 1.00-Ω shunt resistance installed to convert it to an ammeter. It is then used to measure the current in a circuit consisting of a 15.0-Ω resistor connected across the terminals of a 25.0-V battery having no appreciable internal resistance. (a) What current does the ammeter measure? (b) What should be the *true* current in the circuit (that is, the current without the ammeter present)? (c) By what percentage is the ammeter reading in error from the *true* current?

26.39 • In the ohmmeter in Fig. E26.39 M is a 2.50-mA meter of resistance 65.0 Ω. (A 2.50-mA meter deflects full scale when the current through it is 2.50 mA.) The battery B has an emf of 1.52 V and negligible internal resistance. R is chosen so that when the terminals a and b are shorted ($R_x = 0$), the meter reads full scale. When a and b are open ($R_x = \infty$), the meter reads zero. (a) What is the resistance of the resistor R? (b) What current indicates a resistance R_x of 200 Ω? (c) What values of R_x correspond to meter deflections of $\frac{1}{4}$, $\frac{1}{2}$, and $\frac{3}{4}$ of full scale if the deflection is proportional to the current through the galvanometer?

Figure **E26.39**

Section 26.4 *R-C* Circuits

26.40 • A 4.60-μF capacitor that is initially uncharged is connected in series with a 7.50-kΩ resistor and an emf source with $\mathcal{E} = 245$ V and negligible internal resistance. Just after the circuit is completed, what are (a) the voltage drop across the capacitor;

(b) the voltage drop across the resistor; (c) the charge on the capacitor; (d) the current through the resistor? (e) A long time after the circuit is completed (after many time constants) what are the values of the quantities in parts (a)–(d)?

26.41 • A capacitor is charged to a potential of 12.0 V and is then connected to a voltmeter having an internal resistance of 3.40 MΩ. After a time of 4.00 s the voltmeter reads 3.0 V. What are (a) the capacitance and (b) the time constant of the circuit?

26.42 • A 12.4-μF capacitor is connected through a 0.895-MΩ resistor to a constant potential difference of 60.0 V. (a) Compute the charge on the capacitor at the following times after the connections are made: 0, 5.0 s, 10.0 s, 20.0 s, and 100.0 s. (b) Compute the charging currents at the same instants. (c) Graph the results of parts (a) and (b) for t between 0 and 20 s.

26.43 •• CP In the circuit shown in Fig. E26.43 both capacitors are initially charged to 45.0 V. (a) How long after closing the switch S will the potential across each capacitor be reduced to 10.0 V, and (b) what will be the current at that time?

Figure **E26.43**

26.44 • A resistor and a capacitor are connected in series to an emf source. The time constant for the circuit is 0.870 s. (a) A second capacitor, identical to the first, is added in series. What is the time constant for this new circuit? (b) In the original circuit a second capacitor, identical to the first, is connected in parallel with the first capacitor. What is the time constant for this new circuit?

26.45 • An emf source with $\mathcal{E}$ = 120 V, a resistor with R = 80.0 Ω, and a capacitor with C = 4.00 μF are connected in series. As the capacitor charges, when the current in the resistor is 0.900 A, what is the magnitude of the charge on each plate of the capacitor?

26.46 • A 1.50-μF capacitor is charging through a 12.0-Ω resistor using a 10.0-V battery. What will be the current when the capacitor has acquired $\frac{1}{4}$ of its maximum charge? Will it be $\frac{1}{4}$ of the maximum current?

26.47 •• CP In the circuit shown in Fig. E26.47 each capacitor initially has a charge of magnitude 3.50 nC on its plates. After the switch S is closed, what will be the current in the circuit at the instant that the capacitors have lost 80.0% of their initial stored energy?

Figure **E26.47**

26.48 • A 12.0-μF capacitor is charged to a potential of 50.0 V and then discharged through a 175-Ω resistor. How long does it take the capacitor to lose (a) half of its charge and (b) half of its stored energy?

26.49 • In the circuit in Fig. E26.49 the capacitors are all initially uncharged, the battery has no internal resistance, and the ammeter is idealized. Find the reading of the ammeter (a) just after the switch S is closed and (b) after the switch has been closed for a very long time.

Figure **E26.49**

26.50 • In the circuit shown in Fig. E26.50, C = 5.90 μF, $\mathcal{E}$ = 28.0 V, and the emf has negligible resistance. Initially the capacitor is uncharged and the switch S is in position 1. The switch is then moved to position 2, so that the capacitor begins to charge. (a) What will be the charge on the capacitor a long time after the switch is moved to position 2? (b) After the switch has been in position 2 for 3.00 ms, the charge on the capacitor is measured to be 110 μC. What is the value of the resistance R? (c) How long after the switch is moved to position 2 will the charge on the capacitor be equal to 99.0% of the final value found in part (a)?

Figure **E26.50**

26.51 • A capacitor with C = 1.50×10^{-5} F is connected as shown in Fig. E26.50 with a resistor with R = 980 Ω and an emf source with $\mathcal{E}$ = 18.0 V and negligible internal resistance. Initially the capacitor is uncharged and the switch S is in position 1. The switch is then moved to position 2, so that the capacitor begins to charge. After the switch has been in position 2 for 10.0 ms, the switch is moved back to position 1 so that the capacitor begins to discharge. (a) Compute the charge on the capacitor just *before* the switch is thrown from position 2 back to position 1. (b) Compute the voltage drops across the resistor and across the capacitor at the instant described in part (a). (c) Compute the voltage drops across the resistor and across the capacitor just *after* the switch is thrown from position 2 back to position 1. (d) Compute the charge on the capacitor 10.0 ms after the switch is thrown from position 2 back to position 1.

Section 26.5 Power Distribution Systems

26.52 • The heating element of an electric dryer is rated at 4.1 kW when connected to a 240-V line. (a) What is the current in the heating element? Is 12-gauge wire large enough to supply this current? (b) What is the resistance of the dryer's heating element at its operating temperature? (c) At 11 cents per kWh, how much does it cost per hour to operate the dryer?

26.53 • A 1500-W electric heater is plugged into the outlet of a 120-V circuit that has a 20-A circuit breaker. You plug an electric hair dryer into the same outlet. The hair dryer has power settings of 600 W, 900 W, 1200 W, and 1500 W. You start with the hair dryer on the 600-W setting and increase the power setting until the circuit breaker trips. What power setting caused the breaker to trip?

26.54 • CP The heating element of an electric stove consists of a heater wire embedded within an electrically insulating material, which in turn is inside a metal casing. The heater wire has a resistance of 20 Ω at room temperature (23.0°C) and a temperature coefficient of resistivity α = $2.8 \times 10^{-3}(\text{C}°)^{-1}$. The heating element operates from a 120-V line. (a) When the heating element is first turned on, what current does it draw and what electrical power does it dissipate? (b) When the heating element has reached an operating temperature of 280°C (536°F), what current does it draw and what electrical power does it dissipate?

PROBLEMS

26.55 •• In Fig. P26.55, the battery has negligible internal resistance and $\mathcal{E}$ = 48.0 V. R_1 = R_2 = 4.00 Ω and R_4 = 3.00 Ω. What must the resistance R_3 be for the resistor network to dissipate electrical energy at a rate of 295 W?

Figure **P26.55**

26.56 • A 400-Ω, 2.4-W resistor is needed, but only several 400-Ω, 1.2-W resistors are available (see Exercise 26.10). (a) What two different combinations of the available units give the required resistance and power rating? (b) For each of the resistor networks from part (a), what power is dissipated in each resistor when 2.4 W is dissipated by the combination?

26.57 • CP A 20.0-m-long cable consists of a solid-inner, cylindrical, nickel core 10.0 cm in diameter surrounded by a solid-outer cylindrical shell of copper 10.0 cm in inside diameter and 20.0 cm in outside diameter. The resistivity of nickel is 7.8×10^{-8} Ω·m. (a) What is the resistance of this cable? (b) If we think of this cable as a single material, what is its equivalent resistivity?

26.58 • Two identical 3.00-Ω wires are laid side by side and soldered together so they touch each other for half of their lengths. What is the equivalent resistance of this combination?

26.59 • The two identical light bulbs in Example 26.2 (Section 26.1) are connected in parallel to a different source, one with $\mathcal{E} = 8.0$ V and internal resistance 0.8 Ω. Each light bulb has a resistance $R = 2.0$ Ω (assumed independent of the current through the bulb). (a) Find the current through each bulb, the potential difference across each bulb, and the power delivered to each bulb. (b) Suppose one of the bulbs burns out, so that its filament breaks and current no longer flows through it. Find the power delivered to the remaining bulb. Does the remaining bulb glow more or less brightly after the other bulb burns out than before?

26.60 •• Each of the three resistors in Fig. P26.60 has a resistance of 2.4 Ω and can dissipate a maximum of 48 W without becoming excessively heated. What is the maximum power the circuit can dissipate?

Figure **P26.60**

26.61 • If an ohmmeter is connected between points a and b in each of the circuits shown in Fig. P26.61, what will it read?

Figure **P26.61**

(a) a 100.0 Ω b
50.0 Ω
75.0 Ω 25.0 Ω
40.0 Ω   50.0 Ω

(b) 7.00 Ω a 10.0 Ω b
60.0 Ω
20.0 Ω 30.0 Ω
45.0 Ω

26.62 •• CP For the circuit shown in Fig. P26.62 a 20.0-Ω resistor is embedded in a large block of ice at 0.00°C, and the battery has negligible internal resistance. At what rate (in g/s) is this circuit melting the ice? (The latent heat of fusion for ice is 3.34×10^5 J/kg.)

Figure **P26.62**

26.63 • Calculate the three currents I_1, I_2, and I_3 indicated in the circuit diagram shown in Fig. P26.63.

Figure **P26.63**

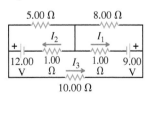
5.00 Ω   8.00 Ω
I_2 I_1
12.00 V 1.00 Ω I_3 1.00 Ω 9.00 V
10.00 Ω

26.64 ••• What must the emf $\mathcal{E}$ in Fig. P26.64 be in order for the current through the 7.00-Ω resistor to be 1.80 A? Each emf source has negligible internal resistance.

Figure **P26.64**

24.0 V $\mathcal{E}$ 7.00 Ω
3.00 Ω   2.00 Ω

Figure **P26.65**

20.0 V   5.00 Ω
2.00 Ω   4.00 Ω   36.0 V
14.0 V

26.65 • Find the current through each of the three resistors of the circuit shown in Fig. P26.65. The emf sources have negligible internal resistance.

26.66 • (a) Find the current through the battery and each resistor in the circuit shown in Fig. P26.66. (b) What is the equivalent resistance of the resistor network?

Figure **P26.66**

$R_1 = 1.00$ Ω $R_2 = 2.00$ Ω
$R_3 = 1.00$ Ω
14.0 V
$R_4 = 2.00$ Ω $R_5 = 1.00$ Ω

26.67 •• (a) Find the potential of point a with respect to point b in Fig. P26.67. (b) If points a and b are connected by a wire with negligible resistance, find the current in the 12.0-V battery.

Figure **P26.67**

1.00 Ω 12.0 V
2.00 Ω a b 1.00 Ω 10.0 V   1.00 Ω
2.00 Ω   1.00 Ω 8.0 V 3.00 Ω 2.00 Ω

26.68 •• Consider the circuit shown in Fig. P26.68. (a) What must the emf $\mathcal{E}$ of the battery be in order for a current of 2.00 A to flow through the 5.00-V battery as shown? Is the polarity of the battery correct as shown? (b) How long does it take for 60.0 J of thermal energy to be produced in the 10.0-Ω resistor?

Figure **P26.68**

10.0 Ω   20.0 Ω
60.0 Ω
60.0 Ω
2.00 A
30.0 Ω   5.0 Ω
5.0 V
10.0 V
5.0 Ω   15.0 Ω $\mathcal{E}$
20.0 Ω

26.69 •• CP A 1.00-km cable having a cross-sectional area of 0.500 cm² is to be constructed out of equal lengths of copper and aluminum. This could be accomplished either by making a 0.50-km cable of each one and welding them together end to end or by making two parallel 1.00-km cables, one of each metal (Fig. P26.69). Calculate the resistance of the 1.00-km cable for both designs to see which one provides the least resistance.

Figure **P26.69**

26.70 ••• In the circuit shown in Fig. P26.70 all the resistors are rated at a maximum power of 2.00 W. What is the maximum emf $\mathcal{E}$ that the battery can have without burning up any of the resistors?

Figure **P26.70**

26.71 • In the circuit shown in Fig. P26.71, the current in the 20.0-V battery is 5.00 A in the direction shown and the voltage across the 8.00-Ω resistor is 16.0 V, with the lower end of the resistor at higher potential. Find (a) the emf (including its polarity) of the battery X; (b) the current I through the 200.0-V battery (including its direction); (c) the resistance R.

Figure **P26.71**

26.72 •• Three identical resistors are connected in series. When a certain potential difference is applied across the combination, the total power dissipated is 36 W. What power would be dissipated if the three resistors were connected in parallel across the same potential difference?

26.73 • A resistor R_1 consumes electrical power P_1 when connected to an emf $\mathcal{E}$. When resistor R_2 is connected to the same emf, it consumes electrical power P_2. In terms of P_1 and P_2, what is the total electrical power consumed when they are both connected to this emf source (a) in parallel and (b) in series?

26.74 • The capacitor in Fig. P26.74 is initially uncharged. The switch is closed at $t = 0$. (a) Immediately after the switch is closed, what is the current through each resistor? (b) What is the final charge on the capacitor?

Figure **P26.74**

26.75 •• A 2.00-μF capacitor that is initially uncharged is connected in series with a 6.00-kΩ resistor and an emf source with $\mathcal{E} = 90.0$ V and negligible internal resistance. The circuit is completed at $t = 0$. (a) Just after the circuit is completed, what is the rate at which electrical energy is being dissipated in the resistor? (b) At what value of t is the rate at which electrical energy is being dissipated in the resistor equal to the rate at which electrical energy is being stored in the capacitor? (c) At the time calculated in part (b), what is the rate at which electrical energy is being dissipated in the resistor?

26.76 •• A 6.00-μF capacitor that is initially uncharged is connected in series with a 5.00-Ω resistor and an emf source with $\mathcal{E} = 50.0$ V and negligible internal resistance. At the instant when the resistor is dissipating electrical energy at a rate of 250 W, how much energy has been stored in the capacitor?

26.77 • Figure P26.77 employs a convention often used in circuit diagrams. The battery (or other power supply) is not shown explicitly. It is understood that the point at the top, labeled "36.0 V," is connected to the positive terminal of a 36.0-V battery having negligible internal resistance, and that the "ground" symbol at the bottom is connected to the negative terminal of the battery. The circuit is completed through the battery, even though it is not shown on the diagram. (a) What is the potential difference V_{ab}, the potential of point a relative to point b, when the switch S is open? (b) What is the current through switch S when it is closed? (c) What is the equivalent resistance when switch S is closed?

Figure **P26.77**

26.78 • (See Problem 26.77.) (a) What is the potential of point a with respect to point b in Fig. P26.78 when switch S is open? (b) Which point, a or b, is at the higher potential? (c) What is the final potential of point b with respect to ground when switch S is closed? (d) How much does the charge on each capacitor change when S is closed?

Figure **P26.78**

26.79 • Point a in Fig. P26.79 is maintained at a constant potential of 400 V above ground. (See Problem 26.77.) (a) What is the reading of a voltmeter with the proper range and with resistance $5.00 \times 10^4 \ \Omega$ when connected between point b and ground? (b) What is the reading of a voltmeter with resistance $5.00 \times 10^6 \ \Omega$? (c) What is the reading of a voltmeter with infinite resistance?

Figure **P26.79**

26.80 •• A 150-V voltmeter has a resistance of 30,000 Ω. When connected in series with a large resistance R across a 110-V line, the meter reads 74 V. Find the resistance R.

26.81 •• **The Wheatstone Bridge.** The circuit shown in Fig. P26.81, called a *Wheatstone bridge,* is used to determine the value of an unknown resistor X by comparison with three resistors M, N, and P whose resistances can be varied. For each setting, the resistance of each resistor is precisely known. With switches K_1 and K_2 closed,

Figure **P26.81**

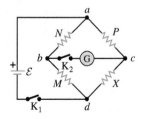

these resistors are varied until the current in the galvanometer G is zero; the bridge is then said to be *balanced*. (a) Show that under this condition the unknown resistance is given by $X = MP/N$. (This method permits very high precision in comparing resistors.) (b) If the galvanometer G shows zero deflection when $M = 850.0 \ \Omega$, $N = 15.00 \ \Omega$, and $P = 33.48 \ \Omega$, what is the unknown resistance X?

26.82 • A 2.36-μF capacitor that is initially uncharged is connected in series with a 5.86-Ω resistor and an emf source with $\mathcal{E} = 120$ V and negligible internal resistance. (a) Just after the connection is made, what are (i) the rate at which electrical energy is being dissipated in the resistor; (ii) the rate at which the electrical energy stored in the capacitor is increasing; (iii) the electrical power output of the source? How do the answers to parts (i), (ii), and (iii) compare? (b) Answer the same questions as in part (a) at a long time after the connection is made. (c) Answer the same questions as in part (a) at the instant when the charge on the capacitor is one-half its final value.

26.83 • A 224-Ω resistor and a 589-Ω resistor are connected in series across a 90.0-V line. (a) What is the voltage across each resistor? (b) A voltmeter connected across the 224-Ω resistor reads 23.8 V. Find the voltmeter resistance. (c) Find the reading of the same voltmeter if it is connected across the 589-Ω resistor. (d) The readings on this voltmeter are lower than the "true" voltages (that is, without the voltmeter present). Would it be possible to design a voltmeter that gave readings *higher* than the "true" voltages? Explain.

26.84 • A resistor with $R = 850 \ \Omega$ is connected to the plates of a charged capacitor with capacitance $C = 4.62 \ \mu$F. Just before the connection is made, the charge on the capacitor is 6.90 mC. (a) What is the energy initially stored in the capacitor? (b) What is the electrical power dissipated in the resistor just after the connection is made? (c) What is the electrical power dissipated in the resistor at the instant when the energy stored in the capacitor has decreased to half the value calculated in part (a)?

26.85 • A capacitor that is initially uncharged is connected in series with a resistor and an emf source with $\mathcal{E} = 110$ V and negligible internal resistance. Just after the circuit is completed, the current through the resistor is 6.5×10^{-5} A. The time constant for the circuit is 5.2 s. What are the resistance of the resistor and the capacitance of the capacitor?

26.86 ••• An R-C circuit has a time constant RC. (a) If the circuit is discharging, how long will it take for its stored energy to be reduced to $1/e$ of its initial value? (b) If it is charging, how long will it take for the stored energy to reach $1/e$ of its maximum value?

26.87 • Strictly speaking, Eq. (26.16) implies that an *infinite* amount of time is required to discharge a capacitor completely. Yet for practical purposes, a capacitor may be considered to be fully discharged after a finite length of time. To be specific, consider a capacitor with capacitance C connected to a resistor R to be fully discharged if its charge q differs from zero by no more than the charge of one electron. (a) Calculate the time required to reach this state if $C = 0.920 \ \mu$F, $R = 670$ kΩ, and $Q_0 = 7.00 \ \mu$C. How many time constants is this? (b) For a given Q_0, is the time required to reach this state always the same number of time constants, independent of the values of C and R? Why or why not?

26.88 • CALC The current in a charging capacitor is given by Eq. (26.13). (a) The instantaneous power supplied by the battery is $\mathcal{E}i$. Integrate this to find the total energy supplied by the battery. (b) The instantaneous power dissipated in the resistor is i^2R. Integrate this to find the total energy dissipated in the resistor. (c) Find the final energy stored in the capacitor, and show that this equals the total energy supplied by the battery less the energy dissipated in

the resistor, as obtained in parts (a) and (b). (d) What fraction of the energy supplied by the battery is stored in the capacitor? How does this fraction depend on R?

26.89 ••• CALC (a) Using Eq. (26.17) for the current in a discharging capacitor, derive an expression for the instantaneous power $P = i^2R$ dissipated in the resistor. (b) Integrate the expression for P to find the total energy dissipated in the resistor, and show that this is equal to the total energy initially stored in the capacitor.

CHALLENGE PROBLEMS

26.90 ••• **A Capacitor Burglar Alarm.** The capacitance of a capacitor can be affected by dielectric material that, although not inside the capacitor, is near enough to the capacitor to be polarized by the fringing electric field that exists near a charged capacitor. This effect is usually of the order of picofarads (pF), but it can be used with appropriate electronic circuitry to detect a change in the dielectric material surrounding the capacitor. Such a dielectric material might be the human body, and the effect described above might be used in the design of a burglar alarm. Consider the simplified circuit shown in Fig. P26.90. The voltage source has emf $\mathcal{E} = 1000$ V, and the capacitor has capacitance $C = 10.0$ pF. The electronic circuitry for detecting the current, represented as an ammeter in the diagram, has negligible resistance and is capable of detecting a current that persists at a level of at least 1.00 μA for at least 200 μs after the capacitance has changed abruptly from C to C'. The burglar alarm is designed to be activated if the capacitance changes by 10%. (a) Determine the charge on the 10.0-pF capacitor when it is fully charged. (b) If the capacitor is fully charged before the intruder is detected, assuming that the time taken for the capacitance to change by 10% is short enough to be ignored, derive an equation that expresses the current through the resistor R as a function of the time t since the capacitance has changed. (c) Determine the range of values of the resistance R that will meet the design specifications of the burglar alarm. What happens if R is too small? Too large? (*Hint:* You will not be able to solve this part analytically but must use numerical methods. Express R as a logarithmic function of R plus known quantities. Use a trial value of R and calculate from the expression a new value. Continue to do this until the input and output values of R agree to within three significant figures.)

Figure **P26.90**

26.91 ••• **An Infinite Network.** As shown in Fig. P26.91, a network of resistors of resistances R_1 and R_2 extends to infinity toward the right. Prove that the total resistance R_T of the infinite network is equal to

$$R_T = R_1 + \sqrt{R_1^2 + 2R_1R_2}$$

Figure **P26.91**

(*Hint:* Since the network is infinite, the resistance of the network to the right of points c and d is also equal to R_T.)

26.92 ••• Suppose a resistor R lies along each edge of a cube (12 resistors in all) with connections at the corners. Find the equivalent resistance between two diagonally opposite corners of the cube (points a and b in Fig. P26.92).

Figure **P26.92**

26.93 ••• BIO **Attenuator Chains and Axons.** The infinite network of resistors shown in Fig. P26.91 is known as an *attenuator chain,* since this chain of resistors causes the potential difference between the upper and lower wires to decrease, or attenuate, along the length of the chain. (a) Show that if the potential difference between the points a and b in Fig. 26.91 is V_{ab}, then the potential difference between points c and d is $V_{cd} = V_{ab}/(1 + \beta)$, where $\beta = 2R_1(R_T + R_2)/R_T R_2$ and R_T, the total resistance of the network, is given in Challenge Problem 26.91. (See the hint given in that problem.) (b) If the potential difference between terminals a and b at the left end of the infinite network is V_0, show that the potential difference between the upper and lower wires n segments from the left end is $V_n = V_0/(1 + \beta)^n$. If $R_1 = R_2$, how many segments are needed to decrease the potential difference V_n to less than 1.0% of V_0? (c) An infinite attenuator chain provides a model of the propagation of a voltage pulse along a nerve fiber, or axon. Each segment of the network in Fig. P26.91 represents a short segment of the axon of length Δx. The resistors R_1 represent the resistance of the fluid inside and outside the membrane wall of the axon. The resistance of the membrane to current flowing through the wall is represented by R_2. For an axon segment of length $\Delta x = 1.0$ μm, $R_1 = 6.4 \times 10^3$ Ω and $R_2 = 8.0 \times 10^8$ Ω (the membrane wall

is a good insulator). Calculate the total resistance R_T and β for an infinitely long axon. (This is a good approximation, since the length of an axon is much greater than its width; the largest axons in the human nervous system are longer than 1 m but only about 10^{-7} m in radius.) (d) By what fraction does the potential difference between the inside and outside of the axon decrease over a distance of 2.0 mm? (e) The attenuation of the potential difference calculated in part (d) shows that the axon cannot simply be a passive, current-carrying electrical cable; the potential difference must periodically be reinforced along the axon's length. This reinforcement mechanism is slow, so a signal propagates along the axon at only about 30 m/s. In situations where faster response is required, axons are covered with a segmented sheath of fatty myelin. The segments are about 2 mm long, separated by gaps called the *nodes of Ranvier.* The myelin increases the resistance of a 1.0-μm-long segment of the membrane to $R_2 = 3.3 \times 10^{12}$ Ω. For such a myelinated axon, by what fraction does the potential difference between the inside and outside of the axon decrease over the distance from one node of Ranvier to the next? This smaller attenuation means the propagation speed is increased.

Answers

Chapter Opening Question ?

The potential difference V is the same across resistors connected in parallel. However, there is a different current I through each resistor if the resistances R are different: $I = V/R$.

Test Your Understanding Questions

26.1 Answer: (a), (c), (d), (b) Here's why: The three resistors in Fig. 26.1a are in series, so $R_{eq} = R + R + R = 3R$. In Fig. 26.1b the three resistors are in parallel, so $1/R_{eq} = 1/R + 1/R + 1/R = 3/R$ and $R_{eq} = R/3$. In Fig. 26.1c the second and third resistors are in parallel, so their equivalent resistance R_{23} is given by $1/R_{23} = 1/R + 1/R = 2/R$; hence $R_{23} = R/2$. This combination is in series with the first resistor, so the three resistors together have equivalent resistance $R_{eq} = R + R/2 = 3R/2$. In Fig. 26.1d the second and third resistors are in series, so their equivalent resistance is $R_{23} = R + R = 2R$. This combination is in parallel with the first resistor, so the equivalent resistance of the three-resistor combination is given by $1/R_{eq} = 1/R + 1/2R = 3/2R$. Hence $R_{eq} = 2R/3$.

26.2 Answer: loop *cbdac* Equation (2) minus Eq. (1) gives $-I_2(1 \ \Omega) - (I_2 + I_3)(2 \ \Omega) + (I_1 - I_3)(1 \ \Omega) + I_1(1 \ \Omega) = 0$. We can obtain this equation by applying the loop rule around the path from c to b to d to a to c in Fig. 26.12. This isn't a new equa-

tion, so it would not have helped with the solution of Example 26.6.

26.3 Answers: (a) (ii), (b) (iii) An ammeter must always be placed in series with the circuit element of interest, and a voltmeter must always be placed in parallel. Ideally the ammeter would have zero resistance and the voltmeter would have infinite resistance so that their presence would have no effect on either the resistor current or the voltage. Neither of these idealizations is possible, but the ammeter resistance should be much less than 2 Ω and the voltmeter resistance should be much greater than 2 Ω.

26.4 Answer: (ii) After one time constant, $t = RC$ and the initial charge Q_0 has decreased to $Q_0 e^{-t/RC} = Q_0 e^{-RC/RC} = Q_0 e^{-1} = Q_0/e$. Hence the stored energy has decreased from $Q_0^2/2C$ to $(Q_0/e)^2/2C = Q_0^2/2Ce^2$, a fraction $1/e^2 = 0.135$ of its initial value. This result doesn't depend on the initial value of the energy.

26.5 Answer: no This is a very dangerous thing to do. The circuit breaker will allow currents up to 40 A, double the rated value of the wiring. The amount of power $P = I^2R$ dissipated in a section of wire can therefore be up to four times the rated value, so the wires could get very warm and start a fire.

Bridging Problem

Answers: (a) 9.39 J **(b)** 2.02×10^4 W **(c)** 4.65×10^{-4} s **(d)** 7.43×10^3 W

MAGNETIC FIELD AND MAGNETIC FORCES

? Magnetic resonance imaging (MRI) makes it possible to see details of soft tissue (such as in the foot shown here) that aren't visible in x-ray images. Yet soft tissue isn't a magnetic material (it's not attracted to a magnet). How does MRI work?

LEARNING GOALS

By studying this chapter, you will learn:

- The properties of magnets, and how magnets interact with each other.

- The nature of the force that a moving charged particle experiences in a magnetic field.

- How magnetic field lines are different from electric field lines.

- How to analyze the motion of a charged particle in a magnetic field.

- Some practical applications of magnetic fields in chemistry and physics.

- How to analyze magnetic forces on current-carrying conductors.

- How current loops behave when placed in a magnetic field.

Everybody uses magnetic forces. They are at the heart of electric motors, microwave ovens, loudspeakers, computer printers, and disk drives. The most familiar examples of magnetism are permanent magnets, which attract unmagnetized iron objects and can also attract or repel other magnets. A compass needle aligning itself with the earth's magnetism is an example of this interaction. But the *fundamental* nature of magnetism is the interaction of moving electric charges. Unlike electric forces, which act on electric charges whether they are moving or not, magnetic forces act only on *moving* charges.

We saw in Chapter 21 that the electric force arises in two stages: (1) a charge produces an electric field in the space around it, and (2) a second charge responds to this field. Magnetic forces also arise in two stages. First, a *moving* charge or a collection of moving charges (that is, an electric current) produces a *magnetic* field. Next, a second current or moving charge responds to this magnetic field, and so experiences a magnetic force.

In this chapter we study the second stage in the magnetic interaction—that is, how moving charges and currents *respond* to magnetic fields. In particular, we will see how to calculate magnetic forces and torques, and we will discover why magnets can pick up iron objects like paper clips. In Chapter 28 we will complete our picture of the magnetic interaction by examining how moving charges and currents *produce* magnetic fields.

27.1 Magnetism

Magnetic phenomena were first observed at least 2500 years ago in fragments of magnetized iron ore found near the ancient city of Magnesia (now Manisa, in western Turkey). These fragments were examples of what are now called **permanent magnets;** you probably have several permanent magnets on your refrigerator

27.1 (a) Two bar magnets attract when opposite poles (N and S, or S and N) are next to each other. (b) The bar magnets repel when like poles (N and N, or S and S) are next to each other.

(a) Opposite poles attract.

(b) Like poles repel.

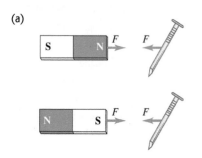

27.2 (a) Either pole of a bar magnet attracts an unmagnetized object that contains iron, such as a nail. (b) A real-life example of this effect.

(a)

(b)

door at home. Permanent magnets were found to exert forces on each other as well as on pieces of iron that were not magnetized. It was discovered that when an iron rod is brought in contact with a natural magnet, the rod also becomes magnetized. When such a rod is floated on water or suspended by a string from its center, it tends to line itself up in a north-south direction. The needle of an ordinary compass is just such a piece of magnetized iron.

Before the relationship of magnetic interactions to moving charges was understood, the interactions of permanent magnets and compass needles were described in terms of *magnetic poles.* If a bar-shaped permanent magnet, or *bar magnet,* is free to rotate, one end points north. This end is called a *north pole* or *N pole;* the other end is a *south pole* or *S pole.* Opposite poles attract each other, and like poles repel each other (Fig. 27.1). An object that contains iron but is not itself magnetized (that is, it shows no tendency to point north or south) is attracted by *either* pole of a permanent magnet (Fig. 27.2). This is the attraction that acts between a magnet and the unmagnetized steel door of a refrigerator. By analogy to electric interactions, we describe the interactions in Figs. 27.1 and 27.2 by saying that a bar magnet sets up a *magnetic field* in the space around it and a second body responds to that field. A compass needle tends to align with the magnetic field at the needle's position.

The earth itself is a magnet. Its north geographic pole is close to a magnetic *south* pole, which is why the north pole of a compass needle points north. The earth's magnetic axis is not quite parallel to its geographic axis (the axis of rotation), so a compass reading deviates somewhat from geographic north. This deviation, which varies with location, is called *magnetic declination* or *magnetic variation.* Also, the magnetic field is not horizontal at most points on the earth's surface; its angle up or down is called *magnetic inclination.* At the magnetic poles the magnetic field is vertical.

Figure 27.3 is a sketch of the earth's magnetic field. The lines, called *magnetic field lines,* show the direction that a compass would point at each location; they are discussed in detail in Section 27.3. The direction of the field at any point can be defined as the direction of the force that the field would exert on a magnetic

27.3 A sketch of the earth's magnetic field. The field, which is caused by currents in the earth's molten core, changes with time; geologic evidence shows that it reverses direction entirely at irregular intervals of 10^4 to 10^6 years.

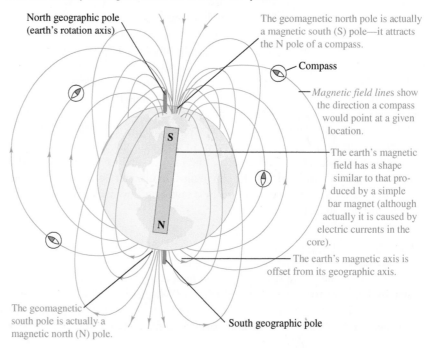

north pole. In Section 27.2 we'll describe a more fundamental way to define the direction and magnitude of a magnetic field.

Magnetic Poles Versus Electric Charge

The concept of magnetic poles may appear similar to that of electric charge, and north and south poles may seem analogous to positive and negative charge. But the analogy can be misleading. While isolated positive and negative charges exist, there is *no* experimental evidence that a single isolated magnetic pole exists; poles always appear in pairs. If a bar magnet is broken in two, each broken end becomes a pole (Fig. 27.4). The existence of an isolated magnetic pole, or **magnetic monopole,** would have sweeping implications for theoretical physics. Extensive searches for magnetic monopoles have been carried out, but so far without success.

The first evidence of the relationship of magnetism to moving charges was discovered in 1820 by the Danish scientist Hans Christian Oersted. He found that a compass needle was deflected by a current-carrying wire, as shown in Fig. 27.5 Similar investigations were carried out in France by André Ampère. A few years later, Michael Faraday in England and Joseph Henry in the United States discovered that moving a magnet near a conducting loop can cause a current in the loop. We now know that the magnetic forces between two bodies shown in Figs. 27.1 and 27.2 are fundamentally due to interactions between moving electrons in the atoms of the bodies. (There are also *electric* interactions between the two bodies, but these are far weaker than the magnetic interactions because the two bodies are electrically neutral.) Inside a magnetized body such as a permanent magnet, there is a *coordinated* motion of certain of the atomic electrons; in an unmagnetized body these motions are not coordinated. (We'll describe these motions further in Section 27.7, and see how the interactions shown in Figs. 27.1 and 27.2 come about.)

Electric and magnetic interactions prove to be intimately connected. Over the next several chapters we will develop the unifying principles of electromagnetism, culminating in the expression of these principles in *Maxwell's equations.* These equations represent the synthesis of electromagnetism, just as Newton's laws of motion are the synthesis of mechanics, and like Newton's laws they represent a towering achievement of the human intellect.

Test Your Understanding of Section 27.1   Suppose you cut off the part of the compass needle shown in Fig. 27.5a that is painted gray. You discard this part, drill a hole in the remaining red part, and place the red part on the pivot at the center of the compass. Will the red part still swing east and west when a current is applied as in Fig. 27.5b?   ❙

27.2   Magnetic Field

To introduce the concept of magnetic field properly, let's review our formulation of *electric* interactions in Chapter 21, where we introduced the concept of *electric* field. We represented electric interactions in two steps:

1. A distribution of electric charge at rest creates an electric field $\vec{E}$ in the surrounding space.
2. The electric field exerts a force $\vec{F} = q\vec{E}$ on any other charge q that is present in the field.

We can describe magnetic interactions in a similar way:

1. A moving charge or a current creates a **magnetic field** in the surrounding space (in addition to its *electric* field).
2. The magnetic field exerts a force $\vec{F}$ on any other moving charge or current that is present in the field.

27.4 Breaking a bar magnet. Each piece has a north and south pole, even if the pieces are different sizes. (The smaller the piece, the weaker its magnetism.)

In contrast to electric charges, magnetic poles always come in pairs and can't be isolated.

Breaking a magnet in two ...

... yields two magnets, not two isolated poles.

27.5 In Oersted's experiment, a compass is placed directly over a horizontal wire (here viewed from above). When the compass is placed directly under the wire, the compass deflection is reversed.

(a)

When the wire carries no current, the compass needle points north.

$I = 0$

(b)

When the wire carries a current, the compass needle deflects. The direction of deflection depends on the direction of the current.

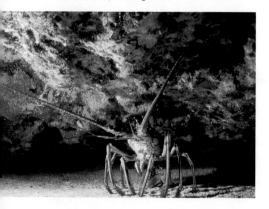

27.6 The magnetic force $\vec{F}$ acting on a positive charge q moving with velocity $\vec{v}$ is perpendicular to both $\vec{v}$ and the magnetic field $\vec{B}$. For given values of the speed v and magnetic field strength B, the force is greatest when $\vec{v}$ and $\vec{B}$ are perpendicular.

(a)

A charge moving **parallel** to a magnetic field experiences **zero magnetic force.**

(b)

A charge moving at an angle ϕ to a magnetic field experiences a magnetic force with magnitude $F = |q|v_\perp B = |q|vB \sin \phi$.

$\vec{F}$ is perpendicular to the plane containing $\vec{v}$ and $\vec{B}$.

(c)

A charge moving **perpendicular** to a magnetic field experiences a maximal magnetic force with magnitude $F_{\max} = qvB$.

In this chapter we'll concentrate on the *second* aspect of the interaction: Given the presence of a magnetic field, what force does it exert on a moving charge or a current? In Chapter 28 we will come back to the problem of how magnetic fields are *created* by moving charges and currents.

Like electric field, magnetic field is a *vector field*—that is, a vector quantity associated with each point in space. We will use the symbol $\vec{B}$ for magnetic field. At any position the direction of $\vec{B}$ is defined as the direction in which the north pole of a compass needle tends to point. The arrows in Fig. 27.3 suggest the direction of the earth's magnetic field; for any magnet, $\vec{B}$ points out of its north pole and into its south pole.

Magnetic Forces on Moving Charges

There are four key characteristics of the magnetic force on a moving charge. First, its magnitude is proportional to the magnitude of the charge. If a 1-μC charge and a 2-μC charge move through a given magnetic field with the same velocity, experiments show that the force on the 2-μC charge is twice as great as the force on the 1-μC charge. Second, the magnitude of the force is also proportional to the magnitude, or "strength," of the field; if we double the magnitude of the field (for example, by using two identical bar magnets instead of one) without changing the charge or its velocity, the force doubles.

A third characteristic is that the magnetic force depends on the particle's velocity. This is quite different from the electric-field force, which is the same whether the charge is moving or not. A charged particle at rest experiences *no* magnetic force. And fourth, we find by experiment that the magnetic force $\vec{F}$ *does not* have the same direction as the magnetic field $\vec{B}$ but instead is always *perpendicular* to both $\vec{B}$ and the velocity $\vec{v}$. The magnitude F of the force is found to be proportional to the component of $\vec{v}$ perpendicular to the field; when that component is zero (that is, when $\vec{v}$ and $\vec{B}$ are parallel or antiparallel), the force is zero.

Figure 27.6 shows these relationships. The direction of $\vec{F}$ is always perpendicular to the plane containing $\vec{v}$ and $\vec{B}$. Its magnitude is given by

$$F = |q|v_\perp B = |q|vB \sin \phi \qquad (27.1)$$

where $|q|$ is the magnitude of the charge and ϕ is the angle measured from the direction of $\vec{v}$ to the direction of $\vec{B}$, as shown in the figure.

This description does not specify the direction of $\vec{F}$ completely; there are always two directions, opposite to each other, that are both perpendicular to the plane of $\vec{v}$ and $\vec{B}$. To complete the description, we use the same right-hand rule that we used to define the vector product in Section 1.10. (It would be a good idea to review that section before you go on.) Draw the vectors $\vec{v}$ and $\vec{B}$ with their tails together, as in Fig. 27.7a. Imagine turning $\vec{v}$ until it points in the direction of $\vec{B}$ (turning through the smaller of the two possible angles). Wrap the fingers of your right hand around the line perpendicular to the plane of $\vec{v}$ and $\vec{B}$ so that they curl around with the sense of rotation from $\vec{v}$ to $\vec{B}$. Your thumb then points in the direction of the force $\vec{F}$ on a *positive* charge. (Alternatively, the direction of the force $\vec{F}$ on a positive charge is the direction in which a right-hand-thread screw would advance if turned the same way.)

This discussion shows that the force on a charge q moving with velocity $\vec{v}$ in a magnetic field $\vec{B}$ is given, both in magnitude and in direction, by

$$\vec{F} = q\vec{v} \times \vec{B} \qquad \text{(magnetic force on a moving charged particle)} \quad (27.2)$$

This is the first of several vector products we will encounter in our study of magnetic-field relationships. It's important to note that Eq. (27.2) was *not* deduced theoretically; it is an observation based on *experiment*.

27.7 Finding the direction of the magnetic force on a moving charged particle.

(a)

Right-hand rule for the direction of magnetic force on a **positive** charge moving in a magnetic field:

① Place the $\vec{v}$ and $\vec{B}$ vectors tail to tail.

② Imagine turning $\vec{v}$ toward $\vec{B}$ in the $\vec{v}$-$\vec{B}$ plane (through the smaller angle).

③ The force acts along a line perpendicular to the $\vec{v}$-$\vec{B}$ plane. Curl the fingers of your *right hand* around this line in the same direction you rotated $\vec{v}$. Your thumb now points in the direction the force acts.

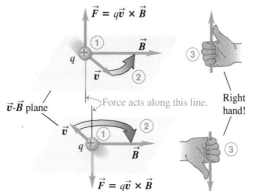

(b)

If the charge is negative, the direction of the force is *opposite* to that given by the right-hand rule.

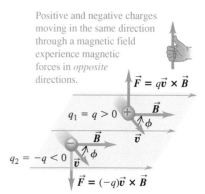

Equation (27.2) is valid for both positive and negative charges. When q is negative, the direction of the force $\vec{F}$ is opposite to that of $\vec{v} \times \vec{B}$ (Fig. 27.7b). If two charges with equal magnitude and opposite sign move in the same $\vec{B}$ field with the same velocity (Fig. 27.8), the forces have equal magnitude and opposite direction. Figures 27.6, 27.7, and 27.8 show several examples of the relationships of the directions of $\vec{F}$, $\vec{v}$, and $\vec{B}$ for both positive and negative charges. Be sure you understand the relationships shown in these figures.

Equation (27.1) gives the magnitude of the magnetic force $\vec{F}$ in Eq. (27.2). We can express this magnitude in a different but equivalent way. Since ϕ is the angle between the directions of vectors $\vec{v}$ and $\vec{B}$, we may interpret $B \sin \phi$ as the component of $\vec{B}$ perpendicular to $\vec{v}$—that is, $B_\perp$. With this notation the force magnitude is

$$F = |q| v B_\perp \qquad (27.3)$$

This form is sometimes more convenient, especially in problems involving *currents* rather than individual particles. We will discuss forces on currents later in this chapter.

From Eq. (27.1) the *units* of B must be the same as the units of F/qv. Therefore the SI unit of B is equivalent to $1 \text{ N} \cdot \text{s}/\text{C} \cdot \text{m}$, or, since one ampere is one coulomb per second ($1 \text{ A} = 1 \text{ C}/\text{s}$), $1 \text{ N}/\text{A} \cdot \text{m}$. This unit is called the **tesla** (abbreviated T), in honor of Nikola Tesla (1856–1943), the prominent Serbian-American scientist and inventor:

$$1 \text{ tesla} = 1 \text{ T} = 1 \text{ N}/\text{A} \cdot \text{m}$$

Another unit of B, the **gauss** ($1 \text{ G} = 10^{-4} \text{ T}$), is also in common use.

The magnetic field of the earth is of the order of 10^{-4} T or 1 G. Magnetic fields of the order of 10 T occur in the interior of atoms and are important in the analysis of atomic spectra. The largest steady magnetic field that can be produced at present in the laboratory is about 45 T. Some pulsed-current electromagnets can produce fields of the order of 120 T for millisecond time intervals.

Measuring Magnetic Fields with Test Charges

To explore an unknown magnetic field, we can measure the magnitude and direction of the force on a *moving* test charge and then use Eq. (27.2) to determine $\vec{B}$. The electron beam in a cathode-ray tube, such as that in an older television set (not a flat screen), is a convenient device for this. The electron gun shoots out a narrow beam of electrons at a known speed. If there is no force to deflect the beam, it strikes the center of the screen.

27.8 Two charges of the same magnitude but opposite sign moving with the same velocity in the same magnetic field. The magnetic forces on the charges are equal in magnitude but opposite in direction.

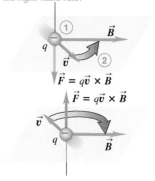

Positive and negative charges moving in the same direction through a magnetic field experience magnetic forces in *opposite* directions.

Application Magnetic Fields of the Body
All living cells are electrically active, and the feeble electric currents within the body produce weak but measurable magnetic fields. The fields produced by skeletal muscles have magnitudes less than 10^{-10} T, about one-millionth as strong as the earth's magnetic field. The brain produces magnetic fields that are far weaker, only about 10^{-12} T.

If a magnetic field is present, in general the electron beam is deflected. But if the beam is parallel or antiparallel to the field, then $\phi = 0$ or π in Eq. (27.1) and $F = 0$; there is no force and hence no deflection. If we find that the electron beam is not deflected when its direction is parallel to a certain axis as in Fig. 27.9a, the $\vec{B}$ vector must point either up or down along that axis.

If we then turn the tube 90° (Fig. 27.9b), $\phi = \pi/2$ in Eq. (27.1) and the magnetic force is maximum; the beam is deflected in a direction perpendicular to the plane of $\vec{B}$ and $\vec{v}$. The direction and magnitude of the deflection determine the direction and magnitude of $\vec{B}$. We can perform additional experiments in which the angle between $\vec{B}$ and $\vec{v}$ is between zero and 90° to confirm Eq. (27.1). We note that the electron has a negative charge; the force in Fig. 27.9b is opposite in direction to the force on a positive charge.

When a charged particle moves through a region of space where *both* electric and magnetic fields are present, both fields exert forces on the particle. The total force $\vec{F}$ is the vector sum of the electric and magnetic forces:

$$\vec{F} = q(\vec{E} + \vec{v} \times \vec{B}) \tag{27.4}$$

ActivPhysics 13.4: Magnetic Force on a Particle

27.9 Determining the direction of a magnetic field using a cathode-ray tube. Because electrons have a negative charge, the magnetic force $\vec{F} = q\vec{v} \times \vec{B}$ in part (b) points opposite to the direction given by the right-hand rule (see Fig. 27.7b).

(a) If the tube axis is parallel to the y-axis, the beam is undeflected, so $\vec{B}$ is in either the $+y$- or the $-y$-direction.

Electron beam

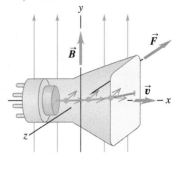

(b) If the tube axis is parallel to the x-axis, the beam is deflected in the $-z$-direction, so $\vec{B}$ is in the $+y$-direction.

Problem-Solving Strategy 27.1 Magnetic Forces

IDENTIFY *the relevant concepts:* The equation $\vec{F} = q\vec{v} \times \vec{B}$ allows you to determine the magnetic force on a moving charged particle.

SET UP *the problem* using the following steps:
1. Draw the velocity $\vec{v}$ and magnetic field $\vec{B}$ with their tails together so that you can visualize the plane that contains them.
2. Determine the angle ϕ between $\vec{v}$ and $\vec{B}$.
3. Identify the target variables.

EXECUTE *the solution* as follows:
1. Express the magnetic force using Eq. (27.2), $\vec{F} = q\vec{v} \times \vec{B}$. Equation (27.1) gives the magnitude of the force, $F = qvB\sin\phi$.

2. Remember that $\vec{F}$ is perpendicular to the plane containing $\vec{v}$ and $\vec{B}$. The right-hand rule (see Fig. 27.7) gives the direction of $\vec{v} \times \vec{B}$. If q is negative, $\vec{F}$ is *opposite* to $\vec{v} \times \vec{B}$.

EVALUATE *your answer:* Whenever possible, solve the problem in two ways to confirm that the results agree. Do it directly from the geometric definition of the vector product. Then find the components of the vectors in some convenient coordinate system and calculate the vector product from the components. Verify that the results agree.

Example 27.1 Magnetic force on a proton

A beam of protons ($q = 1.6 \times 10^{-19}$ C) moves at 3.0×10^5 m/s through a uniform 2.0-T magnetic field directed along the positive z-axis, as in Fig. 27.10. The velocity of each proton lies in the xz-plane and is directed at 30° to the +z-axis. Find the force on a proton.

SOLUTION

IDENTIFY and SET UP: This problem uses the expression $\vec{F} = q\vec{v} \times \vec{B}$ for the magnetic force $\vec{F}$ on a moving charged particle. The target variable is $\vec{F}$.

EXECUTE: The charge is positive, so the force is in the same direction as the vector product $\vec{v} \times \vec{B}$. From the right-hand rule, this direction is along the negative y-axis. The magnitude of the force, from Eq. (27.1), is

27.10 Directions of $\vec{v}$ and $\vec{B}$ for a proton in a magnetic field.

$$F = qvB \sin \phi$$
$$= (1.6 \times 10^{-19}\text{ C})(3.0 \times 10^5\text{ m/s})(2.0\text{ T})(\sin 30°)$$
$$= 4.8 \times 10^{-14}\text{ N}$$

EVALUATE: We check our result by evaluating the force using vector language and Eq. (27.2). We have

$$\vec{v} = (3.0 \times 10^5\text{ m/s})(\sin 30°)\hat{\imath} + (3.0 \times 10^5\text{ m/s})(\cos 30°)\hat{k}$$
$$\vec{B} = (2.0\text{ T})\hat{k}$$
$$\vec{F} = q\vec{v} \times \vec{B}$$
$$= (1.6 \times 10^{-19}\text{ C})(3.0 \times 10^5\text{ m/s})(2.0\text{ T})$$
$$\times (\sin 30°\hat{\imath} + \cos 30°\hat{k}) \times \hat{k}$$
$$= (-4.8 \times 10^{-14}\text{ N})\hat{\jmath}$$

(Recall that $\hat{\imath} \times \hat{k} = -\hat{\jmath}$ and $\hat{k} \times \hat{k} = \mathbf{0}$.) We again find that the force is in the negative y-direction with magnitude 4.8×10^{-14} N.

If the beam consists of *electrons* rather than protons, the charge is negative ($q = -1.6 \times 10^{-19}$ C) and the direction of the force is reversed. The force is now directed along the *positive* y-axis, but the magnitude is the same as before, $F = 4.8 \times 10^{-14}$ N.

Test Your Understanding of Section 27.2 The figure at right shows a uniform magnetic field $\vec{B}$ directed into the plane of the paper (shown by the blue ×'s). A particle with a negative charge moves in the plane. Which of the three paths—1, 2, or 3—does the particle follow?

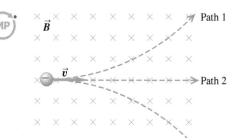

27.3 Magnetic Field Lines and Magnetic Flux

We can represent any magnetic field by **magnetic field lines,** just as we did for the earth's magnetic field in Fig. 27.3. The idea is the same as for the electric field lines we introduced in Section 21.6. We draw the lines so that the line through any point is tangent to the magnetic field vector $\vec{B}$ at that point (Fig. 27.11). Just as with electric field lines, we draw only a few representative lines; otherwise, the lines would fill up all of space. Where adjacent field lines are close together, the field magnitude is large; where these field lines are far apart, the field magnitude is small. Also, because the direction of $\vec{B}$ at each point is unique, field lines never intersect.

CAUTION **Magnetic field lines are not "lines of force"** Magnetic field lines are sometimes called "magnetic lines of force," but that's not a good name for them; unlike electric field lines, they *do not* point in the direction of the force on a charge (Fig. 27.12). Equation (27.2) shows that the force on a moving charged particle is always perpendicular to the magnetic field, and hence to the magnetic field line that passes through the particle's position. The direction of the force depends on the particle's velocity and the sign of its charge, so just looking at magnetic field lines cannot in itself tell you the direction of the force on an arbitrary moving charged particle. Magnetic field lines *do* have the direction that a compass needle would point at each location; this may help you to visualize them. ▮

Figures 27.11 and 27.13 show magnetic field lines produced by several common sources of magnetic field. In the gap between the poles of the magnet shown in Fig. 27.13a, the field lines are approximately straight, parallel, and equally spaced, showing that the magnetic field in this region is approximately *uniform* (that is, constant in magnitude and direction).

27.11 The magnetic field lines of a permanent magnet. Note that the field lines pass through the interior of the magnet.

At each point, the field line is tangent to the magnetic field vector $\vec{B}$.

The more densely the field lines are packed, the stronger the field is at that point.

At each point, the field lines point in the same direction a compass would . . .

. . . therefore, magnetic field lines point *away from* N poles and *toward* S poles.

27.12 Magnetic field lines are *not* "lines of force."

Magnetic field lines are *not* "lines of force." The force on a charged particle is not along the direction of a field line.

The direction of the magnetic force depends on the velocity $\vec{v}$, as expressed by the magnetic force law $\vec{F} = q\vec{v} \times \vec{B}$.

Because magnetic-field patterns are three-dimensional, it's often necessary to draw magnetic field lines that point into or out of the plane of a drawing. To do this we use a dot (·) to represent a vector directed out of the plane and a cross (×) to represent a vector directed into the plane (Fig. 27.13b). To remember these, think of a dot as the head of an arrow coming directly toward you, and think of a cross as the feathers of an arrow flying directly away from you.

Iron filings, like compass needles, tend to align with magnetic field lines. Hence they provide an easy way to visualize field lines (Fig. 27.14).

Magnetic Flux and Gauss's Law for Magnetism

We define the **magnetic flux** Φ_B through a surface just as we defined electric flux in connection with Gauss's law in Section 22.2. We can divide any surface into elements of area dA (Fig. 27.15). For each element we determine $B_\perp$, the component of $\vec{B}$ normal to the surface at the position of that element, as shown. From the figure, $B_\perp = B\cos\phi$, where ϕ is the angle between the direction of $\vec{B}$ and a line perpendicular to the surface. (Be careful not to confuse ϕ with Φ_B.) In general,

27.13 Magnetic field lines produced by some common sources of magnetic field.

(a) Magnetic field of a C-shaped magnet

Between flat, parallel magnetic poles, the magnetic field is nearly uniform.

(b) Magnetic field of a straight current-carrying wire

To represent a field coming out of or going into the plane of the paper, we use dots and crosses, respectively.

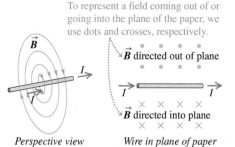

$\vec{B}$ directed out of plane

$\vec{B}$ directed into plane

Perspective view   *Wire in plane of paper*

(c) Magnetic fields of a current-carrying loop and a current-carrying coil (solenoid)

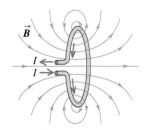

Notice that the field of the loop and, especially, that of the coil look like the field of a bar magnet (see Fig. 27.11).

27.14 (a) Like little compass needles, iron filings line up tangent to magnetic field lines. (b) Drawing of the field lines for the situation shown in (a).

(a)

(b)

this component varies from point to point on the surface. We define the magnetic flux $d\Phi_B$ through this area as

$$d\Phi_B = B_\perp \, dA = B\cos\phi \, dA = \vec{B} \cdot d\vec{A} \qquad (27.5)$$

The *total* magnetic flux through the surface is the sum of the contributions from the individual area elements:

$$\Phi_B = \int B_\perp \, dA = \int B\cos\phi \, dA = \int \vec{B} \cdot d\vec{A} \quad \text{(magnetic flux through a surface)} \qquad (27.6)$$

(This equation uses the concepts of vector area and surface integral that we introduced in Section 22.2; you may want to review that discussion.)

Magnetic flux is a *scalar* quantity. If $\vec{B}$ is uniform over a plane surface with total area A, then $B_\perp$ and ϕ are the same at all points on the surface, and

$$\Phi_B = B_\perp A = BA\cos\phi \qquad (27.7)$$

If $\vec{B}$ happens to be perpendicular to the surface, then $\cos\phi = 1$ and Eq. (27.7) reduces to $\Phi_B = BA$. We will use the concept of magnetic flux extensively during our study of electromagnetic induction in Chapter 29.

The SI unit of magnetic flux is equal to the unit of magnetic field (1 T) times the unit of area (1 m^2). This unit is called the **weber** (1 Wb), in honor of the German physicist Wilhelm Weber (1804–1891):

$$1 \text{ Wb} = 1 \text{ T} \cdot \text{m}^2$$

Also, $1 \text{ T} = 1 \text{ N/A} \cdot \text{m}$, so

$$1 \text{ Wb} = 1 \text{ T} \cdot \text{m}^2 = 1 \text{ N} \cdot \text{m/A}$$

In Gauss's law the total *electric* flux through a closed surface is proportional to the total electric charge enclosed by the surface. For example, if the closed surface encloses an electric dipole, the total electric flux is zero because the total charge is zero. (You may want to review Section 22.3 on Gauss's law.) By analogy, if there were such a thing as a single magnetic charge (magnetic monopole), the total *magnetic* flux through a closed surface would be proportional to the total magnetic charge enclosed. But we have mentioned that no magnetic monopole has ever been observed, despite intensive searches. We conclude:

The total magnetic flux through a closed surface is always zero.

Symbolically,

$$\oint \vec{B} \cdot d\vec{A} = 0 \qquad \text{(magnetic flux through any closed surface)} \qquad (27.8)$$

This equation is sometimes called *Gauss's law for magnetism.* You can verify it by examining Figs. 27.11 and 27.13; if you draw a closed surface anywhere in any of the field maps shown in those figures, you will see that every field line that enters the surface also exits from it; the net flux through the surface is zero. It also follows from Eq. (27.8) that magnetic field lines always form closed loops.

CAUTION **Magnetic field lines have no ends** Unlike electric field lines that begin and end on electric charges, magnetic field lines *never* have end points; such a point would indicate the presence of a monopole. You might be tempted to draw magnetic field lines that begin at the north pole of a magnet and end at a south pole. But as Fig. 27.11 shows, the field lines of a magnet actually continue through the interior of the magnet. Like all other magnetic field lines, they form closed loops.

27.15 The magnetic flux through an area element dA is defined to be $d\Phi_B = B_\perp \, dA$.

PhET: Magnet and Compass
PhET: Magnets and Electromagnets

For Gauss's law, which always deals with *closed* surfaces, the vector area element $d\vec{A}$ in Eq. (27.6) always points *out of* the surface. However, some applications of *magnetic* flux involve an *open* surface with a boundary line; there is then an ambiguity of sign in Eq. (27.6) because of the two possible choices of direction for $d\vec{A}$. In these cases we choose one of the two sides of the surface to be the "positive" side and use that choice consistently.

If the element of area dA in Eq. (27.5) is at right angles to the field lines, then $B_\perp = B$; calling the area $dA_\perp$, we have

$$B = \frac{d\Phi_B}{dA_\perp} \qquad (27.9)$$

That is, the magnitude of magnetic field is equal to *flux per unit area* across an area at right angles to the magnetic field. For this reason, magnetic field $\vec{B}$ is sometimes called **magnetic flux density.**

Example 27.2 **Magnetic flux calculations**

Figure 27.16a is a perspective view of a flat surface with area 3.0 cm² in a uniform magnetic field $\vec{B}$. The magnetic flux through this surface is +0.90 mWb. Find the magnitude of the magnetic field and the direction of the area vector $\vec{A}$.

27.16 (a) A flat area A in a uniform magnetic field $\vec{B}$. (b) The area vector $\vec{A}$ makes a 60° angle with $\vec{B}$. (If we had chosen $\vec{A}$ to point in the opposite direction, ϕ would have been 120° and the magnetic flux Φ_B would have been negative.)

(a) Perspective view   (b) Our sketch of the problem
                              (edge-on view)

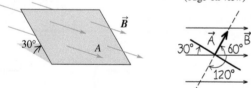

SOLUTION

IDENTIFY and SET UP: Our target variables are the field magnitude B and the direction of the area vector. Because $\vec{B}$ is uniform, B and ϕ are the same at all points on the surface. Hence we can use Eq. (27.7), $\Phi_B = BA\cos\phi$.

EXECUTE: The area A is 3.0×10^{-4} m²; the direction of $\vec{A}$ is perpendicular to the surface, so ϕ could be either 60° or 120°. But Φ_B, B, and A are all positive, so $\cos\phi$ must also be positive. This rules out 120°, so $\phi = 60°$ (Fig. 27.16b). Hence we find

$$B = \frac{\Phi_B}{A\cos\phi} = \frac{0.90 \times 10^{-3} \text{ Wb}}{(3.0 \times 10^{-4} \text{ m}^2)(\cos 60°)} = 6.0 \text{ T}$$

EVALUATE: In many problems we are asked to calculate the flux of a given magnetic field through a given area. This example is somewhat different: It tests your understanding of the definition of magnetic flux.

Test Your Understanding of Section 27.3 Imagine moving along the axis of the current-carrying loop in Fig. 27.13c, starting at a point well to the left of the loop and ending at a point well to the right of the loop. (a) How would the magnetic field strength vary as you moved along this path? (i) It would be the same at all points along the path; (ii) it would increase and then decrease; (iii) it would decrease and then increase. (b) Would the magnetic field direction vary as you moved along the path?

27.4 Motion of Charged Particles in a Magnetic Field

When a charged particle moves in a magnetic field, it is acted on by the magnetic force given by Eq. (27.2), and the motion is determined by Newton's laws. Figure 27.17a shows a simple example. A particle with positive charge q is at point O, moving with velocity $\vec{v}$ in a uniform magnetic field $\vec{B}$ directed into the plane of the figure. The vectors $\vec{v}$ and $\vec{B}$ are perpendicular, so the magnetic force $\vec{F} = q\vec{v} \times \vec{B}$ has magnitude $F = qvB$ and a direction as shown in the figure. The force is *always* perpendicular to $\vec{v}$, so it cannot change the *magnitude* of the velocity, only its direction. To put it differently, the magnetic force never has a component parallel to the particle's motion, so the magnetic force can never do *work* on the particle. This is true even if the magnetic field is not uniform.

> **Motion of a charged particle under the action of a magnetic field alone is always motion with constant speed.**

Using this principle, we see that in the situation shown in Fig. 27.17a the magnitudes of both $\vec{F}$ and $\vec{v}$ are constant. At points such as P and S the directions of force and velocity have changed as shown, but their magnitudes are the same. The particle therefore moves under the influence of a constant-magnitude force that is always at right angles to the velocity of the particle. Comparing the discussion of circular motion in Sections 3.4 and 5.4, we see that the particle's path is a *circle*, traced out with constant speed v. The centripetal acceleration is v^2/R and only the magnetic force acts, so from Newton's second law,

$$F = |q|vB = m\frac{v^2}{R} \tag{27.10}$$

where m is the mass of the particle. Solving Eq. (27.10) for the radius R of the circular path, we find

$$R = \frac{mv}{|q|B} \qquad \text{(radius of a circular orbit in a magnetic field)} \tag{27.11}$$

We can also write this as $R = p/|q|B$, where $p = mv$ is the magnitude of the particle's momentum. If the charge q is negative, the particle moves *clockwise* around the orbit in Fig. 27.17a.

The angular speed ω of the particle can be found from Eq. (9.13), $v = R\omega$. Combining this with Eq. (27.11), we get

$$\omega = \frac{v}{R} = v\frac{|q|B}{mv} = \frac{|q|B}{m} \tag{27.12}$$

The number of revolutions per unit time is $f = \omega/2\pi$. This frequency f is independent of the radius R of the path. It is called the **cyclotron frequency;** in a particle accelerator called a *cyclotron,* particles moving in nearly circular paths are given a boost twice each revolution, increasing their energy and their orbital radii but not their angular speed or frequency. Similarly, one type of *magnetron,* a common source of microwave radiation for microwave ovens and radar systems, emits radiation with a frequency equal to the frequency of circular motion of electrons in a vacuum chamber between the poles of a magnet.

If the direction of the initial velocity is *not* perpendicular to the field, the velocity *component* parallel to the field is constant because there is no force parallel to the field. Then the particle moves in a helix (Fig. 27.18). The radius of the helix is given by Eq. (27.11), where v is now the component of velocity perpendicular to the $\vec{B}$ field.

Motion of a charged particle in a nonuniform magnetic field is more complex. Figure 27.19 shows a field produced by two circular coils separated by some distance. Particles near either coil experience a magnetic force toward the center of the region; particles with appropriate speeds spiral repeatedly from one end of the region to the other and back. Because charged particles can be trapped in such a magnetic field, it is called a *magnetic bottle.* This technique is used to confine very hot plasmas with temperatures of the order of 10^6 K. In a similar way the earth's nonuniform magnetic field traps charged particles coming from the sun in doughnut-shaped regions around the earth, as shown in Fig. 27.20. These regions, called the *Van Allen radiation belts,* were discovered in 1958 using data obtained by instruments aboard the Explorer I satellite.

27.17 A charged particle moves in a plane perpendicular to a uniform magnetic field $\vec{B}$.

(a) The orbit of a charged particle in a uniform magnetic field

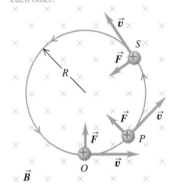

A charge moving at right angles to a uniform $\vec{B}$ field moves in a circle at constant speed because $\vec{F}$ and $\vec{v}$ are always perpendicular to each other.

(b) An electron beam (seen as a white arc) curving in a magnetic field

Video Tutor Demo

27.18 The general case of a charged particle moving in a uniform magnetic field $\vec{B}$. The magnetic field does no work on the particle, so its speed and kinetic energy remain constant.

This particle's motion has components both parallel ($v_{\parallel}$) and perpendicular ($v_{\perp}$) to the magnetic field, so it moves in a helical path.

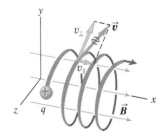

27.19 A magnetic bottle. Particles near either end of the region experience a magnetic force toward the center of the region. This is one way of containing an ionized gas that has a temperature of the order of 10^6 K, which would vaporize any material container.

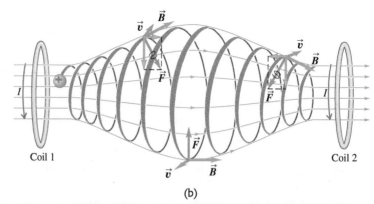

27.20 (a) The Van Allen radiation belts around the earth. Near the poles, charged particles from these belts can enter the atmosphere, producing the aurora borealis ("northern lights") and aurora australis ("southern lights"). (b) A photograph of the aurora borealis.

27.21 This bubble chamber image shows the result of a high-energy gamma ray (which does not leave a track) that collides with an electron in a hydrogen atom. This electron flies off to the right at high speed. Some of the energy in the collision is transformed into a second electron and a positron (a positively charged electron). A magnetic field is directed into the plane of the image, which makes the positive and negative particles curve off in different directions.

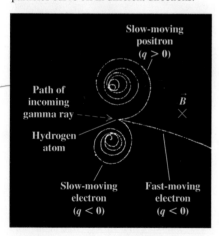

Magnetic forces on charged particles play an important role in studies of elementary particles. Figure 27.21 shows a chamber filled with liquid hydrogen and with a magnetic field directed into the plane of the photograph. A high-energy gamma ray dislodges an electron from a hydrogen atom, sending it off at high speed and creating a visible track in the liquid hydrogen. The track shows the electron curving downward due to the magnetic force. The energy of the collision also produces another electron and a *positron* (a positively charged electron). Because of their opposite charges, the trajectories of the electron and the positron curve in opposite directions. As these particles plow through the liquid hydrogen, they collide with other charged particles, losing energy and speed. As a result, the radius of curvature decreases as suggested by Eq. (27.11). (The electron's speed is comparable to the speed of light, so Eq. (27.11) isn't directly applicable here.) Similar experiments allow physicists to determine the mass and charge of newly discovered particles.

Problem-Solving Strategy 27.2   **Motion in Magnetic Fields**

IDENTIFY *the relevant concepts:* In analyzing the motion of a charged particle in electric and magnetic fields, you will apply Newton's second law of motion, $\sum \vec{F} = m\vec{a}$, with the net force given by $\sum \vec{F} = q(\vec{E} + \vec{v} \times \vec{B})$. Often other forces such as gravity can be neglected. Many of the problems are similar to the trajectory and circular-motion problems in Sections 3.3, 3.4, and 5.4; it would be a good idea to review those sections.

SET UP *the problem* using the following steps:
1. Determine the target variable(s).
2. Often the use of components is the most efficient approach. Choose a coordinate system and then express all vector quanti-

ties (including , and) in terms of their components in this system.

EXECUTE *the solution* as follows:
1. If the particle moves perpendicular to a uniform magnetic field, the trajectory is a circle with a radius and angular speed given by Eqs. (27.11) and (27.12), respectively.
2. If your calculation involves a more complex trajectory, use $\sum \vec{F} = m\vec{a}$ in component form: $\sum F_x = ma_x$, and so forth. This approach is particularly useful when both electric and magnetic fields are present.

EVALUATE *your answer:* Check whether your results are reasonable.

Example 27.3 **Electron motion in a magnetron**

A magnetron in a microwave oven emits electromagnetic waves with frequency f = 2450 MHz. What magnetic field strength is required for electrons to move in circular paths with this frequency?

SOLUTION

IDENTIFY and SET UP: The problem refers to circular motion as shown in Fig. 27.17a. We use Eq. (27.12) to solve for the field magnitude B.

EXECUTE: The angular speed that corresponds to the frequency f is $\omega = 2\pi f = (2\pi)(2450 \times 10^6 \text{ s}^{-1}) = 1.54 \times 10^{10} \text{ s}^{-1}$. Then from Eq. (27.12),

$$B = \frac{m\omega}{|q|} = \frac{(9.11 \times 10^{-31} \text{ kg})(1.54 \times 10^{10} \text{ s}^{-1})}{1.60 \times 10^{-19} \text{ C}} = 0.0877 \text{ T}$$

EVALUATE: This is a moderate field strength, easily produced with a permanent magnet. Incidentally, 2450-MHz electromagnetic waves are useful for heating and cooking food because they are strongly absorbed by water molecules.

Example 27.4 **Helical particle motion in a magnetic field**

In a situation like that shown in Fig. 27.18, the charged particle is a proton ($q = 1.60 \times 10^{-19}$ C, $m = 1.67 \times 10^{-27}$ kg) and the uniform, 0.500-T magnetic field is directed along the x-axis. At $t = 0$ the proton has velocity components $v_x = 1.50 \times 10^5$ m/s, $v_y = 0$, and $v_z = 2.00 \times 10^5$ m/s. Only the magnetic force acts on the proton. (a) At $t = 0$, find the force on the proton and its acceleration. (b) Find the radius of the resulting helical path, the angular speed of the proton, and the *pitch* of the helix (the distance traveled along the helix axis per revolution).

SOLUTION

IDENTIFY and SET UP: The magnetic force is $\vec{F} = q\vec{v} \times \vec{B}$; Newton's second law gives the resulting acceleration. Because $\vec{F}$ is perpendicular to $\vec{v}$, the proton's speed does not change. Hence Eq. (27.11) gives the radius of the helical trajectory if we replace v with the velocity component perpendicular to $\vec{B}$. Equation (27.12) gives the angular speed ω, which yields the time T for one revolution (the *period*). Given the velocity component parallel to the magnetic field, we can then determine the pitch.

EXECUTE: (a) With $\vec{B} = B\hat{\imath}$ and $\vec{v} = v_x\hat{\imath} + v_z\hat{k}$, Eq. (27.2) yields

$$\vec{F} = q\vec{v} \times \vec{B} = q(v_x\hat{\imath} + v_z\hat{k}) \times B\hat{\imath} = qv_zB\hat{\jmath}$$
$$= (1.60 \times 10^{-19} \text{ C})(2.00 \times 10^5 \text{ m/s})(0.500 \text{ T})\hat{\jmath}$$
$$= (1.60 \times 10^{-14} \text{ N})\hat{\jmath}$$

(Recall that that $\hat{\imath} \times \hat{\imath} = 0$ and $\hat{k} \times \hat{\imath} = \hat{\jmath}$.) The resulting acceleration is

$$\vec{a} = \frac{\vec{F}}{m} = \frac{1.60 \times 10^{-14} \text{ N}}{1.67 \times 10^{-27} \text{ kg}}\hat{\jmath} = (9.58 \times 10^{12} \text{ m/s}^2)\hat{\jmath}$$

(b) Since $v_y = 0$, the component of velocity perpendicular to $\vec{B}$ is v_z; then from Eq. (27.11),

$$R = \frac{mv_z}{|q|B} = \frac{(1.67 \times 10^{-27} \text{ kg})(2.00 \times 10^5 \text{ m/s})}{(1.60 \times 10^{-19} \text{ C})(0.500 \text{ T})}$$
$$= 4.18 \times 10^{-3} \text{ m} = 4.18 \text{ mm}$$

From Eq. (27.12) the angular speed is

$$\omega = \frac{|q|B}{m} = \frac{(1.60 \times 10^{-19} \text{ C})(0.500 \text{ T})}{1.67 \times 10^{-27} \text{ kg}} = 4.79 \times 10^7 \text{ rad/s}$$

The period is $T = 2\pi/\omega = 2\pi/(4.79 \times 10^7 \text{ s}^{-1}) = 1.31 \times 10^{-7}$ s. The pitch is the distance traveled along the x-axis in this time, or

$$v_xT = (1.50 \times 10^5 \text{ m/s})(1.31 \times 10^{-7} \text{ s})$$
$$= 0.0197 \text{ m} = 19.7 \text{ mm}$$

EVALUATE: Although the magnetic force has a tiny magnitude, it produces an immense acceleration because the proton mass is so small. Note that the pitch of the helix is almost five times greater than the radius R, so this helix is much more "stretched out" than that shown in Fig. 27.18.

Test Your Understanding of Section 27.4 (a) If you double the speed of the charged particle in Fig. 27.17a while keeping the magnetic field the same (as well as the charge and the mass), how does this affect the radius of the trajectory? (i) The radius is unchanged; (ii) the radius is twice as large; (iii) the radius is four times as large; (iv) the radius is $\frac{1}{2}$ as large; (v) the radius is $\frac{1}{4}$ as large. (b) How does this affect the time required for one complete circular orbit? (i) The time is unchanged; (ii) the time is twice as long; (iii) the time is four times as long; (iv) the time is $\frac{1}{2}$ as long; (v) the time is $\frac{1}{4}$ as long.

27.5 Applications of Motion of Charged Particles

This section describes several applications of the principles introduced in this chapter. Study them carefully, watching for applications of Problem-Solving Strategy 27.2 (Section 27.4).

Velocity Selector

In a beam of charged particles produced by a heated cathode or a radioactive material, not all particles move with the same speed. Many applications, however, require a beam in which all the particle speeds are the same. Particles of a specific speed can be selected from the beam using an arrangement of electric and magnetic fields called a *velocity selector.* In Fig. 27.22a a charged particle with mass m, charge q, and speed v enters a region of space where the electric and magnetic fields are perpendicular to the particle's velocity and to each other. The electric field $\vec{E}$ is to the left, and the magnetic field $\vec{B}$ is into the plane of the figure. If q is positive, the electric force is to the left, with magnitude qE, and the magnetic force is to the right, with magnitude qvB. For given field magnitudes E and B, for a particular value of v the electric and magnetic forces will be equal in magnitude; the total force is then zero, and the particle travels in a straight line with constant velocity. For zero total force, $\Sigma F_y = 0$, we need $-qE + qvB = 0$; solving for the speed v for which there is no deflection, we find

$$v = \frac{E}{B} \qquad (27.13)$$

Only particles with speeds equal to E/B can pass through without being deflected by the fields (Fig. 27.22b). By adjusting E and B appropriately, we can select particles having a particular speed for use in other experiments. Because q divides out in Eq. (27.13), a velocity selector for positively charged particles also works for electrons or other negatively charged particles.

Thomson's e/m Experiment

In one of the landmark experiments in physics at the end of the 19th century, J. J. Thomson (1856–1940) used the idea just described to measure the ratio of charge to mass for the electron. For this experiment, carried out in 1897 at the Cavendish Laboratory in Cambridge, England, Thomson used the apparatus shown in Fig. 27.23. In a highly evacuated glass container, electrons from the hot cathode are accelerated and formed into a beam by a potential difference V between the two anodes A and A'. The speed v of the electrons is determined by the accelerating

27.22 (a) A velocity selector for charged particles uses perpendicular $\vec{E}$ and $\vec{B}$ fields. Only charged particles with $v = E/B$ move through undeflected. (b) The electric and magnetic forces on a positive charge. The forces are reversed if the charge is negative.

(a) Schematic diagram of velocity selector

Source of charged particles

By the right-hand rule, the force of the $\vec{B}$ field on the charge points to the right.

The force of the $\vec{E}$ field on the charge points to the left.

For a negative charge, the directions of *both* forces are reversed.

(b) Free-body diagram for a positive particle

$F_E = qE$ $F_B = qvB$

Only if a charged particle has $v = E/B$ do the electric and magnetic forces cancel. All other particles are deflected.

27.23 Thomson's apparatus for measuring the ratio e/m for the electron.

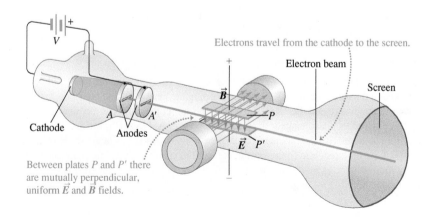

Electrons travel from the cathode to the screen.

Electron beam

Screen

Cathode

Anodes

Between plates P and P' there are mutually perpendicular, uniform $\vec{E}$ and $\vec{B}$ fields.

potential V. The gained kinetic energy $\frac{1}{2}mv^2$ equals the lost electric potential energy eV, where e is the magnitude of the electron charge:

$$\frac{1}{2}mv^2 = eV \quad \text{or} \quad v = \sqrt{\frac{2eV}{m}} \qquad (27.14)$$

The electrons pass between the plates P and P' and strike the screen at the end of the tube, which is coated with a material that fluoresces (glows) at the point of impact. The electrons pass straight through the plates when Eq. (27.13) is satisfied; combining this with Eq. (27.14), we get

$$\frac{E}{B} = \sqrt{\frac{2eV}{m}} \quad \text{so} \quad \frac{e}{m} = \frac{E^2}{2VB^2} \qquad (27.15)$$

All the quantities on the right side can be measured, so the ratio e/m of charge to mass can be determined. It is *not* possible to measure e or m separately by this method, only their ratio.

The most significant aspect of Thomson's e/m measurements was that he found a *single value* for this quantity. It did not depend on the cathode material, the residual gas in the tube, or anything else about the experiment. This independence showed that the particles in the beam, which we now call electrons, are a common constituent of all matter. Thus Thomson is credited with the first discovery of a subatomic particle, the electron.

The most precise value of e/m available as of this writing is

$$e/m = 1.758820150(44) \times 10^{11} \text{ C/kg}$$

In this expression, (44) indicates the likely uncertainty in the last two digits, 50.

Fifteen years after Thomson's experiments, the American physicist Robert Millikan succeeded in measuring the charge of the electron precisely (see Challenge Problem 23.91). This value, together with the value of e/m, enables us to determine the *mass* of the electron. The most precise value available at present is

$$m = 9.10938215(45) \times 10^{-31} \text{ kg}$$

Mass Spectrometers

Techniques similar to Thomson's e/m experiment can be used to measure masses of ions and thus measure atomic and molecular masses. In 1919, Francis Aston (1877–1945), a student of Thomson's, built the first of a family of instruments called **mass spectrometers.** A variation built by Bainbridge is shown in Fig. 27.24. Positive ions from a source pass through the slits S_1 and S_2, forming a narrow beam. Then the ions pass through a velocity selector with crossed $\vec{E}$ and $\vec{B}$ fields, as we have described, to block all ions except those with speeds v equal to E/B. Finally, the ions pass into a region with a magnetic field $\vec{B}'$ perpendicular to the figure, where they move in circular arcs with radius R determined by Eq. (27.11): $R = mv/qB'$. Ions with different masses strike the detector (in Bainbridge's design, a photographic plate) at different points, and the values of R can be measured. We assume that each ion has lost one electron, so the net charge of each ion is just $+e$. With everything known in this equation except m, we can compute the mass m of the ion.

One of the earliest results from this work was the discovery that neon has two species of atoms, with atomic masses 20 and 22 g/mol. We now call these species **isotopes** of the element. Later experiments have shown that many elements have several isotopes, atoms that are identical in their chemical behavior but different in mass owing to differing numbers of neutrons in their nuclei. This is just one of the many applications of mass spectrometers in chemistry and physics.

ActivPhysics 13.8: Velocity Selector

27.24 Bainbridge's mass spectrometer utilizes a velocity selector to produce particles with uniform speed v. In the region of magnetic field B', particles with greater mass ($m_2 > m_1$) travel in paths with larger radius ($R_2 > R_1$).

Velocity selector selects particles with speed v.

Particle detector

$\vec{E}, \vec{B}$

m_2 m_1

S_1
S_2

S_3

R_1
R_2

$\vec{B}'$

Magnetic field separates particles by mass; the greater a particle's mass, the larger is the radius of its path.

Example 27.5 An e/m demonstration experiment

You set out to reproduce Thomson's e/m experiment with an accelerating potential of 150 V and a deflecting electric field of magnitude 6.0×10^6 N/C. (a) At what fraction of the speed of light do the electrons move? (b) What magnetic-field magnitude will yield zero beam deflection? (c) With this magnetic field, how will the electron beam behave if you increase the accelerating potential above 150 V?

SOLUTION

IDENTIFY and SET UP: This is the situation shown in Fig. 27.23. We use Eq. (27.14) to determine the electron speed and Eq. (27.13) to determine the required magnetic field B.

EXECUTE: (a) From Eq. (27.14), the electron speed v is

$$v = \sqrt{2(e/m)V} = \sqrt{2(1.76 \times 10^{11} \text{ C/kg})(150 \text{ V})}$$
$$= 7.27 \times 10^6 \text{ m/s} = 0.024c$$

(b) From Eq. (27.13), the required field strength is

$$B = \frac{E}{v} = \frac{6.00 \times 10^6 \text{ N/C}}{7.27 \times 10^6 \text{ m/s}} = 0.83 \text{ T}$$

(c) Increasing the accelerating potential V increases the electron speed v. In Fig. 27.23 this doesn't change the upward electric force eE, but it increases the downward magnetic force evB. Therefore the electron beam will turn *downward* and will hit the end of the tube below the undeflected position.

EVALUATE: The required magnetic field is relatively large because the electrons are moving fairly rapidly (2.4% of the speed of light). If the maximum available magnetic field is less than 0.83 T, the electric field strength E would have to be reduced to maintain the desired ratio E/B in Eq. (27.15).

Example 27.6 Finding leaks in a vacuum system

There is almost no helium in ordinary air, so helium sprayed near a leak in a vacuum system will quickly show up in the output of a vacuum pump connected to such a system. You are designing a leak detector that uses a mass spectrometer to detect He^+ ions (charge $+e = +1.60 \times 10^{-19}$ C, mass 6.65×10^{-27} kg). The ions emerge from the velocity selector with a speed of 1.00×10^5 m/s. They are curved in a semicircular path by a magnetic field B' and are detected at a distance of 10.16 cm from the slit S_3 in Fig. 27.24. Calculate the magnitude of the magnetic field B'.

SOLUTION

IDENTIFY and SET UP: After it passes through the slit, the ion follows a circular path as described in Section 27.4 (see Fig. 27.17). We solve Eq. (27.11) for B'.

EXECUTE: The distance given is the *diameter* of the semicircular path shown in Fig. 27.24, so the radius is $R = \frac{1}{2}(10.16 \times 10^{-2}$ m). From Eq. (27.11), $R = mv/qB'$, we get

$$B' = \frac{mv}{qR} = \frac{(6.65 \times 10^{-27} \text{ kg})(1.00 \times 10^5 \text{ m/s})}{(1.60 \times 10^{-19} \text{ C})(5.08 \times 10^{-2} \text{ m})}$$
$$= 0.0818 \text{ T}$$

EVALUATE: Helium leak detectors are widely used with high-vacuum systems. Our result shows that only a small magnetic field is required, so leak detectors can be relatively compact.

ActivPhysics 13.7: Mass Spectrometer

27.25 Forces on a moving positive charge in a current-carrying conductor.

Test Your Understanding of Section 27.5 In Example 27.6 He^+ ions with charge $+e$ move at 1.00×10^5 m/s in a straight line through a velocity selector. Suppose the He^+ ions were replaced with He^{2+} ions, in which both electrons have been removed from the helium atom and the ion charge is $+2e$. At what speed must the He^{2+} ions travel through the same velocity selector in order to move in a straight line? (i) about 4.00×10^5 m/s; (ii) about 2.00×10^5 m/s; (iii) 1.00×10^5 m/s; (iv) about 0.50×10^5 m/s; (v) about 0.25×10^5 m/s.

27.6 Magnetic Force on a Current-Carrying Conductor

What makes an electric motor work? Within the motor are conductors that carry currents (that is, whose charges are in motion), as well as magnets that exert forces on the moving charges. Hence there is a magnetic force along the length of each current-carrying conductor, and these forces make the motor turn. The moving-coil galvanometer that we described in Section 26.3 also uses magnetic forces on conductors.

We can compute the force on a current-carrying conductor starting with the magnetic force $\vec{F} = q\vec{v} \times \vec{B}$ on a single moving charge. Figure 27.25 shows a straight segment of a conducting wire, with length l and cross-sectional area A; the current is from bottom to top. The wire is in a uniform magnetic field $\vec{B}$, perpendicular to the plane of the diagram and directed *into* the plane. Let's assume first that the moving charges are positive. Later we'll see what happens when they are negative.

The drift velocity $\vec{v}_d$ is upward, perpendicular to $\vec{B}$. The average force on each charge is $\vec{F} = q\vec{v}_d \times \vec{B}$, directed to the left as shown in the figure; since $\vec{v}_d$ and $\vec{B}$ are perpendicular, the magnitude of the force is $F = qv_d B$.

We can derive an expression for the *total* force on all the moving charges in a length l of conductor with cross-sectional area A using the same language we used in Eqs. (25.2) and (25.3) of Section 25.1. The number of charges per unit volume is n; a segment of conductor with length l has volume Al and contains a number of charges equal to nAl. The total force $\vec{F}$ on *all* the moving charges in this segment has magnitude

$$F = (nAl)(qv_d B) = (nqv_d A)(lB) \qquad (27.16)$$

From Eq. (25.3) the current density is $J = nqv_d$. The product JA is the total current I, so we can rewrite Eq. (27.16) as

$$F = IlB \qquad (27.17)$$

If the $\vec{B}$ field is not perpendicular to the wire but makes an angle ϕ with it, we handle the situation the same way we did in Section 27.2 for a single charge. Only the component of $\vec{B}$ perpendicular to the wire (and to the drift velocities of the charges) exerts a force; this component is $B_\perp = B \sin \phi$. The magnetic force on the wire segment is then

$$F = IlB_\perp = IlB \sin \phi \qquad (27.18)$$

The force is always perpendicular to both the conductor and the field, with the direction determined by the same right-hand rule we used for a moving positive charge (Fig. 27.26). Hence this force can be expressed as a vector product, just like the force on a single moving charge. We represent the segment of wire with a vector $\vec{l}$ along the wire in the direction of the current; then the force $\vec{F}$ on this segment is

$$\boxed{\vec{F} = I\vec{l} \times \vec{B}} \qquad \text{(magnetic force on a straight wire segment)} \qquad (27.19)$$

Figure 27.27 illustrates the directions of $\vec{B}$, $\vec{l}$, and $\vec{F}$ for several cases.

If the conductor is not straight, we can divide it into infinitesimal segments $d\vec{l}$. The force $d\vec{F}$ on each segment is

$$\boxed{d\vec{F} = I\,d\vec{l} \times \vec{B}} \quad \text{(magnetic force on an infinitesimal wire section)} \qquad (27.20)$$

Then we can integrate this expression along the wire to find the total force on a conductor of any shape. The integral is a *line integral,* the same mathematical operation we have used to define work (Section 6.3) and electric potential (Section 23.2).

CAUTION **Current is not a vector** Recall from Section 25.1 that the current I is not a vector. The direction of current flow is described by $d\vec{l}$, not I. If the conductor is curved, the current I is the same at all points along its length, but $d\vec{l}$ changes direction so that it is always tangent to the conductor.

Finally, what happens when the moving charges are negative, such as electrons in a metal? Then in Fig. 27.25 an upward current corresponds to a downward drift velocity. But because q is now negative, the direction of the force $\vec{F}$ is the same as before. Thus Eqs. (27.17) through (27.20) are valid for *both* positive and negative charges and even when *both* signs of charge are present at once. This happens in some semiconductor materials and in ionic solutions.

A common application of the magnetic forces on a current-carrying wire is found in loudspeakers (Fig. 27.28). The radial magnetic field created by the permanent

Video Tutor Demo

27.26 A straight wire segment of length $\vec{l}$ carries a current I in the direction of $\vec{l}$. The magnetic force on this segment is perpendicular to both $\vec{l}$ and the magnetic field $\vec{B}$.

Force $\vec{F}$ on a straight wire carrying a positive current and oriented at an angle ϕ to a magnetic field $\vec{B}$:
- Magnitude is $F = IlB_\perp = IlB \sin \phi$.
- Direction of $\vec{F}$ is given by the right-hand rule.

27.27 Magnetic field $\vec{B}$, length $\vec{l}$, and force $\vec{F}$ vectors for a straight wire carrying a current I.

(a)

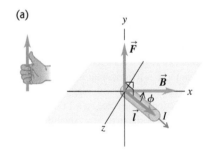

(b)

Reversing $\vec{B}$ reverses the force direction.

(c)

Reversing the current [relative to (b)] reverses the force direction.

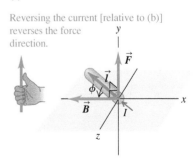

27.28 (a) Components of a loudspeaker. (b) The permanent magnet creates a magnetic field that exerts forces on the current in the voice coil; for a current I in the direction shown, the force is to the right. If the electric current in the voice coil oscillates, the speaker cone attached to the voice coil oscillates at the same frequency.

(a)

(b)

ActivPhysics 13.5: Magnetic Force on Wire

magnet exerts a force on the voice coil that is proportional to the current in the coil; the direction of the force is either to the left or to the right, depending on the direction of the current. The signal from the amplifier causes the current to oscillate in direction and magnitude. The coil and the speaker cone to which it is attached respond by oscillating with an amplitude proportional to the amplitude of the current in the coil. Turning up the volume knob on the amplifier increases the current amplitude and hence the amplitudes of the cone's oscillation and of the sound wave produced by the moving cone.

Example 27.7 | **Magnetic force on a straight conductor**

A straight horizontal copper rod carries a current of 50.0 A from west to east in a region between the poles of a large electromagnet. In this region there is a horizontal magnetic field toward the northeast (that is, 45° north of east) with magnitude 1.20 T. (a) Find the magnitude and direction of the force on a 1.00-m section of rod. (b) While keeping the rod horizontal, how should it be oriented to maximize the magnitude of the force? What is the force magnitude in this case?

SOLUTION

IDENTIFY and SET UP: Figure 27.29 shows the situation. This is a straight wire segment in a uniform magnetic field, as in Fig. 27.26. Our target variables are the force $\vec{F}$ on the segment and the angle ϕ for which the force magnitude F is greatest. We find the magnitude of the magnetic force using Eq. (27.18) and the direction from the right-hand rule.

EXECUTE: (a) The angle ϕ between the directions of current and field is 45°. From Eq. (27.18) we obtain

27.29 Our sketch of the copper rod as seen from overhead.

$F = IlB \sin\phi = (50.0 \text{ A})(1.00 \text{ m})(1.20 \text{ T})(\sin 45°) = 42.4 \text{ N}$

The direction of the force is perpendicular to the plane of the current and the field, both of which lie in the horizontal plane. Thus the force must be vertical; the right-hand rule shows that it is vertically *upward* (out of the plane of the figure).

(b) From $F = IlB \sin\phi$, F is maximum for $\phi = 90°$, so that $\vec{l}$ and $\vec{B}$ are perpendicular. To keep $\vec{F} = I\vec{l} \times \vec{B}$ upward, we rotate the rod *clockwise* by 45° from its orientation in Fig. 27.29, so that the current runs toward the southeast. Then $F = IlB = (50.0 \text{ A})(1.00 \text{ m})(1.20 \text{ T}) = 60.0 \text{ N}$.

EVALUATE: You can check the result in part (a) by using Eq. (27.19) to calculate the force vector. If we use a coordinate system with the x-axis pointing east, the y-axis north, and the z-axis upward, we have $\vec{l} = (1.00 \text{ m})\hat{i}$, $\vec{B} = (1.20 \text{ T})[(\cos 45°)\hat{i} + (\sin 45°)\hat{j}]$, and

$$\vec{F} = I\vec{l} \times \vec{B}$$
$$= (50 \text{ A})(1.00 \text{ m})\hat{i} \times (1.20 \text{ T})[(\cos 45°)\hat{i} + (\sin 45°)\hat{j}]$$
$$= (42.4 \text{ N})\hat{k}$$

Note that the maximum upward force of 60.0 N can hold the conductor in midair against the force of gravity—that is, *magnetically levitate* the conductor—if its weight is 60.0 N and its mass is $m = w/g = (60.0 \text{ N})/(9.8 \text{ m/s}^2) = 6.12 \text{ kg}$. Magnetic levitation is used in some high-speed trains to suspend the train over the tracks. Eliminating rolling friction in this way allows the train to achieve speeds of over 400 km/h.

Example 27.8 Magnetic force on a curved conductor

In Fig. 27.30 the magnetic field $\vec{B}$ is uniform and perpendicular to the plane of the figure, pointing out of the page. The conductor, carrying current I to the left, has three segments: (1) a straight segment with length L perpendicular to the plane of the figure, (2) a semicircle with radius R, and (3) another straight segment with length L parallel to the x-axis. Find the total magnetic force on this conductor.

SOLUTION

IDENTIFY and SET UP: The magnetic field $\vec{B} = B\hat{k}$ is uniform, so we find the forces $\vec{F}_1$ and $\vec{F}_3$ on the straight segments (1) and (3) using Eq. (27.19). We divide the curved segment (2) into infinitesimal straight segments and find the corresponding force $d\vec{F}_2$ on each straight segment using Eq. (27.20). We then integrate to find $\vec{F}_2$. The total magnetic force on the conductor is then $\vec{F} = \vec{F}_1 + \vec{F}_2 + \vec{F}_3$.

27.30 What is the total magnetic force on the conductor?

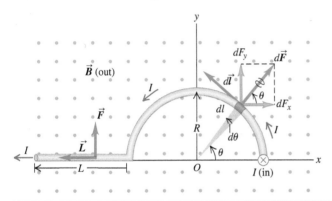

EXECUTE: For segment (1), $\vec{L} = -L\hat{k}$. Hence from Eq. (27.19), $\vec{F}_1 = I\vec{L} \times \vec{B} = 0$. For segment (3), $\vec{L} = -L\hat{i}$, so $\vec{F}_3 = I\vec{L} \times \vec{B} = I(-L\hat{i}) \times (B\hat{k}) = ILB\hat{j}$.

For the curved segment (2), Fig. 27.20 shows a segment $d\vec{l}$ with length $dl = R\,d\theta$, at angle θ. The right-hand rule shows that the direction of $d\vec{l} \times \vec{B}$ is radially outward from the center; make sure you can verify this. Because $d\vec{l}$ and $\vec{B}$ are perpendicular, the magnitude dF_2 of the force on the segment $d\vec{l}$ is just $dF_2 = I\,dl\,B = I(R\,d\theta)B$. The components of the force on this segment are

$$dF_{2x} = IR\,d\theta\,B\cos\theta \qquad dF_{2y} = IR\,d\theta\,B\sin\theta$$

To find the components of the total force, we integrate these expressions with respect to θ from $\theta = 0$ to $\theta = \pi$ to take in the whole semicircle. The results are

$$F_{2x} = IRB \int_0^\pi \cos\theta\,d\theta = 0$$

$$F_{2y} = IRB \int_0^\pi \sin\theta\,d\theta = 2IRB$$

Hence $\vec{F}_2 = 2IRB\hat{j}$. Finally, adding the forces on all three segments, we find that the total force is in the positive y-direction:

$$\vec{F} = \vec{F}_1 + \vec{F}_2 + \vec{F}_3 = 0 + 2IRB\hat{j} + ILB\hat{j} = IB(2R + L)\hat{j}$$

EVALUATE: We could have predicted from symmetry that the x-component of $\vec{F}_2$ would be zero: On the right half of the semicircle the x-component of the force is positive (to the right) and on the left half it is negative (to the left); the positive and negative contributions to the integral cancel. The result is that $\vec{F}_2$ is the force that would be exerted if we replaced the semicircle with a *straight* segment of length $2R$ along the x-axis. Do you see why?

Test Your Understanding of Section 27.6 The figure at right shows a top view of two conducting rails on which a conducting bar can slide. A uniform magnetic field is directed perpendicular to the plane of the figure as shown. A battery is to be connected to the two rails so that when the switch is closed, current will flow through the bar and cause a magnetic force to push the bar to the right. In which orientation, A or B, should the battery be placed in the circuit?

27.7 Force and Torque on a Current Loop

(MP)

Current-carrying conductors usually form closed loops, so it is worthwhile to use the results of Section 27.6 to find the *total* magnetic force and torque on a conductor in the form of a loop. Many practical devices make use of the magnetic force or torque on a conducting loop, including loudspeakers (see Fig. 27.28) and galvanometers (see Section 26.3). Hence the results of this section are of substantial practical importance. These results will also help us understand the behavior of bar magnets described in Section 27.1.

As an example, let's look at a rectangular current loop in a uniform magnetic field. We can represent the loop as a series of straight line segments. We will find

ActivPhysics 13.6: Magnetic Torque on a Loop

27.31 Finding the torque on a current-carrying loop in a uniform magnetic field.

(a)

The two pairs of forces acting on the loop cancel, so no net force acts on the loop.

However, the forces on the a sides of the loop ($\vec{F}$ and $-\vec{F}$) produce a torque $\tau = (IBa)(b\sin\phi)$ on the loop.

ϕ is the angle between a vector normal to the loop and the magnetic field.

(b)

The torque is maximal when $\phi = 90°$ (so $\vec{B}$ is in the plane of the loop).

x (direction normal to loop)

(c)

z (direction normal to loop)

The torque is zero when $\phi = 0°$ (as shown here) or $\phi = 180°$. In both cases, $\vec{B}$ is perpendicular to the plane of the loop.

The loop is in stable equilibrium when $\phi = 0$; it is in unstable equilibrium when $\phi = 180°$.

that the total *force* on the loop is zero but that there can be a net *torque* acting on the loop, with some interesting properties.

Figure 27.31a shows a rectangular loop of wire with side lengths a and b. A line perpendicular to the plane of the loop (i.e., a *normal* to the plane) makes an angle ϕ with the direction of the magnetic field $\vec{B}$, and the loop carries a current I. The wires leading the current into and out of the loop and the source of emf are omitted to keep the diagram simple.

The force $\vec{F}$ on the right side of the loop (length a) is to the right, in the $+x$-direction as shown. On this side, $\vec{B}$ is perpendicular to the current direction, and the force on this side has magnitude

$$F = IaB \qquad (27.21)$$

A force $-\vec{F}$ with the same magnitude but opposite direction acts on the opposite side of the loop, as shown in the figure.

The sides with length b make an angle $(90° - \phi)$ with the direction of $\vec{B}$. The forces on these sides are the vectors $\vec{F}'$ and $-\vec{F}'$; their magnitude F' is given by

$$F' = IbB\sin(90° - \phi) = IbB\cos\phi$$

The lines of action of both forces lie along the y-axis.

The *total* force on the loop is zero because the forces on opposite sides cancel out in pairs.

> **The net force on a current loop in a uniform magnetic field is zero. However, the net torque is not in general equal to zero.**

(You may find it helpful at this point to review the discussion of torque in Section 10.1.) The two forces $\vec{F}'$ and $-\vec{F}'$ in Fig. 27.31a lie along the same line and so give rise to zero net torque with respect to any point. The two forces $\vec{F}$ and $-\vec{F}$ lie along different lines, and each gives rise to a torque about the y-axis. According to the right-hand rule for determining the direction of torques, the vector torques due to $\vec{F}$ and $-\vec{F}$ are both in the $+y$-direction; hence the net vector torque $\vec{\tau}$ is in the $+y$-direction as well. The moment arm for each of these forces (equal to the perpendicular distance from the rotation axis to the line of action of the force) is $(b/2)\sin\phi$, so the torque due to each force has magnitude $F(b/2)\sin\phi$. If we use Eq. (27.21) for F, the magnitude of the net torque is

$$\tau = 2F(b/2)\sin\phi = (IBa)(b\sin\phi) \qquad (27.22)$$

The torque is greatest when $\phi = 90°$, $\vec{B}$ is in the plane of the loop, and the normal to this plane is perpendicular to $\vec{B}$ (Fig. 27.31b). The torque is zero when ϕ is $0°$ or $180°$ and the normal to the loop is parallel or antiparallel to the field (Fig. 27.31c). The value $\phi = 0°$ is a stable equilibrium position because the torque is zero there, and when the loop is rotated slightly from this position, the resulting torque tends to rotate it back toward $\phi = 0°$. The position $\phi = 180°$ is an *unstable* equilibrium position; if displaced slightly from this position, the loop tends to move farther away from $\phi = 180°$. Figure 27.31 shows rotation about the y-axis, but because the net force on the loop is zero, Eq. (27.22) for the torque is valid for *any* choice of axis.

The area A of the loop is equal to ab, so we can rewrite Eq. (27.22) as

$$\tau = IBA\sin\phi \qquad \text{(magnitude of torque on a current loop)} \qquad (27.23)$$

The product IA is called the **magnetic dipole moment** or **magnetic moment** of the loop, for which we use the symbol μ (the Greek letter mu):

$$\mu = IA \qquad (27.24)$$

It is analogous to the electric dipole moment introduced in Section 21.7. In terms of μ, the magnitude of the torque on a current loop is

$$\tau = \mu B\sin\phi \qquad (27.25)$$

where ϕ is the angle between the normal to the loop (the direction of the vector area $\vec{A}$) and $\vec{B}$. The torque tends to rotate the loop in the direction of *decreasing* ϕ—that is, toward its stable equilibrium position in which the loop lies in the xy-plane perpendicular to the direction of the field $\vec{B}$ (Fig. 27.31c). A current loop, or any other body that experiences a magnetic torque given by Eq. (27.25), is also called a **magnetic dipole.**

Magnetic Torque: Vector Form

We can also define a vector magnetic moment $\vec{\mu}$ with magnitude IA: This is shown in Fig. 27.31. The direction of $\vec{\mu}$ is defined to be perpendicular to the plane of the loop, with a sense determined by a right-hand rule, as shown in Fig. 27.32. Wrap the fingers of your right hand around the perimeter of the loop in the direction of the current. Then extend your thumb so that it is perpendicular to the plane of the loop; its direction is the direction of $\vec{\mu}$ (and of the vector area $\vec{A}$ of the loop). The torque is greatest when $\vec{\mu}$ and $\vec{B}$ are perpendicular and is zero when they are parallel or antiparallel. In the stable equilibrium position, $\vec{\mu}$ and $\vec{B}$ are parallel.

Finally, we can express this interaction in terms of the torque vector $\vec{\tau}$, which we used for *electric*-dipole interactions in Section 21.7. From Eq. (27.25) the magnitude of $\vec{\tau}$ is equal to the magnitude of $\vec{\mu} \times \vec{B}$, and reference to Fig. 27.31 shows that the directions are also the same. So we have

$$\vec{\tau} = \vec{\mu} \times \vec{B} \qquad \text{(vector torque on a current loop)} \qquad (27.26)$$

This result is directly analogous to the result we found in Section 21.7 for the torque exerted by an *electric* field $\vec{E}$ on an *electric* dipole with dipole moment $\vec{p}$.

Potential Energy for a Magnetic Dipole

When a magnetic dipole changes orientation in a magnetic field, the field does work on it. In an infinitesimal angular displacement $d\phi$, the work dW is given by

27.32 The right-hand rule determines the direction of the magnetic moment of a current-carrying loop. This is also the direction of the loop's area vector $\vec{A}$; $\vec{\mu} = I\vec{A}$ is a vector equation.

$\tau\,d\phi$, and there is a corresponding change in potential energy. As the above discussion suggests, the potential energy is least when $\vec{\mu}$ and $\vec{B}$ are parallel and greatest when they are antiparallel. To find an expression for the potential energy U as a function of orientation, we can make use of the beautiful symmetry between the electric and magnetic dipole interactions. The torque on an *electric* dipole in an *electric* field is $\vec{\tau} = \vec{p} \times \vec{E}$; we found in Section 21.7 that the corresponding potential energy is $U = -\vec{p} \cdot \vec{E}$. The torque on a *magnetic* dipole in a *magnetic* field is $\vec{\tau} = \vec{\mu} \times \vec{B}$, so we can conclude immediately that the corresponding potential energy is

$$U = -\vec{\mu} \cdot \vec{B} = -\mu B \cos\phi \quad \text{(potential energy for a magnetic dipole)} \quad (27.27)$$

With this definition, U is zero when the magnetic dipole moment is perpendicular to the magnetic field.

Magnetic Torque: Loops and Coils

Although we have derived Eqs. (27.21) through (27.27) for a rectangular current loop, all these relationships are valid for a plane loop of any shape at all. Any planar loop may be approximated as closely as we wish by a very large number of rectangular loops, as shown in Fig. 27.33. If these loops all carry equal currents in the same clockwise sense, then the forces and torques on the sides of two loops adjacent to each other cancel, and the only forces and torques that do not cancel are due to currents around the boundary. Thus all the above relationships are valid for a plane current loop of any shape, with the magnetic moment $\vec{\mu}$ given by $\vec{\mu} = I\vec{A}$.

We can also generalize this whole formulation to a coil consisting of N planar loops close together; the effect is simply to multiply each force, the magnetic moment, the torque, and the potential energy by a factor of N.

An arrangement of particular interest is the **solenoid,** a helical winding of wire, such as a coil wound on a circular cylinder (Fig. 27.34). If the windings are closely spaced, the solenoid can be approximated by a number of circular loops lying in planes at right angles to its long axis. The total torque on a solenoid in a magnetic field is simply the sum of the torques on the individual turns. For a solenoid with N turns in a uniform field B, the magnetic moment is $\mu = NIA$ and

$$\tau = NIAB \sin\phi \quad (27.28)$$

where ϕ is the angle between the axis of the solenoid and the direction of the field. The magnetic moment vector $\vec{\mu}$ is along the solenoid axis. The torque is greatest when the solenoid axis is perpendicular to the magnetic field and zero when they are parallel. The effect of this torque is to tend to rotate the solenoid into a position where its axis is parallel to the field. Solenoids are also useful as *sources* of magnetic field, as we'll discuss in Chapter 28.

The d'Arsonval galvanometer, described in Section 26.3, makes use of a magnetic torque on a coil carrying a current. As Fig. 26.14 shows, the magnetic field is not uniform but is *radial,* so the side thrusts on the coil are always perpendicular to its plane. Thus the angle ϕ in Eq. (27.28) is always 90°, and the magnetic torque is directly proportional to the current, no matter what the orientation of the coil. A restoring torque proportional to the angular displacement of the coil is provided by two hairsprings, which also serve as current leads to the coil. When current is supplied to the coil, it rotates along with its attached pointer until the restoring spring torque just balances the magnetic torque. Thus the pointer deflection is proportional to the current.

An important medical application of the torque on a magnetic dipole is *magnetic resonance imaging* (MRI). A patient is placed in a magnetic field of about 1.5 T, more than 10^4 times stronger than the earth's field. The nucleus of each hydrogen atom in the tissue to be imaged has a magnetic dipole moment,

27.33 The collection of rectangles exactly matches the irregular plane loop in the limit as the number of rectangles approaches infinity and the width of each rectangle approaches zero.

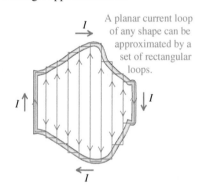

A planar current loop of any shape can be approximated by a set of rectangular loops.

27.34 The torque $\vec{\tau} = \vec{\mu} \times \vec{B}$ on this solenoid in a uniform magnetic field is directed straight into the page. An actual solenoid has many more turns, wrapped closely together.

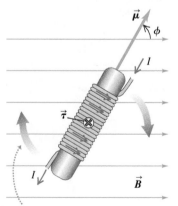

The torque tends to make the solenoid rotate clockwise in the plane of the page, aligning magnetic moment $\vec{\mu}$ with field $\vec{B}$.

which experiences a torque that aligns it with the applied field. The tissue is then illuminated with radio waves of just the right frequency to flip these magnetic moments out of alignment. The extent to which these radio waves are absorbed in the tissue is proportional to the amount of hydrogen present. Hence hydrogen-rich soft tissue looks quite different from hydrogen-deficient bone, which makes MRI ideal for analyzing details in soft tissue that cannot be seen in x-ray images (see the image that opens this chapter).

Example 27.9   Magnetic torque on a circular coil

A circular coil 0.0500 m in radius, with 30 turns of wire, lies in a horizontal plane. It carries a counterclockwise (as viewed from above) current of 5.00 A. The coil is in a uniform 1.20-T magnetic field directed toward the right. Find the magnitudes of the magnetic moment and the torque on the coil.

SOLUTION

IDENTIFY and SET UP: This problem uses the definition of magnetic moment and the expression for the torque on a magnetic dipole in a magnetic field. Figure 27.35 shows the situation. Equation (27.24) gives the magnitude μ of the magnetic moment of a single turn of wire; for N turns, the magnetic moment is N times greater. Equation (27.25) gives the magnitude τ of the torque.

EXECUTE: The area of the coil is $A = \pi r^2$. From Eq. (27.24), the total magnetic moment of all 30 turns is

$$\mu_{total} = NIA = 30(5.00 \text{ A})\pi(0.0500 \text{ m})^2 = 1.18 \text{ A} \cdot \text{m}^2$$

The angle ϕ between the direction of $\vec{B}$ and the direction of $\vec{\mu}$ (which is along the normal to the plane of the coil) is 90°. From Eq. (27.25), the torque on the coil is

$$\tau = \mu_{total}B \sin \phi = (1.18 \text{ A} \cdot \text{m}^2)(1.20 \text{ T})(\sin 90°)$$
$$= 1.41 \text{ N} \cdot \text{m}$$

EVALUATE: The torque tends to rotate the right side of the coil down and the left side up, into a position where the normal to its plane is parallel to $\vec{B}$.

27.35 Our sketch for this problem.

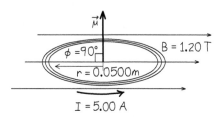

Example 27.10   Potential energy for a coil in a magnetic field

If the coil in Example 27.9 rotates from its initial orientation to one in which its magnetic moment $\vec{\mu}$ is parallel to $\vec{B}$, what is the change in potential energy?

SOLUTION

IDENTIFY and SET UP: Equation (27.27) gives the potential energy for each orientation. The initial position is as shown in Fig. 27.35, with $\phi_1 = 90°$. In the final orientation, the coil has been rotated 90° clockwise so that $\vec{\mu}$ and $\vec{B}$ are parallel, so the angle between these vectors is $\phi_2 = 0$.

EXECUTE: From Eq. (27.27), the potential energy change is

$$\Delta U = U_2 - U_1 = -\mu B \cos \phi_2 - (-\mu B \cos \phi_1)$$
$$= -\mu B(\cos \phi_2 - \cos \phi_1)$$
$$= -(1.18 \text{ A} \cdot \text{m}^2)(1.20 \text{ T})(\cos 0° - \cos 90°) = -1.41 \text{ J}$$

EVALUATE: The potential energy decreases because the rotation is in the direction of the magnetic torque that we found in Example 27.9.

Magnetic Dipole in a Nonuniform Magnetic Field

We have seen that a current loop (that is, a magnetic dipole) experiences zero net force in a uniform magnetic field. Figure 27.36 shows two current loops in the *nonuniform* $\vec{B}$ field of a bar magnet; in both cases the net force on the loop is *not* zero. In Fig. 27.36a the magnetic moment $\vec{\mu}$ is in the direction opposite to the field, and the force $d\vec{F} = I\,d\vec{l} \times \vec{B}$ on a segment of the loop has both a radial component and a component to the right. When these forces are summed to find the net force $\vec{F}$ on the loop, the radial components cancel so that the net force is to the right, away from the magnet. Note that in this case the force is toward the region where the field lines are farther apart and the field magnitude B is less. The polarity of the bar magnet is reversed in Fig. 27.36b, so $\vec{\mu}$ and $\vec{B}$ are parallel;

27.36 Forces on current loops in a nonuniform $\vec{B}$ field. In each case the axis of the bar magnet is perpendicular to the plane of the loop and passes through the center of the loop.

(a) Net force on this coil is away from north pole of magnet.

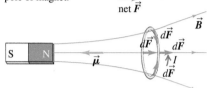

(b) Net force on same coil is toward south pole of magnet.

27.37 (a) An unmagnetized piece of iron. (Only a few representative atomic moments are shown.) (b) A magnetized piece of iron (bar magnet). The net magnetic moment of the bar magnet points from its south pole to its north pole. (c) A bar magnet in a magnetic field.

(a) Unmagnetized iron: magnetic moments are oriented randomly.

(b) In a bar magnet, the magnetic moments are aligned.

(c) A magnetic field creates a torque on the bar magnet that tends to align its dipole moment with the $\vec{B}$ field.

now the net force on the loop is to the left, toward the region of greater field magnitude near the magnet. Later in this section we'll use these observations to explain why bar magnets can pick up unmagnetized iron objects.

Magnetic Dipoles and How Magnets Work

The behavior of a solenoid in a magnetic field (see Fig. 27.34) resembles that of a bar magnet or compass needle; if free to turn, both the solenoid and the magnet orient themselves with their axes parallel to the $\vec{B}$ field. In both cases this is due to the interaction of moving electric charges with a magnetic field; the difference is that in a bar magnet the motion of charge occurs on the microscopic scale of the atom.

Think of an electron as being like a spinning ball of charge. In this analogy the circulation of charge around the spin axis is like a current loop, and so the electron has a net magnetic moment. (This analogy, while helpful, is inexact; an electron isn't really a spinning sphere. A full explanation of the origin of an electron's magnetic moment involves quantum mechanics, which is beyond our scope here.) In an iron atom a substantial fraction of the electron magnetic moments align with each other, and the atom has a nonzero magnetic moment. (By contrast, the atoms of most elements have little or no net magnetic moment.) In an unmagnetized piece of iron there is no overall alignment of the magnetic moments of the atoms; their vector sum is zero, and the net magnetic moment is zero (Fig. 27.37a). But in an iron bar magnet the magnetic moments of many of the atoms are parallel, and there is a substantial net magnetic moment $\vec{\mu}$ (Fig. 27.37b). If the magnet is placed in a magnetic field $\vec{B}$, the field exerts a torque given by Eq. (27.26) that tends to align $\vec{\mu}$ with $\vec{B}$ (Fig. 27.37c). A bar magnet tends to align with a $\vec{B}$ field so that a line from the south pole to the north pole of the magnet is in the direction of $\vec{B}$; hence the real significance of a magnet's north and south poles is that they represent the head and tail, respectively, of the magnet's dipole moment $\vec{\mu}$.

The torque experienced by a current loop in a magnetic field also explains how an unmagnetized iron object like that in Fig. 27.37a becomes magnetized. If an unmagnetized iron paper clip is placed next to a powerful magnet, the magnetic moments of the paper clip's atoms tend to align with the $\vec{B}$ field of the magnet. When the paper clip is removed, its atomic dipoles tend to remain aligned, and the paper clip has a net magnetic moment. The paper clip can be demagnetized by being dropped on the floor or heated; the added internal energy jostles and re-randomizes the atomic dipoles.

The magnetic-dipole picture of a bar magnet explains the attractive and repulsive forces between bar magnets shown in Fig. 27.1. The magnetic moment $\vec{\mu}$ of a bar magnet points from its south pole to its north pole, so the current loops in Figs. 27.36a and 27.36b are both equivalent to a magnet with its north pole on the left. Hence the situation in Fig. 27.36a is equivalent to two bar magnets with their north poles next to each other; the resultant force is repulsive, just as in Fig. 27.1b. In Fig. 27.36b we again have the equivalent of two bar magnets end to end, but with the south pole of the left-hand magnet next to the north pole of the right-hand magnet. The resultant force is attractive, as in Fig. 27.1a.

Finally, we can explain how a magnet can attract an unmagnetized iron object (see Fig. 27.2). It's a two-step process. First, the atomic magnetic moments of the iron tend to align with the $\vec{B}$ field of the magnet, so the iron acquires a net magnetic dipole moment $\vec{\mu}$ parallel to the field. Second, the nonuniform field of the magnet attracts the magnetic dipole. Figure 27.38a shows an example. The north pole of the magnet is closer to the nail (which contains iron), and the magnetic dipole produced in the nail is equivalent to a loop with a current that circulates in a direction opposite to that shown in Fig. 27.36a. Hence the net magnetic force on the nail is opposite to the force on the loop in Fig. 27.36a, and the nail is attracted toward the magnet. Changing the polarity of the magnet, as in Fig. 27.38b, reverses the directions of both $\vec{B}$ and $\vec{\mu}$. The situation is now equivalent to that shown in Fig. 27.36b; like the loop in that figure, the nail is attracted toward the magnet. Hence a previously unmagnetized object containing iron is attracted to *either* pole of a magnet. By contrast, objects made of brass, aluminum, or wood hardly respond at all to a magnet; the atomic magnetic dipoles of these materials, if present at all, have less tendency to align with an external field.

Our discussion of how magnets and pieces of iron interact has just scratched the surface of a diverse subject known as *magnetic properties of materials*. We'll discuss these properties in more depth in Section 28.8.

Test Your Understanding of Section 27.7 Figure 27.13c depicts the magnetic field lines due to a circular current-carrying loop. (a) What is the direction of the magnetic moment of this loop? (b) Which side of the loop is equivalent to the north pole of a magnet, and which side is equivalent to the south pole? ∣

27.8 The Direct-Current Motor

Electric motors play an important role in contemporary society. In a motor a magnetic torque acts on a current-carrying conductor, and electric energy is converted to mechanical energy. As an example, let's look at a simple type of direct-current (dc) motor, shown in Fig. 27.39.

The moving part of the motor is the *rotor*, a length of wire formed into an open-ended loop and free to rotate about an axis. The ends of the rotor wires are attached to circular conducting segments that form a *commutator*. In Fig. 27.39a, each of the two commutator segments makes contact with one of the terminals, or *brushes,* of an external circuit that includes a source of emf. This causes a current to flow into the rotor on one side, shown in red, and out of the rotor on the other side, shown in blue. Hence the rotor is a current loop with a magnetic moment $\vec{\mu}$. The rotor lies between opposing poles of a permanent magnet, so there is a magnetic field $\vec{B}$ that exerts a torque $\vec{\tau} = \vec{\mu} \times \vec{B}$ on the rotor. For the rotor orientation shown in Fig. 27.39a the torque causes the rotor to turn counterclockwise, in the direction that will align $\vec{\mu}$ with $\vec{B}$.

In Fig. 27.39b the rotor has rotated by 90° from its orientation in Fig. 27.39a. If the current through the rotor were constant, the rotor would now be in its equilibrium orientation; it would simply oscillate around this orientation. But here's where the commutator comes into play; each brush is now in contact with *both* segments of the commutator. There is no potential difference between the

27.38 A bar magnet attracts an unmagnetized iron nail in two steps. First, the $\vec{B}$ field of the bar magnet gives rise to a net magnetic moment in the nail. Second, because the field of the bar magnet is not uniform, this magnetic dipole is attracted toward the magnet. The attraction is the same whether the nail is closer to **(a)** the magnet's north pole or **(b)** the magnet's south pole.

(a)

(b)

27.39 Schematic diagram of a simple dc motor. The rotor is a wire loop that is free to rotate about an axis; the rotor ends are attached to the two curved conductors that form the commutator. (The rotor halves are colored red and blue for clarity.) The commutator segments are insulated from one another.

(a) Brushes are aligned with commutator segments.

• Current flows into the red side of the rotor and out of the blue side.
• Therefore the magnetic torque causes the rotor to spin counterclockwise.

(b) Rotor has turned 90°.

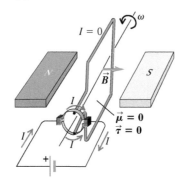

• Each brush is in contact with both commutator segments, so the current bypasses the rotor altogether.
• No magnetic torque acts on the rotor.

(c) Rotor has turned 180°.

• The brushes are again aligned with commutator segments. This time the current flows into the blue side of the rotor and out of the red side.
• Therefore the magnetic torque again causes the rotor to spin counterclockwise.

commutators, so at this instant no current flows through the rotor, and the magnetic moment is zero. The rotor continues to rotate counterclockwise because of its inertia, and current again flows through the rotor as in Fig. 27.39c. But now current enters on the *blue* side of the rotor and exits on the *red* side, just the opposite of the situation in Fig. 27.39a. While the direction of the current has reversed with respect to the rotor, the rotor itself has rotated 180° and the magnetic moment $\vec{\mu}$ is in the same direction with respect to the magnetic field. Hence the magnetic torque $\vec{\tau}$ is in the same direction in Fig. 27.39c as in Fig. 27.39a. Thanks to the commutator, the current reverses after every 180° of rotation, so the torque is always in the direction to rotate the rotor counterclockwise. When the motor has come "up to speed," the average magnetic torque is just balanced by an opposing torque due to air resistance, friction in the rotor bearings, and friction between the commutator and brushes.

The simple motor shown in Fig. 27.39 has only a single turn of wire in its rotor. In practical motors, the rotor has many turns; this increases the magnetic moment and the torque so that the motor can spin larger loads. The torque can also be increased by using a stronger magnetic field, which is why many motor designs use electromagnets instead of a permanent magnet. Another drawback of the simple design in Fig. 27.39 is that the magnitude of the torque rises and falls as the rotor spins. This can be remedied by having the rotor include several independent coils of wire oriented at different angles (Fig. 27.40).

27.40 This motor from a computer disk drive has 12 current-carrying coils. They interact with permanent magnets on the turntable (not shown) to make the turntable rotate. (This design is the reverse of the design in Fig. 27.39, in which the permanent magnets are stationary and the coil rotates.) Because there are multiple coils, the magnetic torque is very nearly constant and the turntable spins at a very constant rate.

Coils

Power for Electric Motors

Because a motor converts electric energy to mechanical energy or work, it requires electric energy input. If the potential difference between its terminals is V_{ab} and the current is I, then the power input is $P = V_{ab}I$. Even if the motor coils have negligible resistance, there must be a potential difference between the terminals if P is to be different from zero. This potential difference results principally from magnetic forces exerted on the currents in the conductors of the rotor as they rotate through the magnetic field. The associated electromotive force $\mathcal{E}$ is called an *induced* emf; it is also called a *back* emf because its sense is opposite to that of the current. In Chapter 29 we will study induced emfs resulting from motion of conductors in magnetic fields.

In a *series* motor the rotor is connected in series with the electromagnet that produces the magnetic field; in a *shunt* motor they are connected in parallel. In a series motor with internal resistance r, V_{ab} is greater than $\mathcal{E}$, and the difference is the potential drop Ir across the internal resistance. That is,

$$V_{ab} = \mathcal{E} + Ir \qquad (27.29)$$

Because the magnetic force is proportional to velocity, $\mathcal{E}$ is *not* constant but is proportional to the speed of rotation of the rotor.

Example 27.11   **A series dc motor**

A dc motor with its rotor and field coils connected in series has an internal resistance of 2.00 Ω. When running at full load on a 120-V line, it draws a 4.00-A current. (a) What is the emf in the rotor? (b) What is the power delivered to the motor? (c) What is the rate of dissipation of energy in the internal resistance? (d) What is the mechanical power developed? (e) What is the motor's efficiency? (f) What happens if the machine being driven by the motor jams, so that the rotor suddenly stops turning?

SOLUTION

IDENTIFY and SET UP: This problem uses the ideas of power and potential drop in a series dc motor. We are given the internal resistance $r = 2.00$ Ω, the voltage $V_{ab} = 120$ V across the motor, and the current $I = 4.00$ A through the motor. We use Eq. (27.29) to determine the emf $\mathcal{E}$ from these quantities. The power delivered to the motor is $V_{ab}I$, the rate of energy dissipation is I^2r, and the power output by the motor is the difference between the power input and the power dissipated. The efficiency e is the ratio of mechanical power output to electric power input.

EXECUTE: (a) From Eq. (27.29), $V_{ab} = \mathcal{E} + Ir$, we have

120 V = $\mathcal{E}$ + (4.00 A)(2.00 Ω)   and so $\mathcal{E}$ = 112 V

(b) The power delivered to the motor from the source is

$$P_{\text{input}} = V_{ab}I = (120 \text{ V})(4.00 \text{ A}) = 480 \text{ W}$$

(c) The power dissipated in the resistance r is

$$P_{\text{dissipated}} = I^2r = (4.00 \text{ A})^2(2.00 \text{ }\Omega) = 32 \text{ W}$$

(d) The mechanical power output is the electric power input minus the rate of dissipation of energy in the motor's resistance (assuming that there are no other power losses):

$$P_{\text{output}} = P_{\text{input}} - P_{\text{dissipated}} = 480 \text{ W} - 32 \text{ W} = 448 \text{ W}$$

(e) The efficiency e is the ratio of mechanical power output to electric power input:

$$e = \frac{P_{\text{output}}}{P_{\text{input}}} = \frac{448 \text{ W}}{480 \text{ W}} = 0.93 = 93\%$$

(f) With the rotor stalled, the back emf $\mathcal{E}$ (which is proportional to rotor speed) goes to zero. From Eq. (27.29) the current becomes

$$I = \frac{V_{ab}}{r} = \frac{120 \text{ V}}{2.00 \text{ }\Omega} = 60 \text{ A}$$

and the power dissipated in the resistance r becomes

$$P_{\text{dissipated}} = I^2r = (60 \text{ A})^2(2.00 \text{ }\Omega) = 7200 \text{ W}$$

EVALUATE: If this massive overload doesn't blow a fuse or trip a circuit breaker, the coils will quickly melt. When the motor is first turned on, there's a momentary surge of current until the motor picks up speed. This surge causes greater-than-usual voltage drops ($V = IR$) in the power lines supplying the current. Similar effects are responsible for the momentary dimming of lights in a house when an air conditioner or dishwasher motor starts.

Test Your Understanding of Section 27.8 In the circuit shown in Fig. 27.39, you add a switch in series with the source of emf so that the current can be turned on and off. When you close the switch and allow current to flow, will the rotor begin to turn no matter what its original orientation? ❙

27.9 The Hall Effect

The reality of the forces acting on the moving charges in a conductor in a magnetic field is strikingly demonstrated by the *Hall effect,* an effect analogous to the transverse deflection of an electron beam in a magnetic field in vacuum. (The effect was discovered by the American physicist Edwin Hall in 1879 while he was still a graduate student.) To describe this effect, let's consider a conductor in the form of a flat strip, as shown in Fig. 27.41. The current is in the direction of the $+x$-axis and there is a uniform magnetic field $\vec{B}$ perpendicular to the plane of the strip, in the $+y$-direction. The drift velocity of the moving charges (charge magnitude $|q|$) has magnitude v_d. Figure 27.41a shows the case of negative charges, such as electrons in a metal, and Fig. 27.41b shows positive charges. In both cases the magnetic force is upward, just as the magnetic force on a conductor is the same whether the moving charges are positive or negative. In either case a moving charge is driven toward the *upper* edge of the strip by the magnetic force $F_z = |q|v_dB$.

If the charge carriers are electrons, as in Fig. 27.41a, an excess negative charge accumulates at the upper edge of the strip, leaving an excess positive charge at its lower edge. This accumulation continues until the resulting transverse electrostatic field $\vec{E}_e$ becomes large enough to cause a force (magnitude $|q|E_e$) that is equal and opposite to the magnetic force (magnitude $|q|v_dB$). After that, there is no longer any net transverse force to deflect the moving charges. This electric field causes a transverse potential difference between opposite edges of the strip, called the *Hall voltage* or the *Hall emf.* The polarity depends on whether the moving charges are positive or negative. Experiments show that for metals the upper edge of the strip in Fig. 27.41a *does* become negatively charged, showing that the charge carriers in a metal are indeed negative electrons.

However, if the charge carriers are *positive,* as in Fig. 27.41b, then *positive* charge accumulates at the upper edge, and the potential difference is *opposite* to the situation with negative charges. Soon after the discovery of the Hall effect in 1879, it was observed that some materials, particularly some *semiconductors,* show a Hall emf opposite to that of the metals, as if their charge carriers were positively charged. We now know that these materials conduct by a process known as *hole conduction.* Within such a material there are locations, called *holes,* that would normally be occupied by an electron but are actually empty. A missing negative charge is equivalent to a positive charge. When an electron moves in one direction to fill a hole, it leaves another hole behind it. The hole migrates in the direction opposite to that of the electron.

27.41 Forces on charge carriers in a conductor in a magnetic field.

(a) Negative charge carriers (electrons)

The charge carriers are pushed toward the top of the strip ...

... so point a is at a higher potential than point b.

(b) Positive charge carriers

The charge carriers are again pushed toward the top of the strip ...

... so the polarity of the potential difference is opposite to that for negative charge carriers.

In terms of the coordinate axes in Fig. 27.41b, the electrostatic field $\vec{E}_e$ for the positive-q case is in the $-z$-direction; its z-component E_z is negative. The magnetic field is in the $+y$-direction, and we write it as B_y. The magnetic force (in the $+z$-direction) is qv_dB_y. The current density J_x is in the $+x$-direction. In the steady state, when the forces qE_z and qv_dB_y are equal in magnitude and opposite in direction,

$$qE_z + qv_dB_y = 0 \quad \text{or} \quad E_z = -v_dB_y$$

This confirms that when q is positive, E_z is negative. The current density J_x is

$$J_x = nqv_d$$

Eliminating v_d between these equations, we find

$$nq = \frac{-J_xB_y}{E_z} \quad \text{(Hall effect)} \quad (27.30)$$

Note that this result (as well as the entire derivation) is valid for both positive and negative q. When q is negative, E_z is positive, and conversely.

We can measure J_x, B_y, and E_z, so we can compute the product nq. In both metals and semiconductors, q is equal in magnitude to the electron charge, so the Hall effect permits a direct measurement of n, the concentration of current-carrying charges in the material. The *sign* of the charges is determined by the polarity of the Hall emf, as we have described.

The Hall effect can also be used for a direct measurement of electron drift speed v_d in metals. As we saw in Chapter 25, these speeds are very small, often of the order of 1 mm/s or less. If we move the entire conductor in the opposite direction to the current with a speed equal to the drift speed, then the electrons are at rest with respect to the magnetic field, and the Hall emf disappears. Thus the conductor speed needed to make the Hall emf vanish is equal to the drift speed.

Example 27.12 **A Hall-effect measurement**

You place a strip of copper, 2.0 mm thick and 1.50 cm wide, in a uniform 0.40-T magnetic field as shown in Fig. 27.41a. When you run a 75-A current in the $+x$-direction, you find that the potential at the bottom of the slab is 0.81 μV higher than at the top. From this measurement, determine the concentration of mobile electrons in copper.

SOLUTION

IDENTIFY and SET UP: This problem describes a Hall-effect experiment. We use Eq. (27.30) to determine the mobile electron concentration n.

EXECUTE: First we find the current density J_x and the electric field E_z:

$$J_x = \frac{I}{A} = \frac{75\ \text{A}}{(2.0 \times 10^{-3}\ \text{m})(1.50 \times 10^{-2}\ \text{m})} = 2.5 \times 10^6\ \text{A/m}^2$$

$$E_z = \frac{V}{d} = \frac{0.81 \times 10^{-6}\ \text{V}}{1.5 \times 10^{-2}\ \text{m}} = 5.4 \times 10^{-5}\ \text{V/m}$$

Then, from Eq. (27.30),

$$n = \frac{-J_xB_y}{qE_z} = \frac{-(2.5 \times 10^6\ \text{A/m}^2)(0.40\ \text{T})}{(-1.60 \times 10^{-19}\ \text{C})(5.4 \times 10^{-5}\ \text{V/m})}$$

$$= 11.6 \times 10^{28}\ \text{m}^{-3}$$

EVALUATE: The actual value of n for copper is $8.5 \times 10^{28}\ \text{m}^{-3}$. The difference shows that our simple model of the Hall effect, which ignores quantum effects and electron interactions with the ions, must be used with caution. This example also shows that with good conductors, the Hall emf is very small even with large current densities. In practice, Hall-effect devices for magnetic-field measurements use semiconductor materials, for which moderate current densities give much larger Hall emfs.

Test Your Understanding of Section 27.9 A copper wire of square cross section is oriented vertically. The four sides of the wire face north, south, east, and west. There is a uniform magnetic field directed from east to west, and the wire carries current downward. Which side of the wire is at the highest electric potential? (i) north side; (ii) south side; (iii) east side; (iv) west side.

Magnetic forces: Magnetic interactions are fundamentally interactions between moving charged particles. These interactions are described by the vector magnetic field, denoted by $\vec{B}$. A particle with charge q moving with velocity $\vec{v}$ in a magnetic field $\vec{B}$ experiences a force $\vec{F}$ that is perpendicular to both $\vec{v}$ and $\vec{B}$. The SI unit of magnetic field is the tesla $(1\ \mathrm{T} = 1\ \mathrm{N/A \cdot m})$. (See Example 27.1.)

$$\vec{F} = q\vec{v} \times \vec{B} \qquad (27.2)$$

Magnetic field lines and flux: A magnetic field can be represented graphically by magnetic field lines. At each point a magnetic field line is tangent to the direction of $\vec{B}$ at that point. Where field lines are close together the field magnitude is large, and vice versa. Magnetic flux Φ_B through an area is defined in an analogous way to electric flux. The SI unit of magnetic flux is the weber $(1\ \mathrm{Wb} = 1\ \mathrm{T \cdot m^2})$. The net magnetic flux through any closed surface is zero (Gauss's law for magnetism). As a result, magnetic field lines always close on themselves. (See Example 27.2.)

$$\Phi_B = \int B_\perp \, dA$$
$$= \int B \cos\phi \, dA \qquad (27.6)$$
$$= \int \vec{B} \cdot d\vec{A}$$
$$\oint \vec{B} \cdot d\vec{A} = 0 \ \text{(closed surface)} \quad (27.8)$$

Motion in a magnetic field: The magnetic force is always perpendicular to $\vec{v}$; a particle moving under the action of a magnetic field alone moves with constant speed. In a uniform field, a particle with initial velocity perpendicular to the field moves in a circle with radius R that depends on the magnetic field strength B and the particle mass m, speed v, and charge q. (See Examples 27.3 and 27.4.)

Crossed electric and magnetic fields can be used as a velocity selector. The electric and magnetic forces exactly cancel when $v = E/B$. (See Examples 27.5 and 27.6.)

$$R = \frac{mv}{|q|B} \qquad (27.11)$$

Magnetic force on a conductor: A straight segment of a conductor carrying current I in a uniform magnetic field $\vec{B}$ experiences a force $\vec{F}$ that is perpendicular to both $\vec{B}$ and the vector $\vec{l}$, which points in the direction of the current and has magnitude equal to the length of the segment. A similar relationship gives the force $d\vec{F}$ on an infinitesimal current-carrying segment $d\vec{l}$. (See Examples 27.7 and 27.8.)

$$\vec{F} = I\vec{l} \times \vec{B} \qquad (27.19)$$
$$d\vec{F} = I\,d\vec{l} \times \vec{B} \qquad (27.20)$$

Magnetic torque: A current loop with area A and current I in a uniform magnetic field $\vec{B}$ experiences no net magnetic force, but does experience a magnetic torque of magnitude τ. The vector torque $\vec{\tau}$ can be expressed in terms of the magnetic moment $\vec{\mu} = I\vec{A}$ of the loop, as can the potential energy U of a magnetic moment in a magnetic field $\vec{B}$. The magnetic moment of a loop depends only on the current and the area; it is independent of the shape of the loop. (See Examples 27.9 and 27.10.)

$$\tau = IBA \sin\phi \qquad (27.23)$$
$$\vec{\tau} = \vec{\mu} \times \vec{B} \qquad (27.26)$$
$$U = -\vec{\mu} \cdot \vec{B} = -\mu B \cos\phi \qquad (27.27)$$

Electric motors: In a dc motor a magnetic field exerts a torque on a current in the rotor. Motion of the rotor through the magnetic field causes an induced emf called a back emf. For a series motor, in which the rotor coil is in parallel with coils that produce the magnetic field, the terminal voltage is the sum of the back emf and the drop Ir across the internal resistance. (See Example 27.11.)

The Hall effect: The Hall effect is a potential difference perpendicular to the direction of current in a conductor, when the conductor is placed in a magnetic field. The Hall potential is determined by the requirement that the associated electric field must just balance the magnetic force on a moving charge. Hall-effect measurements can be used to determine the sign of charge carriers and their concentration n. (See Example 27.12.)

$$nq = \frac{-J_x B_y}{E_z} \qquad (27.30)$$

BRIDGING PROBLEM   **Magnetic Torque on a Current-Carrying Ring**

A circular ring with area 4.45 cm^2 is carrying a current of 12.5 A. The ring, initially at rest, is immersed in a region of uniform magnetic field given by $\vec{B} = (1.15 \times 10^{-2}\ \text{T})(12\hat{\imath} + 3\hat{\jmath} - 4\hat{k})$. The ring is positioned initially such that its magnetic moment is given by $\vec{\mu}_i = \mu(-0.800\hat{\imath} + 0.600\hat{\jmath})$, where μ is the (positive) magnitude of the magnetic moment. (a) Find the initial magnetic torque on the ring. (b) The ring (which is free to rotate around one diameter) is released and turns through an angle of 90.0°, at which point its magnetic moment is given by $\vec{\mu}_f = -\mu\hat{k}$. Determine the decrease in potential energy. (c) If the moment of inertia of the ring about a diameter is $8.50 \times 10^{-7}\ \text{kg}\cdot\text{m}^2$, determine the angular speed of the ring as it passes through the second position.

2. There are no nonconservative forces acting on the ring as it rotates, so the sum of its rotational kinetic energy (discussed in Section 9.4) and the potential energy is conserved.

EXECUTE

3. Use the vector expression for the torque on a magnetic dipole to find the answer to part (a). (*Hint:* You may want to review Section 1.10.)
4. Find the change in potential energy from the first orientation of the ring to the second orientation.
5. Use your result from step 4 to find the rotational kinetic energy of the ring when it is in the second orientation.
6. Use your result from step 5 to find the ring's angular speed when it is in the second orientation.

EVALUATE

7. If the ring were free to rotate around *any* diameter, in what direction would the magnetic moment point when the ring is in a state of stable equilibrium?

SOLUTION GUIDE

See MasteringPhysics® study area for a Video Tutor solution. **MP**

IDENTIFY and SET UP

1. The current-carrying ring acts as a magnetic dipole, so you can use the equations for a magnetic dipole in a uniform magnetic field.

Problems

For instructor-assigned homework, go to MasteringPhysics®. **MP**

•, ••, •••: Problems of increasing difficulty. **CP**: Cumulative problems incorporating material from earlier chapters. **CALC**: Problems requiring calculus. **BIO**: Biosciences problems.

DISCUSSION QUESTIONS

Q27.1 Can a charged particle move through a magnetic field without experiencing any force? If so, how? If not, why not?

Q27.2 At any point in space, the electric field $\vec{E}$ is defined to be in the direction of the electric force on a positively charged particle at that point. Why don't we similarly define the magnetic field $\vec{B}$ to be in the direction of the magnetic force on a moving, positively charged particle?

Q27.3 Section 27.2 describes a procedure for finding the direction of the magnetic force using your right hand. If you use the same procedure, but with your left hand, will you get the correct direction for the force? Explain.

Q27.4 The magnetic force on a moving charged particle is always perpendicular to the magnetic field $\vec{B}$. Is the trajectory of a moving charged particle always perpendicular to the magnetic field lines? Explain your reasoning.

Q27.5 A charged particle is fired into a cubical region of space where there is a uniform magnetic field. Outside this region, there is no magnetic field. Is it possible that the particle will remain inside the cubical region? Why or why not?

Q27.6 If the magnetic force does no work on a charged particle, how can it have any effect on the particle's motion? Are there other examples of forces that do no work but have a significant effect on a particle's motion?

Q27.7 A charged particle moves through a region of space with constant velocity (magnitude and direction). If the external magnetic field is zero in this region, can you conclude that the external electric field in the region is also zero? Explain. (By "external" we mean fields other than those produced by the charged particle.) If the external electric field is zero in the region, can you conclude that the external magnetic field in the region is also zero?

Q27.8 How might a loop of wire carrying a current be used as a compass? Could such a compass distinguish between north and south? Why or why not?

Q27.9 How could the direction of a magnetic field be determined by making only *qualitative* observations of the magnetic force on a straight wire carrying a current?

Q27.10 A loose, floppy loop of wire is carrying current I. The loop of wire is placed on a horizontal table in a uniform magnetic field $\vec{B}$ perpendicular to the plane of the table. This causes the loop of wire to expand into a circular shape while still lying on the table. In a diagram, show all possible orientations of the current I and magnetic field $\vec{B}$ that could cause this to occur. Explain your reasoning.

Q27.11 Several charges enter a uniform magnetic field directed into the page. (a) What path would a positive charge q moving with a velocity of magnitude v follow through the field? (b) What path would a positive charge q moving with a velocity of magnitude $2v$ follow through the field? (c) What path would a negative charge $-q$ moving with a velocity of magnitude v follow through the field? (d) What path would a neutral particle follow through the field?

Q27.12 Each of the lettered points at the corners of the cube in Fig. Q27.12 represents a positive charge q moving with a velocity of magnitude v in the direction indicated. The region in the figure is in a uniform magnetic field $\vec{B}$, parallel to the x-axis and directed toward the right. Which charges experience a force due to $\vec{B}$? What is the direction of the force on each charge?

Figure **Q27.12**

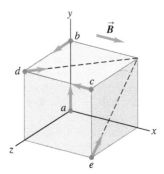

Q27.13 A student claims that if lightning strikes a metal flagpole, the force exerted by the earth's magnetic field on the current in the pole can be large enough to bend it. Typical lightning currents are of the order of 10^4 to 10^5 A. Is the student's opinion justified? Explain your reasoning.

Q27.14 Could an accelerator be built in which *all* the forces on the particles, for steering and for increasing speed, are magnetic forces? Why or why not?

Q27.15 An ordinary loudspeaker such as that shown in Fig. 27.28 should not be placed next to a computer monitor or TV screen. Why not?

Q27.16 The magnetic force acting on a charged particle can never do work because at every instant the force is perpendicular to the velocity. The torque exerted by a magnetic field can do work on a current loop when the loop rotates. Explain how these seemingly contradictory statements can be reconciled.

Q27.17 If an emf is produced in a dc motor, would it be possible to use the motor somehow as a generator or source, taking power out of it rather than putting power into it? How might this be done?

Q27.18 When the polarity of the voltage applied to a dc motor is reversed, the direction of motion does *not* reverse. Why not? How *could* the direction of motion be reversed?

Q27.19 In a Hall-effect experiment, is it possible that *no* transverse potential difference will be observed? Under what circumstances might this happen?

Q27.20 Hall-effect voltages are much greater for relatively poor conductors (such as germanium) than for good conductors (such as copper), for comparable currents, fields, and dimensions. Why?

EXERCISES

Section 27.2 Magnetic Field

27.1 • A particle with a charge of -1.24×10^{-8} C is moving with instantaneous velocity $\vec{v} = (4.19 \times 10^4 \text{ m/s})\hat{\imath} + (-3.85 \times 10^4 \text{ m/s})\hat{\jmath}$. What is the force exerted on this particle by a magnetic field (a) $\vec{B} = (1.40 \text{ T})\hat{\imath}$ and (b) $\vec{B} = (1.40 \text{ T})\hat{k}$?

27.2 • A particle of mass 0.195 g carries a charge of -2.50×10^{-8} C. The particle is given an initial horizontal velocity that is due north and has magnitude 4.00×10^4 m/s. What are the magnitude and direction of the minimum magnetic field that will keep the particle moving in the earth's gravitational field in the same horizontal, northward direction?

27.3 • In a 1.25-T magnetic field directed vertically upward, a particle having a charge of magnitude 8.50 μC and initially moving northward at 4.75 km/s is deflected toward the east. (a) What is the sign of the charge of this particle? Make a sketch to illustrate how you found your answer. (b) Find the magnetic force on the particle.

27.4 • A particle with mass 1.81×10^{-3} kg and a charge of 1.22×10^{-8} C has, at a given instant, a velocity $\vec{v} = (3.00 \times 10^4 \text{ m/s})\hat{\jmath}$. What are the magnitude and direction of the particle's acceleration produced by a uniform magnetic field $\vec{B} = (1.63 \text{ T})\hat{\imath} + (0.980 \text{ T})\hat{\jmath}$?

27.5 • An electron experiences a magnetic force of magnitude 4.60×10^{-15} N when moving at an angle of 60.0° with respect to a magnetic field of magnitude 3.50×10^{-3} T. Find the speed of the electron.

27.6 • An electron moves at 2.50×10^6 m/s through a region in which there is a magnetic field of unspecified direction and magnitude 7.40×10^{-2} T. (a) What are the largest and smallest possible magnitudes of the acceleration of the electron due to the magnetic field? (b) If the actual acceleration of the electron is one-fourth of the largest magnitude in part (a), what is the angle between the electron velocity and the magnetic field?

27.7 •• CP A particle with charge 7.80 μC is moving with velocity $\vec{v} = -(3.80 \times 10^3 \text{ m/s})\hat{\jmath}$. The magnetic force on the particle is measured to be $\vec{F} = +(7.60 \times 10^{-3} \text{ N})\hat{\imath} - (5.20 \times 10^{-3} \text{ N})\hat{k}$. (a) Calculate all the components of the magnetic field you can from this information. (b) Are there components of the magnetic field that are not determined by the measurement of the force? Explain. (c) Calculate the scalar product $\vec{B} \cdot \vec{F}$. What is the angle between $\vec{B}$ and $\vec{F}$?

27.8 •• CP A particle with charge -5.60 nC is moving in a uniform magnetic field $\vec{B} = -(1.25 \text{ T})\hat{k}$. The magnetic force on the particle is measured to be $\vec{F} = -(3.40 \times 10^{-7}\ \text{N})\hat{\imath} + (7.40 \times 10^{-7}\ \text{N})\hat{\jmath}$. (a) Calculate all the components of the velocity of the particle that you can from this information. (b) Are there components of the velocity that are not determined by the measurement of the force? Explain. (c) Calculate the scalar product $\vec{v} \cdot \vec{F}$. What is the angle between $\vec{v}$ and $\vec{F}$?

27.9 •• A group of particles is traveling in a magnetic field of unknown magnitude and direction. You observe that a proton moving at 1.50 km/s in the $+x$-direction experiences a force of 2.25×10^{-16} N in the $+y$-direction, and an electron moving at 4.75 km/s in the $-z$-direction experiences a force of 8.50×10^{-16} N in the $+y$-direction. (a) What are the magnitude and direction of the magnetic field? (b) What are the magnitude and direction of the magnetic force on an electron moving in the $-y$-direction at 3.20 km/s?

Section 27.3 Magnetic Field Lines and Magnetic Flux

27.10 • A flat, square surface with side length 3.40 cm is in the xy-plane at $z = 0$. Calculate the magnitude of the flux through this surface produced by a magnetic field $\vec{B} = (0.200\ \text{T})\hat{\imath} + (0.300\ \text{T})\hat{\jmath} - (0.500\ \text{T})\hat{k}$.

27.11 • A circular area with a radius of 6.50 cm lies in the xy-plane. What is the magnitude of the magnetic flux through this circle due to a uniform magnetic field $B = 0.230$ T (a) in the $+z$-direction; (b) at an angle of 53.1° from the $+z$-direction; (c) in the $+y$-direction?

27.12 • A horizontal rectangular surface has dimensions 2.80 cm by 3.20 cm and is in a uniform magnetic field that is directed at an angle of 30.0° above the horizontal. What must the magnitude of the magnetic field be in order to produce a flux of 4.20×10^{-4} Wb through the surface?

27.13 •• An open plastic soda bottle with an opening diameter of 2.5 cm is placed on a table. A uniform 1.75-T magnetic field directed upward and oriented 25° from vertical encompasses the bottle. What is the total magnetic flux through the plastic of the soda bottle?

27.14 •• The magnetic field $\vec{B}$ in a certain region is 0.128 T, and its direction is that of the $+z$-axis in Fig. E27.14. (a) What is the magnetic flux across the surface *abcd* in the figure? (b) What is the magnetic flux across the surface *befc*? (c) What is the magnetic flux across the surface *aefd*? (d) What is the net flux through all five surfaces that enclose the shaded volume?

Figure **E27.14**

Section 27.4 Motion of Charged Particles in a Magnetic Field

27.15 •• An electron at point A in Fig. E27.15 has a speed v_0 of 1.41×10^6 m/s. Find (a) the magnitude and direction of the magnetic field that will cause the electron to follow the semicircular path from A to B, and (b) the time required for the electron to move from A to B.

Figure **E27.15**

27.16 •• Repeat Exercise 27.15 for the case in which the particle is a proton rather than an electron.

27.17 • CP A 150-g ball containing 4.00×10^8 excess electrons is dropped into a 125-m vertical shaft. At the bottom of the shaft, the ball suddenly enters a uniform horizontal magnetic field that has magnitude 0.250 T and direction from east to west. If air resistance is negligibly small, find the magnitude and direction of the force that this magnetic field exerts on the ball just as it enters the field.

27.18 • An alpha particle (a He nucleus, containing two protons and two neutrons and having a mass of 6.64×10^{-27} kg) traveling horizontally at 35.6 km/s enters a uniform, vertical, 1.10-T magnetic field. (a) What is the diameter of the path followed by this alpha particle? (b) What effect does the magnetic field have on the speed of the particle? (c) What are the magnitude and direction of the acceleration of the alpha particle while it is in the magnetic field? (d) Explain why the speed of the particle does not change even though an unbalanced external force acts on it.

27.19 • CP A particle with charge 6.40×10^{-19} C travels in a circular orbit with radius 4.68 mm due to the force exerted on it by a magnetic field with magnitude 1.65 T and perpendicular to the orbit. (a) What is the magnitude of the linear momentum $\vec{p}$ of the particle? (b) What is the magnitude of the angular momentum $\vec{L}$ of the particle?

27.20 • (a) An ^{16}O nucleus (charge $+8e$) moving horizontally from west to east with a speed of 500 km/s experiences a magnetic force of 0.00320 nN vertically downward. Find the magnitude and direction of the weakest magnetic field required to produce this force. Explain how this same force could be caused by a larger magnetic field. (b) An electron moves in a uniform, horizontal, 2.10-T magnetic field that is toward the west. What must the magnitude and direction of the minimum velocity of the electron be so that the magnetic force on it will be 4.60 pN, vertically upward? Explain how the velocity could be greater than this minimum value and the force still have this same magnitude and direction.

27.21 • A deuteron (the nucleus of an isotope of hydrogen) has a mass of 3.34×10^{-27} kg and a charge of $+e$. The deuteron travels in a circular path with a radius of 6.96 mm in a magnetic field with magnitude 2.50 T. (a) Find the speed of the deuteron. (b) Find the time required for it to make half a revolution. (c) Through what potential difference would the deuteron have to be accelerated to acquire this speed?

27.22 • In an experiment with cosmic rays, a vertical beam of particles that have charge of magnitude $3e$ and mass 12 times the proton mass enters a uniform horizontal magnetic field of 0.250 T and is bent in a semicircle of diameter 95.0 cm, as shown in Fig. E27.22. (a) Find the speed of the particles and the sign of their charge. (b) Is it reasonable to ignore the gravity force on the particles? (c) How does the speed of the particles as they enter the field compare to their speed as they exit the field?

Figure **E27.22**

27.23 • A physicist wishes to produce electromagnetic waves of frequency 3.0 THz (1 THz = 1 terahertz = 10^{12} Hz) using a magnetron (see Example 27.3). (a) What magnetic field would be required? Compare this field with the strongest constant magnetic fields yet produced on earth, about 45 T. (b) Would there be any advantage to using protons instead of electrons in the magnetron? Why or why not?

27.24 •• A beam of protons traveling at 1.20 km/s enters a uniform magnetic field, traveling perpendicular to the field. The beam exits the magnetic field, leaving the field in a direction perpendicular to its original direction (Fig. E27.24). The beam travels a distance of 1.18 cm *while in the field*. What is the magnitude of the magnetic field?

Figure **E27.24**

27.25 • An electron in the beam of a TV picture tube is accelerated by a potential difference of 2.00 kV. Then it passes through a region of transverse magnetic field, where it moves in a circular arc with radius 0.180 m. What is the magnitude of the field?

27.26 • A singly charged ion of ^{7}Li (an isotope of lithium) has a mass of 1.16×10^{-26} kg. It is accelerated through a potential difference of 220 V and then enters a magnetic field with magnitude 0.723 T perpendicular to the path of the ion. What is the radius of the ion's path in the magnetic field?

27.27 •• A proton ($q = 1.60 \times 10^{-19}$ C, $m = 1.67 \times 10^{-27}$ kg) moves in a uniform magnetic field $\vec{B} = (0.500 \text{ T})\hat{\imath}$. At $t = 0$ the proton has velocity components $v_x = 1.50 \times 10^5$ m/s, $v_y = 0$, and $v_z = 2.00 \times 10^5$ m/s (see Example 27.4). (a) What are the magnitude and direction of the magnetic force acting on the proton? In addition to the magnetic field there is a uniform electric field in the +x-direction, $\vec{E} = (+2.00 \times 10^4 \text{ V/m})\hat{\imath}$. (b) Will the proton have a component of acceleration in the direction of the electric field? (c) Describe the path of the proton. Does the electric field affect the radius of the helix? Explain. (d) At $t = T/2$, where T is the period of the circular motion of the proton, what is the x-component of the displacement of the proton from its position at $t = 0$?

Section 27.5 Applications of Motion of Charged Particles

27.28 • (a) What is the speed of a beam of electrons when the simultaneous influence of an electric field of 1.56×10^4 V/m and a magnetic field of 4.62×10^{-3} T, with both fields normal to the beam and to each other, produces no deflection of the electrons? (b) In a diagram, show the relative orientation of the vectors $\vec{v}$, $\vec{E}$, and $\vec{B}$. (c) When the electric field is removed, what is the radius of the electron orbit? What is the period of the orbit?

27.29 • In designing a velocity selector that uses uniform perpendicular electric and magnetic fields, you want to select positive ions of charge +5e that are traveling perpendicular to the fields at 8.75 km/s. The magnetic field available to you has a magnitude of 0.550 T. (a) What magnitude of electric field do you need? (b) Show how the two fields should be oriented relative to each other and to the velocity of the ions. (c) Will your velocity selector also allow the following ions (having the same velocity as the +5e ions) to pass through undeflected: (i) negative ions of charge −5e, (ii) positive ions of charge different from +5e?

27.30 • **Crossed $\vec{E}$ and $\vec{B}$ Fields.** A particle with initial velocity $\vec{v}_0 = (5.85 \times 10^3 \text{ m/s})\hat{\jmath}$ enters a region of uniform electric and magnetic fields. The magnetic field in the region is $\vec{B} = -(1.35 \text{ T})\hat{k}$. Calculate the magnitude and direction of the electric field in the region if the particle is to pass through undeflected, for a particle of charge (a) +0.640 nC and (b) −0.320 nC. You can ignore the weight of the particle.

27.31 •• A 150-V battery is connected across two parallel metal plates of area 28.5 cm^2 and separation 8.20 mm. A beam of alpha particles (charge +2e, mass 6.64×10^{-27} kg) is accelerated from rest through a potential difference of 1.75 kV and enters the region between the plates perpendicular to the electric field, as shown in Fig. E27.31. What magnitude and direction of magnetic field are needed so that the alpha particles emerge undeflected from between the plates?

Figure **E27.31**

27.32 • A singly ionized (one electron removed) ^{40}K atom passes through a velocity selector consisting of uniform perpendicular electric and magnetic fields. The selector is adjusted to allow ions having a speed of 4.50 km/s to pass through undeflected when the magnetic field is 0.0250 T. The ions next enter a second uniform magnetic field (B') oriented at right angles to their velocity. ^{40}K contains 19 protons and 21 neutrons and has a mass of 6.64×10^{-26} kg. (a) What is the magnitude of the electric field in the velocity selector? (b) What must be the magnitude of B' so that the ions will be bent into a semicircle of radius 12.5 cm?

27.33 • Singly ionized (one electron removed) atoms are accelerated and then passed through a velocity selector consisting of perpendicular electric and magnetic fields. The electric field is 155 V/m and the magnetic field is 0.0315 T. The ions next enter a uniform magnetic field of magnitude 0.0175 T that is oriented perpendicular to their velocity. (a) How fast are the ions moving when they emerge from the velocity selector? (b) If the radius of the path of the ions in the second magnetic field is 17.5 cm, what is their mass?

27.34 • In the Bainbridge mass spectrometer (see Fig. 27.24), the magnetic-field magnitude in the velocity selector is 0.650 T, and ions having a speed of 1.82×10^6 m/s pass through undeflected. (a) What is the electric-field magnitude in the velocity selector? (b) If the separation of the plates is 5.20 mm, what is the potential difference between plates P and P'?

27.35 •• **BIO** **Ancient Meat Eating.** The amount of meat in prehistoric diets can be determined by measuring the ratio of the isotopes nitrogen-15 to nitrogen-14 in bone from human remains. Carnivores concentrate ^{15}N, so this ratio tells archaeologists how much meat was consumed by ancient people. Use the spectrometer of Exercise 27.34 to find the separation of the ^{14}N and ^{15}N isotopes at the detector. The measured masses of these isotopes are 2.32×10^{-26} kg (^{14}N) and 2.49×10^{-26} kg (^{15}N).

Section 27.6 Magnetic Force on a Current-Carrying Conductor

27.36 • A straight, 2.5-m wire carries a typical household current of 1.5 A (in one direction) at a location where the earth's magnetic field is 0.55 gauss from south to north. Find the magnitude and direction of the force that our planet's magnetic field exerts on this wire if is oriented so that the current in it is running (a) from west to east, (b) vertically upward, (c) from north to south. (d) Is the magnetic force ever large enough to cause significant effects under normal household conditions?

27.37 • A straight, 2.00-m, 150-g wire carries a current in a region where the earth's magnetic field is horizontal with a magnitude of 0.55 gauss. (a) What is the minimum value of the current in this wire so that its weight is completely supported by the magnetic force due to earth's field, assuming that no other forces except gravity act on it? Does it seem likely that such a wire could support this size of current? (b) Show how the wire would have to be oriented relative to the earth's magnetic field to be supported in this way.

27.38 •• An electromagnet produces a magnetic field of 0.550 T in a cylindrical region of radius 2.50 cm between its poles. A straight wire carrying a current of 10.8 A passes through the center of this region and is perpendicular to both the axis of the cylindrical region and the magnetic field. What magnitude of force is exerted on the wire?

27.39 •• A long wire carrying 4.50 A of current makes two 90° bends, as shown in Fig. E27.39. The bent part of the wire passes through a uniform 0.240-T magnetic field directed as shown in the figure and confined to a limited region of space. Find the magnitude and direction of the force that the magnetic field exerts on the wire.

Figure **E27.39**

27.40 • A straight, vertical wire carries a current of 1.20 A downward in a region between the poles of a large superconducting electromagnet, where the magnetic field has magnitude $B = 0.588$ T and is horizontal. What are the magnitude and direction of the magnetic force on a 1.00-cm section of the wire that is in this uniform magnetic field, if the magnetic field direction is (a) east; (b) south; (c) 30.0°south of west?

27.41 • A thin, 50.0-cm-long metal bar with mass 750 g rests on, but is not attached to, two metallic supports in a uniform 0.450-T magnetic field, as shown in Fig. E27.41. A battery and a 25.0-Ω resistor in series are connected to the supports. (a) What is the highest voltage the battery can have without breaking the circuit at the supports? (b) The battery voltage has the maximum value calculated in part (a). If the resistor suddenly gets partially short-circuited, decreasing its resistance to 2.0 Ω, find the initial acceleration of the bar.

Figure **E27.41**

27.42 • **Magnetic Balance.** The circuit shown in Fig. E27.42 is used to make a magnetic balance to weigh objects. The mass m to be measured is hung from the center of the bar that is in a uniform magnetic field of 1.50 T, directed into the plane of the figure. The battery voltage can be adjusted to vary the current in the circuit. The horizontal bar is 60.0 cm long and is made of extremely light-weight material. It is connected to the battery by thin vertical wires that can support no appreciable tension; all the weight of the suspended mass m is supported by the magnetic force on the bar. A resistor with $R = 5.00$ Ω is in series with the bar; the resistance of the rest of the circuit is much less than this. (a) Which point, a or b, should be the positive terminal of the battery? (b) If the maximum terminal voltage of the battery is 175 V, what is the greatest mass m that this instrument can measure?

Figure **E27.42**

27.43 • Consider the conductor and current in Example 27.8, but now let the magnetic field be parallel to the x-axis. (a) What are the magnitude and direction of the total magnetic force on the conductor? (b) In Example 27.8, the total force is the same as if we replaced the semicircle with a straight segment along the x-axis. Is that still true when the magnetic field is in this different direction? Can you explain why, or why not?

Section 27.7 Force and Torque on a Current Loop

27.44 •• The plane of a 5.0 cm × 8.0 cm rectangular loop of wire is parallel to a 0.19-T magnetic field. The loop carries a current of 6.2 A. (a) What torque acts on the loop? (b) What is the magnetic moment of the loop? (c) What is the maximum torque that can be obtained with the same total length of wire carrying the same current in this magnetic field?

27.45 • The 20.0 cm × 35.0 cm rectangular circuit shown in Fig. E27.45 is hinged along side ab. It carries a clockwise 5.00-A current and is located in a uniform 1.20-T magnetic field oriented perpendicular to two of its sides, as shown. (a) Draw a clear diagram showing the direction of the force that the magnetic field exerts on each segment of the circuit (ab, bc, etc.). (b) Of the four forces you drew in part (a), decide which ones exert a torque about the hinge ab. Then calculate only those forces that exert this torque. (c) Use your results from part (b) to calculate the torque that the magnetic field exerts on the circuit about the hinge axis ab.

Figure **E27.45**

27.46 • A rectangular coil of wire, 22.0 cm by 35.0 cm and carrying a current of 1.40 A, is oriented with the plane of its loop perpendicular to a uniform 1.50-T magnetic field, as shown in Fig. E27.46. (a) Calculate the net force and torque that the magnetic field exerts on the coil. (b) The coil is rotated through a 30.0° angle about the axis shown, with the left side coming out of the plane of the figure and the right side going into the plane. Calculate the net force and torque that the magnetic field now exerts on the coil. (*Hint:* In order to help visualize this three-dimensional problem, make a careful drawing of the coil as viewed along the rotation axis.)

Figure **E27.46**

27.47 • **CP** A uniform rectangular coil of total mass 212 g and dimensions 0.500 m × 1.00 m is oriented with its plane parallel to a uniform 3.00-T magnetic field (Fig. E27.47). A current of 2.00 A is suddenly started in the coil. (a) About which axis (A_1 or A_2) will the coil begin to rotate? Why? (b) Find the initial angular acceleration of the coil just after the current is started.

Figure **E27.47**

27.48 • A circular coil with area A and N turns is free to rotate about a diameter that coincides with the x-axis. Current I is circulating in the coil. There is a uniform magnetic field $\vec{B}$ in the positive y-direction. Calculate the magnitude and direction of the torque $\vec{\tau}$

Figure **E27.48**

and the value of the potential energy U, as given in Eq. (27.27), when the coil is oriented as shown in parts (a) through (d) of Fig. E27.48.

27.49 •• A coil with magnetic moment 1.45 A·m² is oriented initially with its magnetic moment antiparallel to a uniform 0.835-T magnetic field. What is the change in potential energy of the coil when it is rotated 180° so that its magnetic moment is parallel to the field?

Section 27.8 The Direct-Current Motor

27.50 • A dc motor with its rotor and field coils connected in series has an internal resistance of 3.2 Ω. When the motor is running at full load on a 120-V line, the emf in the rotor is 105 V. (a) What is the current drawn by the motor from the line? (b) What is the power delivered to the motor? (c) What is the mechanical power developed by the motor?

27.51 •• In a shunt-wound dc motor with the field coils and rotor connected in parallel (Fig. E27.51), the resistance R_f of the field coils is 106 Ω, and the resistance R_r of the rotor is 5.9 Ω. When a potential difference of 120 V is applied to the brushes and the motor is running at full speed delivering mechanical power, the current supplied to it is 4.82 A. (a) What is the current in the field coils? (b) What is the current in the rotor? (c) What is the induced emf developed by the motor? (d) How much mechanical power is developed by this motor?

Figure **E27.51**

27.52 • A shunt-wound dc motor with the field coils and rotor connected in parallel (see Fig. E27.51) operates from a 120-V dc power line. The resistance of the field windings, R_f, is 218 Ω. The resistance of the rotor, R_r, is 5.9 Ω. When the motor is running, the rotor develops an emf $\mathcal{E}$. The motor draws a current of 4.82 A from the line. Friction losses amount to 45.0 W. Compute (a) the field current; (b) the rotor current; (c) the emf $\mathcal{E}$; (d) the rate of development of thermal energy in the field windings; (e) the rate of development of thermal energy in the rotor; (f) the power input to the motor; (g) the efficiency of the motor.

Section 27.9 The Hall Effect

27.53 • Figure E27.53 shows a portion of a silver ribbon with $z_1 = 11.8$ mm and $y_1 = 0.23$ mm, carrying a current of 120 A in the +x-direction. The ribbon lies in a uniform magnetic field, in the y-direction, with magnitude 0.95 T. Apply the simplified model of the Hall effect presented in Section 27.9. If there are 5.85×10^{28} free electrons per cubic meter, find (a) the magnitude of the drift velocity of the electrons in the x-direction; (b) the magnitude and direction of the electric field in the z-direction due to the Hall effect; (c) the Hall emf.

Figure **E27.53**

27.54 • Let Fig. E27.53 represent a strip of an unknown metal of the same dimensions as those of the silver ribbon in Exercise 27.53. When the magnetic field is 2.29 T and the current is 78.0 A, the Hall emf is found to be 131 μV. What does the simplified model of the Hall effect presented in Section 27.9 give for the density of free electrons in the unknown metal?

PROBLEMS

27.55 • When a particle of charge $q > 0$ moves with a velocity of $\vec{v}_1$ at 45.0° from the +x-axis in the xy-plane, a uniform magnetic field exerts a force $\vec{F}_1$ along the −z-axis (Fig. P27.55). When the same particle moves with a velocity $\vec{v}_2$ with the same magnitude as $\vec{v}_1$ but along the +z-axis, a force $\vec{F}_2$ of magnitude F_2 is exerted on it along the +x-axis. (a) What are the magnitude (in terms of q, v_1, and F_2) and direction of the magnetic field? (b) What is the magnitude of $\vec{F}_1$ in terms of F_2?

Figure **P27.55**

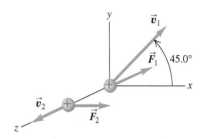

27.56 • A particle with charge 9.45×10^{-8} C is moving in a region where there is a uniform magnetic field of 0.650 T in the +x-direction. At a particular instant of time the velocity of the particle has components $v_x = -1.68 \times 10^4$ m/s, $v_y = -3.11 \times 10^4$ m/s, and $v_z = 5.85 \times 10^4$ m/s. What are the components of the force on the particle at this time?

27.57 ••• **CP Fusion Reactor.** If two deuterium nuclei (charge +e, mass 3.34×10^{-27} kg) get close enough together, the attraction of the strong nuclear force will fuse them to make an isotope of helium, releasing vast amounts of energy. The range of this force is about 10^{-15} m. This is the principle behind the fusion reactor. The deuterium nuclei are moving much too fast to be contained by physical walls, so they are confined magnetically. (a) How fast would two nuclei have to move so that in a head-on collision they would get close enough to fuse? (Assume their speeds are equal. Treat the nuclei as point charges, and assume that a separation of 1.0×10^{-15} is required for fusion.) (b) What strength magnetic field is needed to make deuterium nuclei with this speed travel in a circle of diameter 2.50 m?

27.58 •• **Magnetic Moment of the Hydrogen Atom.** In the Bohr model of the hydrogen atom (see Section 38.5), in the lowest energy state the electron orbits the proton at a speed of 2.2×10^6 m/s in a circular orbit of radius 5.3×10^{-11} m. (a) What is the orbital period of the electron? (b) If the orbiting electron is considered to be a current loop, what is the current I? (c) What is the magnetic moment of the atom due to the motion of the electron?

27.59 •• You wish to hit a target from several meters away with a charged coin having a mass of 4.25 g and a charge of +2500 μC. The coin is given an initial velocity of 12.8 m/s, and a downward, uniform electric field with field strength 27.5 N/C exists throughout the region. If you aim directly at the target and fire the coin horizontally, what magnitude and direction of uniform magnetic field are needed in the region for the coin to hit the target?

27.60 • A cyclotron is to accelerate protons to an energy of 5.4 MeV. The superconducting electromagnet of the cyclotron produces a 2.9-T magnetic field perpendicular to the proton orbits. (a) When the protons have achieved a kinetic energy of 2.7 MeV, what is the radius of their circular orbit and what is their angular speed? (b) Repeat part (a) when the protons have achieved their final kinetic energy of 5.4 MeV.

27.61 • The magnetic poles of a small cyclotron produce a magnetic field with magnitude 0.85 T. The poles have a radius of 0.40 m, which is the maximum radius of the orbits of the accelerated particles. (a) What is the maximum energy to which protons ($q = 1.60 \times 10^{-19}$ C, $m = 1.67 \times 10^{-27}$ kg) can be accelerated by this cyclotron? Give your answer in electron volts and in joules. (b) What is the time for one revolution of a proton orbiting at this maximum radius? (c) What would the magnetic-field magnitude have to be for the maximum energy to which a proton can be accelerated to be twice that calculated in part (a)? (d) For $B = 0.85$ T, what is the maximum energy to which alpha particles ($q = 3.20 \times 10^{-19}$ C, $m = 6.65 \times 10^{-27}$ kg) can be accelerated by this cyclotron? How does this compare to the maximum energy for protons?

27.62 •• A particle with charge q is moving with speed v in the $-y$-direction. It is moving in a uniform magnetic field $\vec{B} = B_x \hat{i} + B_y \hat{j} + B_z \hat{k}$. (a) What are the components of the force $\vec{F}$ exerted on the particle by the magnetic field? (b) If $q > 0$, what must the signs of the components of $\vec{B}$ be if the components of $\vec{F}$ are all nonnegative? (c) If $q < 0$ and $B_x = B_y = B_z > 0$, find the direction of $\vec{F}$ and find the magnitude of $\vec{F}$ in terms of $|q|$, v, and B_x.

27.63 •• A particle with negative charge q and mass $m = 2.58 \times 10^{-15}$ kg is traveling through a region containing a uniform magnetic field $\vec{B} = -(0.120 \text{ T})\hat{k}$. At a particular instant of time the velocity of the particle is $\vec{v} = (1.05 \times 10^6 \text{ m/s})(-3\hat{i} + 4\hat{j} + 12\hat{k})$ and the force $\vec{F}$ on the particle has a magnitude of 2.45 N. (a) Determine the charge q. (b) Determine the acceleration $\vec{a}$ of the particle. (c) Explain why the path of the particle is a helix, and determine the radius of curvature R of the circular component of the helical path. (d) Determine the cyclotron frequency of the particle. (e) Although helical motion is not periodic in the full sense of the word, the x- and y-coordinates do vary in a periodic way. If the coordinates of the particle at $t = 0$ are $(x, y, z) = (R, 0, 0)$, determine its coordinates at a time $t = 2T$, where T is the period of the motion in the xy-plane.

27.64 •• **BIO** **Medical Uses of Cyclotrons.** The largest cyclotron in the United States is the *Tevatron* at Fermilab, near Chicago, Illinois. It is called a Tevatron because it can accelerate particles to energies in the TeV range: 1 tera-eV $= 10^{12}$ eV. Its circumference is 6.4 km, and it currently can produce a maximum energy of 2.0 TeV. In a certain medical experiment, protons will be accelerated to energies of 1.25 MeV and aimed at a tumor to destroy its cells. (a) How fast are these protons moving when they hit the tumor? (b) How strong must the magnetic field be to bend the protons in the circle indicated?

27.65 • A magnetic field exerts a torque τ on a round current-carrying loop of wire. What will be the torque on this loop (in terms of τ) if its diameter is tripled?

27.66 •• A particle of charge $q > 0$ is moving at speed v in the $+z$-direction through a region of uniform magnetic field $\vec{B}$. The magnetic force on the particle is $\vec{F} = F_0(3\hat{i} + 4\hat{j})$, where F_0 is a positive constant. (a) Determine the components B_x, B_y, and B_z, or at least as many of the three components as is possible from the information given. (b) If it is given in addition that the magnetic field has magnitude $6F_0/qv$, determine as much as you can about the remaining components of $\vec{B}$.

27.67 •• Suppose the electric field between the plates in Fig. 27.24 is 1.88×10^4 V/m and the magnetic field in both regions is 0.682 T. If the source contains the three isotopes of krypton, ^{82}Kr, ^{84}Kr, and ^{86}Kr, and the ions are singly charged, find the distance between the lines formed by the three isotopes on the particle detector. Assume the atomic masses of the isotopes (in atomic mass units) are equal to their mass numbers, 82, 84, and 86. (One atomic mass unit $= 1$ u $= 1.66 \times 10^{-27}$ kg.)

27.68 •• **Mass Spectrograph.** A mass spectrograph is used to measure the masses of ions, or to separate ions of different masses (see Section 27.5). In one design for such an instrument, ions with mass m and charge q are accelerated through a potential difference V. They then enter a uniform magnetic field that is perpendicular to their velocity, and they are deflected in a semicircular path of radius R. A detector measures where the ions complete the semicircle and from this it is easy to calculate R. (a) Derive the equation for calculating the mass of the ion from measurements of B, V, R, and q. (b) What potential difference V is needed so that singly ionized ^{12}C atoms will have $R = 50.0$ cm in a 0.150-T magnetic field? (c) Suppose the beam consists of a mixture of ^{12}C and ^{14}C ions. If v and B have the same values as in part (b), calculate the separation of these two isotopes at the detector. Do you think that this beam separation is sufficient for the two ions to be distinguished? (Make the assumption described in Problem 27.67 for the masses of the ions.)

27.69 •• A straight piece of conducting wire with mass M and length L is placed on a frictionless incline tilted at an angle θ from the horizontal (Fig. P27.69). There is a uniform, vertical magnetic field $\vec{B}$ at all points (produced by an arrangement of magnets not shown in the figure). To keep the wire from sliding down the incline, a voltage source is attached to the ends of the wire. When just the right amount of current flows through the wire, the wire remains at rest. Determine the magnitude and direction of the current in the wire that will cause the wire to remain at rest. Copy the figure and draw the direction of the current on your copy. In addition, show in a free-body diagram all the forces that act on the wire.

Figure **P27.69**

$\vec{B}$ (vertical)

Wire, mass M

θ

L

27.70 •• **CP** A 2.60-N metal bar, 1.50 m long and having a resistance of 10.0 Ω, rests horizontally on conducting wires connecting it to the circuit shown in Fig. P27.70. The bar is in a uniform, horizontal, 1.60-T magnetic field and is not attached to the wires in the circuit. What is the acceleration of the bar just after the switch S is closed?

Figure **P27.70**

25.0 Ω

S

120.0 V

10.0 Ω

$\vec{B}$

27.71 •• **Using Gauss's Law for Magnetism.** In a certain region of space, the magnetic field $\vec{B}$ is not uniform. The magnetic field has both a z-component and a component that points radially away from or toward the z-axis. The z-component is given by $B_z(z) = \beta z$, where β is a positive constant. The radial component B_r depends only on r, the radial distance from the z-axis. (a) Use Gauss's law for magnetism, Eq. (27.8), to find the radial component B_r as a function of r. (*Hint:* Try a cylindrical Gaussian surface of radius r concentric with the z-axis, with one end at $z = 0$ and the other at $z = L$.) (b) Sketch the magnetic field lines.

27.72 ·· **CP** A plastic circular loop has radius R, and a positive charge q is distributed uniformly around the circumference of the loop. The loop is then rotated around its central axis, perpendicular to the plane of the loop, with angular speed ω. If the loop is in a region where there is a uniform magnetic field $\vec{B}$ directed parallel to the plane of the loop, calculate the magnitude of the magnetic torque on the loop.

27.73 ·· **BIO Determining Diet.** One method for determining the amount of corn in early Native American diets is the *stable isotope ratio analysis* (SIRA) technique. As corn photosynthesizes, it concentrates the isotope carbon-13, whereas most other plants concentrate carbon-12. Overreliance on corn consumption can then be correlated with certain diseases, because corn lacks the essential amino acid lysine. Archaeologists use a mass spectrometer to separate the ^{12}C and ^{13}C isotopes in samples of human remains. Suppose you use a velocity selector to obtain singly ionized (missing one electron) atoms of speed 8.50 km/s, and you want to bend them within a uniform magnetic field in a semicircle of diameter 25.0 cm for the ^{12}C. The measured masses of these isotopes are 1.99×10^{-26} kg (^{12}C) and 2.16×10^{-26} kg (^{13}C). (a) What strength of magnetic field is required? (b) What is the diameter of the ^{13}C semicircle? (c) What is the separation of the ^{12}C and ^{13}C ions at the detector at the end of the semicircle? Is this distance large enough to be easily observed?

27.74 ·· **CP An Electromagnetic Rail Gun.** A conducting bar with mass m and length L slides over horizontal rails that are connected to a voltage source. The voltage source maintains a constant current I in the rails and bar, and a constant, uniform, vertical magnetic field $\vec{B}$ fills the region between the rails (Fig. P27.74). (a) Find the magnitude and direction of the net force on the conducting bar. Ignore friction, air resistance, and electrical resistance. (b) If the bar has mass m, find the distance d that the bar must move along the rails from rest to attain speed v. (c) It has been suggested that rail guns based on this principle could accelerate payloads into earth orbit or beyond. Find the distance the bar must travel along the rails if it is to reach the escape speed for the earth (11.2 km/s). Let $B = 0.80$ T, $I = 2.0 \times 10^3$ A, $m = 25$ kg, and $L = 50$ cm. For simplicity assume the net force on the object is equal to the magnetic force, as in parts (a) and (b), even though gravity plays an important role in an actual launch in space.

Figure **P27.74**

27.75 · A long wire carrying a 6.00-A current reverses direction by means of two right-angle bends, as shown in Fig. P27.75. The part of the wire where the bend occurs is in a magnetic field of 0.666 T confined to the circular region of diameter 75 cm, as shown. Find the magnitude and direction of the net force that the magnetic field exerts on this wire.

Figure **P27.75**

27.76 · A wire 25.0 cm long lies along the z-axis and carries a current of 7.40 A in the $+z$-direction. The magnetic field is uniform and has components $B_x = -0.242$ T, $B_y = -0.985$ T, and $B_z = -0.336$ T. (a) Find the components of the magnetic force on the wire. (b) What is the magnitude of the net magnetic force on the wire?

27.77 ·· **CP** The rectangular loop of wire shown in Fig. P27.77 has a mass of 0.15 g per centimeter of length and is pivoted about side *ab* on a frictionless axis. The current in the wire is 8.2 A in the direction shown. Find the magnitude and direction of the magnetic field parallel to the y-axis that will cause the loop to swing up until its plane makes an angle of 30.0° with the yz-plane.

Figure **P27.77**

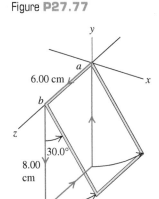

27.78 ·· The rectangular loop shown in Fig. P27.78 is pivoted about the y-axis and carries a current of 15.0 A in the direction indicated. (a) If the loop is in a uniform magnetic field with magnitude 0.48 T in the $+x$-direction, find the magnitude and direction of the torque required to hold the loop in the position shown. (b) Repeat part (a) for the case in which the field is in the $-z$-direction. (c) For each of the above magnetic fields, what torque would be required if the loop were pivoted about an axis through its center, parallel to the y-axis?

Figure **P27.78**

27.79 ·· **CP CALC** A thin, uniform rod with negligible mass and length 0.200 m is attached to the floor by a frictionless hinge at point P (Fig. P27.79). A horizontal spring with force constant $k = 4.80$ N/m connects the other end of the rod to a vertical wall. The rod is in a uniform magnetic field $B = 0.340$ T directed into the plane of the figure. There is current $I = 6.50$ A in the rod, in the direction shown. (a) Calculate the torque due to the magnetic force on the rod, for an axis at P. Is it correct to take the total magnetic force to act at the center of gravity of the rod when calculating the torque? Explain. (b) When the rod is in equilibrium and makes an angle of 53.0° with the floor, is the spring stretched or compressed? (c) How much energy is stored in the spring when the rod is in equilibrium?

Figure **P27.79**

27.80 ·· The loop of wire shown in Fig. P27.80 forms a right triangle and carries a current $I = 5.00$ A in the direction shown. The loop is in a uniform magnetic field that has magnitude $B = 3.00$ T and the same direction as the current in side PQ of the loop. (a) Find the force exerted by the magnetic field on each side of the triangle. If the force is not zero, specify its direction. (b) What is the net force on the loop? (c) The loop is pivoted about an axis that lies along side *PR*. Use the forces calculated in part (a) to calculate the torque on each side of the loop (see Problem 27.79). (d) What is the magnitude of the net torque on the loop? Calculate the net torque from the torques calculated in part (c) and also from Eq. (27.28). Do these two results agree? (e) Is the net torque directed to rotate point *Q* into the plane of the figure or out of the plane of the figure?

Figure **P27.80**

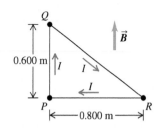

27.81 •• **CP** A uniform, 458-g metal bar 75.0 cm long carries a current *I* in a uniform, horizontal 1.25-T magnetic field as shown in Fig. P27.81. The directions of *I* and $\vec{B}$ are shown in the figure. The bar is free to rotate about a frictionless hinge at point *b*. The other end of the bar rests on a conducting support at point *a* but is not attached there. The bar rests at an angle of 60.0° above the horizontal. What is the largest value the current *I* can have without breaking the electrical contact at *a*? (See Problem 27.77.)

Figure **P27.81**

27.82 •• **Paleoclimate.** Climatologists can determine the past temperature of the earth by comparing the ratio of the isotope oxygen-18 to the isotope oxygen-16 in air trapped in ancient ice sheets, such as those in Greenland. In one method for separating these isotopes, a sample containing both of them is first singly ionized (one electron is removed) and then accelerated from rest through a potential difference *V*. This beam then enters a magnetic field *B* at right angles to the field and is bent into a quarter-circle. A particle detector at the end of the path measures the amount of each isotope. (a) Show that the separation Δr of the two isotopes at the detector is given by

$$\Delta r = \frac{\sqrt{2eV}}{eB}\left(\sqrt{m_{18}} - \sqrt{m_{16}}\right)$$

where m_{16} and m_{18} are the masses of the two oxygen isotopes, (b) The measured masses of the two isotopes are 2.66×10^{-26} kg (^{16}O) and 2.99×10^{-26} kg (^{18}O). If the magnetic field is 0.050 T, what must be the accelerating potential *V* so that these two isotopes will be separated by 4.00 cm at the detector?

27.83 •• **CALC A Voice Coil.** It was shown in Section 27.7 that the net force on a current loop in a *uniform* magnetic field is zero. The magnetic force on the voice coil of a loudspeaker (see Fig. 27.28) is nonzero because the magnetic field at the coil is not uniform. A voice coil in a loudspeaker has 50 turns of wire and a diameter of 1.56 cm, and the current in the coil is 0.950 A. Assume that the magnetic field at each point of the coil has a constant magnitude of 0.220 T and is directed at an angle of 60.0° outward from the normal to the plane of the coil (Fig. P27.83). Let the axis of the coil be in the *y*-direction. The current in the coil is in the direction shown (counterclockwise as viewed from a point above the coil on the *y*-axis). Calculate the magnitude and direction of the net magnetic force on the coil.

Figure **P27.83**

27.84 •• **Quark Model of the Neutron.** The neutron is a particle with zero charge. Nonetheless, it has a nonzero magnetic moment with *z*-component 9.66×10^{-27} A·m². This can be explained by the internal structure of the neutron. A substantial body of evidence indicates that a neutron is composed of three fundamental particles called *quarks*: an "up" (*u*) quark, of charge $+2e/3$, and two "down" (*d*) quarks, each of charge $-e/3$. The combination of the three quarks produces a net charge of $2e/3 - e/3 - e/3 = 0$. If the quarks are in motion, they can produce a nonzero magnetic moment. As a very simple model, suppose the *u* quark moves in a counterclockwise circular path and the *d* quarks move in a clockwise circular path, all of radius *r* and all with the same speed *v* (Fig. P27.84). (a) Determine the current due to the circulation of the *u* quark. (b) Determine the magnitude of the magnetic moment due to the circulating *u* quark. (c) Determine the magnitude of the magnetic moment of the three-quark system. (Be careful to use the correct magnetic moment directions.) (d) With what speed *v* must the quarks move if this model is to reproduce the magnetic moment of the neutron? Use $r = 1.20 \times 10^{-15}$ m (the radius of the neutron) for the radius of the orbits.

Figure **P27.84**

27.85 •• **CALC Force on a Current Loop in a Nonuniform Magnetic Field.** It was shown in Section 27.7 that the net force on a current loop in a *uniform* magnetic field is zero. But what if $\vec{B}$ is *not* uniform? Figure P27.85 shows a square loop of wire that lies in the *xy*-plane. The loop has corners at (0, 0), (0, *L*), (*L*, 0), and (*L*, *L*) and carries a constant current *I* in the clockwise direction. The magnetic field has no *x*-component but has both *y*- and *z*-components: $\vec{B} = (B_0 z/L)\hat{\jmath} + (B_0 y/L)\hat{k}$, where B_0 is a positive constant. (a) Sketch the magnetic field lines in the *yz*-plane. (b) Find the magnitude and direction of the magnetic force exerted on each of the sides of the loop by integrating Eq. (27.20). (c) Find the magnitude and direction of the net magnetic force on the loop.

Figure **P27.85**

27.86 • **CALC Torque on a Current Loop in a Nonuniform Magnetic Field.** In Section 27.7 the expression for the torque on a current loop was derived assuming that the magnetic field $\vec{B}$ was uniform. But what if $\vec{B}$ is *not* uniform? Figure P27.85 shows a square loop of wire that lies in the *xy*-plane. The loop has corners at (0, 0), (0, *L*), (*L*, 0), and (*L*, *L*) and carries a constant current *I* in the clockwise direction. The magnetic field has no *z*-component but has both *x*- and *y*-components: $\vec{B} = (B_0 y/L)\hat{\imath} + (B_0 x/L)\hat{\jmath}$, where B_0 is a positive constant. (a) Sketch the magnetic field lines in the *xy*-plane. (b) Find the magnitude and direction of the magnetic force exerted on each of the sides of the loop by integrating Eq. (27.20). (c) If the loop is free to rotate about the *x*-axis, find the magnitude and direction of the magnetic torque on the loop. (d) Repeat part (c) for the case in which the loop is free to rotate about the *y*-axis. (e) Is Eq. (27.26), $\vec{\tau} = \vec{\mu} \times \vec{B}$, an appropriate description of the torque on this loop? Why or why not?

27.87 •• **CP** An insulated wire with mass $m = 5.40 \times 10^{-5}$ kg is bent into the shape of an inverted U such that the horizontal part has a length $l = 15.0$ cm. The bent ends of the wire are partially

immersed in two pools of mercury, with 2.5 cm of each end below the mercury's surface. The entire structure is in a region containing a uniform 0.00650-T magnetic field directed into the page (Fig. P27.87). An electrical connection from the mercury pools is made through the ends of the wires. The mercury pools are connected to a 1.50-V battery and a switch S. When switch S is closed, the wire jumps 35.0 cm into the air, measured from its initial position. (a) Determine the speed v of the wire as it leaves the mercury. (b) Assuming that the current I through the wire was constant from the time the switch was closed until the wire left the mercury, determine I. (c) Ignoring the resistance of the mercury and the circuit wires, determine the resistance of the moving wire.

Figure **P27.87**

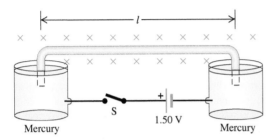

27.88 ⋅⋅ A circular loop of wire with area A lies in the xy-plane. As viewed along the z-axis looking in the $-z$-direction toward the origin, a current I is circulating clockwise around the loop. The torque produced by an external magnetic field $\vec{B}$ is given by $\vec{\tau} = D(4\hat{i} - 3\hat{j})$, where D is a positive constant, and for this orientation of the loop the magnetic potential energy $U = -\vec{\mu} \cdot \vec{B}$ is negative. The magnitude of the magnetic field is $B_0 = 13D/IA$. (a) Determine the vector magnetic moment of the current loop. (b) Determine the components B_x, B_y, and B_z of $\vec{B}$.

CHALLENGE PROBLEMS

27.89 ⋅⋅⋅ A particle with charge 2.15 μC and mass 3.20 × 10^{-11} kg is initially traveling in the $+y$-direction with a speed $v_0 = 1.45 \times 10^5$ m/s. It then enters a region containing a uniform magnetic field that is directed into, and perpendicular to, the page in Fig. P27.89. The magnitude of the field is 0.420 T. The

Figure **P27.89**

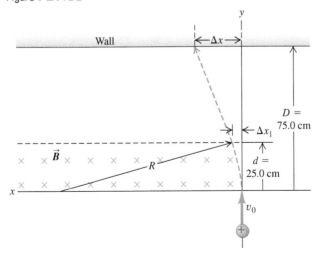

region extends a distance of 25.0 cm along the initial direction of travel; 75.0 cm from the point of entry into the magnetic field region is a wall. The length of the field-free region is thus 50.0 cm. When the charged particle enters the magnetic field, it follows a curved path whose radius of curvature is R. It then leaves the magnetic field after a time t_1, having been deflected a distance Δx_1. The particle then travels in the field-free region and strikes the wall after undergoing a total deflection Δx. (a) Determine the radius R of the curved part of the path. (b) Determine t_1, the time the particle spends in the magnetic field. (c) Determine Δx_1, the horizontal deflection at the point of exit from the field. (d) Determine Δx, the total horizontal deflection.

27.90 ⋅⋅⋅ **The Electromagnetic Pump.** Magnetic forces acting on conducting fluids provide a convenient means of pumping these fluids. For example, this method can be used to pump blood without the damage to the cells that can be caused by a mechanical pump. A horizontal tube with rectangular cross section (height h, width w) is placed at right angles to a uniform magnetic field with magnitude B so that a length l is in the field (Fig. P27.90). The tube is filled with a conducting liquid, and an electric current of density J is maintained in the third mutually perpendicular direction. (a) Show that the difference of pressure between a point in the liquid on a vertical plane through ab and a point in the liquid on another vertical plane through cd, under conditions in which the liquid is prevented from flowing, is $\Delta p = JlB$. (b) What current density is needed to provide a pressure difference of 1.00 atm between these two points if $B = 2.20$ T and $l = 35.0$ mm?

Figure **P27.90**

27.91 ⋅⋅⋅ **CP A Cycloidal Path.** A particle with mass m and positive charge q starts from rest at the origin shown in Fig. P27.91. There is a uniform electric field $\vec{E}$ in the $+y$-direction and a uniform magnetic field $\vec{B}$ directed out of the page. It is shown in more advanced books that the path is a *cycloid* whose radius of curvature at the top points is twice the y-coordinate at that level. (a) Explain why the path has this general shape and why it is_repetitive. (b) Prove that the speed at any point is equal to $\sqrt{2qEy/m}$. (*Hint:* Use energy conservation.) (c) Applying Newton's second law at the top point and taking as given that the radius of curvature here equals $2y$, prove that the speed at this point is $2E/B$.

Figure **P27.91**

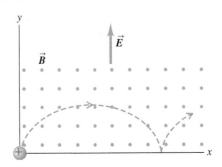

Answers

Chapter Opening Question ?

In MRI the nuclei of hydrogen atoms within soft tissue act like miniature current loops whose magnetic moments align with an applied field. See Section 27.7 for details.

Test Your Understanding Questions

27.1 Answer: yes When a magnet is cut apart, each part has a north and south pole (see Fig. 27.4). Hence the small red part behaves much like the original, full-sized compass needle.

27.2 Answer: path 3 Applying the right-hand rule to the vectors $\vec{v}$ (which points to the right) and $\vec{B}$ (which points into the plane of the figure) says that the force $\vec{F} = q\vec{v} \times \vec{B}$ on a *positive* charge would point *upward*. Since the charge is *negative,* the force points *downward* and the particle follows a trajectory that curves downward.

27.3 Answers: (a) (ii), (b) no The magnitude of $\vec{B}$ would increase as you moved to the right, reaching a maximum as you pass through the plane of the loop. As you moved beyond the plane of the loop, the field magnitude would decrease. You can tell this from the spacing of the field lines: The closer the field lines, the stronger the field. The direction of the field would be to the right at all points along the path, since the path is along a field line and the direction of $\vec{B}$ at any point is tangent to the field line through that point.

27.4 Answers: (a) (ii), (b) (i) The radius of the orbit as given by Eq. (27.11) is directly proportional to the speed, so doubling the particle speed causes the radius to double as well. The particle has twice as far to travel to complete one orbit but is traveling at double the speed, so the time for one orbit is unchanged. This result also follows from Eq. (27.12), which states that the angular speed ω is independent of the linear speed v. Hence the time per orbit, $T = 2\pi/\omega$, likewise does not depend on v.

27.5 Answer: (iii) From Eq. (27.13), the speed $v = E/B$ at which particles travel straight through the velocity selector does not depend on the magnitude or sign of the charge or the mass of the particle. All that is required is that the particles (in this case, ions) have a nonzero charge.

27.6 Answer: A This orientation will cause current to flow clockwise around the circuit and hence through the conducting bar in the direction from the top to the bottom of the figure. From the right-hand rule, the magnetic force $\vec{F} = I\vec{l} \times \vec{B}$ on the bar will then point to the right.

27.7 Answers: (a) to the right; (b) north pole on the right, south pole on the left If you wrap the fingers of your right hand around the coil in the direction of the current, your right thumb points to the right (perpendicular to the plane of the coil). This is the direction of the magnetic moment $\vec{\mu}$. The magnetic moment points from the south pole to the north pole, so the right side of the loop is equivalent to a north pole and the left side is equivalent to a south pole.

27.8 Answer: no The rotor will not begin to turn when the switch is closed if the rotor is initially oriented as shown in Fig. 27.39b. In this case there is no current through the rotor and hence no magnetic torque. This situation can be remedied by using multiple rotor coils oriented at different angles around the rotation axis. With this arrangement, there is always a magnetic torque no matter what the orientation.

27.9 Answer: (ii) The mobile charge carriers in copper are negatively charged electrons, which move upward through the wire to give a downward current. From the right-hand rule, the force on a positively charged particle moving upward in a westward-pointing magnetic field would be to the south; hence the force on a negatively charged particle is to the north. The result is an excess of negative charge on the north side of the wire, leaving an excess of positive charge—and hence a higher electric potential—on the south side.

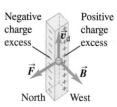

Bridging Problem

Answers: (a) $\tau_x = -1.54 \times 10^{-4} \, \text{N} \cdot \text{m},$

$\tau_y = -2.05 \times 10^{-4} \, \text{N} \cdot \text{m},$

$\tau_z = -6.14 \times 10^{-4} \, \text{N} \cdot \text{m}$

(b) $-7.55 \times 10^{-4} \, \text{J}$ (c) 42.1 rad/s

SOURCES OF MAGNETIC FIELD

? The immense cylinder in this photograph is actually a current-carrying coil, or solenoid, that generates a uniform magnetic field in its interior as part of an experiment at CERN, the European Organization for Nuclear Research. If two such solenoids were joined end to end, how much stronger would the magnetic field become?

I n Chapter 27 we studied the forces exerted on moving charges and on current-carrying conductors in a magnetic field. We didn't worry about how the magnetic field got there; we simply took its existence as a given fact. But how are magnetic fields *created*? We know that both permanent magnets and electric currents in electromagnets create magnetic fields. In this chapter we will study these sources of magnetic field in detail.

We've learned that a charge creates an electric field and that an electric field exerts a force on a charge. But a *magnetic* field exerts a force only on a *moving* charge. Is it also true that a charge *creates* a magnetic field only when the charge is moving? In a word, yes.

Our analysis will begin with the magnetic field created by a single moving point charge. We can use this analysis to determine the field created by a small segment of a current-carrying conductor. Once we can do that, we can in principle find the magnetic field produced by *any* shape of conductor.

Then we will introduce Ampere's law, which plays a role in magnetism analogous to the role of Gauss's law in electrostatics. Ampere's law lets us exploit symmetry properties in relating magnetic fields to their sources.

Moving charged particles within atoms respond to magnetic fields and can also act as sources of magnetic field. We'll use these ideas to understand how certain magnetic materials can be used to intensify magnetic fields as well as why some materials such as iron act as permanent magnets.

28.1 Magnetic Field of a Moving Charge

Let's start with the basics, the magnetic field of a single point charge q moving with a constant velocity $\vec{v}$. In practical applications, such as the solenoid shown in the photo that opens this chapter, magnetic fields are produced by tremendous

923

numbers of charged particles moving together in a current. But once we understand how to calculate the magnetic field due to a single point charge, it's a small leap to calculate the field due to a current-carrying wire or collection of wires.

As we did for electric fields, we call the location of the moving charge at a given instant the **source point** and the point P where we want to find the field the **field point.** In Section 21.4 we found that at a field point a distance r from a point charge q, the magnitude of the *electric* field $\vec{E}$ caused by the charge is proportional to the charge magnitude $|q|$ and to $1/r^2$, and the direction of $\vec{E}$ (for positive q) is along the line from source point to field point. The corresponding relationship for the *magnetic* field $\vec{B}$ of a point charge q moving with constant velocity has some similarities and some interesting differences.

Experiments show that the magnitude of $\vec{B}$ is also proportional to $|q|$ and to $1/r^2$. But the *direction* of $\vec{B}$ is *not* along the line from source point to field point. Instead, $\vec{B}$ is perpendicular to the plane containing this line and the particle's velocity vector $\vec{v}$, as shown in Fig. 28.1. Furthermore, the field *magnitude* B is also proportional to the particle's speed v and to the sine of the angle ϕ. Thus the magnetic field magnitude at point P is given by

$$ B = \frac{\mu_0}{4\pi} \frac{|q|v \sin\phi}{r^2} \tag{28.1} $$

where $\mu_0/4\pi$ is a proportionality constant (μ_0 is read as "mu-nought" or "mu-sub-zero"). The reason for writing the constant in this particular way will emerge shortly. We did something similar with Coulomb's law in Section 21.3.

Moving Charge: Vector Magnetic Field

We can incorporate both the magnitude and direction of $\vec{B}$ into a single vector equation using the vector product. To avoid having to say "the direction from the source q to the field point P" over and over, we introduce a *unit* vector $\hat{r}$ ("r-hat") that points from the source point to the field point. (We used $\hat{r}$ for the same purpose in Section 21.4.) This unit vector is equal to the vector $\vec{r}$ from the source to the field point divided by its magnitude: $\hat{r} = \vec{r}/r$. Then the $\vec{B}$ field of a moving point charge is

$$ \vec{B} = \frac{\mu_0}{4\pi} \frac{q\vec{v} \times \hat{r}}{r^2} \qquad \text{(magnetic field of a point charge with constant velocity)} \tag{28.2} $$

Figure 28.1 shows the relationship of $\hat{r}$ to P and also shows the magnetic field $\vec{B}$ at several points in the vicinity of the charge. At all points along a line through the charge parallel to the velocity $\vec{v}$, the field is zero because $\sin\phi = 0$ at all such points. At any distance r from q, $\vec{B}$ has its greatest magnitude at points lying in the plane perpendicular to $\vec{v}$, because there $\phi = 90°$ and $\sin\phi = 1$. If q is negative, the directions of $\vec{B}$ are opposite to those shown in Fig. 28.1.

Moving Charge: Magnetic Field Lines

A point charge in motion also produces an *electric* field, with field lines that radiate outward from a positive charge. The *magnetic* field lines are completely different. For a point charge moving with velocity $\vec{v}$, the magnetic field lines are *circles* centered on the line of $\vec{v}$ and lying in planes perpendicular to this line. The field-line directions for a positive charge are given by the following *right-hand rule,* one of several that we will encounter in this chapter: Grasp the velocity vector $\vec{v}$ with your right hand so that your right thumb points in the direction of $\vec{v}$; your fingers then curl around the line of $\vec{v}$ in the same sense as the magnetic field lines, assuming q is positive. Figure 28.1a shows parts of a few field lines; Fig. 28.1b shows some field lines in a plane through q, perpendicular to $\vec{v}$. If the point charge is negative, the directions of the field and field lines are the opposite of those shown in Fig. 28.1.

28.1 (a) Magnetic-field vectors due to a moving positive point charge q. At each point, $\vec{B}$ is perpendicular to the plane of $\vec{r}$ and $\vec{v}$, and its magnitude is proportional to the sine of the angle between them. (b) Magnetic field lines in a plane containing a moving positive charge.

(a) Perspective view

Right-hand rule for the magnetic field due to a positive charge moving at constant velocity: Point the thumb of your right hand in the direction of the velocity. Your fingers now curl around the charge in the direction of the magnetic field lines. (If the charge is negative, the field lines are in the opposite direction.)

For these field points, $\vec{r}$ and $\vec{v}$ both lie in the beige plane, and $\vec{B}$ is perpendicular to this plane.

For these field points, $\vec{r}$ and $\vec{v}$ both lie in the gold plane, and $\vec{B}$ is perpendicular to this plane.

(b) View from behind the charge

The × symbol indicates that the charge is moving into the plane of the page (away from you).

Equations (28.1) and (28.2) describe the $\vec{B}$ field of a point charge moving with *constant* velocity. If the charge *accelerates,* the field can be much more complicated. We won't need these more complicated results for our purposes. (The moving charged particles that make up a current in a wire accelerate at points where the wire bends and the direction of $\vec{v}$ changes. But because the magnitude v_d of the drift velocity in a conductor is typically very small, the centripetal acceleration v_d^2/r is so small that we can ignore its effects.)

As we discussed in Section 27.2, the unit of B is one tesla (1 T):

$$1\,T = 1\,N\cdot s/C\cdot m = 1\,N/A\cdot m$$

Using this with Eq. (28.1) or (28.2), we find that the units of the constant μ_0 are

$$1\,N\cdot s^2/C^2 = 1\,N/A^2 = 1\,Wb/A\cdot m = 1\,T\cdot m/A$$

In SI units the numerical value of μ_0 is exactly $4\pi \times 10^{-7}$. Thus

$$\mu_0 = 4\pi \times 10^{-7}\,N\cdot s^2/C^2 = 4\pi \times 10^{-7}\,Wb/A\cdot m$$

$$= 4\pi \times 10^{-7}\,T\cdot m/A \qquad (28.3)$$

It may seem incredible that μ_0 has *exactly* this numerical value! In fact this is a *defined* value that arises from the definition of the ampere, as we'll discuss in Section 28.4.

We mentioned in Section 21.3 that the constant $1/4\pi\epsilon_0$ in Coulomb's law is related to the speed of light c:

$$k = \frac{1}{4\pi\epsilon_0} = (10^{-7}\,N\cdot s^2/C^2)c^2$$

When we study electromagnetic waves in Chapter 32, we will find that their speed of propagation in vacuum, which is equal to the speed of light c, is given by

$$c^2 = \frac{1}{\epsilon_0\mu_0} \qquad (28.4)$$

If we solve the equation $k = 1/4\pi\epsilon_0$ for ϵ_0, substitute the resulting expression into Eq. (28.4), and solve for μ_0, we indeed get the value of μ_0 stated above. This discussion is a little premature, but it may give you a hint that electric and magnetic fields are intimately related to the nature of light.

Example 28.1 Forces between two moving protons

Two protons move parallel to the x-axis in opposite directions (Fig. 28.2) at the same speed v (small compared to the speed of light c). At the instant shown, find the electric and magnetic forces on the upper proton and compare their magnitudes.

SOLUTION

IDENTIFY and SET UP: Coulomb's law [Eq. (21.2)] gives the electric force F_E on the upper proton. The magnetic force law [Eq. (27.2)] gives the magnetic force on the upper proton; to use it, we must first use Eq. (28.2) to find the magnetic field that the lower proton produces at the position of the upper proton. The unit vector from the lower proton (the source) to the position of the upper proton is $\hat{r} = \hat{j}$.

EXECUTE: From Coulomb's law, the magnitude of the electric force on the upper proton is

$$F_E = \frac{1}{4\pi\epsilon_0}\frac{q^2}{r^2}$$

28.2 Electric and magnetic forces between two moving protons.

Continued

The forces are repulsive, and the force on the upper proton is vertically upward (in the +y-direction).

The velocity of the lower proton is $\vec{v} = v\hat{\imath}$. From the right-hand rule for the cross product $\vec{v} \times \hat{r}$ in Eq. (28.2), the $\vec{B}$ field due to the lower proton at the position of the upper proton is in the +z-direction (see Fig. 28.2). From Eq. (28.2), the field is

$$\vec{B} = \frac{\mu_0}{4\pi} \frac{q(v\hat{\imath}) \times \hat{\jmath}}{r^2} = \frac{\mu_0}{4\pi} \frac{qv}{r^2} \hat{k}$$

The velocity of the upper proton is $-\vec{v} = -v\hat{\imath}$, so the magnetic force on it is

$$\vec{F}_B = q(-\vec{v}) \times \vec{B} = q(-v\hat{\imath}) \times \frac{\mu_0}{4\pi} \frac{qv}{r^2} \hat{k} = \frac{\mu_0}{4\pi} \frac{q^2v^2}{r^2} \hat{\jmath}$$

The magnetic interaction in this situation is also repulsive. The ratio of the force magnitudes is

$$\frac{F_B}{F_E} = \frac{\mu_0 q^2 v^2 / 4\pi r^2}{q^2/4\pi\epsilon_0 r^2} = \frac{\mu_0 v^2}{1/\epsilon_0} = \epsilon_0 \mu_0 v^2$$

With the relationship $\epsilon_0 \mu_0 = 1/c^2$, Eq. (28.4), this becomes

$$\frac{F_B}{F_E} = \frac{v^2}{c^2}$$

When v is small in comparison to the speed of light, the magnetic force is much smaller than the electric force.

EVALUATE: We have described the velocities, fields, and forces as they are measured by an observer who is stationary in the coordinate system of Fig. 28.2. In a coordinate system that moves with one of the charges, one of the velocities would be zero, so there would be *no* magnetic force. The explanation of this apparent paradox provided one of the paths that led to the special theory of relativity.

Test Your Understanding of Section 28.1   (a) If two protons are traveling parallel to each other in the *same* direction and at the same speed, is the magnetic force between them (i) attractive or (ii) repulsive? (b) Is the net force between them (i) attractive, (ii) repulsive, or (iii) zero? (Assume that the protons' speed is much slower than the speed of light.)

28.2 Magnetic Field of a Current Element

Just as for the electric field, there is a **principle of superposition of magnetic fields:**

> The total magnetic field caused by several moving charges is the vector sum of the fields caused by the individual charges.

We can use this principle with the results of Section 28.1 to find the magnetic field produced by a current in a conductor.

We begin by calculating the magnetic field caused by a short segment $d\vec{l}$ of a current-carrying conductor, as shown in Fig. 28.3a. The volume of the segment is $A\,dl$, where A is the cross-sectional area of the conductor. If there are n moving charged particles per unit volume, each of charge q, the total moving charge dQ in the segment is

$$dQ = nqA\,dl$$

The moving charges in this segment are equivalent to a single charge dQ, traveling with a velocity equal to the *drift* velocity $\vec{v}_d$. (Magnetic fields due to the *random* motions of the charges will, on average, cancel out at every point.) From Eq. (28.1) the magnitude of the resulting field $d\vec{B}$ at any field point P is

$$dB = \frac{\mu_0}{4\pi} \frac{|dQ| v_d \sin\phi}{r^2} = \frac{\mu_0}{4\pi} \frac{n|q| v_d A\,dl \sin\phi}{r^2}$$

But from Eq. (25.2), $n|q| v_d A$ equals the current I in the element. So

$$dB = \frac{\mu_0}{4\pi} \frac{I\,dl \sin\phi}{r^2} \qquad (28.5)$$

Current Element: Vector Magnetic Field

In vector form, using the unit vector $\hat{r}$ as in Section 28.1, we have

$$d\vec{B} = \frac{\mu_0}{4\pi} \frac{I\,d\vec{l} \times \hat{r}}{r^2} \qquad \text{(magnetic field of a current element)} \qquad (28.6)$$

28.3 (a) Magnetic-field vectors due to a current element $d\vec{l}$. (b) Magnetic field lines in a plane containing the current element $d\vec{l}$. Compare this figure to Fig. 28.1 for the field of a moving point charge.

(a) Perspective view

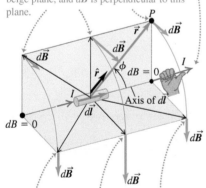

Right-hand rule for the magnetic field due to a current element: Point the thumb of your right hand in the direction of the current. Your fingers now curl around the current element in the direction of the magnetic field lines.

For these field points, $\vec{r}$ and $d\vec{l}$ both lie in the beige plane, and $d\vec{B}$ is perpendicular to this plane.

For these field points, $\vec{r}$ and $d\vec{l}$ both lie in the gold plane, and $d\vec{B}$ is perpendicular to this plane.

(b) View along the axis of the current element

Current directed into the plane of the page

where $d\vec{l}$ is a vector with length dl, in the same direction as the current in the conductor.

Equations (28.5) and (28.6) are called the **law of Biot and Savart** (pronounced "Bee-oh" and "Suh-var"). We can use this law to find the total magnetic field $\vec{B}$ at any point in space due to the current in a complete circuit. To do this, we integrate Eq. (28.6) over all segments $d\vec{l}$ that carry current; symbolically,

$$\vec{B} = \frac{\mu_0}{4\pi} \int \frac{I\, d\vec{l} \times \hat{r}}{r^2} \qquad (28.7)$$

In the following sections we will carry out this vector integration for several examples.

Current Element: Magnetic Field Lines

As Fig. 28.3 shows, the field vectors $d\vec{B}$ and the magnetic field lines of a current element are exactly like those set up by a positive charge dQ moving in the direction of the drift velocity $\vec{v}_d$. The field lines are circles in planes perpendicular to $d\vec{l}$ and centered on the line of $d\vec{l}$. Their directions are given by the same right-hand rule that we introduced for point charges in Section 28.1.

We can't verify Eq. (28.5) or (28.6) directly because we can never experiment with an isolated segment of a current-carrying circuit. What we measure experimentally is the *total* $\vec{B}$ for a complete circuit. But we can still verify these equations indirectly by calculating $\vec{B}$ for various current configurations using Eq. (28.7) and comparing the results with experimental measurements.

If matter is present in the space around a current-carrying conductor, the field at a field point P in its vicinity will have an additional contribution resulting from the *magnetization* of the material. We'll return to this point in Section 28.8. However, unless the material is iron or some other ferromagnetic material, the additional field is small and is usually negligible. Additional complications arise if time-varying electric or magnetic fields are present or if the material is a superconductor; we'll return to these topics later.

Problem-Solving Strategy 28.1   **Magnetic-Field Calculations**

IDENTIFY *the relevant concepts:* The Biot–Savart law [Eqs. (28.5) and (28.6)] allows you to calculate the magnetic field at a field point P due to a current-carrying wire of any shape. The idea is to calculate the field element $d\vec{B}$ at P due to a representative current element in the wire and integrate all such field elements to find the field $\vec{B}$ at P.

SET UP *the problem* using the following steps:
1. Make a diagram showing a representative current element and the field point P.
2. Draw the current element $d\vec{l}$, being careful that it points in the direction of the current.
3. Draw the unit vector $\hat{r}$ directed *from* the current element (the source point) to P.
4. Identify the target variable (usually $\vec{B}$).

EXECUTE *the solution* as follows:
1. Use Eq. (28.5) or (28.6) to express the magnetic field $d\vec{B}$ at P from the representative current element.
2. Add up all the $d\vec{B}$'s to find the total field at point P. In some situations the $d\vec{B}$'s at point P have the same direction for all the current elements; then the magnitude of the total $\vec{B}$ field is the

sum of the magnitudes of the $d\vec{B}$'s. But often the $d\vec{B}$'s have different directions for different current elements. Then you have to set up a coordinate system and represent each $d\vec{B}$ in terms of its components. The integral for the total $\vec{B}$ is then expressed in terms of an integral for each component.
3. Sometimes you can use the symmetry of the situation to prove that one component of $\vec{B}$ must vanish. Always be alert for ways to use symmetry to simplify the problem.
4. Look for ways to use the principle of superposition of magnetic fields. Later in this chapter we'll determine the fields produced by certain simple conductor shapes; if you encounter a conductor of a complex shape that can be represented as a combination of these simple shapes, you can use superposition to find the field of the complex shape. Examples include a rectangular loop and a semicircle with straight line segments on both sides.

EVALUATE *your answer:* Often your answer will be a mathematical expression for $\vec{B}$ as a function of the position of the field point. Check the answer by examining its behavior in as many limits as you can.

Example 28.2   Magnetic field of a current segment

A copper wire carries a steady 125-A current to an electroplating tank (Fig. 28.4). Find the magnetic field due to a 1.0-cm segment of this wire at a point 1.2 m away from it, if the point is (a) point P_1, straight out to the side of the segment, and (b) point P_2, in the xy-plane and on a line at 30° to the segment.

SOLUTION

IDENTIFY and SET UP: Although Eqs. (28.5) and (28.6) apply only to infinitesimal current elements, we may use either of them here because the segment length is much less than the distance to the field point. The current element is shown in red in Fig. 28.4 and points in the $-x$-direction (the direction of the current), so $d\vec{l} = dl(-\hat{i})$. The unit vector $\hat{r}$ for each field point is directed from the current element toward that point: $\hat{r}$ is in the $+y$-direction for point P_1 and at an angle of 30° above the $-x$-direction for point P_2.

28.4 Finding the magnetic field at two points due to a 1.0-cm segment of current-carrying wire (not shown to scale).

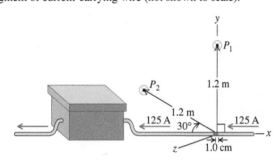

EXECUTE: (a) At point P_1, $\hat{r} = \hat{j}$, so

$$\vec{B} = \frac{\mu_0}{4\pi}\frac{I\,d\vec{l} \times \hat{r}}{r^2} = \frac{\mu_0}{4\pi}\frac{I\,dl(-\hat{i}) \times \hat{j}}{r^2} = -\frac{\mu_0}{4\pi}\frac{I\,dl}{r^2}\hat{k}$$

$$= -(10^{-7}\,\text{T}\cdot\text{m/A})\frac{(125\,\text{A})(1.0 \times 10^{-2}\,\text{m})}{(1.2\,\text{m})^2}\hat{k}$$

$$= -(8.7 \times 10^{-8}\,\text{T})\hat{k}$$

The direction of $\vec{B}$ at P_1 is into the xy-plane of Fig. 28.4.

(b) At P_2, the unit vector is $\hat{r} = (-\cos 30°)\hat{i} + (\sin 30°)\hat{j}$. From Eq. (28.6),

$$\vec{B} = \frac{\mu_0}{4\pi}\frac{I\,d\vec{l} \times \hat{r}}{r^2} = \frac{\mu_0}{4\pi}\frac{I\,dl(-\hat{i}) \times (-\cos 30°\hat{i} + \sin 30°\hat{j})}{r^2}$$

$$= -\frac{\mu_0 I}{4\pi}\frac{dl\sin 30°}{r^2}\hat{k}$$

$$= -(10^{-7}\,\text{T}\cdot\text{m/A})\frac{(125\,\text{A})(1.0 \times 10^{-2}\,\text{m})(\sin 30°)}{(1.2\,\text{m})^2}\hat{k}$$

$$= -(4.3 \times 10^{-8}\,\text{T})\hat{k}$$

The direction of $\vec{B}$ at P_2 is also into the xy-plane of Fig. 28.4.

EVALUATE: We can check our results for the direction of $\vec{B}$ by comparing them with Fig. 28.3. The xy-plane in Fig. 28.4 corresponds to the beige plane in Fig. 28.3, but here the direction of the current and hence of $d\vec{l}$ is the reverse of that shown in Fig. 28.3. Hence the direction of the magnetic field is reversed as well. Hence the field at points in the xy-plane in Fig. 28.4 must point *into*, not out of, that plane. This is just what we concluded above.

Test Your Understanding of Section 28.2 An infinitesimal current element located at the origin ($x = y = z = 0$) carries current I in the positive y-direction. Rank the following locations in order of the strength of the magnetic field that the current element produces at that location, from largest to smallest value. (i) $x = L, y = 0, z = 0$; (ii) $x = 0, y = L, z = 0$; (iii) $x = 0, y = 0, z = L$; (iv) $x = L/\sqrt{2}, y = L/\sqrt{2}, z = 0$. ❙

28.5 Magnetic field produced by a straight current-carrying conductor of length $2a$.

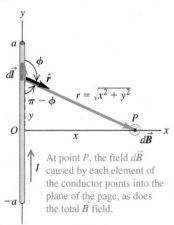

At point P, the field $d\vec{B}$ caused by each element of the conductor points into the plane of the page, as does the total B field.

28.3 Magnetic Field of a Straight Current-Carrying Conductor

Let's use the law of Biot and Savart to find the magnetic field produced by a straight current-carrying conductor. This result is useful because straight conducting wires are found in essentially all electric and electronic devices. Figure 28.5 shows such a conductor with length $2a$ carrying a current I. We will find $\vec{B}$ at a point a distance x from the conductor on its perpendicular bisector.

We first use the law of Biot and Savart, Eq. (28.5), to find the field $d\vec{B}$ caused by the element of conductor of length $dl = dy$ shown in Fig. 28.5. From the figure, $r = \sqrt{x^2 + y^2}$ and $\sin\phi = \sin(\pi - \phi) = x/\sqrt{x^2 + y^2}$. The right-hand rule for the vector product $d\vec{l} \times \hat{r}$ shows that the *direction* of $d\vec{B}$ is into the plane of the figure, perpendicular to the plane; furthermore, the directions of the $d\vec{B}$'s from *all* elements of the conductor are the same. Thus in integrating Eq. (28.7), we can just add the *magnitudes* of the $d\vec{B}$'s, a significant simplification.

Putting the pieces together, we find that the magnitude of the total $\vec{B}$ field is

$$B = \frac{\mu_0 I}{4\pi} \int_{-a}^{a} \frac{x\,dy}{(x^2 + y^2)^{3/2}}$$

We can integrate this by trigonometric substitution or by using an integral table:

$$B = \frac{\mu_0 I}{4\pi} \frac{2a}{x\sqrt{x^2 + a^2}} \qquad (28.8)$$

When the length $2a$ of the conductor is very great in comparison to its distance x from point P, we can consider it to be infinitely long. When a is much larger than x, $\sqrt{x^2 + a^2}$ is approximately equal to a; hence in the limit $a \to \infty$, Eq. (28.8) becomes

$$B = \frac{\mu_0 I}{2\pi x}$$

The physical situation has axial symmetry about the y-axis. Hence $\vec{B}$ must have the same *magnitude* at all points on a circle centered on the conductor and lying in a plane perpendicular to it, and the *direction* of $\vec{B}$ must be everywhere tangent to such a circle (Fig. 28.6). Thus, at all points on a circle of radius r around the conductor, the magnitude B is

$$B = \frac{\mu_0 I}{2\pi r} \qquad \text{(near a long, straight, current-carrying conductor)} \quad (28.9)$$

The geometry of this problem is similar to that of Example 21.10 (Section 21.5), in which we solved the problem of the *electric* field caused by an infinite line of charge. The same integral appears in both problems, and the field magnitudes in both problems are proportional to $1/r$. But the lines of $\vec{B}$ in the magnetic problem have completely different shapes than the lines of $\vec{E}$ in the analogous electrical problem. Electric field lines radiate outward from a positive line charge distribution (inward for negative charges). By contrast, magnetic field lines *encircle* the current that acts as their source. Electric field lines due to charges begin and end at those charges, but magnetic field lines always form closed loops and *never* have end points, irrespective of the shape of the current-carrying conductor that sets up the field. As we discussed in Section 27.3, this is a consequence of Gauss's law for magnetism, which states that the total magnetic flux through *any* closed surface is always zero:

$$\oint \vec{B} \cdot d\vec{A} = 0 \qquad \text{(magnetic flux through any closed surface)} \quad (28.10)$$

Any magnetic field line that enters a closed surface must also emerge from that surface.

28.6 Magnetic field around a long, straight, current-carrying conductor. The field lines are circles, with directions determined by the right-hand rule.

Right-hand rule for the magnetic field around a current-carrying wire: Point the thumb of your right hand in the direction of the current. Your fingers now curl around the wire in the direction of the magnetic field lines.

ActivPhysics 13.1: Magnetic Field of a Wire

Example 28.3   Magnetic field of a single wire

A long, straight conductor carries a 1.0-A current. At what distance from the axis of the conductor does the resulting magnetic field have magnitude $B = 0.5 \times 10^{-4}$ T (about that of the earth's magnetic field in Pittsburgh)?

SOLUTION

IDENTIFY and SET UP: The length of a "long" conductor is much greater than the distance from the conductor to the field point. Hence we can use the ideas of this section. The geometry is the same as that of Fig. 28.6, so we use Eq. (28.9). All of the quantities in this equation are known except the target variable, the distance r.

EXECUTE: We solve Eq. (28.9) for r:

$$r = \frac{\mu_0 I}{2\pi B} = \frac{(4\pi \times 10^{-7}\,\text{T}\cdot\text{m/A})(1.0\,\text{A})}{(2\pi)(0.5 \times 10^{-4}\,\text{T})}$$

$$= 4 \times 10^{-3}\,\text{m} = 4\,\text{mm}$$

EVALUATE: As we saw in Example 26.14, currents of an ampere or more are typical of those found in the wiring of home appliances. This example shows that the magnetic fields produced by these appliances are very weak even very close to the wire; the fields are proportional to $1/r$, so they become even weaker at greater distances.

Example 28.4 | **Magnetic field of two wires**

Figure 28.7a is an end-on view of two long, straight, parallel wires perpendicular to the xy-plane, each carrying a current I but in opposite directions. (a) Find $\vec{B}$ at points P_1, P_2, and P_3. (b) Find an expression for $\vec{B}$ at any point on the x-axis to the right of wire 2.

SOLUTION

IDENTIFY and SET UP: We can find the magnetic fields $\vec{B}_1$ and $\vec{B}_2$ due to wires 1 and 2 at each point using the ideas of this section. By the superposition principle, the magnetic field at each point is then $\vec{B} = \vec{B}_1 + \vec{B}_2$. We use Eq. (28.9) to find the magnitudes B_1 and B_2 of these fields and the right-hand rule to find the corresponding directions. Figure 28.7a shows $\vec{B}_1$, $\vec{B}_2$, and $\vec{B} = \vec{B}_{\text{total}}$ at each point; you should confirm that the directions and relative magnitudes shown are correct. Figure 28.7b shows some of the magnetic field lines due to this two-wire system.

EXECUTE: (a) Since point P_1 is a distance $2d$ from wire 1 and a distance $4d$ from wire 2, $B_1 = \mu_0 I/2\pi(2d) = \mu_0 I/4\pi d$ and $B_2 = \mu_0 I/2\pi(4d) = \mu_0 I/8\pi d$. The right-hand rule shows that $\vec{B}_1$ is in the negative y-direction and $\vec{B}_2$ is in the positive y-direction, so

$$\vec{B}_{\text{total}} = \vec{B}_1 + \vec{B}_2 = -\frac{\mu_0 I}{4\pi d}\hat{\boldsymbol{j}} + \frac{\mu_0 I}{8\pi d}\hat{\boldsymbol{j}} = -\frac{\mu_0 I}{8\pi d}\hat{\boldsymbol{j}} \quad \text{(point } P_1)$$

At point P_2, a distance d from both wires, $\vec{B}_1$ and $\vec{B}_2$ are both in the positive y-direction, and both have the same magnitude $B_1 = B_2 = \mu_0 I/2\pi d$. Hence

$$\vec{B}_{\text{total}} = \vec{B}_1 + \vec{B}_2 = \frac{\mu_0 I}{2\pi d}\hat{\boldsymbol{j}} + \frac{\mu_0 I}{2\pi d}\hat{\boldsymbol{j}} = \frac{\mu_0 I}{\pi d}\hat{\boldsymbol{j}} \quad \text{(point } P_2)$$

Finally, at point P_3 the right-hand rule shows that $\vec{B}_1$ is in the positive y-direction and $\vec{B}_2$ is in the negative y-direction. This point is a distance $3d$ from wire 1 and a distance d from wire 2, so $B_1 = \mu_0 I/2\pi(3d) = \mu_0 I/6\pi d$ and $B_2 = \mu_0 I/2\pi d$. The total field at P_3 is

$$\vec{B}_{\text{total}} = \vec{B}_1 + \vec{B}_2 = \frac{\mu_0 I}{6\pi d}\hat{\boldsymbol{j}} - \frac{\mu_0 I}{2\pi d}\hat{\boldsymbol{j}} = -\frac{\mu_0 I}{3\pi d}\hat{\boldsymbol{j}} \quad \text{(point } P_3)$$

The same technique can be used to find $\vec{B}_{\text{total}}$ at any point; for points off the x-axis, caution must be taken in vector addition, since $\vec{B}_1$ and $\vec{B}_2$ need no longer be simply parallel or antiparallel.

(b) At any point on the x-axis to the right of wire 2 (that is, for $x > d$), $\vec{B}_1$ and $\vec{B}_2$ are in the same directions as at P_3. Such a point is a distance $x + d$ from wire 1 and a distance $x - d$ from wire 2, so the total field is

$$\vec{B}_{\text{total}} = \vec{B}_1 + \vec{B}_2 = \frac{\mu_0 I}{2\pi(x + d)}\hat{\boldsymbol{j}} - \frac{\mu_0 I}{2\pi(x - d)}\hat{\boldsymbol{j}}$$
$$= -\frac{\mu_0 I d}{\pi(x^2 - d^2)}\hat{\boldsymbol{j}}$$

where we combined the two terms using a common denominator.

EVALUATE: Consider our result from part (b) at a point very far from the wires, so that x is much larger than d. Then the d^2 term in the denominator can be neglected, and the magnitude of the total field is approximately $B_{\text{total}} = \mu_0 I d/\pi x^2$. For a single wire, Eq. (28.9) shows that the magnetic field decreases with distance in proportion to $1/x$; for two wires carrying opposite currents, $\vec{B}_1$ and $\vec{B}_2$ partially cancel each other, and so B_{total} decreases more rapidly, in proportion to $1/x^2$. This effect is used in communication systems such as telephone or computer networks. The wiring is arranged so that a conductor carrying a signal in one direction and the conductor carrying the return signal are side by side, as in Fig. 28.7a, or twisted around each other (Fig. 28.8). As a result, the magnetic field due to these signals *outside* the conductors is very small, making it less likely to exert unwanted forces on other information-carrying currents.

28.8 Computer cables, or cables for audio-video equipment, create little or no magnetic field. This is because within each cable, closely spaced wires carry current in both directions along the length of the cable. The magnetic fields from these opposing currents cancel each other.

28.7 (a) Two long, straight conductors carrying equal currents in opposite directions. The conductors are seen end-on. (b) Map of the magnetic field produced by the two conductors. The field lines are closest together between the conductors, where the field is strongest.

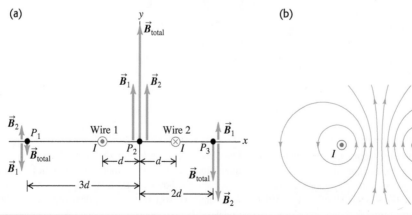

Test Your Understanding of Section 28.3 The figure at right shows a circuit that lies on a horizontal table. A compass is placed on top of the circuit as shown. A battery is to be connected to the circuit so that when the switch is closed, the compass needle deflects counterclockwise. In which orientation, A or B, should the battery be placed in the circuit?

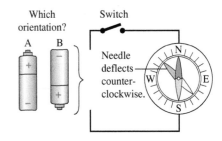

28.4 Force Between Parallel Conductors

In Example 28.4 (Section 28.3) we showed how to use the principle of superposition of magnetic fields to find the total field due to two long current-carrying conductors. Another important aspect of this configuration is the *interaction force* between the conductors. This force plays a role in many practical situations in which current-carrying wires are close to each other. Figure 28.9 shows segments of two long, straight, parallel conductors separated by a distance r and carrying currents I and I' in the same direction. Each conductor lies in the magnetic field set up by the other, so each experiences a force. The figure shows some of the field lines set up by the current in the lower conductor.

From Eq. (28.9) the lower conductor produces a $\vec{B}$ field that, at the position of the upper conductor, has magnitude

$$B = \frac{\mu_0 I}{2\pi r}$$

From Eq. (27.19) the force that this field exerts on a length L of the upper conductor is $\vec{F} = I'\vec{L} \times \vec{B}$, where the vector $\vec{L}$ is in the direction of the current I' and has magnitude L. Since $\vec{B}$ is perpendicular to the length of the conductor and hence to $\vec{L}$, the magnitude of this force is

$$F = I'LB = \frac{\mu_0 II'L}{2\pi r}$$

and the force *per unit length F/L* is

$$\frac{F}{L} = \frac{\mu_0 II'}{2\pi r} \quad \text{(two long, parallel, current-carrying conductors)} \quad (28.11)$$

Applying the right-hand rule to $\vec{F} = I'\vec{L} \times \vec{B}$ shows that the force on the upper conductor is directed *downward*.

The current in the *upper* conductor also sets up a field at the position of the *lower* one. Two successive applications of the right-hand rule for vector products (one to find the direction of the $\vec{B}$ field due to the upper conductor, as in Section 28.2, and one to find the direction of the force that this field exerts on the lower conductor, as in Section 27.6) show that the force on the lower conductor is *upward*. Thus *two parallel conductors carrying current in the same direction attract each other*. If the direction of either current is reversed, the forces also reverse. *Parallel conductors carrying currents in opposite directions repel each other.*

Magnetic Forces and Defining the Ampere

The attraction or repulsion between two straight, parallel, current-carrying conductors is the basis of the official SI definition of the **ampere:**

> **One ampere** is that unvarying current that, if present in each of two parallel conductors of infinite length and one meter apart in empty space, causes each conductor to experience a force of exactly 2×10^{-7} newtons per meter of length.

From Eq. (28.11) you can see that this definition of the ampere is what leads us to choose the value of $4\pi \times 10^{-7}$ T·m/A for μ_0. It also forms the basis of the SI

28.9 Parallel conductors carrying currents in the same direction attract each other. The diagrams show how the magnetic field $\vec{B}$ caused by the current in the lower conductor exerts a force $\vec{F}$ on the upper conductor.

The magnetic field of the lower wire exerts an attractive force on the upper wire. By the same token, the upper wire attracts the lower one.

If the wires had currents in *opposite* directions, they would *repel* each other.

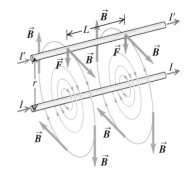

definition of the coulomb, which is the amount of charge transferred in one second by a current of one ampere.

This is an *operational definition;* it gives us an actual experimental procedure for measuring current and defining a unit of current. For high-precision standardization of the ampere, coils of wire are used instead of straight wires, and their separation is only a few centimeters. Even more precise measurements of the standardized ampere are possible using a version of the Hall effect (see Section 27.9).

Mutual forces of attraction exist not only between *wires* carrying currents in the same direction, but also between the longitudinal elements of a single current-carrying conductor. If the conductor is a liquid or an ionized gas (a plasma), these forces result in a constriction of the conductor. This is called the *pinch effect*. The high temperature produced by the pinch effect in a plasma has been used in one technique to bring about nuclear fusion.

Example 28.5 | **Forces between parallel wires**

Two straight, parallel, superconducting wires 4.5 mm apart carry equal currents of 15,000 A in opposite directions. What force, per unit length, does each wire exert on the other?

SOLUTION

IDENTIFY and SET UP: Figure 28.10 shows the situation. We find F/L, the magnetic force per unit length of wire, using Eq. (28.11).

28.10 Our sketch for this problem.

$I = 15,000\ A$

L

$r = 4.5\ mm$

$I' = 15,000\ A$

EXECUTE: The conductors *repel* each other because the currents are in opposite directions. From Eq. (28.11) the force per unit length is

$$\frac{F}{L} = \frac{\mu_0 II'}{2\pi r} = \frac{(4\pi \times 10^{-7}\ \text{T} \cdot \text{m/A})(15{,}000\ \text{A})^2}{(2\pi)(4.5 \times 10^{-3}\ \text{m})}$$

$$= 1.0 \times 10^4\ \text{N/m}$$

EVALUATE: This is a large force, more than one ton per meter. Currents and separations of this magnitude are used in superconducting electromagnets in particle accelerators, and mechanical stress analysis is a crucial part of the design process.

28.11 This electromagnet contains a current-carrying coil with numerous turns of wire. The resulting magnetic field can pick up large quantities of steel bars and other iron-bearing items.

Test Your Understanding of Section 28.4 A solenoid is a wire wound into a helical coil. The figure at left shows a solenoid that carries a current I. (a) Is the *magnetic* force that one turn of the coil exerts on an adjacent turn (i) attractive, (ii) repulsive, or (iii) zero? (b) Is the *electric* force that one turn of the coil exerts on an adjacent turn (i) attractive, (ii) repulsive, or (iii) zero? (c) Is the *magnetic* force between opposite sides of the same turn of the coil (i) attractive, (ii) repulsive, or (iii) zero? (d) Is the *electric* force between opposite sides of the same turn of the coil (i) attractive, (ii) repulsive, or (iii) zero?

28.5 Magnetic Field of a Circular Current Loop

If you look inside a doorbell, a transformer, an electric motor, or an electromagnet (Fig. 28.11), you will find coils of wire with a large number of turns, spaced so closely that each turn is very nearly a planar circular loop. A current in such a coil is used to establish a magnetic field. So it is worthwhile to derive an expression for the magnetic field produced by a single circular conducting loop carrying a current or by N closely spaced circular loops forming a coil. In Section 27.7 we considered the force and torque on such a current loop placed in an external magnetic field produced by other currents; we are now about to find the magnetic field produced by the loop itself.

Figure 28.12 shows a circular conductor with radius a. A current I is led into and out of the loop through two long, straight wires side by side; the currents in these straight wires are in opposite directions, and their magnetic fields very nearly cancel each other (see Example 28.4 in Section 28.3).

We can use the law of Biot and Savart, Eq. (28.5) or (28.6), to find the magnetic field at a point P on the axis of the loop, at a distance x from the center. As the figure shows, $d\vec{l}$ and $\hat{r}$ are perpendicular, and the direction of the field $d\vec{B}$ caused by this particular element $d\vec{l}$ lies in the xy-plane. Since $r^2 = x^2 + a^2$, the magnitude dB of the field due to element $d\vec{l}$ is

$$dB = \frac{\mu_0 I}{4\pi} \frac{dl}{(x^2 + a^2)} \qquad (28.12)$$

The components of the vector $d\vec{B}$ are

$$dB_x = dB\cos\theta = \frac{\mu_0 I}{4\pi} \frac{dl}{(x^2 + a^2)} \frac{a}{(x^2 + a^2)^{1/2}} \qquad (28.13)$$

$$dB_y = dB\sin\theta = \frac{\mu_0 I}{4\pi} \frac{dl}{(x^2 + a^2)} \frac{x}{(x^2 + a^2)^{1/2}} \qquad (28.14)$$

The *total* field $\vec{B}$ at P has only an x-component (it is perpendicular to the plane of the loop). Here's why: For every element $d\vec{l}$ there is a corresponding element on the opposite side of the loop, with opposite direction. These two elements give equal contributions to the x-component of $d\vec{B}$, given by Eq. (28.13), but *opposite* components perpendicular to the x-axis. Thus all the perpendicular components cancel and only the x-components survive.

To obtain the x-component of the total field $\vec{B}$, we integrate Eq. (28.13), including all the $d\vec{l}$'s around the loop. Everything in this expression except dl is constant and can be taken outside the integral, and we have

$$B_x = \int \frac{\mu_0 I}{4\pi} \frac{a\, dl}{(x^2 + a^2)^{3/2}} = \frac{\mu_0 Ia}{4\pi(x^2 + a^2)^{3/2}} \int dl$$

The integral of dl is just the circumference of the circle, $\int dl = 2\pi a$, and we finally get

$$B_x = \frac{\mu_0 Ia^2}{2(x^2 + a^2)^{3/2}} \qquad \text{(on the axis of a circular loop)} \qquad (28.15)$$

The *direction* of the magnetic field on the axis of a current-carrying loop is given by a right-hand rule. If you curl the fingers of your right hand around the loop in the direction of the current, your right thumb points in the direction of the field (Fig. 28.13).

Magnetic Field on the Axis of a Coil

Now suppose that instead of the single loop in Fig. 28.12 we have a coil consisting of N loops, all with the same radius. The loops are closely spaced so that the plane of each loop is essentially the same distance x from the field point P. Then the total field is N times the field of a single loop:

$$B_x = \frac{\mu_0 NIa^2}{2(x^2 + a^2)^{3/2}} \qquad \text{(on the axis of } N \text{ circular loops)} \qquad (28.16)$$

The factor N in Eq. (28.16) is the reason coils of wire, not single loops, are used to produce strong magnetic fields; for a desired field strength, using a single loop might require a current I so great as to exceed the rating of the loop's wire.

Figure 28.14 shows a graph of B_x as a function of x. The maximum value of the field is at $x = 0$, the center of the loop or coil:

$$B_x = \frac{\mu_0 NI}{2a} \qquad \text{(at the center of } N \text{ circular loops)} \qquad (28.17)$$

As we go out along the axis, the field decreases in magnitude.

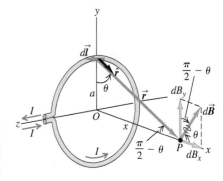

28.12 Magnetic field on the axis of a circular loop. The current in the segment $d\vec{l}$ causes the field $d\vec{B}$, which lies in the xy-plane. The currents in other $d\vec{l}$'s cause $d\vec{B}$'s with different components perpendicular to the x-axis; these components add to zero. The x-components of the $d\vec{B}$'s combine to give the total $\vec{B}$ field at point P.

PhET: Faraday's Electromagnetic Lab
PhET: Magnets and Electromagnets
ActivPhysics 13.2: Magnetic Field of a Loop

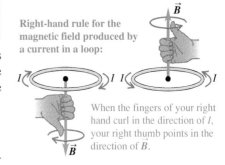

28.13 The right-hand rule for the direction of the magnetic field produced on the axis of a current-carrying coil.

Right-hand rule for the magnetic field produced by a current in a loop:

When the fingers of your right hand curl in the direction of I, your right thumb points in the direction of $\vec{B}$.

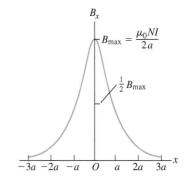

28.14 Graph of the magnetic field along the axis of a circular coil with N turns. When x is much larger than a, the field magnitude decreases approximately as $1/x^3$.

28.15 Magnetic field lines produced by the current in a circular loop. At points on the axis the $\vec{B}$ field has the same direction as the magnetic moment of the loop.

In Section 27.7 we defined the *magnetic dipole moment* μ (or *magnetic moment*) of a current-carrying loop to be equal to IA, where A is the cross-sectional area of the loop. If there are N loops, the total magnetic moment is NIA. The circular loop in Fig. 28.12 has area $A = \pi a^2$, so the magnetic moment of a single loop is $\mu = I\pi a^2$; for N loops, $\mu = NI\pi a^2$. Substituting these results into Eqs. (28.15) and (28.16), we find that both of these expressions can be written as

$$B_x = \frac{\mu_0\mu}{2\pi(x^2 + a^2)^{3/2}} \qquad \text{(on the axis of any number of circular loops)} \qquad (28.18)$$

We described a magnetic dipole in Section 27.7 in terms of its response to a magnetic field produced by currents outside the dipole. But a magnetic dipole is also a *source* of magnetic field; Eq. (28.18) describes the magnetic field *produced* by a magnetic dipole for points along the dipole axis. This field is directly proportional to the magnetic dipole moment μ. Note that the field along the x-axis is in the same direction as the vector magnetic moment $\vec{\mu}$; this is true on both the positive and negative x-axis.

CAUTION **Magnetic field of a coil** Equations (28.15), (28.16), and (28.18) are valid only on the *axis* of a loop or coil. Don't attempt to apply these equations at other points! ▌

Figure 28.15 shows some of the magnetic field lines surrounding a circular current loop (magnetic dipole) in planes through the axis. The directions of the field lines are given by the same right-hand rule as for a long, straight conductor. Grab the conductor with your right hand, with your thumb in the direction of the current; your fingers curl around in the same direction as the field lines. The field lines for the circular current loop are closed curves that encircle the conductor; they are *not* circles, however.

Example 28.6 **Magnetic field of a coil**

A coil consisting of 100 circular loops with radius 0.60 m carries a 5.0-A current. (a) Find the magnetic field at a point along the axis of the coil, 0.80 m from the center. (b) Along the axis, at what distance from the center of the coil is the field magnitude $\frac{1}{8}$ as great as it is at the center?

SOLUTION

IDENTIFY and SET UP: This problem concerns the magnetic field magnitude B along the axis of a current-carrying coil, so we can use the ideas of this section, and in particular Eq. (28.16). We are given $N = 100$, $I = 5.0$ A, and $a = 0.60$ m. In part (a) our target variable is B_x at a given value of x. In part (b) the target variable is the value of x at which the field has $\frac{1}{8}$ of the magnitude that it has at the origin.

EXECUTE: (a) Using $x = 0.80$ m, from Eq. (28.16) we have

$$B_x = \frac{(4\pi \times 10^{-7}\,\text{T}\cdot\text{m/A})(100)(5.0\,\text{A})(0.60\,\text{m})^2}{2[(0.80\,\text{m})^2 + (0.60\,\text{m})^2]^{3/2}}$$

$$= 1.1 \times 10^{-4}\,\text{T}$$

(b) Considering Eq. (28.16), we want to find a value of x such that

$$\frac{1}{(x^2 + a^2)^{3/2}} = \frac{1}{8}\frac{1}{(0^2 + a^2)^{3/2}}$$

To solve this for x, we take the reciprocal of the whole thing and then take the 2/3 power of both sides; the result is

$$x = \pm\sqrt{3}a = \pm 1.04\,\text{m}$$

EVALUATE: We check our answer in part (a) by finding the coil's magnetic moment and substituting the result into Eq. (28.18):

$$\mu = NI\pi a^2 = (100)(5.0\,\text{A})\pi(0.60\,\text{m})^2 = 5.7 \times 10^2\,\text{A}\cdot\text{m}^2$$

$$B_x = \frac{(4\pi \times 10^{-7}\,\text{T}\cdot\text{m/A})(5.7 \times 10^2\,\text{A}\cdot\text{m}^2)}{2\pi[(0.80\,\text{m})^2 + (0.60\,\text{m})^2]^{3/2}} = 1.1 \times 10^{-4}\,\text{T}$$

The magnetic moment μ is relatively large, yet it produces a rather small field, comparable to that of the earth. This illustrates how difficult it is to produce strong fields of 1 T or more.

Test Your Understanding of Section 28.5 Figure 28.12 shows the magnetic field $d\vec{B}$ produced at point P by a segment $d\vec{l}$ that lies on the positive y-axis (at the top of the loop). This field has components $dB_x > 0$, $dB_y > 0$, $dB_z = 0$. (a) What are the signs of the components of the field $d\vec{B}$ produced at P by a segment $d\vec{l}$ on the negative y-axis (at the bottom of the loop)? (i) $dB_x > 0$, $dB_y > 0$, $dB_z = 0$; (ii) $dB_x > 0$, $dB_y < 0$, $dB_z = 0$; (iii) $dB_x < 0$, $dB_y > 0$, $dB_z = 0$; (iv) $dB_x < 0$, $dB_y < 0$, $dB_z = 0$; (v) none of these. (b) What are the signs of the components of the field $d\vec{B}$ produced at P by a segment $d\vec{l}$ on the negative z-axis (at the right-hand side of the loop)? (i) $dB_x > 0$, $dB_y > 0$, $dB_z = 0$; (ii) $dB_x > 0$, $dB_y < 0$, $dB_z = 0$; (iii) $dB_x < 0$, $dB_y > 0$, $dB_z = 0$; (iv) $dB_x < 0$, $dB_y < 0$, $dB_z = 0$; (v) none of these.

28.6 Ampere's Law

So far our calculations of the magnetic field due to a current have involved finding the infinitesimal field $d\vec{B}$ due to a current element and then summing all the $d\vec{B}$'s to find the total field. This approach is directly analogous to our *electric-field* calculations in Chapter 21.

For the electric-field problem we found that in situations with a highly symmetric charge distribution, it was often easier to use Gauss's law to find $\vec{E}$. There is likewise a law that allows us to more easily find the *magnetic* fields caused by highly symmetric *current* distributions. But the law that allows us to do this, called *Ampere's law,* is rather different in character from Gauss's law.

Gauss's law for electric fields involves the flux of $\vec{E}$ through a closed surface; it states that this flux is equal to the total charge enclosed within the surface, divided by the constant ϵ_0. Thus this law relates electric fields and charge distributions. By contrast, Gauss's law for *magnetic* fields, Eq. (28.10), is *not* a relationship between magnetic fields and current distributions; it states that the flux of $\vec{B}$ through *any* closed surface is always zero, whether or not there are currents within the surface. So Gauss's law for $\vec{B}$ can't be used to determine the magnetic field produced by a particular current distribution.

Ampere's law is formulated not in terms of magnetic flux, but rather in terms of the *line integral* of $\vec{B}$ around a closed path, denoted by

$$\oint \vec{B} \cdot d\vec{l}$$

We used line integrals to define work in Chapter 6 and to calculate electric potential in Chapter 23. To evaluate this integral, we divide the path into infinitesimal segments $d\vec{l}$, calculate the scalar product of $\vec{B} \cdot d\vec{l}$ for each segment, and sum these products. In general, $\vec{B}$ varies from point to point, and we must use the value of $\vec{B}$ at the location of each $d\vec{l}$. An alternative notation is $\oint B_\parallel \, dl$, where $B_\parallel$ is the component of $\vec{B}$ parallel to $d\vec{l}$ at each point. The circle on the integral sign indicates that this integral is always computed for a *closed* path, one whose beginning and end points are the same.

Ampere's Law for a Long, Straight Conductor

To introduce the basic idea of Ampere's law, let's consider again the magnetic field caused by a long, straight conductor carrying a current I. We found in Section 28.3 that the field at a distance r from the conductor has magnitude

$$B = \frac{\mu_0 I}{2\pi r}$$

The magnetic field lines are circles centered on the conductor. Let's take the line integral of $\vec{B}$ around one such circle with radius r, as in Fig. 28.16a. At every point on the circle, $\vec{B}$ and $d\vec{l}$ are parallel, and so $\vec{B} \cdot d\vec{l} = B \, dl$; since r is constant around the circle, B is constant as well. Alternatively, we can say that $B_\parallel$ is constant and equal to B at every point on the circle. Hence we can take B

28.16 Three integration paths for the line integral of $\vec{B}$ in the vicinity of a long, straight conductor carrying current I *out* of the plane of the page (as indicated by the circle with a dot). The conductor is seen end-on.

(a) Integration path is a circle centered on the conductor; integration goes around the circle counterclockwise.

Result: $\oint \vec{B} \cdot d\vec{l} = \mu_0 I$

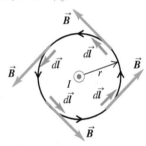

(b) Same integration path as in (a), but integration goes around the circle clockwise.

Result: $\oint \vec{B} \cdot d\vec{l} = -\mu_0 I$

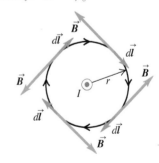

(c) An integration path that does not enclose the conductor

Result: $\oint \vec{B} \cdot dl = 0$

outside of the integral. The remaining integral is just the circumference of the circle, so

$$\oint \vec{B} \cdot d\vec{l} = \oint B_\parallel \, dl = B \oint dl = \frac{\mu_0 I}{2\pi r}(2\pi r) = \mu_0 I$$

The line integral is thus independent of the radius of the circle and is equal to μ_0 multiplied by the current passing through the area bounded by the circle.

In Fig. 28.16b the situation is the same, but the integration path now goes around the circle in the opposite direction. Now $\vec{B}$ and $d\vec{l}$ are antiparallel, so $\vec{B} \cdot d\vec{l} = -B \, dl$ and the line integral equals $-\mu_0 I$. We get the same result if the integration path is the same as in Fig. 28.16a, but the direction of the current is reversed. Thus $\oint \vec{B} \cdot d\vec{l}$ equals μ_0 multiplied by the current passing through the area bounded by the integration path, with a positive or negative sign depending on the direction of the current relative to the direction of integration.

There's a simple rule for the sign of the current; you won't be surprised to learn that it uses your right hand. Curl the fingers of your right hand around the integration path so that they curl in the direction of integration (that is, the direction that you use to evaluate $\oint \vec{B} \cdot d\vec{l}$). Then your right thumb indicates the positive current direction. Currents that pass through the integration path in this direction are positive; those in the opposite direction are negative. Using this rule, you should be able to convince yourself that the current is positive in Fig. 28.16a and negative in Fig. 28.16b. Here's another way to say the same thing: Looking at the surface bounded by the integration path, integrate counterclockwise around the path as in Fig. 28.16a. Currents moving toward you through the surface are positive, and those going away from you are negative.

An integration path that does *not* enclose the conductor is used in Fig. 28.16c. Along the circular arc ab of radius r_1, $\vec{B}$ and $d\vec{l}$ are parallel, and $B_\parallel = B_1 = \mu_0 I/2\pi r_1$; along the circular arc cd of radius r_2, $\vec{B}$ and $d\vec{l}$ are antiparallel and $B_\parallel = -B_2 = -\mu_0 I/2\pi r_2$. The $\vec{B}$ field is perpendicular to $d\vec{l}$ at each point on the straight sections bc and da, so $B_\parallel = 0$ and these sections contribute zero to the line integral. The total line integral is then

$$\oint \vec{B} \cdot d\vec{l} = \oint B_\parallel \, dl = B_1 \int_a^b dl + (0)\int_b^c dl + (-B_2)\int_c^d dl + (0)\int_d^a dl$$

$$= \frac{\mu_0 I}{2\pi r_1}(r_1\theta) + 0 - \frac{\mu_0 I}{2\pi r_2}(r_2\theta) + 0 = 0$$

The magnitude of $\vec{B}$ is greater on arc cd than on arc ab, but the arc length is less, so the contributions from the two arcs exactly cancel. Even though there is a magnetic field everywhere along the integration path, the line integral $\oint \vec{B} \cdot d\vec{l}$ is zero if there is no current passing through the area bounded by the path.

We can also derive these results for more general integration paths, such as the one in Fig. 28.17a. At the position of the line element $d\vec{l}$, the angle between $d\vec{l}$ and $\vec{B}$ is ϕ, and

$$\vec{B} \cdot d\vec{l} = B \, dl \cos \phi$$

From the figure, $dl \cos \phi = r \, d\theta$, where $d\theta$ is the angle subtended by $d\vec{l}$ at the position of the conductor and r is the distance of $d\vec{l}$ from the conductor. Thus

$$\oint \vec{B} \cdot d\vec{l} = \oint \frac{\mu_0 I}{2\pi r}(r \, d\theta) = \frac{\mu_0 I}{2\pi} \oint d\theta$$

But $\oint d\theta$ is just equal to 2π, the total angle swept out by the radial line from the conductor to $d\vec{l}$ during a complete trip around the path. So we get

28.17 (a) A more general integration path for the line integral of $\vec{B}$ around a long, straight conductor carrying current I *out* of the plane of the page. The conductor is seen end-on. (b) A more general integration path that does not enclose the conductor.

(a)

(b)

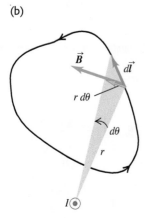

$$\oint \vec{B} \cdot d\vec{l} = \mu_0 I \qquad (28.19)$$

This result doesn't depend on the shape of the path or on the position of the wire inside it. If the current in the wire is opposite to that shown, the integral has the opposite sign. But if the path doesn't enclose the wire (Fig. 28.17b), then the net change in θ during the trip around the integration path is zero; $\oint d\theta$ is zero instead of 2π and the line integral is zero.

Ampere's Law: General Statement

Equation (28.19) is almost, but not quite, the general statement of Ampere's law. To generalize it even further, suppose *several* long, straight conductors pass through the surface bounded by the integration path. The total magnetic field $\vec{B}$ at any point on the path is the vector sum of the fields produced by the individual conductors. Thus the line integral of the total $\vec{B}$ equals μ_0 times the *algebraic sum* of the currents. In calculating this sum, we use the sign rule for currents described above. If the integration path does not enclose a particular wire, the line integral of the $\vec{B}$ field of that wire is zero, because the angle θ for that wire sweeps through a net change of zero rather than 2π during the integration. Any conductors present that are not enclosed by a particular path may still contribute to the value of $\vec{B}$ at every point, but the *line integrals* of their fields around the path are zero.

Thus we can replace I in Eq. (28.19) with I_{encl}, the algebraic sum of the currents *enclosed* or *linked* by the integration path, with the sum evaluated by using the sign rule just described (Fig. 28.18). Our statement of **Ampere's law** is then

$$\oint \vec{B} \cdot d\vec{l} = \mu_0 I_{encl} \qquad \text{(Ampere's law)} \qquad (28.20)$$

While we have derived Ampere's law only for the special case of the field of several long, straight, parallel conductors, Eq. (28.20) is in fact valid for conductors and paths of *any* shape. The general derivation is no different in principle from what we have presented, but the geometry is more complicated.

If $\oint \vec{B} \cdot d\vec{l} = 0$, it *does not* necessarily mean that $\vec{B} = 0$ everywhere along the path, only that the total current through an area bounded by the path is zero. In Figs. 28.16c and 28.17b, the integration paths enclose no current at all; in Fig. 28.19 there are positive and negative currents of equal magnitude through the area enclosed by the path. In both cases, $I_{encl} = 0$ and the line integral is zero.

CAUTION **Line integrals of electric and magnetic fields** In Chapter 23 we saw that the line integral of the electrostatic field $\vec{E}$ around any closed path is equal to zero; this is a statement that the electrostatic force $\vec{F} = q\vec{E}$ on a point charge q is conservative, so this force does zero work on a charge that moves around a closed path that returns to the starting point. You might think that the value of the line integral $\oint \vec{B} \cdot d\vec{l}$ is similarly related to the question of whether the *magnetic* force is conservative. This isn't the case at all. Remember that the magnetic force $\vec{F} = q\vec{v} \times \vec{B}$ on a moving charged particle is always *perpendicular* to $\vec{B}$, so $\oint \vec{B} \cdot d\vec{l}$ is *not* related to the work done by the magnetic force; as stated in Ampere's law, this integral is related only to the total current through a surface bounded by the integration path. In fact, the magnetic force on a moving charged particle is *not* conservative. A conservative force depends only on the position of the body on which the force is exerted, but the magnetic force on a moving charged particle also depends on the *velocity* of the particle.

Equation (28.20) turns out to be valid only if the currents are steady and if no magnetic materials or time-varying electric fields are present. In Chapter 29 we will see how to generalize Ampere's law for time-varying fields.

28.18 Ampere's law.

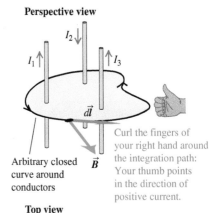

Perspective view

Arbitrary closed curve around conductors

Curl the fingers of your right hand around the integration path: Your thumb points in the direction of positive current.

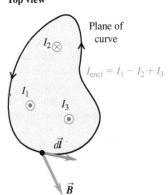

Top view

Plane of curve

$I_{encl} = I_1 - I_2 + I_3$

Ampere's law: If we calculate the line integral of the magnetic field around a closed curve, the result equals μ_0 times the total enclosed current: $\oint \vec{B} \cdot d\vec{l} = \mu_0 I_{encl}$.

28.19 Two long, straight conductors carrying equal currents in opposite directions. The conductors are seen end-on, and the integration path is counterclockwise. The line integral $\oint \vec{B} \cdot d\vec{l}$ gets zero contribution from the upper and lower segments, a positive contribution from the left segment, and a negative contribution from the right segment; the net integral is zero.

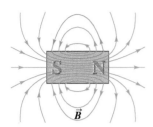

$\vec{B}$

Test Your Understanding of Section 28.6 The figure at left shows magnetic field lines through the center of a permanent magnet. The magnet is not connected to a source of emf. One of the field lines is colored red. What can you conclude about the currents inside the permanent magnet within the region enclosed by this field line? (i) There are no currents inside the magnet; (ii) there are currents directed out of the plane of the page; (iii) there are currents directed into the plane of the page; (iv) not enough information is given to decide.

28.7 Applications of Ampere's Law

Ampere's law is useful when we can exploit the symmetry of a situation to evaluate the line integral of $\vec{B}$. Several examples are given below. Problem-Solving Strategy 28.2 is directly analogous to Problem-Solving Strategy 22.1 (Section 22.4) for applications of Gauss's law; we suggest you review that strategy now and compare the two methods.

Problem-Solving Strategy 28.2 | **Ampere's Law**

IDENTIFY *the relevant concepts:* Like Gauss's law, Ampere's law is most useful when the magnetic field is highly symmetric. In the form $\oint \vec{B} \cdot d\vec{l} = \mu_0 I_{\text{encl}}$, it can yield the magnitude of $\vec{B}$ as a function of position if we are given the magnitude and direction of the field-generating electric current.

SET UP *the problem* using the following steps:
1. Determine the target variable(s). Usually one will be the magnitude of the $\vec{B}$ field as a function of position.
2. Select the integration path you will use with Ampere's law. If you want to determine the magnetic field at a certain point, then the path must pass through that point. The integration path doesn't have to be any actual physical boundary. Usually it is a purely geometric curve; it may be in empty space, embedded in a solid body, or some of each. The integration path has to have enough *symmetry* to make evaluation of the integral possible. Ideally the path will be tangent to $\vec{B}$ in regions of interest; elsewhere the path should be perpendicular to $\vec{B}$ or should run through regions in which $\vec{B} = 0$.

EXECUTE *the solution* as follows:
1. Carry out the integral $\oint \vec{B} \cdot d\vec{l}$ along the chosen path. If $\vec{B}$ is tangent to all or some portion of the path and has the same

magnitude B at every point, then its line integral is the product of B and the length of that portion of the path. If $\vec{B}$ is perpendicular to some portion of the path, or if $\vec{B} = 0$, that portion makes no contribution to the integral.
2. In the integral $\oint \vec{B} \cdot d\vec{l}$, $\vec{B}$ is the *total* magnetic field at each point on the path; it can be caused by currents enclosed *or not enclosed* by the path. If *no* net current is enclosed by the path, the field at points on the path need not be zero, but the integral $\oint \vec{B} \cdot d\vec{l}$ is always zero.
3. Determine the current I_{encl} enclosed by the integration path. A right-hand rule gives the sign of this current: If you curl the fingers of your right hand so that they follow the path in the direction of integration, then your right thumb points in the direction of positive current. If $\vec{B}$ is tangent to the path everywhere and I_{encl} is positive, the direction of $\vec{B}$ is the same as the direction of integration. If instead I_{encl} is negative, $\vec{B}$ is in the direction opposite to that of the integration.
4. Use Ampere's law $\oint \vec{B} \cdot d\vec{l} = \mu_0 I$ to solve for the target variable.

EVALUATE *your answer:* If your result is an expression for the field magnitude as a function of position, check it by examining how the expression behaves in different limits.

Example 28.7 | **Field of a long, straight, current-carrying conductor**

In Section 28.6 we derived Ampere's law using Eq. (28.9) for the field $\vec{B}$ of a long, straight, current-carrying conductor. Reverse this process, and use Ampere's law to find $\vec{B}$ for this situation.

SOLUTION

IDENTIFY and SET UP: The situation has cylindrical symmetry, so in Ampere's law we take our integration path to be a circle with radius r centered on the conductor and lying in a plane perpendicular to it, as in Fig. 28.16a. The field $\vec{B}$ is everywhere tangent to this circle and has the same magnitude B everywhere on the circle.

EXECUTE: With our choice of integration path, Ampere's law [Eq. (28.20)] becomes

$$\oint \vec{B} \cdot d\vec{l} = \oint B_{\parallel} \, dl = B(2\pi r) = \mu_0 I$$

Equation (28.9), $B = \mu_0 I / 2\pi r$, follows immediately.

Ampere's law determines the direction of $\vec{B}$ as well as its magnitude. Since we chose to go counterclockwise around the integration path, the positive direction for current is out of the plane of Fig. 28.16a; this is the same as the actual current direction in the figure, so I is positive and the integral $\oint \vec{B} \cdot d\vec{l}$ is also positive. Since the $d\vec{l}$'s run counterclockwise, the direction of $\vec{B}$ must be counterclockwise as well, as shown in Fig. 28.16a.

EVALUATE: Our results are consistent with those in Section 28.6.

Example 28.8 Field of a long cylindrical conductor

A cylindrical conductor with radius R carries a current I (Fig. 28.20). The current is uniformly distributed over the cross-sectional area of the conductor. Find the magnetic field as a function of the distance r from the conductor axis for points both inside ($r < R$) and outside ($r > R$) the conductor.

SOLUTION

IDENTIFY and SET UP: As in Example 28.7, the current distribution has cylindrical symmetry, and the magnetic field lines must be circles concentric with the conductor axis. To find the magnetic field inside and outside the conductor, we choose circular integration paths with radii $r < R$ and $r > R$, respectively (see Fig. 28.20).

EXECUTE: In either case the field $\vec{B}$ has the same magnitude at every point on the circular integration path and is tangent to the path. Thus the magnitude of the line integral is simply $B(2\pi r)$. To find the current I_{encl} enclosed by a circular integration path inside the conductor ($r < R$,), note that the current density (current per unit area) is $J = I/\pi R^2$, so $I_{encl} = J(\pi r^2) = Ir^2/R^2$. Hence Ampere's law gives $B(2\pi r) = \mu_0 Ir^2/R^2$, or

28.20 To find the magnetic field at radius $r < R$, we apply Ampere's law to the circle enclosing the gray area. The current through the red area is $(r^2/R^2)I$. To find the magnetic field at radius $r > R$, we apply Ampere's law to the circle enclosing the entire conductor.

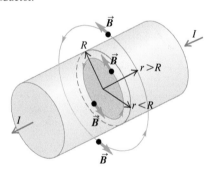

$$B = \frac{\mu_0 I}{2\pi} \frac{r}{R^2} \qquad \text{(inside the conductor, } r < R) \qquad (28.21)$$

A circular integration path outside the conductor encloses the total current in the conductor, so $I_{encl} = I$. Applying Ampere's law gives the same equation as in Example 28.7, with the same result for B:

$$B = \frac{\mu_0 I}{2\pi r} \qquad \text{(outside the conductor, } r > R) \qquad (28.22)$$

Outside the conductor, the magnetic field is the same as that of a long, straight conductor carrying current I, independent of the radius R over which the current is distributed. Indeed, the magnetic field outside *any* cylindrically symmetric current distribution is the same as if the entire current were concentrated along the axis of the distribution. This is analogous to the results of Examples 22.5 and 22.9 (Section 22.4), in which we found that the *electric* field outside a spherically symmetric *charged* body is the same as though the entire charge were concentrated at the center.

EVALUATE: Note that at the surface of the conductor ($r = R$), Eqs. (28.21) and (28.22) agree, as they must. Figure 28.21 shows a graph of B as a function of r.

28.21 Magnitude of the magnetic field inside and outside a long, straight cylindrical conductor with radius R carrying a current I.

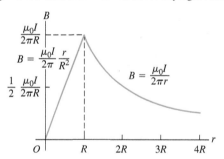

Example 28.9 Field of a solenoid

A solenoid consists of a helical winding of wire on a cylinder, usually circular in cross section. There can be thousands of closely spaced turns (often in several layers), each of which can be regarded as a circular loop. For simplicity, Fig. 28.22 shows a solenoid with only a few turns. All turns carry the same current I, and the total $\vec{B}$ field at every point is the vector sum of the fields caused by the individual turns. The figure shows field lines in the *xy*- and *xz*-planes. We draw field lines that are uniformly spaced at the center of the solenoid. Exact calculations show that for a long, closely wound solenoid, half of these field lines emerge from the ends and half "leak out" through the windings between the center and the end, as the figure suggests.

If the solenoid is long in comparison with its cross-sectional diameter and the coils are tightly wound, the field inside the solenoid near its midpoint is very nearly uniform over the cross section and parallel to the axis; the *external* field near the midpoint is very small.

28.22 Magnetic field lines produced by the current in a solenoid. For clarity, only a few turns are shown.

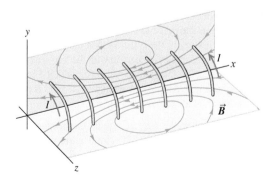

Continued

Use Ampere's law to find the field at or near the center of such a solenoid if it has n turns per unit length and carries current I.

SOLUTION

IDENTIFY and SET UP: We assume that $\vec{B}$ is uniform inside the solenoid and zero outside. Figure 28.23 shows the situation and our chosen integration path, rectangle $abcd$. Side ab, with length L, is parallel to the axis of the solenoid. Sides bc and da are taken to be very long so that side cd is far from the solenoid; then the field at side cd is negligibly small.

EXECUTE: Along side ab, $\vec{B}$ is parallel to the path and is constant. Our Ampere's-law integration takes us along side ab in the same direction as $\vec{B}$, so here $B_{\parallel} = +B$ and

$$\int_a^b \vec{B} \cdot d\vec{l} = BL$$

Along sides bc and da, $\vec{B}$ is perpendicular to the path and so $B_{\parallel} = 0$; along side cd, $\vec{B} = 0$ and so $B_{\parallel} = 0$. Around the entire closed path, then, we have $\oint \vec{B} \cdot d\vec{l} = BL$.

In a length L there are nL turns, each of which passes once through $abcd$ carrying current I. Hence the total current enclosed by the rectangle is $I_{encl} = nLI$. The integral $\oint \vec{B} \cdot d\vec{l}$ is

28.23 Our sketch for this problem.

Central part of solenoid

positive, so from Ampere's law I_{encl} must be positive as well. This means that the current passing through the surface bounded by the integration path must be in the direction shown in Fig. 28.23. Ampere's law then gives $BL = \mu_0 nLI$, or

$$B = \mu_0 nI \qquad \text{(solenoid)} \qquad (28.23)$$

Side ab need not lie on the axis of the solenoid, so this result demonstrates that the field is uniform over the entire cross section at the center of the solenoid's length.

EVALUATE: Note that the *direction* of $\vec{B}$ inside the solenoid is in the same direction as the solenoid's vector magnetic moment $\vec{\mu}$, as we found in Section 28.5 for a single current-carrying loop.

For points along the axis, the field is strongest at the center of the solenoid and drops off near the ends. For a solenoid very long in comparison to its diameter, the field magnitude at each end is exactly half that at the center. This is approximately the case even for a relatively short solenoid, as Fig. 28.24 shows.

28.24 Magnitude of the magnetic field at points along the axis of a solenoid with length $4a$, equal to four times its radius a. The field magnitude at each end is about half its value at the center. (Compare with Fig. 28.14 for the field of N circular loops.)

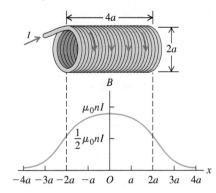

Example 28.10 | **Field of a toroidal solenoid**

Figure 28.25a shows a doughnut-shaped **toroidal solenoid**, tightly wound with N turns of wire carrying a current I. (In a practical solenoid the turns would be much more closely spaced than they are in the figure.) Find the magnetic field at all points.

SOLUTION

IDENTIFY and SET UP: Ignoring the slight pitch of the helical windings, we can consider each turn of a tightly wound toroidal solenoid as a loop lying in a plane perpendicular to the large, circular axis of the toroid. The symmetry of the situation then tells us that the magnetic field lines must be circles concentric with the toroid axis. Therefore we choose circular integration paths (of which Fig. 28.25b shows three) for use with Ampere's law, so that the field $\vec{B}$ (if any) is tangent to each path at all points along the path.

EXECUTE: Along each path, $\oint \vec{B} \cdot d\vec{l}$ equals the product of B and the path circumference $l = 2\pi r$. The total current enclosed by path 1 is zero, so from Ampere's law the field $\vec{B} = \mathbf{0}$ everywhere on this path.

Each turn of the winding passes *twice* through the area bounded by path 3, carrying equal currents in opposite directions. The *net*

28.25 (a) A toroidal solenoid. For clarity, only a few turns of the winding are shown. (b) Integration paths (black circles) used to compute the magnetic field $\vec{B}$ set up by the current (shown as dots and crosses).

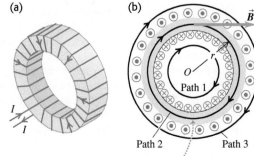

The magnetic field is confined almost entirely to the space enclosed by the windings (in blue).

current enclosed is therefore zero, and hence $\vec{B} = \mathbf{0}$ at all points on this path as well. We conclude that *the field of an ideal toroidal solenoid is confined to the space enclosed by the windings.* We can think of such a solenoid as a tightly wound, straight solenoid that has been bent into a circle.

For path 2, we have $\oint \vec{B} \cdot d\vec{l} = 2\pi r B$. Each turn of the winding passes *once* through the area bounded by this path, so $I_{encl} = NI$. We note that I_{encl} is positive for the clockwise direction of integration in Fig. 28.25b, so $\vec{B}$ is in the direction shown. Ampere's law then says that $2\pi r B = \mu_0 NI$, so

$$B = \frac{\mu_0 NI}{2\pi r} \qquad \text{(toroidal solenoid)} \qquad (28.24)$$

EVALUATE: Equation (28.24) indicates that B is *not* uniform over the interior of the core, because different points in the interior are difference distances r from the toroid axis. However, if the radial extent of the core is small in comparison to r, the variation is slight. In that case, considering that $2\pi r$ is the circumferential length of the toroid and that $N/2\pi r$ is the number of turns per unit length n, the field may be written as $B = \mu_0 nI$, just as it is at the center of a long, *straight* solenoid.

In a real toroidal solenoid the turns are not precisely circular loops but rather segments of a bent helix. As a result, the external field is not exactly zero. To estimate its magnitude, we imagine Fig. 28.25a as being *very* roughly equivalent, for points outside the torus, to a *single-turn* circular loop with radius r. At the center of such a loop, Eq. (28.17) gives $B = \mu_0 I/2r$; this is smaller than the field inside the solenoid by the factor N/π.

The equations we have derived for the field in a closely wound straight or toroidal solenoid are strictly correct only for windings in *vacuum*. For most practical purposes, however, they can be used for windings in air or on a core of any nonmagnetic, nonsuperconducting material. In the next section we will show how these equations are modified if the core is a magnetic material.

Test Your Understanding of Section 28.7 Consider a conducting wire that runs along the central axis of a hollow conducting cylinder. Such an arrangement, called a *coaxial cable,* has many applications in telecommunications. (The cable that connects a television set to a local cable provider is an example of a coaxial cable.) In such a cable a current I runs in one direction along the hollow conducting cylinder and is spread uniformly over the cylinder's cross-sectional area. An equal current runs in the opposite direction along the central wire. How does the magnitude B of the magnetic field outside such a cable depend on the distance r from the central axis of the cable? (i) B is proportional to $1/r$; (ii) B is proportional to $1/r^2$; (iii) B is zero at all points outside the cable.

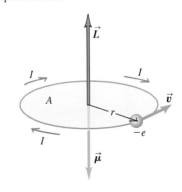

Hollow conducting cylinder   Insulator   Central wire

28.8 Magnetic Materials

In discussing how currents cause magnetic fields, we have assumed that the conductors are surrounded by vacuum. But the coils in transformers, motors, generators, and electromagnets nearly always have iron cores to increase the magnetic field and confine it to desired regions. Permanent magnets, magnetic recording tapes, and computer disks depend directly on the magnetic properties of materials; when you store information on a computer disk, you are actually setting up an array of microscopic permanent magnets on the disk. So it is worthwhile to examine some aspects of the magnetic properties of materials. After describing the atomic origins of magnetic properties, we will discuss three broad classes of magnetic behavior that occur in materials; these are called *paramagnetism, diamagnetism,* and *ferromagnetism.*

The Bohr Magneton

As we discussed briefly in Section 27.7, the atoms that make up all matter contain moving electrons, and these electrons form microscopic current loops that produce magnetic fields of their own. In many materials these currents are randomly oriented and cause no net magnetic field. But in some materials an external field (a field produced by currents outside the material) can cause these loops to become oriented preferentially with the field, so their magnetic fields *add* to the external field. We then say that the material is *magnetized.*

Let's look at how these microscopic currents come about. Figure 28.26 shows a primitive model of an electron in an atom. We picture the electron (mass m, charge $-e$) as moving in a circular orbit with radius r and speed v. This moving charge is equivalent to a current loop. In Section 27.7 we found that a current loop with area A and current I has a magnetic dipole moment μ given by $\mu = IA$; for the orbiting electron the area of the loop is $A = \pi r^2$. To find the current

28.26 An electron moving with speed v in a circular orbit of radius r has an angular momentum $\vec{L}$ and an oppositely directed orbital magnetic dipole moment $\vec{\mu}$. It also has a spin angular momentum and an oppositely directed spin magnetic dipole moment.

associated with the electron, we note that the orbital period T (the time for the electron to make one complete orbit) is the orbit circumference divided by the electron speed: $T = 2\pi r/v$. The equivalent current I is the total charge passing any point on the orbit per unit time, which is just the magnitude e of the electron charge divided by the orbital period T:

$$I = \frac{e}{T} = \frac{ev}{2\pi r}$$

The magnetic moment $\mu = IA$ is then

$$\mu = \frac{ev}{2\pi r}(\pi r^2) = \frac{evr}{2} \tag{28.25}$$

It is useful to express μ in terms of the *angular momentum L* of the electron. For a particle moving in a circular path, the magnitude of angular momentum equals the magnitude of momentum mv multiplied by the radius r—that is, $L = mvr$ (see Section 10.5). Comparing this with Eq. (28.25), we can write

$$\mu = \frac{e}{2m}L \tag{28.26}$$

Equation (28.26) is useful in this discussion because atomic angular momentum is *quantized;* its component in a particular direction is always an integer multiple of $h/2\pi$, where h is a fundamental physical constant called *Planck's constant.* The numerical value of h is

$$h = 6.626 \times 10^{-34} \text{ J} \cdot \text{s}$$

The quantity $h/2\pi$ thus represents a fundamental unit of angular momentum in atomic systems, just as e is a fundamental unit of charge. Associated with the quantization of $\vec{L}$ is a fundamental uncertainty in the *direction* of $\vec{L}$ and therefore of $\vec{\mu}$. In the following discussion, when we speak of the magnitude of a magnetic moment, a more precise statement would be "maximum component in a given direction." Thus, to say that a magnetic moment $\vec{\mu}$ is aligned with a magnetic field $\vec{B}$ really means that $\vec{\mu}$ has its maximum possible component in the direction of $\vec{B}$; such components are always quantized.

Equation (28.26) shows that associated with the fundamental unit of angular momentum is a corresponding fundamental unit of magnetic moment. If $L = h/2\pi$, then

$$\mu = \frac{e}{2m}\left(\frac{h}{2\pi}\right) = \frac{eh}{4\pi m} \tag{28.27}$$

This quantity is called the **Bohr magneton,** denoted by μ_B. Its numerical value is

$$\mu_B = 9.274 \times 10^{-24} \text{ A} \cdot \text{m}^2 = 9.274 \times 10^{-24} \text{ J/T}$$

You should verify that these two sets of units are consistent. The second set is useful when we compute the potential energy $U = -\vec{\mu} \cdot \vec{B}$ for a magnetic moment in a magnetic field.

Electrons also have an intrinsic angular momentum, called *spin,* that is not related to orbital motion but that can be pictured in a classical model as spinning on an axis. This angular momentum also has an associated magnetic moment, and its magnitude turns out to be almost exactly one Bohr magneton. (Effects having to do with quantization of the electromagnetic field cause the spin magnetic moment to be about 1.001 μ_B.)

Paramagnetism

In an atom, most of the various orbital and spin magnetic moments of the electrons add up to zero. However, in some cases the atom has a net magnetic moment that is of the order of μ_B. When such a material is placed in a magnetic field, the field exerts a torque on each magnetic moment, as given by Eq. (27.26): $\vec{\tau} = \vec{\mu} \times \vec{B}$. These torques tend to align the magnetic moments with the field, as we discussed in Section 27.7. In this position, the directions of the current loops are such as to *add* to the externally applied magnetic field.

We saw in Section 28.5 that the $\vec{B}$ field produced by a current loop is proportional to the loop's magnetic dipole moment. In the same way, the additional $\vec{B}$ field produced by microscopic electron current loops is proportional to the total magnetic moment $\vec{\mu}_{total}$ per unit volume V in the material. We call this vector quantity the **magnetization** of the material, denoted by $\vec{M}$:

$$\vec{M} = \frac{\vec{\mu}_{total}}{V} \qquad (28.28)$$

The additional magnetic field due to magnetization of the material turns out to be equal simply to $\mu_0 \vec{M}$, where μ_0 is the same constant that appears in the law of Biot and Savart and Ampere's law. When such a material completely surrounds a current-carrying conductor, the total magnetic field $\vec{B}$ in the material is

$$\vec{B} = \vec{B}_0 + \mu_0 \vec{M} \qquad (28.29)$$

where $\vec{B}_0$ is the field caused by the current in the conductor.

To check that the units in Eq. (28.29) are consistent, note that magnetization $\vec{M}$ is magnetic moment per unit volume. The units of magnetic moment are current times area $(A \cdot m^2)$, so the units of magnetization are $(A \cdot m^2)/m^3 = A/m$. From Section 28.1, the units of the constant μ_0 are $T \cdot m/A$. So the units of $\mu_0 \vec{M}$ are the same as the units of $\vec{B}$: $(T \cdot m/A)(A/m) = T$.

A material showing the behavior just described is said to be **paramagnetic.** The result is that the magnetic field at any point in such a material is greater by a dimensionless factor K_m, called the **relative permeability** of the material, than it would be if the material were replaced by vacuum. The value of K_m is different for different materials; for common paramagnetic solids and liquids at room temperature, K_m typically ranges from 1.00001 to 1.003.

All of the equations in this chapter that relate magnetic fields to their sources can be adapted to the situation in which the current-carrying conductor is embedded in a paramagnetic material. All that need be done is to replace μ_0 by $K_m \mu_0$. This product is usually denoted as μ and is called the **permeability** of the material:

$$\mu = K_m \mu_0 \qquad (28.30)$$

CAUTION **Two meanings of the symbol μ** Equation (28.30) involves some really dangerous notation because we have also used μ for magnetic dipole moment. It's customary to use μ for both quantities, but beware: From now on, every time you see a μ, make sure you know whether it is permeability or magnetic moment. You can usually tell from the context.

The amount by which the relative permeability differs from unity is called the **magnetic susceptibility,** denoted by χ_m:

$$\chi_m = K_m - 1 \qquad (28.31)$$

Both K_m and χ_m are dimensionless quantities. Table 28.1 lists values of magnetic susceptibility for several materials. For example, for aluminum, $\chi_m = 2.2 \times 10^{-5}$ and $K_m = 1.000022$. The first group of materials in the table are paramagnetic; we'll discuss the second group of materials, which are called *diamagnetic,* very shortly.

The tendency of atomic magnetic moments to align themselves parallel to the magnetic field (where the potential energy is minimum) is opposed by random thermal motion, which tends to randomize their orientations. For this reason, paramagnetic susceptibility always decreases with increasing temperature.

Table 28.1 Magnetic Susceptibilities of Paramagnetic and Diamagnetic Materials at $T = 20°C$

Material	$\chi_m = K_m - 1 \ (\times 10^{-5})$
Paramagnetic	
Iron ammonium alum	66
Uranium	40
Platinum	26
Aluminum	2.2
Sodium	0.72
Oxygen gas	0.19
Diamagnetic	
Bismuth	−16.6
Mercury	−2.9
Silver	−2.6
Carbon (diamond)	−2.1
Lead	−1.8
Sodium chloride	−1.4
Copper	−1.0

In many cases it is inversely proportional to the absolute temperature T, and the magnetization M can be expressed as

$$M = C\frac{B}{T} \qquad (28.32)$$

This relationship is called *Curie's law,* after its discoverer, Pierre Curie (1859–1906). The quantity C is a constant, different for different materials, called the *Curie constant.*

As we described in Section 27.7, a body with atomic magnetic dipoles is attracted to the poles of a magnet. In most paramagnetic substances this attraction is very weak due to thermal randomization of the atomic magnetic moments. But at very low temperatures the thermal effects are reduced, the magnetization increases in accordance with Curie's law, and the attractive forces are greater.

Example 28.11 **Magnetic dipoles in a paramagnetic material**

Nitric oxide (NO) is a paramagnetic compound. The magnetic moment of each NO molecule has a maximum component in any direction of about one Bohr magneton. Compare the interaction energy of such magnetic moments in a 1.5-T magnetic field with the average translational kinetic energy of molecules at 300 K.

SOLUTION

IDENTIFY and SET UP: This problem involves the energy of a magnetic moment in a magnetic field and the average thermal kinetic energy. We have Eq. (27.27), $U = -\vec{\mu} \cdot \vec{B}$, for the interaction energy of a magnetic moment $\vec{\mu}$ with a $\vec{B}$ field, and Eq. (18.16), $K = \frac{3}{2}kT$, for the average translational kinetic energy of a molecule at temperature T.

EXECUTE: We can write $U = -\mu_{\parallel}B$, where $\mu_{\parallel}$ is the component of the magnetic moment $\vec{\mu}$ in the direction of the $\vec{B}$ field. Here the maximum value of $\mu_{\parallel}$ is about μ_B, so

$$|U|_{max} \approx \mu_B B = (9.27 \times 10^{-24}\,\text{J/T})(1.5\,\text{T})$$
$$= 1.4 \times 10^{-23}\,\text{J} = 8.7 \times 10^{-5}\,\text{eV}$$

The average translational kinetic energy K is

$$K = \tfrac{3}{2}kT = \tfrac{3}{2}(1.38 \times 10^{-23}\,\text{J/K})(300\,\text{K})$$
$$= 6.2 \times 10^{-21}\,\text{J} = 0.039\,\text{eV}$$

EVALUATE: At 300 K the magnetic interaction energy is only about 0.2% of the thermal kinetic energy, so we expect only a slight degree of alignment. This is why paramagnetic susceptibilities at ordinary temperature are usually very small.

Diamagnetism

In some materials the total magnetic moment of all the atomic current loops is zero when no magnetic field is present. But even these materials have magnetic effects because an external field alters electron motions within the atoms, causing additional current loops and induced magnetic dipoles comparable to the induced *electric* dipoles we studied in Section 28.5. In this case the additional field caused by these current loops is always *opposite* in direction to that of the external field. (This behavior is explained by Faraday's law of induction, which we will study in Chapter 29. An induced current always tends to cancel the field change that caused it.)

Such materials are said to be **diamagnetic.** They always have negative susceptibility, as shown in Table 28.1, and relative permeability K_m slightly *less* than unity, typically of the order of 0.99990 to 0.99999 for solids and liquids. Diamagnetic susceptibilities are very nearly temperature independent.

Ferromagnetism

There is a third class of materials, called **ferromagnetic** materials, that includes iron, nickel, cobalt, and many alloys containing these elements. In these materials, strong interactions between atomic magnetic moments cause them to line up parallel to each other in regions called **magnetic domains,** even when no external field is present. Figure 28.27 shows an example of magnetic domain structure. Within each domain, nearly all of the atomic magnetic moments are parallel.

When there is no externally applied field, the domain magnetizations are randomly oriented. But when a field $\vec{B}_0$ (caused by external currents) is present, the domains tend to orient themselves parallel to the field. The domain boundaries also shift; the domains that are magnetized in the field direction grow, and those that are magnetized in other directions shrink. Because the total magnetic moment of a domain may be many thousands of Bohr magnetons, the torques that tend to align the domains with an external field are much stronger than occur with paramagnetic materials. The relative permeability K_m is *much* larger than unity, typically of the order of 1000 to 100,000. As a result, an object made of a ferromagnetic material such as iron is strongly magnetized by the field from a permanent magnet and is attracted to the magnet (see Fig. 27.38). A paramagnetic material such as aluminum is also attracted to a permanent magnet, but K_m for paramagnetic materials is so much smaller for such a material than for ferromagnetic materials that the attraction is very weak. Thus a magnet can pick up iron nails, but not aluminum cans.

As the external field is increased, a point is eventually reached at which nearly *all* the magnetic moments in the ferromagnetic material are aligned parallel to the external field. This condition is called *saturation magnetization;* after it is reached, further increase in the external field causes no increase in magnetization or in the additional field caused by the magnetization.

Figure 28.28 shows a "magnetization curve," a graph of magnetization M as a function of external magnetic field B_0, for soft iron. An alternative description of this behavior is that K_m is not constant but decreases as B_0 increases. (Paramagnetic materials also show saturation at sufficiently strong fields. But the magnetic fields required are so large that departures from a linear relationship between M and B_0 in these materials can be observed only at very low temperatures, 1 K or so.)

For many ferromagnetic materials the relationship of magnetization to external magnetic field is different when the external field is increasing from when it is decreasing. Figure 28.29a shows this relationship for such a material. When the material is magnetized to saturation and then the external field is reduced to zero, some magnetization remains. This behavior is characteristic of permanent magnets, which retain most of their saturation magnetization when the magnetizing field is removed. To reduce the magnetization to zero requires a magnetic field in the reverse direction.

This behavior is called **hysteresis,** and the curves in Fig. 28.29 are called *hysteresis loops.* Magnetizing and demagnetizing a material that has hysteresis involve the dissipation of energy, and the temperature of the material increases during such a process.

28.27 In this drawing adapted from a magnified photo, the arrows show the directions of magnetization in the domains of a single crystal of nickel. Domains that are magnetized in the direction of an applied magnetic field grow larger.

(a) No field

(b) Weak field

(c) Stronger field

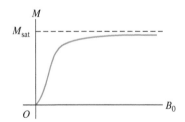

28.28 A magnetization curve for a ferromagnetic material. The magnetization M approaches its saturation value M_{sat} as the magnetic field B_0 (caused by external currents) becomes large.

28.29 Hysteresis loops. The materials of both **(a)** and **(b)** remain strongly magnetized when B_0 is reduced to zero. Since **(a)** is also hard to demagnetize, it would be good for permanent magnets. Since **(b)** magnetizes and demagnetizes more easily, it could be used as a computer memory material. The material of **(c)** would be useful for transformers and other alternating-current devices where zero hysteresis would be optimal.

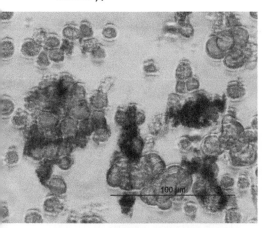

Ferromagnetic materials are widely used in electromagnets, transformer cores, and motors and generators, in which it is desirable to have as large a magnetic field as possible for a given current. Because hysteresis dissipates energy, materials that are used in these applications should usually have as narrow a hysteresis loop as possible. Soft iron is often used; it has high permeability without appreciable hysteresis. For permanent magnets a broad hysteresis loop is usually desirable, with large zero-field magnetization and large reverse field needed to demagnetize. Many kinds of steel and many alloys, such as Alnico, are commonly used for permanent magnets. The remaining magnetic field in such a material, after it has been magnetized to near saturation, is typically of the order of 1 T, corresponding to a remaining magnetization $M = B/\mu_0$ of about 800,000 A/m.

Example 28.12 A ferromagnetic material

A cube-shaped permanent magnet is made of a ferromagnetic material with a magnetization M of about 8×10^5 A/m. The side length is 2 cm. (a) Find the magnetic dipole moment of the magnet. (b) Estimate the magnetic field due to the magnet at a point 10 cm from the magnet along its axis.

SOLUTION

IDENTIFY and SET UP: This problem uses the relationship between magnetization M and magnetic dipole moment μ_{total} and the idea that a magnetic dipole produces a magnetic field. We find μ_{total} using Eq. (28.28). To estimate the field, we approximate the magnet as a current loop with this same magnetic moment and use Eq. (28.18).

EXECUTE: (a) From Eq. (28.28),

$$\mu_{total} = MV = (8 \times 10^5 \text{ A/m})(2 \times 10^{-2} \text{ m})^3 = 6 \text{ A} \cdot \text{m}^2$$

(b) From Eq. (28.18), the magnetic field on the axis of a current loop with magnetic moment μ_{total} is

$$B = \frac{\mu_0 \mu_{total}}{2\pi(x^2 + a^2)^{3/2}}$$

where x is the distance from the loop and a is its radius. We can use this expression here if we take a to refer to the size of the permanent magnet. Strictly speaking, there are complications because our magnet does not have the same geometry as a circular current loop. But because $x = 10$ cm is fairly large in comparison to the 2-cm size of the magnet, the term a^2 is negligible in comparison to x^2 and can be ignored. So

$$B \approx \frac{\mu_0 \mu_{total}}{2\pi x^3} = \frac{(4\pi \times 10^{-7} \text{ T} \cdot \text{m/A})(6 \text{ A} \cdot \text{m}^2)}{2\pi(0.1 \text{ m})^3}$$
$$= 1 \times 10^{-3} \text{ T} = 10 \text{ G}$$

which is about ten times stronger than the earth's magnetic field.

EVALUATE: We calculated B at a point *outside* the magnetic material and therefore used μ_0, not the permeability μ of the magnetic material, in our calculation. You would substitute permeability μ for μ_0 if you were calculating B *inside* a material with relative permeability K_m, for which $\mu = K_m\mu_0$.

Test Your Understanding of Section 28.8 Which of the following materials are attracted to a magnet? (i) sodium; (ii) bismuth; (iii) lead; (iv) uranium.

Magnetic field of a moving charge: The magnetic field $\vec{B}$ created by a charge q moving with velocity $\vec{v}$ depends on the distance r from the source point (the location of q) to the field point (where $\vec{B}$ is measured). The $\vec{B}$ field is perpendicular to $\vec{v}$ and to $\hat{r}$, the unit vector directed from the source point to the field point. The principle of superposition of magnetic fields states that the total $\vec{B}$ field produced by several moving charges is the vector sum of the fields produced by the individual charges. (See Example 28.1.)

$$\vec{B} = \frac{\mu_0}{4\pi}\frac{q\vec{v} \times \hat{r}}{r^2} \qquad (28.2)$$

Magnetic field of a current-carrying conductor: The law of Biot and Savart gives the magnetic field $d\vec{B}$ created by an element $d\vec{l}$ of a conductor carrying current I. The field $d\vec{B}$ is perpendicular to both $d\vec{l}$ and $\hat{r}$, the unit vector from the element to the field point. The $\vec{B}$ field created by a finite current-carrying conductor is the integral of $d\vec{B}$ over the length of the conductor. (See Example 28.2.)

$$d\vec{B} = \frac{\mu_0}{4\pi}\frac{I\,d\vec{l} \times \hat{r}}{r^2} \qquad (28.6)$$

Magnetic field of a long, straight, current-carrying conductor: The magnetic field $\vec{B}$ at a distance r from a long, straight conductor carrying a current I has a magnitude that is inversely proportional to r. The magnetic field lines are circles coaxial with the wire, with directions given by the right-hand rule. (See Examples 28.3 and 28.4.)

$$B = \frac{\mu_0 I}{2\pi r} \qquad (28.9)$$

Magnetic force between current-carrying conductors: Two long, parallel, current-carrying conductors attract if the currents are in the same direction and repel if the currents are in opposite directions. The magnetic force per unit length between the conductors depends on their currents I and I' and their separation r. The definition of the ampere is based on this relationship. (See Example 28.5.)

$$\frac{F}{L} = \frac{\mu_0 II'}{2\pi r} \qquad (28.11)$$

Magnetic field of a current loop: The law of Biot and Savart allows us to calculate the magnetic field produced along the axis of a circular conducting loop of radius a carrying current I. The field depends on the distance x along the axis from the center of the loop to the field point. If there are N loops, the field is multiplied by N. At the center of the loop, $x = 0$. (See Example 28.6.)

$$B_x = \frac{\mu_0 I a^2}{2(x^2 + a^2)^{3/2}} \qquad (28.15)$$
(circular loop)

$$B_x = \frac{\mu_0 NI}{2a} \qquad (28.17)$$
(center of N circular loops)

Ampere's law: Ampere's law states that the line integral of $\vec{B}$ around any closed path equals μ_0 times the net current through the area enclosed by the path. The positive sense of current is determined by a right-hand rule. (See Examples 28.7–28.10.)

$$\oint \vec{B} \cdot d\vec{l} = \mu_0 I_{\text{encl}} \qquad (28.20)$$

Magnetic fields due to current distributions: The table lists magnetic fields caused by several current distributions. In each case the conductor is carrying current I.

Current Distribution	Point in Magnetic Field	Magnetic-Field Magnitude
Long, straight conductor	Distance r from conductor	$B = \dfrac{\mu_0 I}{2\pi r}$
Circular loop of radius a	On axis of loop	$B = \dfrac{\mu_0 I a^2}{2(x^2 + a^2)^{3/2}}$
	At center of loop	$B = \dfrac{\mu_0 I}{2a}$ (for N loops, multiply these expressions by N)
Long cylindrical conductor of radius R	Inside conductor, $r < R$	$B = \dfrac{\mu_0 I}{2\pi}\dfrac{r}{R^2}$
	Outside conductor, $r > R$	$B = \dfrac{\mu_0 I}{2\pi r}$
Long, closely wound solenoid with n turns per unit length, near its midpoint	Inside solenoid, near center	$B = \mu_0 n I$
	Outside solenoid	$B \approx 0$
Tightly wound toroidal solenoid (toroid) with N turns	Within the space enclosed by the windings, distance r from symmetry axis	$B = \dfrac{\mu_0 N I}{2\pi r}$
	Outside the space enclosed by the windings	$B \approx 0$

Magnetic materials: When magnetic materials are present, the magnetization of the material causes an additional contribution to $\vec{B}$. For paramagnetic and diamagnetic materials, μ_0 is replaced in magnetic-field expressions by $\mu = K_m \mu_0$, where μ is the permeability of the material and K_m is its relative permeability. The magnetic susceptibility χ_m is defined as $\chi_m = K_m - 1$. Magnetic susceptibilities for paramagnetic materials are small positive quantities; those for diamagnetic materials are small negative quantities. For ferromagnetic materials, K_m is much larger than unity and is not constant. Some ferromagnetic materials are permanent magnets, retaining their magnetization even after the external magnetic field is removed. (See Examples 28.11 and 28.12.)

BRIDGING PROBLEM | **Magnetic Field of a Charged, Rotating Dielectric Disk**

A thin dielectric disk with radius a has a total charge $+Q$ distributed uniformly over its surface. It rotates n times per second about an axis perpendicular to the surface of the disk and passing through its center. Find the magnetic field at the center of the disk.

SOLUTION GUIDE

See MasteringPhysics® study area for a Video Tutor solution.

IDENTIFY and SET UP

1. Think of the rotating disk as a series of concentric rotating rings. Each ring acts as a circular current loop that produces a magnetic field at the center of the disk.
2. Use the results of Section 28.5 to find the magnetic field due to a single ring. Then integrate over all rings to find the total field.

EXECUTE

3. Find the charge on a ring with inner radius r and outer radius $r + dr$.

4. How long does it take the charge found in step 3 to make a complete trip around the rotating ring? Use this to find the current of the rotating ring.
5. Use a result from Section 28.5 to determine the magnetic field that this ring produces at the center of the disk.
6. Integrate your result from step 5 to find the total magnetic field from all rings with radii from $r = 0$ to $r = a$.

EVALUATE

7. Does your answer have the correct units?
8. Suppose all of the charge were concentrated at the rim of the disk (at $r = a$). Would this increase or decrease the field at the center of the disk?

Problems

•, ••, •••: Problems of increasing difficulty. **CP**: Cumulative problems incorporating material from earlier chapters. **CALC**: Problems requiring calculus. **BIO**: Biosciences problems.

DISCUSSION QUESTIONS

Q28.1 A topic of current interest in physics research is the search (thus far unsuccessful) for an isolated magnetic pole, or magnetic *monopole*. If such an entity were found, how could it be recognized? What would its properties be?

Q28.2 Streams of charged particles emitted from the sun during periods of solar activity create a disturbance in the earth's magnetic field. How does this happen?

Q28.3 The text discussed the magnetic field of an infinitely long, straight conductor carrying a current. Of course, there is no such thing as an infinitely long *anything*. How do you decide whether a particular wire is long enough to be considered infinite?

Q28.4 Two parallel conductors carrying current in the same direction attract each other. If they are permitted to move toward each other, the forces of attraction do work. From where does the energy come? Does this contradict the assertion in Chapter 27 that magnetic forces on moving charges do no work? Explain.

Q28.5 Pairs of conductors carrying current into or out of the power-supply components of electronic equipment are sometimes twisted together to reduce magnetic-field effects. Why does this help?

Q28.6 Suppose you have three long, parallel wires arranged so that in cross section they are at the corners of an equilateral triangle. Is there any way to arrange the currents so that all three wires attract each other? So that all three wires repel each other? Explain.

Q28.7 In deriving the force on one of the long, current-carrying conductors in Section 28.4, why did we use the magnetic field due to only one of the conductors? That is, why didn't we use the *total* magnetic field due to *both* conductors?

Q28.8 Two concentric, coplanar, circular loops of wire of different diameter carry currents in the same direction. Describe the nature of the force exerted on the inner loop by the outer loop and on the outer loop by the inner loop.

Q28.9 A current was sent through a helical coil spring. The spring contracted, as though it had been compressed. Why?

Q28.10 What are the relative advantages and disadvantages of Ampere's law and the law of Biot and Savart for practical calculations of magnetic fields?

Q28.11 Magnetic field lines never have a beginning or an end. Use this to explain why it is reasonable for the field of a toroidal solenoid to be confined entirely to its interior, while a straight solenoid *must* have some field outside.

Q28.12 If the magnitude of the magnetic field a distance R from a very long, straight, current-carrying wire is B, at what distance from the wire will the field have magnitude $3B$?

Q28.13 Two very long, parallel wires carry equal currents in opposite directions. (a) Is there any place that their magnetic fields completely cancel? If so, where? If not, why not? (b) How would the answer to part (a) change if the currents were in the same direction?

Q28.14 In the circuit shown in Fig. Q28.14, when switch S is suddenly closed, the wire L is pulled toward the lower wire carrying current I. Which (a or b) is the positive terminal of the battery? How do you know?

Figure **Q28.14**

Q28.15 A metal ring carries a current that causes a magnetic field B_0 at the center of the ring and a field B at point P a distance x from the center along the axis of the ring. If the radius of the ring is doubled, find the magnetic field at the center. Will the field at point P change by the same factor? Why?

Q28.16 Why should the permeability of a paramagnetic material be expected to decrease with increasing temperature?

Q28.17 If a magnet is suspended over a container of liquid air, it attracts droplets to its poles. The droplets contain only liquid oxygen; even though nitrogen is the primary constituent of air, it is not attracted to the magnet. Explain what this tells you about the magnetic susceptibilities of oxygen and nitrogen, and explain why a magnet in ordinary, room-temperature air doesn't attract molecules of oxygen *gas* to its poles.

Q28.18 What features of atomic structure determine whether an element is diamagnetic or paramagnetic? Explain.

Q28.19 The magnetic susceptibility of paramagnetic materials is quite strongly temperature dependent, but that of diamagnetic materials is nearly independent of temperature. Why the difference?

Q28.20 A cylinder of iron is placed so that it is free to rotate around its axis. Initially the cylinder is at rest, and a magnetic field is applied to the cylinder so that it is magnetized in a direction parallel to its axis. If the direction of the *external* field is suddenly reversed, the direction of magnetization will also reverse and the cylinder will begin rotating around its axis. (This is called the *Einstein–de Haas effect.*) Explain why the cylinder begins to rotate.

Q28.21 The discussion of magnetic forces on current loops in Section 27.7 commented that no net force is exerted on a complete loop in a uniform magnetic field, only a torque. Yet magnetized materials that contain atomic current loops certainly *do* experience net forces in magnetic fields. How is this discrepancy resolved?

Q28.22 Show that the units $A \cdot m^2$ and J/T for the Bohr magneton are equivalent.

EXERCISES

Section 26.1 Magnetic Field of a Moving Charge

28.1 •• A $+6.00\text{-}\mu C$ point charge is moving at a constant 8.00×10^6 m/s in the $+y$-direction, relative to a reference frame. At the instant when the point charge is at the origin of this reference frame, what is the magnetic-field vector $\vec{B}$ it produces at the following points: (a) $x = 0.500$ m, $y = 0$, $z = 0$; (b) $x = 0$, $y = -0.500$ m, $z = 0$; (c) $x = 0$, $y = 0$, $z = +0.500$ m; (d) $x = 0$, $y = -0.500$ m, $z = +0.500$ m?

28.2 • **Fields Within the Atom.** In the Bohr model of the hydrogen atom, the electron moves in a circular orbit of radius 5.3×10^{-11} m with a speed of 2.2×10^6 m/s. If we are viewing the atom in such a way that the electron's orbit is in the plane of the paper with the electron moving clockwise, find the magnitude and direction of the electric and magnetic fields that the electron produces at the location of the nucleus (treated as a point).

28.3 • An electron moves at $0.100c$ as shown in Fig. E28.3. Find the magnitude and direction of the magnetic field this electon produces at the following points, each 2.00 μm from the electron: (a) points A and B; (b) point C; (c) point D.

Figure **E28.3**

28.4 •• An alpha particle (charge $+2e$) and an electron move in opposite directions from the same point, each with the speed of 2.50×10^5 m/s (Fig. E28.4). Find the magnitude and direction of the total magnetic field these charges produce at point P, which is 1.75 nm from each of them.

Figure **E28.4**

28.5 • A $-4.80\text{-}\mu$C charge is moving at a constant speed of 6.80×10^5 m/s in the $+x$-direction relative to a reference frame. At the instant when the point charge is at the origin, what is the magnetic-field vector it produces at the following points: (a) $x = 0.500$ m, $y = 0$, $z = 0$; (b) $x = 0$, $y = 0.500$ m, $z = 0$; (c) $x = 0.500$ m, $y = 0.500$ m, $z = 0$; (d) $x = 0$, $y = 0$, $z = 0.500$ m?

28.6 • Positive point charges $q = +8.00 \mu$C and $q' = +3.00 \mu$C are moving relative to an observer at point P, as shown in Fig. E28.6. The distance d is 0.120 m, $v = 4.50 \times 10^6$ m/s, and $v' = 9.00 \times 10^6$ m/s. (a) When the two charges are at the locations shown in the figure, what are the magnitude and direction of the net magnetic field they produce at point P? (b) What are the magnitude and direction of the electric and magnetic forces that each charge exerts on the other, and what is the ratio of the magnitude of the electric force to the magnitude of the magnetic force? (c) If the direction of $\vec{v}'$ is reversed, so both charges are moving in the same direction, what are the magnitude and direction of the magnetic forces that the two charges exert on each other?

Figure **E28.6**

28.7 •• Figure E28.6 shows two point charges, q and q', moving relative to an observer at point P. Suppose that the lower charge is actually *negative*, with $q' = -q$. (a) Find the magnetic field (magnitude and direction) produced by the two charges at point P if (i) $v' = v/2$; (ii) $v' = v$; (iii) $v' = 2v$. (b) Find the direction of the magnetic force that q exerts on q', and find the direction of the magnetic force that q' exerts on q. (c) If $v = v' = 3.00 \times 10^5$ m/s, what is the ratio of the magnitude of the magnetic force acting on each charge to that of the Coulomb force acting on each charge?

28.8 •• An electron and a proton are each moving at 845 km/s in perpendicular paths as shown in Fig. E28.8. At the instant when they are at the positions shown in the figure, find the magnitude and direction of (a) the total magnetic field they produce at the origin; (b) the magnetic field the electron produces at the location of the proton; (c) the total electric force and the total magnetic force that the electron exerts on the proton.

Figure **E28.8**

28.9 • A negative charge $q = -3.60 \times 10^{-6}$ C is located at the origin and has velocity $\vec{v} = (7.50 \times 10^4$ m/s$)\hat{\imath} + (-4.90 \times 10^4$ m/s$)\hat{\jmath}$. At this instant what are the magnitude and direction of

the magnetic field produced by this charge at the point $x = 0.200$ m, $y = -0.300$ m, $z = 0$?

Section 28.2 Magnetic Field of a Current Element

28.10 • A short current element $d\vec{l} = (0.500$ mm$)\hat{\jmath}$ carries a current of 8.20 A in the same direction as $d\vec{l}$. Point P is located at $\vec{r} = (-0.730$ m$)\hat{\imath} + (0.390$ m$)\hat{k}$. Use unit vectors to express the magnetic field at P produced by this current element.

28.11 • A straight wire carries a 10.0-A current (Fig. E28.11). $ABCD$ is a rectangle with point D in the middle of a 1.10-mm segment of the wire and point C in the wire. Find the magnitude and direction of the magnetic field due to this segment at (a) point A; (b) point B; (c) point C.

Figure **E28.11**

28.12 • A long, straight wire, carrying a current of 200 A, runs through a cubical wooden box, entering and leaving through holes in the centers of opposite faces (Fig. E28.12). The length of each side of the box is 20.0 cm. Consider an element dl of the wire 0.100 cm long at the center of the box. Compute the magnitude dB of the magnetic field produced by this element at the points a, b, c, d, and e in Fig. E28.12. Points a, c, and d are at the centers of the faces of the cube; point b is at the midpoint of one edge; and point e is at a corner. Copy the figure and show the directions and relative magnitudes of the field vectors. (*Note:* Assume that the length dl is small in comparison to the distances from the current element to the points where the magnetic field is to be calculated.)

Figure **E28.12**

28.13 •• A long, straight wire lies along the z-axis and carries a 4.00-A current in the $+z$-direction. Find the magnetic field (magnitude and direction) produced at the following points by a 0.500-mm segment of the wire centered at the origin: (a) $x = 2.00$ m, $y = 0$, $z = 0$; (b) $x = 0$, $y = 2.00$ m, $z = 0$; (c) $x = 2.00$ m, $y = 2.00$ m, $z = 0$; (d) $x = 0$, $y = 0$, $z = 2.00$ m.

28.14 •• Two parallel wires are 5.00 cm apart and carry currents in opposite directions, as shown in Fig. E28.14. Find the magnitude and direction of the magnetic field at point P due to two 1.50-mm segments of wire that are opposite each other and each 8.00 cm from P.

Figure **E28.14**

28.15 • A wire carrying a 28.0-A current bends through a right angle. Consider two 2.00-mm segments of wire, each 3.00 cm from the bend (Fig. E28.15). Find the magnitude and direction of the magnetic field these two segments produce at point P, which is midway between them.

Figure **E28.15**

28.16 •• A square wire loop 10.0 cm on each side carries a clockwise current of 15.0 A. Find the magnitude and direction of the magnetic field at its center due to the four 1.20-mm wire segments at the midpoint of each side.

Section 28.3 Magnetic Field of a Straight Current-Carrying Conductor

28.17 • **The Magnetic Field from a Lightning Bolt.** Lightning bolts can carry currents up to approximately 20 kA. We can model such a current as the equivalent of a very long, straight wire. (a) If you were unfortunate enough to be 5.0 m away from such a lightning bolt, how large a magnetic field would you experience? (b) How does this field compare to one you would experience by being 5.0 cm from a long, straight household current of 10 A?

28.18 • A very long, straight horizontal wire carries a current such that 3.50×10^{18} electrons per second pass any given point going from west to east. What are the magnitude and direction of the magnetic field this wire produces at a point 4.00 cm directly above it?

28.19 • **BIO Currents in the Heart.** The body contains many small currents caused by the motion of ions in the organs and cells. Measurements of the magnetic field around the chest due to currents in the heart give values of about 10 μG. Although the actual currents are rather complicated, we can gain a rough understanding of their magnitude if we model them as a long, straight wire. If the surface of the chest is 5.0 cm from this current, how large is the current in the heart?

28.20 • **BIO Bacteria Navigation.** Certain bacteria (such as *Aquaspirillum magnetotacticum*) tend to swim toward the earth's geographic north pole because they contain tiny particles, called magnetosomes, that are sensitive to a magnetic field. If a transmission line carrying 100 A is laid underwater, at what range of distances would the magnetic field from this line be great enough to interfere with the migration of these bacteria? (Assume that a field less than 5 percent of the earth's field would have little effect on the bacteria. Take the earth's field to be 5.0×10^{-5} T and ignore the effects of the seawater.)

28.21 • (a) How large a current would a very long, straight wire have to carry so that the magnetic field 2.00 cm from the wire is equal to 1.00 G (comparable to the earth's northward-pointing magnetic field)? (b) If the wire is horizontal with the current running from east to west, at what locations would the magnetic field of the wire point in the same direction as the horizontal component of the earth's magnetic field? (c) Repeat part (b) except the wire is vertical with the current going upward.

28.22 • Two long, straight wires, one above the other, are separated by a distance $2a$ and are parallel to the x-axis. Let the $+y$-axis be in the plane of the wires in the direction from the lower wire to the upper wire. Each wire carries current I in the $+x$-direction. What are the magnitude and direction of the net magnetic field of the two wires at a point in the plane of the wires (a) midway between them; (b) at a distance a above the upper wire; (c) at a distance a below the lower wire?

28.23 •• A long, straight wire lies along the y-axis and carries a current $I = 8.00$ A in the $-y$-direction (Fig. E28.23). In addition to the magnetic field due to the current in the wire, a uniform magnetic field $\vec{B}_0$ with magnitude 1.50×10^{-6} T is in the $+x$-direction What is the total field (magnitude and direction) at the following points in the xz-plane: (a) $x = 0$, $z = 1.00$ m; (b) $x = 1.00$ m, $z = 0$; (c) $x = 0$, $z = -0.25$ m?

Figure **E28.23**

28.24 •• **BIO EMF.** Currents in dc transmission lines can be 100 A or more. Some people have expressed concern that the electromagnetic fields (EMFs) from such lines near their homes could cause health dangers. For a line with current 150 A and at a height of 8.0 m above the ground, what magnetic field does the line produce at ground level? Express your answer in teslas and as a percent of the earth's magnetic field, which is 0.50 gauss. Does this seem to be cause for worry?

28.25 • Two long, straight, parallel wires, 10.0 cm apart, carry equal 4.00-A currents in the same direction, as shown in Fig. E28.25. Find the magnitude and direction of the magnetic field at (a) point P_1, midway between the wires; (b) point P_2, 25.0 cm to the right of P_1; (c) point P_3, 20.0 cm directly above P_1.

Figure **E28.25**

28.26 •• A rectangular loop with dimensions 4.20 cm by 9.50 cm carries current I. The current in the loop produces a magnetic field at the center of the loop that has magnitude 5.50×10^{-5} T and direction away from you as you view the plane of the loop. What are the magnitude and direction (clockwise or counterclockwise) of the current in the loop?

28.27 • Four, long, parallel power lines each carry 100-A currents. A cross-sectional diagram of these lines is a square, 20.0 cm on each side. For each of the three cases shown in Fig. E28.27, calculate the magnetic field at the center of the square.

Figure **E28.27**

(a)   (b)   (c)

28.28 • Four very long, current-carrying wires in the same plane intersect to form a square 40.0 cm on each side, as shown in Fig. E28.28. Find the magnitude and direction of the current I so that the magnetic field at the center of the square is zero.

Figure **E28.28**   Figure **E28.29**

28.29 •• Two insulated wires perpendicular to each other in the same plane carry currents as shown in Fig. E28.29. Find the magnitude of the *net* magnetic field these wires produce at points P and Q if the 10.0 A-current is (a) to the right or (b) to the left.

Section 28.4 Force Between Parallel Conductors

28.30 • Three parallel wires each carry current I in the directions shown in Fig. E28.30. If the separation between adjacent wires is d, calculate the magnitude and direction of the net magnetic force per unit length on each wire.

Figure **E28.30**

28.31 • Two long, parallel wires are separated by a distance of 0.400 m (Fig. E28.31). The currents I_1 and I_2 have the directions shown. (a) Calculate the magnitude of the force exerted by each wire on a 1.20-m length of the other. Is the force attractive or repulsive? (b) Each current is doubled, so that I_1 becomes 10.0 A and I_2 becomes 4.00 A. Now what is the magnitude of the force that each wire exerts on a 1.20-m length of the other?

Figure **E28.31**

$I_1 =$
5.00 A
0.400 m
$I_2 =$
2.00 A

28.32 • Two long, parallel wires are separated by a distance of 2.50 cm. The force per unit length that each wire exerts on the other is 4.00×10^{-5} N/m, and the wires repel each other. The current in one wire is 0.600 A. (a) What is the current in the second wire? (b) Are the two currents in the same direction or in opposite directions?

28.33 • **Lamp Cord Wires.** The wires in a household lamp cord are typically 3.0 mm apart center to center and carry equal currents in opposite directions. If the cord carries current to a 100-W light bulb connected across a 120-V potential difference, what force per meter does each wire of the cord exert on the other? Is the force attractive or repulsive? Is this force large enough so it should be considered in the design of the lamp cord? (Model the lamp cord as a very long straight wire.)

28.34 • A long, horizontal wire *AB* rests on the surface of a table and carries a current *I*. Horizontal wire *CD* is vertically above wire *AB* and is free to slide up and down on the two vertical metal guides *C* and *D* (Fig. E28.34). Wire *CD* is connected through the sliding contacts to another wire that also carries a current *I*, opposite in direction to the current in wire *AB*. The mass per unit length of the wire *CD* is λ. To what equilibrium height *h* will the wire *CD* rise, assuming that the magnetic force on it is due entirely to the current in the wire *AB*?

Figure **E28.34**

I
C D
h
I
A B

Section 28.5 Magnetic Field of a Circular Current Loop

28.35 • **BIO Currents in the Brain.** The magnetic field around the head has been measured to be approximately 3.0×10^{-8} G. Although the currents that cause this field are quite complicated, we can get a rough estimate of their size by modeling them as a single circular current loop 16 cm (the width of a typical head) in diameter. What is the current needed to produce such a field at the center of the loop?

28.36 • Calculate the magnitude and direction of the magnetic field at point *P* due to the current in the semicircular section of wire shown in Fig. E28.36. (*Hint:* Does the current in the long, straight section of the wire produce any field at *P*?)

Figure **E28.36**

R
P
I I

Figure **E28.37**

28.37 •• Calculate the magnitude of the magnetic field at point *P* of Fig. E28.37 in terms of *R*, I_1, and I_2. What does your expression give when $I_1 = I_2$?

I_1 R I_1
R P
I_2 I_2

28.38 •• A closely wound, circular coil with radius 2.40 cm has 800 turns. (a) What must the current in the coil be if the magnetic field at the center of the coil is 0.0580 T? (b) At what distance *x* from the center of the coil, on the axis of the coil, is the magnetic field half its value at the center?

28.39 •• A closely wound, circular coil with a diameter of 4.00 cm has 600 turns and carries a current of 0.500 A. What is the magnitude of the magnetic field (a) at the center of the coil and (b) at a point on the axis of the coil 8.00 cm from its center?

28.40 •• A closely wound coil has a radius of 6.00 cm and carries a current of 2.50 A. How many turns must it have if, at a point on the coil axis 6.00 cm from the center of the coil, the magnetic field is 6.39×10^{-4} T?

28.41 •• Two concentric circular loops of wire lie on a tabletop, one inside the other. The inner wire has a diameter of 20.0 cm and carries a clockwise current of 12.0 A, as viewed from above, and the outer wire has a diameter of 30.0 cm. What must be the magnitude and direction (as viewed from above) of the current in the outer wire so that the net magnetic field due to this combination of wires is zero at the common center of the wires?

Section 28.6 Ampere's Law

28.42 • Figure E28.42 shows, in cross section, several conductors that carry currents through the plane of the figure. The currents have the magnitudes $I_1 = 4.0$ A, $I_2 = 6.0$ A, and $I_3 = 2.0$ A, and the directions shown. Four paths, labeled *a* through *d*, are shown. What is the line integral $\oint \vec{B} \cdot d\vec{l}$ for each path? Each integral involves going around the path in the counterclockwise direction. Explain your answers.

Figure **E28.42**

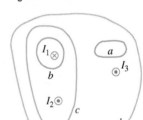
$I_1 \otimes$
a
b
$I_3 \odot$
$I_2 \odot$
c
d

28.43 • A closed curve encircles several conductors. The line integral $\oint \vec{B} \cdot d\vec{l}$ around this curve is 3.83×10^{-4} T·m. (a) What is the net current in the conductors? (b) If you were to integrate around the curve in the opposite direction, what would be the value of the line integral? Explain.

Section 28.7 Applications of Ampere's Law

28.44 •• As a new electrical technician, you are designing a large solenoid to produce a uniform 0.150-T magnetic field near the center of the solenoid. You have enough wire for 4000 circular turns. This solenoid must be 1.40 m long and 2.80 cm in diameter. What current will you need to produce the necessary field?

28.45 • **Coaxial Cable.** A solid conductor with radius *a* is supported by insulating disks on the axis of a conducting tube with inner radius *b* and outer radius *c* (Fig. E28.45). The central conductor and tube carry equal currents *I* in opposite directions. The currents are distributed uniformly over the cross sections of each conductor. Derive an expression for the magnitude of the magnetic field (a) at points outside the central, solid conductor but inside the tube ($a < r < b$) and (b) at points outside the tube ($r > c$).

Figure **E28.45**

a
I
I
c
b

28.46 • Repeat Exercise 28.45 for the case in which the current in the central, solid conductor is I_1, the current in the tube is I_2, and these currents are in the same direction rather than in opposite directions.

28.47 • A long, straight, cylindrical wire of radius R carries a current uniformly distributed over its cross section. At what locations is the magnetic field produced by this current equal to half of its largest value? Consider points inside and outside the wire.

28.48 •• A 15.0-cm-long solenoid with radius 0.750 cm is closely wound with 600 turns of wire. The current in the windings is 8.00 A. Compute the magnetic field at a point near the center of the solenoid.

28.49 •• A solenoid is designed to produce a magnetic field of 0.0270 T at its center. It has radius 1.40 cm and length 40.0 cm, and the wire can carry a maximum current of 12.0 A. (a) What minimum number of turns per unit length must the solenoid have? (b) What total length of wire is required?

28.50 • A toroidal solenoid has an inner radius of 12.0 cm and an outer radius of 15.0 cm. It carries a current of 1.50 A. How many equally spaced turns must it have so that it will produce a magnetic field of 3.75 mT at points within the coils 14.0 cm from its center?

28.51 • A magnetic field of 37.2 T has been achieved at the MIT Francis Bitter National Magnetic Laboratory. Find the current needed to achieve such a field (a) 2.00 cm from a long, straight wire; (b) at the center of a circular coil of radius 42.0 cm that has 100 turns; (c) near the center of a solenoid with radius 2.40 cm, length 32.0 cm, and 40,000 turns.

28.52 • A toroidal solenoid (see Example 28.10) has inner radius $r_1 = 15.0$ cm and outer radius $r_2 = 18.0$ cm. The solenoid has 250 turns and carries a current of 8.50 A. What is the magnitude of the magnetic field at the following distances from the center of the torus: (a) 12.0 cm; (b) 16.0 cm; (c) 20.0 cm?

28.53 •• A wooden ring whose mean diameter is 14.0 cm is wound with a closely spaced toroidal winding of 600 turns. Compute the magnitude of the magnetic field at the center of the cross section of the windings when the current in the windings is 0.650 A.

Section 28.8 Magnetic Materials

28.54 •• A toroidal solenoid with 400 turns of wire and a mean radius of 6.0 cm carries a current of 0.25 A. The relative permeability of the core is 80. (a) What is the magnetic field in the core? (b) What part of the magnetic field is due to atomic currents?

28.55 • A toroidal solenoid with 500 turns is wound on a ring with a mean radius of 2.90 cm. Find the current in the winding that is required to set up a magnetic field of 0.350 T in the ring (a) if the ring is made of annealed iron ($K_m = 1400$) and (b) if the ring is made of silicon steel ($K_m = 5200$).

28.56 • The current in the windings of a toroidal solenoid is 2.400 A. There are 500 turns, and the mean radius is 25.00 cm. The toroidal solenoid is filled with a magnetic material. The magnetic field inside the windings is found to be 1.940 T. Calculate (a) the relative permeability and (b) the magnetic susceptibility of the material that fills the toroid.

28.57 • A long solenoid with 60 turns of wire per centimeter carries a current of 0.15 A. The wire that makes up the solenoid is wrapped around a solid core of silicon steel ($K_m = 5200$). (The wire of the solenoid is jacketed with an insulator so that none of the current flows into the core.) (a) For a point inside the core, find the magnitudes of (i) the magnetic field $\vec{B}_0$ due to the solenoid current; (ii) the magnetization $\vec{M}$; (iii) the total magnetic field $\vec{B}$. (b) In a sketch of the solenoid and core, show the directions of the vectors $\vec{B}$, $\vec{B}_0$, and $\vec{M}$ inside the core.

28.58 • When a certain paramagnetic material is placed in an external magnetic field of 1.5000 T, the field inside the material is measured to be 1.5023 T. Find (a) the relative permeability and (b) the magnetic permeability of this material.

PROBLEMS

28.59 •• A pair of point charges, $q = +8.00$ μC and $q' = -5.00$ μC, are moving as shown in Fig. P28.59 with speeds $v = 9.00 \times 10^4$ m/s and $v' = 6.50 \times 10^4$ m/s. When the charges are at the locations shown in the figure, what are the magnitude and direction of (a) the magnetic field produced at the origin and (b) the magnetic force that q' exerts on q?

Figure **P28.59**

28.60 •• At a particular instant, charge $q_1 = +4.80 \times 10^{-6}$ C is at the point (0, 0.250 m, 0) and has velocity $\vec{v}_1 = (9.20 \times 10^5 \text{ m/s})\hat{\imath}$. Charge $q_2 = -2.90 \times 10^{-6}$ C is at the point (0.150 m, 0, 0) and has velocity $\vec{v}_2 = (-5.30 \times 10^5 \text{ m/s})\hat{\jmath}$. At this instant, what are the magnitude and direction of the magnetic force that q_1 exerts on q_2?

28.61 ••• Two long, parallel transmission lines, 40.0 cm apart, carry 25.0-A and 75.0-A currents. Find all locations where the net magnetic field of the two wires is zero if these currents are in (a) the same direction and (b) the opposite direction.

28.62 • A long, straight wire carries a current of 5.20 A. An electron is traveling in the vicinity of the wire. At the instant when the electron is 4.50 cm from the wire and traveling with a speed of 6.00×10^4 m/s directly toward the wire, what are the magnitude and direction (relative to the direction of the current) of the force that the magnetic field of the current exerts on the electron?

28.63 • CP A long, straight wire carries a 13.0-A current. An electron is fired parallel to this wire with a velocity of 250 km/s in the same direction as the current, 2.00 cm from the wire. (a) Find the magnitude and direction of the electron's initial acceleration. (b) What should be the magnitude and direction of a uniform electric field that will allow the electron to continue to travel parallel to the wire? (c) Is it necessary to include the effects of gravity? Justify your answer.

28.64 • Two very long, straight wires carry currents as shown in Fig. P28.64. For each case, find all locations where the net magnetic field is zero.

Figure **P28.64**

(a)   (b)   (c)

28.65 •• CP Two identical circular, wire loops 40.0 cm in diameter each carry a current of 3.80 A in the same direction. These loops are parallel to each other and are 25.0 cm apart. Line ab is normal to the plane of the loops and passes through their centers.

A proton is fired at 2400 km/s perpendicular to line *ab* from a point midway between the centers of the loops. Find the magnitude of the magnetic force these loops exert on the proton just after it is fired.

28.66 • A negative point charge $q = -7.20$ mC is moving in a reference frame. When the point charge is at the origin, the magnetic field it produces at the point $x = 25.0$ cm, $y = 0$, $z = 0$ is $\vec{B} = (6.00\ \mu\text{T})\hat{j}$, and its speed is 800 m/s. (a) What are the x-, y-, and z-components of the velocity $\vec{v}_0$ of the charge? (b) At this same instant, what is the magnitude of the magnetic field that the charge produces at the point $x = 0$, $y = 25.0$ cm, $z = 0$?

28.67 • Two long, straight, parallel wires are 1.00 m apart (Fig. P28.67). The wire on the left carries a current I_1 of 6.00 A into the plane of the paper. (a) What must the magnitude and direction of the current I_2 be for the net field at point P to be zero? (b) Then what are the magnitude and direction of the net field at Q? (c) Then what is the magnitude of the net field at S?

Figure **P28.67**

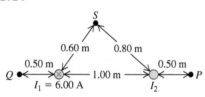

28.68 •• Figure P28.68 shows an end view of two long, parallel wires perpendicular to the *xy*-plane, each carrying a current *I* but in opposite directions. (a) Copy the diagram, and draw vectors to show the $\vec{B}$ field of each wire and the net $\vec{B}$ field at point *P*. (b) Derive the expression for the magnitude of $\vec{B}$ at any point on the *x*-axis in terms of the *x*-coordinate of the point. What is the direction of $\vec{B}$? (c) Graph the magnitude of $\vec{B}$ at points on the *x*-axis. (d) At what value of *x* is the magnitude of $\vec{B}$ a maximum? (e) What is the magnitude of $\vec{B}$ when $x \gg a$?

Figure **P28.68**

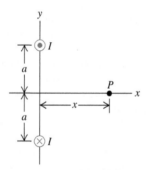

28.69 • Refer to the situation in Problem 28.68. Suppose that a third long, straight wire, parallel to the other two, passes through point *P* (see Fig. P28.68) and that each wire carries a current $I = 6.00$ A. Let $a = 40.0$ cm and $x = 60.0$ cm. Find the magnitude and direction of the force per unit length on the third wire, (a) if the current in it is directed into the plane of the figure, and (b) if the current in it is directed out of the plane of the figure.

28.70 •• **CP** A pair of long, rigid metal rods, each of length *L*, lie parallel to each other on a perfectly smooth table. Their ends are connected by identical, very light conducting springs of force constant *k* (Fig. P28.70) and negligible unstretched length. If a current *I* runs through this circuit, the springs will stretch. At what separation will the rods remain at rest? Assume that *k* is large enough so that the separation of the rods will be much less than *L*.

Figure **P28.70**

28.71 ••• **CP** Two long, parallel wires hang by 4.00-cm-long cords from a common axis (Fig. P28.71). The wires have a mass per unit length of 0.0125 kg/m and carry the same current in opposite directions. What is the current in each wire if the cords hang at an angle of 6.00° with the vertical?

Figure **P28.71**

28.72 • The long, straight wire *AB* shown in Fig. P28.72 carries a current of 14.0 A. The rectangular loop whose long edges are parallel to the wire carries a current of 5.00 A. Find the magnitude and direction of the net force exerted on the loop by the magnetic field of the wire.

Figure **P28.72**

28.73 •• **CP** A flat, round iron ring 5.00 cm in diameter has a current running through it that produces a magnetic field of 75.4 μT at its center. This ring is placed in a uniform external magnetic field of 0.375 T. What is the maximum torque the external field can exert on the ring? Show how the ring should be oriented relative to the field for the torque to have its maximum value.

28.74 • The wire semicircles shown in Fig. P28.74 have radii *a* and *b*. Calculate the net magnetic field (magnitude and direction) that the current in the wires produces at point *P*.

Figure **P28.74**

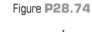

28.75 • **CALC** **Helmholtz Coils.** Figure 28.75 is a sectional view of two circular coils with radius *a*, each wound with *N* turns of wire carrying a current *I*, circulating in the same direction in both coils. The coils are separated by a distance *a* equal to their radii. In this configuration the coils are called Helmholtz coils; they produce a very uniform magnetic field in the region between them. (a) Derive the expression for the magnitude *B* of the magnetic field at a point on the axis a distance *x* to the right of point *P*, which is midway between the coils. (b) Graph *B* versus *x* for $x = 0$ to $x = a/2$. Compare this graph to one for the magnetic field due to the right-hand coil alone. (c) From part (a), obtain an expression for the magnitude of the magnetic field at point *P*. (d) Calculate the magnitude of the magnetic field at *P* if $N = 300$ turns, $I = 6.00$ A, and $a = 8.00$ cm. (e) Calculate dB/dx and d^2B/dx^2 at $P(x = 0)$. Discuss how your results show that the field is very uniform in the vicinity of *P*.

Figure **P28.75**   Figure **P28.76**

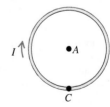

28.76 • A circular wire of diameter *D* lies on a horizontal table and carries a current *I*. In Fig. P28.76 point *A* marks the center of the circle and point *C* is on its rim. (a) Find the magnitude and direction of the magnetic field at point A. (b) The wire is now unwrapped so it is straight, centered on point C, and perpendicular to the line AC, but the same current is maintained in it. Now find the magnetic field at point A. (c) Which field is greater: the one in part (a) or in part (b)? By what factor? Why is this result physically reasonable?

28.77 • **CALC** A long, straight wire with a circular cross section of radius R carries a current I. Assume that the current density is not constant across the cross section of the wire, but rather varies as $J = \alpha r$, where α is a constant. (a) By the requirement that J integrated over the cross section of the wire gives the total current I, calculate the constant α in terms of I and R. (b) Use Ampere's law to calculate the magnetic field $B(r)$ for (i) $r \leq R$ and (ii) $r \geq R$. Express your answers in terms of I.

28.78 • **CALC** The wire shown in Fig. P28.78 is infinitely long and carries a current I. Calculate the magnitude and direction of the magnetic field that this current produces at point P.

Figure **P28.78**

28.79 • A conductor is made in the form of a hollow cylinder with inner and outer radii a and b, respectively. It carries a current I uniformly distributed over its cross section. Derive expressions for the magnitude of the magnetic field in the regions (a) $r < a$; (b) $a < r < b$; (c) $r > b$.

28.80 • A circular loop has radius R and carries current I_2 in a clockwise direction (Fig. P28.80). The center of the loop is a distance D above a long, straight wire. What are the magnitude and direction of the current I_1 in the wire if the magnetic field at the center of the loop is zero?

Figure **P28.80**

28.81 • **CALC** A long, straight, solid cylinder, oriented with its axis in the z-direction, carries a current whose current density is $\vec{J}$. The current density, although symmetric about the cylinder axis, is not constant but varies according to the relationship

$$\vec{J} = \frac{2I_0}{\pi a^2}\left[1 - \left(\frac{r}{a}\right)^2\right]\hat{k} \quad \text{for } r \leq a$$

$$= 0 \quad \text{for } r \geq a$$

where a is the radius of the cylinder, r is the radial distance from the cylinder axis, and I_0 is a constant having units of amperes. (a) Show that I_0 is the total current passing through the entire cross section of the wire. (b) Using Ampere's law, derive an expression for the magnitude of the magnetic field $\vec{B}$ in the region $r \geq a$. (c) Obtain an expression for the current I contained in a circular cross section of radius $r \leq a$ and centered at the cylinder axis. (d) Using Ampere's law, derive an expression for the magnitude of the magnetic field $\vec{B}$ in the region $r \leq a$. How do your results in parts (b) and (d) compare for $r = a$?

28.82 • A long, straight, solid cylinder, oriented with its axis in the z-direction, carries a current whose current density is $\vec{J}$. The current density, although symmetric about the cylinder axis, is not constant and varies according to the relationship

$$\vec{J} = \left(\frac{b}{r}\right)e^{(r-a)/\delta}\hat{k} \quad \text{for } r \leq a$$

$$= 0 \quad \text{for } r \geq a$$

where the radius of the cylinder is $a = 5.00$ cm, r is the radial distance from the cylinder axis, b is a constant equal to 600 A/m, and δ is a constant equal to 2.50 cm. (a) Let I_0 be the total current passing

through the entire cross section of the wire. Obtain an expression for I_0 in terms of b, δ, and a. Evaluate your expression to obtain a numerical value for I_0. (b) Using Ampere's law, derive an expression for the magnetic field $\vec{B}$ in the region $r \geq a$. Express your answer in terms of I_0 rather than b. (c) Obtain an expression for the current I contained in a circular cross section of radius $r \leq a$ and centered at the cylinder axis. Express your answer in terms of I_0 rather than b. (d) Using Ampere's law, derive an expression for the magnetic field $\vec{B}$ in the region $r \leq a$. (e) Evaluate the magnitude of the magnetic field at $r = \delta$, $r = a$, and $r = 2a$.

28.83 • **An Infinite Current Sheet.** Long, straight conductors with square cross sections and each carrying current I are laid side by side to form an infinite current sheet (Fig. P28.83). The conductors lie in the xy-plane, are parallel to the y-axis, and carry current in the +y-direction There are n conductors per unit length measured along the x-axis. (a) What are the magnitude and direction of the magnetic field a distance a below the current sheet? (b) What are the magnitude and direction of the magnetic field a distance a above the current sheet?

Figure **P28.83**

28.84 • Long, straight conductors with square cross section, each carrying current I, are laid side by side to form an infinite current sheet with current directed out of the plane of the page (Fig. P28.84). A second infinite current sheet is a distance d below the first and is parallel to it. The second sheet carries current into the plane of the page. Each sheet has n conductors per unit length. (Refer to Problem 28.83.) Calculate the magnitude and direction of the net magnetic field at (a) point P (above the upper sheet); (b) point R (midway between the two sheets); (c) point S (below the lower sheet).

Figure **P28.84**

28.85 • **CP** A piece of iron has magnetization $M = 6.50 \times 10^4$ A/m. Find the average magnetic dipole moment *per atom* in this piece of iron. Express your answer both in A·m² and in Bohr magnetons. The density of iron is given in Table 14.1, and the atomic mass of iron (in grams per mole) is given in Appendix D. The chemical symbol for iron is Fe.

CHALLENGE PROBLEMS

28.86 ••• A wide, long, insulating belt has a uniform positive charge per unit area σ on its upper surface. Rollers at each end move the belt to the right at a constant speed v. Calculate the magnitude and direction of the magnetic field produced by the moving belt at a point just above its surface. (*Hint:* At points near the surface and far from its edges or ends, the moving belt can be considered to be an infinite current sheet like that in Problem 28.83.)

28.87 ••• **CP** Two long, straight conducting wires with linear mass density λ are suspended from cords so that they are each horizontal, parallel to each other, and a distance d apart. The back ends of the wires are connected to each other by a slack, low-resistance connecting wire. A charged capacitor (capacitance C) is now added to the system; the positive plate of the capacitor (initial charge $+Q_0$) is connected to the front end of one of the wires, and the negative plate of the capacitor (initial charge $-Q_0$) is connected to the front end of the other wire (Fig. P28.87). Both of these connections are also made by slack, low-resistance wires. When the connection is made, the wires are pushed aside by the repulsive force between the wires, and each wire has an initial horizontal velocity of magnitude v_0. Assume that the time constant for the capacitor to discharge is negligible compared to the time it takes for any appreciable displacement in the position of the wires to occur. (a) Show that the initial speed v_0 of either wire is given by

$$v_0 = \frac{\mu_0 Q_0^2}{4\pi \lambda RCd}$$

Figure **P28.87**

where R is the total resistance of the circuit. (b) To what height h will each wire rise as a result of the circuit connection?

28.88 ••• **CALC** A wire in the shape of a semicircle with radius a is oriented in the yz-plane with its center of curvature at the origin (Fig. P28.88). If the current in the wire is I, calculate the magnetic-field components produced at point P, a distance x out along the x-axis. (*Note:* Do not forget the contribution from the straight wire at the bottom of the semicircle that runs from $z = -a$ to $z = +a$. You may use the fact that the fields of the two antiparallel currents at $z > a$ cancel, but you must explain *why* they cancel.)

Figure **P28.88**

Answers

Chapter Opening Question ?

There would be *no* change in the magnetic field strength. From Example 28.9 (Section 28.7), the field inside a solenoid has magnitude $B = \mu_0 n I$, where n is the number of turns of wire per unit length. Joining two solenoids end to end doubles both the number of turns and the length, so the number of turns per unit length is unchanged.

Test Your Understanding Questions

28.1 Answers: (a) (i), (b) (ii) The situation is the same as shown in Fig. 28.2 except that the upper proton has velocity $\vec{v}$ rather than $-\vec{v}$. The magnetic field due to the lower proton is the same as shown in Fig. 28.2, but the direction of the magnetic force $\vec{F} = q\vec{v} \times \vec{B}$ on the upper proton is reversed. Hence the magnetic force is attractive. Since the speed v is small compared to c, the magnetic force is much smaller in magnitude than the repulsive electric force and the net force is still repulsive.

28.2 Answer: (i) and (iii) (tie), (iv), (ii) From Eq. (28.5), the magnitude of the field dB due to a current element of length dl carrying current I is $dB = (\mu/4\pi)(I\,dl\sin\phi/r^2)$. In this expression r is the distance from the element to the field point, and ϕ is the angle between the direction of the current and a vector from the current element to the field point. All four points are the same distance $r = L$ from the current element, so the value of dB is proportional to the value of $\sin\phi$. For the four points the angle is (i) $\phi = 90°$, (ii) $\phi = 0$, (iii) $\phi = 90°$, and (iv) $\phi = 45°$, so the values of $\sin\phi$ are (i) 1, (ii) 0, (iii) 1, and (iv) $1/\sqrt{2}$.

28.3 Answer: A This orientation will cause current to flow clockwise around the circuit. Hence current will flow south through the wire that lies under the compass. From the right-hand rule for the magnetic field produced by a long, straight, current-carrying conductor, this will produce a magnetic field that points to the left at the position of the compass (which lies atop the wire). The combination of the northward magnetic field of the earth and the westward field produced by the current gives a net magnetic field to the northwest, so the compass needle will swing counterclockwise to align with this field.

28.4 Answers: (a) (i), (b) (iii), (c) (ii), (d) (iii) Current flows in the same direction in adjacent turns of the coil, so the magnetic forces between these turns are attractive. Current flows in opposite directions on opposite sides of the same turn, so the magnetic forces between these sides are repulsive. Thus the magnetic forces on the

solenoid turns squeeze them together in the direction along its axis but push them apart radially. The *electric* forces are zero because the wire is electrically neutral, with as much positive charge as there is negative charge.

28.5 Answers: (a) (ii), (b) (v) The vector $d\vec{B}$ is in the direction of $d\vec{l} \times \vec{r}$. For a segment on the negative y-axis, $d\vec{l} = -\hat{k}\,dl$ points in the negative z-direction and $\vec{r} = x\hat{i} + a\hat{j}$. Hence $d\vec{l} \times \vec{r} = (a\,dl)\hat{i} - (x\,dl)\hat{j}$, which has a positive x-component, a negative y-component, and zero z-component. For a segment on the negative z-axis, $d\vec{l} = \hat{j}\,dl$ points in the positive y-direction and $\vec{r} = x\hat{i} + a\hat{k}$. Hence $d\vec{l} \times \vec{r} = 1(a\,dl)\hat{i} - 1(x\,dl)\hat{k}$, which has a positive x-component, zero y-component, and a negative z-component.

28.6 Answer: (ii) Imagine carrying out the integral $\oint \vec{B} \cdot d\vec{l}$ along an integration path that goes counterclockwise around the red magnetic field line. At each point along the path the magnetic field $\vec{B}$ and the infinitesimal segment $d\vec{l}$ are both tangent to the path, so $\vec{B} \cdot d\vec{l}$ is positive at each point and the integral $\oint \vec{B} \cdot d\vec{l}$ is likewise positive. It follows from Ampere's law $\oint \vec{B} \cdot d\vec{l} = \mu_0 I_{encl}$ and the right-hand rule that the integration path encloses a current directed out of the plane of the page. There are no currents in the empty space outside the magnet, so there must be currents inside the magnet (see Section 28.8).

28.7 Answer: (iii) By symmetry, any $\vec{B}$ field outside the cable must circulate around the cable, with circular field lines like those surrounding the solid cylindrical conductor in Fig. 28.20. Choose an integration path like the one shown in Fig. 28.20 with radius $r > R$, so that the path completely encloses the cable. As in Example 28.8, the integral $\oint \vec{B} \cdot d\vec{l}$ for this path has magnitude $B(2\pi r)$. From Ampere's law this is equal to $\mu_0 I_{encl}$. The net enclosed current I_{encl} is zero because it includes two currents of equal magnitude but opposite direction: one in the central wire and one in the hollow cylinder. Hence $B(2\pi r) = 0$, and so $B = 0$ for any value of r outside the cable. (The field is nonzero *inside* the cable; see Exercise 28.45.)

28.8 Answer: (i), (iv) Sodium and uranium are paramagnetic materials and hence are attracted to a magnet, while bismuth and lead are diamagnetic materials that are repelled by a magnet. (See Table 28.1.)

Bridging Problem

Answer: $B = \dfrac{\mu_0 n Q}{a}$

ELECTROMAGNETIC INDUCTION

? When a credit card is "swiped" through a card reader, the information coded in a magnetic pattern on the back of the card is transmitted to the cardholder's bank. Why is it necessary to swipe the card rather than holding it motionless in the card reader's slot?

LEARNING GOALS

By studying this chapter, you will learn:

• The experimental evidence that a changing magnetic field induces an emf.

• How Faraday's law relates the induced emf in a loop to the change in magnetic flux through the loop.

• How to determine the direction of an induced emf.

• How to calculate the emf induced in a conductor moving through a magnetic field.

• How a changing magnetic flux generates an electric field that is very different from that produced by an arrangement of charges.

• The four fundamental equations that completely describe both electricity and magnetism.

Almost every modern device or machine, from a computer to a washing machine to a power drill, has electric circuits at its heart. We learned in Chapter 25 that an electromotive force (emf) is required for a current to flow in a circuit; in Chapters 25 and 26 we almost always took the source of emf to be a battery. But for the vast majority of electric devices that are used in industry and in the home (including any device that you plug into a wall socket), the source of emf is *not* a battery but an electric generating station. Such a station produces electric energy by converting other forms of energy: gravitational potential energy at a hydroelectric plant, chemical energy in a coal- or oil-fired plant, nuclear energy at a nuclear plant. But how is this energy conversion done?

The answer is a phenomenon known as *electromagnetic induction:* If the magnetic flux through a circuit changes, an emf and a current are induced in the circuit. In a power-generating station, magnets move relative to coils of wire to produce a changing magnetic flux in the coils and hence an emf. Other key components of electric power systems, such as transformers, also depend on magnetically induced emfs.

The central principle of electromagnetic induction, and the keystone of this chapter, is *Faraday's law.* This law relates induced emf to changing magnetic flux in any loop, including a closed circuit. We also discuss Lenz's law, which helps us to predict the directions of induced emfs and currents. These principles will allow us to understand electrical energy-conversion devices such as motors, generators, and transformers.

Electromagnetic induction tells us that a time-varying magnetic field can act as a source of electric field. We will also see how a time-varying *electric* field can act as a source of *magnetic* field. These remarkable results form part of a neat package of formulas, called *Maxwell's equations,* that describe the behavior of electric and magnetic fields in *any* situation. Maxwell's equations pave the way toward an understanding of electromagnetic waves, the topic of Chapter 32.

29.1 Induction Experiments

During the 1830s, several pioneering experiments with magnetically induced emf were carried out in England by Michael Faraday and in the United States by Joseph Henry (1797–1878), later the first director of the Smithsonian Institution. Figure 29.1 shows several examples. In Fig. 29.1a, a coil of wire is connected to a galvanometer. When the nearby magnet is stationary, the meter shows no current. This isn't surprising; there is no source of emf in the circuit. But when we *move* the magnet either toward or away from the coil, the meter shows current in the circuit, but *only* while the magnet is moving (Fig. 29.1b). If we keep the magnet stationary and move the coil, we again detect a current during the motion. We call this an **induced current,** and the corresponding emf required to cause this current is called an **induced emf.**

In Fig. 29.1c we replace the magnet with a second coil connected to a battery. When the second coil is stationary, there is no current in the first coil. However, when we move the second coil toward or away from the first or move the first toward or away from the second, there is current in the first coil, but again *only* while one coil is moving relative to the other.

Finally, using the two-coil setup in Fig. 29.1d, we keep both coils stationary and vary the current in the second coil, either by opening and closing the switch or by changing the resistance of the second coil with the switch closed (perhaps by changing the second coil's temperature). We find that as we open or close the switch, there is a momentary current pulse in the first circuit. When we vary the resistance (and thus the current) in the second coil, there is an induced current in the first circuit, but only while the current in the second circuit is changing.

To explore further the common elements in these observations, let's consider a more detailed series of experiments (Fig. 29.2). We connect a coil of wire to a galvanometer and then place the coil between the poles of an electromagnet whose magnetic field we can vary. Here's what we observe:

1. When there is no current in the electromagnet, so that $\vec{B} = 0$, the galvanometer shows no current.
2. When the electromagnet is turned on, there is a momentary current through the meter as $\vec{B}$ increases.
3. When $\vec{B}$ levels off at a steady value, the current drops to zero, no matter how large $\vec{B}$ is.
4. With the coil in a horizontal plane, we squeeze it so as to decrease the cross-sectional area of the coil. The meter detects current only *during* the

29.1 Demonstrating the phenomenon of induced current.

(a) A stationary magnet does NOT induce a current in a coil.

All these actions DO induce a current in the coil. What do they have in common?*

(b) Moving the magnet toward or away from the coil

(c) Moving a second, current-carrying coil toward or away from the coil

(d) Varying the current in the second coil (by closing or opening a switch)

Meter shows zero current.

Meter shows induced current.

*They cause the magnetic field through the coil to *change*.

deformation, not before or after. When we increase the area to return the coil to its original shape, there is current in the opposite direction, but only while the area of the coil is changing.

5. If we rotate the coil a few degrees about a horizontal axis, the meter detects current during the rotation, in the same direction as when we decreased the area. When we rotate the coil back, there is a current in the opposite direction during this rotation.
6. If we jerk the coil out of the magnetic field, there is a current during the motion, in the same direction as when we decreased the area.
7. If we decrease the number of turns in the coil by unwinding one or more turns, there is a current during the unwinding, in the same direction as when we decreased the area. If we wind more turns onto the coil, there is a current in the opposite direction during the winding.
8. When the magnet is turned off, there is a momentary current in the direction opposite to the current when it was turned on.
9. The faster we carry out any of these changes, the greater the current.
10. If all these experiments are repeated with a coil that has the same shape but different material and different resistance, the current in each case is inversely proportional to the total circuit resistance. This shows that the induced emfs that are causing the current do not depend on the material of the coil but only on its shape and the magnetic field.

29.2 A coil in a magnetic field. When the $\vec{B}$ field is constant and the shape, location, and orientation of the coil do not change, no current is induced in the coil. A current is induced when any of these factors change.

The common element in all these experiments is changing *magnetic flux* Φ_B through the coil connected to the galvanometer. In each case the flux changes either because the magnetic field changes with time or because the coil is moving through a nonuniform magnetic field. Faraday's law of induction, the subject of the next section, states that in all of these situations the induced emf is proportional to the *rate of change* of magnetic flux Φ_B through the coil. The *direction* of the induced emf depends on whether the flux is increasing or decreasing. If the flux is constant, there is no induced emf.

Induced emfs are not mere laboratory curiosities but have a tremendous number of practical applications. If you are reading these words indoors, you are making use of induced emfs right now! At the power plant that supplies your neighborhood, an electric generator produces an emf by varying the magnetic flux through coils of wire. (In the next section we'll see in detail how this is done.) This emf supplies the voltage between the terminals of the wall sockets in your home, and this voltage supplies the power to your reading lamp. Indeed, any appliance that you plug into a wall socket makes use of induced emfs.

Magnetically induced emfs, just like the emfs discussed in Section 25.4, are the result of *nonelectrostatic* forces. We have to distinguish carefully between the electrostatic electric fields produced by charges (according to Coulomb's law) and the nonelectrostatic electric fields produced by changing magnetic fields. We'll return to this distinction later in this chapter and the next.

29.2 Faraday's Law

The common element in all induction effects is changing magnetic flux through a circuit. Before stating the simple physical law that summarizes all of the kinds of experiments described in Section 29.1, let's first review the concept of magnetic flux Φ_B (which we introduced in Section 27.3). For an infinitesimal-area element $d\vec{A}$ in a magnetic field $\vec{B}$ (Fig. 29.3), the magnetic flux $d\Phi_B$ through the area is

$$d\Phi_B = \vec{B} \cdot d\vec{A} = B_\perp \, dA = B \, dA \cos\phi$$

where $B_\perp$ is the component of $\vec{B}$ perpendicular to the surface of the area element and ϕ is the angle between $\vec{B}$ and $d\vec{A}$. (As in Chapter 27, be careful to distinguish

29.3 Calculating the magnetic flux through an area element.

Magnetic flux through element of area $d\vec{A}$:
$d\Phi_B = \vec{B} \cdot d\vec{A} = B_\perp dA = B \, dA \cos\phi$

29.4 Calculating the flux of a uniform magnetic field through a flat area. (Compare to Fig. 22.6, which shows the rules for calculating the flux of a uniform *electric* field.)

Surface is face-on to magnetic field:
• $\vec{B}$ and $\vec{A}$ are parallel (the angle between $\vec{B}$ and $\vec{A}$ is $\phi = 0$).
• The magnetic flux $\Phi_B = \vec{B} \cdot \vec{A} = BA$.

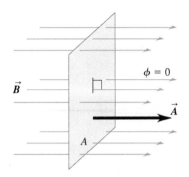

Surface is tilted from a face-on orientation by an angle ϕ:
• The angle between $\vec{B}$ and $\vec{A}$ is ϕ.
• The magnetic flux $\Phi_B = \vec{B} \cdot \vec{A} = BA \cos \phi$.

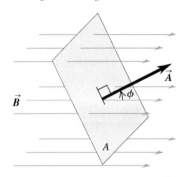

Surface is edge-on to magnetic field:
• $\vec{B}$ and $\vec{A}$ are perpendicular (the angle between $\vec{B}$ and $\vec{A}$ is $\phi = 90°$).
• The magnetic flux $\Phi_B = \vec{B} \cdot \vec{A} = BA \cos 90° = 0$.

between two quantities named "phi," ϕ and Φ_B.) The total magnetic flux Φ_B through a finite area is the integral of this expression over the area:

$$\Phi_B = \int \vec{B} \cdot d\vec{A} = \int B \, dA \cos \phi \qquad (29.1)$$

If $\vec{B}$ is uniform over a flat area $\vec{A}$, then

$$\Phi_B = \vec{B} \cdot \vec{A} = BA \cos \phi \qquad (29.2)$$

Figure 29.4 reviews the rules for using Eq. (29.2).

CAUTION **Choosing the direction of $d\vec{A}$ or $\vec{A}$** In Eqs. (29.1) and (29.2) we have to be careful to define the direction of the vector area $d\vec{A}$ or $\vec{A}$ unambiguously. There are always two directions perpendicular to any given area, and the sign of the magnetic flux through the area depends on which one we choose to be positive. For example, in Fig. 29.3 we chose $d\vec{A}$ to point upward so ϕ is less than 90° and $\vec{B} \cdot d\vec{A}$ is positive. We could have chosen instead to have $d\vec{A}$ point downward, in which case ϕ would have been greater than 90° and $\vec{B} \cdot d\vec{A}$ would have been negative. Either choice is equally good, but once we make a choice we must stick with it. ∎

Faraday's law of induction states:

> **The induced emf in a closed loop equals the negative of the time rate of change of magnetic flux through the loop.**

In symbols, Faraday's law is

$$\mathcal{E} = -\frac{d\Phi_B}{dt} \qquad \text{(Faraday's law of induction)} \qquad (29.3)$$

To understand the negative sign, we have to introduce a sign convention for the induced emf $\mathcal{E}$. But first let's look at a simple example of this law in action.

Example 29.1 **Emf and current induced in a loop**

The magnetic field between the poles of the electromagnet in Fig. 29.5 is uniform at any time, but its magnitude is increasing at the rate of 0.020 T/s. The area of the conducting loop in the field is 120 cm², and the total circuit resistance, including the meter, is 5.0 Ω. (a) Find the induced emf and the induced current in the circuit. (b) If the loop is replaced by one made of an insulator, what effect does this have on the induced emf and induced current?

SOLUTION

IDENTIFY and SET UP: The magnetic flux Φ_B through the loop changes as the magnetic field changes. Hence there will be an induced emf $\mathcal{E}$ and an induced current I in the loop. We calculate Φ_B using Eq. (29.2), then find $\mathcal{E}$ using Faraday's law. Finally, we calculate I using $\mathcal{E} = IR$, where R is the total resistance of the circuit that includes the loop.

EXECUTE: (a) The area vector $\vec{A}$ for the loop is perpendicular to the plane of the loop; we take $\vec{A}$ to be vertically upward. Then $\vec{A}$ and $\vec{B}$ are parallel, and because $\vec{B}$ is uniform the magnetic flux through the loop is $\Phi_B = \vec{B} \cdot \vec{A} = BA \cos 0 = BA$. The area $A = 0.012 \text{ m}^2$ is constant, so the rate of change of magnetic flux is

29.5 A stationary conducting loop in an increasing magnetic field.

$$\frac{d\Phi_B}{dt} = \frac{d(BA)}{dt} = \frac{dB}{dt} A = (0.020 \text{ T/s})(0.012 \text{ m}^2)$$
$$= 2.4 \times 10^{-4} \text{ V} = 0.24 \text{ mV}$$

This, apart from a sign that we haven't discussed yet, is the induced emf $\mathcal{E}$. The corresponding induced current is

$$I = \frac{\mathcal{E}}{R} = \frac{2.4 \times 10^{-4} \text{ V}}{5.0 \ \Omega} = 4.8 \times 10^{-5} \text{A} = 0.048 \text{ mA}$$

(b) By changing to an insulating loop, we've made the resistance of the loop very high. Faraday's law, Eq. (29.3), does not involve the resistance of the circuit in any way, so the induced *emf* does not change. But the *current* will be smaller, as given by the equation $I = \mathcal{E}/R$. If the loop is made of a perfect insulator with infinite resistance, the induced current is zero. This situation is analogous to an isolated battery whose terminals aren't connected to anything: An emf is present, but no current flows.

EVALUATE: Let's verify unit consistency in this calculation. One way to do this is to note that the magnetic-force relationship $\vec{F} = q\vec{v} \times \vec{B}$ implies that the units of $\vec{B}$ are the units of force divided by the units of (charge times velocity): $1 \text{ T} = (1 \text{ N})/(1 \text{ C} \cdot \text{m/s})$. The units of magnetic flux are then $(1 \text{ T})(1 \text{ m}^2) = 1 \text{ N} \cdot \text{s} \cdot \text{m/C}$, and the rate of change of magnetic flux is $1 \text{ N} \cdot \text{m/C} = 1 \text{ J/C} = 1 \text{ V}$. Thus the unit of $d\Phi_B/dt$ is the volt, as required by Eq. (29.3). Also recall that the unit of magnetic flux is the weber (Wb): $1 \text{ T} \cdot \text{m}^2 = 1 \text{ Wb}$, so $1 \text{ V} = 1 \text{ Wb/s}$.

Direction of Induced emf

We can find the direction of an induced emf or current by using Eq. (29.3) together with some simple sign rules. Here's the procedure:

1. Define a positive direction for the vector area $\vec{A}$.
2. From the directions of $\vec{A}$ and the magnetic field $\vec{B}$, determine the sign of the magnetic flux Φ_B and its rate of change $d\Phi_B/dt$. Figure 29.6 shows several examples.
3. Determine the sign of the induced emf or current. If the flux is increasing, so $d\Phi_B/dt$ is positive, then the induced emf or current is negative; if the flux is decreasing, $d\Phi_B/dt$ is negative and the induced emf or current is positive.
4. Finally, determine the direction of the induced emf or current using your right hand. Curl the fingers of your right hand around the $\vec{A}$ vector, with your right thumb in the direction of $\vec{A}$. If the induced emf or current in the circuit is *positive*, it is in the same direction as your curled fingers; if the induced emf or current is *negative*, it is in the opposite direction.

In Example 29.1, in which $\vec{A}$ is upward, a positive $\mathcal{E}$ would be directed counterclockwise around the loop, as seen from above. Both $\vec{A}$ and $\vec{B}$ are upward in this example, so Φ_B is positive; the magnitude B is increasing, so $d\Phi_B/dt$ is positive. Hence by Eq. (29.3), $\mathcal{E}$ in Example 29.1 is *negative*. Its actual direction is thus *clockwise* around the loop, as seen from above.

If the loop in Fig. 29.5 is a conductor, an induced current results from this emf; this current is also clockwise, as Fig. 29.5 shows. This induced current produces an additional magnetic field through the loop, and the right-hand rule described in Section 28.6 shows that this field is *opposite* in direction to the increasing field produced by the electromagnet. This is an example of a general rule called *Lenz's law*, which says that any induction effect tends to oppose the change that caused it; in this case the change is the increase in the flux of the

Application Exploring the Brain with Induced emfs

Transcranial magnetic stimulation (TMS) is a technique for studying the function of various parts of the brain. A coil held to the subject's head carries a varying electric current, and so produces a varying magnetic field. This field causes an induced emf, and that triggers electric activity in the region of the brain underneath the coil. By observing how the TMS subject responds (for instance, which muscles move as a result of stimulating a certain part of the brain), a physician can test for various neurological conditions.

29.6 The magnetic flux is becoming (a) more positive, (b) less positive, (c) more negative, and (d) less negative. Therefore Φ_B is increasing in (a) and (d) and decreasing in (b) and (c). In (a) and (d) the emfs are negative (they are opposite to the direction of the curled fingers of your right hand when your right thumb points along $\vec{A}$). In (b) and (c) the emfs are positive (in the same direction as the curled fingers).

(a)

• Flux is positive ($\Phi_B > 0$) ...
• ... and becoming more positive ($d\Phi_B/dt > 0$).
• Induced emf is negative ($\mathcal{E} < 0$).

(b)

• Flux is positive ($\Phi_B > 0$) ...
• ... and becoming less positive ($d\Phi_B/dt < 0$).
• Induced emf is positive ($\mathcal{E} > 0$).

(c)

• Flux is negative ($\Phi_B < 0$) ...
• ... and becoming more negative ($d\Phi_B/dt < 0$).
• Induced emf is positive ($\mathcal{E} > 0$).

(d)

• Flux is negative ($\Phi_B < 0$) ...
• ... and becoming less negative ($d\Phi_B/dt > 0$).
• Induced emf is negative ($\mathcal{E} < 0$).

electromagnet's field through the loop. (We'll study this law in detail in the next section.)

You should check out the signs of the induced emfs and currents for the list of experiments in Section 29.1. For example, when the loop in Fig. 29.2 is in a constant field and we tilt it or squeeze it to *decrease* the flux through it, the induced emf and current are counterclockwise, as seen from above.

CAUTION **Induced emfs are caused by changes in flux** Since magnetic flux plays a central role in Faraday's law, it's tempting to think that *flux* is the cause of induced emf and that an induced emf will appear in a circuit whenever there is a magnetic field in the region bordered by the circuit. But Eq. (29.3) shows that only a *change* in flux through a circuit, not flux itself, can induce an emf in a circuit. If the flux through a circuit has a constant value, whether positive, negative, or zero, there is no induced emf.

If we have a coil with N identical turns, and if the flux varies at the same rate through each turn, the *total* rate of change through all the turns is N times as large as for a single turn. If Φ_B is the flux through each turn, the total emf in a coil with N turns is

$$\mathcal{E} = -N\frac{d\Phi_B}{dt}$$ (29.4)

As we discussed in this chapter's introduction, induced emfs play an essential role in the generation of electric power for commercial use. Several of the following examples explore different methods of producing emfs by the motion of a conductor relative to a magnetic field, giving rise to a changing flux through a circuit.

Problem-Solving Strategy 29.1 Faraday's Law

IDENTIFY *the relevant concepts:* Faraday's law applies when there is a changing magnetic flux. To use the law, identify an area through which there is a flux of magnetic field. This will usually be the area enclosed by a loop made of a conducting material (though not always—see part (b) of Example 29.1). Identify the target variables.

SET UP *the problem* using the following steps:
1. Faraday's law relates the induced emf to the rate of change of magnetic flux. To calculate this rate of change, you first have to understand what is making the flux change. Is the conductor moving? Is it changing orientation? Is the magnetic field changing? Remember that it's not the flux itself that counts, but its *rate of change*.
2. The area vector $\vec{A}$ (or $d\vec{A}$) must be perpendicular to the plane of the area. You always have two choices of its direction; for example, if the area is in a horizontal plane, $\vec{A}$ could point up or

down. Choose a direction and use it consistently throughout the problem.

EXECUTE *the solution* as follows:
1. Calculate the magnetic flux using Eq. (29.2) if $\vec{B}$ is uniform over the area of the loop or Eq. (29.1) if it isn't uniform. Remember the direction you chose for the area vector.
2. Calculate the induced emf using Eq. (29.3) or (if your conductor has N turns in a coil) Eq. (29.4). Apply the sign rule (described just after Example 29.1) to determine the positive direction of emf.
3. If the circuit resistance is known, you can calculate the magnitude of the induced current I using $\mathcal{E} = IR$.

EVALUATE *your answer:* Check your results for the proper units, and double-check that you have properly implemented the sign rules for magnetic flux and induced emf.

Example 29.2 Magnitude and direction of an induced emf

A 500-loop circular wire coil with radius 4.00 cm is placed between the poles of a large electromagnet. The magnetic field is uniform and makes an angle of 60° with the plane of the coil; it decreases at 0.200 T/s. What are the magnitude and direction of the induced emf?

SOLUTION

IDENTIFY and SET UP: Our target variable is the emf induced by a varying magnetic flux through the coil. The flux varies because the magnetic field decreases in amplitude. We choose the area vector $\vec{A}$ to be in the direction shown in Fig. 29.7. With this choice, the geometry is similar to that of Fig. 29.6b. That figure will help us determine the direction of the induced emf.

29.7 Our sketch for this problem.

EXECUTE: The magnetic field is uniform over the loop, so we can calculate the flux using Eq. (29.2): $\Phi_B = BA\cos\phi$, where $\phi = 30°$. In this expression, the only quantity that changes with time is the magnitude B of the field, so $d\Phi_B/dt = (dB/dt)A\cos\phi$.

CAUTION **Remember how ϕ is defined** You may have been tempted to say that $\phi = 60°$ in this problem. If so, remember that ϕ is the angle between $\vec{A}$ and $\vec{B}$, *not* the angle between $\vec{B}$ and the plane of the loop.

From Eq. (29.4), the induced emf in the coil of $N = 500$ turns is

$$\mathcal{E} = -N\frac{d\Phi_B}{dt} = N\frac{dB}{dt}A\cos\phi$$
$$= 500(-0.200 \text{ T/s})\pi(0.0400 \text{ m})^2(\cos 30°) = 0.435 \text{ V}$$

The positive answer means that when you point your right thumb in the direction of the area vector $\vec{A}$ (30° below the magnetic field $\vec{B}$ in Fig. 29.7), the positive direction for $\mathcal{E}$ is in the direction of the curled fingers of your right hand. If you viewed the coil from the left in Fig. 29.7 and looked in the direction of $\vec{A}$, the emf would be clockwise.

EVALUATE: If the ends of the wire are connected, the direction of current in the coil is in the same direction as the emf—that is, clockwise as seen from the left side of the coil. A clockwise current increases the magnetic flux through the coil, and therefore tends to oppose the decrease in total flux. This is an example of Lenz's law, which we'll discuss in Section 29.3.

Example 29.3 Generator I: A simple alternator

Figure 29.8a shows a simple *alternator,* a device that generates an emf. A rectangular loop is rotated with constant angular speed ω about the axis shown. The magnetic field $\vec{B}$ is uniform and constant. At time $t = 0$, $\phi = 0$. Determine the induced emf.

SOLUTION

IDENTIFY and SET UP: The magnetic field $\vec{B}$ and the area A of the loop are both constant, but the flux through the loop varies because the loop rotates and so the angle ϕ between $\vec{B}$ and the area vector

Continued

29.8 (a) Schematic diagram of an alternator. A conducting loop rotates in a magnetic field, producing an emf. Connections from each end of the loop to the external circuit are made by means of that end's slip ring. The system is shown at the time when the angle $\phi = \omega t = 90°$. (b) Graph of the flux through the loop and the resulting emf between terminals a and b, along with the corresponding positions of the loop during one complete rotation.

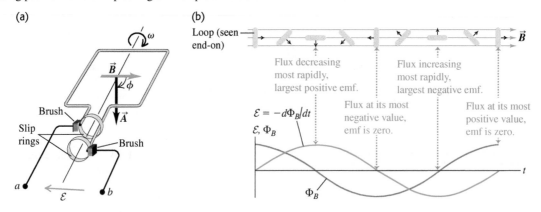

(a)

(b)

$\vec{A}$ changes (Fig. 29.8a). Because the angular speed is constant and $\phi = 0$ at $t = 0$, the angle as a function of time is given by $\phi = \omega t$.

EXECUTE: The magnetic field is uniform over the loop, so the magnetic flux is $\Phi_B = BA \cos\phi = BA \cos\omega t$. Hence, by Faraday's law [Eq. (29.3)] the induced emf is

$$\mathcal{E} = -\frac{d\Phi_B}{dt} = -\frac{d}{dt}(BA \cos\omega t) = \omega BA \sin\omega t$$

EVALUATE: The induced emf $\mathcal{E}$ varies sinusoidally with time (Fig. 29.8b). When the plane of the loop is perpendicular to $\vec{B}$ ($\phi = 0$ or 180°), Φ_B reaches its maximum and minimum values. At these times, its instantaneous rate of change is zero and $\mathcal{E}$ is zero. Conversely, $\mathcal{E}$ reaches its maximum and minimum values when the plane of the loop is parallel to $\vec{B}$ ($\phi = 90°$ or 270°) and Φ_B is changing most rapidly. We note that the induced emf does not depend on the *shape* of the loop, but only on its area.

We can use the alternator as a source of emf in an external circuit by using two *slip rings* that rotate with the loop, as shown in Fig. 29.8a. The rings slide against stationary contacts called *brushes*, which are connected to the output terminals a and b. Since the emf varies sinusoidally, the current that results in the circuit is an *alternating* current that also varies sinusoidally in magnitude and direction. The amplitude of the emf can be increased by increasing the rotation speed, the field magnitude, or the loop area or by using N loops instead of one, as in Eq. (29.4).

Alternators are used in automobiles to generate the currents in the ignition, the lights, and the entertainment system. The arrangement is a little different than in this example; rather than having a rotating loop in a magnetic field, the loop stays fixed and an electromagnet rotates. (The rotation is provided by a mechanical connection between the alternator and the engine.) But the result is the same; the flux through the loop varies sinusoidally, producing a sinusoidally varying emf. Larger alternators of this same type are used in electric power plants (Fig. 29.9).

29.9 A commercial alternator uses many loops of wire wound around a barrel-like structure called an armature. The armature and wire remain stationary while electromagnets rotate on a shaft (not shown) through the center of the armature. The resulting induced emf is far larger than would be possible with a single loop of wire.

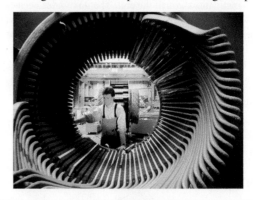

Example 29.4 **Generator II: A DC generator and back emf in a motor**

The alternator in Example 29.3 produces a sinusoidally varying emf and hence an alternating current. Figure 29.10a shows a *direct-current* (dc) *generator* that produces an emf that always has the same sign. The arrangement of split rings, called a *commutator*, reverses the connections to the external circuit at angular positions at which the emf reverses. Figure 29.10b shows the resulting emf. Commercial dc generators have a large number of coils and commutator segments, smoothing out the bumps in the emf so that the terminal voltage is not only one-directional but also practically constant. This brush-and-commutator arrangement is the same as that in the direct-current motor discussed in Section 27.8. The

motor's *back emf* is just the emf induced by the changing magnetic flux through its rotating coil. Consider a motor with a square, 500-turn coil 10.0 cm on a side. If the magnetic field has magnitude 0.200 T, at what rotation speed is the *average* back emf of the motor equal to 112 V?

SOLUTION

IDENTIFY and SET UP: As far as the rotating loop is concerned, the situation is the same as in Example 29.3 except that we now have N turns of wire. Without the commutator, the emf would alternate between positive and negative values and have an average value of zero (see Fig. 29.8b). With the commutator, the emf is never negative and its average value is positive (Fig. 29.10b). We'll use our result from Example 29.3 to obtain an expression for this average value and solve it for the rotational speed ω.

EXECUTE: Comparison of Figs. 29.8b and 29.10b shows that the back emf of the motor is just N times the absolute value of the emf found for an alternator in Example 29.3, as in Eq. (29.4): $|\mathcal{E}| = N\omega BA|\sin\omega t|$. To find the *average* back emf, we must replace $|\sin\omega t|$ by its average value. We find this by integrating $|\sin\omega t|$ over half a cycle, from $t = 0$ to $t = T/2 = \pi/\omega$, and dividing by the elapsed time π/ω. During this half cycle, the sine function is positive, so $|\sin\omega t| = \sin\omega t$, and we find

$$(|\sin\omega t|)_{\text{av}} = \frac{\int_0^{\pi/\omega} \sin\omega t \, dt}{\pi/\omega} = \frac{2}{\pi}$$

The average back emf is then

$$\mathcal{E}_{\text{av}} = \frac{2N\omega BA}{\pi}$$

This confirms that the back emf is proportional to the rotation speed ω, as we stated without proof in Section 27.8. Solving for ω, we obtain

$$\omega = \frac{\pi\mathcal{E}_{\text{av}}}{2NBA}$$
$$= \frac{\pi(112 \text{ V})}{2(500)(0.200 \text{ T})(0.100 \text{ m})^2} = 176 \text{ rad/s}$$

(We used the unit relationships $1 \text{ V} = 1 \text{ Wb/s} = 1 \text{ T} \cdot \text{m}^2/\text{s}$ from Example 29.1.)

EVALUATE: The average back emf is directly proportional to ω. Hence the slower the rotation speed, the less the back emf and the greater the possibility of burning out the motor, as we described in Example 27.11 (Section 27.8).

29.10 (a) Schematic diagram of a dc generator, using a split-ring commutator. The ring halves are attached to the loop and rotate with it. (b) Graph of the resulting induced emf between terminals a and b. Compare to Fig. 29.8b.

| **Example 29.5** | **Generator III: The slidewire generator** |

Figure 29.11 shows a U-shaped conductor in a uniform magnetic field $\vec{B}$ perpendicular to the plane of the figure and directed *into* the page. We lay a metal rod (the "slidewire") with length L across the two arms of the conductor, forming a circuit, and move it to the right with constant velocity $\vec{v}$. This induces an emf and a current, which is why this device is called a *slidewire generator.* Find the magnitude and direction of the resulting induced emf.

SOLUTION

IDENTIFY and SET UP: The magnetic flux changes because the area of the loop—bounded on the right by the moving rod—is

29.11 A slidewire generator. The magnetic field $\vec{B}$ and the vector area $\vec{A}$ are both directed into the figure. The increase in magnetic flux (caused by an increase in area) induces the emf and current.

increasing. Our target variable is the emf $\mathcal{E}$ induced in this expanding loop. The magnetic field is uniform over the area of the loop, so we can find the flux using $\Phi_B = BA\cos\phi$. We choose the area vector $\vec{A}$ to point straight into the page, in the same direction as $\vec{B}$. With this choice a positive emf will be one that is directed clockwise around the loop. (You can check this with the right-hand rule: Using your right hand, point your thumb into the page and curl your fingers as in Fig. 29.6.)

EXECUTE: Since $\vec{B}$ and $\vec{A}$ point in the same direction, the angle $\phi = 0$ and $\Phi_B = BA$. The magnetic field magnitude B is constant, so the induced emf is

$$\mathcal{E} = -\frac{d\Phi_B}{dt} = -B\frac{dA}{dt}$$

To calculate dA/dt, note that in a time dt the sliding rod moves a distance $v \, dt$ (Fig. 29.11) and the loop area increases by an amount $dA = Lv \, dt$. Hence the induced emf is

$$\mathcal{E} = -B\frac{Lv \, dt}{dt} = -BLv$$

The minus sign tells us that the emf is directed *counterclockwise* around the loop. The induced current is also counterclockwise, as shown in the figure.

Continued

EVALUATE: The emf of a slidewire generator is constant if $\vec{v}$ is constant. Hence the slidewire generator is a *direct-current* generator. It's not a very practical device because the rod eventually moves beyond the U-shaped conductor and loses contact, after which the current stops.

Example 29.6 Work and power in the slidewire generator

In the slidewire generator of Example 29.5, energy is dissipated in the circuit owing to its resistance. Let the resistance of the circuit (made up of the moving slidewire and the U-shaped conductor that connects the ends of the slidewire) at a given point in the slidewire's motion be R. Find the rate at which energy is dissipated in the circuit and the rate at which work must be done to move the rod through the magnetic field.

SOLUTION

IDENTIFY and SET UP: Our target variables are the *rates* at which energy is dissipated and at which work is done. Energy is dissipated in the circuit at the rate $P_{\text{dissipated}} = I^2 R$. The current I in the circuit equals $|\mathcal{E}|/R$; we found an expression for the induced emf $\mathcal{E}$ in this circuit in Example 29.5. There is a magnetic force $\vec{F} = I\vec{L} \times \vec{B}$ on the rod, where $\vec{L}$ points along the rod in the direction of the current. Figure 29.12 shows that this force is opposite to the rod velocity $\vec{v}$; to maintain the motion, whoever is pushing the rod must apply a force of equal magnitude in the direction of $\vec{v}$. This force does work at the rate $P_{\text{applied}} = Fv$.

29.12 The magnetic force $\vec{F} = I\vec{L} \times \vec{B}$ that acts on the rod due to the induced current is to the left, opposite to $\vec{v}$.

EXECUTE: First we'll calculate $P_{\text{dissipated}}$. From Example 29.5, $\mathcal{E} = -BLv$, so the current in the rod is $I = |\mathcal{E}|/R = Blv/R$. Hence

$$P_{\text{dissipated}} = I^2 R = \left(\frac{BLv}{R}\right)^2 R = \frac{B^2 L^2 v^2}{R}$$

To calculate P_{applied}, we first calculate the magnitude of $\vec{F} = I\vec{L} \times \vec{B}$. Since $\vec{L}$ and $\vec{B}$ are perpendicular, this magnitude is

$$F = ILB = \frac{BLv}{R}LB = \frac{B^2 L^2 v}{R}$$

The applied force has the same magnitude and does work at the rate

$$P_{\text{applied}} = Fv = \frac{B^2 L^2 v^2}{R}$$

EVALUATE: The rate at which work is done is exactly *equal* to the rate at which energy is dissipated in the resistance.

CAUTION **You can't violate energy conservation** You might think that reversing the direction of $\vec{B}$ or of $\vec{v}$ might make it possible to have the magnetic force $\vec{F} = I\vec{L} \times \vec{B}$ be in the *same* direction as $\vec{v}$. This would be a pretty neat trick. Once the rod was moving, the changing magnetic flux would induce an emf and a current, and the magnetic force on the rod would make it move even faster, increasing the emf and current; this would go on until the rod was moving at tremendous speed and producing electric power at a prodigious rate. If this seems too good to be true, not to mention a violation of energy conservation, that's because it is. Reversing $\vec{B}$ also reverses the sign of the induced emf and current and hence the direction of $\vec{L}$, so the magnetic force still opposes the motion of the rod; a similar result holds true if we reverse $\vec{v}$.

Generators As Energy Converters

Example 29.6 shows that the slidewire generator doesn't produce electric energy out of nowhere; the energy is supplied by whatever body exerts the force that keeps the rod moving. All that the generator does is *convert* that energy into a different form. The equality between the rate at which *mechanical* energy is supplied to a generator and the rate at which *electric* energy is generated holds for all types of generators. This is true in particular for the alternator described in Example 29.3. (We are neglecting the effects of friction in the bearings of an alternator or between the rod and the U-shaped conductor of a slidewire generator. If these are included, the conservation of energy demands that the energy lost to friction is not available for conversion to electric energy. In real generators the friction is kept to a minimum to keep the energy-conversion process as efficient as possible.)

In Chapter 27 we stated that the magnetic force on moving charges can never do work. But you might think that the magnetic force $\vec{F} = I\vec{L} \times \vec{B}$ in Example 29.6 *is* doing (negative) work on the current-carrying rod as it moves, contradicting our earlier statement. In fact, the work done by the magnetic force is actually zero. The moving charges that make up the current in the rod in Fig. 29.12 have a vertical component of velocity, causing a horizontal component of force on these charges. As a result, there is a horizontal displacement of charge within the rod, the left side acquiring a net positive charge and the right side a net negative charge. The result is a horizontal component of electric field, perpendicular to the length of the rod (analogous to the Hall effect, described in Section 27.9). It is this field, in the direction of motion of the rod, that does work on the mobile charges in the rod and hence indirectly on the atoms making up the rod.

Test Your Understanding of Section 29.2 The figure at right shows a wire coil being squeezed in a uniform magnetic field. (a) While the coil is being squeezed, is the induced emf in the coil (i) clockwise, (ii) counterclockwise, or (iii) zero? (b) Once the coil has reached its final squeezed shape, is the induced emf in the coil (i) clockwise, (ii) counterclockwise, or (iii) zero?

Circular wire coil   Coil squeezed
                            into oval

29.3 Lenz's Law

Lenz's law is a convenient alternative method for determining the direction of an induced current or emf. Lenz's law is not an independent principle; it can be derived from Faraday's law. It always gives the same results as the sign rules we introduced in connection with Faraday's law, but it is often easier to use. Lenz's law also helps us gain intuitive understanding of various induction effects and of the role of energy conservation. H. F. E. Lenz (1804–1865) was a Russian scientist who duplicated independently many of the discoveries of Faraday and Henry. **Lenz's law** states:

> **The direction of any magnetic induction effect is such as to oppose the cause of the effect.**

The "cause" may be changing flux through a stationary circuit due to a varying magnetic field, changing flux due to motion of the conductors that make up the circuit, or any combination. If the flux in a stationary circuit changes, as in Examples 29.1 and 29.2, the induced current sets up a magnetic field of its own. Within the area bounded by the circuit, this field is *opposite* to the original field if the original field is *increasing* but is in the *same* direction as the original field if the latter is *decreasing*. That is, the induced current opposes the *change in flux* through the circuit (*not* the flux itself).

If the flux change is due to motion of the conductors, as in Examples 29.3 through 29.6, the direction of the induced current in the moving conductor is such that the direction of the magnetic-field force on the conductor is opposite in direction to its motion. Thus the motion of the conductor, which caused the induced current, is opposed. We saw this explicitly for the slidewire generator in Example 29.6. In all these cases the induced current tries to preserve the *status quo* by opposing motion or a change of flux.

Lenz's law is also directly related to energy conservation. If the induced current in Example 29.6 were in the direction opposite to that given by Lenz's law, the magnetic force on the rod would accelerate it to ever-increasing speed with no external energy source, even though electric energy is being dissipated in the circuit. This would be a clear violation of energy conservation and doesn't happen in nature.

Conceptual Example 29.7   **Lenz's law and the slidewire generator**

In Fig. 29.11, the induced current in the loop causes an additional magnetic field in the area bounded by the loop. The direction of the induced current is counterclockwise, so from the discussion of Section 28.2, this additional magnetic field is directed *out of* the plane of the figure. That direction is opposite that of the original magnetic field, so it tends to cancel the effect of that field. This is just what Lenz's law predicts.

Conceptual Example 29.8   **Lenz's law and the direction of induced current**

In Fig. 29.13 there is a uniform magnetic field $\vec{B}$ through the coil. The magnitude of the field is increasing, so there is an induced emf. Use Lenz's law to determine the direction of the resulting induced current.

SOLUTION

This situation is the same as in Example 29.1 (Section 29.2). By Lenz's law the induced current must produce a magnetic field $\vec{B}_{induced}$ inside the coil that is downward, opposing the change in flux. From the right-hand rule we described in Section 28.5 for the direction of the magnetic field produced by a circular loop, $\vec{B}_{induced}$ will be in the desired direction if the induced current flows as shown in Fig. 29.13.

Figure 29.14 shows several applications of Lenz's law to the similar situation of a magnet moving near a conducting loop. In each case, the induced current produces a magnetic field whose

29.13 The induced current due to the change in $\vec{B}$ is clockwise, as seen from above the loop. The added field $\vec{B}_{induced}$ that it causes is downward, opposing the change in the upward field $\vec{B}$.

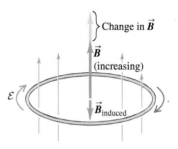

direction opposes the change in flux through the loop due to the magnet's motion.

29.14 Directions of induced currents as a bar magnet moves along the axis of a conducting loop. If the bar magnet is stationary, there is no induced current.

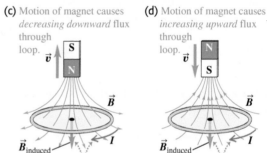

(a) Motion of magnet causes *increasing downward* flux through loop.

(b) Motion of magnet causes *decreasing upward* flux through loop.

The induced magnetic field is *upward* to oppose the flux change. To produce this induced field, the induced current must be *counterclockwise* as seen from above the loop.

(c) Motion of magnet causes *decreasing downward* flux through loop.

(d) Motion of magnet causes *increasing upward* flux through loop.

The induced magnetic field is *downward* to oppose the flux change. To produce this induced field, the induced current must be *clockwise* as seen from above the loop.

Lenz's Law and the Response to Flux Changes

Since an induced current always opposes any change in magnetic flux through a circuit, how is it possible for the flux to change at all? The answer is that Lenz's law gives only the *direction* of an induced current; the *magnitude* of the current depends on the resistance of the circuit. The greater the circuit resistance, the less the induced current that appears to oppose any change in flux and the easier it is for a flux change to take effect. If the loop in Fig. 29.14 were made out of wood (an insulator), there would be almost no induced current in response to changes in the flux through the loop.

Conversely, the less the circuit resistance, the greater the induced current and the more difficult it is to change the flux through the circuit. If the loop in Fig. 29.14 is a good conductor, an induced current flows as long as the magnet moves relative to the loop. Once the magnet and loop are no longer in relative motion, the induced current very quickly decreases to zero because of the nonzero resistance in the loop.

The extreme case occurs when the resistance of the circuit is *zero*. Then the induced current in Fig. 29.14 will continue to flow even after the induced emf has disappeared—that is, even after the magnet has stopped moving relative to the loop. Thanks to this *persistent current*, it turns out that the flux through the loop is exactly the same as it was before the magnet started to move, so the flux through a loop of zero resistance *never* changes. Exotic materials called *superconductors* do indeed have zero resistance; we discuss these further in Section 29.8.

29.4 Motional Electromotive Force

We've seen several situations in which a conductor moves in a magnetic field, as in the generators discussed in Examples 29.3 through 29.6. We can gain additional insight into the origin of the induced emf in these situations by considering the magnetic forces on mobile charges in the conductor. Figure 29.15a shows the same moving rod that we discussed in Example 29.5, separated for the moment from the U-shaped conductor. The magnetic field $\vec{B}$ is uniform and directed into the page, and we move the rod to the right at a constant velocity $\vec{v}$. A charged particle q in the rod then experiences a magnetic force $\vec{F} = q\vec{v} \times \vec{B}$ with magnitude $F = |q|vB$. We'll assume in the following discussion that q is positive; in that case the direction of this force is upward along the rod, from b toward a.

This magnetic force causes the free charges in the rod to move, creating an excess of positive charge at the upper end a and negative charge at the lower end b. This in turn creates an electric field $\vec{E}$ within the rod, in the direction from a toward b (opposite to the magnetic force). Charge continues to accumulate at the ends of the rod until $\vec{E}$ becomes large enough for the downward electric force (with magnitude qE) to cancel exactly the *upward* magnetic force (with magnitude qvB). Then $qE = qvB$ and the charges are in equilibrium.

The magnitude of the potential difference $V_{ab} = V_a - V_b$ is equal to the electric-field magnitude E multiplied by the length L of the rod. From the above discussion, $E = vB$, so

$$V_{ab} = EL = vBL \qquad (29.5)$$

with point a at higher potential than point b.

Now suppose the moving rod slides along a stationary U-shaped conductor, forming a complete circuit (Fig. 29.15b). No *magnetic* force acts on the charges in the stationary U-shaped conductor, but the charge that was near points a and b redistributes itself along the stationary conductor, creating an *electric* field within it. This field establishes a current in the direction shown. The moving rod has become a source of electromotive force; within it, charge moves from lower to higher potential, and in the remainder of the circuit, charge moves from higher to lower potential. We call this emf a **motional electromotive force,** denoted by $\mathcal{E}$. From the above discussion, the magnitude of this emf is

$$\mathcal{E} = vBL \qquad \text{(motional emf; length and velocity perpendicular to uniform } \vec{B}) \qquad (29.6)$$

corresponding to a force per unit charge of magnitude vB acting for a distance L along the moving rod. If the total circuit resistance of the U-shaped conductor and the sliding rod is R, the induced current I in the circuit is given by $vBL = IR$. This is the same result we obtained in Section 29.2 using Faraday's law, and indeed motional emf is a particular case of Faraday's law, one of the several examples described in Section 29.2.

The emf associated with the moving rod in Fig. 29.15 is analogous to that of a battery with its positive terminal at a and its negative terminal at b, although the origins of the two emfs are quite different. In each case a nonelectrostatic force acts on the charges in the device, in the direction from b to a, and the emf is the work per unit charge done by this force when a charge moves from b to a in the device. When the device is connected to an external circuit, the direction of

29.15 A conducting rod moving in a uniform magnetic field. (a) The rod, the velocity, and the field are mutually perpendicular. (b) Direction of induced current in the circuit.

(a) Isolated moving rod

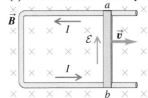

(b) Rod connected to stationary conductor

The motional emf $\mathcal{E}$ in the moving rod creates an electric field in the stationary conductor.

ActivPhysics 13.10: Motional EMF

current is from b to a in the device and from a to b in the external circuit. While we have discussed motional emf in terms of a closed circuit like that in Fig. 29.15b, a motional emf is also present in the isolated moving rod in Fig. 29.15a, in the same way that a battery has an emf even when it's not part of a circuit.

The direction of the induced emf in Fig. 29.15 can be deduced by using Lenz's law, even if (as in Fig. 29.15a) the conductor does not form a complete circuit. In this case we can mentally complete the circuit between the ends of the conductor and use Lenz's law to determine the direction of the current. From this we can deduce the polarity of the ends of the open-circuit conductor. The direction from the $-$ end to the $+$ end within the conductor is the direction the current would have if the circuit were complete.

You should verify that if we express v in meters per second, B in teslas, and L in meters, then $\mathcal{E}$ is in volts. (Recall that $1 \text{ V} = 1 \text{ J/C.}$)

Motional emf: General Form

We can generalize the concept of motional emf for a conductor with *any* shape, moving in any magnetic field, uniform or not (assuming that the magnetic field at each point does not vary with time). For an element $d\vec{l}$ of the conductor, the contribution $d\mathcal{E}$ to the emf is the magnitude dl multiplied by the component of $\vec{v} \times \vec{B}$ (the magnetic force per unit charge) parallel to $d\vec{l}$; that is,

$$d\mathcal{E} = (\vec{v} \times \vec{B}) \cdot d\vec{l}$$

For any closed conducting loop, the total emf is

$$\mathcal{E} = \oint (\vec{v} \times \vec{B}) \cdot d\vec{l} \qquad \text{(motional emf; closed conducting loop)} \quad (29.7)$$

This expression looks very different from our original statement of Faraday's law, Eq. (29.3), which stated that $\mathcal{E} = -d\Phi_B/dt$. In fact, though, the two statements are equivalent. It can be shown that the rate of change of magnetic flux through a moving conducting loop is always given by the negative of the expression in Eq. (29.7). Thus this equation gives us an alternative formulation of Faraday's law. This alternative is often more convenient than the original one in problems with *moving* conductors. But when we have *stationary* conductors in changing magnetic fields, Eq. (29.7) *cannot* be used; in this case, $\mathcal{E} = -d\Phi_B/dt$ is the only correct way to express Faraday's law.

Example 29.9   Motional emf in the slidewire generator

Suppose the moving rod in Fig. 29.15b is 0.10 m long, the velocity v is 2.5 m/s, the total resistance of the loop is 0.030 Ω, and B is 0.60 T. Find the motional emf, the induced current, and the force acting on the rod.

SOLUTION

IDENTIFY and SET UP: The first target variable is the motional emf $\mathcal{E}$ due to the rod's motion, which we'll find using Eq. (29.6). We'll find the current from the values of $\mathcal{E}$ and the resistance R. The force on the rod is a *magnetic* force, exerted by $\vec{B}$ on the current in the rod; we'll find this force using $\vec{F} = I\vec{L} \times \vec{B}$.

EXECUTE: From Eq. (29.6) the motional emf is

$$\mathcal{E} = vBL = (2.5 \text{ m/s})(0.60 \text{ T})(0.10 \text{ m}) = 0.15 \text{ V}$$

The induced current in the loop is

$$I = \frac{\mathcal{E}}{R} = \frac{0.15 \text{ V}}{0.030 \text{ Ω}} = 5.0 \text{ A}$$

In the expression for the magnetic force, $\vec{F} = I\vec{L} \times \vec{B}$, the vector $\vec{L}$ points in the same direction as the induced current in the rod (from b to a in Fig. 29.15). Applying the right-hand rule for vector products shows that this force is directed *opposite* to the rod's motion. Since $\vec{L}$ and $\vec{B}$ are perpendicular, the magnetic force has magnitude

$$F = ILB = (5.0 \text{ A})(0.10 \text{ m})(0.60 \text{ T}) = 0.30 \text{ N}$$

EVALUATE: We can check our answer for the direction of $\vec{F}$ by using Lenz's law. If we take the area vector $\vec{A}$ to point into the plane of the loop, the magnetic flux is positive and increasing as the rod moves to the right and increases the area of the loop. Lenz's law tells us that a force appears to oppose this increase in flux. Hence the force on the rod is to the left, opposite its motion.

Example 29.10 **The Faraday disk dynamo**

Figure 29.16 shows a conducting disk with radius R that lies in the xy-plane and rotates with constant angular velocity ω about the z-axis. The disk is in a uniform, constant $\vec{B}$ field in the z-direction. Find the induced emf between the center and the rim of the disk.

SOLUTION

IDENTIFY and SET UP: A motional emf arises because the conducting disk moves relative to $\vec{B}$. The complication is that different

29.16 A conducting disk with radius R rotating at an angular speed ω in a magnetic field $\vec{B}$. The emf is induced along radial lines of the disk and is applied to an external circuit through the two sliding contacts labeled b.

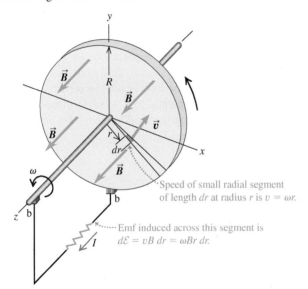

Speed of small radial segment of length dr at radius r is $v = \omega r$.

Emf induced across this segment is $d\mathcal{E} = vB\,dr = \omega Br\,dr$.

parts of the disk move at different speeds v, depending on their distance from the rotation axis. We'll address this by considering small segments of the disk and integrating their contributions to determine our target variable, the emf between the center and the rim. Consider the small segment of the disk shown in red in Fig. 29.16 and labeled by its velocity vector $\vec{v}$. The magnetic force per unit charge on this segment is $\vec{v} \times \vec{B}$, which points radially outward from the center of the disk. Hence the induced emf tends to make a current flow radially outward, which tells us that the moving conducting path to think about here is a straight line from the center to the rim. We can find the emf from each small disk segment along this line using $d\mathcal{E} = (\vec{v} \times \vec{B}) \cdot d\vec{l}$ and then integrate to find the total emf.

EXECUTE: The length vector $d\vec{l}$ (of length dr) associated with the segment points radially outward, in the same direction as $\vec{v} \times \vec{B}$. The vectors $\vec{v}$ and $\vec{B}$ are perpendicular, and the magnitude of $\vec{v}$ is $v = \omega r$. The emf from the segment is then $d\mathcal{E} = \omega Br\,dr$. The total emf is the integral of $d\mathcal{E}$ from the center ($r = 0$) to the rim ($r = R$):

$$\mathcal{E} = \int_0^R \omega Br\,dr = \tfrac{1}{2}\omega BR^2$$

EVALUATE: We can use this device as a source of emf in a circuit by completing the circuit through two stationary brushes (labeled b in the figure) that contact the disk and its conducting shaft as shown. Such a disk is called a *Faraday disk dynamo* or a *homopolar generator.* Unlike the alternator in Example 29.3, the Faraday disk dynamo is a direct-current generator; it produces an emf that is constant in time. Can you use Lenz's law to show that for the direction of rotation in Fig. 29.16, the current in the external circuit must be in the direction shown?

Test Your Understanding of Section 29.4 The earth's magnetic field points toward (magnetic) north. For simplicity, assume that the field has no vertical component (as is the case near the earth's equator). (a) If you hold a metal rod in your hand and walk toward the east, how should you orient the rod to get the maximum motional emf between its ends? (i) east–west; (ii) north–south; (iii) up–down; (iv) you get the same motional emf with all of these orientations. (b) How should you hold it to get *zero* emf as you walk toward the east? (i) east–west; (ii) north–south; (iii) up–down; (iv) none of these. (c) In which direction should you travel so that the motional emf across the rod is zero no matter how the rod is oriented? (i) west; (ii) north; (iii) south; (iv) straight up; (v) straight down.

29.5 Induced Electric Fields

When a conductor moves in a magnetic field, we can understand the induced emf on the basis of magnetic forces on charges in the conductor, as described in Section 29.4. But an induced emf also occurs when there is a changing flux through a stationary conductor. What is it that pushes the charges around the circuit in this type of situation?

As an example, let's consider the situation shown in Fig. 29.17. A long, thin solenoid with cross-sectional area A and n turns per unit length is encircled at its center by a circular conducting loop. The galvanometer G measures the current in the loop. A current I in the winding of the solenoid sets up a magnetic field $\vec{B}$ along the solenoid axis, as shown, with magnitude B as calculated in Example 28.9 (Section 28.7): $B = \mu_0 nI$, where n is the number of turns per unit length.

29.17 (a) The windings of a long solenoid carry a current I that is increasing at a rate dI/dt. The magnetic flux in the solenoid is increasing at a rate $d\Phi_B/dt$, and this changing flux passes through a wire loop. An emf $\mathcal{E} = -d\Phi_B/dt$ is induced in the loop, inducing a current I' that is measured by the galvanometer G. (b) Cross-sectional view.

(a)

(b)

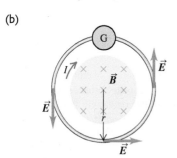

If we neglect the small field outside the solenoid and take the area vector $\vec{A}$ to point in the same direction as $\vec{B}$, then the magnetic flux Φ_B through the loop is

$$\Phi_B = BA = \mu_0 nIA$$

When the solenoid current I changes with time, the magnetic flux Φ_B also changes, and according to Faraday's law the induced emf in the loop is given by

$$\mathcal{E} = -\frac{d\Phi_B}{dt} = -\mu_0 nA \frac{dI}{dt} \tag{29.8}$$

If the total resistance of the loop is R, the induced current in the loop, which we may call I', is $I' = \mathcal{E}/R$.

But what *force* makes the charges move around the wire loop? It can't be a magnetic force because the loop isn't even *in* a magnetic field. We are forced to conclude that there has to be an **induced electric field** in the conductor *caused by the changing magnetic flux*. This may be a little jarring; we are accustomed to thinking about electric field as being caused by electric charges, and now we are saying that a changing magnetic field somehow acts as a source of electric field. Furthermore, it's a strange sort of electric field. When a charge q goes once around the loop, the total work done on it by the electric field must be equal to q times the emf $\mathcal{E}$. That is, the electric field in the loop *is not conservative*, as we used the term in Chapter 23, because the line integral of $\vec{E}$ around a closed path is not zero. Indeed, this line integral, representing the work done by the induced $\vec{E}$ field per unit charge, is equal to the induced emf $\mathcal{E}$:

$$\oint \vec{E} \cdot d\vec{l} = \mathcal{E} \tag{29.9}$$

From Faraday's law the emf $\mathcal{E}$ is also the negative of the rate of change of magnetic flux through the loop. Thus for this case we can restate Faraday's law as

$$\oint \vec{E} \cdot d\vec{l} = -\frac{d\Phi_B}{dt} \quad \text{(stationary integration path)} \tag{29.10}$$

Note that Faraday's law is *always* true in the form $\mathcal{E} = -d\Phi_B/dt$; the form given in Eq. (29.10) is valid *only* if the path around which we integrate is *stationary*.

As an example of a situation to which Eq. (29.10) can be applied, consider the stationary circular loop in Fig. 29.17b, which we take to have radius r. Because of cylindrical symmetry, the electric field $\vec{E}$ has the same magnitude at every point on the circle and is tangent to it at each point. (Symmetry would also permit the field to be *radial*, but then Gauss's law would require the presence of a net charge inside the circle, and there is none.) The line integral in Eq. (29.10) becomes simply the magnitude E times the circumference $2\pi r$ of the loop, $\oint \vec{E} \cdot d\vec{l} = 2\pi rE$, and Eq. (29.10) gives

$$E = \frac{1}{2\pi r}\left|\frac{d\Phi_B}{dt}\right| \tag{29.11}$$

The directions of $\vec{E}$ at points on the loop are shown in Fig. 29.17b. We know that $\vec{E}$ has to have the direction shown when $\vec{B}$ in the solenoid is increasing, because $\oint \vec{E} \cdot d\vec{l}$ has to be negative when $d\Phi_B/dt$ is positive. The same approach can be used to find the induced electric field *inside* the solenoid when the solenoid $\vec{B}$ field is changing; we leave the details to you (see Exercise 29.35).

Nonelectrostatic Electric Fields

Now let's summarize what we've learned. Faraday's law, Eq. (29.3), is valid for two rather different situations. In one, an emf is induced by magnetic forces on charges when a conductor moves through a magnetic field. In the other, a time-varying magnetic field induces an electric field in a stationary conductor and hence induces an emf; in fact, the $\vec{E}$ field is induced even when no conductor is present. This $\vec{E}$ field differs from an electro*static* field in an important way. It is *nonconservative;* the line integral $\oint \vec{E} \cdot d\vec{l}$ around a closed path is not zero, and when a charge moves around a closed path, the field does a nonzero amount of work on it. It follows that for such a field the concept of *potential* has no meaning. We call such a field a **nonelectrostatic field.** In contrast, an *electrostatic* field is *always* conservative, as we discussed in Section 23.1, and always has an associated potential function. Despite this difference, the fundamental effect of *any* electric field is to exert a force $\vec{F} = q\vec{E}$ on a charge q. This relationship is valid whether $\vec{E}$ is a conservative field produced by a charge distribution or a nonconservative field caused by changing magnetic flux.

So a changing magnetic field acts as a source of electric field of a sort that we *cannot* produce with any static charge distribution. This may seem strange, but it's the way nature behaves. What's more, we'll see in Section 29.7 that a changing *electric* field acts as a source of *magnetic* field. We'll explore this symmetry between the two fields in greater detail in our study of electromagnetic waves in Chapter 32.

If any doubt remains in your mind about the reality of magnetically induced electric fields, consider a few of the many practical applications (Fig. 29.18). Pickups in electric guitars use currents induced in stationary pickup coils by the vibration of nearby ferromagnetic strings. Alternators in most cars use rotating magnets to induce currents in stationary coils. Whether we realize it or not, magnetically induced electric fields play an important role in everyday life.

29.18 Applications of induced electric fields. **(a)** Data are stored on a computer hard disk in a pattern of magnetized areas on the surface of the disk. To read these data, a coil on a movable arm is placed next to the spinning disk. The coil experiences a changing magnetic flux, inducing a current whose characteristics depend on the pattern coded on the disk. **(b)** This hybrid automobile has both a gasoline engine and an electric motor. As the car comes to a halt, the spinning wheels run the motor backward so that it acts as a generator. The resulting induced current is used to recharge the car's batteries. **(c)** The rotating crankshaft of a piston-engine airplane spins a magnet, inducing an emf in an adjacent coil and generating the spark that ignites fuel in the engine cylinders. This keeps the engine running even if the airplane's other electrical systems fail.

Example 29.11 **Induced electric fields**

Suppose the long solenoid in Fig. 29.17a has 500 turns per meter and cross-sectional area 4.0 cm². The current in its windings is increasing at 100 A/s. (a) Find the magnitude of the induced emf in the wire loop outside the solenoid. (b) Find the magnitude of the induced electric field within the loop if its radius is 2.0 cm.

SOLUTION

IDENTIFY and SET UP: As in Fig. 29.17b, the increasing magnetic field inside the solenoid causes a change in the magnetic flux through the wire loop and hence induces an electric field $\vec{E}$ around the loop. Our target variables are the induced emf $\mathcal{E}$ and the electric-field magnitude E. We use Eq. (29.8) to determine the emf.

Determining the field magnitude E is simplified because the loop and the solenoid share the same central axis. Hence, by symmetry, the electric field is tangent to the loop and has the same magnitude all the way around its circumference. We can therefore use Eq. (29.9) to find E.

EXECUTE: (a) From Eq. (29.8), the induced emf is

$$\mathcal{E} = -\frac{d\Phi_B}{dt} = -\mu_0 n A \frac{dI}{dt}$$
$$= -(4\pi \times 10^{-7}\,\text{Wb/A} \cdot \text{m})(500\,\text{turns/m})$$
$$\times (4.0 \times 10^{-4}\,\text{m}^2)(100\,\text{A/s})$$
$$= -25 \times 10^{-6}\,\text{Wb/s} = -25 \times 10^{-6}\,\text{V} = -25\,\mu\text{V}$$

Continued

(b) By symmetry the line integral $\oint \vec{E} \cdot d\vec{l}$ has absolute value $2\pi r E$ no matter which direction we integrate around the loop. This is equal to the absolute value of the emf, so

$$E = \frac{|\mathcal{E}|}{2\pi r} = \frac{25 \times 10^{-6}\,\text{V}}{2\pi(2.0 \times 10^{-2}\,\text{m})} = 2.0 \times 10^{-4}\,\text{V/m}$$

EVALUATE: In Fig. 29.17b the magnetic flux *into* the plane of the figure is increasing. According to the right-hand rule for induced emf (illustrated in Fig. 29.6), a positive emf would be clockwise around the loop; the negative sign of $\mathcal{E}$ shows that the emf is in the counterclockwise direction. Can you also show this using Lenz's law?

Test Your Understanding of Section 29.5 If you wiggle a magnet back and forth in your hand, are you generating an electric field? If so, is this electric field conservative?

29.6 Eddy Currents

29.19 Eddy currents induced in a rotating metal disk.

(a) Metal disk rotating through a magnetic field

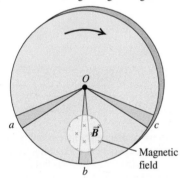

(b) Resulting eddy currents and braking force

Video Tutor Demo

In the examples of induction effects that we have studied, the induced currents have been confined to well-defined paths in conductors and other components forming a circuit. However, many pieces of electrical equipment contain masses of metal moving in magnetic fields or located in changing magnetic fields. In situations like these we can have induced currents that circulate throughout the volume of a material. Because their flow patterns resemble swirling eddies in a river, we call these **eddy currents.**

As an example, consider a metallic disk rotating in a magnetic field perpendicular to the plane of the disk but confined to a limited portion of the disk's area, as shown in Fig. 29.19a. Sector *Ob* is moving across the field and has an emf induced in it. Sectors *Oa* and *Oc* are not in the field, but they provide return conducting paths for charges displaced along *Ob* to return from *b* to *O*. The result is a circulation of eddy currents in the disk, somewhat as sketched in Fig. 29.19b.

We can use Lenz's law to decide on the direction of the induced current in the neighborhood of sector *Ob*. This current must experience a magnetic force $\vec{F} = I\vec{L} \times \vec{B}$ that *opposes* the rotation of the disk, and so this force must be to the right in Fig. 29.19b. Since $\vec{B}$ is directed into the plane of the disk, the current and hence $\vec{L}$ have downward components. The return currents lie outside the field, so they do not experience magnetic forces. The interaction between the eddy currents and the field causes a braking action on the disk. Such effects can be used to stop the rotation of a circular saw quickly when the power is turned off. Some sensitive balances use this effect to damp out vibrations. Eddy current braking is used on some electrically powered rapid-transit vehicles. Electromagnets mounted in the cars induce eddy currents in the rails; the resulting magnetic fields cause braking forces on the electromagnets and thus on the cars.

Eddy currents have many other practical uses. The shiny metal disk in the electric power company's meter outside your house rotates as a result of eddy currents. These currents are induced in the disk by magnetic fields caused by sinusoidally varying currents in a coil. In induction furnaces, eddy currents are used to heat materials in completely sealed containers for processes in which it is essential to avoid the slightest contamination of the materials. The metal detectors used at airport security checkpoints (Fig. 29.20a) operate by detecting eddy currents induced in metallic objects. Similar devices (Fig. 29.20b) are used to find buried treasure such as bottlecaps and lost pennies.

Eddy currents also have undesirable effects. In an alternating-current transformer, coils wrapped around an iron core carry a sinusoidally varying current. The resulting eddy currents in the core waste energy through I^2R heating and themselves set up an unwanted opposing emf in the coils. To minimize these effects, the core is designed so that the paths for eddy currents are as narrow as possible. We'll describe how this is done when we discuss transformers in detail in Section 31.6.

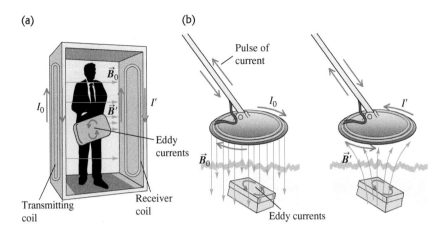

(a)

(b)

Pulse of current

$\vec{B}_0$

I_0

$\vec{B}'$

I'

Eddy currents

Transmitting coil

Receiver coil

I_0

I'

$\vec{B}_0$

$\vec{B}'$

Eddy currents

29.20 (a) A metal detector at an airport security checkpoint generates an alternating magnetic field $\vec{B}_0$. This induces eddy currents in a conducting object carried through the detector. The eddy currents in turn produce an alternating magnetic field $\vec{B}'$, and this field induces a current in the detector's receiver coil. (b) Portable metal detectors work on the same principle.

Test Your Understanding of Section 29.6 Suppose that the magnetic field in Fig. 29.19 were directed out of the plane of the figure and the disk were rotating counterclockwise. Compared to the directions of the force $\vec{F}$ and the eddy currents shown in Fig. 29.19b, what would the new directions be? (i) The force $\vec{F}$ and the eddy currents would both be in the same direction; (ii) the force $\vec{F}$ would be in the same direction, but the eddy currents would be in the opposite direction; (iii) the force $\vec{F}$ would be in the opposite direction, but the eddy currents would be in the same direction; (iv) the force $\vec{F}$ and the eddy currents would be in the opposite directions.

29.7 Displacement Current and Maxwell's Equations

We have seen that a varying magnetic field gives rise to an induced electric field. In one of the more remarkable examples of the symmetry of nature, it turns out that a varying *electric* field gives rise to a *magnetic* field. This effect is of tremendous importance, for it turns out to explain the existence of radio waves, gamma rays, and visible light, as well as all other forms of electromagnetic waves.

Generalizing Ampere's Law

To see the origin of the relationship between varying electric fields and magnetic fields, let's return to Ampere's law as given in Section 28.6, Eq. (28.20):

$$\oint \vec{B} \cdot d\vec{l} = \mu_0 I_{encl}$$

The problem with Ampere's law in this form is that it is *incomplete*. To see why, let's consider the process of charging a capacitor (Fig. 29.21). Conducting wires lead current i_C into one plate and out of the other; the charge Q increases, and the electric field $\vec{E}$ between the plates increases. The notation i_C indicates *conduction* current to distinguish it from another kind of current we are about to encounter, called *displacement* current i_D. We use lowercase i's and v's to denote instantaneous values of currents and potential differences, respectively, that may vary with time.

Let's apply Ampere's law to the circular path shown. The integral $\oint \vec{B} \cdot d\vec{l}$ around this path equals $\mu_0 I_{encl}$. For the plane circular area bounded by the circle, I_{encl} is just the current i_C in the left conductor. But the surface that bulges out to the right is bounded by the same circle, and the current through that surface is zero. So $\oint \vec{B} \cdot d\vec{l}$ is equal to $\mu_0 i_C$, and at the same time it is equal to zero! This is a clear contradiction.

But something else is happening on the bulged-out surface. As the capacitor charges, the electric field $\vec{E}$ and the electric *flux* Φ_E through the surface are increasing. We can determine their rates of change in terms of the charge and

Application Eddy Currents Help Power Io's Volcanoes

Jupiter's moon Io is slightly larger than the earth's moon. It moves at more than 60,000 km/h through Jupiter's intense magnetic field (about ten times stronger than the earth's field), which sets up strong eddy currents within Io that dissipate energy at a rate of 10^{12} W. This dissipated energy helps to heat Io's interior and causes volcanic eruptions on its surface, as shown in the lower close-up image. (Gravitational effects from Jupiter cause even more heating.)

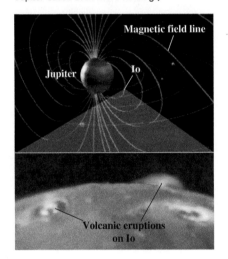

Magnetic field line

Jupiter

Io

Volcanic eruptions on Io

29.21 Parallel-plate capacitor being charged. The conduction current through the plane surface is i_C, but there is no conduction current through the surface that bulges out to pass between the plates. The two surfaces have a common boundary, so this difference in I_{encl} leads to an apparent contradiction in applying Ampere's law.

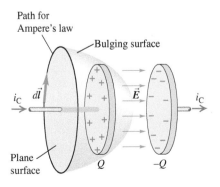

Path for Ampere's law

Bulging surface

i_C

$d\vec{l}$

$\vec{E}$

i_C

Plane surface

Q

$-Q$

current. The instantaneous charge is $q = Cv$, where C is the capacitance and v is the instantaneous potential difference. For a parallel-plate capacitor, $C = \epsilon_0 A/d$, where A is the plate area and d is the spacing. The potential difference v between plates is $v = Ed$, where E is the electric-field magnitude between plates. (We neglect fringing and assume that $\vec{E}$ is uniform in the region between the plates.) If this region is filled with a material with permittivity ϵ, we replace ϵ_0 by ϵ everywhere; we'll use ϵ in the following discussion.

Substituting these expressions for C and v into $q = Cv$, we can express the capacitor charge q as

$$q = Cv = \frac{\epsilon A}{d}(Ed) = \epsilon EA = \epsilon \Phi_E \tag{29.12}$$

where $\Phi_E = EA$ is the electric flux through the surface.

As the capacitor charges, the rate of change of q is the conduction current, $i_C = dq/dt$. Taking the derivative of Eq. (29.12) with respect to time, we get

$$i_C = \frac{dq}{dt} = \epsilon \frac{d\Phi_E}{dt} \tag{29.13}$$

Now, stretching our imagination a little, we invent a fictitious **displacement current** i_D in the region between the plates, defined as

$$i_D = \epsilon \frac{d\Phi_E}{dt} \quad \text{(displacement current)} \tag{29.14}$$

That is, we imagine that the changing flux through the curved surface in Fig. 29.21 is somehow equivalent, in Ampere's law, to a conduction current through that surface. We include this fictitious current, along with the real conduction current i_C, in Ampere's law:

$$\oint \vec{B} \cdot d\vec{l} = \mu_0(i_C + i_D)_{encl} \quad \text{(generalized Ampere's law)} \tag{29.15}$$

Ampere's law in this form is obeyed no matter which surface we use in Fig. 29.21. For the flat surface, i_D is zero; for the curved surface, i_C is zero; and i_C for the flat surface equals i_D for the curved surface. Equation (29.15) remains valid in a magnetic material, provided that the magnetization is proportional to the external field and we replace μ_0 by μ.

The fictitious current i_D was invented in 1865 by the Scottish physicist James Clerk Maxwell (1831–1879), who called it displacement current. There is a corresponding *displacement current density* $j_D = i_D/A$; using $\Phi_E = EA$ and dividing Eq. (29.14) by A, we find

$$j_D = \epsilon \frac{dE}{dt} \tag{29.16}$$

We have pulled the concept out of thin air, as Maxwell did, but we see that it enables us to save Ampere's law in situations such as that in Fig. 29.21.

Another benefit of displacement current is that it lets us generalize Kirchhoff's junction rule, discussed in Section 26.2. Considering the left plate of the capacitor, we have conduction current into it but none out of it. But when we include the displacement current, we have conduction current coming in one side and an equal displacement current coming out the other side. With this generalized meaning of the term "current," we can speak of current going *through* the capacitor.

The Reality of Displacement Current

You might well ask at this point whether displacement current has any real physical significance or whether it is just a ruse to satisfy Ampere's law and Kirchhoff's junction rule. Here's a fundamental experiment that helps to answer that question. We take a plane circular area between the capacitor plates (Fig. 29.22). If displacement current really plays the role in Ampere's law that we have claimed, then there ought to be a magnetic field in the region between the plates while the capacitor is charging. We can use our generalized Ampere's law, including displacement current, to predict what this field should be.

To be specific, let's picture round capacitor plates with radius R. To find the magnetic field at a point in the region between the plates at a distance r from the axis, we apply Ampere's law to a circle of radius r passing through the point, with $r < R$. This circle passes through points a and b in Fig. 29.22. The total current enclosed by the circle is j_D times its area, or $(i_D/\pi R^2)(\pi r^2)$. The integral $\oint \vec{B} \cdot d\vec{l}$ in Ampere's law is just B times the circumference $2\pi r$ of the circle, and because $i_D = i_C$ for the charging capacitor, Ampere's law becomes

$$\oint \vec{B} \cdot d\vec{l} = 2\pi r B = \mu_0 \frac{r^2}{R^2} i_C \qquad \text{or}$$

$$B = \frac{\mu_0}{2\pi} \frac{r}{R^2} i_C \qquad (29.17)$$

This result predicts that in the region between the plates $\vec{B}$ is zero at the axis and increases linearly with distance from the axis. A similar calculation shows that *outside* the region between the plates (that is, for $r > R$), $\vec{B}$ is the same as though the wire were continuous and the plates not present at all.

When we *measure* the magnetic field in this region, we find that it really is there and that it behaves just as Eq. (29.17) predicts. This confirms directly the role of displacement current as a source of magnetic field. It is now established beyond reasonable doubt that displacement current, far from being just an artifice, is a fundamental fact of nature. Maxwell's discovery was the bold step of an extraordinary genius.

Maxwell's Equations of Electromagnetism

We are now in a position to wrap up in a single package *all* of the relationships between electric and magnetic fields and their sources. This package consists of four equations, called **Maxwell's equations.** Maxwell did not discover all of these equations single-handedly (though he did develop the concept of displacement current). But he did put them together and recognized their significance, particularly in predicting the existence of electromagnetic waves.

For now we'll state Maxwell's equations in their simplest form, for the case in which we have charges and currents in otherwise empty space. In Chapter 32 we'll discuss how to modify these equations if a dielectric or a magnetic material is present.

Two of Maxwell's equations involve an integral of $\vec{E}$ or $\vec{B}$ over a closed surface. The first is simply Gauss's law for electric fields, Eq. (22.8), which states that the surface integral of $E_\perp$ over any closed surface equals $1/\epsilon_0$ times the total charge Q_{encl} enclosed within the surface:

$$\oint \vec{E} \cdot d\vec{A} = \frac{Q_{encl}}{\epsilon_0} \qquad \text{(Gauss's law for } \vec{E}) \qquad (29.18)$$

The second is the analogous relationship for *magnetic* fields, Eq. (27.8), which states that the surface integral of $B_\perp$ over any closed surface is always zero:

$$\oint \vec{B} \cdot d\vec{A} = 0 \qquad \text{(Gauss's law for } \vec{B}) \qquad (29.19)$$

This statement means, among other things, that there are no magnetic monopoles (single magnetic charges) to act as sources of magnetic field.

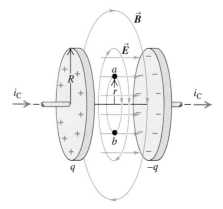

29.22 A capacitor being charged by a current i_C has a displacement current equal to i_C between the plates, with displacement-current density $j_D = \epsilon \, dE/dt$. This can be regarded as the source of the magnetic field between the plates.

The third equation is Ampere's law including displacement current. This states that both conduction current i_C and displacement current $\epsilon_0 d\Phi_E/dt$, where Φ_E is electric flux, act as sources of magnetic field:

$$\oint \vec{B} \cdot d\vec{l} = \mu_0 \left(i_C + \epsilon_0 \frac{d\Phi_E}{dt} \right)_{\text{encl}} \quad \text{(Ampere's law)} \quad (29.20)$$

The fourth and final equation is Faraday's law. It states that a changing magnetic field or magnetic flux induces an electric field:

$$\oint \vec{E} \cdot d\vec{l} = -\frac{d\Phi_B}{dt} \quad \text{(Faraday's law)} \quad (29.21)$$

If there is a changing magnetic flux, the line integral in Eq. (29.21) is not zero, which shows that the $\vec{E}$ field produced by a changing magnetic flux is not conservative. Recall that this line integral must be carried out over a *stationary* closed path.

It's worthwhile to look more carefully at the electric field $\vec{E}$ and its role in Maxwell's equations. In general, the total $\vec{E}$ field at a point in space can be the superposition of an electrostatic field $\vec{E}_c$ caused by a distribution of charges at rest and a magnetically induced, nonelectrostatic field $\vec{E}_n$. (The subscript c stands for Coulomb or conservative; the subscript n stands for non-Coulomb, nonelectrostatic, or nonconservative.) That is,

$$\vec{E} = \vec{E}_c + \vec{E}_n$$

The electrostatic part $\vec{E}_c$ is *always* conservative, so $\oint \vec{E}_c \cdot d\vec{l} = 0$. This conservative part of the field does not contribute to the integral in Faraday's law, so we can take $\vec{E}$ in Eq. (29.21) to be the *total* electric field $\vec{E}$, including both the part $\vec{E}_c$ due to charges and the magnetically induced part $\vec{E}_n$. Similarly, the nonconservative part $\vec{E}_n$ of the $\vec{E}$ field does not contribute to the integral in Gauss's law, because this part of the field is not caused by static charges. Hence $\oint \vec{E}_n \cdot d\vec{A}$ is always zero. We conclude that in all the Maxwell equations, $\vec{E}$ is the total electric field; these equations don't distinguish between conservative and nonconservative fields.

Symmetry in Maxwell's Equations

There is a remarkable symmetry in Maxwell's four equations. In empty space where there is no charge, the first two equations (Eqs. (29.18) and (29.19)) are identical in form, one containing $\vec{E}$ and the other containing $\vec{B}$. When we compare the second two equations, Eq. (29.20) says that a changing electric flux creates a magnetic field, and Eq. (29.21) says that a changing magnetic flux creates an electric field. In empty space, where there is no conduction current, $i_C = 0$ and the two equations have the same form, apart from a numerical constant and a negative sign, with the roles of $\vec{E}$ and $\vec{B}$ exchanged in the two equations.

We can rewrite Eqs. (29.20) and (29.21) in a different but equivalent form by introducing the definitions of electric and magnetic flux, $\Phi_E = \int \vec{E} \cdot d\vec{A}$ and $\Phi_B = \int \vec{B} \cdot d\vec{A}$, respectively. In empty space, where there is no charge or conduction current, $i_C = 0$ and $Q_{\text{encl}} = 0$, and we have

$$\oint \vec{B} \cdot d\vec{l} = \epsilon_0 \mu_0 \frac{d}{dt} \int \vec{E} \cdot d\vec{A} \quad (29.22)$$

$$\oint \vec{E} \cdot d\vec{l} = -\frac{d}{dt} \int \vec{B} \cdot d\vec{A} \quad (29.23)$$

Again we notice the symmetry between the roles of $\vec{E}$ and $\vec{B}$ in these expressions.

The most remarkable feature of these equations is that a time-varying field of *either* kind induces a field of the other kind in neighboring regions of space. Maxwell recognized that these relationships predict the existence of electromagnetic disturbances consisting of time-varying electric and magnetic fields that travel or *propagate* from one region of space to another, even if no matter is present in the intervening space. Such disturbances, called *electromagnetic waves,* provide the physical basis for light, radio and television waves, infrared, ultraviolet, x rays, and the rest of the electromagnetic spectrum. We will return to this vitally important topic in Chapter 32.

Although it may not be obvious, *all* the basic relationships between fields and their sources are contained in Maxwell's equations. We can derive Coulomb's law from Gauss's law, we can derive the law of Biot and Savart from Ampere's law, and so on. When we add the equation that defines the $\vec{E}$ and $\vec{B}$ fields in terms of the forces that they exert on a charge q, namely,

$$\vec{F} = q(\vec{E} + \vec{v} \times \vec{B}) \qquad (29.24)$$

we have *all* the fundamental relationships of electromagnetism!

Finally, we note that Maxwell's equations would have even greater symmetry between the $\vec{E}$ and $\vec{B}$ fields if single magnetic charges (magnetic monopoles) existed. The right side of Eq. (29.19) would contain the total *magnetic* charge enclosed by the surface, and the right side of Eq. (29.21) would include a magnetic monopole current term. Perhaps you can begin to see why some physicists wish that magnetic monopoles existed; they would help to perfect the mathematical poetry of Maxwell's equations.

The discovery that electromagnetism can be wrapped up so neatly and elegantly is a very satisfying one. In conciseness and generality, Maxwell's equations are in the same league with Newton's laws of motion and the laws of thermodynamics. Indeed, a major goal of science is learning how to express very broad and general relationships in a concise and compact form. Maxwell's synthesis of electromagnetism stands as a towering intellectual achievement, comparable to the Newtonian synthesis we described at the end of Section 13.5 and to the development of relativity and quantum mechanics in the 20th century.

Test Your Understanding of Section 29.7   (a) Which of Maxwell's equations explains how a credit card reader works? (b) Which one describes how a wire carrying a steady current generates a magnetic field?   ❙

29.8 Superconductivity

The most familiar property of a superconductor is the sudden disappearance of all electrical resistance when the material is cooled below a temperature called the *critical temperature,* denoted by T_c. We discussed this behavior and the circumstances of its discovery in Section 25.2. But superconductivity is far more than just the absence of measurable resistance. As we'll see in this section, superconductors also have extraordinary *magnetic* properties.

The first hint of unusual magnetic properties was the discovery that for any superconducting material the critical temperature T_c changes when the material is placed in an externally produced magnetic field $\vec{B}_0$. Figure 29.23 shows this dependence for mercury, the first element in which superconductivity was observed. As the external field magnitude B_0 increases, the superconducting transition occurs at lower and lower temperature. When B_0 is greater than 0.0412 T, *no* superconducting transition occurs. The minimum magnitude of magnetic field that is needed to eliminate superconductivity at a temperature below T_c is called the *critical field,* denoted by B_c.

The Meissner Effect

Another aspect of the magnetic behavior of superconductors appears if we place a homogeneous sphere of a superconducting material in a uniform applied magnetic field $\vec{B}_0$ at a temperature T greater than T_c. The material is then in the normal phase, not the superconducting phase (Fig. 29.24a). Now we lower the temperature until the superconducting transition occurs. (We assume that the magnitude of $\vec{B}_0$ is not large enough to prevent the phase transition.) What happens to the field?

29.23 Phase diagram for pure mercury, showing the critical magnetic field B_c and its dependence on temperature. Superconductivity is impossible above the critical temperature T_c. The curves for other superconducting materials are similar but with different numerical values.

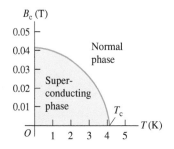

29.24 A superconducting material (a) above the critical temperature and (b), (c) below the critical temperature.

(a) Superconducting material in an external magnetic field $\vec{B}_0$ at $T > T_c$.

The field inside the material is very nearly equal to $\vec{B}_0$.

(b) The temperature is lowered to $T < T_c$, so the material becomes superconducting.

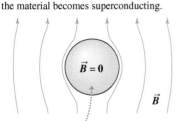

Magnetic flux is expelled from the material, and the field inside it is zero (Meissner effect).

(c) When the external field is turned off at $T < T_c$, the field is zero everywhere.

There is no change in magnetic flux in the material.

29.25 A superconductor (the black slab) exerts a repulsive force on a magnet (the metallic cylinder), supporting the magnet in midair.

Measurements of the field outside the sphere show that the field lines become distorted as in Fig. 29.24b. There is no longer any field inside the material, except possibly in a very thin surface layer a hundred or so atoms thick. If a coil is wrapped around the sphere, the emf induced in the coil shows that during the superconducting transition the magnetic flux through the coil decreases from its initial value to zero; this is consistent with the absence of field inside the material. Finally, if the field is now turned off while the material is still in its superconducting phase, no emf is induced in the coil, and measurements show no field outside the sphere (Fig. 29.24c).

We conclude that during a superconducting transition in the presence of the field $\vec{B}_0$, all of the magnetic flux is expelled from the bulk of the sphere, and the magnetic flux Φ_B through the coil becomes zero. This expulsion of magnetic flux is called the *Meissner effect*. As Fig. 29.24b shows, this expulsion crowds the magnetic field lines closer together to the side of the sphere, increasing $\vec{B}$ there.

Superconductor Levitation and Other Applications

The diamagnetic nature of a superconductor has some interesting *mechanical* consequences. A paramagnetic or ferromagnetic material is attracted by a permanent magnet because the magnetic dipoles in the material align with the nonuniform magnetic field of the permanent magnet. (We discussed this in Section 27.7.) For a diamagnetic material the magnetization is in the opposite sense, and a diamagnetic material is *repelled* by a permanent magnet. By Newton's third law the magnet is also repelled by the diamagnetic material. Figure 29.25 shows the repulsion between a specimen of a high-temperature superconductor and a magnet; the magnet is supported ("levitated") by this repulsive magnetic force.

The behavior we have described is characteristic of what are called *type-I superconductors*. There is another class of superconducting materials called *type-II superconductors*. When such a material in the superconducting phase is placed in a magnetic field, the bulk of the material remains superconducting, but thin filaments of material, running parallel to the field, may return to the normal phase. Currents circulate around the boundaries of these filaments, and there *is* magnetic flux inside them. Type-II superconductors are used for electromagnets because they usually have much larger values of B_c than do type-I materials, permitting much larger magnetic fields without destroying the superconducting state. Type-II superconductors have *two* critical magnetic fields: The first, B_{c1}, is the field at which magnetic flux begins to enter the material, forming the filaments just described, and the second, B_{c2}, is the field at which the material becomes normal.

Many important and exciting applications of superconductors are under development. Superconducting electromagnets have been used in research laboratories for several years. Their advantages compared to conventional electromagnets include greater efficiency, compactness, and greater field magnitudes. Once a current is established in the coil of a superconducting electromagnet, no additional power input is required because there is no resistive energy loss. The coils can also be made more compact because there is no need to provide channels for the circulation of cooling fluids. Superconducting magnets routinely attain steady fields of the order of 10 T, much larger than the maximum fields that are available with ordinary electromagnets.

Superconductors are attractive for long-distance electric power transmission and for energy-conversion devices, including generators, motors, and transformers. Very sensitive measurements of magnetic fields can be made with superconducting quantum interference devices (SQUIDs), which can detect changes in magnetic flux of less than 10^{-14} Wb; these devices have applications in medicine, geology, and other fields. The number of potential uses for superconductors has increased greatly since the discovery in 1987 of high-temperature superconductors. These materials have critical temperatures that are above the temperature of liquid nitrogen (about 77 K) and so are comparatively easy to attain. Development of practical applications of superconductor science promises to be an exciting chapter in contemporary technology.

Faraday's law: Faraday's law states that the induced emf in a closed loop equals the negative of the time rate of change of magnetic flux through the loop. This relationship is valid whether the flux change is caused by a changing magnetic field, motion of the loop, or both. (See Examples 29.1–29.6.)

$$\mathcal{E} = -\frac{d\Phi_B}{dt} \qquad (29.3)$$

The magnet's motion causes a *changing* magnetic field through the coil, inducing a current in the coil.

Lenz's law: Lenz's law states that an induced current or emf always tends to oppose or cancel out the change that caused it. Lenz's law can be derived from Faraday's law and is often easier to use. (See Examples 29.7 and 29.8.)

Motional emf: If a conductor moves in a magnetic field, a motional emf is induced. (See Examples 29.9 and 29.10.)

$$\mathcal{E} = vBL \qquad (29.6)$$

(conductor with length L moves in uniform $\vec{B}$ field, $\vec{L}$ and $\vec{v}$ both perpendicular to $\vec{B}$ and to each other)

$$\mathcal{E} = \oint (\vec{v} \times \vec{B}) \cdot d\vec{l} \qquad (29.7)$$

(all or part of a closed loop moves in a $\vec{B}$ field)

Induced electric fields: When an emf is induced by a changing magnetic flux through a stationary conductor, there is an induced electric field $\vec{E}$ of nonelectrostatic origin. This field is nonconservative and cannot be associated with a potential. (See Example 29.11.)

$$\oint \vec{E} \cdot d\vec{l} = -\frac{d\Phi_B}{dt} \qquad (29.10)$$

$\vec{B}$ increasing

Displacement current and Maxwell's equations: A time-varying electric field generates a displacement current i_D, which acts as a source of magnetic field in exactly the same way as conduction current. The relationships between electric and magnetic fields and their sources can be stated compactly in four equations, called Maxwell's equations. Together they form a complete basis for the relationship of $\vec{E}$ and $\vec{B}$ fields to their sources.

$$i_D = \epsilon \frac{d\Phi_E}{dt} \qquad (29.14)$$

(displacement current)

$$\oint \vec{E} \cdot d\vec{A} = \frac{Q_{encl}}{\epsilon_0} \qquad (29.18)$$

(Gauss's law for $\vec{E}$ fields)

$$\oint \vec{B} \cdot d\vec{A} = 0 \qquad (29.19)$$

(Gauss's law for $\vec{B}$ fields)

$$\oint \vec{B} \cdot d\vec{l} = \mu_0 \left(i_C + \epsilon_0 \frac{d\Phi_E}{dt} \right)_{encl} \qquad (29.20)$$

(Ampere's law including displacement current)

$$\oint \vec{E} \cdot d\vec{l} = -\frac{d\Phi_B}{dt} \qquad (29.21)$$

(Faraday's law)

BRIDGING PROBLEM | **A Falling Square Loop**

A vertically oriented square loop of copper wire falls from rest in a region in which the field $\vec{B}$ is horizontal, uniform, and perpendicular to the plane of the loop, into a field-free region. The side length of the loop is s and the wire diameter is d. The resistivity of copper is ρ_R and the density of copper is ρ_m. If the loop reaches its terminal speed while its upper segment is still in the magnetic-field region, find an expression for the terminal speed.

SOLUTION GUIDE

See MasteringPhysics® study area for a Video Tutor solution. (MP)

IDENTIFY and SET UP

1. The motion of the loop through the magnetic field induces an emf and a current in the loop. The field then gives rise to a magnetic force on this current that opposes the downward force of gravity.
2. Consider the case in which the entire loop is in the magnetic-field region. Is there an induced emf in this case? If so, what is its direction?

3. Consider the case in which only the upper segment of the loop is in the magnetic-field region. Is there an induced emf in this case? If so, what is its direction?
4. For the case in which there is an induced emf and hence an induced current, what is the direction of the magnetic force on each of the four sides of the loop? What is the direction of the *net* magnetic force on the loop?

EXECUTE

5. For the case in which the loop is falling at speed v and there is an induced emf, find (i) the emf, (ii) the induced current, and (iii) the magnetic force on the loop in terms of its resistance R.
6. Find R and the mass of the loop in terms of the given information about the loop.
7. Use your results from steps 5 and 6 to find an expression for the terminal speed.

EVALUATE

8. How does the terminal speed depend on the magnetic-field magnitude B? Explain why this makes sense.

Problems

For instructor-assigned homework, go to MasteringPhysics®. (MP)

•, ••, •••: Problems of increasing difficulty. **CP**: Cumulative problems incorporating material from earlier chapters. **CALC**: Problems requiring calculus. **BIO**: Biosciences problems.

DISCUSSION QUESTIONS

Q29.1 A sheet of copper is placed between the poles of an electromagnet with the magnetic field perpendicular to the sheet. When the sheet is pulled out, a considerable force is required, and the force required increases with speed. Explain.

Q29.2 In Fig. 29.8, if the angular speed ω of the loop is doubled, then the frequency with which the induced current changes direction doubles, and the maximum emf also doubles. Why? Does the torque required to turn the loop change? Explain.

Q29.3 Two circular loops lie side by side in the same plane. One is connected to a source that supplies an increasing current; the other is a simple closed ring. Is the induced current in the ring in the same direction as the current in the loop connected to the source, or opposite? What if the current in the first loop is decreasing? Explain.

Q29.4 For Eq. (29.6), show that if v is in meters per second, B in teslas, and L in meters, then the units of the right-hand side of the equation are joules per coulomb or volts (the correct SI units for $\mathcal{E}$).

Q29.5 A long, straight conductor passes through the center of a metal ring, perpendicular to its plane. If the current in the conductor increases, is a current induced in the ring? Explain.

Q29.6 A student asserted that if a permanent magnet is dropped down a vertical copper pipe, it eventually reaches a terminal velocity even if there is no air resistance. Why should this be? Or should it?

Q29.7 An airplane is in level flight over Antarctica, where the magnetic field of the earth is mostly directed upward away from

the ground. As viewed by a passenger facing toward the front of the plane, is the left or the right wingtip at higher potential? Does your answer depend on the direction the plane is flying?

Q29.8 Consider the situation in Exercise 29.19. In part (a), find the direction of the force that the large circuit exerts on the small one. Explain how this result is consistent with Lenz's law.

Q29.9 A metal rectangle is close to a long, straight, current-carrying wire, with two of its sides parallel to the wire. If the current in the long wire is decreasing, is the rectangle repelled by or attracted to the wire? Explain why this result is consistent with Lenz's law.

Q29.10 A square conducting loop is in a region of uniform, constant magnetic field. Can the loop be rotated about an axis along one side and no emf be induced in the loop? Discuss, in terms of the orientation of the rotation axis relative to the magnetic-field direction.

Q29.11 Example 29.6 discusses the external force that must be applied to the slidewire to move it at constant speed. If there were a break in the left-hand end of the U-shaped conductor, how much force would be needed to move the slidewire at constant speed? As in the example, you can ignore friction.

Q29.12 In the situation shown in Fig. 29.17, would it be appropriate to ask how much *energy* an electron gains during a complete trip around the wire loop with current I'? Would it be appropriate to ask what *potential difference* the electron moves through during such a complete trip? Explain your answers.

Q29.13 A metal ring is oriented with the plane of its area perpendicular to a spatially uniform magnetic field that increases at a steady rate. If the radius of the ring is doubled, by what factor do (a) the emf induced in the ring and (b) the electric field induced in the ring change?

Q29.14 • A type-II superconductor in an external field between B_{c1} and B_{c2} has regions that contain magnetic flux and have resistance, and also has superconducting regions. What is the resistance of a long, thin cylinder of such material?

Q29.15 Can one have a displacement current as well as a conduction current within a conductor? Explain.

Q29.16 Your physics study partner asks you to consider a parallel-plate capacitor that has a dielectric completely filling the volume between the plates. He then claims that Eqs. (29.13) and (29.14) show that the conduction current in the dielectric equals the displacement current in the dielectric. Do you agree? Explain.

Q29.17 Match the mathematical statements of Maxwell's equations as given in Section 29.7 to these verbal statements. (a) Closed electric field lines are evidently produced only by changing magnetic flux. (b) Closed magnetic field lines are produced both by the motion of electric charge and by changing electric flux. (c) Electric field lines can start on positive charges and end on negative charges. (d) Evidently there are no magnetic monopoles on which to start and end magnetic field lines.

Q29.18 If magnetic monopoles existed, the right-hand side of Eq. (29.21) would include a term proportional to the current of magnetic monopoles. Suppose a steady monopole current is moving in a long straight wire. Sketch the *electric* field lines that such a current would produce.

EXERCISES

Section 29.2 Faraday's Law

29.1 • A single loop of wire with an area of 0.0900 m^2 is in a uniform magnetic field that has an initial value of 3.80 T, is perpendicular to the plane of the loop, and is decreasing at a constant rate of 0.190 T/s. (a) What emf is induced in this loop? (b) If the loop has a resistance of $0.600 \ \Omega$, find the current induced in the loop.

29.2 •• In a physics laboratory experiment, a coil with 200 turns enclosing an area of 12 cm^2 is rotated in 0.040 s from a position where its plane is perpendicular to the earth's magnetic field to a position where its plane is parallel to the field. The earth's magnetic field at the lab location is 6.0×10^{-5} T. (a) What is the total magnetic flux through the coil before it is rotated? After it is rotated? (b) What is the average emf induced in the coil?

29.3 •• **Search Coils and Credit Cards.** One practical way to measure magnetic field strength uses a small, closely wound coil called a *search coil*. The coil is initially held with its plane perpendicular to a magnetic field. The coil is then either quickly rotated a quarter-turn about a diameter or quickly pulled out of the field. (a) Derive the equation relating the total charge Q that flows through a search coil to the magnetic-field magnitude B. The search coil has N turns, each with area A, and the flux through the coil is decreased from its initial maximum value to zero in a time Δt. The resistance of the coil is R, and the total charge is $Q = I\Delta t$, where I is the average current induced by the change in flux. (b) In a credit card reader, the magnetic strip on the back of a credit card is rapidly "swiped" past a coil within the reader. Explain, using the same ideas that underlie the operation of a search coil, how the reader can decode the information stored in the pattern of magnetization on the strip. (c) Is it necessary that the credit card be "swiped" through the reader at exactly the right speed? Why or why not?

29.4 • A closely wound search coil (see Exercise 29.3) has an area of 3.20 cm^2, 120 turns, and a resistance of $60.0 \ \Omega$. It is connected to a charge-measuring instrument whose resistance is $45.0 \ \Omega$. When the coil is rotated quickly from a position parallel to a uniform magnetic field to a position perpendicular to the field, the instrument indicates a charge of 3.56×10^{-5} C. What is the magnitude of the field?

29.5 • A circular loop of wire with a radius of 12.0 cm and oriented in the horizontal xy-plane is located in a region of uniform magnetic field. A field of 1.5 T is directed along the positive z-direction, which is upward. (a) If the loop is removed from the field region in a time interval of 2.0 ms, find the average emf that will be induced in the wire loop during the extraction process. (b) If the coil is viewed looking down on it from above, is the induced current in the loop clockwise or counterclockwise?

29.6 • **CALC** A coil 4.00 cm in radius, containing 500 turns, is placed in a uniform magnetic field that varies with time according to $B = (0.0120 \text{ T/s})t + (3.00 \times 10^{-5} \text{ T/s}^4)t^4$. The coil is connected to a 600-Ω resistor, and its plane is perpendicular to the magnetic field. You can ignore the resistance of the coil. (a) Find the magnitude of the induced emf in the coil as a function of time. (b) What is the current in the resistor at time $t = 5.00$ s?

29.7 • **CALC** The current in the long, straight wire AB shown in Fig. E29.7 is upward and is increasing steadily at a rate di/dt. (a) At an instant when the current is i, what are the magnitude and direction of the field $\vec{B}$ at a distance r to the right of the wire? (b) What is the flux $d\Phi_B$ through the narrow, shaded strip? (c) What is the total flux through the loop? (d) What is the induced emf in the loop? (e) Evaluate the numerical value of the induced emf if $a = 12.0$ cm, $b = 36.0$ cm, $L = 24.0$ cm, and $di/dt = 9.60$ A/s.

Figure **E29.7**

29.8 • **CALC** A flat, circular, steel loop of radius 75 cm is at rest in a uniform magnetic field, as shown in an edge-on view in Fig. E29.8. The field is changing with time, according to $B(t) = (1.4 \text{ T})e^{-(0.057 \text{ s}^{-1})t}$. (a) Find the emf induced in the loop as a function of time. (b) When is the induced emf equal to $\frac{1}{10}$ of its initial value? (c) Find the direction of the current induced in the loop, as viewed from above the loop.

Figure **E29.8**

29.9 • **Shrinking Loop.** A circular loop of flexible iron wire has an initial circumference of 165.0 cm, but its circumference is decreasing at a constant rate of 12.0 cm/s due to a tangential pull on the wire. The loop is in a constant, uniform magnetic field oriented perpendicular to the plane of the loop and with magnitude 0.500 T. (a) Find the emf induced in the loop at the instant when 9.0 s have passed. (b) Find the direction of the induced current in the loop as viewed looking along the direction of the magnetic field.

29.10 • A closely wound rectangular coil of 80 turns has dimensions of 25.0 cm by 40.0 cm. The plane of the coil is rotated from a position where it makes an angle of 37.0° with a magnetic field of 1.10 T to a position perpendicular to the field. The rotation takes 0.0600 s. What is the average emf induced in the coil?

29.11 • **CALC** In a region of space, a magnetic field points in the +x-direction (toward the right). Its magnitude varies with position according to the formula $B_x = B_0 + bx$, where B_0 and b are positive constants, for $x \geq 0$. A flat coil of area A moves with uniform speed v from right to left with the plane of its area always perpendicular to this field. (a) What is the emf induced in this coil while it is to the right of the origin? (b) As viewed from the origin, what is the direction (clockwise or counterclockwise) of the current induced in the coil? (c) If instead the coil moved from left to right, what would be the answers to parts (a) and (b)?

29.12 • **Back emf.** A motor with a brush-and-commutator arrangement, as described in Example 29.4, has a circular coil with radius 2.5 cm and 150 turns of wire. The magnetic field has magnitude 0.060 T, and the coil rotates at 440 rev/min. (a) What is the maximum emf induced in the coil? (b) What is the average back emf?

29.13 •• The armature of a small generator consists of a flat, square coil with 120 turns and sides with a length of 1.60 cm. The coil rotates in a magnetic field of 0.0750 T. What is the angular speed of the coil if the maximum emf produced is 24.0 mV?

29.14 • A flat, rectangular coil of dimensions l and w is pulled with uniform speed v through a uniform magnetic field B with the plane of its area perpendicular to the field (Fig. E29.14). (a) Find the emf induced in this coil. (b) If the speed and magnetic field are both tripled, what is the induced emf?

Figure **E29.14**

Section 29.3 Lenz's Law

29.15 • A circular loop of wire is in a region of spatially uniform magnetic field, as shown in Fig. E29.15. The magnetic field is directed into the plane of the figure. Determine the direction (clockwise or counterclockwise) of the induced current in the loop when (a) B is increasing; (b) B is decreasing; (c) B is constant with value B_0. Explain your reasoning.

Figure **E29.15**

29.16 • The current in Fig. E29.16 obeys the equation $I(t) = I_0 e^{-bt}$, where $b > 0$. Find the direction (clockwise or counterclockwise) of the current induced in the round coil for $t > 0$.

Figure **E29.16**

29.17 • Using Lenz's law, determine the direction of the current in resistor ab of Fig. E29.17 when (a) switch S is opened after having been closed for several minutes; (b) coil B is brought closer to coil A with the switch closed; (c) the resistance of R is decreased while the switch remains closed.

Figure **E29.17**

29.18 • A cardboard tube is wrapped with two windings of insulated wire wound in opposite directions, as shown in Fig. E29.18. Terminals a and b of winding A may be connected to a battery through a reversing switch. State whether the induced current in the resistor R is from left to right or from right to left in the following circumstances: (a) the current in winding A is from a to b and is increasing; (b) the current in winding A is from b to a and is decreasing; (c) the current in winding A is from b to a and is increasing.

Figure **E29.18**

29.19 • A small, circular ring is inside a larger loop that is connected to a battery and a switch, as shown in Fig. E29.19. Use Lenz's law to find the direction of the current induced in the small ring (a) just after switch S is closed; (b) after S has been closed a long time; (c) just after S has been reopened after being closed a long time.

Figure **E29.19**

29.20 • A circular loop of wire with radius $r = 0.0480$ m and resistance $R = 0.160 \ \Omega$ is in a region of spatially uniform magnetic field, as shown in Fig. E29.20. The magnetic field is directed out of the plane of the figure. The magnetic field has an initial value of 8.00 T and is decreasing at a rate of $dB/dt = -0.680$ T/s. (a) Is the induced current in the loop clockwise or counterclockwise? (b) What is the rate at which electrical energy is being dissipated by the resistance of the loop?

Figure **E29.20**

29.21 • **CALC** A circular loop of wire with radius $r = 0.0250$ m and resistance $R = 0.390 \ \Omega$ is in a region of spatially uniform magnetic field, as shown in Fig. E29.21. The magnetic field is directed into the plane of the figure. At $t = 0$, $B = 0$. The magnetic field then begins increasing, with $B(t) = (0.380 \ \text{T/s}^3)t^3$. What is the current in the loop (magnitude and direction) at the instant when $B = 1.33$ T?

Figure **E29.21**

Section 29.4 Motional Electromotive Force

29.22 • A rectangular loop of wire with dimensions 1.50 cm by 8.00 cm and resistance $R = 0.600 \ \Omega$ is being pulled to the right out of a region of uniform magnetic field. The magnetic field has magnitude $B = 3.50$ T and is directed into the plane of Fig. E29.22. At

Figure **E29.22**

the instant when the speed of the loop is 3.00 m/s and it is still partially in the field region, what force (magnitude and direction) does the magnetic field exert on the loop?

29.23 • In Fig. E29.23 a conducting rod of length $L = 30.0$ cm moves in a magnetic field $\vec{B}$ of magnitude 0.450 T directed into the plane of the figure. The rod moves with speed $v = 5.00$ m/s in the direction shown. (a) What is the potential difference between the ends of the rod? (b) Which point, a or b, is at higher potential? (c) When the charges in the rod are in equilibrium, what are the magnitude and direction of the electric field within the rod? (d) When the charges in the rod are in equilibrium, which point, a or b, has an excess of positive charge? (e) What is the potential difference across the rod if it moves (i) parallel to ab and (ii) directly out of the page?

Figure **E29.23**

29.24 • A rectangle measuring 30.0 cm by 40.0 cm is located inside a region of a spatially uniform magnetic field of 1.25 T, with the field perpendicular to the plane of the coil (Fig. E29.24). The coil is pulled out at a steady rate of 2.00 cm/s traveling perpendicular to the field lines. The region of the field ends abruptly as shown. Find the emf induced in this coil when it is (a) all inside the field; (b) partly inside the field; (c) all outside the field.

Figure **E29.24**

29.25 • **Are Motional emfs a Practical Source of Electricity?** How fast (in m/s and mph) would a 5.00-cm copper bar have to move at right angles to a 0.650-T magnetic field to generate 1.50 V (the same as a AA battery) across its ends? Does this seem like a practical way to generate electricity?

29.26 • **Motional emfs in Transportation.** Airplanes and trains move through the earth's magnetic field at rather high speeds, so it is reasonable to wonder whether this field can have a substantial effect on them. We shall use a typical value of 0.50 G for the earth's field (a) The French TGV train and the Japanese "bullet train" reach speeds of up to 180 mph moving on tracks about 1.5 m apart. At top speed moving perpendicular to the earth's magnetic field, what potential difference is induced across the tracks as the wheels roll? Does this seem large enough to produce noticeable effects? (b) The Boeing 747-400 aircraft has a wingspan of 64.4 m and a cruising speed of 565 mph. If there is no wind blowing (so that this is also their speed relative to the ground), what is the maximum potential difference that could be induced between the opposite tips of the wings? Does this seem large enough to cause problems with the plane?

29.27 • The conducting rod ab shown in Fig. E29.27 makes contact with metal rails ca and db. The apparatus is in a uniform magnetic field of 0.800 T, perpendicular to the plane of the figure (a) Find the magnitude of the emf induced in the rod when it is moving toward the right with a speed 7.50 m/s. (b) In what direction does the current flow in the rod? (c) If the resistance of the circuit $abdc$ is 1.50 Ω (assumed to be constant), find the force (magnitude and direction) required to keep the rod moving to the right with a constant speed of 7.50 m/s. You can

Figure **E29.27**

ignore friction. (d) Compare the rate at which mechanical work is done by the force (Fv) with the rate at which thermal energy is developed in the circuit (I^2R).

29.28 • A 1.50-m-long metal bar is pulled to the right at a steady 5.0 m/s perpendicular to a uniform, 0.750-T magnetic field. The bar rides on parallel metal rails connected through a 25.0-Ω resistor, as shown in Fig. E29.28, so the apparatus makes a complete circuit. You can ignore the resistance of the bar and the rails. (a) Calculate the magnitude of the emf induced in the circuit. (b) Find the direction of the current induced in the circuit (i) using the magnetic force on the charges in the moving bar; (ii) using Faraday's law; (iii) using Lenz's law. (c) Calculate the current through the resistor.

Figure **E29.28**

29.29 • A 0.360-m-long metal bar is pulled to the left by an applied force F. The bar rides on parallel metal rails connected through a 45.0-Ω resistor, as shown in Fig. E29.29, so the apparatus makes a complete circuit. You can ignore the resistance of the bar and rails. The circuit is in a uniform 0.650-T magnetic field that is directed out of the plane of the figure. At the instant when the bar is moving to the left at 5.90 m/s, (a) is the induced current in the circuit clockwise or counterclockwise and (b) what is the rate at which the applied force is doing work on the bar?

Figure **E29.29**

29.30 • Consider the circuit shown in Fig. E29.29, but with the bar moving to the right with speed v. As in Exercise 29.29, the bar has length 0.360 m, $R = 45.0$ Ω, and $B = 0.650$ T. (a) Is the induced current in the circuit clockwise or counterclockwise? (b) At an instant when the 45.0-Ω resistor is dissipating electrical energy at a rate of 0.840 J/s, what is the speed of the bar?

29.31 • A 0.250-m-long bar moves on parallel rails that are connected through a 6.00-Ω resistor, as shown in Fig. E29.31, so the apparatus makes a complete circuit. You can ignore the resistance of the bar and rails. The circuit is in a uniform magnetic field $B = 1.20$ T that is directed into the plane of the figure. At an instant when the induced current in the circuit is counterclockwise and equal to 1.75 A, what is the velocity of the bar (magnitude and direction)?

Figure **E29.31**

29.32 •• **BIO Measuring Blood Flow.** Blood contains positive and negative ions and thus is a conductor. A blood vessel, therefore, can be viewed as an electrical wire. We can even picture the flowing blood as a series of parallel conducting slabs whose thickness is the diameter d of the vessel moving with speed v. (See Fig. E29.32.) (a) If the blood vessel is placed in a magnetic field B perpendicular to the vessel, as in the figure, show that the motional potential difference induced across it is $\mathcal{E} = vBd$. (b) If you expect that the blood will be flowing at 15 cm/s for a vessel

Figure **E29.32**

5.0 mm in diameter, what strength of magnetic field will you need to produce a potential difference of 1.0 mV? (c) Show that the volume rate of flow (R) of the blood is equal to $R = \pi \mathcal{E} d / 4B$. (*Note:* Although the method developed here is useful in measuring the rate of blood flow in a vessel, it is limited to use in surgery because measurement of the potential $\mathcal{E}$ must be made directly across the vessel.)

29.33 • A 1.41-m bar moves through a uniform, 1.20-T magnetic field with a speed of 2.50 m/s (Fig. E29.33). In each case, find the emf induced between the ends of this bar and identify which, if any, end (*a* or *b*) is at the higher potential. The bar moves in the direction of (a) the +*x*-axis; (b) the −*y*-axis; (c) the +*z*-axis. (d)

Figure **E29.33**

How should this bar move so that the emf across its ends has the greatest possible value with *b* at a higher potential than *a*, and what is this maximum emf?

29.34 •• A rectangular circuit is moved at a constant velocity of 3.0 m/s into, through, and then out of a uniform 1.25-T magnetic field, as shown in Fig. E29.34. The magnetic-field region is considerably wider than 50.0 cm. Find the magnitude and direction (clockwise or counterclockwise) of the current induced in the circuit as it is (a) going into the magnetic field; (b) totally within the magnetic field, but still moving; and (c) moving out of the field. (d) Sketch a graph of the current in this circuit as a function of time, including the preceding three cases.

Figure **E29.34**

Section 29.5 Induced Electric Fields

29.35 • The magnetic field within a long, straight solenoid with a circular cross section and radius R is increasing at a rate of dB/dt. (a) What is the rate of change of flux through a circle with radius r_1 inside the solenoid, normal to the axis of the solenoid, and with center on the solenoid axis? (b) Find the magnitude of the induced electric field inside the solenoid, at a distance r_1 from its axis. Show the direction of this field in a diagram. (c) What is the magnitude of the induced electric field *outside* the solenoid, at a distance r_2 from the axis? (d) Graph the magnitude of the induced electric field as a function of the distance r from the axis from $r = 0$ to $r = 2R$. (e) What is the magnitude of the induced emf in a circular turn of radius $R/2$ that has its center on the solenoid axis? (f) What is the magnitude of the induced emf if the radius in part (e) is R? (g) What is the induced emf if the radius in part (e) is $2R$?

29.36 •• A long, thin solenoid has 900 turns per meter and radius 2.50 cm. The current in the solenoid is increasing at a uniform rate of 60.0 A/s. What is the magnitude of the induced electric field at a point near the center of the solenoid and (a) 0.500 cm from the axis of the solenoid; (b) 1.00 cm from the axis of the solenoid?

29.37 •• A long, thin solenoid has 400 turns per meter and radius 1.10 cm. The current in the solenoid is increasing at a uniform rate di/dt. The induced electric field at a point near the center of the solenoid and 3.50 cm from its axis is 8.00×10^{-6} V/m. Calculate di/dt.

29.38 • A metal ring 4.50 cm in diameter is placed between the north and south poles of large magnets with the plane of its area perpendicular to the magnetic field. These magnets produce an initial uniform field of 1.12 T between them but are gradually pulled apart, causing this field to remain uniform but decrease steadily at 0.250 T/s. (a) What is the magnitude of the electric field induced in the ring? (b) In which direction (clockwise or counterclockwise) does the current flow as viewed by someone on the south pole of the magnet?

29.39 • A long, straight solenoid with a cross-sectional area of 8.00 cm^2 is wound with 90 turns of wire per centimeter, and the windings carry a current of 0.350 A. A second winding of 12 turns encircles the solenoid at its center. The current in the solenoid is turned off such that the magnetic field of the solenoid becomes zero in 0.0400 s. What is the average induced emf in the second winding?

29.40 • The magnetic field $\vec{B}$ at all points within the colored circle shown in Fig. E29.15 has an initial magnitude of 0.750 T. (The circle could represent approximately the space inside a long, thin solenoid.) The magnetic field is directed into the plane of the diagram and is decreasing at the rate of −0.0350 T/s. (a) What is the shape of the field lines of the induced electric field shown in Fig. E29.15, within the colored circle? (b) What are the magnitude and direction of this field at any point on the circular conducting ring with radius 0.100 m? (c) What is the current in the ring if its resistance is 4.00 Ω? (d) What is the emf between points *a* and *b* on the ring? (e) If the ring is cut at some point and the ends are separated slightly, what will be the emf between the ends?

Section 29.7 Displacement Current and Maxwell's Equations

29.41 • **CALC** The electric flux through a certain area of a dielectric is $(8.76 \times 10^3 \text{ V} \cdot \text{m/s}^4)t^4$. The displacement current through that area is 12.9 pA at time $t = 26.1$ ms. Calculate the dielectric constant for the dielectric.

29.42 • A parallel-plate, air-filled capacitor is being charged as in Fig. 29.22. The circular plates have radius 4.00 cm, and at a particular instant the conduction current in the wires is 0.280 A. (a) What is the displacement current density j_D in the air space between the plates? (b) What is the rate at which the electric field between the plates is changing? (c) What is the induced magnetic field between the plates at a distance of 2.00 cm from the axis? (d) At 1.00 cm from the axis?

29.43 • **Displacement Current in a Dielectric.** Suppose that the parallel plates in Fig. 29.22 have an area of 3.00 cm^2 and are separated by a 2.50-mm-thick sheet of dielectric that completely fills the volume between the plates. The dielectric has dielectric constant 4.70. (You can ignore fringing effects.) At a certain instant, the potential difference between the plates is 120 V and the conduction current i_C equals 6.00 mA. At this instant, what are (a) the charge q on each plate; (b) the rate of change of charge on the plates; (c) the displacement current in the dielectric?

29.44 • **CALC** In Fig. 29.22 the capacitor plates have area 5.00 cm^2 and separation 2.00 mm. The plates are in vacuum. The charging current i_C has a *constant* value of 1.80 mA. At $t = 0$ the charge on the plates is zero. (a) Calculate the charge on the plates, the electric field between the plates, and the potential difference between the plates when $t = 0.500$ μs. (b) Calculate dE/dt, the time rate of change of the electric field between the plates. Does dE/dt vary in time? (c) Calculate the displacement current density j_D between the plates, and from this the total displacement current i_D. How do i_C and i_D compare?

29.45 · CALC **Displacement Current in a Wire.** A long, straight, copper wire with a circular cross-sectional area of 2.1 mm² carries a current of 16 A. The resistivity of the material is $2.0 \times 10^{-8} \ \Omega \cdot m$. (a) What is the uniform electric field in the material? (b) If the current is changing at the rate of 4000 A/s, at what rate is the electric field in the material changing? (c) What is the displacement current density in the material in part (b)? (*Hint:* Since K for copper is very close to 1, use $\epsilon = \epsilon_0$.) (d) If the current is changing as in part (b), what is the magnitude of the magnetic field 6.0 cm from the center of the wire? Note that both the conduction current and the displacement current should be included in the calculation of B. Is the contribution from the displacement current significant?

Section 29.8 Superconductivity

29.46 · At temperatures near absolute zero, B_c approaches 0.142 T for vanadium, a type-I superconductor. The normal phase of vanadium has a magnetic susceptibility close to zero. Consider a long, thin vanadium cylinder with its axis parallel to an external magnetic field $\vec{B}_0$ in the $+x$-direction. At points far from the ends of the cylinder, by symmetry, all the magnetic vectors are parallel to the x-axis. At temperatures near absolute zero, what are the resultant magnetic field $\vec{B}$ and the magnetization $\vec{M}$ inside and outside the cylinder (far from the ends) for (a) $\vec{B}_0 = (0.130 \ T)\hat{\imath}$ and (b) $\vec{B}_0 = (0.260 \ T)\hat{\imath}$?

29.47 · The compound SiV₃ is a type-II superconductor. At temperatures near absolute zero the two critical fields are $B_{c1} = 55.0$ mT and $B_{c2} = 15.0$ T. The normal phase of SiV₃ has a magnetic susceptibility close to zero. A long, thin SiV₃ cylinder has its axis parallel to an external magnetic field $\vec{B}_0$ in the $+x$-direction. At points far from the ends of the cylinder, by symmetry, all the magnetic vectors are parallel to the x-axis. At a temperature near absolute zero, the external magnetic field is slowly increased from zero. What are the resultant magnetic field $\vec{B}$ and the magnetization $\vec{M}$ inside the cylinder at points far from its ends (a) just before the magnetic flux begins to penetrate the material, and (b) just after the material becomes completely normal?

PROBLEMS

29.48 ··· CALC **A Changing Magnetic Field.** You are testing a new data-acquisition system. This system allows you to record a graph of the current in a circuit as a function of time. As part of the test, you are using a circuit made up of a 4.00-cm-radius, 500-turn coil of copper wire connected in series to a 600-Ω resistor. Copper has resistivity $1.72 \times 10^{-8} \ \Omega \cdot m$, and the wire used for the coil has diameter 0.0300 mm. You place the coil on a table that is tilted 30.0° from the horizontal and that lies between the poles of an electromagnet. The electromagnet generates a vertically upward magnetic field that is zero for $t < 0$, equal to $(0.120 \ T) \times [1 - (\cos \pi \ rad/s)t]$ for $0 \le t \le 1.00$ s, and equal to 0.240 T for $t > 1.00$ s. (a) Draw the graph that should be produced by your data-acquisition system. (This is a full-featured system, so the graph will include labels and numerical values on its axes.) (b) If you were looking vertically downward at the coil, would the current be flowing clockwise or counterclockwise?

29.49 ·· CP CALC In the circuit shown in Fig. P29.49 the capacitor has capacitance $C = 20 \ \mu F$ and is initially charged to 100 V with the polarity shown. The resistor R_0 has resistance 10 Ω. At time $t = 0$ the switch is closed. The small circuit is not connected in any way to the large one. The wire of the small circuit has a resistance of 1.0 Ω/m and contains 25 loops. The large circuit is a rectangle 2.0 m by 4.0 m, while the small one has dimensions $a = 10.0$ cm and $b = 20.0$ cm. The distance c is 5.0 cm. (The figure is not drawn to scale.) Both circuits are held stationary. Assume that only the wire nearest the small circuit produces an appreciable magnetic field through it. (a) Find the current in the large circuit 200 μs after S is closed. (b) Find the current in the small circuit 200 μs after S is closed. (*Hint:* See Exercise 29.7.) (c) Find the direction of the current in the small circuit. (d) Justify why we can ignore the magnetic field from all the wires of the large circuit except for the wire closest to the small circuit.

Figure **P29.49**

29.50 ·· CP CALC In the circuit in Fig. P29.49, an emf of 90.0 V is added in series with the capacitor and the resistor, and the capacitor is initially uncharged. The emf is placed between the capacitor and the switch, with the positive terminal of the emf adjacent to the capacitor. Otherwise, the two circuits are the same as in Problem 29.49. The switch is closed at $t = 0$. When the current in the large circuit is 5.00 A, what are the magnitude and direction of the induced current in the small circuit?

29.51 ·· CALC A very long, straight solenoid with a cross-sectional area of 2.00 cm² is wound with 90.0 turns of wire per centimeter. Starting at $t = 0$, the current in the solenoid is increasing according to $i(t) = (0.160 \ A/s^2)t^2$. A secondary winding of 5 turns encircles the solenoid at its center, such that the secondary winding has the same cross-sectional area as the solenoid. What is the magnitude of the emf induced in the secondary winding at the instant that the current in the solenoid is 3.20 A?

29.52 · A flat coil is oriented with the plane of its area at right angles to a spatially uniform magnetic field. The magnitude of this field varies with time according to the graph in Fig. P29.52. Sketch a qualitative (but accurate!) graph of the emf induced in the coil as a function of time. Be sure to identify the times t_1, t_2, and t_3 on your graph.

Figure **P29.52**

29.53 · In Fig. P29.53 the loop is being pulled to the right at constant speed v. A constant current I flows in the long wire, in the direction shown. (a) Calculate the magnitude of the net emf $\mathcal{E}$ induced in the loop. Do this two ways: (i) by using Faraday's law of induction (*Hint:* See Exercise 29.7) and (ii) by looking at the emf induced in each segment of the loop due to its motion. (b) Find the direction (clockwise or counterclockwise) of the current induced in the loop. Do this two ways: (i) using Lenz's law and (ii) using the magnetic force on charges in the loop. (c) Check your answer for the emf in part (a) in the following special cases to see whether it is physically reasonable: (i) The loop is stationary; (ii) the loop is very thin, so $a \to 0$; (iii) the loop gets very far from the wire.

Figure **P29.53**

29.54 • Suppose the loop in Fig. P29.54 is (a) rotated about the y-axis; (b) rotated about the x-axis; (c) rotated about an edge parallel to the z-axis. What is the maximum induced emf in each case if $A = 600 \text{ cm}^2$, $\omega = 35.0 \text{ rad/s}$, and $B = 0.450 \text{ T}$?

Figure **P29.54**

29.55 ••• As a new electrical engineer for the local power company, you are assigned the project of designing a generator of sinusoidal ac voltage with a maximum voltage of 120 V. Besides plenty of wire, you have two strong magnets that can produce a constant uniform magnetic field of 1.5 T over a square area of 10.0 cm on a side when they are 12.0 cm apart. The basic design should consist of a square coil turning in the uniform magnetic field. To have an acceptable coil resistance, the coil can have at most 400 loops. What is the minimum rotation rate (in rpm) of the coil so it will produce the required voltage?

29.56 • **Make a Generator?** You are shipwrecked on a deserted tropical island. You have some electrical devices that you could operate using a generator but you have no magnets. The earth's magnetic field at your location is horizontal and has magnitude $8.0 \times 10^{-5} \text{ T}$, and you decide to try to use this field for a generator by rotating a large circular coil of wire at a high rate. You need to produce a peak emf of 9.0 V and estimate that you can rotate the coil at 30 rpm by turning a crank handle. You also decide that to have an acceptable coil resistance, the maximum number of turns the coil can have is 2000. (a) What area must the coil have? (b) If the coil is circular, what is the maximum translational speed of a point on the coil as it rotates? Do you think this device is feasible? Explain.

29.57 • A flexible circular loop 6.50 cm in diameter lies in a magnetic field with magnitude 1.35 T, directed into the plane of the page as shown in Fig. P29.57. The loop is pulled at the points indicated by the arrows, forming a loop of zero area in 0.250 s. (a) Find the average induced emf in the circuit. (b) What is the direction of the current in R: from a to b or from b to a? Explain your reasoning.

Figure **P29.57**

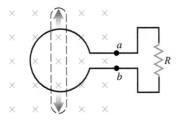

29.58 ••• **CALC** A conducting rod with length $L = 0.200 \text{ m}$, mass $m = 0.120 \text{ kg}$, and resistance $R = 80.0 \ \Omega$ moves without friction on metal rails as shown in Fig. 29.11. A uniform magnetic field with magnitude $B = 1.50 \text{ T}$ is directed into the plane of the figure. The rod is initially at rest, and then a constant force with magnitude $F = 1.90 \text{ N}$ and directed to the right is applied to the bar. How many seconds after the force is applied does the bar reach a speed of 25.0 m/s?

29.59 ••• **Terminal Speed.** A conducting rod with length L, mass m, and resistance R moves without friction on metal rails as shown in Fig. 29.11. A uniform magnetic field $\vec{B}$ is directed into the plane of the figure. The rod starts from rest and is acted on by a constant force $\vec{F}$ directed to the right. The rails are infinitely long and have negligible resistance. (a) Graph the speed of the rod as a function of time. (b) Find an expression for the terminal speed (the speed when the acceleration of the rod is zero).

29.60 •• **CP CALC Terminal Speed.** A bar of length $L = 0.36 \text{ m}$ is free to slide without friction on horizontal rails, as shown in Fig. P29.60. There is a uniform magnetic field $B = 1.5 \text{ T}$ directed into the plane of the figure. At one end of the rails there is a battery with emf $\mathcal{E} = 12 \text{ V}$ and a switch. The bar has mass 0.90 kg and resistance 5.0 Ω, and all other resistance in the circuit can be ignored. The switch is closed at time $t = 0$. (a) Sketch the speed of the bar as a function of time. (b) Just after the switch is closed, what is the acceleration of the bar? (c) What is the acceleration of the bar when its speed is 2.0 m/s? (d) What is the terminal speed of the bar?

Figure **P29.60**

29.61 • **CP Antenna emf.** A satellite, orbiting the earth at the equator at an altitude of 400 km, has an antenna that can be modeled as a 2.0-m-long rod. The antenna is oriented perpendicular to the earth's surface. At the equator, the earth's magnetic field is essentially horizontal and has a value of $8.0 \times 10^{-5} \text{ T}$; ignore any changes in B with altitude. Assuming the orbit is circular, determine the induced emf between the tips of the antenna.

29.62 • **emf in a Bullet.** At the equator, the earth's magnetic field is approximately horizontal, is directed toward the north, and has a value of $8 \times 10^{-5} \text{ T}$. (a) Estimate the emf induced between the top and bottom of a bullet shot horizontally at a target on the equator if the bullet is shot toward the east. Assume the bullet has a length of 1 cm and a diameter of 0.4 cm and is traveling at 300 m/s. Which is at higher potential: the top or bottom of the bullet? (b) What is the emf if the bullet travels south? (c) What is the emf induced between the front and back of the bullet for any horizontal velocity?

29.63 •• **CALC** A very long, cylindrical wire of radius R carries a current I_0 uniformly distributed across the cross section of the wire. Calculate the magnetic flux through a rectangle that has one side of length W running down the center of the wire and another side of length R, as shown in Fig. P29.63 (see Exercise 29.7).

Figure **P29.63**

29.64 • **CALC** A circular conducting ring with radius $r_0 = 0.0420 \text{ m}$ lies in the xy-plane in a region of uniform magnetic field $\vec{B} = B_0[1 - 3(t/t_0)^2 + 2(t/t_0)^3]\hat{k}$. In this expression, $t_0 = 0.0100 \text{ s}$ and is constant, t is time, $\hat{k}$ is the unit vector in the +z-direction, and $B_0 = 0.0800 \text{ T}$ and is constant. At points a and b (Fig. P29.64) there is a small gap in the ring with wires leading to an external circuit of resistance $R = 12.0 \ \Omega$. There is no magnetic field at the location of the external circuit. (a) Derive an expression, as a function of time, for the total magnetic flux Φ_B through the ring. (b) Determine the emf

Figure **P29.64**

induced in the ring at time $t = 5.00 \times 10^{-3}$ s. What is the polarity of the emf? (c) Because of the internal resistance of the ring, the current through R at the time given in part (b) is only 3.00 mA. Determine the internal resistance of the ring. (d) Determine the emf in the ring at a time $t = 1.21 \times 10^{-2}$ s. What is the polarity of the emf? (e) Determine the time at which the current through R reverses its direction.

29.65 • **CALC** The long, straight wire shown in Fig. P29.65a carries constant current I. A metal bar with length L is moving at constant velocity $\vec{v}$, as shown in the figure. Point a is a distance d from the wire. (a) Calculate the emf induced in the bar. (b) Which point, a or b, is at higher potential? (c) If the bar is replaced by a rectangular wire loop of resistance R (Fig. P29.65b), what is the magnitude of the current induced in the loop?

Figure **P29.65**

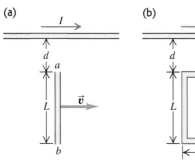

29.66 • The cube shown in Fig. P29.66, 50.0 cm on a side, is in a uniform magnetic field of 0.120 T, directed along the positive y-axis. Wires A, C, and D move in the directions indicated, each with a speed of 0.350 m/s. (Wire A moves parallel to the xy-plane, C moves at an angle of 45.0° below the xy-plane, and D moves parallel to the xz-plane.) What is the potential difference between the ends of each wire?

Figure **P29.66**

29.67 • **CALC** A slender rod, 0.240 m long, rotates with an angular speed of 8.80 rad/s about an axis through one end and perpendicular to the rod. The plane of rotation of the rod is perpendicular to a uniform magnetic field with a magnitude of 0.650 T. (a) What is the induced emf in the rod? (b) What is the potential difference between its ends? (c) Suppose instead the rod rotates at 8.80 rad/s about an axis through its center and perpendicular to the rod. In this case, what is the potential difference between the ends of the rod? Between the center of the rod and one end?

29.68 • **A Magnetic Exercise Machine.** You have designed a new type of exercise machine with an extremely simple mechanism (Fig. E29.28). A vertical bar of silver (chosen for its low resistivity and because it makes the machine look cool) with length $L = 3.0$ m is free to move left or right without friction on silver rails. The entire apparatus is placed in a horizontal, uniform magnetic field of strength 0.25 T. When you push the bar to the left or right, the bar's motion sets up a current in the circuit that includes the bar. The resistance of the bar and the rails can be neglected. The magnetic field exerts a force on the current-carrying bar, and this force opposes the bar's motion. The health benefit is from the exercise that you do in working against this force. (a) Your design

goal is that the person doing the exercise is to do work at the rate of 25 watts when moving the bar at a steady 2.0 m/s. What should be the resistance R? (b) You decide you want to be able to vary the power required from the person, to adapt the machine to the person's strength and fitness. If the power is to be increased to 50 W by altering R while leaving the other design parameters constant, should R be increased or decreased? Calculate the value of R for 50 W. (c) When you start to construct a prototype machine, you find it is difficult to produce a 0.25-T magnetic field over such a large area. If you decrease the length of the bar to 0.20 m while leaving B, v, and R the same as in part (a), what will be the power required of the person?

29.69 •• **CP CALC** A rectangular loop with width L and a slide wire with mass m are as shown in Fig. P29.69. A uniform magnetic field $\vec{B}$ is directed perpendicular to the plane of the loop into the plane of the figure. The slide wire is given an initial speed of v_0 and then released. There is no friction between the slide wire and the loop, and the resistance of the loop is negligible in comparison to the resistance R of the slide wire. (a) Obtain an expression for F, the magnitude of the force exerted on the wire while it is moving at speed v. (b) Show that the distance x that the wire moves before coming to rest is $x = mv_0R/L^2B^2$.

Figure **P29.69**

29.70 •• A 25.0-cm-long metal rod lies in the xy-plane and makes an angle of 36.9° with the positive x-axis and an angle of 53.1° with the positive y-axis. The rod is moving in the $+x$-direction with a speed of 6.80 m/s. The rod is in a uniform magnetic field $\vec{B} = (0.120 \text{ T})\hat{i} - (0.220 \text{ T})\hat{j} - (0.0900 \text{ T})\hat{k}$. (a) What is the magnitude of the emf induced in the rod? (b) Indicate in a sketch which end of the rod is at higher potential.

29.71 • The magnetic field $\vec{B}$, at all points within a circular region of radius R, is uniform in space and directed into the plane of the page as shown in Fig. P29.71. (The region could be a cross section inside the windings of a long, straight solenoid.) If the magnetic field is increasing at a rate dB/dt, what are the magnitude and direction of the force on a stationary positive point charge q located at points a, b, and c? (Point a is a distance r above the center of the region, point b is a distance r to the right of the center, and point c is at the center of the region.)

Figure **P29.71**

29.72 • **CALC** An airplane propeller of total length L rotates around its center with angular speed ω in a magnetic field that is perpendicular to the plane of rotation. Modeling the propeller as a thin, uniform bar, find the potential difference between (a) the center and either end of the propeller and (b) the two ends. (c) If the field is the earth's field of 0.50 G and the propeller turns at 220 rpm and is 2.0 m long, what is the potential difference between the middle and either end? It this large enough to be concerned about?

29.73 ••• **CALC** A dielectric of permittivity 3.5×10^{-11} F/m completely fills the volume between two capacitor plates. For $t > 0$ the electric flux through the dielectric is $(8.0 \times 10^3 \text{ V} \cdot \text{m/s}^3)t^3$. The dielectric is ideal and nonmagnetic; the conduction current in the dielectric is zero. At what time does the displacement current in the dielectric equal 21 μA?

29.74 •• **CP CALC** A capacitor has two parallel plates with area A separated by a distance d. The space between plates is filled with a material having dielectric constant K. The material is not a perfect insulator but has resistivity ρ. The capacitor is initially charged with charge of magnitude Q_0 on each plate that gradually discharges by conduction through the dielectric. (a) Calculate the conduction current density $j_C(t)$ in the dielectric. (b) Show that at any instant the displacement current density in the dielectric is equal in magnitude to the conduction current density but opposite in direction, so the total current density is zero at every instant.

29.75 •• **CALC** A rod of pure silicon (resistivity $\rho = 2300 \ \Omega \cdot m$) is carrying a current. The electric field varies sinusoidally with time according to $E = E_0 \sin \omega t$, where $E_0 = 0.450 \ V/m$, $\omega = 2\pi f$, and the frequency $f = 120 \ Hz$. (a) Find the magnitude of the maximum conduction current density in the wire. (b) Assuming $\mathcal{E} = \mathcal{E}_0$, find the maximum displacement current density in the wire, and compare with the result of part (a). (c) At what frequency f would the maximum conduction and displacement densities become equal if $\mathcal{E} = \mathcal{E}_0$ (which is not actually the case)? (d) At the frequency determined in part (c), what is the relative *phase* of the conduction and displacement currents?

CHALLENGE PROBLEMS

29.76 ••• **CP CALC** A square, conducting, wire loop of side L, total mass m, and total resistance R initially lies in the horizontal xy-plane, with corners at $(x, y, z) = (0, 0, 0)$, $(0, L, 0)$, $(L, 0, 0)$, and $(L, L, 0)$. There is a uniform, upward magnetic field $\vec{B} = B\hat{k}$ in the space within and around the loop. The side of the loop that extends from $(0, 0, 0)$ to $(L, 0, 0)$ is held in place on the x-axis; the rest of the loop is free to pivot around this axis. When the loop is released, it begins to rotate due to the gravitational torque. (a)

Find the *net* torque (magnitude and direction) that acts on the loop when it has rotated through an angle ϕ from its original orientation and is rotating downward at an angular speed ω. (b) Find the angular acceleration of the loop at the instant described in part (a). (c) Compared to the case with zero magnetic field, does it take the loop a longer or shorter time to rotate through 90°? Explain. (d) Is mechanical energy conserved as the loop rotates downward? Explain.

29.77 ••• A metal bar with length L, mass m, and resistance R is placed on frictionless metal rails that are inclined at an angle ϕ above the horizontal. The rails have negligible resistance. A uniform magnetic field of magnitude B is directed downward as shown in Fig. P29.77. The bar is released from rest and slides down the rails. (a) Is the direction of the current induced in the bar from a to b or from b to a? (b) What is the terminal speed of the bar? (c) What is the induced current in the bar when the terminal speed has been reached? (d) After the terminal speed has been reached, at what rate is electrical energy being converted to thermal energy in the resistance of the bar? (e) After the terminal speed has been reached, at what rate is work being done on the bar by gravity? Compare your answer to that in part (d).

Figure **P29.77**

Answers

INDUCTANCE

? Many traffic lights change when a car rolls up to the intersection. How does the light sense the presence of the car?

LEARNING GOALS

By studying this chapter, you will learn:

- How a time-varying current in one coil can induce an emf in a second, unconnected coil.
- How to relate the induced emf in a circuit to the rate of change of current in the same circuit.
- How to calculate the energy stored in a magnetic field.
- How to analyze circuits that include both a resistor and an inductor (coil).
- Why electrical oscillations occur in circuits that include both an inductor and a capacitor.
- Why oscillations decay in circuits with an inductor, a resistor, and a capacitor.

Take a length of copper wire and wrap it around a pencil to form a coil. If you put this coil in a circuit, does it behave any differently than a straight piece of wire? Remarkably, the answer is yes. In an ordinary gasoline-powered car, a coil of this kind makes it possible for the 12-volt car battery to provide thousands of volts to the spark plugs, which in turn makes it possible for the plugs to fire and make the engine run. Other coils of this type are used to keep fluorescent light fixtures shining. Larger coils placed under city streets are used to control the operation of traffic signals. All of these applications, and many others, involve the *induction* effects that we studied in Chapter 29.

A changing current in a coil induces an emf in an adjacent coil. The coupling between the coils is described by their *mutual inductance*. A changing current in a coil also induces an emf in that same coil. Such a coil is called an *inductor,* and the relationship of current to emf is described by the *inductance* (also called *self-inductance*) of the coil. If a coil is initially carrying a current, energy is released when the current decreases; this principle is used in automotive ignition systems. We'll find that this released energy was stored in the magnetic field caused by the current that was initially in the coil, and we'll look at some of the practical applications of magnetic-field energy.

We'll also take a first look at what happens when an inductor is part of a circuit. In Chapter 31 we'll go on to study how inductors behave in alternating-current circuits; in that chapter we'll learn why inductors play an essential role in modern electronics, including communication systems, power supplies, and many other devices.

30.1 Mutual Inductance

In Section 28.4 we considered the magnetic interaction between two wires carrying *steady* currents; the current in one wire causes a magnetic field, which exerts a force on the current in the second wire. But an additional interaction arises

30.1 A current i_1 in coil 1 gives rise to a magnetic flux through coil 2.

Mutual inductance: If the current in coil 1 is changing, the changing flux through coil 2 induces an emf in coil 2.

Coil 1
N_1 turns

Coil 2
N_2 turns

i_1

$\vec{B}$

Φ_{B2}

i_1

between two circuits when there is a *changing* current in one of the circuits. Consider two neighboring coils of wire, as in Fig. 30.1. A current flowing in coil 1 produces a magnetic field $\vec{B}$ and hence a magnetic flux through coil 2. If the current in coil 1 changes, the flux through coil 2 changes as well; according to Faraday's law, this induces an emf in coil 2. In this way, a change in the current in one circuit can induce a current in a second circuit.

Let's analyze the situation shown in Fig. 30.1 in more detail. We will use lowercase letters to represent quantities that vary with time; for example, a time-varying current is i, often with a subscript to identify the circuit. In Fig. 30.1 a current i_1 in coil 1 sets up a magnetic field (as indicated by the blue lines), and some of these field lines pass through coil 2. We denote the magnetic flux through *each* turn of coil 2, caused by the current i_1 in coil 1, as Φ_{B2}. (If the flux is different through different turns of the coil, then Φ_{B2} denotes the *average* flux.) The magnetic field is proportional to i_1, so Φ_{B2} is also proportional to i_1. When i_1 changes, Φ_{B2} changes; this changing flux induces an emf $\mathcal{E}_2$ in coil 2, given by

$$\mathcal{E}_2 = -N_2 \frac{d\Phi_{B2}}{dt} \qquad (30.1)$$

We could represent the proportionality of Φ_{B2} and i_1 in the form $\Phi_{B2} = (\text{constant})i_1$, but instead it is more convenient to include the number of turns N_2 in the relationship. Introducing a proportionality constant M_{21}, called the **mutual inductance** of the two coils, we write

$$N_2\Phi_{B2} = M_{21}i_1 \qquad (30.2)$$

where Φ_{B2} is the flux through a *single* turn of coil 2. From this,

$$N_2 \frac{d\Phi_{B2}}{dt} = M_{21}\frac{di_1}{dt}$$

and we can rewrite Eq. (30.1) as

$$\mathcal{E}_2 = -M_{21}\frac{di_1}{dt} \qquad (30.3)$$

That is, a change in the current i_1 in coil 1 induces an emf in coil 2 that is directly proportional to the rate of change of i_1 (Fig. 30.2).

We may also write the definition of mutual inductance, Eq. (30.2), as

$$M_{21} = \frac{N_2\Phi_{B2}}{i_1}$$

If the coils are in vacuum, the flux Φ_{B2} through each turn of coil 2 is directly proportional to the current i_1. Then the mutual inductance M_{21} is a constant that depends only on the geometry of the two coils (the size, shape, number of turns, and orientation of each coil and the separation between the coils). If a magnetic material is present, M_{21} also depends on the magnetic properties of the material. If the material has nonlinear magnetic properties—that is, if the relative permeability K_m (defined in Section 28.8) is not constant and magnetization is not proportional to magnetic field—then Φ_{B2} is no longer directly proportional to i_1. In that case the mutual inductance also depends on the value of i_1. In this discussion we will assume that any magnetic material present has constant K_m so that flux *is* directly proportional to current and M_{21} depends on geometry only.

We can repeat our discussion for the opposite case in which a changing current i_2 in coil 2 causes a changing flux Φ_{B1} and an emf $\mathcal{E}_1$ in coil 1. We might expect that the corresponding constant M_{12} would be different from M_{21} because in general the two coils are not identical and the flux through them is not the same. It turns out, however, that M_{12} is *always* equal to M_{21}, even when the two coils are not symmetric. We call this common value simply the mutual inductance,

30.2 This electric toothbrush makes use of mutual inductance. The base contains a coil that is supplied with alternating current from a wall socket. This varying current induces an emf in a coil within the toothbrush itself, which is used to recharge the toothbrush battery.

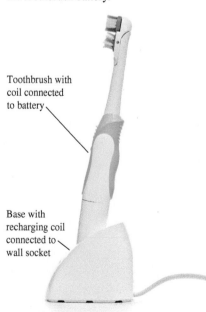

Toothbrush with coil connected to battery

Base with recharging coil connected to wall socket

denoted by the symbol M without subscripts; it characterizes completely the induced-emf interaction of two coils. Then we can write

$$\mathcal{E}_2 = -M\frac{di_1}{dt} \quad \text{and} \quad \mathcal{E}_1 = -M\frac{di_2}{dt} \qquad \text{(mutually induced emfs)} \qquad \text{(30.4)}$$

where the mutual inductance M is

$$M = \frac{N_2\Phi_{B2}}{i_1} = \frac{N_1\Phi_{B1}}{i_2} \qquad \text{(mutual inductance)} \qquad \text{(30.5)}$$

The negative signs in Eq. (30.4) are a reflection of Lenz's law. The first equation says that a change in current in coil 1 causes a change in flux through coil 2, inducing an emf in coil 2 that opposes the flux change; in the second equation the roles of the two coils are interchanged.

CAUTION **Only a time-varying current induces an emf** Note that only a *time-varying* current in a coil can induce an emf and hence a current in a second coil. Equations (30.4) show that the induced emf in each coil is directly proportional to the *rate of change* of the current in the other coil, not to the value of the current. A steady current in one coil, no matter how strong, cannot induce a current in a neighboring coil.

The SI unit of mutual inductance is called the **henry** (1 H), in honor of the American physicist Joseph Henry (1797–1878), one of the discoverers of electromagnetic induction. From Eq. (30.5), one henry is equal to *one weber per ampere*. Other equivalent units, obtained by using Eq. (30.4), are *one volt-second per ampere, one ohm-second,* and *one joule per ampere squared:*

$$1\text{ H} = 1\text{ Wb/A} = 1\text{ V}\cdot\text{s/A} = 1\,\Omega\cdot\text{s} = 1\text{ J/A}^2$$

Just as the farad is a rather large unit of capacitance (see Section 24.1), the henry is a rather large unit of mutual inductance. As Example 30.1 shows, typical values of mutual inductance can be in the millihenry (mH) or microhenry (μH) range.

Drawbacks and Uses of Mutual Inductance

Mutual inductance can be a nuisance in electric circuits, since variations in current in one circuit can induce unwanted emfs in other nearby circuits. To minimize these effects, multiple-circuit systems must be designed so that M is as small as possible; for example, two coils would be placed far apart or with their planes perpendicular.

Happily, mutual inductance also has many useful applications. A *transformer,* used in alternating-current circuits to raise or lower voltages, is fundamentally no different from the two coils shown in Fig. 30.1. A time-varying alternating current in one coil of the transformer produces an alternating emf in the other coil; the value of M, which depends on the geometry of the coils, determines the amplitude of the induced emf in the second coil and hence the amplitude of the output voltage. (We'll describe transformers in more detail in Chapter 31 after we've discussed alternating current in greater depth.)

| **Example 30.1** | **Calculating mutual inductance** |

In one form of Tesla coil (a high-voltage generator popular in science museums), a long solenoid with length l and cross-sectional area A is closely wound with N_1 turns of wire. A coil with N_2 turns surrounds it at its center (Fig. 30.3). Find the mutual inductance M.

SOLUTION

IDENTIFY and SET UP: Mutual inductance occurs here because a current in either coil sets up a magnetic field that causes a flux through the other coil. From Example 28.9 (Section 28.7) we have

Continued

30.3 A long solenoid with cross-sectional area A and N_1 turns is surrounded at its center by a coil with N_2 turns.

Cross-sectional area A

N_1 turns N_2 turns

an expression [Eq. (28.23)] for the field magnitude B_1 at the center of the solenoid (coil 1) in terms of the solenoid current i_1. This allows us to determine the flux through a cross section of the solenoid. Since there is no magnetic field outside a very long solenoid, this is also equal to the flux Φ_{B2} through each turn of the *outer* coil (2). We then use Eq. (30.5), in the form $M = N_2\Phi_{B2}/i_1$, to determine M.

EXECUTE: Equation (28.23) is expressed in terms of the number of turns per unit length, which for solenoid (1) is $n_1 = N_1/L$. We then have

$$B_1 = \mu_0 n_1 i_1 = \frac{\mu_0 N_1 i_1}{l}$$

The flux through a cross section of the solenoid equals B_1A. As we mentioned above, this also equals the flux Φ_{B2} through each turn of the outer coil, independent of its cross-sectional area. From Eq. (30.5), the mutual inductance M is then

$$M = \frac{N_2\Phi_{B2}}{i_1} = \frac{N_2 B_1 A}{i_1} = \frac{N_2}{i_1}\frac{\mu_0 N_1 i_1}{l}A = \frac{\mu_0 A N_1 N_2}{l}$$

EVALUATE: The mutual inductance M of any two coils is proportional to the product N_1N_2 of their numbers of turns. Notice that M depends only on the geometry of the two coils, not on the current.

Here's a numerical example to give you an idea of magnitudes. Suppose $l = 0.50$ m, $A = 10$ cm$^2 = 1.0 \times 10^{-3}$ m^2, $N_1 = 1000$ turns, and $N_2 = 10$ turns. Then

$$M = \frac{(4\pi \times 10^{-7}\ \text{Wb/A}\cdot\text{m})(1.0 \times 10^{-3}\ \text{m}^2)(1000)(10)}{0.50\ \text{m}}$$
$$= 25 \times 10^{-6}\ \text{Wb/A} = 25 \times 10^{-6}\ \text{H} = 25\ \mu\text{H}$$

Example 30.2 **Emf due to mutual inductance**

In Example 30.1, suppose the current i_2 in the outer coil is given by $i_2 = (2.0 \times 10^6\ \text{A/s})t$. (Currents in wires can indeed increase this rapidly for brief periods.) (a) At $t = 3.0\ \mu$s, what is the average magnetic flux through each turn of the solenoid (coil 1) due to the current in the outer coil? (b) What is the induced emf in the solenoid?

SOLUTION

IDENTIFY and SET UP: In Example 30.1 we found the mutual inductance by relating the current in the solenoid to the flux produced in the outer coil; to do that, we used Eq. (30.5) in the form $M = N_2\Phi_{B2}/i_1$. Here we are given the current i_2 in the outer coil and want to find the resulting flux Φ_1 in the solenoid. The mutual inductance is the *same* in either case, and we have $M = 25\ \mu$H from Example 30.1. We use Eq. (30.5) in the form $M = N_1\Phi_{B1}/i_2$ to determine the average flux Φ_{B1} through each turn of the solenoid caused by a given current i_2 in the outer coil. We then use Eq. (30.4) to determine the emf induced in the solenoid by the time variation of i_2.

EXECUTE: (a) At $t = 3.0\ \mu$s $= 3.0 \times 10^{-6}$ s, the current in the outer coil is $i_2 = (2.0 \times 10^6\ \text{A/s})(3.0 \times 10^{-6}\ \text{s}) = 6.0$ A. We

solve Eq. (30.5) for the flux Φ_{B1} through each turn of the solenoid (coil 1):

$$\Phi_{B1} = \frac{Mi_2}{N_1} = \frac{(25 \times 10^{-6}\ \text{H})(6.0\ \text{A})}{1000} = 1.5 \times 10^{-7}\ \text{Wb}$$

We emphasize that this is an *average* value; the flux can vary considerably between the center and the ends of the solenoid.

(b) We are given $i_2 = (2.0 \times 10^6\ \text{A/s})t$, so $di_2/dt = 2.0 \times 10^6$ A/s; then, from Eq. (30.4), the induced emf in the solenoid is

$$\mathcal{E}_1 = -M\frac{di_2}{dt} = -(25 \times 10^{-6}\ \text{H})(2.0 \times 10^6\ \text{A/s}) = -50\ \text{V}$$

EVALUATE: This is a substantial induced emf in response to a very rapid current change. In an operating Tesla coil, there is a high-frequency alternating current rather than a continuously increasing current as in this example; both di_2/dt and $\mathcal{E}_1$ alternate as well, with amplitudes that can be thousands of times larger than in this example.

Test Your Understanding of Section 30.1 Consider the Tesla coil described in Example 30.1. If you make the solenoid out of twice as much wire, so that it has twice as many turns and is twice as long, how much larger is the mutual inductance? (i) M is four times greater; (ii) M is twice as great; (iii) M is unchanged; (iv) M is $\frac{1}{2}$ as great; (v) M is $\frac{1}{4}$ as great.

30.2 Self-Inductance and Inductors

In our discussion of mutual inductance we considered two separate, independent circuits: A current in one circuit creates a magnetic field that gives rise to a flux through the second circuit. If the current in the first circuit changes, the flux through the second circuit changes and an emf is induced in the second circuit.

An important related effect occurs even if we consider only a *single* isolated circuit. When a current is present in a circuit, it sets up a magnetic field that causes a magnetic flux through the *same* circuit; this flux changes when the current changes. Thus any circuit that carries a varying current has an emf induced in it by the variation in *its own* magnetic field. Such an emf is called a **self-induced emf.** By Lenz's law, a self-induced emf always opposes the change in the current that caused the emf and so tends to make it more difficult for variations in current to occur. For this reason, self-induced emfs can be of great importance whenever there is a varying current.

Self-induced emfs can occur in *any* circuit, since there is always some magnetic flux through the closed loop of a current-carrying circuit. But the effect is greatly enhanced if the circuit includes a coil with N turns of wire (Fig. 30.4). As a result of the current i, there is an average magnetic flux Φ_B through each turn of the coil. In analogy to Eq. (30.5) we define the **self-inductance** L of the circuit as

$$L = \frac{N\Phi_B}{i} \qquad \text{(self-inductance)} \qquad (30.6)$$

When there is no danger of confusion with mutual inductance, the self-inductance is called simply the **inductance.** Comparing Eqs. (30.5) and (30.6), we see that the units of self-inductance are the same as those of mutual inductance; the SI unit of self-inductance is the henry.

If the current i in the circuit changes, so does the flux Φ_B; from rearranging Eq. (30.6) and taking the derivative with respect to time, the rates of change are related by

$$N\frac{d\Phi_B}{dt} = L\frac{di}{dt}$$

From Faraday's law for a coil with N turns, Eq. (29.4), the self-induced emf is $\mathcal{E} = -N\,d\Phi_B/dt$, so it follows that

$$\mathcal{E} = -L\frac{di}{dt} \qquad \text{(self-induced emf)} \qquad (30.7)$$

The minus sign in Eq. (30.7) is a reflection of Lenz's law; it says that the self-induced emf in a circuit opposes any change in the current in that circuit. (Later in this section we'll explore in greater depth the significance of this minus sign.)

Equation (30.7) also states that the self-inductance of a circuit is the magnitude of the self-induced emf per unit rate of change of current. This relationship makes it possible to measure an unknown self-inductance in a relatively simple way: Change the current in the circuit at a known rate di/dt, measure the induced emf, and take the ratio to determine L.

Inductors As Circuit Elements

A circuit device that is designed to have a particular inductance is called an **inductor,** or a *choke*. The usual circuit symbol for an inductor is

Like resistors and capacitors, inductors are among the indispensable circuit elements of modern electronics. Their purpose is to oppose any variations in the current through the circuit. An inductor in a direct-current circuit helps to maintain a steady current despite any fluctuations in the applied emf; in an alternating-current circuit, an inductor tends to suppress variations of the current that are more rapid than desired. In this chapter and the next we will explore the behavior and applications of inductors in circuits in more detail.

To understand the behavior of circuits containing inductors, we need to develop a general principle analogous to Kirchhoff's loop rule (discussed in

30.4 The current i in the circuit causes a magnetic field $\vec{B}$ in the coil and hence a flux through the coil.

Self-inductance: If the current i in the coil is changing, the changing flux through the coil induces an emf in the coil.

Application Inductors, Power Transmission, and Lightning Strikes
If lightning strikes part of an electrical power transmission system, it causes a sudden spike in voltage that can damage the components of the system as well as anything connected to that system (for example, home appliances). To minimize these effects, large inductors are incorporated into the transmission system. These use the principle that an inductor opposes and suppresses any rapid changes in the current.

30.5 A circuit containing a source of emf and an inductor. The source is variable, so the current i and its rate of change di/dt can be varied.

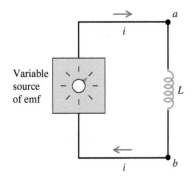

30.6 (a) The potential difference across a resistor depends on the current. (b), (c), (d) The potential difference across an inductor depends on the rate of change of the current.

(a) Resistor with current i flowing from a to b: potential drops from a to b.

$$V_{ab} = iR > 0$$

(b) Inductor with *constant* current i flowing from a to b: no potential difference.

i constant: $di/dt = 0$

$\mathcal{E} = 0$

$$V_{ab} = L\frac{di}{dt} = 0$$

(c) Inductor with *increasing* current i flowing from a to b: potential drops from a to b.

i increasing: $di/dt > 0$

$\mathcal{E}$

$$V_{ab} = L\frac{di}{dt} > 0$$

(d) Inductor with *decreasing* current i flowing from a to b: potential increases from a to b.

i decreasing: $di/dt < 0$

$\mathcal{E}$

$$V_{ab} = L\frac{di}{dt} < 0$$

Section 26.2). To apply that rule, we go around a conducting loop, measuring potential differences across successive circuit elements as we go. The algebraic sum of these differences around any closed loop must be zero because the electric field produced by charges distributed around the circuit is *conservative*. In Section 29.7 we denoted such a conservative field as $\vec{E}_c$.

When an inductor is included in the circuit, the situation changes. The magnetically induced electric field within the coils of the inductor is *not* conservative; as in Section 29.7, we'll denote it by $\vec{E}_n$. We need to think very carefully about the roles of the various fields. Let's assume we are dealing with an inductor whose coils have negligible resistance. Then a negligibly small electric field is required to make charge move through the coils, so the *total* electric field $\vec{E}_c + \vec{E}_n$ within the coils must be zero, even though neither field is individually zero. Because $\vec{E}_c$ is nonzero, there have to be accumulations of charge on the terminals of the inductor and the surfaces of its conductors to produce this field.

Consider the circuit shown in Fig. 30.5; the box contains some combination of batteries and variable resistors that enables us to control the current i in the circuit. According to Faraday's law, Eq. (29.10), the line integral of $\vec{E}_n$ around the circuit is the negative of the rate of change of flux through the circuit, which in turn is given by Eq. (30.7). Combining these two relationships, we get

$$\oint \vec{E}_n \cdot d\vec{l} = -L\frac{di}{dt}$$

where we integrate clockwise around the loop (the direction of the assumed current). But $\vec{E}_n$ is different from zero only within the inductor. Therefore the integral of $\vec{E}_n$ around the whole loop can be replaced by its integral only from a to b through the inductor; that is,

$$\int_a^b \vec{E}_n \cdot d\vec{l} = -L\frac{di}{dt}$$

Next, because $\vec{E}_c + \vec{E}_n = 0$ at each point within the inductor coils, we can rewrite this as

$$\int_a^b \vec{E}_c \cdot d\vec{l} = L\frac{di}{dt}$$

But this integral is just the potential V_{ab} of point a with respect to point b, so we finally obtain

$$V_{ab} = V_a - V_b = L\frac{di}{dt} \qquad (30.8)$$

We conclude that there is a genuine potential difference between the terminals of the inductor, associated with conservative, electrostatic forces, despite the fact that the electric field associated with the magnetic induction effect is nonconservative. Thus we are justified in using Kirchhoff's loop rule to analyze circuits that include inductors. Equation (30.8) gives the potential difference across an inductor in a circuit.

CAUTION **Self-induced emf opposes changes in current** Note that the self-induced emf does not oppose the current i itself; rather, it opposes any *change* (di/dt) in the current. Thus the circuit behavior of an inductor is quite different from that of a resistor. Figure 30.6 compares the behaviors of a resistor and an inductor and summarizes the sign relationships.

Applications of Inductors

Because an inductor opposes changes in current, it plays an important role in fluorescent light fixtures (Fig. 30.7). In such fixtures, current flows from the wiring into the gas that fills the tube, ionizing the gas and causing it to glow. However, an ionized gas or *plasma* is a highly nonohmic conductor: The greater the current, the more highly ionized the plasma becomes and the lower its resistance. If a sufficiently large voltage is applied to the plasma, the current can grow so much that it damages the circuitry outside the fluorescent tube. To prevent this problem, an inductor or *magnetic ballast* is put in series with the fluorescent tube to keep the current from growing out of bounds.

The ballast also makes it possible for the fluorescent tube to work with the alternating voltage provided by household wiring. This voltage oscillates sinusoidally with a frequency of 60 Hz, so that it goes momentarily to zero 120 times per second. If there were no ballast, the plasma in the fluorescent tube would rapidly deionize when the voltage went to zero and the tube would shut off. With a ballast present, a self-induced emf sustains the current and keeps the tube lit. Magnetic ballasts are also used for this purpose in streetlights (which obtain their light from a glowing vapor of mercury or sodium atoms) and in neon lights. (In compact fluorescent lamps, the magnetic ballast is replaced by a more complicated scheme for regulating current. This scheme utilizes transistors, discussed in Chapter 42.)

The self-inductance of a circuit depends on its size, shape, and number of turns. For N turns close together, it is always proportional to N^2. It also depends on the magnetic properties of the material enclosed by the circuit. In the following examples we will assume that the circuit encloses only vacuum (or air, which from the standpoint of magnetism is essentially vacuum). If, however, the flux is concentrated in a region containing a magnetic material with permeability μ, then in the expression for B we must replace μ_0 (the permeability of vacuum) by $\mu = K_m\mu_0$, as discussed in Section 28.8. If the material is diamagnetic or paramagnetic, this replacement makes very little difference, since K_m is very close to 1. If the material is *ferromagnetic,* however, the difference is of crucial importance. A solenoid wound on a soft iron core having $K_m = 5000$ can have an inductance approximately 5000 times as great as that of the same solenoid with an air core. Ferromagnetic-core inductors are very widely used in a variety of electronic and electric-power applications.

An added complication is that with ferromagnetic materials the magnetization is in general not a linear function of magnetizing current, especially as saturation is approached. As a result, the inductance is not constant but can depend on current in a fairly complicated way. In our discussion we will ignore this complication and assume always that the inductance is constant. This is a reasonable assumption even for a ferromagnetic material if the magnetization remains well below the saturation level.

Because automobiles contain steel, a ferromagnetic material, driving an automobile over a coil causes an appreciable increase in the coil's inductance. This effect is used in traffic light sensors, which use a large, current-carrying coil embedded under the road surface near an intersection. The circuitry connected to the coil detects the inductance change as a car drives over. When a preprogrammed number of cars have passed over the coil, the light changes to green to allow the cars through the intersection.

30.7 These fluorescent light tubes are wired in series with an inductor, or ballast, that helps to sustain the current flowing through the tubes.

Example 30.3 Calculating self-inductance

Determine the self-inductance of a toroidal solenoid with cross-sectional area A and mean radius r, closely wound with N turns of wire on a nonmagnetic core (Fig. 30.8). Assume that B is uniform across a cross section (that is, neglect the variation of B with distance from the toroid axis).

SOLUTION

IDENTIFY and SET UP: Our target variable is the self-inductance L of the toroidal solenoid. We can find L using Eq. (30.6), which requires knowing the flux Φ_B through each turn and the current i in

Continued

30.8 Determining the self-inductance of a closely wound toroidal solenoid. For clarity, only a few turns of the winding are shown. Part of the toroid has been cut away to show the cross-sectional area A and radius r.

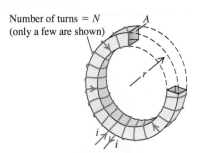

Number of turns = N (only a few are shown)

the coil. For this, we use the results of Example 28.10 (Section 28.7), in which we found the magnetic field in the interior of a toroidal solenoid as a function of the current.

EXECUTE: From Eq. (30.6), the self-inductance is $L = N\Phi_B/i$. From Example 28.10, the field magnitude at a distance r from the toroid axis is $B = \mu_0 Ni/2\pi r$. If we assume that the field has this magnitude over the entire cross-sectional area A, then

$$\Phi_B = BA = \frac{\mu_0 NiA}{2\pi r}$$

The flux Φ_B is the same through each turn, and the self-inductance L is

$$L = \frac{N\Phi_B}{i} = \frac{\mu_0 N^2 A}{2\pi r} \quad \text{(self-inductance of a toroidal solenoid)}$$

EVALUATE: Suppose $N = 200$ turns, $A = 5.0$ cm^2 $= 5.0 \times 10^{-4}$ m^2, and $r = 0.10$ m; then

$$L = \frac{(4\pi \times 10^{-7}\ \text{Wb/A}\cdot\text{m})(200)^2(5.0 \times 10^{-4}\ \text{m}^2)}{2\pi(0.10\ \text{m})}$$
$$= 40 \times 10^{-6}\ \text{H} = 40\ \mu\text{H}$$

Example 30.4 Calculating self-induced emf

If the current in the toroidal solenoid in Example 30.3 increases uniformly from 0 to 6.0 A in 3.0 μs, find the magnitude and direction of the self-induced emf.

SOLUTION

IDENTIFY and SET UP: We are given L, the self-inductance, and di/dt, the rate of change of the solenoid current. We find the magnitude of self-induced emf $\mathcal{E}$ using Eq. (30.7) and its direction using Lenz's law.

EXECUTE: We have $di/dt = (6.0\ \text{A})/(3.0 \times 10^{-6}\ \text{s}) = 2.0 \times 10^6$ A/s. From Eq. (30.7), the magnitude of the induced emf is

$$|\mathcal{E}| = L\left|\frac{di}{dt}\right| = (40 \times 10^{-6}\ \text{H})(2.0 \times 10^6\ \text{A/s}) = 80\ \text{V}$$

The current is increasing, so according to Lenz's law the direction of the emf is opposite to that of the current. This corresponds to the situation in Fig. 30.6c; the emf is in the direction from b to a, like a battery with a as the $+$ terminal and b the $-$ terminal, tending to oppose the current increase from the external circuit.

EVALUATE: This example shows that even a small inductance L can give rise to a substantial induced emf if the current changes rapidly.

Test Your Understanding of Section 30.2 Rank the following inductors in order of the potential difference v_{ab}, from most positive to most negative. In each case the inductor has zero resistance and the current flows from point a through the inductor to point b. (i) The current through a 2.0-μH inductor increases from 1.0 A to 2.0 A in 0.50 s; (ii) the current through a 4.0-μH inductor decreases from 3.0 A to 0 in 2.0 s; (iii) the current through a 1.0-μH inductor remains constant at 4.0 A; (iv) the current through a 1.0-μH inductor increases from 0 to 4.0 A in 0.25 s.

30.3 Magnetic-Field Energy

Establishing a current in an inductor requires an input of energy, and an inductor carrying a current has energy stored in it. Let's see how this comes about. In Fig. 30.5, an increasing current i in the inductor causes an emf $\mathcal{E}$ between its terminals and a corresponding potential difference V_{ab} between the terminals of the source, with point a at higher potential than point b. Thus the source must be adding energy to the inductor, and the instantaneous power P (rate of transfer of energy into the inductor) is $P = V_{ab}i$.

Energy Stored in an Inductor

We can calculate the total energy input U needed to establish a final current I in an inductor with inductance L if the initial current is zero. We assume that the inductor has zero resistance, so no energy is dissipated within the inductor. Let the current at some instant be i and let its rate of change be di/dt; the current is increasing, so $di/dt > 0$. The voltage between the terminals a and b of the inductor at this instant is $V_{ab} = L\,di/dt$, and the rate P at which energy is being delivered to the inductor (equal to the instantaneous power supplied by the external source) is

$$P = V_{ab}i = Li\frac{di}{dt}$$

The energy dU supplied to the inductor during an infinitesimal time interval dt is $dU = P\,dt$, so

$$dU = Li\,di$$

The total energy U supplied while the current increases from zero to a final value I is

$$U = L\int_0^I i\,di = \tfrac{1}{2}LI^2 \quad \text{(energy stored in an inductor)} \quad (30.9)$$

After the current has reached its final steady value I, $di/dt = 0$ and no more energy is input to the inductor. When there is no current, the stored energy U is zero; when the current is I, the energy is $\tfrac{1}{2}LI^2$.

When the current decreases from I to zero, the inductor acts as a source that supplies a total amount of energy $\tfrac{1}{2}LI^2$ to the external circuit. If we interrupt the circuit suddenly by opening a switch or yanking a plug from a wall socket, the current decreases very rapidly, the induced emf is very large, and the energy may be dissipated in an arc across the switch contacts. This large emf is the electrical analog of the large force exerted by a car running into a brick wall and stopping very suddenly.

CAUTION **Energy, resistors, and inductors** It's important not to confuse the behavior of resistors and inductors where energy is concerned (Fig. 30.9). Energy flows into a resistor whenever a current passes through it, whether the current is steady or varying; this energy is dissipated in the form of heat. By contrast, energy flows into an ideal, zero-resistance inductor only when the current in the inductor *increases*. This energy is not dissipated; it is stored in the inductor and released when the current *decreases*. When a steady current flows through an inductor, there is no energy flow in or out. ∎

Magnetic Energy Density

The energy in an inductor is actually stored in the magnetic field within the coil, just as the energy of a capacitor is stored in the electric field between its plates. We can develop relationships for magnetic-field energy analogous to those we obtained for electric-field energy in Section 24.3 [Eqs. (24.9) and (24.11)]. We will concentrate on one simple case, the ideal toroidal solenoid. This system has the advantage that its magnetic field is confined completely to a finite region of space within its core. As in Example 30.3, we assume that the cross-sectional area A is small enough that we can pretend that the magnetic field is uniform over the area. The volume V enclosed by the toroidal solenoid is approximately equal to the circumference $2\pi r$ multiplied by the area A: $V = 2\pi rA$. From Example 30.3, the self-inductance of the toroidal solenoid with vacuum within its coils is

$$L = \frac{\mu_0 N^2 A}{2\pi r}$$

From Eq. (30.9), the energy U stored in the toroidal solenoid when the current is I is

$$U = \tfrac{1}{2}LI^2 = \tfrac{1}{2}\frac{\mu_0 N^2 A}{2\pi r}I^2$$

30.9 A resistor is a device in which energy is irrecoverably dissipated. By contrast, energy stored in a current-carrying inductor can be recovered when the current decreases to zero.

Resistor with current i: energy is *dissipated*.

Inductor with current i: energy is *stored*.

This composite of two images of the sun shows a coronal mass ejection, a dramatic event in which about 10^{12} kg (a billion tons) of material from the sun's outer atmosphere is ejected into space at speeds of 500 km/s or faster. Such ejections happen at intervals of a few hours to a few days. These immense eruptions are powered by the energy stored in the sun's magnetic field. Unlike the earth's relatively steady magnetic field, the sun's field is constantly changing, and regions of unusually strong field (and hence unusually high magnetic energy density) frequently form. A coronal mass ejection occurs when the energy stored in such a region is suddenly released.

The magnetic field and therefore this energy are localized in the volume $V = 2\pi rA$ enclosed by the windings. The energy *per unit volume*, or *magnetic energy density,* is $u = U/V$:

$$u = \frac{U}{2\pi rA} = \tfrac{1}{2}\mu_0 \frac{N^2 I^2}{(2\pi r)^2}$$

We can express this in terms of the magnitude B of the magnetic field inside the toroidal solenoid. From Eq. (28.24) in Example 28.10 (Section 28.7), this is

$$B = \frac{\mu_0 NI}{2\pi r}$$

and so

$$\frac{N^2 I^2}{(2\pi r)^2} = \frac{B^2}{\mu_0^2}$$

When we substitute this into the above equation for u, we finally find the expression for **magnetic energy density** in vacuum:

$$u = \frac{B^2}{2\mu_0} \qquad \text{(magnetic energy density in vacuum)} \qquad (30.10)$$

This is the magnetic analog of the energy per unit volume in an *electric* field in vacuum, $u = \tfrac{1}{2}\epsilon_0 E^2$, which we derived in Section 24.3. As an example, the energy density in the 1.5-T magnetic field of an MRI scanner (see Section 27.7) is $u = B^2/2\mu_0 = (1.5\ \text{T})^2/(2 \times 4\pi \times 10^{-7}\ \text{T}\cdot\text{m/A}) = 9.0 \times 10^5\ \text{J/m}^3$.

When the material inside the toroid is not vacuum but a material with (constant) magnetic permeability $\mu = K_m\mu_0$, we replace μ_0 by μ in Eq. (30.10). The energy per unit volume in the magnetic field is then

$$u = \frac{B^2}{2\mu} \qquad \text{(magnetic energy density in a material)} \qquad (30.11)$$

Although we have derived Eq. (30.11) only for one special situation, it turns out to be the correct expression for the energy per unit volume associated with *any* magnetic-field configuration in a material with constant permeability. For vacuum, Eq. (30.11) reduces to Eq. (30.10). We will use the expressions for electric-field and magnetic-field energy in Chapter 32 when we study the energy associated with electromagnetic waves.

Magnetic-field energy plays an important role in the ignition systems of gasoline-powered automobiles. A primary coil of about 250 turns is connected to the car's battery and produces a strong magnetic field. This coil is surrounded by a secondary coil with some 25,000 turns of very fine wire. When it is time for a spark plug to fire (see Fig. 20.5 in Section 20.3), the current to the primary coil is interrupted, the magnetic field quickly drops to zero, and an emf of tens of thousands of volts is induced in the secondary coil. The energy stored in the magnetic field thus goes into a powerful pulse of current that travels through the secondary coil to the spark plug, generating the spark that ignites the fuel–air mixture in the engine's cylinders (Fig. 30.10).

30.10 The energy required to fire an automobile spark plug is derived from magnetic-field energy stored in the ignition coil.

Example 30.5 **Storing energy in an inductor**

The electric-power industry would like to find efficient ways to store electrical energy generated during low-demand hours to help meet customer requirements during high-demand hours. Could a large inductor be used? What inductance would be needed to store 1.00 kW · h of energy in a coil carrying a 200-A current?

IDENTIFY and SET UP: We are given the required amount of stored energy U and the current $I = 200$ A. We use Eq. (30.9) to find the self-inductance L.

EXECUTE: We have $I = 200$ A and $U = 1.00$ kW$\cdot$h $= (1.00 \times 10^3$ W$)(3600$ s$) = 3.60 \times 10^6$ J. Solving Eq. (30.9) for L, we find

$$L = \frac{2U}{I^2} = \frac{2(3.60 \times 10^6 \text{ J})}{(200 \text{ A})^2} = 180 \text{ H}$$

EVALUATE: The required inductance is more than a million times greater than the self-inductance of the toroidal solenoid of Example 30.3. Conventional wires that are to carry 200 A would have to be of large diameter to keep the resistance low and avoid unacceptable energy losses due to I^2R heating. As a result, a 180-H inductor using conventional wire would be very large (room-size). A superconducting inductor could be much smaller, since the resistance of a superconductor is zero and much thinner wires could be used; but the wires would have to be kept at low temperature to remain superconducting, and maintaining this temperature would itself require energy. This scheme is impractical with present technology.

Test Your Understanding of Section 30.3 The current in a solenoid is reversed in direction while keeping the same magnitude. (a) Does this change the magnetic field within the solenoid? (b) Does this change the magnetic energy density in the solenoid?

30.4 The *R-L* Circuit

Let's look at some examples of the circuit behavior of an inductor. One thing is clear already; an inductor in a circuit makes it difficult for rapid changes in current to occur, thanks to the effects of self-induced emf. Equation (30.7) shows that the greater the rate of change of current di/dt, the greater the self-induced emf and the greater the potential difference between the inductor terminals. This equation, together with Kirchhoff's rules (see Section 26.2), gives us the principles we need to analyze circuits containing inductors.

ActivPhysics 14.1: The *RL* Circuit

Problem-Solving Strategy 30.1 **Inductors in Circuits**

IDENTIFY *the relevant concepts:* An inductor is just another circuit element, like a source of emf, a resistor, or a capacitor. One key difference is that when an inductor is included in a circuit, all the voltages, currents, and capacitor charges are in general functions of time, not constants as they have been in most of our previous circuit analysis. But Kirchhoff's rules (see Section 26.2) are still valid. When the voltages and currents vary with time, Kirchhoff's rules hold at each instant of time.

SET UP *the problem* using the following steps:
1. Follow the procedure described in Problem-Solving Strategy 26.2 (Section 26.2). Draw a circuit diagram and label all quantities, known and unknown. Apply the junction rule immediately so as to express the currents in terms of as few quantities as possible.
2. Determine which quantities are the target variables.

EXECUTE *the solution* as follows:
1. As in Problem-Solving Strategy 26.2, apply Kirchhoff's loop rule to each loop in the circuit.

2. Review the sign rules given in Problem-Solving Strategy 26.2. To get the correct sign for the potential difference between the terminals of an inductor, apply Lenz's law and the sign rule described in Section 30.2 in connection with Eq. (30.7) and Fig. 30.6. In Kirchhoff's loop rule, when we go through an inductor in the *same* direction as the assumed current, we encounter a voltage *drop* equal to $L\,di/dt$, so the corresponding term in the loop equation is $-L\,di/dt$. When we go through an inductor in the *opposite* direction from the assumed current, the potential difference is reversed and the term to use in the loop equation is $+L\,di/dt$.
3. Solve for the target variables.

EVALUATE *your answer:* Check whether your answer is consistent with the behavior of inductors. By Lenz's law, if the current through an inductor is changing, your result should indicate that the potential difference across the inductor opposes the change.

Current Growth in an *R-L* Circuit

We can learn several basic things about inductor behavior by analyzing the circuit of Fig. 30.11. A circuit that includes both a resistor and an inductor, and possibly a source of emf, is called an ***R-L* circuit.** The inductor helps to prevent rapid changes in current, which can be useful if a steady current is required but the external source has a fluctuating emf. The resistor R may be a separate circuit

30.11 An *R-L* circuit.

Closing switch S_1 connects the *R-L* combination in series with a source of emf $\mathcal{E}$.

Closing switch S_2 while opening switch S_1 disconnnects the combination from the source.

element, or it may be the resistance of the inductor windings; every real-life inductor has some resistance unless it is made of superconducting wire. By closing switch S_1, we can connect the *R-L* combination to a source with constant emf $\mathcal{E}$. (We assume that the source has zero internal resistance, so the terminal voltage equals the emf.)

Suppose both switches are open to begin with, and then at some initial time $t = 0$ we close switch S_1. The current cannot change suddenly from zero to some final value, since di/dt and the induced emf in the inductor would both be infinite. Instead, the current begins to grow at a rate that depends only on the value of *L* in the circuit.

Let *i* be the current at some time *t* after switch S_1 is closed, and let di/dt be its rate of change at that time. The potential difference v_{ab} across the resistor at that time is

$$v_{ab} = iR$$

and the potential difference v_{bc} across the inductor is

$$v_{bc} = L\frac{di}{dt}$$

Note that if the current is in the direction shown in Fig. 30.11 and is increasing, then both v_{ab} and v_{bc} are positive; *a* is at a higher potential than *b*, which in turn is at a higher potential than *c*. (Compare to Figs. 30.6a and c.) We apply Kirchhoff's loop rule, starting at the negative terminal and proceeding counterclockwise around the loop:

$$\mathcal{E} - iR - L\frac{di}{dt} = 0 \qquad (30.12)$$

Solving this for di/dt, we find that the rate of increase of current is

$$\frac{di}{dt} = \frac{\mathcal{E} - iR}{L} = \frac{\mathcal{E}}{L} - \frac{R}{L}i \qquad (30.13)$$

At the instant that switch S_1 is first closed, $i = 0$ and the potential drop across *R* is zero. The initial rate of change of current is

$$\left(\frac{di}{dt}\right)_{\text{initial}} = \frac{\mathcal{E}}{L}$$

As we would expect, the greater the inductance *L*, the more slowly the current increases.

As the current increases, the term $(R/L)i$ in Eq. (30.13) also increases, and the *rate* of increase of current given by Eq. (30.13) becomes smaller and smaller. This means that the current is approaching a final, steady-state value *I*. When the current reaches this value, its rate of increase is zero. Then Eq. (30.13) becomes

$$\left(\frac{di}{dt}\right)_{\text{final}} = 0 = \frac{\mathcal{E}}{L} - \frac{R}{L}I \quad \text{and}$$

$$I = \frac{\mathcal{E}}{R}$$

The *final* current *I* does not depend on the inductance *L*; it is the same as it would be if the resistance *R* alone were connected to the source with emf $\mathcal{E}$.

Figure 30.12 shows the behavior of the current as a function of time. To derive the equation for this curve (that is, an expression for current as a function of time), we proceed just as we did for the charging capacitor in Section 26.4. First we rearrange Eq. (30.13) to the form

$$\frac{di}{i - (\mathcal{E}/R)} = -\frac{R}{L}dt$$

30.12 Graph of *i* versus *t* for growth of current in an *R-L* circuit with an emf in series. The final current is $I = \mathcal{E}/R$; after one time constant τ, the current is $1 - 1/e$ of this value.

Switch S_1 is closed at $t = 0$.

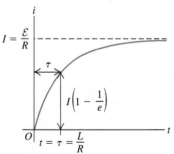

This separates the variables, with i on the left side and t on the right. Then we integrate both sides, renaming the integration variables i' and t' so that we can use i and t as the upper limits. (The lower limit for each integral is zero, corresponding to zero current at the initial time $t = 0$.) We get

$$\int_0^i \frac{di'}{i' - (\mathcal{E}/R)} = -\int_0^t \frac{R}{L} dt'$$

$$\ln\left(\frac{i - (\mathcal{E}/R)}{-\mathcal{E}/R}\right) = -\frac{R}{L}t$$

Now we take exponentials of both sides and solve for i. We leave the details for you to work out; the final result is

$$i = \frac{\mathcal{E}}{R}(1 - e^{-(R/L)t}) \qquad \text{(current in an } R\text{-}L \text{ circuit with emf)} \qquad (30.14)$$

This is the equation of the curve in Fig. 30.12. Taking the derivative of Eq. (30.14), we find

$$\frac{di}{dt} = \frac{\mathcal{E}}{L}e^{-(R/L)t} \qquad\qquad (30.15)$$

At time $t = 0$, $i = 0$ and $di/dt = \mathcal{E}/L$. As $t \to \infty$, $i \to \mathcal{E}/R$ and $di/dt \to 0$, as we predicted.

As Fig. 30.12 shows, the instantaneous current i first rises rapidly, then increases more slowly and approaches the final value $I = \mathcal{E}/R$ asymptotically. At a time equal to L/R, the current has risen to $(1 - 1/e)$, or about 63%, of its final value. The quantity L/R is therefore a measure of how quickly the current builds toward its final value; this quantity is called the **time constant** for the circuit, denoted by τ:

$$\tau = \frac{L}{R} \qquad \text{(time constant for an } R\text{-}L \text{ circuit)} \qquad (30.16)$$

In a time equal to 2τ, the current reaches 86% of its final value; in 5τ, 99.3%; and in 10τ, 99.995%. (Compare the discussion in Section 26.4 of charging a capacitor of capacitance C that was in series with a resistor of resistance R; the time constant for that situation was the product RC.)

The graphs of i versus t have the same general shape for all values of L. For a given value of R, the time constant τ is greater for greater values of L. When L is small, the current rises rapidly to its final value; when L is large, it rises more slowly. For example, if $R = 100\ \Omega$ and $L = 10\ \text{H}$,

$$\tau = \frac{L}{R} = \frac{10\ \text{H}}{100\ \Omega} = 0.10\ \text{s}$$

and the current increases to about 63% of its final value in 0.10 s. (Recall that $1\ \text{H} = 1\ \Omega \cdot \text{s}$.) But if $L = 0.010\ \text{H}$, $\tau = 1.0 \times 10^{-4}\ \text{s} = 0.10\ \text{ms}$, and the rise is much more rapid.

Energy considerations offer us additional insight into the behavior of an $R\text{-}L$ circuit. The instantaneous rate at which the source delivers energy to the circuit is $P = \mathcal{E}i$. The instantaneous rate at which energy is dissipated in the resistor is i^2R, and the rate at which energy is stored in the inductor is $iv_{bc} = Li\,di/dt$ [or, equivalently, $(d/dt)(\frac{1}{2}Li^2) = Li\,di/dt$]. When we multiply Eq. (30.12) by i and rearrange, we find

$$\mathcal{E}i = i^2R + Li\frac{di}{dt} \qquad\qquad (30.17)$$

Of the power $\mathcal{E}i$ supplied by the source, part (i^2R) is dissipated in the resistor and part $(Li\,di/dt)$ goes to store energy in the inductor. This discussion is completely analogous to our power analysis for a charging capacitor, given at the end of Section 26.4.

Example 30.6   Analyzing an *R-L* circuit

A sensitive electronic device of resistance $R = 175 \ \Omega$ is to be connected to a source of emf (of negligible internal resistance) by a switch. The device is designed to operate with a 36-mA current, but to avoid damage to the device, the current can rise to no more than 4.9 mA in the first 58 μs after the switch is closed. An inductor is therefore connected in series with the device, as in Fig. 30.11; the switch in question is S_1. (a) What is the required source emf $\mathcal{E}$? (b) What is the required inductance L? (c) What is the *R-L* time constant τ?

SOLUTION

IDENTIFY and SET UP: This problem concerns current and current growth in an *R-L* circuit, so we can use the ideas of this section. Figure 30.12 shows the current i versus the time t that has elapsed since closing S_1. The graph shows that the final current is $I = \mathcal{E}/R$; we are given $R = 175 \ \Omega$, so the emf is determined by the requirement that the final current be $I = 36$ mA. The other requirement is that the current be no more than $i = 4.9$ mA at $t = 58$ μs; to satisfy this, we use Eq. (30.14) for the current as a function of time and solve for the inductance, which is the only unknown quantity. Equation (30.16) then tells us the time constant.

EXECUTE: (a) We solve $I = \mathcal{E}/R$ for $\mathcal{E}$:

$$\mathcal{E} = IR = (0.036 \ \text{A})(175 \ \Omega) = 6.3 \ \text{V}$$

(b) To find the required inductance, we solve Eq. (30.14) for L. First we multiply through by $(-R/\mathcal{E})$ and then add 1 to both sides to obtain

$$1 - \frac{iR}{\mathcal{E}} = e^{-(R/L)t}$$

Then we take natural logs of both sides, solve for L, and insert the numbers:

$$L = \frac{-Rt}{\ln(1 - iR/\mathcal{E})}$$

$$= \frac{-(175 \ \Omega)(58 \times 10^{-6} \ \text{s})}{\ln[1 - (4.9 \times 10^{-3} \ \text{A})(175 \ \Omega)/(6.3 \ \text{V})]} = 69 \ \text{mH}$$

(c) From Eq. (30.16),

$$\tau = \frac{L}{R} = \frac{69 \times 10^{-3} \ \text{H}}{175 \ \Omega} = 3.9 \times 10^{-4} \ \text{s} = 390 \ \mu\text{s}$$

EVALUATE: Note that 58 μs is much less than the time constant. In 58 μs the current builds up from zero to 4.9 mA, a small fraction of its final value of 36 mA; after 390 μs the current equals $(1 - 1/e)$ of its final value, or about $(0.63)(36 \ \text{mA}) = 23$ mA.

30.13 Graph of i versus t for decay of current in an *R-L* circuit. After one time constant τ, the current is $1/e$ of its initial value.

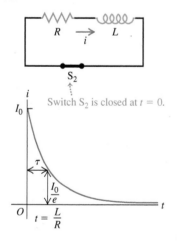

Current Decay in an *R-L* Circuit

Now suppose switch S_1 in the circuit of Fig. 30.11 has been closed for a while and the current has reached the value I_0. Resetting our stopwatch to redefine the initial time, we close switch S_2 at time $t = 0$, bypassing the battery. (At the same time we should open S_1 to save the battery from ruin.) The current through R and L does not instantaneously go to zero but decays smoothly, as shown in Fig. 30.13. The Kirchhoff's-rule loop equation is obtained from Eq. (30.12) by simply omitting the $\mathcal{E}$ term. We challenge you to retrace the steps in the above analysis and show that the current i varies with time according to

$$i = I_0 e^{-(R/L)t} \tag{30.18}$$

where I_0 is the initial current at time $t = 0$. The time constant, $\tau = L/R$, is the time for current to decrease to $1/e$, or about 37%, of its original value. In time 2τ it has dropped to 13.5%, in time 5τ to 0.67%, and in 10τ to 0.0045%.

The energy that is needed to maintain the current during this decay is provided by the energy stored in the magnetic field of the inductor. The detailed energy analysis is simpler this time. In place of Eq. (30.17) we have

$$0 = i^2 R + Li\frac{di}{dt} \tag{30.19}$$

In this case, $Li \ di/dt$ is negative; Eq. (30.19) shows that the energy stored in the inductor *decreases* at a rate equal to the rate of dissipation of energy $i^2 R$ in the resistor.

This entire discussion should look familiar; the situation is very similar to that of a charging and discharging capacitor, analyzed in Section 26.4. It would be a good idea to compare that section with our discussion of the *R-L* circuit.

Example 30.7 **Energy in an *R-L* circuit**

When the current in an *R-L* circuit is decaying, what fraction of the original energy stored in the inductor has been dissipated after 2.3 time constants?

SOLUTION

IDENTIFY and SET UP: This problem concerns current decay in an *R-L* circuit as well as the relationship between the current in an inductor and the amount of stored energy. The current i at any time t is given by Eq. (30.18); the stored energy associated with this current is given by Eq. (30.9), $U = \frac{1}{2}Li^2$.

EXECUTE: From Eq. (30.18), the current i at any time t is

$$i = I_0 e^{-(R/L)t}$$

We substitute this into $U = \frac{1}{2}Li^2$ to obtain an expression for the stored energy at any time:

$$U = \frac{1}{2}LI_0^2 e^{-2(R/L)t} = U_0 e^{-2(R/L)t}$$

where $U_0 = \frac{1}{2}LI_0^2$ is the energy at the initial time $t = 0$. When $t = 2.3\tau = 2.3L/R$, we have

$$U = U_0 e^{-2(2.3)} = U_0 e^{-4.6} = 0.010 U_0$$

That is, only 0.010 or 1.0% of the energy initially stored in the inductor remains, so 99.0% has been dissipated in the resistor.

EVALUATE: To get a sense of what this result means, consider the *R-L* circuit we analyzed in Example 30.6, for which $\tau = 390 \ \mu$s. With $L = 69$ mH and $I_0 = 36$ mA, we have $U_0 = \frac{1}{2}LI_0^2 = \frac{1}{2}(0.069 \ \text{H})(0.036 \ \text{A})^2 = 4.5 \times 10^{-5}$ J. Of this, 99.0% or 4.4×10^{-5} J is dissipated in $2.3(390 \ \mu\text{s}) = 9.0 \times 10^{-4}$ s $= 0.90$ ms. In other words, this circuit can be almost completely powered off (or powered on) in 0.90 ms, so the minimum time for a complete on–off cycle is 1.8 ms. Even shorter cycle times are required for many purposes, such as in fast switching networks for telecommunications. In such cases a smaller time constant $\tau = L/R$ is needed.

Test Your Understanding of Section 30.4   (a) In Fig. 30.11, what are the algebraic signs of the potential differences v_{ab} and v_{bc} when switch S_1 is closed and switch S_2 is open? (i) $v_{ab} > 0$, $v_{bc} > 0$; (ii) $v_{ab} > 0$, $v_{bc} < 0$; (iii) $v_{ab} < 0$, $v_{bc} > 0$; (iv) $v_{ab} < 0$, $v_{bc} < 0$. (b) What are the signs of v_{ab} and v_{bc} when S_1 is open, S_2 is closed, and current is flowing in the direction shown? (i) $v_{ab} > 0$, $v_{bc} > 0$; (ii) $v_{ab} > 0$, $v_{bc} < 0$; (iii) $v_{ab} < 0$, $v_{bc} > 0$; (iv) $v_{ab} < 0$, $v_{bc} < 0$. ❙

30.5 The *L-C* Circuit

ActivPhysics 14.2: AC Circuits: The *RLC* Oscillator (Questions 1–6)

A circuit containing an inductor and a capacitor shows an entirely new mode of behavior, characterized by *oscillating* current and charge. This is in sharp contrast to the *exponential* approach to a steady-state situation that we have seen with both *R-C* and *R-L* circuits. In the **L-C circuit** in Fig. 30.14a we charge the capacitor to a potential difference V_m and initial charge $Q = CV_m$ on its left-hand plate and then close the switch. What happens?

The capacitor begins to discharge through the inductor. Because of the induced emf in the inductor, the current cannot change instantaneously; it starts at zero and eventually builds up to a maximum value I_m. During this buildup the capacitor is discharging. At each instant the capacitor potential equals the induced emf, so as the capacitor discharges, the *rate of change* of current decreases. When the capacitor potential becomes zero, the induced emf is also zero, and the current has leveled off at its maximum value I_m. Figure 30.14b shows this situation; the capacitor has completely discharged. The potential difference between its terminals (and those of the inductor) has decreased to zero, and the current has reached its maximum value I_m.

During the discharge of the capacitor, the increasing current in the inductor has established a magnetic field in the space around it, and the energy that was initially stored in the capacitor's electric field is now stored in the inductor's magnetic field.

Although the capacitor is completely discharged in Fig. 30.14b, the current persists (it cannot change instantaneously), and the capacitor begins to charge with polarity opposite to that in the initial state. As the current decreases, the magnetic field also decreases, inducing an emf in the inductor in the *same* direction as the current; this slows down the decrease of the current. Eventually, the

30.14 In an oscillating *L-C* circuit, the charge on the capacitor and the current through the inductor both vary sinusoidally with time. Energy is transferred between magnetic energy in the inductor (U_B) and electric energy in the capacitor (U_E). As in simple harmonic motion, the total energy E remains constant. (Compare Fig. 14.14 in Section 14.3.)

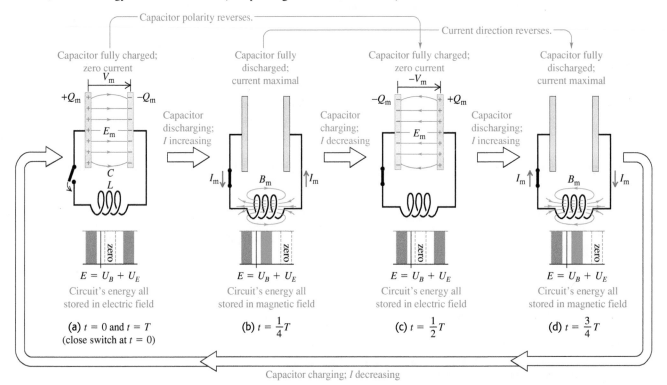

current and the magnetic field reach zero, and the capacitor has been charged in the sense *opposite* to its initial polarity (Fig. 30.14c), with potential difference $-V_m$ and charge $-Q$ on its left-hand plate.

The process now repeats in the reverse direction; a little later, the capacitor has again discharged, and there is a current in the inductor in the opposite direction (Fig. 30.14d). Still later, the capacitor charge returns to its original value (Fig. 30.14a), and the whole process repeats. If there are no energy losses, the charges on the capacitor continue to oscillate back and forth indefinitely. This process is called an **electrical oscillation.**

From an energy standpoint the oscillations of an electrical circuit transfer energy from the capacitor's electric field to the inductor's magnetic field and back. The *total* energy associated with the circuit is constant. This is analogous to the transfer of energy in an oscillating mechanical system from potential energy to kinetic energy and back, with constant total energy. As we will see, this analogy goes much further.

Electrical Oscillations in an *L-C* Circuit

To study the flow of charge in detail, we proceed just as we did for the *R-L* circuit. Figure 30.15 shows our definitions of q and i.

30.15 Applying Kirchhoff's loop rule to the *L-C* circuit. The direction of travel around the loop in the loop equation is shown. Just after the circuit is completed and the capacitor first begins to discharge, as in Fig. 30.14a, the current is negative (opposite to the direction shown).

CAUTION **Positive current in an *L-C* circuit** After examining Fig. 30.14, the positive direction for current in Fig. 30.15 may seem backward to you. In fact we've chosen this direction to simplify the relationship between current and capacitor charge. We define the current at each instant to be $i = dq/dt$, the rate of change of the charge on the left-hand capacitor plate. Hence if the capacitor is initially charged and begins to discharge as in Figs. 30.14a and 30.14b, then $dq/dt < 0$ and the initial current i is negative; the direction of the current is then opposite to the (positive) direction shown in Fig. 30.15. ▌

We apply Kirchhoff's loop rule to the circuit in Fig. 30.15. Starting at the lower-right corner of the circuit and adding voltages as we go clockwise around the loop, we obtain

$$-L\frac{di}{dt} - \frac{q}{C} = 0$$

Since $i = dq/dt$, it follows that $di/dt = d^2q/dt^2$. We substitute this expression into the above equation and divide by $-L$ to obtain

$$\frac{d^2q}{dt^2} + \frac{1}{LC}q = 0 \qquad (L\text{-}C \text{ circuit}) \qquad (30.20)$$

Equation (30.20) has exactly the same form as the equation we derived for simple harmonic motion in Section 14.2, Eq. (14.4). That equation is $d^2x/dt^2 = -(k/m)x$, or

$$\frac{d^2x}{dt^2} + \frac{k}{m}x = 0$$

(You should review Section 14.2 before going on with this discussion.) In the *L-C* circuit the capacitor charge q plays the role of the displacement x, and the current $i = dq/dt$ is analogous to the particle's velocity $v_x = dx/dt$. The inductance L is analogous to the mass m, and the reciprocal of the capacitance, $1/C$, is analogous to the force constant k.

Pursuing this analogy, we recall that the angular frequency $\omega = 2\pi f$ of the harmonic oscillator is equal to $(k/m)^{1/2}$, and the position is given as a function of time by Eq. (14.13),

$$x = A\cos(\omega t + \phi)$$

where the amplitude A and the phase angle ϕ depend on the initial conditions. In the analogous electrical situation the capacitor charge q is given by

$$q = Q\cos(\omega t + \phi) \qquad (30.21)$$

and the angular frequency ω of oscillation is given by

$$\omega = \sqrt{\frac{1}{LC}} \qquad \begin{array}{l}\text{(angular frequency of oscillation}\\ \text{in an } L\text{-}C \text{ circuit)}\end{array} \qquad (30.22)$$

You should verify that Eq. (30.21) satisfies the loop equation, Eq. (30.20), when ω has the value given by Eq. (30.22). In doing this, you will find that the instantaneous current $i = dq/dt$ is given by

$$i = -\omega Q\sin(\omega t + \phi) \qquad (30.23)$$

Thus the charge and current in an *L-C* circuit oscillate sinusoidally with time, with an angular frequency determined by the values of L and C. The ordinary frequency f, the number of cycles per second, is equal to $\omega/2\pi$ as always. The constants Q and ϕ in Eqs. (30.21) and (30.23) are determined by the initial conditions. If at time $t = 0$ the left-hand capacitor plate in Fig. 30.15 has its maximum charge Q and the current i is zero, then $\phi = 0$. If $q = 0$ at time $t = 0$, then $\phi = \pm\pi/2$ rad.

Energy in an *L-C* Circuit

We can also analyze the *L-C* circuit using an energy approach. The analogy to simple harmonic motion is equally useful here. In the mechanical problem a body with mass m is attached to a spring with force constant k. Suppose we displace the body a distance A from its equilibrium position and release it from rest at time $t = 0$. The kinetic energy of the system at any later time is $\frac{1}{2}mv_x^2$, and its elastic potential energy is $\frac{1}{2}kx^2$. Because the system is conservative, the sum of these energies equals the initial energy of the system, $\frac{1}{2}kA^2$. We find the velocity v_x at any position x just as we did in Section 14.3, Eq. (14.22):

$$v_x = \pm\sqrt{\frac{k}{m}}\sqrt{A^2 - x^2} \qquad (30.24)$$

The L-C circuit is also a conservative system. Again let Q be the maximum capacitor charge. The magnetic-field energy $\frac{1}{2}Li^2$ in the inductor at any time corresponds to the kinetic energy $\frac{1}{2}mv^2$ of the oscillating body, and the electric-field energy $q^2/2C$ in the capacitor corresponds to the elastic potential energy $\frac{1}{2}kx^2$ of the spring. The sum of these energies equals the total energy $Q^2/2C$ of the system:

$$\frac{1}{2}Li^2 + \frac{q^2}{2C} = \frac{Q^2}{2C} \qquad (30.25)$$

The total energy in the L-C circuit is *constant;* it oscillates between the magnetic and the electric forms, just as the constant total mechanical energy in simple harmonic motion is constant and oscillates between the kinetic and potential forms.

Solving Eq. (30.25) for i, we find that when the charge on the capacitor is q, the current i is

$$i = \pm\sqrt{\frac{1}{LC}}\sqrt{Q^2 - q^2} \qquad (30.26)$$

You can verify this equation by substituting q from Eq. (30.21) and i from Eq. (30.23). Comparing Eqs. (30.24) and (30.26), we see that current $i = dq/dt$ and charge q are related in the same way as are velocity $v_x = dx/dt$ and position x in the mechanical problem.

Table 30.1 summarizes the analogies between simple harmonic motion and L-C circuit oscillations. The striking parallels shown there are so close that we can solve complicated mechanical and acoustical problems by setting up analogous electric circuits and measuring the currents and voltages that correspond to the mechanical and acoustical quantities to be determined. This is the basic principle of many analog computers. This analogy can be extended to *damped* oscillations, which we consider in the next section. In Chapter 31 we will extend the analogy further to include *forced* electrical oscillations, which occur in all alternating-current circuits.

Table 30.1 Oscillation of a Mass-Spring System Compared with Electrical Oscillation in an L-C Circuit

Mass-Spring System

Kinetic energy $= \frac{1}{2}mv_x^2$

Potential energy $= \frac{1}{2}kx^2$

$\frac{1}{2}mv_x^2 + \frac{1}{2}kx^2 = \frac{1}{2}kA^2$

$v_x = \pm\sqrt{k/m}\sqrt{A^2 - x^2}$

$v_x = dx/dt$

$\omega = \sqrt{\dfrac{k}{m}}$

$x = A\cos(\omega t + \phi)$

Inductor-Capacitor Circuit

Magnetic energy $= \frac{1}{2}Li^2$

Electric energy $= q^2/2C$

$\frac{1}{2}Li^2 + q^2/2C = Q^2/2C$

$i = \pm\sqrt{1/LC}\sqrt{Q^2 - q^2}$

$i = dq/dt$

$\omega = \sqrt{\dfrac{1}{LC}}$

$q = Q\cos(\omega t + \phi)$

Example 30.8 | **An oscillating circuit**

A 300-V dc power supply is used to charge a 25-μF capacitor. After the capacitor is fully charged, it is disconnected from the power supply and connected across a 10-mH inductor. The resistance in the circuit is negligible. (a) Find the frequency and period of oscillation of the circuit. (b) Find the capacitor charge and the circuit current 1.2 ms after the inductor and capacitor are connected.

SOLUTION

IDENTIFY and SET UP: Our target variables are the oscillation frequency f and period T, as well as the charge q and current i at a particular time t. We are given the capacitance C and the inductance L, from which we can calculate the frequency and period using Eq. (30.22). We find the charge and current using Eqs. (30.21) and (30.23). Initially the capacitor is fully charged and the current is zero, as in Fig. 30.14a, so the phase angle is $\phi = 0$ [see the discussion that follows Eq. (30.23)].

EXECUTE: (a) The natural angular frequency is

$$\omega = \sqrt{\frac{1}{LC}} = \sqrt{\frac{1}{(10\times10^{-3}\text{ H})(25\times10^{-6}\text{ F})}}$$
$$= 2.0\times10^3\text{ rad/s}$$

The frequency f and period T are then

$$f = \frac{\omega}{2\pi} = \frac{2.0\times10^3\text{ rad/s}}{2\pi\text{ rad/cycle}} = 320\text{ Hz}$$

$$T = \frac{1}{f} = \frac{1}{320\text{ Hz}} = 3.1\times10^{-3}\text{ s} = 3.1\text{ ms}$$

(b) Since the period of the oscillation is $T = 3.1$ ms, $t = 1.2$ ms equals $0.38T$; this corresponds to a situation intermediate between Fig. 30.14b ($t = T/4$) and Fig. 30.14c ($t = T/2$). Comparing those figures with Fig. 30.15, we expect the capacitor charge q to be negative (that is, there will be negative charge on the left-hand plate of the capacitor) and the current i to be negative as well (that is, current will flow counterclockwise).

To find the value of q, we use Eq. (30.21), $q = Q\cos(\omega t + \phi)$. The charge is maximum at $t = 0$, so $\phi = 0$ and $Q = C\mathcal{E} = (25 \times 10^{-6}\text{ F})(300\text{ V}) = 7.5 \times 10^{-3}$ C. Hence Eq. (30.21) becomes

$$q = (7.5 \times 10^{-3}\text{ C})\cos\omega t$$

At time $t = 1.2 \times 10^{-3}$ s,

$$\omega t = (2.0 \times 10^3\text{ rad/s})(1.2 \times 10^{-3}\text{ s}) = 2.4\text{ rad}$$

$$q = (7.5 \times 10^{-3}\text{ C})\cos(2.4\text{ rad}) = -5.5 \times 10^{-3}\text{ C}$$

From Eq. (30.23), the current i at any time is $i = -\omega Q\sin\omega t$. At $t = 1.2 \times 10^{-3}$ s,

$$i = -(2.0 \times 10^3\text{ rad/s})(7.5 \times 10^{-3}\text{ C})\sin(2.4\text{ rad}) = -10\text{ A}$$

EVALUATE: The signs of q and i are both negative, as predicted.

Example 30.9   Energy in an oscillating circuit

For the *L-C* circuit of Example 30.8, find the magnetic and electric energies (a) at $t = 0$ and (b) at $t = 1.2$ ms.

SOLUTION

IDENTIFY and SET UP: We must calculate the magnetic energy U_B (stored in the inductor) and the electric energy U_E (stored in the capacitor) at two times during the *L-C* circuit oscillation. From Example 30.8 we know the values of the capacitor charge q and circuit current i for both times. We use them to calculate $U_B = \frac{1}{2}Li^2$ and $U_E = q^2/2C$.

EXECUTE: (a) At $t = 0$ there is no current and $q = Q$. Hence there is no magnetic energy, and all the energy in the circuit is in the form of electric energy in the capacitor:

$$U_B = \tfrac{1}{2}Li^2 = 0 \qquad U_E = \frac{Q^2}{2C} = \frac{(7.5 \times 10^{-3}\text{ C})^2}{2(25 \times 10^{-6}\text{ F})} = 1.1\text{ J}$$

(b) From Example 30.8, at $t = 1.2$ ms we have $i = -10$ A and $q = -5.5 \times 10^{-3}$ C. Hence

$$U_B = \tfrac{1}{2}Li^2 = \tfrac{1}{2}(10 \times 10^{-3}\text{ H})(-10\text{ A})^2 = 0.5\text{ J}$$

$$U_E = \frac{q^2}{2C} = \frac{(-5.5 \times 10^{-3}\text{ C})^2}{2(25 \times 10^{-6}\text{ F})} = 0.6\text{ J}$$

EVALUATE: The magnetic and electric energies are the same at $t = 3T/8 = 0.375T$, halfway between the situations in Figs. 30.14b and 30.14c. We saw in Example 30.8 that the time considered in part (b), $t = 1.2$ ms, equals $0.38T$; this is slightly later than $0.375T$, so U_B is slightly less than U_E. At *all* times the *total* energy $E = U_B + U_E$ has the same value, 1.1 J. An *L-C* circuit without resistance is a conservative system; no energy is dissipated.

Test Your Understanding of Section 30.5 One way to think about the energy stored in an *L-C* circuit is to say that the circuit elements do positive or negative work on the charges that move back and forth through the circuit. (a) Between stages (a) and (b) in Fig. 30.14, does the capacitor do positive work or negative work on the charges? (b) What kind of force (electric or magnetic) does the capacitor exert on the charges to do this work? (c) During this process, does the inductor do positive or negative work on the charges? (d) What kind of force (electric or magnetic) does the inductor exert on the charges?

30.6 The *L-R-C* Series Circuit

In our discussion of the *L-C* circuit we assumed that there was no *resistance* in the circuit. This is an idealization, of course; every real inductor has resistance in its windings, and there may also be resistance in the connecting wires. Because of resistance, the electromagnetic energy in the circuit is dissipated and converted to other forms, such as internal energy of the circuit materials. Resistance in an electric circuit is analogous to friction in a mechanical system.

Suppose an inductor with inductance L and a resistor of resistance R are connected in series across the terminals of a charged capacitor, forming an **L-R-C series circuit.** As before, the capacitor starts to discharge as soon as the circuit is completed. But because of i^2R losses in the resistor, the magnetic-field energy acquired by the inductor when the capacitor is completely discharged is *less* than the original electric-field energy of the capacitor. In the same way, the energy of the capacitor when the magnetic field has decreased to zero is still smaller, and so on.

If the resistance R is relatively small, the circuit still oscillates, but with **damped harmonic motion** (Fig. 30.16a), and we say that the circuit is

ActivPhysics 14.2: AC Circuits: The *RLC* Oscillator (Questions 7–10)

30.16 Graphs of capacitor charge as a function of time in an *L-R-C* series circuit with initial charge *Q*.

(a) Underdamped circuit (small resistance *R*)

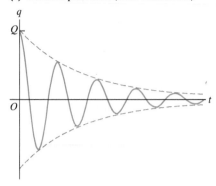

(b) Critically damped circuit (larger resistance *R*)

(c) Overdamped circuit (very large resistance *R*)

30.17 An *L-R-C* series circuit.

When switch S is in this position, the emf charges the capacitor.

When switch S is moved to this position, the capacitor discharges through the resistor and inductor.

underdamped. If we increase *R*, the oscillations die out more rapidly. When *R* reaches a certain value, the circuit no longer oscillates; it is **critically damped** (Fig. 30.16b). For still larger values of *R*, the circuit is **overdamped** (Fig. 30.16c), and the capacitor charge approaches zero even more slowly. We used these same terms to describe the behavior of the analogous mechanical system, the damped harmonic oscillator, in Section 14.7.

Analyzing an *L-R-C* Series Circuit

To analyze *L-R-C* series circuit behavior in detail, we consider the circuit shown in Fig. 30.17. It is like the *L-C* circuit of Fig. 30.15 except for the added resistor *R*; we also show the source that charges the capacitor initially. The labeling of the positive senses of *q* and *i* are the same as for the *L-C* circuit.

First we close the switch in the upward position, connecting the capacitor to a source of emf $\mathcal{E}$ for a long enough time to ensure that the capacitor acquires its final charge $Q = C\mathcal{E}$ and any initial oscillations have died out. Then at time $t = 0$ we flip the switch to the downward position, removing the source from the circuit and placing the capacitor in series with the resistor and inductor. Note that the initial current is negative, opposite to the direction of *i* shown in Fig. 30.17.

To find how *q* and *i* vary with time, we apply Kirchhoff's loop rule. Starting at point *a* and going around the loop in the direction *abcda*, we obtain the equation

$$-iR - L\frac{di}{dt} - \frac{q}{C} = 0$$

Replacing *i* with dq/dt and rearranging, we get

$$\frac{d^2q}{dt^2} + \frac{R}{L}\frac{dq}{dt} + \frac{1}{LC}q = 0 \qquad (30.27)$$

Note that when $R = 0$, this reduces to Eq. (30.20) for an *L-C* circuit.

There are general methods for obtaining solutions of Eq. (30.27). The form of the solution is different for the underdamped (small *R*) and overdamped (large *R*) cases. When R^2 is less than $4L/C$, the solution has the form

$$q = Ae^{-(R/2L)t}\cos\left(\sqrt{\frac{1}{LC} - \frac{R^2}{4L^2}}\, t + \phi\right) \qquad (30.28)$$

where *A* and ϕ are constants. We invite you to take the first and second derivatives of this function and show by direct substitution that it does satisfy Eq. (30.27).

This solution corresponds to the *underdamped* behavior shown in Fig. 30.16a; the function represents a sinusoidal oscillation with an exponentially decaying amplitude. (Note that the exponential factor $e^{-(R/2L)t}$ is *not* the same as the factor $e^{-(R/L)t}$ that we encountered in describing the *R-L* circuit in Section 30.4.) When $R = 0$, Eq. (30.28) reduces to Eq. (30.21) for the oscillations in an *L-C* circuit. If *R* is not zero, the angular frequency of the oscillation is *less* than $1/(LC)^{1/2}$ because of the term containing *R*. The angular frequency ω' of the damped oscillations is given by

$$\omega' = \sqrt{\frac{1}{LC} - \frac{R^2}{4L^2}} \qquad \text{(underdamped *L-R-C* series circuit)} \qquad (30.29)$$

When $R = 0$, this reduces to Eq. (30.22), $\omega = (1/LC)^{1/2}$. As *R* increases, ω' becomes smaller and smaller. When $R^2 = 4L/C$, the quantity under the radical becomes zero; the system no longer oscillates, and the case of *critical damping* (Fig. 30.16b) has been reached. For still larger values of *R* the system behaves as in Fig. 30.16c. In this case the circuit is *overdamped*, and *q* is given as a function of time by the sum of two decreasing exponential functions.

In the *underdamped* case the phase constant ϕ in the cosine function of Eq. (30.28) provides for the possibility of both an initial charge and an initial current at time $t = 0$, analogous to an underdamped harmonic oscillator given both an initial displacement and an initial velocity (see Exercise 30.40).

We emphasize once more that the behavior of the *L-R-C* series circuit is completely analogous to that of the damped harmonic oscillator studied in Section 14.7. We invite you to verify, for example, that if you start with Eq. (14.41) and substitute q for x, L for m, $1/C$ for k, and R for the damping constant b, the result is Eq. (30.27). Similarly, the cross-over point between underdamping and over-damping occurs at $b^2 = 4km$ for the mechanical system and at $R^2 = 4L/C$ for the electrical one. Can you find still other aspects of this analogy?

The practical applications of the *L-R-C* series circuit emerge when we include a sinusoidally varying source of emf in the circuit. This is analogous to the *forced oscillations* that we discussed in Section 14.7, and there are analogous *resonance* effects. Such a circuit is called an *alternating-current (ac) circuit;* the analysis of ac circuits is the principal topic of the next chapter.

Example 30.10   An underdamped *L-R-C* series circuit

What resistance R is required (in terms of L and C) to give an *L-R-C* series circuit a frequency that is one-half the undamped frequency?

SOLUTION

IDENTIFY and SET UP: This problem concerns an underdamped *L-R-C* series circuit (Fig. 30.16a). We want just enough resistance to reduce the oscillation frequency to one-half of the undamped value. Equation (30.29) gives the angular frequency ω' of an underdamped *L-R-C* series circuit; Eq. (30.22) gives the angular frequency ω of an undamped *L-C* circuit. We use these two equations to solve for R.

EXECUTE: From Eqs. (30.29) and (30.22), the requirement $\omega' = \omega/2$ yields

$$\sqrt{\frac{1}{LC} - \frac{R^2}{4L^2}} = \frac{1}{2}\sqrt{\frac{1}{LC}}$$

We square both sides and solve for R:

$$R = \sqrt{\frac{3L}{C}}$$

For example, adding 35 Ω to the circuit of Example 30.8 ($L = 10$ mH, $C = 25\ \mu$F) would reduce the frequency from 320 Hz to 160 Hz.

EVALUATE: The circuit becomes critically damped with no oscillations when $R = \sqrt{4L/C}$. Our result for R is smaller than that, as it should be; we want the circuit to be *under*damped.

Test Your Understanding of Section 30.6   An *L-R-C* series circuit includes a 2.0-Ω resistor. At $t = 0$ the capacitor charge is 2.0 μC. For which of the following values of the inductance and capacitance will the charge on the capacitor *not* oscillate? (i) $L = 3.0\ \mu$H, $C = 6.0\ \mu$F; (ii) $L = 6.0\ \mu$H, $C = 3.0\ \mu$F; (iii) $L = 3.0\ \mu$H, $C = 3.0\ \mu$F.

Video Tutor Solutions

Mutual inductance: When a changing current i_1 in one circuit causes a changing magnetic flux in a second circuit, an emf $\mathcal{E}_2$ is induced in the second circuit. Likewise, a changing current i_2 in the second circuit induces an emf $\mathcal{E}_1$ in the first circuit. If the circuits are coils of wire with N_1 and N_2 turns, the mutual inductance M can be expressed in terms of the average flux Φ_{B2} through each turn of coil 2 caused by the current i_1 in coil 1, or in terms of the average flux Φ_{B1} through each turn of coil 1 caused by the current i_2 in coil 2. The SI unit of mutual inductance is the henry, abbreviated H. (See Examples 30.1 and 30.2.)

$$\mathcal{E}_2 = -M\frac{di_1}{dt} \quad \text{and}$$

$$\mathcal{E}_1 = -M\frac{di_2}{dt} \qquad (30.4)$$

$$M = \frac{N_2\Phi_{B2}}{i_1} = \frac{N_1\Phi_{B1}}{i_2} \qquad (30.5)$$

Self-inductance: A changing current i in any circuit causes a self-induced emf $\mathcal{E}$. The inductance (or self-inductance) L depends on the geometry of the circuit and the material surrounding it. The inductance of a coil of N turns is related to the average flux Φ_B through each turn caused by the current i in the coil. An inductor is a circuit device, usually including a coil of wire, intended to have a substantial inductance. (See Examples 30.3 and 30.4.)

$$\mathcal{E} = -L\frac{di}{dt} \qquad (30.7)$$

$$L = \frac{N\Phi_B}{i} \qquad (30.6)$$

Magnetic-field energy: An inductor with inductance L carrying current I has energy U associated with the inductor's magnetic field. The magnetic energy density u (energy per unit volume) is proportional to the square of the magnetic field magnitude. (See Example 30.5.)

$$U = \tfrac{1}{2}LI^2 \qquad (30.9)$$

$$u = \frac{B^2}{2\mu_0} \quad \text{(in vacuum)} \qquad (30.10)$$

$$u = \frac{B^2}{2\mu} \quad \begin{array}{l}\text{(in a material}\\ \text{with magnetic}\\ \text{permeability } \mu)\end{array} \qquad (30.11)$$

Stored energy $\qquad$ Energy density
$U = \tfrac{1}{2}LI^2 \qquad u = B^2/2\mu_0$

R-L circuits: In a circuit containing a resistor R, an inductor L, and a source of emf, the growth and decay of current are exponential. The time constant τ is the time required for the current to approach within a fraction $1/e$ of its final value. (See Examples 30.6 and 30.7.)

$$\tau = \frac{L}{R} \qquad (30.16)$$

L-C circuits: A circuit that contains inductance L and capacitance C undergoes electrical oscillations with an angular frequency ω that depends on L and C. This is analogous to a mechanical harmonic oscillator, with inductance L analogous to mass m, the reciprocal of capacitance $1/C$ to force constant k, charge q to displacement x, and current i to velocity v_x. (See Examples 30.8 and 30.9.)

$$\omega = \sqrt{\frac{1}{LC}} \qquad (30.22)$$

L-R-C series circuits: A circuit that contains inductance, resistance, and capacitance undergoes damped oscillations for sufficiently small resistance. The frequency ω' of damped oscillations depends on the values of L, R, and C. As R increases, the damping increases; if R is greater than a certain value, the behavior becomes overdamped and no longer oscillates. (See Example 30.10.)

$$\omega' = \sqrt{\frac{1}{LC} - \frac{R^2}{4L^2}} \qquad (30.29)$$

Underdamped circuit (small R)

BRIDGING PROBLEM **Analyzing an *L-C* Circuit**

An *L-C* circuit consists of a 60.0-mH inductor and a 250-μF capacitor. The initial charge on the capacitor is 6.00 μC, and the initial current in the inductor is 0.400 mA. (a) What is the maximum energy stored in the inductor? (b) What is the maximum current in the inductor? (c) What is the maximum voltage across the capacitor? (d) When the current in the inductor has half its maximum value, what is the energy stored in the inductor and the voltage across the capacitor?

SOLUTION GUIDE

See MasteringPhysics® study area for a Video Tutor solution.

IDENTIFY and SET UP:

1. An *L-C* circuit is a conservative system because there is no resistance to dissipate energy. The energy oscillates between electric energy in the capacitor and magnetic energy stored in the inductor.

2. Which key equations are needed to describe the capacitor? To describe the inductor?

EXECUTE:

3. Find the initial total energy in the *L-C* circuit. Use this to determine the maximum energy stored in the inductor during the oscillation.

4. Use the result of step 3 to find the maximum current in the inductor.

5. Use the result of step 3 to find the maximum energy stored in the capacitor during the oscillation. Then use this to find the maximum capacitor voltage.

6. Find the energy in the inductor and the capacitor charge when the current has half the value that you found in step 4.

EVALUATE:

7. Initially, what fraction of the total energy is in the inductor? Is it possible to tell whether this is initially increasing or decreasing?

Problems

For instructor-assigned homework, go to MasteringPhysics®.

•, ••, •••: Problems of increasing difficulty. **CP**: Cumulative problems incorporating material from earlier chapters. **CALC**: Problems requiring calculus. **BIO**: Biosciences problems.

DISCUSSION QUESTIONS

Q30.1 In an electric trolley or bus system, the vehicle's motor draws current from an overhead wire by means of a long arm with an attachment at the end that slides along the overhead wire. A brilliant electric spark is often seen when the attachment crosses a junction in the wires where contact is momentarily lost. Explain this phenomenon.

Q30.2 From Eq. (30.5) 1 H = 1 Wb/A, and from Eq. (30.4) 1 H = 1 $\Omega \cdot$ s. Show that these two definitions are equivalent.

Q30.3 In Fig. 30.1, if coil 2 is turned 90° so that its axis is vertical, does the mutual inductance increase or decrease? Explain.

Q30.4 The tightly wound toroidal solenoid is one of the few configurations for which it is easy to calculate self-inductance. What features of the toroidal solenoid give it this simplicity?

Q30.5 Two identical, closely wound, circular coils, each having self-inductance L, are placed next to each other, so that they are coaxial and almost touching. If they are connected in series, what is the self-inductance of the combination? What if they are connected in parallel? Can they be connected so that the total inductance is zero? Explain.

Q30.6 Two closely wound circular coils have the same number of turns, but one has twice the radius of the other. How are the self-inductances of the two coils related? Explain your reasoning.

Q30.7 You are to make a resistor by winding a wire around a cylindrical form. To make the inductance as small as possible, it is proposed that you wind half the wire in one direction and the other half in the opposite direction. Would this achieve the desired result? Why or why not?

Q30.8 For the same magnetic field strength B, is the energy density greater in vacuum or in a magnetic material? Explain. Does

Eq. (30.11) imply that for a long solenoid in which the current is I the energy stored is proportional to $1/\mu$? And does this mean that for the same current less energy is stored when the solenoid is filled with a ferromagnetic material rather than with air? Explain.

Q30.9 In Section 30.5 Kirchhoff's loop rule is applied to an *L-C* circuit where the capacitor is initially fully charged and the equation $-L \, di/dt - q/C = 0$ is derived. But as the capacitor starts to discharge, the current increases from zero. The equation says $L \, di/dt = -q/C$, so it says $L \, di/dt$ is negative. Explain how $L \, di/dt$ can be negative when the current is increasing.

Q30.10 In Section 30.5 the relationship $i = dq/dt$ is used in deriving Eq. (30.20). But a flow of current corresponds to a decrease in the charge on the capacitor. Explain, therefore, why this is the correct equation to use in the derivation, rather than $i = -dq/dt$.

Q30.11 In the *R-L* circuit shown in Fig. 30.11, when switch S_1 is closed, the potential v_{ab} changes suddenly and discontinuously, but the current does not. Explain why the voltage can change suddenly but the current can't.

Q30.12 In the *R-L* circuit shown in Fig. 30.11, is the current in the resistor always the same as the current in the inductor? How do you know?

Q30.13 Suppose there is a steady current in an inductor. If you attempt to reduce the current to zero instantaneously by quickly opening a switch, an arc can appear at the switch contacts. Why? Is it physically possible to stop the current instantaneously? Explain.

Q30.14 In an *L-R-C* series circuit, what criteria could be used to decide whether the system is overdamped or underdamped? For example, could we compare the maximum energy stored during one cycle to the energy dissipated during one cycle? Explain.

EXERCISES

Section 30.1 Mutual Inductance

30.1 • Two coils have mutual inductance $M = 3.25 \times 10^{-4}$ H. The current i_1 in the first coil increases at a uniform rate of 830 A/s. (a) What is the magnitude of the induced emf in the second coil? Is it constant? (b) Suppose that the current described is in the second coil rather than the first. What is the magnitude of the induced emf in the first coil?

30.2 • Two coils are wound around the same cylindrical form, like the coils in Example 30.1. When the current in the first coil is decreasing at a rate of -0.242 A/s, the induced emf in the second coil has magnitude 1.65×10^{-3} V. (a) What is the mutual inductance of the pair of coils? (b) If the second coil has 25 turns, what is the flux through each turn when the current in the first coil equals 1.20 A? (c) If the current in the second coil increases at a rate of 0.360 A/s, what is the magnitude of the induced emf in the first coil?

30.3 • A 10.0-cm-long solenoid of diameter 0.400 cm is wound uniformly with 800 turns. A second coil with 50 turns is wound around the solenoid at its center. What is the mutual inductance of the combination of the two coils?

30.4 • A solenoidal coil with 25 turns of wire is wound tightly around another coil with 300 turns (see Example 30.1). The inner solenoid is 25.0 cm long and has a diameter of 2.00 cm. At a certain time, the current in the inner solenoid is 0.120 A and is increasing at a rate of 1.75×10^3 A/s. For this time, calculate: (a) the average magnetic flux through each turn of the inner solenoid; (b) the mutual inductance of the two solenoids; (c) the emf induced in the outer solenoid by the changing current in the inner solenoid.

30.5 • Two toroidal solenoids are wound around the same form so that the magnetic field of one passes through the turns of the other. Solenoid 1 has 700 turns, and solenoid 2 has 400 turns. When the current in solenoid 1 is 6.52 A, the average flux through each turn of solenoid 2 is 0.0320 Wb. (a) What is the mutual inductance of the pair of solenoids? (b) When the current in solenoid 2 is 2.54 A, what is the average flux through each turn of solenoid 1?

30.6 •• A toroidal solenoid with mean radius r and cross-sectional area A is wound uniformly with N_1 turns. A second toroidal solenoid with N_2 turns is wound uniformly on top of the first, so that the two solenoids have the same cross-sectional area and mean radius. (a) What is the mutual inductance of the two solenoids? Assume that the magnetic field of the first solenoid is uniform across the cross section of the two solenoids. (b) If $N_1 = 500$ turns, $N_2 = 300$ turns, $r = 10.0$ cm, and $A = 0.800$ cm^2, what is the value of the mutual inductance?

Section 30.2 Self-Inductance and Inductors

30.7 • A 2.50-mH toroidal solenoid has an average radius of 6.00 cm and a cross-sectional area of 2.00 cm^2. (a) How many coils does it have? (Make the same assumption as in Example 30.3.) (b) At what rate must the current through it change so that a potential difference of 2.00 V is developed across its ends?

30.8 • A toroidal solenoid has 500 turns, cross-sectional area 6.25 cm^2, and mean radius 4.00 cm. (a) Calculate the coil's self-inductance. (b) If the current decreases uniformly from 5.00 A to 2.00 A in 3.00 ms, calculate the self-induced emf in the coil. (c) The current is directed from terminal a of the coil to terminal b. Is the direction of the induced emf from a to b or from b to a?

30.9 • At the instant when the current in an inductor is increasing at a rate of 0.0640 A/s, the magnitude of the self-induced emf is 0.0160 V. (a) What is the inductance of the inductor? (b) If the

inductor is a solenoid with 400 turns, what is the average magnetic flux through each turn when the current is 0.720 A?

30.10 •• When the current in a toroidal solenoid is changing at a rate of 0.0260 A/s, the magnitude of the induced emf is 12.6 mV. When the current equals 1.40 A, the average flux through each turn of the solenoid is 0.00285 Wb. How many turns does the solenoid have?

30.11 • The inductor in Fig. E30.11 has inductance 0.260 H and carries a current in the direction shown that is decreasing at a uniform rate, $di/dt = -0.0180$ A/s. (a) Find the self-induced emf. (b) Which end of the inductor, a or b, is at a higher potential?

Figure **E30.11**

30.12 • The inductor shown in Fig. E30.11 has inductance 0.260 H and carries a current in the direction shown. The current is changing at a constant rate. (a) The potential between points a and b is $V_{ab} = 1.04$ V, with point a at higher potential. Is the current increasing or decreasing? (b) If the current at $t = 0$ is 12.0 A, what is the current at $t = 2.00$ s?

30.13 •• A toroidal solenoid has mean radius 12.0 cm and cross-sectional area 0.600 cm^2. (a) How many turns does the solenoid have if its inductance is 0.100 mH? (b) What is the resistance of the solenoid if the wire from which it is wound has a resistance per unit length of 0.0760 Ω/m?

30.14 • A long, straight solenoid has 800 turns. When the current in the solenoid is 2.90 A, the average flux through each turn of the solenoid is 3.25×10^{-3} Wb. What must be the magnitude of the rate of change of the current in order for the self-induced emf to equal 7.50 mV?

30.15 •• **Inductance of a Solenoid.** (a) A long, straight solenoid has N turns, uniform cross-sectional area A, and length l. Show that the inductance of this solenoid is given by the equation $L = \mu_0 A N^2 / l$. Assume that the magnetic field is uniform inside the solenoid and zero outside. (Your answer is approximate because B is actually smaller at the ends than at the center. For this reason, your answer is actually an upper limit on the inductance.) (b) A metallic laboratory spring is typically 5.00 cm long and 0.150 cm in diameter and has 50 coils. If you connect such a spring in an electric circuit, how much self-inductance must you include for it if you model it as an ideal solenoid?

Section 30.3 Magnetic-Field Energy

30.16 • An inductor used in a dc power supply has an inductance of 12.0 H and a resistance of 180 Ω. It carries a current of 0.300 A. (a) What is the energy stored in the magnetic field? (b) At what rate is thermal energy developed in the inductor? (c) Does your answer to part (b) mean that the magnetic-field energy is decreasing with time? Explain.

30.17 • An air-filled toroidal solenoid has a mean radius of 15.0 cm and a cross-sectional area of 5.00 cm^2. When the current is 12.0 A, the energy stored is 0.390 J. How many turns does the winding have?

30.18 • An air-filled toroidal solenoid has 300 turns of wire, a mean radius of 12.0 cm, and a cross-sectional area of 4.00 cm^2. If the current is 5.00 A, calculate: (a) the magnetic field in the solenoid; (b) the self-inductance of the solenoid; (c) the energy stored in the magnetic field; (d) the energy density in the magnetic field. (e) Check your answer for part (d) by dividing your answer to part (c) by the volume of the solenoid.

30.19 •• A solenoid 25.0 cm long and with a cross-sectional area of 0.500 cm^2 contains 400 turns of wire and carries a current of 80.0 A. Calculate: (a) the magnetic field in the solenoid; (b) the energy density in the magnetic field if the solenoid is filled with air; (c) the total energy contained in the coil's magnetic field (assume the field is uniform); (d) the inductance of the solenoid.

30.20 • It has been proposed to use large inductors as energy storage devices. (a) How much electrical energy is converted to light and thermal energy by a 200-W light bulb in one day? (b) If the amount of energy calculated in part (a) is stored in an inductor in which the current is 80.0 A, what is the inductance?

30.21 •• In a proton accelerator used in elementary particle physics experiments, the trajectories of protons are controlled by bending magnets that produce a magnetic field of 4.80 T. What is the magnetic-field energy in a 10.0-cm^3 volume of space where $B = 4.80$ T?

30.22 • It is proposed to store 1.00 kW·h $= 3.60 \times 10^6$ J of electrical energy in a uniform magnetic field with magnitude 0.600 T. (a) What volume (in vacuum) must the magnetic field occupy to store this amount of energy? (b) If instead this amount of energy is to be stored in a volume (in vacuum) equivalent to a cube 40.0 cm on a side, what magnetic field is required?

Section 30.4 The *R-L* Circuit

30.23 • An inductor with an inductance of 2.50 H and a resistance of 8.00 Ω is connected to the terminals of a battery with an emf of 6.00 V and negligible internal resistance. Find (a) the initial rate of increase of current in the circuit; (b) the rate of increase of current at the instant when the current is 0.500 A; (c) the current 0.250 s after the circuit is closed; (d) the final steady-state current.

30.24 • In Fig. 30.11, $R = 15.0$ Ω and the battery emf is 6.30 V. With switch S_2 open, switch S_1 is closed. After several minutes, S_1 is opened and S_2 is closed. (a) At 2.00 ms after S_1 is opened, the current has decayed to 0.320 A. Calculate the inductance of the coil. (b) How long after S_1 is opened will the current reach 1.00% of its original value?

30.25 • A 35.0-V battery with negligible internal resistance, a 50.0-Ω resistor, and a 1.25-mH inductor with negligible resistance are all connected in series with an open switch. The switch is suddenly closed. (a) How long after closing the switch will the current through the inductor reach one-half of its maximum value? (b) How long after closing the switch will the energy stored in the inductor reach one-half of its maximum value?

30.26 • In Fig. 30.11, switch S_1 is closed while switch S_2 is kept open. The inductance is $L = 0.115$ H, and the resistance is $R = 120$ Ω. (a) When the current has reached its final value, the energy stored in the inductor is 0.260 J. What is the emf $\mathcal{E}$ of the battery? (b) After the current has reached its final value, S_1 is opened and S_2 is closed. How much time does it take for the energy stored in the inductor to decrease to 0.130 J, half the original value?

30.27 • In Fig. 30.11, suppose that $\mathcal{E} = 60.0$ V, $R = 240$ Ω, and $L = 0.160$ H. With switch S_2 open, switch S_1 is left closed until a constant current is established. Then S_2 is closed and S_1 opened, taking the battery out of the circuit. (a) What is the initial current in the resistor, just after S_2 is closed and S_1 is opened? (b) What is the current in the resistor at $t = 4.00 \times 10^{-4}$ s? (c) What is the potential difference between points *b* and *c* at $t = 4.00 \times 10^{-4}$ s? Which point is at a higher potential? (d) How long does it take the current to decrease to half its initial value?

30.28 • In Fig. 30.11, suppose that $\mathcal{E} = 60.0$ V, $R = 240$ Ω, and $L = 0.160$ H. Initially there is no current in the circuit. Switch S_2 is left open, and switch S_1 is closed. (a) Just after S_1 is closed, what are the potential differences v_{ab} and v_{bc}? (b) A long time (many time constants) after S_1 is closed, what are v_{ab} and v_{bc}? (c) What are v_{ab} and v_{bc} at an intermediate time when $i = 0.150$ A?

30.29 • Refer to the circuit in Exercise 30.23. (a) What is the power input to the inductor from the battery as a function of time if the circuit is completed at $t = 0$? (b) What is the rate of dissipation of energy in the resistance of the inductor as a function of time? (c) What is the rate at which the energy of the magnetic field in the inductor is increasing, as a function of time? (d) Compare the results of parts (a), (b), and (c).

30.30 • In Fig. 30.11 switch S_1 is closed while switch S_2 is kept open. The inductance is $L = 0.380$ H, the resistance is $R = 48.0$ Ω, and the emf of the battery is 18.0 V. At time t after S_1 is closed, the current in the circuit is increasing at a rate of $di/dt = 7.20$ A/s. At this instant what is v_{ab}, the voltage across the resistor?

Section 30.5 The *L-C* Circuit

30.31 • CALC Show that the differential equation of Eq. (30.20) is satisfied by the function $q = Q \cos(\omega t + \phi)$, with ω given by $1/\sqrt{LC}$.

30.32 •• A 20.0-μF capacitor is charged by a 150.0-V power supply, then disconnected from the power and connected in series with a 0.280-mH inductor. Calculate: (a) the oscillation frequency of the circuit; (b) the energy stored in the capacitor at time $t = 0$ ms (the moment of connection with the inductor); (c) the energy stored in the inductor at $t = 1.30$ ms.

30.33 • A 7.50-nF capacitor is charged up to 12.0 V, then disconnected from the power supply and connected in series through a coil. The period of oscillation of the circuit is then measured to be 8.60×10^{-5} s. Calculate: (a) the inductance of the coil; (b) the maximum charge on the capacitor; (c) the total energy of the circuit; (d) the maximum current in the circuit.

30.34 •• A 18.0-μF capacitor is placed across a 22.5-V battery for several seconds and is then connected across a 12.0-mH inductor that has no appreciable resistance. (a) After the capacitor and inductor are connected together, find the maximum current in the circuit. When the current is a maximum, what is the charge on the capacitor? (b) How long after the capacitor and inductor are connected together does it take for the capacitor to be completely discharged for the first time? For the second time? (c) Sketch graphs of the charge on the capacitor plates and the current through the inductor as functions of time.

30.35 • **L-C Oscillations.** A capacitor with capacitance 6.00×10^{-5} F is charged by connecting it to a 12.0-V battery. The capacitor is disconnected from the battery and connected across an inductor with $L = 1.50$ H. (a) What are the angular frequency ω of the electrical oscillations and the period of these oscillations (the time for one oscillation)? (b) What is the initial charge on the capacitor? (c) How much energy is initially stored in the capacitor? (d) What is the charge on the capacitor 0.0230 s after the connection to the inductor is made? Interpret the sign of your answer. (e) At the time given in part (d), what is the current in the inductor? Interpret the sign of your answer. (f) At the time given in part (d), how much electrical energy is stored in the capacitor and how much is stored in the inductor?

30.36 • **A Radio Tuning Circuit.** The minimum capacitance of a variable capacitor in a radio is 4.18 pF. (a) What is the inductance of a coil connected to this capacitor if the oscillation frequency of the *L-C* circuit is 1600×10^3 Hz, corresponding to one end of the AM radio broadcast band, when the capacitor is set to its minimum capacitance? (b) The frequency at the other end of the broadcast band is 540×10^3 Hz. What is the maximum capacitance of the capacitor if the oscillation frequency is adjustable over the range of the broadcast band?

30.37 •• An *L-C* circuit containing an 80.0-mH inductor and a 1.25-nF capacitor oscillates with a maximum current of 0.750 A. Calculate: (a) the maximum charge on the capacitor and (b) the oscillation frequency of the circuit. (c) Assuming the capacitor had its maximum charge at time $t = 0$, calculate the energy stored in the inductor after 2.50 ms of oscillation.

30.38 • In an *L-C* circuit, $L = 85.0$ mH and $C = 3.20$ μF. During the oscillations the maximum current in the inductor is 0.850 mA. (a) What is the maximum charge on the capacitor? (b) What is the magnitude of the charge on the capacitor at an instant when the current in the inductor has magnitude 0.500 mA?

Section 30.6 The *L-R-C* Series Circuit

30.39 • An *L-R-C* series circuit has $L = 0.450$ H, $C = 2.50 \times 10^{-5}$ F, and resistance R. (a) What is the angular frequency of the circuit when $R = 0$? (b) What value must R have to give a 5.0% decrease in angular frequency compared to the value calculated in part (a)?

30.40 • For the circuit of Fig. 30.17, let $C = 15.0$ nF, $L = 22$ mH, and $R = 75.0$ Ω. (a) Calculate the oscillation frequency of the circuit once the capacitor has been charged and the switch has been connected to point a. (b) How long will it take for the amplitude of the oscillation to decay to 10.0% of its original value? (c) What value of R would result in a critically damped circuit?

30.41 • CP (a) In Eq. (14.41), substitute q for x, L for m, $1/C$ for k, and R for the damping constant b. Show that the result is Eq. (30.27). (b) Make these same substitutions in Eq. (14.43) and show that Eq. (30.29) results. (c) Make these same substitutions in Eq. (14.42) and show that Eq. (30.28) results.

30.42 • CALC (a) Take first and second derivatives with respect to time of q given in Eq. (30.28), and show that it is a solution of Eq. (30.27). (b) At $t = 0$ the switch shown in Fig. 30.17 is thrown so that it connects points d and a; at this time, $q = Q$ and $i = dq/dt = 0$. Show that the constants ϕ and A in Eq. (30.28) are given by

$$\tan\phi = -\frac{R}{2L\sqrt{(1/LC) - (R^2/4L^2)}} \quad \text{and} \quad A = \frac{Q}{\cos\phi}$$

PROBLEMS

30.43 • One solenoid is centered inside another. The outer one has a length of 50.0 cm and contains 6750 coils, while the coaxial inner solenoid is 3.0 cm long and 0.120 cm in diameter and contains 15 coils. The current in the outer solenoid is changing at 49.2 A/s. (a) What is the mutual inductance of these solenoids? (b) Find the emf induced in the innner solenoid.

30.44 •• CALC A coil has 400 turns and self-inductance 4.80 mH. The current in the coil varies with time according to $i = (680$ mA$)\cos(\pi t/0.0250$ s$)$. (a) What is the maximum emf induced in the coil? (b) What is the maximum average flux through each turn of the coil? (c) At $t = 0.0180$ s, what is the magnitude of the induced emf?

30.45 • A Differentiating Circuit. The current in a resistanceless inductor is caused to vary with time as shown in the graph of Fig. P30.45. (a) Sketch the pattern that would be observed on the screen of an oscilloscope connected to the terminals of the inductor. (The oscilloscope spot sweeps horizontally across the screen at a constant speed, and its vertical deflection is proportional to the potential difference between the inductor terminals.) (b) Explain why a circuit with an inductor can be described as a "differentiating circuit."

Figure **P30.45**

30.46 •• CALC A 0.250-H inductor carries a time-varying current given by the expression $i = (124$ mA$)\cos[(240\pi/\text{s})t]$. (a) Find an expression for the induced emf as a function of time. Graph the current and induced emf as functions of time for $t = 0$ to $t = \frac{1}{60}$ s. (b) What is the maximum emf? What is the current when the induced emf is a maximum? (c) What is the maximum current? What is the induced emf when the current is a maximum?

30.47 •• **Solar Magnetic Energy.** Magnetic fields within a sunspot can be as strong as 0.4 T. (By comparison, the earth's magnetic field is about 1/10,000 as strong.) Sunspots can be as large as 25,000 km in radius. The material in a sunspot has a density of about 3×10^{-4} kg/m^3. Assume μ for the sunspot material is μ_0. If 100% of the magnetic-field energy stored in a sunspot could be used to eject the sunspot's material away from the sun's surface, at what speed would that material be ejected? Compare to the sun's escape speed, which is about 6×10^5 m/s. (*Hint:* Calculate the kinetic energy the magnetic field could supply to 1 m^3 of sunspot material.)

30.48 •• CP CALC A Coaxial Cable. A small solid conductor with radius a is supported by insulating, nonmagnetic disks on the axis of a thin-walled tube with inner radius b. The inner and outer conductors carry equal currents i in opposite directions. (a) Use Ampere's law to find the magnetic field at any point in the volume between the conductors. (b) Write the expression for the flux $d\Phi_B$ through a narrow strip of length l parallel to the axis, of width dr, at a distance r from the axis of the cable and lying in a plane containing the axis. (c) Integrate your expression from part (b) over the volume between the two conductors to find the total flux produced by a current i in the central conductor. (d) Show that the inductance of a length l of the cable is

$$L = l\frac{\mu_0}{2\pi}\ln\left(\frac{b}{a}\right)$$

(e) Use Eq. (30.9) to calculate the energy stored in the magnetic field for a length l of the cable.

30.49 •• CP CALC Consider the coaxial cable of Problem 30.48. The conductors carry equal currents i in opposite directions. (a) Use Ampere's law to find the magnetic field at any point in the volume between the conductors. (b) Use the energy density for a magnetic field, Eq. (30.10), to calculate the energy stored in a thin, cylindrical shell between the two conductors. Let the cylindrical shell have inner radius r, outer radius $r + dr$, and length l. (c) Integrate your result in part (b) over the volume between the two conductors to find the total energy stored in the magnetic field for a length l of the cable. (d) Use your result in part (c) and Eq. (30.9) to calculate the inductance L of a length l of the cable. Compare your result to L calculated in part (d) of Problem 30.48.

30.50 •• A toroidal solenoid has a mean radius r and a cross-sectional area A and is wound uniformly with N_1 turns. A second toroidal solenoid with N_2 turns is wound uniformly around the first. The two coils are wound in the same direction. (a) Derive an expression for the inductance L_1 when only the first coil is used and an expression for L_2 when only the second coil is used. (b) Show that $M^2 = L_1 L_2$.

30.51 • (a) What would have to be the self-inductance of a solenoid for it to store 10.0 J of energy when a 2.00-A current runs through it? (b) If this solenoid's cross-sectional diameter is 4.00 cm, and if you could wrap its coils to a density of 10 coils/mm, how long would the solenoid be? (See Exercise 30.15.) Is this a realistic length for ordinary laboratory use?

30.52 • An inductor is connected to the terminals of a battery that has an emf of 12.0 V and negligible internal resistance. The current is 4.86 mA at 0.940 ms after the connection is completed. After a long time the current is 6.45 mA. What are (a) the resistance R of the inductor and (b) the inductance L of the inductor?

30.53 •• **CALC** Continuation of Exercises 30.23 and 30.29. (a) How much energy is stored in the magnetic field of the inductor one time constant after the battery has been connected? Compute this both by integrating the expression in Exercise 30.29(c) and by using Eq. (30.9), and compare the results. (b) Integrate the expression obtained in Exercise 30.29(a) to find the *total* energy supplied by the battery during the time interval considered in part (a). (c) Integrate the expression obtained in Exercise 30.29(b) to find the *total* energy dissipated in the resistance of the inductor during the same time period. (d) Compare the results obtained in parts (a), (b), and (c).

30.54 •• **CALC** Continuation of Exercise 30.27. (a) What is the total energy initially stored in the inductor? (b) At $t = 4.00 \times 10^{-4}$ s, at what rate is the energy stored in the inductor decreasing? (c) At $t = 4.00 \times 10^{-4}$ s, at what rate is electrical energy being converted into thermal energy in the resistor? (d) Obtain an expression for the rate at which electrical energy is being converted into thermal energy in the resistor as a function of time. Integrate this expression from $t = 0$ to $t = \infty$ to obtain the total electrical energy dissipated in the resistor. Compare your result to that of part (a).

30.55 • **CALC** The equation preceding Eq. (30.27) may be converted into an energy relationship. Multiply both sides of this equation by $-i = -dq/dt$. The first term then becomes i^2R. Show that the second term can be written as $d\left(\frac{1}{2}Li^2\right)/dt$, and that the third term can be written as $d(q^2/2C)/dt$. What does the resulting equation say about energy conservation in the circuit?

30.56 • A 7.00-μF capacitor is initially charged to a potential of 16.0 V. It is then connected in series with a 3.75-mH inductor. (a) What is the total energy stored in this circuit? (b) What is the maximum current in the inductor? What is the charge on the capacitor plates at the instant the current in the inductor is maximal?

30.57 • An Electromagnetic Car Alarm. Your latest invention is a car alarm that produces sound at a particularly annoying frequency of 3500 Hz. To do this, the car-alarm circuitry must produce an alternating electric current of the same frequency. That's why your design includes an inductor and a capacitor in series. The maximum voltage across the capacitor is to be 12.0 V (the same voltage as the car battery). To produce a sufficiently loud sound, the capacitor must store 0.0160 J of energy. What values of capacitance and inductance should you choose for your car-alarm circuit?

30.58 • An L-C circuit consists of a 60.0-mH inductor and a 250-μF capacitor. The initial charge on the capacitor is 6.00 μC, and the initial current in the inductor is zero. (a) What is the maximum voltage across the capacitor? (b) What is the maximum current in the inductor? (c) What is the maximum energy stored in the inductor? (d) When the current in the inductor has half its maximum value, what is the charge on the capacitor and what is the energy stored in the inductor?

30.59 •• A 84.0-nF capacitor is charged to 12.0 V, then disconnected from the power supply and connected in series with a coil that has $L = 0.0420$ H and negligible resistance. At an instant when the charge on the capacitor is 0.650 μC, what is the magnitude of the current in the inductor and what is the magnitude of the rate of change of this current?

30.60 •• A charged capacitor with $C = 590\ \mu$F is connected in series to an inductor that has $L = 0.330$ H and negligible resistance.

At an instant when the current in the inductor is $i = 2.50$ A, the current is increasing at a rate of $di/dt = 89.0$ A/s. During the current oscillations, what is the maximum voltage across the capacitor?

30.61 ••• **CP** In the circuit shown in Fig. P30.61, the switch has been open for a long time and is suddenly closed. Neither the battery nor the inductors have any appreciable resistance. (a) What do the ammeter and voltmeter read just after S is closed? (b) What do the ammeter and the voltmeter read after S has been closed a very long time? (c) What do the ammeter and the voltmeter read 0.115 ms after S is closed?

Figure **P30.61**

30.62 •• While studying a coil of unknown inductance and internal resistance, you connect it in series with a 25.0-V battery and a 150-Ω resistor. You then place an oscilloscope across one of these circuit elements and use the oscilloscope to measure the voltage across the circuit element as a function of time. The result is shown in Fig. P30.62.

Figure **P30.62**

(a) Across which circuit element (coil or resistor) is the oscilloscope connected? How do you know this? (b) Find the inductance and the internal resistance of the coil. (c) Carefully make a quantitative sketch showing the voltage versus time you would observe if you put the oscilloscope across the other circuit element (resistor or coil).

30.63 •• In the lab, you are trying to find the inductance and internal resistance of a solenoid. You place it in series with a battery of negligible internal resistance, a 10.0-Ω resistor, and a switch. You then put an oscilloscope across one of these circuit elements to measure the voltage across that circuit element as a function of time. You close the switch, and the oscilloscope shows voltage versus time as shown in Fig. P30.63. (a) Across which circuit element (solenoid or resistor) is the oscilloscope connected? How do you know this? (b) Why doesn't the graph approach zero as $t \rightarrow \infty$? (c) What is the emf of the battery? (d) Find the maximum current in the circuit. (e) What are the internal resistance and self-inductance of the solenoid?

Figure **P30.63**

30.64 •• **CP** In the circuit shown in Fig. P30.64, find the reading in each ammeter and voltmeter (a) just after switch S is closed and (b) after S has been closed a very long time.

30.65 •• **CP** In the circuit shown in Fig. P30.65, switch S is closed at time $t = 0$ with no charge initially on the capacitor. (a) Find the reading of each ammeter and each voltmeter just after S is closed. (b) Find the

Figure **P30.64**

reading of each meter after a long time has elapsed. (c) Find the maximum charge on the capacitor. (d) Draw a qualitative graph of the reading of voltmeter V_2 as a function of time.

Figure **P30.65**

30.66 · In the circuit shown in Fig. P30.66 the battery and the inductor have no appreciable internal resistance and there is no current in the circuit. After the switch is closed, find the readings of the ammeter (A) and voltmeters (V_1 and V_2) (a) the instant after the switch is closed and (b) after the switch has been closed for a very long time. (c) Which answers in parts (a) and (b) would change if the inductance were 24.0 mH instead?

Figure **P30.66**

30.67 ·· CP In the circuit shown in Fig. P30.67, switch S is closed at time $t = 0$. (a) Find the reading of each meter just after S is closed. (b) What does each meter read long after S is closed?

Figure **P30.67**

30.68 ·· In the circuit shown in Fig. P30.68, switch S_1 has been closed for a long enough time so that the current reads a steady 3.50 A. Suddenly, switch S_2 is closed and S_1 is opened at the same instant. (a) What is the maximum charge that the capacitor will receive? (b) What is the current in the inductor at this time?

Figure **P30.68**

30.69 ·· CP In the circuit shown in Fig. P30.69, $\mathcal{E} = 60.0$ V, $R_1 = 40.0$ Ω, $R_2 = 25.0$ Ω, and $L = 0.300$ H. Switch S is closed at $t = 0$. Just after the switch is closed, (a) what is the potential difference v_{ab} across the resistor R_1; (b) which point, a or b, is at a higher potential; (c) what is the

Figure **P30.69**

potential difference v_{cd} across the inductor L; (d) which point, c or d, is at a higher potential? The switch is left closed a long time and then opened. Just after the switch is opened, (e) what is the potential difference v_{ab} across the resistor R_1; (f) which point, a or b, is at a higher potential; (g) what is the potential difference v_{cd} across the inductor L; (h) which point, c or d, is at a higher potential?

30.70 ·· CP In the circuit shown in Fig. P30.69, $\mathcal{E} = 60.0$ V, $R_1 = 40.0$ Ω, $R_2 = 25.0$ Ω, and $L = 0.300$ H. (a) Switch S is closed. At some time t afterward, the current in the inductor is increasing at a rate of $di/dt = 50.0$ A/s. At this instant, what are the current i_1 through R_1 and the current i_2 through R_2? (*Hint:* Analyze two separate loops: one containing $\mathcal{E}$ and R_1 and the other containing $\mathcal{E}$, R_2, and L.) (b) After the switch has been closed a long time, it is opened again. Just after it is opened, what is the current through R_1?

30.71 ·· CALC Consider the circuit shown in Fig. P30.71. Let $\mathcal{E} = 36.0$ V, $R_0 = 50.0$ Ω, $R = 150$ Ω, and $L = 4.00$ H. (a) Switch S_1 is closed and switch S_2 is left open. Just after S_1 is closed, what are the current i_0 through R_0 and the potential differences v_{ac} and v_{cb}? (b) After S_1 has been closed a long time (S_2 is still open) so that the current has reached its final, steady value, what are i_0, v_{ac}, and v_{cb}? (c) Find the expressions for i_0, v_{ac}, and v_{cb} as functions of the time t since S_1 was closed. Your results should agree with part (a) when $t = 0$ and with part (b) when $t \to \infty$. Graph i_0, v_{ac}, and v_{cb} versus time.

Figure **P30.71**

30.72 ·· After the current in the circuit of Fig. P30.71 has reached its final, steady value with switch S_1 closed and S_2 open, switch S_2 is closed, thus short-circuiting the inductor. (Switch S_1 remains closed. See Problem 30.71 for numerical values of the circuit elements.) (a) Just after S_2 is closed, what are v_{ac} and v_{cb}, and what are the currents through R_0, R, and S_2? (b) A long time after S_2 is closed, what are v_{ac} and v_{cb}, and what are the currents through R_0, R, and S_2? (c) Derive expressions for the currents through R_0, R, and S_2 as functions of the time t that has elapsed since S_2 was closed. Your results should agree with part (a) when $t = 0$ and with part (b) when $t \to \infty$. Graph these three currents versus time.

30.73 ··· CP CALC We have ignored the variation of the magnetic field across the cross section of a toroidal solenoid. Let's now examine the validity of that approximation. A certain toroidal solenoid has a rectangular cross section (Fig. P30.73). It has N uniformly spaced turns, with air inside. The magnetic field at a point inside the toroid is given by the equation derived in Example 28.10 (Section 28.7). *Do not* assume the field is uniform over the cross section. (a) Show that the magnetic flux through a cross section of the toroid is

Figure **P30.73**

$$\Phi_B = \frac{\mu_0 N i h}{2\pi} \ln\left(\frac{b}{a}\right)$$

(b) Show that the inductance of the toroidal solenoid is given by

$$L = \frac{\mu_0 N^2 h}{2\pi} \ln\left(\frac{b}{a}\right)$$

(c) The fraction b/a may be written as

$$\frac{b}{a} = \frac{a + b - a}{a} = 1 + \frac{b - a}{a}$$

Use the power series expansion $\ln(1 + z) = z + z^2/2 + \cdots$, valid for $|z| < 1$, to show that when $b - a$ is much less than a, the inductance is approximately equal to

$$L = \frac{\mu_0 N^2 h(b - a)}{2\pi a}$$

Compare this result with the result given in Example 30.3 (Section 30.2).

30.74 ••• **CP** In the circuit shown in Fig. P30.74, neither the battery nor the inductors have any appreciable resistance, the capacitors are initially uncharged, and the switch S has been in position 1 for a very long time. (a) What is the current in the circuit? (b) The switch is now suddenly flipped to position 2. Find the maximum charge that each capacitor will receive, and how much time after the switch is flipped it will take them to acquire this charge.

Figure **P30.74**

30.75 ••• **CP CALC Demonstrating Inductance.** A common demonstration of inductance employs a circuit such as the one shown in Fig. P30.69. Switch S is closed, and the light bulb (represented by resistance R_1) just barely glows. After a period of time, switch S is opened, and the bulb lights up brightly for a short period of time. To understand this effect, think of an inductor as a device that imparts an "inertia" to the current, preventing a discontinuous change in the current through it. (a) Derive, as explicit functions of time, expressions for i_1 (the current through the light bulb) and i_2 (the current through the inductor) after switch S is closed. (b) After a long period of time, the currents i_1 and i_2 reach their steady-state values. Obtain expressions for these steady-state currents. (c) Switch S is now opened. Obtain an expression for the current through the inductor and light bulb as an explicit function of time. (d) You have been asked to design a demonstration apparatus using the circuit shown in Fig. P30.69 with a 22.0-H inductor and a 40.0-W light bulb. You are to connect a resistor in series with the inductor, and R_2 represents the sum of that resistance plus the internal resistance of the inductor. When switch S is opened, a transient current is to be set up that starts at 0.600 A and is not to fall below 0.150 A until after 0.0800 s. For simplicity, assume that the resistance of the light bulb is constant and equals the resistance the bulb must have to dissipate 40.0 W at 120 V. Determine R_2 and $\mathcal{E}$ for the given design considerations. (e) With the numerical values determined in part (d), what is the current through the light bulb just before the switch is opened? Does this result confirm the qualitative description of what is observed in the demonstration?

CHALLENGE PROBLEMS

30.76 ••• **CP CALC** Consider the circuit shown in Fig. P30.76. The circuit elements are as follows: $\mathcal{E} = 32.0$ V, $L = 0.640$ H, $C = 2.00$ μF, and $R = 400$ Ω. At time $t = 0$, switch S is closed. The current through the inductor is i_1, the current through the capacitor branch is i_2, and the charge on the capacitor is q_2. (a) Using Kirchhoff's rules, verify the circuit equations

$$R(i_1 + i_2) + L\left(\frac{di_1}{dt}\right) = \mathcal{E}$$

$$R(i_1 + i_2) + \frac{q_2}{C} = \mathcal{E}$$

(b) What are the initial values of i_1, i_2, and q_2? (c) Show by direct substitution that the following solutions for i_1 and q_2 satisfy the circuit equations from part (a). Also, show that they satisfy the initial conditions

$$i_1 = \left(\frac{\mathcal{E}}{R}\right)[1 - e^{-\beta t}\{(2\omega RC)^{-1} \sin(\omega t) + \cos(\omega t)\}]$$

$$q_2 = \left(\frac{\mathcal{E}}{\omega R}\right)e^{-\beta t} \sin(\omega t)$$

where $\beta = (2RC)^{-1}$ and $\omega = [(LC)^{-1} - (2RC)^{-2}]^{1/2}$. (d) Determine the time t_1 at which i_2 first becomes zero.

Figure **P30.76**

30.77 ••• **CP A Volume Gauge.** A tank containing a liquid has turns of wire wrapped around it, causing it to act like an inductor. The liquid content of the tank can be measured by using its inductance to determine the height of the liquid in the tank. The inductance of the tank changes from a value of L_0 corresponding to a relative permeability of 1 when the tank is empty to a value of L_f corresponding to a relative permeability of K_m (the relative permeability of the liquid) when the tank is full. The appropriate electronic circuitry can determine the inductance to five significant figures and thus the effective relative permeability of the combined air and liquid within the rectangular cavity of the tank. The four sides of the tank each have width W and height D (Fig. P30.77). The height of the liquid in the tank is d. You can ignore any fringing effects and assume that the relative permeability of the material of which the tank is made can be ignored. (a) Derive an expression for d as a function of L, the inductance corresponding to a certain fluid height, L_0, L_f, and D. (b) What is the inductance (to five significant figures) for a tank $\frac{1}{4}$ full, $\frac{1}{2}$ full, $\frac{3}{4}$ full, and completely full if the tank contains liquid oxygen? Take $L_0 = 0.63000$ H. The magnetic susceptibility of liquid oxygen is $\chi_m = 1.52 \times 10^{-3}$. (c) Repeat part (b) for mercury. The magnetic susceptibility of mercury is given in Table 28.1. (d) For which material is this volume gauge more practical?

Figure **P30.77**

30.78 ••• Two coils are wrapped around each other as shown in Fig. 30.3. The current travels in the same sense around each coil. One coil has self-inductance L_1, and the other coil has self-inductance L_2. The mutual inductance of the two coils is M. (a) Show that if the two coils are connected in series, the equivalent inductance of the combination is $L_{eq} = L_1 + L_2 + 2M$. (b) Show that if the two coils are connected in parallel, the equivalent inductance of the combination is

$$L_{eq} = \frac{L_1 L_2 - M^2}{L_1 + L_2 - 2M}$$

30.79 ••• **CP CALC** Consider the circuit shown in Fig. P30.79. Switch S is closed at time $t = 0$, causing a current i_1 through the inductive branch and a current i_2 through the capacitive branch.

The initial charge on the capacitor is zero, and the charge at time t is q_2. (a) Derive expressions for i_1, i_2, and q_2 as functions of time. Express your answers in terms of $\mathcal{E}$, L, C, R_1, R_2, and t. For the remainder of the problem let the circuit elements have the following values: $\mathcal{E} = 48$ V, $L = 8.0$ H, $C = 20 \mu$F, $R_1 = 25 \Omega$, and $R_2 = 5000 \Omega$. (b) What is the initial current through the inductive branch? What is the initial current

Figure **P30.79**

through the capacitive branch? (c) What are the currents through the inductive and capacitive branches a long time after the switch has been closed? How long is a "long time"? Explain. (d) At what time t_1 (accurate to two significant figures) will the currents i_1 and i_2 be equal? (*Hint:* You might consider using series expansions for the exponentials.) (e) For the conditions given in part (d), determine i_1. (f) The total current through the battery is $i = i_1 + i_2$. At what time t_2 (accurate to two significant figures) will i equal one-half of its final value? (*Hint:* The numerical work is greatly simplified if one makes suitable approximations. A sketch of i_1 and i_2 versus t may help you decide what approximations are valid.)

Answers

Chapter Opening Question ?

As explained in Section 30.2, traffic light sensors work by measuring the change in inductance of a coil embedded under the road surface when a car drives over it.

Test Your Understanding Questions

30.1 Answer: (iii) Doubling both the length of the solenoid (l) and the number of turns of wire in the solenoid (N_1) would have *no* effect on the mutual inductance M. Example 30.1 shows that M depends on the ratio of these quantities, which would remain unchanged. This is because the magnetic field produced by the solenoid depends on the number of turns *per unit length*, and the proposed change has no effect on this quantity.

30.2 Answer: (iv), (i), (iii), (ii) From Eq. (30.8), the potential difference across the inductor is $V_{ab} = L \, di/dt$. For the four cases we find (i) $V_{ab} = (2.0 \mu\text{H})(2.0 \text{ A} - 1.0 \text{ A})/(0.50 \text{ s}) = 4.0 \mu\text{V}$; (ii) $V_{ab} = (4.0 \mu\text{H})(0 - 3.0 \text{ A})/(2.0 \text{ s}) = -6.0 \mu\text{V}$; (iii) $V_{ab} = 0$ because the rate of change of current is zero; and (iv) $V_{ab} = (1.0 \mu\text{H})(4.0 \text{ A} - 0)/(0.25 \text{ s}) = 16 \mu\text{V}$.

30.3 Answers: (a) yes, (b) no Reversing the direction of the current has no effect on the magnetic field magnitude, but it causes the direction of the magnetic field to reverse. It has no effect on the magnetic-field energy density, which is proportional to the square of the *magnitude* of the magnetic field.

30.4 Answers: (a) (i), (b) (ii) Recall that v_{ab} is the potential at a minus the potential at b, and similarly for v_{bc}. For either arrangement of the switches, current flows through the resistor from a to

b. The upstream end of the resistor is always at the higher potential, so v_{ab} is positive. With S_1 closed and S_2 open, the current through the inductor flows from b to c and is increasing. The self-induced emf opposes this increase and is therefore directed from c toward b, which means that b is at the higher potential. Hence v_{bc} is positive. With S_1 open and S_2 closed, the inductor current again flows from b to c but is now decreasing. The self-induced emf is directed from b to c in an effort to sustain the decaying current, so c is at the higher potential and v_{bc} is negative.

30.5 Answers: (a) positive, (b) electric, (c) negative, (d) electric The capacitor loses energy between stages (a) and (b), so it does positive work on the charges. It does this by exerting an electric force that pushes current away from the positively charged left-hand capacitor plate and toward the negatively charged right-hand plate. At the same time, the inductor gains energy and does negative work on the moving charges. Although the inductor stores magnetic energy, the force that the inductor exerts is *electric*. This force comes about from the inductor's self-induced emf (see Section 30.2).

30.6 Answer: (i) and (iii) There are no oscillations if $R^2 \geq 4L/C$. In each case $R^2 = (2.0 \Omega)^2 = 4.0 \Omega^2$. In case (i) $4L/C = 4(3.0 \mu\text{H})/(6.0 \mu\text{F}) = 2.0 \Omega^2$, so there are no oscillations (the system is overdamped); in case (ii) $4L/C = 4(6.0 \mu\text{H})/(3.0 \mu\text{F}) = 8.0 \Omega^2$, so there are oscillations (the system is underdamped); and in case (iii) $4L/C = 4(3.0 \mu\text{H})/(3.0 \mu\text{F}) = 4.0 \Omega^2$, so there are no oscillations (the system is critically damped).

Bridging Problem

Answers: (a) 7.68×10^{-8} J   (b) 1.60 mA   (c) 24.8 mV
(d) 1.92×10^{-8} J, 21.5 mV

ALTERNATING CURRENT

? Waves from a broadcasting station produce an alternating current in the circuits of a radio (like the one in this classic car). If a radio is tuned to a station at a frequency of 1000 kHz, does it also detect the transmissions from a station broadcasting at 600 kHz?

LEARNING GOALS

By studying this chapter, you will learn:

- How phasors make it easy to describe sinusoidally varying quantities.

- How to use reactance to describe the voltage across a circuit element that carries an alternating current.

- How to analyze an *L-R-C* series circuit with a sinusoidal emf.

- What determines the amount of power flowing into or out of an alternating-current circuit.

- How an *L-R-C* series circuit responds to sinusoidal emfs of different frequencies.

- Why transformers are useful, and how they work.

During the 1880s in the United States there was a heated and acrimonious debate between two inventors over the best method of electric-power distribution. Thomas Edison favored direct current (dc)—that is, steady current that does not vary with time. George Westinghouse favored **alternating current (ac),** with sinusoidally varying voltages and currents. He argued that transformers (which we will study in this chapter) can be used to step the voltage up and down with ac but not with dc; low voltages are safer for consumer use, but high voltages and correspondingly low currents are best for long-distance power transmission to minimize i^2R losses in the cables.

Eventually, Westinghouse prevailed, and most present-day household and industrial power-distribution systems operate with alternating current. Any appliance that you plug into a wall outlet uses ac, and many battery-powered devices such as radios and cordless telephones make use of the dc supplied by the battery to create or amplify alternating currents. Circuits in modern communication equipment, including pagers and television, also make extensive use of ac.

In this chapter we will learn how resistors, inductors, and capacitors behave in circuits with sinusoidally varying voltages and currents. Many of the principles that we found useful in Chapters 25, 28, and 30 are applicable, along with several new concepts related to the circuit behavior of inductors and capacitors. A key concept in this discussion is *resonance,* which we studied in Chapter 14 for mechanical systems.

31.1 Phasors and Alternating Currents

To supply an alternating current to a circuit, a source of alternating emf or voltage is required. An example of such a source is a coil of wire rotating with constant angular velocity in a magnetic field, which we discussed in Example 29.3 (Section 29.2). This develops a sinusoidal alternating emf and is the prototype of the commercial alternating-current generator or *alternator* (see Fig. 29.8).

We use the term **ac source** for any device that supplies a sinusoidally varying voltage (potential difference) v or current i. The usual circuit-diagram symbol for an ac source is

A sinusoidal voltage might be described by a function such as

$$v = V\cos\omega t \qquad (31.1)$$

31.1 The voltage across a sinusoidal ac source.

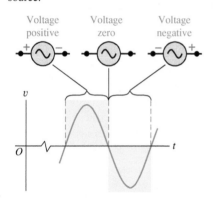

In this expression, v (lowercase) is the *instantaneous* potential difference; V (uppercase) is the maximum potential difference, which we call the **voltage amplitude;** and ω is the *angular frequency,* equal to 2π times the frequency f (Fig. 31.1).

In the United States and Canada, commercial electric-power distribution systems always use a frequency of $f = 60\,\text{Hz}$, corresponding to $\omega = (2\pi\,\text{rad})(60\,\text{s}^{-1}) = 377\,\text{rad/s}$; in much of the rest of the world, $f = 50\,\text{Hz}$ ($\omega = 314\,\text{rad/s}$) is used. Similarly, a sinusoidal current might be described as

$$i = I\cos\omega t \qquad (31.2)$$

where i (lowercase) is the instantaneous current and I (uppercase) is the maximum current or **current amplitude.**

Phasor Diagrams

31.2 A phasor diagram.

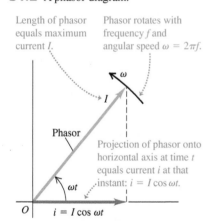

To represent sinusoidally varying voltages and currents, we will use rotating vector diagrams similar to those we used in the study of simple harmonic motion in Section 14.2 (see Figs. 14.5b and 14.6). In these diagrams the instantaneous value of a quantity that varies sinusoidally with time is represented by the *projection* onto a horizontal axis of a vector with a length equal to the amplitude of the quantity. The vector rotates counterclockwise with constant angular speed ω. These rotating vectors are called **phasors,** and diagrams containing them are called **phasor diagrams.** Figure 31.2 shows a phasor diagram for the sinusoidal current described by Eq. (31.2). The projection of the phasor onto the horizontal axis at time t is $I\cos\omega t$; this is why we chose to use the cosine function rather than the sine in Eq. (31.2).

CAUTION **Just what is a phasor?** A phasor is not a real physical quantity with a direction in space, such as velocity, momentum, or electric field. Rather, it is a *geometric* entity that helps us to describe and analyze physical quantities that vary sinusoidally with time. In Section 14.2 we used a single phasor to represent the position of a point mass undergoing simple harmonic motion. In this chapter we will use phasors to *add* sinusoidal voltages and currents. Combining sinusoidal quantities with phase differences then becomes a matter of vector addition. We will find a similar use for phasors in Chapters 35 and 36 in our study of interference effects with light.

Rectified Alternating Current

How do we measure a sinusoidally varying current? In Section 26.3 we used a d'Arsonval galvanometer to measure steady currents. But if we pass a *sinusoidal* current through a d'Arsonval meter, the torque on the moving coil varies sinusoidally, with one direction half the time and the opposite direction the other half. The needle may wiggle a little if the frequency is low enough, but its average deflection is zero. Hence a d'Arsonval meter by itself isn't very useful for measuring alternating currents.

To get a measurable one-way current through the meter, we can use *diodes*, which we described in Section 25.3. A diode is a device that conducts better in one direction than in the other; an ideal diode has zero resistance for one direction of current and infinite resistance for the other. Figure 31.3a shows one possible arrangement, called a *full-wave rectifier circuit*. The current through the galvanometer G is always upward, regardless of the direction of the current from the ac source (i.e., which part of the cycle the source is in). The graph in Fig. 31.3b shows the current through G: It pulsates but always has the same direction, and the average meter deflection is *not* zero.

The **rectified average current** I_{rav} is defined so that during any whole number of cycles, the total charge that flows is the same as though the current were constant with a value equal to I_{rav}. The notation I_{rav} and the name *rectified average current* emphasize that this is *not* the average of the original sinusoidal current. In Fig. 31.3b the total charge that flows in time t corresponds to the area under the curve of i versus t (recall that $i = dq/dt$, so q is the integral of t); this area must equal the rectangular area with height I_{rav}. We see that I_{rav} is less than the maximum current I; the two are related by

$$I_{rav} = \frac{2}{\pi} I = 0.637I \qquad \text{(rectified average value of a sinusoidal current)} \qquad (31.3)$$

(The factor of $2/\pi$ is the average value of $|\cos \omega t|$ or of $|\sin \omega t|$; see Example 29.4 in Section 29.2.) The galvanometer deflection is proportional to I_{rav}. The galvanometer scale can be calibrated to read I, I_{rav}, or, most commonly, I_{rms} (discussed below).

Root-Mean-Square (rms) Values

A more useful way to describe a quantity that can be either positive or negative is the *root-mean-square (rms) value*. We used rms values in Section 18.3 in connection with the speeds of molecules in a gas. We *square* the instantaneous current i, take the *average* (mean) value of i^2, and finally take the *square root* of that average. This procedure defines the **root-mean-square current**, denoted as I_{rms} (Fig. 31.4). Even when i is negative, i^2 is always positive, so I_{rms} is never zero (unless i is zero at every instant).

Here's how we obtain I_{rms} for a sinusoidal current, like that shown in Fig. 31.4. If the instantaneous current is given by $i = I \cos \omega t$, then

$$i^2 = I^2 \cos^2 \omega t$$

Using a double-angle formula from trigonometry,

$$\cos^2 A = \tfrac{1}{2}(1 + \cos 2A)$$

we find

$$i^2 = I^2 \tfrac{1}{2}(1 + \cos 2\omega t) = \tfrac{1}{2}I^2 + \tfrac{1}{2}I^2 \cos 2\omega t$$

The average of $\cos 2\omega t$ is zero because it is positive half the time and negative half the time. Thus the average of i^2 is simply $I^2/2$. The square root of this is I_{rms}:

$$I_{rms} = \frac{I}{\sqrt{2}} \qquad \text{(root-mean-square value of a sinusoidal current)} \qquad (31.4)$$

31.3 (a) A full-wave rectifier circuit. (b) Graph of the resulting current through the galvanometer G.

(a) A full-wave rectifier circuit

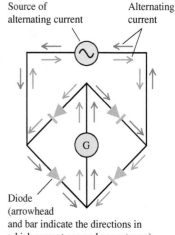

Source of alternating current

Alternating current

Diode (arrowhead and bar indicate the directions in which current can and cannot pass)

(b) Graph of the full-wave rectified current and its average value, the rectified average current I_{rav}

Rectified current through galvanometer G

Area under curve = total charge that flows through galvanometer in time t.

31.4 Calculating the root-mean-square (rms) value of an alternating current.

Meaning of the rms value of a sinusoidal quantity (here, ac current with $I = 3$ A):

① Graph current i versus time.

② *Square* the instantaneous current i.

③ Take the *average* (mean) value of i^2.

④ Take the *square root* of that average.

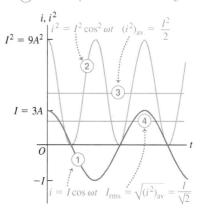

i, i^2

$i^2 = I^2 \cos^2 \omega t$ $(i^2)_{av} = \dfrac{I^2}{2}$

$I^2 = 9A^2$

$I = 3A$

$i = I \cos \omega t$ $I_{rms} = \sqrt{(i^2)_{av}} = \dfrac{I}{\sqrt{2}}$

31.5 This wall socket delivers a root-mean-square voltage of 120 V. Sixty times per second, the instantaneous voltage across its terminals varies from $(\sqrt{2})(120\text{ V}) = 170$ V to -170 V and back again.

In the same way, the root-mean-square value of a sinusoidal voltage with amplitude (maximum value) V is

$$V_{rms} = \frac{V}{\sqrt{2}} \quad \text{(root-mean-square value of a sinusoidal voltage)} \quad (31.5)$$

We can convert a rectifying ammeter into a voltmeter by adding a series resistor, just as for the dc case discussed in Section 26.3. Meters used for ac voltage and current measurements are nearly always calibrated to read rms values, not maximum or rectified average. Voltages and currents in power distribution systems are always described in terms of their rms values. The usual household power supply, "120-volt ac," has an rms voltage of 120 V (Fig. 31.5). The voltage amplitude is

$$V = \sqrt{2}V_{rms} = \sqrt{2}(120\text{ V}) = 170\text{ V}$$

Example 31.1 Current in a personal computer

The plate on the back of a personal computer says that it draws 2.7 A from a 120-V, 60-Hz line. For this computer, what are (a) the average current, (b) the average of the square of the current, and (c) the current amplitude?

SOLUTION

IDENTIFY and SET UP: This example is about alternating current. In part (a) we find the average, over a complete cycle, of the alternating current. In part (b) we recognize that the 2.7-A current draw of the computer is the rms value I_{rms}—that is, the *square root* of the *mean* (average) of the *square* of the current, $(i^2)_{av}$. In part (c) we use Eq. (31.4) to relate I_{rms} to the current amplitude.

EXECUTE: (a) The average of *any* sinusoidally varying quantity, over any whole number of cycles, is zero.

(b) We are given $I_{rms} = 2.7$ A. From the definition of rms value,

$$I_{rms} = \sqrt{(i^2)_{av}} \text{ so } (i^2)_{av} = (I_{rms})^2 = (2.7\text{ A})^2 = 7.3\text{ A}^2$$

(c) From Eq. (31.4), the current amplitude I is

$$I = \sqrt{2}I_{rms} = \sqrt{2}(2.7\text{ A}) = 3.8\text{ A}$$

Figure 31.6 shows graphs of i and i^2 versus time t.

31.6 Our graphs of the current i and the square of the current i^2 versus time t.

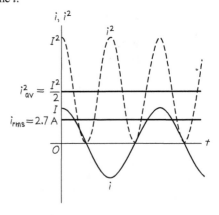

EVALUATE: Why would we be interested in the average of the square of the current? Recall that the rate at which energy is dissipated in a resistor R equals i^2R. This rate varies if the current is alternating, so it is best described by its average value $(i^2)_{av}R = I_{rms}^2R$. We'll use this idea in Section 31.4.

Test Your Understanding of Section 31.1 The figure at left shows four different current phasors with the same angular frequency ω. At the time shown, which phasor corresponds to (a) a positive current that is becoming more positive; (b) a positive current that is decreasing toward zero; (c) a negative current that is becoming more negative; (d) a negative current that is decreasing in magnitude toward zero?

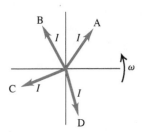

31.2 Resistance and Reactance

In this section we will derive voltage–current relationships for individual circuit elements carrying a sinusoidal current. We'll consider resistors, inductors, and capacitors.

Resistor in an ac Circuit

First let's consider a resistor with resistance R through which there is a sinusoidal current given by Eq. (31.2): $i = I\cos\omega t$. The positive direction of current is counterclockwise around the circuit, as in Fig. 31.7a. The current amplitude (maximum current) is I. From Ohm's law the instantaneous potential v_R of point a with respect to point b (that is, the instantaneous voltage across the resistor) is

$$v_R = iR = (IR)\cos\omega t \tag{31.6}$$

The maximum voltage V_R, the *voltage amplitude,* is the coefficient of the cosine function:

$$V_R = IR \quad \text{(amplitude of voltage across a resistor, ac circuit)} \tag{31.7}$$

Hence we can also write

$$v_R = V_R\cos\omega t \tag{31.8}$$

The current i and voltage v_R are both proportional to $\cos\omega t$, so the current is *in phase* with the voltage. Equation (31.7) shows that the current and voltage amplitudes are related in the same way as in a dc circuit.

Figure 31.7b shows graphs of i and v_R as functions of time. The vertical scales for current and voltage are different, so the relative heights of the two curves are not significant. The corresponding phasor diagram is given in Fig. 31.7c. Because i and v_R are *in phase* and have the same frequency, the current and voltage phasors rotate together; they are parallel at each instant. Their projections on the horizontal axis represent the instantaneous current and voltage, respectively.

Inductor in an ac Circuit

Next, we replace the resistor in Fig. 31.7 with a pure inductor with self-inductance L and zero resistance (Fig. 31.8a). Again we assume that the current is $i = I\cos\omega t$, with the positive direction of current taken as counterclockwise around the circuit.

Although there is no resistance, there is a potential difference v_L between the inductor terminals a and b because the current varies with time, giving rise to a self-induced emf. The induced emf in the direction of i is given by Eq. (30.7), $\mathcal{E} = -L\,di/dt$; however, the voltage v_L is *not* simply equal to $\mathcal{E}$. To see why, notice that if the current in the inductor is in the positive (counterclockwise) direction from a to b and is increasing, then di/dt is positive and the induced emf is directed to the left to oppose the increase in current; hence point a is at higher potential than is point b. Thus the potential of point a with respect to point b is positive and is given by $v_L = +L\,di/dt$, the *negative* of the induced emf. (You

31.7 Resistance R connected across an ac source.

(a) Circuit with ac source and resistor

(b) Graphs of current and voltage versus time

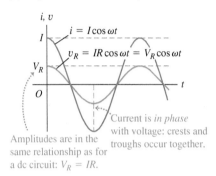

Amplitudes are in the same relationship as for a dc circuit: $V_R = IR$.

Current is *in phase* with voltage: crests and troughs occur together.

(c) Phasor diagram

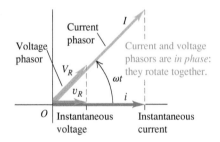

Current and voltage phasors are *in phase:* they rotate together.

31.8 Inductance L connected across an ac source.

(a) Circuit with ac source and inductor

(b) Graphs of current and voltage versus time

Voltage curve *leads* current curve by a quarter-cycle (corresponding to $\phi = \pi/2$ rad $= 90°$).

(c) Phasor diagram

Voltage phasor *leads* current phasor by $\phi = \pi/2$ rad $= 90°$.

ActivPhysics 14.3: AC Circuits: The Driven Oscillator (Questions 1–5)

should convince yourself that this expression gives the correct sign of v_L in *all* cases, including i counterclockwise and decreasing, i clockwise and increasing, and i clockwise and decreasing; you should also review Section 30.2.) So we have

$$v_L = L\frac{di}{dt} = L\frac{d}{dt}(I\cos\omega t) = -I\omega L\sin\omega t \qquad (31.9)$$

The voltage v_L across the inductor at any instant is proportional to the *rate of change* of the current. The points of maximum voltage on the graph correspond to maximum steepness of the current curve, and the points of zero voltage are the points where the current curve instantaneously levels off at its maximum and minimum values (Fig. 31.8b). The voltage and current are "out of step" or *out of phase* by a quarter-cycle. Since the voltage peaks occur a quarter-cycle earlier than the current peaks, we say that the voltage *leads* the current by 90°. The phasor diagram in Fig. 31.8c also shows this relationship; the voltage phasor is ahead of the current phasor by 90°.

We can also obtain this phase relationship by rewriting Eq. (31.9) using the identity $\cos(A + 90°) = -\sin A$:

$$v_L = I\omega L\cos(\omega t + 90°) \qquad (31.10)$$

This result shows that the voltage can be viewed as a cosine function with a "head start" of 90° relative to the current.

As we have done in Eq. (31.10), we will usually describe the phase of the *voltage* relative to the *current*, not the reverse. Thus if the current i in a circuit is

$$i = I\cos\omega t$$

and the voltage v of one point with respect to another is

$$v = V\cos(\omega t + \phi)$$

we call ϕ the **phase angle;** it gives the phase of the *voltage* relative to the *current*. For a pure resistor, $\phi = 0$, and for a pure inductor, $\phi = 90°$.

From Eq. (31.9) or (31.10) the amplitude V_L of the inductor voltage is

$$V_L = I\omega L \qquad (31.11)$$

We define the **inductive reactance** X_L of an inductor as

$$X_L = \omega L \qquad \text{(inductive reactance)} \qquad (31.12)$$

Using X_L, we can write Eq. (31.11) in a form similar to Eq. (31.7) for a resistor ($V_R = IR$):

$$V_L = IX_L \qquad \text{(amplitude of voltage across an inductor, ac circuit)} \qquad (31.13)$$

Because X_L is the ratio of a voltage and a current, its SI unit is the ohm, the same as for resistance.

CAUTION **Inductor voltage and current are not in phase** Keep in mind that Eq. (31.13) is a relationship between the *amplitudes* of the oscillating voltage and current for the inductor in Fig. 31.8a. It does *not* say that the voltage at any instant is equal to the current at that instant multiplied by X_L. As Fig. 31.8b shows, the voltage and current are 90° out of phase. Voltage and current are in phase only for resistors, as in Eq. (31.6). █

The Meaning of Inductive Reactance

The inductive reactance X_L is really a description of the self-induced emf that opposes any change in the current through the inductor. From Eq. (31.13), for a given current amplitude I the voltage $v_L = +L\,di/dt$ across the inductor and the self-induced emf $\mathcal{E} = -L\,di/dt$ both have an amplitude V_L that is directly proportional to X_L. According to Eq. (31.12), the inductive reactance and self-induced emf increase with more rapid variation in current (that is, increasing angular frequency ω) and increasing inductance L.

If an oscillating voltage of a given amplitude V_L is applied across the inductor terminals, the resulting current will have a smaller amplitude I for larger values of X_L. Since X_L is proportional to frequency, a high-frequency voltage applied to the inductor gives only a small current, while a lower-frequency voltage of the same amplitude gives rise to a larger current. Inductors are used in some circuit applications, such as power supplies and radio-interference filters, to block high frequencies while permitting lower frequencies or dc to pass through. A circuit device that uses an inductor for this purpose is called a *low-pass filter* (see Problem 31.52).

Example 31.2   An inductor in an ac circuit

The current amplitude in a pure inductor in a radio receiver is to be 250 μA when the voltage amplitude is 3.60 V at a frequency of 1.60 MHz (at the upper end of the AM broadcast band). (a) What inductive reactance is needed? What inductance? (b) If the voltage amplitude is kept constant, what will be the current amplitude through this inductor at 16.0 MHz? At 160 kHz?

SOLUTION

IDENTIFY and SET UP: There may be other elements of this circuit, but in this example we don't care: All they do is provide the inductor with an oscillating voltage, so the other elements are lumped into the ac source shown in Fig. 31.8a. We are given the current amplitude I and the voltage amplitude V. Our target variables in part (a) are the inductive reactance X_L at 1.60 MHz and the inductance L, which we find using Eqs. (31.13) and (31.12). Knowing L, we use these equations in part (b) to find X_L and I at any frequency.

EXECUTE: (a) From Eq. (31.13),

$$X_L = \frac{V_L}{I} = \frac{3.60 \text{ V}}{250 \times 10^{-6} \text{ A}} = 1.44 \times 10^4 \ \Omega = 14.4 \text{ k}\Omega$$

From Eq. (31.12), with $\omega = 2\pi f$,

$$L = \frac{X_L}{2\pi f} = \frac{1.44 \times 10^4 \ \Omega}{2\pi(1.60 \times 10^6 \text{ Hz})}$$

$$= 1.43 \times 10^{-3} \text{ H} = 1.43 \text{ mH}$$

(b) Combining Eqs. (31.12) and (31.13), we find $I = V_L/X_L = V_L/\omega L = V_L/2\pi f L$. Thus the current amplitude is inversely proportional to the frequency f. Since $I = 250 \ \mu$A at $f = 1.60$ MHz, the current amplitudes at 16.0 MHz ($10f$) and 160 kHz = 0.160 MHz ($f/10$) will be, respectively, one-tenth as great (25.0 μA) and ten times as great (2500 μA = 2.50 mA).

EVALUATE: In general, the lower the frequency of an oscillating voltage applied across an inductor, the greater the amplitude of the resulting oscillating current.

Capacitor in an ac Circuit

Finally, we connect a capacitor with capacitance C to the source, as in Fig. 31.9a, producing a current $i = I\cos\omega t$ through the capacitor. Again, the positive direction of current is counterclockwise around the circuit.

CAUTION   Alternating current through a capacitor You may object that charge can't really move through the capacitor because its two plates are insulated from each other. True enough, but as the capacitor charges and discharges, there is at each instant a current i into one plate, an equal current out of the other plate, and an equal *displacement* current between the plates just as though the charge were being conducted through the capacitor. (You may want to review the discussion of displacement current in Section 29.7.) Thus we often speak about alternating current *through* a capacitor.

To find the instantaneous voltage v_C across the capacitor—that is, the potential of point a with respect to point b—we first let q denote the charge on the left-hand plate of the capacitor in Fig. 31.9a (so $-q$ is the charge on the right-hand plate). The current i is related to q by $i = dq/dt$; with this definition, positive current corresponds to an increasing charge on the left-hand capacitor plate. Then

$$i = \frac{dq}{dt} = I\cos\omega t$$

Integrating this, we get

$$q = \frac{I}{\omega}\sin\omega t \qquad \text{(31.14)}$$

31.9 Capacitor C connected across an ac source.

(a) Circuit with ac source and capacitor

(b) Graphs of current and voltage versus time

Voltage curve *lags* current curve by a quarter-cycle (corresponding to $\phi = -\pi/2$ rad $= -90°$).

(c) Phasor diagram

Also, from Eq. (24.1) the charge q equals the voltage v_C multiplied by the capacitance, $q = Cv_C$. Using this in Eq. (31.14), we find

$$v_C = \frac{I}{\omega C} \sin \omega t \qquad (31.15)$$

The instantaneous current i is equal to the rate of change dq/dt of the capacitor charge q; since $q = Cv_C$, i is also proportional to the rate of change of voltage. (Compare to an inductor, for which the situation is reversed and v_L is proportional to the rate of change of i.) Figure 31.9b shows v_C and i as functions of t. Because $i = dq/dt = C \, dv_C/dt$, the current has its greatest magnitude when the v_C curve is rising or falling most steeply and is zero when the v_C curve instantaneously levels off at its maximum and minimum values.

The capacitor voltage and current are out of phase by a quarter-cycle. The peaks of voltage occur a quarter-cycle *after* the corresponding current peaks, and we say that the voltage *lags* the current by 90°. The phasor diagram in Fig. 31.9c shows this relationship; the voltage phasor is behind the current phasor by a quarter-cycle, or 90°.

We can also derive this phase difference by rewriting Eq. (31.15) using the identity $\cos(A - 90°) = \sin A$:

$$v_C = \frac{I}{\omega C} \cos(\omega t - 90°) \qquad (31.16)$$

This corresponds to a phase angle $\phi = -90°$. This cosine function has a "late start" of 90° compared with the current $i = I \cos \omega t$.

Equations (31.15) and (31.16) show that the *maximum* voltage V_C (the voltage amplitude) is

$$V_C = \frac{I}{\omega C} \qquad (13.17)$$

To put this expression in a form similar to Eq. (31.7) for a resistor, $V_R = IR$, we define a quantity X_C, called the **capacitive reactance** of the capacitor, as

$$X_C = \frac{1}{\omega C} \qquad \text{(capacitive reactance)} \qquad (31.18)$$

Then

$$V_C = IX_C \qquad \text{(amplitude of voltage across a capacitor, ac circuit)} \qquad (31.19)$$

The SI unit of X_C is the ohm, the same as for resistance and inductive reactance, because X_C is the ratio of a voltage and a current.

CAUTION **Capacitor voltage and current are not in phase** Remember that Eq. (31.19) for a capacitor, like Eq. (31.13) for an inductor, is *not* a statement about the instantaneous values of voltage and current. The instantaneous values are actually 90° out of phase, as Fig. 31.9b shows. Rather, Eq. (31.19) relates the *amplitudes* of the voltage and current.

The Meaning of Capacitive Reactance

The capacitive reactance of a capacitor is inversely proportional both to the capacitance C and to the angular frequency ω; the greater the capacitance and the higher the frequency, the *smaller* the capacitive reactance X_C. Capacitors tend to pass high-frequency current and to block low-frequency currents and dc, just the opposite of inductors. A device that preferentially passes signals of high frequency is called a *high-pass filter* (see Problem 31.51).

Example 31.3 A resistor and a capacitor in an ac circuit

A 200-Ω resistor is connected in series with a 5.0-μF capacitor. The voltage across the resistor is $v_R = (1.20\ \text{V})\cos(2500\ \text{rad/s})t$ (Fig. 31.10). (a) Derive an expression for the circuit current. (b) Determine the capacitive reactance of the capacitor. (c) Derive an expression for the voltage across the capacitor.

SOLUTION

IDENTIFY and SET UP: Since this is a series circuit, the current is the same through the capacitor as through the resistor. Our target variables are the current i, the capacitive reactance X_C, and the capacitor voltage v_C. We use Eq. (31.6) to find an expression for i in terms of the angular frequency $\omega = 2500\ \text{rad/s}$, Eq. (31.18) to find X_C, Eq. (31.19) to find the capacitor voltage amplitude V_C, and Eq. (31.16) to write an expression for v_C.

31.10 Our sketch for this problem.

EXECUTE: (a) From Eq. (31.6), $v_R = iR$, we find

$$i = \frac{v_R}{R} = \frac{(1.20\ \text{V})\cos(2500\ \text{rad/s})t}{200\ \Omega}$$

$$= (6.0 \times 10^{-3}\ \text{A})\cos(2500\ \text{rad/s})t$$

(b) From Eq. (31.18), the capacitive reactance at $\omega = 2500\ \text{rad/s}$ is

$$X_C = \frac{1}{\omega C} = \frac{1}{(2500\ \text{rad/s})(5.0 \times 10^{-6}\ \text{F})} = 80\ \Omega$$

(c) From Eq. (31.19), the capacitor voltage amplitude is

$$V_C = IX_C = (6.0 \times 10^{-3}\ \text{A})(80\ \Omega) = 0.48\ \text{V}$$

(The 80-Ω reactance of the capacitor is 40% of the resistor's 200-Ω resistance, so V_C is 40% of V_R.) The instantaneous capacitor voltage is given by Eq. (31.16):

$$v_C = V_C\cos(\omega t - 90°)$$

$$= (0.48\ \text{V})\cos[(2500\ \text{rad/s})t - \pi/2\ \text{rad}]$$

EVALUATE: Although the same *current* passes through both the capacitor and the resistor, the *voltages* across them are different in both amplitude and phase. Note that in the expression for v_C we converted the 90° to $\pi/2$ rad so that all the angular quantities have the same units. In ac circuit analysis, phase angles are often given in degrees, so be careful to convert to radians when necessary.

Comparing ac Circuit Elements

Table 31.1 summarizes the relationships of voltage and current amplitudes for the three circuit elements we have discussed. Note again that *instantaneous* voltage and current are proportional in a resistor, where there is zero phase difference between v_R and i (see Fig. 31.7b). The instantaneous voltage and current are *not* proportional in an inductor or capacitor, because there is a 90° phase difference in both cases (see Figs. 31.8b and 31.9b).

Figure 31.11 shows how the resistance of a resistor and the reactances of an inductor and a capacitor vary with angular frequency ω. Resistance R is independent of frequency, while the reactances X_L and X_C are not. If $\omega = 0$, corresponding to a dc circuit, there is *no* current through a capacitor because $X_C \to \infty$, and there is no inductive effect because $X_L = 0$. In the limit $\omega \to \infty$, X_L also approaches infinity, and the current through an inductor becomes vanishingly small; recall that the self-induced emf opposes rapid changes in current. In this same limit, X_C and the voltage across a capacitor both approach zero; the current changes direction so rapidly that no charge can build up on either plate.

Figure 31.12 shows an application of the above discussion to a loudspeaker system. Low-frequency sounds are produced by the *woofer*, which is a speaker with large diameter; the *tweeter*, a speaker with smaller diameter, produces high-frequency sounds. In order to route signals of different frequency to the appropriate speaker, the woofer and tweeter are connected in parallel across the amplifier

31.11 Graphs of R, X_L, and X_C as functions of angular frequency ω.

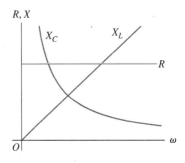

Table 31.1 Circuit Elements with Alternating Current

Circuit Element	Amplitude Relationship	Circuit Quantity	Phase of v
Resistor	$V_R = IR$	R	In phase with i
Inductor	$V_L = IX_L$	$X_L = \omega L$	Leads i by 90°
Capacitor	$V_C = IX_C$	$X_C = 1/\omega C$	Lags i by 90°

31.12 (a) The two speakers in this loudspeaker system are connected in parallel to the amplifier. (b) Graphs of current amplitude in the tweeter and woofer as functions of frequency for a given amplifier voltage amplitude.

(a) A crossover network in a loudspeaker system

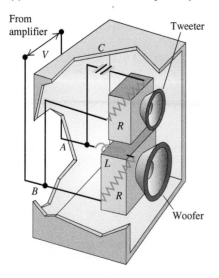

(b) Graphs of rms current as functions of frequency for a given amplifier voltage

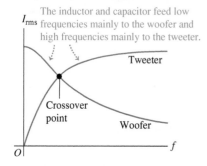

output. The capacitor in the tweeter branch blocks the low-frequency components of sound but passes the higher frequencies; the inductor in the woofer branch does the opposite.

Test Your Understanding of Section 31.2 An oscillating voltage of fixed amplitude is applied across a circuit element. If the frequency of this voltage is increased, will the amplitude of the current through the element (i) increase, (ii) decrease, or (iii) remain the same if it is (a) a resistor, (b) an inductor, or (c) a capacitor?

31.3 The *L-R-C* Series Circuit

Many ac circuits used in practical electronic systems involve resistance, inductive reactance, and capacitive reactance. Figure 31.13a shows a simple example: A series circuit containing a resistor, an inductor, a capacitor, and an ac source. (In Section 30.6 we considered the behavior of the current in an *L-R-C* series circuit *without* a source.)

To analyze this and similar circuits, we will use a phasor diagram that includes the voltage and current phasors for each of the components. In this circuit, because of Kirchhoff's loop rule, the instantaneous *total* voltage v_{ad} across all three components is equal to the source voltage at that instant. We will show that the phasor representing this total voltage is the *vector sum* of the phasors for the individual voltages.

Figures 31.13b and 31.13c show complete phasor diagrams for the circuit of Fig. 31.13a. We assume that the source supplies a current i given by $i = I\cos\omega t$. Because the circuit elements are connected in series, the current at any instant is the same at every point in the circuit. Thus a *single phasor I*, with length proportional to the current amplitude, represents the current in *all* circuit elements.

As in Section 31.2, we use the symbols v_R, v_L, and v_C for the instantaneous voltages across R, L, and C, and the symbols V_R, V_L, and V_C for the maximum voltages. We denote the instantaneous and maximum *source* voltages by v and V. Then, in Fig. 31.13a, $v = v_{ad}$, $v_R = v_{ab}$, $v_L = v_{bc}$, and $v_C = v_{cd}$.

We have shown that the potential difference between the terminals of a resistor is *in phase* with the current in the resistor and that its maximum value V_R is given by Eq. (31.7):

$$V_R = IR$$

31.13 An *L-R-C* series circuit with an ac source.

(a) *L-R-C* series circuit

(b) Phasor diagram for the case $X_L > X_C$

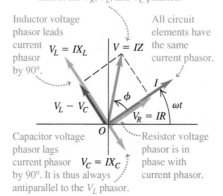

Source voltage phasor is the vector sum of the V_R, V_L, and V_C phasors.

Inductor voltage phasor leads current phasor by 90°.

All circuit elements have the same current phasor.

Capacitor voltage phasor lags current phasor by 90°. It is thus always antiparallel to the V_L phasor.

Resistor voltage phasor is in phase with current phasor.

(c) Phasor diagram for the case $X_L < X_C$

If $X_L < X_C$, the source voltage phasor lags the current phasor, $X < 0$, and ϕ is a negative angle between 0 and −90°.

The phasor V_R in Fig. 31.13b, in phase with the current phasor I, represents the voltage across the resistor. Its projection onto the horizontal axis at any instant gives the instantaneous potential difference v_R.

The voltage across an inductor *leads* the current by 90°. Its voltage amplitude is given by Eq. (31.13):

$$V_L = IX_L$$

The phasor V_L in Fig. 31.13b represents the voltage across the inductor, and its projection onto the horizontal axis at any instant equals v_L.

The voltage across a capacitor *lags* the current by 90°. Its voltage amplitude is given by Eq. (31.19):

$$V_C = IX_C$$

The phasor V_C in Fig. 31.13b represents the voltage across the capacitor, and its projection onto the horizontal axis at any instant equals v_C.

The instantaneous potential difference v between terminals a and d is equal at every instant to the (algebraic) sum of the potential differences v_R, v_L, and v_C. That is, it equals the sum of the *projections* of the phasors V_R, V_L, and V_C. But the sum of the projections of these phasors is equal to the *projection* of their *vector sum*. So the vector sum V must be the phasor that represents the source voltage v and the instantaneous total voltage v_{ad} across the series of elements.

To form this vector sum, we first subtract the phasor V_C from the phasor V_L. (These two phasors always lie along the same line, with opposite directions.) This gives the phasor $V_L - V_C$. This is always at right angles to the phasor V_R, so from the Pythagorean theorem the magnitude of the phasor V is

$$V = \sqrt{V_R^2 + (V_L - V_C)^2} = \sqrt{(IR)^2 + (IX_L - IX_C)^2} \quad \text{or}$$
$$V = I\sqrt{R^2 + (X_L - X_C)^2} \tag{31.20}$$

We define the **impedance** Z of an ac circuit as the ratio of the voltage amplitude across the circuit to the current amplitude in the circuit. From Eq. (31.20) the impedance of the *L-R-C* series circuit is

$$Z = \sqrt{R^2 + (X_L - X_C)^2} \tag{31.21}$$

so we can rewrite Eq. (31.20) as

$$V = IZ \quad \text{(amplitude of voltage across an ac circuit)} \tag{31.22}$$

While Eq. (31.21) is valid only for an *L-R-C* series circuit, we can use Eq. (31.22) to define the impedance of *any* network of resistors, inductors, and capacitors as the ratio of the amplitude of the voltage across the network to the current amplitude. The SI unit of impedance is the ohm.

The Meaning of Impedance and Phase Angle

Equation (31.22) has a form similar to $V = IR$, with impedance Z in an ac circuit playing the role of resistance R in a dc circuit. Just as direct current tends to follow the path of least resistance, so alternating current tends to follow the path of lowest impedance (Fig. 31.14). Note, however, that impedance is actually a function of R, L, and C, as well as of the angular frequency ω. We can see this by substituting Eq. (31.12) for X_L and Eq. (31.18) for X_C into Eq. (31.21), giving the following complete expression for Z for a series circuit:

$$\begin{aligned} Z &= \sqrt{R^2 + (X_L - X_C)^2} \\ &= \sqrt{R^2 + [\omega L - (1/\omega C)]^2} \end{aligned} \quad \begin{array}{l}\text{(impedance of an } L\text{-}R\text{-}C \\ \text{series circuit)}\end{array} \tag{31.23}$$

PhET: Circuit Construction Kit (AC+DC)
PhET: Faraday's Electromagnetic Lab
ActivPhysics 14.3: AC Circuits: The Driven Oscillator (Questions 6, 7, and 10)

31.14 This gas-filled glass sphere has an alternating voltage between its surface and the electrode at its center. The glowing streamers show the resulting alternating current that passes through the gas. When you touch the outside of the sphere, your fingertips and the inner surface of the sphere act as the plates of a capacitor, and the sphere and your body together form an *L-R-C* series circuit. The current (which is low enough to be harmless) is drawn to your fingers because the path through your body has a low impedance.

Hence for a given amplitude V of the source voltage applied to the circuit, the amplitude $I = V/Z$ of the resulting current will be different at different frequencies. We'll explore this frequency dependence in detail in Section 31.5.

In the phasor diagram shown in Fig. 31.13b, the angle ϕ between the voltage and current phasors is the phase angle of the source voltage v with respect to the current i; that is, it is the angle by which the source voltage leads the current. From the diagram,

$$\tan\phi = \frac{V_L - V_C}{V_R} = \frac{I(X_L - X_C)}{IR} = \frac{X_L - X_C}{R}$$

$$\tan\phi = \frac{\omega L - 1/\omega C}{R} \qquad \text{(phase angle of an } L\text{-}R\text{-}C \text{ series circuit)} \qquad (31.24)$$

If the current is $i = I\cos\omega t$, then the source voltage v is

$$v = V\cos(\omega t + \phi) \qquad (31.25)$$

Figure 31.13b shows the behavior of a circuit in which $X_L > X_C$. Figure 31.13c shows the behavior when $X_L < X_C$; the voltage phasor V lies on the opposite side of the current phasor I and the voltage *lags* the current. In this case, $X_L - X_C$ is *negative,* tan ϕ is negative, and ϕ is a negative angle between 0 and $-90°$. Since X_L and X_C depend on frequency, the phase angle ϕ depends on frequency as well. We'll examine the consequences of this in Section 31.5.

All of the expressions that we've developed for an L-R-C series circuit are still valid if one of the circuit elements is missing. If the resistor is missing, we set $R = 0$; if the inductor is missing, we set $L = 0$. But if the capacitor is missing, we set $C = \infty$, corresponding to the absence of any potential difference ($v_C = q/C = 0$) or any capacitive reactance ($X_C = 1/\omega C = 0$).

In this entire discussion we have described magnitudes of voltages and currents in terms of their *maximum* values, the voltage and current *amplitudes.* But we remarked at the end of Section 31.1 that these quantities are usually described in terms of rms values, not amplitudes. For any sinusoidally varying quantity, the rms value is always $1/\sqrt{2}$ times the amplitude. All the relationships between voltage and current that we have derived in this and the preceding sections are still valid if we use rms quantities throughout instead of amplitudes. For example, if we divide Eq. (31.22) by $\sqrt{2}$, we get

$$\frac{V}{\sqrt{2}} = \frac{I}{\sqrt{2}}Z$$

which we can rewrite as

$$V_{\text{rms}} = I_{\text{rms}}Z \qquad (31.26)$$

We can translate Eqs. (31.7), (31.13), and (31.19) in exactly the same way.

We have considered only ac circuits in which an inductor, a resistor, and a capacitor are in series. You can do a similar analysis for an L-R-C *parallel* circuit; see Problem 31.56.

Finally, we remark that in this section we have been describing the *steady-state* condition of a circuit, the state that exists after the circuit has been connected to the source for a long time. When the source is first connected, there may be additional voltages and currents, called *transients,* whose nature depends on the time in the cycle when the circuit is initially completed. A detailed analysis of transients is beyond our scope. They always die out after a sufficiently long time, and they do not affect the steady-state behavior of the circuit. But they can cause dangerous and damaging surges in power lines, which is why delicate electronic systems such as computers are often provided with power-line surge protectors.

Problem-Solving Strategy 31.1   **Alternating-Current Circuits**

IDENTIFY *the relevant concepts:* In analyzing ac circuits, we can apply all of the concepts used to analyze direct-current circuits, particularly those in Problem-Solving Strategies 26.1 and 26.2. But now we must distinguish between the amplitudes of alternating currents and voltages and their instantaneous values, and among resistance (for resistors), reactance (for inductors or capacitors), and impedance (for composite circuits).

SET UP *the problem* using the following steps:
1. Draw a diagram of the circuit and label all known and unknown quantities.
2. Identify the target variables.

EXECUTE *the solution* as follows:
1. Use the relationships derived in Sections 31.2 and 31.3 to solve for the target variables, using the following hints.
2. It's almost always easiest to work with angular frequency $\omega = 2\pi f$ rather than ordinary frequency f.
3. Keep in mind the following phase relationships: For a resistor, voltage and current are *in phase,* so the corresponding phasors always point in the same direction. For an inductor, the voltage *leads* the current by 90° (i.e., $\phi = +90° = \pi/2$ radians), so the voltage phasor points 90° counterclockwise from the current phasor. For a capacitor, the voltage *lags* the current by 90° (i.e., $\phi = -90° = -\pi/2$ radians), so the voltage phasor points 90° clockwise from the current phasor.

4. Kirchhoff's rules hold *at each instant.* For example, in a series circuit, the instantaneous current is the same in all circuit elements; in a parallel circuit, the instantaneous potential difference is the same across all circuit elements.
5. Inductive reactance, capacitive reactance, and impedance are analogous to resistance; each represents the ratio of voltage amplitude V to current amplitude I in a circuit element or combination of elements. However, phase relationships are crucial. In applying Kirchhoff's loop rule, you must combine the effects of resistance and reactance by *vector* addition of the corresponding voltage phasors, as in Figs. 31.13b and 31.13c. When you have several circuit elements in series, for example, you can't just *add* all the numerical values of resistance and reactance to get the impedance; that would ignore the phase relationships.

EVALUATE *your answer:* When working with an *L-R-C series* circuit, you can check your results by comparing the values of the inductive and capacitive reactances X_L and X_C. If $X_L > X_C$, then the voltage amplitude across the inductor is greater than that across the capacitor and the phase angle ϕ is positive (between 0 and 90°). If $X_L < X_C$, then the voltage amplitude across the inductor is less than that across the capacitor and the phase angle ϕ is negative (between 0 and −90°).

Example 31.4   **An *L-R-C* series circuit I**

In the series circuit of Fig. 31.13a, suppose $R = 300\ \Omega$, $L = 60\ \text{mH}$, $C = 0.50\ \mu\text{F}$, $V = 50\ \text{V}$, and $\omega = 10{,}000\ \text{rad/s}$. Find the reactances X_L and X_C, the impedance Z, the current amplitude I, the phase angle ϕ, and the voltage amplitude across each circuit element.

SOLUTION

IDENTIFY and SET UP: This problem uses the ideas developed in Section 31.2 and this section about the behavior of circuit elements in an ac circuit. We use Eqs. (31.12) and (31.18) to determine X_L and X_C, and Eq. (31.23) to find Z. We then use Eq. (31.22) to find the current amplitude and Eq. (31.24) to find the phase angle. The relationships in Table 31.1 then yield the voltage amplitudes.

EXECUTE: The inductive and capacitive reactances are

$$X_L = \omega L = (10{,}000\ \text{rad/s})(60\ \text{mH}) = 600\ \Omega$$

$$X_C = \frac{1}{\omega C} = \frac{1}{(10{,}000\ \text{rad/s})(0.50 \times 10^{-6}\ \text{F})} = 200\ \Omega$$

The impedance Z of the circuit is then

$$Z = \sqrt{R^2 + (X_L - X_C)^2} = \sqrt{(300\ \Omega)^2 + (600\ \Omega - 200\ \Omega)^2}$$
$$= 500\ \Omega$$

With source voltage amplitude $V = 50\ \text{V}$, the current amplitude I and phase angle ϕ are

$$I = \frac{V}{Z} = \frac{50\ \text{V}}{500\ \Omega} = 0.10\ \text{A}$$

$$\phi = \arctan \frac{X_L - X_C}{R} = \arctan \frac{400\ \Omega}{300\ \Omega} = 53°$$

From Table 31.1, the voltage amplitudes V_R, V_L, and V_C across the resistor, inductor, and capacitor, respectively, are

$$V_R = IR = (0.10\ \text{A})(300\ \Omega) = 30\ \text{V}$$

$$V_L = IX_L = (0.10\ \text{A})(600\ \Omega) = 60\ \text{V}$$

$$V_C = IX_C = (0.10\ \text{A})(200\ \Omega) = 20\ \text{V}$$

EVALUATE: As in Fig. 31.13b, $X_L > X_C$; hence the voltage amplitude across the inductor is greater than that across the capacitor and ϕ is positive. The value $\phi = 53°$ means that the voltage *leads* the current by 53°.

Note that the source voltage amplitude $V = 50\ \text{V}$ is *not* equal to the sum of the voltage amplitudes across the separate circuit elements: $50\ \text{V} \neq 30\ \text{V} + 60\ \text{V} + 20\ \text{V}$. Instead, V is the *vector sum* of the V_R, V_L, and V_C phasors. If you draw the phasor diagram like Fig. 31.13b for this particular situation, you'll see that V_R, $V_L - V_C$, and V constitute a 3-4-5 right triangle.

Example 31.5 An *L-R-C* series circuit II

For the *L-R-C* series circuit of Example 31.4, find expressions for the time dependence of the instantaneous current i and the instantaneous voltages across the resistor (v_R), inductor (v_L), capacitor (v_C), and ac source (v).

SOLUTION

IDENTIFY and SET UP: We describe the current using Eq. (31.2), which assumes that the current is maximum at $t = 0$. The voltages are then given by Eq. (31.8) for the resistor, Eq. (31.10) for the inductor, Eq. (31.16) for the capacitor, and Eq. (31.25) for the source.

EXECUTE: The current and the voltages all oscillate with the same angular frequency, $\omega = 10{,}000$ rad/s, and hence with the same period, $2\pi/\omega = 2\pi/(10{,}000 \text{ rad/s}) = 6.3 \times 10^{-4}$ s $= 0.63$ ms. From Eq. (31.2), the current is

$$i = I\cos\omega t = (0.10 \text{ A})\cos(10{,}000 \text{ rad/s})t$$

The resistor voltage is *in phase* with the current, so

$$v_R = V_R\cos\omega t = (30 \text{ V})\cos(10{,}000 \text{ rad/s})t$$

The inductor voltage *leads* the current by 90°, so

$$v_L = V_L\cos(\omega t + 90°) = -V_L\sin\omega t$$
$$= -(60 \text{ V})\sin(10{,}000 \text{ rad/s})t$$

The capacitor voltage *lags* the current by 90°, so

$$v_C = V_C\cos(\omega t - 90°) = V_C\sin\omega t$$
$$= (20 \text{ V})\sin(10{,}000 \text{ rad/s})t$$

We found in Example 31.4 that the source voltage (equal to the voltage across the entire combination of resistor, inductor, and capacitor) *leads* the current by $\phi = 53°$, so

$$v = V\cos(\omega t + \phi)$$
$$= (50 \text{ V})\cos\left[(10{,}000 \text{ rad/s})t + \left(\frac{2\pi \text{ rad}}{360°}\right)(53°)\right]$$
$$= (50 \text{ V})\cos[(10{,}000 \text{ rad/s})t + 0.93 \text{ rad}]$$

EVALUATE: Figure 31.15 graphs the four voltages versus time. The inductor voltage has a larger amplitude than the capacitor voltage because $X_L > X_C$. The *instantaneous* source voltage v is always equal to the sum of the instantaneous voltages v_R, v_L, and v_C. You should verify this by measuring the values of the voltages shown in the graph at different values of the time t.

31.15 Graphs of the source voltage v, resistor voltage v_R, inductor voltage v_L, and capacitor voltage v_C as functions of time for the situation of Example 31.4. The current, which is not shown, is in phase with the resistor voltage.

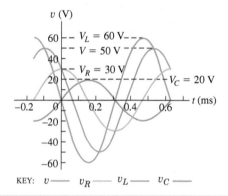

KEY: v —— v_R —— v_L —— v_C ——

Test Your Understanding of Section 31.3 Rank the following ac circuits in order of their current amplitude, from highest to lowest value. (i) the circuit in Example 31.4; (ii) the circuit in Example 31.4 with the capacitor and inductor both removed; (iii) the circuit in Example 31.4 with the resistor and capacitor both removed; (iv) the circuit in Example 31.4 with the resistor and inductor both removed.

31.4 Power in Alternating-Current Circuits

Alternating currents play a central role in systems for distributing, converting, and using electrical energy, so it's important to look at power relationships in ac circuits. For an ac circuit with instantaneous current i and current amplitude I, we'll consider an element of that circuit across which the instantaneous potential difference is v with voltage amplitude V. The instantaneous power p delivered to this circuit element is

$$p = vi$$

Let's first see what this means for individual circuit elements. We'll assume in each case that $i = I\cos\omega t$.

Power in a Resistor

Suppose first that the circuit element is a *pure resistor* R, as in Fig. 31.7a; then $v = v_R$ and i are *in phase*. We obtain the graph representing p by multiplying the heights of the graphs of v and i in Fig. 31.7b at each instant. This graph is shown by the black curve in Fig. 31.16a. The product vi is always positive because v and i are always either both positive or both negative. Hence energy is supplied *to* the resistor at every instant for both directions of i, although the power is not constant.

The power curve for a pure resistor is symmetrical about a value equal to one-half its maximum value VI, so the *average power* P_{av} is

$$P_{av} = \tfrac{1}{2}VI \qquad \text{(for a pure resistor)} \qquad (31.27)$$

An equivalent expression is

$$P_{av} = \frac{V}{\sqrt{2}}\frac{I}{\sqrt{2}} = V_{rms}I_{rms} \qquad \text{(for a pure resistor)} \qquad (31.28)$$

Also, $V_{rms} = I_{rms}R$, so we can express P_{av} by any of the equivalent forms

$$P_{av} = I_{rms}{}^2R = \frac{V_{rms}{}^2}{R} = V_{rms}I_{rms} \qquad \text{(for a pure resistor)} \qquad (31.29)$$

Note that the expressions in Eq. (31.29) have the same form as the corresponding relationships for a dc circuit, Eq. (25.18). Also note that they are valid only for pure resistors, not for more complicated combinations of circuit elements.

Power in an Inductor

Next we connect the source to a pure inductor L, as in Fig. 31.8a. The voltage $v = v_L$ leads the current i by 90°. When we multiply the curves of v and i, the product vi is *negative* during the half of the cycle when v and i have *opposite* signs. The power curve, shown in Fig. 31.16b, is symmetrical about the horizontal axis; it is positive half the time and negative the other half, and the average power is zero. When p is positive, energy is being supplied to set up the magnetic field in the inductor; when p is negative, the field is collapsing and the inductor is returning energy to the source. The net energy transfer over one cycle is zero.

Power in a Capacitor

Finally, we connect the source to a pure capacitor C, as in Fig. 31.9a. The voltage $v = v_C$ lags the current i by 90°. Figure 31.16c shows the power curve; the average power is again zero. Energy is supplied to charge the capacitor and is returned

31.16 Graphs of current, voltage, and power as functions of time for (a) a pure resistor, (b) a pure inductor, (c) a pure capacitor, and (d) an arbitrary ac circuit that can have resistance, inductance, and capacitance.

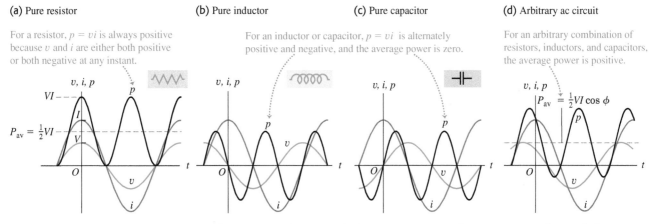

to the source when the capacitor discharges. The net energy transfer over one cycle is again zero.

Power in a General ac Circuit

In *any* ac circuit, with any combination of resistors, capacitors, and inductors, the voltage v across the entire circuit has some phase angle ϕ with respect to the current i. Then the instantaneous power p is given by

$$p = vi = [V\cos(\omega t + \phi)][I\cos\omega t] \qquad (31.30)$$

The instantaneous power curve has the form shown in Fig. 31.16d. The area between the positive loops and the horizontal axis is greater than the area between the negative loops and the horizontal axis, and the average power is positive.

We can derive from Eq. (31.30) an expression for the *average* power P_{av} by using the identity for the cosine of the sum of two angles:

$$p = [V(\cos\omega t\cos\phi - \sin\omega t\sin\phi)][I\cos\omega t]$$
$$= VI\cos\phi\cos^2\omega t - VI\sin\phi\cos\omega t\sin\omega t$$

From the discussion in Section 31.1 that led to Eq. (31.4), we see that the average value of $\cos^2\omega t$ (over one cycle) is $\frac{1}{2}$. The average value of $\cos\omega t\sin\omega t$ is zero because this product is equal to $\frac{1}{2}\sin 2\omega t$, whose average over a cycle is zero. So the average power P_{av} is

$$P_{av} = \tfrac{1}{2}VI\cos\phi = V_{rms}I_{rms}\cos\phi \qquad \begin{array}{l}\text{(average power into a}\\\text{general ac circuit)}\end{array} \qquad (31.31)$$

31.17 Using phasors to calculate the average power for an arbitrary ac circuit.

Average power $= \frac{1}{2}I(V\cos\phi)$, where $V\cos\phi$ is the component of V in phase with I.

When v and i are in phase, so $\phi = 0$, the average power equals $\frac{1}{2}VI = V_{rms}I_{rms}$; when v and i are 90° out of phase, the average power is zero. In the general case, when v has a phase angle ϕ with respect to i, the average power equals $\frac{1}{2}I$ multiplied by $V\cos\phi$, the component of the voltage phasor that is *in phase* with the current phasor. Figure 31.17 shows the general relationship of the current and voltage phasors. For the L-R-C series circuit, Figs. 31.13b and 31.13c show that $V\cos\phi$ equals the voltage amplitude V_R for the resistor; hence Eq. (31.31) is the average power dissipated in the resistor. On average there is no energy flow into or out of the inductor or capacitor, so none of P_{av} goes into either of these circuit elements.

The factor $\cos\phi$ is called the **power factor** of the circuit. For a pure resistance, $\phi = 0$, $\cos\phi = 1$, and $P_{av} = V_{rms}I_{rms}$. For a pure inductor or capacitor, $\phi = \pm 90°$, $\cos\phi = 0$, and $P_{av} = 0$. For an L-R-C series circuit the power factor is equal to R/Z; we leave the proof of this statement to you (see Exercise 31.21).

A low power factor (large angle ϕ of lag or lead) is usually undesirable in power circuits. The reason is that for a given potential difference, a large current is needed to supply a given amount of power. This results in large i^2R losses in the transmission lines. Your electric power company may charge a higher rate to a client with a low power factor. Many types of ac machinery draw a *lagging* current; that is, the current drawn by the machinery lags the applied voltage. Hence the voltage leads the current, so $\phi > 0$ and $\cos\phi < 1$. The power factor can be corrected toward the ideal value of 1 by connecting a capacitor in parallel with the load. The current drawn by the capacitor *leads* the voltage (that is, the voltage across the capacitor lags the current), which compensates for the lagging current in the other branch of the circuit. The capacitor itself absorbs no net power from the line.

Example 31.6 **Power in a hair dryer**

An electric hair dryer is rated at 1500 W (the *average* power) at 120 V (the *rms* voltage). Calculate (a) the resistance, (b) the rms current, and (c) the maximum instantaneous power. Assume that the dryer is a pure resistor. (The heating element acts as a resistor.)

Continued

IDENTIFY and SET UP: We are given $P_{av} = 1500$ W and $V_{rms} = 120$ V. Our target variables are the resistance R, the rms current I_{rms}, and the maximum value p_{max} of the instantaneous power p. We solve Eq. (31.29) to find R, Eq. (31.28) to find I_{rms} from V_{rms} and P_{av}, and Eq. (31.30) to find p_{max}.

EXECUTE: (a) From Eq. (31.29), the resistance is

$$R = \frac{V_{rms}^2}{P_{av}} = \frac{(120 \text{ V})^2}{1500 \text{ W}} = 9.6 \ \Omega$$

(b) From Eq. (31.28),

$$I_{rms} = \frac{P_{av}}{V_{rms}} = \frac{1500 \text{ W}}{120 \text{ V}} = 12.5 \text{ A}$$

(c) For a pure resistor, the voltage and current are in phase and the phase angle ϕ is zero. Hence from Eq. (31.30), the instantaneous power is $p = VI\cos^2 \omega t$ and the maximum instantaneous power is $p_{max} = VI$. From Eq. (31.27), this is twice the average power P_{av}, so

$$p_{max} = VI = 2P_{av} = 2(1500 \text{ W}) = 3000 \text{ W}$$

EVALUATE: We can confirm our result in part (b) by using Eq. (31.7): $I_{rms} = V_{rms}/R = (120 \text{ V})/(9.6 \ \Omega) = 12.5$ A. Note that some unscrupulous manufacturers of stereo amplifiers advertise the *peak* power output rather than the lower average value.

Example 31.7 **Power in an *L-R-C* series circuit**

For the *L-R-C* series circuit of Example 31.4, (a) calculate the power factor and (b) calculate the average power delivered to the entire circuit and to each circuit element.

IDENTIFY and SET UP: We can use the results of Example 31.4. The power factor is the cosine of the phase angle ϕ, and we use Eq. (31.31) to find the average power delivered in terms of ϕ and the amplitudes of voltage and current.

EXECUTE: (a) The power factor is $\cos\phi = \cos 53° = 0.60$.
(b) From Eq. (31.31),

$$P_{av} = \tfrac{1}{2}VI\cos\phi = \tfrac{1}{2}(50 \text{ V})(0.10 \text{ A})(0.60) = 1.5 \text{ W}$$

EVALUATE: Although P_{av} is the average power delivered to the *L-R-C* combination, all of this power is dissipated in the *resistor*. As Figs. 31.16b and 31.16c show, the average power delivered to a pure inductor or pure capacitor is always zero.

Test Your Understanding of Section 31.4 Figure 31.16d shows that during part of a cycle of oscillation, the instantaneous power delivered to the circuit is negative. This means that energy is being extracted from the circuit. (a) Where is the energy extracted from? (i) the resistor; (ii) the inductor; (iii) the capacitor; (iv) the ac source; (v) more than one of these. (b) Where does the energy go? (i) the resistor; (ii) the inductor; (iii) the capacitor; (iv) the ac source; (v) more than one of these.

31.5 Resonance in Alternating-Current Circuits

ActivPhysics 14.3: AC Circuits: The Driven Oscillator (Questions 8, 9, and 11)

Much of the practical importance of *L-R-C* series circuits arises from the way in which such circuits respond to sources of different angular frequency ω. For example, one type of tuning circuit used in radio receivers is simply an *L-R-C* series circuit. A radio signal of any given frequency produces a current of the same frequency in the receiver circuit, but the amplitude of the current is *greatest* if the signal frequency equals the particular frequency to which the receiver circuit is "tuned." This effect is called *resonance*. The circuit is designed so that signals at other than the tuned frequency produce currents that are too small to make an audible sound come out of the radio's speakers.

To see how an *L-R-C* series circuit can be used in this way, suppose we connect an ac source with constant voltage amplitude V but adjustable angular frequency ω across an *L-R-C* series circuit. The current that appears in the circuit has the same angular frequency as the source and a current amplitude $I = V/Z$, where Z is the impedance of the *L-R-C* series circuit. This impedance depends on the frequency, as Eq. (31.23) shows. Figure 31.18a shows graphs of R, X_L, X_C, and Z as functions of ω. We have used a logarithmic angular frequency scale so that we can cover a wide range of frequencies. As the frequency increases, X_L increases and X_C decreases; hence there is always one frequency at which

31.18 How variations in the angular frequency of an ac circuit affect (a) reactance, resistance, and impedance, and (b) impedance, current amplitude, and phase angle.

(a) Reactance, resistance, and impedance as functions of angular frequency

Impedance Z is least at the angular frequency at which $X_C = X_L$.

R, X, Z

$Z = \sqrt{R^2 + (X_L - X_C)^2}$

X_C

R

X_L

O ω_0 $\log \omega$

$X_L - X_C$ Logarithmic scale

(b) Impedance, current, and phase angle as functions of angular frequency

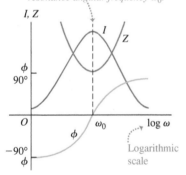

Current peaks at the angular frequency at which impedance is least. This is the *resonance angular frequency* ω_0.

I, Z

ϕ
$90°$

I
Z

O ω_0 $\log \omega$

ϕ

$-90°$
ϕ

Logarithmic scale

31.19 Graph of current amplitude I as a function of angular frequency ω for an L-R-C series circuit with $V = 100$ V, $L = 2.0$ H, $C = 0.50$ μF, and three different values of the resistance R.

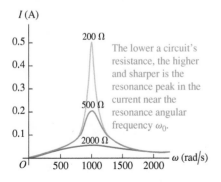

I (A)

0.5 $200\ \Omega$

0.4

0.3

0.2 $500\ \Omega$

0.1

$2000\ \Omega$

O 500 1000 1500 2000 ω (rad/s)

The lower a circuit's resistance, the higher and sharper is the resonance peak in the current near the resonance angular frequency ω_0.

X_L and X_C are equal and $X_L - X_C$ is zero. At this frequency the impedance $Z = \sqrt{R^2 + (X_L - X_C)^2}$ has its *smallest* value, equal simply to the resistance R.

Circuit Behavior at Resonance

As we vary the angular frequency ω of the source, the current amplitude $I = V/Z$ varies as shown in Fig. 31.18b; the *maximum* value of I occurs at the frequency at which the impedance Z is *minimum*. This peaking of the current amplitude at a certain frequency is called **resonance**. The angular frequency ω_0 at which the resonance peak occurs is called the **resonance angular frequency.** This is the angular frequency at which the inductive and capacitive reactances are equal, so at resonance,

$$X_L = X_C \qquad \omega_0 L = \frac{1}{\omega_0 C} \qquad \omega_0 = \frac{1}{\sqrt{LC}} \qquad \begin{matrix} (L\text{-}R\text{-}C \text{ series circuit} \\ \text{at resonance}) \end{matrix} \qquad (31.32)$$

Note that this is equal to the natural angular frequency of oscillation of an L-C circuit, which we derived in Section 30.5, Eq. (30.22). The **resonance frequency** f_0 is $\omega_0/2\pi$. This is the frequency at which the greatest current appears in the circuit for a given source voltage amplitude; in other words, f_0 is the frequency to which the circuit is "tuned."

It's instructive to look at what happens to the *voltages* in an L-R-C series circuit at resonance. The current at any instant is the same in L and C. The voltage across an inductor always *leads* the current by 90°, or $\frac{1}{4}$ cycle, and the voltage across a capacitor always *lags* the current by 90°. Therefore the instantaneous voltages across L and C always differ in phase by 180°, or $\frac{1}{2}$ cycle; they have opposite signs at each instant. At the resonance frequency, and *only* at the resonance frequency, $X_L = X_C$ and the voltage amplitudes $V_L = IX_L$ and $V_C = IX_C$ are *equal*; then the instantaneous voltages across L and C add to zero at each instant, and the *total* voltage v_{bd} across the L-C combination in Fig. 31.13a is exactly zero. The voltage across the resistor is then equal to the source voltage. So at the resonance frequency the circuit behaves as if the inductor and capacitor weren't there at all!

The *phase* of the voltage relative to the current is given by Eq. (31.24). At frequencies below resonance, X_C is greater than X_L; the capacitive reactance dominates, the voltage *lags* the current, and the phase angle ϕ is between zero and −90°. Above resonance, the inductive reactance dominates, the voltage *leads* the current, and the phase angle ϕ is between zero and +90°. Figure 31.18b shows this variation of ϕ with angular frequency.

Tailoring an ac Circuit

If we can vary the inductance L or the capacitance C of a circuit, we can also vary the resonance frequency. This is exactly how a radio or television receiving set is "tuned" to receive a particular station. In the early days of radio this was accomplished by the use of capacitors with movable metal plates whose overlap could be varied to change C. (This is what is being done with the radio tuning knob shown in the photograph that opens this chapter.) A more modern approach is to vary L by using a coil with a ferrite core that slides in or out.

In an L-R-C series circuit the impedance reaches its minimum value and the current its maximum value at the resonance frequency. The middle curve in Fig. 31.19 is a graph of current as a function of frequency for such a circuit, with source voltage amplitude $V = 100$ V, $L = 2.0$ H, $C = 0.50$ μF, and $R = 500$ Ω. This curve is called a *response curve* or a *resonance curve*. The resonance angular frequency is $\omega_0 = (LC)^{-1/2} = 1000$ rad/s. As we expect, the curve has a peak at this angular frequency.

The resonance frequency is determined by L and C; what happens when we change R? Figure 31.19 also shows graphs of I as a function of ω for $R = 200$ Ω and for $R = 2000$ Ω. The curves are similar for frequencies far away from resonance, where the impedance is dominated by X_L or X_C. But near resonance, where X_L and X_C nearly cancel each other, the curve is higher and more sharply peaked for small values of R and broader and flatter for large values of R. At resonance, $Z = R$ and $I = V/R$, so the maximum height of the curve is inversely proportional to R.

The shape of the response curve is important in the design of radio and television receiving circuits. The sharply peaked curve is what makes it possible to discriminate between two stations broadcasting on adjacent frequency bands. But if the peak is *too* sharp, some of the information in the received signal is lost, such as the high-frequency sounds in music. The shape of the resonance curve is also related to the overdamped and underdamped oscillations that we described in Section 30.6. A sharply peaked resonance curve corresponds to a small value of R and a lightly damped oscillating system; a broad, flat curve goes with a large value of R and a heavily damped system.

In this section we have discussed resonance in an *L-R-C series* circuit. Resonance can also occur in an ac circuit in which the inductor, resistor, and capacitor are connected in *parallel*. We leave the details to you (see Problem 31.57).

Resonance phenomena occur not just in ac circuits, but in all areas of physics. We discussed examples of resonance in *mechanical* systems in Sections 13.8 and 16.5. The amplitude of a mechanical oscillation peaks when the driving-force frequency is close to a natural frequency of the system; this is analogous to the peaking of the current in an *L-R-C* series circuit. We suggest that you review the sections on mechanical resonance now, looking for the analogies.

Example 31.8 **Tuning a radio**

The series circuit in Fig. 31.20 is similar to some radio tuning circuits. It is connected to a variable-frequency ac source with an rms terminal voltage of 1.0 V. (a) Find the resonance frequency. At the resonance frequency, find (b) the inductive reactance X_L, the capacitive reactance X_C, and the impedance Z; (c) the rms current I_{rms}; (d) the rms voltage across each circuit element.

SOLUTION

IDENTIFY and SET UP: Figure 31.20 shows an *L-R-C* series circuit, with ideal meters inserted to measure the rms current and voltages, our target variables. Equations (31.32) include the formula for the resonance angular frequency ω_0, from which we find the resonance frequency f_0. We use Eqs. (31.12) and (31.18) to find X_L and X_C, which are equal at resonance; at resonance, from Eq. (31.23), we

have $Z = R$. We use Eqs. (31.7), (31.13), and (31.19) to find the voltages across the circuit elements.

EXECUTE: (a) The values of ω_0 and f_0 are

$$\omega_0 = \frac{1}{\sqrt{LC}} = \frac{1}{\sqrt{(0.40 \times 10^{-3} \text{ H})(100 \times 10^{-12} \text{ F})}}$$

$$= 5.0 \times 10^6 \text{ rad/s}$$

$$f_0 = 8.0 \times 10^5 \text{ Hz} = 800 \text{ kHz}$$

This frequency is in the lower part of the AM radio band.
(b) At this frequency,

$$X_L = \omega L = (5.0 \times 10^6 \text{ rad/s})(0.40 \times 10^{-3} \text{ H}) = 2000 \ \Omega$$

$$X_C = \frac{1}{\omega C} = \frac{1}{(5.0 \times 10^6 \text{ rad/s})(100 \times 10^{-12} \text{ F})} = 2000 \ \Omega$$

Since $X_L = X_C$ at resonance as stated above, $Z = R = 500 \ \Omega$.
(c) From Eq. (31.26) the rms current at resonance is

$$I_{rms} = \frac{V_{rms}}{Z} = \frac{V_{rms}}{R} = \frac{1.0 \text{ V}}{500 \ \Omega} = 0.0020 \text{ A} = 2.0 \text{ mA}$$

(d) The rms potential difference across the resistor is

$$V_{R\text{-rms}} = I_{rms}R = (0.0020 \text{ A})(500 \ \Omega) = 1.0 \text{ V}$$

The rms potential differences across the inductor and capacitor are

$$V_{L\text{-rms}} = I_{rms}X_L = (0.0020 \text{ A})(2000 \ \Omega) = 4.0 \text{ V}$$

$$V_{C\text{-rms}} = I_{rms}X_C = (0.0020 \text{ A})(2000 \ \Omega) = 4.0 \text{ V}$$

EVALUATE: The potential differences across the inductor and the capacitor have equal rms values and amplitudes, but are 180° out of phase and so add to zero at each instant. Note also that at resonance, $V_{R\text{-rms}}$ is equal to the source voltage V_{rms}, while in this example, $V_{L\text{-rms}}$ and $V_{C\text{-rms}}$ are both considerably *larger* than V_{rms}.

31.20 A radio tuning circuit at resonance. The circles denote rms current and voltages.

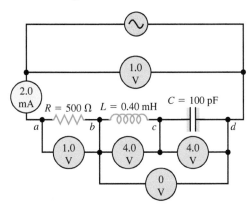

Test Your Understanding of Section 31.5 How does the resonance frequency of an *L-R-C* series circuit change if the plates of the capacitor are brought closer together? (i) It increases; (ii) it decreases; (iii) it is unaffected. ❙

31.6 Transformers

One of the great advantages of ac over dc for electric-power distribution is that it is much easier to step voltage levels up and down with ac than with dc. For long-distance power transmission it is desirable to use as high a voltage and as small a current as possible; this reduces i^2R losses in the transmission lines, and smaller wires can be used, saving on material costs. Present-day transmission lines routinely operate at rms voltages of the order of 500 kV. On the other hand, safety considerations and insulation requirements dictate relatively low voltages in generating equipment and in household and industrial power distribution. The standard voltage for household wiring is 120 V in the United States and Canada and 240 V in many other countries. The necessary voltage conversion is accomplished by the use of **transformers.**

How Transformers Work

Figure 31.21 shows an idealized transformer. The key components of the transformer are two coils or *windings,* electrically insulated from each other but wound on the same core. The core is typically made of a material, such as iron, with a very large relative permeability K_m. This keeps the magnetic field lines due to a current in one winding almost completely within the core. Hence almost all of these field lines pass through the other winding, maximizing the *mutual inductance* of the two windings (see Section 30.1). The winding to which power is supplied is called the **primary;** the winding from which power is delivered is called the **secondary.** The circuit symbol for a transformer with an iron core, such as those used in power distribution systems, is

Here's how a transformer works. The ac source causes an alternating current in the primary, which sets up an alternating flux in the core; this induces an emf in each winding, in accordance with Faraday's law. The induced emf in the secondary gives rise to an alternating current in the secondary, and this delivers energy to the device to which the secondary is connected. All currents and emfs have the same frequency as the ac source.

Let's see how the voltage across the secondary can be made larger or smaller in amplitude than the voltage across the primary. We neglect the resistance of the windings and assume that all the magnetic field lines are confined to the iron core, so at any instant the magnetic flux Φ_B is the same in each turn of the primary and secondary windings. The primary winding has N_1 turns and the secondary winding has N_2 turns. When the magnetic flux changes because of changing currents in the two coils, the resulting induced emfs are

$$\mathcal{E}_1 = -N_1 \frac{d\Phi_B}{dt} \quad \text{and} \quad \mathcal{E}_2 = -N_2 \frac{d\Phi_B}{dt} \tag{31.33}$$

The flux *per turn* Φ_B is the same in both the primary and the secondary, so Eqs. (31.33) show that the induced emf *per turn* is the same in each. The ratio of the secondary emf $\mathcal{E}_2$ to the primary emf $\mathcal{E}_1$ is therefore equal at any instant to the ratio of secondary to primary turns:

$$\frac{\mathcal{E}_2}{\mathcal{E}_1} = \frac{N_2}{N_1} \tag{31.34}$$

Since $\mathcal{E}_1$ and $\mathcal{E}_2$ both oscillate with the same frequency as the ac source, Eq. (31.34) also gives the ratio of the amplitudes or of the rms values of the induced

31.21 Schematic diagram of an idealized step-up transformer. The primary is connected to an ac source; the secondary is connected to a device with resistance *R*.

The induced emf *per turn* is the same in both coils, so we adjust the ratio of terminal voltages by adjusting the ratio of turns:

$$\frac{V_2}{V_1} = \frac{N_2}{N_1}$$

emfs. If the windings have zero resistance, the induced emfs $\mathcal{E}_1$ and $\mathcal{E}_2$ are equal to the terminal voltages across the primary and the secondary, respectively; hence

$$\frac{V_2}{V_1} = \frac{N_2}{N_1} \qquad \text{(terminal voltages of transformer primary and secondary)} \qquad (31.35)$$

where V_1 and V_2 are either the amplitudes or the rms values of the terminal voltages. By choosing the appropriate turns ratio N_2/N_1, we may obtain any desired secondary voltage from a given primary voltage. If $N_2 > N_1$, as in Fig. 31.21, then $V_2 > V_1$ and we have a *step-up* transformer; if $N_2 < N_1$, then $V_2 < V_1$ and we have a *step-down* transformer. At a power generating station, step-up transformers are used; the primary is connected to the power source and the secondary is connected to the transmission lines, giving the desired high voltage for transmission. Near the consumer, step-down transformers lower the voltage to a value suitable for use in home or industry (Fig. 31.22).

Even the relatively low voltage provided by a household wall socket is too high for many electronic devices, so a further step-down transformer is necessary. This is the role of an "ac adapter" such as those used to recharge a mobile phone or laptop computer from line voltage. Such adapters contain a step-down transformer that converts line voltage to a lower value, typically 3 to 12 volts, as well as diodes to convert alternating current to the direct current that small electronic devices require (Fig. 31.23).

Energy Considerations for Transformers

If the secondary circuit is completed by a resistance R, then the amplitude or rms value of the current in the secondary circuit is $I_2 = V_2/R$. From energy considerations, the power delivered to the primary equals that taken out of the secondary (since there is no resistance in the windings), so

$$V_1 I_1 = V_2 I_2 \qquad \text{(currents in transformer primary and secondary)} \qquad (31.36)$$

We can combine Eqs. (31.35) and (31.36) and the relationship $I_2 = V_2/R$ to eliminate V_2 and I_2; we obtain

$$\frac{V_1}{I_1} = \frac{R}{(N_2/N_1)^2} \qquad (31.37)$$

This shows that when the secondary circuit is completed through a resistance R, the result is the same as if the *source* had been connected directly to a resistance equal to R divided by the square of the turns ratio, $(N_2/N_1)^2$. In other words, the transformer "transforms" not only voltages and currents, but resistances as well. More generally, we can regard a transformer as "transforming" the *impedance* of the network to which the secondary circuit is completed.

Equation (31.37) has many practical consequences. The power supplied by a source to a resistor depends on the resistances of both the resistor and the source. It can be shown that the power transfer is greatest when the two resistances are *equal*. The same principle applies in both dc and ac circuits. When a high-impedance ac source must be connected to a low-impedance circuit, such as an audio amplifier connected to a loudspeaker, the source impedance can be *matched* to that of the circuit by the use of a transformer with an appropriate turns ratio N_2/N_1.

Real transformers always have some energy losses. (That's why an ac adapter like the one shown in Fig. 31.23 feels warm to the touch after it's been in use for a while; the transformer is heated by the dissipated energy.) The windings have some resistance, leading to i^2R losses. There are also energy losses through hysteresis in the core (see Section 28.8). Hysteresis losses are minimized by the use of soft iron with a narrow hysteresis loop.

Another important mechanism for energy loss in a transformer core involves eddy currents (see Section 29.6). Consider a section AA through an iron transformer core (Fig. 31.24a). Since iron is a conductor, any such section can be pictured as

31.22 The cylindrical can near the top of this power pole is a step-down transformer. It converts the high-voltage ac in the power lines to low-voltage (120 V) ac, which is then distributed to the surrounding homes and businesses.

31.23 An ac adapter like this one converts household ac into low-voltage dc for use in electronic devices. It contains a step-down transformer to lower the voltage and diodes to rectify the output current (see Fig. 31.3).

31.24 (a) Primary and secondary windings in a transformer. (b) Eddy currents in the iron core, shown in the cross section at *AA*. (c) Using a laminated core reduces the eddy currents.

(a) Schematic transformer

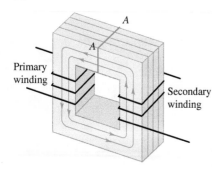

(b) Large eddy currents in solid core

(c) Smaller eddy currents in laminated core

several conducting circuits, one within the other (Fig. 31.24b). The flux through each of these circuits is continually changing, so eddy currents circulate in the entire volume of the core, with lines of flow that form planes perpendicular to the flux. These eddy currents are very undesirable; they waste energy through i^2R heating and themselves set up an opposing flux.

The effects of eddy currents can be minimized by the use of a *laminated* core— that is, one built up of thin sheets or laminae. The large electrical surface resistance of each lamina, due either to a natural coating of oxide or to an insulating varnish, effectively confines the eddy currents to individual laminae (Fig. 31.24c). The possible eddy-current paths are narrower, the induced emf in each path is smaller, and the eddy currents are greatly reduced. The alternating magnetic field exerts forces on the current-carrying laminae that cause them to vibrate back and forth; this vibration causes the characteristic "hum" of an operating transformer. You can hear this same "hum" from the magnetic ballast of a fluorescent light fixture (see Section 30.2).

Thanks to the use of soft iron cores and lamination, transformer efficiencies are usually well over 90%; in large installations they may reach 99%.

Example 31.9   **"Wake up and smell the (transformer)!"**

A friend returns to the United States from Europe with a 960-W coffeemaker, designed to operate from a 240-V line. (a) What can she do to operate it at the USA-standard 120 V? (b) What current will the coffeemaker draw from the 120-V line? (c) What is the resistance of the coffeemaker? (The voltages are rms values.)

SOLUTION

IDENTIFY and SET UP: Our friend needs a step-up transformer to convert 120-V ac to the 240-V ac that the coffeemaker requires. We use Eq. (31.35) to determine the transformer turns ratio N_2/N_1, $P_{av} = V_{rms}I_{rms}$ for a resistor to find the current draw, and Eq. (31.37) to calculate the resistance.

EXECUTE: (a) To get $V_2 = 240$ V from $V_1 = 120$ V, the required turns ratio is $N_2/N_1 = V_2/V_1 = (240 \text{ V})/(120 \text{ V}) = 2$. That is, the secondary coil (connected to the coffeemaker) should have twice as many turns as the primary coil (connected to the 120-V line).

(b) We find the rms current I_1 in the 120-V primary by using $P_{av} = V_1I_1$, where P_{av} is the average power drawn by the coffeemaker and hence the power supplied by the 120-V line. (We're assuming that no energy is lost in the transformer.) Hence $I_1 = P_{av}/V_1 = (960 \text{ W})/(120 \text{ V}) = 8.0$ A. The secondary current is then $I_2 = P_{av}/V_2 = (960 \text{ W})/(240 \text{ V}) = 4.0$ A.

(c) We have $V_1 = 120$ V, $I_1 = 8.0$ A, and $N_2/N_1 = 2$, so

$$\frac{V_1}{I_1} = \frac{120 \text{ V}}{8.0 \text{ A}} = 15 \ \Omega$$

From Eq. (31.37),

$$R = 2^2(15 \ \Omega) = 60 \ \Omega$$

EVALUATE: As a check, $V_2/R = (240 \text{ V})/(60 \ \Omega) = 4.0$ A $= I_2$, the same value obtained previously. You can also check this result for R by using the expression $P_{av} = V_2^2/R$ for the power drawn by the coffeemaker.

Test Your Understanding of Section 31.6   Each of the following four transformers has 1000 turns in its primary coil. Rank the transformers from largest to smallest number of turns in the secondary coil. (i) converts 120-V ac into 6.0-V ac; (ii) converts 120-V ac into 240-V ac; (iii) converts 240-V ac into 6.0-V ac; (iv) converts 240-V ac into 120-V ac. ∎

Phasors and alternating current: An alternator or ac source produces an emf that varies sinusoidally with time. A sinusoidal voltage or current can be represented by a phasor, a vector that rotates counterclockwise with constant angular velocity ω equal to the angular frequency of the sinusoidal quantity. Its projection on the horizontal axis at any instant represents the instantaneous value of the quantity.

For a sinusoidal current, the rectified average and rms (root-mean-square) currents are proportional to the current amplitude I. Similarly, the rms value of a sinusoidal voltage is proportional to the voltage amplitude V. (See Example 31.1.)

$$I_{\mathrm{rav}} = \frac{2}{\pi}I = 0.637I \qquad (31.3)$$

$$I_{\mathrm{rms}} = \frac{I}{\sqrt{2}} \qquad (31.4)$$

$$V_{\mathrm{rms}} = \frac{V}{\sqrt{2}} \qquad (31.5)$$

Voltage, current, and phase angle: In general, the instantaneous voltage between two points in an ac circuit is not in phase with the instantaneous current passing through those points. The quantity ϕ is called the phase angle of the voltage relative to the current.

$$i = I\cos\omega t \qquad (31.2)$$

$$v = V\cos(\omega t + \phi) \qquad (31.2)$$

Resistance and reactance: The voltage across a resistor R is in phase with the current. The voltage across an inductor L leads the current by 90° ($\phi = +90°$), while the voltage across a capacitor C lags the current by 90° ($\phi = -90°$). The voltage amplitude across each type of device is proportional to the current amplitude I. An inductor has inductive reactance $X_L = \omega L$, and a capacitor has capacitive reactance $X_C = 1/\omega C$. (See Examples 31.2 and 31.3.)

$$V_R = IR \qquad (31.7)$$

$$V_L = IX_L \qquad (31.13)$$

$$V_C = IX_C \qquad (31.19)$$

Impedance and the L-R-C series circuit: In a general ac circuit, the voltage and current amplitudes are related by the circuit impedance Z. In an L-R-C series circuit, the values of L, R, C, and the angular frequency ω determine the impedance and the phase angle ϕ of the voltage relative to the current. (See Examples 31.4 and 31.5.)

$$V = IZ \qquad (31.22)$$

$$Z = \sqrt{R^2 + (X_L - X_C)^2}$$
$$= \sqrt{R^2 + [\omega L - (1/\omega C)]^2} \qquad (31.23)$$

$$\tan\phi = \frac{\omega L - 1/\omega C}{R} \qquad (31.24)$$

Power in ac circuits: The average power input P_{av} to an ac circuit depends on the voltage and current amplitudes (or, equivalently, their rms values) and the phase angle ϕ of the voltage relative to the current. The quantity $\cos\phi$ is called the power factor. (See Examples 31.6 and 31.7.)

$$P_{\mathrm{av}} = \tfrac{1}{2}VI\cos\phi \qquad (31.31)$$

$$= V_{\mathrm{rms}}I_{\mathrm{rms}}\cos\phi$$

Resonance in ac circuits: In an L-R-C series circuit, the current becomes maximum and the impedance becomes minimum at an angular frequency called the resonance angular frequency. This phenomenon is called resonance. At resonance the voltage and current are in phase, and the impedance Z is equal to the resistance R. (See Example 31.8.)

$$\omega_0 = \frac{1}{\sqrt{LC}} \qquad (31.32)$$

Transformers: A transformer is used to transform the voltage and current levels in an ac circuit. In an ideal transformer with no energy losses, if the primary winding has N_1 turns and the secondary winding has N_2 turns, the amplitudes (or rms values) of the two voltages are related by Eq. (31.35). The amplitudes (or rms values) of the primary and secondary voltages and currents are related by Eq. (31.36). (See Example 31.9.)

$$\frac{V_2}{V_1} = \frac{N_2}{N_1} \qquad (31.35)$$

$$V_1 I_1 = V_2 I_2 \qquad (31.36)$$

BRIDGING PROBLEM **An Alternating-Current Circuit**

A series circuit consists of a 1.50-mH inductor, a 125-Ω resistor, and a 25.0-nF capacitor connected across an ac source having an rms voltage of 35.0 V and variable frequency. (a) At what angular frequencies will the current amplitude be equal to $\frac{1}{3}$ of its maximum possible value? (b) At the frequencies in part (a), what are the current amplitude and the voltage amplitude across each circuit element (including the ac source)?

SOLUTION GUIDE

See MasteringPhysics® study area for a Video Tutor solution. (MP)

IDENTIFY and SET UP

1. The maximum current amplitude occurs at the resonance angular frequency. This problem concerns the angular frequencies at which the current amplitude is one-third of that maximum.
2. Choose the equation that will allow you to find the angular frequencies in question, and choose the equations that you will

then use to find the current and voltage amplitudes at each angular frequency.

EXECUTE

3. Find the impedance at the angular frequencies in part (a); then solve for the values of angular frequency.
4. Find the voltage amplitude across the source and the current amplitude for each of the angular frequencies in part (a). (*Hint:* Be careful to distinguish between *amplitude* and *rms value*.)
5. Use the results of steps 3 and 4 to find the reactances at each angular frequency. Then calculate the voltage amplitudes for the resistor, inductor, and capacitor.

EVALUATE

6. Are there any voltage amplitudes that are greater than the voltage amplitude of the source? If so, does this mean your results are in error?

Problems

For instructor-assigned homework, go to MasteringPhysics®. (MP)

•, ••, •••: Problems of increasing difficulty. **CP:** Cumulative problems incorporating material from earlier chapters. **CALC:** Problems requiring calculus. **BIO:** Biosciences problems.

DISCUSSION QUESTIONS

Q31.1 Household electric power in most of western Europe is supplied at 240 V, rather than the 120 V that is standard in the United States and Canada. What are the advantages and disadvantages of each system?

Q31.2 The current in an ac power line changes direction 120 times per second, and its average value is zero. Explain how it is possible for power to be transmitted in such a system.

Q31.3 In an ac circuit, why is the average power for an inductor and a capacitor zero, but not for a resistor?

Q31.4 Equation (31.14) was derived by using the relationship $i = dq/dt$ between the current and the charge on the capacitor. In Fig. 31.9a the positive counterclockwise current increases the charge on the capacitor. When the charge on the left plate is positive but decreasing in time, is $i = dq/dt$ still correct or should it be $i = -dq/dt$? Is $i = dq/dt$ still correct when the right-hand plate has positive charge that is increasing or decreasing in magnitude? Explain.

Q31.5 Fluorescent lights often use an inductor, called a ballast, to limit the current through the tubes. Why is it better to use an inductor rather than a resistor for this purpose?

Q31.6 Equation (31.9) says that $v_{ab} = L\, di/dt$ (see Fig. 31.8a). Using Faraday's law, explain why point a is at higher potential than point b when i is in the direction shown in Fig. 31.8a and is increasing in magnitude. When i is counterclockwise and decreasing in magnitude, is $v_{ab} = L\, di/dt$ still correct, or should it be $v_{ab} = -L\, di/dt$? Is $v_{ab} = L\, di/dt$ still correct when i is clockwise and increasing or decreasing in magnitude? Explain.

Q31.7 Is it possible for the power factor of an L-R-C series ac circuit to be zero? Justify your answer on *physical* grounds.

Q31.8 In an L-R-C series circuit, can the instantaneous voltage across the capacitor exceed the source voltage at that same instant? Can this be true for the instantaneous voltage across the inductor? Across the resistor? Explain.

Q31.9 In an L-R-C series circuit, what are the phase angle ϕ and power factor $\cos\phi$ when the resistance is much smaller than the inductive or capacitive reactance and the circuit is operated far from resonance? Explain.

Q31.10 When an *L-R-C* series circuit is connected across a 120-V ac line, the voltage rating of the capacitor may be exceeded even if it is rated at 200 or 400 V. How can this be?

Q31.11 In Example 31.6 (Section 31.4), a hair dryer is treated as a pure resistor. But because there are coils in the heating element and in the motor that drives the blower fan, a hair dryer also has inductance. Qualitatively, does including an inductance increase or decrease the values of R, I_{rms}, and P?

Q31.12 A light bulb and a parallel-plate capacitor with air between the plates are connected in series to an ac source. What happens to the brightness of the bulb when a dielectric is inserted between the plates of the capacitor? Explain.

Q31.13 A coil of wire wrapped on a hollow tube and a light bulb are connected in series to an ac source. What happens to the brightness of the bulb when an iron rod is inserted in the tube?

Q31.14 A circuit consists of a light bulb, a capacitor, and an inductor connected in series to an ac source. What happens to the brightness of the bulb when the inductor is removed? When the inductor is left in the circuit but the capacitor is removed? Explain.

Q31.15 A circuit consists of a light bulb, a capacitor, and an inductor connected in series to an ac source. Is it possible for both the capacitor and the inductor to be removed and the brightness of the bulb to remain the same? Explain.

Q31.16 Can a transformer be used with dc? Explain. What happens if a transformer designed for 120-V ac is connected to a 120-V dc line?

Q31.17 An ideal transformer has N_1 windings in the primary and N_2 windings in its secondary. If you double only the number of secondary windings, by what factor does (a) the voltage amplitude in the secondary change, and (b) the effective resistance of the secondary circuit change?

Q31.18 Some electrical appliances operate equally well on ac or dc, and others work only on ac or only on dc. Give examples of each, and explain the differences.

EXERCISES

Section 31.1 Phasors and Alternating Currents

31.1 · You have a special light bulb with a *very* delicate wire filament. The wire will break if the current in it ever exceeds 1.50 A, even for an instant. What is the largest root-mean-square current you can run through this bulb?

31.2 · A sinusoidal current $i = I\cos\omega t$ has an rms value $I_{rms} = 2.10$ A. (a) What is the current amplitude? (b) The current is passed through a full-wave rectifier circuit. What is the rectified average current? (c) Which is larger: I_{rms} or I_{rav}? Explain, using graphs of i^2 and of the rectified current.

31.3 · The voltage across the terminals of an ac power supply varies with time according to Eq. (31.1). The voltage amplitude is $V = 45.0$ V. What are (a) the root-mean-square potential difference V_{rms} and (b) the average potential difference V_{av} between the two terminals of the power supply?

Section 31.2 Resistance and Reactance

31.4 · A capacitor is connected across an ac source that has voltage amplitude 60.0 V and frequency 80.0 Hz. (a) What is the phase angle ϕ for the source voltage relative to the current? Does the source voltage lag or lead the current? (b) What is the capacitance C of the capacitor if the current amplitude is 5.30 A?

31.5 · An inductor with $L = 9.50$ mH is connected across an ac source that has voltage amplitude 45.0 V. (a) What is the phase angle ϕ for the source voltage relative to the current? Does the source voltage lag or lead the current? (b) What value for the frequency of the source results in a current amplitude of 3.90 A?

31.6 · A capacitance C and an inductance L are operated at the same angular frequency. (a) At what angular frequency will they have the same reactance? (b) If $L = 5.00$ mH and $C = 3.50$ μF, what is the numerical value of the angular frequency in part (a), and what is the reactance of each element?

31.7 · **Kitchen Capacitance.** The wiring for a refrigerator contains a starter capacitor. A voltage of amplitude 170 V and frequency 60.0 Hz applied across the capacitor is to produce a current amplitude of 0.850 A through the capacitor. What capacitance C is required?

31.8 · (a) Compute the reactance of a 0.450-H inductor at frequencies of 60.0 Hz and 600 Hz. (b) Compute the reactance of a 2.50-μF capacitor at the same frequencies. (c) At what frequency is the reactance of a 0.450-H inductor equal to that of a 2.50-μF capacitor?

31.9 · (a) What is the reactance of a 3.00-H inductor at a frequency of 80.0 Hz? (b) What is the inductance of an inductor whose reactance is 120 Ω at 80.0 Hz? (c) What is the reactance of a 4.00-μF capacitor at a frequency of 80.0 Hz? (d) What is the capacitance of a capacitor whose reactance is 120 Ω at 80.0 Hz?

31.10 · **A Radio Inductor.** You want the current amplitude through a 0.450-mH inductor (part of the circuitry for a radio receiver) to be 2.60 mA when a sinusoidal voltage with amplitude 12.0 V is applied across the inductor. What frequency is required?

31.11 ·· A 0.180-H inductor is connected in series with a 90.0-Ω resistor and an ac source. The voltage across the inductor is $v_L = -(12.0\text{ V})\sin[(480\text{ rad/s})t]$. (a) Derive an expression for the voltage v_R across the resistor. (b) What is v_R at $t = 2.00$ ms?

31.12 ·· A 250-Ω resistor is connected in series with a 4.80-μF capacitor and an ac source. The voltage across the capacitor is $v_C = (7.60\text{ V})\sin[(120\text{ rad/s})t]$. (a) Determine the capacitive reactance of the capacitor. (b) Derive an expression for the voltage v_R across the resistor.

31.13 ·· A 150-Ω resistor is connected in series with a 0.250-H inductor and an ac source. The voltage across the resistor is $v_R = (3.80\text{ V})\cos[(720\text{ rad/s})t]$. (a) Derive an expression for the circuit current. (b) Determine the inductive reactance of the inductor. (c) Derive an expression for the voltage v_L across the inductor.

Section 31.3 The *L-R-C* Series Circuit

31.14 · You have a 200-Ω resistor, a 0.400-H inductor, and a 6.00-μF capacitor. Suppose you take the resistor and inductor and make a series circuit with a voltage source that has voltage amplitude 30.0 V and an angular frequency of 250 rad/s. (a) What is the impedance of the circuit? (b) What is the current amplitude? (c) What are the voltage amplitudes across the resistor and across the inductor? (d) What is the phase angle ϕ of the source voltage with respect to the current? Does the source voltage lag or lead the current? (e) Construct the phasor diagram.

31.15 · The resistor, inductor, capacitor, and voltage source described in Exercise 31.14 are connected to form an *L-R-C* series circuit. (a) What is the impedance of the circuit? (b) What is the current amplitude? (c) What is the phase angle of the source voltage with respect to the current? Does the source voltage lag or lead the current? (d) What are the voltage amplitudes across the resistor, inductor, and capacitor? (e) Explain how it is possible for the voltage amplitude across the capacitor to be greater than the voltage amplitude across the source.

31.16 •• A 200-Ω resistor, a 0.900-H inductor, and a 6.00-μF capacitor are connected in series across a voltage source that has voltage amplitude 30.0 V and an angular frequency of 250 rad/s. (a) What are v, v_R, v_L, and v_C at $t = 20.0$ ms? Compare $v_R + v_L + v_C$ to v at this instant. (b) What are V_R, V_L, and V_C? Compare V to $V_R + V_L + V_C$. Explain why these two quantities are not equal.

31.17 • In an *L-R-C* series circuit, the rms voltage across the resistor is 30.0 V, across the capacitor it is 90.0 V, and across the inductor it is 50.0 V. What is the rms voltage of the source?

Section 31.4 Power in Alternating-Current Circuits

31.18 •• A resistor with $R = 300\ \Omega$ and an inductor are connected in series across an ac source that has voltage amplitude 500 V. The rate at which electrical energy is dissipated in the resistor is 216 W. (a) What is the impedance Z of the circuit? (b) What is the amplitude of the voltage across the inductor? (c) What is the power factor?

31.19 • The power of a certain CD player operating at 120 V rms is 20.0 W. Assuming that the CD player behaves like a pure resistor, find (a) the maximum instantaneous power; (b) the rms current; (c) the resistance of this player.

31.20 •• In an *L-R-C* series circuit, the components have the following values: $L = 20.0$ mH, $C = 140$ nF, and $R = 350\ \Omega$. The generator has an rms voltage of 120 V and a frequency of 1.25 kHz. Determine (a) the power supplied by the generator and (b) the power dissipated in the resistor.

31.21 • (a) Show that for an *L-R-C* series circuit the power factor is equal to R/Z. (b) An *L-R-C* series circuit has phase angle $-31.5°$. The voltage amplitude of the source is 90.0 V. What is the voltage amplitude across the resistor?

31.22 • (a) Use the results of part (a) of Exercise 31.21 to show that the average power delivered by the source in an *L-R-C* series circuit is given by $P_{av} = I_{rms}^2 R$. (b) An *L-R-C* series series circuit has $R = 96.0\ \Omega$, and the amplitude of the voltage across the resistor is 36.0 V. What is the average power delivered by the source?

31.23 • An *L-R-C* series circuit with $L = 0.120$ H, $R = 240\ \Omega$, and $C = 7.30\ \mu$F carries an rms current of 0.450 A with a frequency of 400 Hz. (a) What are the phase angle and power factor for this circuit? (b) What is the impedance of the circuit? (c) What is the rms voltage of the source? (d) What average power is delivered by the source? (e) What is the average rate at which electrical energy is converted to thermal energy in the resistor? (f) What is the average rate at which electrical energy is dissipated (converted to other forms) in the capacitor? (g) In the inductor?

31.24 •• An *L-R-C* series circuit is connected to a 120-Hz ac source that has $V_{rms} = 80.0$ V. The circuit has a resistance of 75.0 Ω and an impedance at this frequency of 105 Ω. What average power is delivered to the circuit by the source?

31.25 •• A series ac circuit contains a 250-Ω resistor, a 15-mH inductor, a 3.5-μF capacitor, and an ac power source of voltage amplitude 45 V operating at an angular frequency of 360 rad/s, (a) What is the power factor of this circuit? (b) Find the average power delivered to the entire circuit. (c) What is the average power delivered to the resistor, to the capacitor, and to the inductor?

Section 31.5 Resonance in Alternating-Current Circuits

31.26 •• In an *L-R-C* series circuit the source is operated at its resonant angular frequency. At this frequency, the reactance X_C of

the capacitor is 200 Ω and the voltage amplitude across the capacitor is 600 V. The circuit has $R = 300\ \Omega$. What is the voltage amplitude of the source?

31.27 • **Analyzing an *L-R-C* Circuit.**   You have a 200-Ω resistor, a 0.400-H inductor, a 5.00-μF capacitor, and a variable-frequency ac source with an amplitude of 3.00 V. You connect all four elements together to form a series circuit. (a) At what frequency will the current in the circuit be greatest? What will be the current amplitude at this frequency? (b) What will be the current amplitude at an angular frequency of 400 rad/s? At this frequency, will the source voltage lead or lag the current?

31.28 • An *L-R-C* series circuit is constructed using a 175-Ω resistor, a 12.5-μF capacitor, and an 8.00-mH inductor, all connected across an ac source having a variable frequency and a voltage amplitude of 25.0 V. (a) At what angular frequency will the impedance be smallest, and what is the impedance at this frequency? (b) At the angular frequency in part (a), what is the maximum current through the inductor? (c) At the angular frequency in part (a), find the potential difference across the ac source, the resistor, the capacitor, and the inductor at the instant that the current is equal to one-half its greatest positive value. (d) In part (c), how are the potential differences across the resistor, inductor, and capacitor related to the potential difference across the ac source?

31.29 • In an *L-R-C* series circuit, $R = 300\ \Omega$, $L = 0.400$ H, and $C = 6.00 \times 10^{-8}$ F. When the ac source operates at the resonance frequency of the circuit, the current amplitude is 0.500 A. (a) What is the voltage amplitude of the source? (b) What is the amplitude of the voltage across the resistor, across the inductor, and across the capacitor? (c) What is the average power supplied by the source?

31.30 • An *L-R-C* series circuit consists of a source with voltage amplitude 120 V and angular frequency 50.0 rad/s, a resistor with $R = 400\ \Omega$, an inductor with $L = 9.00$ H, and a capacitor with capacitance C. (a) For what value of C will the current amplitude in the circuit be a maximum? (b) When C has the value calculated in part (a), what is the amplitude of the voltage across the inductor?

31.31 • In an *L-R-C* series circuit, $R = 150\ \Omega$, $L = 0.750$ H, and $C = 0.0180\ \mu$F. The source has voltage amplitude $V = 150$ V and a frequency equal to the resonance frequency of the circuit. (a) What is the power factor? (b) What is the average power delivered by the source? (c) The capacitor is replaced by one with $C = 0.0360\ \mu$F and the source frequency is adjusted to the new resonance value. Then what is the average power delivered by the source?

31.32 • In an *L-R-C* series circuit, $R = 400\ \Omega$, $L = 0.350$ H, and $C = 0.0120\ \mu$F. (a) What is the resonance angular frequency of the circuit? (b) The capacitor can withstand a peak voltage of 550 V. If the voltage source operates at the resonance frequency, what maximum voltage amplitude can it have if the maximum capacitor voltage is not exceeded?

31.33 • A series circuit consists of an ac source of variable frequency, a 115-Ω resistor, a 1.25-μF capacitor, and a 4.50-mH inductor. Find the impedance of this circuit when the angular frequency of the ac source is adjusted to (a) the resonance angular frequency; (b) twice the resonance angular frequency; (c) half the resonance angular frequency.

31.34 •• In an *L-R-C* series circuit, $L = 0.280$ H and $C = 4.00\ \mu$F. The voltage amplitude of the source is 120 V. (a) What is the resonance angular frequency of the circuit? (b) When the source operates at the resonance angular frequency, the current amplitude in the circuit is 1.70 A. What is the resistance R of the resistor? (c) At the resonance angular frequency, what are the peak voltages across the inductor, the capacitor, and the resistor?

Section 31.6 Transformers

31.35 · **A Step-Down Transformer.** A transformer connected to a 120-V (rms) ac line is to supply 12.0 V (rms) to a portable electronic device. The load resistance in the secondary is 5.00 Ω. (a) What should the ratio of primary to secondary turns of the transformer be? (b) What rms current must the secondary supply? (c) What average power is delivered to the load? (d) What resistance connected directly across the 120-V line would draw the same power as the transformer? Show that this is equal to 5.00 Ω times the square of the ratio of primary to secondary turns.

31.36 · **A Step-Up Transformer.** A transformer connected to a 120-V (rms) ac line is to supply 13,000 V (rms) for a neon sign. To reduce shock hazard, a fuse is to be inserted in the primary circuit; the fuse is to blow when the rms current in the secondary circuit exceeds 8.50 mA. (a) What is the ratio of secondary to primary turns of the transformer? (b) What power must be supplied to the transformer when the rms secondary current is 8.50 mA? (c) What current rating should the fuse in the primary circuit have?

31.37 · **Off to Europe!** You plan to take your hair dryer to Europe, where the electrical outlets put out 240 V instead of the 120 V seen in the United States. The dryer puts out 1600 W at 120 V. (a) What could you do to operate your dryer via the 240-V line in Europe? (b) What current will your dryer draw from a European outlet? (c) What resistance will your dryer appear to have when operated at 240 V?

PROBLEMS

31.38 ·· Figure 31.12a shows the crossover network in a loudspeaker system. One branch consists of a capacitor C and a resistor R in series (the tweeter). This branch is in parallel with a second branch (the woofer) that consists of an inductor L and a resistor R in series. The same source voltage with angular frequency ω is applied across each parallel branch. (a) What is the impedance of the tweeter branch? (b) What is the impedance of the woofer branch? (c) Explain why the currents in the two branches are equal when the impedances of the branches are equal. (d) Derive an expression for the frequency f that corresponds to the crossover point in Fig. 31.12b.

31.39 · A coil has a resistance of 48.0 Ω. At a frequency of 80.0 Hz the voltage across the coil leads the current in it by 52.3°. Determine the inductance of the coil.

31.40 ·· Five infinite-impedance voltmeters, calibrated to read rms values, are connected as shown in Fig. P31.40. Let $R =$ 200 Ω, $L = 0.400$ H, $C = 6.00$ μF, and $V = 30.0$ V. What is the reading of each voltmeter if (a) $\omega = 200$ rad/s and (b) $\omega =$ 1000 rad/s?

Figure **P31.40**

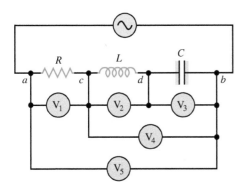

31.41 ·· CP A parallel-plate capacitor having square plates 4.50 cm on each side and 8.00 mm apart is placed in series with an ac source of angular frequency 650 rad/s and voltage amplitude 22.5 V, a 75.0-Ω resistor, and an ideal solenoid that is 9.00 cm long, has a circular cross section 0.500 cm in diameter, and carries 125 coils per centimeter. What is the resonance angular frequency of this circuit? (See Exercise 30.15.)

31.42 ·· CP A toroidal solenoid has 2900 closely wound turns, cross-sectional area 0.450 cm², mean radius 9.00 cm, and resistance $R = 2.80$ Ω. The variation of the magnetic field across the cross section of the solenoid can be neglected. What is the amplitude of the current in the solenoid if it is connected to an ac source that has voltage amplitude 24.0 V and frequency 365 Hz?

31.43 ·· An L-R-C series circuit has $C = 4.80$ μF, $L = 0.520$ H, and source voltage amplitude $V = 56.0$ V. The source is operated at the resonance frequency of the circuit. If the voltage across the capacitor has amplitude 80.0 V, what is the value of R for the resistor in the circuit?

31.44 · A large electromagnetic coil is connected to a 120-Hz ac source. The coil has resistance 400 Ω, and at this source frequency the coil has inductive reactance 250 Ω. (a) What is the inductance of the coil? (b) What must the rms voltage of the source be if the coil is to consume an average electrical power of 800 W?

31.45 ·· A series circuit has an impedance of 60.0 Ω and a power factor of 0.720 at 50.0 Hz. The source voltage lags the current. (a) What circuit element, an inductor or a capacitor, should be placed in series with the circuit to raise its power factor? (b) What size element will raise the power factor to unity?

31.46 ·· An L-R-C series circuit has $R = 300$ Ω. At the frequency of the source, the inductor has reactance $X_L = 900$ Ω and the capacitor has reactance $X_C = 500$ Ω. The amplitude of the voltage across the inductor is 450 V. (a) What is the amplitude of the voltage across the resistor? (b) What is the amplitude of the voltage across the capacitor? (c) What is the voltage amplitude of the source? (d) What is the rate at which the source is delivering electrical energy to the circuit?

31.47 ·· In an L-R-C series circuit, $R = 300$ Ω, $X_C = 300$ Ω, and $X_L = 500$ Ω. The average power consumed in the resistor is 60.0 W. (a) What is the power factor of the circuit? (b) What is the rms voltage of the source?

31.48 · A circuit consists of a resistor and a capacitor in series with an ac source that supplies an rms voltage of 240 V. At the frequency of the source the reactance of the capacitor is 50.0 Ω. The rms current in the circuit is 3.00 A. What is the average power supplied by the source?

31.49 · An L-R-C series circuit consists of a 50.0-Ω resistor, a 10.0-μF capacitor, a 3.50-mH inductor, and an ac voltage source of voltage amplitude 60.0 V operating at 1250 Hz. (a) Find the current amplitude and the voltage amplitudes across the inductor, the resistor, and the capacitor. Why can the voltage amplitudes add up to *more* than 60.0 V? (b) If the frequency is now doubled, but nothing else is changed, which of the quantities in part (a) will change? Find the new values for those that do change.

31.50 · At a frequency ω_1 the reactance of a certain capacitor equals that of a certain inductor. (a) If the frequency is changed to $\omega_2 = 2\omega_1$, what is the ratio of the reactance of the inductor to that of the capacitor? Which reactance is larger? (b) If the frequency is changed to $\omega_3 = \omega_1/3$, what is the ratio of the reactance of the inductor to that of the capacitor? Which reactance is larger? (c) If the capacitor and inductor are placed in series with a resistor of resistance R to form an L-R-C series circuit, what will be the resonance angular frequency of the circuit?

31.51 •• **A High-Pass Filter.** Figure **P31.51**
One application of L-R-C series circuits is to high-pass or low-pass filters, which filter out either the low- or high-frequency components of a signal. A high-pass filter is shown in Fig. P31.51, where the output voltage is taken across the L-R combination. (The L-R combination represents an inductive coil that also has resistance due to the large length of wire in the coil.) Derive an expression for V_{out}/V_s, the ratio of the output and source voltage amplitudes, as a function of the angular frequency ω of the source. Show that when ω is small, this ratio is proportional to ω and thus is small, and show that the ratio approaches unity in the limit of large frequency.

Figure **P31.51**

31.52 •• **A Low-Pass Filter.** Figure P31.52 shows a low-pass filter (see Problem 31.51); the output voltage is taken across the capacitor in an L-R-C series circuit. Derive an expression for V_{out}/V_s, the ratio of the output and source voltage amplitudes, as a function of the angular frequency ω of the source. Show that when ω is large, this ratio is proportional to ω^{-2} and thus is very small, and show that the ratio approaches unity in the limit of small frequency.

Figure **P31.52**

31.53 ••• An L-R-C series circuit is connected to an ac source of constant voltage amplitude V and variable angular frequency ω. (a) Show that the current amplitude, as a function of ω, is

$$I = \frac{V}{\sqrt{R^2 + (\omega L - 1/\omega C)^2}}$$

(b) Show that the average power dissipated in the resistor is

$$P = \frac{V^2 R/2}{R^2 + (\omega L - 1/\omega C)^2}$$

(c) Show that I and P are *both* maximum when $\omega = 1/\sqrt{LC}$, the resonance frequency of the circuit. (d) Graph P as a function of ω for $V = 100$ V, $R = 200 \; \Omega$, $L = 2.0$ H, and $C = 0.50 \; \mu$F. Compare to the light purple curve in Fig. 31.19. Discuss the behavior of I and P in the limits $\omega = 0$ and $\omega \to \infty$.

31.54 •• An L-R-C series circuit is connected to an ac source of constant voltage amplitude V and variable angular frequency ω. Using the results of Problem 31.53, find an expression for (a) the amplitude V_L of the voltage across the inductor as a function of ω and (b) the amplitude V_C of the voltage across the capacitor as a function of ω. (c) Graph V_L and V_C as functions of ω for $V = 100$ V, $R = 200 \; \Omega$, $L = 2.0$ H, and $C = 0.50 \; \mu$F. (d) Discuss the behavior of V_L and V_C in the limits $\omega = 0$ and $\omega \to \infty$. For what value of ω is $V_L = V_C$? What is the significance of this value of ω?

31.55 •• In an L-R-C series circuit the magnitude of the phase angle is $54.0°$, with the source voltage lagging the current. The reactance of the capacitor is $350 \; \Omega$, and the resistor resistance is $180 \; \Omega$. The average power delivered by the source is 140 W. Find

(a) the reactance of the inductor; (b) the rms current; (c) the rms voltage of the source.

31.56 •• **The L-R-C Parallel Circuit.** A resistor, inductor, and capacitor are connected in parallel to an ac source with voltage amplitude V and angular frequency ω. Let the source voltage be given by $v = V\cos\omega t$. (a) Show that the instantaneous voltages v_R, v_L, and v_C at any instant are each equal to v and that $i = i_R + i_L + i_C$, where i is the current through the source and i_R, i_L, and i_C are the currents through the resistor, the inductor, and the capacitor, respectively. (b) What are the phases of i_R, i_L, and i_C with respect to v? Use current phasors to represent i, i_R, i_L, and i_C. In a phasor diagram, show the phases of these four currents with respect to v. (c) Use the phasor diagram of part (b) to show that the current amplitude I for the current i through the source is given by $I = \sqrt{I_R^2 + (I_C - I_L)^2}$. (d) Show that the result of part (c) can be written as $I = V/Z$, with $1/Z = \sqrt{1/R^2 + (\omega C - 1/\omega L)^2}$.

31.57 •• **Parallel Resonance.** The impedance of an L-R-C parallel circuit was derived in Problem 31.56. (a) Show that at the resonance angular frequency $\omega_0 = 1/\sqrt{LC}$, $I_C = I_L$, and I is a *minimum*. (b) Since I is a minimum at resonance, is it correct to say that the power delivered to the resistor is also a minimum at $\omega = \omega_0$? Explain. (c) At resonance, what is the phase angle of the source current with respect to the source voltage? How does this compare to the phase angle for an L-R-C *series* circuit at resonance? (d) Draw the circuit diagram for an L-R-C parallel circuit. Arrange the circuit elements in your diagram so that the resistor is closest to the ac source. Justify the following statement: When the angular frequency of the source is $\omega = \omega_0$, there is *no* current flowing between (i) the part of the circuit that includes the source and the resistor and (ii) the part that includes the inductor and the capacitor, so you could cut the wires connecting these two parts of the circuit without affecting the currents. (e) Is the statement in part (d) still valid if we consider that any real inductor or capacitor also has some resistance of its own? Explain.

31.58 •• A 400-Ω resistor and a 6.00-μF capacitor are connected in parallel to an ac generator that supplies an rms voltage of 220 V at an angular frequency of 360 rad/s. Use the results of Problem 31.56. Note that since there is no inductor in the circuit, the $1/\omega L$ term is not present in the expression for Z. Find (a) the current amplitude in the resistor; (b) the current amplitude in the capacitor; (c) the phase angle of the source current with respect to the source voltage; (d) the amplitude of the current through the generator. (e) Does the source current lag or lead the source voltage?

31.59 •• An L-R-C parallel circuit is connected to an ac source of constant voltage amplitude V and variable angular frequency ω. (a) Using the results of Problem 31.56, find expressions for the amplitudes I_R, I_L, and I_C of the currents through the resistor, inductor, and capacitor as functions of ω. (b) Graph I_R, I_L, and I_C as functions of ω for $V = 100$ V, $R = 200 \; \Omega$, $L = 2.0$ H, and $C = 0.50 \; \mu$F. (c) Discuss the behavior of I_L and I_C in the limits $\omega = 0$ and $\omega \to \infty$. Explain why I_L and I_C behave as they do in these limits. (d) Calculate the resonance frequency (in Hz) of the circuit, and sketch the phasor diagram at the resonance frequency. (e) At the resonance frequency, what is the current amplitude through the source? (f) At the resonance frequency, what is the current amplitude through the resistor, through the inductor, and through the capacitor?

31.60 •• A 100-Ω resistor, a 0.100-μF capacitor, and a 0.300-H inductor are connected in parallel to a voltage source with amplitude 240 V. (a) What is the resonance angular frequency? (b) What is the maximum current through the source at the resonance frequency? (c) Find the maximum current in the resistor at resonance. (d) What is the maximum current in the inductor at resonance? (e) What is the maximum current in the branch containing the capacitor at resonance? (f) Find the maximum energy stored in the inductor and in the capacitor at resonance.

31.61 • You want to double the resonance angular frequency of an L-R-C series circuit by changing only the *pertinent* circuit elements all by the same factor. (a) Which ones should you change? (b) By what factor should you change them?

31.62 ••• An L-R-C series circuit consists of a 2.50-μF capacitor, a 5.00-mH inductor, and a 75.0-Ω resistor connected across an ac source of voltage amplitude 15.0 V having variable frequency. (a) Under what circumstances is the average power delivered to the circuit equal to $\frac{1}{2}V_{rms}I_{rms}$? (b) Under the conditions of part (a), what is the average power delivered to each circuit element and what is the maximum current through the capacitor?

31.63 •• In an L-R-C series circuit, the source has a voltage amplitude of 120 V, $R = 80.0\ \Omega$, and the reactance of the capacitor is 480 Ω. The voltage amplitude across the capacitor is 360 V. (a) What is the current amplitude in the circuit? (b) What is the impedance? (c) What two values can the reactance of the inductor have? (d) For which of the two values found in part (c) is the angular frequency less than the resonance angular frequency? Explain.

31.64 • An L-R-C series circuit has $R = 500\ \Omega$, $L = 2.00$ H, $C = 0.500\ \mu$F, and $V = 100$ V. (a) For $\omega = 800$ rad/s, calculate V_R, V_L, V_C, and ϕ. Using a single set of axes, graph v, v_R, v_L, and v_C as functions of time. Include two cycles of v on your graph. (b) Repeat part (a) for $\omega = 1000$ rad/s. (c) Repeat part (a) for $\omega = 1250$ rad/s.

31.65 •• **CALC** The current in a certain circuit varies with time as shown in Fig. P31.65. Find the average current and the rms current in terms of I_0.

Figure **P31.65**

31.66 •• **The Resonance Width.** Consider an L-R-C series circuit with a 1.80-H inductor, a 0.900-μF capacitor, and a 300-Ω resistor. The source has terminal rms voltage $V_{rms} = 60.0$ V and variable angular frequency ω. (a) What is the resonance angular frequency ω_0 of the circuit? (b) What is the rms current through the circuit at resonance, $I_{rms\text{-}0}$? (c) For what two values of the angular frequency, ω_1 and ω_2, is the rms current half the resonance value? (d) The quantity $|\omega_1 - \omega_2|$ defines the *resonance width*. Calculate $I_{rms\text{-}0}$ and the resonance width for $R = 300\ \Omega$, 30.0 Ω, and 3.00 Ω. Describe how your results compare to the discussion in Section 31.5.

31.67 •• An inductor, a capacitor, and a resistor are all connected in series across an ac source. If the resistance, inductance, and capacitance are all doubled, by what factor does each of the following quantities change? Indicate whether they increase or decrease: (a) the resonance angular frequency; (b) the inductive reactance; (c) the capacitive reactance. (d) Does the impedance double?

31.68 • A resistance R, capacitance C, and inductance L are connected in series to a voltage source with amplitude V and variable angular frequency ω. If $\omega = \omega_0$, the resonance angular frequency, find (a) the maximum current in the resistor; (b) the maximum voltage across the capacitor; (c) the maximum voltage across the inductor; (d) the maximum energy stored in the capacitor; (e) the maximum energy stored in the inductor. Give your answers in terms of R, C, L, and V.

31.69 • Repeat Problem 31.68 for the case $\omega = \omega_0/2$.

31.70 • Repeat Problem 31.68 for the case $\omega = 2\omega_0$.

31.71 • A transformer consists of 275 primary windings and 834 secondary windings. If the potential difference across the primary coil is 25.0 V, (a) what is the voltage across the secondary coil, and (b) what is the effective load resistance of the secondary coil if it is connected across a 125-Ω resistor?

31.72 •• An L-R-C series circuit draws 220 W from a 120-V (rms), 50.0-Hz ac line. The power factor is 0.560, and the source voltage leads the current. (a) What is the net resistance R of the circuit? (b) Find the capacitance of the series capacitor that will result in a power factor of unity when it is added to the original circuit. (c) What power will then be drawn from the supply line?

31.73 •• **CALC** In an L-R-C series circuit the current is given by $i = I \cos \omega t$. The voltage amplitudes for the resistor, inductor, and capacitor are V_R, V_L, and V_C. (a) Show that the instantaneous power into the resistor is $p_R = V_R I \cos^2 \omega t = \frac{1}{2}V_R I(1 + \cos 2\omega t)$. What does this expression give for the average power into the resistor? (b) Show that the instantaneous power into the inductor is $p_L = -V_L I \sin \omega t \cos \omega t = -\frac{1}{2}V_L I \sin 2\omega t$. What does this expression give for the average power into the inductor? (c) Show that the instantaneous power into the capacitor is $p_C = V_C I \sin \omega t \cos \omega t = \frac{1}{2}V_C I \sin 2\omega t$. What does this expression give for the average power into the capacitor? (d) The instantaneous power delivered by the source is shown in Section 31.4 to be $p = VI \cos \omega t (\cos \phi \cos \omega t - \sin \phi \sin \omega t)$. Show that $p_R + p_L + p_C$ equals p at each instant of time.

CHALLENGE PROBLEMS

31.74 ••• **CALC** (a) At what angular frequency is the voltage amplitude across the *resistor* in an L-R-C series circuit at maximum value? (b) At what angular frequency is the voltage amplitude across the *inductor* at maximum value? (c) At what angular frequency is the voltage amplitude across the *capacitor* at maximum value? (You may want to refer to the results of Problem 31.53.)

31.75 ••• **Complex Numbers in a Circuit.** The voltage across a circuit element in an ac circuit is not necessarily in phase with the current through that circuit element. Therefore the voltage amplitudes across the circuit elements in a branch in an ac circuit do not add algebraically. A method that is commonly employed to simplify the analysis of an ac circuit driven by a sinusoidal source is to represent the impedance Z as a *complex* number. The resistance R is taken to be the real part of the impedance, and the reactance $X = X_L - X_C$ is taken to be the imaginary part. Thus, for a branch containing a resistor, inductor, and capacitor in series, the complex impedance is $Z_{cpx} = R + iX$, where $i^2 = -1$. If the voltage amplitude across the branch is V_{cpx}, we define a *complex* current amplitude by $I_{cpx} = V_{cpx}/Z_{cpx}$. The *actual* current amplitude is the absolute value of the complex current amplitude; that is, $I = (I_{cpx}{}^* I_{cpx})^{1/2}$. The phase angle ϕ of the current with respect to the source voltage is given by $\tan \phi = \text{Im}(I_{cpx})/\text{Re}(I_{cpx})$. The voltage amplitudes $V_{R\text{-}cpx}$, $V_{L\text{-}cpx}$, and $V_{C\text{-}cpx}$ across the resistance, inductance, and capacitance, respectively, are found by multiplying I_{cpx} by R, iX_L, and $-iX_C$, respectively. From the complex representation for the voltage amplitudes, the voltage across a branch is just the algebraic sum of the voltages across each circuit element: $V_{cpx} = V_{R\text{-}cpx} + V_{L\text{-}cpx} + V_{C\text{-}cpx}$. The actual value of any current amplitude or voltage amplitude is the absolute value of the corresponding complex

Figure **P31.75**

$L = 0.500$ H

$V = 200$ V
$\omega = 1000$ rad/s

$C = 1.25\ \mu$F

$R = 400\ \Omega$

quantity. Consider the L-R-C series circuit shown in Fig. P31.75. The values of the circuit elements, the source voltage amplitude, and the source angular frequency are as shown. Use the phasor diagram techniques presented in Section 31.1 to solve for (a) the current amplitude and (b) the phase angle ϕ of the current with respect to the source voltage. (Note that this angle is the negative of the phase angle defined in Fig. 31.13.) Now analyze the same circuit using the complex-number approach. (c) Determine the complex impedance of the circuit, Z_{cpx}. Take the absolute value to obtain Z, the actual impedance of the circuit. (d) Take the voltage amplitude of the source, V_{cpx}, to be real, and find the complex current amplitude I_{cpx}. Find the actual current amplitude by taking the absolute value of I_{cpx}. (e) Find the phase angle ϕ of the current with respect to the source voltage by using the real and imaginary parts of I_{cpx}, as explained above. (f) Find the complex representations of the voltages across the resistance, the inductance, and the capacitance. (g) Adding the answers found in part (f), verify that the sum of these complex numbers is real and equal to 200 V, the voltage of the source.

Answers

Chapter Opening Question ?

Yes. In fact, the radio simultaneously detects transmissions at *all* frequencies. However, a radio is an L-R-C series circuit, and at any given time it is tuned to have a resonance at just one frequency. Hence the response of the radio to that frequency is much greater than its response to any other frequency, which is why you hear only one broadcasting station through the radio's speaker. (You can sometimes hear a second station if its frequency is sufficiently close to the tuned frequency.)

Test Your Understanding Questions

31.1 Answers: (a) D; (b) A; (c) B; (d) C For each phasor, the actual current is represented by the projection of that phasor onto the horizontal axis. The phasors all rotate counterclockwise around the origin with angular speed ω, so at the instant shown the projection of phasor A is positive but trending toward zero; the projection of phasor B is negative and becoming more negative; the projection of phasor C is negative but trending toward zero; and the projection of phasor D is positive and becoming more positive.

31.2 Answers: (a) (iii); (b) (ii); (c) (i) For a resistor, $V_R = IR$, so $I = V_R/R$. The voltage amplitude V_R and resistance R do not change with frequency, so the current amplitude I remains constant. For an inductor, $V_L = IX_L = I\omega L$, so $I = V_L/\omega L$. The voltage amplitude V_L and inductance L are constant, so the current amplitude I decreases as the frequency increases. For a capacitor, $V_C = IX_C = I/\omega C$, so $I = V_C\omega C$. The voltage amplitude V_C and capacitance C are constant, so the current amplitude I increases as the frequency increases.

31.3 Answer: (iv), (ii), (i), (iii) For the circuit in Example 31.4, $I = V/Z = (50 \text{ V})/(500 \text{ }\Omega) = 0.10$ A. If the capacitor and inductor are removed so that only the ac source and resistor remain, the circuit is like that shown in Fig. 31.7a; then $I = V/R = (50 \text{ V})/(300 \text{ }\Omega) = 0.17$ A. If the resistor and capacitor are removed so that only the ac source and inductor remain, the circuit is like that shown in Fig. 31.8a; then $I = V/X_L = (50 \text{ V})/(600 \text{ }\Omega) = 0.083$ A. Finally, if the resistor and inductor are removed so that only the ac source and capacitor remain, the circuit is like that shown in Fig. 31.9a; then $I = V/X_C = (50 \text{ V})/(200 \text{ }\Omega) = 0.25$ A.

31.4 Answers: (a) (v); (b) (iv) The energy cannot be extracted from the resistor, since energy is dissipated in a resistor and cannot be recovered. Instead, the energy must be extracted from either the inductor (which stores magnetic-field energy) or the capacitor (which stores electric-field energy). Positive power means that energy is being transferred from the ac source to the circuit, so *negative* power implies that energy is being transferred back into the source.

31.5 Answer: (ii) The capacitance C increases if the plate spacing is decreased (see Section 24.1). Hence the resonance frequency $f_0 = \omega_0/2\pi = 1/2\pi\sqrt{LC}$ decreases.

31.6 Answer: (ii), (iv), (i), (iii) From Eq. (31.35) the turns ratio is $N_2/N_1 = V_2/V_1$, so the number of turns in the secondary is $N_2 = N_1V_2/V_1$. Hence for the four cases we have (i) $N_2 = (1000)(6.0 \text{ V})/(120 \text{ V}) = 50$ turns; (ii) $N_2 = (1000)(240 \text{ V})/(120 \text{ V}) = 2000$ turns; (iii) $N_2 = (1000)(6.0 \text{ V})/(240 \text{ V}) = 25$ turns; and (iv) $N_2 = (1000)(120 \text{ V})/(240 \text{ V}) = 500$ turns. Note that (i), (iii), and (iv) are step-down transformers with fewer turns in the secondary than in the primary, while (ii) is a step-up transformer with more turns in the secondary than in the primary.

Bridging Problem

Answers: (a) 8.35×10^4 rad/s and 3.19×10^5 rad/s
(b) At 8.35×10^4 rad/s: $V_{source} = 49.5$ V,
$I = 0.132$ A, $V_R = 16.5$ V, $V_L = 16.5$ V,
$V_C = 63.2$ V.
At 3.19×10^5 rad/s: $V_{source} = 49.5$ V,
$I = 0.132$ A, $V_R = 16.5$ V, $V_L = 63.2$ V,
$V_C = 16.5$ V.

ELECTROMAGNETIC WAVES

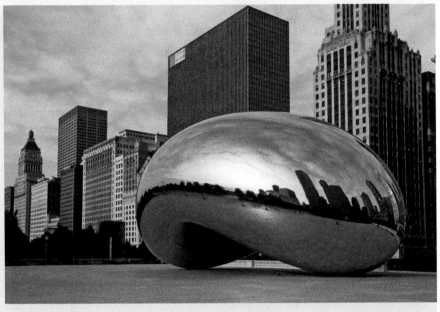

? Metal objects reflect not only visible light but also radio waves. What aspect of metals makes them so reflective?

LEARNING GOALS

By studying this chapter, you will learn:

• Why there are both electric and magnetic fields in a light wave.

• How the speed of light is related to the fundamental constants of electricity and magnetism.

• How to describe the propagation of a sinusoidal electromagnetic wave.

• What determines the amount of power carried by an electromagnetic wave.

• How to describe standing electromagnetic waves.

What is light? This question has been asked by humans for centuries, but there was no answer until electricity and magnetism were unified into *electromagnetism*, as described by Maxwell's equations. These equations show that a time-varying magnetic field acts as a source of electric field and that a time-varying electric field acts as a source of magnetic field. These $\vec{E}$ and $\vec{B}$ fields can sustain each other, forming an *electromagnetic wave* that propagates through space. Visible light emitted by the glowing filament of a light bulb is one example of an electromagnetic wave; other kinds of electromagnetic waves are produced by TV and radio stations, x-ray machines, and radioactive nuclei.

In this chapter we'll use Maxwell's equations as the theoretical basis for understanding electromagnetic waves. We'll find that these waves carry both energy and momentum. In sinusoidal electromagnetic waves, the $\vec{E}$ and $\vec{B}$ fields are sinusoidal functions of time and position, with a definite frequency and wavelength. Visible light, radio, x rays, and other types of electromagnetic waves differ only in their frequency and wavelength. Our study of optics in the following chapters will be based in part on the electromagnetic nature of light.

Unlike waves on a string or sound waves in a fluid, electromagnetic waves do not require a material medium; the light that you see coming from the stars at night has traveled without difficulty across tens or hundreds of light-years of (nearly) empty space. Nonetheless, electromagnetic waves and mechanical waves have much in common and are described in much the same language. Before reading further in this chapter, you should review the properties of mechanical waves as discussed in Chapters 15 and 16.

32.1 Maxwell's Equations and Electromagnetic Waves

In the last several chapters we studied various aspects of electric and magnetic fields. We learned that when the fields don't vary with time, such as an electric field produced by charges at rest or the magnetic field of a steady current, we can analyze the electric and magnetic fields independently without considering interactions between them. But when the fields vary with time, they are no longer independent. Faraday's law (see Section 29.2) tells us that a time-varying magnetic field acts as a source of electric field, as shown by induced emfs in inductors and transformers. Ampere's law, including the displacement current discovered by Maxwell (see Section 29.7), shows that a time-varying electric field acts as a source of magnetic field. This mutual interaction between the two fields is summarized in Maxwell's equations, presented in Section 29.7.

Thus, when *either* an electric or a magnetic field is changing with time, a field of the other kind is induced in adjacent regions of space. We are led (as Maxwell was) to consider the possibility of an electromagnetic disturbance, consisting of time-varying electric and magnetic fields, that can propagate through space from one region to another, even when there is no matter in the intervening region. Such a disturbance, if it exists, will have the properties of a *wave,* and an appropriate term is **electromagnetic wave.**

Such waves do exist; radio and television transmission, light, x rays, and many other kinds of radiation are examples of electromagnetic waves. Our goal in this chapter is to see how such waves are explained by the principles of electromagnetism that we have studied thus far and to examine the properties of these waves.

Electricity, Magnetism, and Light

As often happens in the development of science, the theoretical understanding of electromagnetic waves evolved along a considerably more devious path than the one just outlined. In the early days of electromagnetic theory (the early 19th century), two different units of electric charge were used: one for electrostatics and the other for magnetic phenomena involving currents. In the system of units used at that time, these two units of charge had different physical dimensions. Their *ratio* had units of velocity, and measurements showed that the ratio had a numerical value that was precisely equal to the speed of light, 3.00×10^8 m/s. At the time, physicists regarded this as an extraordinary coincidence and had no idea how to explain it.

In searching to understand this result, Maxwell (Fig. 32.1) proved in 1865 that an electromagnetic disturbance should propagate in free space with a speed equal to that of light and hence that light waves were likely to be electromagnetic in nature. At the same time, he discovered that the basic principles of electromagnetism can be expressed in terms of the four equations that we now call **Maxwell's equations,** which we discussed in Section 29.7. These four equations are (1) Gauss's law for electric fields; (2) Gauss's law for magnetic fields, showing the absence of magnetic monopoles; (3) Ampere's law, including displacement current; and (4) Faraday's law:

$$\oint \vec{E} \cdot d\vec{A} = \frac{Q_{\text{encl}}}{\epsilon_0} \qquad \text{(Gauss's law)} \tag{29.18}$$

$$\oint \vec{B} \cdot d\vec{A} = 0 \qquad \text{(Gauss's law for magnetism)} \tag{29.19}$$

$$\oint \vec{B} \cdot d\vec{l} = \mu_0 \left(i_C + \epsilon_0 \frac{d\Phi_E}{dt} \right)_{\text{encl}} \qquad \text{(Ampere's law)} \tag{29.20}$$

$$\oint \vec{E} \cdot d\vec{l} = -\frac{d\Phi_B}{dt} \qquad \text{(Faraday's law)} \tag{29.21}$$

32.1 James Clerk Maxwell (1831–1879) was the first person to truly understand the fundamental nature of light. He also made major contributions to thermodynamics, optics, astronomy, and color photography. Albert Einstein described Maxwell's accomplishments as "the most profound and the most fruitful that physics has experienced since the time of Newton."

These equations apply to electric and magnetic fields *in vacuum*. If a material is present, the permittivity ϵ_0 and permeability μ_0 of free space are replaced by the permittivity ϵ and permeability μ of the material. If the values of ϵ and μ are different at different points in the regions of integration, then ϵ and μ have to be transferred to the left sides of Eqs. (29.18) and (29.20), respectively, and placed inside the integrals. The ϵ in Eq. (29.20) also has to be included in the integral that gives $d\Phi_E/dt$.

According to Maxwell's equations, a point charge at rest produces a static $\vec{E}$ field but no $\vec{B}$ field; a point charge moving with a constant velocity (see Section 28.1) produces both $\vec{E}$ and $\vec{B}$ fields. Maxwell's equations can also be used to show that in order for a point charge to produce electromagnetic waves, the charge must *accelerate*. In fact, it's a general result of Maxwell's equations that *every* accelerated charge radiates electromagnetic energy (Fig. 32.2).

Generating Electromagnetic Radiation

One way in which a point charge can be made to emit electromagnetic waves is by making it oscillate in simple harmonic motion, so that it has an acceleration at almost every instant (the exception is when the charge is passing through its equilibrium position). Figure 32.3 shows some of the electric field lines produced by such an oscillating point charge. Field lines are *not* material objects, but you may nonetheless find it helpful to think of them as behaving somewhat like strings that extend from the point charge off to infinity. Oscillating the charge up and down makes waves that propagate outward from the charge along these "strings." Note that the charge does not emit waves equally in all directions; the waves are strongest at 90° to the axis of motion of the charge, while there are *no* waves along this axis. This is just what the "string" picture would lead you to conclude. There is also a *magnetic* disturbance that spreads outward from the charge; this is not shown in Fig. 32.3. Because the electric and magnetic disturbances spread or radiate away from the source, the name **electromagnetic radiation** is used interchangeably with the phrase "electromagnetic waves."

Electromagnetic waves with macroscopic wavelengths were first produced in the laboratory in 1887 by the German physicist Heinrich Hertz. As a source of waves, he used charges oscillating in *L-C* circuits of the sort discussed in Section 30.5; he detected the resulting electromagnetic waves with other circuits tuned to the same frequency. Hertz also produced electromagnetic *standing waves* and measured the distance between adjacent nodes (one half-wavelength) to determine the wavelength. Knowing the resonant frequency of his circuits, he then found the speed of the waves from the wavelength–frequency relationship $v = \lambda f$. He established that their speed was the same as that of light; this verified Maxwell's theoretical prediction directly. The SI unit of frequency is named in honor of Hertz: One hertz (1 Hz) equals one cycle per second.

32.2 (Top) Every mobile phone, wireless modem, or radio transmitter emits signals in the form of electromagnetic waves that are made by accelerating charges. (Bottom) Power lines carry a strong alternating current, which means that a substantial amount of charge is accelerating back and forth and generating electromagnetic waves. These waves can produce a buzzing sound from your car radio when you drive near the lines.

32.3 Electric field lines of a point charge oscillating in simple harmonic motion, seen at five instants during an oscillation period T. The charge's trajectory is in the plane of the drawings. At $t = 0$ the point charge is at its maximum upward displacement. The arrow shows one "kink" in the lines of $\vec{E}$ as it propagates outward from the point charge. The magnetic field (not shown) comprises circles that lie in planes perpendicular to these figures and concentric with the axis of oscillation.

(a) $t = 0$

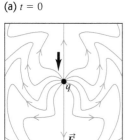

$\vec{E}$

(b) $t = T/4$

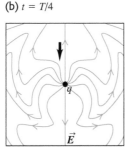

$\vec{E}$

(c) $t = T/2$

$\vec{E}$

(d) $t = 3T/4$

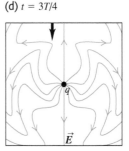

$\vec{E}$

(e) $t = T$

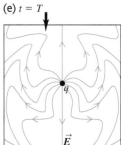

$\vec{E}$

The modern value of the speed of light, which we denote by the symbol c, is 299,792,458 m/s. (Recall from Section 1.3 that this value is the basis of our standard of length: One meter is defined to be the distance that light travels in 1/299,792,458 second.) For our purposes, $c = 3.00 \times 10^8$ m/s is sufficiently accurate.

The possible use of electromagnetic waves for long-distance communication does not seem to have occurred to Hertz. It was left to Marconi and others to make radio communication a familiar household experience. In a radio *transmitter*, electric charges are made to oscillate along the length of the conducting antenna, producing oscillating field disturbances like those shown in Fig. 32.3. Since many charges oscillate together in the antenna, the disturbances are much stronger than those of a single oscillating charge and can be detected at a much greater distance. In a radio *receiver* the antenna is also a conductor; the fields of the wave emanating from a distant transmitter exert forces on free charges within the receiver antenna, producing an oscillating current that is detected and amplified by the receiver circuitry.

For the remainder of this chapter our concern will be with electromagnetic waves themselves, not with the rather complex problem of how they are produced.

The Electromagnetic Spectrum

The **electromagnetic spectrum** encompasses electromagnetic waves of all frequencies and wavelengths. Figure 32.4 shows approximate wavelength and frequency ranges for the most commonly encountered portion of the spectrum. Despite vast differences in their uses and means of production, these are all electromagnetic waves with the same propagation speed (in vacuum) $c = 299,792,458$ m/s. Electromagnetic waves may differ in frequency f and wavelength λ, but the relationship $c = \lambda f$ in vacuum holds for each.

We can detect only a very small segment of this spectrum directly through our sense of sight. We call this range **visible light.** Its wavelengths range from about 380 to 750 nm (380 to 750×10^{-9} m), with corresponding frequencies from about 790 to 400 THz (7.9 to 4.0×10^{14} Hz). Different parts of the visible spectrum evoke in humans the sensations of different colors. Table 32.1 gives the approximate wavelengths for colors in the visible spectrum.

Ordinary white light includes all visible wavelengths. However, by using special sources or filters, we can select a narrow band of wavelengths within a range of a few nm. Such light is approximately *monochromatic* (single-color) light. Absolutely monochromatic light with only a single wavelength is an unattainable idealization. When we use the expression "monochromatic light with $\lambda = 550$ nm" with reference to a laboratory experiment, we really mean a small band

Table 32.1 Wavelengths of Visible Light

380–450 nm	Violet
450–495 nm	Blue
495–570 nm	Green
570–590 nm	Yellow
590–620 nm	Orange
620–750 nm	Red

32.4 The electromagnetic spectrum. The frequencies and wavelengths found in nature extend over such a wide range that we have to use a logarithmic scale to show all important bands. The boundaries between bands are somewhat arbitrary.

of wavelengths *around* 550 nm. Light from a *laser* is much more nearly monochromatic than is light obtainable in any other way.

Invisible forms of electromagnetic radiation are no less important than visible light. Our system of global communication, for example, depends on radio waves: AM radio uses waves with frequencies from 5.4×10^5 Hz to 1.6×10^6 Hz, while FM radio broadcasts are at frequencies from 8.8×10^7 Hz to 1.08×10^8 Hz. (Television broadcasts use frequencies that bracket the FM band.) Microwaves are also used for communication (for example, by cellular phones and wireless networks) and for weather radar (at frequencies near 3×10^9 Hz). Many cameras have a device that emits a beam of infrared radiation; by analyzing the properties of the infrared radiation reflected from the subject, the camera determines the distance to the subject and automatically adjusts the focus. X rays are able to penetrate through flesh, which makes them invaluable in dentistry and medicine. Gamma rays, the shortest-wavelength type of electromagnetic radiation, are used in medicine to destroy cancer cells.

Test Your Understanding of Section 32.1 (a) Is it possible to have a purely electric wave propagate through empty space—-that is, a wave made up of an electric field but no magnetic field? (b) What about a purely magnetic wave, with a magnetic field but no electric field?

Application Ultraviolet Vision
Many insects and birds can see ultraviolet wavelengths that humans cannot. As an example, the left-hand photo shows how black-eyed Susans (genus *Rudbeckia*) look to us. The right-hand photo (in false color), taken with an ultraviolet-sensitive camera, shows how these same flowers appear to the bees that pollinate them. Note the prominent central spot that is invisible to humans. Similarly, many birds with ultraviolet vision—including budgies, parrots, and peacocks—have ultraviolet patterns on their bodies that make them even more vivid to each other than they appear to us.

32.2 Plane Electromagnetic Waves and the Speed of Light

We are now ready to develop the basic ideas of electromagnetic waves and their relationship to the principles of electromagnetism. Our procedure will be to postulate a simple field configuration that has wavelike behavior. We'll assume an electric field $\vec{E}$ that has only a *y*-component and a magnetic field $\vec{B}$ with only a *z*-component, and we'll assume that both fields move together in the +*x*-direction with a speed *c* that is initially unknown. (As we go along, it will become clear why we choose $\vec{E}$ and $\vec{B}$ to be perpendicular to the direction of propagation as well as to each other.) Then we will test whether these fields are physically possible by asking whether they are consistent with Maxwell's equations, particularly Ampere's law and Faraday's law. We'll find that the answer is yes, provided that *c* has a particular value. We'll also show that the *wave equation,* which we encountered during our study of mechanical waves in Chapter 15, can be derived from Maxwell's equations.

A Simple Plane Electromagnetic Wave

Using an *xyz*-coordinate system (Fig. 32.5), we imagine that all space is divided into two regions by a plane perpendicular to the *x*-axis (parallel to the *yz*-plane). At every point to the left of this plane there are a uniform electric field $\vec{E}$ in the +*y*-direction and a uniform magnetic field $\vec{B}$ in the +*z*-direction, as shown. Furthermore, we suppose that the boundary plane, which we call the *wave front,* moves to the right in the +*x*-direction with a constant speed *c*, the value of which we'll leave undetermined for now. Thus the $\vec{E}$ and $\vec{B}$ fields travel to the right into previously field-free regions with a definite speed. This is a rudimentary electromagnetic wave. A wave such as this, in which at any instant the fields are uniform over any plane perpendicular to the direction of propagation, is called a **plane wave.** In the case shown in Fig. 32.5, the fields are zero for planes to the right of the wave front and have the same values on all planes to the left of the wave front; later we will consider more complex plane waves.

We won't concern ourselves with the problem of actually *producing* such a field configuration. Instead, we simply ask whether it is consistent with the laws of electromagnetism—-that is, with Maxwell's equations. We'll consider each of these four equations in turn.

32.5 An electromagnetic wave front. The plane representing the wave front moves to the right (in the positive *x*-direction) with speed *c*.

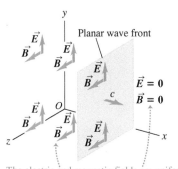

The electric and magnetic fields are uniform behind the advancing wave front and zero in front of it.

32.6 Gaussian surface for a transverse plane electromagnetic wave.

The electric field is the same on the top and bottom sides of the Gaussian surface, so the total electric flux through the surface is zero.

The magnetic field is the same on the left and right sides of the Gaussian surface, so the total magnetic flux through the surface is zero.

32.7 (a) Applying Faraday's law to a plane wave. (b) In a time dt, the magnetic flux through the rectangle in the xy-plane increases by an amount $d\Phi_B$. This increase equals the flux through the shaded rectangle with area $ac\,dt$; that is, $d\Phi_B = Bac\,dt$. Thus $d\Phi_B/dt = Bac$.

(a) In time dt, the wave front moves a distance $c\,dt$ in the $+x$-direction.

(b) Side view of situation in **(a)**

Let us first verify that our wave satisfies Maxwell's first and second equations—that is, Gauss's laws for electric and magnetic fields. To do this, we take as our Gaussian surface a rectangular box with sides parallel to the xy, xz, and yz coordinate planes (Fig. 32.6). The box encloses no electric charge. The total electric flux and magnetic flux through the box are both zero, even if part of the box is in the region where $E = B = 0$. This would *not* be the case if $\vec{E}$ or $\vec{B}$ had an x-component, parallel to the direction of propagation; if the wave front were inside the box, there would be flux through the left-hand side of the box (at $x = 0$) but not the right-hand side (at $x > 0$). Thus to satisfy Maxwell's first and second equations, the electric and magnetic fields must be perpendicular to the direction of propagation; that is, the wave must be **transverse.**

The next of Maxwell's equations to be considered is Faraday's law:

$$\oint \vec{E} \cdot d\vec{l} = -\frac{d\Phi_B}{dt} \qquad (32.1)$$

To test whether our wave satisfies Faraday's law, we apply this law to a rectangle $efgh$ that is parallel to the xy-plane (Fig. 32.7a). As shown in Fig. 32.7b, a cross section in the xy-plane, this rectangle has height a and width Δx. At the time shown, the wave front has progressed partway through the rectangle, and $\vec{E}$ is zero along the side ef. In applying Faraday's law we take the vector area $d\vec{A}$ of rectangle $efgh$ to be in the $+z$-direction. With this choice the right-hand rule requires that we integrate $\vec{E} \cdot d\vec{l}$ *counterclockwise* around the rectangle. At every point on side ef, $\vec{E}$ is zero. At every point on sides fg and he, $\vec{E}$ is either zero or perpendicular to $d\vec{l}$. Only side gh contributes to the integral. On this side, $\vec{E}$ and $d\vec{l}$ are opposite, and we obtain

$$\oint \vec{E} \cdot d\vec{l} = -Ea \qquad (32.2)$$

Hence, the left-hand side of Eq. (32.1) is nonzero.

To satisfy Faraday's law, Eq. (32.1), there must be a component of $\vec{B}$ in the z-direction (perpendicular to $\vec{E}$) so that there can be a nonzero magnetic flux Φ_B through the rectangle $efgh$ and a nonzero derivative $d\Phi_B/dt$. Indeed, in our wave, $\vec{B}$ has *only* a z-component. We have assumed that this component is in the *positive* z-direction; let's see whether this assumption is consistent with Faraday's law. During a time interval dt the wave front moves a distance $c\,dt$ to the right in Fig. 32.7b, sweeping out an area $ac\,dt$ of the rectangle $efgh$. During this interval the magnetic flux Φ_B through the rectangle $efgh$ increases by $d\Phi_B = B(ac\,dt)$, so the rate of change of magnetic flux is

$$\frac{d\Phi_B}{dt} = Bac \qquad (32.3)$$

Now we substitute Eqs. (32.2) and (32.3) into Faraday's law, Eq. (32.1); we get

$$-Ea = -Bac$$

$$E = cB \qquad \text{(electromagnetic wave in vacuum)} \qquad (32.4)$$

This shows that our wave is consistent with Faraday's law only if the wave speed c and the magnitudes of the perpendicular vectors $\vec{E}$ and $\vec{B}$ are related as in Eq. (32.4). Note that if we had assumed that $\vec{B}$ was in the *negative* z-direction, there would have been an additional minus sign in Eq. (32.4); since E, c, and B are all positive magnitudes, no solution would then have been possible. Furthermore, any component of $\vec{B}$ in the y-direction (parallel to $\vec{E}$) would not contribute to the changing magnetic flux Φ_B through the rectangle $efgh$ (which is parallel to the xy-plane) and so would not be part of the wave.

Finally, we carry out a similar calculation using Ampere's law, the remaining member of Maxwell's equations. There is no conduction current $(i_C = 0)$, so Ampere's law is

$$\oint \vec{B} \cdot d\vec{l} = \mu_0 \epsilon_0 \frac{d\Phi_E}{dt} \qquad (32.5)$$

To check whether our wave is consistent with Ampere's law, we move our rectangle so that it lies in the xz-plane, as shown in Fig. 32.8, and we again look at the situation at a time when the wave front has traveled partway through the rectangle. We take the vector area $d\vec{A}$ in the $+y$-direction, and so the right-hand rule requires that we integrate $\vec{B} \cdot d\vec{l}$ counterclockwise around the rectangle. The $\vec{B}$ field is zero at every point along side ef, and at each point on sides fg and he it is either zero or perpendicular to $d\vec{l}$. Only side gh, where $\vec{B}$ and $d\vec{l}$ are parallel, contributes to the integral, and we find

$$\oint \vec{B} \cdot d\vec{l} = Ba \qquad (32.6)$$

Hence, the left-hand side of Ampere's law, Eq. (32.5), is nonzero; the right-hand side must be nonzero as well. Thus $\vec{E}$ must have a y-component (perpendicular to $\vec{B}$) so that the electric flux Φ_E through the rectangle and the time derivative $d\Phi_E/dt$ can be nonzero. We come to the same conclusion that we inferred from Faraday's law: In an electromagnetic wave, $\vec{E}$ and $\vec{B}$ must be mutually perpendicular.

In a time interval dt the electric flux Φ_E through the rectangle increases by $d\Phi_E = E(ac\,dt)$. Since we chose $d\vec{A}$ to be in the $+y$-direction, this flux change is positive; the rate of change of electric field is

$$\frac{d\Phi_E}{dt} = Eac \qquad (32.7)$$

Substituting Eqs. (32.6) and (32.7) into Ampere's law, Eq. (32.5), we find

$$Ba = \epsilon_0 \mu_0 Eac$$

$$B = \epsilon_0 \mu_0 cE \qquad \text{(electromagnetic wave in vacuum)} \qquad (32.8)$$

Thus our assumed wave obeys Ampere's law only if B, c, and E are related as in Eq. (32.8).

Our electromagnetic wave must obey *both* Ampere's law and Faraday's law, so Eqs. (32.4) and (32.8) must both be satisfied. This can happen only if $\epsilon_0 \mu_0 c = 1/c$, or

$$c = \frac{1}{\sqrt{\epsilon_0 \mu_0}} \qquad \text{(speed of electromagnetic waves in vacuum)} \qquad (32.9)$$

Inserting the numerical values of these quantities, we find

$$c = \frac{1}{\sqrt{(8.85 \times 10^{-12} \text{ C}^2/\text{N} \cdot \text{m}^2)(4\pi \times 10^{-7} \text{ N/A}^2)}}$$

$$= 3.00 \times 10^8 \text{ m/s}$$

Our assumed wave is consistent with all of Maxwell's equations, provided that the wave front moves with the speed given above, which you should recognize as the speed of light! Note that the *exact* value of c is defined to be 299,792,458 m/s; the modern value of ϵ_0 is defined to agree with this when used in Eq. (32.9) (see Section 21.3).

32.8 (a) Applying Ampere's law to a plane wave. (Compare to Fig. 32.7a.) (b) In a time dt, the electric flux through the rectangle in the xz-plane increases by an amount $d\Phi_E$. This increase equals the flux through the shaded rectangle with area $ac\,dt$; that is, $d\Phi_E = Eac\,dt$. Thus $d\Phi_E/dt = Eac$.

(a) In time dt, the wave front moves a distance $c\,dt$ in the $+x$-direction.

(b) Top view of situation in (a)

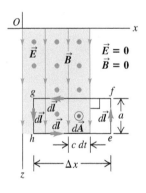

32.9 A right-hand rule for electromagnetic waves relates the directions of $\vec{E}$ and $\vec{B}$ and the direction of propagation.

Right-hand rule for an electromagnetic wave:

① Point the thumb of your right hand in the wave's direction of propagation.

② Imagine rotating the $\vec{E}$-field vector 90° in the sense your fingers curl.

That is the direction of the $\vec{B}$ field.

Direction of propagation = direction of $\vec{E} \times \vec{B}$.

Key Properties of Electromagnetic Waves

We chose a simple wave for our study in order to avoid mathematical complications, but this special case illustrates several important features of *all* electromagnetic waves:

1. The wave is *transverse;* both $\vec{E}$ and $\vec{B}$ are perpendicular to the direction of propagation of the wave. The electric and magnetic fields are also perpendicular to each other. The direction of propagation is the direction of the vector product $\vec{E} \times \vec{B}$ (Fig. 32.9).
2. There is a definite ratio between the magnitudes of $\vec{E}$ and $\vec{B}$: $E = cB$.
3. The wave travels in vacuum with a definite and unchanging speed.
4. Unlike mechanical waves, which need the oscillating particles of a medium such as water or air to transmit a wave, electromagnetic waves require no medium.

We can generalize this discussion to a more realistic situation. Suppose we have several wave fronts in the form of parallel planes perpendicular to the x-axis, all of which are moving to the right with speed c. Suppose that the $\vec{E}$ and $\vec{B}$ fields are the same at all points within a single region between two planes, but that the fields differ from region to region. The overall wave is a plane wave, but one in which the fields vary in steps along the x-axis. Such a wave could be constructed by superposing several of the simple step waves we have just discussed (shown in Fig. 32.5). This is possible because the $\vec{E}$ and $\vec{B}$ fields obey the superposition principle in waves just as in static situations: When two waves are superposed, the total $\vec{E}$ field at each point is the vector sum of the $\vec{E}$ fields of the individual waves, and similarly for the total $\vec{B}$ field.

We can extend the above development to show that a wave with fields that vary in steps is also consistent with Ampere's and Faraday's laws, provided that the wave fronts all move with the speed c given by Eq. (32.9). In the limit that we make the individual steps infinitesimally small, we have a wave in which the $\vec{E}$ and $\vec{B}$ fields at any instant vary *continuously* along the x-axis. The entire field pattern moves to the right with speed c. In Section 32.3 we will consider waves in which $\vec{E}$ and $\vec{B}$ are *sinusoidal* functions of x and t. Because at each point the magnitudes of $\vec{E}$ and $\vec{B}$ are related by $E = cB$, the periodic variations of the two fields in any periodic traveling wave must be *in phase*.

Electromagnetic waves have the property of **polarization.** In the above discussion the choice of the y-direction for $\vec{E}$ was arbitrary. We could just as well have specified the z-axis for $\vec{E}$; then $\vec{B}$ would have been in the $-y$-direction. A wave in which $\vec{E}$ is always parallel to a certain axis is said to be **linearly polarized** along that axis. More generally, *any* wave traveling in the x-direction can be represented as a superposition of waves linearly polarized in the y- and z-directions. We will study polarization in greater detail in Chapter 33.

Derivation of the Electromagnetic Wave Equation

Here is an alternative derivation of Eq. (32.9) for the speed of electromagnetic waves. It is more mathematical than our other treatment, but it includes a derivation of the wave equation for electromagnetic waves. This part of the section can be omitted without loss of continuity in the chapter.

During our discussion of mechanical waves in Section 15.3, we showed that a function $y(x, t)$ that represents the displacement of any point in a mechanical wave traveling along the x-axis must satisfy a differential equation, Eq. (15.12):

$$\frac{\partial^2 y(x, t)}{\partial x^2} = \frac{1}{v^2} \frac{\partial^2 y(x, t)}{\partial t^2} \tag{32.10}$$

This equation is called the **wave equation,** and v is the speed of propagation of the wave.

To derive the corresponding equation for an electromagnetic wave, we again consider a plane wave. That is, we assume that at each instant, E_y and B_z are uniform over any plane perpendicular to the x-axis, the direction of propagation. But now we let E_y and B_z vary continuously as we go along the x-axis; then each is a function of x and t. We consider the values of E_y and B_z on two planes perpendicular to the x-axis, one at x and one at $x + \Delta x$.

Following the same procedure as previously, we apply Faraday's law to a rectangle lying parallel to the xy-plane, as in Fig. 32.10. This figure is similar to Fig. 32.7. Let the left end gh of the rectangle be at position x, and let the right end ef be at position $(x + \Delta x)$. At time t, the values of E_y on these two sides are $E_y(x, t)$ and $E_y(x + \Delta x, t)$, respectively. When we apply Faraday's law to this rectangle, we find that instead of $\oint \vec{E} \cdot d\vec{l} = -Ea$ as before, we have

$$\oint \vec{E} \cdot d\vec{l} = -E_y(x, t)a + E_y(x + \Delta x, t)a$$

$$= a[E_y(x + \Delta x, t) - E_y(x, t)] \qquad (32.11)$$

To find the magnetic flux Φ_B through this rectangle, we assume that Δx is small enough that B_z is nearly uniform over the rectangle. In that case, $\Phi_B = B_z(x, t)A = B_z(x, t)a\,\Delta x$, and

$$\frac{d\Phi_B}{dt} = \frac{\partial B_z(x, t)}{\partial t} a\,\Delta x$$

We use partial-derivative notation because B_z is a function of both x and t. When we substitute this expression and Eq. (32.11) into Faraday's law, Eq. (32.1), we get

$$a[E_y(x + \Delta x, t) - E_y(x, t)] = -\frac{\partial B_z}{\partial t} a\,\Delta x$$

$$\frac{E_y(x + \Delta x, t) - E_y(x, t)}{\Delta x} = -\frac{\partial B_z}{\partial t}$$

Finally, imagine shrinking the rectangle down to a sliver so that Δx approaches zero. When we take the limit of this equation as $\Delta x \to 0$, we get

$$\frac{\partial E_y(x, t)}{\partial x} = -\frac{\partial B_z(x, t)}{\partial t} \qquad (32.12)$$

This equation shows that if there is a time-varying component B_z of magnetic field, there must also be a component E_y of electric field that varies with x, and conversely. We put this relationship on the shelf for now; we'll return to it soon.

Next we apply Ampere's law to the rectangle shown in Fig. 32.11. The line integral $\oint \vec{B} \cdot d\vec{l}$ becomes

$$\oint \vec{B} \cdot d\vec{l} = -B_z(x + \Delta x, t)a + B_z(x, t)a \qquad (32.13)$$

Again assuming that the rectangle is narrow, we approximate the electric flux Φ_E through it as $\Phi_E = E_y(x, t)A = E_y(x, t)a\,\Delta x$. The rate of change of Φ_E, which we need for Ampere's law, is then

$$\frac{d\Phi_E}{dt} = \frac{\partial E_y(x, t)}{\partial t} a\,\Delta x$$

Now we substitute this expression and Eq. (32.13) into Ampere's law, Eq. (32.5):

$$-B_z(x + \Delta x, t)a + B_z(x, t)a = \epsilon_0 \mu_0 \frac{\partial E_y(x, t)}{\partial t} a\,\Delta x$$

Again we divide both sides by $a\,\Delta x$ and take the limit as $\Delta x \to 0$. We find

$$-\frac{\partial B_z(x, t)}{\partial x} = \epsilon_0 \mu_0 \frac{\partial E_y(x, t)}{\partial t} \qquad (32.14)$$

32.10 Faraday's law applied to a rectangle with height a and width Δx parallel to the xy-plane.

(a)

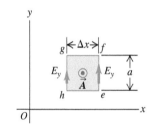

(b) Side view of the situation in (a)

32.11 Ampere's law applied to a rectangle with height a and width Δx parallel to the xz-plane.

(a)

(b) Top view of the situation in (a)

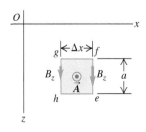

Now comes the final step. We take the partial derivatives with respect to x of both sides of Eq. (32.12), and we take the partial derivatives with respect to t of both sides of Eq. (32.14). The results are

$$-\frac{\partial^2 E_y(x, t)}{\partial x^2} = \frac{\partial^2 B_z(x, t)}{\partial x \partial t}$$

$$-\frac{\partial^2 B_z(x, t)}{\partial x \partial t} = \epsilon_0 \mu_0 \frac{\partial^2 E_y(x, t)}{\partial t^2}$$

Combining these two equations to eliminate B_z, we finally find

$$\frac{\partial^2 E_y(x, t)}{\partial x^2} = \epsilon_0 \mu_0 \frac{\partial^2 E_y(x, t)}{\partial t^2} \qquad \begin{array}{l}\text{(electromagnetic wave}\\ \text{equation in vacuum)}\end{array} \qquad \text{(32.15)}$$

This expression has the same form as the general wave equation, Eq. (32.10). Because the electric field E_y must satisfy this equation, it behaves as a wave with a pattern that travels through space with a definite speed. Furthermore, comparison of Eqs. (32.15) and (32.10) shows that the wave speed v is given by

$$\frac{1}{v^2} = \epsilon_0 \mu_0 \qquad \text{or} \qquad v = \frac{1}{\sqrt{\epsilon_0 \mu_0}}$$

This agrees with Eq. (32.9) for the speed c of electromagnetic waves.

We can show that B_z also must satisfy the same wave equation as E_y, Eq. (32.15). To prove this, we take the partial derivative of Eq. (32.12) with respect to t and the partial derivative of Eq. (32.14) with respect to x and combine the results. We leave this derivation for you to carry out.

Test Your Understanding of Section 32.2   For each of the following electromagnetic waves, state the direction of the magnetic field. (a) The wave is propagating in the positive z-direction, and $\vec{E}$ is in the positive x-direction; (b) the wave is propagating in the positive y-direction, and $\vec{E}$ is in the negative z-direction; (c) the wave is propagating in the negative x-direction, and $\vec{E}$ is in the positive z-direction.

32.3 Sinusoidal Electromagnetic Waves

Sinusoidal electromagnetic waves are directly analogous to sinusoidal transverse mechanical waves on a stretched string, which we studied in Section 15.3. In a sinusoidal electromagnetic wave, $\vec{E}$ and $\vec{B}$ at any point in space are sinusoidal functions of time, and at any instant of time the *spatial* variation of the fields is also sinusoidal.

Some sinusoidal electromagnetic waves are *plane waves;* they share with the waves described in Section 32.2 the property that at any instant the fields are uniform over any plane perpendicular to the direction of propagation. The entire pattern travels in the direction of propagation with speed c. The directions of $\vec{E}$ and $\vec{B}$ are perpendicular to the direction of propagation (and to each other), so the wave is *transverse*. Electromagnetic waves produced by an oscillating point charge, shown in Fig. 32.3, are an example of sinusoidal waves that are *not* plane waves. But if we restrict our observations to a relatively small region of space at a sufficiently great distance from the source, even these waves are well approximated by plane waves (Fig. 32.12). In the same way, the curved surface of the (nearly) spherical earth appears flat to us because of our small size relative to the earth's radius. In this section we'll restrict our discussion to plane waves.

The frequency f, the wavelength λ, and the speed of propagation c of any periodic wave are related by the usual wavelength–frequency relationship $c = \lambda f$. If the frequency f is 10^8 Hz (100 MHz), typical of commercial FM radio broadcasts, the wavelength is

$$\lambda = \frac{3 \times 10^8 \text{ m/s}}{10^8 \text{ Hz}} = 3 \text{ m}$$

Figure 32.4 shows the inverse proportionality between wavelength and frequency.

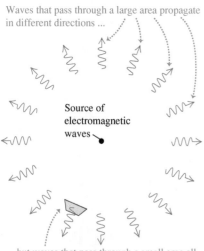

32.12 Waves passing through a small area at a sufficiently great distance from a source can be treated as plane waves.

Waves that pass through a large area propagate in different directions ...

Source of electromagnetic waves

... but waves that pass through a small area all propagate in nearly the same direction, so we can treat them as plane waves.

Fields of a Sinusoidal Wave

Figure 32.13 shows a linearly polarized sinusoidal electromagnetic wave traveling in the $+x$-direction. The $\vec{E}$ and $\vec{B}$ vectors are shown for only a few points on the positive x-axis. Note that the electric and magnetic fields oscillate in phase: $\vec{E}$ is maximum where $\vec{B}$ is maximum and $\vec{E}$ is zero where $\vec{B}$ is zero. Note also that where $\vec{E}$ is in the $+y$-direction, $\vec{B}$ is in the $+z$-direction; where $\vec{E}$ is in the $-y$-direction, $\vec{B}$ is in the $-z$-direction. At all points the vector product $\vec{E} \times \vec{B}$ is in the direction in which the wave is propagating (the $+x$-direction). We mentioned this in Section 32.2 in the list of characteristics of electromagnetic waves.

CAUTION In a plane wave, $\vec{E}$ and $\vec{B}$ are everywhere Figure 32.13 may give you the erroneous impression that the electric and magnetic fields exist only along the x-axis. In fact, in a sinusoidal plane wave there are electric and magnetic fields at *all* points in space. Imagine a plane perpendicular to the x-axis (that is, parallel to the yz-plane) at a particular point, at a particular time; the fields have the same values at all points in that plane. The values are different on different planes.

We can describe electromagnetic waves by means of *wave functions,* just as we did in Section 15.3 for waves on a string. One form of the wave function for a transverse wave traveling in the $+x$-direction along a stretched string is Eq. (15.7):

$$y(x, t) = A \cos(kx - \omega t)$$

where $y(x, t)$ is the transverse displacement from its equilibrium position at time t of a point with coordinate x on the string. The quantity A is the maximum displacement, or *amplitude,* of the wave; ω is its *angular frequency,* equal to 2π times the frequency f; and k is the *wave number,* equal to $2\pi/\lambda$, where λ is the wavelength.

Let $E_y(x, t)$ and $B_z(x, t)$ represent the instantaneous values of the y-component of $\vec{E}$ and the z-component of $\vec{B}$, respectively, in Fig. 32.13, and let E_{max} and B_{max} represent the maximum values, or *amplitudes,* of these fields. The wave functions for the wave are then

$$E_y(x, t) = E_{max} \cos(kx - \omega t) \qquad B_z(x, t) = B_{max} \cos(kx - \omega t) \qquad \text{(32.16)}$$

(sinusoidal electromagnetic plane wave, propagating in $+x$-direction)

We can also write the wave functions in vector form:

$$\vec{E}(x, t) = \hat{\jmath} E_{max} \cos(kx - \omega t)$$
$$\vec{B}(x, t) = \hat{k} B_{max} \cos(kx - \omega t) \qquad \text{(32.17)}$$

CAUTION The symbol k has two meanings Note the two different k's: the unit vector $\hat{k}$ in the z-direction and the wave number k. Don't get these confused!

The sine curves in Fig. 32.13 represent instantaneous values of the electric and magnetic fields as functions of x at time $t = 0$—that is, $\vec{E}(x, t = 0)$ and $\vec{B}(x, t = 0)$. As time goes by, the wave travels to the right with speed c. Equations (32.16) and (32.17) show that at any point the sinusoidal oscillations of $\vec{E}$ and $\vec{B}$ are *in phase.* From Eq. (32.4) the amplitudes must be related by

$$E_{max} = cB_{max} \qquad \text{(electromagnetic wave in vacuum)} \qquad \text{(32.18)}$$

These amplitude and phase relationships are also required for $E(x, t)$ and $B(x, t)$ to satisfy Eqs. (32.12) and (32.14), which came from Faraday's law and Ampere's law, respectively. Can you verify this statement? (See Problem 32.38.)

32.13 Representation of the electric and magnetic fields as functions of x for a linearly polarized sinusoidal plane electromagnetic wave. One wavelength of the wave is shown at time $t = 0$. The fields are shown only for points along the x-axis.

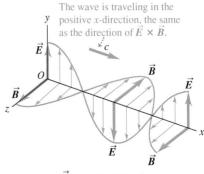

$\vec{E}$: y-component only
$\vec{B}$: z-component only

PhET: Radio Waves & Electromagnetic Fields
ActivPhysics 10.1: Properties of Mechanical Waves

32.14 Representation of one wavelength of a linearly polarized sinusoidal plane electromagnetic wave traveling in the negative x-direction at $t = 0$. The fields are shown only for points along the x-axis. (Compare with Fig. 32.13.)

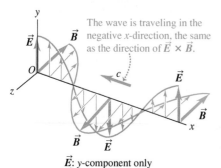

The wave is traveling in the negative x-direction, the same as the direction of $\vec{E} \times \vec{B}$.

$\vec{E}$: y-component only
$\vec{B}$: z-component only

Figure 32.14 shows the electric and magnetic fields of a wave traveling in the *negative x*-direction. At points where $\vec{E}$ is in the positive y-direction, $\vec{B}$ is in the *negative z*-direction; where $\vec{E}$ is in the negative y-direction, $\vec{B}$ is in the *positive z*-direction. The wave functions for this wave are

$$E_y(x, t) = E_{max}\cos(kx + \omega t) \quad B_z(x, t) = -B_{max}\cos(kx + \omega t) \quad (32.19)$$

(sinusoidal electromagnetic plane wave, propagating in $-x$-direction)

As with the wave traveling in the $+x$-direction, at any point the sinusoidal oscillations of the $\vec{E}$ and $\vec{B}$ fields are *in phase,* and the vector product $\vec{E} \times \vec{B}$ points in the direction of propagation.

The sinusoidal waves shown in Figs. 32.13 and 32.14 are both linearly polarized in the y-direction; the $\vec{E}$ field is always parallel to the y-axis. Example 32.1 concerns a wave that is linearly polarized in the z-direction.

Problem-Solving Strategy 32.1   Electromagnetic Waves

IDENTIFY *the relevant concepts:* Many of the same ideas that apply to mechanical waves apply to electromagnetic waves. One difference is that electromagnetic waves are described by two quantities (in this case, electric field $\vec{E}$ and magnetic field $\vec{B}$), rather than by a single quantity, such as the displacement of a string.

SET UP *the problem* using the following steps:
1. Draw a diagram showing the direction of wave propagation and the directions of $\vec{E}$ and $\vec{B}$.
2. Identify the target variables.

EXECUTE *the solution* as follows:
1. Review the treatment of sinusoidal mechanical waves in Chapters 15 and 16, and particularly the four problem-solving strategies suggested there.
2. Keep in mind the basic relationships for periodic waves: $v = \lambda f$ and $\omega = vk$. For electromagnetic waves in vacuum,

$v = c$. Distinguish between ordinary frequency f, usually expressed in hertz, and angular frequency $\omega = 2\pi f$, expressed in rad/s. Remember that the wave number is $k = 2\pi/\lambda$.

3. Concentrate on basic relationships, such as those between $\vec{E}$ and $\vec{B}$ (magnitude, direction, and relative phase), how the wave speed is determined, and the transverse nature of the waves.

EVALUATE *your answer:* Check that your result is reasonable. For electromagnetic waves in vacuum, the magnitude of the magnetic field in teslas is much smaller (by a factor of 3.00×10^8) than the magnitude of the electric field in volts per meter. If your answer suggests otherwise, you probably made an error using the relationship $E = cB$. (We'll see later in this section that the relationship between E and B is different for electromagnetic waves in a material medium.)

Example 32.1   Electric and magnetic fields of a laser beam

A carbon dioxide laser emits a sinusoidal electromagnetic wave that travels in vacuum in the negative x-direction. The wavelength is 10.6 μm (in the infrared; see Fig. 32.4) and the $\vec{E}$ field is parallel to the z-axis, with $E_{max} = 1.5$ MV/m. Write vector equations for $\vec{E}$ and $\vec{B}$ as functions of time and position.

SOLUTION

IDENTIFY and SET UP: Equations (32.19) describe a wave traveling in the negative x-direction with $\vec{E}$ along the y-axis—that is, a wave that is linearly polarized along the y-axis. By contrast, the wave in this example is linearly polarized along the z-axis. At points where $\vec{E}$ is in the positive z-direction, $\vec{B}$ must be in the positive y-direction for the vector product $\vec{E} \times \vec{B}$ to be in the negative x-direction (the direction of propagation). Figure 32.15 shows a wave that satisfies these requirements.

EXECUTE: A possible pair of wave functions that describe the wave shown in Fig. 32.15 are

32.15 Our sketch for this problem.

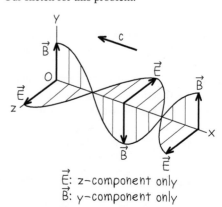

$\vec{E}$: z-component only
$\vec{B}$: y-component only

$$\vec{E}(x, t) = \hat{k}E_{max}\cos(kx + \omega t)$$
$$\vec{B}(x, t) = \hat{j}B_{max}\cos(kx + \omega t)$$

The plus sign in the arguments of the cosine functions indicates that the wave is propagating in the negative x-direction, as it should. Faraday's law requires that $E_{max} = cB_{max}$ [Eq. (32.18)], so

$$B_{max} = \frac{E_{max}}{c} = \frac{1.5 \times 10^6 \text{ V/m}}{3.0 \times 10^8 \text{ m/s}} = 5.0 \times 10^{-3} \text{ T}$$

To check unit consistency, note that $1 \text{ V} = 1 \text{ Wb/s}$ and $1 \text{ Wb/m}^2 = 1 \text{ T}$.

We have $\lambda = 10.6 \times 10^{-6}$ m, so the wave number and angular frequency are

$$k = \frac{2\pi}{\lambda} = \frac{2\pi \text{ rad}}{10.6 \times 10^{-6} \text{ m}} = 5.93 \times 10^5 \text{ rad/m}$$

$$\omega = ck = (3.00 \times 10^8 \text{ m/s})(5.93 \times 10^5 \text{ rad/m})$$
$$= 1.78 \times 10^{14} \text{ rad/s}$$

Substituting these values into the above wave functions, we get

$$\vec{E}(x, t) = \hat{k}(1.5 \times 10^6 \text{ V/m})$$
$$\times \cos[(5.93 \times 10^5 \text{ rad/m})x + (1.78 \times 10^{14} \text{ rad/s})t]$$

$$\vec{B}(x, t) = \hat{j}(5.0 \times 10^{-3} \text{ T})$$
$$\times \cos[(5.93 \times 10^5 \text{ rad/m})x + (1.78 \times 10^{14} \text{ rad/s})t]$$

EVALUATE: As we expect, the magnitude B_{max} in teslas is much smaller than the magnitude E_{max} in volts per meter. To check the directions of $\vec{E}$ and $\vec{B}$, note that $\vec{E} \times \vec{B}$ is in the direction of $\hat{k} \times \hat{j} = -\hat{i}$. This is as it should be for a wave that propagates in the negative x-direction.

Our expressions for $\vec{E}(x, t)$ and $\vec{B}(x, t)$ are not the only possible solutions. We could always add a phase angle ϕ to the arguments of the cosine function, so that $kx + \omega t$ would become $kx + \omega t + \phi$. To determine the value of ϕ we would need to know $\vec{E}$ and $\vec{B}$ either as functions of x at a given time t or as functions of t at a given coordinate x. However, the statement of the problem doesn't include this information.

Electromagnetic Waves in Matter

So far, our discussion of electromagnetic waves has been restricted to waves in *vacuum*. But electromagnetic waves can also travel in *matter;* think of light traveling through air, water, or glass. In this subsection we extend our analysis to electromagnetic waves in nonconducting materials—that is, *dielectrics.*

In a dielectric the wave speed is not the same as in vacuum, and we denote it by v instead of c. Faraday's law is unaltered, but in Eq. (32.4), derived from Faraday's law, the speed c is replaced by v. In Ampere's law the displacement current is given not by $\epsilon_0 \, d\Phi_E/dt$, where Φ_E is the flux of $\vec{E}$ through a surface, but by $\epsilon \, d\Phi_E/dt = K\epsilon_0 \, d\Phi_E/dt$, where K is the dielectric constant and ϵ is the permittivity of the dielectric. (We introduced these quantities in Section 24.4.) Also, the constant μ_0 in Ampere's law must be replaced by $\mu = K_m\mu_0$, where K_m is the relative permeability of the dielectric and μ is its permeability (see Section 28.8). Hence Eqs. (32.4) and (32.8) are replaced by

$$E = vB \qquad \text{and} \qquad B = \epsilon\mu vE \qquad (32.20)$$

Following the same procedure as for waves in vacuum, we find that the wave speed v is

$$v = \frac{1}{\sqrt{\epsilon\mu}} = \frac{1}{\sqrt{KK_m}}\frac{1}{\sqrt{\epsilon_0\mu_0}} = \frac{c}{\sqrt{KK_m}} \qquad \begin{array}{l}\text{(speed of electromagnetic} \\ \text{waves in a dielectric)}\end{array} \qquad (32.21)$$

For most dielectrics the relative permeability K_m is very nearly equal to unity (except for insulating ferromagnetic materials). When $K_m \cong 1$,

$$v = \frac{1}{\sqrt{K}}\frac{1}{\sqrt{\epsilon_0\mu_0}} = \frac{c}{\sqrt{K}}$$

Because K is always greater than unity, the speed v of electromagnetic waves in a dielectric is always *less* than the speed c in vacuum by a factor of $1/\sqrt{K}$ (Fig. 32.16). The ratio of the speed c in vacuum to the speed v in a material is known in optics as the **index of refraction** n of the material. When $K_m \cong 1$,

$$\frac{c}{v} = n = \sqrt{KK_m} \cong \sqrt{K} \qquad (32.22)$$

Usually, we can't use the values of K in Table 24.1 in this equation because those values are measured using *constant* electric fields. When the fields oscillate rapidly,

32.16 The dielectric constant K of water is about 1.8 for visible light, so the speed of visible light in water is slower than in vacuum by a factor of $1/\sqrt{K} = 1/\sqrt{1.8} = 0.75$.

there is usually not time for the reorientation of electric dipoles that occurs with steady fields. Values of K with rapidly varying fields are usually much *smaller* than the values in the table. For example, K for water is 80.4 for steady fields but only about 1.8 in the frequency range of visible light. Thus the dielectric "constant" K is actually a function of frequency (the *dielectric function*).

Example 32.2 Electromagnetic waves in different materials

(a) Visiting a jewelry store one evening, you hold a diamond up to the light of a sodium-vapor street lamp. The heated sodium vapor emits yellow light with a frequency of 5.09×10^{14} Hz. Find the wavelength in vacuum and the wave speed and wavelength in diamond, for which $K = 5.84$ and $K_m = 1.00$ at this frequency. (b) A 90.0-MHz radio wave (in the FM radio band) passes from vacuum into an insulating ferrite (a ferromagnetic material used in computer cables to suppress radio interference). Find the wavelength in vacuum and the wave speed and wavelength in the ferrite, for which $K = 10.0$ and $K_m = 1000$ at this frequency.

SOLUTION

IDENTIFY and SET UP: In each case we find the wavelength in vacuum using $c = \lambda f$. To use the corresponding equation $v = \lambda f$ to find the wavelength in a material medium, we find the speed v of electromagnetic waves in the medium using Eq. (32.21), which relates v to the values of dielectric constant K and relative permeability K_m for the medium.

EXECUTE: (a) The wavelength in vacuum of the sodium light is

$$\lambda_{\text{vacuum}} = \frac{c}{f} = \frac{3.00 \times 10^8 \text{ m/s}}{5.09 \times 10^{14} \text{ Hz}} = 5.89 \times 10^{-7} \text{ m} = 589 \text{ nm}$$

The wave speed and wavelength in diamond are

$$v_{\text{diamond}} = \frac{c}{\sqrt{KK_m}} = \frac{3.00 \times 10^8 \text{ m/s}}{\sqrt{(5.84)(1.00)}} = 1.24 \times 10^8 \text{ m/s}$$

$$\lambda_{\text{diamond}} = \frac{v_{\text{diamond}}}{f} = \frac{1.24 \times 10^8 \text{ m/s}}{5.09 \times 10^{14} \text{ Hz}}$$
$$= 2.44 \times 10^{-7} \text{ m} = 244 \text{ nm}$$

(b) Following the same steps as in part (a), we find

$$\lambda_{\text{vacuum}} = \frac{c}{f} = \frac{3.00 \times 10^8 \text{ m/s}}{90.0 \times 10^6 \text{ Hz}} = 3.33 \text{ m}$$

$$v_{\text{ferrite}} = \frac{c}{\sqrt{KK_m}} = \frac{3.00 \times 10^8 \text{ m/s}}{\sqrt{(10.0)(1000)}} = 3.00 \times 10^6 \text{ m/s}$$

$$\lambda_{\text{ferrite}} = \frac{v_{\text{ferrite}}}{f} = \frac{3.00 \times 10^6 \text{ m/s}}{90.0 \times 10^6 \text{ Hz}}$$
$$= 3.33 \times 10^{-2} \text{ m} = 3.33 \text{ cm}$$

EVALUATE: The speed of light in transparent materials is typically between $0.2c$ and c; our result in part (a) shows that $v_{\text{diamond}} = 0.414c$. As our results in part (b) show, the speed of electromagnetic waves in dense materials like ferrite (for which $v_{\text{ferrite}} = 0.010c$) can be *far* slower than in vacuum.

Test Your Understanding of Section 32.3 The first of Eqs. (32.17) gives the electric field for a plane wave as measured at points along the x-axis. For this plane wave, how does the electric field at points *off* the x-axis differ from the expression in Eqs. (32.17)? (i) The amplitude is different; (ii) the phase is different; (iii) both the amplitude and phase are different; (iv) none of these.

32.4 Energy and Momentum in Electromagnetic Waves

It is a familiar fact that energy is associated with electromagnetic waves; think of the energy in the sun's radiation. Microwave ovens, radio transmitters, and lasers for eye surgery all make use of the energy that these waves carry. To understand how to utilize this energy, it's helpful to derive detailed relationships for the energy in an electromagnetic wave.

We begin with the expressions derived in Sections 24.3 and 30.3 for the **energy densities** in electric and magnetic fields; we suggest you review those derivations now. Equations (24.11) and (30.10) show that in a region of empty space where $\vec{E}$ and $\vec{B}$ fields are present, the total energy density u is given by

$$u = \tfrac{1}{2}\epsilon_0 E^2 + \frac{1}{2\mu_0}B^2 \tag{32.23}$$

where ϵ_0 and μ_0 are, respectively, the permittivity and permeability of free space. For electromagnetic waves in vacuum, the magnitudes E and B are related by

$$B = \frac{E}{c} = \sqrt{\epsilon_0\mu_0}E \qquad (32.24)$$

Combining Eqs. (32.23) and (32.24), we can also express the energy density u in a simple electromagnetic wave in vacuum as

$$u = \tfrac{1}{2}\epsilon_0 E^2 + \frac{1}{2\mu_0}(\sqrt{\epsilon_0\mu_0}E)^2 = \epsilon_0 E^2 \qquad (32.25)$$

This shows that in vacuum, the energy density associated with the $\vec{E}$ field in our simple wave is equal to the energy density of the $\vec{B}$ field. In general, the electric-field magnitude E is a function of position and time, as for the sinusoidal wave described by Eqs. (32.16); thus the energy density u of an electromagnetic wave, given by Eq. (32.25), also depends in general on position and time.

Electromagnetic Energy Flow and the Poynting Vector

Electromagnetic waves such as those we have described are *traveling* waves that transport energy from one region to another. We can describe this energy transfer in terms of energy transferred *per unit time per unit cross-sectional area,* or *power per unit area,* for an area perpendicular to the direction of wave travel.

To see how the energy flow is related to the fields, consider a stationary plane, perpendicular to the x-axis, that coincides with the wave front at a certain time. In a time dt after this, the wave front moves a distance $dx = c\,dt$ to the right of the plane. Considering an area A on this stationary plane (Fig. 32.17), we note that the energy in the space to the right of this area must have passed through the area to reach the new location. The volume dV of the relevant region is the base area A times the length $c\,dt$, and the energy dU in this region is the energy density u times this volume:

$$dU = u\,dV = (\epsilon_0 E^2)(Ac\,dt)$$

This energy passes through the area A in time dt. The energy flow per unit time per unit area, which we will call S, is

$$S = \frac{1}{A}\frac{dU}{dt} = \epsilon_0 c E^2 \qquad \text{(in vacuum)} \qquad (32.26)$$

Using Eqs. (32.4) and (32.9), we can derive the alternative forms

$$S = \frac{\epsilon_0}{\sqrt{\epsilon_0\mu_0}}E^2 = \sqrt{\frac{\epsilon_0}{\mu_0}}E^2 = \frac{EB}{\mu_0} \qquad \text{(in vacuum)} \qquad (32.27)$$

We leave the derivation of Eq. (32.27) from Eq. (32.26) as an exercise for you. The units of S are energy per unit time per unit area, or power per unit area. The SI unit of S is 1 J/s·m² or 1 W/m².

We can define a *vector* quantity that describes both the magnitude and direction of the energy flow rate:

$$\vec{S} = \frac{1}{\mu_0}\vec{E} \times \vec{B} \qquad \text{(Poynting vector in vacuum)} \qquad (32.28)$$

The vector $\vec{S}$ is called the **Poynting vector;** it was introduced by the British physicist John Poynting (1852–1914). Its direction is in the direction of propagation of the wave (Fig. 32.18). Since $\vec{E}$ and $\vec{B}$ are perpendicular, the magnitude of $\vec{S}$ is $S = EB/\mu_0$; from Eqs. (32.26) and (32.27) this is the energy flow per unit area and per unit time through a cross-sectional area perpendicular to the propagation direction. The total energy flow per unit time (power, P) out of any closed surface is the integral of $\vec{S}$ over the surface:

$$P = \oint \vec{S}\cdot d\vec{A}$$

32.17 A wave front at a time dt after it passes through the stationary plane with area A.

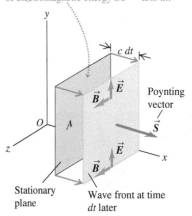

At time dt, the volume between the stationary plane and the wave front contains an amount of electromagnetic energy $dU = uAc\,dt$.

32.18 These rooftop solar panels are tilted to be face-on to the sun—that is, face-on to the Poynting vector of electromagnetic waves from the sun, so that the panels can absorb the maximum amount of wave energy.

For the sinusoidal waves studied in Section 32.3, as well as for other more complex waves, the electric and magnetic fields at any point vary with time, so the Poynting vector at any point is also a function of time. Because the frequencies of typical electromagnetic waves are very high, the time variation of the Poynting vector is so rapid that it's most appropriate to look at its *average* value. The magnitude of the average value of $\vec{S}$ at a point is called the **intensity** of the radiation at that point. The SI unit of intensity is the same as for S, 1 W/m² (watt per square meter).

Let's work out the intensity of the sinusoidal wave described by Eqs. (32.17). We first substitute $\vec{E}$ and $\vec{B}$ into Eq. (32.28):

$$\vec{S}(x, t) = \frac{1}{\mu_0}\vec{E}(x, t) \times \vec{B}(x, t)$$

$$= \frac{1}{\mu_0}[\hat{j}E_{max}\cos(kx - \omega t)] \times [\hat{k}B_{max}\cos(kx - \omega t)]$$

The vector product of the unit vectors is $\hat{j} \times \hat{k} = \hat{i}$ and $\cos^2(kx - \omega t)$ is never negative, so $\vec{S}(x, t)$ always points in the positive x-direction (the direction of wave propagation). The x-component of the Poynting vector is

$$S_x(x, t) = \frac{E_{max}B_{max}}{\mu_0}\cos^2(kx - \omega t) = \frac{E_{max}B_{max}}{2\mu_0}[1 + \cos 2(kx - \omega t)]$$

The time average value of $\cos 2(kx - \omega t)$ is zero because at any point, it is positive during one half-cycle and negative during the other half. So the average value of the Poynting vector over a full cycle is $\vec{S}_{av} = \hat{i}S_{av}$, where

$$S_{av} = \frac{E_{max}B_{max}}{2\mu_0}$$

That is, the magnitude of the average value of $\vec{S}$ for a sinusoidal wave (the intensity I of the wave) is $\frac{1}{2}$ the maximum value. By using the relationships $E_{max} = B_{max}c$ and $\epsilon_0\mu_0 = 1/c^2$, we can express the intensity in several equivalent forms:

$$I = S_{av} = \frac{E_{max}B_{max}}{2\mu_0} = \frac{E_{max}^2}{2\mu_0 c}$$

$$= \frac{1}{2}\sqrt{\frac{\epsilon_0}{\mu_0}}E_{max}^2 = \frac{1}{2}\epsilon_0 c E_{max}^2$$

(intensity of a sinusoidal wave in vacuum)   (32.29)

We invite you to verify that these expressions are all equivalent.

For a wave traveling in the $-x$-direction, represented by Eqs. (32.19), the Poynting vector is in the $-x$-direction at every point, but its magnitude is the same as for a wave traveling in the $+x$-direction. Verifying these statements is left to you (see Exercise 32.24).

CAUTION   **Poynting vector vs. intensity** At any point x, the magnitude of the Poynting vector varies with time. Hence, the *instantaneous* rate at which electromagnetic energy in a sinusoidal plane wave arrives at a surface is not constant. This may seem to contradict everyday experience; the light from the sun, a light bulb, or the laser in a grocery-store scanner appears steady and unvarying in strength. In fact the Poynting vector from these sources *does* vary in time, but the variation isn't noticeable because the oscillation frequency is so high (around 5×10^{14} Hz for visible light). All that you sense is the *average* rate at which energy reaches your eye, which is why we commonly use intensity (the average value of S) to describe the strength of electromagnetic radiation. ▮

Throughout this discussion we have considered only electromagnetic waves propagating in vacuum. If the waves are traveling in a dielectric medium, however,

Application Laser Surgery

Lasers are used widely in medicine as ultra-precise, bloodless "scalpels." They can reach and remove tumors with minimal damage to neighboring healthy tissues, as in the brain surgery shown here. The power output of the laser is typically below 40 W, less than that of a typical light bulb. However, this power is concentrated into a spot from 0.1 to 2.0 mm in diameter, so the intensity of the light (equal to the average value of the Poynting vector) can be as high as 5×10^9 W/m².

the expressions for energy density [Eq. (32.23)], the Poynting vector [Eq. (32.28)], and the intensity of a sinusoidal wave [Eq. (32.29)] must be modified. It turns out that the required modifications are quite simple: Just replace ϵ_0 with the permittivity ϵ of the dielectric, replace μ_0 with the permeability μ of the dielectric, and replace c with the speed v of electromagnetic waves in the dielectric. Remarkably, the energy densities in the $\vec{E}$ and $\vec{B}$ fields are equal even in a dielectric.

Video Tutor Demo

Example 32.3 **Energy in a nonsinusoidal wave**

For the nonsinusoidal wave described in Section 32.2, suppose that $E = 100$ V/m $= 100$ N/C. Find the value of B, the energy density u, and the rate of energy flow per unit area S.

SOLUTION

IDENTIFY and SET UP: In this wave $\vec{E}$ and $\vec{B}$ are uniform behind the wave front (and zero ahead of it). Hence the target variables B, u, and S must also be uniform behind the wave front. Given the magnitude E, we use Eq. (32.4) to find B, Eq. (32.25) to find u, and Eq. (32.27) to find S. (We cannot use Eq. (32.29), which applies to sinusoidal waves only.)

EXECUTE: From Eq. (32.4),

$$B = \frac{E}{c} = \frac{100 \text{ V/m}}{3.00 \times 10^8 \text{ m/s}} = 3.33 \times 10^{-7} \text{ T}$$

From Eq. (32.25),

$$u = \epsilon_0 E^2 = (8.85 \times 10^{-12} \text{ C}^2/\text{N} \cdot \text{m}^2)(100 \text{ N/C})^2$$
$$= 8.85 \times 10^{-8} \text{ N/m}^2 = 8.85 \times 10^{-8} \text{ J/m}^3$$

The magnitude of the Poynting vector is

$$S = \frac{EB}{\mu_0} = \frac{(100 \text{ V/m})(3.33 \times 10^{-7} \text{ T})}{4\pi \times 10^{-7} \text{ T} \cdot \text{m/A}}$$
$$= 26.5 \text{ V} \cdot \text{A/m}^2 = 26.5 \text{ W/m}^2$$

EVALUATE: We can check our result for S by using Eq. (32.26):

$$S = \epsilon_0 c E^2 = (8.85 \times 10^{-12} \text{ C}^2/\text{N} \cdot \text{m}^2)(3.00 \times 10^8 \text{ m/s})$$
$$\times (100 \text{ N/C})^2 = 26.5 \text{ W/m}^2$$

Since $\vec{E}$ and $\vec{B}$ have the same values at all points behind the wave front, u and S likewise have the same value everywhere behind the wave front. In front of the wave front, $\vec{E} = 0$ and $\vec{B} = 0$, and so $u = 0$ and $S = 0$; where there are no fields, there is no field energy.

Example 32.4 **Energy in a sinusoidal wave**

A radio station on the earth's surface emits a sinusoidal wave with average total power 50 kW (Fig. 32.19). Assuming that the transmitter radiates equally in all directions above the ground (which is unlikely in real situations), find the electric-field and magnetic-field amplitudes E_{max} and B_{max} detected by a satellite 100 km from the antenna.

SOLUTION

IDENTIFY and SET UP: We are given the transmitter's average total power P. The intensity I is just the average power per unit area, so to find I at 100 km from the transmitter we divide P by the surface area of the hemisphere shown in Fig. 32.19. For a sinusoidal wave, I is also equal to the magnitude of the average value S_{av} of the Poynting vector, so we can use Eqs. (32.29) to find E_{max}; Eq. (32.4) then yields B_{max}.

32.19 A radio station radiates waves into the hemisphere shown.

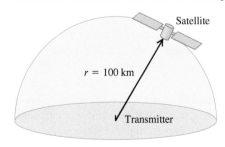
Satellite
$r = 100$ km
Transmitter

EXECUTE: The surface area of a hemisphere of radius $r = 100$ km $= 1.00 \times 10^5$ m is

$$A = 2\pi R^2 = 2\pi (1.00 \times 10^5 \text{ m})^2 = 6.28 \times 10^{10} \text{ m}^2$$

All the radiated power passes through this surface, so the average power per unit area (that is, the intensity) is

$$I = \frac{P}{A} = \frac{P}{2\pi R^2} = \frac{5.00 \times 10^4 \text{ W}}{6.28 \times 10^{10} \text{ m}^2} = 7.96 \times 10^{-7} \text{ W/m}^2$$

From Eqs. (32.29), $I = S_{av} = E_{max}^2/2\mu_0 c$, so

$$E_{max} = \sqrt{2\mu_0 c S_{av}}$$
$$= \sqrt{2(4\pi \times 10^{-7} \text{ T} \cdot \text{m/A})(3.00 \times 10^8 \text{ m/s})(7.96 \times 10^{-7} \text{ W/m}^2)}$$
$$= 2.45 \times 10^{-2} \text{ V/m}$$

Then from Eq. (32.4),

$$B_{max} = \frac{E_{max}}{c} = 8.17 \times 10^{-11} \text{ T}$$

EVALUATE: Note that E_{max} is comparable to fields commonly seen in the laboratory, but B_{max} is extremely small in comparison to $\vec{B}$ fields we saw in previous chapters. For this reason, most detectors of electromagnetic radiation respond to the effect of the electric field, not the magnetic field. Loop radio antennas are an exception (see the Bridging Problem at the end of this chapter).

Electromagnetic Momentum Flow and Radiation Pressure

By using the observation that energy is required to establish electric and magnetic fields, we have shown that electromagnetic waves transport energy. It can also be shown that electromagnetic waves carry *momentum p*, with a corresponding momentum density (momentum dp per volume dV) of magnitude

$$\frac{dp}{dV} = \frac{EB}{\mu_0 c^2} = \frac{S}{c^2} \qquad (32.30)$$

This momentum is a property of the field; it is not associated with the mass of a moving particle in the usual sense.

There is also a corresponding momentum flow rate. The volume dV occupied by an electromagnetic wave (speed c) that passes through an area A in time dt is $dV = Ac\,dt$. When we substitute this into Eq. (32.30) and rearrange, we find that the momentum flow rate per unit area is

$$\frac{1}{A}\frac{dp}{dt} = \frac{S}{c} = \frac{EB}{\mu_0 c} \qquad \text{(flow rate of electromagnetic momentum)} \qquad (32.31)$$

This is the momentum transferred per unit surface area per unit time. We obtain the *average* rate of momentum transfer per unit area by replacing S in Eq. (32.31) by $S_{av} = I$.

This momentum is responsible for **radiation pressure.** When an electromagnetic wave is completely absorbed by a surface, the wave's momentum is also transferred to the surface. For simplicity we'll consider a surface perpendicular to the propagation direction. Using the ideas developed in Section 8.1, we see that the rate dp/dt at which momentum is transferred to the absorbing surface equals the *force* on the surface. The average force per unit area due to the wave, or *radiation pressure* p_{rad}, is the average value of dp/dt divided by the absorbing area A. (We use the subscript "rad" to distinguish pressure from momentum, for which the symbol p is also used.) From Eq. (32.31) the radiation pressure is

$$p_{rad} = \frac{S_{av}}{c} = \frac{I}{c} \qquad \text{(radiation pressure, wave totally absorbed)} \qquad (32.32)$$

If the wave is totally reflected, the momentum change is twice as great, and the pressure is

$$p_{rad} = \frac{2S_{av}}{c} = \frac{2I}{c} \qquad \text{(radiation pressure, wave totally reflected)} \qquad (32.33)$$

For example, the value of I (or S_{av}) for direct sunlight, before it passes through the earth's atmosphere, is approximately 1.4 kW/m^2. From Eq. (32.32) the corresponding average pressure on a completely absorbing surface is

$$p_{rad} = \frac{I}{c} = \frac{1.4 \times 10^3 \text{ W/m}^2}{3.0 \times 10^8 \text{ m/s}} = 4.7 \times 10^{-6} \text{ Pa}$$

From Eq. (32.33) the average pressure on a totally *reflecting* surface is twice this: $2I/c$ or 9.4×10^{-6} Pa. These are very small pressures, of the order of 10^{-10} atm, but they can be measured with sensitive instruments.

The radiation pressure of sunlight is much greater *inside* the sun than at the earth (see Problem 32.45). Inside stars that are much more massive and luminous than the sun, radiation pressure is so great that it substantially augments the gas pressure within the star and so helps to prevent the star from collapsing under its own gravity. In some cases the radiation pressure of stars can have dramatic effects on the material surrounding them (Fig. 32.20).

32.20 At the center of this interstellar gas cloud is a group of intensely luminous stars that exert tremendous radiation pressure on their surroundings. Aided by a "wind" of particles emanating from the stars, over the past million years the radiation pressure has carved out a bubble within the cloud 70 light-years across.

Example 32.5 **Power and pressure from sunlight**

An earth-orbiting satellite has solar energy–collecting panels with a total area of 4.0 m² (Fig. 32.21). If the sun's radiation is perpendicular to the panels and is completely absorbed, find the average solar power absorbed and the average radiation-pressure force.

SOLUTION

IDENTIFY and SET UP: This problem uses the relationships among intensity, power, radiation pressure, and force. In the above discussion we calculated the intensity I (power per unit area) of sunlight as well as the radiation pressure p_{rad} (force per unit area) of sunlight on an absorbing surface. (We calculated these values for

32.21 Solar panels on a satellite.

Sun sensor (to keep panels facing the sun)
$\vec{S}$
$\vec{S}$
Solar panels

points above the atmosphere, which is where the satellite orbits.) Multiplying each value by the area of the solar panels gives the average power absorbed and the net radiation force on the panels.

EXECUTE: The intensity I (power per unit area) is 1.4×10^3 W/m². Although the light from the sun is not a simple sinusoidal wave, we can still use the relationship that the average power P is the intensity I times the area A:

$$P = IA = (1.4 \times 10^3 \text{ W/m}^2)(4.0 \text{ m}^2)$$
$$= 5.6 \times 10^3 \text{ W} = 5.6 \text{ kW}$$

The radiation pressure of sunlight on an absorbing surface is $p_{rad} = 4.7 \times 10^{-6}$ Pa $= 4.7 \times 10^{-6}$ N/m². The total force F is the pressure p_{rad} times the area A:

$$F = p_{rad}A = (4.7 \times 10^{-6} \text{ N/m}^2)(4.0 \text{ m}^2) = 1.9 \times 10^{-5} \text{ N}$$

EVALUATE: The absorbed power is quite substantial. Part of it can be used to power the equipment aboard the satellite; the rest goes into heating the panels, either directly or due to inefficiencies in the photocells contained in the panels.

The total radiation force is comparable to the weight (on earth) of a single grain of salt. Over time, however, this small force can have a noticeable effect on the orbit of a satellite like that in Fig. 32.21, and so radiation pressure must be taken into account.

Test Your Understanding of Section 32.4 Figure 32.13 shows one wavelength of a sinusoidal electromagnetic wave at time $t = 0$. For which of the following four values of x is (a) the energy density a maximum; (b) the energy density a minimum; (c) the magnitude of the instantaneous (not average) Poynting vector a maximum; (d) the magnitude of the instantaneous (not average) Poynting vector a minimum? (i) $x = 0$; (ii) $x = \lambda/4$; (iii) $x = \lambda/2$; (iv) $x = 3\lambda/4$.

32.5 Standing Electromagnetic Waves

Electromagnetic waves can be *reflected;* the surface of a conductor (like a polished sheet of metal) or of a dielectric (such as a sheet of glass) can serve as a reflector. The superposition principle holds for electromagnetic waves just as for electric and magnetic fields. The superposition of an incident wave and a reflected wave forms a **standing wave.** The situation is analogous to standing waves on a stretched string, discussed in Section 15.7; you should review that discussion.

Suppose a sheet of a perfect conductor (zero resistivity) is placed in the yz-plane of Fig. 32.22 and a linearly polarized electromagnetic wave, traveling in the negative x-direction, strikes it. As we discussed in Section 23.4, $\vec{E}$ cannot have a component parallel to the surface of a perfect conductor. Therefore in the present situation, $\vec{E}$ must be zero everywhere in the yz-plane. The electric field of the *incident* electromagnetic wave is *not* zero at all times in the yz-plane. But this incident wave induces oscillating currents on the surface of the conductor, and these currents give rise to an additional electric field. The *net* electric field, which is the vector sum of this field and the incident $\vec{E}$, *is* zero everywhere inside and on the surface of the conductor.

The currents induced on the surface of the conductor also produce a *reflected* wave that travels out from the plane in the $+x$-direction. Suppose the incident wave is described by the wave functions of Eqs. (32.19) (a sinusoidal wave traveling in the $-x$-direction) and the reflected wave by the negative of Eqs. (32.16) (a sinusoidal wave traveling in the $+x$-direction). We take the *negative* of the

32.22 Representation of the electric and magnetic fields of a linearly polarized electromagnetic standing wave when $\omega t = 3\pi/4$ rad. In any plane perpendicular to the x-axis, E is maximum (an antinode) where B is zero (a node), and vice versa. As time elapses, the pattern does *not* move along the x-axis; instead, at every point the $\vec{E}$ and $\vec{B}$ vectors simply oscillate.

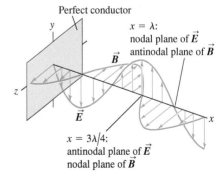

Perfect conductor
$x = \lambda$: nodal plane of $\vec{E}$ antinodal plane of $\vec{B}$
$\vec{B}$
$\vec{E}$
$x = 3\lambda/4$: antinodal plane of $\vec{E}$ nodal plane of $\vec{B}$

wave given by Eqs. (32.16) so that the incident and reflected electric fields cancel at $x = 0$ (the plane of the conductor, where the total electric field must be zero). The superposition principle states that the total $\vec{E}$ field at any point is the vector sum of the $\vec{E}$ fields of the incident and reflected waves, and similarly for the $\vec{B}$ field. Therefore the wave functions for the superposition of the two waves are

$$E_y(x, t) = E_{max}[\cos(kx + \omega t) - \cos(kx - \omega t)]$$
$$B_z(x, t) = B_{max}[-\cos(kx + \omega t) - \cos(kx - \omega t)]$$

We can expand and simplify these expressions, using the identities

$$\cos(A \pm B) = \cos A \cos B \mp \sin A \sin B$$

The results are

$$E_y(x, t) = -2E_{max} \sin kx \sin \omega t \qquad (32.34)$$
$$B_z(x, t) = -2B_{max} \cos kx \cos \omega t \qquad (32.35)$$

Equation (32.34) is analogous to Eq. (15.28) for a stretched string. We see that at $x = 0$ the electric field $E_y(x = 0, t)$ is *always* zero; this is required by the nature of the ideal conductor, which plays the same role as a fixed point at the end of a string. Furthermore, $E_y(x, t)$ is zero at *all* times at points in those planes perpendicular to the x-axis for which $\sin kx = 0$—that is, $kx = 0, \pi, 2\pi, \ldots$. Since $k = 2\pi/\lambda$, the positions of these planes are

$$x = 0, \frac{\lambda}{2}, \lambda, \frac{3\lambda}{2}, \ldots \qquad \text{(nodal planes of } \vec{E}) \qquad (32.36)$$

These planes are called the **nodal planes** of the $\vec{E}$ field; they are the equivalent of the nodes, or nodal points, of a standing wave on a string. Midway between any two adjacent nodal planes is a plane on which $\sin kx = \pm 1$; on each such plane, the magnitude of $E(x, t)$ equals the maximum possible value of $2E_{max}$ twice per oscillation cycle. These are the **antinodal planes** of $\vec{E}$, corresponding to the antinodes of waves on a string.

The total magnetic field is zero at all times at points in planes on which $\cos kx = 0$. This occurs where

$$x = \frac{\lambda}{4}, \frac{3\lambda}{4}, \frac{5\lambda}{4}, \ldots \qquad \text{(nodal planes of } \vec{B}) \qquad (32.37)$$

These are the nodal planes of the $\vec{B}$ field; there is an antinodal plane of $\vec{B}$ midway between any two adjacent nodal planes.

Figure 32.22 shows a standing-wave pattern at one instant of time. The magnetic field is *not* zero at the conducting surface ($x = 0$). The surface currents that must be present to make $\vec{E}$ exactly zero at the surface cause magnetic fields at the surface. The nodal planes of each field are separated by one half-wavelength. The nodal planes of one field are midway between those of the other; hence the nodes of $\vec{E}$ coincide with the antinodes of $\vec{B}$, and conversely. Compare this situation to the distinction between pressure nodes and displacement nodes in Section 16.4.

The total electric field is a *sine* function of t, and the total magnetic field is a *cosine* function of t. The sinusoidal variations of the two fields are therefore 90° out of phase at each point. At times when $\sin \omega t = 0$, the electric field is zero *everywhere,* and the magnetic field is maximum. When $\cos \omega t = 0$, the magnetic field is zero everywhere, and the electric field is maximum. This is in contrast to a wave traveling in one direction, as described by Eqs. (32.16) or (32.19) separately, in which the sinusoidal variations of $\vec{E}$ and $\vec{B}$ at any particular point are *in phase*. You can show that Eqs. (32.34) and (32.35) satisfy the wave equation, Eq. (32.15). You can also show that they satisfy Eqs. (32.12) and (32.14), the equivalents of Faraday's and Ampere's laws (see Exercise 32.36).

Standing Waves in a Cavity

Let's now insert a second conducting plane, parallel to the first and a distance L from it, along the $+x$-axis. The cavity between the two planes is analogous to a stretched string held at the points $x = 0$ and $x = L$. Both conducting planes must be nodal planes for $\vec{E}$; a standing wave can exist only when the second plane is placed at one of the positions where $E(x, t) = 0$, so L must be an integer multiple of $\lambda/2$. The wavelengths that satisfy this condition are

$$\lambda_n = \frac{2L}{n} \qquad (n = 1, 2, 3, \dots) \qquad (32.38)$$

The corresponding frequencies are

$$f_n = \frac{c}{\lambda_n} = n\frac{c}{2L} \qquad (n = 1, 2, 3, \dots) \qquad (32.39)$$

Thus there is a set of *normal modes,* each with a characteristic frequency, wave shape, and node pattern (Fig. 32.23). By measuring the node positions, we can measure the wavelength. If the frequency is known, the wave speed can be determined. This technique was first used by Hertz in the 1880s in his pioneering investigations of electromagnetic waves.

Conducting surfaces are not the only reflectors of electromagnetic waves. Reflections also occur at an interface between two insulating materials with different dielectric or magnetic properties. The mechanical analog is a junction of two strings with equal tension but different linear mass density. In general, a wave incident on such a boundary surface is partly transmitted into the second material and partly reflected back into the first. For example, light is transmitted through a glass window, but its surfaces also reflect light.

32.23 A typical microwave oven sets up a standing electromagnetic wave with $\lambda = 12.2$ cm, a wavelength that is strongly absorbed by the water in food. Because the wave has nodes spaced $\lambda/2 = 6.1$ cm apart, the food must be rotated while cooking. Otherwise, the portion that lies at a node—where the electric-field amplitude is zero—will remain cold.

Example 32.6 | **Intensity in a standing wave**

Calculate the intensity of the standing wave represented by Eqs. (32.34) and (32.35).

SOLUTION

IDENTIFY and SET UP: The intensity I of the wave is the time-averaged value S_{av} of the magnitude of the Poynting vector $\vec{S}$. To find S_{av}, we first use Eq. (32.28) to find the instantaneous value of $\vec{S}$ and then average it over a whole number of cycles of the wave.

EXECUTE: Using the wave functions of Eqs. (32.34) and (32.35) in Eq. (32.28) for the Poynting vector $\vec{S}$, we find

$$\vec{S}(x, t) = \frac{1}{\mu_0}\vec{E}(x, t) \times \vec{B}(x, t)$$

$$= \frac{1}{\mu_0}[-2\hat{\jmath}E_{max}\sin kx \cos \omega t] \times [-2\hat{k}B_{max}\cos kx \sin \omega t]$$

$$= \hat{\imath}\frac{E_{max}B_{max}}{\mu_0}(2\sin kx \cos kx)(2\sin \omega t \cos \omega t)$$

$$= \hat{\imath}S_x(x, t)$$

Using the identity $\sin 2A = 2\sin A \cos A$, we can rewrite $S_x(x, t)$ as

$$S_x(x, t) = \frac{E_{max}B_{max}\sin 2kx \sin 2\omega t}{\mu_0}$$

The average value of a sine function over any whole number of cycles is zero. Thus *the time average of $\vec{S}$ at any point is zero;* $I = S_{av} = 0$.

EVALUATE: This result is what we should expect. The standing wave is a superposition of two waves with the same frequency and amplitude, traveling in opposite directions. All the energy transferred by one wave is cancelled by an equal amount transferred in the opposite direction by the other wave. When we use electromagnetic waves to transmit power, it is important to avoid reflections that give rise to standing waves.

Example 32.7 | **Standing waves in a cavity**

Electromagnetic standing waves are set up in a cavity with two parallel, highly conducting walls 1.50 cm apart. (a) Calculate the longest wavelength λ and lowest frequency f of these standing waves. (b) For a standing wave of this wavelength, where in the cavity does $\vec{E}$ have maximum magnitude? Where is $\vec{E}$ zero? Where does $\vec{B}$ have maximum magnitude? Where is $\vec{B}$ zero?

Continued

IDENTIFY and SET UP: Only certain normal modes are possible for electromagnetic waves in a cavity, just as only certain normal modes are possible for standing waves on a string. The longest possible wavelength and lowest possible frequency correspond to the $n = 1$ mode in Eqs. (32.38) and (32.39); we use these to find λ and f. Equations (32.36) and (32.37) then give the locations of the nodal planes of $\vec{E}$ and $\vec{B}$. The antinodal planes of each field are midway between adjacent nodal planes.

EXECUTE: (a) From Eqs. (32.38) and (32.39), the $n = 1$ wavelength and frequency are

$$\lambda_1 = 2L = 2(1.50 \text{ cm}) = 3.00 \text{ cm}$$

$$f_1 = \frac{c}{2L} = \frac{3.00 \times 10^8 \text{ m/s}}{2(1.50 \times 10^{-2} \text{ m})} = 1.00 \times 10^{10} \text{ Hz} = 10 \text{ GHz}$$

(b) With $n = 1$ there is a single half-wavelength between the walls. The electric field has nodal planes ($\vec{E} = 0$) at the walls and an antinodal plane (where $\vec{E}$ has its maximum magnitude) midway between them. The magnetic field has *antinodal* planes at the walls and a nodal plane midway between them.

EVALUATE: One application of such standing waves is to produce an oscillating $\vec{E}$ field of definite frequency, which is used to probe the behavior of a small sample of material placed in the cavity. To subject the sample to the strongest possible field, it should be placed near the center of the cavity, at the antinode of $\vec{E}$.

Test Your Understanding of Section 32.5 In the standing wave described in Example 32.7, is there any point in the cavity where the energy density is zero at all times? If so, where? If not, why not?

Maxwell's equations and electromagnetic waves:
Maxwell's equations predict the existence of electromagnetic waves that propagate in vacuum at the speed of light c. The electromagnetic spectrum covers frequencies from at least 1 to 10^{24} Hz and a correspondingly broad range of wavelengths. Visible light, with wavelengths from 380 to 750 nm, is only a very small part of this spectrum. In a plane wave, $\vec{E}$ and $\vec{B}$ are uniform over any plane perpendicular to the propagation direction. Faraday's law and Ampere's law both give relationships between the magnitudes of $\vec{E}$ and $\vec{B}$; requiring both of these relationships to be satisfied gives an expression for c in terms of ϵ_0 and μ_0. Electromagnetic waves are transverse; the $\vec{E}$ and $\vec{B}$ fields are perpendicular to the direction of propagation and to each other. The direction of propagation is the direction of $\vec{E} \times \vec{B}$.

$$E = cB \qquad (32.4)$$

$$B = \epsilon_0 \mu_0 c E \qquad (32.8)$$

$$c = \frac{1}{\sqrt{\epsilon_0 \mu_0}} \qquad (32.9)$$

Sinusoidal electromagnetic waves: Equations (32.17) and (32.18) describe a sinusoidal plane electromagnetic wave traveling in vacuum in the $+x$-direction. If the wave is propagating in the $-x$-direction, replace $kx - \omega t$ by $kx + \omega t$. (See Example 32.1.)

$$\vec{E}(x, t) = \hat{j} E_{max} \cos(kx - \omega t)$$
$$\vec{B}(x, t) = \hat{k} B_{max} \cos(kx - \omega t) \qquad (32.17)$$

$$E_{max} = c B_{max} \qquad (32.18)$$

Electromagnetic waves in matter: When an electromagnetic wave travels through a dielectric, the wave speed v is less than the speed of light in vacuum c. (See Example 32.2.)

$$v = \frac{1}{\sqrt{\epsilon \mu}} = \frac{1}{\sqrt{K K_m}} \frac{1}{\sqrt{\epsilon_0 \mu_0}}$$
$$= \frac{c}{\sqrt{K K_m}} \qquad (32.21)$$

Energy and momentum in electromagnetic waves: The energy flow rate (power per unit area) in an electromagnetic wave in vacuum is given by the Poynting vector $\vec{S}$. The magnitude of the time-averaged value of the Poynting vector is called the intensity I of the wave. Electromagnetic waves also carry momentum. When an electromagnetic wave strikes a surface, it exerts a radiation pressure p_{rad}. If the surface is perpendicular to the wave propagation direction and is totally absorbing, $p_{rad} = I/c$; if the surface is a perfect reflector, $p_{rad} = 2I/c$. (See Examples 32.3–32.5.)

$$\vec{S} = \frac{1}{\mu_0} \vec{E} \times \vec{B} \qquad (32.28)$$

$$I = S_{av} = \frac{E_{max} B_{max}}{2\mu_0} = \frac{E_{max}^2}{2\mu_0 c}$$

$$= \frac{1}{2}\sqrt{\frac{\epsilon_0}{\mu_0}} E_{max}^2$$

$$= \frac{1}{2}\epsilon_0 c E_{max}^2 \qquad (32.29)$$

$$\frac{1}{A}\frac{dp}{dt} = \frac{S}{c} = \frac{EB}{\mu_0 c} \qquad (32.31)$$

(flow rate of electromagnetic momentum)

Standing electromagnetic waves: If a perfect reflecting surface is placed at $x = 0$, the incident and reflected waves form a standing wave. Nodal planes for $\vec{E}$ occur at $kx = 0, \pi, 2\pi, \dots$, and nodal planes for $\vec{B}$ at $kx = \pi/2, 3\pi/2, 5\pi/2, \dots$. At each point, the sinusoidal variations of $\vec{E}$ and $\vec{B}$ with time are 90° out of phase. (See Examples 32.6 and 32.7.)

BRIDGING PROBLEM | **Detecting Electromagnetic Waves**

A circular loop of wire can be used as a radio antenna. If an 18.0-cm-diameter antenna is located 2.50 km from a 95.0-MHz source with a total power of 55.0 kW, what is the maximum emf induced in the loop? Assume that the plane of the antenna loop is perpendicular to the direction of the radiation's magnetic field and that the source radiates uniformly in all directions.

SOLUTION GUIDE

See MasteringPhysics® study area for a Video Tutor solution.

IDENTIFY and SET UP:

1. The electromagnetic wave has an oscillating magnetic field. This causes a magnetic flux through the loop antenna that varies sinusoidally with time. By Faraday's law, this produces an emf equal in magnitude to the rate of change of the flux. The target variable is the magnitude of this emf.

2. Select the equations that you will need to find (i) the intensity of the wave at the position of the loop, a distance $r = 2.50$ km

from the source of power $P = 55.0$ kW; (ii) the amplitude of the sinusoidally varying magnetic field at that position; (iii) the magnetic flux through the loop as a function of time; and (iv) the emf produced by the flux.

EXECUTE

3. Find the wave intensity at the position of the loop.

4. Use your result from step 3 to write expressions for the time-dependent magnetic field at this position and the time-dependent magnetic flux through the loop.

5. Use the results of step 4 to find the time-dependent induced emf in the loop. The amplitude of this emf is your target variable.

EVALUATE

6. Is the induced emf large enough to detect? (If it is, a receiver connected to this antenna will be able to pick up signals from the source.)

Problems

•, ••, •••: Problems of increasing difficulty. **CP**: Cumulative problems incorporating material from earlier chapters. **CALC**: Problems requiring calculus. **BIO**: Biosciences problems.

DISCUSSION QUESTIONS

Q32.1 By measuring the electric and magnetic fields at a point in space where there is an electromagnetic wave, can you determine the direction from which the wave came? Explain.

Q32.2 According to Ampere's law, is it possible to have both a conduction current and a displacement current at the same time? Is it possible for the effects of the two kinds of current to cancel each other exactly so that *no* magnetic field is produced? Explain.

Q32.3 Give several examples of electromagnetic waves that are encountered in everyday life. How are they all alike? How do they differ?

Q32.4 Sometimes neon signs located near a powerful radio station are seen to glow faintly at night, even though they are not turned on. What is happening?

Q32.5 Is polarization a property of all electromagnetic waves, or is it unique to visible light? Can sound waves be polarized? What fundamental distinction in wave properties is involved? Explain.

Q32.6 Suppose that a positive point charge q is initially at rest on the x-axis, in the path of the electromagnetic plane wave described in Section 32.2. Will the charge move after the wave front reaches it? If not, why not? If the charge does move, describe its motion qualitatively. (Remember that $\vec{E}$ and $\vec{B}$ have the same value at all points behind the wave front.)

Q32.7 The light beam from a searchlight may have an electric-field magnitude of 1000 V/m, corresponding to a potential difference of 1500 V between the head and feet of a 1.5-m-tall person on whom the light shines. Does this cause the person to feel a strong electric shock? Why or why not?

Q32.8 For a certain sinusoidal wave of intensity I, the amplitude of the magnetic field is B. What would be the amplitude (in terms of B) in a similar wave of twice the intensity?

Q32.9 The magnetic-field amplitude of the electromagnetic wave from the laser described in Example 32.1 (Section 32.3) is about 100 times greater than the earth's magnetic field. If you illuminate a compass with the light from this laser, would you expect the compass to deflect? Why or why not?

Q32.10 Most automobiles have vertical antennas for receiving radio broadcasts. Explain what this tells you about the direction of polarization of $\vec{E}$ in the radio waves used in broadcasting.

Q32.11 If a light beam carries momentum, should a person holding a flashlight feel a recoil analogous to the recoil of a rifle when it is fired? Why is this recoil not actually observed?

Q32.12 A light source radiates a sinusoidal electromagnetic wave uniformly in all directions. This wave exerts an average pressure p on a perfectly reflecting surface a distance R away from it. What average pressure (in terms of p) would this wave exert on a perfectly absorbing surface that was twice as far from the source?

Q32.13 Does an electromagnetic *standing* wave have energy? Does it have momentum? Are your answers to these questions the same as for a *traveling* wave? Why or why not?

Q32.14 When driving on the upper level of the Bay Bridge, westbound from Oakland to San Francisco, you can easily pick up a number of radio stations on your car radio. But when driving eastbound on the lower level of the bridge, which has steel girders on either side to support the upper level, the radio reception is much worse. Why is there a difference?

EXERCISES

Section 32.2 Plane Electromagnetic Waves and the Speed of Light

32.1 · (a) How much time does it take light to travel from the moon to the earth, a distance of 384,000 km? (b) Light from the star Sirius takes 8.61 years to reach the earth. What is the distance from earth to Sirius in kilometers?

32.2 · Consider each of the electric- and magnetic-field orientations given next. In each case, what is the direction of propagation of the wave? (a) $\vec{E}$ in the $+x$-direction, $\vec{B}$ in the $+y$-direction; (b) $\vec{E}$ in the $-y$-direction, $\vec{B}$ in the $+x$-direction; (c) $\vec{E}$ in the $+z$-direction, $\vec{B}$ in the $-x$-direction; (d) $\vec{E}$ in the $+y$-direction, $\vec{B}$ in the $-z$-direction.

32.3 · A sinusoidal electromagnetic wave is propagating in vacuum in the $+z$-direction. If at a particular instant and at a certain point in space the electric field is in the $+x$-direction and has magnitude 4.00 V/m, what are the magnitude and direction of the magnetic field of the wave at this same point in space and instant in time?

32.4 · Consider each of the following electric- and magnetic-field orientations. In each case, what is the direction of propagation of the wave? (a) $\vec{E} = E\hat{\imath}$, $\vec{B} = -B\hat{\jmath}$; (b) $\vec{E} = E\hat{\jmath}$, $\vec{B} = B\hat{\imath}$; (c) $\vec{E} = -E\hat{k}$, $\vec{B} = -B\hat{\imath}$; (d) $\vec{E} = E\hat{\imath}$, $\vec{B} = -B\hat{k}$.

Section 32.3 Sinusoidal Electromagnetic Waves

32.5 · BIO **Medical X rays.** Medical x rays are taken with electromagnetic waves having a wavelength of around 0.10 nm. What are the frequency, period, and wave number of such waves?

32.6 · BIO **Ultraviolet Radiation.** There are two categories of ultraviolet light. Ultraviolet A (UVA) has a wavelength ranging from 320 nm to 400 nm. It is not harmful to the skin and is necessary for the production of vitamin D. UVB, with a wavelength between 280 nm and 320 nm, is much more dangerous because it causes skin cancer. (a) Find the frequency ranges of UVA and UVB. (b) What are the ranges of the wave numbers for UVA and UVB?

32.7 · A sinusoidal electromagnetic wave having a magnetic field of amplitude 1.25 μT and a wavelength of 432 nm is traveling in the $+x$-direction through empty space. (a) What is the frequency of this wave? (b) What is the amplitude of the associated electric field? (c) Write the equations for the electric and magnetic fields as functions of x and t in the form of Eqs. (32.17).

32.8 · An electromagnetic wave of wavelength 435 nm is traveling in vacuum in the $-z$-direction. The electric field has amplitude 2.70×10^{-3} V/m and is parallel to the x-axis. What are (a) the frequency and (b) the magnetic-field amplitude? (c) Write the vector equations for $\vec{E}(z, t)$ and $\vec{B}(z, t)$.

32.9 · Consider electromagnetic waves propagating in air. (a) Determine the frequency of a wave with a wavelength of (i) 5.0 km, (ii) 5.0 μm, (iii) 5.0 nm. (b) What is the wavelength (in meters and nanometers) of (i) gamma rays of frequency 6.50×10^{21} Hz and (ii) an AM station radio wave of frequency 590 kHz?

32.10 · The electric field of a sinusoidal electromagnetic wave obeys the equation $E = (375 \text{ V/m}) \cos[(1.99 \times 10^7 \text{ rad/m})x + (5.97 \times 10^{15} \text{ rad/s})t]$. (a) What are the amplitudes of the electric and magnetic fields of this wave? (b) What are the frequency, wavelength, and period of the wave? Is this light visible to humans? (c) What is the speed of the wave?

32.11 · An electromagnetic wave has an electric field given by $\vec{E}(y, t) = (3.10 \times 10^5 \text{ V/m})\hat{k} \cos[ky - (12.65 \times 10^{12} \text{ rad/s})t]$. (a) In which direction is the wave traveling? (b) What is the wavelength of the wave? (c) Write the vector equation for $\vec{B}(y, t)$.

32.12 · An electromagnetic wave has a magnetic field given by $\vec{B}(x, t) = -(8.25 \times 10^{-9} \text{ T})\hat{\jmath} \cos[(1.38 \times 10^4 \text{ rad/m})x + \omega t]$. (a) In which direction is the wave traveling? (b) What is the frequency f of the wave? (c) Write the vector equation for $\vec{E}(x, t)$.

32.13 · Radio station WCCO in Minneapolis broadcasts at a frequency of 830 kHz. At a point some distance from the transmitter, the magnetic-field amplitude of the electromagnetic wave from WCCO is 4.82×10^{-11} T. Calculate (a) the wavelength; (b) the wave number; (c) the angular frequency; (d) the electric-field amplitude.

32.14 · An electromagnetic wave with frequency 65.0 Hz travels in an insulating magnetic material that has dielectric constant 3.64 and relative permeability 5.18 at this frequency. The electric field has amplitude 7.20×10^{-3} V/m. (a) What is the speed of propagation of the wave? (b) What is the wavelength of the wave? (c) What is the amplitude of the magnetic field?

32.15 · An electromagnetic wave with frequency 5.70×10^{14} Hz propagates with a speed of 2.17×10^8 m/s in a certain piece of glass. Find (a) the wavelength of the wave in the glass; (b) the wavelength of a wave of the same frequency propagating in air; (c) the index of refraction n of the glass for an electromagnetic wave with this frequency; (d) the dielectric constant for glass at this frequency, assuming that the relative permeability is unity.

Section 32.4 Energy and Momentum in Electromagnetic Waves

32.16 · BIO **High-Energy Cancer Treatment.** Scientists are working on a new technique to kill cancer cells by zapping them with ultrahigh-energy (in the range of 10^{12} W) pulses of light that last for an extremely short time (a few nanoseconds). These short pulses scramble the interior of a cell without causing it to explode, as long pulses would do. We can model a typical such cell as a disk 5.0 μm in diameter, with the pulse lasting for 4.0 ns with an average power of 2.0×10^{12} W. We shall assume that the energy is spread uniformly over the faces of 100 cells for each pulse. (a) How much energy is given to the cell during this pulse? (b) What is the intensity (in W/m^2) delivered to the cell? (c) What are the maximum values of the electric and magnetic fields in the pulse?

32.17 ·· **Fields from a Light Bulb.** We can reasonably model a 75-W incandescent light bulb as a sphere 6.0 cm in diameter. Typically, only about 5% of the energy goes to visible light; the rest goes largely to nonvisible infrared radiation. (a) What is the visible-light intensity (in W/m^2) at the surface of the bulb? (b) What are the amplitudes of the electric and magnetic fields at this surface, for a sinusoidal wave with this intensity?

32.18 ·· A sinusoidal electromagnetic wave from a radio station passes perpendicularly through an open window that has area 0.500 m^2. At the window, the electric field of the wave has rms value 0.0200 V/m. How much energy does this wave carry through the window during a 30.0-s commercial?

32.19 ·· **Testing a Space Radio Transmitter.** You are a NASA mission specialist on your first flight aboard the space shuttle. Thanks to your extensive training in physics, you have been assigned to evaluate the performance of a new radio transmitter on board the International Space Station (ISS). Perched on the shuttle's movable arm, you aim a sensitive detector at the ISS, which is 2.5 km away. You find that the electric-field amplitude of the radio waves coming from the ISS transmitter is 0.090 V/m and that the frequency of the waves is 244 MHz. Find the following: (a) the intensity of the radio wave at your location; (b) the magnetic-field amplitude of the wave at your location; (c) the total power output of the ISS radio transmitter. (d) What assumptions, if any, did you make in your calculations?

32.20 • The intensity of a cylindrical laser beam is 0.800 W/m². The cross-sectional area of the beam is 3.0×10^{-4} m² and the intensity is uniform across the cross section of the beam. (a) What is the average power output of the laser? (b) What is the rms value of the electric field in the beam?

32.21 • A space probe 2.0×10^{10} m from a star measures the total intensity of electromagnetic radiation from the star to be 5.0×10^3 W/m². If the star radiates uniformly in all directions, what is its total average power output?

32.22 • A sinusoidal electromagnetic wave emitted by a cellular phone has a wavelength of 35.4 cm and an electric-field amplitude of 5.40×10^{-2} V/m at a distance of 250 m from the phone. Calculate (a) the frequency of the wave; (b) the magnetic-field amplitude; (c) the intensity of the wave.

32.23 • A monochromatic light source with power output 60.0 W radiates light of wavelength 700 nm uniformly in all directions. Calculate E_{max} and B_{max} for the 700-nm light at a distance of 5.00 m from the source.

32.24 • For the electromagnetic wave represented by Eqs. (32.19), show that the Poynting vector (a) is in the same direction as the propagation of the wave and (b) has average magnitude given by Eqs. (32.29).

32.25 •• An intense light source radiates uniformly in all directions. At a distance of 5.0 m from the source, the radiation pressure on a perfectly absorbing surface is 9.0×10^{-6} Pa. What is the total average power output of the source?

32.26 • **Television Broadcasting.** Public television station KQED in San Francisco broadcasts a sinusoidal radio signal at a power of 316 kW. Assume that the wave spreads out uniformly into a hemisphere above the ground. At a home 5.00 km away from the antenna, (a) what average pressure does this wave exert on a totally reflecting surface, (b) what are the amplitudes of the electric and magnetic fields of the wave, and (c) what is the average density of the energy this wave carries? (d) For the energy density in part (c), what percentage is due to the electric field and what percentage is due to the magnetic field?

32.27 •• **BIO Laser Safety.** If the eye receives an average intensity greater than 1.0×10^2 W/m², damage to the retina can occur. This quantity is called the *damage threshold* of the retina. (a) What is the largest average power (in mW) that a laser beam 1.5 mm in diameter can have and still be considered safe to view head-on? (b) What are the maximum values of the electric and magnetic fields for the beam in part (a)? (c) How much energy would the beam in part (a) deliver per second to the retina? (d) Express the damage threshold in W/cm².

32.28 • In the 25-ft Space Simulator facility at NASA's Jet Propulsion Laboratory, a bank of overhead arc lamps can produce light of intensity 2500 W/m² at the floor of the facility. (This simulates the intensity of sunlight near the planet Venus.) Find the average radiation pressure (in pascals and in atmospheres) on (a) a totally absorbing section of the floor and (b) a totally reflecting section of the floor. (c) Find the average momentum density (momentum per unit volume) in the light at the floor.

32.29 • **Laboratory Lasers.** He–Ne lasers are often used in physics demonstrations. They produce light of wavelength 633 nm and a power of 0.500 mW spread over a cylindrical beam 1.00 mm in diameter (although these quantities can vary). (a) What is the intensity of this laser beam? (b) What are the maximum values of the electric and magnetic fields? (c) What is the average energy density in the laser beam?

32.30 •• **Solar Sail 1.** During 2004, Japanese scientists successfully tested two solar sails. One had a somewhat complicated shape that we shall model as a disk 9.0 m in diameter and 7.5 μm thick. The intensity of solar energy at that location was about 1400 W/m². (a) What force did the sun's light exert on this sail, assuming that it struck perpendicular to the sail and that the sail was perfectly reflecting? (b) If the sail was made of magnesium, of density 1.74 g/cm³, what acceleration would the sun's radiation give to the sail? (c) Does the acceleration seem large enough to be feasible for space flight? In what ways could the sail be modified to increase its acceleration?

Section 32.5 Standing Electromagnetic Waves

32.31 • **Microwave Oven.** The microwaves in a certain microwave oven have a wavelength of 12.2 cm. (a) How wide must this oven be so that it will contain five antinodal planes of the electric field along its width in the standing-wave pattern? (b) What is the frequency of these microwaves? (c) Suppose a manufacturing error occurred and the oven was made 5.0 cm longer than specified in part (a). In this case, what would have to be the frequency of the microwaves for there still to be five antinodal planes of the electric field along the width of the oven?

32.32 • An electromagnetic standing wave in air of frequency 750 MHz is set up between two conducting planes 80.0 cm apart. At which positions between the planes could a point charge be placed at rest so that it would *remain* at rest? Explain.

32.33 • A standing electromagnetic wave in a certain material has frequency 2.20×10^{10} Hz. The nodal planes of $\vec{B}$ are 3.55 mm apart. Find (a) the wavelength of the wave in this material; (b) the distance between adjacent nodal planes of the $\vec{E}$ field; (c) the speed of propagation of the wave.

32.34 • An electromagnetic standing wave in air has frequency 75.0 MHz. (a) What is the distance between nodal planes of the $\vec{E}$ field? (b) What is the distance between a nodal plane of $\vec{E}$ and the closest nodal plane of $\vec{B}$?

32.35 • An electromagnetic standing wave in a certain material has frequency 1.20×10^{10} Hz and speed of propagation 2.10×10^8 m/s. (a) What is the distance between a nodal plane of $\vec{B}$ and the closest antinodal plane of $\vec{B}$? (b) What is the distance between an antinodal plane of $\vec{E}$ and the closest antinodal plane of $\vec{B}$? (c) What is the distance between a nodal plane of $\vec{E}$ and the closest nodal plane of $\vec{B}$?

32.36 • **CALC** Show that the electric and magnetic fields for standing waves given by Eqs. (32.34) and (32.35) (a) satisfy the wave equation, Eq. (32.15), and (b) satisfy Eqs. (32.12) and (32.14).

PROBLEMS

32.37 •• **BIO Laser Surgery.** Very short pulses of high-intensity laser beams are used to repair detached portions of the retina of the eye. The brief pulses of energy absorbed by the retina weld the detached portions back into place. In one such procedure, a laser beam has a wavelength of 810 nm and delivers 250 mW of power spread over a circular spot 510 μm in diameter. The vitreous humor (the transparent fluid that fills most of the eye) has an index of refraction of 1.34. (a) If the laser pulses are each 1.50 ms long, how much energy is delivered to the retina with each pulse? (b) What average pressure does the pulse of the laser beam exert on the retina as it is fully absorbed by the circular spot? (c) What are the wavelength and frequency of the laser light inside the vitreous humor of the eye? (d) What are the maximum values of the electric and magnetic fields in the laser beam?

32.38 •• **CALC** Consider a sinusoidal electromagnetic wave with fields $\vec{E} = E_{max}\hat{j}\cos(kx - \omega t)$ and $\vec{B} = B_{max}\hat{k}\cos(kx - \omega t + \phi)$, with $-\pi \le \phi \le \pi$. Show that if $\vec{E}$ and $\vec{B}$ are to satisfy Eqs. (32.12) and (32.14), then $E_{max} = cB_{max}$ and $\phi = 0$. (The result $\phi = 0$ means the $\vec{E}$ and $\vec{B}$ fields oscillate in phase.)

32.39 •• You want to support a sheet of fireproof paper horizontally, using only a vertical upward beam of light spread uniformly over the sheet. There is no other light on this paper. The sheet measures 22.0 cm by 28.0 cm and has a mass of 1.50 g. (a) If the paper is black and hence absorbs all the light that hits it, what must be the intensity of the light beam? (b) For the light in part (a), what are the amplitudes of its electric and magnetic fields? (c) If the paper is white and hence reflects all the light that hits it, what intensity of light beam is needed to support it? (d) To see if it is physically reasonable to expect to support a sheet of paper this way, calculate the intensity in a typical 0.500-mW laser beam that is 1.00 mm in diameter, and compare this value with your answer in part (a).

32.40 •• For a sinusoidal electromagnetic wave in vacuum, such as that described by Eq. (32.16), show that the *average* energy density in the electric field is the same as that in the magnetic field.

32.41 • A satellite 575 km above the earth's surface transmits sinusoidal electromagnetic waves of frequency 92.4 MHz uniformly in all directions, with a power of 25.0 kW. (a) What is the intensity of these waves as they reach a receiver at the surface of the earth directly below the satellite? (b) What are the amplitudes of the electric and magnetic fields at the receiver? (c) If the receiver has a totally absorbing panel measuring 15.0 cm by 40.0 cm oriented with its plane perpendicular to the direction the waves travel, what average force do these waves exert on the panel? Is this force large enough to cause significant effects?

32.42 • A plane sinusoidal electromagnetic wave in air has a wavelength of 3.84 cm and an $\vec{E}$-field amplitude of 1.35 V/m. (a) What is the frequency? (b) What is the $\vec{B}$-field amplitude? (c) What is the intensity? (d) What average force does this radiation exert on a totally absorbing surface with area 0.240 m^2 perpendicular to the direction of propagation?

32.43 • A small helium–neon laser emits red visible light with a power of 4.60 mW in a beam that has a diameter of 2.50 mm. (a) What are the amplitudes of the electric and magnetic fields of the light? (b) What are the average energy densities associated with the electric field and with the magnetic field? (c) What is the total energy contained in a 1.00-m length of the beam?

32.44 •• The electric-field component of a sinusoidal electromagnetic wave traveling through a plastic cylinder is given by the equation $E = (5.35 \text{ V/m}) \cos[(1.39 \times 10^7 \text{ rad/m})x - (3.02 \times 10^{15} \text{ rad/s})t]$. (a) Find the frequency, wavelength, and speed of this wave in the plastic. (b) What is the index of refraction of this plastic? (c) Assuming that the amplitude of the electric field does not change, write a comparable equation for the electric field if the light is traveling in air instead of in plastic.

32.45 • The sun emits energy in the form of electromagnetic waves at a rate of 3.9×10^{26} W. This energy is produced by nuclear reactions deep in the sun's interior. (a) Find the intensity of electromagnetic radiation and the radiation pressure on an absorbing object at the surface of the sun (radius $r = R = 6.96 \times 10^5$ km) and at $r = R/2$, in the sun's interior. Ignore any scattering of the waves as they move radially outward from the center of the sun. Compare to the values given in Section 32.4 for sunlight just before it enters the earth's atmosphere. (b) The gas pressure at the sun's surface is about 1.0×10^4 Pa; at $r = R/2$, the gas pressure is calculated from solar models to be about 4.7×10^{13} Pa. Comparing with your results in part (a), would you expect that radiation pressure is an important factor in determining the structure of the sun? Why or why not?

32.46 •• A source of sinusoidal electromagnetic waves radiates uniformly in all directions. At 10.0 m from this source, the amplitude of the electric field is measured to be 1.50 N/C. What is the electric-field amplitude at a distance of 20.0 cm from the source?

32.47 •• CP Two square reflectors, each 1.50 cm on a side and of mass 4.00 g, are located at opposite ends of a thin, extremely light, 1.00-m rod that can rotate without friction and in vacuum about an axle perpendicular to it through its center (Fig. P32.47). These reflectors are small enough to be treated as point masses in moment-of-inertia calculations. Both reflectors are illuminated on one face by a sinusoidal light wave having an electric field of amplitude 1.25 N/C that falls uniformly on both surfaces and always strikes them perpendicular to the plane of their surfaces. One reflector is covered with a perfectly absorbing coating, and the other is covered with a perfectly reflecting coating. What is the angular acceleration of this device?

Figure **P32.47**

32.48 •• CP A circular loop of wire has radius 7.50 cm. A sinusoidal electromagnetic plane wave traveling in air passes through the loop, with the direction of the magnetic field of the wave perpendicular to the plane of the loop. The intensity of the wave at the location of the loop is 0.0195 W/m^2, and the wavelength of the wave is 6.90 m. What is the maximum emf induced in the loop?

32.49 • CALC CP A cylindrical conductor with a circular cross section has a radius a and a resistivity ρ and carries a constant current I. (a) What are the magnitude and direction of the electric-field vector $\vec{E}$ at a point just inside the wire at a distance a from the axis? (b) What are the magnitude and direction of the magnetic-field vector $\vec{B}$ at the same point? (c) What are the magnitude and direction of the Poynting vector $\vec{S}$ at the same point? (The direction of $\vec{S}$ is the direction in which electromagnetic energy flows into or out of the conductor.) (d) Use the result in part (c) to find the rate of flow of energy into the volume occupied by a length l of the conductor. (*Hint:* Integrate $\vec{S}$ over the surface of this volume.) Compare your result to the rate of generation of thermal energy in the same volume. Discuss why the energy dissipated in a current-carrying conductor, due to its resistance, can be thought of as entering through the cylindrical sides of the conductor.

32.50 • In a certain experiment, a radio transmitter emits sinusoidal electromagnetic waves of frequency 110.0 MHz in opposite directions inside a narrow cavity with reflectors at both ends, causing a standing-wave pattern to occur. (a) How far apart are the nodal planes of the magnetic field? (b) If the standing-wave pattern is determined to be in its eighth harmonic, how long is the cavity?

32.51 •• CP **Flashlight to the Rescue.** You are the sole crew member of the interplanetary spaceship *T:1339 Vorga*, which makes regular cargo runs between the earth and the mining colonies in the asteroid belt. You are working outside the ship one day while at a distance of 2.0 AU from the sun. [1 AU (astronomical unit) is the average distance from the earth to the sun, 149,600,000 km.] Unfortunately, you lose contact with the ship's hull and begin to drift away into space. You use your spacesuit's rockets to try to push yourself back toward the ship, but they run out of fuel and stop working before you can return to the ship. You find yourself in an awkward position, floating 16.0 m from the spaceship with zero velocity relative to it. Fortunately, you are carrying a 200-W flashlight. You turn on the flashlight and use its beam as a "light rocket" to push yourself back toward the ship. (a) If you, your spacesuit, and the flashlight have a combined mass of 150 kg, how long will it take you to get back to the ship? (b) Is there another way you could use the flashlight to accomplish the same job of returning you to the ship?

32.52 • The 19th-century inventor Nikola Tesla proposed to transmit electric power via sinusoidal electromagnetic waves. Suppose power is to be transmitted in a beam of cross-sectional area 100 m². What electric- and magnetic-field amplitudes are required to transmit an amount of power comparable to that handled by modern transmission lines (that carry voltages and currents of the order of 500 kV and 1000 A)?

32.53 •• **CP Global Positioning System (GPS).** The GPS network consists of 24 satellites, each of which makes two orbits around the earth per day. Each satellite transmits a 50.0-W (or even less) sinusoidal electromagnetic signal at two frequencies, one of which is 1575.42 MHz. Assume that a satellite transmits half of its power at each frequency and that the waves travel uniformly in a downward hemisphere. (a) What average intensity does a GPS receiver on the ground, directly below the satellite, receive? (*Hint:* First use Newton's laws to find the altitude of the satellite.) (b) What are the amplitudes of the electric and magnetic fields at the GPS receiver in part (a), and how long does it take the signal to reach the receiver? (c) If the receiver is a square panel 1.50 cm on a side that absorbs all of the beam, what average pressure does the signal exert on it? (d) What wavelength must the receiver be tuned to?

32.54 •• **CP Solar Sail 2.** NASA is giving serious consideration to the concept of *solar sailing*. A solar sailcraft uses a large, low-mass sail and the energy and momentum of sunlight for propulsion. (a) Should the sail be absorbing or reflective? Why? (b) The total power output of the sun is 3.9×10^{26} W. How large a sail is necessary to propel a 10,000-kg spacecraft against the gravitational force of the sun? Express your result in square kilometers. (c) Explain why your answer to part (b) is independent of the distance from the sun.

32.55 •• **CP** Interplanetary space contains many small particles referred to as *interplanetary dust*. Radiation pressure from the sun sets a lower limit on the size of such dust particles. To see the origin of this limit, consider a spherical dust particle of radius R and mass density ρ. (a) Write an expression for the gravitational force exerted on this particle by the sun (mass M) when the particle is a distance r from the sun. (b) Let L represent the luminosity of the sun, equal to the rate at which it emits energy in electromagnetic radiation. Find the force exerted on the (totally absorbing) particle due to solar radiation pressure, remembering that the intensity of the sun's radiation also depends on the distance r. The relevant area is the cross-sectional area of the particle, *not* the total surface area of the particle. As part of your answer, explain why this is so. (c) The mass density of a typical interplanetary dust particle is about 3000 kg/m³. Find the particle radius R such that the gravitational and radiation forces acting on the particle are equal in magnitude. The luminosity of the sun is 3.9×10^{26} W. Does your answer depend on the distance of the particle from the sun? Why or why not? (d) Explain why dust particles with a radius less than

that found in part (c) are unlikely to be found in the solar system. [*Hint:* Construct the ratio of the two force expressions found in parts (a) and (b).]

CHALLENGE PROBLEMS

32.56 ••• **CALC** Electromagnetic waves propagate much differently in *conductors* than they do in dielectrics or in vacuum. If the resistivity of the conductor is sufficiently low (that is, if it is a sufficiently good conductor), the oscillating electric field of the wave gives rise to an oscillating conduction current that is much larger than the displacement current. In this case, the wave equation for an electric field $\vec{E}(x, t) = E_y(x, t)\hat{\jmath}$ propagating in the +x-direction within a conductor is

$$\frac{\partial^2 E_y\,(x, t)}{\partial x^2} = \frac{\mu}{\rho}\,\frac{\partial E_y(x, t)}{\partial t}$$

where μ is the permeability of the conductor and ρ is its resistivity. (a) A solution to this wave equation is

$$E_y(x, t) = E_{\max} e^{-k_C x}\cos(k_C x - \omega t)$$

where $k_C = \sqrt{\omega\mu/2\rho}$. Verify this by substituting $E_y(x, t)$ into the above wave equation. (b) The exponential term shows that the electric field decreases in amplitude as it propagates. Explain why this happens. (*Hint:* The field does work to move charges within the conductor. The current of these moving charges causes i^2R heating within the conductor, raising its temperature. Where does the energy to do this come from?) (c) Show that the electric-field amplitude decreases by a factor of $1/e$ in a distance $1/k_C = \sqrt{2\rho/\omega\mu}$, and calculate this distance for a radio wave with frequency $f =1.0$ MHz in copper (resistivity 1.72×10^{-8} $\Omega\cdot$m; permeability $\mu = \mu_0$). Since this distance is so short, electromagnetic waves of this frequency can hardly propagate at all into copper. Instead, they are reflected at the surface of the metal. This is why radio waves cannot penetrate through copper or other metals, and why radio reception is poor inside a metal structure.

32.57 ••• **CP** Electromagnetic radiation is emitted by accelerating charges. The rate at which energy is emitted from an accelerating charge that has charge q and acceleration a is given by

$$\frac{dE}{dt} = \frac{q^2 a^2}{6\pi\epsilon_0 c^3}$$

where c is the speed of light. (a) Verify that this equation is dimensionally correct. (b) If a proton with a kinetic energy of 6.0 MeV is traveling in a particle accelerator in a circular orbit of radius 0.750 m, what fraction of its energy does it radiate per second? (c) Consider an electron orbiting with the same speed and radius. What fraction of its energy does it radiate per second?

32.58 ••• **CP The Classical Hydrogen Atom.** The electron in a hydrogen atom can be considered to be in a circular orbit with a radius of 0.0529 nm and a kinetic energy of 13.6 eV. If the electron behaved classically, how much energy would it radiate per second (see Challenge Problem 32.57)? What does this tell you about the use of classical physics in describing the atom?

Answers

Chapter Opening Question ?

Metals are reflective because they are good conductors of electricity. When an electromagnetic wave strikes a conductor, the electric field of the wave sets up currents on the conductor surface that generate a reflected wave. For a perfect conductor, this reflected wave is just as intense as the incident wave. Tarnished metals are less shiny because their surface is oxidized and less conductive; polishing the metal removes the oxide and exposes the conducting metal.

Test Your Understanding Questions

32.1 Answers: (a) no, (b) no A purely electric wave would have a varying electric field. Such a field necessarily generates a magnetic field through Ampere's law, Eq. (29.20), so a purely electric wave is impossible. In the same way, a purely magnetic wave is impossible: The varying magnetic field in such a wave would automatically give rise to an electric field through Faraday's law, Eq. (29.21).

32.2 Answers: (a) positive y-direction, (b) negative x-direction, (c) positive y-direction You can verify these answers by using the right-hand rule to show that $\vec{E} \times \vec{B}$ in each case is in the direction of propagation, or by using the rule shown in Fig. 32.9.

32.3 Answer: (iv) In an ideal electromagnetic plane wave, at any instant the fields are the same anywhere in a plane perpendicular to the direction of propagation. The plane wave described by Eqs. (32.17) is propagating in the x-direction, so the fields depend on the coordinate x and time t but do *not* depend on the coordinates y and z.

32.4 Answers: (a) (i) and (iii), (b) (ii) and (iv), (c) (i) and (iii), (d) (ii) and (iv) Both the energy density u and the Poynting vector magnitude S are maximum where the $\vec{E}$ and $\vec{B}$ fields have their maximum magnitudes. (The directions of the fields doesn't matter.) From Fig. 32.13, this occurs at $x = 0$ and $x = \lambda/2$. Both u and S have a minimum value of zero; that occurs where $\vec{E}$ and $\vec{B}$ are both zero. From Fig. 32.13, this occurs at $x = \lambda/4$ and $x = 3\lambda/4$.

32.5 Answer: no There are places where $\vec{E} = 0$ at all times (at the walls) and the electric energy density $\frac{1}{2}\epsilon_0 E^2$ is always zero. There are also places where $\vec{B} = 0$ at all times (on the plane midway between the walls) and the magnetic energy density $B^2/2\mu_0$ is always zero. However, there are *no* locations where both $\vec{E}$ and $\vec{B}$ are always zero. Hence the energy density at any point in the standing wave is always nonzero.

Bridging Problem

Answer: 0.0368 V

PHOTONS: LIGHT WAVES BEHAVING AS PARTICLES

38

? This plastic surgeon is using two light sources: a headlamp that emits a beam of visible light and a handheld laser that emits infrared light. The light from both sources is emitted in the form of packets of energy called photons. For which source are the photons more energetic: the headlamp or the laser?

LEARNING GOALS

By studying this chapter, you will learn:

- How experiments involving the photoelectric effect and x rays pointed the way to a radical reinterpretation of the nature of light.

- How Einstein's photon picture of light explains the photoelectric effect.

- How experiments with x rays and gamma rays helped confirm the photon picture of light.

- How the wave and particle pictures of light complement each other.

- How the Heisenberg uncertainty principle imposes fundamental limits on what can be measured.

In Chapter 32 we saw how Maxwell, Hertz, and others established firmly that light is an electromagnetic wave. Interference, diffraction, and polarization, discussed in Chapters 35 and 36, further demonstrate this *wave nature* of light.

When we look more closely at the emission, absorption, and scattering of electromagnetic radiation, however, we discover a completely different aspect of light. We find that the energy of an electromagnetic wave is *quantized;* it is emitted and absorbed in particle-like packages of definite energy, called *photons.* The energy of a single photon is proportional to the frequency of the radiation.

We'll find that light and other electromagnetic radiation exhibits *wave–particle duality:* Light acts sometimes like waves and sometimes like particles. Interference and diffraction demonstrate wave behavior, while emission and absorption of photons demonstrate the particle behavior. This radical reinterpretation of light will lead us in the next chapter to no less radical changes in our views of the nature of matter.

38.1 Light Absorbed as Photons: The Photoelectric Effect

A phenomenon that gives insight into the nature of light is the **photoelectric effect,** in which a material emits electrons from its surface when illuminated (Fig. 38.1). To escape from the surface, an electron must absorb enough energy from the incident light to overcome the attraction of positive ions in the material. These attractions constitute a potential-energy barrier; the light supplies the "kick" that enables the electron to escape.

The photoelectric effect has a number of applications. Digital cameras and night-vision scopes use it to convert light energy into an electric signal that is

38.1 The photoelectric effect.

Light

Photoelectric effect: Light absorbed by a surface causes electrons to be ejected.

Electrons

To eject an electron the light must supply enough energy to overcome the forces holding the electron in the material.

38.2 (a) A night-vision scope makes use of the photoelectric effect. Photons entering the scope strike a plate, ejecting electrons that pass through a thin disk in which there are millions of tiny channels. The current through each channel is amplified electronically and then directed toward a screen that glows when hit by electrons. (b) The image formed on the screen, which is a combination of these millions of glowing spots, is thousands of times brighter than the naked-eye view.

(a)

(b)

PhET: Photoelectric Effect
ActivPhysics 17.3: Photoelectric Effect

reconstructed into an image (Fig. 38.2). On the moon, sunlight striking the surface causes surface dust to eject electrons, leaving the dust particles with a positive charge. The mutual electric repulsion of these charged dust particles causes them to rise above the moon's surface, a phenomenon that was observed from lunar orbit by the Apollo astronauts.

Threshold Frequency and Stopping Potential

In Section 32.1 we explored the wave model of light, which Maxwell formulated two decades before the photoelectric effect was observed. Is the photoelectric effect consistent with this model? Figure 38.3a shows a modern version of one of the experiments that explored this question. Two conducting electrodes are enclosed in an evacuated glass tube and connected by a battery, and the cathode is illuminated. Depending on the potential difference V_{AC} between the two electrodes, electrons emitted by the illuminated cathode (called *photoelectrons*) may travel across to the anode, producing a *photocurrent* in the external circuit. (The tube is evacuated to a pressure of 0.01 Pa or less to minimize collisions between the electrons and gas molecules.)

The illuminated cathode emits photoelectrons with various kinetic energies. If the electric field points toward the cathode, as in Fig. 38.3a, all the electrons are accelerated toward the anode and contribute to the photocurrent. But by reversing the field and adjusting its strength as in Fig. 38.3b, we can prevent the less energetic electrons from reaching the anode. In fact, we can determine the *maximum* kinetic energy K_{max} of the emitted electrons by making the potential of the anode relative to the cathode, V_{AC}, just negative enough so that the current stops. This occurs for $V_{AC} = -V_0$, where V_0 is called the **stopping potential.** As an electron moves from the cathode to the anode, the potential decreases by V_0 and negative work $-eV_0$ is done on the (negatively charged) electron. The most energetic electron leaves the cathode with kinetic energy $K_{max} = \frac{1}{2}mv_{max}^2$ and has zero kinetic energy at the anode. Using the work–energy theorem, we have

$$W_{tot} = -eV_0 = \Delta K = 0 - K_{max}$$
$$K_{max} = \tfrac{1}{2}mv_{max}^2 = eV_0$$

(maximum kinetic energy of photoelectrons)   (38.1)

Hence by measuring the stopping potential V_0, we can determine the maximum kinetic energy with which electrons leave the cathode. (We are ignoring any effects due to differences in the materials of the cathode and anode.)

In this experiment, how do we expect the photocurrent to depend on the voltage across the electrodes and on the frequency and intensity of the light? Based on Maxwell's picture of light as an electromagnetic wave, here is what we *would* expect:

Wave-Model Prediction 1: We saw in Section 32.4 that the intensity of an electromagnetic wave depends on its amplitude but not on its frequency. So the photoelectric effect should occur for light of any frequency, and *the magnitude of the photocurrent should not depend on the frequency of the light.*

Wave-Model Prediction 2: It takes a certain minimum amount of energy, called the **work function,** to eject a single electron from a particular surface (see Fig. 38.1). If the light falling on the surface is very faint, some time may elapse before the total energy absorbed by the surface equals the work function. Hence, for faint illumination, *we expect a time delay* between when we switch on the light and when photoelectrons appear.

Wave-Model Prediction 3: Because the energy delivered to the cathode surface depends on the intensity of illumination, *we expect the stopping potential to increase with increasing light intensity.* Since intensity does not depend on frequency, we further expect that *the stopping potential should not depend on the frequency of the light.*

The experimental results proved to be *very* different from these predictions. Here is what was found in the years between 1877 and 1905:

Experimental Result 1: *The photocurrent depends on the light frequency.* For a given material, monochromatic light with a frequency below a minimum **threshold frequency** produces *no* photocurrent, regardless of intensity. For most metals the threshold frequency is in the ultraviolet (corresponding to wavelengths λ between 200 and 300 nm), but for other materials like potassium oxide and cesium oxide it is in the visible spectrum (λ between 380 and 750 nm).

Experimental Result 2: There is *no measurable time delay* between when the light is turned on and when the cathode emits photoelectrons (assuming the frequency of the light exceeds the threshold frequency). This is true no matter how faint the light is.

Experimental Result 3: *The stopping potential does not depend on intensity, but does depend on frequency.* Figure 38.4 shows graphs of photocurrent as a function of potential difference V_{AC} for light of a given frequency and two different intensities. The reverse potential difference $-V_0$ needed to reduce the current to zero is the same for both intensities. The only effect of increasing the intensity is to increase the number of electrons per second and hence the photocurrent i. (The curves level off when V_{AC} is large and positive because at that point all the emitted electrons are being collected by the anode.) If the intensity is held constant but the frequency is increased, the stopping potential also increases. In other words, the greater the light frequency, the higher the energy of the ejected photoelectrons.

These results directly contradict Maxwell's description of light as an electromagnetic wave. A solution to this dilemma was provided by Albert Einstein in 1905. His proposal involved nothing less than a new picture of the nature of light.

Einstein's Photon Explanation

Einstein made the radical postulate that a beam of light consists of small packages of energy called **photons** or *quanta.* This postulate was an extension of an idea developed five years earlier by Max Planck to explain the properties of blackbody radiation, which we discussed in Section 17.7. (We'll explore Planck's ideas in Section 39.5.) In Einstein's picture, the energy E of an individual photon is equal to a constant h times the photon frequency f. From the relationship $f = c/\lambda$ for electromagnetic waves in vacuum, we have

$$E = hf = \frac{hc}{\lambda} \quad \text{(energy of a photon)} \quad (38.2)$$

where h is a universal constant called **Planck's constant.** The numerical value of this constant, to the accuracy known at present, is

$$h = 6.62606896(33) \times 10^{-34} \text{ J} \cdot \text{s}$$

CAUTION **Photons are not "particles" in the usual sense** It's common to envision photons as miniature billiard balls or pellets. While that's a convenient mental picture, it's not very accurate. For one thing, billiard balls and bullets have a rest mass and travel slower than the speed of light c, while photons travel at the speed of light and have *zero* rest mass. For another thing, photons have wave aspects (frequency and wavelength) that are easy to observe. The fact is that the photon concept is a very strange one, and the true nature of photons is difficult to visualize in a simple way. We'll discuss the dual personality of photons in more detail in Section 38.4.

In Einstein's picture, an individual photon arriving at the surface in Fig. 38.1a or 38.2 is absorbed by a single electron. This energy transfer is an all-or-nothing process, in contrast to the continuous transfer of energy in the wave theory of

38.3 An experiment testing whether the photoelectric effect is consistent with the wave model of light.

(a)

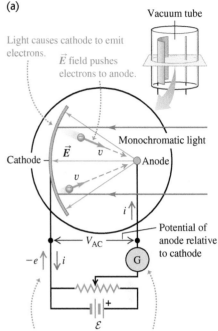

Light causes cathode to emit electrons.
$\vec{E}$ field pushes electrons to anode.

Vacuum tube

Cathode

Monochromatic light

Anode

Potential of anode relative to cathode

Electrons return to cathode via circuit; galvanometer measures current.

(b) We now reverse the electric field so that it tends to repel electrons from the anode. Above a certain field strength, electrons no longer reach the anode.

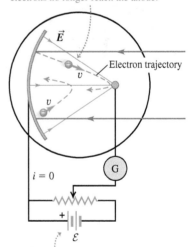

Electron trajectory

$i = 0$

The **stopping potential** at which the current ceases has absolute value V_0.

38.4 Photocurrent i for a constant light frequency f as a function of the potential V_{AC} of the anode with respect to the cathode.

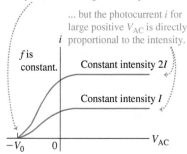

The stopping potential V_0 is independent of the light intensity ...

... but the photocurrent i for large positive V_{AC} is directly proportional to the intensity.

f is constant.

Constant intensity $2I$

Constant intensity I

$-V_0$ 0 V_{AC}

38.5 Stopping potential as a function of frequency for a particular cathode material.

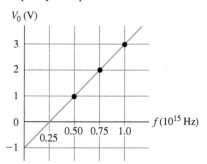

V_0 (V)

3

2

1

0 $f (10^{15}$ Hz)

0.25 0.50 0.75 1.0

−1

Table 38.1 Work Functions of Several Elements

Element	Work Function (eV)
Aluminum	4.3
Carbon	5.0
Copper	4.7
Gold	5.1
Nickel	5.1
Silicon	4.8
Silver	4.3
Sodium	2.7

38.6 Stopping potential as a function of frequency for two cathode materials having different work functions ϕ.

Stopping potential V_0

Material 1

Material 2 $\phi_2 > \phi_1$

0 Frequency f

$-\phi_1/e$

Threshold frequency

$-\phi_2/e$

Stopping potential is zero at threshold frequency (electrons emerge with zero kinetic energy).

For each material,

$eV = hf - \phi$ or $V_0 = \dfrac{h}{e} - \dfrac{\phi}{e}$

so the plots have same slope h/e but different intercepts $-f/e$ on the vertical axis.

light; the electron gets all of the photon's energy or none at all. The electron can escape from the surface only if the energy it acquires is greater than the work function ϕ. Thus photoelectrons will be ejected only if $hf > \phi$, or $f > \phi/h$. Einstein's postulate therefore explains why the photoelectric effect occurs only for frequencies greater than a minimum threshold frequency. This postulate is also consistent with the observation that greater intensity causes a greater photocurrent (Fig. 38.4). Greater intensity at a particular frequency means a greater number of photons per second absorbed, and thus a greater number of electrons emitted per second and a greater photocurrent.

Einstein's postulate also explains why there is no delay between illumination and the emission of photoelectrons. As soon as photons of sufficient energy strike the surface, electrons can absorb them and be ejected.

Finally, Einstein's postulate explains why the stopping potential for a given surface depends only on the light frequency. Recall that ϕ is the *minimum* energy needed to remove an electron from the surface. Einstein applied conservation of energy to find that the *maximum* kinetic energy $K_{max} = \frac{1}{2}mv_{max}^2$ for an emitted electron is the energy hf gained from a photon minus the work function ϕ:

$$K_{max} = \tfrac{1}{2}mv_{max}^2 = hf - \phi \qquad (38.3)$$

Substituting $K_{max} = eV_0$ from Eq. (38.1), we find

$$eV_0 = hf - \phi \quad \text{(photoelectric effect)} \qquad (38.4)$$

Equation (38.4) shows that the stopping potential V_0 increases with increasing frequency f. The intensity doesn't appear in Eq. (38.4), so V_0 is independent of intensity. As a check of Eq. (38.4), we can measure the stopping potential V_0 for each of several values of frequency f for a given cathode material (Fig. 38.5). A graph of V_0 as a function of f turns out to be a straight line, verifying Eq. (38.4), and from such a graph we can determine both the work function ϕ for the material and the value of the quantity h/e. After the electron charge $-e$ was measured by Robert Millikan in 1909, Planck's constant h could also be determined from these measurements.

Electron energies and work functions are usually expressed in electron volts (eV), defined in Section 23.2. To four significant figures,

$$1 \text{ eV} = 1.602 \times 10^{-19} \text{ J}$$

To this accuracy, Planck's constant is

$$h = 6.626 \times 10^{-34} \text{ J} \cdot \text{s} = 4.136 \times 10^{-15} \text{ eV} \cdot \text{s}$$

Table 38.1 lists the work functions of several elements. These values are approximate because they are very sensitive to surface impurities. The greater the work function, the higher the minimum frequency needed to emit photoelectrons (Fig. 38.6).

The photon picture explains a number of other phenomena in which light is absorbed. One example is a *suntan*, which is caused when the energy in sunlight triggers a chemical reaction in skin cells that leads to increased production of the pigment melanin. This reaction can occur only if a specific molecule in the cell absorbs a certain minimum amount of energy. A short-wavelength ultraviolet photon has enough energy to trigger the reaction, but a longer-wavelength visible-light photon does not. Hence ultraviolet light causes tanning, while visible light cannot.

Photon Momentum

Einstein's photon concept applies to *all* regions of the electromagnetic spectrum, including radio waves, x rays, and so on. A photon of any electromagnetic radiation with frequency f and wavelength λ has energy E given by Eq. (38.2).

Furthermore, according to the special theory of relativity, every particle that has energy must also have momentum, even if it has no rest mass. Photons have zero rest mass. As we saw in Eq. (37.40), a particle with zero rest mass and energy E has momentum with magnitude p given by $E = pc$. Thus the wavelength λ of a photon and the magnitude of its momentum p are related simply by

$$p = \frac{E}{c} = \frac{hf}{c} = \frac{h}{\lambda} \qquad \text{(momentum of a photon)} \qquad (38.5)$$

The direction of the photon's momentum is simply the direction in which the electromagnetic wave is moving.

Problem-Solving Strategy 38.1   Photons

IDENTIFY *the relevant concepts:* The energy and momentum of an individual photon are proportional to the frequency and inversely proportional to the wavelength. Einstein's interpretation of the photoelectric effect is that energy is conserved as a photon ejects an electron from a material surface.

SET UP *the problem:* Identify the target variable. It could be the photon's wavelength λ, frequency f, energy E, or momentum p. If the problem involves the photoelectric effect, the target variable could be the maximum kinetic energy of photoelectrons K_{max}, the stopping potential V_0, or the work function ϕ.

EXECUTE *the solution* as follows:
1. Use Eqs. (38.2) and (38.5) to relate the energy and momentum of a photon to its wavelength and frequency. If the problem involves the photoelectric effect, use Eqs. (38.1), (38.3), and

(38.4) to relate the photon frequency, stopping potential, work function, and maximum photoelectron kinetic energy.
2. The electron volt (eV), which we introduced in Section 23.2, is a convenient unit. It is the kinetic energy gained by an electron when it moves freely through an increase of potential of one volt: 1 eV = 1.602×10^{-19} J. If the photon energy E is given in electron volts, use $h = 4.136 \times 10^{-15}$ eV·s; if E is in joules, use $h = 6.626 \times 10^{-34}$ J·s.

EVALUATE *your answer:* In problems involving photons, at first the numbers will be unfamiliar to you and errors will not be obvious. It helps to remember that a visible-light photon with $\lambda = 600$ nm and $f = 5 \times 10^{14}$ Hz has an energy E of about 2 eV, or about 3×10^{-19} J.

Example 38.1   Laser-pointer photons

A laser pointer with a power output of 5.00 mW emits red light ($\lambda = 650$ nm). (a) What is the magnitude of the momentum of each photon? (b) How many photons does the laser pointer emit each second?

SOLUTION

IDENTIFY and SET UP: This problem involves the ideas of (a) photon momentum and (b) photon energy. In part (a) we'll use Eq. (38.5) and the given wavelength to find the magnitude of each photon's momentum. In part (b), Eq. (38.2) gives the energy per photon, and the power output tells us the energy emitted per second. We can combine these quantities to calculate the number of photons emitted per second.

EXECUTE: (a) We have $\lambda = 650$ nm $= 6.50 \times 10^{-7}$ m, so from Eq. (38.5) the photon momentum is

$$p = \frac{h}{\lambda} = \frac{6.626 \times 10^{-34} \text{ J·s}}{6.50 \times 10^{-7} \text{ m}}$$
$$= 1.02 \times 10^{-27} \text{ kg·m/s}$$

(Recall that 1 J = 1 kg·m²/s².)

(b) From Eq. (38.2), the energy of a single photon is

$$E = pc = (1.02 \times 10^{-27} \text{ kg·m/s})(3.00 \times 10^8 \text{ m/s})$$
$$= 3.06 \times 10^{-19} \text{ J} = 1.91 \text{ eV}$$

The laser pointer emits energy at the rate of 5.00×10^{-3} J/s, so it emits photons at the rate of

$$\frac{5.00 \times 10^{-3} \text{ J/s}}{3.06 \times 10^{-19} \text{ J/photon}} = 1.63 \times 10^{16} \text{ photons/s}$$

EVALUATE: The result in part (a) is very small; a typical oxygen molecule in room-temperature air has 2500 times more momentum. As a check on part (b), we can calculate the photon energy using Eq. (38.2):

$$E = hf = \frac{hc}{\lambda} = \frac{(6.626 \times 10^{-34} \text{ J·s})(3.00 \times 10^8 \text{ m/s})}{6.50 \times 10^{-7} \text{ m}}$$
$$= 3.06 \times 10^{-19} \text{ J} = 1.91 \text{ eV}$$

Our result in part (b) shows that a huge number of photons leave the laser pointer each second, each of which has an infinitesimal amount of energy. Hence the discreteness of the photons isn't noticed, and the radiated energy appears to be a continuous flow.

Example 38.2 A photoelectric-effect experiment

While conducting a photoelectric-effect experiment with light of a certain frequency, you find that a reverse potential difference of 1.25 V is required to reduce the current to zero. Find (a) the maximum kinetic energy and (b) the maximum speed of the emitted photoelectrons.

SOLUTION

IDENTIFY and SET UP: The value of 1.25 V is the stopping potential V_0 for this experiment. We'll use this in Eq. (38.1) to find the maximum photoelectron kinetic energy K_{max}, and from this we'll find the maximum photoelectron speed.

EXECUTE: (a) From Eq. (38.1),

$$K_{max} = eV_0 = (1.60 \times 10^{-19}\ \text{C})(1.25\ \text{V}) = 2.00 \times 10^{-19}\ \text{J}$$

(Recall that $1\ \text{V} = 1\ \text{J/C}$.) In terms of electron volts,

$$K_{max} = eV_0 = e(1.25\ \text{V}) = 1.25\ \text{eV}$$

since the electron volt (eV) is the magnitude of the electron charge e times one volt (1 V).

(b) From $K_{max} = \frac{1}{2}mv_{max}^2$ we get

$$v_{max} = \sqrt{\frac{2K_{max}}{m}} = \sqrt{\frac{2(2.00 \times 10^{-19}\ \text{J})}{9.11 \times 10^{-31}\ \text{kg}}}$$
$$= 6.63 \times 10^5\ \text{m/s}$$

EVALUATE The value of v_{max} is about 0.2% of the speed of light, so we are justified in using the nonrelativistic expression for kinetic energy. (An equivalent justification is that the electron's 1.25-eV kinetic energy is much less than its rest energy $mc^2 = 0.511\ \text{MeV} = 5.11 \times 10^5\ \text{eV}$.)

Example 38.3 Determining ϕ and h experimentally

For a particular cathode material in a photoelectric-effect experiment, you measure stopping potentials $V_0 = 1.0$ V for light of wavelength $\lambda = 600$ nm, 2.0 V for 400 nm, and 3.0 V for 300 nm. Determine the work function ϕ for this material and the implied value of Planck's constant h.

SOLUTION

IDENTIFY and SET UP: This example uses the relationship among stopping potential V_0, frequency f, and work function ϕ in the photoelectric effect. According to Eq. (38.4), a graph of V_0 versus f should be a straight line as in Fig. 38.5 or 38.6. Such a graph is completely determined by its slope and the value at which it intercepts the vertical axis; we will use these to determine the values of the target variables ϕ and h.

EXECUTE: We rewrite Eq. (38.4) as

$$V_0 = \frac{h}{e}f - \frac{\phi}{e}$$

In this form we see that the slope of the line is h/e and the vertical-axis intercept (corresponding to $f = 0$) is $-\phi/e$. The frequencies,

obtained from $f = c/\lambda$ and $c = 3.00 \times 10^8$ m/s, are 0.50×10^{15} Hz, 0.75×10^{15} Hz, and 1.0×10^{15} Hz, respectively. From a graph of these data (see Fig. 38.6), we find

$$-\frac{\phi}{e} = \text{vertical intercept} = -1.0\ \text{V}$$
$$\phi = 1.0\ \text{eV} = 1.6 \times 10^{-19}\ \text{J}$$

and

$$\text{Slope} = \frac{\Delta V_0}{\Delta f} - \frac{3.0\ \text{V} - (-1.0\ \text{V})}{1.00 \times 10^{15}\ \text{s}^{-1} - 0} = 4.0 \times 10^{-15}\ \text{J} \cdot \text{s/C}$$
$$h = \text{slope} \times e = (4.0 \times 10^{-15}\ \text{J} \cdot \text{s/C})(1.60 \times 10^{-19}\ \text{C})$$
$$= 6.4 \times 10^{-34}\ \text{J} \cdot \text{s}$$

EVALUATE: The value of Planck's constant h determined from your experiment differs from the accepted value by only about 3%. The small value $\phi = 1.0$ eV tells us that the cathode surface is not composed solely of one of the elements in Table 38.1.

Application Sterilizing with High-Energy Photons
One technique for killing harmful microorganisms is to illuminate them with ultraviolet light with a wavelength shorter than 254 nm. If a photon of such short wavelength strikes a DNA molecule within a microorganism, the energy of the photon is great enough to break the bonds within the molecule. This renders the microorganism unable to grow or reproduce. Such ultraviolet germicidal irradiation is used for medical sanitation, to keep laboratories sterile (as shown here), and to treat both drinking water and wastewater.

Test Your Understanding of Section 38.1 Silicon films become better electrical conductors when illuminated by photons with energies of 1.14 eV or greater, an effect called *photoconductivity*. Which of the following wavelengths of electromagnetic radiation can cause photoconductivity in silicon films? (i) ultraviolet light with $\lambda = 300$ nm; (ii) red light with $\lambda = 600$ nm; (iii) infrared light with $\lambda = 1200$ nm. ∎

38.2 Light Emitted as Photons: X-Ray Production

The photoelectric effect provides convincing evidence that light is *absorbed* in the form of photons. For physicists to accept Einstein's radical photon concept, however, it was also necessary to show that light is *emitted* as photons. An experiment that demonstrates this convincingly is the inverse of the photoelectric effect: Instead of releasing electrons from a surface by shining electromagnetic radiation on it, we cause a surface to emit radiation—specifically, *x rays*—by bombarding it with fast-moving electrons.

X-Ray Photons

X rays were first produced in 1895 by the German physicist Wilhelm Röntgen, using an apparatus similar in principle to the setup shown in Fig. 38.7. Electrons are released from the cathode by *thermionic emission,* in which the escape energy is supplied by heating the cathode to a very high temperature. (As in the photoelectric effect, the minimum energy that an individual electron must be given to escape from the cathode's surface is equal to the work function for the surface. In this case the energy is provided to the electrons by heat rather than by light.) The electrons are then accelerated toward the anode by a potential difference V_{AC}. The bulb is evacuated (residual pressure 10^{-7} atm or less), so the electrons can travel from the cathode to the anode without colliding with air molecules. When V_{AC} is a few thousand volts or more, x rays are emitted from the anode surface.

The anode produces x rays in part simply by slowing the electrons abruptly. (Recall from Section 32.1 that accelerated charges emit electromagnetic waves.) This process is called *bremsstrahlung* (German for "braking radiation"). Because the electrons undergo accelerations of very great magnitude, they emit much of their radiation at short wavelengths in the x-ray range, about 10^{-9} to 10^{-12} m (1 nm to 1 pm). (X-ray wavelengths can be measured quite precisely by crystal diffraction techniques, which we discussed in Section 36.6.) Most electrons are braked by a series of collisions and interactions with anode atoms, so bremsstrahlung produces a continuous spectrum of electromagnetic radiation.

Just as we did for the photoelectric effect in Section 38.1, let's compare what Maxwell's wave theory of electromagnetic radiation would predict about this radiation to what is observed experimentally.

> **Wave-Model Prediction:** The electromagnetic waves produced when an electron slams into the anode should be analogous to the sound waves produced by crashing cymbals together. These waves include sounds of all frequencies. By analogy, the x rays produced by bremsstrahlung should have a spectrum that includes *all* frequencies and hence *all* wavelengths.

> **Experimental Result:** Figure 38.8 shows bremsstrahlung spectra using the same cathode and anode with four different accelerating voltages. We see that *not* all x-ray frequencies and wavelengths are emitted: Each spectrum has a maximum frequency f_{max} and a corresponding minimum wavelength λ_{min}. The greater the potential difference V_{AC}, the higher the maximum frequency and the shorter the minimum wavelength.

The wave model of electromagnetic radiation cannot explain these experimental results. But we can readily understand them using the photon model. An electron has charge $-e$ and gains kinetic energy eV_{AC} when accelerated through a potential increase V_{AC}. The most energetic photon (highest frequency and shortest wavelength) is produced if the electron is braked to a stop all at once when it hits the anode, so that all of its kinetic energy goes to produce one photon; that is,

$$eV_{AC} = hf_{max} = \frac{hc}{\lambda_{min}} \qquad \text{(bremsstrahlung)} \qquad (38.6)$$

(In this equation we neglect the work function of the target anode and the initial kinetic energy of the electrons "boiled off" from the cathode. These energies are very small compared to the kinetic energy eV_{AC} gained due to the potential

38.7 An apparatus used to produce x rays, similar to Röntgen's 1895 apparatus.

Electrons are emitted thermionically from the heated cathode and are accelerated toward the anode; when they strike it, x rays are produced.

38.8 The continuous spectrum of x rays produced when a tungsten target is struck by electrons accelerated through a voltage V_{AC}. The curves represent different values of V_{AC}; points *a*, *b*, *c*, and *d* show the minimum wavelength for each voltage.

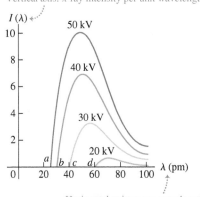

difference.) If only a portion of an electron's kinetic energy goes into producing a photon, the photon energy will be less than eV_{AC} and the wavelength will be greater than λ_{min}. As further support for the photon model, the measured values for λ_{min} for different values of eV_{AC} (see Fig. 38.8) agree with Eq. (38.6). Note that according to Eq. (38.6), the maximum frequency and minimum wavelength in the bremsstrahlung process do not depend on the target material; this also agrees with experiment. So we can conclude that the photon picture of electromagnetic radiation is valid for the *emission* as well as the absorption of radiation.

The apparatus shown in Fig. 38.7 can also produce x rays by a second process in which electrons transfer their kinetic energy partly or completely to individual atoms within the target. It turns out that this process not only is consistent with the photon model of electromagnetic radiation, but also provides insight into the structure of atoms. We'll return to this process in Section 41.5.

Example 38.4 **Producing x rays**

Electrons in an x-ray tube accelerate through a potential difference of 10.0 kV before striking a target. If an electron produces one photon on impact with the target, what is the minimum wavelength of the resulting x rays? Find the answer by expressing energies in both SI units and electron volts.

SOLUTION

IDENTIFY and SET UP: To produce an x-ray photon with minimum wavelength and hence maximum energy, all of the electron's kinetic energy must go into producing a single x-ray photon. We'll use Eq. (38.6) to determine the wavelength.

EXECUTE: From Eq. (38.6), using SI units we have

$$\lambda_{min} = \frac{hc}{eV_{AC}} = \frac{(6.626 \times 10^{-34} \text{ J} \cdot \text{s})(3.00 \times 10^8 \text{ m/s})}{(1.602 \times 10^{-19} \text{ C})(10.0 \times 10^3 \text{ V})}$$

$$= 1.24 \times 10^{-10} \text{ m} = 0.124 \text{ nm}$$

Using electron volts, we have

$$\lambda_{min} = \frac{hc}{eV_{AC}} = \frac{(4.136 \times 10^{-15} \text{ eV} \cdot \text{s})(3.00 \times 10^8 \text{ m/s})}{e(10.0 \times 10^3 \text{ V})}$$

$$= 1.24 \times 10^{-10} \text{ m} = 0.124 \text{ nm}$$

In the second calculation, the "e" for the magnitude of the electron charge cancels the "e" in the unit "eV," because the electron volt (eV) is the magnitude of the electron charge e times one volt (1 V).

EVALUATE: To check our result, recall from Example 38.1 that a 1.91-eV photon has a wavelength of 650 nm. Here the electron energy, and therefore the x-ray photon energy, is 10.0×10^3 eV = 10.0 keV, about 5000 times greater than in Example 38.1, and the wavelength is about $\frac{1}{5000}$ as great as in Example 38.1. This makes sense, since wavelength and photon energy are inversely proportional.

38.9 This radiologist is operating a CT scanner (seen through the window) from a separate room to avoid repeated exposure to x rays.

Applications of X Rays

X rays have many practical applications in medicine and industry. Because x-ray photons are of such high energy, they can penetrate several centimeters of solid matter. Hence they can be used to visualize the interiors of materials that are opaque to ordinary light, such as broken bones or defects in structural steel. The object to be visualized is placed between an x-ray source and an electronic detector (like that used in a digital camera) or a piece of photographic film. The darker an area in the image recorded by such a detector, the greater the radiation exposure. Bones are much more effective x-ray absorbers than soft tissue, so bones appear as light areas. A crack or air bubble allows greater transmission and shows as a dark area.

A widely used and vastly improved x-ray technique is *computed tomography;* the corresponding instrument is called a *CT scanner.* The x-ray source produces a thin, fan-shaped beam that is detected on the opposite side of the subject by an array of several hundred detectors in a line. Each detector measures absorption along a thin line through the subject. The entire apparatus is rotated around the subject in the plane of the beam, and the changing photon-counting rates of the detectors are recorded digitally. A computer processes this information and reconstructs a picture of absorption over an entire cross section of the subject (see Fig. 38.9). Differences in absorption as small as 1% or less can be detected with CT scans, and tumors and other anomalies that are much too small to be seen with older x-ray techniques can be detected.

X rays cause damage to living tissues. As x-ray photons are absorbed in tissues, their energy breaks molecular bonds and creates highly reactive free radicals (such as neutral H and OH), which in turn can disturb the molecular structure of proteins and especially genetic material. Young and rapidly growing cells are particularly susceptible, which is why x rays are useful for selective destruction of cancer cells. Conversely, however, a cell may be damaged by radiation but survive, continue dividing, and produce generations of defective cells; thus x rays can *cause* cancer.

Even when the organism itself shows no apparent damage, excessive exposure to x rays can cause changes in the organism's reproductive system that will affect its offspring. A careful assessment of the balance between risks and benefits of radiation exposure is essential in each individual case.

Test Your Understanding of Section 38.2 In the apparatus shown in Fig. 38.7, suppose you increase the number of electrons that are emitted from the cathode per second while keeping the potential difference V_{AC} the same. How will this affect the intensity I and minimum wavelength λ_{min} of the emitted x rays? (i) I and λ_{min} will both increase; (ii) I will increase but λ_{min} will be unchanged; (iii) I will increase but λ_{min} will decrease; (iv) I will remain the same but λ_{min} will decrease; (v) none of these. ▌

38.3 Light Scattered as Photons: Compton Scattering and Pair Production

The final aspect of light that we must test against Einstein's photon model is its behavior after the light is produced and before it is eventually absorbed. We can do this by considering the *scattering* of light. As we discussed in Section 33.6, scattering is what happens when light bounces off particles such as molecules in the air.

Compton Scattering

Let's see what Maxwell's wave model and Einstein's photon model predict for how light behaves when it undergoes scattering by a single electron, such as an individual electron within an atom.

Wave-Model Prediction: In the wave description, scattering would be a process of absorption and re-radiation. Part of the energy of the light wave would be absorbed by the electron, which would oscillate in response to the oscillating electric field of the wave. The oscillating electron would act like a miniature antenna (see Section 32.1), re-radiating its acquired energy as *scattered* waves in a variety of directions. The frequency at which the electron oscillates would be the same as the frequency of the incident light, and the re-radiated light would have the same frequency as the oscillations of the electron. So, *in the wave model, the scattered light and incident light have the same frequency and same wavelength.*

Photon-Model Prediction: In the photon model we imagine the scattering process as a collision of two *particles,* the incident photon and an electron that is initially at rest (Fig. 38.10a). The incident photon would give up part of its energy and momentum to the electron, which recoils as a result of this impact. The scattered photon that remains can fly off at a variety of angles ϕ with respect to the incident direction, but it has less energy and less momentum than the incident photon (Fig. 38.10b). The energy and momentum of a photon are given by $E = hf = hc/\lambda$ (Eq. 38.2) and $p = hf/c = h/\lambda$ (Eq. 38.5). Therefore, *in the photon model, the scattered light has a lower frequency f and longer wavelength λ than the incident light.*

38.10 The photon model of light scattering by an electron.

(a) Before collision: The target electron is at rest.

Incident photon: wavelength λ, momentum $\vec{p}$ Target electron (at rest)

(b) After collision: The angle between the directions of the scattered photon and incident photon is ϕ.

Scattered photon: wavelength λ', momentum $\vec{p}'$

ϕ

Recoiling electron: momentum $\vec{P}_e$

38.11 A Compton-effect experiment.

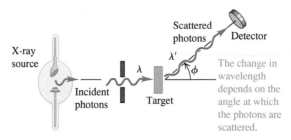

The change in wavelength depends on the angle at which the photons are scattered.

The definitive experiment that tested these predictions of the wave and photon models was carried out in 1922 by the American physicist Arthur H. Compton. In his experiment Compton aimed a beam of x rays at a solid target and measured the wavelength of the radiation scattered from the target (Fig. 38.11). He discovered that some of the scattered radiation has smaller frequency (longer wavelength) than the incident radiation and that the change in wavelength depends on the angle through which the radiation is scattered. This is precisely what the photon model predicts for light scattered from electrons in the target, a process that is now called **Compton scattering.**

Specifically, if the scattered radiation emerges at an angle ϕ with respect to the incident direction, as shown in Fig. 38.11, and if λ and λ' are the wavelengths of the incident and scattered radiation, respectively, Compton found that

$$\lambda' - \lambda = \frac{h}{mc}(1 - \cos\phi) \qquad \text{(Compton scattering)} \qquad (38.7)$$

where m is the electron rest mass. In other words, λ' is greater than λ. The quantity h/mc that appears in Eq. (38.7) has units of length. Its numerical value is

$$\frac{h}{mc} = \frac{6.626 \times 10^{-34} \text{ J}\cdot\text{s}}{(9.109 \times 10^{-31} \text{ kg})(2.998 \times 10^8 \text{ m/s})} = 2.426 \times 10^{-12} \text{ m}$$

Compton showed that Einstein's photon theory, combined with the principles of conservation of energy and conservation of momentum, provides a beautifully clear explanation of his experimental results. We outline the derivation below. The electron recoil energy may be in the relativistic range, so we have to use the relativistic energy–momentum relationships, Eqs. (37.39) and (37.40). The incident photon has momentum $\vec{p}$, with magnitude p and energy pc. The scattered photon has momentum $\vec{p}'$, with magnitude p' and energy $p'c$. The electron is initially at rest, so its initial momentum is zero and its initial energy is its rest energy mc^2. The final electron momentum $\vec{P}_e$ has magnitude P_e, and the final electron energy is given by $E_e^2 = (mc^2)^2 + (P_e c)^2$. Then energy conservation gives us the relationship

$$pc + mc^2 = p'c + E_e$$

38.12 Vector diagram showing conservation of momentum in Compton scattering.

Conservation of momentum during Compton scattering

Rearranging, we find

$$(pc - p'c + mc^2)^2 = E_e^2 = (mc^2)^2 + (P_e c)^2 \qquad (38.8)$$

We can eliminate the electron momentum $\vec{P}_e$ from Eq. (38.8) by using momentum conservation. From Fig. 38.12 we see that $\vec{p} = \vec{p}' + \vec{P}_e$, or

$$\vec{P}_e = \vec{p} - \vec{p}' \qquad (38.9)$$

By taking the scalar product of each side of Eq. (38.9) with itself, we find

$$P_e^2 = p^2 + p'^2 - 2pp' \cos \phi \qquad (38.10)$$

We now substitute this expression for P_e^2 into Eq. (38.8) and multiply out the left side. We divide out a common factor c^2; several terms cancel, and when the resulting equation is divided through by (pp'), the result is

$$\frac{mc}{p'} - \frac{mc}{p} = 1 - \cos \phi \qquad (38.11)$$

Finally, we substitute $p' = h/\lambda'$ and $p = h/\lambda$, then multiply by h/mc to obtain Eq. (38.7).

When the wavelengths of x rays scattered at a certain angle are measured, the curve of intensity per unit wavelength as a function of wavelength has two peaks (Fig. 38.13). The longer-wavelength peak represents Compton scattering. The shorter-wavelength peak, labeled λ_0, is at the wavelength of the incident x rays and corresponds to x-ray scattering from tightly bound electrons. In such scattering processes the entire atom must recoil, so the m in Eq. (38.7) is the mass of the entire atom rather than of a single electron. The resulting wavelength shifts are negligible.

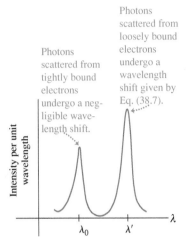

38.13 Intensity as a function of wavelength for photons scattered at an angle of 135° in a Compton-scattering experiment.

Photons scattered from tightly bound electrons undergo a negligible wavelength shift.

Photons scattered from loosely bound electrons undergo a wavelength shift given by Eq. (38.7).

Example 38.5 Compton scattering

You use 0.124-nm x-ray photons in a Compton-scattering experiment. (a) At what angle is the wavelength of the scattered x rays 1.0% longer than that of the incident x rays? (b) At what angle is it 0.050% longer?

SOLUTION

IDENTIFY and SET UP: We'll use the relationship between scattering angle and wavelength shift in the Compton effect. In each case our target variable is the angle ϕ (see Fig. 38.10b). We solve for ϕ using Eq. (38.7).

EXECUTE: (a) In Eq. (38.7) we want $\Delta\lambda = \lambda' - \lambda$ to be 1.0% of 0.124 nm, so $\Delta\lambda = 0.00124$ nm $= 1.24 \times 10^{-12}$ m. Using the value $h/mc = 2.426 \times 10^{-12}$ m, we find

$$\Delta\lambda = \frac{h}{mc}(1 - \cos \phi)$$

$$\cos \phi = 1 - \frac{\Delta\lambda}{h/mc} = 1 - \frac{1.24 \times 10^{-12} \text{ m}}{2.426 \times 10^{-12} \text{ m}} = 0.4889$$

$$\phi = 60.7°$$

(b) For $\Delta\lambda$ to be 0.050% of 0.124 nm, or 6.2×10^{-14} m,

$$\cos \phi = 1 - \frac{6.2 \times 10^{-14} \text{ m}}{2.426 \times 10^{-12} \text{ m}} = 0.9744$$

$$\phi = 13.0°$$

EVALUATE: Our results show that smaller scattering angles give smaller wavelength shifts. Thus in a grazing collision the photon energy loss and the electron recoil energy are smaller than when the scattering angle is larger. This is just what we would expect for an elastic collision, whether between a photon and an electron or between two billiard balls.

Pair Production

Another effect that can be explained only with the photon picture involves *gamma rays,* the shortest-wavelength and highest-frequency variety of electromagnetic radiation. If a gamma-ray photon of sufficiently short wavelength is fired at a target, it may not scatter. Instead, as depicted in Fig. 38.14, it may disappear completely and be replaced by two new particles: an electron and a **positron** (a particle that has the same rest mass m as an electron but has a positive charge $+e$ rather than the negative charge $-e$ of the electron). This process, called **pair production,** was first observed by the physicists Patrick Blackett and Giuseppe Occhialini in 1933. The electron and positron have to be produced in pairs in order to conserve electric charge: The incident photon has zero charge, and the electron–positron pair has net charge $(-e) + (+e) = 0$. Enough energy must be available to account for the rest energy $2mc^2$ of the two particles. To four significant figures, this minimum energy is

38.14 (a) Photograph of bubble-chamber tracks of electron–positron pairs that are produced when 300-MeV photons strike a lead sheet. A magnetic field directed out of the photograph made the electrons (e^-) and positrons (e^+) curve in opposite directions. (b) Diagram showing the pair-production process for two of the gamma-ray photons (γ).

(a)

Electron–positron pair

(b)

$$E_{min} = 2mc^2 = 2(9.109 \times 10^{-31} \text{ kg})(2.998 \times 10^8 \text{ m/s})^2$$

$$= 1.637 \times 10^{-13} \text{ J} = 1.022 \text{ MeV}$$

Thus the photon must have at least this much energy to produce an electron–positron pair. From Eq. (38.2), $E = hc/\lambda$, the photon wavelength has to be shorter than

$$\lambda_{max} = \frac{hc}{E_{min}} = \frac{(6.626 \times 10^{-34} \text{ J} \cdot \text{s})(2.998 \times 10^8 \text{ m/s})}{1.637 \times 10^{-13} \text{ J}}$$

$$= 1.213 \times 10^{-12} \text{ m} = 1.213 \times 10^{-3} \text{ nm} = 1.213 \text{ pm}$$

This is a very short wavelength, about $\frac{1}{1000}$ as large as the x-ray wavelengths that Compton used in his scattering experiments. (The requisite minimum photon energy is actually a bit higher than 1.022 MeV, so the photon wavelength must be a bit shorter than 1.213 pm. The reason is that when the incident photon encounters an atomic nucleus in the target, some of the photon energy goes into the kinetic energy of the recoiling nucleus.) Just as for the photoelectric effect, the wave model of electromagnetic radiation cannot explain why pair production occurs only when very short wavelengths are used.

The inverse process, *electron–positron pair annihilation*, occurs when a positron and an electron collide. Both particles disappear, and two (or occasionally three) photons can appear, with total energy of at least $2m_ec^2 = 1.022$ MeV. Decay into a *single* photon is impossible because such a process could not conserve both energy and momentum. It's easiest to analyze this annihilation process in the frame of reference called the *center-of-momentum system*, in which the total momentum is zero. It is the relativistic generalization of the center-of-mass system that we discussed in Section 8.5.

Example 38.6 **Pair annihilation**

An electron and a positron, initially far apart, move toward each other with the same speed. They collide head-on, annihilating each other and producing two photons. Find the energies, wavelengths, and frequencies of the photons if the initial kinetic energies of the electron and positron are (a) both negligible and (b) both 5.000 MeV. The electron rest energy is 0.511 MeV.

SOLUTION

IDENTIFY and SET UP: Just as in the elastic collisions we studied in Chapter 8, both momentum and energy are conserved in pair annihilation. The electron and positron are initially far apart, so the initial electric potential energy is zero and the initial energy is the sum of the particle kinetic and rest energies. The final energy is the sum of the photon energies. The total initial momentum is zero; the total momentum of the two photons must likewise be zero. We find the photon energy E using conservation of energy, conservation of momentum, and the relationship $E = pc$ (see Section 38.1). We then calculate the wavelengths and frequencies using $E = hc/\lambda = hf$.

EXECUTE: If the total momentum of the two photons is to be zero, their momenta must have equal magnitudes p and opposite directions. From $E = pc = hc/\lambda = hf$, the two photons must also have the same energy E, wavelength λ, and frequency f.

Before the collision the energy of each electron is $K + mc^2$, where K is its kinetic energy and $mc^2 = 0.511$ MeV. Conservation of energy then gives

$$(K + mc^2) + (K + mc^2) = E + E$$

Hence the energy of each photon is $E = K + mc^2$.

(a) In this case the electron kinetic energy K is negligible compared to its rest energy mc^2, so each photon has energy $E = mc^2 = 0.511$ MeV. The corresponding photon wavelength and frequency are

$$\lambda = \frac{hc}{E} = \frac{(4.136 \times 10^{-15} \text{ eV} \cdot \text{s})(3.00 \times 10^8 \text{ m/s})}{0.511 \times 10^6 \text{ eV}}$$

$$= 2.43 \times 10^{-12} \text{ m} = 2.43 \text{ pm}$$

$$f = \frac{E}{h} = \frac{0.511 \times 10^6 \text{ eV}}{4.136 \times 10^{-15} \text{ eV} \cdot \text{s}} = 1.24 \times 10^{20} \text{ Hz}$$

(b) In this case $K = 5.000$ MeV, so each photon has energy $E = 5.000 \text{ MeV} + 0.511 \text{ MeV} = 5.511 \text{ MeV}$. Proceeding as in part (a), you can show that the photon wavelength is 0.2250 pm and the frequency is 1.333×10^{21} Hz.

EVALUATE: As a check, recall from Example 38.1 that a 650-nm visible-light photon has energy 1.91 eV and frequency 4.62×10^{14} Hz. The photon energy in part (a) is about 2.5×10^5 times greater. As expected, the photon's wavelength is shorter and its frequency higher than those for a visible-light photon by the same factor. You can check the results for part (b) in the same way.

Test Your Understanding of Section 38.3 If you used visible-light photons in the experiment shown in Fig. 38.11, would the photons undergo a wavelength shift due to the scattering? If so, is it possible to detect the shift with the human eye? ▮

38.4 Wave–Particle Duality, Probability, and Uncertainty

We have studied many examples of the behavior of light and other electromagnetic radiation. Some, including the interference and diffraction effects described in Chapters 35 and 36, demonstrate conclusively the *wave* nature of light. Others, the subject of the present chapter, point with equal force to the *particle* nature of light. At first glance these two aspects seem to be in direct conflict. How can light be a wave and a particle at the same time?

We can find the answer to this apparent wave–particle conflict in the **principle of complementarity,** first stated by the Danish physicist Niels Bohr in 1928. The wave descriptions and the particle descriptions are complementary. That is, we need both to complete our model of nature, but we will never need to use both at the same time to describe a single part of an occurrence.

Diffraction and Interference in the Photon Picture

Let's start by considering again the diffraction pattern for a single slit, which we analyzed in Sections 36.2 and 36.3. Instead of recording the pattern on a digital camera chip or photographic film, we use a detector called a *photomultiplier* that can actually detect individual photons. Using the setup shown in Fig. 38.15, we place the photomultiplier at various positions for equal time intervals, count the photons at each position, and plot out the intensity distribution.

We find that, on average, the distribution of photons agrees with our predictions from Section 36.3. At points corresponding to the maxima of the pattern, we count many photons; at minimum points, we count almost none; and so on. The graph of the counts at various points gives the same diffraction pattern that we predicted with Eq. (36.7).

But suppose we now reduce the intensity to such a low level that only a few photons per second pass through the slit. We now record a series of discrete strikes, each representing a single photon. While we *cannot predict* where any given photon will strike, over time the accumulating strikes build up the familiar diffraction pattern we expect for a wave. To reconcile the wave and particle aspects of this pattern, we have to regard the pattern as a *statistical* distribution that tells us how many photons, on average, go to each spot. Equivalently, the pattern tells us the *probability* that any individual photon will land at a given spot. If we shine our faint light beam on a two-slit apparatus, we get an analogous result (Fig. 38.16). Again we can't predict exactly where an individual photon will go; the interference pattern is a statistical distribution.

How does the principle of complementarity apply to these diffraction and interference experiments? The wave description, not the particle description, explains the single- and double-slit patterns. But the particle description, not the wave description, explains why the photomultiplier records discrete packages of energy. The two descriptions complete our understanding of the results. For instance, suppose we consider an individual photon and ask how it knows "which way to go" when passing through the slit. This question seems like a conundrum, but that is because it is framed in terms of a *particle* description—whereas it is the *wave* nature of light that determines the distribution of photons. Conversely,

38.15 Single-slit diffraction pattern of light observed with a movable photomultiplier. The curve shows the intensity distribution predicted by the wave picture. The photon distribution is shown by the numbers of photons counted at various positions.

38.16 These images record the positions where individual photons in a two-slit interference experiment strike the screen. As more photons reach the screen, a recognizable interference pattern appears.

After 21 photons reach the screen

After 1000 photons reach the screen

After 10,000 photons reach the screen

the fact that the photomultiplier detects faint light as a sequence of individual "spots" can't be explained in wave terms.

Probability and Uncertainty

Although photons have energy and momentum, they are nonetheless very different from the particle model we used for Newtonian mechanics in Chapters 4 through 8. The Newtonian particle model treats an object as a point mass. We can describe the location and state of motion of such a particle at any instant with three spatial coordinates and three components of momentum, and we can then predict the particle's future motion. This model doesn't work at all for photons, however: We *cannot* treat a photon as a point object. This is because there are fundamental limitations on the precision with which we can simultaneously determine the position and momentum of a photon. Many aspects of a photon's behavior can be stated only in terms of *probabilities*. (In Chapter 39 we will find that the non-Newtonian ideas we develop for photons in this section also apply to particles such as electrons.)

To get more insight into the problem of measuring a photon's position and momentum simultaneously, let's look again at the single-slit diffraction of light (Fig. 38.17). Suppose the wavelength λ is much less than the slit width a. Then most (85%) of the photons go into the central maximum of the diffraction pattern, and the remainder go into other parts of the pattern. We use θ_1 to denote the angle between the central maximum and the first minimum. Using Eq. (36.2) with $m = 1$, we find that θ_1 is given by $\sin \theta_1 = \lambda/a$. Since we assume $\lambda = a$, it follows that θ_1 is very small, $\sin \theta_1$ is very nearly equal to θ_1 (in radians), and

$$\theta_1 = \frac{\lambda}{a} \tag{38.12}$$

Even though the photons all have the same initial state of motion, they don't all follow the same path. We can't predict the exact trajectory of any individual photon from knowledge of its initial state; we can only describe the *probability* that an individual photon will strike a given spot on the screen. This fundamental indeterminacy has no counterpart in Newtonian mechanics.

Furthermore, there are fundamental *uncertainties* in both the position and the momentum of an individual particle, and these uncertainties are related inseparably. To clarify this point, let's go back to Fig. 38.17. A photon that strikes the screen at the outer edge of the central maximum, at angle θ_1, must have a component of momentum p_y in the y-direction, as well as a component p_x in the x-direction, despite the fact that initially the beam was directed along the x-axis. From the geometry of the situation the two components are related by $p_y/p_x = \tan \theta_1$. Since θ_1 is small, we may use the approximation $\tan \theta_1 = \theta_1$, and

38.17 Interpreting single-slit diffraction in terms of photon momentum.

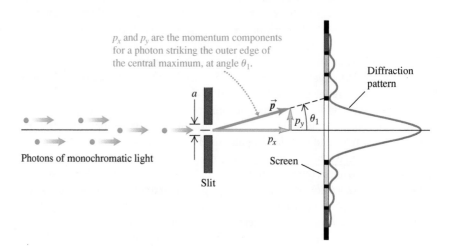

$$p_y = p_x \theta_1 \qquad (38.13)$$

Substituting Eq. (38.12), $\theta_1 = \lambda/a$, into Eq. (38.13) gives

$$p_y = p_x \frac{\lambda}{a} \qquad (38.14)$$

Equation (38.14) says that for the 85% of the photons that strike the detector within the central maximum (that is, at angles between $-\lambda/a$ and $+\lambda/a$), the y-component of momentum is spread out over a range from $-p_x\lambda/a$ to $+p_x\lambda/a$. Now let's consider *all* the photons that pass through the slit and strike the screen. Again, they may hit above or below the center of the pattern, so their component p_y may be positive or negative. However the symmetry of the diffraction pattern shows us the average value $(p_y)_{av} = 0$. There will be an *uncertainty* Δp_y in the y-component of momentum at least as great as $p_x\lambda/a$. That is,

$$\Delta p_y \geq p_x \frac{\lambda}{a} \qquad (38.15)$$

The narrower the slit width a, the broader is the diffraction pattern and the greater is the uncertainty in the y-component of momentum p_y.

The photon wavelength λ is related to the momentum p_x by Eq. (38.5), which we can rewrite as $\lambda = h/p_x$. Using this relationship in Eq. (38.15) and simplifying, we find

$$\Delta p_y \geq p_x \frac{h}{p_x a} = \frac{h}{a}$$

$$\Delta p_y a \geq h \qquad (38.16)$$

What does Eq. (38.16) mean? The slit width a represents an uncertainty in the y-component of the *position* of a photon as it passes through the slit. We don't know exactly *where* in the slit each photon passes through. So both the y-position and the y-component of momentum have uncertainties, and the two uncertainties are related by Eq. (38.16). We can reduce the *momentum* uncertainty Δp_y only by reducing the width of the diffraction pattern. To do this, we have to increase the slit width a, which increases the *position* uncertainty. Conversely, when we *decrease* the position uncertainty by narrowing the slit, the diffraction pattern broadens and the corresponding momentum uncertainty *increases*.

You may protest that it doesn't seem to be consistent with common sense for a photon not to have a definite position and momentum. We reply that what we call *common sense* is based on familiarity gained through experience. Our usual experience includes very little contact with the microscopic behavior of particles like photons. Sometimes we have to accept conclusions that violate our intuition when we are dealing with areas that are far removed from everyday experience.

The Uncertainty Principle

In more general discussions of uncertainty relationships, the uncertainty of a quantity is usually described in terms of the statistical concept of *standard deviation,* which is a measure of the spread or dispersion of a set of numbers around their average value. Suppose we now begin to describe uncertainties in this way [neither Δp_y nor a in Eq. (38.16) is a standard deviation]. If a coordinate x has an uncertainty Δx and if the corresponding momentum component p_x has an uncertainty Δp_x, then those standard-deviation uncertainties are found to be related in general by the inequality

$$\Delta x \, \Delta p_x \geq \hbar/2 \qquad \begin{array}{l}\text{(Heisenberg uncertainty principle} \\ \text{for position and momentum)}\end{array} \qquad (38.17)$$

In this expression the quantity $\hbar$ (pronounced "h-bar") is Planck's constant divided by 2π:

$$\hbar = \frac{h}{2\pi} = 1.054571628(53) \times 10^{-34} \text{ J} \cdot \text{s}$$

We will use this quantity frequently to avoid writing a lot of factors of 2π in later equations.

CAUTION   **h versus h-bar**   It's common for students to plug in the value of h when what they really wanted was $\hbar = h/2\pi$, or vice versa. Be careful not to make the same mistake, or you'll find yourself wondering why your answer is off by a factor of 2π!

38.18 The Heisenberg uncertainty principle for position and momentum components. It is impossible for the product $\Delta x \Delta p_x$ to be less than $\hbar/2 = h/4\pi$.

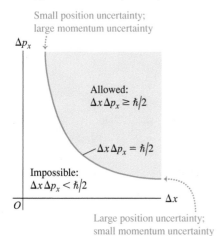

Small position uncertainty; large momentum uncertainty

Δp_x

Allowed:
$\Delta x \Delta p_x \geq \hbar/2$

$\Delta x \Delta p_x = \hbar/2$

Impossible:
$\Delta x \Delta p_x < \hbar/2$

O Δx

Large position uncertainty; small momentum uncertainty

Equation (38.17) is one form of the **Heisenberg uncertainty principle,** first discovered by the German physicist Werner Heisenberg (1901–1976). It states that, in general, it is impossible to simultaneously determine both the position and the momentum of a particle with arbitrarily great precision, as classical physics would predict. Instead, the uncertainties in the two quantities play complementary roles, as we have described. Figure 38.18 shows the relationship between the two uncertainties. Our derivation of Eq. (38.16), a less refined form of the uncertainty principle given by Eq. (38.17), shows that this principle has its roots in the wave aspect of photons. We will see in Chapter 39 that electrons and other subatomic particles also have a wave aspect, and the same uncertainty principle applies to them as well.

It is tempting to suppose that we could get greater precision by using more sophisticated detectors of position and momentum. This turns out not to be possible. To detect a particle, the detector must *interact* with it, and this interaction unavoidably changes the state of motion of the particle, introducing uncertainty about its original state. For example, we could imagine placing an electron at a certain point in the middle of the slit in Fig. 38.17. If the photon passes through the middle, we would see the electron recoil. We would then know that the photon passed through that point in the slit, and we would be much more certain about the x-coordinate of the photon. However, the collision between the photon and the electron would change the photon momentum, giving us greater uncertainty in the value of that momentum. A more detailed analysis of such hypothetical experiments shows that the uncertainties we have described are fundamental and intrinsic. They *cannot* be circumvented *even in principle* by any experimental technique, no matter how sophisticated.

There is nothing special about the x-axis. In a three-dimensional situation with coordinates (x, y, z) there is an uncertainty relationship for each coordinate and its corresponding momentum component: $\Delta x \Delta p_x \geq \hbar/2$, $\Delta y \Delta p_y \geq \hbar/2$, and $\Delta z \Delta p_z \geq \hbar/2$. However, the uncertainty in one coordinate is *not* related to the uncertainty in a different component of momentum. For example, Δx is not related directly to Δp_y.

Waves and Uncertainty

Here's an alternative way to understand the Heisenberg uncertainty principle in terms of the properties of waves. Consider a sinusoidal electromagnetic wave propagating in the positive x-direction with its electric field polarized in the y-direction. If the wave has wavelength λ, frequency f, and amplitude A, we can write the wave function as

$$E_y(x, t) = A\sin(kx - \omega t) \tag{38.18}$$

In this expression the wave number is $k = 2\pi/\lambda$ and the angular frequency is $\omega = 2\pi f$. We can think of the wave function in Eq. (38.18) as a description of a photon with a definite wavelength and a definite frequency. In terms of k and ω we can express the momentum and energy of the photon as

$$p_x = \frac{h}{\lambda} = \frac{h}{2\pi}\frac{2\pi}{\lambda} = \hbar k \qquad \text{(photon momentum in terms of wave number)} \tag{38.19a}$$

$$E = hf = \frac{h}{2\pi} 2\pi f = \hbar\omega \qquad \text{(photon energy in terms of angular frequency)} \qquad (38.19b)$$

Using Eqs. (38.19) in Eq. (38.18), we can rewrite our photon wave equation as

$$E_y(x, t) = A \sin[(p_x x - Et)/\hbar] \qquad \begin{array}{l}\text{(wave function for a}\\ \text{photon with } x\text{-momentum}\\ p_x \text{ and energy } E)\end{array} \qquad (38.20)$$

Since this wave function has a definite value of x-momentum p_x, there is *no* uncertainty in the value of this quantity: $\Delta p_x = 0$. The Heisenberg uncertainty principle, Eq. (38.17), says that $\Delta x \Delta p_x \geq \hbar/2$. If Δp_x is zero, then Δx must be infinite. Indeed, the wave described by Eq. (38.20) extends along the entire x-axis and has the same amplitude everywhere. The price we pay for knowing the photon's momentum precisely is that we have no idea *where* the photon is!

In practical situations we always have *some* idea where a photon is. To describe this situation, we need a wave function that is more localized in space. We can create one by superimposing two or more sinusoidal functions. To keep things simple, we'll consider only waves propagating in the positive x-direction. For example, let's add together two sinusoidal wave functions like those in Eqs. (38.18) and (38.20), but with slightly different wavelengths and frequencies and hence slightly different values p_{x1} and p_{x2} of x-momentum and slightly different values E_1 and E_2 of energy. The total wave function is

$$E_y(x, t) = A_1 \sin[(p_{1x} x - E_1 t)/\hbar] + A_2 \sin[(p_{2x} x - E_2 t)/\hbar] \qquad (38.21)$$

Consider what this wave function looks like at a particular instant of time, say $t = 0$. At this instant Eq. (38.21) becomes

$$E_y(x, t = 0) = A_1 \sin(p_{1x} x/\hbar) + A_2 \sin(p_{2x} x/\hbar) \qquad (38.22)$$

Figure 38.19a is a graph of the individual wave functions at $t = 0$ for the case $A_2 = -A_1$, and Fig. 38.19b graphs the combined wave function $E_y(x, t = 0)$ given by Eq. (38.22). We saw something very similar to Fig. 38.19b in our discussion of beats in Section 16.7: When we superimposed two sinusoidal waves with slightly different frequencies (see Fig. 16.24), the resulting wave exhibited amplitude variations not present in the original waves. In the same way, a photon represented by the wave function in Eq. (38.21) is most likely to be found in the regions where the wave function's amplitude is greatest. That is, the photon is *localized*. However, the photon's momentum no longer has a definite value because we began with two different x-momentum values, p_{x1} and p_{x2}. This agrees with the Heisenberg uncertainty principle: By decreasing the uncertainty in the photon's position, we have increased the uncertainty in its momentum.

38.19 (a) Two sinusoidal waves with slightly different wave numbers k and hence slightly different values of momentum $p_x = \hbar k$ shown at one instant of time. (b) The superposition of these waves has a momentum equal to the average of the two individual values of momentum. The amplitude varies, giving the total wave a lumpy character not possessed by either individual wave.

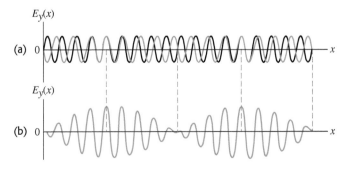

Uncertainty in Energy

Our discussion of combining waves also shows that there is an uncertainty principle that involves *energy* and *time*. To see why this is so, imagine measuring the combined wave function described by Eq. (38.21) at a certain position, say $x = 0$, over a period of time. At $x = 0$, the wave function from Eq. (38.21) becomes

$$E_y(x, t) = A_1 \sin(-E_1 t/\hbar) + A_2 \sin(-E_2 t/\hbar)$$
$$= -A_1 \sin(E_1 t/\hbar) - A_2 \sin(E_2 t/\hbar) \qquad (38.23)$$

What we measure at $x = 0$ is a combination of two oscillating electric fields with slightly different angular frequencies $\omega_1 = E_1/\hbar$ and $\omega_2 = E_2/\hbar$. This is exactly the phenomenon of beats that we discussed in Section 16.7 (compare Fig. 16.24). The amplitude of the combined field rises and falls, so the photon described by this field is localized in *time* as well as in position. The photon is most likely to be found at the times when the amplitude is large. The price we pay for localizing the photon in time is that the wave does not have a definite energy. By contrast, if the photon is described by a sinusoidal wave like that in Eq. (38.20) that *does* have a definite energy E but that has the same amplitude at all times, we have no idea when the photon will appear at $x = 0$. So the better we know the photon's energy, the less certain we are of when we will observe the photon.

Just as for the momentum–position uncertainty principle, we can write a mathematical expression for the uncertainty principle that relates energy and time. In fact, except for an overall minus sign, Eq. (38.23) is identical to Eq. (38.22) if we replace the x-momentum p_x by energy E and the position x by time t. This tells us that in the momentum–position uncertainty relation, Eq. (38.17), we can replace the momentum uncertainty Δp_x with the energy uncertainty ΔE and replace the position uncertainty Δx with the time uncertainty Δt. The result is

$$\Delta t \, \Delta E \geq \hbar/2 \qquad \begin{array}{l}\text{(Heisenberg uncertainty principle} \\ \text{for energy and time)}\end{array} \qquad (38.24)$$

In practice, any real photon has a limited spatial extent and hence passes any point in a limited amount of time. The following example illustrates how this affects the momentum and energy of the photon.

Example 38.7 Ultrashort laser pulses and the uncertainty principle

Many varieties of lasers emit light in the form of pulses rather than a steady beam. A tellurium–sapphire laser can produce light at a wavelength of 800 nm in ultrashort pulses that last only 4.00×10^{-15} s (4.00 femtoseconds, or 4.00 fs). The energy in a single pulse produced by one such laser is $2.00 \ \mu\text{J} = 2.00 \times 10^{-6}$ J, and the pulses propagate in the positive x-direction. Find (a) the frequency of the light; (b) the energy and minimum energy uncertainty of a single photon in the pulse; (c) the minimum frequency uncertainty of the light in the pulse; (d) the spatial length of the pulse, in meters and as a multiple of the wavelength; (e) the momentum and minimum momentum uncertainty of a single photon in the pulse; and (f) the approximate number of photons in the pulse.

SOLUTION

IDENTIFY and SET UP: It's important to distinguish between the light pulse as a whole (which contains a very large number of photons) and an individual photon within the pulse. The 5.00-fs pulse duration represents the time it takes the pulse to emerge from the laser; it is also the time *uncertainty* for an individual photon within

the pulse, since we don't know when during the pulse that photon emerges. Similarly, the position uncertainty of a photon is the spatial length of the pulse, since a given photon could be found anywhere within the pulse. To find our target variables, we'll use the relationships for photon energy and momentum from Section 38.1 and the two Heisenberg uncertainty principles, Eqs. (38.17) and (38.24).

EXECUTE: (a) From the relationship $c = \lambda f$, the frequency of 800-nm light is

$$f = \frac{c}{\lambda} = \frac{3.00 \times 10^8 \ \text{m/s}}{8.00 \times 10^{-7} \ \text{m}} = 3.75 \times 10^{14} \ \text{Hz}$$

(b) From Eq. (38.2) the energy of a single 800-nm photon is

$$E = hf = (6.626 \times 10^{-34} \ \text{J} \cdot \text{s})(3.75 \times 10^{14} \ \text{Hz})$$
$$= 2.48 \times 10^{-19} \ \text{J}$$

The time uncertainty equals the pulse duration, $\Delta t = 4.00 \times 10^{-15}$ s. From Eq. (38.24) the minimum uncertainty in energy corresponds to the case $\Delta t \, \Delta E = \hbar/2$, so

$$\Delta E = \frac{\hbar}{2\Delta t} = \frac{1.055 \times 10^{-34} \text{ J} \cdot \text{s}}{2(4.00 \times 10^{-15} \text{ s})} = 1.32 \times 10^{-20} \text{ J}$$

This is 5.3% of the photon energy $E = 2.48 \times 10^{-19}$ J, so the energy of a given photon is uncertain by at least 5.3%. The uncertainty could be greater, depending on the shape of the pulse.

(c) From the relationship $f = E/h$, the minimum frequency uncertainty is

$$\Delta f = \frac{\Delta E}{h} = \frac{1.32 \times 10^{-20} \text{ J}}{6.626 \times 10^{-34} \text{ J} \cdot \text{s}} = 1.99 \times 10^{13} \text{ Hz}$$

This is 5.3% of the frequency $f = 3.75 \times 10^{14}$ Hz we found in part (a). Hence these ultrashort pulses do not have a definite frequency; the average frequency of many such pulses will be 3.75×10^{14} Hz, but the frequency of any individual pulse can be anywhere from 5.3% higher to 5.3% lower.

(d) The spatial length Δx of the pulse is the distance that the front of the pulse travels during the time $\Delta t = 4.00 \times 10^{-15}$ s it takes the pulse to emerge from the laser:

$$\Delta x = c\Delta t = (3.00 \times 10^8 \text{ m/s})(4.00 \times 10^{-15} \text{ s})$$

$$= 1.20 \times 10^{-6} \text{ m}$$

$$\Delta x = \frac{1.20 \times 10^{-6} \text{ m}}{8.00 \times 10^{-7} \text{ m/wavelength}} = 1.50 \text{ wavelengths}$$

This justifies the term *ultrashort*. The pulse is less than two wavelengths long!

(e) From Eq. (38.5), the momentum of an average photon in the pulse is

$$p_x = \frac{E}{c} = \frac{2.48 \times 10^{-19} \text{ J}}{3.00 \times 10^8 \text{ m/s}} = 8.28 \times 10^{-28} \text{ kg} \cdot \text{m/s}$$

The spatial uncertainty is $\Delta x = 1.20 \times 10^{-6}$ m. From Eq. (38.17) minimum momentum uncertainty corresponds to $\Delta x \, \Delta p_x = \hbar/2$, so

$$\Delta p_x = \frac{\hbar}{2\Delta x} = \frac{1.055 \times 10^{-34} \text{ J} \cdot \text{s}}{2(1.20 \times 10^{-6} \text{ m})} = 4.40 \times 10^{-29} \text{ kg} \cdot \text{m/s}$$

This is 5.3% of the average photon momentum p_x. An individual photon within the pulse have a momentum that is 5.3% greater or less than the average.

(f) To estimate the number of photons in the pulse, we divide the total pulse energy by the average photon energy:

$$\frac{2.00 \times 10^{-6} \text{ J/pulse}}{2.48 \times 10^{-19} \text{ J/photon}} = 8.06 \times 10^{12} \text{ photons/pulse}$$

The energy of an individual photon is uncertain, so this is the *average* number of photons per pulse.

EVALUATE: The percentage uncertainties in energy and momentum are large because this laser pulse is so short. If the pulse were longer, both Δt and Δx would be greater and the corresponding uncertainties in photon energy and photon momentum would be smaller.

Our calculation in part (f) shows an important distinction between photons and other kinds of particles. In principle it is possible to make an exact count of the number of electrons, protons, and neutrons in an object such as this book. If you repeated the count, you would get the same answer as the first time. By contrast, if you counted the number of photons in a laser pulse you would *not* necessarily get the same answer every time! The uncertainty in photon energy means that on each count there could be a different number of photons whose individual energies sum to 2.00×10^{-6} J. That's yet another of the many strange properties of photons.

Test Your Understanding of Section 38.4 Through which of the following angles is a photon of wavelength λ most likely to be deflected after passing through a slit of width a? Assume that λ is much less than a. (i) $\theta = \lambda/a$; (ii) $\theta = 3\lambda/2a$; (iii) $\theta = 2\lambda/a$; (iv) $\theta = 3\lambda/a$; (v) not enough information given to decide. ❙

Photons: Electromagnetic radiation behaves as both waves and particles. The energy in an electromagnetic wave is carried in units called photons. The energy E of one photon is proportional to the wave frequency f and inversely proportional to the wavelength λ, and is proportional to a universal quantity h called Planck's constant. The momentum of a photon has magnitude E/c. (See Example 38.1.)

$$E = hf = \frac{hc}{\lambda} \qquad (38.2)$$

$$p = \frac{E}{c} = \frac{hf}{c} = \frac{h}{\lambda} \qquad (38.5)$$

The photoelectric effect: In the photoelectric effect, a surface can eject an electron by absorbing a photon whose energy hf is greater than or equal to the work function ϕ of the material. The stopping potential V_0 is the voltage required to stop a current of ejected electrons from reaching an anode. (See Examples 38.2 and 38.3.)

$$eV_0 = hf - \phi \qquad (38.4)$$

Photon production, photon scattering, and pair production: X rays can be produced when electrons accelerated to high kinetic energy across a potential increase V_{AC} strike a target. The photon model explains why the maximum frequency and minimum wavelength produced are given by Eq. (38.6). (See Example 38.4.) In Compton scattering a photon transfers some of its energy and momentum to an electron with which it collides. For free electrons (mass m), the wavelengths of incident and scattered photons are related to the photon scattering angle ϕ by Eq. (38.7). (See Example 38.5.) In pair production a photon of sufficient energy can disappear and be replaced by an electron–positron pair. In the inverse process, an electron and a positron can annihilate and be replaced by a pair of photons. (See Example 38.6.)

$$eV_{AC} = hf_{max} = \frac{hc}{\lambda_{min}} \qquad (38.6)$$
(bremsstrahlung)

$$\lambda' - \lambda = \frac{h}{mc}(1 - \cos\phi) \qquad (38.7)$$
(Compton scattering)

The Heisenberg uncertainty principle: It is impossible to determine both a photon's position and its momentum at the same time to arbitrarily high precision. The precision of such measurements for the x-components is limited by the Heisenberg uncertainty principle, Eq. (38.17); there are corresponding relationships for the y- and z-components. The uncertainty ΔE in the energy of a state that is occupied for a time Δt is given by Eq. (38.24). In these expressions, $\hbar = h/2\pi$. (See Example 38.7.)

$$\Delta x \, \Delta p_x \geq \hbar/2 \qquad (38.17)$$
(Heisenberg uncertainty principle for position and momentum)

$$\Delta t \, \Delta E \geq \hbar/2 \qquad (38.24)$$
(Heisenberg uncertainty principle for energy and time)

BRIDGING PROBLEM | Compton Scattering and Electron Recoil

An incident x-ray photon is scattered from a free electron that is initially at rest. The photon is scattered straight back at an angle of 180° from its initial direction. The wavelength of the scattered photon is 0.0830 nm. (a) What is the wavelength of the incident photon? (b) What are the magnitude of the momentum and the speed of the electron after the collision? (c) What is the kinetic energy of the electron after the collision?

SOLUTION GUIDE

See MasteringPhysics® study area for a Video Tutor solution.

IDENTIFY and SET UP

1. In this problem a photon is scattered by an electron initially at rest. In Section 38.3 you learned how to relate the wavelengths of the incident and scattered photons; in this problem you must also find the momentum, speed, and kinetic energy of the recoiling electron. You can find these because momentum and energy are conserved in the collision.
2. Which key equation can be used to find the incident photon wavelength? What is the photon scattering angle ϕ in this problem?

EXECUTE

3. Use the equation you selected in step 2 to find the wavelength of the incident photon.
4. Use momentum conservation and your result from step 3 to find the momentum of the recoiling electron. (*Hint:* All of the momentum vectors are along the same line, but not all point in the same direction. Be careful with signs.)
5. Find the speed of the recoiling electron from your result in step 4. (*Hint:* Assume that the electron is nonrelativistic, so you can use the relationship between momentum and speed from Chapter 8. This is acceptable if the speed of the electron is less than about $0.1c$. Is it?)
6. Use your result from step 4 or step 5 to find the electron kinetic energy.

EVALUATE

7. You can check your answer in step 6 by finding the difference between the energies of the incident and scattered photons. Is your result consistent with conservation of energy?

Problems

For instructor-assigned homework, go to MasteringPhysics®.

•, ••, •••: Problems of increasing difficulty. **CP**: Cumulative problems incorporating material from earlier chapters. **CALC**: Problems requiring calculus. **BIO**: Biosciences problems.

DISCUSSION QUESTIONS

Q38.1 In what ways do photons resemble other particles such as electrons? In what ways do they differ? Do photons have mass? Do they have electric charge? Can they be accelerated? What mechanical properties do they have?

Q38.2 There is a certain probability that a single electron may simultaneously absorb *two* identical photons from a high-intensity laser. How would such an occurrence affect the threshold frequency and the equations of Section 38.1? Explain.

Q38.3 According to the photon model, light carries its energy in packets called quanta or photons. Why then don't we see a series of flashes when we look at things?

Q38.4 Would you expect effects due to the photon nature of light to be generally more important at the low-frequency end of the electromagnetic spectrum (radio waves) or at the high-frequency end (x rays and gamma rays)? Why?

Q38.5 During the photoelectric effect, light knocks electrons out of metals. So why don't the metals in your home lose their electrons when you turn on the lights?

Q38.6 Most black-and-white photographic film (with the exception of some special-purpose films) is less sensitive to red light than blue light and has almost no sensitivity to infrared. How can these properties be understood on the basis of photons?

Q38.7 Human skin is relatively insensitive to visible light, but ultraviolet radiation can cause severe burns. Does this have anything to do with photon energies? Explain.

Q38.8 Explain why Fig. 38.4 shows that most photoelectrons have kinetic energies less than $hf - \phi$, and also explain how these smaller kinetic energies occur.

Q38.9 In a photoelectric-effect experiment, the photocurrent i for large positive values of V_{AC} has the same value no matter what the light frequency f (provided that f is higher than the threshold frequency f_0). Explain why.

Q38.10 In an experiment involving the photoelectric effect, if the intensity of the incident light (having frequency higher than the threshold frequency) is reduced by a factor of 10 without changing anything else, which (if any) of the following statements about this process will be true? (a) The number of photoelectrons will most likely be reduced by a factor of 10. (b) The maximum kinetic energy of the ejected photoelectrons will most likely be reduced by a factor of 10. (c) The maximum speed of the ejected photoelectrons will most likely be reduced by a factor of 10. (d) The maximum speed of the ejected photoelectrons will most likely be reduced by a factor of $\sqrt{10}$. (e) The time for the first photoelectron to be ejected will be increased by a factor of 10.

Q38.11 The materials called *phosphors* that coat the inside of a fluorescent lamp convert ultraviolet radiation (from the mercury-vapor discharge inside the tube) into visible light. Could one also make a phosphor that converts visible light to ultraviolet? Explain.

Q38.12 In a photoelectric-effect experiment, which of the following will increase the maximum kinetic energy of the photoelectrons? (a) Use light of greater intensity; (b) use light of higher frequency; (c) use light of longer wavelength; (d) use a metal surface with a larger work function. In each case justify your answer.

Q38.13 A photon of frequency f undergoes Compton scattering from an electron at rest and scatters through an angle ϕ. The frequency of the scattered photon is f'. How is f' related to f? Does your answer depend on ϕ? Explain.

Q38.14 Can Compton scattering occur with protons as well as electrons? For example, suppose a beam of x rays is directed at a target of liquid hydrogen. (Recall that the nucleus of hydrogen consists of a single proton.) Compared to Compton scattering with electrons, what similarities and differences would you expect? Explain.

Q38.15 Why must engineers and scientists shield against x-ray production in high-voltage equipment?

Q38.16 In attempting to reconcile the wave and particle models of light, some people have suggested that the photon rides up and down on the crests and troughs of the electromagnetic wave. What things are *wrong* with this description?

Q38.17 Some lasers emit light in pulses that are only 10^{-12} s in duration. The length of such a pulse is $(3 \times 10^8 \text{ m/s})(10^{-12} \text{ s}) = 3 \times 10^{-4} \text{ m} = 0.3 \text{ mm}$. Can pulsed laser light be as monochromatic as light from a laser that emits a steady, continuous beam? Explain.

EXERCISES

Section 38.1 Light Absorbed as Photons: The Photoelectric Effect

38.1 •• (a) A proton is moving at a speed much slower than the speed of light. It has kinetic energy K_1 and momentum p_1. If the momentum of the proton is doubled, so $p_2 = 2p_1$, how is its new kinetic energy K_2 related to K_1? (b) A photon with energy E_1 has momentum p_1. If another photon has momentum p_2 that is twice p_1, how is the energy E_2 of the second photon related to E_1?

38.2 • BIO **Response of the Eye.** The human eye is most sensitive to green light of wavelength 505 nm. Experiments have found that when people are kept in a dark room until their eyes adapt to the darkness, a *single* photon of green light will trigger receptor cells in the rods of the retina. (a) What is the frequency of this photon? (b) How much energy (in joules and electron volts) does it deliver to the receptor cells? (c) To appreciate what a small amount of energy this is, calculate how fast a typical bacterium of mass 9.5×10^{-12} g would move if it had that much energy.

38.3 • A photon of green light has a wavelength of 520 nm. Find the photon's frequency, magnitude of momentum, and energy. Express the energy in both joules and electron volts.

38.4 • BIO A laser used to weld detached retinas emits light with a wavelength of 652 nm in pulses that are 20.0 ms in duration. The average power during each pulse is 0.600 W. (a) How much energy is in each pulse in joules? In electron volts? (b) What is the energy of one photon in joules? In electron volts? (c) How many photons are in each pulse?

38.5 • A 75-W light source consumes 75 W of electrical power. Assume all this energy goes into emitted light of wavelength 600 nm. (a) Calculate the frequency of the emitted light. (b) How many photons per second does the source emit? (c) Are the answers to parts (a) and (b) the same? Is the frequency of the light the same thing as the number of photons emitted per second? Explain.

38.6 • A photon has momentum of magnitude 8.24×10^{-28} kg · m/s. (a) What is the energy of this photon? Give your answer in joules and in electron volts. (b) What is the wavelength of this photon? In what region of the electromagnetic spectrum does it lie?

38.7 • The graph in Fig. E38.7 shows the stopping potential as a function of the frequency of the incident light falling on a metal surface. (a) Find the photoelectric work function for this metal. (b) What value of Planck's constant does the graph yield? (c) Why does the graph *not* extend below the x-axis? (d) If a different metal were used, which characteristics of the graph would you expect to be the same and which ones would be different?

Figure **E38.7**

38.8 • The photoelectric threshold wavelength of a tungsten surface is 272 nm. Calculate the maximum kinetic energy of the electrons ejected from this tungsten surface by ultraviolet radiation of frequency 1.45×10^{15} Hz. Express the answer in electron volts.

38.9 •• A clean nickel surface is exposed to light of wavelength 235 nm. What is the maximum speed of the photoelectrons emitted from this surface? Use Table 38.1.

38.10 •• What would the minimum work function for a metal have to be for visible light (380–750 nm) to eject photoelectrons?

38.11 •• When ultraviolet light with a wavelength of 400.0 nm falls on a certain metal surface, the maximum kinetic energy of the emitted photoelectrons is measured to be 1.10 eV. What is the maximum kinetic energy of the photoelectrons when light of wavelength 300.0 nm falls on the same surface?

38.12 •• The photoelectric work function of potassium is 2.3 eV. If light having a wavelength of 250 nm falls on potassium, find (a) the stopping potential in volts; (b) the kinetic energy in electron volts of the most energetic electrons ejected; (c) the speed of these electrons.

38.13 • When ultraviolet light with a wavelength of 254 nm falls on a clean copper surface, the stopping potential necessary to stop emission of photoelectrons is 0.181 V. (a) What is the photoelectric threshold wavelength for this copper surface? (b) What is the work function for this surface, and how does your calculated value compare with that given in Table 38.1?

Section 38.2 Light Emitted as Photons: X-Ray Production

38.14 • The cathode-ray tubes that generated the picture in early color televisions were sources of x rays. If the acceleration voltage in a television tube is 15.0 kV, what are the shortest-wavelength x rays produced by the television? (Modern televisions contain shielding to stop these x rays.)

38.15 • Protons are accelerated from rest by a potential difference of 4.00 kV and strike a metal target. If a proton produces one photon on impact, what is the minimum wavelength of the resulting x rays? How does your answer compare to the minimum wavelength if 4.00-keV electrons are used instead? Why do x-ray tubes use electrons rather than protons to produce x rays?

38.16 •• (a) What is the minimum potential difference between the filament and the target of an x-ray tube if the tube is to produce x rays with a wavelength of 0.150 nm? (b) What is the shortest wavelength produced in an x-ray tube operated at 30.0 kV?

Section 38.3 Light Scattered as Photons: Compton Scattering and Pair Production

38.17 • An x ray with a wavelength of 0.100 nm collides with an electron that is initially at rest. The x ray's final wavelength is 0.110 nm. What is the final kinetic energy of the electron?

38.18 • X rays are produced in a tube operating at 18.0 kV. After emerging from the tube, x rays with the minimum wavelength produced strike a target and are Compton-scattered through an angle of 45.0°. (a) What is the original x-ray wavelength? (b) What is the wavelength of the scattered x rays? (c) What is the energy of the scattered x rays (in electron volts)?

38.19 •• X rays with initial wavelength 0.0665 nm undergo Compton scattering. What is the longest wavelength found in the scattered x rays? At which scattering angle is this wavelength observed?

38.20 • A beam of x rays with wavelength 0.0500 nm is Compton-scattered by the electrons in a sample. At what angle from the incident beam should you look to find x rays with a wavelength of (a) 0.0542 nm; (b) 0.0521 nm; (c) 0.0500 nm?

38.21 •• If a photon of wavelength 0.04250 nm strikes a free electron and is scattered at an angle of 35.0° from its original direction, find (a) the change in the wavelength of this photon; (b) the wavelength of the scattered light; (c) the change in energy of the photon (is it a loss or a gain?); (d) the energy gained by the electron.

38.22 •• A photon scatters in the backward direction ($\phi = 180°$) from a free proton that is initially at rest. What must the wavelength of the incident photon be if it is to undergo a 10.0% change in wavelength as a result of the scattering?

38.23 •• X rays with an initial wavelength of 0.900×10^{-10} m undergo Compton scattering. For what scattering angle is the wavelength of the scattered x rays greater by 1.0% than that of the incident x rays?

38.24 •• A photon with wavelength $\lambda = 0.1385$ nm scatters from an electron that is initially at rest. What must be the angle between the direction of propagation of the incident and scattered photons if the speed of the electron immediately after the collision is 8.90×10^6 m/s?

38.25 • An electron and a positron are moving toward each other and each has speed $0.500c$ in the lab frame. (a) What is the kinetic energy of each particle? (b) The e^+ and e^- meet head-on and annihilate. What is the energy of each photon that is produced? (c) What is the wavelength of each photon? How does the wavelength compare to the photon wavelength when the initial kinetic energy of the e^+ and e^- is negligibly small (see Example 38.6)?

Section 38.4 Wave–Particle Duality, Probability, and Uncertainty

38.26 • A laser produces light of wavelength 625 nm in an ultrashort pulse. What is the minimum duration of the pulse if the minimum uncertainty in the energy of the photons is 1.0%?

38.27 • An ultrashort pulse has a duration of 9.00 fs and produces light at a wavelength of 556 nm. What are the momentum and momentum uncertainty of a single photon in the pulse?

38.28 • A horizontal beam of laser light of wavelength 585 nm passes through a narrow slit that has width 0.0620 mm. The intensity of the light is measured on a vertical screen that is 2.00 m from the slit. (a) What is the minimum uncertainty in the vertical component of the momentum of each photon in the beam after the

photon has passed through the slit? (b) Use the result of part (a) to estimate the width of the central diffraction maximum that is observed on the screen.

PROBLEMS

38.29 • **Exposing Photographic Film.** The light-sensitive compound on most photographic films is silver bromide, AgBr. A film is "exposed" when the light energy absorbed dissociates this molecule into its atoms. (The actual process is more complex, but the quantitative result does not differ greatly.) The energy of dissociation of AgBr is 1.00×10^5 J/mol. For a photon that is just able to dissociate a molecule of silver bromide, find (a) the photon energy in electron volts; (b) the wavelength of the photon; (c) the frequency of the photon. (d) What is the energy in electron volts of a photon having a frequency of 100 MHz? (e) Light from a firefly can expose photographic film, but the radiation from an FM station broadcasting 50,000 W at 100 MHz cannot. Explain why this is so.

38.30 •• (a) If the average frequency emitted by a 200-W light bulb is 5.00×10^{14} Hz, and 10.0% of the input power is emitted as visible light, approximately how many visible-light photons are emitted per second? (b) At what distance would this correspond to 1.00×10^{11} visible-light photons per square centimeter per second if the light is emitted uniformly in all directions?

38.31 • When a certain photoelectric surface is illuminated with light of different wavelengths, the following stopping potentials are observed:

Wavelength (nm)	Stopping potential (V)
366	1.48
405	1.15
436	0.93
492	0.62
546	0.36
579	0.24

Plot the stopping potential on the vertical axis against the frequency of the light on the horizontal axis. Determine (a) the threshold frequency; (b) the threshold wavelength; (c) the photoelectric work function of the material (in electron volts); (d) the value of Planck's constant h (assuming that the value of e is known).

38.32 • A 2.50-W beam of light of wavelength 124 nm falls on a metal surface. You observe that the maximum kinetic energy of the ejected electrons is 4.16 eV. Assume that each photon in the beam ejects a photoelectron. (a) What is the work function (in electron volts) of this metal? (b) How many photoelectrons are ejected each second from this metal? (c) If the power of the light beam, but not its wavelength, were reduced by half, what would be the answer to part (b)? (d) If the wavelength of the beam, but not its power, were reduced by half, what would be the answer to part (b)?

38.33 •• CP BIO **Removing Vascular Lesions.** A pulsed dye laser emits light of wavelength 585 nm in 450-μs pulses. Because this wavelength is strongly absorbed by the hemoglobin in the blood, the method is especially effective for removing various types of blemishes due to blood, such as port-wine–colored birthmarks. To get a reasonable estimate of the power required for such laser surgery, we can model the blood as having the same specific heat and heat of vaporization as water (4190 J/kg·K, 2.256×10^6 J/kg). Suppose that each pulse must remove 2.0 μg of blood by evaporating it, starting at 33°C. (a) How much energy must each pulse deliver to the blemish? (b) What must be the power output of this laser? (c) How many photons does each pulse deliver to the blemish?

38.34 • The photoelectric work functions for particular samples of certain metals are as follows: cesium, 2.1 eV; copper, 4.7 eV;

potassium, 2.3 eV; and zinc, 4.3 eV. (a) What is the threshold wavelength for each metal surface? (b) Which of these metals could *not* emit photoelectrons when irradiated with visible light (380–750 nm)?

38.35 •• An incident x-ray photon of wavelength 0.0900 nm is scattered in the backward direction from a free electron that is initially at rest. (a) What is the magnitude of the momentum of the scattered photon? (b) What is the kinetic energy of the electron after the photon is scattered?

38.36 •• CP A photon with wavelength $\lambda = 0.0900$ nm is incident on an electron that is initially at rest. If the photon scatters in the backward direction, what is the magnitude of the linear momentum of the electron just after the collision with the photon?

38.37 •• CP A photon with wavelength $\lambda = 0.1050$ nm is incident on an electron that is initially at rest. If the photon scatters at an angle of 60.0° from its original direction, what are the magnitude and direction of the linear momentum of the electron just after the collision with the photon?

38.38 •• CP An x-ray tube is operating at voltage V and current I. (a) If only a fraction p of the electric power supplied is converted into x rays, at what rate is energy being delivered to the target? (b) If the target has mass m and specific heat c (in J/kg · K), at what average rate would its temperature rise if there were no thermal losses? (c) Evaluate your results from parts (a) and (b) for an x-ray tube operating at 18.0 kV and 60.0 mA that converts 1.0% of the electric power into x rays. Assume that the 0.250-kg target is made of lead ($c = 130$ J/kg · K). (d) What must the physical properties of a practical target material be? What would be some suitable target elements?

38.39 •• Nuclear fusion reactions at the center of the sun produce gamma-ray photons with energies of about 1 MeV (10^6 eV). By contrast, what we see emanating from the sun's surface are visible-light photons with wavelengths of about 500 nm. A simple model that explains this difference in wavelength is that a photon undergoes Compton scattering many times—in fact, about 10^{26} times, as suggested by models of the solar interior—as it travels from the center of the sun to its surface. (a) Estimate the increase in wavelength of a photon in an average Compton-scattering event. (b) Find the angle in degrees through which the photon is scattered in the scattering event described in part (a). (*Hint:* A useful approximation is $\cos \phi \approx 1 - \phi^2/2$, which is valid for $\phi \ll 1$. Note that ϕ is in radians in this expression.) (c) It is estimated that a photon takes about 10^6 years to travel from the core to the surface of the sun. Find the average distance that light can travel within the interior of the sun without being scattered. (This distance is roughly equivalent to how far you could see if you were inside the sun and could survive the extreme temperatures there. As your answer shows, the interior of the sun is *very* opaque.)

38.40 •• (a) Derive an expression for the total shift in photon wavelength after two successive Compton scatterings from electrons at rest. The photon is scattered by an angle θ_1 in the first scat-

tering and by θ_2 in the second. (b) In general, is the total shift in wavelength produced by two successive scatterings of an angle $\theta/2$ the same as by a single scattering of θ? If not, are there any specific values of θ, other than $\theta = 0°$, for which the total shifts are the same? (c) Use the result of part (a) to calculate the total wavelength shift produced by two successive Compton scatterings of 30.0° each. Express your answer in terms of h/mc. (d) What is the wavelength shift produced by a single Compton scattering of 60.0°? Compare to the answer in part (c).

38.41 •• A photon with wavelength 0.1100 nm collides with a free electron that is initially at rest. After the collision the wavelength is 0.1132 nm. (a) What is the kinetic energy of the electron after the collision? What is its speed? (b) If the electron is suddenly stopped (for example, in a solid target), all of its kinetic energy is used to create a photon. What is the wavelength of this photon?

38.42 •• An x-ray photon is scattered from a free electron (mass m) at rest. The wavelength of the scattered photon is λ', and the final speed of the struck electron is v. (a) What was the initial wavelength λ of the photon? Express your answer in terms of λ', v, and m. (*Hint:* Use the relativistic expression for the electron kinetic energy.) (b) Through what angle ϕ is the photon scattered? Express your answer in terms of λ, λ', and m. (c) Evaluate your results in parts (a) and (b) for a wavelength of 5.10×10^{-3} nm for the scattered photon and a final electron speed of 1.80×10^8 m/s. Give ϕ in degrees.

38.43 •• (a) Calculate the maximum increase in photon wavelength that can occur during Compton scattering. (b) What is the energy (in electron volts) of the lowest-energy x-ray photon for which Compton scattering could result in doubling the original wavelength?

CHALLENGE PROBLEM

38.44 ••• Consider Compton scattering of a photon by a *moving* electron. Before the collision the photon has wavelength λ and is moving in the $+x$-direction, and the electron is moving in the $-x$-direction with total energy E (including its rest energy mc^2). The photon and electron collide head-on. After the collision, both are moving in the $-x$-direction (that is, the photon has been scattered by 180°). (a) Derive an expression for the wavelength λ' of the scattered photon. Show that if $E \gg mc^2$, where m is the rest mass of the electron, your result reduces to

$$\lambda' = \frac{hc}{E}\left(1 + \frac{m^2c^4\lambda}{4hcE}\right)$$

(b) A beam of infrared radiation from a CO_2 laser ($\lambda = 10.6$ μm) collides head-on with a beam of electrons, each of total energy $E = 10.0$ GeV (1 GeV = 10^9 eV). Calculate the wavelength λ' of the scattered photons, assuming a 180° scattering angle. (c) What kind of scattered photons are these (infrared, microwave, ultraviolet, etc.)? Can you think of an application of this effect?

Answers

Chapter Opening Question ?

The energy of a photon E is inversely proportional to its wavelength λ: The shorter the wavelength, the more energetic is the photon. Since visible light has shorter wavelengths than infrared light,

the headlamp emits photons of greater energy. However, the light from the infrared laser is far more *intense* (delivers much more energy per second per unit area to the patient's skin) because it emits many more photons per second than does the headlamp and concentrates them onto a very small spot.

Test Your Understanding Questions

38.1 Answers: (i) and (ii) From Eq. (38.2), a photon of energy $E = 1.14$ eV has wavelength $\lambda = hc/E = (4.136 \times 10^{-15}$ eV$)$ $\cdot (3.00 \times 10^8$ m/s$)/(1.14$ eV$) = 1.09 \times 10^{-6}$ m $= 1090$ nm. This is in the infrared part of the spectrum. Since wavelength is inversely proportional to photon energy, the *minimum* photon energy of 1.14 eV corresponds to the *maximum* wavelength that causes photoconductivity in silicon. Thus the wavelength must be 1090 nm or less.

38.2 Answer: (ii) Equation (38.6) shows that the minimum wavelength of x rays produced by bremsstrahlung depends on the potential difference V_{AC} but does *not* depend on the rate at which electrons strike the anode. Each electron produces at most one photon, so increasing the number of electrons per second causes an increase in the number of x-ray photons emitted per second (that is, the x-ray intensity).

38.3 Answers: yes, no Equation (38.7) shows that the wavelength shift $\Delta\lambda = \lambda' - \lambda$ depends only on the photon scattering angle ϕ, not on the wavelength of the incident photon. So a visible-light photon scattered through an angle ϕ undergoes the same wavelength shift as an x-ray photon. Equation (38.7) also shows that this shift is of the order of $h/mc = 2.426 \times 10^{-12}$ m = 0.002426 nm. This is a few percent of the wavelength of x rays (see Example 38.5), so the effect is noticeable in x-ray scattering. However, h/mc is a tiny fraction of the wavelength of visible light (between 380 and 750 nm). The human eye cannot distinguish such minuscule differences in wavelength (that is, differences in color).

38.4 Answer: (ii) There is *zero* probability that a photon will be deflected by one of the angles where the diffraction pattern has zero intensity. These angles are given by $a \sin\theta = m\lambda$ with $m = \pm 1$, $\pm 2, \pm 3, \ldots$. Since λ is much less than a, we can write these angles as $\theta = m\lambda/a = \pm\lambda/a, \pm 2\lambda/a, \pm 3\lambda/a, \ldots$. These values include answers (i), (iii), and (iv), so it is impossible for a photon to be deflected through any of these angles. The intensity is not zero at $\theta = 3\lambda/2a$ (located between two zeros in the diffraction pattern), so there is some probability that a photon will be deflected through this angle.

Bridging Problem

Answers: **(a)** 0.0781 nm
(b) 1.65×10^{-23} kg $\cdot$ m/s, 1.81×10^7 m/s
(c) 1.49×10^{-16} J

APPENDIX A

THE INTERNATIONAL SYSTEM OF UNITS

The Système International d'Unités, abbreviated SI, is the system developed by the General Conference on Weights and Measures and adopted by nearly all the industrial nations of the world. The following material is adapted from the National Institute of Standards and Technology (**http://physics.nist.gov/cuu**).

Quantity	Name of unit	Symbol	
SI base units			
length	meter	m	
mass	kilogram	kg	
time	second	s	
electric current	ampere	A	
thermodynamic temperature	kelvin	K	
amount of substance	mole	mol	
luminous intensity	candela	cd	
SI derived units			**Equivalent units**
area	square meter	m^2	
volume	cubic meter	m^3	
frequency	hertz	Hz	s^{-1}
mass density (density)	kilogram per cubic meter	kg/m^3	
speed, velocity	meter per second	m/s	
angular velocity	radian per second	rad/s	
acceleration	meter per second squared	m/s^2	
angular acceleration	radian per second squared	rad/s^2	
force	newton	N	$kg \cdot m/s^2$
pressure (mechanical stress)	pascal	Pa	N/m^2
kinematic viscosity	square meter per second	m^2/s	
dynamic viscosity	newton-second per square meter	$N \cdot s/m^2$	
work, energy, quantity of heat	joule	J	$N \cdot m$
power	watt	W	J/s
quantity of electricity	coulomb	C	$A \cdot s$
potential difference, electromotive force	volt	V	J/C, W/A
electric field strength	volt per meter	V/m	N/C
electric resistance	ohm	Ω	V/A
capacitance	farad	F	$A \cdot s/V$
magnetic flux	weber	Wb	$V \cdot s$
inductance	henry	H	$V \cdot s/A$
magnetic flux density	tesla	T	Wb/m^2
magnetic field strength	ampere per meter	A/m	
magnetomotive force	ampere	A	
luminous flux	lumen	lm	$cd \cdot sr$
luminance	candela per square meter	cd/m^2	
illuminance	lux	lx	lm/m^2
wave number	1 per meter	m^{-1}	
entropy	joule per kelvin	J/K	
specific heat capacity	joule per kilogram-kelvin	$J/kg \cdot K$	
thermal conductivity	watt per meter-kelvin	$W/m \cdot K$	

Quantity	Name of unit	Symbol	Equivalent units
radiant intensity	watt per steradian	W/sr	
activity (of a radioactive source)	becquerel	Bq	s^{-1}
radiation dose	gray	Gy	J/kg
radiation dose equivalent	sievert	Sv	J/kg
	SI supplementary units		
plane angle	radian	rad	
solid angle	steradian	sr	

Definitions of SI Units

meter (m)   The *meter* is the length equal to the distance traveled by light, in vacuum, in a time of 1/299,792,458 second.

kilogram (kg)   The *kilogram* is the unit of mass; it is equal to the mass of the international prototype of the kilogram. (The international prototype of the kilogram is a particular cylinder of platinum-iridium alloy that is preserved in a vault at Sévres, France, by the International Bureau of Weights and Measures.)

second (s)   The *second* is the duration of 9,192,631,770 periods of the radiation corresponding to the transition between the two hyperfine levels of the ground state of the cesium-133 atom.

ampere (A)   The *ampere* is that constant current that, if maintained in two straight parallel conductors of infinite length, of negligible circular cross section, and placed 1 meter apart in vacuum, would produce between these conductors a force equal to 2×10^{-7} newton per meter of length.

kelvin (K)   The *kelvin,* unit of thermodynamic temperature, is the fraction 1/273.16 of the thermodynamic temperature of the triple point of water.

ohm (Ω)   The *ohm* is the electric resistance between two points of a conductor when a constant difference of potential of 1 volt, applied between these two points, produces in this conductor a current of 1 ampere, this conductor not being the source of any electromotive force.

coulomb (C)   The *coulomb* is the quantity of electricity transported in 1 second by a current of 1 ampere.

candela (cd)   The *candela* is the luminous intensity, in a given direction, of a source that emits monochromatic radiation of frequency 540×10^{12} hertz and that has a radiant intensity in that direction of 1/683 watt per steradian.

mole (mol)   The *mole* is the amount of substance of a system that contains as many elementary entities as there are carbon atoms in 0.012 kg of carbon 12. The elementary entities must be specified and may be atoms, molecules, ions, electrons, other particles, or specified groups of such particles.

newton (N)   The *newton* is that force that gives to a mass of 1 kilogram an acceleration of 1 meter per second per second.

joule (J)   The *joule* is the work done when the point of application of a constant force of 1 newton is displaced a distance of 1 meter in the direction of the force.

watt (W)   The *watt* is the power that gives rise to the production of energy at the rate of 1 joule per second.

volt (V)   The *volt* is the difference of electric potential between two points of a conducting wire carrying a constant current of 1 ampere, when the power dissipated between these points is equal to 1 watt.

weber (Wb)   The *weber* is the magnetic flux that, linking a circuit of one turn, produces in it an electromotive force of 1 volt as it is reduced to zero at a uniform rate in 1 second.

lumen (lm)   The *lumen* is the luminous flux emitted in a solid angle of 1 steradian by a uniform point source having an intensity of 1 candela.

farad (F)   The *farad* is the capacitance of a capacitor between the plates of which there appears a difference of potential of 1 volt when it is charged by a quantity of electricity equal to 1 coulomb.

henry (H)   The *henry* is the inductance of a closed circuit in which an electromotive force of 1 volt is produced when the electric current in the circuit varies uniformly at a rate of 1 ampere per second.

radian (rad)   The *radian* is the plane angle between two radii of a circle that cut off on the circumference an arc equal in length to the radius.

steradian (sr)   The *steradian* is the solid angle that, having its vertex in the center of a sphere, cuts off an area of the surface of the sphere equal to that of a square with sides of length equal to the radius of the sphere.

SI Prefixes   To form the names of multiples and submultiples of SI units, apply the prefixes listed in Appendix F.

APPENDIX B

USEFUL MATHEMATICAL RELATIONS

Algebra

$$a^{-x} = \frac{1}{a^x} \qquad a^{(x+y)} = a^x a^y \qquad a^{(x-y)} = \frac{a^x}{a^y}$$

Logarithms: If $\log a = x$, then $a = 10^x$. $\log a + \log b = \log(ab)$ $\log a - \log b = \log(a/b)$ $\log(a^n) = n \log a$

If $\ln a = x$, then $a = e^x$. $\ln a + \ln b = \ln(ab)$ $\ln a - \ln b = \ln(a/b)$ $\ln(a^n) = n \ln a$

Quadratic formula: If $ax^2 + bx + c = 0$, $x = \dfrac{-b \pm \sqrt{b^2 - 4ac}}{2a}$.

Binomial Theorem

$$(a + b)^n = a^n + na^{n-1}b + \frac{n(n-1)a^{n-2}b^2}{2!} + \frac{n(n-1)(n-2)a^{n-3}b^3}{3!} + \cdots$$

Trigonometry
In the right triangle ABC, $x^2 + y^2 = r^2$.

Definitions of the trigonometric functions:
$\sin\alpha = y/r \qquad \cos\alpha = x/r \qquad \tan\alpha = y/x$

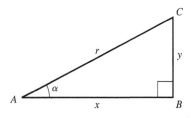

Identities: $\sin^2\alpha + \cos^2\alpha = 1$ $\tan\alpha = \dfrac{\sin\alpha}{\cos\alpha}$

$\sin 2\alpha = 2\sin\alpha\cos\alpha$ $\cos 2\alpha = \cos^2\alpha - \sin^2\alpha = 2\cos^2\alpha - 1$
$$= 1 - 2\sin^2\alpha$$

$\sin\tfrac{1}{2}\alpha = \sqrt{\dfrac{1 - \cos\alpha}{2}}$ $\cos\tfrac{1}{2}\alpha = \sqrt{\dfrac{1 + \cos\alpha}{2}}$

$\sin(-\alpha) = -\sin\alpha$ $\sin(\alpha \pm \beta) = \sin\alpha\cos\beta \pm \cos\alpha\sin\beta$

$\cos(-\alpha) = \cos\alpha$ $\cos(\alpha \pm \beta) = \cos\alpha\cos\beta \mp \sin\alpha\sin\beta$

$\sin(\alpha \pm \pi/2) = \pm\cos\alpha$ $\sin\alpha + \sin\beta = 2\sin\tfrac{1}{2}(\alpha + \beta)\cos\tfrac{1}{2}(\alpha - \beta)$

$\cos(\alpha \pm \pi/2) = \mp\sin\alpha$ $\cos\alpha + \cos\beta = 2\cos\tfrac{1}{2}(\alpha + \beta)\cos\tfrac{1}{2}(\alpha - \beta)$

For *any* triangle $A'B'C'$ (not necessarily a right triangle) with sides a, b, and c and angles α, β, and γ:

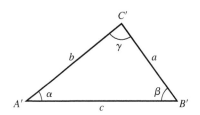

Law of sines: $\dfrac{\sin\alpha}{a} = \dfrac{\sin\beta}{b} = \dfrac{\sin\gamma}{c}$

Law of cosines: $c^2 = a^2 + b^2 - 2ab\cos\gamma$

Geometry

Circumference of circle of radius r:	$C = 2\pi r$	Surface area of sphere of radius r:	$A = 4\pi r^2$
Area of circle of radius r:	$A = \pi r^2$	Volume of cylinder of radius r and height h:	$V = \pi r^2 h$
Volume of sphere of radius r:	$V = 4\pi r^3/3$		

Calculus

Derivatives:

$$\frac{d}{dx}x^n = nx^{n-1}$$

$$\frac{d}{dx}\ln ax = \frac{1}{x}$$

$$\frac{d}{dx}e^{ax} = ae^{ax}$$

$$\frac{d}{dx}\sin ax = a\cos ax$$

$$\frac{d}{dx}\cos ax = -a\sin ax$$

Integrals:

$$\int x^n\,dx = \frac{x^{n+1}}{n+1} \quad (n \neq -1)$$

$$\int \frac{dx}{x} = \ln x$$

$$\int e^{ax}\,dx = \frac{1}{a}e^{ax}$$

$$\int \sin ax\,dx = -\frac{1}{a}\cos ax$$

$$\int \cos ax\,dx = \frac{1}{a}\sin ax$$

$$\int \frac{dx}{\sqrt{a^2 - x^2}} = \arcsin\frac{x}{a}$$

$$\int \frac{dx}{\sqrt{x^2 + a^2}} = \ln\left(x + \sqrt{x^2 + a^2}\right)$$

$$\int \frac{dx}{x^2 + a^2} = \frac{1}{a}\arctan\frac{x}{a}$$

$$\int \frac{dx}{(x^2 + a^2)^{3/2}} = \frac{1}{a^2}\frac{x}{\sqrt{x^2 + a^2}}$$

$$\int \frac{x\,dx}{(x^2 + a^2)^{3/2}} = -\frac{1}{\sqrt{x^2 + a^2}}$$

Power series (convergent for range of x shown):

$$(1 + x)^n = 1 + nx + \frac{n(n-1)x^2}{2!} + \frac{n(n-1)(n-2)}{3!}x^3 + \cdots \quad (|x| < 1)$$

$$\tan x = x + \frac{x^3}{3} + \frac{2x^2}{15} + \frac{17x^7}{315} + \cdots \quad (|x| < \pi/2)$$

$$e^x = 1 + x + \frac{x^2}{2!} + \frac{x^3}{3!} + \cdots \quad (\text{all } x)$$

$$\sin x = x - \frac{x^3}{3!} + \frac{x^5}{5!} - \frac{x^7}{7!} + \cdots \quad (\text{all } x)$$

$$\ln(1 + x) = x - \frac{x^2}{2} + \frac{x^3}{3} - \frac{x^4}{4} + \cdots \quad (|x| < 1)$$

$$\cos x = 1 - \frac{x^2}{2!} + \frac{x^4}{4!} - \frac{x^6}{6!} + \cdots \quad (\text{all } x)$$

APPENDIX C

THE GREEK ALPHABET

Name	Capital	Lowercase	Name	Capital	Lowercase	Name	Capital	Lowercase
Alpha	A	α	Iota	I	ι	Rho	P	ρ
Beta	B	β	Kappa	K	κ	Sigma	Σ	σ
Gamma	Γ	γ	Lambda	Λ	λ	Tau	T	τ
Delta	Δ	δ	Mu	M	μ	Upsilon	Υ	υ
Epsilon	E	ϵ	Nu	N	ν	Phi	Φ	ϕ
Zeta	Z	ζ	Xi	Ξ	ξ	Chi	X	χ
Eta	H	η	Omicron	O	o	Psi	Ψ	ψ
Theta	Θ	θ	Pi	Π	π	Omega	Ω	ω

APPENDIX D

PERIODIC TABLE OF THE ELEMENTS

Group →	1	2	3	4	5	6	7	8	9	10	11	12	13	14	15	16	17	18
Period ↓																		
1	1 **H** 1.008																	2 **He** 4.003
2	3 **Li** 6.941	4 **Be** 9.012											5 **B** 10.811	6 **C** 12.011	7 **N** 14.007	8 **O** 15.999	9 **F** 18.998	10 **Ne** 20.180
3	11 **Na** 22.990	12 **Mg** 24.305											13 **Al** 26.982	14 **Si** 28.086	15 **P** 30.974	16 **S** 32.065	17 **Cl** 35.453	18 **Ar** 39.948
4	19 **K** 39.098	20 **Ca** 40.078	21 **Sc** 44.956	22 **Ti** 47.867	23 **V** 50.942	24 **Cr** 51.996	25 **Mn** 54.938	26 **Fe** 55.845	27 **Co** 58.933	28 **Ni** 58.693	29 **Cu** 63.546	30 **Zn** 65.409	31 **Ga** 69.723	32 **Ge** 72.64	33 **As** 74.922	34 **Se** 78.96	35 **Br** 79.904	36 **Kr** 83.798
5	37 **Rb** 85.468	38 **Sr** 87.62	39 **Y** 88.906	40 **Zr** 91.224	41 **Nb** 92.906	42 **Mo** 95.94	43 **Tc** (98)	44 **Ru** 101.07	45 **Rh** 102.906	46 **Pd** 106.42	47 **Ag** 107.868	48 **Cd** 112.411	49 **In** 114.818	50 **Sn** 118.710	51 **Sb** 121.760	52 **Te** 127.60	53 **I** 126.904	54 **Xe** 131.293
6	55 **Cs** 132.905	56 **Ba** 137.327	71 **Lu** 174.967	72 **Hf** 178.49	73 **Ta** 180.948	74 **W** 183.84	75 **Re** 186.207	76 **Os** 190.23	77 **Ir** 192.217	78 **Pt** 195.078	79 **Au** 196.967	80 **Hg** 200.59	81 **Tl** 204.383	82 **Pb** 207.2	83 **Bi** 208.980	84 **Po** (209)	85 **At** (210)	86 **Rn** (222)
7	87 **Fr** (223)	88 **Ra** (226)	103 **Lr** (262)	104 **Rf** (261)	105 **Db** (262)	106 **Sg** (266)	107 **Bh** (264)	108 **Hs** (269)	109 **Mt** (268)	110 **Ds** (271)	111 **Rg** (272)	112 **Uub** (285)	113 **Uut** (284)	114 **Uuq** (289)	115 **Uup** (288)	116 **Uuh** (292)	117 **Uus** (294)	118 **Uuo**

Lanthanoids

57 **La** 138.905	58 **Ce** 140.116	59 **Pr** 140.908	60 **Nd** 144.24	61 **Pm** (145)	62 **Sm** 150.36	63 **Eu** 151.964	64 **Gd** 157.25	65 **Tb** 158.925	66 **Dy** 162.500	67 **Ho** 164.930	68 **Er** 167.259	69 **Tm** 168.934	70 **Yb** 173.04

Actinoids

89 **Ac** (227)	90 **Th** (232)	91 **Pa** (231)	92 **U** (238)	93 **Np** (237)	94 **Pu** (244)	95 **Am** (243)	96 **Cm** (247)	97 **Bk** (247)	98 **Cf** (251)	99 **Es** (252)	100 **Fm** (257)	101 **Md** (258)	102 **No** (259)

For each element the average atomic mass of the mixture of isotopes occurring in nature is shown. For elements having no stable isotope, the approximate atomic mass of the longest-lived isotope is shown in parentheses. For elements that have been predicted but not yet confirmed, no atomic mass is given. All atomic masses are expressed in atomic mass units ($1\ u = 1.660538782(83) \times 10^{-27}$ kg), equivalent to grams per mole (g/mol).

APPENDIX E

UNIT CONVERSION FACTORS

Length
$1 \text{ m} = 100 \text{ cm} = 1000 \text{ mm} = 10^6 \, \mu\text{m} = 10^9 \text{ nm}$
$1 \text{ km} = 1000 \text{ m} = 0.6214 \text{ mi}$
$1 \text{ m} = 3.281 \text{ ft} = 39.37 \text{ in.}$
$1 \text{ cm} = 0.3937 \text{ in.}$
$1 \text{ in.} = 2.540 \text{ cm}$
$1 \text{ ft} = 30.48 \text{ cm}$
$1 \text{ yd} = 91.44 \text{ cm}$
$1 \text{ mi} = 5280 \text{ ft} = 1.609 \text{ km}$
$1 \text{ Å} = 10^{-10} \text{ m} = 10^{-8} \text{ cm} = 10^{-1} \text{ nm}$
$1 \text{ nautical mile} = 6080 \text{ ft}$
$1 \text{ light year} = 9.461 \times 10^{15} \text{ m}$

Area
$1 \text{ cm}^2 = 0.155 \text{ in.}^2$
$1 \text{ m}^2 = 10^4 \text{ cm}^2 = 10.76 \text{ ft}^2$
$1 \text{ in.}^2 = 6.452 \text{ cm}^2$
$1 \text{ ft}^2 = 144 \text{ in.}^2 = 0.0929 \text{ m}^2$

Volume
$1 \text{ liter} = 1000 \text{ cm}^3 = 10^{-3} \text{ m}^3 = 0.03531 \text{ ft}^3 = 61.02 \text{ in.}^3$
$1 \text{ ft}^3 = 0.02832 \text{ m}^3 = 28.32 \text{ liters} = 7.477 \text{ gallons}$
$1 \text{ gallon} = 3.788 \text{ liters}$

Time
$1 \text{ min} = 60 \text{ s}$
$1 \text{ h} = 3600 \text{ s}$
$1 \text{ d} = 86{,}400 \text{ s}$
$1 \text{ y} = 365.24 \text{ d} = 3.156 \times 10^7 \text{ s}$

Angle
$1 \text{ rad} = 57.30° = 180°/\pi$
$1° = 0.01745 \text{ rad} = \pi/180 \text{ rad}$
$1 \text{ revolution} = 360° = 2\pi \text{ rad}$
$1 \text{ rev/min (rpm)} = 0.1047 \text{ rad/s}$

Speed
$1 \text{ m/s} = 3.281 \text{ ft/s}$
$1 \text{ ft/s} = 0.3048 \text{ m/s}$
$1 \text{ mi/min} = 60 \text{ mi/h} = 88 \text{ ft/s}$
$1 \text{ km/h} = 0.2778 \text{ m/s} = 0.6214 \text{ mi/h}$
$1 \text{ mi/h} = 1.466 \text{ ft/s} = 0.4470 \text{ m/s} = 1.609 \text{ km/h}$
$1 \text{ furlong/fortnight} = 1.662 \times 10^{-4} \text{ m/s}$

Acceleration
$1 \text{ m/s}^2 = 100 \text{ cm/s}^2 = 3.281 \text{ ft/s}^2$
$1 \text{ cm/s}^2 = 0.01 \text{ m/s}^2 = 0.03281 \text{ ft/s}^2$
$1 \text{ ft/s}^2 = 0.3048 \text{ m/s}^2 = 30.48 \text{ cm/s}^2$
$1 \text{ mi/h} \cdot \text{s} = 1.467 \text{ ft/s}^2$

Mass
$1 \text{ kg} = 10^3 \text{ g} = 0.0685 \text{ slug}$
$1 \text{ g} = 6.85 \times 10^{-5} \text{ slug}$
$1 \text{ slug} = 14.59 \text{ kg}$
$1 \text{ u} = 1.661 \times 10^{-27} \text{ kg}$
1 kg has a weight of 2.205 lb when $g = 9.80 \text{ m/s}^2$

Force
$1 \text{ N} = 10^5 \text{ dyn} = 0.2248 \text{ lb}$
$1 \text{ lb} = 4.448 \text{ N} = 4.448 \times 10^5 \text{ dyn}$

Pressure
$1 \text{ Pa} = 1 \text{ N/m}^2 = 1.450 \times 10^{-4} \text{ lb/in.}^2 = 0.209 \text{ lb/ft}^2$
$1 \text{ bar} = 10^5 \text{ Pa}$
$1 \text{ lb/in.}^2 = 6895 \text{ Pa}$
$1 \text{ lb/ft}^2 = 47.88 \text{ Pa}$
$1 \text{ atm} = 1.013 \times 10^5 \text{ Pa} = 1.013 \text{ bar}$
$\qquad = 14.7 \text{ lb/in.}^2 = 2117 \text{ lb/ft}^2$
$1 \text{ mm Hg} = 1 \text{ torr} = 133.3 \text{ Pa}$

Energy
$1 \text{ J} = 10^7 \text{ ergs} = 0.239 \text{ cal}$
$1 \text{ cal} = 4.186 \text{ J (based on 15° calorie)}$
$1 \text{ ft} \cdot \text{lb} = 1.356 \text{ J}$
$1 \text{ Btu} = 1055 \text{ J} = 252 \text{ cal} = 778 \text{ ft} \cdot \text{lb}$
$1 \text{ eV} = 1.602 \times 10^{-19} \text{ J}$
$1 \text{ kWh} = 3.600 \times 10^6 \text{ J}$

Mass–Energy Equivalence
$1 \text{ kg} \leftrightarrow 8.988 \times 10^{16} \text{ J}$
$1 \text{ u} \leftrightarrow 931.5 \text{ MeV}$
$1 \text{ eV} \leftrightarrow 1.074 \times 10^{-9} \text{ u}$

Power
$1 \text{ W} = 1 \text{ J/s}$
$1 \text{ hp} = 746 \text{ W} = 550 \text{ ft} \cdot \text{lb/s}$
$1 \text{ Btu/h} = 0.293 \text{ W}$

APPENDIX F

NUMERICAL CONSTANTS

Fundamental Physical Constants*

Name	Symbol	Value
Speed of light in vacuum	c	2.99792458×10^8 m/s
Magnitude of charge of electron	e	$1.602176487(40) \times 10^{-19}$ C
Gravitational constant	G	$6.67428(67) \times 10^{-11}$ N $\cdot$ m^2/kg^2
Planck's constant	h	$6.62606896(33) \times 10^{-34}$ J $\cdot$ s
Boltzmann constant	k	$1.3806504(24) \times 10^{-23}$ J/K
Avogadro's number	N_A	$6.02214179(30) \times 10^{23}$ molecules/mol
Gas constant	R	$8.314472(15)$ J/mol $\cdot$ K
Mass of electron	m_e	$9.10938215(45) \times 10^{-31}$ kg
Mass of proton	m_p	$1.672621637(83) \times 10^{-27}$ kg
Mass of neutron	m_n	$1.674927211(84) \times 10^{-27}$ kg
Permeability of free space	μ_0	$4\pi \times 10^{-7}$ Wb/A $\cdot$ m
Permittivity of free space	$\epsilon_0 = 1/\mu_0 c^2$	$8.854187817\ldots \times 10^{-12}$ C^2/N $\cdot$ m^2
	$1/4\pi\epsilon_0$	$8.987551787\ldots \times 10^9$ N $\cdot$ m^2/C^2

Other Useful Constants*

Name	Symbol	Value
Mechanical equivalent of heat		4.186 J/cal (15° calorie)
Standard atmospheric pressure	1 atm	1.01325×10^5 Pa
Absolute zero	0 K	$-273.15°$C
Electron volt	1 eV	$1.602176487(40) \times 10^{-19}$ J
Atomic mass unit	1 u	$1.660538782(83) \times 10^{-27}$ kg
Electron rest energy	$m_e c^2$	0.510998910(13) MeV
Volume of ideal gas (0°C and 1 atm)		22.413996(39) liter/mol
Acceleration due to gravity (standard)	g	9.80665 m/s^2

*Source: National Institute of Standards and Technology (**http://physics.nist.gov/cuu**). Numbers in parentheses show the uncertainty in the final digits of the main number; for example, the number 1.6454(21) means 1.6454 $\pm$ 0.0021. Values shown without uncertainties are exact.

Astronomical Data[†]

Body	Mass (kg)	Radius (m)	Orbit radius (m)	Orbit period
Sun	1.99×10^{30}	6.96×10^{8}	—	—
Moon	7.35×10^{22}	1.74×10^{6}	3.84×10^{8}	27.3 d
Mercury	3.30×10^{23}	2.44×10^{6}	5.79×10^{10}	88.0 d
Venus	4.87×10^{24}	6.05×10^{6}	1.08×10^{11}	224.7 d
Earth	5.97×10^{24}	6.38×10^{6}	1.50×10^{11}	365.3 d
Mars	6.42×10^{23}	3.40×10^{6}	2.28×10^{11}	687.0 d
Jupiter	1.90×10^{27}	6.91×10^{7}	7.78×10^{11}	11.86 y
Saturn	5.68×10^{26}	6.03×10^{7}	1.43×10^{12}	29.45 y
Uranus	8.68×10^{25}	2.56×10^{7}	2.87×10^{12}	84.02 y
Neptune	1.02×10^{26}	2.48×10^{7}	4.50×10^{12}	164.8 y
Pluto[‡]	1.31×10^{22}	1.15×10^{6}	5.91×10^{12}	247.9 y

[†]Source: NASA Jet Propulsion Laboratory Solar System Dynamics Group (**http://ssd.jpl.nasa.gov**), and P. Kenneth Seidelmann, ed., ***Explanatory Supplement to the Astronomical Almanac*** (University Science Books, Mill Valley, CA, 1992), pp. 704–706. For each body, "radius" is its radius at its equator and "orbit radius" is its average distance from the sun or (for the moon) from the earth.

[‡]In August 2006, the International Astronomical Union reclassified Pluto and other small objects that orbit the sun as "dwarf planets."

Prefixes for Powers of 10

Power of ten	Prefix	Abbreviation	Pronunciation
10^{-24}	yocto-	y	*yoc*-toe
10^{-21}	zepto-	z	*zep*-toe
10^{-18}	atto-	a	*at*-toe
10^{-15}	femto-	f	*fem*-toe
10^{-12}	pico-	p	*pee*-koe
10^{-9}	nano-	n	*nan*-oe
10^{-6}	micro-	μ	*my*-crow
10^{-3}	milli-	m	*mil*-i
10^{-2}	centi-	c	*cen*-ti
10^{3}	kilo-	k	*kil*-oe
10^{6}	mega-	M	*meg*-a
10^{9}	giga-	G	*jig*-a or *gig*-a
10^{12}	tera-	T	*ter*-a
10^{15}	peta-	P	*pet*-a
10^{18}	exa-	E	*ex*-a
10^{21}	zetta-	Z	*zet*-a
10^{24}	yotta-	Y	*yot*-a

Examples:

1 femtometer = 1 fm = 10^{-15} m

1 picosecond = 1 ps = 10^{-12} s

1 nanocoulomb = 1 nC = 10^{-9} C

1 microkelvin = 1 μK = 10^{-6} K

1 millivolt = 1 mV = 10^{-3} V

1 kilopascal = 1 kPa = 10^{3} Pa

1 megawatt = 1 MW = 10^{6} W

1 gigahertz = 1 GHz = 10^{9} Hz

ANSWERS TO ODD-NUMBERED PROBLEMS

Chapter 21

21.1 a) 2.00×10^{10} b) 8.59×10^{-13}
21.3 2.1×10^{28}, -3.35×10^9 C
21.5 1.3 nC
21.7 3.7 km
21.9 a) 0.742 μC on each b) 0.371 μC, 1.48 μC
21.11 1.43×10^{13}, away from each other
21.13 a) 2.21×10^4 m/s^2
21.15 0.750 nC
21.17 1.8×10^{-4} N, in the $+x$-direction
21.19 $x = -0.144$ m
21.21 2.58 μN, in the $-y$-direction
21.23 a) 8.80×10^{-9} N, attractive
b) 8.22×10^{-8} N, about 10 times larger than the bonding force
21.25 a) 4.40×10^{-16} N b) 2.63×10^{11} m/s^2
c) 2.63×10^5 m/s
21.27 a) 3.30×10^6 N/C, to the left b) 14.2 ns
c) 1.80×10^3 N/C, to the right
21.29 a) -21.9 μC b) 1.02×10^{-7} N/C
21.31 a) 8740 N/C, to the right
b) 6540 N/C, to the right c) 1.40×10^{-15} N, to the right
21.33 a) 364 N/C b) no, 2.73 μm, downward
21.35 1.79×10^6 m/s
21.37 1.73×10^{-8} N, toward a point midway between the two electrons
21.39 a) $-\hat{\jmath}$ b) $\dfrac{\sqrt{2}}{2}\hat{\imath} + \dfrac{\sqrt{2}}{2}\hat{\jmath}$
c) $-0.39\hat{\imath} + 0.92\hat{\jmath}$
21.41 a) 633 km/s b) 15.9 km/s
21.43 a) 0
b) for $|x| < a$: $E_x = -\dfrac{q}{\pi\epsilon_0}\dfrac{ax}{(x^2 - a^2)^2}$;
for $x > a$: $E_x = \dfrac{q}{2\pi\epsilon_0}\dfrac{x^2 + a^2}{(x^2 - a^2)^2}$;
for $x < -a$: $E_x = -\dfrac{q}{2\pi\epsilon_0}\dfrac{x^2 + a^2}{(x^2 - a^2)^2}$
21.45 a) (i) 574 N/C, $+x$-direction (ii) 268 N/C, $-x$-direction (iii) 404 N/C, $-x$-direction
b) (i) 9.20×10^{-17} N, $-x$-direction
(ii) 4.30×10^{-17} N, $+x$-direction
(iii) 6.48×10^{-17} N, $+x$-direction
21.47 1.04×10^7 N/C, toward the -2.00-μC charge
21.49 a) $E_x = E_y = E = 0$ b) $E_x = 2660$ N/C, $E_y = 0$, $E = 2660$ N/C, $+x$-direction
c) $E_x = 129$ N/C, $E_y = 510$ N/C, $E = 526$ N/C, 284° counterclockwise from the $+x$-axis d) $E_x = 0$, $E_y = 1380$ N/C, $E = 1380$ N/C, $+y$-direction
21.51 a) $E_x = -4790$ N/C, $E_y = 0$, $E = 4790$ N/C, $-x$-direction b) $E_x = 2130$ N/C, $E_y = 0$, $E = 2130$ N/C, $+x$-direction c) $E_x = -129$ N/C, $E_y = -164$ N/C, $E = 209$ N/C, 232° counterclockwise from the $+x$-axis
d) $E_x = -1040$ N/C, $E_y = 0$, $E = 1040$ N/C, $-x$-direction
21.53 a) $(7.0 \text{ N/C})\hat{\imath}$ b) $(1.75 \times 10^{-5} \text{ N})\hat{\imath}$
21.55 a) 1.14×10^5 N/C, toward the center of the disk b) 8.92×10^4 N/C, toward the center of the disk c) 1.46×10^5 N/C, toward the charge
21.57 a) 1.4×10^{-11} C·m, from q_1 toward q_2
b) 860 N/C
21.59 a) $\vec{p}$ is aligned in either the same or the opposite direction as $\vec{E}$. b) $\vec{p}$ is aligned in the same direction as $\vec{E}$.
21.61 a) 1680 N, from the $+5.00$-μC charge toward the -5.00-μC charge
b) 22.3 N·m, clockwise

21.63 b) $\dfrac{Q^2}{8\pi\epsilon_0 L^2}(1 + 2\sqrt{2})$, away from the center of the square
21.65 a) 3.17 nC b) $+x$-direction c) $x = -1.76$ m
21.67 a) $\dfrac{1}{2\pi}\sqrt{\dfrac{qQ}{\pi\epsilon_0 ma^3}}$ b) accelerates away from the origin along the y-axis
21.69 b) 2.80 μC c) 39.5°
21.71 a) 2.09×10^{21} N b) 5.90×10^{23} m/s^2
c) no
21.73 3.41×10^4 N/C, to the left
21.75 between the charges, 0.24 m from the 0.500-nC charge
21.77 a) $\dfrac{6q^2}{4\pi\epsilon_0 L^2}$, away from the vacant corner
b) $\dfrac{3q^2}{4\pi\epsilon_0 L^2}\left(\sqrt{2} + \dfrac{1}{2}\right)$, toward the center of the square
21.79 a) 6.0×10^{23}
b) 510 kN (electric), 4.1×10^{-31} N (gravitation)
c) yes for electric force, no for gravitation
21.81 a) $\approx$480 C b) 8.3×10^{13} N, repulsive
21.83 2190 km/s
21.85 a) 3.5×10^{20} b) 1.6 C, 2.3×10^{10} N
21.87 a) $\dfrac{mv_0^2 \sin^2\alpha}{2eE}$ b) $\dfrac{mv_0^2 \sin 2\alpha}{eE}$
d) 0.418 m, 2.89 m
21.89 a) $E_x = \dfrac{Q}{4\pi\epsilon_0 a}\left(\dfrac{1}{x - a} - \dfrac{1}{x}\right)$, $E_y = 0$
b) $\dfrac{qQ}{4\pi\epsilon_0 a}\left(\dfrac{1}{r} - \dfrac{1}{r + a}\right)\hat{\imath}$
21.91 a) $(-6110 \text{ N/C})\hat{\imath}$ b) smaller c) 0.177 m
21.93 a) 1.56 N/C, $+x$-direction c) smaller
d) 4.7%
21.95 a) $-\dfrac{qQ}{2\pi\epsilon_0 a}\left(\dfrac{1}{y} - \dfrac{1}{\sqrt{a^2 + y^2}}\right)\hat{\imath}$
b) $\dfrac{qQ}{4\pi\epsilon_0 a}\left(\dfrac{1}{x - a} + \dfrac{1}{x + a} - \dfrac{2}{x}\right)\hat{\imath}$
21.97 $E_x = E_y = \dfrac{Q}{2\pi^2\epsilon_0 a^2}$
21.99 a) 6.25×10^4 N/C, 225° counterclockwise from an axis pointing to the right at the point P
b) 1.00×10^{-14} N, opposite the electric field direction
21.101 a) 1.19×10^6 N/C, to the left
b) 1.19×10^5 N/C, to the left
c) 1.19×10^5 N/C, to the right
21.103 $\dfrac{\sigma}{2\epsilon_0}\left(-\dfrac{x}{|x|}\hat{\imath} + \dfrac{z}{|z|}\hat{k}\right)$
21.105 b) $q_1 < 0, q_2 > 0$ c) 0.843 μC d) 56.2 N
21.107 a) $\dfrac{Q}{2\pi\epsilon_0 L}\left(\dfrac{1}{2x + a} - \dfrac{1}{2L + 2x + a}\right)$

Chapter 22

22.1 a) 1.8 N·m^2/C b) no c) (i) 0° (ii) 90°
22.3 a) 3.53×10^5 N·m^2/C b) 3.13 μC
22.5 $\pi r^2 E$
22.7 0.977 N·m^2/C, inward
22.9 a) 0 b) 8.74×10^7 N/C
c) 2.60×10^7 N/C

22.11 a) 1.17×10^5 N·m^2/C b) no change
22.13 a) 4.50×10^4 N/C b) 918 N/C
22.15 0.0810 N
22.17 2.04×10^{10}
22.19 a) 6.47×10^5 N/C, $+y$-direction
b) 7.2×10^4 N/C, $-y$-direction
22.21 a) 5.73 μC/m^2 b) 6.47×10^5 N/C
c) -5.65×10^4 N·m^2/C
22.23 a) 0.260 μC/m^3 b) 1960 N/C
22.25 1.16 km/s
22.27 23.6 μJ
22.29 0 (outside the plates), σ/ϵ_0 (between the plates)
22.31 a) $2\pi R\sigma$ b) $\sigma R/\epsilon_0 r$ c) $\lambda/2\pi\epsilon_0 r$
22.33 a) yes, $+Q$ b) no c) yes d) no, no
e) no, yes, no
22.35 a) 750 N·m^2/C b) 0
c) 577 N/C, $+x$-direction d) charges both within and outside
22.37 a) -0.598 nC b) charges both within and outside
22.39 a) $\lambda/2\pi\epsilon_0 r$, radially outward b) $\lambda/2\pi\epsilon_0 r$, radially outward
d) $-\lambda$ (inner surface), $+\lambda$ (outer surface)
22.41 a) (i) $\dfrac{\alpha}{2\pi\epsilon_0 r}$, radially outward (ii) 0 (iii) 0
b) (i) $-\alpha$ (ii) 0
22.43 10.2°
22.45 a) 0 $(r < R)$; $\dfrac{1}{4\pi\epsilon_0}\dfrac{Q}{r^2}$ $(R < r < 2R)$, radially outward; $\dfrac{1}{4\pi\epsilon_0}\dfrac{2Q}{r^2}$ $(r > 2R)$, radially outward
22.47 a) (i) 0 (ii) 0 (iii) $\dfrac{q}{2\pi\epsilon_0 r^2}$, radially outward
(iv) 0 (v) $\dfrac{3q}{2\pi\epsilon_0 r^2}$, radially outward
b) (i) 0 (ii) $+2q$ (iii) $-2q$ (iv) $+6q$
22.49 a) (i) 0 (ii) 0 (iii) $\dfrac{q}{2\pi\epsilon_0 r^2}$, radially outward
(iv) 0 (v) $\dfrac{q}{2\pi\epsilon_0 r^2}$, radially inward
b) (i) 0 (ii) $+2q$ (iii) $-2q$ (iv) $-2q$
22.51 a) $\dfrac{qQ}{4\pi\epsilon_0 r^2}$, toward the center of the shell
b) 0
22.53 a) $\dfrac{\alpha}{2\epsilon_0}\left(1 - \dfrac{a^2}{r^2}\right)$
b) $q = 2\pi\alpha a^2, E = \dfrac{\alpha}{2\epsilon_0}$
22.55 $R/2$
22.57 b) $|x| > d$ (outside the slab): $\dfrac{\rho_0 d}{3\epsilon_0}\dfrac{x}{|x|}\hat{\imath}$; $|x| < d$ (inside the slab): $\dfrac{\rho_0 x^3}{3\epsilon_0 d^2}\hat{\imath}$
22.61 b) $\rho\vec{b}/3\epsilon_0$
22.63 a) $-\dfrac{Q}{16\pi\epsilon_0 R^2}\hat{\imath}$ b) $\dfrac{Q}{72\pi\epsilon_0 R^2}\hat{\imath}$
c) 0 d) $\dfrac{5Q}{18\pi\epsilon_0 R^2}\hat{\imath}$
22.65 c) $\dfrac{Qr}{4\pi\epsilon_0 R^3}\left(4 - \dfrac{3r}{R}\right)$ e) $2R/3$, $\dfrac{Q}{3\pi\epsilon_0 R^2}$
22.67 a) $\dfrac{480Q}{233\pi R^3}$

b) $r \le R/2$: $E = \dfrac{180Qr^2}{233\pi\epsilon_0 R^4}$; $R/2 \le r \le R$:

$E = \dfrac{480Q}{233\pi\epsilon_0 r^2}\left[\dfrac{1}{3}\left(\dfrac{r}{R}\right)^3 - \dfrac{1}{5}\left(\dfrac{r}{R}\right)^5 - \dfrac{23}{1920}\right]$;

$r \ge R$: $E = \dfrac{Q}{4\pi\epsilon_0 r^2}$ c) 0.807

d) $E = \dfrac{180}{233}\dfrac{Q}{4\pi\epsilon_0 R^2}$

Chapter 23

23.1 -0.356 J
23.3 3.46×10^{-13} J $= 2.16$ MeV
23.5 a) 12.5 m/s b) 0.323 m
23.7 -1.42×10^{-18} J
23.9 a) 13.6 km/s b) 2.45×10^{17} m/s^2
23.11 $-q/2$
23.13 7.42 m/s, faster
23.15 a) 0 b) 0.750 mJ c) -2.06 mJ
23.17 a) 0 b) -175 kV c) -0.875 J
23.19 a) -737 V b) -704 V c) 8.2×10^{-8} J
23.21 b) $V = \dfrac{q}{4\pi\epsilon_0}\left(\dfrac{1}{|x|} - \dfrac{2}{|x-a|}\right)$

  c) $x = -a, a/3$
23.23 a) 156 V b) -182 V
23.25 a) point b b) 800 V/m c) $-48.0\ \mu$J
23.27 a) (i) 180 V (ii) -270 V (iii) -450 V
  b) 719 V, inner shell
23.29 a) oscillatory b) 1.67×10^7 m/s
23.31 a) 94.9 nC/m b) less c) zero
23.33 a) 78.2 kV b) zero
23.35 0.474 J
23.37 a) 9.3×10^6 V/m, inward
  b) outer surface
23.39 a) 8.00 kV/m b) 19.2 μN c) 0.864 μJ
  d) $-0.864\ \mu$J
23.41 b) -20 nC c) no
23.43 -760 V
23.45 a) $E_x = -Ay + 2Bx, E_y = -Ax - C, E_z = 0$
  b) $x = -C/A, y = -2BC/A^2$, any value of z
23.47 a) (i) $V = \dfrac{q}{4\pi\epsilon_0}\left(\dfrac{1}{r_a} - \dfrac{1}{r_b}\right)$

  (ii) $V = \dfrac{q}{4\pi\epsilon_0}\left(\dfrac{1}{r} - \dfrac{1}{r_b}\right)$ (iii) $V = 0$

  d) 0 e) $E = \dfrac{q-Q}{4\pi\epsilon_0 r^2}$

23.49 a) cylinders coaxial with the given cylinder
  b) 2.90 cm, 4.20 cm, 6.08 cm
  c) get farther apart
23.51 a) $-0.360\ \mu$J b) $x = 0.074$ m
23.53 a) 7.66×10^{-13} J b) 5.17×10^{-14} m
23.55 a) $-21.5\ \mu$J b) -2.83 kV c) 35.4 kV/m
23.57 a) 7.85×10^4 V/m$^{4/3}$
  b) $E_x = -(1.05 \times 10^5$ V/m$^{4/3})x^{1/3}$
  c) 3.13×10^{-15} N, toward the positive anode
23.59 a) $-\dfrac{1.46q^2}{\pi\epsilon_0 d}$

23.61 a) -8.60×10^{-18} J $= -53.7$ eV
  b) 2.88×10^{-11} m
23.63 a) (i) $V = (\lambda/2\pi\epsilon_0)\ln(b/a)$
  (ii) $V = (\lambda/2\pi\epsilon_0)\ln(b/r)$ (iii) $V = 0$
  d) $(\lambda/2\pi\epsilon_0)\ln(b/a)$
23.65 a) 1.76×10^{-16} N, downward
  b) 1.93×10^{14} m/s^2, downward
  c) 0.822 cm d) 15.3° e) 3.29 cm
23.67 a) 97.1 kV/m b) 30.3 pC
23.69 a) $r > R$: $V_r = -\dfrac{\lambda}{2\pi\epsilon_0}\ln\left(\dfrac{r}{R}\right)$;

  $r < R$: $V_r = \dfrac{\lambda}{4\pi\epsilon_0}\left[1 - \left(\dfrac{r}{R}\right)^2\right]$

23.71 $\dfrac{3}{5}\left(\dfrac{Q^2}{4\pi\epsilon_0 R}\right)$

23.73 360 kV
23.75 b) yes c) no, no
23.77 $\dfrac{Q}{8\pi\epsilon_0 R}$

23.79 a) $\dfrac{Q}{4\pi\epsilon_0 a}\ln\left(\dfrac{x+a}{x}\right)$

  b) $\dfrac{Q}{4\pi\epsilon_0 a}\ln\left(\dfrac{a + \sqrt{a^2 + y^2}}{y}\right)$

  c) part (a): $\dfrac{Q}{4\pi\epsilon_0 x}$, part (b): $\dfrac{Q}{4\pi\epsilon_0 y}$

23.81 a) 1/3 b) 3

23.83 a) $E = \dfrac{Q_1}{4\pi\epsilon_0 R_1^2}, V = \dfrac{Q_1}{4\pi\epsilon_0 R_1}$

  b) $q_1 = \dfrac{Q_1 R_1}{R_1 + R_2}, q_2 = \dfrac{Q_1 R_2}{R_1 + R_2}$

  c) $V = \dfrac{Q_1}{4\pi\epsilon_0(R_1 + R_2)}$ for either sphere

  d) $E_1 = \dfrac{Q_1}{4\pi\epsilon_0 R_1(R_1 + R_2)}$,

  $E_2 = \dfrac{Q_1}{4\pi\epsilon_0 R_2(R_1 + R_2)}$

23.85 a) 7580 km/s b) 7260 km/s
  c) 2.3×10^9 K (protons), 6.4×10^9 K
  (helium)
23.87 a) 5.9×10^{-15} m b) 20.7 pJ
  c) 1.06×10^{15} J $= 253$ kilotons of TNT
23.89 1.01×10^{-12} m, 1.11×10^{-13} m,
  2.54×10^{-14} m
23.91 c) 3, 0.507 μm

Chapter 24

24.1 a) 10.0 kV b) 22.6 cm^2 c) 8.00 pF
24.3 a) 604 V b) 90.8 cm^2 c) 1840 kV/m
  d) 16.3 μC/m^2
24.5 a) 120 μC b) 60 μC c) 480 μC
24.7 2.8 mm, yes
24.9 a) 1.05 mm b) 84.0 V
24.11 a) 4.35 pF b) 2.30 V
24.13 a) 15.0 pF b) 3.09 cm c) 31.2 kN/C
24.15 a) series b) 5000
24.17 a) $Q_1 = Q_2 = 22.4\ \mu$C, $Q_3 = 44.8\ \mu$C,
  $Q_4 = 67.2\ \mu$C
  b) $V_1 = V_2 = 5.6$ V, $V_3 = 11.2$ V, $V_4 = 16.8$ V
  c) 11.2 V
24.19 a) $Q_1 = 156\ \mu$C, $Q_2 = 260\ \mu$C
  b) $V_1 = V_2 = 52.0$ V
24.21 a) 19.3 nF b) 482 nC c) 162 nC
  d) 25 V
24.23 57 μF
24.25 0.0283 J/m^3
24.27 a) $\dfrac{xQ^2}{2\epsilon_0 A}$ b) $\left(\dfrac{Q^2}{2\epsilon_0 A}\right)dx$ c) $\dfrac{Q^2}{2\epsilon_0 A}$

24.29 a) $U_p = 4U_s$ b) $Q_p = 2Q_s$ c) $E_p = 2E_s$
24.31 a) 24.2 μC b) $Q_{35} = 7.7\ \mu$C, $Q_{75} = 16.5\ \mu$C
  c) 2.66 mJ d) $U_{35} = 0.85$ mJ, $U_{75} = 1.81$ mJ
  e) 220 V for each capacitor
24.33 a) 1.60 nC b) 8.05
24.35 a) 3.60 mJ (before), 13.5 mJ (after)
  b) increased by 9.9 mJ
24.37 a) 0.620 μC/m^2 b) 1.28
24.39 0.0135 m^2
24.41 a) 2.31×10^{-11} C^2/N$\cdot$m^2
  b) 4.0×10^4 V
  c) $\sigma = 4.6 \times 10^{-4}$ C/m^2,
  $\sigma_i = 2.8 \times 10^{-4}$ C/m^2
24.43 a) 10.1 V b) 2.25

24.45 a) $\dfrac{Q}{\epsilon_0 AK}$ b) $\dfrac{Qd}{\epsilon_0 AK}$ c) $K\dfrac{\epsilon_0 A}{d} = KC_0$

24.47 a) 421 J b) 0.054 F
24.49 a) 31 pF b) 0.37 nC c) 1.6 kV/m
  d) 2.2 nJ
24.51 133 kV/m
24.53 a) 0.0160 C b) 533 V c) 4.26 J d) 2.14 J
24.55 a) 158 μJ b) 72.1 μJ
24.57 a) 2.5 μF
  b) $Q_1 = 550\ \mu$C, $Q_2 = 370\ \mu$C, $Q_3 = Q_4 =$
  180 μC, $Q_5 = 550\ \mu$C; $V_1 = 65$ V, $V_2 = 87$ V,
  $V_3 = V_4 = 43$ V, $V_5 = 65$ V
24.59 $C_2 = 6.00\ \mu$F, $C_3 = 4.50\ \mu$F
24.61 a) 76 μC b) 1.4 mJ
  c) 11 V across each capacitor d) 1.3 mJ
24.63 a) 2.3 μF b) $Q_1 = 970\ \mu$C, $Q_2 = 640\ \mu$C
  c) 47 V
24.65 3.91 b) 22.8 V
24.67 a) $C = 4\pi\epsilon_0 R$ b) 710 μF
24.69 a) 0.065 F b) 23,000 C
  c) 4.0×10^9 J
24.71 48.3 μF
24.73 0.185 μJ
24.75 b) 2.38 nF

24.77 a) $\dfrac{\epsilon_0 L}{D}[L + (K-1)x]$

  c) $Q = \dfrac{\epsilon_0 LV}{D}[L + (K-1)x]$

Chapter 25

25.1 1.0 C
25.3 a) 3.12×10^{19} b) 1.51×10^6 A/m^2
  c) 0.111 mm/s d) both J and v_d would
  decrease
25.5 a) 110 min b) 440 min c) $v_d \propto 1/d^2$
25.7 a) 330 C b) 41 A
25.9 9.0 μA
25.11 a) $1.06 \times 10^{-5}\ \Omega \cdot$m
  b) 0.00105 (C°)$^{-1}$
25.13 a) 0.206 mV b) 0.176 mV
25.15 a) 1.21 V/m b) 0.0145 Ω c) 0.182 V
25.17 0.125 Ω
25.19 15 g
25.21 $1.53 \times 10^{-8}\ \Omega$
25.23 a) 11 A b) 3.1 V c) 0.28 Ω
25.25 a) 99.54 Ω b) 0.0158 Ω
25.27 a) $4.67 \times 10^{-8}\ \Omega$ b) $6.72 \times 10^{-4}\ \Omega$
25.29 a) 27.4 V b) 12.3 MJ
25.31 a) zero b) 5.0 V c) 5.0 V
25.33 3.08 V, 0.067 Ω, 1.80 Ω
25.35 a) 1.41 A, clockwise b) 13.7 V c) -1.0 V
25.37 b) yes c) 3.88 Ω
25.39 a) 144 Ω b) 240 Ω c) 0.833 A, 0.500 A
25.41 a) 29.8 W b) 0.248 A
25.43 a) EJ b) ρJ^2 c) E^2/ρ
25.45 a) 300 W b) 0.90 J
25.47 a) 2.6 MJ b) 0.063 L c) 1.6 h
25.49 12.3%
25.51 a) 24.0 W b) 4.0 W c) 20.0 W
25.53 a) 26.7 Ω b) 4.50 A c) 453 W d) larger
25.55 a) $3.65 \times 10^{-8}\ \Omega \cdot$m b) 172 A
  c) 2.58 mm/s
25.57 0.060 Ω
25.59 a) 2.5 mA b) 2.14×10^{-5} V/m
  c) 8.55×10^{-5} V/m d) 0.180 mV
25.61 42.0 s
25.63 a) 80 C° b) no
25.65 a) $\dfrac{\rho h}{\pi r_1 r_2}$

25.67 a) 0.057 Ω b) $3.34 \times 10^{-8}\ \Omega \cdot$m
  c) 0.86 mm d) 0.00240 Ω
  e) 0.0011 (C°)$^{-1}$
25.69 a) 0.20 Ω b) 8.7 V
25.71 a) 1.0 kΩ b) 100 V c) 10 W
25.73 1.42 A

25.75 a) $I_A\left(1 + \dfrac{R_A}{r+R}\right)$ b) 0.0429 Ω

25.77 b) 8-gauge   c) 106 W   d) $19.25
25.79 a) 0.40 A   b) 1.6 W
       c) 4.8 W, in the 12.0-V battery
       d) 3.2 W, in the 8.0-V battery
25.81 a) 14.4 V   b) 2.59 MJ   c) 0.432 MJ
       d) 0.96 Ω e) 1.73 MJ   f) 0.432 MJ
25.83 6.67 V
25.85 a) a/E b) aL/V_{bc} c) point c
       d) 3.5×10^8 m/s^2
25.87 a) $R = \dfrac{\rho_0 L}{A}\left(1 - \dfrac{1}{e}\right), I = \dfrac{V_0 A}{\rho_0 L\left(1 - \dfrac{1}{e}\right)}$

       b) $E(x) = \dfrac{V_0 e^{-x/L}}{L\left(1 - \dfrac{1}{e}\right)}$,

       c) $V(x) = \dfrac{V_0\left(e^{-x/L} - \dfrac{1}{e}\right)}{1 - \dfrac{1}{e}}$

Chapter 26

26.1 $3R/4$
26.3   22.5 W
26.5   a) 3.50 A   b) 4.50 A   c) 3.15 A   d) 3.25 A
26.7   0.769 A
26.9   a) 8.80 Ω b) 3.18 A   c) 3.18 A   d) 5.09 V,
       7.63 V, 15.3 V   e) 16.2 W, 24.3 W, 48.5 W
       f) resistor with greater resistance
26.11 a) 8.00 A, 12.0 A   b) 84.0 V
26.13 5.00 Ω; $I_3 = 8.00$ A, $I_4 = 9.00$ A,
       $I_6 = 4.00$ A, $I_{12} = 3.00$ A
26.15 a) $I_1 = 1.50$ A, $I_2 = I_3 = I_4 = 0.500$ A
       b) $P_1 = 10.1$ W, $P_2 = P_3 = P_4 = 1.12$ W; R_1
       glows brightest   c) $I_1 = 1.33$ A, $I_2 = I_3 =$
       0.667 A   d) $P_1 = 8.00$ W, $P_2 = P_3 = 2.00$ W
       e) R_1 glows less brightly; R_2 and R_3 glow
       brighter
26.17 18.0 V, 3.00 A
26.19 a) 2 resistors in parallel and that combination
       in series with 3 more resistors   b) 10 resistors
       in parallel   c) 3 resistors in parallel
       d) 2 resistors in parallel and that combination
       in series with 4 resistors in parallel
26.21 a) 0.100 A   b) 4.0 W, 8.0 W   c) 12.0 W
       d) 0.300 A, 0.150 A   e) 36.0 W, 18.0 W
       f) 54.0 W   g) in series, the 800-Ω bulb is
       brighter; in parallel, the 400-Ω bulb is brighter
       h) parallel connection
26.23 1010 s
26.25 a) 2.00 A   b) 5.00 Ω c) 42.0 V
       d) 3.50 A
26.27 a) 8.00 A   b) $\varepsilon_1 = 36.0$ V, $\varepsilon_2 = 54.0$ V
       c) 9.00 Ω
26.29 a) 1.60 A, 1.40 A, 0.20 A   b) 10.4 V
26.31 a) 36.4 V   b) 0.500 A
26.33 a) 2.14 V, a is higher
       b) 0.050 A, downward; 0
26.35 a) 0.641 Ω b) 975 Ω
26.37 a) 17.9 V   b) 22.7 V   c) 21.4%
26.39 a) 543 Ω b) 1.88 mA
       c) 1824 Ω, 608 Ω, 203 Ω
26.41 a) 0.849 μF   b) 2.89 s
26.43 a) 4.21 ms   b) 0.125 A
26.45 192 μC
26.47 13.6 A
26.49 a) 0.937 A   b) 0.606 A
26.51 a) 133 μC   b) 8.87 V, 9.13 V
       c) 8.87 V for both   d) 67.4 μC
26.53 900 W
26.55 12.1 Ω
26.57 a) 13.6 $\mu\Omega$ b) 2.14×10^{-8} $\Omega \cdot$m
26.59 a) 2.2 A, 4.4 V, 9.7 W   b) 16.3 W, brighter
26.61 a) 18.7 Ω b) 7.5 Ω
26.63 $I_1 = 0.848$ A, $I_2 = 2.14$ A, $I_3 = 0.171$ A
26.65 $I_2 = 5.21$ A, $I_4 = 1.11$ A, $I_5 = 6.32$ A
26.67 a) +0.22 V   b) 0.464 A

26.69 0.447 Ω (end-to-end), 0.423 Ω (in parallel)
26.71 a) 186 V, upper terminal positive
       b) 3.00 A, upward   c) 20.0 Ω
26.73 a) $P_1 + P_2$ b) $\dfrac{P_1 P_2}{P_1 + P_2}$
26.75 a) 1.35 W   b) 8.31 ms   c) 0.337 W
26.77 a) -12.0 V   b) 1.71 A   c) 4.21 Ω
26.79 a) 114 V   b) 263 V   c) 266 V
26.81 b) 1897 Ω
26.83 a) 24.8 V, 65.2 V   b) 3840 Ω c) 62.6 V
       d) no
26.85 1.7 MΩ, 3.1 μF
26.87 a) 19.4 s, 31.4 time constants   b) yes
26.89 a) $P = \dfrac{Q_0^2}{RC^2} e^{-2t/RC}$
26.93 b) 4 segments   c) 3.2 MΩ, 4.0×10^{-3}
       d) 3.4×10^{-4} e) 0.88

Chapter 27

27.1   a) $(-6.68 \times 10^{-4}\text{ N})\hat{k}$
       b) $(6.68 \times 10^{-4}\text{ N})\hat{\imath} + (7.27 \times 10^{-4}\text{ N})\hat{\jmath}$
27.3   a) positive   b) 0.0505 N
27.5   9490 km/s
27.7   a) $B_x = -0.175$ T, $B_z = -0.256$ T
       b) B_y is not determined   c) 0, 90°
27.9   a) 1.46 T, in the xz-plane at 40° from the $+x$-axis
       toward the $-z$-axis   b) 7.47×10^{-16} N, in the
       xz-plane at 50° from the $-x$-axis toward the
       $-z$-axis.
27.11 a) 3.05 mWb   b) 1.83 mWb   c) 0
27.13 -0.78 mWb
27.15 a) 0.160 mT, into the page   b) 0.111 μs
27.17 7.93×10^{-10} N, toward the south
27.19 a) 4.94×10^{-21} kg $\cdot$ m/s
       b) 2.31×10^{-23} kg $\cdot$ m^2/s
27.21 a) 835 km/s   b) 26.2 ns   c) 7.27 kV
27.23 a) 107 T   b) no
27.25 0.838 mT
27.27 a) $(1.60 \times 10^{-14}\text{ N})\hat{\jmath}$ b) yes
       c) helix, no   d) 1.40 cm
27.29 a) 4.81 kN/C   c) yes
27.31 0.0445 T, out of the page
27.33 a) 4.92 km/s   b) 9.96×10^{-26} kg
27.35 2.0 cm
27.37 a) 13.4 kA, no
27.39 0.724 N, 63.4° below the direction of the
       current in the upper wire segment
27.41 a) 817 V   b) 113 m/s^2
27.43 a) $-ILB\hat{\jmath}$ b) yes
27.45 b) $F_{cd} = 1.20$ N   b) 0.420 N $\cdot$ m
27.47 a) A_2 b) 290 rad/s^2
27.49 -2.42 J
27.51 a) 1.13 A   b) 3.69 A   c) 98.2 V
       d) 362 W
27.53 a) 4.7 mm/s   b) $+4.5 \times 10^{-3}$ V/m,
       $+z$-direction   c) 53 μV
27.55 a) $-\dfrac{F_2}{qv_1}\hat{\jmath}$; $F_2/2$
27.57 a) 8.3×10^6 m/s   b) 0.14 T
27.59 3.45 T, perpendicular to the initial velocity of
       the coin
27.61 a) 8.9×10^{-13} J $= 5.5$ MeV   b) 77 ns
       c) 1.2 T   d) same as in (a)
27.63 a) -3.89 μC
       b) $(7.60 \times 10^{14}\text{ m/s}^2)\hat{\imath} +$
       $(5.70 \times 10^{14}\text{ m/s}^2)\hat{\jmath}$
       c) 2.90 cm   d) 2.88×10^7 Hz
       e) $(0.0290\text{ m}, 0, 0.874\text{ m})$
27.65 9τ
27.67 1.6 mm
27.69 $\dfrac{Mg\tan\theta}{LB}$, right to left
27.71 $B_r(r) = -\beta r/2$
27.73 a) 8.46 mT   b) 27.2 cm   c) 2.2 cm, yes
27.75 1.80 N, to the left
27.77 0.024 T, $+y$-direction
27.79 a) 0.0442 N $\cdot$ m, clockwise   b) stretched
       c) 7.98 mJ

27.81 2.39 A
27.83 $-(0.444$ N$)\hat{\jmath}$
27.85 b) $(0, 0)$ to $(0, L)$: $\dfrac{1}{2}B_0 LI\hat{\imath}$
       $(0, L)$ to (L, L): $-IB_0 L\hat{\jmath}$
       (L, L) to $(L, 0)$: $-\dfrac{1}{2}B_0 LI\hat{\imath}$
       $(L, 0)$ to $(0, 0)$: 0
       c) $-IB_0 L\hat{\jmath}$
27.87 a) 2.52 m/s   b) 7.58 A   c) 0.198 Ω
27.89 a) 5.14 m   b) 1.72 μs   c) 6.08 mm
       d) 3.05 cm

Chapter 28

28.1   a) $-(19.2\ \mu\text{T})\hat{k}$ b) 0   c) $(19.2\ \mu\text{T})\hat{\imath}$
       d) $(6.79\ \mu\text{T})\hat{\imath}$
28.3   a) 60.0 nT, out of the page, at A and B
       b) 0.120 μT, out of the page   c) 0
28.5   a) 0   b) $-(1.31\ \mu\text{T})\hat{k}$ c) $-(0.462\ \mu\text{T})\hat{k}$
       d) $(1.31\ \mu\text{T})\hat{\jmath}$
28.7   a) (i) $\dfrac{\mu_0 qv}{8\pi d^2}$, into the page   (ii) 0
       (iii) $\dfrac{\mu_0 qv}{4\pi d^2}$, out of the page
       b) $\dfrac{\mu_0 q^2 v'v}{16\pi d^2}$, attractive   c) 1.00×10^{-6}
28.9 $(97.5$ nT$)\hat{k}$
28.11 a) 0.440 μT, out of the page
       b) 16.7 nT, out of the page   c) 0
28.13 a) $(5.00 \times 10^{-11}$ T$)\hat{\jmath}$
       b) $-(5.00 \times 10^{-11}$ T$)\hat{\imath}$
       c) $(-1.77 \times 10^{-11}$ T$)(\hat{\imath} - \hat{\jmath})$ d) 0
28.15 17.6 μT, into the page
28.17 a) 0.8 mT   b) 40 mT, 20 times larger
28.19 25 μA
28.21 a) 10.0 A
       b) at all points directly above the wire
       c) at all points directly east of the wire
28.23 a) $-(0.10\ \mu\text{T})\hat{\imath}$
       b) 2.19 μT, at 46.8° from the x-axis to the
       z-axis   c) $(7.9\ \mu\text{T})\hat{\imath}$
28.25 a) 0   b) 6.67 μT, toward the top of the page
       c) 7.54 μT, to the left
28.27 a) 0   b) 0   c) 0.40 mT, to the left
28.29 a) at P: 41 μT, into the page; at Q: 41 μT, out
       of the page   b) at P: 9.0 μT, out of the page;
       at Q: 9.0 μT, into the page
28.31 a) 6.00 μN, repulsive   b) 24.0 μN
28.33 46 μN/m, repulsive, no
28.35 0.38 μA
28.37 $\dfrac{\mu_0|I_1 - I_2|}{4R}$, 0
28.39 a) 9.42 mT   b) 0.134 mT
28.41 18.0 A, counterclockwise
28.43 a) 305 A   b) -3.83×10^{-4} T $\cdot$ m
28.45 a) $\mu_0 I/2\pi r$ b) 0
28.47 $r = R/2$ and $2R$
28.49 a) 1790 turns/m   b) 63.0 m
28.51 a) 3.72 MA   b) 124 kA   c) 237 A
28.53 1.11 mT
28.55 a) 72.5 mA   b) 19.5 mA
28.57 a) (i) 1.13 mT   (ii) 4.68 MA/m   (iii) 5.88 T
28.59 a) 1.00 μT, into the page
       b) $(7.49 \times 10^{-8}$ N$)\hat{\jmath}$
28.61 a) in the plane of the wires, between them,
       0.300 m from the 75.0-A wire
       b) in the plane of the wires, 0.200 m from the
       25.0-A wire and 0.600 m from the 75.0-A wire
28.63 a) 5.7×10^{12} m/s^2, away from the wire
       b) 32.5 N/C, away from the wire   c) no
28.65 5.59×10^{-18} N
28.67 a) 2.00 A, out of the page
       b) 2.13 μT, to the right   c) 2.06 μT
28.69 a) 11.1 μN/m, $-y$-direction
       b) 11.1 μN/m, $+y$-direction

28.71 23.2 A

28.73 2.21×10^{-3} N·m

28.75 a) $\dfrac{\mu_0 N I a^2}{2}\Bigg\{ \dfrac{1}{[(x+a/2)^2+a^2]^{3/2}} + \dfrac{1}{[(x-a/2)^2+a^2]^{3/2}} \Bigg\}$

c) $\left(\dfrac{4}{5}\right)^{3/2}\dfrac{\mu_0 N I}{a}$ d) 20.2 mT e) 0, 0

28.77 a) $\dfrac{3I}{2\pi R^3}$ b) (i) $B=\dfrac{\mu_0 I r}{2\pi R^3}$ (ii) $B=\dfrac{\mu_0 I}{2\pi r}$

28.79 a) 0 b) $B=\dfrac{\mu_0 I}{2\pi r}\dfrac{r^2-a^2}{b^2-a^2}$ c) $B=\dfrac{\mu_0 I}{2\pi r}$

28.81 b) $B=\dfrac{\mu_0 I_0}{2\pi r}$ c) $\dfrac{I_0 r^2}{a^2}\left(2-\dfrac{r^2}{a^2}\right)$

d) $B=\dfrac{\mu_0 I_0 r}{2\pi a^2}\left(2-\dfrac{r^2}{a^2}\right)$

28.83 a) $B=\dfrac{1}{2}\mu_0 I n$, $+x$-direction

b) $B=\dfrac{1}{2}\mu_0 I n$, $-x$-direction

28.85 7.73×10^{-25} A·m^2 = $0.0834\mu_B$

28.87 b) $\dfrac{1}{2g}\left(\dfrac{\mu_0 Q_0^2}{4\pi\lambda R C d}\right)^2$

Chapter 29

29.1 a) 17.1 mV b) 28.5 mA

29.3 a) $Q=NBA/R$ c) no

29.5 a) 34 V b) counterclockwise

29.7 a) $\mu_0 i/2\pi r$, into the page b) $\dfrac{\mu_0 i}{2\pi r}L\,dr$

c) $\dfrac{\mu_0 i L}{2\pi}\ln(b/a)$ d) $\dfrac{\mu_0 L}{2\pi}\ln(b/a)\dfrac{di}{dt}$

e) 0.506 μV

29.9 a) 5.44 mV b) clockwise

29.11 a) bAv b) clockwise

c) bAv, counterclockwise

29.13 10.4 rad/s

29.15 a) counterclockwise b) clockwise

c) no induced current

29.17 a) a to b b) b to a c) b to a

29.19 a) clockwise b) no induced current

c) counterclockwise

29.21 13.2 mA, counterclockwise

29.23 a) 0.675 V b) point b c) 2.25 V/m, b to a

d) point b e) (i) 0 (ii) 0

29.25 46.2 m/s = 103 mph, no

29.27 a) 3.00 V b) b to a c) 0.800 N, to the right

d) 6.00 W for each

29.29 a) counterclockwise b) 42.4 mW

29.31 35.0 m/s, to the right

29.33 a) 2.55 V, point a b) 3.38 V, point a c) 0

d) 4.23 V

29.35 a) $\pi r_1^2\dfrac{dB}{dt}$ b) $\dfrac{r_1}{2}\dfrac{dB}{dt}$ c) $\dfrac{R^2}{2r_2}\dfrac{dB}{dt}$

e) $\dfrac{\pi R^2}{4}\dfrac{dB}{dt}$ f) $\pi R^2\dfrac{dB}{dt}$ g) $\pi R^2\dfrac{dB}{dt}$

29.37 9.21 A/s

29.39 0.950 mV

29.41 2.34

29.43 a) 0.599 nC b) 6.00 mA c) 6.00 mA

29.45 a) 0.15 V/m b) 38 V/m·s

c) 3.4×10^{-10} A/m^2 d) 53.3 μT

29.47 a) $B=0, \vec{M}=-(4.38\times10^4\text{ A/m})\hat{\imath}$

b) $\vec{B}=(15.0\text{ T})\hat{\imath}, M=0$

29.49 a) 3.7 A b) 1.33 mA c) counterclockwise

29.51 16.2 μV

29.53 a) $\dfrac{\mu_0 I a b v}{2\pi r(r+a)}$ b) clockwise

29.55 190 rpm

29.57 a) 17.9 mV b) a to b

29.59 b) $\dfrac{RF}{B^2 L^2}$

29.61 1.2 V

29.63 $\mu_0 IW/4\pi$

29.65 a) $\dfrac{\mu_0 I v}{2\pi}\ln(1+L/d)$ b) point a c) 0

29.67 a) 0.165 V b) 0.165 V c) 0, 0.0412 V

29.69 a) B^2L^2v/R

29.71 point a: $\dfrac{qr}{2}\dfrac{dB}{dt}$, to the left; point b: $\dfrac{qr}{2}\dfrac{dB}{dt}$,

toward the top of the page; point c: 0

29.73 5.0 s

29.75 a) 196 μA/m^2 b) 3.00 nA/m^2 c) 7.82 MHz

d) 90°

29.77 a) a to b b) $\dfrac{Rmg\tan\phi}{L^2B^2\cos\phi}$ c) $\dfrac{mg\tan\phi}{LB}$

d) $\dfrac{Rm^2g^2\tan^2\phi}{L^2B^2}$ e) $\dfrac{Rm^2g^2\tan^2\phi}{L^2B^2}$

Chapter 30

30.1 a) 0.270 V, yes b) 0.270 V

30.3 6.32 μH

30.5 a) 1.96 H b) 7.11 mWb

30.7 a) 1940 b) 800 A/s

30.9 a) 0.250 H b) 0.450 mWb

30.11 a) 4.68 mV b) point a

30.13 a) 1000 b) 2.09 Ω

30.15 b) 0.111 μH

30.17 2850

30.19 a) 0.161 T b) 10.3 kJ/m^3 c) 0.129 J

d) 40.2 μH

30.21 91.7 J

30.23 a) 2.40 A/s b) 0.800 A/s c) 0.413 A

d) 0.750 A

30.25 a) 17.3 μs b) 30.7 μs

30.27 a) 0.250 A b) 0.137 A c) 32.9 V, point c

d) 0.462 ms

30.29 a) $P=(4.50\text{ W})(1-e^{-(3.20\text{ s}^{-1})t})$

b) $P_R=(4.50\text{ W})(1-e^{-(3.20\text{ s}^{-1})t})^2$

c) $P_L=(4.50\text{ W})(e^{-(3.20\text{ s}^{-1})t}-e^{-(6.40\text{ s}^{-1})t})$

30.33 a) 25.0 mH b) 90.0 nC c) 0.540 μJ

d) 6.58 mA

30.35 a) 105 rad/s, 0.0596 s b) 0.720 mC

c) 4.32 mJ d) -0.542 mC

e) -0.050 A, counterclockwise

f) $U_C=2.45$ mJ, $U_L=1.87$ mJ

30.37 a) 7.50 μC b) 15.9 kHz c) 0.0212 J

30.39 a) 298 rad/s b) 83.8 Ω

30.43 a) 0.288 μH b) 14.2 μV

30.47 20 km/s, about 30 times smaller

30.49 a) $\dfrac{\mu_0 i}{2\pi r}$ b) $\dfrac{\mu_0 i^2 l}{4\pi r}dr$ c) $\dfrac{\mu_0 i^2 l}{4\pi}\ln(b/a)$

d) $\dfrac{\mu_0 l}{2\pi}\ln(b/a)$

30.51 a) 5.00 H b) 31.7 m, no

30.53 a) 0.281 J b) 0.517 J c) 0.236 J

30.57 222 μF, 9.31 μH

30.59 13.0 mA, 184 A/s

30.61 a) 0 A, 20.0 V b) 0.267 A, 0 V

c) 0.147 A, 9.0 V

30.63 a) solenoid c) 50 V d) 3.5 A

e) 4.3 Ω, 43 mH

30.65 a) $A_1=A_4=0.800$ A, $A_2=A_3=0$;

$V_1=40.0$ V, $V_2=V_3=V_4=V_5=0$

b) $A_1=0.480$ A, $A_2=0.160$ A, $A_3=0.320$ A,

$A_4=0$; $V_1=24.0$ V, $V_2=0, V_3=V_4=V_5=$

16.0 V c) 192 μC

30.67 a) $A_1=A_4=0.455$ A, $A_2=A_3=0$

b) $A_1=0.585$ A, $A_2=0.320$ A,

$A_3=0.160$ A, $A_4=0.107$ A

30.69 a) 60.0 V b) point a c) 60.0 V d) point c

e) -96.0 V f) point b g) 156 V h) point d

30.71 a) 0; $v_{ac}=0, v_{cb}=36.0$ V

b) 0.180 A; $v_{ac}=9.0$ V, $v_{cb}=27.0$ V

c) $i_0=(0.180\text{ A})(1-e^{-t/(0.020\text{ s})})$,

$v_{ac}=(9.0\text{ V})(1-e^{-t/(0.020\text{ s})})$,

$v_{cb}=(9.0\text{ V})(3.00+e^{-t/(0.020\text{ s})})$

30.75 a) $i_1=\dfrac{\varepsilon}{R_1}, i_2=\dfrac{\varepsilon}{R_2}(1-e^{-R_2 t/L})$

b) $i_1=\dfrac{\varepsilon}{R_1}, i_2=\dfrac{\varepsilon}{R_2}$ c) $i=\dfrac{\varepsilon}{R_2}e^{-(R_1+R_2)t/L}$

d) 21.2 Ω, 12.7 V e) 35.3 mA

30.77 a) $d=D\left(\dfrac{L-L_0}{L_f-L_0}\right)$

b) 0.63024 H, 0.63048 H, 0.63072 H, 0.63096 H

c) 0.63000 H, 0.62999 H, 0.62999 H, 0.62998 H

d) oxygen

30.79 a) $i_1=\dfrac{\varepsilon}{R_1}(1-e^{-R_1 t/L}), i_2=\dfrac{\varepsilon}{R_2}e^{-t/R_2 C}$

$q_2=\varepsilon C(1-e^{-t/R_2 C})$

b) $i_1=0, i_2=9.60$ mA c) $i_1=1.92$ A,

$i_2=0$ d) 1.6 ms e) 9.4 mA f) 0.22 s

Chapter 31

31.1 1.06 A

31.3 a) 31.8 V b) 0

31.5 a) 90°, leads b) 193 Hz

31.7 13.3 μF

31.9 a) 1510 Ω b) 0.239 H c) 497 Ω

d) 16.6 μF

31.11 a) $(12.5\text{ V})\cos[(480\text{ rad/s})t]$ b) 7.17 V

31.13 a) $i=(0.0253\text{ A})\cos[(720\text{ rad/s})t]$

b) 180 Ω

c) $v_L=-(4.56\text{ V})\sin[(720\text{ rad/s})t]$

31.15 a) 601 Ω b) 0.0499 A c) $-70.6°$, lags

d) 9.98 V, 4.99 V, 33.3 V

31.17 50.0 V

31.19 a) 40.0 W b) 0.167 A c) 720 Ω

31.21 b) 76.7 V

31.23 a) 45.8°, 0.697 b) 344 Ω c) 155 V

d) 48.6 W e) 48.6 W f) 0 g) 0

31.25 a) 0.302 b) 0.370 W c) 0.370 W, 0, 0

31.27 a) 113 Hz, 15.0 mA b) 7.61 mA, lag

31.29 a) 150 V b) 150 V, 1290 V, 1290 V

c) 37.5 W

31.31 a) 1.00 b) 75.0 W c) 75.0 W

31.33 a) 115 Ω b) 146 Ω c) 146 Ω

31.35 a) 10 b) 2.40 A c) 28.8 W d) 500 Ω

31.37 a) use a step-down transformer with $N_2/N_1=\frac{1}{2}$

b) 6.67 A b) 36.0 Ω

31.39 0.124 H

31.41 3.59×10^7 rad/s

31.43 230 Ω

31.45 a) inductor b) 0.133 H

31.47 a) 0.831 b) 161 V

31.49 a) inductor: 1.15 A, 31.6 V; resistor: 1.15 A,

57.5 V; capacitor: 1.15 A, 14.6 V

b) all change; inductor: 0.860 A, 47.3 V; resistor:

0.860 A, 43.0 V; capacitor: 0.860 A, 5.46 V

31.51 $\dfrac{V_{out}}{V_s}=\sqrt{\dfrac{R^2+\omega^2 L^2}{R^2+\left(\omega L-\dfrac{1}{\omega C}\right)^2}}$

31.55 a) 102 Ω b) 0.882 A c) 270 V

31.57 b) yes c) 0 e) no

31.59 a) $I_R=V/R, I_C=V\omega C, I_L=V/\omega L$

d) 159 Hz e) 0.50 A

f) 0.50 A, 0.050 A, 0.050 A

31.61 a) L and C b) $\frac{1}{2}$ for each

31.63 a) 0.750 A b) 160 Ω c) 341 Ω, 619 Ω

d) 341 Ω

31.65 $0, I_0/\sqrt{3}$

31.67 a) decreases by $\frac{1}{2}$ b) increases by 2

c) decreases by $\frac{1}{2}$ d) no

31.69 a) $\dfrac{V}{\sqrt{R^2+\dfrac{9L}{4C}}}$ b) $\sqrt{\dfrac{L}{C}}\dfrac{2V}{\sqrt{R^2+\dfrac{9L}{4C}}}$

c) $\sqrt{\dfrac{L}{C}}\dfrac{V/2}{\sqrt{R^2+\dfrac{9L}{4C}}}$ d) $\dfrac{2LV^2}{R^2+\dfrac{9L}{4C}}$

e) $\dfrac{1}{2}\dfrac{LV^2}{R^2+\dfrac{9L}{4C}}$

31.71 a) 75.8 V   b) 13.6 Ω
31.73 a) $V_R I/2$ b) 0   c) 0
31.75 a) 0.400 A   b) 36.9°   c) $(400 - 300i)\ \Omega$,
500 Ω d) $(0.320 + 0.240i)$ A, 0.400 A
e) 36.9°   f) $V_{R\text{-cpx}} = (128 + 96i)$V,
$V_{L\text{-cpx}} = (-120 + 160i)$V,
$V_{C\text{-cpx}} = (192 - 256i)$V

Chapter 32

32.1 a) 1.28 s   b) 8.15×10^{13} km
32.3 13.3 nT, +y-direction
32.5 3.0×10^{18} Hz, 3.3×10^{-19} s,
6.3×10^{10} rad/m
32.7 a) 6.94×10^{14} Hz b) 375 V/m c) $E(x,t) =$
$(375\ \text{V/m})\cos[(1.45 \times 10^7\ \text{rad/m})x -$
$(4.36 \times 10^{15}\ \text{rad/s})t]$, $B(x,t) =$
$(1.25\ \mu\text{T})\cos[(1.45 \times 10^7\ \text{rad/m})x -$
$(4.36 \times 10^{15}\ \text{rad/s})t]$
32.9 a) (i) 60 kHz   (ii) 6.0×10^{13} Hz
(iii) 6.0×10^{16} Hz   b) (i) 4.62×10^{-14} m =
4.62×10^{-5} nm
(ii) 508 m = 5.08×10^{11} nm
32.11 a) +y-direction   b) 0.149 mm   c) $\vec{B} =$
$(1.03\ \text{mT})\hat{\imath}\cos[(4.22 \times 10^4\ \text{rad/m})y -$
$(1.265 \times 10^{13}\ \text{rad/s})t]$
32.13 a) 361 m   b) 0.0174 rad/m
c) 5.22×10^6 rad/s   d) 0.0144 V/m
32.15 a) 0.381 μm   b) 0.526 μm   c) 1.38
d) 1.90
32.17 a) 330 W/m²   b) 500 V/m, 1.7 μT
32.19 a) 11 μW/m²   b) 0.30 nT   c) 840 W
32.21 2.5×10^{25} W
32.23 12.0 V/m, 40.0 nT
32.25 850 kW

32.27 a) 0.18 mW   b) 274 V/m, 0.913 μT
c) 0.18 mJ/s   d) 0.010 W/cm²
32.29 a) 637 W/m²   b) 693 V/m, 2.31 μT
c) 2.12 μJ/m³
32.31 a) 30.5 cm   b) 2.46 GHz   c) 2.11 GHz
32.33 a) 7.10 mm   b) 3.55 mm
c) 1.56×10^8 m/s
32.35 a) 4.38 mm   b) 4.38 mm   c) 4.38 mm
32.37 a) 0.375 mJ   b) 4.08 mPa
c) 604 nm, 3.70×10^{14} Hz
d) 30.3 kV/m, 101 μT
32.39 a) 71.6 MW/m²   b) 232 kV/m, 774 μT
c) 35.8 MW/m²   d) 637 W/m²
32.41 a) 0.00602 W/m²   b) 2.13 V/m, 7.10 nT
c) 1.20 pN, no
32.43 a) 840 V/m, 2.80 μT
b) 1.56 μJ/m³ for each   c) 15.3 pJ
32.45 a) at $r = R$: 64 MW/m², 0.21 Pa; at $r = R/2$:
260 MW/m², 0.85 Pa   b) no
32.47 3.89×10^{-13} rad/s²
32.49 a) $\rho I/\pi a^2$, in the direction of the current
b) $\mu_0 I/2\pi a$, counterclockwise if the current is
out of the page
c) $\dfrac{\rho I^2}{2\pi^2 a^3}$, radially inward
d) $\dfrac{\rho l I^2}{\pi a^2} = I^2 R$
32.51 a) 23.6 h   b) throw it
32.53 a) 9.75×10^{-15} W/m²
b) 2.71 μV/m, 9.03×10^{-15} T, 67.3 ms
c) 3.25×10^{-23} Pa
d) 0.190 m
32.55 a) $\dfrac{4\rho G \pi MR^3}{3r^2}$ b) $\dfrac{LR^2}{4cr^2}$ c) 0.19 μm, no
32.57 b) 1.39×10^{-11} c) 2.54×10^{-8}

Chapter 38

38.1 a) $K_2 = 4K_1$ b) $E_2 = 2E_1$
38.3 5.77×10^{14} Hz, 1.28×10^{-27} kg·m/s,
3.84×10^{-19} J = 2.40 eV
38.5 a) 5.00×10^{14} Hz   b) 1.13×10^{19} photons/s
c) no
38.7 a) 4.8 eV   b) 6.1×10^{-34} J·s
d) f_{th}, ϕ, and the horizontal-axis intercept are
different, the slope is the same
38.9 249 km/s
38.11 2.14 eV
38.13 a) 264 nm   b) 4.70 eV
38.15 0.311 nm, same
38.17 1.13 keV
38.19 0.0714 nm, 180°
38.21 a) 4.39×10^{-4} nm   b) 0.04294 nm
c) 300 eV, loss   d) 300 eV
38.23 51.0°
38.25 a) 1.27×10^{-14} J   b) 9.46×10^{-14} J
c) 2.10 pm, less
38.27 1.19×10^{-27} kg·m/s, 1.96×10^{-29} kg·m/s
38.29 a) 1.04 eV   b) 1200 nm   c) 2.50×10^{14} Hz
d) 4.14×10^{-7} eV
38.31 a) 4.56×10^{14} Hz   b) 658 nm
c) 1.89 eV   d) 6.58×10^{-34} J·s
38.33 a) 5.07 mJ   b) 11.3 W
c) 1.49×10^{16} photons/s
38.35 a) 6.99×10^{-24} kg·m/s   b) 705 eV
38.37 6.28×10^{-24} kg·m/s, 59.4°
38.39 a) 5×10^{-33} m   b) 4×10^{-9} deg
c) 0.1 mm
38.41 a) 319 eV, 1.06×10^7 m/s   b) 3.89 nm
38.43 a) 4.85 pm   b) 0.256 MeV

PHOTO CREDITS

INDEX

For users of the three-volume edition: pages 1–686 are in Volume 1; pages 687–1260 are in Volume 2; and pages 1223–1522 are in Volume 3. Pages 1261–1522 are not in the Standard Edition.

Note: Page numbers followed by f indicate figures; those followed by t indicate tables.